The Coming Last Days Temple

Randall Price

HARVEST HOUSE PUBLISHERS
EUGENE, OREGON 97402

Unless otherwise indicated, all Scripture quotations are taken from the New American Standard Bible, © 1960, 1962, 1963, 1968, 1971, 1972, 1973, 1975, 1977, 1995 by The Lockman Foundation. Used by permission.

Scripture quotations marked KJV are taken from the King James Version of the Bible.

Cover by Terry Dugan Design, Minneapolis, Minnesota

For a free copy of Dr. Price's newsletter about biblical archaeology, biblical backgrounds, and biblical prophecy, write to:

World of the Bible Ministries, Inc.
P.O. Box 827
San Marcos, TX 78667-0827

(512) 396-3799, FAX (512) 392-9080
www.worldofthebible.com
E-mail: wbmrandl@itouch.net

THE COMING LAST DAYS TEMPLE

Copyright © 1999 by World of the Bible Ministries, Inc.
Published by Harvest House Publishers
Eugene, Oregon 97402

Library of Congress Cataloging-in-Publication Data
    Price, Randall.
        The coming last days Temple / Randall Price
            p. cm.
        Includes bibliographical references and index.
        ISBN 1-56507-901-9
        1. Bible—Prophecies—Temple of Jerusalem. 2. Temple of Jerusalem (Jerusalem)—Biblical teaching. I. Title.
    BS649.J4P75   1999
    236'.9—dc21
                                                                                    99-15415
                                                                                        CIP

99 00 01 02 03 / BP / 10 9 8 7 6 5 4 3 2 1

To

Gordon ("Chief") and Alice Whitelock—
Founders of Camp Peniel, Inc.,
in whose lives I, and countless others,
have "seen God face to face" (Genesis 32:30)

Acknowledgments

When the Gentile courtier of Ptolemy II Philadelphus, Aristeas, toured the Temple Mount during the later half of the second century B.C., he wrote concerning the Temple: "And there is an endless supply of water, as if indeed a strongly flowing natural spring were issuing forth from within" *(Letter of Aristeas* 88). In writing this book on the Temple I often felt like my sources of supply were inexhaustible. During the ten years of research that have gone into this book I have been helped by such an overwhelming number of people that acknowledgment of all of them here would be quite impossible. For each one who has had a part I owe a great debt and pray that as they have been a part of that "spring" of knowledge which has refreshed my understanding of the Temple, that they will share in the joys of the Coming Last Days Temple when a life-giving stream will again flow from the Sanctuary (Ezekiel 47:1-12; Joel 3:18; Zechariah 14:8). Two individuals who have refreshed me throughout my Christian life are Rev. Gordon ("Chief") and Alice Whitelock, the founders of Camp Peniel, Inc., to whom this book is dedicated. Above all I must thank and give love to my wife, Beverlee, who has supported my studies and given me new insights into God's Word, and to my always patient-children, Elisabeth, Eleisha, Erin, Jon, and Emilee, who have prayed for their Dad through one more book! My mother, Maurine Price, has also given sacrificially of her time and her home to allow me a refuge to write—thanks always, Mother!

My sincere thanks is also extended to Dr. John F. Walvoord, one of this century's foremost prophetic authorities, who has not only been my teacher but a good friend, and has graciously contributed the foreword to this work. I am also grateful to those in Israel who have willingly given interviews and discussed biblical and rabbinic details concerning the Temple, including the late Rabbi Shlomo Goren and Rabbi Meir Yehuda Getz, Rabbi Yisrael Ariel, Rabbi Chaim Richman, Danny Zachariah, Rabbi Yosef Elboim, Rabbi Nachman Kahane, Gershon Salomon, Ze'ev Bar-Tov, Yehuda Etzion, Shoshi Harrari, Yohanan Ramati, Dan Bahat, Ronny Reich, Hillel Geva, Rami Arav, Meir Ben-Dov, Tuvia Sugiv, Dr. Asher Kaufman, Reuven Prager, Noam Hendren, Dave Dolan, Clarence Wagner, Palestinian Mufti Ikrama Sabri, and Wakf Administrator Adnan Husseini. Many thanks are also given to Meno Kalisher and Binyamin Lalizou for Hebrew translations; Gary, Debra, and Jeremy Collett for transportation, accommodations, and technical assistance in Israel; John and Janice Carness for film footage; and Susan Magaña and Debbie Smith for interview transcriptions. I would also like to express my gratitude to Mrs. Ann Dixon, who was instrumental in making possible my trip for Succot 1998, during which I first came into contact with the Temple movement, to my longtime friend and director of the Pre-Trib Research Center, Thomas Ice, for encouraging me to publish my research on the Temple movement and for writing with me my first book on the subject, and to my doctoral advisor Harold Liebowitz for allowing me to do the initial research that forms parts of this present work.

My sincerest thanks is also extended to friends and colleagues in ministry (and in many cases their families), who have continually prayed for me and given me spiritual support during this writing process: Dr. Tim LaHaye, Dave Hunt, Steve Sullivan, Dr. Harry Leafe, Gordon Franz (who also assisted in research), Richard Short (who also assisted with "The Temple in Prophecy" chronological research), Dr. H. Wayne House, Rev. Tommy Jenkins and Steve Hager, and to Paul Streber for his assistance in filming interviews and his friendship through many trips to Israel.

Special thanks also goes to Harvest House Publishers for accepting my longer-than-expected manuscript and for their professional execution in its published form. From their staff, particular thanks must be given to Steve Miller, who faithfully and meticulously edited the manuscript and offered both encouragement and needed criticism, and to President Bob Hawkins, Jr., Vice President of Editorial Carolyn McCready, and LaRae Weikert, Barbara Sherrill, and Betty Fletcher.

Finally, I must acknowledge that my every effort has been enabled and guided by my sovereign God, to whom is due not only my thanks but all my praise. To Him be the honor and glory forever!

Contents

Illustrations and Charts

Foreword

John F. Walvoord

This volume has been made possible by years of careful research on the part of its author, whom I have known for many years. His studies in Israel and many trips to the Land, interviews with top officials, and the detailed research that can be found on every page of the book support his view of the Temples of Scripture. It is doubtful whether there has ever been or ever will be another volume on the Temple as comprehensive and complete as this volume. Those who are accustomed to scholarly research and writings will find this book an incredible compilation of facts on the subject.

Any interpreter of the Bible becomes aware of the fact that the Temple and its history and prophecy are a decisive factor in the fulfillment of God's program. For Jews, the Temple and the activities toward its rebuilding are part of their expectation that their messiah will return in this generation. For Christians, it represents a different factor, that of indication that the rapture of the church, which will occur before the time of the end time trouble which precedes the second coming of Christ, may be near.

For those who share the evangelical point of view that the rapture is imminent, this volume provides evidence that the stage is being set for events that will follow the rapture. If this is the case, then the rapture itself could be very near. And the doctrine of the Temple becomes an integral part of prophetic outlook for those who seek to interpret prophecy in a literal way.

The scholarly analysis of the doctrine of the Temple will prove to be of great benefit both to Christian theologians and to those of Jewish faith, especially those who are part of the Orthodox movement. This volume is highly recommended as an integral part of the scholarly presentation of biblical truth.

—John F. Walvoord
Chancellor
Dallas Theological Seminary

Preface

Almost a decade ago I wrote with Thomas Ice a book entitled *Ready to Rebuild: The Imminent Plan to Rebuild the Last Days Temple.*[1] At that time I made the observation that "something is happening in the Middle East today that will soon affect the destiny of our entire planet. It has not been extensively reported in our major newspapers, and few of our political analysts have connected it with the events...that are rapidly changing the course of future history." Perhaps I should have thought better at the time, but I added to that observation a prediction: "Nevertheless, we believe that it will soon become the focal point of world controversy and usher in dramatic days of war and peace foretold long ago by the ancient Hebrew prophets."[2] When those words were written the Temple movement was in its infancy and our book was one of the first to bring to a Christian audience the significant facts behind these budding efforts to see the Jerusalem Temple rebuilt for the first time in nearly 2,000 years. Since that book was published I have continued to research the subject of the Temple, having completed a doctoral dissertation on the topic,[3] written a book on the treasures of the Temple,[4] contributed chapters on the archaeology and theology of the Temple to five different books[5] and articles on its role in history and prophecy to a theological dictionary,[6] as well as having written a regular feature called "Temple Times" for the past seven years.[7] My lectures on the subject of the Temple have taken me to audiences ranging from seminary professors and students to church laymen and businessmen in over seven countries around the world. From all of these people I have received many questions which have challenged me to continue my search for answers.

I have also continued and cultivated my relationships with both the leaders and opponents of Temple movement organizations in Israel and have spent countless hours discussing and debating with them various aspects of the coming Temple. Complementing this has been the exceptional access I have been given to the Islamic authorities who maintain control over the Temple Mount and their permission to enter sites under their jurisdiction, usually restricted to Muslims. Access has been granted as well to the extensive Israeli excavations above and beneath the Temple Mount by the archaeologists in charge. These sites have shed new light on the past (and prompted heated riots in the present), and for me have been rich experiences that have enlarged considerably my own knowledge in the field. Throughout these years, too, my original excitement concerning the significance of the current efforts to rebuild the Temple has not waned but grown in proportion to my increasing understanding of its purpose in the past and in prophecy. Contrary to critics who have dismissed renewed Jewish activity toward rebuilding the Temple as the insignificant fantasy of a handful of upstart Jews, the closing days of the twentieth century and the beginning of the sixth millennium in human history have proved the Temple Mount to be at the center of international controversy and the Arab-Israeli conflict. If, as the political scene indicates, the Temple Mount continues its present course toward prophetic fulfillment, this generation may indeed be that which sees the event of the rebuilding of the Temple change the course of history.

For these reasons, rather than revise and update *Ready to Rebuild*, which continues to offer the most extensive introduction to Christians concerning the Jewish preparations for rebuilding the Temple, I have written an entirely new book, taking into account not only new developments in the Temple movement, but also treating in greater detail the historical and prophetic texts as well as the theological concepts that support the argument for a Last Days Temple. Over my years of interaction with the topic of the Temple I have been repeatedly impressed with two facts: The first is that this subject ranks at the top of the biblical prophecies. The signal event in Jesus' teaching on the Tribulation is the Temple, whose desecration by the "abomination of desolation" serves as a warning of the wrath to come (Matthew 24:15; Mark 13:14). In the Old Testament predictions about the period of Israel's restoration, called by Christians the "Millennium" or "Millennial kingdom," the Temple occupies center stage (Isaiah 2:2-3; 56:6-7; 65:25; 66:1-6,18-21; Ezekiel 37:26-28; 40–48; Daniel 9:24,27; 11:45; 12:11; Jeremiah 3:16-17; 31:38-40; 33:18; Hosea 3:4-5; Joel 2:1; 3:18; Obadiah 21; Micah 4:1-8; Zephaniah 3:10-11; Haggai 2:7-9; Zechariah 1:16; 6:12-15; 8:3; 14:10,16-21). In like manner, the New Testament also expects a future fulfillment for the Old Testament prophecies of the Temple, while adding new revelation of its own (Matthew 23:38-39; 24:15; Mark 13:14; 2 Thessalonians 2:4; Revelation 11:1-2; 21:3,22).

The second fact is that the literal interpretation of these prophecies of the Temple have generated much confusion and opposition. For the past 2,000 years, Christendom has generally viewed the Old Testament prophecies concerning a future Temple as a symbolic prefigurement of the church, rejecting any idea of rebuilding a physical structure and restoring sacrifices as Judaistic and non-Christian. One reason for this is that from the earliest disputations between Christianity and Judaism a central tenet of the Christian argument has been that the Temple's destruction proved not only Jesus' status as a prophet (see Matthew 23:38; Luke 19:43-44), but also the superior status of Christianity. This gave rise to the belief that the church superceded or replaced Israel as the final fulfillment of God's divine design, and that Christians rather than Jews were now the chosen people of God. Although these tenets were contested in Scripture (see Romans 11:11-12,15,25-32), they became so dogmatically established in many denominations that to challenge them in any part has invited the charge, even in this age of tolerance, of blasphemy or worse. This was brought home to me when I wrote my doctoral dissertation on the Temple in prophecy at a secular university under an Orthodox Jewish advisor. With genuine concern for my future in light of my defense of the Temple's restoration, he cautioned me that I "would never get a job in a Christian institution!"

Adding insult to injury, I have also received adverse reactions from the Jewish community. For a Christian to write on a topic that is considered the provenance of Judaism strikes some Jewish people as odd, and their first suspicion is that I am probably ill-informed. I have had rabbis dismiss my questions simply because I was considered undeserving to receive their answers. Others have doubted the sincerity of my study because I was a Christian and they assumed my motives to be suspect. Surely, one rabbi told me, the only reason I cared about the rebuilding of the future Temple was because it would make Jesus come back sooner and convert the Jews! I have also had to deal with critical reactions from Jewish-Christians, some of whom have fervently warned me that a Third Temple is against the gospel because it will be built by unbelieving Jews who will reinstate the sacrificial system in rejection of Messiah's finished atonement.

These encounters and others like them have convinced me that the Temple needs to be better understood by both Gentiles and Jews in the full scope of its revelation from the beginning of time to the end times, which encompasses both the Old and New Testaments. Only by tracing the divine design of the Creator to dwell in the midst of His creatures can the greater purpose for which the Temple was created be grasped.

In light of this greater purpose, our present assumptions concerning future fulfillment should be tempered by the realization that we have a limited perspective of the overall plan of God. The church must become aware that, to a large extent, it has come to adopt the placid perspective of a jaded world that mockingly says, "Where is the promise of His coming?…all continues just as it was from the beginning of creation" (2 Peter 3:4). Yet history has revealed that change is the eternal constant. Although the Jewish Temple has not existed for the past 2,000 years, it is presumptuous to assume that it could not return in the future. For nearly the same amount of time, the nation of Israel itself was but a footnote in history, leading many to conclude that it was a fossil civilization, forever abandoned by God. Yet, in the last half of the twentieth century a new national Israel has returned to their biblical homeland to command the world's attention. In this same vein, when Christopher Columbus left the Old World some five centuries ago, the focus of history shifted to the New World and its expanding economy, which launched the United States to world prominence. Today, however, the Old World has returned economically and politically with the establishment of the economic and monetary union developed in Europe, and the eurodollar is challenging the U.S. dollar as the new global standard. Is it only coincidence that the center of international focus is again in Europe, where the end-time world ruler is destined to arise (Daniel 7:23-26; 9:26-27)? Such a turning of the times from the west back to the east was predicted by the Bible, for this is the stage upon which the events of the last days drama will be enacted. Following this pattern, the rise of a Temple movement in Israel at this critical juncture in their history may also be a part of the turning of the times in preparation for the predicted days climaxing God's purpose for the Jewish nation and the world.

As an evangelical Christian, my own introduction to the subject of the Temple and the Temple movement began providentially many years ago and has continued with many surprises ever since. I had just entered a doctoral program at the University of Texas when, in the second month of classes, I was offered a free trip to Israel. The trip came at the expense of a woman who had to cancel her own trip but could not get a refund for her ticket. Because the trip came during the Jewish high holidays, one of my favorite seasons when I had lived in the Land, I was eager to accept. However, I knew that leaving for two weeks at the start of my studies might create a negative impression on my department chairman, jeopardizing my future in this competitive academic arena. Nevertheless, I felt compelled to explain my opportunity to him. To my surprise he said, "Go for it!" And, just like that, I was off to Jerusalem. The last week of my stay in the city was during the week-long celebration of Succot (the Feast of Tabernacles), a time pregnant with prophetic fulfillment (see Zechariah 14:16; Matthew 17:4; Mark 9:5; Luke 9:33). Early on the morning of the day before my departure I happened to see a newspaper clipping about a group called the Temple Mount Faithful. Ironically, the clipping was tacked to the wall of the Arab house on the Mount of Olives where I was staying. This group, whose interest was in rebuilding the Temple, planned to meet at the Dung Gate in the Old City for a public demonstration. Because this event was scheduled for that very morning, I hurried on foot down the slope of the Mount of Olives, crossed the Kidron Valley, and then followed the road around to the meeting place. Soon I found I had joined a strange group of Orthodox Jews carrying flags, banners, and ritual vessels, with one man dressed in priestly attire! Little did I known then—as I followed the march of this band of throwbacks to the biblical period—that this was to be my introduction to a decade of discoveries concerning the Temple. Since that day I have journeyed back to Jerusalem over 40 times and have had many unusual encounters on the Temple Mount. Some of these include the unprecedented experience of scaling the outside of the Dome of the Rock, and an unforgettable meeting at 2:00 A.M. deep beneath the Temple Mount with the late Rabbi Meir Yehuda Getz, who had rediscovered an ancient gate in the very tunnel in which we met and had searched within it for the lost Ark of the Covenant!

Former U.S. President Dwight D. Eisenhower once defined an intellectual as a man who takes more words than necessary to tell more than he knows. Although I have taken many words in this book to tell about the Temple, and am aware that there is much more to know, it is my conviction that all of it is necessary. It has not been intellectualism, but my love of biblical history (fulfilled and unfulfilled), coupled with a quest for the unexplored, that has driven me to delve deeper into the Scriptures in my search for the significance of the Temple. There I have discovered the prophetic path that leads to the coming Last Days Temple. It promises a new journey into an adventure that has today only just begun. It is my privilege to share it with you as we move toward these most momentous days in God's prohetic plan.

—Randall Price, *Pesach* (Passover) 1999

PART I

The Perspective
of the
Last Days Temple

This people says, "The time has not come, even the time for the House of the Lord [Temple] to be rebuilt...Is it time for you yourselves to dwell in paneled houses while this House lies desolate? Now therefore, thus says the LORD of hosts, 'Consider your ways...Go up...and rebuild the Temple that I may be pleased with it and be glorified, says the Lord."

—Haggai 1:2,4,8

[We should] probe the issue not as an exercise in apocalyptic forecasting, but with an eye toward those aspects of the Temple's rebuilding that may contribute to "the fear of God and the love of Him."

—Joshua Berman

CHAPTER 1

Time for a Temple

Rebuilding the Temple in This Generation

Each generation in which the Temple is not rebuilt is considered as if they destroyed the Temple.

—JERUSALEM TALMUD, *YOMA* 1:1

I believe that the preparations for the rebuilding of the Temple today are extremely significant. . . I think we're seeing a time when in the hearts of people they're saying the time has come.

—ELWOOD McQUAID

As the numbers on the millennial clock counted down toward the long-awaited climatic hour signaling the change to the year 2000, numbers of people were moving toward Jerusalem. These were religious groups, mostly Christian millennialists, camped out on the Mount of Olives in anticipation of prophetic events coming to fulfillment. Some were arrested and deported by Israeli police, who feared that these detractors were plotting to commit a mass suicide on the Temple Mount, or incite anti-Muslim provocation, or destroy the Al-Aqsa mosque.[1] Most, however, simply wanted front row seats for the last days' most climatic events—the return of Christ and the rebuilding of the Temple. This expectation was so pervasive that it was even voiced by such surprising a source as the popular Muslim Egyptian writer Said Ayyub, who said, "The countdown to the hour of judgment will begin in 2000, when the Al-Aqsa Mosque will be destroyed and the Temple rebuilt."[2] Yet even before all these people descended on Jerusalem, thousands of Orthodox Jews had long been resident and making plans of their own to realize the expected day of the Temple's rebuilding.

The Will to Rebuild

Because ancient Israel originally had sovereignty over the Temple Mount, Orthodox Jews around the world have placed unrelenting pressure on the Israeli government to create a Jewish presence there. The attempts to rebuild the Temple have come as a natural result of the modern-day Jewish return to Israel and Jerusalem. Irving Greenberg, former Chairman of the Department of Jewish Studies at City College of New York's City University and founder and director of the National Jewish Resource Center, said:

> Now in our lifetime, the period of exile and powerlessness of Jewry is coming to an end. The Holocaust and the rebirth of the State of Israel have ended the period of exilic Judaism. *Tisha B'Av* [the time of mourning for the destruction of the Temple and of prayer for its rebuilding] cannot be unaffected by the miracle of Israel and the reunification of Jerusalem. The prophet Zechariah told Israel in God's name that after the return, Tisha B'Av and the three other fasts will become days of celebration and joy (Zechariah 8:19). While it is too early to claim that the Messianic fulfillment is here, the process of redemption now underway is discernable.[3]

The sentiments driving the Israeli will to rebuild were expressed by Israel Defense Forces Chief Rabbi General Shlomo Goren on the day of the Temple Mount's liberation:

> We have taken the city of God, we are entering the Messianic era for the Jewish people....We took an oath today, while capturing the city....on our blood we took an oath that we will never give it up, we will never leave this place. The Wailing Wall belongs to us. The holy place [Temple Mount] was our place first, and our God's place. From here we do not move. Never, never![4]

In response to the unification of their ancient capital, and reclamation of the site of the Temple, Jewish groups in Israel and throughout the world began organizing efforts to raise funds and promote a movement to rebuild.[5] From the evangelical premillennial Christian camp articles appeared in evangelical magazines and theological journals analyzing the biblical statements concerning a future Temple and the prospects of proposed Jewish efforts.[6] The secular press appeared to expect an imminent erection of the Temple. At the time, Jewish historian Israel Eldad prescribed a positive yet more cautious posture: "We are at the stage where David was when he liberated Jerusalem. From that time until the construction of the Temple by Solomon, only one generation passed. So will it be with us."

However, a delay in Jewish expectation came abruptly when General Moshe Dayan returned the jurisdiction of the Temple Mount to the *Wakf*, the Muslim Supreme Council, as a peaceful gesture of Israeli intentions to the Arab League. The Dayan agreement restricted non-Muslim access to the Temple Mount for religious ceremonies of any kind. Immediately, efforts to reverse this decision began in the form of legal suits and illegal and violent protests (see chapter 19). Until recently, these have been infrequent and marginal, but as a generation passed, Arab jurisdiction of the Temple Mount became a *de facto* claim of sovereignty over the Temple Mount. Then in 1987, this Arab presumption of sovereignty erupted in the Palestinian *Intifada* ("uprising"), claiming rights to all of Judea and Samaria (the West Bank) and ultimately the total land possessed by the present State of Israel.[7] Graffiti used by Palestinians as a symbol of the *Intifada* since 1987 has depicted the Dome of the Rock as the base of an upraised clenched fist. Anne Marie Oliver and Paul Steinberg, who have extensively studied such graffiti, have noted that "it functions as a proclamation of Moslem possession of the most contentious site in the Arab-Israel conflict, and by extension, to Jerusalem and the land as a whole."[8] A similar statement has appeared on the walls of the Temple Mount in the aftermath of Israeli-Arab conflicts in Jerusalem and Hebron, in the form of Arab handprints stained with blood. In light of these aggressive demands by the Palestinians, Israeli political activism has increased dramatically, and some felt that physical preparations for a Temple were necessary in order to help reverse the secular Israeli governments tendency toward making concessions with the Muslim enemy. Thus was born the Temple movement—non-aligned groups actively working toward the common goal of seeing the Temple rebuilt in this generation. Commenting on the rise of this Temple movement back in 1989, *Time* magazine religion reporter Richard Ostling startled readers in the October 16 issue by asking the long unasked question in the title of his feature article: "Time for a Temple?"[9]

The Movement to Rebuild the Temple

At the very same time Richard Ostling's article was being read around the world, a group known as *Tenu'at Ne'emani Har-Habayit ve'aretz Yisrael* ("Temple Mount and Land of Israel Faithful Movement") was staging a demonstration near the Temple Mount—a demonstration that would set their organization at the forefront of international conflict. They performed an ancient Jewish ritual not seen since the days of the Second Temple (see chapter 19), which concluded with an attempt to place a cornerstone for the Third Temple near the ascent to the Temple Mount. Although the Israeli police stopped this demonstration just outside the Dung Gate entrance to the Western Wall Plaza, the group vowed that next time they would be successful. The next time came on October 8, 1990. As in the previous year, the Temple Mount Faithful were turned away at the Dung Gate—but not before thousands of Palestinian Arabs had gathered to riot on the Temple Mount, hurling a shower of stones down upon some 20,000 Jewish worshipers gathered at the Western Wall area. The Israeli police's attempts to quell the riot only escalated it, with the result that 17 Palestinians were killed.

The "Temple Mount incident," as it was called, not only made international headlines and brought the condemnation of the United Nations for "Israeli aggression," but was also used to advantage by Saddam Hussein, who, having invaded Kuwait just two months earlier, launched SCUD missiles against Israel for its "imperialistic occupation" of Arab lands. Later intelligence reports revealed that Israeli police had prohibited the Temple Mount Faithful from coming to the Temple Mount and that the police had assured the Islamic authorities of this. Despite these assurances, that morning the loudspeakers that normally sound the Muslim call to prayer exhorted tens of thousands of Muslims to "come to the Mount and sacrifice soul and blood to save the land" and to "prevent the occupation of Islam's holy places."[10] Israeli witnesses have claimed that there were also explicit calls to "kill the Jews." Intelligence reports also reveal that the Palestinian attack on the Jewish worshipers at the Western Wall was part of an Iraqi plot to deflect world attention away from Saddam Hussein's invasion and rally the Arab league behind his call for *Jihad* ("holy war"). So, attempting to portray Israel as the real "invader" in the Middle East,[11] Saddam announced to the press immediately after the Temple Mount incident that he would not consider the Kuwaiti issue until the greater Palestinian problem was resolved. It was his bold plan to emerge as the new champion of the Palestinian people (and all Muslims) by taking the mantle of former "Iraqi" (Babylonian) king Nebuchadnezzar against Israel, the ancient enemy of all Arab nations.

Fortunately, Operation Desert Storm ended the Gulf War and prevented a premature Armageddon. While war was averted on this occasion, it is important to note that to the Arabs, Israel's desire to return to the Temple Mount constitutes a war against Islam and their claim to the land. This was made clear on September 25, 1996 as violence again erupted on the Temple Mount. The cause this time was the Netanyahu government's decision to open an exit tunnel for tourists at the end of a 2,000 plus year-old Hasmonean tunnel located more than 50 feet below and more than 1,000 feet to the north of the Temple Mount (see chapter 19). Allegedly the Muslim Wakf had given its approval to the former Rabin government for this project—in exchange for Israeli permission for Muslims to hold prayer services at Ramadan within the so-called "Solomon's Stables" on the Temple Mount. However, when it was learned by the Arabs that the exit tunnel had been opened, a massive riot broke out on the Temple Mount, and additional riots occurred throughout Jerusalem and Hebron and other areas of Palestinian occupation. The result was 58 deaths, the highest death toll in connection with the Temple Mount since the early part of the twentieth century.

Such incidents reveal that the tension over matters related to the Temple Mount are escalating. They also demonstrate the reality that every riot and protest in the struggle for the Temple Mount has the potential to ignite a worldwide conflagration. Today the Temple Mount is at the center stage of negotiations between Israel and the Palestinians (as representatives of the Muslim world), and is destined to be the center of military conflict in the days ahead. But what is it about the Temple Mount that makes it of such importance to the Jewish people?

The Magnitude of the Mount

Based on mere geography, the Temple Mount hardly constitutes a wonder of the world. It is set on a scant 35 acres in a corner of the Old City, on a mount only 2,580 feet high. By contrast, the abode of the Hellenic gods, Mount Olympus, towers a majestic 9,750 feet. However, physical magnitude was never of greatest importance for the Temple Mount. Rather, the key is its religious role as the physical locus of God's manifestation on earth, the "camp of the *Shekinah.*" The Temple Mount is traditionally identified with Mount Moriah, the place where Abraham intended to offer his son Isaac as a sacrifice to God (Genesis 22), yet its sacredness derives from the fact that it was once the site of the Temple, with its Holy of Holies. Here the Ark of the Covenant once rested on the *'Even Shetiyyah* ("Foundation Stone"), which is recorded in Jewish tradition to be "the rock from which the world was woven"—the very center of creation. For more than a millennium the Jewish Sanctuary occupied this spot, then was destroyed by the Roman general Titus on the ninth of the Jewish month of Av, 2,000 years ago. Yet, despite the Roman, Christian, and Muslim presence thereafter on the Mount, the hope for the rebuilding of the Temple has remained at the epicenter of Jewish religious consciousness. Dr. Y.I. Hayutman expresses well the feelings not only of the Jews in Israel and the Diaspora, but also of the Gentiles of various religious persuasions:

> The hope to return to Jerusalem and to rebuild the Temple has been a dream of the Jewish people for the last two thousand years. Millions of evangelical Christians pray for it, as well as "Free Masons" and other people. In the Jewish tradition the Temple represents the heart of God, Israel, and the heart in each of us where the Divine dwells....As Israel celebrates its 50th year of rebirth, the Jewish world remains split and unwell. How can it be healed when its heart remains broken and ignored?[12]

The heartbreak among those who long for but live without a Temple is compounded by a realization that the destiny of the Jewish Nation and the world hinges on the fulfillment of the biblical prophecies concerning the Temple. The spiritual redemption of Israel, as described by the prophets, revolves around ascent to the rebuilt Temple in the Messianic age (Isaiah 2:2-3; 56:6-7; 60:3-7; Micah 4:1-2; Haggai 2:7; Zechariah 14:16). Living in light of this future reality, Rabbi Nachman Kahane of the Young Israel Synagogue and Director of the Institute for Talmudic Commentary explains: "All Jewish history, as far as we're concerned, is one big parenthesis until the Temple is returned. Life without the

Temple is not really living."[13] With the "real life" of the modern nation facing the threat of annihilation from neighboring Muslim countries, and Jews around the world becoming more assimilated into pagan cultures and religions, redemption has never seemed more necessary, yet further from fulfillment. Added to this is the sense of guilt felt by many Orthodox Jews for failing to fulfill the commandment to rebuild the Temple (Exodus 25:8) since the Temple Mount came under Israeli sovereignty in 1967. Such guilt is also fostered by the harsh verdict of the Jerusalem Talmud: "Each generation in which the *Beit HaMikdash* [Temple] is not rebuilt is considered as if they destroyed the *Beit HaMikdash* [Temple]" (*Yoma* 1:1). Since one of the greatest of sins is to destroy the holy Temple, if this generation of Jews has incurred such a sin, it is incumbent for them to atone for it by fulfilling the divine commandment, which in turn, they believe, will start the process of national and universal redemption.

The Means to Messiah

Another reason for the fervent desire to see the Temple rebuilt is because its rebuilding is thought to be a necessary prerequisite to the coming of the Messiah. This belief is fervently held by both Jews and Christians alike. The Jews refer to the prophecy in Malachi 3:1: "The Lord, whom you seek, will suddenly come to His temple." For the Messiah to be able to come to His Temple requires, of course, that it must already be built. This is reflected in the Jewish commentaries: "Our rabbis taught: When the King, the Messiah arrives, he will stand on the roof of the Holy Temple, and shout out to Israel: 'Humble ones! The time of your redemption is at hand!'" (*Yalkut Shimoni Isaiah* 499). Orthodox Jews who believe that the next Temple, the Third Temple, will be the final Temple, have the difficulty of resolving how this Temple can be built before Messiah arrives and yet, how, according to the prophecy of Zechariah, Messiah will build the final Temple (Zechariah 6:12-14).

Christians who interpret the prophecies of the New Testament in a consistently futuristic manner resolve this by understanding that two Temples will be constructed in the last days. Jesus' words in the Olivet Discourse (Matthew 24:15; Mark 13:14), Paul's statement in 2 Thessalonians 2:4, and John's vision in the Book of Revelation (Revelation 11:1-2) are taken to refer to a Third Temple that will be built, according to Daniel's prophecy (Daniel 9:27), during the time just before the second coming of Christ. This will be an interim Temple, as the Second Temple before it. When Jesus as Messiah delivers and restores Jerusalem at His coming, He will then build a fourth and final Temple in accordance with the restoration promised by the Old Testament prophets (Isaiah 2:2-3; 56:7-8; Ezekiel 40–48). That is why the present-day preparations for a new Temple are generating excitement, for they seem to indicate that the events that herald Messiah's coming and reign are near at hand.

The "Prophecy" of Rebuilding in This Generation

A tradition is recorded in the Jewish Midrash that even though the Second Temple was destroyed at the conclusion of a Sabbath (a Saturday night), the Levites sang on that day a Temple song normally reserved for Wednesdays. This song, preserved by Jewish oral tradition, includes the words, "O God, to whom vengeance belongs, shine forth!" Ever since the Second Temple's destruction, Jewish people have asked, "Why did the Levites sing a Wednesday song on a Saturday?" One possible answer is that the calamity surrounding the destruction called for this specific song as a prayer for deliverance or retribution.

Yet another explanation has been proposed by modern rabbis. They contend that in this last desperate hour the Levites received a prophetic revelation that foretold the time of the future rebuilding of the Temple. Ironically, according to the rabbis, it was a Wednesday, June 7, 1967, that marked a major turning point in Jewish history in relation to the rebuilding of the Temple. This was the day the Jewish people recaptured the Temple Mount in Jerusalem after an almost 2,000-year hiatus. Most Orthodox Jews believe that this act was the first step toward the greater redemption of the Land of Israel, which they say will be climaxed by the rebuilding of the Third Temple. Even secular historians reflecting on the capture of the Temple Mount echoed the rabbis' interpretation. Israel Eldad, one of Israel's most prominent historians, declared, "We are at the stage where David was when he liberated Jerusalem. From that time until the construction of the Temple by Solomon, only one generation passed. So will it be with us."[14] Clearly, the generation that returned to their most holy site and reunited the holy city of Jerusalem expected to complete this return by rebuilding the Temple.

But how many modern Israelis actually want the Temple to be rebuilt? While some have said the Jewish people are eager to see the Temple rebuilt, others downplay the preparatory activities taking place among Temple movement groups, saying that a rebuilt Temple is of only marginal concern to the Jewish people.

Who Wants a Temple?

Since the destruction of the Second Temple by the Romans in A.D. 70, Jewish people have prayed for its rebuilding. Such a precedent was set by the prophet Daniel while he was in Babylonian exile (Daniel 6:10). Today's Orthodox Jews, the denomination most desirous for a Third Temple, recite three times daily the words, "May it be Thy will that the Temple be speedily rebuilt in our own time." Even so, almost 2,000 years have passed, modern-day Israel is largely a secular state, and many understand this thrice-recited prayer as being metaphorical. Given this largely non-religious climate, what does the modern Israeli public think of the idea of rebuilding the Temple?

I put this question to Clarence Wagner, a 20-year resident of Jerusalem and International Director of Bridges for Peace and host of the television program "Jerusalem Mosaic":

> When I was teaching a course at Jerusalem University College, one of my students was very much interested in this subject. So I had him prepare a survey and go out into the streets of Jerusalem and just question all kinds of Israelis to find out what is the general view. He came up with some very interesting conclusions. Heretofore, I thought that many more Israelis and Jews would be in favor of rebuilding of a Temple, but what we actually found with the survey is that even between secular and religious they weren't that interested in necessarily seeing a physical building again. Here were the reasons that they gave. The secular Israeli said, "We've been going fine for 2,000 years without the Temple; why do we need it now, particularly if such a thing would cause a terrible explosion within the Muslim world? Where would you put it, how would you do it, and who needs it? We don't need it!" [This same thing was said by] the religious Jews because Rabbinical Judaism adapted itself to life without a Temple and found other ways of showing a sacrifice to God by fasting on *Yom Kippur,* and various other things. Since Rabbinical Judaism has found this accommodation, they also are not necessarily interested. But then there were some who reflectively thought, "It would be good to have this again, it would be good to have a central place and a central focus. Much of Judaism is very fragmented, just as much of Christianity is, so there needs to be a centralized focus that would draw people together and turn their attention towards God...." So we find what we have is a very broad spectrum and that there are only a very few who would really get the stones and go build it

tomorrow. Yet I don't believe that, in general, anybody would be against it if the possibility was there.[15]

In addition to this student survey, other more "official" studies on the question of rebuilding have been published. Back in 1989 at the beginning of the Temple movement, *Time* magazine reported that a 1983 newspaper poll had shown "that a surprising 18.3% of Israelis thought it was time to rebuild."[16] However, since that time Israel has suffered through the *Intifada*, the "peace process," and numerous riots provoked by the tensions over the Temple Mount. When I recently put the question to Ehud Olmert, the current mayor of Jerusalem, he replied that most people were not in favor, stating that such an act was associated with fanatics wanting to destroy the peace process. However, on February 11, 1996 The Temple Mount and Land of Israel Faithful Movement, an Israeli activist organization that publicly demonstrates in favor of rebuilding the Temple, commissioned a poll of Israelis of all age groups conducted by the international Gallup organization. The question asked was this: "The Temple Mount and Land of Israel Faithful Movement, headed by Gershon Salomon, put forth its main ideology on the struggle for Israeli sovereignty and the Jewish future of the Temple Mount, Jerusalem, and Land of Israel, and the rebuilding of the Temple. How likely would you be to support the idea of this movement?" The results, according to the Temple Mount Faithful, were the largest show of support any organization in Israel had ever received (58.5%). Of the polled group, the highest percentage came from young Israelis. Depending on the usual variables in statistical surveys, this indicates a substantial increase in the readiness of Israelis to see Jewish sovereignty reasserted over the Temple Mount and a new Temple erected.

One evidence of such an increase was the 1998 Annual Conference of the Movement for Rebuilding the Temple, which took place at Binyane Ha'uma (the International Convention Center) in Jerusalem. When the conference first began in 1990 only 65 attended, but this year 1,500 Jews of every sort (traditional, national-religious, haredi) each paid 65 New Israeli Shekels (about $22) to attend. The participants had no personal or vested interest and no commercial motivation. For their money they were treated to an evening of speeches, poetry reading, music, and film on the theme of the Temple. The growing attendance figures at this conference, as well as the growth of established Temple movement organizations and the proliferation of new ones, indicate that an increasing number of Jews are coming to support the efforts to rebuild the Temple. This conference also revealed a change in the public attitude of government officials toward the rebuilding of the Temple. While many such officials have been known to have privately sympathized with the goals of the Temple movement, this conference marked the first time that a government figure was willing to give his official endorsement and blessing to an event calling for the re-establishment of the Temple. Deputy Education Minister Moshe Peled of the Tsomet party, in a pre-recorded appearance, called for the "inculcation of the values of the Temple in the educational system and among the country's youth."[17] This, in part, indicates that a more favorable view of rebuilding is becoming apparent in some of the higher echelons of power.

Minority Rule in Israel

Regardless of how many people in Israel want a Temple rebuilt today, it has always been a religious minority, not the secular majority, that has made policy in the country. Despite a secular society comprising about 85% of the population and a secular government in control of the state, the religious parties represented in the Israeli Knesset (Parliament) have managed to force conformity to Jewish law since the founding of the state. Therefore, the traditional observance of the Sabbath as well as the national observance of the many biblical and extrabiblical festivals of Judaism are part of the fabric of modern Israeli society. As well, foreign restaurant chains and businesses that have come to Israel have made the painful discovery that most have to conform to Kosher laws and other restrictions to survive. Although secular Jews have long battled against some of the prohibitions connected with these observances (for example, no public transportation, open businesses, or movies on the Sabbath), they have, for the most part, been ineffective in instigating change. If anything, the religious minority has gained greater control in recent elections and has become more demanding and successful in enforcing existing laws. What's more, Israeli politicians have always courted the religious parties, knowing that their political futures depend on their support. Therefore, if this religious minority ever decided that a Temple should be rebuilt, and that it could be rebuilt without being a threat to national security, it would not matter what the rest of the Israeli population thought on the matter. Interestingly, the description of the Tribulation Temple in the New Testament exhibits the kind of situation that now exists. Matthew 24:15-16 reveals that the Sabbath is being observed (verse 16), and Revelation 11:1-2 seems to imply that only a portion of the Jewish community is represented at the Temple by the command to "measure those who worship in it" (verse 1).[18]

What Is Being Done Today?

At one time, most people around the world had no awareness at all of the efforts to rebuild the Temple. But today, everywhere I go, people ask me if the Israelis have already begun to rebuild the Temple. They find it hard to understand why this is not the case if in fact the Temple Mount has been under Israeli sovereignty for more than 30 years. Of course any Israeli government in power who had the will to do so could have asserted itself and removed the Islamic presence from the Temple Mount and rebuilt the Temple. However, the expected repercussions from the more than one billion Muslims worldwide and pressure from the international community, whose members have strategic investments in oil and military alliances with the Muslims, has outweighed Israel's will to rebuild. Thus many in the Temple movement believe the process of restoring Jewish sovereignty over the Temple Mount is going to take place gradually. As Yirimayhu Fischer, editor of *Mikdash-Build* journal, explains:

> Although the Temple Mount is still de facto under the Wakf's dominion (although officially under Israeli sovereignty), and Jews are prevented from praying there, preparations [to rebuild the Temple] are being made. The vessels are being prepared, *Kohanim* ["priests"] are studying how to offer sacrifices, and *Kohanim* children are about to be raised in purity, so that they may be fit to slaughter the red heifer....as more and more Jews ascend the Temple Mount in purity, the Temple Mount becomes de facto more Jewish [and] we hope its status will be changed little by little, so that we may be able to rebuild the *Beit HaMikdash* ["Temple"] there.[19]

In many of the chapters that follow I will reveal the details of these preparations as well as the activities the Temple movement is using to further move the Israeli populace, as well as the world, toward the goal of rebuilding. Even though many in the movement feel resigned to a lengthy process of redemption, the present political situation is moving rapidly toward a resolution of its own, which may bring unexpected changes and increase the likelihood that rebuilding will occur soon. It is because of the realization that a climatic day is dawning that many of the more activist elements in the Temple movement are speaking of a new imperative to rebuild.

The Imperative for Rebuilding

With the continuing tensions in the Israeli-Palestinian "peace process" and Israel being pressured by the Arab League, the European Union, and the United States to make concessions for Palestinian statehood (with its capital in Jerusalem), a new point of imperative has been reached that has led some groups in the Temple movement to make plans to use more forceful measures to achieve their ends. Where will such plans propel the current state of intense feeling? Some recent examples may predict the outcome. International newpapers published photographs of Yasser Arafat holding up an artist's depiction of a restored Temple on the Temple Mount and telling his people to "get ready for the next battle [for Jerusalem]." When Israel's Supreme Court decided that Jews were legally permitted to pray on the Temple Mount, the Islamic sheikh of the Al-Aqsa Mosque said, "We refuse to obey the decisions of this racist court. The rabbis will not enter Al-Aqsa, not [unless] over our dead bodies and shrouds." While no one can know when such a conflict will come or if it will move the Jews closer or further from the realization of their goal of rebuilding, its seeming imminence in the present political crisis should lead us to understand the future plans God has for the Temple. To this end Elwood McQuaid, Executive Director of the Friends of Israel, encourages our study of this subject when he says:

> I believe that the preparations for the rebuilding of the Temple today are extremely significant because first of all it demonstrates what is in the hearts and minds at least of a segment of the Jewish nation; that there is a significant portion of the conservative-thinking Jewish people who believe that a Temple should be on Mount Moriah. It also demonstrates the prophetic aspect of the Word of God that tells us there will be a Temple built on Mount Moriah in the last days, during the Tribulation period. I think we're seeing the preparation for that. I think we're seeing a time when in the hearts of people they're saying the time has come. And it also reflects the desire, I believe, for the coming of the Messiah. So for those reasons, and many more, I believe we're seeing something that is historic and something certainly significant.[20]

In order to understand the coming Last Days Temple, it is necessary to understand what the Temple was originally intended to be—a purpose it scarcely achieved in past history—and how it will eventually fulfill this purpose on earth in the future. To gain this understanding, let us explore the meaning of the Temple and its divine design for the Nation of Israel and ultimately, the world.

CHAPTER 2

The Purpose
of the Temple

Recognizing the Reasons
for Restoration

The Holy Temple was not just some magnificent building or synagogue rooted in Jerusalem's ancient Biblical past; it was an arena of cosmic themes; a place where man could meet with his Creator . . . It is the reality of the living memory of that relationship as it once was, and the dream of its renewal—as promised by G-d Himself— that keeps the fires of the Temple altar burning within the collective heart of the nation of Israel, and the hearts of all those who cherish Israel's G-d and His message for humanity.[1]

—RABBI CHAIM RICHMAN

For many Jews the Temple is a relic of ancient history, a shameful reminder of a primitive period when bloody sacrifices paved the way to a bloodthirsty God who punished them with epidemics and exile if they did not obey. To them, a more evolved, more enlightened society would never consider abandoning a promising future to return to such a problematic past. For some Christians the Temple is nothing more than an object lesson of sin—a shadow whose preparatory purpose has long since been eclipsed by a greater spiritual substance. Any thought of reviving this structure, or worse—the sacrifical system—is in the category of Judaizing apostasy. For Muslims, the Temple, if it ever existed except as Israeli propaganda, was part of an old order, long since corrupted and replaced by Islam for the last 1,300 years. To hear Jews or Christians speaking about rebuilding the Temple is the greatest affront to Allah, since it would necessitate abdicating sovereignty over Muslim property and mosques sacred to his name.

If such disparaging thoughts are voiced by members of the three world religions whose history touches the Temple Mount, and even lays claim there, why should the rebuilding of a future Temple even be considered? It's important to recognize that much of the dispute over the propriety of a future Temple results from an inadequate understanding of the Temple's purpose in the plan of God. If God has a future for the Nation of Israel in His plan, and that plan is to be realized in the same place as it was in the past, then the Temple whose destruction served as a prominent symbol of that nation's past failure should be expected to return as a part of its future restoration. As we will see in chapters 9–14, the biblical prophets reveal that the greater purpose of the Temple is yet unfulfilled, for it will function in the future as "a house of prayer for all the peoples" (Isaiah 56:7). The coming Last Days Temple will enlarge upon all of God's purposes for the Temple through time. Therefore, all of us have a vested interest in the purpose of the Temple in the fulfillment of God's plan for human history. In order to understand God's purpose for the Temple as it was and will be revealed in history, let us first consider the meaning of the word *temple* and its usage in both the Old and New Testaments.

The Meaning of a Temple

In defining the concept of a temple, the languages of the Bible employ various terms. The general Hebrew term for *temple,* although rarely used in the Bible, is the word *hekal.*[2] This term probably derived from an original Sumerian word (*e-gal*) meaning "big house."[3] From another Sumerian term, *temen,*[4] comes the Old Greek term *temenos* ("precinct"), which denotes "a piece of land marked off from common uses and dedicated to a god."[5] These terms define a special place of theophany where a deity appeared as revealer, healer, or giver of fertility, but *did not dwell there*. Thus, the term may be generally used with reference to any ancient Near Eastern center of worship, whether pagan or Israelite. In this sense it could be rendered in English as "shrine," and today has this meaning in modern Hebrew, as in *Hekal Ha-Sefer* ("the Shrine of the Book"), the name of Israel's museum of the Dead Sea Scrolls.

The Bible, however, preferred to describe the Jerusalem Temple as *Beit 'Adonai* (the "house of the Lord"), or *Beit 'Elohim* (the "house of God").[6] This expression better denotes the basic idea of the Temple as "a place where God dwells," a connotation expressed by the earliest Hebrew term for God's abode, *Mishkan* ("Tabernacle," literally, "dwelling").[7] Another biblical Hebrew term for the Temple (and the one used today in modern Hebrew)[8] is *Beit Hamikdash* ("the Sanctuary"—literally "house of holiness," but usually translated as "sanctuary") or simply *Mikdash* ("Holy [Place]," "Sanctuary").[9] This latter term appears in the Old Testament primarily with reference to the only legitimate Israelite Temple in Jerusalem (Isaiah 63:18; Ezekiel 5:11; 9:6; Psalm 74:7; 96:6; Lamentations 1:10; 2:7,20). In this regard it may denote either the entire Tabernacle compound (Leviticus 19:30; 26:2), the entire district of the Temple (Ezekiel 43:21; 44:1 5,7-8), or exclusively the Holy of Holies (Leviticus 16:33). However, it could also be used of rival Israelite temples both inside and outside the Land (Amos 7:9,13; Isaiah 16:12).

The Septuagint (the Greek version of the Old Testament) follows the Hebrew Bible in its understanding of *Beit Hamikdash* ("Sanctuary") by its selective use of the term *naos*, a noun derived from the verb *naio* ("to dwell" or "inhabit"). In classical Greek *naos* referred to the "abode of the gods," with specific reference to the innermost part of a shrine which contained the image of a god.[10] The Septuagint uses this term 55 out of 61 times to translate the Hebrew *hekal*, the nonspecific sense of a "palace" or "a temple." If the Septuagint had wished to indicate "a temple" in general, it might have used the Greek term *heiron* ("holy place").[11] As a result of this usage by the Greek Old Testament, the term takes on a technical significance referring exclusively to the "Temple of God" in Jerusalem.[12] This usage was adopted by the Greek New Testament[13] and often denotes the inner part of the Temple (the Holy of Holies) in distinction to the outer part of the Temple (the Temple complex) by the more common Greek word *heiron*, the term for a sacred edifice. An example of this in the New Testament can be seen in *naos* being used as a metaphor for the church or the believer's body as "a temple." In these two cases the term is used because the emphasis in the text is on the indwelling presence of God (within the Holy of Holies), which corresponds to the indwelling Holy Spirit. Further, in the book of Revelation, *naos* is used of both the earthly and heavenly Temples, where in the latter reference, the Holy of Holies is usually indicated by God's presence or the mention of incense or the Ark of the Covenant (Revelation 11:19; 15:8; 21:22).[14]

Our English Bibles do not adequately reflect the distinctions that are apparent in the original biblical languages. They translate the primary Hebrew and Greek terms by using the word "temple," which is itself derived from the Latin *templum*, after the Greek *temenos*. While in most cases the English translation "temple" refers to the Jerusalem Temple, I prefer to capitalize this reference to distinguish it from references to rival Jewish and non-Jewish temples.[15] This capitalization will also be used with reference to the Heavenly Temple, the Tabernacle (which as a portable structure was later incorporated into the Temple), and the Sanctuary (as a general synonym). Therefore, what I have in mind in this use of *Temple* is the permanent aspect of God's dwelling with His people, which includes all intermediate and future forms.

The Plan for the Temple

God's plan for the Temple was first revealed at the foot of Mount Sinai. Concerning this historical event and its connection with the Temple Rabbi Shmuel Bar Abba explained in the Jewish Midrash: "The Holy One, Blessed be He, desired to have an abode below, just as He has one above ... and when Israel stood before Him at Sinai, He told them: 'There is only one reason I delivered you out of Egypt—in order for you to erect for Me a Tabernacle so that My presence will dwell amongst you'" (*Tanhuma Bechukoti* 65). The biblical text behind this statement is Exodus 25:8: "Let them construct a sanctuary for Me that I may dwell among them." According to the Jewish Sage Rambam, "This commandment is to build the Temple and all its vessels" (*Hilchot Beit HaBechirah*, chapter 1). Although the Tabernacle was the initial fulfillment of this plan, in time it was superseded by the more permanent structure of the Temple (see chapter 4).

The full emotional impact of God's plan to manifest Himself in the midst of His people can be felt only when we observe the context. Just a few chapters earlier in Exodus (19:16-24), the Lord had majestically descended upon Mt. Sinai.

His descent had been accompanied by smoke, fire, thunder, and lightning, trumpet sounds, and earthquakes. The holy mountain had been cordoned off to prevent people from coming near and being consumed by God's holy presence. Moses later wrote of this event: "... the mountain burned with fire to the very heart of the heavens: darkness, cloud, and thick gloom" (Deuteronomy 4:11; see also Exodus 19:9,18; 20:18). Terrified by this awesome display of theophany, the Israelites begged Moses to keep God from even speaking to them lest they die (Exodus 20:19). Instead, Moses announced to the people the words of our text (Exodus 25:8). In effect Moses was saying to them, "God wants to move from the mountain into *your* camp!" Can you imagine their feelings? This God who destroyed the land of Egypt by plagues, drowned the mighty Egyptian army in the Red Sea, and appeared as a mountain-consuming fire warning them not to even approach His presence, He was coming down right into their midst!

The fear the Israelites felt came from an innate consciousness that God and man could not co-exist. Although God had once walked with man in the Garden of Eden, the change that had taken place in man's constitution now distanced a holy God from an unholy humanity. Because of the Fall, man could no longer go to God. But God had a way He could return to man. God's way required that a safeguard be set up in the form of a structure that would keep Israel from being consumed. Perhaps the people did not immediately comprehend the moment, but this command "to build a sanctuary for Me" represented a pivotal point in Israel's history to that time. Here God was returning to them at Sinai what had been lost in Eden—a personal relationship manifested by His presence. The long exile from God's ideal was now to be ended, and the Sanctuary was the means of restoration. With God's plan for the Temple understood, we may now consider the purpose for the Temple in God's plan.

The Purpose for the Temple

When King David charged the people of Israel concerning the preparations for the First Temple, he declared, " ... the work is great; for the Temple is not for man, but for the Lord God" (1 Chronicles 29:1). This statement reflects the Israelite distinction that while the Temple would certainly be a place where the needs of man were met, it was first and foremost a witness to the fact of God's existence, His covenant with Israel, and His purpose through the Nation of Israel as a kingdom of priests to manifest God's glory to the world. In order to fulfill this holy mandate, the Jewish people had to fulfill the terms of the covenant given to them (see 1 Kings 2:3). The commandments contained in this covenant have been numbered at 613. In order to accomplish these in their entirety the Temple and its service was required. Because at least one-third of these commandments depends upon a functioning Temple for their completion, one purpose of the Temple was to enable Israel to function as a kingdom of priests. In like manner, the prophecies of Israel's restoration, at which time it will fulfill its purpose to bless the world, depends on the existence of the Temple. This is particularly true for Messianic prophecies that describe the Messiah as building the Temple (Zechariah 6:12-13) and coming to His Temple (Malachi 3:1). Others, such as Rabbi Chaim Richman, explain that the Temple's purpose is part of God's grand design for human creation. He states:

> The key to understanding the Holy Temple's functioning in all its detail
> is a concept which takes in an entire world-view.... The Temple is a
> microcosm; a cosmic blueprint.... Within the Holy Temple, all forces
> unite to acknowledge Him who brought them all into being as the only
> reality, the Supreme Force which drives the universe.

While many purposes of the Temple could be explored in light of Rabbi Richman's observation, and although Kabbalistic Judaism has its own unique interpretation of the Temple's purpose, let us examine eight purposes that are set forth in Scripture.

A Station of the Divine Presence

While the concept of God dwelling in the midst of His people may have been symbolized in Eden, the first historical promise of the Temple occurs in the "Song of Moses," recorded in Exodus 15:17. There we read, "Thou wilt bring them and plant them in the mountain of Thine inheritance, the place, O LORD, which Thou hast made for Thy dwelling, the sanctuary, O Lord, which Thy hands have established." In time the Temple in Jerusalem became the only place on earth where God's presence was manifested among His people.[16] The theological statement in Solomon's dedicatory prayer of 1 Kings 8:27 that God could not be contained on earth by any structure meant that God Himself could not be localized on earth. The Temple rather stood as the visible station of His invisible, though manifest, presence. For this reason the divine presence was expressed by a circumlocution that He had caused His *name* to dwell there (cf. Jeremiah 7:12; Deuteronomy 12:11; 2 Chronicles 7:16; Ezra 6:12; Nehemiah 1:9). Thus, while God Himself did not even temporarily dwell in the Temple, it was a fixed place where

God in His transcendence and incomparability was accessible to man. The Jewish sages called this divine manifestation the *Shekinah* (from the Hebrew verb *shakan*, "to dwell"), explaining that this concentration of the divine presence in a given place did not imply divine reduction, for "the more limited the space, the greater is His might."[17] Jesus acknowledged this aspect of the Temple's purpose when He affirmed this concerning oaths: "He who swears by the temple, swears both by the temple and by Him who dwells within it" (Matthew 23:21). Eschatologically, the final portrait painted of the millennial Jerusalem in the book of Ezekiel underscores this reality: "The name of the city from that day shall be *'Adonai Shammah* ("The LORD is there," Ezekiel 48:35).

A Sign of the Covenant

The Tabernacle and the Temple functioned as witnesses to God's covenants with Israel. The presence of God in the Temple presupposed a covenant relationship, based on the Hittite model of the legal arrangement between a sovereign ruler and subject people, which was known as the suzerain-vassal treaty. In this relationship God, as the suzerain, would conditionally protect and prosper Israel as His vassals. The Temple was an evident witness to the Mosaic Covenant, for it had been built to house the Ark, which served as a repository of the tablets of the law (Exodus 25:9 with 2 Samuel 7:2,5). Its placement on "the Mount of the Lord" in Jerusalem (the Land of Moriah) was confirmation of the Abrahamic Covenant and God's promise to make spiritual provision there (Genesis 22:14). It was also confirmation of the Davidic Covenant and the promise of a son (Solomon) who would build God's house and whose house God would build until the Messianic Son would establish His throne there forever (1 Chronicles 17:14). The religious impact of the Temple was directly related to it being understood as a sign of covenantal security.[18] This is seen in the denunciations against covenant-breaking made in the prophetic literature.[19] For example, in Jeremiah 7:7-15 the prophet begins by referring to the people's trust in the promise of the Abrahamic and Mosaic Covenants that Israel would dwell in the Land forever (verse 7) as a false security, because the promise was conditional, resting upon covenant obedience (verse 8). Each destruction of the Temple proved this point, for the destructions were prophesied as retributive judgments for violating the covenants.

In the prophetic context of the Last Days the Temple will again serve as the place to which the world will come to learn God's law as the basis of millennial government:

The mountain of the house of the LORD [the Millennial Temple erected on the Temple Mount] will be established as the chief of the mountains … and all the nations will stream to it… many peoples will come and say, "Come let us go up to the mountain of the LORD [the Temple Mount], to the house of the God of Jacob [the Temple]; that He may teach us concerning His ways, and that we may walk in His paths." For the law will go forth from Zion, and the word of the LORD from Jerusalem (Isaiah 2:2-3).

In this future age the Temple will serve as a sign of the New Covenant and Israel will be protected and prosper under its terms (Isaiah 59:20-21; Jeremiah 31:27-40; 32:37-40; Ezekiel 16:60-63; 37:21-28), but this time without threat of possible violating the covenant because the people will all have new hearts and new spirits that will cause them to obey the Lord (Ezekiel 36:26-27).

A Signal of the End of Exile

Israel's experience of Exile and Diaspora, whether in Egypt, Assyria, or Babylon, ended only when she was able to establish or restore her center of worship. The motif of national rest in relationship to entrance to the Land and the establishment of a central sanctuary is presented in Deuteronomy 12:9-11:

You have not yet come to *the resting place* and to the inheritance which the LORD your God is giving you. When you cross the Jordan and live in the land which the LORD your God is giving you to inherit, and He *gives you rest* from all your enemies around you so that you live in security, then it shall come about that *the place* in which the LORD your God shall choose for His name to dwell, there you shall bring all that I command you: your burnt offerings and your sacrifices, your tithes and the contribution of your hand, and all your choice votive offerings which you vow unto the LORD (emphasis added).

In verse 9 the *promise* of "rest" is found with the definite article (indicating a specific rest ("the rest"), and is paired with "the inheritance" as a gift from the Lord.[20] With verse 10, the *time* of "rest" is connected with settlement in the Land, and in verse 11 the *place* of rest is connected with building of the Temple. This relationship to the Temple is confirmed in Solomon's dedicatory prayer[21]: "Blessed be the LORD who has given *rest* to His people Israel, according to all that He promised; not one word has failed of all His good promise, which He promised through Moses His servant" (1 Kings 8:56). These words join the building of the Temple with the fulfillment of the "rest" envisioned by Moses for the Nation in Deuteronomy 12:9.[22]

The prophets announced an *eschatological* rest, which was expected because the exile had interrupted the promise of a permanent rest within the Land, and the destruction of the Temple had removed the symbol of that rest connected with the presence of the Lord, the giver of rest.[23] Isaiah anticipated a future "rest" for Israel after her last exile (Isaiah 11:10; 14:3-4,7; 28:12; 32:17), and associated the longing for it (in remembrance of the former "rest") with a spiritual purification that will bring eschatological restoration and rest (Isaiah 63:11-14). This rest will be maintained, according to Ezekiel, through the restoration of the Temple and its priestly service—literally "to rest in blessing" (see Ezekiel 44:30). Just as the destruction of the Temple caused a loss of rest, so will its rebuilding restore that rest.

A Socio-Political Institution

The Temple was not only prominent as a religious institution to the Jewish people, but (especially in Second Temple times) also played a significant role in the political life of the people. In addition, the Temple was extremely important to Jewish national unity, and Jews in the Diaspora fought for the right to send their contributions to Jerusalem, despite many attempts to deny them that right. In fact, all other institutions, even those unrelated to the Temple service, gained moral stature from their association with the Temple.[24]

The Temple, then, governed the daily life of the Jew, since this life was lived in view of the festivals, the pilgrimages, the sacrificial rites, and the reading and study of the Torah—all of which centered on the Temple. Though later, and especially after A.D. 70, the synagogue, which probably began in the Temple Court, took precedence, it was with the Temple that this institution (and all others) were organically connected. The Temple was the channel by which the religious institutions of Israel became a part of the people's lives. Stipulated hours of prayer were set according to the times of the sacrifices, and even those in the Diaspora were to turn their faces toward Jerusalem and the Temple. All legal matters were decided by the Sanhedrin, who had their full prerogatives of office only when seated in the Temple, and only when the sacrificial system was operational.[25]

This general introduction to the significance of the Temple to Jewish life will be augmented and expanded in the later chapters of this book; for now, it is sufficient to emphasize the importance of the institution—an importance that will now be seen in the religious, historical, and cultural continuity that was imbued in the concept of the Temple.

A Symbol of National Sovereignty

The Temple was also a symbol of Israel's national sovereignty. This was apparent when enemies who had her under hegemony and considered her guilty of political disloyalty demonstrated their (and their gods') sovereignty by ending Israel's independence through the destruction of the Temple. This was also seen by the Israelites' desire to rebuild the Temple and their enemies' desire to thwart rebuilding (such as in Ezra 4), and the Romans' exercise of control over the Jewish Nation through political appointments to the office of high priest.[26] The Temple was also essential to establishing and preserving national unity. The Davidic-Solomonic state united for the first time the political and spiritual centers in one capital through the construction of the Temple. This act not only unified the tribal groups inhabiting the highlands from Upper Galilee to the Northern Negev, but also extended the Nation's domain to the surrounding regions of Syria and Transjordan. Thus, the Temple brought a unique measure of stability to the Israelites throughout the Levant. The return from exile, considered a disunifying experience, was completed in a true sense only when the Temple was rebuilt. It stood as the unifying institution for the Nation as well as the national rallying point in times of distress.

Even though today political independence has been achieved through the Zionist movement and military might, spiritual independence has not yet been realized, since Jews are forbidden access to the Temple Mount for prayer or religious activity of any kind by the Muslim Wakf, which has control of the site. Those in the present Temple movement contend that the lack of unity among Jews today (the schism between secular and religious as well as among the religious factions) is a result of the Temple's absence. It is believed by some that once the Temple returns, its presence will not only unite world Jewry, but also all the peoples of the earth.

The Millennial Temple will return not only as a symbol of national sovereignty (under the Messiah), but to fulfill this need for unity. In Ezekiel 48:1-35, this unity is attained through the Land of Israel being allotted among the tribes of Israel, with the Temple as the central reference point. Unity will also be encouraged by the Temple's river of life, which will flow to and refresh all the Land (Ezekiel 47:1-12), as well as the annual visits by the nations who assemble in Jerusalem for the Feast of Booths (Zechariah 14:16).

It Secured National Blessings

When the foundations for the Second Temple were laid during the Persian period, the prophet Haggai announced, "Consider from this day onward: before one stone was placed on another in the temple of the LORD. ... Is the seed still in the barn? Even including the vine, the fig tree, the pomegranate, and the olive tree, it has not borne fruit. Yet from this day on I will bless you" (Haggai 2:15,19). This connection between the Temple and national blessing is well defined in the dedicatory prayer of Solomon (1 Kings 8). The prayer reveals a cause-effect relationship between the Temple and the bestowal of rain, relief from famine, military security, and help in foreign distress (verses 35-49, cf. 2 Chronicles 6:24-30). In the parallel account in 2 Chronicles 7:12-14, a passage often misapplied to our own American nation, fidelity toward God through the Temple is the immediate cause of national prosperity or its lack. So in the familiar words of verse 14 we read, "[If] My people who are called by My name humble themselves *and pray [toward the Temple]*, and seek My face and turn from their wicked ways, then I will hear from heaven [i.e., the Heavenly Temple], will forgive their sin, and *will heal their land*" (emphasis added). Non-Israelite temples were places where man, through the service of the cultus, attempted to meet the needs of the gods. By contrast, through the Jerusalem Temple, God was able to meet the needs of man. Because the Lord is at the center of the Nation at the Temple, those who look toward the Temple via prayer will find protection (individually), as will the Nation (corporately).

In the millennial kingdom the future blessings of restoration include not only the renewal of the Land as a result of the river flowing from under the altar of the Temple (Ezekiel 47:1-12; Zechariah 14:8), but also agricultural blessings connected with the divine bestowal of rain (Zechariah 14:16-17). This rain, so vital to an agrarian society, will be provided based on Israelite and non-Israelite faithfulness to worship at the Temple at the appointed feasts. Thus, the national blessings secured by the future Temple will be extended internationally to all of the inhabitants of the kingdom, fulfilling the mandate of the Abrahamic Covenant that all of the families of the earth would be blessed through Israel (Genesis 12:3).

A Source of Worldwide Blessing

In his dedicatory prayer, Solomon indicated that the Temple was to be a source of universal appeal and blessing. In 1 Kings 8:41-43 we read:

Concerning the foreigner who is not of Thy people Israel, when he comes from a far country for Thy name's sake (for they will hear of Thy great name and Thy mighty hand, and Thy outstretched arm); when he comes and prays toward this house, hear Thou in heaven Thy dwelling place, and do according to all for which the foreigner calls to Thee, in order that all the peoples of the earth may know Thy name, to fear Thee, as do Thy people Israel, and that they may know that this house which I have built is called by Thy name.

While this potential existed during the First and Second Temple periods, the covenantal failure of Israel left this promise unfulfilled.

The prophets depicted the Millennial Temple as the fulfillment of international blessing. In such texts as Isaiah 2:2-4; 11:1-11 (cf. 65:25) and chapters 60–66, Zechariah 8:23; 14:16; and Micah 4:1-5, the Temple is envisioned as the center of world renewal, drawing all nations and peoples to the covenant people and to Temple worship.[27] In Isaiah 56:6-7 the prophet declared that the Temple would serve as a sacrificial center and a "house of prayer for all the peoples." Jesus Himself employed this verse with reference to the money-changers in the Temple, understanding their activities as a sign of how far that Temple was from the fulfillment of this great purpose.

It Served as the Focal Point of Prayer

Since Israel's God was the true God—the God of the covenant—and only He could answer prayer, those who wanted their prayers answered had to come to the Temple (or pray toward the Temple). The Mishnah, based on 1 Kings 8:48-49 and Daniel 6:11, stated that prayer should be made by directing the heart towards the Holy of Holies. The last Tannaitic sages had a difference of opinion concerning the interpretation of these Mishnaic instructions concerning the Holy of Holies: "To which Holy of Holies? R. Hiyya Rabba said: 'Towards the heavenly Holy of Holies'; R. Simeon b. Halafta said: 'Towards the earthly Holy of Holies.'"[28] This divergence was reconciled by the Amora R. Phinehas bar Hama, who said, "They do not disagree: the earthly Holy of Holies faces the heavenly Holy of Holies."[29] Thus, according to the Jewish sages, in orienting oneself towards the earthly Holy of Holies, one orients himself at the same time to the Holy of Holies in the Heavenly Temple.

This understanding of the orientation of the heavenly and earthly sanctuaries became especially important after the destruction of the Temple in A.D. 70. During Temple times, the only earthly access for both Jew and non-Jew to the divine presence was through association with the Temple. Without the regular Temple service, there was no direct link between the people and their God, and no longer any possibility of atoning for sins, as one of the sages observed after the destruction of the Second Temple: "Since the day that the Temple was destroyed, an iron wall has intervened between Israel and their Father in heaven" (*Berakhot* 32b; cf. Isaiah 59:2). In like manner, Simeon the Just underscored the pivotal position of the Temple in Jewish life: "The world is based upon three things: the Torah, *Avodah* [the Temple service] and the practice of *gemilut hasadim* ["charity"]" (*Pirke Avot* 1.2). Given this perspective, the destruction of the Temple undermined one of the pillars of the Jewish universe—Temple service—and caused a complete imbalance in the life of the religious Jew, whose very existence was determined by its order.

This explains why the rabbinic concept concerning the orientation of the earthly Temple facing the Heavenly Temple was formulated. If prayer depended upon orienting oneself towards the *Shekinah*, whose presence was within the Holy of Holies, then even after the destruction of the Jerusalem Temple prayer could be continued (especially the Eighteen Benedictions) in the direction of the desolated Sanctuary.[30] Later, however, an argument based on Song of Solomon 2:9, "Behold, he is standing behind our wall," stated that the *Shekinah* never left the Temple Mount, and remained at the Kotel (Western Wall), which for them was a remnant of the Sanctuary site.[31]

While prayer is not specifically mentioned in those texts which describe the Millennial Temple, prayer is nevertheless a part of the worship that is indicated to take place there. In Zechariah 14:16 the command for "all the families of the earth" to ascend to the Temple Mount to "worship the King, the LORD of hosts" certainly parallels the previous function of the Temple as the place to which all earthly prayer was to be directed (1 Kings 8:29,41-43). This correspondence is made certain in the fact that just as the blessing of rain once depended on this orientation to the Lord (1 Kings 8:35), so will it do so again in the future (Zechariah 14:17-19).

A Purpose that Must Be Performed

Six million Jewish people have ended their physical exile and returned to the Land of Israel, and one day all of the Jewish people will be regathered and end their spiritual exile (Isaiah 27:12-13; 59:20-21; Ezekiel 36:24-28; Matthew 24:31; Romans 11:25-26). The Messiah will come and the divine presence will return

(Zechariah 14:4; Ezekiel 37:1-4; Matthew 24:27; Luke 21:27). Then Israel will be established as a political and religious entity in her Land under the New Covenant (Jeremiah 31). All of these future events are in accord with the Temple's past purposes, and therefore it is evident that the Temple must also return to serve these future purposes. The Temple must be restored to maintain Israel's national blessings, extend them to the nations of the world, and become the focal point of prayer for the peoples when the Lord again dwells in their midst (Isaiah 2:4; 56:5-9; 66:18-20; Matthew 25:31-32). However, to fully explain the purpose of the Temple in God's plan, we must go back to a time before the command at Sinai to build a Sanctuary—and even before time itself. In the next chapter we will look away from earth and up to heaven, where there exists the Temple that gave its plan and purpose to Israel's earthly Temples.

CHAPTER 3

The Temple Before Time

The Heavenly Pattern
for the Earthly Temple

[Jewish] literature avers that in heaven there is a Temple that is the counterpart of the Temple on earth. The same sacrifices are said to be offered there and the same hymns sung as in the earthly Temple. Just as the Temple below is located in terrestrial Jerusalem so the Temple above is located in celestial Jerusalem.[1]

—VICTOR APTOWITZER

One of the most famous of Christian prayers is known as "The Lord's Prayer."[2] In the opening of the prayer we find these words: "Our Father who art in heaven, hallowed be Thy name. Thy kingdom come. Thy will be done, on earth as it is in heaven" (Matthew 6:9-10). These words, part of a model prayer that Jesus taught His disciples, center on God's great prophetic plan to one day conform earth to heaven. God in heaven is holy, and holiness is His goal for both humanity and the world in which we live. Ultimately, the coming creation of a new heaven and a new earth will fulfill this divine ideal (Isaiah 65:17; 66:22; 2 Peter 3:10-13; Revelation 21:1), but in history it is the Temple that God ordained as the place for His heavenly presence on earth. That brings us to ask: Why did God choose the Temple as the means for manifesting His will on earth as in heaven? Having seen God's earthly purpose for the Temple *in* time, let us consider the answer to this question through an exploration of the Temple *before* time.

The Heavenly Temple in the Old Testament

The Heavenly Temple as the holy dwelling place of God appears in both the Old and the New Testaments as well as in discussions in the Apocrypha, Pseudepigrapha, and Jewish writings such as the Talmud and Midrash. In the Old Testament many passages reveal that God's proper place is in the heavens (1 Kings 8:39; Psalm 115:3).[3] The psalmist explicity refers to the Heavenly Temple when he declares: "The LORD is in His holy temple; the LORD's throne is in heaven" (Psalm 11:4). Because David's psalms predated the building of the First Temple, his references to "Temple" and "the house of the Lord" are difficult to interpret. For example, when David says, "I will bow down toward Thy holy temple" (Psalm 138:2), we might assume that he means the Tabernacle, but such an interpretation is complicated by Psalm 27, where he mentions both meditating "in His temple," being hidden from trouble "in His tabernacle," and offering sacrifices "in His tent" (verses 4-6). All of these references may refer to the earthly Sanctuary; however, in this same text David declares, "One thing have I asked from the LORD, that I shall seek: That I may dwell in the house of the LORD all the days of my life, to behold the beauty of the LORD" (verse 4). The word translated "behold" literally means "to have a fixed gaze." Since David was not a Levite and had no access to the place in the Sanctuary where God's presence was manifest, he is either speaking metaphorically, or his focus is the Heavenly Temple.

The same question is present in the closing words of David's famous twenty-third Psalm: "I will dwell in the house of the LORD forever [literally "for length of days"]" (verse 6), which corresponds to the previous text (compare Psalm 27:4). In other psalms the Heavenly Temple is clearly in view as God is seen in "His holy Temple" or on "His holy mountain" (Psalm 3:4), from which He looks down to test men (Psalm 11:5) and hears their cries of distress or praise (Psalm 18:6; 102:18-19; 1 Kings 8:30). The Temple depicted in Ezekiel 40–48 has also been proposed as a description of the Heavenly Temple (or the church) by Christian commentators who deny a literal interpretation of this text. However, a number of factors make this connection implausible (see chapter 23 of this book).

The earliest mention of the Temple in the Bible is in Exodus 15:17, where Moses, in his praise to God for the miracle at the Red Sea, declares, "You will bring them [the people of Israel] in and plant them on the mountain of your inheritance—the place, O LORD, you made for your dwelling, the sanctuary, O LORD, your hands established." While this is best interpreted with reference to the building of the First Temple by Solomon in Jerusalem, some rabbinical sages also saw in it an allusion to the Heavenly Temple. For example, Rabbi Pinchas said, "The Holy of Holies below (on the Temple Mount) is positioned parallel to the Holy of Holies above (in heaven), as the Torah states, *Machon leshivtecha* ["the place for Your dwelling"] is interpreted as *mechuvan leshivtecha* ["the position parallel to Your sitting"]" (Jerusalem Talmud, *Brachot* 4:5). Based on this interpretation, the traditional Jewish view of the Heavenly Temple has been that it is aligned in sync with the earthly Temple so that God's presence can be in both the heavenly and earthly Holy of Holies simultaneously. Therefore, even with the earthly Temple's removal, the site remains sanctified by this terrestrial-celestial position.

In the Old Testament, Moses, Aaron and his sons, and 70 of the elders of Israel were permitted a view into the Heavenly Temple. In Exodus 24:10 we read the remarkable words, "[They] saw the God of Israel; and under His feet there appeared to be a pavement of sapphire, as clear as the sky itself." From this description God's presence (rather than His person) is seen, with the emphasis being on the details of the pavement beneath the throne. Such privileged peeks into the heavenly realm were also granted several of the prophets by similar theophanic ("appearances of God") experiences or through visions of God's presence. During the reign of the Israelite king Ahab, a prophet named Micaiah was permitted to see the Heavenly Temple (1 Kings 22:19), as was the prophet Isaiah after entering the earthly Temple to seek the Lord upon the death of the Judean king Uzziah (Isaiah 6:1-5). The prophet Ezekiel, while in residence by the river Chebar in Babylon during the time of his captivity with the Judean exiles, likewise saw a vision of the Lord enthroned in the Heavenly Temple (Ezekiel 1:1-28).[4] From these references we can understand that the Heavenly Temple is the place where God dwells, where His counsel may be sought, and from which His revelation goes forth.

The Heavenly Temple in the New Testament

In the New Testament we find a clear distinction and contrast made between the "earthly sanctuary" and a "greater and more perfect tabernacle, not made with hands, that is to say, not of this creation" (Hebrews 9:1,11). This place is located in "heaven itself...in the presence of God" (verse 24). It is the place where holy, heavenly vessels are found and where Christ officiates as High Priest (verses 21-25). In the book of Revelation the Heavenly Temple appears frequently as the place where John receives revelation about the future. In these texts it is clearly defined as the Temple that is in heaven (Revelation 7:15; 14:17; 15:5; 16:17). When the apostle John was transported to this Heavenly Temple in a vision (Revelation 4:1), he beheld a scene similar to that previously described by Isaiah and Ezekiel (verses 2-3). Thereafter, throughout the rest of the book, the scene shifts back and forth between the terrestrial (often Jerusalem) and the celestial (the Heavenly Temple).

From the various scenes in the Heavenly Temple it is revealed that it contains the same ascending degrees of sanctity as the earthly Temple (Revelation 4:1-10), and the same essential furniture and sacred vessels. In Revelation we find that these include the sacrificial altar (Revelation 6:9; 8:3,5; 9:13; 14:18; 16:7), God's throne (Revelation 16:17), the *menorot* or seven-branched lampstands (Revelation 1:12), trumpets (Revelation 8:2,6), the incense altar (Revelation 5:8; 8:3-4), the golden censer (Revelation 8:3-5), incense bowls (Revelation 5:8), priestly vestments (Revelation 4:4; 6:11; 15:6), and the heavenly Ark of the Covenant (Revelation 11:19). In addition, we could add the veil, which separated the Holy Place from the Holy of Holies—as implied in those texts that depict an "opening" to the innermost room of the Heavenly Temple, through which angelic beings or John himself passes immediately into the divine presence (Revelation 4:1-3; 6:14-17; 15:5; 16:1,17).[5] Furthermore, the Heavenly Temple is the place where the saints will serve God. In Revelation 7:15 we read, " ... they are before the throne of God; and they serve Him day and night in His temple; and He who sits on the throne shall spread His tabernacle over them." We will deal in greater detail with this passage in chapter 14, but here we can see that the throne of God, at whose center is the Lamb of God (Revelation 7:17), is at the heart of the Heavenly Temple—and that heavenly priestly service (note the white robes of verse 14) will be the constant occupation of the redeemed. These similarities prepare us for the function of the Heavenly Temple as the pattern for its counterpart on earth.

The Heavenly Temple Between the Testaments

More than 400 years passed between the close of the Old Testament canon and the writing of the New Testament. During that time, Jewish interpreters in the context of political and religious upheaval sought to explain certain issues raised in the prophetic sections of the Old Testament. The apocalyptic literature that resulted shows us how Jewish interpretation of the Old Testament prophetic material developed, preparing us for the eschatological debates and statements of New Testament times. The subject of the Temple was of special concern in apocalyptic literature,[6] motivated in part because the Second Temple had not fulfilled the grand design of the prophets. As the writers considered the contrasts between the Temple that existed in their day and the divine ideal of the prophets, their focus frequently was drawn to the original model for all earthly Temples, the Heavenly Temple. For instance, in Testament of Levi 3:6 a description of the Heavenly Temple is given, with God dwelling in the celestial Holy of Holies, where archangels offer sacrifices. There also appears to be a heavenly altar of incense, since the Lord is said to smell a pleasing odor from the propitiatory sacrifices offered by His celestial attendants.

In the *Sibylline Oracles* (150 B.C.) the Heavenly Temple (in its position over the earthly Jerusalem) is in view: "...there shines a Temple with a gigantic tower that touches the clouds, and all can see it." The use of the Heavenly Temple as an archetype for the earthly Sanctuary was also considered. In Wisdom 9:8 we read: "...and you said that I would build a Temple for Your holy name and an altar in the city where You dwell, in the likeness of Your holy Tabernacle, that You prepared from the beginning." This pattern of the Heavenly Temple was said to have been revealed to the great figures in Jewish faith beginning with Adam in the Garden of Eden:

> Do you think that this is that city of which I said, "On the palms of my hands I have graven you"? This building which is now built in your midst is it not that which is revealed to me, that which was prepared beforehand here from the time I took counsel to make paradise, and

showed it to Adam before he sinned, but when he transgressed the commandment, it was removed from him, as also paradise. And after these things I showed it to my servant Abraham by night among the portions of the victims. And again I showed it to Moses on Mount Sinai, when I showed him the likeness of the Tabernacle and all its vessels. And now, behold it is preserved with me, as also paradise (2 Baruch 4:2-6).

This intertestamental concept of the Heavenly Temple as a "pattern" for the earthly Sanctuary was not new, but based on several references in the Old Testament (later alluded to in the New Testament).

The Heavenly Pattern for the Earthly Sanctuary

A Prototype from God

Have you ever wondered who drew up the blueprint for the earthly Sanctuary? Where did Moses find hidden in the desert his amazing architect for the Tabernacle? Where did Solomon discover his elaborate plans for the building of the First Temple? According to the Bible, the blueprint originated in heaven, not on earth. Both the Old and New Testaments maintain that the Heavenly Temple served as the basis for the revelation of the form of the earthly sanctuaries. The earliest references to the Heavenly Temple as an archetype or prototype for the Tabernacle appear in the book of Exodus in the construction details following God's command to Moses to build a Sanctuary (Exodus 25:8). In the introduction to these instructions for the Tabernacle and its vessels the text specifies: "According to all that I am going to show you, as the pattern of the tabernacle and the pattern of all its furniture, just so you shall construct it . . . . and see that you make them after the pattern for them, which was shown to you on the mountain" (verses 9,40; compare Exodus 26:30; 27:8; Numbers 8:4). Here we are told that when Moses ascended Mount Sinai, where the Lord revealed His plan for Israel's future, he was shown a "pattern" for making all of the intricate parts of the Sanctuary.

The next time these words appear in the context of building instructions occurs when King David bequeaths to his son Solomon the plans for the First Temple. In 1 Chronicles 28 we read: "Then David gave to his son Solomon the plan of the porch of the temple, its buildings, its storehouses, its upper rooms, its inner rooms, and the room for the mercy seat, and the plan of all that he had in mind, for the courts of the house of the LORD. . . . 'All this,' said David, 'the LORD made me understand in writing by His hand upon me, all the details of this pattern'" (verses 11,19). Like Moses, King David had been shown by God the "pattern" for the Sanctuary's construction and had passed this on to Solomon in the form of divinely inspired "plans." The term translated "pattern" in both of these accounts is the Hebrew word *tabnit*. The Hebrew dictionaries list as many as eight separate meanings for this term: "original, prototype, copy, duplicate, model, image, something like an architect's plan."[7] This "pattern" was communicated to Moses and David orally, by vision, and by superintended writing.[8]

In the New Testament it is said that the earthly Temple and its vessels were "copies" of those in heaven. In the book of Hebrews it is written, "... the true tabernacle, which the Lord pitched, not man. ... on earth ... [is] a copy and shadow of the heavenly things" (Hebrews 8:2,4,5), and "it was necessary for the copies of the things in the heavens to be cleansed with these, but the heavenly things themselves with better sacrifices than these. For Christ did not enter a holy place made with hands, a mere copy of the true one, but into heaven itself, now to appear in the presence of God" (Hebrews 9:23-24). The connection with the Old Testament is made in the first of these verses (Hebrews 8:5), where the author quotes from Exodus 25:40, the command to Moses to build the earthly Sanctuary exactly according to the heavenly design. In the book of Revelation the author depicts the Heavenly Temple as the source for the earthly Sanctuary in all its forms by combining them all into one as typifying the ideal heavenly model: "After these things I looked, and the temple of the tabernacle of testimony in heaven was opened" (Revelation 15:5).

The Character of the Copy

What exactly was it that Moses and David were shown when they produced their copies of the original? The answer to this question has been the subject of some debate. Based on the uses of the Hebrew word *tabnit*, interpreters have suggested it was an original miniature model of the Sanctuary, a miniature model that was a copy of the original,[9] an architect's blueprint or plan, or the original itself—the Heavenly Temple.[10] According to several rabbinic sources, Moses was shown a miniature model of the Tabernacle and its furnishings,[11] which was necessary because of the complexity of the instructions.[12] Others argue that it was an exact copy of the Sanctuary,[13] contending that the basic meaning of *tabnit* denotes a "replica"[14] in Exodus 28:9,40 and in 1 Chronicles 28:11,12,19 "a written blueprint."[15] However, in most of the references to the "pattern" there seems to be an indication of an actual object, not an architect's plan.[16] This view is found in Jewish and Christian non-canonical sources from the Hellenistic period onwards,[17] and supports the view that Moses was shown the Heavenly Temple of which the Tabernacle and later the First Temple were the earthly counterparts. In like manner, the New Testament's use of the Greek term *tupos* ("model, copy") in Hebrews, following the Old Testament concept, has been variously debated. However, after careful evaluation, the evidence supports the view of the Heavenly Temple itself as an archetype. As one commentator on the book of Hebrews has concluded: "… what Moses is shown is constituted a *tupos* simply by the fact that he is told to copy it. It is assumed that the copy is inferior to the original (Hebrews 8:6)."[18] One Old Testament scholar explains this when he writes concerning Moses' ascent of the mountain in Exodus 24 : "It was on this mountain that Yahweh's palace stood, a palace made by Yahweh for himself with its throne room and throne, on which he is seated, king forever (v. 18).…. This heavenly temple or sanctuary with its throne room or holy of holies where the deity was seated on his cherubim throne constituted the *tabnit* or structure seen by Moses during his sojourn on that same mountain."[19] There-fore, it may be concluded that the actual Heavenly Temple served as an original archetype for the Sanctuaries constructed on earth.[20]

A Heavenly Distinction

It is important to remember that the true and eternal Temple is the Heavenly Temple and that although the God of Israel manifested His presence on earth in the earthly Temple, His actual abode was in the heavens. This was made clear when David first desired to build the Lord a permanent dwelling place. In 2 Samuel 7 David stated that because he now lived in a house of cedar, God should move from tent curtains to a house like his (verses 1-2). David made his request through the prophet Nathan, who himself thought the idea seemed appropriate (verse 3). However, the statement reflected an inaccurate concept of God's relationship with Israel. First, God reminds David that He is the builder of houses (or dynasties), and that He never issued a command for David to build for Him a house of cedar that was on par with the royal palaces or the temples of the pagan nations. God would pick the person who would build for Him "a house for My name" (verse 13; see also 1 Kings 8:20). In stating the manner of God's dwelling with Israel in this way ("My name"), the point is made that God never lived in the Temple, as though His being was confined to that place, but filled the Tabernacle (Exodus 25:22) and later the Temple (1 Kings 8:10-12) with His *Shek-inah* glory as a demonstration of His presence. While the gods of the nations lived in their temples and were fed and clothed by their priests, the God of Israel, the Creator of all things, could not be confined to anything that He has made.

David must have passed on this important distinction to his son Solomon when he informed him that he was God's choice to build the First Temple and instructed him on its construction (1 Chronicles 28:6,10-21), for in Solomon's dedicatory prayer for the Temple we hear him say, "Will God indeed dwell on earth? Behold, heaven and the highest heaven cannot contain Thee, how much less this house which I have built!" (1 Kings 8:27). Solomon's focus was on God's immensity and omnipresence. Putting this in conceptual terms, we might say that God is like a circle who is at every point the center. Because His presence fills all that He has made He cannot be limited, reduced, or compromised by time or space.

However, God can choose to *manifest* His presence temporally, spacially and locally as He did at the Tabernacle and in the First Temple. Israel sometimes forgot this important distinction and treated God as their local deity in keeping with the fashion of the nations that surrounded them, or acted as though God was obligated to them because of their service in building and maintaining His house. In opposition to this way of thinking, Stephen in the book of Acts reminded his audience of the Heavenly Temple: "The Most High does not dwell in houses made by human hands; as the prophet says: 'Heaven is My throne, and earth is the footstool of My feet; what kind of house will you build for Me?' says the Lord, 'Or what place is there for my repose? Was it not My hand which made all these things?'" (Acts 7:48-50).

The apostle Paul makes the same point in Acts 17:24-25: "God who made the world and all things in it, since He is Lord of heaven and earth, does not dwell in temples made with hands ... as though He needed anything, since He gives to all life and breath and all things." Both of these texts argue that the proper place of God is in the Heavenly Temple and that the earthly Temple, in contrast to the temples of all other peoples, does not contain God, but only manifests Him.

The Purpose of the Heavenly Temple

Just as the earthly Temple has its purposes in relation to God revealing His presence among men, so the Heavenly Temple has purposes that bring a necessary corrective to the false thinking that God is resident in the earthly Temple, that Israel is simply like the other nations in their possession of an earthly Temple, and that its destruction is a conquest of Israel's God. Four significant distinctions of the Heavenly Temple reveal its purpose:

1. *The Heavenly Temple is the place of perfect holiness.* Whereas the Temple and its priesthood had no sanctity in themselves, the Heavenly Temple is the place of perfect holiness: "Thus says the high and exalted One who lives forever, whose name is Holy, I dwell on a high and holy place" (Isaiah 57:15). A holy God cannot dwell in an unholy place (Habakkuk 1:13), therefore the Heavenly Temple serves as the place where God and His holy ones (angels and saints) remain untouched by the things of earth. It is this condition of holiness and the functional correspondence between God and Israel as a holy nation that required the structural correspondence between the Heavenly Temple and the earthly Temple (for the significance of this, see chapter 24). Before the Temple's existence it would appear that this heavenly-earthly connection was demonstrated in the Garden of Eden (see the next chapter) and to Israel at Mount Sinai. While Israel remained at Mount Sinai, the Heavenly Temple was manifested on the mountain's top with its earthly counterpart, the Tabernacle at its base.[21] Thereafter, it was represented by the *Shekinah* glory, who directed Israel's way and returned to the Tabernacle when Israel was encamped in the wilderness. The Israelites, then, were distinct as a holy nation among all the nations on earth because they had the Holy God (whose *Shekinah* linked the earthly Temple and its priesthood to the Heavenly Temple) dwelling in their midst (Deuteronomy 4:7; 1 Kings 8:60).

2. *The Heavenly Temple is the ideal and undefilable Sanctuary* in contrast to the profaned earthly Sanctuary. This at once offered a contrasting model of holiness to the existing corruptible Temple and priesthood, offering a symbol of permanence and inviolability in the wake of the desecration and destruction of the earthly Temple. This was a consolation theologically, since there existed a Temple that could not be invaded, conquered, or defiled (either by Israel or the nations). This significance, after the Roman destruction of the Temple in A.D. 70, was developed in post-biblical Judaism as one rabbinic response to the loss of their spiritual center. In like manner, while the church functions as a spiritual temple for believers in Christ during the present age, Christians have a relationship with their great High Priest, Jesus, who entered the Heavenly Temple through His blood to become the mediator of the New Covenant (Hebrews 4:14-15; 8:1,3-4; 9:11-15).[22]

3. *The Heavenly Temple is the source of divine revelation.* As we have already seen, Moses (Exodus 24:18; 34:28; Deuteronomy 9:9,18), Aaron and his sons, the 70 elders of Israel (Exodus 24:9), several of the Old Testament prophets (1 Kings

22:19; Isaiah 6:1-4; Ezekiel 1:4-28), and the apostle John in the New Testament (Revelation 4:1-11), received revelation from an encounter or vision of God on His throne in the holy Temple. We might add to this list Jacob, who apparently saw something of the Heavenly Temple in a dream, saying, "How awesome is this place! This is none other than the house of God, and this is the gate of heaven" (Genesis 28:12-17). He consequently gave the name *Bethel* ("the house of God") to the place where the experience occurred (Genesis 28:19). King David understood that the answers to his prayers were dispensed from the Heavenly Temple (Psalm 18:6), and Stephen, as he was being stoned to death, saw the heavens open to reveal the glorious throne room of the Heavenly Temple (Acts 7:55-56). In like manner, the prophets often entered God's earthly Temple to receive a divine message. The prophet Samuel received his call when, as a boy, he served with the high priest Eli and was sleeping in the tabernacle near the place of the Ark of the Covenant (1 Samuel 3:1-21). King Solomon was at the high place in Gibeon when God met him in a dream, and Isaiah was in the Temple when the Lord appeared to him (Isaiah 6:1). Although the prophet Jeremiah is not said to have received a revelation in the Temple, the Lord directed him on two occasions to stand at the gate of the Temple and in the Temple's court to give God's revelation to those who came to worship (Jeremiah 7:1; 26:2). Thus, while revelation is received at the earthly Temple, it originates in the Heavenly Temple.

4. *The Heavenly Temple is the source of true righteousness and justice.* In the earthly Temples the Sanhedrin sat to dispense justice for Israel according to the law, and in the millennial kingdom the Messianic Temple will be the center of law and justice for the world (Isaiah 2:3-4). Yet the standard for the earthly is the heavenly, from which righteousness falls down like rain (Hosea 10:12). This served as a motivation for righteousness and continued fidelity in the face of persecution and loss as well as an answer to the quest for theodicy (the vindication of God). In the New Testament and particularly in the book of Revelation, the Heavenly Temple is the place from which the angels carry the judgments of God to be poured out on the world's rebellious unbelievers (Revelation 11:19; 14:15,17; 15:5-6,8; 16:1-2). The constant view given into this heavenly realm and the realization that God, on His throne in the Heavenly Temple, hears the martyred saints' cries for justice (Revelation 6:9-10; 16:6-7) enables believers in the church age, and especially the Tribulation saints, to persevere despite their sufferings on earth.

Significantly, the Heavenly Temple is also the setting for the victorious celebration song commemorating God's judgments (patterned after the song of the Red Sea deliverance in Exodus 15 and 32). Here, God's subduing of the Gentile nations and bringing them to worship before Him is an encouragement to those on earth who have yet to realize the final deliverance. Isaiah 66:23 says that all the nations will bow down and worship God—including those that formerly opposed God and His people. In addition, if the New Jerusalem is a part of the Heavenly Temple (more on this in chapter 25), then the references in Revelation 21:24,26 to the glory and honor of the nations may also be part of this resolution through the Heavenly Temple. The final resolution in theodicy appears in the climatic battle of Armageddon when Christ, as Judge (not just angels with judgments), emerges from the Heavenly Temple to wage war and smite the nations (Revelation 19:11-15).

We have seen, then, that the earthly Temple has a heavenly counterpart that served as the pattern for its construction. This Temple before time set the stage for our understanding of the Temple within time. The next steps of our journey will take us to the Tabernacle of Moses, and the Temples of Solomon, Zerubbabel, and Herod, covering a span of some 1,500 years. Come with me, and let's walk together through history and discover the preeminent place of God's Temple on earth.

Elements Common to the Earthly and Heavenly Temples

	Earthly Temple		Heavenly Temple
Description	**References**	**Description**	**References**
called "worldly sanctuary"	Heb. 9:1-2	called "Temple in heaven" or "true Tabernacle"	Rev. 7:15; 14:17; 15:5; 16:17; Heb. 8:2
seven-branched lampstand	Ex. 26:35	seven-branched lampstand	Rev. 1:12
trumpet	Ex. 19:13,16,19	trumpet	Rev. 8:2,6
altar of sacrifice	Ex. 27:1-2; 39:39	altar of sacrifice	Rev. 6:9
sacral vestments	Ex. 29, 39	sacral vestments	Rev. 4:4; 6:11; 15:6
altar of incense	Ex. 30:1-6; 39:38	altar of incense	Rev. 8:3-5
four horns of the altar	Ex. 30:10	four horns of the altar	Rev. 9:13
Ark of the Covenant	Ex. 25	Ark of the Covenant	Rev. 11:19
golden censer	1 Kgs. 7:50	golden censer	Rev. 8:3-5
incense	Ex. 30:34-36	incense	Rev. 5:8; 8:3-4
incense bowls	1 Kgs. 7:50; Num. 7:13,19,25,31,37	incense bowls	Rev. 5:8
throne (mercy seat)	Ex. 25:22; Lev. 16:2	throne	Ps. 11:4; Rev. 7:9; 16:17
Holy Place	1 Kgs. 7:50	Holy Place	Heb. 9:11-12,24
Holy of Holies	Ex. 26:25-33	Holy of Holies	Rev. 4:1-10
high priest	Heb. 4:14	high priest	Heb. 9:6-7
priestly officiants	Ps. 110:4; Heb. 7:17	priestly officials	Rev. 8:2-5
rites	Lev. 1–10; 16,23–35	rites	Rev. 4:8-11; 8:2-5; 15:1-8
24 priestly courses	1 Chr. 23:3-6	24 elders	Rev. 4:4,10; 5:8
cherubim	Ex. 25:18,22; 1 Kgs. 6:23-28	four living creatures	Rev. 4:6-8
worshipers	2 Chr. 7:3	worshipers	Rev. 5:11; 7:9; 19:6
sacrifice of lambs	Ex. 29:39	slain Lamb of God	Rev. 5:6

Adapted from the chart by J.A. and Donald Parry in *Temples of the Ancient World*, p. 521.

CHAPTER 4

The Temple Through Time

The History of the Temple

How did an old wall become a shrine so revered and longed for? What made the broad Haram area above it a treasury of tradition for three great faiths of the western world? For the answers, we trace back three thousand years.[1]

—MINA AND ARTHUR KLEIN

W e live in a brief moment of time, unconnected for most of us, with what has been or what will be. The study of history reconnects us to the forgotten past, which has produced our present and gives us a glimpse into the unknown future based on repeating patterns in antiquity. If the Temple is to reappear in the future, we must search the past to understand why it disappeared and why it should appear again. In doing so we will find a divine design of predicted destruction that has been coupled with a promised restoration. So let us move backward into history to explore the previous Temples and understand God's purpose in the Temple through time.

The Succession of Sanctuaries

When we consider the past history of the Temple, one difficulty we must face is that not one, but four different sanctuaries existed in Jerusalem over a nearly 1,000-year period.[2] Even though one of these was pitched as a Tabernacle and three were constructed as distinct Temples on the Temple Mount, these latter buildings are conventionally referred to as the *First* and *Second* Temples. The reason for this is that while the Second Temple was begun by Zerubbabel in 515 B.C., and was completely reconstructed from its foundations upward by Herod the Great in c. 20 B.C., the latter is not considered a *Third* Temple. According to Jewish understanding, a new Temple only follows the destruction of a previous Temple and an intervening period in which the priestly (sacrificial) service is unable to be performed within the Temple precincts. The reason Herod's rebuilding did not constitute a new Temple (even though it was a new structure) was because during the period of reconstruction the sacrifices remained uninterrupted.[3]

The Tabernacle, God's Sanctuary in Motion

After Moses received the command and pattern for the Sanctuary on Mount Sinai (Exodus 25:2,8-9,40), he commissioned two craftsmen chosen by the Lord—named Bezalel and Oholiab—to supervise the skilled workers in making the structural framework, tent curtains, and ritual furniture that comprised the Tabernacle. The materials for this construction were derived from the voluntary contributions of the people (Exodus 25:2-7), who had received much of the costly articles of metals, skins, and fabrics as "plunder from the Egyptians" (Exodus 3:22; 12:35-36). The result was an ingenious, prefabricated building that could be

The Temple Through Time

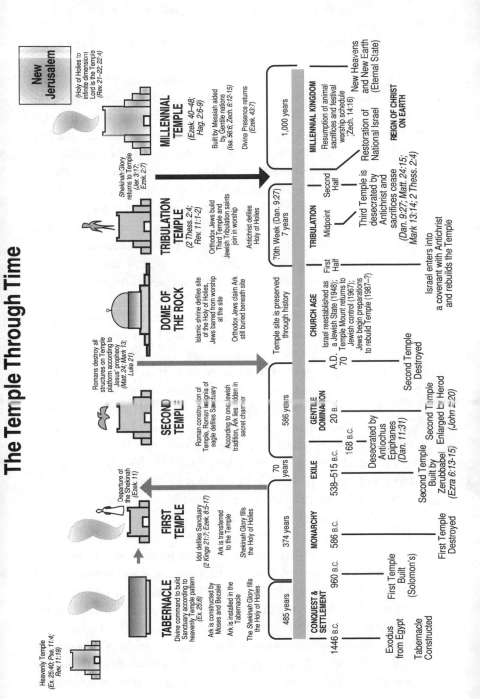

Heavenly Temple
(Ex. 25:40; Psa. 11:4; Rev. 11:19)

New Jerusalem
(Holy of Holies to infinite dimension)
Lord is the Temple
(Rev. 21–22; 22:4)

TABERNACLE
Divine command to build Sanctuary according to heavenly Temple pattern (Ex. 25:8)

Ark is constructed by Moses and Bezalel

Ark is installed in the Tabernacle

The Shekinah Glory fills the Holy of Holies

Departure of the Shekinah (Ezek. 11)

FIRST TEMPLE
Idol defiles Sanctuary (2 Kings 21:7; Ezek. 8:5–17)

Ark is transferred to the Temple

Shekinah Glory fills the Holy of Holies

Romans destroy all structures on Temple platform according to Jesus' prophecy (Matt. 24; Mark 13; Luke 21)

SECOND TEMPLE
Roman construction of Temple, Roman insignia of eagle defiles Sanctuary

According to one Jewish tradition, Ark lies hidden in secret chamber

DOME OF THE ROCK
Islamic shrine defiles site of the Holy of Holies, Jews barred from worship at the site

Orthodox Jews claim Ark still buried beneath site

Temple site is preserved through history

Shekinah Glory returns to Temple (Jer. 3:17; Ezek. 2:7)

TRIBULATION TEMPLE
(2 Thess. 2:4; Rev. 11:1–2)

Orthodox Jews build Third Temple and Jewish Tribulation saints join in worship

Antichrist defiles Holy of Holies

MILLENNIAL TEMPLE
(Ezek. 40–48; Hag. 2:6–9)

Built by Messiah aided by Gentile nations (Isa. 56:6; Zech. 6:12–15)

Divine Presence returns (Ezek. 43:7)

New Heavens and New Earth (Eternal State)

485 years	374 years	70 years	586 years	1,000 years
CONQUEST & SETTLEMENT	**MONARCHY**	**EXILE**	**GENTILE DOMINATION**	**CHURCH AGE**	**70th Week (Dan. 9:27) 7 years** / **TRIBULATION**	**MILLENNIAL KINGDOM**

1446 B.C.

960 B.C.

586 B.C.

538–515 B.C.

168 B.C.

20 B.C.

A.D. 70

Exodus from Egypt

Tabernacle Constructed

First Temple Built (Solomon's)

First Temple Destroyed

Second Temple Built by Zerubbabel (Ezra 6:13–15)

Desecrated by Antiochus Epiphanes (Dan. 11:31)

Second Temple Enlarged by Herod (John 2:20)

Second Temple Destroyed

Israel reestablished as a Jewish State (1948); Temple Mount returns to Jewish control (1967); Jews begin preparations to rebuild Temple (1987–?)

Israel enters into a covenant with Antichrist and rebuilds the Temple

First Half

Midpoint

Second Half

Third Temple is desecrated by Antichrist and sacrifices cease (Dan. 9:27; Matt. 24:15; Mark 13:14; 2 Thess. 2:4)

REIGN OF CHRIST ON EARTH

Resumption of animal sacrifices and festival worship schedule (Zech. 14:16)

Restoration of National Israel

collapsed and transported with the Israelites as they journeyed to and in the Promised Land.

During the time of the Tabernacle's construction a "Tent of Meeting" was erected by Moses outside the camp so that Moses could privately enter into the presence of God (the *Shekinah*) and receive divine guidance and answers to the people's prayers (Exodus 33:7-11). While some see this as a provisional structure that was replaced by the Tabernacle,[4] others see it as one and the same, for both terms are used interchangeably after the Tabernacle's completion (Leviticus 1:3; 12:6; 14:23; 15:14; Numbers 11:26; 12:4; Deuteronomy 31:14-15). It is preferable to see "the Tent of Meeting" and "the Tabernacle" as two parts of a single structure—the outer "tent" (Hebrew, *'ohel*) and the inner "Tabernacle" (Hebrew, *mishkan*). For this reason 2 Samuel 7:6 notes that God moved about "in a tent, even in a tabernacle."[5] When the First Temple was dedicated, the portable Tent of Meeting/Tabernacle was incorporated within the new permanent structure (1 Kings 8:4).[6]

The form of the Tabernacle was relatively simple, with one outer court defined by a rectangle 75 feet wide and 150 feet long. Its structure consisted of linen curtains 7½ feet high set on 60 posts made of acacia wood overlaid with bronze and spaced 7½ feet apart. The entrance was at the eastern end, and as one moved westward, the degree of sanctity increased. Toward the center of this court was the brazen altar of sacrifice, and just west of it a bronze washbasin called the *laver*. At the far western end of this court was pitched a rectangular tent 15 feet wide and 30 feet long. This structure was divided into two sections, again moving in a westward direction: a Holy Place and a Most Holy Place, separated from one another by a curtain or veil (Hebrew, *paroket*). Within the Holy Place were housed three ritual objects: the golden table for the shewbread on the right, the golden lampstand on the left, and the golden altar of incense directly in the middle, close to the separating curtain. Within the Most Holy Place or the Holy of Holies, a square room 15 feet in width and length, was only one ritual object; the Ark of the Covenant. While the high priest and his priests officiated in the outer court and the Holy Place, only the high priest was permitted within the Most Holy Place to perform the annual act of atonement on behalf of the people of Israel (see next page).

The Tabernacle as a whole was situated in the very midst of the encampment of the tribes of Israel (Numbers 2:17; 10:14-28), which is estimated to have stretched approximately 12 square miles.[7] This central location was not because

The Tabernacle

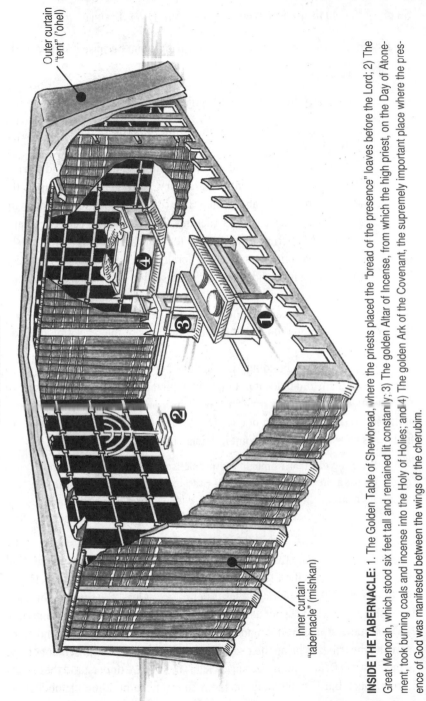

Outer curtain "tent" ('ohel)

Inner curtain "tabernacle" (mishkan)

INSIDE THE TABERNACLE: 1. The Golden Table of Shewbread, where the priests placed the "bread of the presence" loaves before the Lord; 2) The Great Menorah, which stood six feet tall and remained lit constantly; 3) The golden Altar of Incense, from which the high priest, on the Day of Atonement, took burning coals and incense into the Holy of Holies; and 4) The golden Ark of the Covenant, the supremely important place where the presence of God was manifested between the wings of the cherubim.

the Tabernacle needed to be guarded by the people, but because it served as the focal point of Israel's daily life.

The History of the First Temple

For 485 years (from Moses to Solomon)[8] the Tabernacle served Israel as a temporary structure, moving from place to place. However, when the Israelites finally settled in the Promised Land and became unified politically and spiritually, it was time to make the central Sanctuary more permanent. When the Temple was finally built the Tabernacle was incorporated within it and established a continuity between the two structures. Concerning this connection and continuation of the Tabernacle within the Temple, the Rambam (Rav Moshe Nachmanides), in his commentary on the Torah, makes a comparison between Exodus 24:15-16 and a nearly identical set of verses in 1 Kings 8:10-11. He comes to the conclusion that the city of Jerusalem is, in terms of holiness, the permanent continuation of the camp of the Israelites in the desert, and the Temple was the permanent continuation of Mount Sinai in terms of the revelation of God's holiness and glory.[9]

The possibility of building the Temple began when David conquered Jebusite Jerusalem and made it not only the capital of Israel, but also the site for the Sanctuary. For the first time in Israel's history the civil and the religious authority were centralized in one geographical location. In 1 Kings 8:16-17 we find God's view of this pivotal point in Israel's history:

> Since the day that I brought My people Israel from Egypt, I did not choose a city out of all the tribes of Israel in which to build a house that My name might be there, but I chose David to be over My people Israel. Now it was in the heart of my father David to build a house for the name of the LORD, the God of Israel.

These verses declare that since the time of the exodus until David's day, God had not chosen a specific city in which to build the Temple. Is this correct? Had not God chosen Mount Moriah in Jerusalem since at least the time of Abraham (Genesis 22:2,14)? Did He not tell Moses to plant His people on the mountain of His inheritance, the place He made for His Sanctuary (Exodus 15:17), and command all the tribes to bring their sacrifices to this central site chosen out of one of their tribes (Deuteronomy 12:1-14)? That is the way we understand these texts in retrospect, but actually none of them connect the building of the Temple

Jerusalem During the Time of Solomon

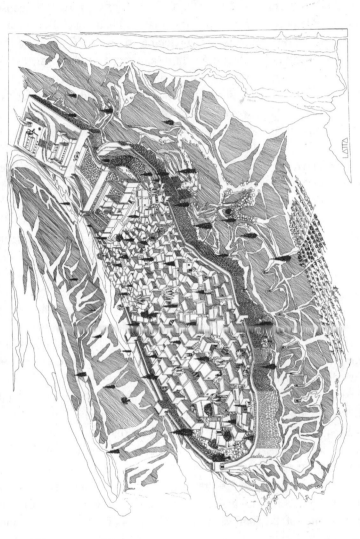

JERUSALEM DURING THE TIME OF SOLOMON: View of Jerusalem from the southwest during the time of Solomon (962–922 B.C.), showing the Temple (upper right), Solomon's Palace (at the left edge of the Temple platform), the Citadel fortress (center), and the city of David (left, center). The Tyropœon Valley (top, center) and the Kidron Valley (lower right) flank each side of the city perched high on the escarpment of Zion. Used with per- mission of © Biblical Illustrator.

directly with Jerusalem. Furthermore, we do not find God specifically telling David the place of His choice.

Yet, David deduced this was God's will. The words of the text "but I chose David to be over My people Israel" may mean that God had not chosen a place *until* He chose David. However, it is more preferable to see here God choosing a man who knew His choice (1 Samuel 13:14; Psalm 78:70-72; 89:20-21,24-29). David was said to be "a man after [God's] own heart" (1 Samuel 13:14), and in this passage we see that it was "in the heart of David to build a house for the name of the LORD." So David was chosen by God (who knew all the while that David would choose what He had chosen) to choose the site for the central Sanctuary.[10]

In consideration of why David chose Jerusalem, several reasons are possible: 1) As we have noted, it had a historic connection with the people of Israel from the time of Abraham with the *Akedah*, or binding of Isaac, and according to a late midrash, Moriah was traditionally assumed to be "the mountain of God's inheritance" (2 Chronicles 3:1; Exodus 15:17),[11] and the place God had chosen (Deuteronomy 12); 2) it was territory that had not belonged to any of the northern or southern tribes, and thus represented a neutral region that would not provoke jealousy among the tribes; 3) it was strategically located and could serve as a central location for civil administration. Thus, Jerusalem, thought to have been prepared by God as the designated site for the central Sanctuary and the unfolding of the eternal purpose, became not only the capital of Israel, but Mount Zion, the eternal capital and holy habitation of God, from which His blessings would flow to all the earth. For this reason the Psalms, composed for Israel's worship, frequently extol the choice, virtues, and divine destiny of Zion as God's house (Psalm 48:1-3,11-14; 50:2-3; 53:6; 68:29; 87; 102:16; 110:2; 125:1-2; cf. Psalms 2:6-9; 5:7; 9:11-14,20; 15:1; 20:1-3; 23:6; 24:7-10; 27:4-6; 29:9-10; 51:18-19; 65:4; 76:2; 78:68-69; 84:5-12; 96:6-10; 99:9; 114:2; 122:1-9; 128:5-6; 129:5-8; 134; 138:1-3; 147:12-20).

David was forbidden to build the First Temple because he had been a man of war (1 Kings 8:18-19; 1 Chronicles 28:3-4) and the Temple was to be a place of peace. The building of the Temple waited until Israel's warfare ended and Solomon had established the kingdom. Although the First Temple was built by David's son Solomon, David was able to provide for its initial building expenses during his last years through the royal treasury and a collection taken from the people of Israel (1 Chronicles 29:1-9). Following David's death, Solomon built the Temple through foreign expertise, but largely through forced labor from the native Israelites (1 Kings 5:13-16; 2 Chronicles 2:2). While expedient, the hardships it created seriously cracked the foundation of trust David had established. When Solomon's son and successor Rehoboam threatened to increase the hardships, the foundation broke and the kingdom divided (1 Kings 12:14-19; 2 Chronicles 10:14-19). Nevertheless, the First Temple endured for another 300 years.

The Design of the First Temple

The architectural pattern of temples in the ancient Near East was the *tripartite*, or three-room temple. Common examples are the Egyptian long-room temple with direct access to the innermost room, which housed a statue of the deity. The closest models to the Solomonic style in the ancient near East are those from Syria (the temple at Tel Ta'anat) and Phoenicia. In keeping with the custom of his age, Solomon constructed the Temple using the Phoenician expertise of his father David's materials supplier, Hiram (Huram), king of Tyre (2 Samuel 5:11; 1 Kings 5; 2 Chronicles 2:3-18). The biblical text records that besides materials, Hiram sent his Phoenician architects and craftsmen to advise their Israelite counterparts on building the Temple to contemporary specifications. One of these was a half-Jewish, half-Phoenician artisan named Huramabi, who was given oversight of the Temple craftsmen.[12] Credit is given to him for the vast array of decorative, cast, and overlaid objects in the Temple (1 Kings 7:13-45; 2 Chronicles 2:13-14). The construction of the Second Temple, under Zerubbabel, also involved Phoenician workmen (Ezra 3:7-10),[13] in harmony with the decree from the Persian king Darius to "rebuild" the Temple. The Jewish exiles who had returned were long removed from the original construction and could only rebuild (rather than replace) this Temple with the aid of skilled Phoenicians.

While few examples of Phoenician temples exist (or have yet to be found) to confirm this design, it is certain that their constructions were descendants of the same long-room temple.[14] One Phoenician temple two centuries older than Solomon's was excavated in Hazor. It was 84 feet by 56 feet and tripartite. At each side of the entrance to the main hall was a round pillar, like those in Solomon's Temple. Also, ivory panels and sculptures in several Phoenician temples bear pattern decorations similar to the cherubim, palm trees, and open flowers carved in the paneling of the Jerusalem Temple (1 Kings 6:35).[15] In addition, the fourth-century A.D. church father Eusebius preserved in his writings the record of a Phoenician priest named Sanchuniathon, who gave details of how King

Solomon's Temple

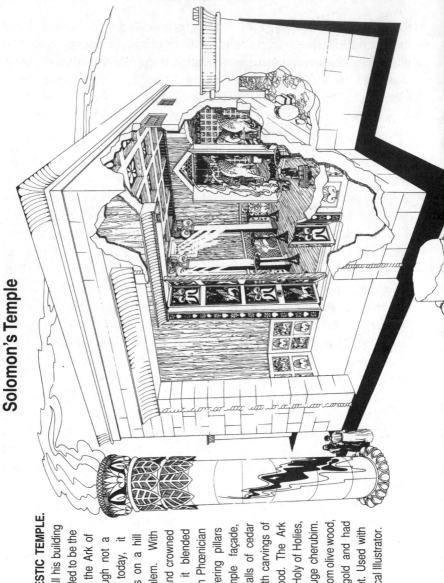

SOLOMON'S MAJESTIC TEMPLE.

The culmination of all his building projects—was intended to be the permanent home of the Ark of the Covenant. Though not a fragment remains today, it stood for 400 years on a hill overlooking Jerusalem. With walls 10 feet thick and crowned with a battlement, it blended fortress strength with Phoenician elegance. Two towering pillars dominated the temple façade, while the interior walls of cedar were resplendent with carvings of ivory, gold, and wood. The Ark stood in front of the Holy of Holies, at the feet of two huge cherubim. These were carved from olive wood, covered with pure gold and had wingspans of 15 feet. Used with permission of © Biblical Illustrator.

Hiram of Tyre had supplied Solomon with materials for the building of the Temple. Such archaeological information concerning comparative temples makes it possible to reconstruct a reasonably accurate portrait of the Solomonic Temple.[16]

A Description of the First Temple

In appearance the First Temple was a modest building (see diagram on previous page). It was about the size of a small church or synagogue: 90 feet long by 30 feet wide by 45 feet high, or about 3,500 square feet,[17] and situated on a platform approximately 10 feet high. This was ascended by ten steps leading up between the twin bronze pillars, named *Jachin* ("He [God] establishes") and *Boaz* ("in Him [God] is strength"), each about 40 feet high and 12 feet in circumference. Beyond an entrance porch lay the first, and smallest room of the Temple (Hebrew, *Ulam*), which led into the main room, called "the Holy Place" (Hebrew, *Hekal*). This was the largest room in the Temple—the interior walls were covered with elaborately carved cedar panels overlaid or inlaid with gold, and the floors were covered with boards of cypress so that no stonework remained visible. In addition, Solomon is said to have adorned this room with beautiful precious stones. Housed within this awe-inspiring central chamber were the sacred ritual objects from the Tabernacle: the golden seven-branched candelabrum (Hebrew, *Menorah*), and the table bearing the sacred presence bread (Hebrew, *Shulkan*). Elements made for this room, and originally not in the Tabernacle, were ten tables (five on the north side and five on the south) that were accompanied by ten lamps on lampstands, as well as the numerous implements used in the priestly service.

The innermost room (Hebrew, *Devir*) was separated from the Holy Place by a double veil of fabric and by a wall whose only door was kept closed, except on rare occasions. Access to this room, called also "the Holy of Holies" (Hebrew, *Qodesh Qodashim*) was forbidden to all except the high priest, and to him only once a year at the high, holy Day of Atonement (Hebrew, *Yom Kippur*). In this room, a perfect cube (about 35 feet square), gilded throughout with 23 tons of gold, stood the central sacred object, variously called "the Ark of the Covenant" and "the Ark of the Testimony." The Ark rested on a bedrock platform that protruded within the Holy of Holies, called in Jewish tradition the "Foundation Stone" (Hebrew, *'Even Shetiyyah*). In front of the Ark was the golden altar of incense. Finally, at this westernmost end of the Temple complex was a belt of storerooms surrounding the holy places.

In the front of the Temple to the east was an open courtyard, in which stood the brazen altar. Not far away was located an immense basin called "the Brazen Sea," or "the Molten Sea." This water-basin, which contained an estimated 15,000 gallons of water and rested on the backs of a dozen bronze bulls, was used for the ritual purification and cleansing of the priests engaged in offering sacrifices. Ten ornamented bronze basins or lavers with wheels were stationed nearby on both the north and south sides of the courtyard; they were used to transport water to various places around the Temple.

Only a couple of items related to Solomon's Temple have been discovered by archaeologists. One that is connected with the priestly service is a tiny ivory pomegranate that was once attached to the tip of a scepter. Dated to the eighth-century B.C., its relation to the Temple is indicated by an inscription on the scepter head that reads, "Belonging to the hou[se of...]. A holy thing of the priests" (or "Holy to the priests"). The "house" it mentions is the "house of the Lord," or the Temple. Another item is a fragmentary text preserved on a small piece of potsherd that contains a receipt for an obligatory contribution to the "house of the Lord."[18] This inscription also mentions a "Zechariah," which it indicates was a ritual civil servant. This may be the Levitical priest Zechariah, who served as an official in the First Temple during the reign of King Josiah from 640–609 B.C. (2 Chronicles 35:8).[19] These scant archaeological remains from the First Temple confirm its existence, yet their very scarcity also confirms its destruction.

The Destruction of the First Temple

God warned Solomon about the future destruction of the Temple shortly after its completion. In 1 Kings 9:6-9 God told the king, "If you or your sons shall indeed turn away from following Me, and shall not keep My commandments and My statutes which I have set before you and shall go and serve other gods and worship them, then I will cut off Israel from the land which I have given them, and the house which I have consecrated for My name, I will cast out of My sight....and this house will become a heap of ruins." Throughout the history of Israel's monarchy people continued to set up pagan cultic installations in the Land. But what set in motion the fall of the kingdom was a divided spiritual loyalty within the hearts of the kings. The seeds of the Temple's destruction were first sown when Solomon established multiple centers for idolatrous worship. His political marriages had a part in this—as part of his contractual agreement,

Solomon had to provide for the worship practices of his 1,000 foreign wives and concubines (1 Kings 11:1-3). This included the construction of idolatrous high places (Hebrew, *bamot*). What was unforseen by Solomon, but inevitable, was his own turning away from God to adopt his wives' idolatrous practices and invoke God's wrath (1 Kings 11:3-9).

With the practice of idolatry dividing people's hearts spiritually, God announced through His prophets that the kingdom would be divided politically (1 Kings 11:10-13).[20] Solomon's son Rehoboam fomented an insurrection that split the kingdom into two: Judah to the south, and Israel (Ephraim) to the north. The presence of the Temple in the south stabilized the spiritual decline in that region, but it continued unabated in the north. This was because the kings of the Northern Kingdom, beginning with Jeroboam, built alternate worship sites to keep the people from returning to the Temple and coming back under the southern administration of Judah. These actions fostered syncretism and henotheism and brought the Northern Kingdom to judgment under the Assyrians in 721 B.C.

The presence of the Temple in Judah, and of kings in the Davidic dynasty that attempted occasional reforms from idolatry, delayed divine judgment on the Southern Kingdom for 135 years. During this period, the people of Judah were made aware that the punishment for their sin would find its expression in the Temple. Evidence of this impending judgment came shortly after Rehoboam had divided the kingdom. Pharaoh Shishak of Egypt attacked Jerusalem, specifically targeting the Temple and Solomon's Palace, which housed 300 shields of beaten gold. These and other treasures from the Temple were carried back to Egypt (1 Kings 14:25-26; 2 Chronicles 12:2,9). Only because the royal court "humbled" itself at the instigation of God's prophet was the Temple and Jerusalem spared further plunder (2 Chronicles 12:5-8).

After this, the south went through a series of unsuccessful reforms accompanied by political alliances that demanded Judah pay monetary tribute to superior states. This tribute came largely from the Temple treasury and the material wealth adorning the Temple. The attempt to meet these economic obligations actually set about the destruction of the Temple piece by piece. King Ahaz, for example, stripped the Temple of a portion of its silver and gold, broke up the Temple furniture and utensils, and removed the bronze oxen from the Brazen Sea in order to satisfy his obligations to the Assyrian king Tiglath-Pileser III (2 Chronicles 28:21,24). When Ahaz went to pay his tribute in Damascus, he offered sacrifices to the Assyrian gods, and desiring to honor them in place of the God of Israel, had a replica of the Damascus altar made for the Temple courtyard in Jerusalem. This being done, he closed the Temple doors and constructed idolatrous altars throughout Jerusalem.

Even though Ahaz's son, Hezekiah, brought spiritual and military reform to Judah, he also set in motion the final act that would bring about the Temple's destruction. In 2 Kings 20:12-18 the account is given of Hezekiah's tour of the remaining Temple treasures, which was given to Assyria's future successors, the Babylonians. The Temple was held like bait in front of the hungry eyes of the Babylonians, and it was only a matter of time before the bait was seized. Therefore, God announced through His prophets in 2 Kings 23:27: "I will remove Judah also from My sight, as I have removed Israel. And I will cast off Jerusalem, this city which I have chosen, *and the temple of which I have said: 'My name shall be there'*"(emphasis added). The idolatrous offense culminated with King Manasseh, whose acts of violence against the Temple (2 Kings 21:4-8) were used as a prediction of its ultimate destruction (2 Kings 21:11-15). The long history of Sabbath violation (2 Chronicles 36:21), coupled with Manasseh's desecration of the Holy Place, could not even be quelled by good King Josiah's reforms to the Temple and its worship (2 Kings 22–23, see especially 23:26-27).

Josiah's untimely death at the hands of the Egyptian Pharaoh Neco (2 Kings 23:29-30) forced payment of tribute to Neco as well as the reversal of Josiah's reforms (2 Kings 23:34-37). This signaled that the time for the execution of the predicted judgment was near. It came under Jehoiakim's reign in 605 B.C., when the Babylonian king Nebuchadnezzar took Jehoiakim and thousands of his nobles and skilled laborers (including Daniel and his friends) to Babylon.

A second invasion and deportation followed in 597 B.C., this time removing all of the remaining Temple treasures to Babylon (2 Kings 24:13). The prophet Ezekiel was taken captive in this deportation, and he predicted the soon collapse of Jerusalem and the slaughter of its inhabitants (Ezekiel 9:1-8). In this same prophetic context, Ezekiel saw a vision of the *Shekinah* glory (the presence of God) departing from the Temple and vanishing over the Mount of Olives to the East (Ezekiel 10:18-19). With the departure of God's presence, the Temple was set apart as a common thing, ready for destruction.[21]

The final Babylonian invasion came in 587/586 B.C. and with it the total destruction predicted by Ezekiel.[22] The Temple was burned, along with the palace complex, and all the houses of the city (2 Kings 25:8-9; 2 Chronicles 36:18-19). The sorrowful attitude of the Judeans toward the ruined Temple is well presented by the prophet Jeremiah: "The adversary has stretched out his hand over all her precious things, *for she has seen the nations enter her sanctuary*...whom Thou didst command that they should not enter into Thy congregation....*the Lord has rejected His altar, He has abandoned His sanctuary;* He has delivered into the hands of the enemy the walls of her palaces" (Lamentations 1:10; 2:7, emphasis added).

The History of the Second Temple

The First Temple had stood for some 374 years, but the apostasy of the people in violating God's ordinances had brought it to an end. One of the ordinances that had been forsaken was the sabbatical rest that was to be given to the land every seven years. This had gone on for 490 years, or a total of 70 sabbath rests. To compensate for this violation, God mandated that the Land of Israel would be desolate for an equivalent period (70 years of captivity for the 70 sabbath rests that had gone unobserved over the course of 490 years). Jeremiah explained this divine reckoning in his writing, and Daniel used this information when he prayed for his people's promised return to Israel and the restoration of the Temple (Jeremiah 25:10-12; Daniel 6:10; 9:2-19). So that the captive Jews would know that God would keep His promise, He demonstrated to them that the sanctity of the Temple still remained. When King Belshazzar of Babylon brought out the captured Temple vessels for use in a pagan feast (for the purpose of desecrating them by using them for a libation to his gods and to boast of his victory over Jerusalem), God's hand appeared in the room and spelled out Babylon's doom (Daniel 5). That very night the city fell to the Persians, an empire that would serve as a divine instrument for the later return of the Jews and the rebuilding of the Temple (2 Chronicles 36:20-21).

Long before this happened, the prophet Isaiah had prophesied that the Persian king Cyrus would be the specific instrument God used for the Temple's rebuilding: "It is I [the Lord] who says of Cyrus, 'He is My shepherd! And he will perform all My desire.' And he declares of Jerusalem, 'She will be built,' and of the temple, 'Your foundation will be laid'" (Isaiah 44:28). Just as Daniel had understood from Jeremiah's prophecy the time of Israel's return, so Cyrus learned of his role from Isaiah's prophecy (Ezra 1:1-2). Josephus Flavius, the first-century Jewish historian who wrote an account of Jewish history for the Romans, recorded the tradition that the Jews' return and the Temple's rebuilding were prompted by Isaiah's prophecy: "...by reading the book which Isaiah left behind of his prophecies; for this prophet had spoken thus to him in a secret vision: 'My will is, that Cyrus…send back My people to their own land, and build My temple.' Accordingly, when Cyrus read this, and admired the divine power, an earnest desire and ambition seized upon him to fulfill what was so written."[23]

The Second Temple of Zerubbabel

Little is known about the actual physical structure of the Second Temple,[24] however, from the biblical record we can well outline the history of its rebuilding. Under the leadership of Zerubbabel, about 50,000 Jews returned to Jerusalem in 538 B.C. and began to lay the foundation for the Temple with the help of Phœnician workmen. An altar was constructed, sacrifices begun, and the observance of the biblical festivals restored (Ezra 3:1-5). The Temple vessels and utensils that had been taken by the Babylonians were also returned in 538 B.C. However, the construction of the Temple itself met with opposition from Samaritan residents of the Northern Kingdom and was not resumed for another 15 years. The work was finally completed (more than 20 years after it was begun) in 515 B.C. after a decree from the Persian king Darius not only permitted the rebuilding, but prescribed local taxes be paid to the Jews to finance the construction (Ezra 6:1-15).

When the foundation of the Second Temple was laid in 538 B.C., many of the priests and Levites who were old enough to have seen the First Temple wept upon the realization that this edifice would only be a shadow of the former (Ezra 3:12-13). No doubt this impression persisted and grew as the years passed, especially since there was a delay in erecting the Temple on these seemingly inferior foundations. However, as the people completed the rebuilding the prophet Haggai issued a word of encouragement promising that the "latter glory" of the Temple would be even greater than it was during the former times of the renowned Solomonic Temple (see chapter 10). Therefore, while the expected restoration surrounding the rebuilt Temple appeared postponed to the future, hope continued while life returned to its central focus around the Second Temple.

The Desecration of Zerubbabel's Temple

For 200 years the Second Temple served as the official center of worship for the Jews—both those in the Land of Israel and those in the Diaspora. Although during this time, at least two other rival Jewish temples were known to have existed at Leontopolis and Elephantine (as well as the Samaritan temple on Mount Gerizim), the Diaspora Jews respected the superlative sanctity of the Jerusalem Temple. Josephus accurately represented the viewpoint of Jewry at this time when he wrote, "One Temple for the One God."[25] Despite this universal recognition, the Second Temple had not yet received the universal "peace" predicted for it by the prophet Haggai. The non-canonical documents that record this period of time tell us that under Persian rule the high priests had become the governing authority in Judea. The transformation of the priestly office to a political office had degraded the spiritual and moral character of the priesthood. Stories of political rivalries, intrigue, and murder color the narratives concerning the struggles for the high priest's office. An instance of this spiritual morass may be seen in the case of Yohanan (Johanan), the son of Joiada (Nehemiah 12:22), who assassinated his own brother in the Temple itself.

During this period, Judea came under the control of the Greeks through Alexander the Great and later his generals Ptolemy and Seleucis, yielding the Egyptian Greeks (Ptolemies) and the Syrian Greeks (Seleucids). Alexander and Ptolemy treated the Jews favorably and allowed continued governorship by the high priests, but during the reign of the Syrian Greek ruler Antiochus IV Epiphanes (175–164 B.C.), strife broke out. As a result, two Jewish factions, Orthodox and Hellenist (Jews who adopted Greek culture), contended for the high priesthood. Antiochus IV naturally sided with the Hellenistic party, and appointed a high priest who permitted pagan worship. The events surrounding this man's successor brought an invasion of Jerusalem in 170 B.C., in which many Jews were killed and the Temple—along with its restored treasures—was plundered. Antiochus further desecrated the Temple by sacrificing an unclean animal (a pig) on the Temple altar and by erecting a statute of Zeus Olympias in the Holy of Holies in 168 B.C. This action had been predicted by the prophet Daniel (Daniel 8:23-25; 11:21-35) and served as a partial fulfillment of the type of desecration the Temple would one day suffer under the Antichrist (Daniel 7:24-26; 9:24-27; 11:36-45).

The Purification of Zerubbabel's Temple

After the Jews suffered numerous atrocities—including the burning of copies of the Torah, forced consumption of pork (treif) contrary to the Mosaic law, and compulsory sacrifices to pagan idols, an Orthodox priest named Mattathias started a revolt, which his son Judas Maccabeas successfully completed.

In December 164 B.C., Judas Maccabeas liberated Jerusalem and purified the Temple, reinstituting the *tamid* (daily offerings). That day has been celebrated ever since as Hanukkah, or the Feast of Dedication (John 10:22). In time, the rule of the Maccabean (Hasmonean) dynasty was established over all Judea and lasted for a century.

Further desecration came to the Temple when the independent Jewish rule of Judea ended in the year 63 B.C. with the entrance of the Roman general Pompey into Jerusalem. When it became apparent that Pompey intended to enter the Temple, it was reported that thousands of Jews threw themselves to the ground before the general and begged him not to desecrate the Holy Place. Such a display only convinced Pompey that the Temple must contain great riches or some hidden secret, so not only did he enter the Holy Place, but he also tore away its veil of separation and marched into the Holy of Holies itself. A record of the event was preserved by the Roman historian Tacitus: "By right of conquest he [Pompey] entered their Temple. It is a fact well known, that he found no image, no statue, no symbolical representation of the Deity: the whole presented a naked dome; the sanctuary was unadorned and simple."[26] Tradition has further recorded that when Pompey emerged from the Temple he looked around at the Jews in wonder and exclaimed, "It is empty; there is nothing there but darkness!" Pompey's statement typified the confusion of Gentile rulers toward the Temple and its service of the invisible God, yet, when he ordered the walls of the city to be torn down, he left the Temple intact.

The Second Temple of Herod

The Plans for Enlarging the Temple

Rome was now in possession of the Land, and in 37 B.C. it placed in rulership over the Jews a despotic self-made former slave of Edomite ancestry by the name of Herod. This began a dynasty that would continue its tyrannical rule for another 100 years. In 23 B.C., Herod proposed a massive reconstruction of the almost 500-year-old Temple of Zerubbabel, which by this time had fallen into a state of disrepair. Because Herod's plans entailed the complete demolition of the Temple, the people feared that he might tear it down and not rebuild it. He therefore had to prepare and transport to the Temple Mount all the stones for the rebuilding project before touching the Temple itself. Herod began construction on the Temple in 19 B.C., and although the work on the central part of the sacrificial area was completed in seven years and dedicated, detail work continued on the Temple complex for the next 75 years.[27] His expansion project involved creating a new platform enclosing Mount Moriah, on whose pinnacle the Temple rested.

To accomplish this feat, Herod's engineers had to construct enormous retaining walls, some towering more than 150 feet from the bedrock foundation that sloped upward from the south to the north. A portion of one of these walls still stands today and is known as the Western (or Wailing) Wall (Hebrew, *Kotel*). The dimensions of these walls as exposed today are more than 1,500 feet in length (north to south) and 900 feet in width (east to west). Once these walls were in place thousands of tons of backfill was added and built over with level stones to form a platform encompassing some 40 acres.[28]

The Temple itself was doubled in height and its width was significantly increased.[29] New compartments were added to the original design, as well as a second story above the innermost chambers. A monumental royal basilica was constructed to serve as a meeting place for Jews buying animals for the offerings. Herod also transformed the Hasmonean fortress *(birah)* on the northwest corner into the Antonia (named in honor of Mark Anthony). In this was placed the Roman garrison, positioned to quell disturbances on the Temple Mount. The Antonia also had quarters for housing the Roman procurator when he was in residence (e.g., Pontius Pilate in A.D. 26–36).

The Herodian Temple reveals Herod's conflict of interests in its construction—namely, he tried to demonstrate to the Jews his support of Judaism, and at the same time he tried to prove his loyalty to Rome. This conflict was embodied in the display of the Roman eagle above the doorway of the Temple. As a bird of prey it symbolized the character of Rome, but it corrupted the character of the Temple as a place of peace. Its presence was also considered a violation of the Mosaic injunction against the making of graven images (whether of men or animals). Shortly after this image was placed on the Temple, a riot occurred (in 4 B.C.) and the Roman eagle was torn down and hacked to pieces. Herod severely punished those involved—then some months later died himself of an excruciatingly painful disease. This was interpreted as a divine verdict on Herod, who never lived to see the completion of the work he had begun. This was also the case with the dynastic successor Herod Antipas, who ruled during the time of Jesus and Paul (Acts 12:21-23).

At the time of the Second Temple, Jerusalem was considered, even by non-Jews, to be among the great cities of the East, and the Second Temple was regarded as one of the engineering marvels of the ancient world. Josephus tells us that the Temple was made of marble overlaid with gold, and appeared from a

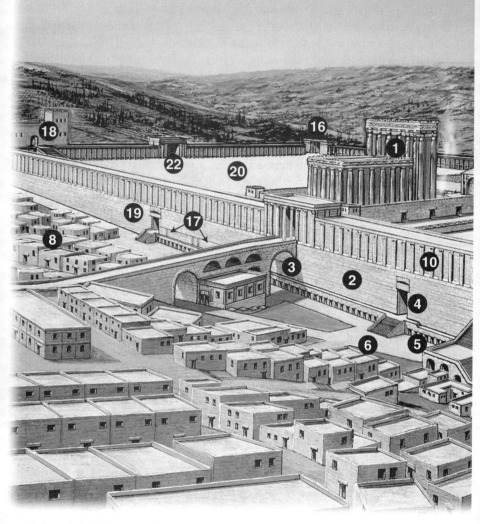

1. Second Temple (Herod's)
2. Western Wall
3. Wilson's Arch*
4. Barclay's Gate*
5. Small shops
6. Main N-S Street
7. Robinson's Arch*
8. Upper city
9. Royal porch
10. Pilasters
11. Double Gate

* Named after nineteenth-century explorer

Late Second Temple Period

12. Triple Gate
13. Plaza
14. Ritual bathhouse
15. Council House

16. Herodian Tower
17. Largest Ashlars
18. Antonia Fortress
19. Warren's Gate*

20. Court of the Gentiles
21. Eastern Gate
22. Tadi Gate
23. Hanuyot (moneychangers' area)

distance as a mountain of snow glistening in the sun. A commentary on the splendor of the Temple may be seen in the words of the sages who wrote, "He who has not seen Herod's building has not seen a beautiful building in his life" (Succah 51b). The New Testament records that Jesus' disciples were so impressed by the Temple's construction that they sought to point out to Him its latest additions and adornments when they were together at the site (Matthew 24:1; Luke 21:5). The significance that the Herodian Temple had to the Jews of that period has been well described by Talmudic scholar Rabbi Jacob Neusner:

> From near and far pilgrims climbed the paths to Jerusalem. Distant lands sent their annual tribute, taxes imposed by a spiritual rather than a worldly sovereignty. Everywhere Jews turned to the Temple mountain when they prayed. Although Jews differed about matters of law and theology, the meaning of history and the timing of the Messiah's arrival, most affirmed the holiness of Ariel, Jerusalem, the faithful city. It was here that the sacred drama of the day must be enacted.[30]

The awesome presence of the Temple seemed to render Jerusalem inviolable, and many Jews of the time were convinced that the prophetic promises of restoration had been fulfilled and therefore removed any further threat of the Temple being desecrated or destroyed. Some, however, held the view (such as the Dead Sea sect at Qumran) that the Herodian Temple was destined to be destroyed and replaced by a Temple that better conformed to the prophetic expectation. Among those who had the latter view were some Jewish-Christians who, warned by prophetic revelation (probably based on Jesus' prediction in Luke 19:43-44; 21:20-24), fled to the non-Jewish city of Pella several years before the Roman destruction[31] (an area beyond the Jordan that was safe from Roman attack).

The Destruction of Herod's Temple

According to Jewish, Roman, and Christian sources, the destruction of the Second Temple was divinely predicted. Various records preserve accounts of miraculous portents that were interpreted as signaling the impending doom of the Temple.[32] For example, Josephus (*Jewish Wars* 6:293-96) noted that at the time of the Passover *c.* A.D. 66, as the Roman seige was about to begin, the huge Nicanor gate that secured the inner court of the Eastern (Shushan) Gate was observed at the sixth hour to open of its own accord. This event was ultimately interpreted negatively as evidence of divine displeasure: "This again to the

The Temple Mount in the Late Second Temple Period

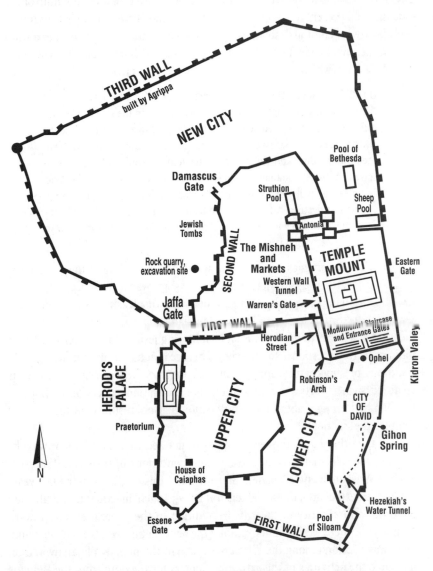

uninitiated seemed to be the best of omens, as they supposed that God had opened to them the gate of blessing; but the learned understood that the security of the Temple was dissolving of its own accord and that the opening of the gate meant a present to the enemy, interpreting the portent in their own minds as indicative of coming desolation."[33] This interpretation is also given in a story told in the Babylonian Talmud (*Yoma* 39b), along with another concerning the Temple service, which reflected the problem of divine favor:

> Our Rabbis taught: During the last forty years before the destruction of the Temple the lot "for the Lord" did not come up in the right hand; nor did the crimson-colored string [suspended in the Temple to show the acceptance of the pascal sacrifice] become white; nor did the westernmost light shine; and the doors of the Temple would open by themselves, until R. Yohanan b. Zakkai rebuked them, saying: "Temple, Temple, why will you yourself be the alarmer? I know about you that you will be destroyed, for Zechariah b. Ido has already prophesied concerning you: 'Open your doors, O Lebanon, that the fire may devour your cedars'" (Zechariah 11:1).

The New Testament's record of the spontaneous rending of the Temple veil in A.D. 33 (Matthew 27:51; Mark 15:38; Luke 23:45) was also interpreted by the Jewish-Christian community as a sign of divine displeasure as a result of the Jewish leadership's rejection of Jesus as Messiah. In fact, the torn veil is placed at the head of a series of miraculous signs following Jesus' death—signs meant to indicate heaven's response to the event. This account agrees in kind with Jewish traditions of supernatural manifestations, and the early Christian apologists regarded such reports as confirmation that the Nation's rejection of Jesus as Messiah had brought about its own rejection by God, resulting in the city and Temple's destruction.[34]

On the other hand, the Jewish sages contended that the problem was the result of the schismatic social and religious conditions of the time. Professors Michael Avi-Yonah and Menahem Stern write of this conflict: "In the last years before the destruction, the social tension grew to such an extent that it affected the order and security of the city. In addition to the general enmity toward Roman rule, there were conflicts among the Jews themselves. On the one hand, there was friction among the different groups in the priestly oligarchy and on the other, the activities of the extremist fighters for freedom from the Romans (the Sicarii), who used violence and were not averse to killing their opponents."[35]

Because of such internal contention, the Jewish sages felt that God was displeased and had allowed their own facetiousness to bring the calamity.[36] Another warning of the impending destruction came with the attempted desecration of the Temple under the notorious Roman emperor Gaius Caligula around A.D. 40–41. Josephus records that Caligula ordered his own image to be placed in the Holy of Holies, and mandated that any Jews who resisted his efforts were to be slaughtered or taken captive. So great was the resistance by both the Pharisees and the more radical Zealots that the edict was never carried out. A short time later, Caligula was assassinated.

The inevitable path to destruction began in A.D. 66 when riots against Rome erupted over the misrule of the procurators. A sensational act of defiance took place in the Temple when Eleazar, son of the captain of the Temple, ordered an end to the imperial sacrifice (which had been offered to the emperor alongside the traditional Jewish service during the period of Roman rule). The formidable Tenth Legion attempted to retake the Temple Mount but failed, losing much equipment to the Jewish defenders. This defiance, which by now had escalated to a full-scale revolt, soon secured all of Judea in Jewish hands. Enraged by the success of this revolt, the emperor, Nero, sent Rome's best commander, Vespasian, with Rome's finest legions and instructed them to crush the rebellion at all costs. In A.D. 68 the Roman army destroyed the Jewish sect at Qumran and turned their priestly enclave into a military outpost. By the following year the Romans had retaken all areas lost in the revolt except Jerusalem. Vespasian, who by this time had succeeded Nero as emperor, put his son, Titus, in charge of the Tenth Legion to oversee the Jerusalem campaign.[37]

Following the siege of Jerusalem, Titus took counsel with the officers of his army concerning the fate of the Temple. While there are conflicting reports as to the orders given, according to the Roman historian Tacitus, the majority of the officers were in agreement that nothing less than the total destruction of the Temple would secure a lasting peace. Therefore, on the ninth day of the Jewish month of Av, the city and the Temple were set ablaze, with the Roman soldiers slaughtering both priests and people.[38] Josephus says that Titus had given specific orders that the Temple be left intact, but evidently a soldier acting on impulse threw a torch through an archway of the Temple and set the tapestries inside on fire. It is said that when the building burned, the decorative gold on the walls melted and ran into the seams between the stones. Afterward, in a frenzied attempt to recover the gold, the Roman soldiers tore apart the stones of the Temple's walls, resulting in a complete desolation of the Temple (see Jesus' prophecy in Luke 19:43-44). A large number of the stones of the uppermost course of the outside retaining walls of the Temple were also forcibly torn down as a show of Roman vengeance. Today archaeologists have uncovered a section of the street where these stones fell along the southern end of the Western Wall. Most of the stones weighed 2–4 tons each, but some were in excess of 15 tons, and at several points the flagstones of the street were caved in by the force of the impact.[39] The Israelis purposely left this stone-littered street to remind modern-day visitors of the magnitude of the awful devastation suffered under the Romans.

The next year, Titus made a triumphal procession into Rome before his father Vespasian. In front of Titus were paraded 700 Jewish captives as well as some of the vessels from the Temple, a menorah, a table of shewbread, and some silver trumpets. Rome had conquered, the Temple was in ruins, and the Jewish people were scattered in exile.

The Lessons of History

The destructions of the First and Second Temples forced Judaism to assess the cause of their calamity and see what lessons could be learned. According to the Jewish Mishnah it was discovered by the rabbis that five things had happened to the Jewish forefathers on the ninth of Av (the Jewish month when these events occurred): 1) the Jews were sentenced not to enter Eretz-Yisrael; 2) the First Temple was destroyed; 3) the Second Temple was destroyed; 4) Bethar (the city in the Judean hills where Bar Kokhba made his final stand against the Romans) was captured; and 5) the Temple Mount was plowed over by the Romans (Mishnah, *Ta'anit* 4:6). The discovery that the two Temples were destroyed on the very same day was proof to the rabbis that the destruction had been part of God's predetermined plan rather than a historical coincidence. The lesson that emerged was that God was just as much in control of the Temple's destruction as He had been in its construction. If that were indeed the case, then the Jewish people knew they had reason to be hopeful, for they knew that God's plans included the rebuilding of yet another Temple. In the next chapter we will move ahead in time through the transition period of the past two millennia to the present day to see how this belief in the restoration of the Temple has motivated repeated attempts to rebuild the Temple whenever conditions have seemed favorable.

CHAPTER 5

The Temple in Transition

The Last 2,000 Years on the Temple Mount

The disappearance of the Temple created a revolutionary situation in the life of the contemporary Jew. Never having experienced such a situation, he did not know if it would be possible for him to continue to live as a Jew without the sacrificial services of the Temple.

Even though the Temple today is still in ruins because of our sins, one is still commanded to fear it even as it was when it was in all its glory. One is prohibited from entering anywhere that was previously prohibited, nor can one sit in the courtyard nor may he act in a light-hearted manner near the eastern wall. As is written "you shall keep the Sabbath and fear my Temple." Just as the Sabbath must be kept forever, so too must the Temple be feared forever, even though it may have been destroyed, the holiness surrounding it still stands.[1]

—RAMBAM

With the destruction of the Second Temple in A.D. 70 Judaism in the Land of Israel was faced with a crisis of spiritual and national survival. The problem was three-fold: 1) The question of how Jews could exist spiritually without the divinely sanctioned means of sacrifice to atone for sin; 2) the danger that the frameworks that had formerly assured the continuation of orderly society would disappear; and 3) the threat of the collapse of the Nation's central institutions of leadership, which had derived their legitimacy from the Temple. The religious replacement for atonement would come only after generations of halakhic development in which repentance and prayer temporarily substituted for the sacrifices, so for a time many Jews continued in a state of despair. The continuance of orderly life was also an issue because Rome had conferred upon the Jews of the Land of Israel the status of *dediticii* (defeated subjects or captives) and stripped them of all rights of self-government. Coming at a time when religious instability reigned, the loss of the central religious and political institutions of the Sanhedrin and high priesthood meant that there was no national leadership to guide the people.

Down but Not Destroyed

This crisis of post-Temple Judaism was indeed significant, and the threat to the continued national existence of Israel brought on by the loss of the Temple should not be underestimated. Jerusalem, as a city that depended politically and commercially upon the religious life centered on the Temple, suffered stagnation and decline, and its Jewish population was, for a period, in despair. However, it is a common misconception (especially amongst Christians who hold to the Preterist view) that the Roman destruction totally vanquished the Jews politically and religiously, thus ending the Jewish era. Although after the destruction many of the Jews in Jerusalem and Judea were dispersed, a great many Jews continued their life in the Land. Furthermore, it must be remembered that at the time of the destruction the majority of world Jewry had been living outside of the Land for more than 700 years. This community of Jews, especially those in Babylonia and Alexandria, were regarded by those in the Land as living in the exile or dispersion (Hebrew, *galut*; Greek, *diaspora*). Even so, this larger community of Diaspora Jews maintained connections with its historic homeland and financially supported the Temple. While its loss had consequences for them, their life was not radically affected. The greater adjustment came to the community of Jews that continued their residence in the Land.

Some of them apparently attempted to resume sacrifices after the Temple's destruction,[2] but with a dysfunctional priesthood and with Roman authorities opposed to any sign of independence represented by a revival of Temple ritual, the practice soon was discontinued.

Nevertheless, national leadership was restored under Rabbi Yohanan ben Zakk'ai, who, before the destruction, had been a leading member of an academy of priests and sages that had existed in Yavneh (a city west of Jerusalem near the Mediterranean coast). He and other sages continued this academy after the destruction as a national institution, although most priests and many highly prominent sages would not be a part because of Rabbi Yohanan ben Zakk'ai's controversial act of abandoning Jerusalem and surrendering to the Romans on the eve of the Temple's destruction. The leadership of this academy and the regulations (*takkanot*) promulgated by Rabbi Yohanan ben Zakk'ai and these sages helped rebuild the Jewish Nation and restore societal order. While the Jewish people could not judge criminal cases nor civil proceedings under the Roman edict, they could legislate in the area of religion and religious law (*halakha*). In this way the academy continued the institution of the Sanhedrin, which, by the time of his successor, Rabbi Gamaliel (A.D. 85–115), was said to have been functioning with all its original powers and to have resumed ties with the Diaspora communities.

Therefore, while the destruction of Jerusalem and the Temple had been a divine judgment (like the destruction of the First Temple), and a fulfillment of Jesus' prophecy regarding the national rejection of His Messianic status (Matthew 23:37-38; Luke 19:41-44; 21:6, 20-24), it was not meant to be an irreversible or irrevocable judgment, as the New Testament affirms (Matthew 23:39; Acts 1:6-7; 2:17-21; Romans 11:1-32). The Nation survived and Judaism continued, although Israel was not an independent Nation, and the Judaism was not the type predicted by the prophets. This would await a future time of Jewish national repentance and the coming of the Messiah (Zechariah 12:10-14; 14:4-11; Matthew 24:29-31; Romans 11:25-27).

Preserving the Priority of the Temple

Having regained control of its national existence in the Land, post-Temple Judaism further sought to restore its spiritual life by shifting its focus from the literal fulfillment of the Temple ritual (which was now impossible) to its inherently spiritual dimension. Yet the people still held to the hope of a restored Temple, which they believed would attend the return of national sovereignty in Jerusalem. F.E. Peters makes this comment concerning this preservation of the Temple:

> The city and its Temple were permanently and untouchably enshrined in the Mishnah more than a century after their destruction, where in the tractate Middoth the Temple's buildings and rituals were as lovingly and as carefully detailed as if there were still Jews passing daily in and out of those precincts. And in Kelim 1:6-9 the holiness of Jerusalem and the Temple are mapped and guaranteed. In both texts the conviction is enormous that in reality neither Jerusalem nor the house of the Lord had been destroyed, as in fact they had not, in the sense that the rabbis intended and that many subsequent generations of Jews understood.[3]

Rabbi Yohanan ben Zakk'ai had maintained the memory of the Temple as the major Sanctuary by transferring its rites and ceremonies to the synagogue as a "minor sanctuary" (see *Ro'sh ha-Shanah* 4.1-3; *Sukkah* 3.12). This deliberate act served to preserve the Temple's function for the future. Therefore, ceremonies such as the morning and evening synagogue services, which replaced the Temple's daily sacrifices, and the Musaf service, which commemorated the additional sacrifices on the days on which these used to be offered, reminded worshipers that a semblance of the past Temple service was still present while encouraging hope for its complete restoration in the future. This is evident in that the biblical verses which pertained to the sacrifices for that day were combined in the synagogue with prayers for the restoration of Israel to the Land and the rebuilding of the Temple. This can also be seen in the development of the *Shemoneh Esreh*, the "Eighteen Benedictions," which every Jew was required, according to the Mishnah (*Berekoth* 4:1), to pray three times daily. Benediction 14, in particular, is a prayer for the restoration of Jerusalem and the rebuilding of the Temple:

> Be merciful, O Lord our God, in Thy great mercy, towards Israel Thy people, and towards Jerusalem Thy city, and towards Zion the abiding place of Thy glory, and towards the Temple and Thy habitation, and towards the kingdom of the house of David, Thy righteous anointed one. Blessed art Thou, O Lord God of David, the builder of Jerusalem (*Shemoneh Esreh*, Benediction 14).

In this manner a "Temple consciousness" was maintained throughout the period of exile. This "Temple consciousness" also expressed itself in tangible

ways Whenever circumstances favored the rebuilding of the Temple, there
existed in Jerusalem an activist movement that would attempt this effort.

The Temple of Bar Kokhba

The earliest movement among Jews in the Land to rebuild the Temple
occurred only 60 years after the Temple's destruction. Although the Temple
Mount and much of the city of Jerusalem had remained in ruins during this
time, there was no ban on Jewish settlement in the city. As a result, 75 Jewish
communities had been established in Judea and seven synagogues were built at
the foot of Mount Zion. Even though politically the means did not exist to
rebuild the Temple, a fervent religious desire for its restoration continued. These
hopes were excited when the Roman emperor Publius Aelius Hadrian began his
reign in A.D. 117. Initially, Hadrian did not appear to entertain any hostility
toward the Jews, leading them to believe their situation would soon improve.
This belief may appear in the *Sibylline Oracles*, a Jewish pseudepigraphal
writing that states, "After him another will reign, a silver-headed man. He will
have the name of a sea. He will also be a most excellent man and he will consider
everything…" (*Sibylline Oracles* 5:46-50). This poetic description appears to be
of Hadrian because his name was like that of a sea (H-adrian—Adriatic), and
implied that he would act favorably toward the Jews.

The Jewish Midrash also indicates that official contacts between the Judean
Jews and the Roman government under Hadrian led the former to believe that
the emperor was even willing to grant permission for rebuilding the Temple
(*Genesis Rabbah* 64:10). Early Christian sources also seem to confirm this by
recording that the Jews attempted to raise funds for such a project. But, whatever plans were made for the rebuilding effort ended in A.D. 130 when Hadrian
came to Jerusalem to establish a Roman colony on the ruins of the Jewish city
and renamed it *Aelia Capitolina* (in honor of the family name of the emperor
and the Capitoline triad of deities—Jupiter, Juno, and Minerva). To make matters worse, on the very day that commemorated the Temple's destruction, the
Ninth of Av, the Roman governor of Judea, Tinneius Rufus, plowed up the Sanctuary of the Temple Mount and its environs in the name of the emperor (see
Eruchin 27a; *Ta'anit* 29a; Eusebius, *Ecclesiastical History* 4:6, 1). Also, during the
next two years, Hadrian issued harsh decrees against Jewish life and religious
observance (such as an edict prohibiting circumcision).

As a result, in A.D. 132 the Second Jewish Revolt against Rome erupted under the leadership of Shimon ben Kosiba—largely, it is believed by most historians, because of Hadrian's unkept promise to rebuild the Temple.[4] This revolt was successful in liberating Jerusalem. In recognition of the victory, the leading sage of the time, Rabbi Akiva, heralded Shimon as the Messiah and renamed him *Bar Kokhba* ("Son of the Star"), a Messianic title based on the prophecy of Numbers 24:17: "…a star shall come forth from Jacob, and a scepter shall rise from Israel, and shall crush through the forehead of Moab, and tear down all the sons of Sheth." From Jewish reckoning, Shimon seemed to fit this role, for he not only had managed to repulse the Roman garrisons but ruled as king of an independent Jerusalem for the next three years. He, too, was apparently convinced of his Messianic status, for he announced that his conquest of Jerusalem had begun the Messianic era and he began a new calendar system of counting the years from the date of his victory. However, the capstone of Messianic identity, as later the sage Maimonides would affirm (*Melochim* 11:4), was rebuilding the Temple.

According to the nineteenth-century Lithuanian rabbi, Samuel Shtrashun (R'shash), who claimed his source was the Roman historian of the period, Dio Casius, Bar Kokhba rebuilt the Temple and resumed the sacrificial system (commentary on *Pesachim* 74a). Rabbi Leibel Reznick, who has published a reassessment of the historical and theological events of the Bar Kokhba era,[5] believes that there may have been a Bar Kokhba dynasty that lasted 21 years and that Shimon ben Kosiba led the Second Revolt under the rule of the emperor Trajan and built the Third Temple. He then believes that Trajan quelled this revolt after a few years and sacked Bar Kokhba's Temple treasury. However, a Third Revolt (second Bar Kokhba uprising) occurred under Hadrian, and the Bar Kokhba Temple was rededicated and sacrifices resumed until Hadrian subdued this rebellion and again sacked the Temple treasury. Whichever historical reconstruction one accepts, the question of the rebuilding of the Temple under Bar Kokhba still exists. Let's consider some of the evidence that has been put forth in support of this proposal.

Evidence for the Third Temple of Bar Kokhba

Rabbi Reznick finds literary evidence for Bar Kokhba's rebuilding of the Temple in the *Sibylline Oracles,* where the advent of a heaven-sent Messianic figure who rebuilds the Temple is described: "For there came from the heavenly realm a man, one blessed, with a scepter in his hands which God gave him, and he ruled all things well and restored the riches the previous men had seized....and the city which God desired he made more brilliant than stars and sun and moon, and he provided ornament and made a holy temple..." (*Sibylline Oracles* 5:414-417, 420-422). Rabbi Reznick suggests that the "blessed man with a scepter" is Bar Kokhba, the "previous men" who had "seized" the riches are the Romans, the "city which God desired" is Jerusalem, and "a holy temple" is the Third Temple. In addition, he argues that other historical accounts concerning Hadrian's actions toward the Jewish Temple would be better understood given the existence of the Bar Kokhba Temple. For example, the Midrash states, "When Hadrian entered the Holy of Holies, he showed great arrogance and blasphemed God" (*Exodus Rabbah* 51:5). Since the Second Temple had been destroyed 60 years earlier by Titus, what Holy of Holies did Hadrian enter? While Hadrian may have entered the ruins where the Holy of Holies once stood, Rabbi Reznick argues that the language more properly understands the defiling of an existing Temple. In like manner, the seventh-century Byzantine historian known as Chronicum Paschale, who says he drew from earlier records, wrote in his *History of the Jews*: "Hadrian tore down the Temple of the Jews in Jerusalem and built two public baths, a theatre, and the Temple of Jupiter."[6] How could Hadrian tear down a Temple that did not exist in his time? Paschale's words would make sense only if the Bar Kokhba Temple were in view. In addition, there is the statement of the fourth-century Roman emperor Julian in his *Fragment of a Letter to a Priest*: "...what have they [the Jews] to say about their own temple, which was overthrown *three times* and even now is not being raised up again?..." (emphasis added). To what three historical destructions of the Jerusalem Temple could Julian be referring? History only records two: the Babylonian destruction of 586 B.C. and the Roman destruction of A.D. 70. Julian's remark was made in A.D. 362. Could he have had in mind Hadrian's destruction in A.D. 135?

Another source of evidence is coins minted by Bar Kokhba that bear an image of the Holy Temple. It was common practice among the Gentile nations in those times to picture a temple on coins, but it was never the practice to depict a nonexisting temple. On some of these coins there also appears the name of Eleazar, the high priest appointed by Bar Kokhba. In light of this numismatic evidence, Rabbi Leibel Reznick asks:

> Why would Bar Kokhba issue coins of a Jewish Temple that had been destroyed sixty years earlier, a Temple no longer standing, a Temple

whose façade would not be recognized?...If there was no Temple, there was no service. Why then did Bar Kokhba appoint a High Priest? A primary function of the Jewish Messiah is to rebuild the Temple as described in the Book of Ezekiel (Ezekiel 40–47). Since Bar Kokhba believed himself to be the Messiah, why didn't he at least begin rebuilding the Temple of the Jews during his two-and-a-half-year reign? These questions almost suggest their own obvious solution. Bar Kokhba did in fact rebuild the Temple during the years he ruled in Jerusalem. The Temple façade that Bar Kokhba built was represented on the Bar Kokhba coins.[7]

The Coin of Bar Kokhba

Silver tetradrachma coin of the Bar Kokhba period, depicting the façade of the Temple, the star of the messiah (top), and the name "Simon" written in two parts on each side. In the center of the Temple is the Torah shrine with two scrolls of the Law.

Additional support for this argument comes from an almost identical but much more detailed image of the Temple façade that appears in a fresco (see below) at the ancient synagogue (about A.D. 225) in Dura-Europos. If this image was borrowed from that found on the coins, how could the additional details, not shown on the coins because they were too small, be explained? One idea is that the image was that of Hadrian's temple to Jupiter erected on the Temple Mount. But why would a Jewish synagogue depict a pagan temple? An alternate theory is that when Hadrian recaptured Jerusalem he did not tear down Bar Kokhba's Temple, but simply converted it into a pagan shrine. If this is the case, then the painter of the synagogue fresco was copying an image that still existed when his work was commissioned.

There is also evidence of the resumption of the sacrificial system in a reference to Rabbi Gamaliel's concern that Passover would arrive too early that year for the sacrificial lambs and doves to reach maturity (*Sanhedrin* 11b). Since the dates for Rabbi Gamaliel, the head of the academy at Yavne, appear to have been well after the Second Temple's destruction, the only Temple in which such sacrifices could have been offered was the Bar Kokhba Temple. In addition, Rabbi Gamaliel's own sacrifice is mentioned in the Talmud in answer to a question

Image of the Temple in a fresco

about the method of roasting the sacrificial Pascal lamb. It states that Rabbi Gamaliel ordered his servant to grill this sacrifice over a metal grill. Again, the only possible place this could have happened is the Bar Kokhba Temple.

Rabbi Reznick also believes that the Temple Mount bears archaeological evidence for the Bar Kokhba Temple. When he compared the measurements of the elevated platform (Azurah) on which the Dome of the Rock presently sits, a platform which is considered by most Orthodox Jews and Israeli archaeologists to be a remnant of the Second Temple's flooring, he discovered that it was too large to have been the flooring of the Azurah Courtyard of the Second Temple. If it did not fit the dimensions of this courtyard, as preserved by the Mishnah tractate *Middot,* then to what Temple would it conform? To his surprise he found that its measurements conformed exactly to the dimensions of the Azurah Courtyard of Ezekiel's Temple as given by Rabbi Yom Tov Lipman Heller in his commentary *Trzurat HaBayit* ("Structure of the Temple"). This calculation was arrived at by using a cubit measurement of 19.07 inches, which produced the identical dimensions of 550 feet x 540 feet. He also noted that Maimonides described this courtyard in the Temple as having an elevated floor surrounded by a retaining wall—which also matches the platform under the Dome of the Rock.[8] His explanation for this is that since Messiah was expected to build the Temple of Ezekiel's vision, and Bar Kokhba was proclaimed as Messiah, that the Temple he rebuilt would have employed Ezekiel's measurements. Therefore, the elevated platform on which the Dome of the Rock was built is actually the remains of the Messianic Temple of Bar Kokhba.[9]

Bar Kokhba's reign ended when Hadrian recaptured Jerusalem in A.D. 135. The emperor issued restrictive edicts against Jewish study of the Torah and made all Jewish observances or religious practices a capital offense. In order to demonstrate that the Jews had not succeeded in saving their people or their Temple, Hadrian probably destroyed the Bar Kokhba Temple.[10] This act of destruction may be that referred to in the Midrash when it says, "Hadrian, may his bones be turned to dust, came and dashed the Temple stones" (*Deuteronomy Rabbah* 3:13). In its place he erected a temple to the Roman trinity of Juno, Jupiter, and Minerva, along with an equestrian statue of himself on the Temple Mount.[11] This served as an official statement of the continuing triumph of the Roman Empire. The evidence for this comes from an inscription on a Roman gate from that time period (located near the present American Consulate), which states that "a holy place" stood on the Temple Mount. Most scholars assume that this "holy place" was Hadrian's pagan temple and that it was built on the site of the Jewish Temple because Hadrian built similar shrines on Christian holy sites as well. The early church father Jerome was of the opinion that the equestrian statue was over the site of the Holy of Holies.[12] John Wilkinson, however, disagrees: "It is clear that a political and religious statement was being made...in the statue, undoubtedly of Hadrian, *overlooking* the ruins on the Temple Mount...."[13] Wilkinson further argues that Hadrian was an astute ruler who realized that the time might come when the Empire would wish to allow the Jews to rebuild their Temple. Leaving the site in ruins while erecting the Roman temple elsewhere allowed for this possibility and, at the same time, attested to the absoluteness of the Roman victory. Any rebuilding of the Jewish Temple would be by Roman right of decision and generous forgiveness. Though Hadrian turned the city of Jerusalem into the Roman colony of Aelia Capitolina, Rome did little more than maintain civil order. It was satisfied that it had made its point and that it had prevented Jerusalem from continuing to serve as a focal point for Jewish nationalism and revolt.

The Jews continued their life under Roman rule until the Roman emperor Constantine (A.D. 288–337) replaced paganism as the state religion with Christianity. With Christianity now the official and favored religion, all pagan temples and statues were destroyed and replaced by Christian places of worship. The Temple Mount became a focal point of Christian theological superiority. It had been argued in Jewish/Christian disputations for two centuries that the destruction of the Second Temple had proven the end of the old Jewish covenant. Now that an institutional Christianity had risen to supplant national Judaism as the "true and accepted faith," it could visibly demonstrate its contention of Israel's divine rejection. This was accomplished in two ways: one, by leaving the Temple Mount in ruins and progressively turning it into a dung heap; and two, by building the Church of the Holy Sepulchre in a structural layout identical to the Temple and setting it on higher ground overlooking the Temple Mount (see chapter 7).

During the Roman Byzantine period (A.D. 324–637) which followed, Jews in the Land suffered even greater restrictions under Christian rule. Both the Jews who remained in Israel or visited on pilgrimages were prohibited from gathering on the Temple Mount except for one day a year, the Ninth of Av (the day commemorating the destruction of the Temple). On that day, they were allowed to visit what was known as the *lapis pertusus* ("pierced stone")—the place considered by most scholars today to be the rock within the Muslim Dome of the Rock. The early church father Jerome records that the Jews even had to purchase a permit to weep on this day.[14] Otherwise, prayers were made from a distance on the Mount of Olives. Not until later did a new development in the Roman succession of rulers offer the Jewish community a new hope for rebuilding the Temple.

The Temple of Julian

Upon the death of the first Christian emperor Constantine in A.D. 361, his nephew, Flavius Claudius Julianus, or Julian, became the undisputed ruler of the Roman Empire at the age of 30. Julian had been raised as a Christian and educated in Christian truth by the renowned bishop of Caesarea, Eusebius. But upon his ascension to the throne he revealed what he had been keeping a secret for years: that he had converted to paganism around his twentieth birthday. His syncretistic paganism included being an initiate in at least three mystery religions, including Mithraism, and a reverence for the gods and goddesses of Homeric tradition. Out of his desire for religious pluralism he issued an edict of universal religious toleration. However, this toleration did not extend to Christianity because he had grown up witnessing Christians persecuting those of other beliefs. As a result, he referred to Christians as "demented" and to Christianity as a "disease."

By contrast, Julian favored Judaism because he viewed Christianity as a defection from Judaism. He also saw Judaism as being more in harmony with his concept of religious pluralism, since Judaism practiced the offering of sacrifices, as did the pagan religions. As Jeffrey Brodd notes: "Julian knew that the Jews had sacrificed animals in the Jerusalem Temple. By allowing the Temple to be rebuilt, he was ensuring that Jews would resume their practice of offering animal sacrifices—to a god Julian regarded as his own!"[15] Furthermore, Julian's belief that the god of the Jews "is worshiped by us also under other names"[16] enabled him to support it while isolating Christianity, which claimed exclusivity and superiority with their one true God, Christ. Thus, Julian issued numerous edicts that restricted Christian worship and favored Judaism. These actions were regarded by Christians with disdain and horror, but they were nothing compared to Julian's decision to rebuild the Jewish Temple—an action designed to replace Christianity with paganism as the dominant religion. It was an effective polemic against Jesus' role as a prophet, since He had prophesied that after the Temple was destroyed, "not one stone would be left upon another." Because Christians thought this prophecy would stand forever, Julian's plan countered

The Temple Mount in the Roman Period (A.D. 70–132)

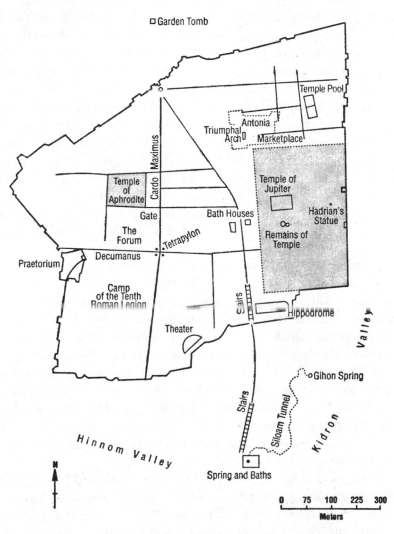

□ Garden Tomb

Temple Pool

Antonia

Triumphal Arch

Marketplace

Cardo Maximus

Temple of Aphrodite

Temple of Jupiter

Hadrian's Statue

Gate

Bath Houses

The Forum

Tetrapylon

Remains of Temple

Decumanus

Praetorium

Camp of the Tenth Roman Legion

Stairs

Hippodrome

Theater

Valley

Stairs

Gihon Spring

Siloam Tunnel

Kidron

Hinnom Valley

N

Spring and Baths

0   75   100   225   300

Meters

the central Christian tenet that the Temple's destruction proved that Christians, not Jews, were the chosen people of God. Julian's intentions to rebuild the Temple were made known prior to his Persian campaign, when, in his *Letter to the Community of the Jews* (A.D. 362), he promised to abolish anti-Jewish laws and to rebuild "the sacred city of Jerusalem" (which included the Temple), where he would join them in worship: "When I have successfully concluded the war with Persia, I may rebuild by my own efforts the sacred city of Jerusalem, which for so many years you have longed to see inhabited, and may bring settlers there, and together with you, may glorify the Most High God therein."[17] He explicitly referred to the Temple elsewhere when he said, "I raise with the utmost zeal the Temple of the Highest God."[18] The last great Roman historian, Ammianus Marcellinus (A.D. 330–395), a pagan who was a member of Julian's expedition to Persia, gave a detailed account of Julian's Temple project in his work entitled *Rex Gestae* (Book XXIII). He records that Julian was "eager to extend the memory of his reign by great works...[and] planned to restore at vast cost the once splendid temple at Jerusalem."[19] Julian therefore arranged for funds and building materials for the Temple project to be provided, and appointed his friend and general Alypius of Antioch to oversee the reconstruction.

The pagan Romans had no interest in Julian's plans, for they viewed Julian's efforts merely as a way for him to establish a memorial to his rule. However, the Jews were ecstatic over Julian's announcement. Although initially Jewish religious leaders raised the question of whether it was appropriate to rebuild the Temple with the help of a pagan ruler, any reluctance was overruled by the reminder that the Second Temple had been rebuilt under Cyrus and then Herod. Rabbi Acha pointed this out, contending that since certain sacred objects were absent from the Second Temple when it was rebuilt, then the Third Temple (of Julian) could be built without them,[20] and that the Temple could even be built before the coming of the Messiah.[21] The Jewish religious authorities then led the way in acquiring building materials. According to the church father Gregory of Nazianzus, who wrote in Asia Minor within a year of the rebuilding project, the Jews "in large number and with great zeal set about the work." Women contributed ornaments and carried dirt in their gowns,[22] and, according to the Christian monk Ephraem of Syria, the people "raged and raved and sounded trumpets" and "all of them...were without restraint."[23] As Jews throughout the Land and in the Diaspora heard that the Temple was being erected, a wave of immigration to Jerusalem began. Christian sources tell of multitudes of Jews returning to Jerusalem to assist in the project, and evidence for this was found in an inscription discovered beneath Robinson's Arch on the southern end of the Western Wall in 1969. Probably written by one of those returning to rebuild the Temple, the Hebrew inscription is based on Isaiah 66:14: "Then you shall see [this], and your heart shall rejoice, and their bones shall flourish like grass...." The inscription reveals that those returning to Jerusalem expected the Messianic era to begin soon. This is affirmed by the writer's deliberate change in the wording of the passage. Whereas Isaiah had written, "When you see this... *your* bones shall flourish like grass," the inscription reads "*their* bones like grass." Israeli archaeologist Meir Ben-Dov says, "The explanation seems quite logical: 'And when ye see this' refers to the people who will behold the inscription, whereas 'their bones' are those of the dead about to be resurrected."[24] With the rebuilding of the Temple under way, the Jews apparently expected that last days were at hand, and with them the national resurrection of the Jewish people as predicted by the prophets.

While the Jews rejoiced over the rebuilding as a fulfillment of Isaiah's prophecy, Christians saw it as a fulfillment of Daniel's prophecy. They interpreted the event in light of Daniel 11:34 and they concluded that the emperor's act was the "abomination of desolation" and therefore branded him "Julian the Apostate." Christians felt that God would avenge this blasphemous act, and soon an event took place that seemed to support their belief. According to the accounts left to us by historians of the time, an earthquake interrupted the building plans and destroyed the site materials. Philip Hammond, who has studied this earthquake, which also destroyed the Nabatean city of Petra, describes what happened:

> The stones were piled and ready. Costly wood had been purchased. The necessary metal was at hand. The Jews of Jerusalem were rejoicing. Tomorrow—May 20, 363 A.D.—the rebuilding of the Temple would begin!...Suddenly, and without warning, at the third hour of the night...the streets of Jerusalem trembled and buckled, crushing two hundred years of hope in a pile of dust. No longer would there be any possibility of rebuilding the Temple.[25]

The Roman historian Ammianus Marcellinus, who may have personally witnessed the incident, wrote, "Terrifying balls of flame kept bursting forth near the foundations of the Temple," burning some of the workers to death.[26] Apparently the earthquake ignited reservoirs of gasses trapped underground or ignited volatile materials that were on hand for the building project, resulting in a violent explosion. Christian sources told the story with some embellishments drawn from the punishment of Korah in Numbers 16, claiming that earthquakes, furious winds, lightning, and fire fell from heaven—accompanied by a vision of Christ—as a judgment on those who sought to blaspheme the verdict of God and history. This account has in modern times been used by Christian polemicists as a "proof" of Christianity.[27] While we might understand this earthquake to have been an act of divine intervention, it does not follow that it was meant as a sign that the Jews were never to build their Temple. That the Temple was not meant to be rebuilt in A.D. 363 is obvious, yet this does not deny that God Himself has a decreed time for the Temple's rebuilding and Israel's restoration. At this time the emperor had just begun his Persian campaign, so his supervisor Alypius suspended the work. However, it was never to be renewed, for Julian died in the war (June 26, 363), and was succeeded by the Christian emperor Jovian, who put an end to both Julian's favorable edicts toward the Jews and any hope of rebuilding.

Lost Opportunities to Rebuild

During the remaining centuries under Roman Byzantine rule, other unsuccessful attempts were made to organize a Temple rebuilding effort. Only 75 years after the Julian catastrophe, Jewish hopes for rebuilding were again aroused through the Empress Eudocia's show of kindness to the Jews in the Land. Eudocia was a Greek woman born in Athens as Athenais and raised as a pagan by her father Leontius, an Athenian sophist and professor of rhetoric. She converted to Christianity in Constantinople (receiving her Christian name *Eudocia* at her baptism) in order to marry the emperor Theodosius II who had been attracted by her great beauty. Theodosius II (A.D. 408-450) continued the strict prohibition against Jews entering Jerusalem except to pray on the one day of Tisha B'Av. He further persecuted the Jews in the Land by forbidding them the right to hold public positions or construct synagogues. However, when Eudocia made her first pilgrimage to Jerusalem in A.D. 438, she intervened for the Jews so that they could again return to the Holy City and resume prayer on the Temple Mount. This act was viewed by them as a first step toward rebuilding the Temple itself. In light of the fact that none of these Jews had never before set foot on the Temple Mount, it is understandable that they would interpret the empress' clemency as a sign of divine restoration. Therefore, the heads of the Galilean Jews immediately sent a letter to the Diaspora Jewish community in Egypt, calling them back to the Land in preparation for the imminent Messianic age:

To the great and mighty Jewish people; from the priests and elders in Galilee—many greetings! Know that the end of the exile of our people is near and all our tribes shall be gathered together. Lo, the rulers of Rome have decreed that our city, Jerusalem, shall be returned to us. Come quickly to Jerusalem for the Feast of Tabernacles, for the kingdom is at hand in Jerusalem.[28]

But to the Jews' disappointment, the day of deliverance was not to come. When the delegates from these Jewish communities assembled at the Temple Mount, a riot ensued, and a number of people were stoned to death by Christians. A Christian record of this incident reports that a miracle occurred and that the stones descended from heaven in order to prevent the Jews from rebuilding the Temple. However, the Jews who were struck by the stones interpreted the matter quite differently. Those who survived the stoning brought accusations against the disciples of an anti-Semitic monk named Barsauma, who were subsequently arrested for murder. Even so, Juvenal, the bishop of Jerusalem, protected Barsauma from harm, and under his political influence the issue was turned against the Jews.

Furthermore, in A.D. 443 Eudocia was exiled to Jerusalem after being accused of having aspirations for the government of the Eastern empire. While the reason for her exile is uncertain, her benevolence toward the Jews may have been used by her enemies in the court to bring about this accusation and her husband's disfavor. Although her banishment in Jerusalem (where she died in A.D. 460) ended Jewish aspirations, the empress spent lavishly on the restoration of churches and was responsible for numerous building projects in the city, such as a church and a hospital above the Pool of Siloam.

The next opportunity would not come until A.D. 614, when the Persians shattered the Byzantine defenses and entered Jerusalem. The Jews of Jerusalem helped the Persians defeat the Christian emperor Heraclius, and as a result the Persian king Chosroes II appointed a Jew named Nehemiah as governor of the city. The Jews believed it was more than a coincidence that the Persians of Bible times had also named a Nehemiah as governor of Jerusalem. That earlier Nehemiah had rebuilt the city's walls to protect the newly built Temple of Zerubbabel. The Jews took this as a sign that king Chosroes would likewise grant them permission to rebuild Jerusalem and the Temple. In this they were not disappointed, for Chosroes II apparently gave his approval and the Jews enjoyed a brief hegemony from A.D. 614-617 in which they resumed the ritual service atop the Temple Mount. The Jewish pseudepigraphal work entitled the *Book of*

Zerubbabel confirms this when it remarks that the Jewish leader "made sacrifices."[29] It is unclear how far the work of rebuilding progressed during these years, but whatever work was begun was soon halted when the Persian king changed his mind and rescinded the permission. This change may have been caused by political pressure from the substantial Christian influence that existed at that time in the Persian court in Iraq. The Persians further dashed any possibility of reprieve by installing their own governor and expelling all Jews from Jerusalem.

This situation worsened for the Jews when, some 15 years later, the Byzantine emperor Heraclius recaptured the city and built an octagonal church on the Temple Mount.[29] Even so, the Temple Mount remained largely unoccupied until, in A.D. 691, the Umayyad Caliph 'Abd of Malik constructed the Dome of the Rock on a raised platform in the middle of the Herodian esplanade, and his successors built the Al-Aqsa Mosque at the southern end over the Byzantine church. This act suppressed any hope of regaining or restoring the Temple Mount to the Jews.

Zionism—A First Step Toward Restoration

The Zionist movement, which began in 1897, reawakened hopes that one day Jews would return not only to Eretz-Yisrael but also to the Temple Mount.

This movement led to the several waves of Jewish immigrants who desired to reclaim the ancient Jewish homeland and place the capital in Jerusalem. A watching world took notice as the Jews streamed back in what seemed to many observers a fulfillment of the prophetic dream. One of these observers, American President Warren G. Harding, stated on June 1, 1921, "It is impossible for one who has studied at all the services of the Hebrew people to avoid the faith that they will one day be restored to their historic national home and there enter on a new and yet greater phase of their contribution to the advance of humanity."[30] On May 15, 1948 that "faith" became reality when the British ended their mandate of Palestine and opened the door for the Jews to form the independent State of Israel. The Arab nations that surrounded the newly declared state went to war in an attempt to end its birth just as quickly as it had begun. But with an unexpected vigor that stunned the world, the Jews fought and won against overwhelming odds. However, the eastern section of the city of Jerusalem, which includes the Temple Mount and Western Wall, fell under the control of the Hashemite Kingdom of Jordan. Although Jews continued to live in the western

The Temple Mount in the Byzantine Period (A.D. 324–638)

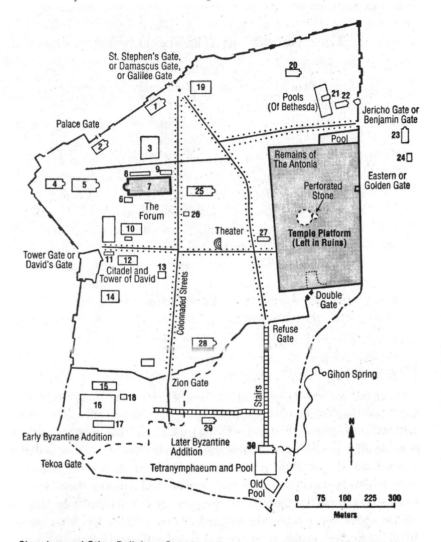

Churches and Other Religious Structures

1. Serapion Church
2. St. Georges Church
3. Patriarch's Hospice or the Smith's Market
4. Theodorus Monastery
5. Spondaean Monastery
6. Baptistry
7. Church of the Holy Sepulchre
8. Priest's House
9. Patriarch's Palace
10. Greek Monastery Church of John the Baptist
11. Monastery of St. Sabas
12. Iberian Monastery
13. Syrian Monastery
14. Church of St. James
15. House of Caiaphas
16. Basilica of Mt. Zion
17. St. Stephen's Church
18. Priest's House
19. Eudocia's Palace
20. Church of Mary Magdalene
21. Church of the Paralytic
22. Church of the Nativity of St. Mary
23. Tomb of the Virgin
24. Gethsemane
25. Church of SS Cosmos and Damianus
26. Home of the Aged
27. St. Sophia's Church
28. Nea (New) Church
29. Monastery of St. Peter
30. Eudocia's Church

section of the city, just meters away from these holy sites, they were again forbidden access to them.

The "Defeat" in the Six-Day War

The modern Jewish Nation's loss of access to its most holy site continued for the next 19 years. Then in June 1967 Israel was again attacked by the neighboring Arab countries. Again Israel was victorious, but this time with an unexpected triumph: The Jordanian eastern section of Jerusalem was captured, and the Temple Mount was finally under the control of the independent Jewish state. It seemed that a great circle of history had been closed and the time of restoration was at hand. Indeed, that would have been the conclusion of previous generations of Jews who had longed for just such a return. However, this victory turned into the greatest of all lost opportunities, one of the worst religious "defeats." As it turned out, the city of Jerusalem, finally reunited, ended up religiously divided, with the control of the Temple Mount returned to the very enemies from whom it was captured! Through the ages Jewish people had longed to ascend the Temple Mount, but when the opportunity finally came, it was turned down. Why? In order to understand this surprising turn of events, we must briefly reconstruct the events that occurred on that fateful day of June 7, 1967, when Israel regained possession of the Temple Mount.

Returning the Temple Mount

After the unplanned capture of the Temple Mount, the Jewish authorities had to take time to think about the political and religious ramifications of what they had done. During the conquest military officers had attempted to safeguard Muslim sensibilities by controlling the zealousness of the soldiers who crowded onto the site of the Dome of the Rock. An Israeli flag that had been hoisted up to the top of the Dome had been ordered removed. Rabbi Shlomo Goren, the chief rabbi of the Israeli Defense Forces, had urged that the Muslim buildings be blown up, but he was repeatedly rebuffed. In the days following the capture of the Temple Mount, the site was closed to the Jewish population, and only the Western Wall was made accessible to those who sought to pray at the Mount. Nevertheless, Rabbi Goren, who was the first to lead public prayer at the Western Wall, held jurisdiction of the Temple Mount for a month after its capture. He recounts the opportunities he had in those early days and what the site meant to him as an Orthodox Jew:

With the first military deployment in the liberated and united Jerusalem, I decided that the time has come to establish facts on the ground, and I started to organize Jewish prayer services on the Temple Mount, in areas permissible for those defiled by contact with the dead to enter. In these great days, I could not free myself from the thought that, from historical perspective, the designation of the Western Wall Plaza for Jewish prayer is only the result of Jews being banned from the Temple Mount by the Crusaders and by Moslems together. Hence, an intolerable situation has been created, that even after the liberation of the Temple Mount, the Moslems remained up on the Temple Mount, and we stayed down below, them inside and us outside. Prayer by the Western Wall is a sign of destruction and exile, and not freedom and redemption, since Jewish prayer by the Western Wall started only in the 16th century. Before that, Jews had prayed on the Temple Mount for centuries, and when they were expelled, they prayed on the Mountain of Olives, across from the Eastern Gate. Jews have been praying by the Western Wall for only about three hundred years. In the framework of the function of the Military Rabbinate, we held organized study and prayer on the Temple Mount—*Shacharit* (morning service), *Mincha* (afternoon service), and *Ma'ariv* (evening service), and Torah reading on Shabbat, Monday, and Thursday on the Temple Mount Plaza itself, inside the Mugrabi Gate, near our study center. Once, the Wakf people tried to close the Shevatim Gate, on the northeastern end of the Temple Mount, from a gathering of officers of the Military Rabbinate that was held on the Temple Mount. We broke through the gate and entered. That taught them the Temple Mount is ours officially and practically. On the 9th of Av, 5727 [1967], I held a *Mincha* (afternoon) service for a small group on the Temple Mount Plaza across from the steps going up south of the Dome of the Rock, a place that is permissible to enter according to all halachic authorities. This *Mincha* service on the 9th of Av on the Temple Mount raised many reactions in the media in Israel and abroad. Jewish writers hostile to religion in the State started incitement against our efforts to renew Jewish prayer on the Temple Mount.[31]

But Rabbi Goren's presence on the Temple Mount was to be short-lived. A little more than a month after its capture, General Moshe Dayan, who had commanded the Israeli forces in the war, came up to Rabbi Goren and told him that the government had decided to return the jurisdiction of the Temple Mount to the Muslim Wakf. Rabbi Goren recounts the events of that day:

In the midst of deliberations, in both governmental and religious frameworks, about renewing Jewish prayer on the Temple Mount and building a permanent synagogue on the open southern plain, the Minister of Defense told me, to my great surprise, that he decided to pass the auspices and responsibilities for all arrangements on the Temple Mount to the Islamic Wakf. He ordered me to take the Torah study center of the Military Rabbinate down from the Temple Mount and to remove all officers of the Temple Mount. From then on, according to him, the Military Rabbinate has no responsibility for the arrangements there, and I should stop organizing Jewish prayer on the Temple Mount. I accepted the order with anger and pain, and I told the Minister of Defense that this is likely to bring about a third destruction, since the key to our sovereignty over Judea, Samaria, and Gaza is the Temple Mount.[32]

Rabbi Goren later told me that this was the private decision of Dayan and not the government, but that the government weakly followed Dayan's decision since the act had already been done. Dayan was a secularist and had long been friends with the Arabs despite his military actions against them. Although he knew the biblical history of the site, he felt it was past history and that the only possible future for Israel lay in its present security—one that was threatened by continued possession of one of Islam's holy sites. Dayan's actions have been criticized by Gershom Salomon, founder and director of The Land of Israel and Temple Mount Faithful Movement and one of the soldiers who was present on the Temple Mount at the time of its capture:

He [Moshe Dayan] thought that if he made a gesture and gave back the Temple Mount, that they [the Arabs] would appreciate it so much that after one hour [sic] they would call him to the Table and make peace. But he acted in dishonor and against the will of God and history, and gave back the Temple Mount, the heart and soul, the center of Israeli life for more than 4,000 years. After God had brought back again His people to His house, the Temple Mount, and He expected His people and the leadership of His people to appreciate it and to build again the Temple, as the prophets said, on the right place, on the Temple Mount, after 1,300 years of Arab imperialistic occupation of the Temple Mount and the Land of Israel. But he [Moshe Dayan] did a terrible thing, and the result of this was that the Arabs did not call him after one hour or even ten years to make peace. They did the opposite and started to fight against the people of Israel and to destroy this people, because they considered this act [of Dayan's] an act of weakness…and the war which came in 1973 [Yom Kippur War] was God's punishment on us for doing this terrible thing….[33]

It is somewhat ironic that Chief of Staff Yitzhak Rabin—who gave the order to Colonel Motta Gur on June 7 to "enter the Old City immediately and capture it!"—should have been assassinated as Prime Minister out of concern that he would give away the holy city to the Arabs, and that General Moshe Dayan died with honors after in fact giving away the Holy of the Holies! So that we can further understand the actions of the Israeli government on that day, let's look at the attitude the Jewish authorities displayed toward the Temple Mount at the time of its capture in 1967.

The Attitude Toward the Temple Mount

On the day of the Temple Mount's "liberation" there occurred a most exciting and odd event. Motta Gur, the conqueror of the Temple Mount, shouted on his two-way radio, "The Temple Mount is in our hands!" (see photo section). Rabbi Shlomo Goren, the chief rabbi of the Israeli Defense Forces, gripped by the emotion of the moment, blew the shofar at the Western Wall (see photo section). Then came renowned Israeli Prime Minister Levi Eshkol, who, before the entire nation, pronounced the *shehechianu* blessing (a prayer given at the arrival of important events). A photographer took a photo of an Israeli soldier pressed against the Wall and bathed in tears. This now-famous photo became the symbol of Israeli victory over their most sacred site. But to an Orthodox Jewish observer of the past, something was wrong with this picture. Israel Eldad, one of Israel's premiere historians, has graphically described the problem:

> What is going on here? At the Wall? Why not on the Temple Mount? Who, at that time, thought of Halachic restrictions? Certainly not Gur and Eshkol and the weeping soldier and those masses that began to flow to the Wall. It was not Halachah that prevented them from ascending and celebrating on the Mount….The [soldiers] break into the Temple square. With their commanders, they storm its length and diagonally cross its wonderful and great expanse. And that search for the way to the Wailing Wall….They ask the Arabs: How does one go down to the Wall?…The Arabs are scared and show them the way, the steep steps to the Mughrabi Quarter, and the liberators descend to the narrow lane. These soldiers, conquerors of the Temple Mount, as if possessed…run down to the Wailing Wall, to the Wall of Tears, and cling to

it in glowing passion and deeply moving tears....We have returned to the Kotel [Wall]! Had we broken through the Jaffa Gate or the Zion Gate, had we reached the Kotel on the way to the liberation of the Temple Mount, then one might understand....But no. The Mount was conquered first. We were on the Temple Mount, and spontaneously, without orders from superiors without thinking or planning, we went down to the Wall. And this Wall is not even a wall of the Temple, but part of the wall with which Herod surrounded it. Its entire sanctity derives from prohibitions forced on us by foreign usurpers, preventing us from ascending the Mount. It is a reminder, a memorial, a substitute. Hence it is a Wailing Wall, for it reminds us only of the destruction, of the disgrace of being below, with our enemies on top. For 2,000 years this fabulous mountain waited for its Jewish liberators....finally they come to it, but what is happening here?...Why do they run down to the Wall? Why, holding the genuine thing, do they want the substitute?...The Temple Mount was conquered and not liberated. We are down below and our enemies sit above as if we are not living in the State of Israel, as if we are not in charge in the age of *Tzahal* [the Israeli Army]. We deal with the recidivism of an exilic soul. Zionism had two sources: a positive root in the sovereign will to redemption, to return, to renew our days as of old, and a second, negative root, in escape from oppression, in the despair of emancipation. It is this second one that won. And so, to the extent that memories and emotions played a role—and they certainly did—they were memories and emotions that went as far as the Wall of Tears. They did not go higher than that Wall, not to the establishment of decisive facts in Jewish redemptive history. The Mount was liberated and abandoned. An intimidated, wavering rabbinate shaped by exilic traditionalism joined hands with a political establishment on which the entire issue had been forced, and who could not forget that its main demand had always been free access to the Wailing Wall. Behold, this was now achieved. There was yet another factor. Was it not clear, as a matter of course, that should the city fall into the hands of Jews, even if the mosques on the Temple Mount should survive the battles that the Temple Mount itself appropriated be removed from the control of the political-religious-nationalist Wakf, with its incitement to kill the Jews, would one not expect that Jews, following both Halachic prescriptions and their generations of longing, renew their prayers on the Mount? Could anything be more natural? After all, the Hasmoneans and the Zealots fought for the Temple Mount, not for the Wall. But no: the Jews abandon the Mount and go down to the Wailing Wall. At that moment, it dawned upon the Muslim Arabs that the battle might be over, but the war was not. There was no decision, and the heart of El Quds ["the Holy"—the Arab name for Jerusalem] remained in their hands.[34]

It is intriguing that the Western Wall, seemingly the sole object of veneration after the capture of the Temple Mount in 1967, should never have been a subject of political or religious debate nor controversy within the Israeli government, despite the fact that the Jewish return to the Wall was viewed by many nations as an act of occupation and usurpation of Muslim territory. The Western Wall, like the Temple Mount, is still claimed by Islam as a holy site—Al Buraq Wall— a site where Al Buraq, the celestial steed of Mohammed, rested before alighting on the rock within the Dome of the Rock. Yet Jerusalem mayor Teddy Kollek had no reservations about bulldozing the masses of Arab homes and shops in the Mughrabi quarter, adjacent to the Western Wall, in order to create the present-day Western Wall plaza. And, no Jewish authorities listened seriously to Muslim protests that thousands of Jews were coming to conduct religious services at the Wall once it was opened to the public. If the rabbinic and governmental authorities could act in this way toward the Western Wall, why not toward the Temple Mount?

The answer lies again in the attitude of both the secular and religious Jews of that time. Will that attitude change? Is it changing today? To understand this better, we need to look at how modern-day Judaism perceives the Temple Mount and the hope of the coming Last Days Temple.

CHAPTER 6

The Holy Hope

Judaism and the Temple

The hope for the rebuilding of the Temple was born on the very day of its destruction almost 2,000 years ago. Rabbi Akiva comforted his weeping colleagues by proclaiming that if the prophecies of destruction have come to pass, the fulfillment of the prophecy of redemption and rebuilding is certainly to follow. In the course of 2,000 years, the Jewish people have never forgotten the Temple.... The dream of rebuilding the Temple spans 50 generations of Jews, five continents and innumerable seas and oceans. The prayer for rebuilding is recited in as many languages as are known to humanity. These prayers recited in prisons and ghettos, study halls and synagogues, homes and fields everyday for 2,000 years of exile... now gain a new dimension with the return of the people to the Land of Israel.... this new dimension is: a possibility [of rebuilding the Temple].[1]

—RABBI CHAIM RICHMAN

The sages referred to the synagogue as *Miqdash Me'at*, "a small or minor temple" (Babylonian Talmud, *Megilla* 29a), and Rav Hazal taught that the day the Temple was destroyed God was left nothing in His world but the four cubits of Halacha, the world of Torah study (Babylonian Talmud, *Berakhot* 8a). With the synagogue for practical purposes replacing the Temple in function, and God apparently content with the study of its laws in the Torah, why would any Jew dream of returning to the cold, stone Temples of the ancient past when a more modern and evolved social and spiritual "temple" has now successfully served Judaism for two millennia?

Despite some 50 generations without a Temple, the Temple has remained steadfast in Jewish prayers and prophecy. With the Jewish people's recent return to the Promised Land the hope has been revived that perhaps the Temple would return as well. The one restoration presages the other, for there has always been a link between the physical return to the Land and a literal rebuilding of the Temple. Historian David Salomon affirms, "It [the desire for a rebuilt Temple] was the essence of our Jewish being, the unifying force of our people."[2] Judaism's claim to Jerusalem and the Temple Mount exceeds that of any other rival religion whose history also includes this city and site. Christian New Testament scholar Krister Stendahl affirms this when he writes, "For Christians and Moslems, the term 'Holy Sites' is an adequate expression of what matters. Here [in Jerusalem] are sacred places hallowed by most holy events....But Judaism...is not tied to sites, but to the land; not to what happened in Jerusalem, but to Jerusalem itself."[3]

What happened to Jerusalem is vividly portrayed by the actions of Jews around the world every year on Tisha B'Av, or the ninth of the Jewish month of Av (which is equal to July/August on the Julian calendar). On this day observant Jews fast and refrain from all normal pleasures as a sign of sorrow over the destruction of the First and Second Temples. In Israel, Tisha B'Av has been granted the status of a national day of mourning, and even though the population is largely secular, movie theaters, nightclubs, and other places of entertainment are strictly forbidden from being open during the entire time of the fast.[4] This reveals an almost universal Jewish identification with the loss of the Temple and its effect on Jewish nationalism even though Judaism continued to function without it. However, these widespread feelings about the loss of the Temple do not indicate that there is unanimity concerning the form or function of the Temple, or the way in which it could be restored.

Jewish Viewpoints Concerning the Temple

In the days of the Second Temple the Pharisees, Sadducees, Essenes, Sicarii, and other groups contended politically and religiously with one another. Likewise, modern Judaism continues to exist in a pluralistic form. Because there is no monolithic group that represents all religious Jews and no normative and uniform set of doctrinal beliefs for Judaism, when we consider the Jewish hope for the Temple it is important to distinguish what the different Jewish groups believe on the subject. Although a wider variety of subgroups could also be included, in the United States we find that four dominant groups represent this pluralistic Judaism: Traditional or Orthodox Judaism, Ultra-Orthodox Judaism, Conservative Judaism, and Reform or Progressive Judaism. Let us consider what each of these groups believe and then look at their particular views on the matter of rebuilding the Temple.

The View of Orthodox Judaism

Orthodox Judaism follows the traditional practice of Judaism as it was developed between A.D. 400–500. This includes a strict adherence to the Written Torah (Bible) as the divine law and the Oral Torah (contained in the Talmud and Mishnah) as its commentary, a separated home and lifestyle marked by keeping *Kashrut* (Kosher laws), and a religious education for children. While all Orthodox Jews are "observant Jews," the males alone wear *tallitot* ("prayer shawls") *tzizit* ("fringes"), *kippot* or *yarmulkes* (skullcaps), and *tefillin* or phylacteries when praying. Orthodox Jews accept that a literal, physical Temple will be rebuilt in accordance with the prophets, although they differ as to whether this will be brought about by divine (miraculous) or human (political) means.

Most Orthodox Jews are committed to waiting for the arrival of Elijah and the Messiah to resolve all discrepancies about the location of the Temple, disclose the hiding place of the ashes of the Red Heifer as well as the Ark of the Covenant, and build the altar and the Temple. Some among this group believe that the First Temple was never actually destroyed but translated to heaven, and that it will descend from heaven with fire to take its place upon the Temple Mount in the Messianic Age of Redemption (see photo section). However, others see this as the final heavenly form of the Temple which will exist only in the Age to Come (following the Messianic Age).

Many Orthodox Jews believe it is their responsibility to obey the long-standing biblical injunction to "construct a sanctuary for me" (Exodus 25:8) whenever the opportunity arises. Much of this thinking has been inspired by the teachings of Rabbi Abraham Isaac Kook (1865–1935), the late Chief Rabbi of Israel. He "built the secular Zionist enterprise into his own, entirely religious system of God's plan [in which]...even the most secular activity in building the Land was given religious meaning and value."[5] This was because, as he saw it, "All possessions of Israel are suffused with the indwelling spirit of God: its land, its language, its history and its customs."[6] From this it can be seen why those influenced by Rabbi Kook, which includes the majority of those in the Temple movement, would see the preparation for and the rebuilding of the Temple as a work that can and should be performed at the present time.

All Orthodox Jews further believe that the *Shekinah* never left the Temple Mount, and therefore the ancient place of the Holy of Holies (whose exact location on the Temple Mount is either believed unknown or is debated) is today still a place of ultimate sanctity. For this reason it is strictly forbidden for Orthodox Jews to presently enter the Temple Mount (except *outside* prescribed boundaries of sanctity) for fear that they would enter in an impure state and desecrate the holy site.

The View of Ultra-Orthodox Judaism

Ultra-Orthodox Judaism, known as Hasidic (literally, "pious, devout ones"), Kabbalistic, or Mystical Judaism, is distinguished by outward dress conforming to the traditional clothing of the community (usually Eastern European) from which he or she immigrated and allegiance to a leading rabbi (Rebbe) and his dynastic successors. It refers to itself as the Chabad movement, because the name *Chabad*, which is a Hebrew acrostic for the Mochin (powers of intellect) or the three sefirot: C = *Chokmah* ("wisdom"), B = *Binah* ("understanding"), and D = *Da'at* ("knowledge/intellect"), best characterizes them in their unique adherence to the Zohar (which contains the Kabbalah and its commentary) and their attempt to attain to the levels of existence revealed by the Ten Sefirot (emanations of God). The largest and best-known group among the Hasidim is the Lubavitch Hasidic movement or Lubavitchers, whose modern Rebbe was the late Rabbi Menachem Mendel Schneerson. The Lubavitchers once campaigned actively for the rebuilding of the Temple because they believed that their Rebbe was the Messiah and that upon his immigration to Israel he himself would initiate the rebuilding.

In Ultra-Orthodox Judaism, in keeping with Kabbalistic concepts, Jerusalem and the Temple exist as spiritual, not just material (which often conceals the spiritual) entities. Therefore the rebuilding of the Temple occurs on two levels (material and mystical). On the material level it is the Messiah's responsibility to build the Temple, which will be a physical structure complete with animal sacrifices. On the mystical level, the material Temple will be constructed after mankind has built its own spiritual temple through study, prayer, and the *mitzvah* of charity, and has reached a level of godliness that will bring the Messiah and the expected redemption. As Chaim Kramer writes:

> When analyzing our Sages' statement about *Daat* [knowledge] being synonymous with the Holy Temple, we can better understand what the building of the holy Temple means on several levels. The first is the physical structure. It will contain an altar upon which to offer the various sacrifices. But this Holy Temple will also represent the building of one's mind—to a level of *Daat* and purity. This will be a level at which one is capable of receiving spiritual influx and developing an expanded awareness of God....Every person's individual Holy Temple is slowly—and surely—being put together, to become a natural dwelling place for spirituality....Building one's mind to receive God's divine presence is building the Sanctuary or Temple....when all mankind is ready for *Mashiach* ["Messiah"]...then the building of the Holy Temple will be done by God Himself—a building that will never be destroyed again.[7]

So while the Ultra-Orthodox will rejoice when Messiah comes and the Temple is rebuilt, they will continue waiting for that day while striving to bring themselves and the Jewish world into a proper state of spirituality, regarding with mixed feeling the aspirations and actions of Orthodox Jews who seek to erect a physical Temple.

The View of Conservative Judaism

Conservative Judaism, which is a distinctly American movement, lies along the entire continuum between Reform Judaism and Orthodoxy. Based on the principles of the German Zacharias Frankel (1801–1875), its theological perspective, as articulated by Jewish Theological Seminary's Solomon Schechter (1850–1915), who developed its institutions, is that the legal, moral, and spiritual commandments of the Torah were placed by God in the hands of the Jewish people and may be adjusted in keeping with their own social evolution. While Conservative doctrine states that the decisions of Torah and Talmud must be followed, that Zionism is a fundamental principle, and that the commandments must be practiced, their approach is pragmatic and left open to interpretation and application by individual congregations. This effectively separates them from the Orthodox, who permit no changes to the traditional understanding of the commandments.

Conservative Judaism views the Temple and its service in light of its social importance in strengthening national cohesion. This social-national function also serves a spiritual purpose, offering a spiritual and social ascent of the people of Israel, and of all mankind, which will effectively draw all the peoples of the world closer to each other.

The View of Reform Judaism

Reform Judaism is the most progressive, or liberal, of the three major movements in Judaism. According to the book *Towards a Theology of Judaism* by (Reform) Rabbi Professor Manfred Vogel, "Reform Judaism does not regard the relationship to God through a 'vertical connection' of man to God as achieved through a fulfillment of the commandments between God and man, but through the 'horizontal connection' of the fulfillment of the commandments between man and man. This is expressed in the functioning of the whole community on a high moral and spiritual level." This theological position has historically allowed Reform Judaism to retain the outward form of Judaism but to impute any meaning it has chosen to its observance. As a result, one recent writer to *The Jerusalem Post* described it as "a different religion from Torah Judaism....more distinct theologically from classic Judaism than is Christianity....In the Reform movement, the ultimate authority is the local, contemporary chic: feminism, egalitarianism, Far Eastern meditation, homosexuality, you name it."[8]

Reform Judaism's view of rebuilding the Temple is reflected in its having long ago expunged from its prayer book all prayers for the rebuilding of the Temple and the resumption of the sacrifices. Rather than call their assemblies *synagogues*, Reform Jews call them *temples*, revealing their belief that there is no need for the rebuilding of a literal Temple. As Rabbi Pesach Schindler explains: "We have respect for the past, but [the Temple] has no operational significance. With the establishment of the State of Israel, we have all our spiritual centers within us. That is where the temples should be built."[9] Therefore, while Reform Jews have contributed significantly to the modern rebuilding of the ancient Land of Israel, they have no interest in helping to restore its historic faith and culture surrounding the Temple. The reason is obvious: to do so would restore traditional Judaism, and thereby nullify the cardinal distinctives that define their own movement. This was decided as the founding platform when the Reform movement began in Pittsburgh in 1885, where they rejected many Jewish traditions as "entirely foreign to our mental and spiritual state" and a hindrance "to modern spiritual elevation."[10]

Nevertheless, in May 1999, the governing body of Reform Judaism endorsed a return to traditional practices (keeping kosher, wearing yarmulkes, and prayers in Hebrew). The 1.5-million-member Central Conference of American Rabbis voted 324-68 for the dramatic change because they have seen a yearning for a return to the old ways in their synagogues, especially among the younger rabbis, who have been concerned over the threat of assimilation and the high rate of intermarriage. As Reform Rabbi Deborah Zecher of Great Barring, Massachusetts, confessed: "In our generation, we do not know our history; this brings us back to our history."[11] If this new return to an observant lifestyle continues with a reassessment of the traditional view of restoring the Temple, then a sizeable Jewish community may be waiting in the wings to help when all is ready to rebuild.

Judaism in Israel

These same four groups also exist in Israel, but the only group that is officially recognized is traditional Orthodox Judaism. However, it should be noted that a significant number of non-Orthodox (non-observant) Israeli Jews consider themselves religous even though they are identified as "secular" by the Orthodox. The traditional position is so dominant that even though Reform Judaism maintains a strong presence in the academic institutions in the Land and its support of humanitarian efforts, the status of its members as "religious Jews" under the Law of Return has been continually debated in the Israeli Knesset and repeatedly denied by the Orthodox. Orthodox Judaism has seen growth in the last decade from the ranks of more than one million Russian Jewish immigrants (who came from an atheistic nation, hungry for religion) as well as from a revival of Orthodoxy (and even Kabbalistic Hasidism) among formerly secular Jews. Because Orthodox Judaism alone maintains the prophetic hope of a literal restoration of the Temple, almost all of the Israeli Jews who are active in the Temple Movement identify with Orthodox Judaism in one form or another. Also, Orthodox Israeli prime ministers—such as Menachem Begin and Yitzhak Shamir—in the past have openly shared the aspirations of the Temple movement. For example, when Begin was still the leader of the Irgun in 1947, he is said to have stated, "The Third Temple as outlined by the prophet Ezekiel will assuredly be rebuilt in our generation." And Shamir, during his administration, wrote a letter of encouragement and support to Gershon Salomon, the leader of the Temple Mount Faithful. Even though more recent prime ministers have been secular, those in the Temple movement believe that their viewpoint will one day prevail in the Israeli government.

One reason for the current lack of governmental support is that the majority of Israelis are secular Jews and generally struggle against the imposition of religious laws that curtail their hard-won independence. However, even though they have chosen to distance themselves from Judaism and adopt national values, the Temple remains a very real part of their history, and the Muslim presence on the Temple Mount prohibits the full exercise of their rights as Jews. Though Israel regained control of the Temple Mount in 1967 and has since reunited the city of Jerusalem as its indivisible capital and claimed sovereignty over everything within its boundaries, the lack of Jewish access to the Temple Mount (with exception of the full access to the Western Wall) has remained a visible sign of an incomplete and potentially reversible independence.

Therefore, though the Temple is the ultimate religious symbol in Judaism, it is no less a national symbol for the secular Jew. This was evident during the Second Temple period, when the majority of the Diaspora Jews (who at that time already lived outside the Land for some 600 years) regarded the Temple as a national rallying point. For all practical purposes, these Jews were secular, yet they took great pains to perform what were religious acts—the thrice-annual pilgrimages to the Temple in Jerusalem and payment of the half-shekel Temple tax. This was their way of showing national identification. In the same way, despite the schism that presently exists between religious and secular Jews in modern Israel, there could soon be a consensus on the issue of the Temple— given the proper catalyst of political and social instability. Such a catalyst may be in the making, and could provoke at the present hour a renewed need for the Temple as a statement of Israeli sovereignty.

The Present Need for the Temple in Judaism

Today, Jewish leaders around the world—and especially those in the Temple movement in Israel—believe that the Jewish people, and all humanity, are not living on the spiritual level God intended. This, they argue, is because of the absence of the *Shekinah* (divine presence) from the world. Rabbi Chaim Richman draws the connection between the need for a new level of spiritual attainment and the rebuilding of the Temple: "The *Shekinah* is brought about only through the Temple....in terms of our mission as a people, we cannot in any way reach our spiritual status without the Temple."[12] Yitzhak I. Hayutman also notes in this light that the purpose of the Temple will be to alter society spiritually: "The future mission of the Temple will be individual, social and even national transformation. On a national level the Temple will lead to The New Israel. It will be a passage from the fixation on the familiar old track: Jews vs. Gentiles, to a new federation of twelve New Israeli Tribes (among which "Judah"—in the sense of Orthodox Halakhic-Rabbinic Judaism will be just one, albeit a senior, member), on the way to a future global Israel."[13]

Gershon Salomon, leader of the Temple Mount Faithful, also views the Temple as the harbinger of a new spiritual and moral order, which does not precede, but follows, the actions of the present-day Israeli faithful:

> [Building the Third Temple] is an act which must be done to complete the redemption of the people of the Bible in the Land of the Bible. I cannot imagine an Israeli State or Israeli life in this country without the Temple Mount in the center of this life, without Jerusalem in the center of this country, as the capital of national, spiritual, and moral life. The Temple Mount is for us the place of life, but also a symbol, a vision, the vision of the prophets. The Israeli people must renew their life as God chose for them to be, a people who have a biblical mission to fulfill the principles of God and the vision of the prophets, and the Temple Mount is the very big condition to fulfill this historical mission of the Israeli people. More than this, the Temple Mount, after its redemption and the rebuilding of the Third Temple, will be again as God and the prophets decided it must be, not only a center for the Israeli people, but for all the world, a center of belief in God, of prayer to God....So the redemption of all the world is connected, and the condition [for it], the first step, is the redemption of the Temple Mount, the coming of Israel back to the Temple Mount and the rebuilding of the Third Temple. Then the second step will be the redemption of all the world. We live now in a world that needs such a redemption, it is a materialistic world, and we must bring people close to the principles of the prophets, and then we will have a revolution in humankind....people will live as neighbors in peace and love, and by helping each other will have a spiritual, moral, and happy life which God gave us in this world forever.[14]

The problem that exists today for Judaism is that the majority of Jewish people around the world have lost their religion. While Muslims continue to increase both in numbers and devotion to their religion of Islam, Judaism is fragmented and on the decline. Statistics of Jewry in the United States alone seem to support these facts. A major study by the Council of Jewish Federations has revealed that of America's six million Jews, two million no longer identify themselves as Jews, two million who identify themselves as Jews are not affiliated with any Jewish organization or synagogue, and another 600,000 have converted to other religions and are no longer recognized as Jewish. This means that only 1,400,000 Jews in America are united with the Jewish community or in their Jewish faith. A study commissioned by Harvard University has estimated that by the American Tricentennial year of 2076, there could be as few as 10,000 religious Jews in America.[15] In addition, the increase in pogroms and persecutions against Jews worldwide, unparalleled since the rise of the Third Reich, has motivated many Jews to make *aliyah* ("immigrate") to Israel. However, their numbers are being diminished at a faster pace than they are being replenished because those accustomed to the affluence of Western and European cultures have difficulty adapting to the hardships of Israeli life and language, do not share the Zionistic imperatives or idealism of previous generations, and have a birth rate below the replacement level. As a result, the present generation of Jews, not having experienced the horrors of the Holocaust, long more for world peace and material prosperity than for the uncultivated foreign soil of strife-ridden Israel.

Orthodox Rabbi Ephraim Buchwald of Lincoln Square Synagogue in New York and director of the National Jewish Outreach Program has interpreted these statistics as nothing less than a "death knell." He says, "There has never been a community of Jews that has abandoned ritual and survived."[16] The seriousness of these statistics has prompted attempts to return the younger generation to Judaism through organizations such as Jews for Judaism and the "Discovery Seminars" *(Arachim),* whose approach on college campuses emphasize the divine origin of the Bible through a demonstration of Torah codes and prophetic fulfillments (which have included the present preparations to rebuild the Temple). These are among the reasons that many Jews in Israel believe that rebuilding the Temple is the best means of bringing Jews back to Judaism and to the Land, spiritually unifying the Jewish people, and preserving the identity of the Jewish people.

Messianic Proportions of the Temple Movement

While the *intafada* has stirred the attempts to rebuild the Temple, this fervor has also come as a natural result of the Jewish return to Israel and Jerusalem.

Irving Greenberg, former Chairman of the Department of Jewish Studies at City College of New York's City University and founder and director of the National Jewish Resource Center, explains:

> Now in our lifetime, the period of exile and powerlessness of Jewry is coming to an end. The Holocaust and the rebirth of the State of Israel have ended the period of exilic Judaism. *Tisha B'Av* [the time of mourning for the destruction of the Temple and of prayer for its rebuilding] cannot be unaffected by the miracle of Israel and the reunification of Jerusalem. The prophet Zechariah told Israel in God's name that after the return, *Tisha B'Av* and the three other fasts will become days of celebration and joy (Zechariah 8:19). While it is too early to claim that the Messianic fulfillment is here, the process of redemption now underway is discernable.[17]

Greenberg's citation from Scripture affirms that the return to the Promised Land has been viewed by Jews as the beginning of the fulfillment of the prophetic hope. Never before have world events been interpreted with such prophetic conviction by Jewish rabbis and average Israelis alike, who believe that they are in the final days and about to enter the promised "messianic era." The expectation of the coming Messianic age has grown in some Orthodox circles as a result of the Gulf War, the fall of the Iron Curtain, the collapse of communist control in the Commonwealth of Independent States, the exodus of Ethiopian and Russian Jews, and the Palestinian problem. For these Jews the advent of Messianic redemption has never been more necessary, and they view the rebuilding of the Temple as the predicted means to hastening its arrival.

Why Jews Have Not Rebuilt the Temple

Most Gentiles outside of Israel wonder why, if Israel has been an independent Jewish State for over half a century, it has not yet rebuilt its holiest site. A number of answers have been offered from both Orthodox and Hasidic Judaism: 1) The population of Israel is insufficient for the time prescribed for the rebuilding of the Temple; 2) the Jews are in a condition of ritual impurity and unable to enter the Temple Mount to rebuild; 3) the Muslim presence on *Har Habayit* (the Temple Mount) precludes any attempt at rebuilding; 4) the Israeli government's unwillingness to disrupt the status quo on the Temple Mount; 5) the complacent mindset of establishment Orthodox Judaism; and 6) the belief that the Jewish people must wait for God to rebuild the Temple, including a) the belief that the Temple must await the Messiah, who will rebuild it; b) the belief that the Temple will descend from heaven fully reconstructed by God; and c) the belief that the Temple will be rebuilt when the Gentile nations desire for it to be rebuilt and assist in its rebuilding.

Let's consider each of these views.

The Problem of Israel's Population

According to the Jewish legal expert Maimonides, one of the chief obstacles preventing the rebuilding of the Temple is that it cannot be built until a majority of the Jewish people live in the biblical Land of Israel. This concept was derived from the prophetic passages in the Old Testament which assume that the Jewish Nation is functioning in the Land with the bulk of the Jewish people resident (see Ezekiel 36:37-38; 37:15-28; Zechariah 8:7-8), as well as passages that connect a worldwide pilgrimage of Gentiles who visit the Temple, where the Jewish people are positioned to dispense spiritual knowledge (see Isaiah 2:2-3; Zechariah 8:22-23). Until recently Maimonides' objection was reasonable because only about 30 percent of world Jewry lived in Israel. However, in the past two decades Israel's population has doubled, and in the last decade alone there has been a substantial increase in population with the return of Ethiopian Jews (through Operations Moses and Solomon), Soviet Jews, and other Jews from numerous smaller communities in Islamic countries. Sergio Della Pergola, a Hebrew University demographer, predicted in 1991 that soon the majority of the world's Jews would be living in Israel.[18] In 1999 the Israeli population reached the six-million mark, for the first time replacing in the Jewish homeland the number of Jews who were murdered in the Holocaust. Based on current figures, it is now predicted that by the year 2003 Israel will have the largest Jewish population in the world (today only the United States has a slightly larger Jewish population). At present, the rate of *aliyot* ("immigrations") continue to rise and fall in fairly predictable fashion, but if world conditions worsen for the Jews, a massive influx of new immigrants to Israel could quickly result. Also, those who advocate the rebuilding of the Temple believe that the event of the rebuilding itself will arouse Jews living outside the Land to return and partake in a new era of spiritual and moral blessing.

The Concern over Ritual Impurity

Traditional Orthodox teaching contends that the Jewish people, because of their long exile outside the Land, have incurred several types of ritual impurity (with "corpse impurity" or contact with the dead being the most defiling) and therefore are presently unfit to enter the Temple Mount and begin the work of rebuilding the Temple. The continued sanctity of the Temple Mount itself, according to the Mishnah (*Sotah* 9a), results from the Tabernacle and its treasures, which have been stored under the Temple Mount in a subterranean chamber: "With regard to Moses the Master said: 'After the First Temple was erected, the Tent of Meeting was stored away, its boards, hooks, bars, pillars, and sockets.' Where [were they stored]?—Rabbi Hisda said in the name of Abimi: 'Beneath the crypts of the Temple'." Chief among these hidden objects is the Ark of the Covenant, the most holy of all the treasures of the Tabernacle and First Temple. Because of the sanctity that is believed to still attend the Ark, and therefore, the place of the Holy of Holies, Orthodox Jews are expressly forbidden to enter the Temple Mount because the exact location of this site is unknown and unintentionally treading upon it in an impure state would desecrate it. For this reason the Chief Rabbinate of Israel, as well as the rabbis of the Ultra-Orthodox Eda Charedit, have stressed that Jews entering the Mount while impure risk the punishment of *Kareit* (literally, "cutting off"), social exile, or ostracization from the Jewish community. While this ancient punishment (tantamount to a death sentence) is not enforceable in Israel's modern secular courts, it still could carry severe social consequences in certain religious communities where the guilty party was a member. For many years the Chief Rabbinate posted a sign by the Mughrabi Gate (the only Jewish entrance to the Temple Mount) to warn observant Jews who might be visiting as tourists to avoid entering the site. It read in English: "Notice and Warning: Entrance to the area of the Temple Mount is forbidden to everyone by Jewish law owing to the sacredness of the place."[19]

Even though some rabbis, such as Chief Rabbi Shlomo Goren, published plans showing "safe" areas where entrance was possible, and many Jews today enter the Temple Mount to walk a circuitous path within these prescribed boundaries (see diagram on page 355), most Orthodox Jews have never set foot on the Temple Mount in their lifetime. This was one of the reasons Moshe Dayan gave for relinquishing jurisdiction of the Temple Mount to the Wakf—he believed that neither the rabbis nor the Orthodox wanted to go there anyway! However, there are some Orthodox Jews who, using a different ruling of *halakha*, believe that whenever all or most of the people of Israel are ritually impure, all public sacrifices (including the *Qorban Pesach*, or "Passover sacrifice") can be offered because the *tuma* ("ritual impurity") is overridden (*Hilchot Beit HaMiqdash* 4:9-13). According to this interpretation there is no obstacle to restoring the sacrificial system (except for the lack of an altar and trained priest-hood) even *before* the Temple is rebuilt (see chapter 24). While this viewpoint is not accepted by all Orthodox Jews, some who have adopted it are already practicing sacrifice, although in a symbolic manner because they cannot gain access to the Temple Mount, where such service is to be carried out (see chapter 17).

The Muslim Occupation of the Temple Mount

The fact that the formidable religion of Islam (some billion strong world-wide) has occupied the site of the Temple Mount for over 1,300 years—and that the tiny island of Israel is surrounded by a vast sea of Islamic nations bent on its destruction—has prevented any possibility of recovering the site for Judaism. Although during the period of the Crusades the Muslim presence was removed from the Temple Mount temporarily, and in 1967 Israel regained sovereignty over the site and could remove the Muslim presence at any time, the political reality has been that the international superpowers have never supported and never will support an action by Israel that provokes a war with Islam. The reason for this is that a key resource vital to the world's economy—oil—is held in abundance by nations that are wholly Islamic. Furthermore, not even the super-powers in alliance together would want to go against the raging tide of a united Muslim *Jihad,* which includes an unrelenting horde of terrorists and suicide bombers, as well as access to nuclear, chemical, and biological weapons of mass destruction. So as long as Islam threatens holy war over the Temple Mount, nei-ther secular Israeli politicians nor the greater democracies will permit the status quo on the Temple Mount to be disturbed.

The Israeli Government's Policy on the Temple Mount

When the newly declared State of Israel was under siege by seven Arab armies, an armistice in 1948 ended the conflict, but resulted in Jerusalem becoming a divided city. The eastern section of Jerusalem, with its Old City and the Temple Mount, was held by Jordan, one of the nations that had participated in the attack. The terms of the armistice called for the Jews to have access to the Western Wall for worship, but Jordan denied this right and systematically destroyed 58 of the ancient Jewish synagogues in the Old City's Jewish Quarter. Jordan also dismantled centuries-old Jewish cemeteries, using the gravestones as building materials for private homes and even for latrines. The result was that for the next 19 years, even though Israelis shared the same city and were only hundreds of feet away from the Wall, they were strictly forbidden to come near it to utter even one prayer there.

When the State of Israel ended this intolerable situation by capturing East Jerusalem in the Six-Day War in 1967, it might have been expected that the previous two decades of Jordanian abuse and restrictions on Jewish holy places would have been repaid in kind, according to the law of the desert. But shortly after the city's reunification, Israeli prime minister Levi Eshkol and the Israeli Knesset passed a special law guaranteeing all the various religions (including Islam) free access to all the holy places. This law, known as the "Protection of Holy Places Law," prescribed a punishment of seven years of imprisonment for "desecration or violation of a holy place" and five years of imprisonment to anyone who "violates the freedom of access to the members of the various religions." The implementation and regulation of the law has since been the jurisdiction of the Israeli Minister of Religious Affairs, who is supposed to maintain the equal access status for those whose religions hold these places as sacred. This has held true for the Western Wall, even though it is still claimed by the Islamic Wakf as their possession. However, with the return of the jurisdiction of the Temple Mount to Islam, Jews were again strictly forbidden to have free access to their holy place, even though they had both passed a law guaranteeing it and restored the site to the Wakf as a gesture of peace.

To this day the overriding concern for the Israeli government is the preservation of peace. This is considered more important than enforcing the law that gives Jews the right to worship at the Temple Mount, since it was the Western Wall, not the Temple Mount, that had been the primary focus of the Jewish people for previous centuries. (Of course, this was because the Temple Mount was accessible only to Muslims during the last 1,300 years.) Nevertheless, it was a compromise that allowed for a united city even in spite of the tensions over the holy places. Consequently, Israeli police today will protect Arabs who come to worship on the Temple Mount, but arrest Jews who seek to pray there.

The Orthodox Jewish Mindset Toward Rebuilding

Many Jews today do not place much importance on the Temple because they contend the Bible teaches that the spiritual principle of obedience to the Torah is more relevant than the institution of the Temple. They cite passages such as, "Has the LORD as much delight in burnt offerings and sacrifices...?" (1 Samuel 15:22). In this regard Reform Judaism has taken the reminiscences of the sacrifices from their prayer books and accepted these as sufficient. This spiritualized way of thinking, which sets aside hope in a literal fulfillment of the biblical prophecies regarding a future Temple, has led to a belief that the present political situation on the Temple Mount is acceptable.

The Reform Jews are not the only ones who have neglected the cause of rebuilding the Temple. The Orthodox Jews who support the idea of rebuilding the Temple complain that Establishment Orthodoxy is marked by complacency and spiritual inertia. They argue that Establishment Orthodoxy still has the mentality of *Galut* (Diaspora) Judaism and lacks the ability to disengage itself from the spiritualized form of Torah observance to which Judaism became accustomed in its nearly 2,000-year exile from the Land. Rabbi David Bar Haim says this about the apathy of the majority of Orthodox Jewry:

> The tragic, heartrending truth is that even if the Moslems were to voluntarily vacate *Har Habayit* ["Temple Mount"] tomorrow, Establishment Orthodoxy would not know what to do with the Temple Mount. In its heart, Establishment Orthodoxy recognizes this. The Moslems and the authorities are, in reality, convenient distractions, serving to obviate the need for serious Torah discussion. Thus many Jews are quite content with the present situation.... The Arabs are not the problem; nor is it a question of political machinations and interests. The problem is deepseated and fundamental: do we possess the vision and direction to live a complete and authentic expression of Torah? The problem is within ourselves. As is the solution.[20]

This sentiment is shared by Dr. Yitzhak Hayutman, the dean of research and development at the Academy of Jerusalem, who observes:

> Ironically Israelis recoil from the idea of rebuilding the Temple. Some because it is not relevant to their lives, some out of fear that it will lead to confrontation with the Islamic world, and some from a religious belief that the Third Temple will not be built by human hands but will descend ready-made from heaven.[21] People who care about the Temple mourn on the fact that the access to the Temple Mount, for religious purposes, is barred from Jews. But the bitter truth is that even if we were given free access to the Temple Mount, and even if we would be given all the legal and financial means that are needed to build the Temple, nothing would happen.[22]

The problem, as reflected in this observation, is not the political dominion of Islam, but of the need for the modern, secular State of Israel to see the Temple as relevant. On the one hand, there is nothing that the Jew prays and yearns for more than the rebuilding of the Temple, but on the other hand, the inactivity of most Jews, according to the Temple activists, testifies otherwise, creating a dangerous contradiction since, as Hayutman notes, "it can destroy the credence of our beliefs."[23] Although the complacency of so many Orthodox Jews is discouraging, Gershon Salomon says that the return of many secular Jews back to Orthodoxy is a sign that the time of apathy may be about to end:

> An exciting part of the godly end times in which we are now living in Israel is the return to faith of hundreds of thousands of Israelis who were completely secular. This is one of the biggest signs that we are living in the time of redemption and of the Mashiach. All the prophets of Israel prophesied about this when they spoke about the end times. It has been very well known in the Jewish heritage during the time of the exile. According to this, a short time before the rebuilding of the Temple and the coming of Mashiach ben David, the Jewish nation in Israel will return to the G-d of Israel.... This is now a big wave in Israel, which is becoming bigger and bigger. It is happening in our time because we are blessed to be the generation of the redemption. The State of Israel is again a reality in the Land that G-d promised us, and everything is moving quickly to the accomplishment of this godly process. The return to G-d in Israel means that the Temple Mount is going to be completely opened to Israel and all mankind in our lifetime.

In spite of these signs of change, the reality of the moment is that Orthodox Jewry remains divided. Let's survey some of the factors that have created the impasse over rebuilding the Temple.

Jewish Beliefs that Wait on God to Rebuild

Among the Orthodox there is a marked difference of opinion over when and how the Temple can be rebuilt. Some of the Jewish sages taught that the rebuilding of the Temple is to be an act of divine intervention reserved for the long-awaited Age of Redemption. There are some Orthodox Jews, even in the Temple Movement, who believe that the Temple will not be rebuilt under the present spiritual and moral climate in secular Israel, but rather at a later time of worldwide spiritual revival, during which even Muslims will convert to Judaism. Reuven Prager, founder of *Beged Ivri* (literally, "Hebrew Clothing"), is of this opinion and has told me that he does not support the attempt to wrest the Temple Mount away from the Arabs. He believes that one day the Arabs themselves will come to the Jews and ask them to rebuild the Temple. This view is usually answered by the argument (see below) that the command to rebuild is on-going and has never depended on the Gentile population or even the majority of the Jewish population to have attained a new spiritual level.

The most popular Orthodox objection to rebuilding at the present time is that the timing is not right. The view here is that the Temple will be built when the Messiah arrives or when God sends it directly from heaven. Support for these opinions is drawn from the medieval rabbi Rashi, who declared that the Temple would descend directly from heaven after the coming of the Messiah. Moses Maimonides (Rambam) also argued that the Temple would be built by the Messiah alone. This famous commentator is also said to have set forth the idea that a heaven-sent Temple is seen in Scripture: "I am obliged to pay for the burning that I burnt and the fire that I set in Zion, as it is stated, 'He set a fire in Zion, and it ate its foundations' (Lamentations 4:11); And I will rebuild it with fire, as it is stated, 'And I will be for it, says G-d, a wall of fire around it and for glory within it' (Zechariah 2:11)—Talmud, *Baba Kama* 60b."

The prayer at the afternoon service on *Tisha B'Av* reflects this view that the Temple will be miraculously reconstructed in the coming Restoration: "For You, O Lord, did consume it [the Temple] with fire, and with fire You will in the future restore it." Rabbi Goren, who appealed for the removal of the Dome of the Rock in 1967 in order that the Temple could be rebuilt, nevertheless said, "The Temple will not be built by mortals."[24] Rabbi Nahman Kahane, one of the leaders in the Temple movement, likewise has stated that only "the Messiah can come and tell us where the altar [of sacrifice] is, and where the Temple should be built."[25] This viewpoint is used by the Israeli government to support its prohibition against Jews worshiping on the Temple Mount and their defense against Arab accusations that the government has instigated demonstrations at the Temple Mount in order to get the Temple rebuilt. For example, during the investigation that followed the fire at the Al-Aqsa Mosque in 1969, when an Arab investigative committee reported their conclusion that the Israeli government deliberately set the fire in order to rebuild the Temple, the Israeli government denied the allegation, saying, "The Temple Mount is so holy that the devout amongst us would not even tread on it. According to the *halakha,* the Temple will be rebuilt when the Messiah will have come. It is, therefore, inconceivable that we ourselves should make any plans for the rebuilding of the Temple."[26] Typical of such Jewish responses to those in the Temple Movement is an anonymous comment sent to one of the many Temple-related websites: "When G-d decides He wants another 'Temple,' He'll do it Himself. He does not need you to get others to do it for Him."

Temple Scholars Respond to a Heaven-Sent Temple

The view that the Temple will be heaven-sent or descend from heaven fully formed when God deems it proper is said by Temple movement scholars to be akin to the Jewish belief of the exiles that, while they were in exile, there would appear the wings of an eagle that would scoop them up and whirl them off to the Land of Israel. As one writer put it: "The *Beit HaMikdash* ["Temple"] coming from heaven is the way of the soul from above, but the parents must make the body here on earth....the Temple of Hashem [a substitute for the divine name, literally, "the Name"], which Your hands have established—is the actions of the righteous, as explained in the Talmud, tractate Ketubot." By contrast, Rabbi Yisrael Ariel, founder of the Temple Institute, has stated that a heaven-sent Temple is not a Jewish concept but derived from the Christian book of Revelation and apocryphal sources. He has published an extensive response to this position and the following is a summation of the main points of his argument:[27]

1. There is no trace of the concept of a heaven-sent Temple in either the Written Law or the Prophets. The only source for the concept as a halakhic ruling is based on Aggadic sources which the Jerusalem Talmud forbids being used for this purpose (Jerusalem Talmud, *Pe'a* 2:4).

2. The Temple referred to in the Aggadic sources is for the World to Come (see for example, *Hilkhot T'shuva*), and the sages have stated that this Torah precepts are not valid in this future spiritual world (*Nidda* 61).

3. The biblical prophecies of the future Temple explicitly reveal that it will be built by mortal men, for instance: it will be built of Lebanese cedar (Isaiah 60:9), it will be built with the aid of non-Jews (Isaiah 60, 61, 66), it will be built by human effort (see Rashi's explanation on the following: Jeremiah 30:8; Ezekiel 40ff; Hosea 4:4; Zechariah 2:3; 10:12; Malachi 3:1-3).

4. The rabbis have clearly stated: "Not at all! That is, there will neither be a heaven-sent Temple nor a heaven-sent wall of fire—for that is all a parable" (*Sota* 47a). This view is shared consistently by the Talmudic sages who expressly stated that the Temple would be built by man (see the following tractates: *B'rakhot* 29a; *Ta'anit* 5a; v. Dikdukei *Sofrim*; *Ketubot* 5a' *Middot*; *Shavuot* 15b; 16; *Sukka* 40a; *Tanhuma*,

Vayehi, section 10; B'reshit 49:11; midrash Tanhuma, Vayikra 11:7; Tanhuma, Tazira; Tosafot to Shavuot 15b).

5. The Zohar also affirms that the eternal precept of rebuilding the Temple is entrusted to man (see Vayishlah 170b; B'shallah 59b; Zohar part 3, 147b; Vayehi, part 1, 231a).

6. Both Maimonides and Rashi support that the precept for rebuilding the Temple by man is lasting (see Maimonides in Sefer HaMitzvot ["Book of Precepts"] and Hilkhot Beit HaBehira ["Laws of the Temple"], and Rashi's commentaries to the Torah and Prophets and especially tractate Sukka 41a).

As to Rambam's explanation of the verse cited above, Yirmiyahu Fisher notes: "The Rambam does not mention having to await the Mashiach; such a view is in fact quite the opposite of the Rambam's express approach to such matters: 'And if you should suggest that the Mashiach shall do this, that is impossible, as I have already explained in the introduction that the Mashiach neither adds nor detracts from the Torah' (Commentary to Mishnah, Sanhedrin 1:3). The Rambam's intention is clear—the Mashiach plays no role in 'activating' or performing the Mitzvot ["commandments"]."[28] Therefore, from this analysis of the sources, it is evident that those in the Temple movement do not believe that the Orthodox opinion of a heaven-sent Temple is valid. They follow only the Bible and the rabbinic authorities, and therefore conclude that the responsibility for rebuilding the Temple rests upon the Jewish people and is an ongoing command.

Temple Activists Respond to Waiting on God to Rebuild

Temple Mount activists, in response to the idea of waiting on God before taking action to rebuild, say that the Babylonian Talmud has conflicting opinions about the matter. They also note that the Jerusalem Talmud permits Jews to construct an intermediate edifice before the Messianic era. In support of this, some cite Rambam and the Sifrey on his commentary on Jeremiah 50:5, where, in connection with seeking the house of the Lord, we read, "Seek—means on the instructions of a prophet. You might infer from this that you should wait until the prophet tells you so. But the Torah says 'unto His habitation shall you seek and to there shall you come,' meaning that you should first search for the site and then the prophet is to confirm it for you." Malbim, writing in his 1860 commentary, adds, "The Lord will not reveal His secrets through His prophets about the chosen place unless they make endeavors to locate it, and only after such preparation will He inspire them to disclose it."

In response to statements that only a descendant of the Davidic dynasty can rebuild the Temple, and that it has to be Mashiach ben-David ["Messiah, son of David"], the activists say that rebuilding is commanded to be undertaken by the Jewish people—both in the Torah (Exodus 25:8) and in the instructions of the sages, such as Rambam's *Sefer Hamitzvot* (Positive No. 20) and *Sefer Hachinuch* No. 95. For example, in Rambam's *Mishneh Torah* we read, "The Nation of Israel was commanded to attend to three things upon their entering the Land: to establish a monarchy, to wipe out Amalek…and to build the Temple, as it is written, 'you shall search out a place for Him, and there shall you come…' (Deuteronomy 12:5)" (*Hllkhoth Melakhim* 1:1). The building of the Second Temple by the Jewish exiles upon their return from Babylon was considered to be the proper and commanded course of action despite the lack of being politically independent and having no king (much less a king from the line of David). It was the obvious and natural course of action for the Jews to embark upon: God commanded the Jewish people to do this as soon as it became feasible, which occurred when Cyrus, the King of Persia (a Gentile), had given his permission. Therefore, if all external obstacles are removed, the commandment, which is always in force, awaits fulfillment. As one Temple activist puts it, "It is our duty as Jews to give it [the rebuilding of the Temple] our fullest attention—it is simply incorrect to imagine that the commandment is somehow 'on hold' until further notice, or until the advent of the Mashiach ["Messiah"]."

There is also the concept in Kabbalistic Judaism that a cooperation is expected between the human and the divine spheres. Rabbi Chaim Richman explains:

> You have the concept of the masculine waters and the feminine waters. Feminine waters that rise, masculine waters that descend, in order to elicit a divine response. In an allegorical sense, we [Jews] are the feminine aspect, and God is the masculine aspect. The feminine aspect has to arouse, and the masculine aspect has to respond. A lower arousal awakens an upper arousal. This concept is a blanket policy in Judaism. It always starts with someone wanting to do something. Even in terms of the whole prophetic experience in Jewish mysticism, it always entails a great deal of preparation and purification. A person can't expect any gifts gratis; a person has to expect to put in the effort.[29]

It is also from this perspective that Gershon Salomon, leader of the Temple Mount Faithful movement, defends his activist attempts to rebuild the Temple immediately. He argues that his detractors suffer from a Diaspora mentality: "Physically they are in Israel, but spiritually they are in the Diaspora!" He further states, "The Jewish people have always brought about divine intervention through their own actions. The Red Sea did not split until the children of Israel walked into it."[30]

If the Orthodox proponents of the Temple movement believe that Jewish *halakha* permits the rebuilding of the Temple when conditions permit, then what are those conditions, and when is the right time to rebuild?

The Talmudic Timing for Rebuilding the Temple

According to the Babylonian Talmud, two events were understood to precede the rebuilding of the Temple. The Talmudic passage seems to require a specific order when it states, "The Jewish people were commanded three *mitzvot* ["commandments"] to perform when they entered the Land: 1) to appoint a king, 2) to eradicate the descendants of Amalek, 3) to build the *Beit HaMikdash* ["Temple"]."[31] If the king that is to be appointed must be from the line of David, and this order must be retained, then before the Temple can be rebuilt the Davidic kingdom must have begun, the Messiah (who will appoint this king) must have already arrived, and the Era of Redemption (which follows the period of the Messianic war) will have commenced. The source for the Babylonian Talmud's statement was the prophecy given in Hosea 3:4-5:

> The sons of Israel will remain for many days without king or prince, without sacrifice or sacred pillar, and without ephod or household idols. Afterward the sons of Israel will return and seek the LORD their God and David their king; and they will come trembling to the LORD and to His goodness in the last days.

The Jewish commentator Rashi explained the words of verse 5 this way: "After[ward] they will return to the Temple, they will seek Hashem their G-d and David their King." He clearly held the view that the Temple would be built before the Davidic kingdom. His view is supported by the Babylonian Talmud itself in a different passage (*Megilla* 17b), as well as by the Jerusalem Talmud (*Ma'aser Sheni* 5:2) and other authorities such as Malbim, Rav Kook, Tosafot Yomtov, and the author of the *Gevurot Ari*.[32] There is added to this support the understanding of the commandment in Exodus 25:8 that a Temple is to be built whenever the Jews have returned to the Land. There is also the historical fact that, aside from the First Temple, all succeeding Temples were not built by the Davidic kingdom. The final argument in resolution of this question is a Talmudic statement that every king—not just a king from the Davidic dynasty—is commanded to war with Amalek and to rebuild the Temple. This statement is based on Exodus 17:16: "The LORD has sworn; the LORD will have war against Amalek from generation to generation." One Jewish commentator explains that "this verse refers to Yehoshua ["Joshua"], who was not from the tribe of Yehuda ["Judah," i.e., David's tribe], but was nevertheless called a king for the purpose of these three *mitzvot* ["commandments"] that the Jewish people were commanded—to appoint a king, to wipe out the descendants of Amalek, and to build the *Beit HaMikdash* ["Temple"]. Thus, the *mitzvah* to appoint a king, as well as the order of events, does not only refer to a Davidic king, but also to kings from other tribes."[33] This leaves open the possibility that any king at any time can rebuild the Temple, and that the rebuilding of the Temple still awaits a future time when the Messiah will rebuild it.

The Belief that the Time of the Redemption Is Near

The belief that the time of redemption is at hand and that the rebuilding of the Temple will take place in this generation is articulated well by Gershon Salomon, leader of the Temple Mount and Land of Israel Faithful. Note that "signs of the times" connected with Israel's return to the Land play a significant role in this belief:

> You must [understand] that we live now in a special age in the life of the Israeli people, and I believe, of all humankind. We can feel the spirit of God in everything which happens now in humankind, and especially in Israel. God decided to bring back His people from every corner of the world to Israel, the country of the Bible, and one can see how it happens every day when airplanes open their doors and Jews, after almost 2,000 years, are falling to the ground and kissing it, their historical country. And they are coming from Russia [where for] more than 70 years the gates were closed before Jews, and the communists forced millions of Jews to forget their roots and their connection to their historical country, to Israel. But see what happened—it is a miracle of God—in one moment happened the revolution in East Europe, in Russia, and unbeliev[ably] the gates opened and they were told "Go back to your

historical country," and thousands are coming every day. We are living in the time of the fulfillment of the prophecy of the prophets, which say: "I shall bring on the wings of big birds, of *nesharim* [eagles], my people from all the corners of the world." [This means] on the wings of airplanes, and He brings them from Russia, from Ethiopia, from South America, from America, from Europe, from all the corners of the world they are all coming back to the country. This is a time of God; the Land of Israel is rebuilding, [but] we have so many enemies—22 Arab countries, having more than 300 million population, and control 14½ million square kilometers from the Atlantic Ocean to the Persian Gulf, and greater if we include the Muslim world. [They] will try again and again to destroy this people by wars and to push this people to the [Mediterranean] Sea . [Yet] this little Israel, only 25,000 square kilometers, 4 million people, continues to win wars again and again against them. This again fulfills the words of the prophets that the little people, the minority, will survive against the majority....

We are now very close to the coming of the Messiah himself, and we can feel it in the atmosphere, and in everything in our life through these days. We can feel through those returning to the Land the spirit of the Messiah. Today everything is building here, a new spirit is in the country, every day another house, another building, another brit [circumcision]. An Arab, who helped me build my house, once told me as he looked at all the new buildings of the Israelis that this country was like a desert until we Jews came back, that the color was again green and not yellow. He said, "I must tell you, though I am an Arab, that this land waited for you like a mother waits for her son, and she was sad and ill until the moment she came back and met him, and she again became strong and happy." Ask anyone in the streets today and he will tell you that he feels...that the Messiah is very, very close to coming...not far from now....[34]

One phenomenon inspired by the belief in the imminency of the Messianic age is the Ultra-Orthodox public demonstrations of "Messianic joy." This resulted when the late Lubavitcher Rebbe Menachem Mendel Schneerson encouraged his followers to show their joy on the Sabbath by dancing. Therefore, some hasids play forms of rock 'n' roll music with words that speak of faith in Messiah's coming based on the rabbinic credo "I believe with complete faith in the coming of Mashiach, and even though he may tarry, I will wait for him every day to come." During the music, the Lubavitchers dance feverishly like whirling dervishes. They are applauded by secular Jews who marvel at (and even join in) their religious exuberation. These Lubavitchers were also told to celebrate Sukkot (Feast of Tabernacles) in this manner by dancing on the Temple Mount: "By doing this, may we merit to dance in Jerusalem, in the Third *Beit HaMikdash* [Temple]."[35]

In Judaism today there are mixed reactions to the idea of rebuilding the Temple. Some dance with joy in anticipation of the day, while others march to the Temple Mount in the belief that they are following standing orders by the Lord, the captain of Israel's armies. Still others wait for a future revelation of the Messiah, a celestial Temple on the descent, or a world spiritually remade that longs for a Temple in which to express its newfound desire to worship. Yet as we will see in later chapters (chapters 15–19), the Orthodox proponents of the Temple movement maintain at present a hope for the rebuilding of the Temple, and their organized efforts will most likely affect the political and religious scene on the Temple Mount in days to come. And they are not alone in their differences of opinion on the matter of the Temple. Christianity also has a long history, both past and present, with as many variations as Judaism, ranging from complete rejection and replacement of the Temple to full cooperation and financial support of the Temple movement. In the next chapter we will look at what Christians believe and say about the possibility of a future Temple in connection with the events of the last days.

CHAPTER 7

The Christian Connection

The Jewish Temple in Christian Perspective

The Jews had a peculiar way of consecrating things to God, which we have not. Under the law, God, who was master of all, made choice of a temple to worship in, where he was more especially present: just as the master of the house, who owns all the house, makes choice of one chamber to lie in, which is called the master's chamber. But under the gospel there was no such thing.

—JOHN SELDEN, *TABLE TALK* (1689)

The Christians claimed that the Temple is no longer needed. As far as they were concerned, the Messiah has already arrived, and became himself a Temple, so that the Christian has no more need for an earthly Temple made from material stones.

—JEWISH SCHOLAR (1998)

137

In Christianity, the understanding of the Temple has largely been a history of misunderstanding. This has been because in general, Christians look at the Temple as a part of Jewish history and see no connection with Christianity. Historically, whereas the observant Jew had difficulties with the loss of a Temple, but found a substitute in the Torah study of the Temple rulings, the faithful Christian had difficulty from the beginning with the Temple and its rulings and found a replacement for them in the church and its rituals. Therefore, for the majority of Christendom, the Temple is conceived of as part of an ancient, now rejected and replaced form of worship that will never and can never return. It is this view that Jews have assumed to be *the* Christian position, as evidenced by one writer in the Temple movement's explanation to a Jewish audience: "The Christians claimed that the Temple is no longer needed. As far as they were concerned, the Messiah has already arrived, and became himself a Temple, so that the Christian has no more need for an earthly Temple made from material stones. This was a total spiritualization which brought the negation of the possibility of sanctity of any material whatsoever...."

Today, churches may call themselves "Tabernacle" or "Temple" and refer to the location where the preaching service takes place as "the Sanctuary," but this is not intended to convey the idea that the actual structure or place is "holy." Christians here have borrowed from the language of the Temple and spiritualized the concept of the Temple without always being conscious of the implications of their theological accommodation. This theological viewpoint of replacement has a long history in Christianity and today is generally accepted without question.

Does the Church Replace the Temple?

Although Christianity's roots are in Judaism, Judaism's denial of the Messiahship and Lordship of Jesus and persecution of Christians created a conflict with the early church that, in time, forced the church to seek a separate (though not necessarily non-Jewish, in the case of messianic believers) identity. Initially the identity with Judaism was maintained in order to preserve Christianity under Roman rule, since the Romans would tolerate only what they considered to be old religions that had existed at the time of the Land's conquest (68 B.C.). Judaism was accepted as one of these religions and received the protection of the empire. At first, Christianity did not claim to be a new religion but only a sect of Judaism. However, in official debates between Jews and Christians, the

Christian position argued supercessionism: that in fact it was the true heir of the old religion. Early church apologists like Justin Martyr, in his "Dialogue with Trypho," contended in this vein that Jews were no longer God's people because their Temple had been destroyed on account of their rejection of Jesus as Messiah. God had always had a chosen people, but now they were the "new spiritual Israel"—the church—which had replaced the "old ethnic Israel." This body of believers had been constituted by God as the true spiritual Temple in which God was now dwelling—in contrast to the old physical Temple, which He had abandoned. Early church fathers such as Origen and Chrysostom based the truthfulness of Christianity on this premise, contending that the Jerusalem Temple would never again be rebuilt.

There were, however, voices in the church that recognized a rebuilt Temple in the future as part of God's prophetic plan. One example is the early church father Irenaeus, who in A.D. 185 stated, "But when this Antichrist shall have devastated all things in this world, he will reign for three years and six months, and sit *in the Temple at Jerusalem;* and then the Lord will come from heaven in the clouds, in the glory of the Father, sending this man and those who follow him into the lake of fire; but bringing in for the righteous the times of the kingdom."[1] Irenaeus represented the school of Chiliasm (or Millennarianism) which was later branded a heresy because it agreed too closely with Judaism on certain issues.

When the Roman emperor Constantine confirmed Christianity as the new state religion in A.D. 313, Chiliasm became suppressed. With Constantine's act, a Christian political kingdom came into existence, and many people thought that the spiritual kingdom proclaimed by Jesus had come as well (see John 18:36). Therefore, the Jewish concept of a future earthly kingdom, accepted also by Chiliasts, was now in competition and became a source of conflict. From the time of Constantine onward, the church's supercession of Judaism became the standard polemic of Christian apologists. For example, both Ambrose and Gregory of Nazianzus wrote in the fourth century that the sanctuary into which Christ enters is the souls or hearts of God's people.[2] The increasing splendor of the Byzantine Christian empire, together with the dominance of the allegorical method of interpretation, codified by the chief church historian Eusebius, Bishop of Caesarea, assured replacement theology as a Christian dictim. To the common Christian the contrast between the glory of the Byzantine empire and the wretched condition of the Jews appeared sufficient to prove this point (although this contrast, in part, was imposed by Christian emperial edicts). As one modern historian of this period said, "It appeared then, as it did to later generations, that the beginning of Christianity coincided with the demise of Judaism. As long as Christianity had been in existence, it seemed, the Jews possessed neither the temple nor the city."[3]

In the minds of the Christians of this period, the destruction of the Jerusalem Temple was understood to be permanent. As if to corroborate this conviction, under the direction of Constantine's mother, Queen Helen, Christians began to transform Jerusalem into a completely Christian city. Christian churches were constructed on every site of significance but the Temple Mount. It was deliberately left barren as a sign of the judgment of God. By contrast, the Anastasis Church, built over the traditional site of Jesus' crucifixion and resurrection, was constructed on the same tripartite design as the Jewish Temple and at a higher elevation overlooking the Temple Mount. The polemical value of this was to demonstrate the church's replacement of the Temple and superiority over Judaism. As a result of this new Christian presence in the city, for the first time in history, Jerusalem began to attract Christian pilgrims in significant numbers.[4] When by the seventh century an emperor such as Julian decided to oppose Christian doctrine, he had to counter this doctrine of replacement. As Jeffrey Brodd, a student of the history of Julian's brief reign, notes:

> To Christians, Julian was attacking the fundamental notion that Christianity was the true inheritor of the ancient tradition of the Israelites; they believed the destruction of the Temple was an affirmation of God's favor toward them and, as an inseparable correlate of this, of God's abandonment of the Jews. From the second century on, Christian apologians had particularly emphasized that these events had been prophesied in the Old Testament, thus proving that they were part of God's predetermined plan. The destruction of Jerusalem verified God's condemnation of the Jews for the crucifixion of Christ; it revealed Jesus as a true prophet, for he had specifically predicted the razing of the Temple.[5]

From this time onward, whether in the Eastern or Western church, replacement theology was understood as an official position. And, as we will see below, the reformation church that separated from the Western Church, continued to accept this position, with the result that this position became established within evangelical Christianity.

The Evangelical Christian View of the Temple

Within evangelical Christianity, which accepts the Bible as divinely inspired and the sole authority for faith and practice, two competing views concerning the Temple exist. In general, each view is conditioned by an interpretation of eschatology as consistently literal (grammatical, historical, cultural, literary) or spiritually symbolic (covenantal, christocentric).[6] The consistently literal hermeneutic (method of interpretation) seeks to understand the Old Testament prophecies in their original setting, reading them as historical realities that will be fulfilled in the future for those to whom they were intended in the context. While it recognizes the use of symbolic language and interprets such language in its context (guided as much as possible by the author's explicit intent and original audience), it understands that symbolic language may picture literal events, and therefore interprets figures consistently with the context in mind. By this method, the prophecies relating to the coming of the Messiah that did *not* see literal fulfillment (such as the restoration of Israel, the judgment of the nations, or the reign of universal peace) are understood to await a literal *future* fulfillment at Christ's second coming. Therefore, the Old Testament (and many New Testament) prophecies related to the restoration of the Jewish nation will find historical fulfillment in the end times. The consistently literal school, then, understands the prophecies of the rebuilding of the Temple as part and parcel of the future return of Messiah and the restoration of Israel.

The spiritually symbolic hermeneutic reads the Old Testament prophecies in light of New Testament fulfillment in Christ. By this method, whether or not an Old Testament prophecy uses symbolic language, it is considered to be symbolic of New Testament or church truth. In this light, almost all of the Old Testament prophecies concerning the coming of the Messiah are said to have been fulfilled by the first advent of Jesus 2,000 years ago or in the experience of His church since. This view says that all of the prophecies related to Israel and the physical and spiritual restoration of the Jewish nation have their fulfillment within the church. This means that in most cases, these prophecies were spiritually intended for the church or have found their historical fulfillment within the church (for example, the aggregate of elect Jews added to the spiritual kingdom of God, the church, is equivalent to the "all Israel" that "will be saved" in Romans 11:26). The only exception, and one shared in part with the consistently literal school, is that Christ is expected to return physically a second time before the general resurrection of the dead at the end of the age. In addition, both Puritan and modern Reform theologians (such as John Murray) have held to a spiritual restoration of the Jewish people prior to Christ's return, but always within or as an addition to the church proper. With respect to the prophecies of the future

Temple, the spiritually symbolic school understands these as symbolizing the church and its priestly role under the new covenant.

The fear of holding any other interpretation but that which sees the Temple and its ministry completely fulfilled in Christ is typified by Edmund P. Clowney, a past president of Westminster Theological Seminary: "We dare not promise to a people with the covenant name of Israel second-class citizenship in the kingdom of heaven by way of the restoration of an earthly economy with a temple of stone. To do so is to obscure the gospel."[7] With equally strong words Preterist David Chilton declares, "The Bible does not prophesy any future literal Temple or sacrificial system to be set up in Jerusalem. The Biblical prophecies of the Temple refer to Christ and His church, definitively, progressively, and finally."[8] In a mocking critique of the position espoused by consistent literalists (and this book), Preterist Gary DeMar, in a chapter entitled "The Temple of Doom," writes: "Does the Bible, especially the new Testament, predict that the temple will be rebuilt? It does not....The earthly temple was designed as a temporary edifice that would no longer be needed when the true temple of God, Jesus Christ, was manifested on earth."[9] Clearly, then, within evangelicalism there are diverse and diametrically opposed views on the subject of a future Temple.

As we will see in chapter 25, the problem of replacement theology in Reformed theology is that it promises too much too soon. Christ will indeed be the fulfillment of the Temple, but in the New Jerusalem and in the eternal state (Revelation 21:22). Reformed eschatology really has no need for a second coming of Christ, but only of a resurrection of Christians, for in their scheme it is redemption at the cross that climaxes human history. Yet redemption does not have its climax at Christ's cross but at Christ's coming, when the curse is conquered and our mortal bodies finally realize the promise fulfilled in glorification (Romans 8:18-25). Likewise, while all things must be summed up in Christ, the church is not exclusive to, nor the end of, this purpose, but its first and great exhibition (Ephesians 1:10-12). There is still "all Israel" that "will be saved," after "the fulness [full number] of the Gentiles has come in" (Romans 11:25). If the church is interpreted as the true, new "Israel," who, then, is the "all Israel" that will be saved? They are those described in verse 25 as hardened and in verse 28 as the enemies of the gospel. They are those described in verse 26 as "Jacob" and in verse 28 as "God's choice...for the sake of the fathers [patriarchs]." This description can only suit ethnic Israel and not the church composed of both Jews and Gentiles (Ephesians 2:11-22). Therefore, "the Deliverer [Messiah] will come from Zion [Jerusalem], He will remove ungodliness from Jacob," fulfilling

His "covenant with them, when [He] take[s] away their sins" (Romans 11:26b-27). Isaiah the prophet, from whom Paul quotes these words (Isaiah 59:20-21; 27:9), would have understood this of his own people—the Jewish people of the Nation of Israel—for whom he prophesied that the suffering Servant would be "pierced through for our transgressions" and "crushed for our iniquities" (Isaiah 53:5). He also would have understood that it was for Israel that this Messiah would set up a nondiminishing, ever peaceful, government "on the throne of David and over his [David's] kingdom, to establish it and to uphold it with justice and righteousness from then on and forevermore" (Isaiah 9:7). In order to "[sum] up all things in Christ, things in the heavens and things upon the earth" (Ephesians 1:12), God's purpose must be completed for the church as the mystery of history (elect Jews and Gentiles in the present age), and for national Israel and the nations as the final act of history (elect Jews and Gentiles in the end times).

The question, however, with respect to the church's long history of viewing the Temple as having been replaced by the church, is this: To what extent was this position the belief of the *first* Christian church as it appears in the pages of the New Testament. In order to examine this question, let us look at how the Temple was perceived by the disciples of Jesus in the book of Acts and then by the apostle Paul, who carried the message of Christianity to the Gentiles.

The Attitude Toward the Temple in First-Century Christianity

Did predominately Jewish first-century Christianity, as replacement theologians argue today, abandon the Jewish Temple as a symbolic rejection of the old Israel according to the flesh whose promises now belong to the church, the new Israel according to the Spirit? Was the reason the Temple was destroyed in A.D. 70, as one Christian scholar states, because "...since Jesus' occupation of the Temple, the Jews are improper tenants whose possession of the Temple profanes it; thus it falls under judgment"?[10] In order to consider these claims in the proper context of first-century Christianity, let us look first at the New Testament book of Acts as a primary source for not only the experience of the early church during a time when the Temple was yet standing, but also a presentation of its theological viewpoint toward its status for the Christian community in Jerusalem.

The Status of the Temple in the First Century

During this time period, and especially before the destruction of the Temple, there were many diverse Jewish sects (such as those at Qumran) who either called for or at least expected the destruction of the Herodian Second Temple. The common understanding among them was that the Second Temple had not been the recipient of the restoration promises due to the spiritual failure of Israel, and therefore, was destined for destruction. However, this was not meant as a condemnation of the Temple or of the sacrificial system, but of the ritual abuses such as those that had threatened the existence of the First Temple and of the Gentile domination of Jerusalem with its symbol of authority (the Roman eagle) affixed above the main (eastern) door of the Temple itself. Rather than view the Temple's destruction as the conclusion of a material institution that would be replaced by a spiritual reality, these groups believed that the removal of the existing Temple would allow for the building of an even greater material Temple yet without the spiritual defilements of the past. According to Markus Bockmuehl,[11] first-century Jewish and Roman sources such as Josephus and Tacitus, as well as the early Ta'anitic rabbinic literature, indicate that there was a flourishing hermeneutical tradition before A.D. 70 that predicted the Temple's destruction. He gives two reasons for this view:

1. *Theological.* The first and most important reason was that the restoration promises of the biblical prophets had not been fulfilled. Prophecies about the exile and subsequent return to the Land under ideal conditions had obviously gone unfulfilled. This awareness is found in texts as early as the pre-Maccabean book of Tobit (13:16-18; 14:5), as well as in Daniel 9:17,26-27. The corruption and decline of the Hasmonean dynasty and the subsequent occupation by Roman forces exacerbated doubts that a full restoration of—much less a liberation of—the Jewish Nation would take place. In addition, there were doubts, by groups such as the Essenes and those who frequented the Jewish Temple at Leontopolis, that the Maccabees had effected a complete cleansing of the Temple. If despite its Herodian-restored splendor it was not the eschatological Temple, and if the purity of the Zadokite priestly line was at all a matter of concern, then the only logical conclusion was that the present corrupt system would need to give way to a new one.

2. *Social and Political.* In addition, the degeneration of the priestly aristocracy invited comparison with the earlier prophetic oracles of judgment and destruction (the desecration motif). Of the 28 high priests between 37 B.C. and

A.D. 70, all but two came from illegitimate non-Zadokite families.[12] It became increasing clear to most Jews that the cultic center, which regulated all of Jewish life, was in the hands of a vast network of economic and religious oppression. The legitimate and necessary operation of the Temple was supported by a maze of intrigue, nepotism, and graft (Mishnah *Keritot* 1.7), involving, for example, the well-known priestly family of the house of Kathros (cf. Baraita, B. *Pesahim* 57a). Such social and political factors prompted many Jews to consider the theological perspective that the corrupt system would give way to a new one.

What this attitude of dissent reveals is that in the first-century context, negative expressions concerning the Second Temple (especially in comparison with the Tabernacle and the First Temple), were *not* condemnations of the Temple. Rather, they testified to the importance the Temple played in the nation's very existence and eschatological formulation. There seems to be little doubt that, whether positively or negatively, the Jerusalem Temple was considered to be an essential and central part of Judaism in the first century.[13] As Oxford Professor of Exegesis, E. P. Sanders, affirms: "I think it is impossible to make too much of the Temple in first-century Jewish Palestine."[14]

The Status of the Temple in Early Jewish Christianity

In the book of Acts, which is universally recognized to represent a pre-A.D. 70 viewpoint,[15] the Temple is still standing and the narratives concerning its service are presented in the context of acceptable ritual function. For example, in the opening chapters of Acts we find the apostles and members of the newly birthed Jerusalem church stationed in the Temple precincts (Acts 2:46; 3:1; 5:21). Not only were they keeping the festival of *Shavuot* (Pentecost) as observant Jews (Acts 2:1), but we are told that they met regularly for prayer in the Temple in the *Stoa* or Porticos of Solomon (Acts 2:46; 3:11; 5:12).[16] This prayerful assembly, which coincided with the time of the daily sacrifices, indicates the early Christians' regard for Jewish *halakha* with respect to the Temple. A Christian supercessionist would have expected at least some of these Spirit-filled disciples of Jesus to have discarded old rituals of their former religion, but Acts 2:46 notes that with respect to this daily practice in the Temple they were all "with one mind."

Of course it might be countered that the Temple was the place designated for public teaching (Acts 5:20,25), which is why Jesus frequented the site, and that the disciples were simply following the precedent set by their Lord (Luke 19:47; 21:37). This was certainly the case at times; however, Acts 2:1 and 2:14 imply that the disciples had not come to the Temple precinct to teach but to participate in the regular exercises of devotion prescribed for a feast day (in this case, *Shavuot*). In addition, Acts 3:1 specifically states that Peter and John were going to the Temple to pray at the ninth hour, when the evening sacrifice was offered. The text does not indicate that they were going for any reason other than to pray.[17] Even as late as Acts chapter 10, Peter is still following the Temple-governed time for prescribed prayer (Acts 10:9).[18] Such a unity of devotion to the Temple is remarkable if the disciples had theological objections to the Temple, its priesthood, and sacrifices. That the Temple was regarded by Peter,[19] the leader of the apostles, and by John,[20] the traditional author of the book of Revelation, as a legitimate and holy institution should be remembered by all Christians as they see Temple metaphors, ritualistic language, and even references to the Temple itself appear in the later epistles (1 Peter 1:2,16,19; 2:5-9; 1 John 1:7; Revelation 1:7; 3:4-5,12; 4:4; 7:15; 11:1-2,19; 14:15,17; 15:8; 16:1,17; 21:22). When the members of this group were later arrested by order of the Sanhedrin, it was not their views of the Temple or its service that were in question, but their Messianic claims concerning Jesus and the Sanhedrin's fear of the social consequences resulting from their complicity in Jesus' death (Acts 5:28-33). While the accusation against Stephen was that he spoke "against this holy place [Temple]" (Acts 6:13), the text, as well as Stephen's sermon itself, reveals this claim was unfounded and represented the kind of general accusation (as used against Jesus at His trial) of false witnesses.

The fidelity of the early Christian leadership to Jerusalem and the Temple area is remarkable, especially since most of the individuals were Galileans and most of their ministry with Jesus had taken place in regions outside of Jerusalem. As W. O. E. Oesterley observed, "in Jerusalem the Temple was more important for Christian worship, and the synagogue elsewhere...."[21] If Jesus' words in Matthew 21:43 are taken, as they are by replacement theologians, as a prophecy that the kingdom of God would be taken away from the Jewish nation and given to the church,[22] which would be predominately Gentile in character throughout most of its existence, why should Jerusalem, the very city where their Lord was rejected and crucified, become the center and hub of early Jewish-Christianity (see Acts 1:8; Galatians 1:18-2:2)? Furthermore, in view of Jesus' statements concerning the city (Matthew 23:37-38; Luke 19:41-44), and His own predictions of the Temple's imminent destruction (Matthew 24:2; Mark 13:2; Luke 21:6), it would seem that the disciples might corporately reject Temple worship in favor of their own community as a "new" temple. To do so would not have violated

Jesus' command to begin their witness in Jerusalem (Acts 1:8). However, because they *did* observe the daily Temple services and the festival calendar regulated by the Temple, it would appear that they did *not* see a conflict between the Temple and the church or a contradiction between Jewish worship at the Temple (with its sacrificial system) and the atonement that Christ had made on their behalf. In fact, Hegesippus, who was a member of the Christian leadership a generation after the apostles, recorded that James, the head of the Jerusalem church (and most likely the half-brother of Jesus and the author of the New Testament epistle that bears his name), was renowned for his Temple worship: "He alone was allowed to enter the Sanctuary, for he did not wear wool but linen, and he used to enter alone into the Temple and be found kneeling and praying for forgiveness for the people, so that his knees grew hard like a camel's because of his constant worship of God, kneeling and asking forgiveness for the people."[23]

Another reason for the establishment of the early Jewish-Christian community in Jerusalem and their continued involvement at the Temple is their understanding of God's eschatological plan, which they realized focused on both the city and the Temple in the coming restoration. This understanding had been enforced by Jesus' apocalyptic discourse on the Mount of Olives (Matthew 24:3-31; Mark 13:3-37; Luke 21:5-38), in which He proclaimed the desecration of the Temple as the signal event that would precede His coming. Jesus again evidences this perspective when, before His ascension, He told His disciples to expect the promise of the restoration of the kingdom to Israel, which would come at God's appointed time (Acts 1:6-7). His statement was in accord with the Old Testament prophets, who saw this time of restoration as essential to the completion of God's promises to Israel (Joel 2:28-29 cited in Acts 2:16-21; Ezekiel 36:27; 37:14; 39:29; cf. Jeremiah 31:33; Isaiah 32:15; 44:3). Later, Peter made it clear in a sermon at the Temple (Acts 3:12-26) that he understood Christ's promise of national restoration would occur at the time of His return. Therefore, Peter spoke both of God sending the [heavenly] Messiah "appointed for you" (see Daniel 7:13) who would usher in "the period of restoration of all things" (verses 20-21).[24] Because this employs eschatological language addressed to a Jewish audience at the Temple at the time of the church's birth, we need to give it special attention.

Peter's Temple Sermon

In this passage, two terms are used to express the promise of Israel's future restored kingdom. Both are drawn from the Old Testament prophetic books and

Jesus' teaching in Matthew 19:28 (see Luke 22:30) and Acts 1:6.[25] The term "restoration" (Greek, *apokatastaseos*) in Acts 3:21 is identical to the "restoration" (Greek, *apokathistaneis*) or establishment of Israel's kingdom in Acts 1:6 and parallel in sense to the "renewal" or "regeneration" (Greek, *pallingenesia*) in Matthew 19:28. The prophetic hope here is that the restoration of Israel's blessings—politically and spiritually—would be conditioned upon Israel's repentance, which in turn would bring the Messiah to fulfill the promise of the Messianic age. In Acts 3:19 the term "times of refreshing" (Greek, *kairoi anapsuxeos*) refers to "Israel's renewal when God fully establishes his kingdom on earth."[26] This renewal of man and nature in the Millennial kingdom is presented in part by the two major restoration prophets Isaiah and Ezekiel in conjunction with the rebuilding of the final Temple (Ezekiel 36:24–37:14; Isaiah 2:2-4; 11:6-16; 49:5-13; 56:1-8; 60:1-22; 66:18-24).[27]

The same idea of a renewal of both the Land and the people of Israel is found in the apocalyptic literature (e.g., Tobit 13:16-17; 14:5-6; Jubilees 1:15-17, 26-28; 1QM 2:2-7). Furthermore, in Acts 3:20-21, the disciples are encouraged to look forward to sharing an earthly rule with Jesus as the Messianic King: "When the Son of Man will sit on his glorious throne, you also shall sit upon twelve thrones, judging the twelve tribes of Israel."[28] This may have in view the universal blessings that will flow from the Final Temple.

In Ezekiel 47:1-12, we are told that a river of water will flow from beneath the threshold of the Millennial Temple facing east (verses 1-2), refreshing the eastern region of the Land of Israel, an area known as the Arabah, which formerly was barren and inhospitable. The extent of this restorative work includes even the salty waters of the Dead Sea becoming fresh and hosting life (verses 8-10). If we can see in this passage an ideal reproduction of the heavenly New Jerusalem on earth during the Millennium, then the fruit produced by the trees that grow as a result of this refreshing stream may be for the "healing of the [Gentile] nations" (like that in Revelation 22:1-2).[29] These "times of refreshing" are said by Peter to "come from the presence of the Lord" (Acts 3:19). This may imply the geographical enthronement of the glorified Messiah within the eschatological Temple in the Millennial Jerusalem (see Jeremiah 3:17; Ezekiel 37:27; 43:7; 48:35). The sequence of events spoken of by Peter in Acts 3:19-21 are characteristic of the national restoration promised to Israel: national repentance (verse 19a; see also Zechariah 12:10-14; Ezekiel 37:11-14; Isaiah 59:20-21/Romans 11:25), divine forgiveness and national cleansing (verse 19b; see also Ezekiel 36:25-29; Zechariah 13:1; Romans 11:26-27), the return of *Israel's* Messiah (N.B.

"appointed for *you*") to effect its restoration (verses 20-21; see also Romans 11:12,15), and the blessings of the Millennial kingdom (verse 21; see also Isaiah 11:1-9; 65:17-25). As stated previously, these verses demonstrate that the New Testament continues—*after* the birth of the church—to teach the Old Testament concept of the coming of the Messiah and the Messianic kingdom hinging on Israel's repentance. This also connects Peter's message with Jesus' Olivet Discourse, which predicts an Israelite regathering and repentance during the time of tribulation prior to the Messianic advent (Matthew 24:29-31; Mark 13:24-27).

If, as Acts 3:20-21 implies, the disciples and the early Jewish-Christian community were expecting the arrival of the Messianic kingdom, as was their stated goal (Acts 1:6), they would have originally remained in Jerusalem, since it was to Jerusalem that Christ was expected to return (see Zechariah 14:4) and from where His rule (and theirs) would begin (Jeremiah 3:17; Zechariah 14:9,16-17).[30] Given a Temple and Pentecost setting, a distinct and universally representative Jewish audience (Diaspora Jews on pilgrimage at the feast), and Peter's appeal to the Old Testament predictions of national restoration (Acts 3:19-21), how can it be argued that at this point the Jewish people and their institutions have been rejected and replaced forever by the church? In view of this evidence, E. P. Sanders, Professor of Arts and Sciences in Religion at Duke University, concluded: "The hope that seems to have been most often repeated was that the restoration of the people of Israel...the kingdom expected by Jesus...is like the present world—it has a king, leaders, a temple, and twelve tribes."[31]

In addition, Peter's proximity to the Court of the Gentiles when giving this message may have in view the fulfillment of Israel's destiny to be both a witness to and a spiritual blessing for the Gentile nations. This may be implied from Peter's quotation of the blessing in the Abrahamic Covenant in Genesis 22:18 (which applies to Gentiles): "In your seed [Messiah] all of the families of the earth shall be blessed" (verse 25). In this time of future universal blessing the Temple plays a pivotal role, for the nations are predicted not only to assist in its construction (Zechariah 6:15; Haggai 2:7), but to participate in worship there (Isaiah 2:2-3; 11:10; 56:6-7; Zechariah 14:16-19). Even if the prophetic Temple texts are not directly implied in Peter's message of Israel's restoration, Peter's audience may have very well made the connection between eschatological restoration at the season of Pentecost (the Feast of Ingathering) and the fact that Peter was speaking at the Temple.

Therefore, in light of the disciples' worship at the Temple and their leader's message, it can be seen that the early church in Jerusalem respected the sanctity of the Temple, which they understood to have had continuing relevance for the future age (see Matthew 23:39; Acts 1:6; 15:16-18). This conclusion, however, has been challenged in light of the implied rejection of the Temple by Stephen in his speech in Acts. Therefore, let's examine this objection by looking at the context of the speech itself.

Stephen's Temple Speech

The most extensive speech in the book of Acts is Stephen's discourse delivered before the Sanhedrin (Acts 7:2-53). In a style uncharacteristic of Luke, the Gentile compiler of the account,[32] the speech repeatedly appeals to the Old Testament, citing some 40 passages in its interpretive details of Israel's early history.[33] Commentators on this passage have often assumed that Stephen's speech reflects a Christian attack on the institution of the Temple because of the Jewish accusation against him of speaking "against this holy place" (Acts 6:13). For example, Marcel Simon maintains that "its main characteristic is a strongly anti-ritualistic trend, and a fierce hostility towards the Temple, which he considers almost as a place of idolatry."[34] The justification for this argument is based on Stephen's use in Acts 7:48 of the Greek expression *cheiropoieton* ("made with [human] hands"). Stephen is said to be rejecting the Temple as "made with [human] hands," as against the Tabernacle, which was made according to the heavenly pattern (Acts 7:44).[35] Noting also that the term also appears in the Greek Septuagint to speak of the manufacture of idols,[36] it is argued that Stephen further identified the Temple and its sacrifices with idolatry (see verses 42-43). However, Luke's writings are generally acknowledged to reflect a pro-Temple stance[37] and, despite the use of this term elsewhere, the present context makes it doubtful that Stephen's speech attacks the Temple at all.[38] Several arguments may be offered in defense of this position.

First, while Stephen is accused of speaking against the Temple, Luke takes pains to show that this accusation comes from *false* witnesses.[39] The nature of their charge is that Stephen said Jesus would destroy the Temple and alter the Mosaic tradition (Acts 6:14). This was the same allegation made against Jesus at His trial, which was declared by the Gospel writers to be false (Matthew 26:60-61; 27:40; Mark 14:56-59) because Jesus was talking about His own body and not the physical Temple (John 2:19-21). Luke reveals this continuity by paralleling Stephen's account with that of Jesus' Passion: The testimonies against Stephen are similar to those against Jesus (Acts 6:13 = Mark 14:58) and labeled false (Acts 6:13 = Mark 14:57), and the last three of Stephen's dying words correspond to the three Passion sayings of Jesus (a. Acts 7:55 = Matthew 26:64; Mark 14:62; Luke 22:69; b. Acts 7:59 = Luke 23:46; c. Acts 7:60 = Luke 23:34).[40] While the accusation against Stephen is that he spoke against Moses and the Temple, to the contrary it is Stephen who appeals to Moses and to the Temple against his accusers, whom he states are actually the ones in opposition to both.

Second, the claim that the expression "made without hands" distinguishes the Temple from the Tabernacle and that Stephen thereby views the Temple as an idolatrous institution cannot be supported in comparative usage or the immediate context. The term *cheiropoieton* is also used in Hebrew 9:11,24 in reference to the Tabernacle, and Stephen's usage does not set the Solomonic Temple against the Mosaic Tabernacle, but simply emphasizes that God is not to be defined or confined by reference to a human creation such as a Temple.[41] This, of course, is the same idea expressed by Solomon at the dedication of the First Temple when he said, "Heaven and the highest heaven cannot contain Thee, how much less this house which I have built!" (1 Kings 8:27; 2 Chronicles 6:18). It is also the same point Paul made at the Athenian Areopagus concerning the localization of God in a structure (in the context of the Parthenon) "made with [human] hands" (Acts 17:24). Both speeches have in view the transcendence of God, who, as solitary Creator, is undetermined by His creation.

As to the charge that Stephen associated the Temple with idolatry, we need to recognize that the focus of Stephen's historical review is not idolatry in the sense of worshiping images (which, given the history of Israel, it could have been), but rather the attitude of human self-assertion[42] that refuses to acknowledge divine revelation and thus leads to idolatry (see Romans 1:18-23). In support of this the renowned scholar J.M.P. Sweet further argues that the background for *cheiropoietois* ("made without hands") is drawn from the Old Testament rather than from Hellenistic spiritualizing. He maintains that the word here, in view of its parallel in Acts 17:24-25, is directed against *the Jewish accusers* of Stephen (rather than the Temple itself), who have, by their rejection of Jesus and His witnesses, put themselves in the position of pagans who fail to perceive God's hand at work (see Acts 5:38-39).[43] In addition, notice that Stephen carefully restricted his remarks about disobedience and idolatry to the wilderness wandering (as an example of Israel's rebellion during that initial period—Acts 7:38-43) rather than mention the period of the monarchy, when the First Temple stood.

Third, Stephen's speech develops the historical cycle between God's grants of divine mercy and Israel's acts of human rebellion. In this Old Testament structure, David's desire for a Temple is presented as much as a positive sign of God's favor as the Tabernacle, both of which were revealed to have been made according to the same divinely revealed "blueprint" (Exodus 25:8-9; 1 Chronicles 28:19). This is in harmony with Stephen's citation in Acts 7:46 from Psalm 132:5, which claims that David's original aim for the Temple was that it serve as a "dwelling" for God's presence, and that Solomon succeeded in accomplishing this purpose.[44] Stephen's point is that Solomon, in building a house for *God*, fulfilled his father's ambition to find a habitation for Him. Stephen's declaration that David's desire to build a house "found favor in God's sight" should be applied also to Solomon's completion of the Temple. It is this godly desire to fulfill God's stated intent to "dwell" with His people that led Stephen to the subject of the divine habitation in verses 48-49 rather than any question of the validity of the Temple as a place for the people's worship or God's presence. Stephen knew that his Jewish audience had erred, like their fathers, in transferring the proper desire for the person of God to the place for God, the Temple. Stephen's contrast is between the devotion of David and Solomon, who found God's favor, and the present Jewish Nation, who rejected God Himself (in the person of Jesus) and therefore sided with Israel's apostates rather than with its faithful (see verses 51-52).

Fourth, the problem for Stephen in Acts 7 is not the Temple, but the *actions of the people* to whom God had given the Temple. This, as one scholar commenting on this passage has observed, is in keeping with Jesus' attitude in Luke, where He did not oppose the Temple or its cult, but rather the improper and desecrating behavior of those associated with it.[45] On the one hand, Stephen's concern is to demonstrate that God's revelation of Himself was not always confined to the Temple—thus, God revealed Himself [as a Savior] to Abraham in Mesopotamia, to Joseph in Egypt, to Moses in the burning bush, and likewise through Jesus as Messiah (although He is not mentioned here by name). On the other hand, the rejection of Jesus as a revelation of God, possibly because He did not fulfill the predicted Messianic role of Temple restorer, compelled Stephen to defend the implied thesis that the Messianic purpose required first a restoration of the *hearts* of the Nation to God, a purpose yet unrealized in Israel's history because of its continued rejection of God's prophetic representatives (see Matthew 23:30-35).

This rejection had manifested itself in Stephen's day in a form of worship that relied upon the Temple's existence as proof of God's approval—despite the impropriety of that worship (a point often made by the prophets). Stephen's abrupt shift to an adversarial position in verse 51 makes no sense unless we see a parallel here between the past rebellion of the people (who were given the Tabernacle) and the present rebellion of the people (who were given the Temple). Stephen's implication is that this very attitude characterized Israel in the past during the time it worshiped at the Tabernacle and brought about its destruction at Shiloh, and again during the First Temple period, resulting in the departure of the *Shekinah* and later the Temple's destruction by the Babylonians. Stephen's charge is that by the Jewish authorities' rejection of God's revelation in Jesus, they are in the same company with their rebellious ancestors, who likewise rejected God's revelation in the wilderness.

This rebellion is highlighted by Stephen's use of the phrase "made with [human] hands" (verse 48), for we find similar language used to describe Israel's apostate attitude in verse 41: "rejoicing in the works of their hands" (over the golden calf). Just as "the Most High God" had manifested Himself at Sinai but a portion of the Jewish leadership (and people) had sought "a god" (the golden calf) manifested through the work of their own hands, so now in Stephen's day this same God had manifested Himself in Jesus as the promised Messiah but the Jewish leaders (and people) had again sought God in the work of their hands—in this case, the Temple and its ritual service. The Temple was designed to serve God's purpose in manifesting Himself, not to replace that manifestation (Jesus).

Behind Stephen's words may also be the thought that because Jesus the Messiah would ultimately build the Restoration Temple, involving the Gentile nations and the return of the *Shekinah* (Isaiah 56:7; Ezekiel 43:4; Zechariah 6:12), all acts of rebellion against Him were in fact acts of rebellion against the Most High and His purpose to restore Israel as a witness to the nations. This accords with Stephen's placement of Jesus in verse 52 as standing at the climax of the long line of prophets who were sent to Israel, but were rejected because of the Jewish authorities' misplaced confidence in the Temple. Stephen argues that to seek for God's blessing through the Temple, while at the same time refusing God's Word and the Messiah who is greater than the Temple (Matthew 12:6), is to desecrate the function of the Temple; an act of no less defiance than that displayed at the foot of Mount Horeb. For this reason he can link them in attitude with their ancestors in verses 51-53.

My conclusion, then, is that Stephen did not target the Temple nor argue against its sanctity. His comments concerning the Temple rather concerned the idea of God's presence being restricted to an earthly building, and, like Jesus, of the inadequacy of claiming the Temple of God as a promise of security while at the same time living in rebellion to the God of that Temple (see Matthew 23:16-24).

Stephen's use of Isaiah 66:1-2 confirms that he is thinking in cosmic proportions, like Solomon in 1 Kings 8:27, and fits well within the traditional Jewish perspective that regarded the Temple as the place where God's name dwelt and as the place of prayer. Like the prophets who condemned trusting in the Temple while violating the Law for which the Temple stood, Stephen condemns those who have rejected Jesus, whose purpose was to fulfill the Law (Matthew 5:17-18) and who Himself identified with the prophets in their message against the Law-breakers (see Matthew 12:5-8). Stephen, then, directs his condemnation against those Jewish authorities who rejected God's revelation of Himself and handed Jesus over to the Romans for crucifixion—not against the institution that was meant to reveal and serve Him.[46]

Paul's Attitude Toward the Temple in the Book of Acts

Just as the Temple had been regarded with traditional reverence by the apostles and early church, so it also continued to have a sacred significance for the Jewish Pharisee Saul after he became the apostle Paul.[47] This is evidenced by Luke's mention of Paul's acts of veneration toward the Temple while he ministered outside of the Land. The list of these observant acts include Paul's attendance at the Jewish feasts regulated by the Temple (Acts 20:6),[48] his religious vows, such as the Nazarite vow (Acts 18:18), *miqve* purification rites—in one case involving four Jewish-Christian men under a vow (Acts 21:23-26; 24:18), the payment of ceremonial expenses, which accounted as a *mitzvah* ("a halakhically obligated good deed"—Acts 21:24), participation in the offering of a sacrifice at the Temple (Acts 21:26; 24:17), prayers and worship at the Temple (Acts 22:17; 24:11), proper regard for the high priesthood (Acts 23:5), and payment of the Temple tax (Acts 24:17). Since Paul's work was primarily among Jews in the Diaspora and their Gentile neighbors, the only purpose for Luke's mention of such exceptional acts of Jewish devotion to the Temple would be to demonstrate Paul's fidelity to the Law and the Temple—a point that he himself defended: "I have committed no offense either against the Law of the Jews or against the temple..." (Acts 25:8).

The book of Acts does record Paul as being accused of desecrating the Temple, but it also reveals that he was guiltless of such charges. The events unfold as follows: After a riot at the Temple due to a false rumor that Paul had attempted to desecrate the Temple (Acts 24:6) by bringing a Gentile (Trophimus)[49] beyond the Court of the Gentiles, separated by the boundary fence of sanctity known as the *soreg*,[50] and into the Israelite Court, he was rescued from the incensed Jewish crowd by Roman guards.[51] Paul then addressed his accusers and the crowd in Hebrew and declared himself a Jew (Acts 21:27-39). When his case was finally tried, Paul defended himself (as a Roman citizen) against the anti-Temple charges by affirming his Jewish heritage and professing his ceremonial purification at the Temple (Acts 24:18).

As we come to the end of the book of Acts, despite the persecution of Jewish opponents, Paul still addresses the leaders of the Jews in Rome as "brothers" and declares to them that he had "done nothing against our people or the customs of our fathers [which included all the Temple ritual]" (Acts 28:17), and that he bore no malice against his "nation" (Acts 28:19). These historical accounts in Acts depict Paul as being observant in connection with the laws of the Temple, as one who assisted fellow Jewish believers in performing their Temple obligations, and as one who insisted on regulating his life by the Temple calendar (the feast days)—*even if it meant interrupting his own missionary work* (Acts 20:16). All of these actions are unexplicable coming from one who was commissioned as "the apostle to the Gentiles" (see Romans 1:5; Galatians 2:7-9) if indeed he held to replacement theology and taught the Gentiles that there was no future for ethnic Israel or its ritual institutions![52] Rather, the portrait we see in Acts places Paul in the camp of normative Judaism with respect to his attitude toward the Temple.

John Townsend, who wrote his Harvard University doctoral dissertation on a study of the Temple in the New Testament, agrees with this assessment, saying, "There is little reason to suppose that Paul, after becoming a Christian, radically changed his attitude toward the Jerusalem Temple or that he was opposed to any Christian, Jew, or Gentile taking part in its cult."[53] This cautions us to read Paul's harsh statements toward Jewish legalizers and his comments concerning the Mosaic Law in light of his lifelong adherence to Judaism. Moreover, these examples of Paul's reverence toward the Temple should be sufficient to warrant a reappraisal of his use of Temple and cultic metaphors in his epistles as indicative of replacement by Christ and the church (see chapter 13).[54] This means that when Paul later uses the analogy of the Temple with respect to the believer's body (1 Corinthians 3:16-17; 2 Corinthians 6:16-17) or the body of Christ (Ephesians 2:21-22), he is not seeking to replace the physical Temple with the spiritual church. Rather, he is arguing for the sanctity of the one by analogy with the other (i.e., the presence of God—the Holy Spirit—indwelling the Temple, and also believers individually and collectively).

This survey of the early church in the book of Acts has revealed a different attitude toward the Temple than that assumed by most of Christendom for the past 2,000 years. E.P. Sanders at Oxford University notes this when he says: "We can rely on Acts as showing that they felt that the temple was a fit place of worship (e.g. Acts 3:1; 21:23-26). They may have thought that it was doomed, but not that it was impure or had already been superseded."[55] It reveals that just as Jesus was persecuted by the Sanhedrin because of His activity in the Temple (Luke 22:52-53; 23:5), so also were Peter and John (Acts 4:1-22), Stephen (Acts 7:44-60), and Paul (Acts 21:27-30). Even though these leaders of the church were persecuted by the Jewish establishment, they continued to respect and regulate their lives by the Temple which represented that very establishment. And even though the New Testament portrays Jerusalem and the Temple as the setting in which the Jewish leadership expressed hostility to the purpose of God, to the Messiah, and to His church, we still see that the apostles and the church clearly revered and remained devoted to both. In the book of Acts, written to a Roman official (Theophilus), Luke demonstrated to a Gentile readership that Christianity had not broken with its Israelite origin and become something else. This was to affirm, as Sanders notes, "a direct line of continuity runs from Moses and the prophets to the church....it is not Christianity that has rejected Judaism, but Judaism that has rejected Christianity."[56]

Reconnecting Christianity to the Temple

The perspective that the Temple is part of the old covenant, which has been replaced and abrogated by a new covenant community, the church, needs to be seriously reexamined. We've looked at biblical evidence that has said otherwise. My intention has been to remind us that the early church's expectation was of a restoration of Israel through faith in their Messiah, and that a necessary part of this restoration, according to the Old Testament prophets, Jesus, and Paul, was that a Temple be rebuilt. And, if the Temple was respected as a sacred institution in early Jewish-Christianity, as reflected in the book of Acts, then one should not adduce passages from polemical situations to argue that Christians had rejected the Temple as the spiritual center of life and that the church is the new Temple and that Christians (especially Gentiles) constitute the new Israel.

As a result of our discussion, I would like to suggest the following theological and practical conclusions concerning the Jewish Temple in Christian perspective:

1. The Temple is both a historical institution, divinely given to Israel as a focal point of God's presence and promise of restoration as a nation and a spiri-

tual community, and a symbol of the people of God, which is greater than the church. The Temple is beyond time because its purpose is ultimately to unite Jew and Gentile in the worship of God. The prophets envisioned this when they declared that one day there would come a restored Temple, built by Jewish and Gentile laborers, which would become the house of prayer for all nations. Paul envisioned this when he spoke of the church, made up of both Jews and Gentiles as a temple, unified and indwelt by God's holy presence.

2. Jesus came not to destroy the Temple nor to punish the Jews, but came as a Jew to live an observant Jewish life and to offer the promise of the hope of the consolation of Israel that was tendered by the prophets. To interpret Jesus outside of this context is to do violence to the text and to history, and to sow the seeds of anti-Semitism, which destroys the hope of unity that the imagery of the Temple portrayed.

3. The New Testament affirms the eschatological promise of salvation and national and cultic restoration to Israel as a demonstration of God's covenant faithfulness and power to reverse desecration and bring sanctification. In this respect, the statement of Markus Barth holds true: "The future of the church lies in the salvation of Israel."[57]

4. While the church does not replace Israel, Israel will replace the church as they fulfill their historic destiny to bring the knowledge of the glory of God to all the earth. The church, however, remains with restored Israel as the people of God, enjoying the Messianic kingdom and the eternal state.

5. While Jews have replaced Jesus with the Temple and Christians have replaced the Temple with Jesus, in fact the Temple will one day be built by Jesus and serve to magnify Him. While today the Temple is a matter of division between Jews and Christians, when Messiah is again revealed, all believers (Jew and Gentile) will find the Temple to be a unifying center for their common worship (Isaiah 2:2-3; 56:6-7).

The historian Heinrich Graetz reminds us that "a nation [Israel] which has witnessed the rise and decay of the most ancient empires, and which still continues to hold its place in the present day, deserves the closest attention." When that nation is moving, even in part, to expect its Messiah and to realize its prophetic destiny, we who are Christians and who share in that fulfillment ought, of all people, to pay attention and, moreover, share the good news we have received from the Jewish Messiah. Reuven Doron, the Director of Embrace Israel

Ministries, advises that this is part of our spiritual obligation (see Romans 15:27): "As Israel gave birth to the church in the first century, so the church must give birth to Israel in the last! The historical and biblical debt of love and gratitude is due in this generation, and the Lord is calling for many to give themselves in prayer to see the descendants of Jacob come into their fullness in the kingdom of God...."[58]

Christians and the Temple Today

Today an unprecedented reconnection with Orthodox Judaism in relation to the Temple is taking place within Christianity. For example, in recent years the Lutheran Church (Missouri Synod) has officially asked forgiveness for German Christian complicity in the Holocaust. In addition, Christian Zionism has spread through a broad spectrum of denominational and nondenominational churches. Christian Zionists have, especially for the past decade, embarked upon the road that supports Judaism in its aspirations for a rebuilt Temple. This has been evidenced in the mainstream media's reports on the preparations to rebuild the Temple—reports in which Christians are linked with Jews. For example, one of the first articles on the subject in an international magazine said, "Temple restoration is also a fixation for literal-minded Protestants, who deem a new Temple the precondition for Christ's second coming."[59] In like manner, in 1989 when the Religious News Service sent out a story to local papers about the rebuilding of the Temple in 1989, it stated, "The project...has united ultra-Orthodox Jews with fundamentalist Protestant Christians, both of whom share the dream of a third Jewish temple."[60] In 1988, Wesley Pippert, a former senior UPI Middle East Correspondent, reported, "Some Christian fundamentalists in the United States have raised money to support a project to rebuild the temple. This is the central purpose of a group called 'The Jerusalem Temple Foundation,' which is incorporated in the United States. Its theme is 'Build Thy Temple Speedily'."[61] One group of Christian Zionists, organized as an American branch of the Jerusalem Temple Mount Foundation, operates under the name of Committee of Concerned Evangelicals for Freedom of Worship on the Temple Mount. They purchased a full-page ad in the *Jerusalem Post* condemning the Israeli government for the March 10, 1983 arrest of a group of Temple activists who had sought to penetrate the Temple Mount via the Huldah Gate passageway in the area known as Solomon's Stables. It is rumored that members of this group paid for the legal fees of those arrested, and that they also funded the Lifta Band that tried to blow up the Al Aqsa Mosque and the Dome of the Rock.

In the last decade, evangelical Christians have moved to directly support Jewish efforts to rebuild the Temple. In 1990 Wilem Van der Hoven, director of the Jerusalem-based International Christian Embassy, planned to lead thousands of Christians up to the Temple Mount at the conclusion of their annually sponsored Feast of Tabernacles program in order to pray for the soon rebuilding of the Temple. Although police permits were obtained, then-Mayor Teddy Kollek persuaded Mr. Van der Hoven to cancel these plans. Even so, the fact that such an event was scheduled was witness to a change for the Jewish people of a millennia-old reputation of Christian scorn and supercessionism over the Temple. In recent years, Christian groups have made significant contributions to Temple movement organizations, helped purchase buildings for Ateret Cohanim in the Muslim Quarter near the Temple Mount, and largely financed some Temple activist organizations, such as the Temple Mount Faithful.

This new show of support by Christians has not, of course, gone unnoticed by the Jewish press. The *Jerusalem Post* announced to their international Jewish (and Christian) readership: "There are growing numbers of Christians, many organized into small churches and larger groups, who see the construction of a Third Temple as the cornerstone of their beliefs. Though there is a clear divergence in religious belief between these Christians and Jews who work toward the rebuilding of the Temple, they willingly and enthusiastically cooperate."[62]

This new spirit of Christian cooperation has not escaped the attention of those in the Temple movement, either. As one Israeli scholar and researcher on the Temple reported to an Orthodox Jewish constituency:

Among the fundamentalist Christians, whose number reaches scores of millions, there is a growing conviction that the time has come to realize the biblical prophecies once for all. There are among them Americans and Europeans, and there are others from Japan and Asia, who regard themselves as Zionists and are expecting the building of the temple soon in our times. In Europe there is nowadays a growing interest in the secret societies which were persecuted for centuries by the Inquisition—the Knights Templar—the knights of the Order of the Temple, who ruled the Temple Mount in Jerusalem, and their heirs "The Freemasons," who attribute their organization and teachings to the builders of Solomon's Temple. For all these there must be an interest in the restoration of the temple—and especially in Jerusalem—soon in our lifetime.[63]

Jewish organizations such as the Temple Institute cater to Christian tour groups by providing a visitor's center and lectures about the Temple implements they are preparing. They likewise depend on Christian financial support and exposure through their publications and media. Some, such as the Temple Mount Faithful, have developed even closer ties with Christians, allowing Christians to help in secretarial work and publishing their newsletter and website. One reason for this is because evangelical Christians see the support of Temple-related organizations as one way of fulfilling their general obligation to support Israel. For example, Pentecostal and Charismatic Christian groups have openly joined in showing unqualified support to Temple organizations, both spiritually and tangibly, during annual "Feast of Tabernacle Pilgrimages."

Another reason for this new connection to the Temple is people's heightened awareness of Bible prophecy and its relationship to the times in which we are living. The reality of the State of Israel and the tensions in the Middle East mounting toward a global conflict have produced a generation of Christians who believe they may actually see the fulfillment of end-time prophecies. Since the rebuilding of the Temple is a central feature of the last days, and a Temple movement now exists to bring it to fruition, these Christians see their support of the Temple movement as helping to fulfill, if not hasten, the coming of Christ and the kingdom of God on earth. Surprisingly, these Christian goals are understood by Jews in the Temple movement:

> We have allies among the nations in rebuilding the Temple, allies whose numbers could swell, with some encouragement, many thousands of times. One such possible target for encouragement is the community of Christian fundamentalists, who swear to the literal truth of every word of the Bible. This powerful movement numbers tens of millions in the U.S. and Europe, and its influence and power are rising rapidly. Many among them are friends of Israel; some even call themselves "Zionists." In their own way, they await the Messiah and his appearance in Israel, and some of them see the rise of an independent Jewish sovereignty and the rebuilding of the Temple as connected—and perhaps even a precondition to the Messiah's appearance....I wish to conclude by speculating as to the possible contribution which thousands and tens of thousands of non-Jews could make in expressing their own wish and demand for the rebuilding of the Temple in our day.[64]

For others in the Temple movement, these Christian goals are not enough to warrant excitement for Christian support of the Temple because they still view it as part of a greater Christian agenda to convert Jewish people to Jesus. For example, Rabbi Chaim Richman, the Director of Public Affairs for the Temple Institute, has stated:

> It is interesting at this time in history that both Christians and Jews have an interest in the building of the Temple. What is ironic about this is that these are rather strange bedfellows in that many Christians only want to see the Temple built to fulfill a prophetic scenario that Hal Lindsey has popularized in the Western world. They do not share with the Jews the spiritual aspects of the Temple. The way I see it is that if you want the Temple built only to fulfill a prophetic scenario, you haven't read your scriptures very carefully...that the Temple makes up a very important part of the biblical faith.[65]

Others in the Temple movement, while embracing Christians as fellow supporters of the cause of rebuilding, do so with a conviction that the change in Christian conduct, after so many centuries of advocating replacement theology, is a sure sign that God is turning Gentile hearts to Judaism in preparation for the Messianic age where both Jew and Gentile will serve in the Temple together. However, many of the Christians who are giving their support to Temple organizations are convinced that the Jews they are supporting are coming closer to Christianity because they speak so fervently of God fulfilling His prophetic Word and they believe the Bible's promises of a coming Messiah.

From these polar vewpoints we can see that the contact between Christian and Jew has indeed been made, but that the real connection has yet to be formed. But there's another part of the picture we need to consider: the Muslims. While some Christians and Jews have discovered common ground in the Temple, Muslims and Jews could not be further divided on the topic. In the next chapter we will examine the claims and the control of Islam over the Temple Mount—claims that have eclipsed even the replacement views of Christianity in their assertions for this sacred space.

CHAPTER 8

Only for Islam

Muslims and the Temple Mount

The mosques on the Temple Mount were built by the order of God.... Our sovereignty is not subject to compromise.

—ADNAN HUSSEINI,
SENIOR WAKF OFFICIAL

The Muslims of today want to rule the world. And I mean every word of this.

—YOHANAN RAMATI,
DIRECTOR OF THE JERUSALEM INSTITUTE FOR WESTERN DEFENSE

In front of 200,000 Muslims gathered on the Temple Mount, Sheik Ikrama Sabri, the Palestinian Mufti, demanded the liberation of "Jerusalem and of all the Palestinian territory from the yoke of the Israeli occupiers."[1] He accused the Americans, British, and Israelis of being modern crusaders who "proceed against the Muslims with hate and with blood."[2] Therefore, it was with some trepidation that I, an American, arrived for my interview with this Mufti (literally "decision maker"), the chief Muslim cleric in charge of Islam's holy places on the *Haram al-Sharif* ("Noble Enclosure," i.e., Temple Mount). Although I was punctual, my fear turned to frustration as I was made to wait an additional hour, all the while being questioned and examined concerning my purpose and credentials. This all took place not more than five feet from the Mufti's door! Finally, I was escorted into the office of the Mufti where he sat imposingly at the head of a large desk with long tables on each side filled with well-dressed Muslims. Above his head was prominently displayed a framed picture of Yasser Arafat, while behind him were bookcases filled with volumes on Islamic law.

As we began the interview, I considered again this man who was before me. Here was the Palestinian leader who had recently moved his office from East Jerusalem to the Temple Mount in violation of the Israeli-Palestinian autonomy agreements and against pleas from the Clinton administration. Here was the rival Islamic cleric who had opposed both the Jordanian Mufti and Jordan's claim of official custodianship of Islamic holy places in Jerusalem. Here was the Palestinian leader who called for the death penalty for any Palestinian (or any Arab) who sold land to Jews. Here was the religious spokesman who had publically referred to Jews as "the sons of monkeys and pigs." Here, too, was the voice of Palestinian Muslims who said the Temple never existed on the Temple Mount and that the Arabs would go to war before they would see any Jew pray at the places sacred to Islam. The Mufti did not mince words with me, either. Throughout the interview he fervently affirmed the Muslim jurisdiction of the Temple Mount and claimed that the Jews had no rights whatsoever to touch it (for these comments, see the companion video *The Coming Last Days Temple*).

As I left the Mufti's office I sighed in relief that the interview was over with, but also for the present obstacle that Islam poses for a Jewish return to their Temple Mount today. Yet, even before this Mufti had been appointed by the Palestinians, the conflicting religious claims to the site between Jews and Muslims had long sparked violence that errupted in major confrontations on the Temple Mount.

A Modern History of Muslim Conflict

From 1917–1948, while Jerusalem was under the British Mandate, fierce riots between Arabs and Jews over access and control of the Western Wall was one of the factors forcing political intervention in resolving the problems in Palestine. The Islamic Grand Mufti of Jerusalem, Hajj Amin al-Husseini, an Arab nationalist leader, directed anti-Jewish riots in Jerusalem between 1919–1940, and during World War II collaborated with Adolf Hitler against the Jews and was the Third Reich's chief propogandists to the Arabs, aiding the Nazi program to exterminate the Jewish people.[3] Although Israeli independence was granted on May 14, 1948, no access to the Western Wall or Temple Mount was permitted by Jordan, who took possession of East Jerusalem. Under Jordanian rule 56 Jewish synagogues were destroyed, the Western Wall was turned into a garbage dump, stones from the Western Wall were used to build private houses, and Jewish gravestones were used to construct latrines. In 1951 Jordan's king Abdullah of the Hashemite dynasty was assassinated on the Temple Mount at the Al-Aqsa Mosque by henchmen of Mufti Hajj Amin al-Husseini because of suspected sympathies to the Jews. This event was witnessed by his teenage grandson Hussayn bin Talal (Hussein), who succeeded his mentally-ill father Talal as king in 1953.

Undoubtedly this assassination deeply affected the young King Hussein and was a major factor in his severe treatment of Jewish sites during his control of eastern Jerusalem (1953–1967).

On June 5, 1967 King Hussein joined other Arab states to attack Israel. During this Six-Day War (June 5–7) a battle for the Temple Mount resulted in Jordanian Arabs fleeing the Temple Mount as the Israeli Defense Forces seized the site.[4] Fear of a reprisal by the Arab world over Jewish control returned the jurisdiction of the Temple Mount to the Muslims, who forbade any non-Muslim access to the Temple Mount for religious purposes. However, the Israeli government would not relinquish their control of the Western Wall at the foot of the Temple Mount for Jewish prayers.

On August 23, 1969, Australian Christian cultist Denis Michael Rohan set fire to the Al-Aqsa Mosque, believing that it would hasten the coming of Christ. In response, Muslims demonstrated and accused the Israeli government of deliberately setting the blaze in order to rebuild the Temple. The Islamic Wakf then closed the Temple Mount to non-Muslims for two months.

Several years later, in February 1976, the schools and shops closed in Arab East Jerusalem because of strikes and riots that protested legislation that would permit Jews access to the Temple Mount for prayer. In March 1979 a rumor that a prayer service might be held by a Jewish group on the Temple Mount provoked a general strike among West Bank Arabs as well as 2,000 Arab youths brandishing stones and staves at Temple Mount. In August 1981 the discovery and excavation of a gate in a tunnel from the Jewish Second Temple period incited a riot amongst the Muslims. Arab schools and shops closed once again, and the Islamic authorities demanded that Israeli authorities permanently seal the ancient gate, even though Chief Rabbi Shlomo Goren and Rabbi Meir Yehuda Getz had claimed the Ark of the Covenant was buried within.

More riots occurred in January 1986 when an Israeli Knesset member attempted to pray on the Temple Mount. On October 8, 1990, while more than 20,000 Jewish worshipers were assembled at the Western Wall for prayers during the Feast of Tabernacle services, 3,000 Palestinian Muslims on the Temple Mount hurled stones down upon the crowd. The riot that followed left 18 Arabs dead and brought a missile attack against Israel from Saddam Hussein, who had championed the Palestinian cause.

At the end of October 1991 at the Middle East Peace Conference in Madrid, Spain, Syrian Foreign Minister Farouk Al-Shara accused Israel of attempting to blow up the Al-Aqsa Mosque and proclaimed that there would be no free access for Jews to the religious sites on the Temple Mount unless Israel returned all of East Jerusalem (including the Temple Mount) to the Palestinians. The Temple Mount was again closed to non-Muslims on February 25, 1994 and the months that followed as a result of a shooting in the Hebron mosque.

On September 15, 1993, the day the Israeli-PLO Declaration of Principles was signed, PLO Chairman Yasser Arafat announced that soon all of the mosques, churches, and sacred sites in East Jerusalem would be under the Palestinian flag. In September 1996 the opening of an exit tunnel for tourists in the Western Wall Tunnel sparked Muslim riots on the Temple Mount and spread to outlying Arab villages. The death toll from the riot totalled 58. Muslims then appropriated the area behind the ancient Huldah Gates (dating from the Second Temple period) for Ramadan prayers, ignoring protests from the Israeli government. From 1996–1997 the attempt by Jews to openly pray on the Temple Mount led to additional riots and some closures of the Temple Mount for brief periods.

In 1998 Muslims appropriated the Huldah Gate area and began building a mosque—stating that since the government's opening of the exit tunnel the Wakf no longer recognized the authority of any Israeli agency, including the Antiquities Authority, which supervises all excavations of archaeological sites.

The Mufti further stated that Islamic sovereignty over the sacred sites would not be compromised. In the first few months of 1999 more than five attempts to attack the Temple Mount were thwarted by Jerusalem police, and Palestinians assumed a greater control over the Temple Mount in view of the plans for the whole of East Jerusalem to become the capital of an independent Palestinian state. The Mufti threatened Jewish activists, saying that a Jewish presence on the Temple Mount is an offense to Islam and will not be tolerated. The Hamas spiritual leader Sheik Yassin and the Palestinian Mufti Ikrama Sabri have declared that the Muslims will defend the sacred area to the last drop of blood.

By what right do the Muslims make such a claim that pledges the blood of the whole Muslim religion? Before answering this, let me make it clear that our focus here is upon Muslims, not Arabs per se. While it is true that most of the Arab world is Muslim, many Arabs in the Holy Land, and in Muslim countries, are Christian. The largest Muslim country is the non-Arab country of Indonesia, and of course predominately Muslim countries such as Egypt and Turkey are non-Arab. The conflict with Israel is at heart a religious, not an ethnic, conflict. So, our concern here is with Muslims, not Arabs, even though the Muslims who are involved with the struggle over the Temple Mount are also Arab.[5]

The Islamic Claim to the Temple Mount

It is obvious that the Muslims who presently have control of the Temple Mount will not relinquish it for any reason and have pledged war against Israel if attempts are made to change the status quo. Muslims contend that Jerusalem, to them, is *Al-Quds* ("the Holy") and that it is exclusively sacred to Islam and that Muslims the world over are in solidarity with this claim. Yasser Arafat evidences this mindset when he declares, "Give me one Arab who would betray Jerusalem, one Palestinian who would betray the…Muslim holy places."[6] Indeed, for generations the instruction in Muslim schools has stated that this site has no significance to Israel but only Islam. Jewish historian Gaalyah Cornfield notes this prevailing attitude when he writes:

> It has been said by an eminent contemporary Muslim scholar, Aref el Aref, that the only text needed for a study of the history and present structures of the Temple Mount are the buildings themselves and the Arab inscriptions that both adorn and explain them. But for the Moslems the history of the Mount began with Mohammed's vision of his night's journey from Mecca to Jerusalem and thence, with a spring, that left a mark, much revered, on the surface of the…Temple Mount, up

to heaven. Over that spot, the present "Dome of the Rock" was built, everything lying beneath it being, to the Muslim, irrelevant, even the insights of archaeology in the last hundred years, even the results of contemporary excavations being conducted now. Even these, to the descendants of the Moslems who walled up the historical underground passages and kept "infidels" and curious away, are unimportant.[7]

How did the religion of Islam come to Israel, and what is its claim to Jerusalem and the Temple Mount? Let us briefly survey the history of the early Arab occupation of Jerusalem and the Temple Mount, and then consider what historical and political factors led to the Muslim construction of religious structures on the Temple Mount.

The Religion of Islam

Mohammed, the prophet and founder of Islam, was born in Mecca about A.D. 570. At the time of his birth, Arab tribes in Mecca and throughout the Arabian peninsula were polytheistic, with each tribe having its own local deity. A large black meteor found in the desert and believed to have been sent by astral deities was placed in the southeast corner of a cube-shaped structure (*Ka'aba*) in Mecca and became the central shrine of Hubal, a chief male god among 360 other deities. Among these was al-Hajar al-Aswad, a nature deity, who was symbolized by the black stone. The most prominent Meccan deities besides Hubal were his three sister goddesses al-Lat, al-Manat, and al-Uzza. Mohammed at first acknowledged these goddesses as deities (believing them to be daughters of Allah), but later said his thinking had been corrupted by Satan. *Al-Lat* (or *Allat)* is the feminine form of *Allah,* and is believed to have been the female counterpart of Allah.[8] The chief goddess of Mohammed's tribe of Quraysh was al-Uzza, to whom Mohammed's grandfather almost sacrificed Mohammed's father except for the counsel of a fortune-teller. The head of this pantheon was al-Ilah (literally "the god"), a vague high god (astral deity) who some believe was associated with the moon. Mohammed's father's name was Abd-Allah ("the slave of al-Ilah"), so it is evident that Mohammed was well acquainted with this deity. He was also familiar with the Najran tribe, which was predominately Christian and exercised significant influence in northern Arabia. It is believed that Mohammed was at one time a student of Christianity and that this explains the inclusion of Jesus, as well as the Jewish patriarchs, in the Qur'an.

Beginning in A.D. 610 Mohammed claimed to have received angelic revela-
tions that al-ilah (Allah) was the supreme god and had a message of warning.[9]
Several years later Mohammed began to speak publicly as a prophet of Allah,
but was rejected by the pagan Meccans. The intensity of the persecution to
Mohammed and his followers grew through the years and forced him to flee to
Medina in A.D. 622. This event, known as the *Hijra* ("Migration"), marked the
beginning of the Islamic era. After gaining local favor and amassing an army, in
A.D. 630 Mohammed returned to Mecca, conquered it, and made it the spiritual
center of his new religion of Islam. The city's *Ka'aba* stone was transformed
from a pagan shrine to the focus of Muslim pilgrimage (*Hadj*). The Holy book of
Islam is the Qur'an (or Koran), which is composed of the angelic message to
Mohammed, revelatory books, and selected and "corrected" stories of Abraham,
Joseph, Moses, and David's psalms from the Old Testament and the story of
Jesus (Arabic, *Isa*) from the New Testament. All of these are believed by Muslims
to have been Muslims as well, even though they lived thousands of years before
the birth of Mohammed! [10] The Hadith is another sacred book, which contains
collected sayings and deeds of Mohammed, the last prophet.

Islam's god Allah is not the same as the God of Judaism or Christianity. Neither are its accounts of figures from the Jewish and Christian Bibles the same.
Islam claims its version is correct and that all others have been corrupted.
Christians, in particular, are said to be guilty of the unpardonable sin of *shirk*,
which means to associate partners or companions to Allah. This accusation
results from the Muslim misunderstanding of the Christian doctrine of the
triune nature of the one God.

Islam, from its beginning, has been a religion of the sword (*al Harb*). The
concept of Holy War (*Jihad*), mandated by Allah, requires Islam to completely
subdue the earth through military conquest. The world is thus divided between
Dar al-Islam ("House of Islam") and all areas yet unsubdued by Islam, *Dar al-
Harb* ("House of War"). All other religions and all other prophets after
Mohammed are false, and all non-Muslims are *infidels* or *dhimmi* (tolerated
minorities under Islamic rule—such as Jews and Christians). This controlling
command eventually brought Islam to Israel, and is the reason for the Muslims'
uncompromising control of the Temple Mount.

How Islam Came to Israel

After Mohammed died in A.D. 632, Abu Bakr followed him as the first
Caliph. Soon after, a civil war erupted among Mohammed's descendants over

the right of direct succession. This resulted in the Sunni and Shiite branches of Muslims, as well as lesser-known factions, that continue to war against one another today.[11] Between A.D. 633–643 Syria, Iraq, Egypt, and Persia came under Muslim control, furthering the territorial conquests in honor of Allah and his prophet Mohammed. In A.D. 638 the Muslim invasion moved to Byzantine-Christian governed Israel, and Jerusalem, with its Temple Mount, came under the control of Islam. Historian Steve Runciman recounts the conquest of Jerusalem:

> On a February day in the year A.D. 638 the Caliph Omar entered Jerusalem, riding upon a white camel. He was dressed in worn, filthy robes, and the army that followed him was rough and unkempt; but its discipline was perfect. At his side was the Patriarch Sophronius, as chief magistrate of the surrendered city. Omar rode straight to the site of the Temple of Solomon, whence his friend Mahomet [Mohammed] had ascended into heaven. Watching him stand there, the Patriarch remembered the words of Christ and murmured through his tears: "Behold the abomination of desolation, spoken of by Daniel the prophet."[12]

According to the traditional account, when the second Caliph, Omar (or 'Umar), who reigned from A.D. 634–644, entered Jerusalem in A.D. 638, he caused a mosque to be built on what was considered to be the ancient site of the Temple (or *Masjid*) of David. The position of this site Omar supposedly verified by the re-discovery of the Rock under a dunghill. Caliph Omar was disgusted by the trash and filth that had been strewn upon the abandoned Temple Mount over the centuries as a result of Christian supercessionism. As a show of superiority and in response to the Christian neglect of the sacred site, the Caliph ordered the Christian patriarch to prostrate himself in the refuse and rubble. Then, it is said, Caliph Omar set an example of reverence by personally clearing a handful of garbage from the Rock. In 691 the Umayyad Caliph 'Abd al-Malik built a wooden cupola over the Rock that Caliph Omar had cleared, giving it the misnomer "the mosque of Omar," or as it is properly known, the Dome of the Rock (Arabic, *Qubbet es-Sakhra*). In a further show of conquest over the Christians, Caliph Omar later built a wooden mosque on the compound over the foundations of an early Christian church. This mosque, known as the Al-Aqsa Mosque, was completed in A.D. 715 and has been rebuilt many times since. Today this mosque is regarded as the third holiest place in Islam (after Mecca and Medina), but it is the Dome of the Rock which is considered the crown of the *Haram al-Sharif* (Temple Mount).

Islam and the Temple Mount

When Islam invaded the Holy Land it was faced with the subjugation of both a Christian and Jewish population. As Muslim rulers began erecting Islamic mosques over sites sacred to Judaism and Christianity, such as the Rock on Mount Moriah, Jews and Christians must have wondered what importance Jerusalem had for this newly founded Muslim faith. Their bewilderment was justified, for it is clear that in the beginning Jerusalem had no religious significance for Islam. This is demonstrated by the fact that there is not even one mention of Jerusalem in the Qur'an. In the case of the Temple Mount, Jewish historian Shelomo Dov Goitein explains that "most of the traditions about Jerusalem and its sanctuary were local and largely of foreign origin and had no foundation in old Muhammedian stock."[13] For this reason, Muslim prayer, even today, is in the direction of Mecca, not Jerusalem. According to an early account, when the Muslim cleric Ka'b al-Ahbar proposed to the Caliph Omar that the place of prayer in Jerusalem should be fixed north of the Dome (so that Muslims would turn during their prayers towards the Holy Rock), the Caliph retorted, "You want to adapt yourself to Jewish usage, but we were not told to pray towards the *Sakhra*, but towards the *Ka'aba* alone." There are records of early Caliphs who deliberately avoided the site of the Rock, or who prayed with their backs to it to show their religious indifference. This was done despite the biblical traditions concerning the Rock and Abraham (Arabic: Ibrahim) in the Qur'an. Thus, the only rock that had sanctity for Islam from the beginning was the sacred *Ka'aba* stone in Mecca.

One major factor that compelled the Muslims to focus their building efforts in Jerusalem at this early stage of its Islamic history was that the capital of the new and expanding Islamic empire was Damascus (in Syria). The proximity of the two cities meant that Jerusalem was within the orbit of the many activities evolving from the main center of that time. Although the cradle of Islam was Arabia, and the sacred cities of Mecca and Medina are located there, the whole of Syria and its surroundings held a greater interest for the Muslims as they expanded their conquest efforts.

Miriam Ayalon, professor of Islamic Art and Archaeology at the Hebrew University, has noted some additional factors:

> The first and foremost of these considerations is undoubtedly the religious associations of ideas and events with the city prevailing among both Jews and Christians. Indeed, the fact that Jerusalem was already

important to the two monotheistic faiths from earlier times, and the fact that Islam considered itself as the last of the revelations…made it legitimate for Islam to absorb and identify with former beliefs obtained there. Jerusalem could not be ignored. The Temple area, which had been abandoned after the destruction of the second Temple and turned into the municipal dung center as a deliberate policy of the Byzantines, offered an ideal space to establish the monuments of the new rulers. Moreover, the very fact that some of the preexisting Byzantine buildings remained in Jerusalem and could provoke admiration, or eventually jealousy, required a Muslim response.[14]

This provides for us a motive for the building of the Dome of the Rock some 60 years after the Muslim conquest of Jerusalem. The traditional Muslim view is that it was built to commemorate Mohammed's ascent to heaven on his celestial steed Al-Buraq. Historical explanations range from a competition with a rival caliph in Mecca and an attempt to replace the *Ka'aba* and divert the *Hadj* (Muslim pilgrimage to Mecca) to Jerusalem.[15] However, the Dome of the Rock was designed only as a monument to what had previously existed on the Temple Mount. Therefore, the Dome of the Rock was originally intended as a shrine, or as it has been described, "a precious container for the Holy Rock."[16]

Caliph 'Abd al-Malik's act thus preserved the site and unintentionally honored the sacred tradition of the Temple in Jewish and Christian history. This fact, however, may not have escaped mystically inclined Jews, who saw even Islamic adornment of the Temple Mount as a divine sign. Though the history of this period is sketchy, we know that the Umayyad caliphs were tolerant to the Jewish faith (since they had helped with the conquest of the Byzantine Christians) and that Jews were allowed to take up residence southwest of the Temple area. Some of these Jewish families were even given the responsibility of making lamps for the buildings and lighting and cleaning the Temple Mount. On festival days, Jews were permitted to march around the walls of the Temple Mount and pray at the gates. Such allowances, coupled with the sight of renewed splendor on the Temple Mount, sparked a Jewish messianic movement during 'Abd al-Malik's reign. The height of this messianic fervor was an armed revolt under a self-proclaimed Messiah, Abu 'Isa of Isfahan, which 'Abd al-Malik supressed.

As mentioned above, the political purpose for the Dome's erection was largely an act of propaganda. Islam lacked an established culture and monumental architecture to rival that of centuries-old Byzantine Christianity. This was especially true in Jerusalem, where, from the time of Constantine, magnificent churches, basilicas, and monasteries had been erected to the glory of Christ. The historian Muqaddasi, a native of Jerusalem, supports this:

> So he ['Abd al-Malik's son al-Walid] sought to build for the Muslims [in Damascus] a mosque that should prevent their admiring these [Christian churches] and should be unique and a wonder to the world. And in like manner, is it not evident how Caliph 'Abd al-Malik, noting the greatness of the Dome of the Holy Sepulchre and its magnificence, was moved lest it should dazzle the minds of Muslims and so erected, above the Rock, the Dome which is now seen there.[17]

What we know of the history of the time supports Muqaddasi's statement. We know that the original primitive wooden structure built to house the Rock was satisfactory to the first generation of Muslims who were accustomed to the simplicity of Mohammed's mosque in Mecca. However, the splendor of the Christian churches that filled Jerusalem, which were built in close proximity to the Temple Mount, were feared to be religiously seductive to the second-generation Muslims who had grown up as uncultured conquerors. Indeed the polemical aspect of the Dome of the Rock can be seen to some degree in its architecture, but especially in the many Qur'anic inscriptions decorating its walls, which were written specifically to counter Christian doctrines. This was important because although Jesus is seen as a prophet in Islam, the impressive adornment throughout the city magnified Jesus' divinity, a concept strictly forbidden in Islam. Furthermore, for much of the Muslim period, Jews and Christians were made the objects of scorn and derision. For example, during the reign of the Caliph Harun al-Rashid (A.D. 786–809), Jews and Christians were stripped of religious rights and forced to wear badges that identified their inferior status. Christians had to wear blue badges and Jews had to wear yellow ones. The Muslims thought that if the Jews or Christians were to gain respectability because of their association with a superior architecture or religious history, it would be a grave offense to Allah and his true prophet.

Islam Reinvents the Rock

It was only after many centuries—and most likely to justify the continued Muslim presence in Jerusalem—that the stories of Jerusalem being the place of Mohammed's night journey and his final ascension (supposedly at the time of Byzantine Christian rule when the Rock was under a dung heap!) were invented. This is consistent with the rich collection of Islamic folklore and tradition that emerged in response to the Jewish and Christian history associated with the sacred places the Muslims had occupied. Since there was nothing to compare with or explain the significance of this history in the Qur'an, such connections had to be invented over time. This has occurred for almost all of the ancient sites in and around the Temple Mount.[18] In the case of Mohammed's night journey, this is obvious from the fact that the name of Jerusalem is not mentioned in the Qur'an. While some Muslim authorities have argued that there is a reference to Jerusalem in the night journey of Mohammed when the account says that he went to *Al-Aqsa*, the name of the mosque which today is built south of the Dome of the Rock, the word *Al-Aqsa* simply means "far corner"—a term originally applied to the east corner of Mecca, not Jerusalem. 'Abd al-Malik, who built the mosque (although some say it was Caliph Walid, between A.D. 705–715), did so purely to advance his propagandistic campaign and not because of any historical relevance to Islam. As Gershon Salomon, a former professor of Oriental studies at the Hebrew University and an expert on Islamic history, states:

> They built these two buildings for political reasons. They used a legend that said that Mohammed was taken in a dream by the Angel Gabriel to a mosque called El Aksa in Mecca. They changed the legend to state that the mosque was in Jerusalem, even though no such mosque had ever existed on the Temple Mount during the time of Mohammed. In this way they wanted to give a legitimacy to their imperialistic occupation of Jerusalem and the land of Israel.[19]

The primary motive for building these structures was the need to counter Jewish and Christian traditions displayed in Byzantine art and architecture, and it is believed that both the Dome of the Rock and the Al-Aqsa Mosque were built over the ruins of either synagogues or Byzantine churches. It is fairly certain that the emperor Justinian had built a Christian basilica on the site in the sixth century, and it had the same dimensions as the later Al-Aqsa Mosque. The octagonal shape of the Dome of the Rock, common in Christian architecture of the period, may imply the same or simply be the result of Christian architects employed by 'Abd al-Malik. A similar example of Islamic construction meant to counter the influence of opposing faiths was the modern placement of a Muslim cemetery in front of Jerusalem's Eastern Gate (Golden Gate). This was intended to keep the Jewish (and Christian) Messiah from entering through it (since passage through an unwalled cemetery incurs defilement), and fulfilling the prophecy of rebuilding the Temple on the Temple Mount. Gershon Salomon underscores the Muslim objective to obscure previous religious traditions when he notes:

> The Dome of the Rock was built in an attempt by the ruler of the northern, Omaic part of the Islamic Empire to prevent their people from going to Mecca, which was part of the southern, Abassic part of the empire, and returning with Abassic sympathies while the two parts of the empire were at war. However, when the Abassic ruler died the people continued to go to Mecca and the Dome became almost unknown in the Islamic world. This shows how they used religious terms which they created to progress political goals. In the same way they destroyed or altered Christian churches in all parts of the Islamic empire and built mosques. The most well-known place is the Aya Sophia church in Constantinople, which they renamed as Istanbul. In the same way they changed the name of Jerusalem to Al Quds. They changed the church, which was the focus of Eastern Christianity, into a mosque.[20]

The point to be made by this brief summary of the original construction of the buildings on the Temple Mount is that historically, there does not exist any valid claim for making Jerusalem or the Temple Mount serve as a holy place in Islam. It was not until A.D. 1187—when the Crusaders were finally dislodged by Saladin—that Jerusalem was said to be the third holiest place in Islam (after Mecca and Medina). In fact, in A.D. 1225 the Arab geographer Yakut wrote that the city of Jerusalem was holy to Jews and Christians, as it had been for 3,000 and 2,000 years respectively, but in contrast noted that only Mecca was holy to the Muslims.[21] This attitude was also noted a few decades after Yakut's time, when one of the most orthodox Islamic thinkers, Taqi a-Din, attempted to purify Islam from foreign influences and came out openly against the idea that Jerusalem or the Temple Mount had any sanctity in Islam.[22]

By contrast, the Temple Mount is the one and only holy place in Judaism, and is backed by at least 3,000 years of recorded history. Despite the fact that Islam has dominated the Temple Mount for 1,300 years, Jews have continued to direct their daily prayers toward it and to look forward to the day when the Temple could be rebuilt. An example of this can be seen in the thirteenth-century statement of the Jewish sage Nahmanides in a letter to his son. He wrote:

> What shall I say of this land…the more holy the place the greater the desolation. Jerusalem is the most desolate of all…there are about two thousand inhabitants…but there are no Jews….People regularly come

to Jerusalem, men and women from Damascus and from Aleppo and from all parts of the country, to see the Temple and weep over it. And may He who deemed us worthy to see Jerusalem in her ruins, grant us to see her rebuilt and restored....[23]

It should be apparent that Muslims who lived in Jerusalem realized the prior claim Jews have to the Temple Mount. Even though their modern historians rewrote history to teach that nothing occupied the site before Islam, those who daily passed by the ancient ruins (and today the newly excavated remains of the great entrance stairs to the Temple and the Huldah Gates at the Southern Wall) must have recognized the Jews' glorious past. In this light should be noted the statements in the Qur'an that speak of not only the Temple, but prophesy a Jewish return. For example, in *Night Journey* 8 it is written:

> We sent against you [Israel] our servants to discountenance you, and to enter the Temple, as they entered it the first time, and to destroy utterly which they ascended to. Perchance your Lord will have mercy upon you; but if you [Israel] return, we [Islam] shall return....

Some have said that it was because the Muslims knew these facts and believed that the Jews would one day return to the Temple Mount to rebuild that the Jordanians abandoned the Temple Mount without a fight in 1967. Israel entered into a compromise with the largely Jordanian Wakf in 1967, and later made a Peace Accord with Jordan in 1994 that recognized Jordan's status as the protector of the holy sites on the Temple Mount. For this reason King Hussein of Jordan spent more than 10 million dollars repairing the Dome of the Rock (the repairs were completed in 1997). However, in recent years it has been the Palestinians, not the Jordanians, who have controlled the Wakf and taken domination of the Temple Mount, supplanting the Jordanian Mufti with their own Palestinian Mufti. They now use its universally accepted sacred status in Islam to further their cause and gather international support in favor of their exclusive control of East Jerusalem. Let us, then, consider this new Palestinian Muslim perspective of the Temple Mount.

The Palestinian Perspective of the Temple

Palestinian propaganda has sought to revise the historical facts concerning Jerusalem and the Temple Mount. For instance, Palestinians are now claiming that Jerusalem is singularly important to them. Consider, for example, this state-

ment made by Sheik Isma'il Al-Nawahdah in his sermon at the Al-Aqsa Mosque
on Friday, April 3, 1998:

> Jerusalem is at the top of cities sacred to Islam. No city equals its holi-
> ness, except for Al-Madina and Mecca...Jerusalem is ours and not
> yours [i.e., Israel]; this city is more important to us than it is to
> you....Jerusalem is the key to both war and peace [but] if the Jews
> think that force will allow them [to keep] both the land and the peace—
> they delude themselves.[24]

Muslim revisionist history also teaches that the Jews were simply one of
many peoples who passed through the land originally inhabited by the ancient
Palestinian people whom they identify with the Philistines (and also Jebusites)
and had little or no impact on it. This Muslim revisionist view of Jerusalem and
its holy sites has been influential in turning uncritical and ecumenical modern
Christian thinking against Israel. For example, in June of 1998 the Middle East
Council of Churches, joined by a body called "the Arab Working Group on Chris-
tian-Muslim Dialogue," held a conference in Beirut, Lebanon and issued a statement it called "The Jerusalem Appeal." In this document it is stated, "Jerusalem
is its people. Its people are Palestinians, who, ever since Jerusalem existed and
for countless generations, have lived within it. They...know of no other place as
their capital..."[25] This, of course, is patently false.

The Palestinian Authority, however, even though it has no legal right to make
demands concerning affairs in Jerusalem, has strongly protested archaeological
excavations near the Temple Mount area. In January of 1997 the Palestinian
Authority and Muslim Wakf officials in Jerusalem held a protest meeting
against archaeological digging allegedly carried out by Israel in the vicinity of
the Temple Mount, even though Israel's Antiquities Authority vehemently
denied that any such activity was taking place. Such meetings are considered by
Israelis as violations of the Israeli-PLO agreements (which forbids the Palestinian Authority from conducting diplomatic and political activity within the
borders of the State of Israel), and they reveal the Palestinian Muslim belief that
Israeli archaeologists are politically and religiously motivated in their excavation efforts.

Another reason for this Palestinian fear is that past archaeological excavations have provided abundant material evidence of Israel's historical presence
in Jerusalem and on the Temple Mount 2,000 years ago. These, in addition to the
Western Wall and Temple Mount platform, include the remains of the monumental staircase that ascended to the Temple at the southern end of the Temple

Mount with its blocked Double and Triple Gates, the massive columned hallway behind this area (which the Muslims have used for centuries), the streets and shops that lined the Second Temple thoroughfare on the western side of the Temple Mount and its underground extension (which includes a tunnel used by the priests), and many remnants of Temple architecture with Hebrew inscriptions or reliefs of Jewish ritual objects (such as the Menorah). Such discoveries and their publication to the world make it undeniable that the Jewish people had lived and worshiped for a long period at this very site. Nevertheless, the Palestinians reject this unambiguous evidence of the Jewish Temple as simply "pre-Islamic." Gaayla Cornfield has observed:

> ...everything lying beneath it [the Dome of the Rock] being, to the Muslim, irrelevant, even the insights of archaeology in the last hundred years, even the results of contemporary excavations being conducted now. Even these, to the descendants of the Moslems who walled up all the historical underground passages and kept "infidels" and curious away, are unimportant.[26]

Palestinians have accepted those archaeological discoveries that they believe can work to their advantage. One of the Palestinian claims has been that "the Arabs of Palestine are indigenous inhabitants of the country, who have been in occupation of it since the beginning of history."[27] Recent excavations at the City of David have revealed impressive remains of gates and fortifications of the prior Caananite (Jebusite) occupation there. Some Israeli archaeologists have even revised their former theories concerning Warren's Shaft, believing now that it is of Canaanite, not Israelite, origin. Palestinians have used these findings as proof that *their* ancestors first occupied the site and built the buildings that archaeologists have uncovered, and therefore they have a prior historic claim superior to that of the Jews.

The Palestinians have gone so far as to deny that the Jewish Temple ever existed on Mount Moriah or anywhere else in Jerusalem. According to John Michell:

> A radically different view on the matter is held by the Muslim custodians of the sanctuary area. They point out that [the Jewish figures of] Solomon and David are mythological figures, recorded only by [Jewish and Christian] tradition, and that there is no conclusive evidence that the Jews' Temple stood within the walled enclosure. It could have been elsewhere in the city. It is easy to see and sympathize with one motive behind this attitude, which is to discourage Jewish interest in Islam's

most sacred precinct. But the case for the Temple in its traditional location is quite formidable, and in denying it the Muslim authorities also deny that there is any need for archaeological research in the area.[28]

By preventing any archaeological excavation to confirm the Temple's location, the Palestinians protect their contention that there is no archaeological proof that the Temple existed on the Temple Mount! This attitude is well expressed in the comments of Jeris Soudah, a Palestinian leader who works with Yasser Arafat:

> The Islamic Arab world will not allow the Israelis to mess around in this area because this is a holy place. They cannot do any construction by this area for one reason. It has not been proven that the Temple was ever located there...do the Jews have proof that this is the site of their holy place?...There are the arches and everything [in the Western Wall Tunnel], but are these things from a Jewish Temple being there? How do we know that these are not Muslim or Christian constructions?...Maybe there are certain pieces that prove that something Jewish was there. But there is no absolute proof that a Jewish Temple ever stood there.[29]

When I interviewed the Palestinian Mufti I asked him about an Associated Press news release I had seen, in which Yasser Arafat was shown holding a picture with the Jewish Temple in the place of the Dome of the Rock and which quoted him as saying that no Temple ever existed there. To this the Mufti replied that he had given Arafat the picture and that it was also his firm belief that no Jewish Temple had ever stood at the site. How then do Muslims explain the Jewish obsession over the Temple Mount? They contend that this is merely an attempt to legitimize the Zionist occupation of Jerusalem. Muslim history books teach that "Jews come to pray at *Al-Boraq* wall" (the Western or Wailing Wall), which in Islam is associated only with Mohammed. Thus they tell their people that the only reason Jews want to pray there is because they want to destroy the Islamic mosques and shrines on the *Haram es-Sharif* (Temple Mount). This is also their message to the press regarding the importance of the Al-Aqsa Mosque and the Dome of the Rock, and this revisionist history of the site is further propagated to the undiscerning masses by the mainstream media. History, however, tells a different story.

The Proper Historical Perspective

History reveals that the Arab Muslims who came to Jerusalem in A.D. 638 were of nomadic heritage and cannot prove any direct descendancy from the non-Semitic Canaanite, Amorite, Jebusite, or Philistine peoples who occupied Jerusalem as well as the Land of Canaan before the coming of the Israelites under Joshua. In fact, the historical evidence cannot even connect them with the Ishmaelites (a major claim of Islam).[30] The Palestinian people have never been a national entity, but owe their existence to the displacement and refugee status that followed the allied Arab attack on the newly declared State of Israel in 1948. As we have seen, with regards to the Temple Mount, Islam has not unequivocally regarded the site with the same reverence as today. Muslim prayer even today is only in the direction of Mecca (the opposite direction of the ancient Jewish Temple, toward which Jews pray). Therefore, each year at the major Islamic feast of Ramadan, one can see the area between the Al-Aqsa Mosque and the Dome of the Rock filled with thousands of praying Muslims all turned away from the Dome of the Rock (see photo section). Furthermore, Muslims do not make *hadj* (pilgrimage) to the Al-Aqsa and the Dome of the Rock. In fact, when an acquaintance of mine in Jerusalem sought to specialize in Muslim tours to the city, he had to close up shop because he was unable to get business—partly because other Muslims prevented their fellow Muslims from traveling to Israel.

Today the Muslims call Jerusalem *Al-Quds* ("the Holy"); however, the earliest Arab name for the city was *Iliyia*, derived from the Roman renaming of the city as *Aelia* (*Capitolina*). In the Islamic period the name was *Bayt al Maqdis*, from the Hebrew *Beit Hamiqdash* ("the Holy House," i.e., the Temple), revealing the city's Israelite origin. Only later was the name changed to Al-Quds. This conclusion is supported by the statement of Professor Abdul Hadi Palazzi, Secretary General of the Italian Muslim Association (Rome), an Imam (spiritual teacher) of the Italian Islamic community who holds a Ph.D. in Islamic Sciences by decree of the Grand Mufti of the Kingdom of Saudi Arabia:

> The Arabic name of Jerusalem [al-Quds] comes from the root *q-d-s*, meaning "holiness." It is an abridged form of Bayt al-Maqdis, "the sanctified House" or "the House of the Sanctuary," an exact equivalent of the Hebrew Beth ha-mikdash. The name originally referred only to the Temple Mount, and was afterward extended to the city as a whole. This extension of meaning became common among Arabs from the tenth century C.E. onwards. Earlier Islamic sources use the name Iliyia, an adaptation to Arabic pronunciation of the Roman name Aelia.[31]

Furthermore, the reference to Al-Aqsa in the Qur'an, although later taken to refer to the city, cannot be supported historically, as David Bar-Illan explains:

...while the Qur'an does mention a place called Al-Aqsa, which merely means the endmost, the farthest, the reference has absolutely nothing to do with Jerusalem. [The media] also repeats the canard that the Temple Mount is "Islam's third-holiest shrine." In fact, Iraq, Iran, Turkey, and Syria also claim to have "Islam's third-holiest shrine" on their soil.[32]

The modern objection by Muslims to Jewish sovereignty over Jerusalem and the Temple Mount is based on the Muslim contention that since Al-Quds is a holy place for Muslims, they cannot accept a rule by non-Muslims, which would amount to a betrayal of Islam. Professor Abdul Hadi Palazzi explains why this objection is both incorrect and unnecessary. Although some of his comments are repetitive for us, such a rare opinion by a leading Muslim cleric needs to be heard in full:

> As is well known, the inclusion of Jerusalem among Islamic holy places derives from al-Mi'raj, the Ascension of the Prophet Muhammad to heaven. The Ascension began at the Rock, usually identified by Moslem scholars as the Foundation Stone of the Jewish Temple in Jerusalem referred to in Jewish sources. Recalling this link requires us to admit that there is no connection between al-Miraj [the Ascension] and Moslem sovereign rights over Jerusalem since, in the time that al-Miraj took place, the City was not under Islamic, but under Byzantine administration. Moreover, the Koran expressly recognizes that Jerusalem plays for Jews the same role that Mecca does for Moslems. We read [in the Koran]: "...They would not follow thy direction of prayer (qiblah), nor art thou to follow their direction of prayer; nor indeed will they follow each other's direction of prayer..." (Koran 2:145). All Koranic commentators explain that "thy qiblah" [direction of prayer for Moslems] is clearly the Ka'bah of Mecca, while "their qiblah" [direction of prayer for Jews] refers to the Temple Mount in Jerusalem. To quote only one of the most important Moslem commentators, we read in Qadn Baydawn's Commentary: "Verily, in their prayers Jews orientate themselves toward the Rock (sakhrah), while Christians orientate themselves eastwards..." (M. Shaykh Zadeh *Hashiyyah 'ali Tafsir al-Qadn al-Baydawn*, Istanbul 1979, vol. 1, p. 456). In complete opposition to what "Islamic" fundamentalists continuously claim, the Book of Islam [the Koran]—as we have just now seen—recognizes Jerusalem as the Jewish direction of prayer. After reviewing the relevant Koranic passages concerning this matter, I conclude that, as no one denies Moslems' complete sovereignty over Mecca, from an Islamic point of view—despite opposing, groundless

claims—there is no reason for Moslems to deny the State of Israel—which is a *Jewish* state—complete sovereignty over Jerusalem.[33]

Despite the historic and religious facts affirming the Jewish claim to the Temple Mount, the present Islamic authorities over the Temple Mount seek to prevent Israel from returning to it and enjoy international support from the Western and European communities. Besides political and religious constraints, the Wakf have also attempted to demonstrate their sovereignty by acting independently of the Israeli authorities in their actions on the Temple Mount. Recently, this has taken the form of destroying Jewish structures and constructing Islamic structures—in defiance of government orders to stop their illegal action (more on this in a moment). This was demonstrated in August of 1999 when Muslims cut a door opening in the Southern Wall of the Temple Mount and authorities sought to close it because they feared Muslim worshipers would flood a formerly Jewish-only area. The Islamic Wakf said if the government intervened it would lead to violence paralleling the riots of September 1996, when Israel opened the exit tunnel to the Hasmonean aqueduct.

The Islamic Agenda for the Temple Mount

The Destruction of Jewish Evidence

The Arabs have already destroyed most of the holy remains on the Temple Mount over the last several years, and now they are destroying the marvelous remains of the Huldah Tunnel on the Temple Mount, which had remained intact over the last 2,000 years. This Islamic destruction of Temple-period remains began in the 1980s; Hebrew University physicist Asher Kaufman reported, in the course of his research on the location of the Temple, Muslim attempts to obscure or eliminate traces of ancient evidence at the northern area of the Temple Mount.[34] Photographic support for this accusation was later published in *Biblical Archaeology Review*.[35] This destruction includes tearing down or digging up ancient stones, building new footpaths across lines of walls, and incorporating old Jewish stone structures into new Islamic concrete structures. Remains that were too large to move or not easily destroyed have been covered with tons of earth and planted trees or made into gardens. In 1998 the so-called "Solomon's Stables," which was an important part of the Second Temple complex (used in the Crusader period as stables) was turned into a mosque, altering its ancient Israelite structure. And, within the ancient Huldah Tunnel, yet another mosque is being constructed. This tunnel was the main entrance onto the Temple Mount through the southern Huldah Gates (of the Second Temple), and its walls and ceiling are decorated with ornamental designs of the seven holy fruits chiseled in relief sculpture. These, along with beautiful marble pillars from the middle of the tunnel, were destroyed and covered with cement.[36] The Muslim goal was to remove all the remains from the First and Second Temples that still remained after the destruction in A.D. 70 in order to be able to completely deny the Jewishness of the Temple Mount.

The Construction of Islamic Structures

Just as the destruction of Jewish remains was to remove any historical connection at the site with Israel, so the Islamic constructions are to give the Temple Mount a physical Islamic identity. This is nothing more or less than what the first Islamic caliphs did when they first came to the Temple Mount as conquerors 1,300 years ago. As we have seen, for political purposes they replaced Jewish and Christian holy structures with Islamic ones, just as they replaced Jewish history with new Islamic traditions. In previous centuries the Muslims built Islamic prayer platforms, offices, and cupolas all over the Temple Mount in order to make any unoccupied space exclusively Islamic. In front of the Dome of the Rock, the supposed site of the Holy of Holies, they placed an Arabic stone inscription that commands Muslims to hate the Jews. They closed the Golden Gate and built a cemetery in front of it. They turned the inside of this gate into an Islamic center and library. This is being continued today in order to create a new historical reality for the Palestinians and support their claim that they, not the Jews, are the rightful sovereigns of the sacred site. In 1996 the Wakf completed the construction of a third mosque adjacent to the southern section of the Temple Mount.[37] In that same year they also constructed buildings within the boundaries of the Temple Mount, adjacent to the northern wall, between the Gate of Forgiveness and the Afel Gate. Although Muslims have free access to the site, it still remains a part of Jerusalem that is under Israeli sovereignty. This requires that plans for any new construction activity or alterations to the existing site must be approved by the Israeli authorities. The Palestinian Authority has continually rejected this process and carried on construction as though it has unconditional sovereignty over the site (which it in fact claims to have). Israeli journalist Nadav Shragai reported that the Wakf had not requested permits for the buildings.[38] The Temple Mount Faithful organization appealed to the Supreme Court to order the Jerusalem Municipality, the Attorney General, and the Jerusalem Police to enforce the order that forbids construction on the

Temple Mount; however, Israeli authorities decided not to interfere with the Wakf construction for fear of "instigating unrest."[39]

Muslim Claims vs. Biblical and Historical Evidence

The Muslim claim is that the Temple Mount is only for Islam. To accomplish this objective, which they believe is the command of Allah and his prophet Mohammed, they have sought to replace Israel historically and spiritually at the place destined to be at the center of future fulfillment at the end of the age. However, as we have seen, nothing in the Muslim's own history nor in the Qur'an itself provides any support for the Islamic claim. Elwood McQuaid, executive director of The Friends of Israel, summarizes the case against this Islamic basis for 1,300 years of conflict with the Jewish people:

> It is a fascinating argument that is brought forth by the Islamic people that the Temple Mount had no prior relationship to the Jewish People and that it is sacred to Islam. The Islamic religion did not come into existence until seven centuries after the Lord Jesus Christ was in the world....For them to make the statement that [the Temple Mount] belongs to them contradicts everything that is biblically given to us, archaeologically verified by us, and as far as history is concerned, testified to on almost every page of the history of the Middle East and certainly the city of Jerusalem. [The Temple Mount] is a flashpoint. I think it is reflective of the whole obsession to control the city of Jerusalem and to control the entire area—to succeed in their thought that they are going to drive Israel into the sea. I think it is just one more place that they can use as a ground for controversy and for possible conflict.[40]

Islam has depended on a revisionist- and tradition-laden view of history in order to lay its claim to the Temple Mount. By contrast, the Jewish claim, for the past, present, and future, rests upon a biblical foundation. Let us look in the next several chapters at how the prophecy of the coming Last Days Temple has been preserved within the Old and New Testaments.

PART II

The Predictions of the Last Days Temple

"Let them construct a Sanctuary for Me, that I may dwell among them... and there I will meet with you...from between the two cherubim...."

—Exodus 25:8,22

"Thus says the Lord of hosts, 'Behold, a man whose name is Branch, for He will branch out from where He is; and He will build the Temple of the Lord.'"

—Zechariah 6:12

"Seventy weeks have been decreed for your people and your Holy City, to finish the transgression, to make an end of sin, to make atonement for iniquity, to bring in everlasting righteousness, to seal up vision and prophecy, and to anoint the Most Holy place [Temple]."

—Daniel 9:24

CHAPTER 9

Sanctuary Symbolism

God's Preview of Coming Attractions

The Garden of Eden narrative... may be seen as a prototype of the conditions and environment in which man can intimately encounter God.... Thus, while the story of the Garden and its character is a brief one, it has ramifications for the entire biblical record and can be construed as a paradigm for subsequent discussions concerning the setting in which man encounters the divine presence.[1]

—RABBI JOSHUA BERMAN

While I was talking on the phone recently with a friend of mine who is both a professor of theology and an author, he asked me what I was currently working on. Since I had just started on this chapter, I told him I was writing about the Temple in the book of Genesis. He started laughing and said, "No wonder it's taking you so long to finish that book—there's nothing about the Temple in Genesis!" Before I began my research on this idea I would have been inclined to agree. If the Tabernacle was not even conceived until the time of Moses, how could a Sanctuary have been conceptualized from the dawn of time itself? However, we have already seen in chapter 3 of this book that the Heavenly Temple was in existence from before the creation of the earth and that it served as the original archetype or pattern for God's Sanctuaries on earth. Remember also that the nature of divine revelation (unless it is stated to have been previously unrevealed, such as the teaching concerning the church—Romans 16:25-26; Ephesians 3:3-10) is progressive, with God revealing new information about an important subject in successive time periods. We see this, for example, in God's Messianic program. Most Christian commentators interpret Genesis 3:15 as the first revelation and prediction of the work of the Messiah; for this reason, it is referred to by theologians as the *protevangelium* ("the first proclamation of the gospel").

If the earthly Sanctuary was at the center of God's revelation to the Nation of Israel, as well as a part of the Messianic program, it is not unreasonable to expect that such an important concept might have been revealed at the beginning of God's relationship with man. In this sense, even before the major production was released, Sanctuary symbolism served as God's preview of coming attractions. That such a preview was intended can be seen, for example, in Psalm 36:7-9:

> How precious is Thy lovingkindness, O God!
> And the children of men take refuge in the shadow of Thy wings.
> They drink their fill of the abundance of Thy house;
> And Thou dost give them to drink of the river of Thy delights.
> For with Thee is the fountain of life;
> In Thy light do we see light.

Our English translations obscure this passage's associations between the Sanctuary and the Garden of Eden.[2] King David's usage of the word "house" is a reference to God's Sanctuary. While the heavenly Sanctuary could be in view, the act of "feasting" may imply the experience of abiding in the earthly place of worship. The words "river of Your delights" are literally "river of Thy Edens," since the word "delights" (Hebrew, *'adaneka*) is simply the plural of Eden. If these are understood in this way, then they suggest the parallel between the four rivers of Eden which watered the Garden (Genesis 2:10-14), and the life-giving river which will flow from beneath the Millennial Temple when the earth returns to an Edenic state (Ezekiel 47:1-12). Both of these have their counterpart in the Heavenly Temple, where the "river of the water of life" flows from the throne of God (Revelation 22:1). This background also explains the words "the fountain of life." Following these associations, we can then identify the imagery of the "light" of God as the sacred candlelabras (Hebrew, *menorot*) that made it possible for the priests to see and perform their service of worship in the Tabernacle and Temple.

When we consider the description of the Last Days Temple in the prophets (such as Ezekiel) and in the book of Revelation, we see many literary parallels in the book of Genesis that suggest a connection between the Creation and Garden of Eden and the Temple. Such usage implies that the ultimate fulfillment for the Temple in the future will follow an outline drawn from the beginning of the divine plan. In like manner, as revelation progresses forward in the Pentateuch and Abraham is called to Mount Moriah and Moses to Mount Sinai, we see additional predictions concerning the coming Temple. In this chapter we will search through the first book of the Pentateuch to uncover these preliminary predictions—all made before the Temple's construction. The journey will take us into a study of symbolism and shadow that eventually gave way to substance. And by the end of this chapter, we should have a clearer understanding of God's revelation of a Sanctuary not only for Israel, but for all mankind (Isaiah 56:7).

The Future Is in the Past

The first five books of the Old Testament are known as the Pentateuch (Jews know them as the Torah). The original Torah composed by Moses was stored with the Ark of the Covenant in the Sanctuary, and constituted for the people of Israel one of the most valuable documents of all time. In the Torah are contained all of God's laws for the establishment and maintenance of a holy Nation on earth. In this Torah we also read about the origin of man and the Jewish people, as well as the relationship God and man enjoyed before the Fall. When we look at this divine ideal at the beginning of human history, we also see the goal for mankind at the end of history. Once the intrusion of sin has finally been put away, the earth will revert to its pristine splendor as in the Garden of Eden (Isaiah 11:6-9; 65:17-25; Revelation 22:1-5). The final destiny of redeemed mankind will be worship in the presence of God (Revelation 21:3). This intimate relationship with the Creator was first revealed when God's presence came into the Garden of Eden (Genesis 3:8). It was again revealed at Sinai when God's presence came into the Israelite camp (Exodus 19:11,20). Because this worship at Sinai was centered on God's revelation at the Sanctuary (Exodus 25:8-9; Hebrews 8:5), many biblical scholars have sought a similar pattern in Eden. When we consider this more carefully we find that indeed there are many similarities between the accounts in Genesis and Exodus, and if we take this further to include the New Testament book of Revelation, where similarities also exist, we find that the divine ideal of God dwelling with His people binds together both the beginning and end of time. If the future was indeed hidden in the past, then the symbolism of a first days Sanctuary may reveal the divine pattern for the Last Days Temple.

Looking at the Future from the Past

Why would God have placed patterns of future fulfillment in the past? First, there is in the book of Genesis a concept of time that looks toward the culmination of history from its very creation. This is implied by the introductory words of Genesis: "In the beginning" (Genesis 1:1). The very fact of a "beginning" for the creation indicates that there will be an eventual "ending" of the creation. The apostle Peter warns those who think that "all continues just as it was from the beginning of creation" (2 Peter 3:4) to prepare themselves for the dissolution of the creation that will accompany the coming Day of the Lord (2 Peter 3:10-12).

The Genesis creation account also implies this by the promise of perpetual seasons in Genesis 8:22: "While the earth remains, seed-time and harvest, and cold and heat, and summer and winter, and day and night shall not cease." One day this predictable pattern will be concluded with the creation of a new heavens and earth (Isaiah 65:17; 66:22; Revelation 21:1), but not until God's prophetic purposes have been fulfilled. In fact, this very passage is used by God to confirm to Israel that the prophetic promise of restoration will not be aborted even though it has sinned (see Jeremiah 31:34-37). This text likewise guarantees that the Temple (soon to be destroyed in Jeremiah's day) will never again be defiled or destroyed (Jeremiah 31:38-40). Therefore, the creation account recorded in Genesis contains the kernels of history's completion, allowing a glimpse of the future from the vantage point of the past.

Looking to the End from the Beginning

Genesis also presupposes that there is a goal in the creation toward which all history is moving. On the smaller scale of the creation week, the end of this period is climaxed with the making of man and captioned with the words, "And God saw all that He had made, and behold, it was very good" (Genesis 1:31). This suggests that the goal of history, especially since the Fall of man and the curse upon the ground (Genesis 3:16-19), is to return man and the earth to its original condition of blessing (see Psalm 104:30; Isaiah 43:18; 46:9-10; 62:4; cf. Ezekiel 36:35). According to the apostle Paul, both the believer and the creation groan together in their fallen state, yet in hope of a future day of redemption when both man and nature will finally be set free to a glorified experience (Romans 8:18-23). We may call this goal of history "the divine ideal," since it represents a predestined pattern to which all God's prophetic program conforms. According to this ideal, man in his creation appears as God's representative ruler (Genesis 1:28; cf. Psalm 8:3-8). Therefore the prophetic goal of the last days' restoration is to fulfill this original creation mandate, with all of the created order subject to man as God's representatives (Romans 8:20-21; 1 Corinthians 6:3; Hebrews 2:6-10). The New Testament pictures Christ as the one who has made this possible for man by becoming man Himself. The future fulfillment of this purpose will be literally realized in the Millennium (Isaiah 11:6-9; 65:17-25) and in the re-created order of the new heavens and earth, where righteousness dwells (2 Peter 3:10-13; Revelation 21–22).

Looking at the Big Picture on a Small Screen

Genesis further sets the beginnings of Israel's national history in the context of universal history. Its account begins with all mankind (Genesis 1–11), then telescopes to one man, Abraham (Genesis 12:1-2), and then broadens again through the Abrahamic Covenant and the promises to the Patriarchs to include "all the families of the earth" in blessing (see Genesis 12:3-50). In other words, the big picture of what God is doing in all the ages is being viewed on the small screen of the Nation of Israel. As we see the drama of redemption unfold in Scripture, the story of all mankind appears on a stage in the Middle East—a stage upon which Israel plays out God's grand design.[3] In this way, the outlines drawn at the beginning of history can be progressively filled in until the final picture is portrayed. This understanding not only invites us to carefully consider each detail of the past preparation for the outworking of this plan, but encourages us to look at current events involving Israel and the nations as the present preparation for the completion of the prophetic picture. With this background, we can look back into the beginning of time to see how God first revealed His plot and began setting the stage for His divine drama concerning the Sanctuary.

Symbolism and Substance

In the book of Genesis we find the beginning of God's *spiritual* relationship with man. This relationship, based on the creature's worship of His Creator, reveals how God intended for man to have fellowship with Himself. Outside of the book of Genesis the remaining four books that comprise the Pentateuch (Exodus, Leviticus, Numbers, and Deuteronomy) all focus on this way of approach to God—worship at the Sanctuary (Tabernacle). Therefore, it should not be surprising to find symbols of this divine relationship in Genesis, the first book of that collection. While we cannot go into the details of some of these symbolic settings here,[4] let us briefly survey some of the literary parallels between the creation account and worship at the Sanctuary.

The structure of the creation days of Genesis 1–2 appears to be the literary model for the account of the erection of the Tabernacle in Exodus 25–40. Jewish interpreters[5] have especially noted that the six commands in the instructions for the building of the Tabernacle correspond to the six days of creation. Then the command for the Sabbath, which completes the creation week in Genesis 1:1–2:3, is repeated at the conclusion of the Tabernacle's construction (Exodus 39:43; 40:33). Just as God's rest on the first Sabbath (Genesis 2:2-3) included an inspection of His work and a blessing of it, so God's presence came to rest in the Tabernacle, indicating His blessing of the work (Exodus 40:34-38). In like manner, the consecration ceremony for the priests and Temple vessels was appointed for seven days (see Exodus 29:37; 34:18). This parallel may be comparing the construction of the Sanctuary to the creation of the world. As the first was the divine ideal (a world where God could be worshiped directly by His creatures), the second was the means by which He could rescue and restore a portion of that ideal in the world once the creation had been corrupted by the Fall. The construction of the Tabernacle also appears in Exodus as part of a covenantal process. In Exodus 25–40, the construction of the Tabernacle follows the covenant made at Sinai (Exodus 19–24), which was initiated by God's presence appearing as a covenant witness. In a similar way, the Genesis creation may also be considered a covenantal event as the presence of God ("the Spirit of God") hovers over the primeval waters (Genesis 1:2). Just as the covenant of creation results in the forming of the unformed world, the Sinai covenant results in the formation of an unformed nation. In addition, the literary structure of Genesis 1–11 seems to provide the pattern for the legislation of Israel's laws of purity as presented in Leviticus 11–16, as the order of the animals discussed in relation to their ritually "clean" or "unclean" status follows the order of the creation of animal life in Genesis 1. Furthermore, the first references to the sacrifical system (Genesis 4:3-4) seem to point toward the later Mosaic institution. These symbols of future substance, carefully included within the beginning texts of the Bible, connect the divine ideal to have a relationship with mankind, with the Sanctuary as the place where God could make this possible (Exodus 25:8).

Heaven on Earth

The command to copy the design of the Heavenly Sanctuary, along with the scrupulous rituals of the earthly Sanctuary, indicate that in order for God to bring His presence to earth it must be within a setting that conforms to His dwelling place in heaven. In other words, when God came down to earth He brought a little bit of heaven with Him (Deuteronomy 26:15,19)! That "bit of heaven" is the sacred space (or "holy ground") within which God's presence was manifested (see Exodus 3:5). Just as the Land of Israel was called holy once the Temple was built in Jerusalem (Daniel 9:16), so the land of Eden was once considered holy because God's presence was located there. When we look at the biblical account of the Garden of Eden, its description seems to mirror the court of God in heaven, with God coming into the Garden to commune with His creation (Genesis 3:8). If we examine Edenic geography it appears that the four rivers flowed downward, implying that the Garden was at a higher elevation, a holy mountain. These waters apparently flowed out from the Garden itself. Within the Garden was the "Tree of Life" and the "Tree of the Knowledge of Good and Evil," and at the east two cherubim. This geographical arrangement parallels the arrangement of the Sanctuary with its sacred furniture (see diagram on page 195). This argues that God was originally reproducing on earth a Sanctuary where He could meet with man (Genesis 2:8-14). As author

Donald Parry has noted, "The Garden [of Eden] was not a sanctuary built of cedar or marble, for it is not necessary for a temple to possess an edifice or structure; but rather it was an area of sacred space made holy because God's presence was found there."[6] Such a recognition moved comparative religions scholar Mircea Eliade to propose that "every earthly sanctuary must be considered in some regard a replica of the heavenly abode, and that in worship man seeks to reenact creation."[7]

While pagan religions and their temples may bear faint traces of the original mold of worship cast in Eden, it is in Genesis that we find the true prototype of the Heavenly Sanctuary symbolized. Although the intrusion of sin made it impossible for mankind to continue worshiping God in Eden, God's choice of one man (Abraham) and the covenant made with his descendants (the Jewish people) would enable this to be experienced in a limited and mediated way through the Jewish people and at the Tabernacle and the Temple (see 1 Kings 8:33-34,41-43,60). It will be realized universally in the Millennium with the return of God's presence to the final Temple (Ezekiel 47:1-12; cf. Zechariah 14:8; Isaiah 2:2-4; 56:6-8), and ultimately in the eternal state (Revelation 21:9–22:3). Just as God had given Adam the land of the Garden of Eden, so He gave Abraham the Land of Israel. Just as God's presence once dwelt with Adam in his "Sanctuary," so God's presence dwelt with Israel in the Temple in Jerusalem. Thus, Israel and its Temple become a microcosm for God's dealings with all mankind. Let us now examine some of the symbols that characterize the Garden of Eden as a Sanctuary and type of the Temple to come.

Symbols of the Sanctuary's Presence in Eden

God's purpose for man at creation was to have him rule over the created order and thereby bring glory to the Creator (Genesis 1:28). To this end God gave Adam, the first man, responsibilities in the Garden of Eden, which were to function as acts of service to Him (Genesis 2:15). God's presence also came and went from the Garden and apparently "dwelt" among His people—Adam and Eve (Genesis 2:19-22; 3:8). The coupling of the Garden of Eden and the Temple in Scripture is not meant to be taken as merely symbolic, as though no actual history were behind the allusions. For example, in Ezekiel 28:11-19 imagery from both the Garden of Eden and the Temple are woven together as the King of Tyre is rebuked for his evil pride. However, the very use of this imagery requires us to interpret this event in light of the original setting and see behind this evil king

The Garden of Eden and the Sanctuary

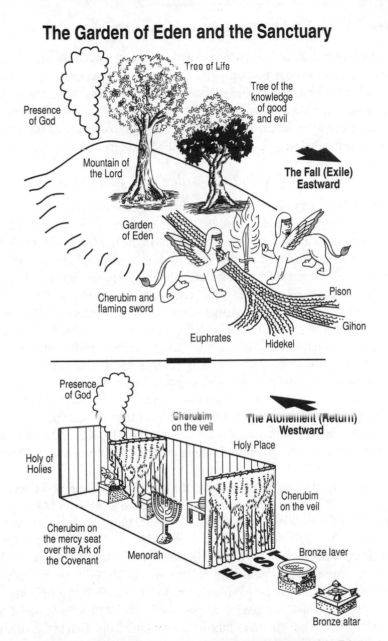

The arrangement of the Garden of Eden's landscape corresponds to that of the Tabernacle and Temple with its furniture. Eastward movement (out of the Garden) is away from God's presence; westward movement (through the Sanctuary) is a return of God. On the Day of Atonement the high priest reverses the people's spiritual exile from God and restores them to a relationship with God (through a blood sacrifice for sin).

the King of Evil, Satan himself, whose actions brought about the first prideful rebellion against God in the Garden (Genesis 3:1-5,14). As we study this imagery we will find it symbolizes the idea of the Garden of Eden as the first Sanctuary on earth. While many of the literary parallels in Genesis 1–3 that give us this insight are complex, we can still see how the creation account serves as the foundation for the Pentateuch's presentation of the Sanctuary and its ordinances.

The Presence of God in the Garden and Tabernacle

In Genesis 3:8 God is said to have "walked" in the Garden of Eden. The Hebrew verb translated "walk" (*mithalek*) is in the form of a *hithpa'el* participle, indicating that God's presence "moved about" in the Garden. This verb, in this construction, appears only here and in texts dealing with God's approach to the Sanctuary. For example, this construction uniquely appears when God's presence came as a cloud to the Tent of Meeting to meet with Moses (Exodus 33:9; 34:5; Numbers 11:25; 12:5,10; Deuteronomy 31:15). In Leviticus 26:11-12 God promised that His presence would continue with Israel when the Nation finally entered the Promised Land and built the Temple. In verse 12 the text states that this will take the form of God "walking among you" (Hebrew, *hithalakti betokekem*). In this same passage (Genesis 3:8) it is said that Adam and Eve "hid themselves from the presence of [literally "from before"] the LORD." This phrase "before the Lord" (Hebrew, *lipne YHWH*) is part of the technical terminology of the Temple, always indicating a Sanctuary setting. Therefore, Adam and Eve were hiding themselves from God, whose presence had come into His Edenic Sanctuary.

This activity of God in the midst of His chosen people was conditioned on obedience to the laws of the Sanctuary (Leviticus 26:1-46), just as God's presence in the Garden was conditioned on obedience to the single law respecting the Tree of the Knowledge of Good and Evil (Genesis 2:17; 3:1-3). In Genesis, disobedience to God's command resulted in man having to toil laboriously with his work producing only thorns and thistles, or weeds (Genesis 3:17-18). In Leviticus 26:16,20 a similar punishment is threatened. There the Israelites are told that they would "sow seed to no purpose" and that their "land would not yield its produce, nor the trees of the land yield their fruit." Finally, this disobedience would result in exile from the presence of God. In Genesis this exile was from the Garden (Genesis 3:23-24), and in Leviticus it was from the Land, which contained the Temple (Leviticus 26:33). The Jewish sages recognized this association and produced a midrash that said when "the Lord God banished him

[Adam] from the Garden of Eden He revealed to him the destruction of the Temple" (*Bereshit Rabbah* 21:8).

The ultimate punishment for the violation in the Garden, of course, is death. It is because of death that man had to leave the Garden, where the Tree of Life grows. Likewise, any form of death is strictly prohibited in the Tabernacle and

Elements Common in Eden and Earthly and Heavenly Temples

Eden	Earthly Temple	Heavenly Temple
East/West Orientation (Gen. 2:8; 3:24)	East/West Orientation (Num. 3:38; Ezek. 43:1-2)	East/West Orientation? (Ex. 26:30)
Holy Mountain? (Gen. 2:10)	Holy Mountain (Ex. 15:17)	Holy Mountain (Ezek. 28:14)
God's Presence (Gen. 3:8-9)	God's Presence (Ex. 16:2; 1 Kgs. 6:23-28)	God's Presence (Rev. 21:3; 22:4)
Paradisial Setting (Gen. 2:8-15)	Sanctified Setting (Lev. 11:44-45)	Paradisial Setting (Rev. 22:1-2)
Cherubim (Gen. 3:24)	Cherubim (Ex. 25:18-22; 1 Kgs. 8:10-12)	Cherubim (Rev. 11:19)
Tree of Life (Gen. 2:10; 3:22)	Menorah (Ex. 25:31-40)	Tree of Life (Rev. 22:2)
River flows out of Eden (Gen. 2:10)	River flows out of Temple (Ezek. 47:1)	River flows from Throne (Rev. 22:1)
No Sin Present (Gen. 2:16-17; 3:3)	No Sin Present (Lev. 21:12,23)	No Sin Present (Rev. 21:27; 22:3)
Priestly Service (Gen. 2:15)	Priestly Service (Ex. 28:1)	Priestly Service (Rev. 7:15; 22:3)
Special Garments (Gen. 3:21)	Special Garments (Ex. 29:29)	Special Garments (Rev. 7:9,13-14)
Direct Revelation (Gen. 2:16; 3:8-22)	Direct Revelation (Jos. 7:6,10; 1 Sam. 3:3-4)	Direct Revelation (Rev. 4:1–16:1)
Sacrifice Offered (Gen. 3:21; 4:3-4)	Sacrifice Offered (1 Kgs. 8:5; Ezek. 43:18)	Sacrifice Offered (Heb. 9:23-26; Rev. 6:9)

Temple. Ritual impurity resulted from contact with things that were dead (Leviticus 11:24-31,39-45), and the people or objects connected with dead bodies were barred from entrance to the Temple complex. Even priests were forbidden to show signs of mourning in the Temple precincts (Leviticus 10:6). In this way, the Sanctuary, like the Garden of Eden, remained a place of life.[8]

The references to the Spirit and *Shekinah* of God in Genesis and other parts of the Pentateuch also have a similar correspondence. In Genesis 1:2 the phrase "the Spirit of God *moved*" is the language later used of the *Shekinah* (cloud) as it "moved" with the Israelites in the wilderness. The function of God's presence in Genesis 1:2 is compared to that of a hovering bird brooding over her young (in this case, the young earth). The Hebrew verb translated "moved" (*merachephet*) occurs elsewhere only in Deuteronomy 32:11,[9] which describes God's care for wandering Israel. In this passage we find the imagery of an eagle preparing its nest for its young and keeping them from harm—a picture of God's protective presence abiding with His people. Since this exact phrase appears in similar imagery at both the beginning and the end of the Torah, it again connects the God of Creation with the God of the covenant. It may also be conjectured that this imagery of a bird protectively spreading its wings corresponds to that of the guardian cherubim of the Temple, who spread their wings over the mercy seat of the Ark within the Holy of Holies.

Based on these associations we can see that God appeared in Eden in the same way that He appeared in only one other place: the Sanctuary. As Rabbi Berman notes, "The aggregate of all these allusions heightens the notion that the Temple is reflective of the Garden of Eden, the first environment in which man encountered God."[10]

The Arrangement of the Garden and the Sanctuary

Another unique association between the Garden of Eden and the Sanctuary is seen in their similar geographical arrangement. In Genesis 2:8 we find that God planted the Garden "toward the east, in Eden." The description of the Garden of Eden "in the east" may be more than a mere geographic indicator. Because the sun rises in the east and light is often used as a metaphor for divine revelation (Psalm 36:10; Isaiah 2:2-4), the use of this term may be symbolic of the place where God dwells.[11] What's more, the Hebrew word for "east" (*qedem*) literally means "faceward" or "frontward." This means that God's presence was specifically located in the western part of the Garden, and when He drove man out from before His face it was in an eastwardly direction. In Genesis 3:24 we read that God stationed guardian cherubim at "the east of the garden of Eden" to prevent man from returning west to the Tree of Life. Note also that when Cain is driven from God's presence, he is sent to a land "east of Eden" (Genesis 4:16). To travel eastward, then, is to go the direction of exile and away from God.[12] This is likewise the direction of idolatry. In Ezekiel 8:16, when Ezekiel was shown the wretched foreign abominations that had infested the Temple, he was shown at its entrance "twenty-five men with their backs to the temple of the LORD and their faces toward the east; and they were prostrating themselves eastward toward the sun." Thus, the way of false worship is the way of the east.

If this orientation represents the proper approach to God, then the arrangement of the Tabernacle and Temple on this same east-west orientation may be attributed to the layout of Eden. In the book of Numbers, this east-west orientation is the basis for the tribal arrangement of those who perform the service of the Sanctuary—Moses, Aaron, and his sons (Numbers 3:38). Also, the altar in the Tabernacle and Temple lay to the east of the edifice, and the only entrance to the Holy of Holies (in the westernmost position) opened eastward in a straight line (Exodus 27:13-16). This indicates that this east-west direction separates the dwelling of man (who has violated God's commandments) from God (whose presence surmounted the Temple). As we saw a moment ago in Ezekiel 8:16, idolaters are described as being in the Temple courtyard with their backs turned to the Temple as they worship in an eastwardly direction toward the rising sun—the direction of pagan prayers. Since the Temple was the holiest place of all, every place in the Tabernacle courtyard or Temple complex outward from the Temple possessed a descending degree of holiness. Therefore, to be "outside the camp" was to be in a place of defilement and estrangement from God (Leviticus 4:21; 16:27). Because this was the region of the "cursed," public executions, including that of Jesus, took place in this area (John 19:17-20; Hebrews 13:11-13; see also Exodus 29:14). Again, the understanding of these orientations depends on the first reference in Scripture—the original arrangement described in Genesis.

Parallels Between Adam and the Priesthood

The symbolism of the Sanctuary in Eden also extends to the Sanctuary's service. When the earthly Sanctuary was established, God appointed a priestly tribe, headed by a high priest, to the holy service (Exodus 28:1). When we examine the role of Adam in the Garden, we find that the terms used to describe his duties are unique to those of the priest in Leviticus, who officiated at the

Tabernacle and Temple. Genesis 2:15 describes for us Adam's responsibility in the Garden of Eden:

> "The LORD God took the man and put him into the garden of Eden to cultivate it and keep it." This translation does not adequately convey the proper sense of the work the man was commanded to perform; the phrase "cultivate it and keep it" would better be translated "serve it [the ground][13] and to guard[14] it [the Garden]."[15]

The terms "work" (Hebrew, *'avodah*) and "keep" (*shemirah*) suggest that Adam had been commissioned to act as a "servant of God" preserving and protecting the holy ground of the Garden-sanctuary from desecration, even as the Levites protected the Tabernacle and Temple.[16] This desecration was certainly the intrusion of sin proceeding from the only possible act of disobedience (Genesis 2:17; 3:3,11), but also to ward off a deceiving presence such as was manifested through the serpent (Genesis 3:1, if this was known). This parallel between Adam and the Levites is supported by the fact that the only other uses of the verbs "serve" and "guard" as a pair are found in Numbers 3:7-8; 8:26; 18:5-6, where they are used to express the duties of the Levites in ministering in and guarding the Sanctuary. The Jewish sages evidently saw this identification, for in their commentary they identified the phrase "to work and to keep it" as "an allusion to sacrifices" (*Genesis Rabbah* 16:5). Apparently, some rabbis saw this charge to Adam as a priestly commission to offer sacrifices (even under perfect conditions; see concerning the Millennial conditions, chapter 23). A further association may be found in the statement in Genesis 3:21 that God made "tunics" for Adam and Eve from animal skins and "clothed them." This act is analogous to the accounts of Moses "clothing" (same verb) the priests in their "tunics" (same noun) at their ordination (Exodus 28:41; 29:8; 40:14; Leviticus 8:13).[17] Adam, then, may have been the first and ideal priest, attending God's presence in the Garden in the same way as the Levites would the Tabernacle and Temple.

Angels at Eden and the Ark

Perhaps the most striking symbolism in the Genesis description is that found in Genesis 4:24 of the two cherubim posted at the east entrance to Eden, guarding access to the Tree of Life in the middle of the Garden. Any Israelite who read this description could not help but think of the two cherubim overshadowing the Mercy Seat on the Ark of the Covenant (Exodus 25:18-22). Symbolic

representations of the cherubim were also embroidered on the veil of the Tabernacle (Exodus 26:31), and carved into the walls, doors, paneling, and lavers of
the First Temple (1 Kings 6:27-35; 7:29,36). Also, Solomon made two 15-foot-high
olivewood cherubim overlaid with gold to overshadow the Ark in the First
Temple (1 Kings 6:23-28; 8:6-7). Cherubim will also adorn the interior of the Millennial Temple (Ezekiel 41:18-25). As with many of the other parallels between
Eden and the Sanctuary, the only other references to the cherubim in the Old
Testament outside of the Genesis account are those found in texts concerning
the Sanctuary. Without the reference to the cherubim in Genesis, there would be
no explanation for their later appearance in the Tabernacle and Temple.

Just as the cherubim in Eden guarded the east entrance to the Garden of
Eden, so God's presence at the Ark was entered from the east, and the cherubim
served as guardians of the divine glory manifested between their wings. Since
cherubim appear only in relation to the earthbound revelation of God, there is
an apparent connection between Adam and Eve's expulsion from God's presence in the Garden and the return of God's presence at Sinai. In the reversal of
this dilemma, the cherubim serve as archetypes for those on the Ark. Consequently, the cherubim on the Ark recall the Edenic angels and the drama of history that had unfolded on both sides of the Garden—the sin inside that led man
away from God, and the Sanctuary outside that led God back to man.

As a result of the Fall, the human couple had to flee from the holy ground in
the Garden to the cursed ground outside, which was now bearing thorns, thistles, the demand of constant toil, and finally, death (Genesis 3:17-19). The temptation to return to the holy Garden in their unholy state was prevented by the
cherubim, or angels of the presence. While the sacred Tree of Life remained, the
Garden had to be guarded from the defiling intrusion of sin, and now of sinners,
in the case of Adam and Eve. Formerly Adam had this responsibility, but having
failed in his duty, God took over the task of preserving His holiness. Man could
not return to God because he could not return to the Garden. Therefore he was
to be a wanderer without rest, seeking God's favor through the same bloody
means that God had performed to kept them alive in His holy presence (Genesis
3:21). It may be misleading to say that man *could not* return to God, for this was
made possible through the rudimentary sacrificial system instituted after the
Fall (Genesis 4:3-4). Return to God was therefore possible *spiritually*, but not
physically. Man could continue to live after sin and could have a promise of
living in God's presence after death, but he could no longer have the hope of
God's presence dwelling with him in life. Furthermore, the divine design of

man's representative rule over the creation and of his service as a priest to God in the earthly sanctuary of Eden was ended.

In the alien world beyond the veil of Eden, God's presence was unwelcome. Therefore the cherubim held flaming swords of fiery judgment, a symbolic warning to sinners of their deserved punishment if they attempted to violate that which was holy. Yet, since the purposes of God will stand, the drama goes forward to Sinai, where God renews His divine ideal around the symbol of the Sanctuary. At Sinai, the Garden of Eden was replaced by the Tabernacle. With its construction, though man could not return to God, God could return to man. And since man needed to fulfill his priestly function, God began to create a priestly nation (Isaiah 61:6; 66:21). Although direct access to God's presence was still forbidden (Exodus 33:20; 34:2-3; see also Leviticus 16:1-2), a dramatic change had taken place in making a mediated entrance into the presence of God possible through the Tabernacle and its priesthood.

After man had been banished from the Garden, God had cherubim placed at the Garden's entrance; they brandished flaming, ever-turning swords that barred a return from any direction. These cherubim functioned, according to the language of Genesis 3:24, as sentinels "stationed" to "guard" the way to the Tree of Life. As already noted, the cherubim reappear in only one other place in the Bible—within the Holy of Holies in the Tabernacle and Temple (Exodus 25:20-21; 26:1,31; 1 Kings 8:4-7). This implies a close analogy between the two appearances, but there is one key difference: The cherubim in Eden face *outward* in order to ward off attempts at re-entry. But in the Holy of Holies, the cherubim stationed atop the Mercy Seat of the Ark face inward toward the place where God's presence was manifested between their wings. These cherubim, rather than turning man away from God's presence, make possible God's presence among men (Exodus 25:8,22). And, just as one man, Adam, served as a representative for the human race and caused all men to be cast out from God's presence, so one man, the high priest, served as a representative for Israel, enabling all the people to enter God's presence representatively.[18]

Having seen the connections between Eden and the Temple, let us conclude by summarizing the theological significance of this comparison.

From Symbolism to Sanctuary

In the Garden of Eden, man had been in God's domain. To remain there man had to remain in a state of purity. At Sinai, God entered man's domain. For God to remain in man's midst, man had to remain in a state of *ritual* purity. When sin affected each domain the result was a separation between God and man. The expulsion from the Garden (Genesis 3:24) is comparable with the later punishment of banishment from the desert camp, and the still later exile from the Land of Israel (Hosea 6:7). Each meant the suffering of a state of perpetual defilement, and a sort of "living death," until ceremonial and spiritual restoration could be effected. In both the expulsion from the Garden and the exile from Israel, the Land, too, was considered "desecrated" (Genesis 3:17-18; Jeremiah 2:7; 16:18; Psalm 106:38; Ezekiel 36:17), and gestures of lamentation were appropriate, as seen with Adam and Eve and all their descendants who have realized their loss of holiness (Leviticus 13:45-46; Numbers 5:2-4; cf. 1 Samuel 15:35 with Lamentations 1:3-4 with Genesis 3:18-19).

The Provision of Purification

The only way of return was a restoration through which the stigma of desecration could be removed. This was alluded to in Eden by the purification ceremony in which the blood of an animal was shed when Adam and Eve were clothed in its skins (Genesis 3:21).[19] From Sinai onward this would be done with the ashes of the Red Heifer (Numbers 19) and the water purification ceremony (Leviticus 14)—both of these rituals ultimately will find fulfillment in the future restoration of Israel (Ezekiel 36:25-27; 37:23,26-28). Too, the act of covering with tunics, as mentioned earlier, might fit with the rite of priestly ordination, for the priest would have to be ritually clean in order to officiate in the Sanctuary, just as the man and woman in leaving Eden to live in a cursed world would have to be sanctified in order to continue serving God. The means to this purification was to be had at the Sanctuary. The high priest, representing the people, went before the Mercy Seat on the Day of Atonement and sprinkled the blood of the offering there. The sins were commuted for another year, and the status of Israel as a priestly nation could continue (Leviticus 16:14-16).

The Provision of Promise

At both Eden and the Sanctuary there was also some promise of future restoration given. In Genesis 3:15 there is the promise in Eden of a reversal or respite from the curse: One day the seed of the woman (the Messiah) would crush the head of the serpent's seed (Satan), though as the Second Adam experiencing the curse Himself ("the bruising of the heel")—i.e., death. This death, however, would reverse the penalty of death and result in life (Romans 5:12-21). Likewise, even while the Temple was under siege by the Babylonians, Jeremiah 25:10-11 provided assurance of a predetermined length of exile (70 years) and promised a return. In other words, though man might sin, and God would punish, He would measure their judgment and restore a remnant in mercy.

When the Tabernacle was erected the promise of a way back to God's presence on earth was provided. Once a year, on the Day of Atonement, the high priest went from outside the camp to inside the Tabernacle, moving in a westwardly direction toward the Holy of Holies, where the *Shekinah* glory was manifested on the Mercy Seat between the wings of the cherubim. The high priest's act of atonement was a reversal of the exile from God experienced by mankind from Adam onward. As he entered the Tabernacle he passed by sacred objects, such as the Menorah, which may have symbolized the Tree of Life. When he finally came into the Holy of Holies, he did so with the blood of the sacrifice to satisfy (propitiate) the wrath that originally drove man away from God in the Garden (Genesis 3:24). In completing this act, the high priest was restoring to Israel the creation mandate given previously to all mankind (Genesis 1:28). This mandate to subdue the earth for the Creator would now be realized only through the shedding of blood—which brought the nation into a proper state of sanctity so they could serve God as priests and bring His light and salvation (Isaiah 49:6) in fulfillment of both the Abrahamic Covenant (as mediators of God's blessings to all the families of the earth—Genesis 12:2-3) and the New Covenant (in the new spiritual order of the Millennium—Jeremiah 31:31-34). In this way, what was left unfulfilled at the beginning of history will find its fulfillment at the end of history.

From Beginning to Ending

When we consider the symbolism in Eden and the substance of the Sanctuary we move from beginning to ending, or in theological terms, from protology to eschatology. *Protology* is the study of the beginning of history while *eschatology* is the study of the end of history. They form a continuity throughout the divine record in promise and fulfillment.[20] That Sanctuary symbolism would be present at the beginning of biblical history is appropriate, for if God should have begun history with symbols of the Sanctuary, should not the end of history expect to find these same elements present to complete God's purpose of dwelling with His creation? We must remember that the Millennial Kingdom is more than a fulfillment of the Jewish Messianic age; it is also a return to the original divine ideal begun in Eden. During this time the Edenic conditions are reproduced and complete their intended purpose, adorning a world in which God reigns with the proper evidence of that reign: prosperity, fruitfulness, and harmony. For this reason, nature is once more subdued to man (see Isaiah 11:1-9) and God's presence is restored to His Sanctuary on earth (see Ezekiel 43:1-12). The Temple's presence in the Millennial Kingdom, besides fulfilling Ezekiel's pattern of exile and return (cf. Ezekiel 10:18-19), will perhaps serve as a witness to the divine purpose being brought full circle, with the earthly exiled nation (Israel) returned and restored to an Eden where, along with the redeemed nations, fellowship with the Creator God will never again be interrupted (Isaiah 60:1-22). We see this completed correspondence suggested in two restoration passages:

> Indeed the LORD will comfort Zion; He will comfort all her waste places. And her wilderness He will make like Eden, And her desert like the garden of the LORD (Isaiah 51:3).

> And they will say, "This desolate land has become like the garden of Eden; and the waste, desolate and ruined cities are fortified and inhabited" (Ezekiel 36:35).

As those who have inherited the spiritual outline of this purpose during the church age, we must keep in mind that the details of the divine design, as originally given, still remain unfulfilled on earth. Such fulfillment awaits the revival of the Jewish nation spiritually, the Temple's restoration physically, and the Lord's return manifestly. When God's presence has one day been restored to His Sanctuary on earth (Ezekiel 37:26-28; 43:1-12), the world will witness that the divine purpose has been brought full circle, with man restored to a worldwide Garden where fellowship with His Creator and Redeemer will never again be interrupted. Ultimately, the final fulfillment will come only when there is a complete correspondence with the Heavenly Temple, which has served as the archetypal model of the Garden of Eden and every earthly Sanctuary.[21] The fulfillment of the divine design is seen in Revelation 22, where we see the original elements of the Heavenly Temple represented in Eden (the river of the water of life, the Tree of Life, the presence of God, the absence of the curse) becoming the heavenly experience of redeemed mankind in the New Jerusalem (see chapter 24).

In Genesis we have seen Sanctuary symbolism as a preview of coming attractions. As we move onward through the rest of the Pentateuch we come to see the first feature (the Tabernacle), which, in the historical books of the Bible, becomes the major production (the Temple). However, the final feature is yet to come (the future Temple). In the next chapter we will explore the prophetic predictions that focus on this future Temple and consider the restoration that accompanies it in fulfillment of Eden's original design.

CHAPTER 10

Predictions in the Prophets

The Promised Last Days Temple

People will not understand these and related ideas until they happen, for they are hidden by the prophets.

—RAMBAM

They [the prophets] had their noble purpose well defined even twenty-five hundred years ago, and to it we of today are heirs. They have left us their plan of endlessly building upward, that we and the generations of Jews who will come after us may unto all future days share in the great task.[1]

—JACOB GOLUB, AUTHOR *IN THE DAYS OF THE FIRST TEMPLE*

The so-called "writing prophets" of the Old Testament encompass a span of time from the final phase of the Jewish monarchy through the Assyrian and Babylonian exiles to the beginning of the post-exilic (Persian) period. The messages of the pre-exilic prophets generally grew out of the crisis that faced their unfaithful nation, whose time of reckoning with God had come. Israel had been constituted as a nation with an unparalleled position: "I will take you for My people, and I will be your God" (Exodus 6:7). The Temple and its priesthood had symbolized this special status before the Gentile nations, regulating Israel's conduct so that its distinctive witness would not be compromised. Yet despite God's own presence dwelling in their midst, the priesthood became corrupted and the Temple itself was invaded by foreign gods in the form of pagan idols. Adding sedition to sin, these idols had been placed there by kings from God's own ordained dynasty, the house of David. Thus the holy union was desecrated and God sent His prophets with the message of divine judgment for the wayward nation. This judgment was centered upon the Temple as the sign that God's presence had been withdrawn and His wrath would come. The Temple's destruction demonstrated the divorce that had occurred between God's people and their God (Isaiah 50:1; Jeremiah 3:8-11), and its ruined state stood as an emblem of the consequences of breaking covenant and of the power of the Lord who enforced it (Lamentations 1:18; 2:1,7).

The problem for the prophets of the exile (Ezekiel, Jeremiah, Daniel) was how to comfort a people who had not only lost their Land but also, as their captors told them, their Lord. The reality was that God went into exile with His people, but only to demonstrate in the midst of their captivity that He was the Lord of lords and that His promise to restore the nation had not suffered the same ruin as their Temple (Psalm 106:44-47). It was the post-exilic prophets who accompanied the return of the exiles to Judah in 538 B.C. that faced the greatest challenge. Were they meant to inherit the promises made by the former prophets? How could their experience of a meager return to a region still under foreign domination, while the majority of their fellow Jews remained outside the Land, be considered a restoration? How could the Temple they rebuilt—which had been financed by a foreign government, erected grudgingly and under duress over an insufferable number of years, and which was pitiable by comparison with the Temple of the past—fulfill the great vision (of Ezekiel) they had been given? When would Elijah come to restore the faithless hearts of those Jews who enjoyed their exile? When would Messiah arrive to return all Jews to the Land, conquer Israel's enemies, restore Jerusalem, and rebuild the Temple into a glorious throne that would draw the nations to worship? These were the questions they had to address while encouraging a nation to seek the Lord and not lose heart over their circumstances.

The prophecies proclaimed by these prophets not only grew out of days of grief and a desire for days of glory, but were first and foremost revelations from God. As such, they had to be studied and interpreted by the prophets themselves so they could discover the meaning and time God intended for their fulfillment (see 1 Peter 1:10-11). This is especially necessary with respect to the Temple, for although its rebuilding was based on obedience to an established command (Exodus 25:8), the extent of its restoration depended on the predetermined plan of God.

The Temple of the Prophets

The majority of modern-day commentators on the prophets assume that the rebuilt Temple mentioned in their prophecies was fulfilled either realistically or idealistically by the Second Temple, which was constructed by the Babylonian exiles upon their return to Jerusalem in 538 B.C. However, the building of the Second Temple, under Zerubabbel's supervision, was done according to the enduring biblical command to rebuild whenever conditions permitted (Ezra 3:2; see also Exodus 25:8), and was not viewed (as far as the Scriptures reveal) by the builders nor by successive generations of Jews as a fulfillment of the restoration prophecies. The reasons for this assessment, despite the historical reality of a lack of literal fulfillment, were the unfavorable spiritual and political conditions as well as the inferior status of the Temple itself. The Rambam gives an evidence of this attitude of Second Temple Judaism when he notes that *Tisha B'Av* (the traditional day of mourning for the destruction of the Temple) continued to be observed as a fast day even though the new (Second) Temple was standing. The people's abiding expression of grief, which should have ended with the rebuilding of the Temple, is indicative of their viewing the Second Temple as inferior to the First (see Ezra 3:12-13; Haggai 2:3, 9), and therefore falling short of prophetic fulfillment. Other rabbinic authorities shared this same opinion:

> The idea that the Second Temple was not a true redemption is expressed in other realms. For example, Rabbi Hasdai Kreskes in his book *'Or Hashem* ["Light of G-d"], maamar 3, volume 1, rule 8, chapter 2 (page 369 in Rabbi Shlomo Fisher's edition) writes, "In the end, the Second Temple Period was as if the King of Egypt who is now ruling Eretz Yisrael ["the Land of Israel"] would give permission to the Jews in some of his lands to go up and rebuild the Temple on the condition that they

remain loyal to his government. It is not surprising that if, after a period of time, they would rebel and be exiled and enslaved....Similarly, in the *Drashot HaRan*, Drash 7 (p. 123 Feldman ed.), "The kings who ruled during the Second Temple Period were not independent rulers at all, only clerks of the Persian, Roman, and other kingdoms."...This was indeed the case for the Second Temple Period, and our current state of Exile is a continuation of the destruction of the First Temple....In the time of Ezra, they were "accounted" (*nifkedu*), as they said, "Since the seventy years of Babylon have been filled, I will account you" (Yirmiyahu [Jeremiah] 29:10). Therefore, it was not a full redemption, but only an accounting.[2]

Although the Second Temple period was regarded as falling short of the promised redemption, it is clear that the Second Temple was still considered to be a legitimate Temple accepted by God (Haggai 1:8) and made possible through God's work of turning the hearts of pagan kings to do His will (Ezra 6:22; see also 2 Chronicles 36:23; Ezra 1:2-4; 6:1-13). But it was not considered to be the Restoration Temple that had been prophesied for the time following the exile and the return to the Land. The problem was not in the Temple but in the Jewish people who had rebuilt the Temple, and whose exile, in the spiritual sense, had not yet ended. This is demonstrated by the fact that the Temple of Zerubbabel had waited more than 15 years to be completed once its foundation was laid because the people feared the Samaritans (Ezra 4:4) and were preoccupied with building their own homes (Haggai 1:2-3). Only after God sent a famine (Haggai 1:5-6), sent the prophets Haggai and Zechariah to preach to the people, and worked through the political efforts of Zerubbabel and Joshua (Ezra 5:1-2; 6:14; Haggai 1:12-15) was the Temple finally completed. Given these dismal circumstances, it is no wonder that the rabbinic sages denied that the prophesied restoration had been fulfilled in the Second Temple period. So that we can more fully understand this viewpoint, let us briefly survey the history of this time from 538 B.C. to A.D. 70.

The Problems of the Second Temple Period

The biblical books of Ezra, Nehemiah, Haggai, Zechariah, and Malachi chronicle the spiritual problems that existed after the return and resettlement of the Judean exiles. The first problem was that only a fraction of the Jewish community in exile cared to return to their ancestral homeland. Most had been born in captivity and were not interested in the pioneering effort required to move their families and rebuild the ruins of what was essentially a "foreign country" (see the book of Esther). Less than 50,000 of the most committed Jewish families, "whose spirit God had stirred to go up" (Ezra 1:5), returned under the edict of Cyrus (Ezra 1:2-4). This lack of spiritual commitment among the exilic community soon appeared in the post-exilic community as well. This condition of covenant complacency was the primary social problem characterizing this period. Upon returning to the Land the faithful remnant under Ezra and Zerubbabel found a spiritually lethargic, uncommitted, compromised resident Jewish population. Some of the violations of covenant committed by this group included idolatrous marriages (Ezra 9:1-4), breaking the Sabbath (Nehemiah 13:16), spiritual apathy and personal indulgence to the exclusion of religious obligation (Haggai 1:3-11), and various social and spiritual abominations (Malachi 1:6-2:17; 3:7-15). From 1000–597 B.C. (the period of the Jewish Monarchy) life in Israel was lived in relation to the Land, which served as a symbol of God's blessing (Deuteronomy 26:9). This blessing (spiritually and socially) could only be experienced through a proper relationship with God through the covenant (Deuteronomy 8:6-18; see also Jeremiah 2:7).[3] The Temple was essential to obtaining and maintaining this blessing, for it enforced and regulated the terms of the covenant. Because most of the sins committed by the post-exilic community were in the realm of violations against the Temple and its services, and the majority of the house of Israel still remained in exile, the faithful remnant developed the conviction that the restoration promised by the prophets could not occur with their generation (Zechariah 10:1-12; 12:10–13:9). However, even when a renewal of the covenant took place (Ezra 3:10; Nehemiah 9:38) it was still observed by only a remnant, even though the threat of non-renewal was exclusion from the assembly (Ezra 10:8).

The third problem faced during this period came as a result of the spiritual and social crisis that continued to divide the post-exilic community. During this time Israel was under the control of Gentile rulers, and crisis turned to conflict when the Syrian ruler Antiochus IV Epiphanes imposed Hellenistic policies (adopted by many of the "non-renewed" Jews). While the committed Jews won a military victory over Antiochus and established an independent state for nearly a century, the priestly dynasty that had won the war (Hasmoneans) eventually corrupted the traditional form of Davidic government by allowing its non-Zadokite clan priests to rule as kings and corrupted the office of the high priest by appointing an illegitimate priesthood. When Rome invaded and conquered Israel in 68 B.C., it appointed kings (under its control) from this same line as well as others (such as Herod) who had no connection to the Davidic line as well as high priests whose credentials were more political than proper (the legitimate Zadokite priesthood). These conditions encouraged the religious and social schisms that had existed from the time of Ezra, eventually developing the different Jewish sects which bitterly contended with one another. Some of these sects simply withdrew from Jerusalem and their fellow Jews (such as the Jewish sect that established itself at Qumran and has become famous for the Dead Sea Scrolls). The Dead Sea Sect (commonly identified with the Essenes) separated from establishment Judaism in Jerusalem, and even though numbers of them were priests, they also separated from the Second Temple. They were opposed to this Temple because they believed its priesthood and offerings were ritually defiled. Since such defilement had brought about the destruction of the First Temple, in their minds it had already doomed the Second. They believed that in the last days, a Third Temple (in which proper sacrifices would be offered) would be built on a restored Temple Mount in Jerusalem. They even had a document prepared that provided the prophetic details for the construction of the end-time Temple (see 11QT, the *Temple Scroll*). They identified their own sect not with the Jews of the Second Temple but with those purer Jews of the First Temple with whom God had made His covenant at Sinai. They believed they were the living continuation of First Temple Judaism and for this reason called themselves the "Community of the Renewed Covenant."[4]

The Second Temple period was never a time of peace. Political conditions worsened under the Roman rule and sectarian groups battled with one another more and more, leading to a Jewish revolt in A.D. 68. This, in turn, led to the Roman destruction of Jerusalem and the Temple in A.D. 70. While the horror of the devastation shocked many, a good number had predicted such an end for an era that had never been right from the beginning.

The Second Temple's Shortcomings

Not only were the conditions of the Second Temple period problematic, but the Second Temple itself suffered from problems that removed it from being the Temple predicted by the prophets. According to the Talmud, several things were missing in the Second Temple that had been in the First Temple. In the Babylonian Talmud, tractate *Yoma* 21b we read: "Why do we read *ve-artza ekavda* (Haggai 1:8), when it is written *ekaved*—missing the letter *he*?!" The words of the Hebrew text cited here are part of God's command to rebuild the Second Temple: "and I will be pleased [with it] and I will be glorified" (Hebrew, *ve-artza-bo ve-ekaved*). The sages in this section of the tractate are debating the different spellings of the Hebrew verb *kaved* ("to honor, glorify"). One is the *Qere*, "what is supposed to read," here, the *plene* ("full") spelling of the word (Hebrew, *ekavda*) and the other is the *Ketib*, "what is written in the biblical text," here, the *defective* ("shorter") spelling of the word (Hebrew, *ekaved*). The difference between the two spellings is the presence or absence of the single Hebrew consonant *he*. The sages' explanation for this was that since the Hebrew letter *he* also stood for the Hebrew numeral "5," its omission was indicating that five things were missing from the rebuilt Temple.[5] The tractate *Yoma* continues the explanation: "These are the five things that were in the First Temple and not in the Second Temple: the Ark with the covering and angelic figures, the heavenly fire (*'esh mᵉhashmayim*), the divine presence (*Shekinah*), Divine Inspiration [or Holy Spirit] (*ruach hakodesh*), and the Urim and the Thummim (*Urim veTumim*)." A variation in the Jerusalem Talmud (*Makkot* 2:6) reads, "Rabbi Shmuel stated in the name of Rabbi Aha, 'Five things were missing in the Second Temple that were in the First Temple: The Fire, The Ark, The Urim and Thummim, the Anointing Oil, and Divine Inspiration.'" Other sources also add to this list the manna, the water of purification (water mixed with the ashes of the Red Heifer), Aaron's rod that budded, the Mosaic menorah, and the treasure chest sent by the Philistines as a tribute (Babylonian Talmud, *Yoma* 52b; Midrash *Numbers Rabbah* 15:10).

According to these sages, then, the glory of God did not return to the Second Temple and will not return until the Temple stands again in its full and final splendor. Following this view the Ritva likewise writes, "The building of the Second Temple was less important because it was merely putting up a fence where it had been broken into." He also added the note concerning the peace that is expected to accompany the restoration: "peace, meaning that Israel dwells on their land, and the Temple is standing." For the Ritva, the fulfillment of these two conditions would merit the promised peace. However, because the Second Temple was built under Persian rule, that period was not considered true peace. In summary, the view advanced by the rabbis—and known as the Babylonian view—was that the Second Temple was fundamentally flawed, its destruction being assured from the day of its construction, and the return under which it was built was still a part of the exile and thus never a true redemption. Those who hold this view maintain that the Exodus from Egypt, not the Second Temple, is the model for the future redemption. They expect the future Temple's advent to be accompanied by miracles and wonders, just as the Exodus was (see Isaiah 63:11-12; Haggai 2:5-7).

By contrast, the Israeli view, generally held by activists in the Temple movement, acknowledges likewise that there were problems in the Second Temple period and with the Temple itself, but still considers the rebuilding of the Temple as a full (though not a Messianic) redemption. The problem, as they see it, is that the Second Temple period did not reach its predicted peak because the Jewish people sinned in not *fully* taking advantage of the opportunity to rebuild. According to this approach, the Second Temple serves as the model for the yet future redemption (see Haggai 2:9). Rather than waiting for the miraculous, the Israeli view emphasizes dealing with the difficult situation at hand and recognizing the activity of God in the normal affairs of government—which have resulted in the return of the Jews to the Land, the establishment of the Jewish State, and the capture of Jerusalem.

Both the Babylonian and Israeli views were developed to explain why redemption had not occurred in the way or to the extent that the prophets had described. The only alternative explanation for this disappointment—other than that the prophets were wrong (as liberal scholars say)—is that the prophets were misunderstood, and that a literal fulfillment was never intended. Let's consider this possibility, which is advocated by the symbolic or spiritual school of interpretation.

Reinterpreting the Prophets

After the Second Temple was destroyed in A.D. 70, the Jewish population was dispersed and forbidden access to the Temple Mount. Centuries went by without a return to the former status and any possibility of rebuilding, so Judaism had to accommodate itself to the historical reality of life without a Temple. Without a Temple or sacrifices, the only way the Jews could fulfill the commandments related to these two former elements of their lives was to spiritualize them and practice them in ways that could be carried out. Thus, the synagogues took the place of the Temple, and sacrifices were transformed into prayers. These changes also brought a reassessment of the eschatological promises of the prophets. Were these prophecies intended to be fulfilled literally, or was God using the medium of historical reference to communicate a more spiritual message? Perhaps the distinctive ideals to which they pointed were not meant to be actualized, but internalized, and then lived out so that the Jews continued to be a distinct people. The majority of Christians down through the millennia have believed that the prophets were speaking to the church, which in Old Testament times contained mostly Jews but was destined to become filled with Gentiles when Jews rejected Jesus as the Messiah. These Christians said the prophets' words were idealistic portraits of the church or heavenly realities to be enjoyed by the church and had nothing to do with the restoration of a political earthly kingdom for the Jews or a physically rebuilt Temple. However, before a spiritual interpretation can be accepted, we must first ask how the prophets intended for us to interpret their messages. Let's look again at their words concerning the Temple, and decide for ourselves their original intent—in the context in which they were first given.

Understanding the Temple Prophecies

In their prophecies, the prophets saw both their day as well as the Day of the Lord. Their expectation of restoration after ruin made it difficult to discern what was to be fulfilled immediately and what was to be fulfilled in the distant future. The detailed descriptions of eschatological renewal have also influenced the interpreters of the prophets to believe that the only practical fulfillment of such details must be immediate. For example, in Zechariah 14:10 the words about the reconstruction of the gates, towers, and walls of the Temple Mount are comparable to those in Ezekiel 40–48. While these would appear to be a description of rebuilding in the prophet's own time, the context makes it clear that we are viewing the time of the Messiah's return and reign as well as the time when unparalleled topographical changes will take place in Jerusalem. Eugene Merrill, professor of Old Testament at Dallas Theological Seminary, explains the proper understanding of such a text:

> The purpose of this description is not so much to give the precise delineations of the eschatological city but to enable Zechariah's own generation (and any other) to understand that the idealism of the future is rooted and grounded in the present, in actual history and geography. The God who led His people through spatial, temporal history will recreate the cosmos in those same categories. This is why a literal hermeneutic is essential in the absence of compelling evidence otherwise.[6]

This "literal hermeneutic" (literal interpretation) understands references such as "Jerusalem," "Zion," "the mountain of the Lord of hosts," and "the Temple of the Lord" as the actual, historical, geographical places and buildings whose desecration or destruction in the past requires a like restoration in the future. Within this prophetic context, then, we are looking at the future (eschatological)

Temple on the Temple Mount in Jerusalem. In order to illustrate this point, let us consider the pattern of desecration and restoration in the prophets, which requires past desecration to have a coming Last Days Temple for the complete fulfillment of restoration.

The Pattern of Ruin and Restoration

The Temple stood as a constant reminder that in the past, God had decreed a specific purpose for the Nation. The Temple was also the focal point of future promise. That's why the prophets balance their warnings of ruin with the reassurance of restoration. Just as the Temple's destruction was to signal the end of the Nation's status as tenants of the Land and the beginning of sorrows, so its rebuilding was to signal the end of sorrows and the return of the Nation's privileged position. In the writings of the prophets, the Temple functions according to this prophetic pattern of the historic promises made to the Jewish people.[7] This pattern is governed by the terms of the covenant,[8] in which God promised both blessing and cursing: if the people sinned, they were punished and the Temple, which was desecrated, was destroyed; if the people repented and returned then both would be restored and rebuilt. This prophetic pattern of desecration and restoration summarizes Israel's history and reveals that the destinies of the Temple and the people are inseparably linked. Furthermore, even though God is faithful to judge unfaithful Israel, the unconditional nature of His oath to the patriarchs (in Genesis) requires the prophets to announce the ultimate fulfillment in a "new covenant" (Jeremiah 31:31) and an "everlasting covenant" (Ezekiel 16:60) which will be signified by a rebuilt, purified, restored, and inviolable future Temple (Jeremiah 31:38-40; 33:18; Ezekiel 40–48). In order to confirm this interpretation of the prophets' original intent, let's examine what the prophets say about the Temple and its connection to Israel's promised restoration (my discussion will leave out the prophet Ezekiel, since his vision is treated separately in chapter 23).

The Last Days Temple in Isaiah

The Temple was particularly significant to the prophet Isaiah for it was in the Temple that he had received his great vision of the Lord's glory and his own recommission as a prophet (Isaiah 6:1-8). This revelation of God's glory in the Temple, which occurred in 740 B.C., served as confirmation of God's promise of restoration despite the days of judgment to come for Israel (722 B.C.) and the Temple (586 B.C.). It may have also set the stage for Isaiah's positive presentation of the Temple in his recommissioned message, although the focus of his book (both in judgment and restoration) is the social and spiritual condition of the Nation, which reflects the theological themes of their sin and salvation. Also at this time—as well as in subsequent years—Isaiah learned that God would be both a Sanctuary (*miqdash*) and a stumbling stone to Israel (Isaiah 8:14-15). Yet even though God would appear to be hiding His face from the Nation, they were to "look eagerly for Him" (Isaiah 8:17). Only in that final eschatological day would they be able to fully say, "Behold, this is our God for whom we have waited that He might save us. This is the LORD for whom we have waited; let us rejoice and be glad in His salvation" (Isaiah 25:9).

Isaiah also learned that the fulfillment he and his people longed for would come as both near and far restorations (Isaiah 6:9-13). The nation would be punished, Jerusalem captured, and the Temple destroyed (Isaiah 63:18; 64:11), and the people would go into exile (Isaiah 1:2-23; 28–31:9), but later a remnant would return (Isaiah 1:24-31; 10:5-34; 40:3-5; 44:28; 48:1-22). Still, the same sins would continue (Isaiah 63:17; compare John 12:37-41) and result in future punishment in a time of tribulation (Isaiah 24:1-23). Only a final restoration under the Messiah (Isaiah 11:11-12) would bring the longed-for release from the cycle of sin and subjugation (Isaiah 9:3-5; 53:1-12; 61:2-3) and establish the throne of David forever (Isaiah 9:6-7; 11:10). This future reign of the Messianic King (Isaiah 2:3; 25:6) would be both universal (Isaiah 56:6-7) and glorious (Isaiah 24:23; 62:2-3), and it is in this eschatological context of God's final program of restoration that we find Isaiah's comments concerning the Last Days Temple.

Isaiah's attitude toward the Temple may be seen in a prayer for the Temple's restoration: "Our holy and beautiful house [the First Temple], where our fathers praised Thee, has been burned by fire; and all our precious things have become a ruin. Wilt Thou restrain Thyself at these things, O LORD? Wilt Thou keep silent and afflict us beyond measure?" (Isaiah 64:11-12). From this prayer we can see that Isaiah shared the Jewish nation's concern over the later loss of the Temple. However, he makes clear that it was not the Temple that was judged but the Jewish people, and that the destruction of the Temple was an act that outraged God and demanded His just and merciful restoration. Indeed, Isaiah pronounces God's accusation against "you who forsake the LORD, who forget My holy mountain [the Temple Mount]" (Isaiah 65:11).

The Tribulation Temple in Isaiah

The historical setting for the Temple described in Isaiah 66:1-6 has been debated among evangelical scholars. For many, the setting is the post-exilic period under Ezra and Zerubbabel, when the Jews built the Second Temple. It was the people's hypocritical worship that had brought the destruction of the First Temple (Isaiah 29:1), and we see the same attitude condemned in Isaiah 66:1-6. Perhaps this was a warning to the new generation of builders to guard against the sins of the past—especially in light of the expected new age of restoration. However, in the post-exilic prophets that document the rebuilding effort, we do not see any censure against improper worship at the Temple. The rebuke in the opening chapter of Haggai (see in text to follow) is against self-centeredness and indolence *before* the Temple was rebuilt, not *after*, as in Isaiah. Furthermore, there is no evidence that God's punishment proceeded from the Temple against any of the builders, as in Isaiah 66:6.

Consistent literalists note that Isaiah 66:1-6 is sandwiched between Isaiah 65:17-25 and Isaiah 66:7-24, where the setting is the Millennial kingdom and eternal state. They therefore contend that an eschatological setting should be expected. Based on the language of the text and comparisons with events in the books of Daniel and Revelation, most have argued that the backdrop for Isaiah 66:1-6 is the Tribulation period. Notice that chronologically, it precedes a description of Israel's national rebirth (in verses 7-9), and observe as well that it's at the *beginning* of the Tribulation period when unbelieving Jews are allowed to rebuild the Temple (Daniel 9:27). So the Temple in Isaiah 66:1-6 is the Tribulation Temple (verses 1, 5-6). Those who receive the rebuke are unbelieving but Orthodox Jews who have rebuilt the Temple and have begun the sacrificial worship system (verses 3-4, see also Revelation 11:1), and their punishment which "they dread" (verse 4) is the Antichrist's desecration of the Temple through the abomination of desolation and the cessation of the ritual offerings (verses 5-6; see also Daniel 9:27).

Does this mean that in Isaiah 66:1-6 God is rejecting the rebuilding and worship of the Third or Tribulation Temple? In Revelation 11:1 the Tribulation Temple is called "the temple *of God*" and John's measurement (spiritual evaluation) of those who worship in the Temple (compared to the nations that trample the outer court, verse 2) appears to be acceptable to God (see chapter 14). The answer for this seeming contradiction is found in a clear understanding of the Isaiah passage. In verses 1-2 we see a statement about God's immensity and incomparability that is later cited in Stephen's sermon in Acts 7:49-50, and also has similarities with the prophet Nathan's statement to King David in 2 Samuel 7:5-7. The point in all of these statements is not that the Temple is illegitimate or that its services were impure, but that the people's motives were wrong and that their allegiance to a structure or system cannot replace following the will of God. For David this meant humbly submitting to God's will and having Solomon build the Temple. For Stephen's audience it meant denying any security in the Temple and humbly repenting of their sin against their Messiah. For those that will build the Third Temple it means not trusting in the rebuilt Temple and its renewed service as a guarantee that they will have God's blessing, for in fact such blessing comes only from humble faith in God's Word and chosen way (verses 2c, 4d). We know from Revelation 11:1 that this Temple will have worshipers who are approved of by God; in Isaiah's text they are called those "who tremble at His word," and whose "brothers hate you, who exclude you for My name's sake" (verse 5). These are believing Jews who are ostracized by the Orthodox Jews for their faith in Jesus as the Messiah. There is, then, a harmony with Revelation 11:1 and no condemnation in Isaiah of the Tribulation Temple or its service.

The Millennial Temple in Isaiah

The primary focus of Isaiah's Temple prophecies, as with all of the prophets, is on the Final or Millennial Temple, since it marks the apex of God's promise of a coming restoration. This Temple is built at the conclusion of the last days' conflict (the campaigns of Armageddon) and will serve as a witness to God's deliverance of Jerusalem or "Ariel" (Isaiah 29:7-8; see also Zechariah 14:2-3). Isaiah also foreshadowed this future event in his careful record of the divine deliverance of Jerusalem from the Assyrian siege of Sennacherib (Isaiah 37:32,35), the release from the Babylonian captivity by Cyrus (Isaiah 44:26–45:6), and the return of the Temple vessels to Jerusalem under the priest Sheshbazzar (Isaiah 52:11-12; see also Jeremiah 27:21-22; Ezra 1:7-11). The Year of Redemption (Isaiah 63:4b) will come with the return of the Redeemer to Zion (Isaiah 4:2; 59:20-21; see also Romans 11:26) and afterward the remnant scattered throughout the nations will return for the purpose of worshiping on the Temple Mount (Isaiah 27:13). After the judgment of the Tribulation period, which Isaiah sees as part of God's means of purifying the nation (Isaiah 4:4), all of the peoples will be invited to the Temple Mount for a Messianic banquet, and God will fulfill His promise of restoration (Isaiah 25:6-8; see also 1 Corinthians 15:54; Revelation 21:4). The rebuilding of the Temple itself will be preceded by topographical changes (Isaiah 2:2a-b; 40:4; see also Zechariah 14:10) that will prepare Jerusalem and the Temple Mount for its Millennial rebuilding (Isaiah 58:12; 61:4).

Once the Temple has been rebuilt, "the LORD of hosts will reign on Mount Zion and in Jerusalem, and His glory will be before His elders" (Isaiah 24:23).

Isaiah adds more details about God's presence when he writes, "Then the LORD will create over the whole area of Mount Zion and over her assemblies a cloud by day, even smoke, and the brightness of a flaming fire by night; for over all the glory will be a canopy" (Isaiah 4:5). Isaiah, with those words, describes the return of the *Shekinah* glory of God to the Temple (see Ezekiel 43:1-7) and to the whole of the Millennial Temple complex (see Jeremiah 3:17). With a reborn Israel in possession of a restored Temple Mount, the promised blessings of the New Covenant will finally be realized (Isaiah 57:13). The age in which this Temple will stand will be one of unparalleled peace (Isaiah 2:4) with the realization of a new harmony in the natural order, especially on the Temple Mount (Isaiah 11:9-10; 65:25).

One of the most significant signs of the Millennial restoration is that formerly unfaithful Jews and the Gentile nations will be involved in the rebuilding of and worship at the Temple. Isaiah pictures the Temple as the center of the Millennial kingdom, serving as "a house of prayer for all the peoples" (Isaiah 56:7) and to which all of the nations of the earth will be drawn to learn the ways of the Lord (Isaiah 2:2c-3; 60:3; 62:2), to see His glory (Isaiah 66:18), to bring tribute to the Temple treasury (Isaiah 66:18-19; see also Revelation 21:24), and to offer sacrifices to the Lord (Isaiah 56:6; 66:20). Among these will be Jews of the Diaspora who formerly had no involvement with the Temple but will become priests and Levites who serve God (Isaiah 66:21). Isaiah 60:1-14 is particularly rich with details about the Millennial Temple—those who will worship in it and its renewed sacrificial system: "The nations will come to your [Jerusalem's] light, and kings to the brightness of your rising....the wealth of the nations will come to you....They [the sacrifices] will go up with acceptance on My altar, and I shall glorify My glorious house....to beautify the place of My sanctuary; and I shall make the place of My feet glorious" (verses 3,5,7,13). When all of these things are accomplished, Isaiah tells the people, "they will call you [Jerusalem] the city of the LORD, the Zion of the Holy One of Israel" (Isaiah 60:14; see also Ezekiel 48:35).

Isaiah's message of Israel's restoration is clear: "They will call them [the Jewish people], 'The holy people, the redeemed of the LORD;' and you [Jerusalem] will be called, 'Sought out, a city not forsaken' " (Isaiah 62:12). We can be absolutely certain that no other people or nation was intended to fulfill these words because Isaiah said that the same people who had experienced the judgment of exile would be the ones who received the promised restoration. Therefore, though Isaiah is used by the church as one of the great books of the Old Testament predicting Christ and His blessings, Isaiah's promises of restoration cannot be said to symbolically predict the church but must literally refer, as they do to Christ, to the future blessing of ethnic Israel.

The Last Days Temple in Jeremiah

Despite Hezekiah and Josiah's attempts at restoration, Judah continued to decline after the pattern of syncretism set by Israel before her fall (722 B.C.). In the autumn of 609 B.C. (Jeremiah 26:1),[9] the prophet Jeremiah, believing that the apostasy was irreversible (see Jeremiah 7:16, 29c-d), stood on the steps to the Temple's main southern entrance and declared that judgment was imminent and unavoidable (Jeremiah 7:1–8:3). First Jeremiah mentioned the ceremonial abuses and idolatry at the Temple (Jeremiah 7:1-15); then he attacked the worship of the Queen of Heaven (7:16-20), and followed that with a condemnation about substituting the ritual of sacrifical offerings for the reality of obedience (7:21-28), child sacrifice and associated evil practices in the Hinnom Valley (7:29-34), and the worship of astral deities (8:1-3). It is difficult to imagine that such violations of God's covenant could have been tolerated so long; yet throughout Jeremiah's harsh sentence we find reminders of restoration. For instance: "Amend your ways[10]...then I will let you dwell in this place, in the land that I gave to your fathers forever and ever" (verses 5a,7). This call to repentance reflects a latent promise of restoration to the Temple and the Land. The phrase "this place" has the extended meaning of "holy site" and was used frequently as a circumlocution for the Temple.[11]

To prove to Israel that the Temple in which it had trusted (Jeremiah 7:4) was not secure without God's protective presence, Jeremiah cited the case of the Tabernacle at Shiloh:[12] "Go now to My place [the Tabernacle] which was in Shiloh, where I made My name dwell at the first, and see what I did to it because of the transgressions[13] of My people Israel" (Jeremiah 7:12). According to 1 Samuel 4:10-11,22, a similar violation proved that God could let even His Sanctuary be defiled when His people's misplaced faith usurped His glory. A summary of what happened is preserved in Psalm 78:60-61: "He [God] abandoned the dwelling place [the Tabernacle], at Shiloh, the tent which He had pitched among men" and "gave up...His glory [the Ark of the Covenant] into the hand of the adversary." Jeremiah's comparison of the Jerusalem Temple with Shiloh obviously had in mind both the spiritual departure of the *Shekinah* glory (as depicted by Ezekiel 10:4,18-19; 11:22-23) and the physical destruction of the edifice (2 Kings 23:27; 25:9; 2 Chronicles 36:19; Psalm 74:3-7).

In the book of Jeremiah the focus is on the sinful spiritual and social disorder and on the Temple's destruction, with the latter being proof of the former. Therefore, Jeremiah's statements about the Temple's restoration are included within his more pointed purpose of dealing with the reversal of the people's condition and the restoration of spiritual and social purity. This can be seen in the conclusion of Jeremiah's mournful petition in the book of Lamentations: "Because of these things our eyes are dim; because of Mount Zion which lies desolate.... Restore us to Thee, O LORD, that we may be restored; renew our days as of old" (Lamentations 5:17-18,21). This reveals Jeremiah's belief that when the Lord once again restores the repentant nation, the Temple itself will be restored.

In the Temple's destruction the Lord acted for the sake of His own divine honor, and it is for this same reason that the Temple's restoration is assured. Jeremiah predicted the Tribulation period, "the time of Jacob's trouble," and Israel's eventual deliverance from it (Jeremiah 30:4-7). Following the Tribulation he saw a national restoration under a resurrected King David (some see here the Messiah) and Israel's renewed service of the Lord (Jeremiah 30:8-9). This will fulfill God's promises that Israel would return to its Land (Jeremiah 24:6; 31:37; 32:41). Jeremiah does not mention specifics about the building of the Millennial Temple, but it is implied in his description of rebuilding Jerusalem from its northeast corner (Tower of Hananel) to its northwest corner (Corner Gate) and the statement that it will all be "holy to the LORD" (Jeremiah 31:38-40). It may also be inferred from Jeremiah's prophecies of the righteous Branch (Messiah) who will sit on David's throne, judge the Land, and make Jerusalem and all Israel secure (Jeremiah 23:5-6; 33:15-16). The Temple is certainly in view in Jeremiah's statement about the coming days when God "will fulfill the good word which [He has] spoken concerning the house of Israel and the house of Judah....and the Levitical priests shall never lack a man before Me to offer burnt offerings, to burn grain offerings, and to prepare sacrifices continually" (Jeremiah 33:14,18). Jeremiah also said that under the new covenant, the knowledge of the Lord will be accessible to all and that Israel will be recognized as the people of God (Jeremiah 31:33-34). It is unclear what Jeremiah meant in Jeremiah 3:16 when he said that the Ark of the Covenant would no longer "come to mind, nor be missed, nor be made again" (some Jewish interpreters take this last phrase as "use again"). But it is clear that Jeremiah expected Jerusalem (the

Temple Mount) to be the center of Messiah's reign, the place to which the nations would be gathered, and the place where a saved and sanctified Israel would serve their Lord (Jeremiah 3:17).

The Last Days Temple in the Post-exilic Prophets

The post-exilic prophetic texts of the Persian period reveal a different attitude toward the restored Temple than that of the prophets who had to announce its ruin. The post-exilic community was marked not only by a revival of interest in the Temple, but also a fear over future violations that might bring about another desecration and destruction. This concern was especially pronounced in the historical books of Ezra and Nehemiah,[14] which chronicled the historical return and rebuilding of the Temple and Jerusalem's walls. This added focus in the messages of the post-exilic prophets grew out of the specific social and religious issues that resulted from the fact that Judah was under foreign rule and that only a partial restoration had been experienced. To be more precise, because Israel was no longer a monarchy, and because the Second Temple had been built primarily by the decree and financial assistance of the dominant Persian government (Ezra 6:4,8), it could not symbolize, as before, the Nation's independence. Furthermore, the accounts of the restoration in Ezra and Nehemiah leave the impression that the restored Temple was viewed as inferior. For instance, we read in Ezra 3:12-13 that the older people in the community, who had seen the glory of the First Temple, wept over the comparatively smaller foundations of the Second Temple. This led the people to realize that the prophecies about the promised restoration were to be pushed into the future.[15] The message of the post-exilic prophets was that the post-exilic stage was the rehearsal of an anticipated eschatological drama to be acted out in complete fulfillment of the original restoration ideal.

If this is so, then the historical events and the figures connected with them may have foreshadowed—for the prophets of this period—future realities and personages that are essential to the final restoration. This may well be what was meant when the high priest Joshua and his friends were told they were to be "signs" (Zechariah 3:8). This word is used of miraculous signs given by God (1 Kings 13:3, 5; 2 Chronicles 32:24; Ezekiel 12:6, 11; 24:24, 27) and as a synonym for "wonders" (Isaiah 8:18; 20:3). It would appear, then, that the term signified "something that astonished or conveyed a deeper, hidden, reality."[16] In a similar way the priest Zerubbabel is called a "seal" (Haggai 2:23).[17] Zerubbabel, as the

Lord's seal, would then be the guarantor of the Temple's completion and would guarantee the ultimate fulfillment of the promises associated with the building of the Temple (Haggai 1:8b; 2:9b,19b).[18] This same analogy appears in Zechariah 3:8; 6:12 for the man whose name is "Branch," who will not only build the Temple, but also rule as a priest on the Davidic throne. Yet it is historically evident that the immediate figures and events associated with this prophecy were not intended to fulfill it. Zerubbabel did not usher in a new independent Davidic dynasty (Haggai 2:22-23), nor did the nations come with their wealth to the Temple (Haggai 2:7-8; Zechariah 8:22), nor did the rebuilt Temple see the return of the *Shekinah* that had been expected at its dedication (Haggai 1:8; Zechariah 1:16; 2:5, 10-13).[19]

At the heart of the post-exilic prophets' messages is the recognition that these aspects of complete fulfillment could not be accomplished except through divine intervention: "This is the word of the LORD to Zerubbabel saying 'Not by might nor by power but by My Spirit,' says the LORD of hosts" (Zechariah 4:6). This, of course, forced a postponement of their expectations of the prophetic restoration being realized in their present experience.[20] This understanding could have caused Israel to despair over the perceived absence of divine intervention in the Nation's condition, but instead, it directed the people to God and the future. As one scholar explained: "The outcome was not a complete collapse of the hopes entertained but rather a reassertion of goals, a rescheduling of the expected millennium."[21]

With this background information in place, we can consider the specific post-exilic prophecies of the Last Days Temple.

The Last Days Temple in the Book of Haggai

In the book of Haggai, the central concern is the Temple. The first major issue raised by this prophet is the spiritual complacency of the restoration community, which slowed down the rebuilding of the Temple (Haggai 1:2). The real danger inherent in this spiritual lethargy, according to one commentator, "was that the people, having become accustomed to life without a Temple, could have 'spiritualized' their religion."[22] Thus Haggai proclaims the need to rebuild the Temple within the covenant framework, including its conditions for blessings (Haggai 1:5, 7-8; 2:19c) and curses (Haggai 1:6, 9-11; 2:15-19b). This call to rebuild the Temple employs the language of King David's original justification for building the Temple (2 Samuel 7:2): "Is it time for you yourselves to dwell in your paneled houses while this house lies desolate?" (Haggai 1:4). By use of the expression "this house," Haggai reminds the people of the biblical concept of the Lord manifesting Himself through the ceremonial system. A "house" is necessary for the priests' and peoples' performance of ritual holiness, through which the Lord will be able to bring His transcendent presence ("glory") to rest once again on His dwelling place (Haggai 1:8). As a result of the people's obedient response to "build a house for the Lord's name," "they feared before the Lord" (the proper expression in covenant terms—see Genesis 22:12; Exodus 18:21; 20:20; Deuteronomy 6:2, et. al.), Haggai announces the divine promise to one day complete the restoration begun with the return to the Land:

> As for the promise which I made you when you came out of Egypt, "My Spirit is abiding in your midst; do not fear!" For thus says the LORD of hosts, "Once more in a little while, I am going to shake the heavens and the earth, the sea also and the dry land. And I will shake all the nations; and they will come with the wealth of all nations; and I will fill this house with glory," says the LORD of hosts. "The silver is Mine, and the gold is Mine," declares the LORD of hosts. "The latter glory of this house will be greater than the former," says the LORD of hosts, "and in this place I shall give peace," declares the LORD of hosts (Haggai 2:5-9).

The specific promise for the future, restored Temple is given in Haggai 2:9. A literal translation of the Hebrew text would read, "Great will be the glory of this house the latter than the former." The term "latter" could be attached to either the word "glory": "the latter glory of this house,"[23] or to "house": "the glory of this latter house."[24] Either way, what Haggai means is that the future Temple will be greater than the one that exists presently. This comparison between the future and the former, however, cannot be a comparison of the Second Temple with the First Temple, since it was the perceived inferior status of the Second Temple that provoked the prophecy in the first place (verses 3-4). Although some have interpreted the latter Temple as being the Herodian expansion of the Second Temple, a careful look at the description given in the context reveals that it cannot mean any form of the Second Temple. First, in verses 5 and 7, this latter Temple apparently will be attended by the *Shekinah*, called here "My Spirit" and "glory," which will be visibly present ("fill this house," verse 7) as in the time of the Exodus (verse 5, see Exodus 19:4; 29:45-46). Second, we read in verses 6-7 that this Temple follows a time of divine judgment in which earthly and heavenly disturbances have forced the Gentile nations to bring their wealth to the Temple (see also Isaiah 60:4-14; Zechariah 14:14).[25] Third, in verse 9 we see that this Temple is one in which God will provide universal peace (see also Isaiah 2:4). All of these spiritual and material elements must be present before any Temple of the future could qualify as fulfilling this prophecy.

Those who employ the symbolic method interpret this as "latter glory" and see it as referring to Christ's entrance "in the days of His flesh" into the Temple courts. In addition, they argue that Jesus as "the Prince of Peace" would be crucified in the area of the Temple Mount, and by His atonement, "in this place give peace" (see Ephesians 2:14-17). However, the force of this passage is with the greater glory of the *house itself* (which was the concern of both the people and the prophets), and not with something separate from the house that enters and "glorifies" it.[26] Since Jesus was not a priest He could not, and did not, ever enter the Temple proper. As to "glorifying" it, His purpose, while respecting its sanctity, was rather to announce its destruction! Furthermore, going with a symbolic interpretation requires that one also spiritualize the other elements in these verses such as shaking the heavens and the earth" (in judgment of the nations), which does violence to Haggai's promise of a greater physical and spiritual restoration for Israel. Yet such a prophecy was clearly taken, by the prophet and his hearers (the Jewish remnant), literally as following an actual overthrow of their enemies (see Haggai 2:21-22, where the same wording is followed by details of human battle).

The Eschatological Character of Haggai's Future Temple

One pattern we frequently see in Scripture is that prophecy will view events simultaneously both near (historical) and far (eschatological). The historical enactment of these events usually has a fulfillment that comes in stages.[27] For example, in Haggai's presentation of the Temple, there are two stages of fulfillment: *stage one* is the immediate rebuilding of the Second Temple under Zerubbabel (including its subsequent enlargement under Herod—Haggai 2:18-19), and *stage two* is the future rebuilding of the Third Temple or Eschatological Final Temple (Haggai 2:21-23). The support for a second stage of fulfillment, as has already been mentioned, is found in the immediate context of the passage. Let's look closer at these details.

First, Haggai describes the eschatological "glory" that will accompany the future rebuilding of the Temple. This "glory" comes in two forms: one physical and the other spiritual. The spiritual glory is first expressed in Haggai 1:8 with the words: [28] "rebuild the temple, that I may be pleased with it and be glorified"—which refers to an active demonstration or manifestation of the divine presence.[29] This spiritual "glory" may also be in view in Haggai 2:5, which reads, "As for the promise I made you when you came out of Egypt, My Spirit is abiding in your midst; do not fear!" Despite the structural problems connected with verse 5a,[30] the intent of the verse is to recall the promise made in Exodus 29:45-46: "I will dwell among the sons of Israel and will be their God. And they shall know that I am the LORD their God who brought them out of the land of Egypt, that I might dwell among them; I am the LORD their God." While the association of "word" with "Spirit" might suggest the idea of the Lord's abiding presence through the prophetic word, it is preferable to interpret "Spirit" as having a reference to the Exodus context with an allusion to the "glory cloud." That would accord well with the verb describing its activity as "abiding."[31]

The physical "glory" that was expected to accompany the rebuilt Temple was described in Haggai 2:7b-8: "They will come with the wealth of all nations; and I will fill this house with glory, says the LORD of hosts. The silver is Mine, and the gold is Mine, declares the LORD of hosts." In this context, verses 6-7a,22 have reference to the spoils of war,[32] which the Lord, as Israel's suzerain, has full right to receive. The wealth of the conquered nations will accrue to the Temple in such a way so as to fill it with abundance (a fitting contrast to the condition of post-exilic poverty and subjugation), increasing its splendor and value (see Zechariah 14:14). We have then a restoration of the Temple that maintains a continuity with the past (the Exodus) and the present experiences (the return from exile) of the restoration community, and goes into the future as well (the end-time exodus, see Revelation 15:2-4).

Second, Haggai depicts the Lord as a divine Warrior who will overcome and conquer the Gentile nations of the world. Haggai's description of the Lord's apocalyptic intervention is given in Haggai 2:6-7a along with verses 21b-22: "For thus says the LORD of hosts, 'Once more in a little while [literally: "again, for once [it is] in a short while"], I am going to shake the heavens and the earth. The sea also and the dry land. And I will shake all nations....I am going to shake the heavens and the earth, And I will overthrow the thrones of kingdoms and destroy the power of the kingdoms of the nations; and I will overthrow the chariots and their riders, and the horses and their riders will go down, everyone by the sword of another.'" In these verses we see the Lord's sovereignty and ownership of the nations' wealth.[33] The terrestrial display of the Lord's sovereignty is described first in verses 6-7a, 21b as a universal shaking by the merisms "the heavens and the earth" and "the sea also and the dry land." The apocalyptic character of these verses is controlled by the recognition that the participle "going to shake" expresses a time in the immediate future,[34] which belongs to the terminology of epiphany during a holy war in which the Lord will violently intervene on behalf of Israel with natural and miraculous disasters (see Exodus 15:16; Judges 5:4; Psalm 18:7; 68:7-8; 2 Samuel 22:8; Isaiah 13:13; 24:18; Ezekiel 38:20; Habakkuk 3:6). A structural analysis of the military elements[35] in verses 21-22 reveals the extent of this holy war—that is, a total defeat of all forces opposed to the Lord and His people. We can know this is a divine judgment not only because of the universality and nature of the description, but also because of the closing words of verse 22: "I will overthrow...everyone by the sword of another"—a scenario that recalls the divinely inspired panics of the Israelite enemies of earlier ages (Judges 7:22; see also Ezekiel 38:21; Zechariah 14:13). The purpose of the shaking will be to upset the nations and harness them for the purpose of rebuilding the Temple (through their material provision, Haggai 2:7).

Third, Haggai declares that universal peace will emanate from the site of the Temple. Haggai's concept, in relation to similar statements in other prophetic texts (Isaiah 2:2-4; 56:6-7; 60:4-14; Micah 4:3b-4), envisions a Temple restored to God's original design with a spiritually regenerate Israel directing the moral leadership of the world from the Temple Mount. This, under the sovereign reign of the Messiah (see Psalm 2:6-9; Zechariah 14:4,9; Matthew 25:31-32), will result in universal peace (Hebrew, *shalom*) as the nations make pilgrimage to the site of the Temple (Haggai 2:9b; see also Ezekiel 47:1-12; Zechariah 14:8). In accord with the establishment of peace under the aegis of Lord, the fact that the nations bring material provisions may imply (as in Isaiah and Ezekiel) that the purpose of divine intervention is to cause the nations to acknowledge God's sovereignty and to bring them to worship Him at the Temple Mount (see Isaiah 2:2-4; 56:7; Ezekiel 36:36; 37:28; see also Revelation 15:4; 21:24).

The Temple in the Book of Zechariah

Zechariah's eschatological oracles about the Second Temple complement and extend those of Haggai.[36] As one scholar has pointed out, "Zechariah represents the implementation of Haggai's expectations for temple reconstruction..."[37] However, unlike Haggai, the focus in Zechariah is not on the rebuilding of the Temple, but starts with the context of an already-rebuilt Temple (Zechariah 3:7) and deals with the theological and eschatological issues affecting the Temple. The prophecy opens with a word to the returnees under Zerubbabel, addressing the spiritual and physical nature of their return (Zechariah 1:1-6). The words of Zechariah 1:3 constitute a call to national repentance based on the conditional aspect of the covenant: "'Return to Me,' declares the LORD of hosts, 'that I may return to you,' says the LORD of hosts." This is followed by an announcement of the Lord's intentions for the future restoration of Jerusalem—which was given through two declarations in Zechariah 1:14-17: "I am exceedingly jealous for Jerusalem and Zion....I will return to Jerusalem with compassion" (verses 14,16a). This is accompanied by the imagery of a builder's line stretched over Jerusalem (verse 16c), which marks off the holy city for constructive blessing, beginning with the restoration of the Temple (verse 16b), and then by a reaffirmation of election and restored prosperity (verse 17). The classic affirmation of restoration by reversal is seen in Zechariah 8:11: "I will not treat the remnant of this people as in the former days."

In Zechariah the Temple is prominently featured, especially in chapters 1–8, and described variously as "the Temple of the Lord" (6:12-15), or "the Temple" (8:9), "My house"/ "this house" (1:16; 3:7; 9:8; see also 4:9), "house of the Almighty Lord"/"the Lord's house" (7:3; 8:9; 11:13; 14:21; see also 14:20). In addition, by metonymy, the Temple is usually implied by the phrase "and I will dwell in her midst" or as "Zion" (Zechariah 2:10; 8:2-3), and "Jerusalem" (Zechariah 1:16; 8:3,8; 14:11,16,21). There is also a reference to the Heavenly Temple, called here "My holy habitation" (Zechariah 2:13).[38] The central importance of the Temple in Zechariah is seen in Zechariah 1:12, where reference is made to the 70-year exile (586–516 B.C.), which, from the vantage point of the writer (October-November 520 B.C., verse 1), had not yet ended. This importance, which is made clearer in chapter 2, is an indication that the exile had ended. This is given support here with the recognition that while the return from Babylonian captivity was a fulfillment of Jeremiah's prophecy "to bring you [Jewish remnant] back to this place [Israel]" (Jeremiah 29:10), the complete experience of the end of the exile for which Daniel had prayed (Daniel 9:17-18) would occur only with the rebuilding of the Second Temple (Zechariah 1:16). Yet this would not be completely realized until the Lord's presence returned with the building of the Final Temple (Zechariah 2:10-11).

The Means of Future Rebuilding

In Zechariah 4:6-7 we see a parallel to the language of Haggai's exhortation (Haggai 2:4-5) concerning divine intervention as the means to fulfillment. In Haggai we saw a contrast between the First and Second Temples; Zechariah uses that comparison (Zechariah 4:10) to reveal that the smaller Second Temple actually contained the eschatological seed of glory that would be brought to fruition by divine might, whereas the larger First Temple, glorious through human construction, was destined for destruction. This is first stated directly in Zechariah 4:6: "Not by might nor by power, but by My Spirit, says the LORD of hosts." This verified that ultimately the Temple would not depend on human or "military strength" (Hebrew, *chayil*), such as the army of workers Solomon had employed to accomplish his building (1 Kings 5:13-18), nor upon available "manpower" (Hebrew, *koach*—see also Nehemiah 4:10), but on the "creative, energizing force of the Lord" (Hebrew, *ruchi*, "My Spirit"). The crowning accomplishment for the Temple would be eschatological, enacted by divine intervention. The future promise of this is expressed in Zechariah 4:7: "What are you, O great mountain? Before Zerubbabel you will become a plain; and he will bring forth the top stone with shouts of 'Grace, grace to it!'" The "mountain" had been the enemies of Israel (Ezra 4:2,4) that had served as one of the main obstacles which had prevented the completion of the Second Temple, but this "mountain" will be leveled so that the work can progress. This future intervention will follow the laying of the last stone in the finished Temple,[39] accompanied by the true estimate of the holy place as seen in the people's exclamation, "Grace, grace to it!" The people here recognized that God had made possible the completion of the Second Temple (which, by contrast, they had neglected for 15 years), and this prompted them to call for God to be gracious to the Temple and by this same might and power bring the Temple to its eschatological goal.

The Builder of the Final Temple

The builder of the Final Temple is identified by Zechariah as "a man whose name is 'Branch,' for He will branch out from where He is; and He will build the temple of the LORD" (Zechariah 6:12). The identification of the "Branch" (Hebrew, *zemach*) with the Messiah is at least as old as the Targum Jonathan (50 B.C.), which at both Zechariah 3:8 and 6:12 translated *zemach* "Branch" as *mashiach* "Messiah." The Messianic connection, especially in association with the term "My servant" (Hebrew, *'evedai*—see Isaiah 42:1; 52:13; Ezekiel 34:23-24), is a natural one in the context of eschatological restoration (see Isaiah 4:2; Jeremiah 23:5). This Messianic figure, described as to His character and purpose (to declare peace to the nations, and to establish His kingly rule over all the earth) is presented in Zechariah 9:9-10. In Zechariah 3:8 and 6:12-13 the high priest Joshua and his fellow priests served as a symbol (literally, "wonder"—Hebrew, *mophet*, used as "a token of a future event," compare Isaiah 8:18),[40] of the Lord's servant called "Branch" (see the comparative term *netzer* in Isaiah 11:1).[41] The ritual duty of this "Branch," symbolized by the high priest Joshua, is restoration of the sacrificial service and the purification of the people, which follows as a consequence of rebuilding the Temple. Therefore, following this correspondence, just as Zerubbabel is the builder of the first restoration Temple (Zechariah 4:9), so the Messiah, whom he foreshadows, will be the builder of the final Restoration Temple. The additional thought in verse 12 is that Messiah as a "Branch" will "sprout up"—that is, He will arise out of obscurity in His native Land to obtain a place of prominence as the seed of promise in the Land of Promise. This prominence will result from His dual role as King and Priest, as typified by Zerubbabel as governor, and Joshua as high priest (wearing the crown—verses 11,13). In the case of Messiah, not only will He build the Temple, but He will also bear the unique "honor" (verse 13) of ruling as an enthroned king-priest.[42] This royal honor will not only be on account of the priestly association with the Temple, but because of His role as the Messiah, a majestic representative of the Lord.[43] Such a reference also implies the dual character of the Messiah as both a humble or submissive servant and a sovereign warrior, as later described in Zechariah 9:9-10. Like the Temples which Zerubbabel and Messiah will build, the complete fulfillment requires a near (historical) and far (eschatological) interpretation—in this case, the first and second advents of Christ.

Zechariah further reveals that this future Temple-builder will be enthroned as "king over all the earth" (Zechariah 14:9: see also Micah 4:7b). Since this Messianic king must be accessible to all at the Temple, there will have to be a topographical alteration of the existing Temple Mount area in order to accommodate this endless parade of worshipers. Indeed, Zechariah 14:10-11 describes how all of the mountains that surround Jerusalem and protectively hide the Temple Mount (Psalm 121:1; 125:2) will be leveled so that the Temple Mount dominates the Land (see Psalm 47:2; 48:2). This accords with the Bible's eschatological descriptions of an elevated Temple Mount, raised high above the hills, to which all worshipers ascend (Isaiah 2:2; Micah 4:1).

In earlier times, access to the Holy City and the Temple Mount was also limited by the imposition of a "ban" (Hebrew, *herem*—see Zechariah 14:11).[44] The removal of this "ban" guarantees that insecurity will be turned to security. The cessation of this ban also implies that the cause for its imposition, ritual impurity, will no longer exist (see Zechariah 13:1-2, see also Ezekiel 36:25-27)—again indicating the Millennial character of this setting.

The Gentiles and Temple Worship

One of the marks of the restoration period is that the formerly oppressive and hostile Gentile nations will no longer be a threat, but will become a part of the worshiping community. This is stated in Zechariah 2:11: "Many nations will join themselves to the LORD in that day and will become My people. Then I will dwell in your midst." Remarkably, the covenantal language of identification "My people" (see Jeremiah 24:7; 30:22; 31:33; 32:38) will include the restored Gentile nations within its provisions (see Isaiah 19:24-25), making them co-participants in both the obligations and benefits of the Temple (see Isaiah 19:21; 27:13; 56:6-8; 60:3,21; 66:20). Because the nations become vassals of the Lord, they have the right to be called "His people," just as He, as their suzerain, can be called "their God." The result of the nations' adherence to cultic purity will permit the Lord's presence in their midst. In addition, Gentiles may also have a part in the building of the eschatological Temple. Zechariah 6:15 states, "Those who are far off will come and build the temple of the LORD." The problem with interpreting the phrase "those who are far off" within the immediate historical context is that it would be limited to the Jews of the Diaspora. However, these Jews could not have been envisioned to be those who would assist in building Zerubbabel's Temple, since it was already under construction and nearing completion. What's more, the reference to the building of the Temple by the "Branch" of verses 12-13 has been seen to have a future fulfillment. Therefore, if we allow this phrase to extend beyond the immediate historical context, in concert with other indicators that point to the future, it becomes possible to include Gentile nations here as part of this building effort, an interpretation that accords with Gentile involvement in the Temple in other prophets (see Isaiah 2:2; 56:6-7; 66:18-20; Micah 4:2; Haggai 2:7).

In Zechariah 14:16-19 an account is given of the particular requirements placed upon the nations in connection with Temple observance. In verse 16a these nations are identified as the remnant from the climatic apocalyptic battle of Zechariah 12:1–14:15: "...all the nations that went up against Jerusalem...." The only nation mentioned by name is Egypt because its geographical situation marked it out for a special condition (more on this in the upcoming text). These that formerly "went up against" Jerusalem, will now "go up to worship [in Jerusalem]," (verse 16b). The prescribed form of worship is the now universal festival uniting all nations, the Feast of Tabernacles or Succot, also known as the Feast of Booths or "Ingathering" (verse 16). The object of the nations' worship is "the King, the LORD of hosts"—a probable reference to the Lord's covenantal status as suzerain and the nations as conquered and incorporated vassals. The obligation of vassal states to be reviewed by the suzerain is here fulfilled by the regional pilgrimage to Jerusalem to observe Succot. This background helps explain the application of the covenantal blessings and curses in the Millennial

Kingdom to the nations in verses 17-19. In these verses, agricultural prosperity, generated by the bestowal of the seasonal rains, was conditioned upon a nation's appearance before the suzerain at Succot. The exception to this was Egypt (verse 18), whose dependence was not upon seasonal rains, but the inundation of the Nile. In their case, failing to appear before the suzerain would bring judgment in the form of a plague (verse 19)—a form of punishment that had been used to secure Egypt's acknowledgment of the Lord's total sovereignty during the time of the exodus. Thus, in the restoration, the nations will recognize the Lord, worship Him annually at the Temple, and be subject to the conditional stipulations of covenant law as His vassals ("His people").

The Future Battle for the Temple Mount

The future battle for Jerusalem in Zechariah chapters 12 and 14 must include the Temple Mount, as indicated by the intended contrast between "all nations of the earth" being "gathered against" Jerusalem *for battle* (Zechariah 12:3; 14:2) and the subsequent restoration context: all the nations gathered to Jerusalem *for worship* (Zechariah 14:16; see also Isaiah 2:2; 56:7). The state of the Temple as desecrated (by the Antichrist) is implied by the geographical reference to the Lord's appearance "on the Mount of Olives, which is in front of Jerusalem on the east," directly across from the Temple Mount. The implication is that the Lord does not proceed directly to the Temple Mount because it has been desecrated by the enemy (Revelation 11:2, see also 2 Thessalonians 2:4).[45] The setting must be eschatological, since this last great invasion and exile of the Holy City will result in the climatic intervention of the Lord to defend it (Zechariah 14:3,12-13), establish it as the governmental and religious center of the earth (Zechariah 14:16-21), the ancient threat of the "ban" (Hebrew, *herem*), will be removed (Zechariah 14:11), and unparalleled topographical changes will occur (Zechariah 14:4-10). In Zechariah 12:2-3, desecration is implied in the defiling presence of the nations that will besiege the sacred places, although the primary intention of these passages is to depict Jerusalem as "a cup that causes reeling to all the peoples" (see Psalm 75:8; Isaiah 51:21-23)—that is, intoxicating the Gentile confederacy so that it attacks and desecrates the city and Temple (see Daniel 9:27), thereby provoking the wrath of the Lord against the nations (see Zechariah 2:8-9; 12:4,8; 14:3,12-15).

The Return of God's Glory to the Temple

The book of Zechariah gives us a vivid description of the restoration following the battle for Jerusalem, Messiah's victory ascent to the Mount of Olives, and the transformation of the Temple Mount and rebuilding of the Millennial Temple. It is evident that the Tribulation Temple will be destroyed and replaced by the effect of the great earthquake and the immense topographical changes that completely transform the Temple Mount and prepare it for the significantly larger Messianic Temple (Zechariah 14:4-5,10; see also Isaiah 2:2; Ezekiel 40:2,48–41:26). The first step in the return of God's glory to this Final Temple is the anointing (consecrating) of the new Holy of Holies (see Daniel 9:24) by the restoration of the divine presence to the Temple. This restoration to the divine ideal, with the Lord dwelling in the midst of His people, is described in Zechariah variously as, "I will be the glory in her midst" (Zechariah 2:5); "I am coming and I will dwell in your midst" (Zechariah 2:10-11), and "I will return to Zion and dwell in the midst of Jerusalem" (Zechariah 8:3; see also Ezekiel 43:1-7; Malachi 3:1). These latter occurrences of "dwell" or "dwelling" employ the traditional advent formula with the Hebrew verb *shakan*, but the first occurrence (2:5) adds the descriptive element of "glory" (Hebrew, *kabod*). This recalls the exodus manifestation of the divine presence (*Shekinah*) as "a wall of fire" and "glory" (see Exodus 13:22; 14:20; 40:34), as well as the prophesied return of the divine presence to the Temple, retracing the route of the departure (Ezekiel 43:2-5; 44:4). Zechariah sees this "glory" extending to the entire city, and later to the whole Land (Zechariah 1:16; 6:12-13;14:20-21), reconstituting Jerusalem as the "City of Truth" and the "Holy Mountain" (Zechariah 8:3). These two epithets describe the new ritual significance of the city as the site of the Temple—a city so characterized by "truth," i.e., *torah* (see Isaiah 2:3), and holiness that all of the nations are spiritually attracted to it (Zecahriah 8:20-23; see also Malachi 3:12).

Zechariah's description of this pervasive purity is given in Zechariah 14:20-21: "In that day there will be inscribed on the bells of the horses, 'Holy to the Lord.' And the cooking pots in the Lord's house will be like the bowls before the altar. And every cooking pot in Jerusalem and in Judah will be holy to the Lord of hosts; and all who sacrifice will come and take of them and boil in them. And there will no longer be a Canaanite in the house of the Lord of hosts in that day." The extent of Jerusalem's purity is shown by ascribing as holy even the common cooking pots—not simply "cooking pots," but *every* "cooking pot" in and around the Holy City! The concept of ceremonial sanctity, one represented by the inscription "Holy to the Lord" on the mitre of the high priest, will now extend to everything in the vicinity of the Temple, for its holiness will be as pervasive as was the contamination caused by defilement—a fact symbolized by the abolition of "the Canaanite," the epitome of unholiness. This extension of sanctity to even the most mundane objects anticipates the extended holiness of the Temple-city (as described in Ezekiel 48:8-22,35, as well as in the extrabiblical Dead Sea document known as the Temple Scroll). At the time of restoration, then, we will see a reversal from pollution to purity, with the Temple as the nexus of a ritual utopianism (see Ezekiel 43:12).

The Coming Temple in Malachi

By the time Malachi rises on the scene (450–400 B.C.), the anticipated promise of a complete restoration under Haggai, Zerubbabel, and Nehemiah had remained unfulfilled for almost a century. Malachi's explanation for a limited restoration and further delay of full realization with respect to the Temple service was that it had been re-established but had not been maintained in ritual purity. Though the Second Temple had not seen a glimpse of the glorious future predicted for it, it had become the prominent institution in Israel. However, the ritual abuses of the past had resurfaced, and therefore Malachi's message is consumed with issues related to the priesthood and the sacrificial system. His focus is the Temple complex, particularly the ritual activity at the altar (Malachi 1:6-14; 2:1-17), and the neglect of the Temple tax, which affected the Temple storehouses (Malachi 3:7-12; see also 2 Chronicles 31:11). Many of the same elements and motifs found in Haggai, Zechariah, and Joel are repeated by Malachi, demonstrating that an imminent though futurist perspective was still the guiding hermeneutic. The eschatological motivation is again presented as a correction for the abuse of the Temple service, with repentance paving the way for the ultimate and last days restoration (Malachi 4:6).

In our studies of Haggai and Zechariah we looked at various eschatological motifs in relation to the Temple; let's do that now with Malachi's prophecy of the Temple's desecration as well as the preparation for the Temple restoration.

The Eschatological Context of Malachi

The use of the Day of the Lord motif in Malachi is predominately apocalyptic and judgmental. In Malachi 4:5 it is called "the great and terrible day of the LORD" (see also Joel 2:11,31; Zephaniah 1:14), and is characterized by "furnaces, fire, chaff," and "ash"—all features of a final conflagration set aflame by the Lord's intervention (Malachi 3:1-5; 4:1-3), called by Jesus "the baptism with fire" (Matthew 3:11). However, Malachi differentiates between a judgment of *purification*, which will take place at the Temple (Malachi 3:2-3), and the *final* judgment, which will destroy the wicked (Malachi 4:1,5). The first judgment is peculiar to the people of Israel (Malachi 3:5-6; see also Ezekiel 20:33-38) because it relates to an eschatological restoration of the Temple service (Zechariah 3:3), and the second judgment is cosmic or universal because it relates to the nations—that is, the annihilation of the wicked (Matthew 25:32-46).

It is important to observe that Malachi's concern over desecration is set within a context of eschatological fulfillment (Malachi 3:1; 4:1-5). The desecration will be relieved only when the Lord intervenes in history, purifies His people and the Temple, and removes the threat of continued contamination by contact with defiling influences (Malachi 3:1-5; 4:3). It is the eschatological element, then, that ties the desecration and restoration motifs together in this context. The vision of apocalyptic intervention here, like the visions in Zechariah 1:7–6:15 and the shaking of all the nations in Haggai 2:7,21, present the theme of judgmental upheaval as a prelude to the establishment of universal ceremonial sanctity.

The Problem of Temple Desecration

In Malachi 2:11, the renewed desecration of the Temple is explicity stated as the reason the promised restoration had not yet taken place: "Judah dealt treacherously; and an abomination has been committed in Israel and Jerusalem; for Judah has profaned the sanctuary of the LORD, which He loves…" This desecration is specifically stated to be because of an "abomination." These are the two terms that define the Temple's profanation by idolatry or ritual impurity, especially when foreign nations are involved (see Deuteronomy 18:9-13). While some have argued that the context is covenantal and suggests Israel as a chosen nation (hence a "holiness to the Lord"), the context is equally ceremonial, as verse 12 reveals in the phrase "presenting an offering to the LORD of hosts." Furthermore, the "abomination" here is clearly ritual defilement through intermarriage with pagan idolaters, the very offense that brought desecration to the First Temple (as introduced by Solomon and climaxed by Manasseh). This sin is especially compounded in view of the historical consequences it brought to "our fathers" (verse 10). Malachi's concern here is that the revival of the sins of the past would put the restoration community at risk of another exile by virtue of desecration. Malachi's list of such defilements include: 1) the desecration of the divine Name (Malachi 1:11c-12a; see also 1:6); 2) the desecration of the altar through defiled offerings (Malachi 1:7-8; see also Leviticus 22:20-25; Deuteronomy 15:21); 3) the desecration of the priestly covenant (Malachi 2:8-9); 4) the desecration of covenantal purity (Malachi 2:10-16); and 5) the desecration of the Temple treasury (Malachi 3:7-12; see also 2 Chronicles 31; Nehemiah 13:10). The result of such Temple desecration is the threat of divine judgment, which Malachi sets at the time of the return of the Lord: "The Lord, whom you seek, will suddenly come to His temple..." (Malachi 3:1). This helps us to understand why the judgments of the Tribulation intensify after the Antichrist's desecration of the Temple at the mid-point of this period (Matthew 24:15, 21; Mark 13:14, 19). These judgments, however, are designed to put away the defiling elements and restore Israel to ceremonial purity (Malachi 3:2-6).

The Preparation for Temple Restoration

The Lord's intervention and revelation before Israel and the nations will be followed by His building of the Temple and reconsecration of its vessels and priesthood. The eschatological dimensions of this are seen in several places. In Malachi 1:11, the Lord's manifested greatness is seen as universal: "From the rising of the sun, even to its setting, My name will be great..." (see Psalm 50:1; 113:3).[46] When eschatological restoration comes to the world, the Temple will be the focal point, as stated in Malachi 1:11: "In every place incense is going to be offered to My name, and a grain offering that is pure." Before the restoration takes place, the Lord will send a priestly mediator to help foster national repentance, the prerequisite to restoration:

> "Behold, I am going to send My messenger, and he will clear the way before Me. And the Lord, whom you seek, will suddenly come to His temple; and the messenger of the covenant, in whom you delight, behold, He is coming," says the LORD of hosts. "But who can endure the day of His coming? And who can stand when He appears? For He is like a refiner's fire and like a fullers' soap. And He will sit as a smelter and purifier of silver, and He will purify the sons of Levi and refine them like gold and silver, so that they may present to the LORD offerings in righteousness" (Malachi 3:1-3).

These verses indicate that the Lord's Sanctuary must be prepared for His coming reign in righteousness. In Malachi the priestly desecration of the Temple apparently foreshadows a future ritual desecration that must be removed prior to the Lord's return to the Temple Mount. Therefore, a "messenger," most likely Elijah (Malachi 4:5), will come to prepare the people for restoration by spiritual repentance: "He will restore the hearts of the fathers to their children, and the hearts of the children to their fathers" (Malachi 4:6). The restoration here is most likely a restoration to the ceremonial and social purity of the covenant, as "fathers" may refer back to the former days mentioned in verse 4 (see also Zechariah 1:5-6). Under a theocracy there was a proper social order: obedience to the covenant brought blessings in every relationship.[47] The terms of purification—"refiner's fire," "fullers' soap," "smelter and purifier of silver" (Malachi 3:2-3)—reveal the extent of purification *outwardly* (removal of the stains of defilement, see Isaiah 4:4; Ezekiel 22:18; Psalm 66:10), and *inwardly* (removal of contaminants that affect the quality of purity, see Psalm 12:6; Proverbs 17:3). The result will be a restored priesthood able to present ritually pure offerings in the Temple (verse 4).

Our survey of the prophets and their messages about the Last Days Temple has revealed that their understanding was that God's promised restoration for Israel and the Temple would take place in the future age. However, according to many Christian interpreters, this eschatological age is said to have arrived with the first advent of the Messiah. In order to get a more complete and accurate picture of God's plans for the Temple, let's focus on one of the prophets who prophesied both the Messiah's advent and the future of the Temple, and provided for us a timetable revealing the proper perspective of end-time events. Join with me as we uncover the predictions made by the prophet Daniel concerning the Last Days Temple.

CHAPTER 11

Predictions in Daniel

The Temple of the Seventieth Week

The Book of Daniel enjoys a special distinction among the Books of the Bible. Nowhere else are the promised redemption [of Israel], the End [time], and the resurrection of the dead, so explicitly spelled out. . . . However, it was not meant for the Book of Daniel to become a secret hidden book. . . . Rather, the matter of the End was meant to be studied. . . . This is all the more true in our generation when the footsteps of the Messianic king are already reverberating in our ears. Indeed, the Book is the clarion call of the Messiah—as Chazon LaMoed relates, in Greek communities it was read [to encourage Messianic expectation] during the three week period of mourning for the Holy Temple.[1]

—RABBI HERSH GOLDWURM

No book in the ancient world or the modern is as enigmatic yet essential to unlocking the mysteries of the prophetic plan for Israel, its Temple, and the nations as the book of Daniel. The late seminary president and author Alva J. McClain once declared: "…with reference to its importance, I am convinced that in the predictions of [Daniel's] 70 weeks, we have the indispensable chronological key to all New Testament prophecy."[2]

The events in the book of Daniel occur during the period of Jewish exile—from the first deportation of Jewish exiles in 605 B.C until after the Persian conquest of Babylon in 538 B.C. Both the internal witness of the book and the external witness (the use of foreign terms, the scarcity of Greek terms, and the evidence of early authorship based on copies of Daniel among the Dead Sea Scrolls) argue in favor of the book being dated to the time of Daniel (sixth century B.C.).[3] The critical view that the book was written pseudonymously (by an unknown Jewish writer) late in the second century B.C. has resulted largely from a prejudice against predictive prophecy.

In the book we see Daniel's concern is over the destruction of the First Temple and his prayer for Israel's restoration to the Land and the building of a Second Temple. The book also records prophecies relating to future earthly kingdoms, both human (Jewish and Gentile) and divine (in chapters 2, 7–12). The prophecy of Daniel's 70 weeks is a part of the last division of the book (which centers on Israel and the Temple's restoration), yet the context is also within a time of Gentile domination that would continue to threaten further invasion and desecration.

Yet, despite the clear prophetic purpose of the book, Daniel does not appear among the prophets in the traditional Jewish division of the Hebrew Scriptures. It is classified as Wisdom Literature and grouped with the "Writings" (Hebrew, *Ketubim*) of the Hebrew Bible, which include the books of Psalms, Proverbs, and Ecclesiastes. In the time of Jesus Daniel was still regarded as a prophet (as Jesus Himself reveals—Matthew 24:15; Mark 13:14), and it wasn't until later that the book was declassified as prophecy. What could explain this change in status for so important a prophetic book?

The Fear of Daniel's Prophecies

The first-century Jewish historian Flavius Josephus[4] revealed not only the uniqueness of Daniel but also provided the motive for why his prophecies might be feared: "He not only predicted the future, like the other prophets, but specified when the events would happen" (*Antiquities* x. 268). The belief that Daniel's prophecy provided information as to the precise time of prediction was no doubt a significant factor in the timing of the war with Rome in A.D. 66–73, since the 70 years of wrath in Daniel 9:3, which figured prominently in the Qumran *War Scroll* (1QM), could have been interpreted as the period between the first outbreak of revolutionary activity in 4 B.C. (the time of Herod's death, and possibly also of Jesus' birth) and the final uprising in A.D. 66. Josephus notes that the Jewish zealots used Daniel's prophecies to support their revolt against Rome:

> But what more than anything else incited them to war was an ambiguous oracle, likewise found in their sacred scriptures, to the effect that at that time one from their country would become ruler of the world. This they understood to mean someone of their own race, and many of their wise men went astray in their interpretation of it. The oracle, however, in reality signified the sovereignty of Vespasian, who was proclaimed Emperor on Jewish soil (*Jewish War* VI).[5]

The prediction to which Josephus referred was probably that depicting the future Messianic king in Daniel 7:13-14 and 9:26. While Josephus indicates the interpretation was misapplied by his kinsmen, his own application was no less inaccurate. However, it was not simply that the book of Daniel exercised an influence based on its own predictions, but that the uniqueness of its prophecies influenced the interpretation of other prophetic books as well. This may be seen by Daniel's use in a Jewish paraphrase of the prophets known as *Targum Jonathan on the Prophets,* written around 50 B.C. It reveals that all of the prophets were interpreted along the lines set out in Daniel.[6] For example, Daniel 9:22-23 reveals the mysteries of Jeremiah's prophecy of the 70 years, Daniel 2:36-38; 7:1-3 interprets the four horns of Zechariah 2:1-4 by means of four successive terrestrial kingdoms, and Daniel 9:27 discloses the eschatological content of the "decreed end" of Isaiah 10:23.[7] More importantly, Daniel was viewed as offering the divine interpretive key to the secret of the determined end and thus to all of Israelite prophecy. With Daniel the biblical revelation was considered to have reached its final stage,[8] since it served as the revealer of the heavenly mysteries (cf. Daniel 2:18-19,27-30), showing that the prophecies of the other prophetic books were to be interpreted for the time of the end (Daniel 12:4,8-10).

The use of Daniel as predictive prophecy by those who waged revolts—with disastrous consequences for the Jewish people—led the rabbis to regard Daniel as a dangerous book, and to fear that people would continue to apply its apocalyptic timetable to contemporary events and thus bring the Nation to ruin. They believed that by separating it from classical prophecy and grouping it with narratives of the exilic period it would no longer exert an interpretive influence on the other prophetic books. Once it was incorporated among the heroes of the exile, the purpose of the book was shifted from prophecy to pedagogy.[9] Now the lessons were of obedience to the Torah, rather than that of figuring out the future. The rabbis further distanced Jews from trying to calculate Daniel's end times by allowing the book to be interpreted allegorically rather than literally.[10] By permitting the prophecies to be allegorized, the inclination to use them as a literal key for prophetically interpreting current events was avoided.

We can understand the rabbis' concern over the misapplication of prophecy not only because erroneous interpretation could provoke an unfounded confidence in a Messianic claimant or incite a revolutionary movement, but also for a more basic spiritual reason: Rambam explains that the sages were troubled lest a predicted time come and go without the expected fulfillment.[11] If that were to happen, people of insufficient faith would probably become more likely to believe that the fulfillment would never come.[12] Had Daniel remained among the prophets, it might have been used as *Haftorah* in the synagogues. This then may explain why Jonathan ben Uziel was said to have been prevented from extending his Targum of the Prophets to include the Writings because it now contained Daniel and the revelation of the End (see *Megilla* 3a).

Nevertheless, the rabbis regarded Daniel as divinely inspired which was in part because the events subsequent to the fall of Jerusalem in A.D. 70 had confirmed to the rabbis (as it had to the early Jewish-Christians and church fathers) that the interpretation of the fourth monarchy in Daniel 2 and 7 was the Roman empire and thus showed Daniel's prophetic timetable was accurate. Therefore, Daniel alone, within the canon of Scripture, contained the key details about the destruction of the Second Temple and about Israel's future restoration after a further exile (Daniel 9:24-27; 12:1-13). The central passage relating to these events is Daniel's prophecy of the 70 weeks, and in order to properly interpret the prophetic program, this text must be clearly understood.

Daniel's Prophecy of the 70 Weeks

Daniel's 70 weeks (verse 24) are to be interpreted according to Hebrew literary convention as 70 weeks of *years*.[13] The resulting period of 490 years (70×7) is divided, according to verses 25-27, as periods of seven weeks (49 years), 62 weeks (434 years), and one week (7 years). Christian interpreters have traditionally accepted the context of this passage as Messianic, with the Messiah coming after the 62 weeks (i.e., after the 7 weeks + the 62 weeks = 483 years) to die. Futurists would see the words in verse 26 concerning the Messiah's being "cut off" (killed) "and have nothing" to mean dying without inheriting the Messianic kingdom,[14] leaving the fulfillment of this purpose to the final week (verse 27), which depicts the resumption of the Messianic promise for Israel (with the overthrow of the Antichrist as a prerequisite to the establishment of the Messianic kingdom). In this regard, Daniel 9:27 serves as the single Old Testament text cited by our Lord in the synoptics as a chronological indicator of eschatological events (Matthew 24:15; Mark 13:14). It is also thought to be the text underlying Paul's eschatological treatise in 2 Thessalonians 2:3-10 concerning "the son of destruction [Antichrist] and the Temple" (language which has no other literary referent but in Daniel 9:27),[15] and also may have served as a literary paradigm for the structure of the book of Revelation,[16] and especially the chronological outline of the Temple in the Tribulation as given in Revelation 11:1-2 (see chapter 14).

The Interpretation of Daniel's Prophecy

Daniel's prophecy of the 70 weeks contains singular terminology[17] that has resulted in a number of different interpretations.[18] The question that has most concerned commentators has been the identification of the historical commencement and the conclusion of the prophecy. Competing interpretations[19] range from past historical to future eschatological fulfillment.[20] In the past historical interpretations, the seventieth week immediately follows the sixty-ninth week, with the events described in Daniel 9:27 having been already fulfilled (with the events in verse 26 already considered part of the seventieth week). The view adopted in this book is that of the eschatological or futurist interpretation,[21] with the commencement in the Persian period (Artaxerxes in 457 or 445 B.C.),[22] and the conclusion in the end times (at the midpoint of the seventieth week, with the desecration of the Temple by the Antichrist). The eschatological interpretation is sometimes combined with both the Maccabean and the Roman interpretations by those who view the passage as having a *dual* reference or fulfillment. The eschatological interpretation, by definition, argues that the nature of the events in Daniel 9:27, which take place only in the seventieth week, have not yet been consummated, but await literal fulfillment in harmony with the eschatological context of verses 2 and 24, the Olivet Discourse, and similarly structured passages in Revelation. If one takes the past historical view, one must conclude that the prophecy of Daniel has either failed in terms of precise historical fulfillment,[23] or that it was intended to be fulfilled other than in a strictly literal

The Temple in Daniel's Prophecy of the 70 Weeks

Jerusalem's Temple Mount serves as the focal point of the prophetic events

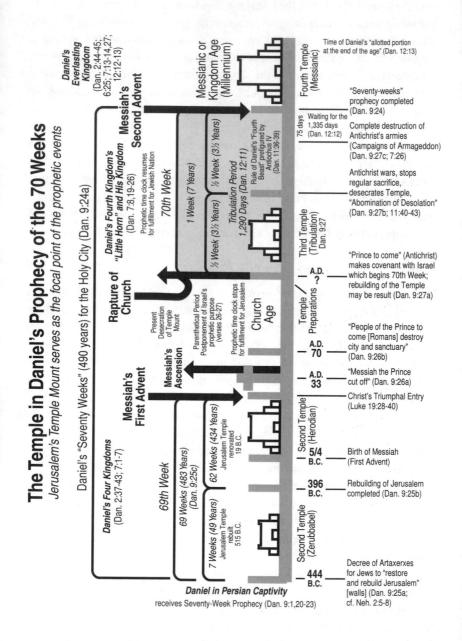

Daniel's "Seventy Weeks" (490 years) for the Holy City (Dan. 9:24a)

Daniel's Four Kingdoms
(Dan. 2:37-43; 7:1-7)

Daniel's Fourth Kingdom's "Little Horn" and His Kingdom
(Dan. 7:8, 19-26)

Daniel's Everlasting Kingdom
(Dan. 2:44-45; 6:25; 7:13-14, 27; 12:12-13)

Messiah's First Advent

Messiah's Ascension

Rapture of Church

Messiah's Second Advent

Messianic or Kingdom Age (Millennium)

70th Week

1 Week (7 Years)

Prophetic time clock resumes for fulfillment for Jewish Nation

½ Week (3½ Years)   ½ Week (3½ Years)

Tribulation Period
1,290 Days (Dan. 12:11)

Rule of Daniel's "Fourth Beast" prefigured by Antiochus IV (Dan. 11:36-39)

Present Desecration of Temple Mount

Parenthetical Period
Postponement of Israel's prophetic purpose (verses 26-27)

Prophetic time clock stops for fulfillment for Jerusalem

Church Age

69th Week

69 Weeks (483 Years) (Dan. 9:25c)

62 Weeks (434 Years)
Jerusalem Temple renovated 19 B.C.

7 Weeks (49 Years)
Jerusalem Temple rebuilt 515 B.C.

Daniel in Persian Captivity
receives Seventy-Week Prophecy (Dan. 9:1, 20-23)

Fourth Temple (Messianic)

Third Temple (Tribulation) Dan. 9:27

Temple / Preparations

Second Temple (Herodian)

Second Temple (Zerubbabel)

75 days   Waiting for the 1,335 days (Dan. 12:12)

Time of Daniel's "allotted portion at the end of the age" (Dan. 12:13)

"Seventy-weeks" prophecy completed (Dan. 9:24)

Complete destruction of Antichrist's armies (Campaigns of Armageddon) (Dan. 9:27c; 7:26)

Antichrist wars, stops regular sacrifice, desecrates Temple, "Abomination of Desolation" (Dan. 9:27b; 11:40-43)

A.D. ?   "Prince to come" (Antichrist) makes covenant with Israel which begins 70th Week; rebuilding of the Temple may be result (Dan. 9:27a)

A.D. 70   "People of the Prince to come [Romans] destroy city and sanctuary" (Dan. 9:26b)

A.D. 33   "Messiah the Prince cut off" (Dan. 9:26a)

Christ's Triumphal Entry (Luke 19:28-40)

5/4 B.C.   Birth of Messiah (First Advent)

396 B.C.   Rebuilding of Jerusalem completed (Dan. 9:25b)

444 B.C.   Decree of Artaxerxes for Jews to "restore and rebuild Jerusalem" [walls] (Dan. 9:25a; cf. Neh. 2:5-8)

fashion. For this reason scholar Lester Grabbe has written, "...much of [Daniel] 9:24-27 does not clearly and easily fit the known historical context. This is highlighted by practically all the major [critical] commentaries which resort to a great deal of emendation [alteration of the text] in order to make the statements correspond with history."[24] Because the historical events do not fit with any known history, amillennial and postmillennial interpreters have sought to find a symbolical or spiritual fulfillment within the uninterrupted scope of the 70 weeks (i.e., the first century). Employing a hermeneutic of replacement (of national Israel by the church), they argue for a Christological fulfillment within the ministry of Christ or, at the latest, the time of the first preaching of the gospel to the Gentiles. However, there are significant reasons why the eschatological, or futurist interpretation, of the prophecy is preferred.

The Basis for the Eschatological Interpretation

Every non-eschatological interpretation fails to explain how the conclusion of the prophecy provides the time of the end of captivity that was said to have been given to Daniel. Since this was the very thing that Daniel was attempting to "understand" (verse 2; cf. 8:17; 9:23), and the motivation behind his prayer in verse 19, the non-eschatological views must find an end to the exile in temporary Jewish revolts. However, all of these were unsuccessful and ultimately led to the destruction of the city of Jerusalem, its Temple, and further Jewish exile. This, of course, offers no solution to Daniel's specific petition for his people's restoration (which included a return to Jerusalem and the rebuilding of the Temple, verses 16-19). By contrast, and in support of the futurist interpretation, verse 27 contains numerous eschatological time markers, such as "end" (*qetz* and *kalah*), "an appointed end" (*necheratzah tittak*), "cause to cease" (*yashebitim*), "until" (*'ad*). These terms indicate that this section belongs to the eschatological period. This is confirmed by the parallels between Daniel 9 and the clearly eschatological context of Daniel 12, with the final resurrection of the dead (verse 2) and an angelic order to seal up the vision until the end time (verses 9, 13). These parallels include a prayer for understanding (9:2 and 12:8), the desolation of the Jewish people (9:27 and 12:7), the three-and-one-half year period (9:27 and 12:7,11), the abolition of sacrifice (9:27 and 12:11), and the abomination of desolation (9:27 and 12:11,13).

Thus, Daniel's prayer for an end to exile will be fulfilled in the eschatological age when all of the elements of his petition are realized. Furthermore, and in direct answer to Daniel's petition concerning the Temple's rebuilding, Daniel is told that the city of Jerusalem and the Temple will be rebuilt (Daniel 9:25-26). Even though in this verse—and others—the city and Temple are predicted to again be destroyed, Daniel understood his prayer for restoration to be answered. This would be possible only if the vision contained eschatological prophecies concerning the Temple's final restoration in the end time. Therefore, Daniel was not discouraged by the words concerning the Temple's destruction after the 69 weeks and its further desecration within the seventieth week because he realized that the final goal of restoration predicted that the Temple would be anointed at the conclusion of the seventieth week (Daniel 9:24).

Let us now look in detail at the 70 weeks prophecy, first giving attention to one of the principal interpretive problems that affects Daniel's prophecy concerning the Temple.

The Postponement of the Events of the Seventieth Week

The eschatological interpretation requires a temporal interval after the sixty-ninth week, postponing the fulfillment of the events of the seventieth week until the end time.[25] The precedence for postponement was announced to Daniel by the angel Gabriel in relation to Jeremiah's 70-year fulfillment in the 70 weeks of years. All commentators accept this postponement; it is simply a question of the length of time. Moreover, temporal intervals have already appeared in chapters 2, 7, 8, and will again in chapter 11. In this light, one might expect to find a similar occurrence in chapter 9. While most Christian interpreters reject a division between the seven and 62 weeks,[26] there is no reason why there should not be one between the sixty-ninth and seventieth week, since the sixty-ninth week is set off as a distinct unit comprised of the seven and 62 weeks. This would imply in itself that the events of the seventieth week are to be treated separately. Further, the events in verse 26—"the cutting off of Messiah" and the destruction of the Temple by "the people of the prince"—are stated to occur *after* the 69 weeks. If this was intended to occur *in* the seventieth week, the text would have read here "during" or "in the midst of" (cf. Daniel's use of *hetzi*, "in the middle of," verse 27). This language implies that these events *precede* the seventieth week, but do not *immediately* follow the sixty-ninth. Therefore, a temporal interval separates the two.[27] It is also important to note that the opening word of verse 27 (*higbbir*, "confirm") is prefixed by the *waw* consecutive, a grammatical connective which indicates a close consequential relationship to a preceding verb. This use indicates that the events of verse 27 are *subsequent* to those of verse 26.

With this interpretative understanding, let us proceed to investigate the context and grammatical features of the Temple prophecy in the 70 weeks prophecy.

The Context of the Temple Prophecy in Daniel 9:27

The prophecy concerning the Temple in Daniel 9:27 concludes the prophecy of the 70 weeks (verses 24-27), which is part of the division of the book that records the visions of future earthly kingdoms (human and divine—chapters 7–12).[28] The reference to the 70 weeks and their predicted fulfillment in this text, points to the purpose for Daniel 9:24-27 in relation to the prayer of Daniel (9:3-19) following his observation of the 70 *years* prophecy in Jeremiah 25:11-12; 29:10 (Daniel 9:2). The prophecy in 9:24-27 is declared to be the divine response to Daniel's prayer as communicated by the heavenly messenger Gabriel (verses 20-23). Since the prophecy comes in answer to Daniel's prayer, it should be noted that 1) Daniel's primary petition is for divine favor toward the desolated Temple (verse 17), the people, and the city (verses 18-19); 2) Daniel uses a number of terms that will be developed in the prophetic response in verses 24-27[29]; and 3) the prayer contains vocabulary similar to the desecration terminology of Jeremiah and Ezekiel:[30] (a) the departure of Israel from covenant (verses 5,10-11,13,14-15); (b) the judgment of the curses written in the Law (verses 11,13); (c) the refusal to hear the prophets (verses 6,10), (d) the sins of the fathers (verses 6,8,16); (e) identification with the holy name (verse 19); (f) exile due to ritual rebellion (verse 7); and (g) the reproach from the nations caused by Israel's exile (verse 16).[31] These similarities are significant in that the concern of Jeremiah and Ezekiel was idolatry and desecration, the very problem faced by Daniel as a captive in exile.

Furthermore, Jeremiah's prophecy concerned the judgment of the Gentile nations, beginning with Babylon (Jeremiah 25:12-14) and extending to all historical oppressors of national Israel (verses 15-38). This judgment is also affirmed in Daniel 9:27. Being more specific, a survey of the terminology of desecration in these prophets reveals that desecration by foreign invaders (as a result of Israelite violations of covenant) form the primary concern of their discourses. Further support may be found in the association of the terms "abomination" (*shiqqutz*) and "desolation" (*shomem*) in Jeremiah and Ezekiel, which most likely influenced Daniel's cryptic construction of "desolating abomination" (*shiqqutzim meshomem*) in Daniel 9:27. If this is so, then Daniel may be attempting to download a theological summation of desecration into this expression to convey in a single thought the entire corpus of prophetic doctrine touching on any future events earmarked by this phrase. This may be helpful in explaining why Jesus, in the Olivet Discourse (Matthew 24:15; Mark 13:14), used this expression to denote the signal event that would serve as a warning of the arrival of apocalyptic fulfillment (Matthew 24:16-31; Mark 13:14-27). The point here is that Daniel's prophecy must be interpreted within the context of his contemporaries, who envisioned fulfillment in eschatological terms (see Jeremiah 31:27-37; Ezekiel 37:23-28).[32]

The Prophetic Goals of the 70 Weeks Prophecy

Equally important to the contextual setting of Daniel 9:27 are six goals given in verse 24 which help to establish the time of the fulfillment of the prophecy. These goals are: 1) "to finish the transgression," 2) "to make an end of sins," 3) "to make atonement for iniquity," 4) "to bring in everlasting righteousness," 5) "to seal up vision and prophecy," and 6) "to anoint the most holy [place]." The interpretation of these goals is germane to the consideration of postponement in the 70 weeks, for if all of these goals could be proven to have been fulfilled historically, then against the eschatological interpretation it can be argued that the 70 weeks were meant to be interpreted as being fulfilled consecutively *without* interruption.

First, it is crucial to observe those for whom this prophecy is to find fulfillment—namely, "your [Daniel's] people and your holy city" (verse 24). In other words, the fulfillment of the 70 weeks prophecy must occur with respect to national Israel and the city of Jerusalem.[33] Because such a Jewish remnant *did* return to Judah to nationally resettle the Land and to rebuild Jerusalem, this prophecy cannot be interpreted other than in terms of literal, historical fulfillment for national Israel.

Setting aside the debate over the arrangement of these goals,[34] it is important to consider the *nature* of these goals to determine whether they could have been fulfilled in past history, or if they require an eschatological fulfillment. The options here include either complete past historical fulfillment or complete eschatological fulfillment,[35] or a partial past historical and partial eschatological fulfillment. In verse 24a we find that the first three goals relate to the sins of national Israel. The terms "finish" (trangression) and "end" (sin) both look at the culmination of a condition.[36] A similar expression is found in an eschatological context in the Dead Sea document known as *Psuedo-Daniel* (4Q243-245).[37] According to the Jewish commentator Abarbanel, the condition of Israelite punishment required the 490 years of this prophecy to complete the sins committed *in addition* to the violation of the sabbatical law (cf. 2 Chronicles 36:21). Other Jewish commentators, such as Rashi and Metzudos, held that this referred to a period following the 490 years (which they believed ended with the destruction of the Second Temple), "the last exile whose purpose it will be to terminate [i.e., *to atone for*] transgression."[38] Thus, according to rabbinic tradition, the return to Jerusalem and the rebuilding of the city and Temple did not historically fulfill this goal, and it still awaits a consummation at the end of time. This final atonement (which, according to Christians, is based on the past work of the Messiah), will be effected for the national remnant of Israel only in the future (Zechariah 12:10; 13:1; Ezekiel 36:25-27; 37:23; Jeremiah 31:33-34; Isaiah 59:20-21, et. al.).[39] It is significant that in the year that the 70 weeks prophecy was given, Cyrus freed the Jews, ending their foreign captivity and their unavoidable contact with idolatry and desecration. However, although a remnant did return to Judah, idolatry and transgression continued (see Ezra 9:1-2; Nehemiah 9:2), and in fact was climaxed in the time of Jesus by the nation's rejection of His messiahship (see Acts 7:51-52). This spiritual failure revealed that this particular prophetic goal for Israel was yet unfulfilled.

The final three goals appear distinctly eschatological, as their terminology is shared by extrabiblical apocalyptic writings whose expectation of fulfillment is the end time.[40] The phrase "everlasting *righteousness*" (or better, "vindication")[41] may have in view an "age of righteousness" (see Isaiah 1:26; 11:2-5; 32:17; Jeremiah 23:5-6; 33:15-18) that resolves the theological scandal (note 9:15-16) of the former age characterized by "the rebellion" (i.e., Israel's rejection of the Messiah). Therefore, this age will be a vindication of God's promise to national Israel (Ezekiel 36:17-23), a reversal of her final judgment in the Tribulation period, and the realization of the "Messianic age" or Messianic kingdom.[42] This eschatological restoration may also be intended in the goal "to seal up the prophetic vision," which probably has the fulfillment (or "confirmation") of Jeremiah's prophecy in view.[43] However, the determining phrase is the final one: "to anoint the Holy of Holies." The Malbim says that this refers to "the Third Temple," since "it will be anointed." This statement reflects the contrast with the Second Temple, which the Mishnah records had *not* been anointed (*Yoma* 21b; compare *Tosefta Sotah* 13:2). The "anointing" refers to the consecration of the chamber that housed the Ark of the Covenant, whose presence sanctified the Temple by virtue of the *Shekinah* (the divine presence). Since neither the Ark nor the *Shekinah* were present in the Second Temple (*Yoma* 21b), rabbinic tradition held that the Ark will be revealed in the future by the Messianic king, who will also build the Third Temple (Zechariah 6:12-13). This will find future fulfillment in the reconsecrated "fourth" Temple prophesied by Ezekiel when the *Shekinah* re-enters its Holy of Holies (Ezekiel 37:26-28; 43:1-7,12—see also chapter 23).

The Structural Divisions of the 70 Weeks Prophecy

The crucial issue for interpreters of this prophecy is the resolution of the structural divisions of the 70 weeks. As we noted earlier, both conservative and critical scholarship have agreed that Gabriel's revelation to Daniel announced an extension of the 70 *years* of Jeremiah's prophecy as seventy *weeks of years*. At the outset let us notice that this extension of the 70 years is itself an example of postponement, a fact often overlooked by opponents of postponement within the 70 weeks. Therefore we have a postponement of the complete restoration promised Jeremiah until *after* the 70 years (initially because of the *past* spiritual condition of the *exiles;* see Daniel 9:5-14; Jeremiah 14:21-23; Esther), but a further postponement until *after* the seventieth week which is to occur only in the eschatological age (in view of the *present* spiritual condition of the *remnant;* see Ezra, Nehemiah, Haggai, Zechariah and the Diaspora Jewish community).[44] In this light, Grelot argues that the 490 years were a "probationary period" granted to Israel to complete the process of restoration from desolation.[45] Though a partial Judean restoration was effected on the *physical* level during this period (the return to the Land of Judah and the rebuilding of the Temple and the city of Jerusalem), Israel failed in its *spiritual* obligation to recognize and accept their Messiah. Thus, the period of desolation was continued (with the A.D. 70 destruction), and ultimate restoration (which depends upon repentance toward the Messiah) was postponed until the events of the seventieth week could be realized historically during the seven years of the Tribulation period. Let us now consider the details of verse 27, which speaks of the Temple that will exist during the Tribulation.

The Tribulation Temple

According to verses 26-27 the Temple will be both destroyed and desecrated. In the chronology of this text, *before* the seventieth week the Messiah comes and is "cut off" (put to death) and the city of Jerusalem and its Temple are destroyed in a war with "the *people* of the prince that shall come" (verse 26). Then during the seventieth week (the final one), the Temple is desecrated by an abomination brought in by "the *prince* who shall come" (verses 26-27), who will later be completely destroyed (verse 27).[46] In part, because the events of verse 27 were interpreted by Jesus in the Olivet Discourse as part of the future time of Tribulation (whose events were *not* fulfilled historically by the A.D. 70 Roman destruction of the Temple; see chapters 12 and 22), the Temple destroyed before the seventieth week must be identified as the Second (Herodian) Temple (of Jesus' day), and the one that will be desecrated at the midpoint of the seventieth week is to be the future Third Temple (Tribulation Temple). Concerning this, John F. Walvoord says:

> The scriptures indicate plainly that there will be a Temple built in the future in which Orthodox Jews will renew the ancient sacrifices prescribed by the Mosaic law. And this Temple will be built sometime before the world government takes over 3½ years before the second coming. And we're told in Daniel 9:27, as well as in other passages, that when that takes place, the Antichrist is going to stop the sacrifices and set the Temple up as a Temple for himself. We anticipate that that could be done soon; we don't know when the Temple will be built, we just know it is going to be in operation at that point when the sacrifices cease.[47]

In the New Testament the apostle Paul described in more detail this desecration and the prince that will come: "The man of lawlessness is revealed, the son of destruction, who opposes and exalts himself above every so-called god or object of worship, so that he takes his seat in the temple of God, displaying himself as being God (2 Thessalonians 2:3-4). Paul's context is the future "day of the Lord" (verse 2), the period of time encompassing the Tribulation and Millennium. We know that the events surrounding the Temple and its desecration occupy the time shortly before the return of Christ (to earth) because the "lawless one" is destroyed by the Lord at His coming (verse 8; see Daniel 9:27). The interpretation of this seems to be that the Antichrist will seek to deify himself by usurping the place of the only true God within the Temple's Holy of Holies[48] (see chapter 22).

Because of this desecration by the Antichrist some Christians have referred to this Temple as "Antichrist's Temple." This is improper, for this Temple must be holy in order to be desecrated, and is called here by Paul "the temple of God" even after its defilement (verse 4). This Temple is also called "the temple of God" by the apostle John, who describes the Jewish worship taking place there at the sacrificial altar (Revelation 11:1). John is told that the outside precinct of the Temple, known as the court of the Gentiles, will be included in the Jerusalem territory invaded by the nations (those under Antichrist) for 42 months (the last three-and-one-half years of the Tribulation period). This agrees with the time period for the abomination of desolation as recorded in Daniel 12:11, the prophecy of the international assault of Jerusalem in Zechariah 12–14, and the Olivet Discourse (Matthew 24; Mark 13; Luke 21).

Based on these texts, and especially Daniel 9:27, it is possible that this future Third Temple may be rebuilt sometime in the future as a result of the covenant made between "the prince who will come" and the Israeli government (Hebrew *rabim*, "many"). In support of this interpretation, Harold Foos, Professor of Bible at Moody Bible Institute, writing before the 1967 capture of the Temple Mount, stated: "…it is the conviction of this writer that the repossession of the Temple site and the rebuilding of the Temple with its renewed worship will be in direct consequence of the covenant that the Antichrist makes with Israel for the 'one week,' the seven years of the Tribulation period."[49] Expanding on Foos' reasons for this connection, the following may be offered to support this conclusion: 1) The Second Temple was rebuilt by the permission and power of a Gentile ruler (Cyrus), setting the precedence for the rebuilding of the Third Temple; 2) if a political power or leader could guarantee the rebuilding of the Temple, any covenant made with Israel would be expected to include this; 3) when the covenant moves from policy to persecution in the middle of the seventieth week, the Antichrist uses his political power to cause the sacrifices to cease (Daniel 9:27; 12:11) and, following the old Roman precedent of conquest, occupies it himself (Matthew 24:15; Mark 13:14; 2 Thessalonians 2:4). This could imply that he had been involved in some prior relationship with the Temple; 4) a pivotal event marked both the beginning and the end of the first 69 weeks and the interval between the end of the sixty-ninth and the beginning of the seventieth (Daniel 9:25-26). Such an event might be expected at the beginning of the seventieth week as well, especially when it would appear to mark a revival of God's direct dealing with the Nation; and 5) since the purpose of the Tribulation is to prepare Israel for the fulfillment of its promises in the Millennium (where the Temple is prominent), and the Temple suffers with the Nation during the Tribulation, its rebuilding should be connected with the beginning of the Tribulation (the signing of the covenant, Daniel 9:27). Later in this book, in chapter 22, we will examine the particulars connected with this covenant, the Temple's rebuilding, and its desecration by the Antichrist. For now, let's look at what rabbinic commentators wrote concerning Daniel's prophetic view of the Temple.

Jewish Interpretation of Daniel's Prophecy

Since the details of the 70 weeks prophecy concern the Jewish people, it is interesting and instructive to read what some of the ancient Jewish interpreters thought about the Temple in this passage. The Malbim referred the last of the restoration goals of Daniel 9:24: "to anoint the most Holy [Place]" to the Third Temple, since *Tosefta Sotah* 13:2 records that the Second Temple had not been anointed. The sages also considered this anointing of the Holy Place to take place in relation to the restoration of the *Shekinah* and the Temple vessels. *Mishnah* tractate *Yoma* 21b recorded that the Ark of the Covenant with the Tablets of the Law, the altars, and the holy vessels were not in the Second Temple. These were to be revealed through the Messianic king at the time He would build and anoint the Third Temple (see Zechariah 6:12-13). With regards to the interpretation of the 70 weeks prophecy, the rabbis also interpreted the weeks as "weeks of *years*" and saw it as having prophesied the Roman destruction of Jerusalem. The seventieth week is not entirely included in that event. Because it predicts the destruction of the Romans, its final statement is retained as a future event.

The Jewish chronological record of Rabbi Jose, known as the *Seder Olam Rabbah*, preserves the oldest rabbinic tradition for interpreting the 70 weeks. In chapter 28 of this work the first seven weeks are related to the exile and return, the next 62 weeks are in the Land, and the final week predicts a period partially spent in the Land and partially spent in exile. Therefore, the seventieth week could include events that occurred *after* A.D. 70.

According to Abarbanel, the Israelites were required to be punished for 490 years in view of the sins they committed *in addition* to their violation of the sabbatical law (see 2 Chronicles 36:21). Other Jewish commentators such as Rashi and Metzudos held that this prophecy referred to a period following the 490 years (which they believed ended with the destruction of the Second Temple), the last exile whose purpose it will be to terminate [i.e., *to atone for*] transgression of the Jewish Nation. Rabbi Hersh Goldwurm, summarizing their views, observes, "Thus, seventy weeks have been decreed upon your people and your city [for relative well-being] after which the Jews will receive the remainder of their punishment in the last exile, whose purpose will be to terminate [i.e., atone for] transgression." One reason for this interpretation is because these commentators believed that Jewish suffering would atone for their transgression. Abarbanel noted that the return to Jerusalem and even the building of the Second Temple did not bring the expected redemption nor atone for past sins, since it was itself a part of the continued exile. He held that the real and complete redemption was still far off in history, awaiting a future fulfillment according to Daniel's prophecy.

According to *Ibn Ezra*, the seventieth week (verse 27) was not included in the 62 weeks of verse 26. He thought it was not counted because of the turmoil and unrest preceding the destruction of the city, during which "an anointed" (Hebrew, *mashiach*) was killed. He arrived at 70 weeks by adding the seven weeks of verse 25 to the 62 of verse 26. This may explain his difficulty in reconciling verse 27 with verse 26. However, Rashi has no difficulty identifying "the people of the prince who is to come" as the Romans (i.e., the legions of Vespasian and Titus). Both Rashi and Rambam are examples of those who ascribe the breaking of the covenant (with the Jewish rulers ["great ones"] rather than "many") to a broken promise of the Romans. However, none of the sages who hold this opinion provide any historical source in support. The Jerusalem Talmud (*Ta'anit* 4:5) apparently attempts to connect this with the Romans substituting pigs for the lambs that were supposed to be used for the daily sacrifice. It states that at that very hour the sacrifices were stopped, and the Temple was destroyed immediately after. Some rabbis believed that the abomination that brings desolation (verse 27) referred to Hadrian's erection of a pagan temple on the site of the Jewish Temple after the Bar-Kokhba war (e.g., Rashi). Even so, when attempting to interpret the final destruction of the desecrator of the Temple in verse 27, Rashi resorted to an eschatological interpretation and stated, "the end of the Romans who destroyed Jerusalem will be a total destruction through the promised Messiah," and the "desolation decreed" for the city is "after the final wars waged by the Messianic king and the war of Gog and Magog."[50]

The Key to the Prophetic Puzzle

Daniel searched the prophets and prayed for an answer to the mystery that surrounded the destruction and desolation of the Temple of his day. The answer he found—both in his study and from divine revelation—was that the times of the Gentiles would not end until the Gentile nations were brought together in an international empire headed by a coming wicked ruler (Daniel 2:28-45; 7:8-28; 11:36-45; 12:1-12). Daniel was told that this would happen in the "latter days" (Daniel 8:28) and "the time of the end" (Daniel 12:4,9), and that with the final act of desecration against the Temple would come the final judgment of God against the Gentile powers that supressed both the Jewish people and their realization of God's promises (Daniel 12:1-12; see also 9:27). He left to us this key to the prophetic puzzle so that we who live closer than Daniel to the times of fulfillment might know what to expect and have confidence in the outworking of God's purpose (Daniel 12:4,10). And it remains for us to follow Daniel's example and search the prophecies and pray (Daniel 9:2-3).

In the next chapters, let us consider how Jesus and the New Testament writers followed Daniel's prophecy and left to us a more sure word concerning God's plan for the coming Last Days Temple.

CHAPTER 12

Predictions in the Gospels

Jesus and the Temple

Jesus, like virtually all other first-century Jews, assumed that there would still be a Temple. . . . Judaism eventually had to give up the idea of returning to the sacrificial worship of God, and Christianity eventually came to see Jesus' death as the complete replacement of the Temple cult. But in Jesus' day these ideas lay in the future. Jesus had either to accept the Temple, oppose it or reform it. He seems to have accepted it, but to have thought that it would be replaced in the new age.[1]

In seeking to understand what the New Testament actually teaches about the subject of the Temple, it is important to begin with Christianity's central figure, Jesus, [2] and His views toward the Temple as recorded in the four Gospels. It has been claimed that in the Gospels, Jesus, as both a Jewish revolutionary and the founder of Christianity, is presented as seeking to overthrow the institution of the Temple and replace its corrupted materialistic ritual with the pure spiritual worship of His church. The picture usually painted is that of a Jesus whose anger was against the worthless sacrifices of apostate Judaism and who pronounced His curse against the Temple as the chief symbol of that old order. On the other hand, the Gospels portray Jesus as an Orthodox Jew with a lifelong devotion to the Temple even calling it "My Father's house" (Luke 2:49; John 2:16).

In chapter 7 we surveyed the attitude Jesus' disciples had toward the Temple after the church came into being. There I concluded that Jesus' followers maintained their Jewish reverence toward the Temple as a legitimate place of worship. In this light, Oxford University Professor of Exegesis E.P. Sanders notes: "After his death and resurrection, his followers continued to worship in the Temple. In Acts, Paul was arrested for trying to take a Gentile into the Temple. Such activities are compatible with Jesus' view...."[3]

But what about Jesus Himself? What exactly was His view of the Temple? Let's see what we can find out by focusing first on Jesus' own involvement with the Temple as a Jew, and then by considering three of His statements about the Temple: the so-called "cleansing of the Temple," His prediction of the Temple's destruction, and His mention of Daniel's "abomination of desolation" in the Temple in His Olivet Discourse.

Jesus' Place Within Judaism

The recent resurgence in Jesus Research[4] has brought a renewed realization to the Christian church that Jesus, as a Jew, was an integral part of, rather than apart from, the Judaism of His time.[5] While this does not imply that either Jesus or the later writers of the New Testament were products of any particular sect of Judaism, it may be assumed that He shared the same reverence and concerns for the Temple as other observant Jews of the time. Historical evidence reveals that until the middle of the first century, the Temple and the priesthood were accepted by both Jews and Jewish Christians solely as religious and spiritual institutions.[6] Research has also attested to the prevalence of predictions about the Temple's eventual destruction—so much so that many religious Jews expected such a destruction (partly because of the past history of Gentile domination, and partly because of the belief that a new Temple was needed).[7] These facts place Jesus' devotion to the Temple, as well as His pronouncements of its destruction, in the context of common action and attitude toward the end of the Second Temple period. This is further confirmed by a survey of Jesus' associations with the Temple throughout His lifetime, which will be the focus of the rest of this chapter.

Jesus' Early Life and the Temple

The Gospel record of Jesus' birth includes the account of His presentation at the Temple (Luke 2:21-38). The text is careful to note the strictly observant conduct of Jesus' family: his circumcision on the eighth day (Luke 2:21) according to the Law (Leviticus 12:3; see also Philippians 3:5), and his mother Mary's ritual *miqve* immersion (Luke 2:22) according to the purification laws (Leviticus 12:4-6). These acts of ritual devotion were followed by Jesus' dedication in the Temple (Luke 2:22), required by Exodus 13:2 (which is cited in Luke 2:23). This dedication was accompanied by the prescribed sacrifice (as noted by the citation of Leviticus 5:11 in Luke 2:24). Luke paints for us not only a picture of a religious family, but of a typically Orthodox family who held the Temple in high esteem and ordered their lives in relation to its services. This fact was underscored by Luke's words in verse 39: "They...performed everything according to the Law of the Lord...." It should not be surprising, then, that the next event recorded by Luke is the family's Passover pilgrimage to the Temple (Luke 2:41-49). Luke emphasizes the family's obedience to the requirement that families make an annual pilgrimage to Jerusalem by stating that this was indeed performed "every year" (verse 41).[8] Luke specifically mentions the visit during Jesus' twelfth year because Jesus was performing the Jewish *mitzvot* connected with arriving at the age of puberty (verse 42),[9] although according to the Law, He would have made such a pilgrimage to the Temple three times a year for the feasts of Yom Kippur ("Day of Atonement"), Pesach ("Passover"), and Shavu'ot ("Pentecost") (Exodus 23:14).

Luke's purpose in the remainder of this account (verses 46-49) is to reveal Jesus' early Messianic consciousness through a contrast between His earthly parents and His heavenly Father (see verse 49). Luke also mentions that Jesus spent several days after Passover in the synagogue (located within the Temple precinct). Here we find Jesus sitting at the feet of the rabbis, exchanging questions in the rabbinical tradition. When found and questioned by His parents Miriam ("Mary") and Yosef ("Joseph") about His continued presence in the

Temple, Jesus replies—in His first recorded words in the Gospels—"I had to be in My Father's house." This statement attests to Jesus' affirmation of the Temple as the house of God (Hebrew, *Beit 'elohim*), a term He continued to use throughout His life (see John 2:16). In addition we see in Luke 2:49 Jesus' declaration that the Temple was the place where He "had to be." The Greek term *dei* ("it is necessary") is used by Luke repeatedly in his Gospel to distinguish key situations critical to Jesus' Messianic ministry.[10] If we accept that the point of His mission here is to identify with His Father's *house* (a word missing in the original text),[11] then this phrase not only indicates that the Temple was an acceptable place of worship and teaching for Jesus (as well as revealing His filial relationship with God as His Father), but that as Messiah He was connected with the Temple as the One who would one day restore its glory in His Millennial kingdom (Jeremiah 3:17; Zechariah 6:13; 14:16).

The Testing of Jesus at the Temple

We can also read about Jesus' attitude toward the Temple in the Gospel accounts about His testing in the Judean desert. This took place at the onset of His public ministry at age 30 and it appears in greatest detail in Matthew 4:1-11 and Luke 4:1-13 (see also Mark 1:12-13).[12] The parallels in these accounts with historic Israel suggest that the writer's purpose was to contrast the testing of Israel in the wilderness with that of Jesus—He as Messiah succeeded where the Nation failed.[13] In the second of these tests (Matthew 4:5-7), the scene is set in the "holy city" (Jerusalem).[14] Luke places this test last (Luke 4:9-13), possibly because he wanted to climax his account in this city where the final test of Jesus' earthly life—the cross—would take place. The specific place of testing is the highest point (literally, "the wing") of the Temple. This place has been identified as either the area on the very top of the Temple itself, where wing-shaped protrusions prevented birds from landing and defiling the Temple's façade, a high Temple gate, or the Royal Porch on the southeastern corner ("wing" = "pinnacle") of the Temple complex, which presented the greatest height/depth ratio in relation to the ravine of the Kidron Valley below.[15] Some have attempted to rule out that Luke was talking about the Temple itself, because Jesus, not being a Levite, would not have approached this area.[16] However, this depends on how literally one takes this transportation to the Temple. Even so, had the Temple not held sanctity there would have been little reason for it to have been chosen as a specific place of Messianic testing. This is confirmed by the fact that Psalm 91:11-12, which is cited (from the Septuagint) in both accounts (Matthew 4:6;

Luke 4:10-11), refers to divine assistance through angelic intervention. Since the Temple is where God's presence was manifested, the assumption is that this test must also take place at the Temple in order for Jesus to demonstrate His claim to a unique relationship with God. There is a Jewish tradition that states the Messiah will stand on the roof of the Temple (*Pesiqta Rabbati* 36.2 [162a]), perhaps as a sign of His Messianic status. If this late text can be adduced in this case, then the idea is that Jesus is being tempted to prematurely and independently assert His messiahship by a dramatic display of power. However, this does not explain the citation from Psalm 91, so a better understanding is that Jesus is being tempted to prove His relationship to God by casting Himself into God's protective care (jumping from the highest point). As one commentator has observed: "The temple is a locale that pictures God's closeness. It is where he is to be found as a refuge of protection....Surely if God will rescue anyone, he will do so at the temple where he is said to dwell."[17]

There are more scriptures that reveal Jesus' positive regard for the Temple, but they are recorded in contexts not related to the Temple. Let's look at three of them, and see what we can learn about Jesus' respect for the Temple.

Jesus' Defense Based on the Temple

In Matthew 12:1-8 (see also Mark 2:23-28 and Luke 6:1-5),[18] the Pharisees accuse Jesus and His disciples of violating the Sabbath by picking and eating grains of wheat (verses 1-2). This was an allowable act (see Deuteronomy 23:25; Ruth 2:2-3), but forbidden on the Sabbath (see Exodus 20:8-11), since no work was to be done on that day. The act of "picking" grain constituted "harvesting," which later rabbinic *halakhah* specifically listed as one of 39 kinds of work that violated the Sabbath. Some have attempted to argue on the basis of new evidence that the word here was actually "rubbing," which constituted "husking," an act permitted on the Sabbath under certain conditions (see Babylonian Talmud, *Sabbath* 128a).[19] However, if Jesus and His disciples were not technically breaking the Sabbath, His subsequent defense concerning the nature of the Sabbath would have been unnecessary.

Jesus' defense for His actions in Matthew 12:3-6 is based on four arguments: 1) the precedent of King David and the sacred bread; 2) the ritual service of the Temple priests on the Sabbath; 3) the priority of compassion (Hosea 6:6); and 4) the purpose of the Sabbath. In making His case, Jesus employs a form of argument known in later rabbinic debate as *Qal va-homer*[20] ("minor and major"). This hermeneutical device reasons that what applies in a less important case

(*Qal*= "minor") will certainly apply in a more important case (*homer* = "major"). By this method Jesus will argue for the validity of profaning the Sabbath in accord with established Jewish *halakhah,* which allowed for exceptions to the general law.

This appears in the first portion of Jesus' defense (in Matthew 12:4-5), which looks to the historical record of King David and his troops entering the House of God (the Tabernacle), possibly on the Sabbath,[21] to eat the "consecrated bread"[22] (1 Samuel 21:3-7). Even though this act usurped the exclusive use of the bread by the priests, David was justified in doing this to preserve the life of the men under his charge, for the laws of hospitality and saving a life were accepted exceptions to the general law (Mishnah, *Sanhedrin* 4:5). Jesus argued that healing on the Sabbath took precedence for the same reason (see in this same context Matthew 12:12-13; see also Luke 6:9).

Jesus' second argument offers another exception based on the command in Numbers 28:9-10, which permitted "the priests in the Temple" to perform the sacrificial service, and as a result "break the Sabbath" yet remain "innocent" (Matthew 12:5). The purpose of this reference is to illustrate the principle of one act superceding another introduced in the account concerning King David. Because the importance of the Temple's service outweighed the importance of the Sabbath, its work did not produce a violation. To complete the connection between the Temple exception and the overriding principle of saving a life, Jesus, in Matthew 12:7, cites Hosea 6:6: "I desire compassion, and not a sacrifice," concluding, "if you had known what this means...you would not have condemned the innocent" (that is, Jesus and His disciples). Just such an interpretation was proposed a century later by Judaism's leading figure of the time, Rabbi Akiba: "If punishment for murder sets aside the Temple service, which itself in turn supercedes the Sabbath, how much more should the duty of saving life supercede the Sabbath laws" (Mekilta de Rabbi Ishmael on Exodus 31:13). Jesus' application of the *Qal va-homer* principle was similar: If David and his men could break the Sabbath laws to preserve their lives, and the Temple priests could break the Sabbath laws because of a higher principle—a principle in which compassion supercedes even sacrifice—then how much more was it appropriate for Jesus and His disciples, who were "hungry" and in need of preserving their lives, to follow this already established and scripturally condoned precedent.

Yet, one problem remains. In verse 6, Jesus said, "I say to you, that something greater than the temple is here." This has been taken as Jesus' own declaration that He is superior to the Temple and therefore replaces it. Therefore, it has been assumed that it was as if He were saying, "No longer will sacrifices be valid, for I will be the final sacrifice and end any need for the Temple and the Law" (represented by the Sabbath). One objection to this interpretation is that the comparative adjective "greater" (Greek, *meizon*) is neuter ("something") rather than masculine ("someone").[23] However, advocates of this position counter that the reference can still be to Jesus, since the neuter can be used to refer to persons when some *quality* is being stressed rather than the individual per se.[24] In this case, the Messianic status (or authority) of Jesus would be that quality in view, a fact said to be supported by the reference to Jesus as the "Son of Man" in Matthew 12:8. Therefore, the use of *Qal va-homer* with this interpretation argues that if the Temple supersedes the Sabbath, even more so does the Messiah, since, as verse 8 states, He is "Lord of the Sabbath."

However, if this were Jesus' argument it would be inadequate, for although Jesus might be exonerated as Messiah, His disciples would not, for they could not claim such a superior status. Rather, the "something greater" that Jesus has in mind is in harmony with the whole of His argument concerning the value of human life. This point has been made by Steven Notley, Assistant Professor of New Testament and Early Christianity at the Jerusalem University College: "If one is able out of necessity, to set aside the Sabbath for the needs of the Temple, then how much more can one set aside the Sabbath in cases of human need? This is not a negation of the prohibition, but a clarification of the relative importance of human need and the Sabbath."[25] Accepting this understanding, Jesus' "something greater" is the needs of His disciples, whose lives, created in the image of God, have a higher priority than laws. This is the meaning of Jesus' conclusion in verse 8—"For the Son of Man is Lord of the Sabbath"—which is clarified in Mark's account with the explanation: "The Sabbath was made for man, and not man for the Sabbath" (Mark 2:27). Matthew, however, also supports this interpretation by adding, after Jesus' conclusion, an account of Jesus healing a man in the synagogue (which occurred on the same day that Jesus and His disciples ate grain on the Sabbath—verses 11-13). Here Jesus justifies His action by the same *Qal va-homer* principle, comparing the accepted action of saving livestock on the Sabbath to saving a human life:[26] "Of how much more value then is a man than a sheep! So, then, it is lawful to do good on the Sabbath" (verse 12).

The proper interpretation of this passage removes the concept that Jesus (and the authors of the Gospels) thought of Himself as replacing the Temple.

Rather, as Northwestern College Professor Michael O. Wise observes in this context, "the Gospel writers thought of the Temple as the special place of God's presence."[27] If Jesus did not accept the Temple and its service as legitimate, His *Qal va-homer* argument would have failed, for His comparison in these cases were with objects of sanctity. It is only because the Temple, its priests, the vessels (represented here by the shewbread), and the services are holy that this case can be argued affirmatively. In fact, in the 1 Samuel account we read that David and his men were permitted to receive the shewbread only if they were ceremonially clean (1 Samuel 21:4). Jesus' statement that "something [is] greater than the temple" and His application of Hosea 6:6 ("compassion and not a sacrifice") cannot be construed to teach replacement through a supercession of the Temple or rejection through a spiritualization of the sacrificial system. Instead, it is an appeal to the higher priority of human life, in which relationship (to one's fellow man) is elevated above ritual (see 1 Samuel 15:22; Psalm 40:6; 50:7-15; 51:16; 69:30-31; Proverbs 21:3).

Jesus on the Sanctity of the Temple

A second incidental remark by Jesus that demonstrates His esteem for the Temple is found in Matthew 5:33-37 and 23:16-21. In these texts, Jesus targets a specific practice that had developed during the late Second Temple period—a practice of substituting, in oaths, lesser objects related to God rather than swearing by the ineffable name of God itself (see, for example, 1 Samuel 14:39). The intention in these substitutions (which had multiplied over time) was to avoid suffering the consequences that would accompany taking the Lord's name in vain (Exodus 20:7; see also Leviticus 19:12; Deuteronomy 19:16-19) if they were unable to fulfill their vow. In Matthew 5:33-37, which is part of the Sermon on the Mount (Matthew 5–7), Jesus stresses the sanctity of oaths and states that the threat of perjury cannot be removed or minimalized by the ploy of substitution. In illustrating His argument He lists examples of some substitutions, including the heavenly Temple ("heaven...the throne of God," Matthew 5:34) and, by circumlocution, the earthly Temple ("the earth...the footstool of His feet," Matthew 5:35; see also Ezekiel 43:7). The point here, based on the warning against ritual presumption in Isaiah 66:1, is that these things have just as great a sanctity as the divine name because they are holy places where God dwells.[28] In the similar text of Matthew 23:16-21, Jesus is engaged in debate with the Pharisees concerning this same issue of substitutionary vows. Jesus again makes reference to some of these substitutions, naming in this instance the Temple (verses 16-17,21), its "gold"[29] (verses 16-17), its "offering" (verses 18-19), and "the altar" (verse 20). The Greek word used here for Temple is *naos* (rather than *heiros*) because this term may distinguish the Temple proper (the Holy Place and especially the Holy of Holies), as opposed to the larger Temple complex (see Luke 1:22).[30] Jesus goes on to say that the Temple sanctifies the gold, the altar, and the offerings, and climaxes His argument by saying, "He who swears by the temple, swears by both the temple and by Him [God] who dwells within it" (verse 21). Jesus presents here an elevated perspective of the Temple as having a unique sanctity that is able to impute sanctity on whatever lesser things are associated with it (its monetary reserves, the sacred vessels, and the sacrificial offering) by virtue of its association with the divine presence. If Jesus had thought otherwise He would have been in agreement with His opponents, who said, "Whoever swears by the temple, that is nothing" (verse 16).

Jesus' Payment of the Temple Tax

A third positive inference to the Temple may be seen in Matthew 17:24-27, where Jesus affirms the validity of paying the yearly Temple tax. The two-drachmas tax (about two days' wages) was levied on all free Jewish males between the ages of 20 and 50 in support of the Temple and its services. This practice originated with the half-shekel levy at the annual census (Exodus 30:11-16).[31] Jews in the Diaspora also paid this tax in order to demonstrate their solidarity with the Temple and the Land. This tax, then, is strictly a Jewish religious obligation rather than a civil tax imposed by Rome.[32]

In Matthew 17:24 we see Simon Peter questioned by Temple tax-collectors about Jesus' payment of this tax. Apparently Jesus' public disputations with the religious authorities led some to question His loyalty to Judaism, and the Temple tax was the standard evidence of such fidelity. Jesus indeed proved His loyalty to the Temple by paying of the tax for both Himself and Peter (verse 27). However, the occasion also offered Jesus the opportunity to test Peter concerning His Messianic status (as in Matthew 12:4 and Luke 6:4). He said, in essence, "If I am the Son of God I should not be taxed for the upkeep of My Father's house. And as King Messiah, I am at least on par with the priests and Levites, who apply such an exemption to themselves" (see Mishnah, *Shekalim* 1:3-4). Moreover, this exemption should rightly extend to Jesus' disciples, who belong to His royal Messianic family as "sons" of the kingdom (verse 26). Nevertheless, Jesus paid the tax. If He thought the Temple was corrupt, He could have refused to pay the tax (as did many Jews after the Romans later confiscated the tax in support of their own pagan temples). However, His willingness to pay shows Jesus regarded the Temple as a legitimate institution properly supported by the Jewish Nation. Matthew's inclusion of this account would have also encouraged his Jewish-Christian audience to continue paying the tax despite the opposition they received from the Temple's officials ("the priests...the temple guard, and the Sadducees"—see Acts 4:1-3). In addition, the fact that the money for Jesus' and Peter's payment of the tax came through miraculous means (verse 27) may further imply heavenly approval of this taxation.

Having surveyed Jesus' positive attitude toward the Temple for background purposes, let us now look at the classic "Cleansing of the Temple" event, in which it is claimed Jesus judged the Temple to be unfit and consequently prophetically proclaimed its destruction.

Jesus' Cleansing of the Temple

Critical scholarship has questioned the historicity of the "Cleansing of the Temple" incident on the grounds that the Mishnah (*Berakot* 9:5) states that the selling of animals for sacrificial purposes was not permitted *within* the Temple walls.[33] Yet the Gospels clearly state that this selling took place within the Temple (John 2:15). Moreover, if such a violent confrontation took place on the Temple Mount, it would have been considered not just a religious demonstration but a political threat, and would have brought an immediate arrest by either the Temple guards or the Roman authorities. Since this did not occur, the critics insist that this incident must be a later redactional insertion. However, this objection can be put to rest in light of the archaeological evidence from the extensive excavations done at the southwest and southern corners of the Temple Mount under the direction of Benjamin Mazar and Meir Ben-Dov (1968–1977).[34] Their work has confirmed certain details in the Gospel account, such as the presence of large animals in the halls of the money changers (see John 2:14).[35] They also have shown that a smaller Temple market was isolated inside the Royal *Stoa* (Hebrew, *Chanuyot*) and did not spread out over into the Court of the Gentiles.[36] In view of this placement of the market *inside* the Temple complex, yet removed from the actual Temple precincts, it can now be understood that Jesus' clash with the Temple vendors was a fairly modest incident, and for this reason permitted His daily return to the Temple precincts to address the Temple crowds (Luke 19:47; see also Matthew 21:14). This location also is thought to approximate the position of the prophet Jeremiah "in the gate of the LORD's house" (Jeremiah 7:2) when, during First Temple times, he gave his "Temple sermon" (Jeremiah 7:1–8:3). This lends support to the interpretation that Jesus was following prophetic precedent in His actions (which agrees with His citation from this very account in Jeremiah).

The Incident as a Sign of Divine Rejection of the Temple

Perhaps no text in the Gospels outside of those predicting the Temple's destruction (Matthew 23:37–24:2; Luke 19:42-44; Mark 13:2) has been used more often to demonstrate an anti-Temple attitude on behalf of Jesus than this "Cleansing[37] of the Temple" account. Recorded in each of the Synoptic Gospels and the Gospel of John (Matthew 21:12-13; Mark 11:15-17; Luke 19:45-46; John 2:14-22),[38] this public demonstration by Jesus in the Temple precinct (accompanied by citations from the prophets and followed by His reply, "Destroy this temple...") provoked questions from Jesus' opponents about His view of the Temple. Indeed, when Jesus was put on trial, His words "destroy this temple" became the grounds for accusations by false witnesses that Jesus had hostile intentions toward the Temple (Matthew 26:61; 27:40; Mark 14:58; 15:29). This has led some commentators to believe that these witnesses were correct, despite the facts that they are clearly called *false* witnesses and the Gospel accounts fully explain Jesus' statement as having no reference to the Jerusalem Temple. Furthermore, because in Mark's Gospel the "cleansing of the Temple" pericope appears between the report of Jesus' "cursing of the fig tree" (Mark 11:12-14,20-21) and the explanation of this miracle, some see the "cleansing" as an "acted parable of judgment" against the Temple, symbolized by the fig tree.[39] However, this case is weakened by Matthew's placement of the account about the fig tree (Matthew 21:18-22) *after* the account of the "cleansing of the Temple" (Matthew 21:12-17).[40]

Various opinions concerning Jesus' motive in the "cleansing" have been offered. These include a formal declaration of opposition to the existence of the Temple, a symbolic enactment of the Temple's destruction, an act of taking possession of the Temple, and an attempt to signal the permanent cessation of the sacrificial system by the temporary interruption of daily sacrifices.[41] In all of these opinions, Jesus is thought to be demonstrating in some way the divine rejection of the ceremonial system embodied in the Temple.

Another group of commentators believe that the problem is not the Temple, but the behavior of those who had assumed control and maintenance of the

Temple.[42] In this interpretation, Jesus is attacking Sadducean enterprise or making a point concerning the priority of worship over commerce. Support for this view is based on Stephen's Temple sermon (Acts 7), in which there appears an abrupt shift in verse 51 from a historical review of the rebellious attitude exhibited by the Israelites who possessed the Tabernacle and First Temple (verses 44-50) to the rebellious attitude displayed by those who possessed the Second Temple (verses 51-53). While this discussion will not permit me to engage these views, my argument of an alternate interpretation (see below) will interact with some of these views. Let us analyze, then, this event in its context and in the light of Jesus' citations from the prophets (Jeremiah 7:11 and Isaiah 56:7), and see what this passage may actually reveal about Jesus' attitude toward the Temple.

Jesus' Citations from the Prophets

In order to understand the purpose of Jesus' actions in the Temple market it is necessary to understand how He interpreted the event based on His citations from the prophets. The prophets were a guiding source for Jesus' public demonstrations, since He identified Himself as the last of the prophets sent to reveal the Nation's spiritual defection (see Matthew 23:29-35; Luke 13:33). Jesus' application of prophetic texts are revealed selectively (and differently) by the Gospel writers in order to emphasize specific aspects of Jesus' theological purpose in His actions and words. For example, the Synoptic accounts in Matthew and Luke both include the composite citation, "My house shall be called a house of prayer; but you are making it a robbers' den," (Matthew 21:13; Luke 19:46).[43] The second part of this citation is a clear reference to Jeremiah's Temple sermon inasmuch as the expression "den of robbers" occurs only in this text.[44] In John's citations, Jesus alludes to Isaiah 56:7 (in the Septuagint version) by using simply the phrase "My Father's house," but adding the phrase "a house of merchandise" in place of "a robber's den" (John 2:16). This is a word play on "house" similar to that in the Synoptic Gospels in contrasting "house" to "den." John's use in verse 16 of the word "merchandise" offers an allusion to Zechariah 14:21, which literally reads: "And there will no longer be a *Canaanite* in the house of the LORD of hosts in that day." If John is alluding to this text, he has taken the Hebrew word *kᵉna'ani* metaphorically to mean "trader," which is an alternate Hebrew meaning.[45] This allusion parallels the Synoptic Gospel's use of Isaiah 56:7 with Zechariah's reference, where in each case the eschatological Temple is the context. The point here is that in this future day of Israel's restoration, there will no longer be a need to have animals certified as ceremonially pure or impure money exchanged, since all will be pure (Zechariah 14:20-21). Therefore, there will be no need for the kind of merchants or traders Jesus complained about. The problem was not what they were doing (which was required by Old Testament law), but the reminder they gave for why they had to be doing it: namely, Israel's lack of spiritual renewal because of its lack of national repentance. John further adds some words from Psalm 69:9 that came to the disciples' minds at this time: "Zeal for Thy house will consume me" (John 2:17). This addition emphasizes Jesus' exceptional concern to maintain the sanctity of the Temple.

The things Jesus said in the Temple cleansing incident had specific theological purpose; that's where we will turn our attention now.

Jeremiah, Jesus, and the Temple

Jesus' citation from Jeremiah's Temple sermon (Jeremiah 7:1–8:3) has provoked numerous suggestions as to the significance of Jeremiah's influence on the thoughts of Jesus and the disciples.[46] As noted earlier, Jeremiah spoke against those defiling the Temple while standing within its precincts (Jeremiah 7:2; 26:2). Did this influence Jesus when He entered the Temple market to identify himself with Jeremiah and to adopt His posture as a prophet, rebuking the abuses of the Second Temple even as Jeremiah had rebuked the abuses of the First Temple? It is interesting that Jeremiah is one of the names the disciples mentioned in response to Jesus' question, "Who do people say that the Son of Man is?" (Matthew 16:13-14; Mark 8:27-28; Luke 9:18-19).[47] Perhaps this opinion developed because Jesus' public actions, such as the incident with the money changers, resembled those of Jeremiah, the prophet most famous for his prophecies concerning Jerusalem and the Temple's destruction.[48] Several parallels between Jeremiah chapters 7 and 26 and Matthew 23:29–24:2 make this suggestion plausible:[49]

1. *The parallel of "sending the prophets."* This phrase appears frequently in Jeremiah (Jeremiah 7:25; 25:4-7; 26:4-6; 29:18-19; 35:15; 44:4-5) and also appears in Matthew 23:34. In Jeremiah 7:25 and 26:4-6 prophets are shown to have been sent to urge the people to repent, but to no avail. Thus Jeremiah was sent a final warning before the destruction of the city and the Temple. In the same way, Jesus refers to His disciples as "prophets" whom He is sending (see Matthew 5:12; 10:16) to a people who have previously rejected the succession of prophets before them (see Jeremiah 7:25-26; Matthew 23:29-34).

2. *The parallel of the "murder of the prophets."* The specific statement that the prophets were "murdered," as opposed to the more general persecution of the prophets,[50] also links the accounts in Jeremiah and Matthew. In Jeremiah's Temple sermon the people are told "do not shed innocent blood in this place [the Temple]" (Jeremiah 7:6). In Jeremiah 26:15 Jeremiah applies the term to himself, warning those who reacted to his sermon that if they kill him the priests, prophets, and people will bring upon themselves "innocent blood." In spite of his denunciation, the people still demand his death in the Temple.[51] In like manner, in Matthew 23:29-37, Jesus applies the accusation of murdering the prophets to the Pharisees, who are said to continue the heinous tradition (verses 29,30,31), and to be planning for Jesus Himself to be their next victim (verse 34). In addition, the coupling of the term "righteous blood" and "upon you" occurs only in Matthew 23:35 and in Jeremiah 26:15.

3. *The parallel of prophetic judgment against the Temple.* Jeremiah 7:4-10 reveals that the people of Judah, when confronted with their sins, felt they were safe from judgment because they were trusting in the inviolability of the Temple. Therefore, they repeated the superlative defense: "The Temple of the LORD, the Temple of the LORD, the Temple of the LORD" (verse 4), even though they had committed all kinds of evil against the Temple themselves (verse 9).[52] Jeremiah then reminded the people that the destruction of the site of the Tabernacle in Shiloh (verses 12-14) was proof that the Lord could carry out His judicial threat on Jerusalem by abandoning it and its Temple. Matthew 23:38 contains similar wording: "Behold, your house is being left to you desolate!"

These parallels serve to demonstrate that Jesus had, in effect, put on the prophetic mantle of Jeremiah when He entered the Temple market, and that He expected His disciples (and especially the Temple personnel), by His citation from Jeremiah's Temple sermon, to recall Jeremiah's rebuke and to count on violent repercussions if the people continued in the path of their predecessors, who had rejected Jeremiah's warnings. Furthermore, in harmony with Jeremiah's position as the final prophet before the sentence of judgment was executed, Jesus' actions establish Him as the last hope for the rebellious Nation before the divine verdict would be poured out (Matthew 21:28–22:14). In addition, just as Jesus identified with Jeremiah's prophetic announcement of Israel's judgment, He also identified with Jeremiah's prophetic proclamation of Israel's restoration (Jeremiah 30:1–33:26). However, Jesus does not cite Jeremiah's restoration prophecies because none of them contained an explicit statement with regard to the Temple.

Instead, He chose to cite the prophet Isaiah—in whose proclamations the eschatological Temple figures prominently in a portrait of proper worship.

Jesus and Isaiah's Eschatological Temple

Jesus' citation from Isaiah 56:7 reveals that He maintains His positive attitude toward the Temple even in the midst of this negative incident (Matthew 21:13; Mark 11:17; Luke 19:46). In citing Isaiah, Jesus affirmed that a central purpose in God's plan for the Temple was that it be a house of prayer for all the nations. The concept of the Temple as a place toward which even Gentile proselytes[53] would direct their prayers was first revealed in Solomon's Temple dedication address (1 Kings 8:41-43). The prophets also envisioned a day when all the nations would worship at the Temple Mount (see chapter 10). Jesus agreed with this design of the Temple's mission, and it is in this light that Jesus' statements in these parallel accounts should be understood. In this case, Jesus' invective is leveled against the present conditions, which prevented the fulfillment of the original spiritual and eschatological function of the Temple for the world. Therefore, Jesus' intent in clearing the Temple market of those who represented the imperfect state of the Second Temple was to draw attention to the prophetic restoration ideal—the Final Temple. This is brought out in Matthew and Luke's abbreviated wording, which contrasts "house of prayer" with "robbers' den." Even though Matthew and Luke omit Isaiah's words "for all the nations," we know from Mark's inclusion of those words that Jesus' purpose was to describe what the Temple should be as opposed to what it had become.[54]

Jesus' focus on Israel's mission to be "a light to the nations" (Isaiah 42:6), which can be properly fulfilled only when the eschatological Temple is built and "all the nations stream to it" to learn God's Word and ways (Isaiah 2:2-3), may have been prompted by His proximity (in this encounter) to the Court of the Gentiles. Jesus' partial statement of Gentile involvement in the Temple ritual understands the fuller content of the verse: "Also the foreigners who join themselves to the LORD...even those I will bring to My holy mountain, and make them joyful in My house of prayer. Their burnt offerings and their sacrifices will be acceptable on My altar; for My house will be called a house of prayer for all the peoples" (Isaiah 56:6-7). Jesus, as the Messiah, is the One who will inaugurate the Messianic age and build the Messianic Temple in which this international worship will be realized. However, in His day the very presence of the *soreg* (a barrier) with warning inscriptions forbidding Gentile passage past the

Court of the Gentiles—on pain of death—stood as an obvious sign that this ideal was far from realized.[55]

Again, if John 2:16 is alluding to Zechariah 14:21, there is additional support for setting Jesus' actions and statements within an eschatological context, for the context in Zechariah 14 is that the Messiah is reigning (verse 9), the last days' Temple has been built (verse 10), the Gentile nations are coming to worship the Lord on the Temple Mount (verses 16-17), and even the commonest of vessels in Jerusalem are consecrated as "Holy to the Lord" (verses 20-21).

Since all of these events depend on Messiah's coming to properly sanctify and build the Temple (Zechariah 6:12-13; Haggai 2:7-9; Malachi 3:1-3), we can say that part of Jesus' Messianic role was to align the Temple and its service to the divine ideal. If this is the case, it is possible to also see an influence here from Malachi 1:10, which was concerned with ritual abuse. In fact, John chapter 1 introduces John the Baptizer with a citation from Malachi 3:1: "Behold, I am going to send My messenger, and he will clear the way before Me." Perhaps the structure of John 2, with Jesus' abrupt entrance to the Temple, implies the completion of this citation: "And the Lord, whom you seek, will suddenly come to His temple." Since the focus of Malachi 3:1-3 is upon the purification of the Temple, there may be in Jesus' actions an implicit witness to Himself as the One predicted in this passage—the One who would ultimately come in the eschatological age to effect ceremonial and spiritual restoration.[56] This further supports the connection between Jesus and Jeremiah as prophets of eschatological restoration. Too, it is hard to believe that Jesus claim to be the Messiah, especially in relation to the Temple (John 10:22-42), would not have been connected by a restoration-anxious people with the expected role of the Messiah as Temple-builder. Furthermore, with regard to Jesus' statement "destroy this temple" (more on this in a moment), if so severe a prophet as Jeremiah could denounce the Temple and announce its destruction yet still be acclaimed as a prophet of restoration, then why couldn't Jesus?

Jesus as the Restorer of the Temple

John's statement that the Jews asked for a "sign" from Jesus (John 2:18) continues the implied theme of Temple restoration. This request was for an authentication of Jesus' prophetic authority to act as He did in the Temple (see Jesus' remarks concerning signs, Matthew 12:38-39; 16:4; Mark 8:11-12; Luke 11:29-30; John 12:37). In response, Jesus states His original motive in connecting the present Temple and Himself with Jeremiah and the other prophets who had questioned the Temple personnel. Jesus said that if they (the Jewish authorities) "destroy this temple [i.e., Jesus' body]," He would "raise it up" in three days (John 2:19).[57] However, Jesus' subtle shift in meaning apparently was lost on His audience. This, in itself, according to John, was a sign of rejection that went back to the pre-exilic prophetic judgment stated by Isaiah 6:9-10 (John 12:37-40). The Jews' reaction to Jesus' words (verse 20) reveals not only that they took His words literally, but also their incredulity at His claim. That Jesus was also misunderstood[58] by the masses is confirmed by the misinterpretation of His words as reported by the false witnesses at Jesus' trial and repeated in the mockery at His crucifixion (Matthew 26:60-61; 27:30,40; Mark 14:57-59; 15:29). Jesus' own disciples apparently also misunderstood Him, for John says that Jesus' true meaning was not perceived until they reflected on His words *after* the resurrection (verse 22).[59] This explains John's interpretive note, "But He was speaking about the temple of His body" (John 2:21). However, the fact that Jesus' words came after He interfered with the buying and selling of animals, which was necessary for the continuance of the Temple services and constituted a direct threat to the Temple establishment, made it humanly impossible for His audience to interpret His words any other way. Therefore, only those who were given special insight by the heavenly Father understood (see Matthew 16:17; Mark 4:11).

What Jesus' audience in the Temple precincts apparently understood was that He had claimed to be the Messianic Temple Restorer who could miraculously tear down and re-erect the Temple in three days. Some of the false witnesses at Jesus' trial disclosed this when they said, "We heard Him say, 'I will destroy this temple made with hands, and in three days I will build another *made without hands*'" (Mark 14:58, emphasis added). Of course, Jesus did not say that *He* would destroy the Temple, but that *they* would.[60] Still, their misunderstanding revealed the correct Jewish tradition at the time of Jesus, based on the prophetic predictions (see 2 Samuel 7:13; 1 Chronicles 17:12; Zechariah 6:12) that the old Temple would be replaced[61] by a new Temple when the Messiah was revealed.[62] However, even though a new Temple was expected to come from God in the eschatological period, the thought of any human destruction of the existing Temple was considered a blasphemous desecration.

Jesus as a Temple Replacement

By contrast, Christian interpretation has historically seen in the words "the temple of His body" an implicit prediction that the physical Temple would be replaced by the spiritual Temple—Christ's body, the church (see Ephesians 2:21;

see also 1 Corinthians 3:16-17). In other words, Jesus would not literally destroy and rebuild the Jerusalem Temple, as John explains, but the literal Temple would be destroyed (by the Romans) and Jesus (by His resurrection) would replace it with a new spiritual building, the temple of His body. This spiritual replacement is thought to be supported by Jesus' prediction of non-localized "spiritual worship" (John 4:21-23) as opposed to Temple worship and John's presentation of Jesus as the spiritual Temple of the New Jerusalem (Revelation 21:22). As one commentator stated: "John points to the fact that, as the place where men used to go in order to meet God, the temple has been supplanted and replaced by Jesus himself...."[63] Such an interpretation is part and parcel to the theological concept of a new spiritual Israel replacing the old ethnic Israel. The hermeneutical device thought to be employed in John's Gospel to make this identification between Jesus' body and the Temple is typological use of the Jerusalem Temple as the type and Jesus' temple as the antitype. This would produce a fulfillment with Jesus replacing the old physical Temple (the shadow) with His new spiritual body (the substance) after the resurrection.

However, according to what we saw in the Synoptic writers, Jesus' attitude does not insinuate a rejection of the physical Temple as either inferior or fading away in light of His advent as the Messiah and head of the church (see Matthew 16:18; Luke 24:44-49). In fact, after the resurrection of Jesus, the fulfillment of Jesus' prediction of the destruction and raising of the Temple, the disciples returned immediately to Jerusalem and the Temple. The closing words of Luke's Gospel say, that "they were continually in the temple, praising God" (Luke 24:52-53). Would not this seem a great incongruity if they understood that this Temple was to be replaced by themselves as the church? And, unless we admit to contradiction in the Gospels, we should expect John's Gospel to be in agreement with this perspective. Some, however, have argued that the Fourth Gospel reflects a Greek perspective, rather than Hebrew, which more readily spiritualizes the concept of a temple. Yet the study of the Dead Sea Scrolls, which are pre-Christian and Orthodox Jewish in origin, has helped to dispel this myth. Professor David Flusser, Professor Emeritus at the Hebrew University, who taught on Judaism in the Second Temple period and Early Christianity, has stated, "In the light of the discovery of the Scrolls, it has been definitely established that Greek influence on early Christianity was but weak, for most of the concepts in the New Testament previously believed to stem from pagan thought are now found to originate with a Jewish sect and in a most definitely Jewish context.[64] Significantly, some of the most striking parallels (mostly theological motifs) between the Dead Sea Scrolls and the New Testament occur in the Gospel of John, which is now recognized by scholars as "the most Jewish Gospel in the Christian canon."[65] While the Dead Sea sect did share with Christianity the concept of their community as a spiritual temple, they also held the physical Temple in high esteem and expected a restored (ceremonially pure) physical Temple to replace the Second Temple in the last days.[66] This reveals that their perspective of the Jerusalem Temple was no different than that of the Jews in John's context, and that their spiritual concept of the Temple was in concert with this.

In this light, a metaphorical usage is preferred. Just as Jesus referred to His body as a temple, so later Paul referred to the Christian's body as a temple (see chapter 13). In this case, just as death "destroyed" Jesus' physical body, so the resurrection would "restore" it again, adding a new spiritual dimension (1 Corinthians 15:42-49,53-54). Since, however, the context of the saying is the Jerusalem Temple, a correspondence is difficult to deny, even if Jesus did not make it explicit. Even so, the correspondence would be the destruction of the physical Temple and its restoration as a physical building with a new spiritual dimension (inviolability) (Ezekiel 37:26-28; 43:7). If the Temple's destruction is accepted as implicit here, then Jesus, rather than announcing the Temple's replacement, was affirming its eschatological restoration![67] This focus may also be present in the future tense used in Jesus' citation of Isaiah 56:7: "My House *shall be called* [in its eschatological fulfillment] a house of prayer for all nations" (Mark 11:17; see also Matthew 21:13; Luke 19:46).

Jesus' Prediction of the Temple's Destruction

Jesus' prediction of Jerusalem's destruction has produced a tremendous volume of scholarly interpretations, most of which fall into the category of a threat or curse by Jesus on the sacrificial institution represented by Jerusalem's Temple.[68] Most of those who assume that Jesus' statements are pronouncements, as though He Himself were judging and condemning the Temple, characterize His prediction of the Temple's fall as unique. This is because they view the Temple's removal as marking the end of the Jewish age and symbolizing the removal of Israel as God's chosen people. However, Jesus was not alone in His expectation that the Temple was doomed; a fairly large percentage of Jews in Jesus' day expected this as well. This point has been argued with substantial evidence from historical sources by Markus Bockmuehl.[69] In his article he cites examples from Josephus, Tacitus, and early rabbinic literature that indicate that there was a flourishing hermeneutical tradition before A.D. 70 that predicted the Temple's destruction.[70] In fact, such a belief was in line with the Mosaic Covenant, under which terms they lived as Jews (Romans 2:17-20), as well as with the Deuteronomic or Land (Palestinian) Covenant (Deuteronomy 29:1–30:20). Since the Second Temple was not the Restoration Temple, its existence was still conditioned upon national Israel's fidelity to God's covenant. The terms for the Temple's continuation were given at the commencement of its original construction (1 Kings 6:12) and repeated shortly thereafter (1 Kings 9:1-9). The "curse" section of this covenant follows the form of the previous covenants and describes what God would do in the event of unfaithfulness:

> If you or your sons shall indeed turn away from following Me, and shall not keep My commandments and My statutes which I have set before you and shall go and serve other gods and worship them, then…the house which I have consecrated for My name, I will cast out of My sight.…And this house will become a heap of ruins; everyone who passes by will be astonished and hiss and say, "Why has the LORD done thus to this land and to this house?" and they will say, "Because they forsook the LORD their God…"(1 Kings 9:6-9).

Even after the destruction and rebuilding of the Second Temple, the Nation had continued in unfaithfulness. Fearing another destruction and return to exile, Ezra led the people to renew the covenant with God (Ezra 10:1-8) and a brief revival was experienced under Nehemiah (Nehemiah 10:28-39). But a century later, the prophet Malachi wrote to redress the violations of the covenant—especially with regards to the Temple, its priesthood, and its services (Malachi 1:3-14; 2:1-9; 3:7-12). Malachi's closing prophecies, which also chronologically close the Old Testament canon, predict a "messenger of the covenant" who will come to His Temple (Malachi 3:1) not only for judgment (Malachi 3:5; 4:1), but also to "purify" the priesthood (Malachi 3:3) and restore Israel spiritually (Malachi 4:6) (see the previous chapter). These words are based on the "blessing" section of the covenant (1 Kings 6:12-13; 9:4-5), which promises that national repentance will be followed by national restoration.

Therefore, Jesus' pronouncements against the Temple are not unique, but are in accord with the "curse" section of the covenant stipulations and follow in the train of similar statements by the prophets that preceded Jesus (see Acts 3:22-24). His indictment of the Nation reviews their covenant unfaithfulness from the time of the return under Ezra (Matthew 23:30-35) to its present climax (as represented by the Jewish leaders) of both failing to recognize the arrival of the

Messiah (Luke 19:44; see also Matthew 27:22, 42; Mark 14:61-65; 15:32; John 7:1; 11:47-53; 12:10-11; 19:7,14-15) and rejecting His offer of the kingdom (Matthew 4:12; 23:37; John 1:11; 6:15,26,41; see also Luke 19:14). However, Jesus also spoke of restoration based on the "blessing" section of the covenant (Matthew 19:28; 25:31-46; 26:29; see also Acts 1:6-7)—which would come when national Israel repented and recognized the Messiah (Matthew 23:39; Luke 24:47; see also Acts 3:19-21; 5:31). Jesus' statements concerning the destruction of the Temple, then, must be read with both sections of the covenant in mind.

Jesus' Proclamation of the Temple's Desolation

In Matthew 23:38 Jesus is thought to have pronounced a climactic judgment on the city of Jerusalem and the Temple: "Behold, your house is being left to you desolate!" Because this text leads directly into the Olivet Discourse, and Jesus' preliminary statement that "not one stone here will be left upon another" (Matthew 24:1-2; Mark 13:1-2; Luke 21:6-7), these words have been interpreted to speak of a divine punishment that finalized God's dealings with ethnic Israel. Indeed, Matthew 23:38 is the verse most cited by church apologists as scriptural proof that the desolation of Jerusalem and the Temple Mount would be permanent and that any attempt to restore the Jewish character of the city or rebuild the Temple would be tantamount to reversing Jesus' prophecy and making void the Word of God. But does this serious charge stand up under a careful scrutiny of this text?

It is important to first limit the extent of the meaning of the word "house" in Matthew 23:38. While various commentators have sought to include in this meaning the Davidic dynasty, the Jewish nation, the city of Jerusalem, and the Temple, the context makes it clear that the Temple is the focal point. Jesus is in the Temple complex when He makes this statement (Matthew 21:23; 24:1) and has been addressing the subject of Temple violations (Matthew 23:16-35), ending with a reference to "the temple and the altar" in verse 35. While Jerusalem is addressed in verse 37, the normal understanding of Jerusalem's "house" (verse 38) is the "house of the Lord," the Temple. Moreover, in the completion of the statement (verse 39), Jesus quotes Psalm 118:26a: "Blessed is the one who comes in the name of the LORD." The remainder of this verse states, "We have blessed you from the house of the LORD," confirming that the Temple alone was what Jesus had in mind when He used the word "house." While the city of Jerusalem is understood to be included in the future event and share the condition of "being left desolate," as the reference to "her [Jerusalem's] desolation" in Luke 21:20 indicates, the focus in Matthew 23:38 here appears to be on to the Temple itself.

To properly interpret Matthew 23:38 we also need to understand the term "desolate" and the duration intended for this condition. In the first place, the desolation spoken of here cannot mean the end of a Jewish presence in Jerusalem, for historically it never ended. It also cannot mean that the Jews would never again possess the city, for today Jerusalem is again under Jewish sovereignty in a national Israel. Rather, it must be a condition specific to the Temple. This is made clear in the meaning of the term "desolate." This is the Greek word *eremos*, which, in the following text of the Olivet Discourse, is the second half of the compound term "abomination of desolation"—that which Jesus says will be in the Temple (Matthew 24:15; Mark 13:14; see chapter 22). The history of the usage of the term "desolate" in this context begins with Jeremiah's prophecy of judicial desolation in a 70-year exile. The prophet Daniel then studied Jeremiah's prophecy (Daniel 9:2) and prayed on the basis of the limited duration of this 70 years for the Temple's restoration from desolation: "O Lord, let Thy face shine on Thy desolate sanctuary" (Daniel 9:17). The response to Daniel's prayer revealed that Israel would endure an extended period of Gentile domination for "seventy weeks [of years]" (Daniel 9:24—see chapter 11). This time, however, would end with the fulfillment of Israel's restoration, climaxed by the anointing of the Most Holy Place (the restoration of the Temple—verse 24). However, in the verses that follow (verses 25-27), a description of the events during this 70-week period predicts the Temple's further desolation. This is said to occur after 69 weeks have elapsed with the destruction of the city and the sanctuary (verse 26). Then in the middle of the seventieth week comes the abomination that desolates (verse 27).

The first desolation, coming after the first advent of the Messiah (verse 25) must be the Roman destruction of Jerusalem and the Temple in A.D. 70. The second, coming just prior to the conclusion of the Gentile dominion defined in verse 27 as a "complete destruction, one that is decreed...on the one who makes desolate," must refer to Israel in the end times (see Daniel 12:9). It is verse 27 that Jesus references in the Olivet Discourse as predicting the "abomination of desolation" within the final period of the Tribulation (Matthew 24:21,29; Mark 13:19,24)—just prior to the advent of Messiah and Israel's national repentance, regathering, and redemption (Matthew 24:30-31; Mark 13:26; Luke 21:27-28).

With this understanding, I would suggest that the desolation of the Temple in Matthew 23:38 was the withdrawal of God's protection (in keeping with the desolation of the First Temple, according to the covenant). This condition of desolation, hypothetically, would not preclude the rebuilding of the Temple many times within this period; however, all of these Temples would still be subject to further acts of desolation and destruction (as was the Second Temple and as the Tribulation Temple will be).

Only Israel's repentance will return God's protection, reverse this condition, and restore the Temple to the divine ideal. This would make the duration of the Temple's desolation "seventy weeks," as anticipated by Daniel. This desolation began with the Roman destruction in A.D. 70 (after the "sixty-nine weeks") and will continue through the Tribulation period (the "seventieth week"). This desolation will end, as depicted in the Olivet Discourse, with Israel's repentance (Matthew 24:30; see Zechariah 12:10-14), an event that will also mark the end of Messiah's absence: "For I say to you, from now on you shall not see Me until you say, 'Blessed is He who comes in the name of the LORD!'" (Matthew 23:39). The words "from now on" describe the unrepentant condition of pre-Messianic Israel ("you"), while the words "shall not see Me" refer to the determined delay of Messiah's coming, despite Israel's many plights and its multiplied prayers. However, this condition is only temporary, as indicated by the word "until." The end is conditioned upon Israel's recognition of and repentance toward Jesus as Messiah, who, as the rejected chief cornerstone in Psalm 118, must be welcomed ("blessed") as one who is identified with "the name of the Lord." This was what the Passover crowds acknowledged as Jesus, upon His first advent to Jerusalem (Luke 19:28-38) fulfilled the first part of the prophecy of Zechariah 9:9. Israel's leaders, however, rejected Jesus, thus eliciting His prediction of the Temple's destruction (Luke 19:41-44). Matthew 23:37-38 takes place at this same time, yet proclaims not only the Temple's desolation but also the promise that when Israel (the "all Israel" of Romans 11:26) joins in the confession of Psalm 118:26, Jesus will fulfill the second part of the prophecy of Zechariah 9:10 (upon His second advent to Jerusalem—Zechariah 14:3-4; see also Romans 11:27; 2 Thessalonians 1:7-10; Revelation 19:11-16). Therefore, Jesus' declaration of desolation here did not end ethnic Israel's future (a teaching promoted by many Christian apologists for centuries), but, reading this statement in light of the context of the Olivet Discourse, we need to say that it simply postponed that future "until the times of the Gentiles be fulfilled" (Luke 21:24) and until Israel repents in mournful recognition of its sin of rejecting Jesus as Messiah (Matthew 24:30).

Jesus' Purpose in the Olivet Discourse

The Olivet Discourse, as interpreted by the schools of Historicism[71] and Preterism,[72] is exclusively a warning of judgment that was fulfilled with the

The Temple's Future According to the Olivet Discourse

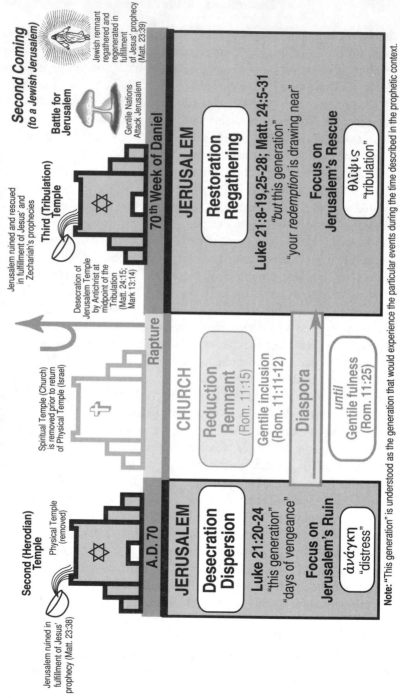

Second (Herodian) Temple

Physical Temple (removed)

Jerusalem ruined in fulfillment of Jesus' prophecy (Matt. 23:38)

Spiritual Temple (Church) is removed prior to return of Physical Temple (Israel)

Desecration of Jerusalem Temple by Antichrist at midpoint of the Tribulation (Matt. 24:15; Mark 13:14)

Jerusalem ruined and rescued in fulfillment of Jesus' and Zechariah's prophecies

Third (Tribulation) Temple

Second Coming (to a Jewish Jerusalem)

Jewish remnant regathered and regenerated in fulfillment of Jesus' prophecy (Matt. 23:39)

Battle for Jerusalem

Gentile Nations Attack Jerusalem

Rapture

A.D. 70

70th Week of Daniel

JERUSALEM

Desecration Dispersion

Luke 21:20-24 "this generation" "days of vengeance"

Focus on Jerusalem's Ruin

ἀνάγκη "distress"

CHURCH

Reduction Remnant (Rom. 11:15)

Gentile inclusion (Rom. 11:11-12)

Diaspora

until Gentile fulness (Rom. 11:25)

JERUSALEM

Restoration Regathering

Luke 21:8-19,25-28; Matt. 24:5-31 *"but this generation"* "your redemption is drawing near"

Focus on Jerusalem's Rescue

θλίψις "tribulation"

Note: "This generation" is understood as the generation that would experience the particular events during the time described in the prophetic context.

Temple's destruction by the Romans in A.D. 70. In the same way as Matthew 23:38 was construed to teach Jesus' rejection of the Jews, this text has been understood to have had a past fulfillment that resulted in an irreversible abandonment of the Jewish people, Jerusalem, and the Temple by God. In Preterism, the basis for this interpretation rests upon understanding the phrase "this generation" as always having reference to the first century generation to whom Jesus spoke. Futurism, by contrast, accepts some uses of "this generation" as having reference to the people of Jesus' day, but only because the immediate context demands this application. Other uses, however, determined by their contexts, may refer to generations of different time periods. For example, the use of "this generation" in Matthew 23:36 is applied as an indictment (in context) to the generation of the scribes and Pharisees (Matthew 23:29) whose actions against Jesus demonstrate their affinity with previous persecutors of the prophets (verses 30-35). Jesus then pronounces judgment with the words "all these things shall come upon this generation." The phrase "these things" must also be interpreted in its context. In this case, the next verse (verse 36) describes "these things" as the future experience of Temple desolation. It is important to observe here that when Jesus' statement was made, "this generation" indicated a *future* generation. It was future from the perspective of the sins "this generation" (in context) would yet commit (complicity in the crucifixion) and the judgment they would receive (the Roman destruction in A.D. 70—see Luke 21:20-24).

Jesus' use of a future sense of "this generation" in a *near* future judgment context sets a precedence for its interpretation in a context of *far* future (eschatological) judgment. Therefore, if the desolation experienced by "this generation" in Matthew 23:36 can be understood as a future fulfillment that came some 40 years later, it should not be a problem to understand the Tribulation judgment of the Olivet Discourse as having a future fulfillment that will come upon the generation that will experience it at the end of the age. However, the difference is not simply the span of time, but the *nature* of that time as eschatological. Consequently, "this generation" (Matthew 24:34, Mark 13:30, and Luke 21:32) and "all these things" (Matthew 24:34; Mark 13:30; Luke 21:28) must refer contextually to the events of the Great Tribulation, the conclusion of "the times of the Gentiles," the coming of Christ in glory, and the regathering and redemption of Israel—all of which Jesus not only declared to be future at the time He spoke (Mark 13:23), but also cast in typical eschatological language (for example, "end of the age," "such as has not occurred since the beginning of the world until now, *nor ever shall,*" "powers of the heavens will be shaken"). Even though in context Jesus may refer to the future "this generation" as "you," this is a conventional usage of language with respect to reference and thus it does not have to apply to a present audience.[73] Such usage may also be found in the Old Testament. For instance, Moses speaks in a way similar to Jesus when he says, "So it shall be when *all of these things* have come upon *you*" (Deuteronomy 30:1a, emphasis added). Even though he is speaking to the present generation ("you"), it is evident from the context that his words speak about a future generation that will live thousands of years later and into the eschatological period. "This generation" (the "you") are those who will have already suffered the judgment of exile (verse 1b) and captivity (verse 3), been regathered and restored (verses 4-5), and received spiritual regeneration "circumcision of heart" (verse 6).

In addition, as an examination of the entire prophecy reveals, Jesus' purpose was not determined solely by thoughts of God's vengeance on Israel nor by a prophetic compulsion to denounce the Temple, but rather, was guided by specific questions that arose from His disciples as a result of His statements about the Temple's future (Matthew 24:2; Mark 13:2; Luke 21:6). Matthew and Mark are generally parallel accounts; however, Luke's account has significant differences. These differences are explained by Jesus' answers to three separate questions posed by the disciples: 1) "Tell us, when will these things [the destruction of the Temple] be?"; 2) "What will be the sign of Your [Messiah's] coming?"; and 3) "What will be the sign...of the end of the [Gentile] age?" From the Futurists' perspective, it should be observed that while all three questions are asked in Matthew 24:3 and Mark 13:4, Jesus only answers questions two and three in these contexts. Luke may have asked only the first question (Luke 21:6-7a), which explains Jesus' answer concerning Jerusalem's desolation being included only here (verses 20-24). However, there are also exegetical reasons for supposing that Luke alone deals with the nearer destruction of Jerusalem and the Temple by Titus in A.D. 70.[74]

What is common to these questions in each account is that they come in response to Jesus' unsolicited statement concerning the Temple that "not one stone here shall be left upon another, which will not be torn down" (Matthew 24:2; Mark 13:2; Luke 21:6). Whether or not we accept the preceding interpretation of the differences between these accounts, each contain Jesus' *predictions* concerning the desecration of the Temple (either in A.D. 70 or at the end of the age).[75] In every question and every account it is the *future* that concerns the disciples, both immediate and especially in terms of the Old Testament prophecies.

Matthew in particular reveals that Jesus' preview of the future was to answer His disciple's questions concerning His (second) coming, and the end of the age (Matthew 24:3). Jesus here explains *why* His coming is necessary (for divine intervention and national repentance, verses 27-31; see also Zechariah 12:9-10) and *when* it will occur: "*after* the tribulation of those days" (verse 29). According to Matthew,[76] the events described in this period prior to the Messianic advent could not have been fulfilled in A.D. 70 with the destruction of Jerusalem, since these events usher in and terminate with the final and climactic coming of Messiah, at which time the heavens will be shaken (Haggai 2:3,6,21; see also Isaiah 13:9-10; Joel 2:31; 3:15).[77]

Moreover, and perhaps most damaging to the Preterist interpretation, is that the Olivet Discourse predicts a *victorious* outcome for Israel and a restoration rather than a defeat that ends its prophetic hopes. This is seen in the provisions of "protection" (Matthew 24:16-17,22; Mark 13:15-16, 20), the promises of "regathering" (Matthew 24:31; Mark 13:27), and "redemption" (Luke 21:28) at the return of Messiah. These are in harmony with other positive expectations of Israel attending Messiah's coming (see Acts 1:6; 3:20-21; Romans 11:26-27). To interpret these positive references as something else or for someone else requires the text to be read in a non-literal way. For Preterism, whose case is argued on the basis of a literal historical fulfillment (in and around the events of A.D. 70), such an approach is inconsistent and fails to reckon with Jesus' eschatological method of interpretation, which is consistently literal and Jewish in character.[78]

Jesus' View in Summary

Our conclusion, then, should be that Jesus accepted the Temple as His "Father's house," and though He predicted that both the Temple and Jerusalem would suffer desolation and destruction, it would only be "until the times of the Gentiles be fulfilled" (Luke 21:28). Then would come Israel's repentance and restoration at the time of Jesus' second coming (Matthew 23:39; see also Matthew 21:13; Mark 11:17; Luke 19:46).

Having seen that Jesus' predictions concerning the Temple follow the pattern established by the prophets, let us now proceed in the next chapter to see if Paul—the apostle to the Gentiles—had a similar understanding of the Temple and its future in the last days.

CHAPTER 13

Predictions in Paul

Jewish Reverence or
Christian Replacement?

The Temple at Jerusalem may have been regarded as the true Temple of God by Paul the Apostle, even as it had formerly been so regarded by Saul the Pharisee...in all of the Apostle's writings there is not a single word against the Temple.[1]

—JOHN TOWNSEND

In the Olivet Discourse, Jesus predicted the trouble that would befall the Jerusalem Temple in the Last Days. The apostle Paul, in 2 Thessalonians 2:2-4, expanded upon Jesus' teaching based on his understanding of Daniel's end-time prophecy about the Temple. These predictions that Paul made for the Last Days Temple will be examined in chapter 21. However, before we can assume that Paul made such predictions, which assumes both the Temple's legitimacy and its future in God's prophetic program, it is first necessary to answer the objections of the critics who say that Paul and the New Testament speak of the Temple only as a spiritual symbol for the church.[2] According to the symbolic school of interpretation, Paul's prediction in 2 Thessalonians 2:3-4 of a "man of sin" who will "sit in the Temple of God" is a description of apostasy in the church. In our study of the Temple, it is not sufficient to simply differ with this interpretation; it must be demonstrated why this view is erroneous both textually and theologically. To do this it is necessary to examine Paul's understanding of the Temple as displayed in his epistles, for the critics' case for the interpretation of the Temple as the church is made there. If it cannot be shown that Paul, as an apostle of Jesus Christ, regarded the Jerusalem Temple as anything more than a symbol of the old legal economy now superceded by a new spiritual and gracious entity—the church—then it will be difficult to argue that he predicted a role for it in the future. Moreover, if Paul's regard for the Temple is, as generally understood today by both Jewish and Christian commentators, entirely negative and seen as a rejection of the Mosaic legislation (which included the Temple construction and service), then it is doubtful that Paul would have interpreted "the temple of God" in 2 Thessalonians 2:4 as the legitimate Jerusalem Temple whose sanctity will be desecrated by the actions of an Antichrist. Therefore, in order to validate the interpretation that Paul predicted the desecration of the Last Days Temple (in concert with Jesus and Daniel), we must first look more carefully at Paul's own concept of the Temple.

The Importance of Understanding Paul

In the New Testament, outside of the four Gospels, more than one-half of the remaining books contain the words of the apostle Paul. How did this former Pharisee conceive of himself in relation to the Temple? Paul's Jewish life had long revolved around the service and schedule of the Temple, and he himself records that his religious training was under Rabbi Gamaliel (Acts 22:3; 23:6), who was known to have met with his students on the southern entrance steps leading to the Temple. However, after Paul came to faith in Jesus as Messiah and

Lord (Acts 9:1-19) and was called to minister to the Gentiles, would he not have disregarded the Temple, if not disdained it, as part of Judaism's false system of salvation by works? In modern Jewish perspective, it was Paul, the renegade Jew, not Jesus, who founded Christianity. According to this viewpoint, Jesus remained a loyal and Orthodox Jew within Judaism and never became a Christian. However, I have heard Jews (and Christians) say that Paul was not Jewish and that he had renounced his former religion and converted to Christianity. For this reason I have heard Jewish rabbis state the opinion that "Jesus would have hated Paul!"

Is it true that Paul defected from Judaism, abandoning and even castigating the Law? Moreover, with respect to our interest, did his theology replace the Jewish Temple with the Gentile church, making impossible any possibility of his writings implying the concept of a rebuilt, physical Temple in the future? Before we explore these questions, let's consider what the New Testament actually reveals concerning Paul's Jewishness and his relationship to traditional Judaism.

Confusion over Paul

We already saw in chapter 7 that the book of Acts gives repeated accounts of Paul's adherence to the Law and his veneration of and pilgrimages to the Temple. Many people are confused over such statements and have suggested that they can be dismissed as mere cultural observances by Paul for the sake of continued relations with his fellow countrymen. They try to back up this claim by pointing to Paul's own statement about his missionary methodology in 1 Corinthians 9:20: "To the Jews I became as a Jew, that I might win Jews; to those who are under the Law, as under the Law, though not being myself under the Law, that I might win those who are under the Law."

Does this mean that Paul was a pretender—that he feigned religious observance as a clever ruse to win over unsuspecting Jews? If this is the case, then what would his converts have thought after they had been "won" and found out that he was living a lie? Would such exposure not impugn Paul's character and ruin his witness? Did Paul think nothing of compromising his Christian commitments in order to live as a lawless pagan, or worse, just to deceive hapless people in order to turn them from their religion?

On the other hand, if the Law really was a bad thing, and worship in the Temple was wrong, then how could Paul confess to the Jews that he had "walk[ed] orderly, keeping the Law" (Acts 21:24), "committed no offense either against the Law of the Jews or against the temple" (Acts 25:8), "done nothing against [the Jewish] people or the customs of [their] fathers" (Acts 28:17), and even offered sacrifices at the Temple (Acts 21:26; 24:17) *after* he was saved and had become a Christian? According to the New Testament and the historical record, Paul was a man of undisputed integrity (Acts 24:16). It should be obvious, then, that he never intended 1 Corinthians 9:20 to mean that he compromised his Christian principles for the sake of reaching either Jew or Gentile with the good news of the Messiah.

Some people are quick to say, Did not Paul say that "Christ is the *end of the law* for righteousness to everyone who believes" (Romans 10:4)? The impression given by this particular English translation is that Christ *cancelled* the Law for Christians! But the meaning of the Greek word *telos*, here translated "end," is better understood as "goal" or "purpose." While this is an accepted meaning of "end," for the average reader this term connotes only the idea of something that is "finished." Paul's idea in this verse (based on the context) is just the opposite: Through Christ the Law has reached its objective, achieving for the believer (whether Jew or Gentile) a divine standard of righteousness that could never be realized by personal observance.

In the same way, despite Paul's affirmations of his Jewishness, there are those who believe that his theological viewpoint of the Temple was that it had been superceded and replaced by the church. Is that really the case? Let's examine Paul's statements about the Temple and decide for ourselves.

Preliminary Considerations

The prevailing view of Paul's attitude toward the Temple—and of his use of Temple imagery in his epistles—is that he sees the Christian church as the true and only Sanctuary of God.[3] However, according to Luke's historical record in Acts, Paul was faithful to the Torah and continued to worship in the Temple. If this is the case, then it would be inconsistent—if not contradictory—to find a contrary attitude revealed in Paul's own epistles. Therefore, it is not incongruous to hear Paul in 2 Thessalonians 2:4 refer to the Jerusalem Temple, even in a state of desecration, as "the temple of God," nor to hear him list with great reverence the Temple as being among Israel's greatest spiritual blessings in Romans 9:4-5: "who are Israelites, to whom belongs the adoption as sons [Exodus 4:22] and the glory [Exodus 16:10] and the covenants [Genesis 12:1-3; Deuteronomy 30; 2 Samuel 7:5-17; Jeremiah 31:31-34] and the giving of the Law [Exodus 20–24] and *the Temple service* [Exodus 25–31] and the promises [Leviticus 26:3-13; Deuteronomy 28:1-14 and Prophets], whose are the Fathers, and from whom is the Christ according to the flesh."

If Paul had rejected the Temple service, then he would also have been rejecting the other listed privileges of Israel, including the Messiah Himself, since they are all part of the same divine blessing. Townsend, whose 1958 Harvard dissertation on the Jerusalem Temple in the New Testament questioned the assumption that Paul rejected the Temple and its service, noted in a 1979 article: "Only occasionally has anyone suggested that, like Saul the Pharisee, Paul the apostle continued to regard the Jerusalem temple as the true temple of God; yet his epistles do not contain a single word against this temple."[4] While this notion runs contrary to some people's presuppositions about Pauline allusions, J.M.P. Sweet has proposed one explanation for this difficulty:

> It is possible, though difficult, to distinguish an attack on an institution from an attack on those who run it, or to distinguish rejection of an institution from the quest for something better which puts it in the shade—as, for Paul, the glory of Moses' dispensation was "de-glorified" by the surpassing glory of the Spirit's (2 Corinthians 3:10). Eschatology, unless it is purely escapist, must seem subversive to those whose stake is in the *status quo*. Thus, it is possible to have respect for the Temple, as the place where God said his name should dwell, and for the Law as holy, just and good, and to combine such respect, on the one hand, with fierce criticism of the present administration whose failure may lead God to demolish his own institution...and on the other hand, with looking for God's "fulfillment" of the earthly institution which (it may be believed) he has already set in motion.[5]

I have already examined Paul's attitude toward the Temple in the book of Acts (see chapter 7), but because some also claim that Paul's attitude was re-cast by Luke as a result of Luke's positive attitude toward the Temple, let's look at some new examples from the Pauline epistles that give additional insight into Paul's view of the Temple. I will begin with a cursory listing of Paul's use of Temple metaphors, and then proceed to deal with the interpretive assumptions drawn from these texts.

Paul's View of the Temple in the Pauline Epistles

Those who believe that Paul rejected the Temple and its service as illegitimate—and that he considered the church (and its worship of Christ) to be the new Temple—base their conclusion on some or all of the following assumptions: 1) Paul referred to the church as the new temple universally (Ephesians 2:19-22), locally (1 Corinthians 3:16-17), and individually (1 Corinthians 6:19); 2) Paul depicted the true Jerusalem (including the Temple) as the heavenly Jerusalem, replacing the earthly Jerusalem (Galatians 4:25-26); 3) Paul used sacrificial and priestly language in relation to Jesus' crucifixion and the Christian's sanctification under the new covenant (Romans 3:25; 12:1; Titus 3:5), referring to the Temple service only depicting this institution as part of the old covenant now superceded in Christ (Romans 9:4; 1 Corinthians 10:18); 4) Paul regarded the Law as a "tutor" to which those justified by faith were no longer subject (Galatians 3:24-25). Since the Law ordained and regulated the Temple and its service, the Temple and its service should have no meaning for those not under the Law.

Let's consider each of these assumptions in their Pauline context, first by looking at why and how Paul used the Jerusalem Temple in his teachings about the church.

Paul's Use of the Temple as a Figure of Speech

Paul used the Temple as a figure of speech in his political and social metaphors.[6] It is significant to note that he employed the Greek distinction between *naos* (as representative of the spiritual aspect of the Temple) and *heiron* (as representative of the physical aspect of the Temple). This is evidenced by the fact that only the former term, which lends itself to a figurative or spiritual idea, is used in his epistles, while the latter term never appears in figurative usage.[7] Yet why did Paul use Temple imagery, especially in epistles written predominately to Gentile churches? Several reasons may be suggested:

1. *Paul's education in Jerusalem as a Pharisee.* Such training would have oriented Paul's concept of worship in terms of the Temple, and because he continued to view it as the central place of Jewish worship and to worship there himself (Acts 21:22-29), it would have been natural for Paul to refer to the Temple in his explanations of worship. The fact that Paul always uses *naos* (the Temple proper and especially the Holy of Holies) rather than *heiron* (the Temple complex and especially the precincts) shows that he is thinking about the *spiritual* nature of the Temple as the place where God's presence dwelt.[8] If Paul was seeking to denigrate the Temple as a defunct institution and promote the view that the church was the new spiritual temple, then we would have expected him to abandon a term (*naos*) that emphasized the Temple's spiritual significance and incomparable holiness. On the other hand, if Paul regarded the Temple with reverence, then he would have found this the ideal term to refer to the Temple when affirming the sanctified nature of the church and its people.

The Eschatological Program of Replacement Theology

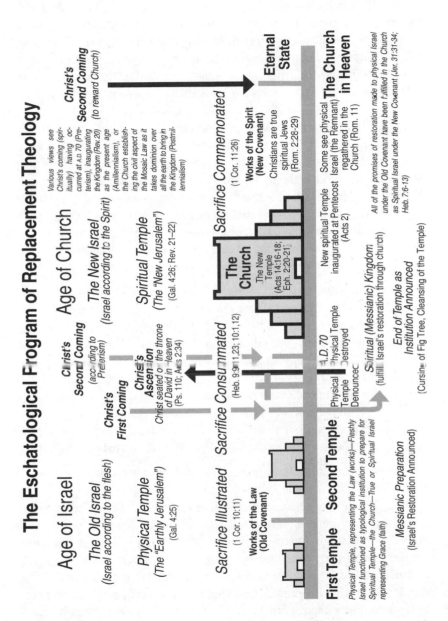

Age of Israel

The Old Israel
(Israel according to the flesh)

Physical Temple
(The "Earthly Jerusalem")
(Gal. 4:25)

Sacrifice Illustrated
(1 Cor. 10:11)

Works of the Law
(Old Covenant)

First Temple   Second Temple

Physical Temple, representing the Law (works)—Fleshly
Israel functioned as typological institution to prepare for
Spiritual Temple—the Church—True or Spiritual Israel
representing Grace (faith)

Messianic Preparation
(Israel's Restoration Announced)

Christ's First Coming

Christ's Second Coming
(according to Preterism)

Christ's Ascension
Christ seated on the throne
of David in Heaven
(Ps. 110; Acts 2:34)

Sacrifice Consummated
(Heb. 9:9-11,23; 10:1,12)

A.D. 70
Physical Temple
Destroyed

Physical Temple
Denounced

Spiritual (Messianic) Kingdom
(fulfill Israel's restoration through church)

End of Temple as
Institution Announced
(Cursing of Fig Tree, Cleansing of the Temple)

Age of Church

The New Israel
(Israel according to the Spirit)

Spiritual Temple
(The "New Jerusalem")
(Gal. 4:26; Rev. 21–22)

Sacrifice Commemorated

The Church
The New
Temple
(Acts 14:16-18;
Eph. 2:20-21)

New spiritual Temple
inaugurated at Pentecost
(Acts 2)

Works of the Spirit
(New Covenant)
(1 Cor. 11:26)

Christians are true
spiritual Jews
(Rom. 2:28-29)

Some see physical
Israel (the Remnant)
regathered in the
Church (Rom. 11)

All of the promises of restoration made to physical Israel
under the Old Covenant have been fulfilled in the Church
as Spiritual Israel under the New Covenant (Jer. 31:31-34;
Heb. 7:6-13)

Christ's Second Coming
(to reward Church)

Various views see
Christ's coming (spir-
itually) having oc-
curred at A.D. 70 (Pre-
terism), inaugurating
the Kingdom (Rev. 20)
as the present age
(Amillennialism), or
the Church establish-
ing the civil aspect of
the Mosaic Law as it
takes dominion over
all the earth to bring in
the Kingdom (Postmil-
lennialism)

**Eternal
State**

**The Church
in Heaven**

2. *Paul's journey to Jerusalem to learn from the apostles.* Paul consulted with Peter and James about the Christian movement centered in the Holy City. Since Peter later used similar Temple-motifs in his epistle (1 Peter 2:4-10),[9] Paul may have learned from these apostles about the positive respect the Jewish-Christian community showed the Temple. Paul would have undoubtedly learned from these apostles of the respect Jesus paid to the Temple (for example, Jesus' reference to the Temple as "My Father's house," John 2:13-17).

In addition, the reverence shown by the early Christians in Jerusalem may have influenced Paul to use the Temple as a motif for his largely Gentile audience, for he would have wanted them to conform to the mother church in Jerusalem (see Acts 15:22-35).[10] It is also significant that in Acts 15, at the Jerusalem Council, that Paul heard James argue the church's position on worship based on the use of a Temple motif (Acts 15:15-18). (James's argument apparently was adapted from the Septuagint text of Amos 9:11-12, which contains variants from the Masoretic Hebrew Text that may have influenced James's selection of this prophecy concerning the Gentiles' eschatological worship in a restored sanctuary.[11])

3. *Paul viewed the church as sharing the same theological distinctives as the Jerusalem Temple.* Paul seems to have thought metaphorically of the church as a dwelling place, corporately and individually, for the *Shekinah* (equated by Paul with the Holy Spirit, see 1 Corinthians 3:16; 6:19; Ephesians 2:22); possessing a cornerstone that lent unity and harmony to the building (Paul's imagery of Christ as the head of the body, see Ephesians 2:20), and containing priests who carried out a holy function in sacrificial worship (Paul's depiction of Christians as a royal priesthood) and who presented themselves as a sacrificial offering in their priestly performance (see Romans 12:2). With this theological correspondence in view, the only appropriate motif Paul could have used was the Temple.

4. *Paul's metaphorical use was consistent with the hermeneutics of first-century Judaism.* The use of the literal/physical Temple to advance the concept of a spiritual Temple was developed from those texts in the Old Testament concerned with the proper motives for the service of the Temple. The pre-exilic prophets' criticism of improper or improperly motivated offerings (see Amos 5:21-27; Isaiah 1:11-17; 66:1-6; Jeremiah 6:20; 7:21-22; Micah 6:6-8; Hosea 6:6) conversely called for pure spiritual motives to accompany the sacrificial rites (see Psalm 51:15-17; Hosea 14:2). Likewise, the exilic and post-exilic prophets, living for a time without a functioning Temple and service, apparently substituted *mizvot* ("[obedience to] commandments") as spiritual sacrifices (Daniel 1:8; 3:12; 6:5,10) until actual sacrifices could be continued (Ezra 3:2-6).[12] In addi-

tion, the spiritual use of the Temple in both the epistle to the Hebrews and the book of Revelation, as well as the later rabbinic orientation of the earthly Jerusalem to the heavenly Jerusalem, suggests that Paul's usage was normative before as well as after the destruction of the Temple.

Pauline Usage and Hellenistic Influence

Some scholars have proposed that the explanation for Paul's Temple imagery, especially with respect to the Christian as a temple (1 Corinthians 6:19), may be the result of exposure to Hellenistic thought (such as the writings of Philo and the Stoics), which viewed man as a temple.[13] However, Paul did not say that the Christian as "man" was a temple, but that the Christian's "body" (Greek, *soma*) was a temple—a tenet that was rejected by Philo and the Stoics.[14] Further, Paul does not say that the body *alone* is a temple, but only as it exists as part of the holy community—the corporate body of Christ, or the universal church. This was an idea that Hellenistic writers could not accept, since they held that a dualism existed between body and mind, with the body being evil. Therefore, their concept of man as a temple was entirely individualistic.[15] Furthermore, in the anthropology of the Hellenistic and the Graeco-Roman humanists, the concept of "temple" had to be spiritualized because their concept of God could not countenance the idea of the divine presence in man-made dwellings or receiving material offerings. Paul's concern, on the other hand, was not with anthropology as much as with eschatology (in its soteriological expression), and therefore he did not spiritualize the Temple, but analogously applied the function of the literal Temple in Jerusalem to illustrate the purification (sanctification) requisite for those "in [union with] Christ."[16]

Pauline Usage and Influence from Qumran

In contrast to Philo and the Stoics, the literature of Qumran or the Dead Sea Scrolls reveals the use of *temple* in a communal sense—that is, of the Qumran community forming a "spiritual" temple. They clearly did not reject the concept or necessity of a literal Temple; rather, in light of the perceived pollution of the Second Temple, and the eschatological purpose accorded their own sect, they found such figurative usage appropriate. Bertil Gärtner, who has authored a work on the figurative usage of *temple* at Qumran, has argued from this that the connection in the Pauline linkage of holiness and the temple indicates that there was a direct dependence upon the Dead Sea texts.[17] However, while Paul was no doubt aware of this community, it is doubtful that he as a non-initiate would have had access to their "secretive" sectarian documents (or that even if he had known their view, that he would have borrowed the concept from them). Although parallel expressions and theological concepts exist[18] between the Pauline and Qumran literature, this is attributable to a common hermeneutical use of the Old Testament, common Messianic orientation, and the similar social and cultural circumstances shared by the Qumran community and the early Jewish-Christian community. Paul's teaching avoided the dualism and determinism reflected in the Qumran sectarian documents, and his Christological perspective would have precluded his being influenced by or directly using such sectarian material. For example, both Paul and the Qumran community held that God dwelt in the faithful, but for the former this was the result of a gracious bestowal by the Spirit based on the work of Christ, whereas for the latter it resulted from adherence to the Torah. Paul's metaphorical usage should be understood as the result of a shared interpretive approach[19] and the similar relationships of the Christian and Qumran communities with respect to the Temple.[20] However, as one study of Paul's metaphorical usage has pointed out,[21] Jesus used the Temple metaphorically with reference to His physical body in John 2:19-22, and this may have been sufficient precedent for Paul to do likewise, since his subject is the spiritual body of Christ.[22]

Having considered some of the possible reasons for Paul's metaphorical use of the Temple as a motif, let us return to the principal texts mentioned earlier (Ephesians 2:19-22; 1 Corinthians 3:16-17; 1 Corinthians 6:19; and Galatians 4:25-26) for an analysis of their argument in support of a positive Pauline attitude toward the Temple.

Paul's Concept of the Church as a Temple

Paul's description of the church as "a temple" does not imply that he viewed the Jerusalem Temple as having been replaced by the church.[23] In fact, the grammar in Paul's analogous use of *naos* indicates that no substitution of the church for the Temple was intended. The Greek noun *naos* is indefinite ("a temple"), rather than definite ("the Temple") in all the occurrences except one. If Paul unambiguously meant to teach that the church was presently or eschatologically *the* New Temple, the definite article would have been expected.[24] Leon Morris suggests that this anartharous (without the article) use was to put emphasis on their *character* as God's temples;[25] however, this would be unnecessary in view of the qualitative adjective "holy," which modifies most of the uses. The single instance (1 Corinthians 3:16)[26] where *naos* may be understood as definite[27] (even though anartharous) with reference to the church still cannot have in view the theological *replacement* of the Jerusalem Temple by the church because, in the very next verse, the effectiveness of Paul's warning depends upon the historic Jerusalem Temple continuing to have sanctity (more on this in a moment). The immediate context addresses the need of the believing members of the Corinthian community to remain undefiled by their pagan culture, symbolized by the temples of Apollo and Aphrodite (at the Agora and Acrocorinth respectively). Paul uses "the temple of God" for the believers as a contrast to the pagan temples that dominated the Corinthian landscape, since the believer's connection was now with the Jerusalem Temple, which represented the holiness of God, as opposed to the impurity of their temple's idols (used in this comparison), from which they were to be separate (1 Corinthians 3:17; see also 1 Thessalonians 1:9). Just as the Jerusalem Temple remained the center of sanctity in the midst of the Gentile domination and its many temples (considered a desecration), so those who had found the *one true God* now represented His *one true temple* in Corinth.[28] Nothing in this analogy requires that their status as the spiritual temple *in Corinth* replace the physical Temple *in Jerusalem*. Rather, it is from the holy *character* of the Jerusalem Temple that their temple derived its sanctity.

Paul's selection of the Jerusalem Temple as a metaphor for the church is justified on account of the spiritual function of the Temple in Judaism. Our source texts demonstrate this, drawing upon six spiritual elements that define the purpose for both structures:[29]

1. *The Temple as a dwelling place for the divine presence*. As we saw in chapter 2, this was the primary significance of the central Sanctuary from its prototype in Eden to the time at Mount Sinai, where the *Shekinah* filled the tent of meeting and the Tabernacle. Even though Solomon articulated the conflict between divine immanence and transcendence at the dedication of the First Temple (1 Kings 8:27), still, the Temple was popularly considered to be the place where God's name dwelt. It is for this reason, and because the *Shekinah* was manifested within the Holy of Holies,[30] that Paul employed *naos* over *heiron*—because it more clearly communicated this reality that Paul now saw as defining the church (whether universal, corporate, or as the believer's body).

This emphasis is seen in Paul's grammatical construction in 1 Corinthians 3:16, where the Greek text reads: *naos theou este* kai *to pneuma tou theou oikei en humin* ("you are a temple of God *and* the Spirit of God dwells in you"). Here the explicative *kai* serves to further explain the previous statement—namely, that the Corinthians were God's temple *because* God's Spirit was dwelling within them. This is also seen in 1 Corinthians 6:19 when Paul writes, "Your body is a temple of the Holy Spirit who is in you." It is the indwelling Holy Spirit that constitutes the believer's "body" as "a temple." Also, in Ephesians 2:21-22 we find Paul paralleling the phrases "holy temple in the Lord" and "a dwelling of God in the Spirit." In this construction, the second phrase explicates the first, showing that the church is a temple because it hosts the presence of God through the Spirit.[31]

2. *The Temple as a place for spiritual offering.* In this instance Paul looks beyond the material sacrifices to the spiritual motives of the person bringing an offering to the altar. Though Paul knew that Jesus had fulfilled the typological significance of the sacrificial system (which was not its only purpose—see chapter 23),[32] he still recognized that offerings served as a spiritual expression of faith, obedience, and devotion. This conclusion may be supported by Paul's application of sacrificial terminology to the Christian's spiritual life. The use of the liturgical metaphors "present," "living and holy sacrifice," and "spiritual service" in Romans 12:1; Paul's description of his own service in relation to the Philippian church's faith as being "poured out [as a libation offering] on [their] sacrifice and [priestly] service" (Philippians 2:17); Paul's description of the Philippians' gift as an "acceptable sacrifice" in Philippians 4:18; and Paul's statement about his own work as a "priest" ministering (as a Temple sacrifice) "the gospel of God" and his Gentile converts as a sacrificial offering (Romans 15:16), all attest to Paul's view of the believer as a priest and his spiritual conduct as priestly service. In addition, Paul's use of certain metaphors for Christian obligations such as "worship" (Philippians 3:3), "prayer" or [priestly] supplication or petition, for example (Philippians 1:4), and the Lord's Supper (see 1 Corinthians 10:14-21, where the Temple service is used for illustration) do not invalidate the Temple ritual, but rather, appeal to it as a model for Christian observance.

3. *The Temple as a witness to the Gentiles.* The Temple and its service were always inclusive of the non-Jewish foreigner, and assurance was given to him of God's presence to hear prayers if they were directed toward the Temple in recognition of it as the established place of God's promise and purpose (1 Kings 8:41-43). For this reason Isaiah had good cause to envision the eschatological Temple as a "house of prayer...for all the peoples" (Isaiah 56:7). The Temple functioned as a witness to the surrounding nations of the glory and power of God (1 Kings 9:6-10; 2 Chronicles 7:19-22). In addition, one of the duties of the priest was to witness to the people through the proclamation of instruction or *Torah* (Leviticus 10:11; Deuteronomy 33:10; Malachi 2:7). Thus, the Temple served as a paradigm for the church (the believing community) to witness to the world of

the glory and power of God as revealed in Jesus as the Messiah (Acts 1:8; 2 Corinthians 5:20).

4. *The Temple as the model for holiness.* Had Paul been thinking about any temple other than the Jerusalem Temple, he could not have written, "...in whom the whole building, being fitted together is growing into *a holy temple* in the Lord" (Ephesians 2:21, emphasis added), or "*The temple of God is holy*, and that is what you are" (1 Corinthians 3:17, emphasis added).[33] To make such an analogy to holiness requires a holy Temple, and only the Jerusalem Temple was the defining *locus* of all sacred space—the center of sanctity to a Jew, and especially to a Pharisee like Paul. Only the Temple could have provided the unique construction metaphors for Paul's exhortation to build spiritually on the proper foundation with permanent materials (see 1 Corinthians 3:10-12). It has been suggested that Paul's depiction of his own role in verse 10 as a "master builder" (Greek, *architekton*) may have been part of the vocabulary of ancient building contracts for temples.[34] Whatever the case, he certainly means more by it than common building construction, as the context reveals.[35] While it is true that Paul's list of six building materials in verse 12 ("gold, silver, precious stones, wood, hay, straw") is given in a descending scale of values, cost is not the issue here, but perishablity (gold being the most imperishable, and straw the most perishable). Yet even here, these represent the permanence of Christ versus the impermanence of Gentile (human) "wisdom" within the context of the Temple imagery.[36] Therefore, the list of materials used in verse 12 anticipates the Temple metaphor of verses 16-17 and must have in mind the materials used to construct the Temple. Indeed, gold and silver would not be reasonable materials for any other type of building; only a temple would contain all of these elements.[37]

This is further confirmed by the manner in which these materials are tested—that is, by fire. Because the context has in view a future judgment by God during which the believer's work will be examined (2 Corinthians 5:10), the context is eschatological, and the use of fire is a standard metaphor for such judgment (see Malachi 3:2; 4:1; 2 Thessalonians 1:7; Hebrews 10:27; 12:29; 2 Peter 3:7)—a metaphor for eschatological judgment.[38] While it is the work (the manner of construction) rather than the building ("temple," see verse 16) that is tested by fire, the association must have in mind the historic destruction of the First Temple by fire, since the desecration of the Temple and the consequence of divine retribution are the subject of verse 17. This punishment owes its severity to the fact that God's *naos* is holy—a punishment that would not make sense if the sanctity and inviolability of the Jerusalem Temple were not in view. The use of the desecration/restoration motif here and in 2 Corinthians 6:14–7:1 further confirms the appropriateness of using the Jerusalem Temple as an analogy for the holiness to be perfected by the church (see 2 Corinthians 7:1).

5. *The Temple as a symbol of unity*. Politically and religiously, the Jerusalem Temple served as a unifying factor for the geographically separated 12 tribes of Israel. When David consolidated the north and south by the placement of his capital (and later, the Ark—2 Samuel 6:17) in Jerusalem, he created this unity, divisible only by cession (political) or apostasy (religious). This was forever fixed thereafter by the placement of the Temple (2 Samuel 7:13). However, it is not to this unity that Paul looks when he seeks to illustrate this theme, but to the uniformity of the building stones and their placement around a cornerstone which unifies the whole. Thus in Ephesians 2:21-22 we read, "…in whom the whole building, being fitted together…into a holy temple in the Lord…built together into a dwelling of God in the Spirit." The unity of the Temple is symbolized here by the verbs *sunarmologoumena* and *sunoikodomiesthe*, which respectively denote a "fitting together" and a "building up together" (of stones) to form a cohesive unit. Based on this analogy, Jesus becomes the cornerstone (after a midrash of Isaiah 28:16; see 1 Peter 2:4-8),[39] and believers become the individual stones, placed together to form a unified church, like the well-constructed holy Temple.

The issue of unity may have also been at the forefront of Paul's thinking in 1 Corinthians 3. While the usual interpretation sees the problem of false wisdom as the focus of the passage, de Lacey has argued that the problem of factiousness was considered an even greater threat to the church by Paul, adding another reason the apostle employed the Temple imagery.[40] He would see this section, if not the whole letter, as an apologetic defense of Paul's apostolic credentials. The Temple-image, then, becomes the ideal means of defusing the threat of the Apollos-group by shifting the attention to the whole church's self-identity as a worshiping community—something not possible within a context of divisiveness. Just as in Ephesians 2:20-21, an appeal to unity based on the functional unity of the Temple's construction and its unification in worship fostered a return to the spiritual cohesiveness that ought to characterize the church, and which was symbolized by the long and ritually regulated process of the careful rebuilding of the Second Temple.[41]

6. *The Temple as a growing community*. Because parts of the Temple were still under construction in Paul's day he could accurately employ the Temple as an image of the growth of the believing community of Christians at Ephesus. This was in spite of the fact that one of the greatest temples in Asia Minor, if not

the entire Graeco-Roman world, was located in Ephesus itself (see Acts 19:27,35). Ephesians 2:21 (see 1 Peter 2:5), in describing the unified building of the Temple, uses the verb "to grow" (Greek, *auxano*) to denote the continuing construction of the Temple structure. The growth is both internal (by the greater cohesion of the individual stones) and external (by the addition of new stones). This is an integral part of the solution to the factions in Corinth, as well, and 1 Corinthians 3:7 also employs the same verb "to grow" in this sense (although in this case, the imagery is taken from horticulture, with each leader of a faction contributing to the overall growth of the church by the addition of new converts). Yet, as previously mentioned, this metaphor is often joined to the construction metaphor in 1 Corinthians 3:9, bringing together the Temple-growth imagery. Paul's picture, then, is of an increased community of believers through the promotion of unity among its members.

Paul's Warnings as Evidence of the Temple's Sanctity

In the Corinthian passages we have just examined there are also practical warnings that assume the sanctity of the Jerusalem Temple and use it to enforce the strength of their exhortations. In order for us to grasp the full extent of Paul's reverence for the Temple, we need to observe the way that Paul used a positive Temple metaphor even in a negative context.

The Warning Against Temple Destruction

The focus of the ominous warning in 1 Corinthians 3:17 that "God will destroy" are moral offenses that result in ritual contamination. The problem we see in 1 Corinthians 3:1-15 is an attitude of spiritual exclusiveness that threatened to destroy the church by splintering it into rival factions—something that in Paul's day was also observable within the political sphere of the Temple. Just as Jewish sectarian rivalries eventually were, in part, responsible for the destruction of the Second Temple, so might a similar "party spirit" affect the analogous "holy place," the church (which theologically is indivisible as the body of Christ—see 1 Corinthians 1:13). Such consequences would bring the wrath of God, as would any desecration of the Temple. Again, Paul's definite reference here to "the temple of God" refers to the Jerusalem Temple, not the church (as in the previous verse, where the indefinite "a temple of God" is used). The language here possesses all the earmarks of a sentence of divine retribution as emphasized by its chiastic (A:B:B:A) structure: "A: the Temple of God B: if anyone destroys B: destroys this person A: will God"[42] Here, then, is a double entendre: the sanctity of the Jerusalem Temple and the church as Christ's own spiritual temple, combined to express the fearful judgment of God in the last days.[43] This expected judgment is patterned after the judicial consequences of Temple desecration and defilement. This is confirmed by its appearances in the formal character of casuistic law (*lex talionis*), where the penalty for such an offense is capital punishment (Exodus 28:43; Leviticus 16:2).[44]

While men who seek to destroy the church may escape judicial review on earth, Paul assures such ones that the heavenly tribunal will execute swift justice in accord with the severity of this crime against holiness. In this announcement of the divine execution of "temple desecrators" we see the *eschatological* nature of the desecration motif, as present desecration invites future retributive response. There may also be in the background of this individual eschatological warning the universal eschatological warning, always latent in Paul, of the coming Temple desecrator, the Antichrist, who will likewise meet with eternal doom as a result of his ultimate sacrilege. Because the text of Daniel 9:27 (which may provide Paul with this eschatological reference) concludes by stating that the one who desolates the Temple of God will be destroyed by God, this famous eschatological judgment may have served to warn potential violators of the true source of such actions typical of antichrists (see 1 John 2:18,22; 4:3).

In 1 Corinthians 6:18-20 the warning against spiritual desecration appears in the imperative: "Flee immorality." The reason for this urgent warning is because of the analogous relationship between the body and the Temple. As the Temple belongs to God by virtue of His dwelling within it—i.e., possessing it—for it is *His* house—so the body of the believer, which has the Spirit of God indwelling it, belongs to God as His possession. Note again that the term Paul uses here for the bodily temple is *naos*, the technical expression used of the inner *sanctum*, especially the *Sanctum Sanctoris*, the Holy of Holies. In the Temple service, to allow foreign objects not legitimately part of the *sancta* into the Holy Place constituted a desecration of the highest magnitude, since it was tantamount to an invasion of idolatry. That this is Paul's meaning here may be seen by the exact same parallel construction in 1 Corinthians 10:14, where there is an injunction against idolatry. Therefore, Paul is saying that because the body is possessed by God as His own "temple," the outside invasion of foreign bodies—i.e., in fornication—disrupts the essential unity and constitutes an idolatrous affront to ownership. The purpose of the Temple was to glorify God through the performance of the Temple service, an activity which, as Scripture states, forged the covenantal relationship between "My people" and "My God" in practical terms. In like manner, the purpose for the bodily "temple" is to glorify God by living a sanctified life, which precludes the commission of defiling acts such as fornication.

The Warning Against Idols in the Temple

Second Corinthians 6 is especially significant for the Pauline use of the Temple desecration imagery, since it contains the only occurrence in the New Testament of the term "Belial" (Greek) or "Beliar" (Hebrew), which also appears in Jewish intertestamental apocalyptic literature, such as the Dead Sea Scrolls (see Hymns Scroll and halakhic letter 4QMMT).[45] As with 1 Corinthians 3 and 6, the problem again is an idolatrous union formed by the holy and the profane. The Pauline imperative bears this out in verse 14: "Do not be bound together with unbelievers." Here Paul's use of the term "bound together" *(heterzugountes)* employs a legal metaphor drawn from Jewish *halakha* and constructed as a midrash on Deuteronomy 22:10, which records the law against mismatching animals (ox and donkey).

Of greater importance to our study, however, is Paul's antithesis section, verses 14b-16a, which is predicated on verse 16b and the assertion that believers are "the temple of the living God." Before considering the antithesis section, let's look at the terminology Paul uses to establish his premise that as a "temple of God" believers are not to participate in any union that would defile God's presence. The analogous relationships he uses to justify his argument are drawn from the legal literature and the prophets. First, citing Exodus 29:45 and Leviticus 26:12, Paul borrows the covenantal language of God's suzerain-vassal relationship to convey the unbreakable bond between the believer and His God: "I will dwell in them and walk among them; and I will be their God, and they shall be My people" (2 Corinthians 6:16). The first part of the clause "I will dwell in them" could very well be a paraphrase of Ezekiel 37:27 (in the Septuagint), which speaks of a dwelling place—literally, "taking up lodging" *(kataskauosis)*. The word *enoikein*, according to commentator Ralph Martin, is a stronger term for habitation than the term *skanoō* (Greek, "tabernacle" = *sheken* [Hebrew], from which both the terms *mishkan* ["Tabernacle"] and *Shekinah* ["Divine Presence"] are derived).[46]

The imagery, then, is of the *Shekinah* within the Holy of Holies—the most exclusive, private, and non-invasive place on earth. The second part of the clause takes us back to the Garden of Eden and the Edenic Sanctuary motif with the words "I will walk among them." Here is a reproduction of the service expression, "walking," used in Genesis 3:8 to speak of God approaching man in Eden and of the activity of a priestly performance in Leviticus. This language, which connects the Pentateuch with the prophets in a continuity of thought, portrays the divine ideal for the Christian community—an ideal that was formerly restricted to the Temple and its service. Such an exceptional comparison, however, can lead commentators to draw unwarranted conclusions, as W.D. Davies explains: "The church is for Paul the fulfillment of the hopes of Judaism for the Temple: the presence of the Lord has moved from the Temple to the church....and the life of the church replaces the Temple service through its own spiritual sacrifices (Rom. 12:1ff.) and the foundation of a new Temple (Ephesians 2:20). It is easy to conclude that there was a deliberate rejection by Paul of the Holy Space in favor of the Holy People—the church."[47]

Again, however, the idea is not one of replacement, but of correspondence, adopting the service motifs (which are pregnant with theological and eschatological meaning) in order to reinforce the concept of spiritual separation from a spatial separation. In other words, the Christian community, the church, is like the ideal eschatological Temple in that it is a "temple" in which God reveals Himself, covenants with His people, promises His abiding presence, and relates to them as priests involved in sacred service. This, then, allows for the church to be *a* temple—and, in the Pauline understanding of the church as the repository of the divine Spirit in this age—*the* (spiritual) Temple, while not displacing the prophetic role of the Jerusalem Temple in the age to come. Davies also acknowledges this, stating that he sees no explicit rejection of the Jerusalem Temple by Paul and supporting his affirmation by referring to 2 Thessalonians 2:3-4, where he observes that the Temple remains "for Paul a centre of eschatological significance."[48]

With Paul's concept of the church in mind, we may return to the antithesis section to consider the significant contrast between "Christ and Belial" in verse 15. Here we read: "...for what partnership have righteousness and lawlessness, or what fellowship has light with darkness? Or what harmony has Christ with Belial, or what has a believer in common with an unbeliever? Or what agreement has the temple of God with idols?" (verse 14-16). These five rhetorical questions, each commencing with the interrogative pronoun "what," are set off in a logical progression to substantiate the conclusion already drawn in the imperatival clause that precedes the section: "Do not be bound together with unbelievers."

Because Paul is addressing a mixed congregation of Jews and Gentiles within one of Asia Minor's most notoriously pagan cities, Corinth, his contrasts are not abstractions, but relate to various concerns for purity in the midst of defilement. It is in this context that we can understand Paul's reference to "Belial" (or "Beliar"), which appears with the word *sugkathathesis* ("harmony") as *hapax legomena* (solitary uses). The word "harmony" is a technical expression for "syncretism," and has in view the coalescing of a true faith (represented in this case by "Christ") with a pagan service (represented by "Belial"). There have been numerous suggestions offered to explain Paul's use of "Belial" instead of the more common (and expected) antonym *Satanos* ("Satan").[49] I am of the opinion, based on the comparative use of the term in the noncanonical Jewish intertestamental writings, that Paul envisioned an eschatological antithesis between *Christos*, the human-divine deliverer of Israel and restorer of the Temple, and *Beliar*, the quasi-human Antichrist figure who is the oppressor of Israel and the desecrator of the Temple.[50] This explanation accords well with the original usage of the term, the pattern of Paul's teaching concerning the Antichrist in Gentile cities,[51] and the eschatological tone that accompanies Temple metaphors in the desecration contexts. Therefore, it may be that Paul's concept of the Antichrist in the Temple (2 Thessalonians 2:4) is in the background of his antithesis in 2 Corinthians 6:16a: "What agreement has the temple of God with idols?"[52] While this could be a general reference against defiling the Holy Place, the preceding contrast between "Christ" and Belial (Antichrist) may intend an allusion to this ultimate eschatological, and in Paul's thinking, possibly near desecration. While the expression "temple of God" is a familiar one with Paul, it is noteworthy that it is exactly this phrase that is used in 2 Thessalonians 2:4 to describe the place of the Antichrist's desecrating presence. Also, the use of the *hapax* "harmony" *(sugkatathesis)* in 1 Corinthians 6:16a may lend to this interpretation, for it goes beyond the idea of mere syncretism to that of "union, agreement," the very kind of blasphemous identification that the Antichrist claims with God by his action of positioning himself in the Holy of Holies in the Temple.

We return to the use of the Temple desecration motif in the appeal to "be separate" in 2 Corinthians 6:17; 7:1. The imperatival phrase "come out from their midst" has an almost escapist tone with the use of *exelthei* ("to go out, escape"—see John 10:39). If the Antichrist teaching were in the background, then such a tone would be an appropriate allusion to the injunction to flee when those in Jerusalem see the "abomination of desolation" in the Temple (Matthew 24:15-16; Mark 13:14). There is also here the idea of ritual-purification in this call to separation (2 Corinthians 6:17). It is apparently a citation in Isaiah 52:11, which records the command to priests who were transporting the sacred Temple vessels back to Jerusalem from Babylon in the day of restoration. When that event occurs, Isaiah's message is to warn the priests to not defile the Temple vessels by making contact with foreign objects. This is an apt analogy for Paul, since as a "temple of God" the church is not to permit "foreign" things (that is, "lawlessness, darkness, unbelievers, idols," etc.) into their holy relationship with God, which would render them defiled, and hence, disqualify them from His service. This liturgical metaphor is reinforced in 2 Corinthians 7:1 with the words: "…let us cleanse ourselves from all defilement of flesh and spirit, perfecting holiness in the fear of God." In the purification process described here, Paul's joining of the indicative ("cleanse") and the imperative ("perfecting") is to call for a *demonstration* of the holiness that is already present in the constitution of the church as a "temple of God." The *hapax* term *molusmos* ("defilement") in this verse connects the thought once again with idolatry (Jeremiah 23:15 LXX; see 1 Esdras 8:80; 2 Maccabees 5:27),[53] and the dual expression "flesh and spirit" may connect with apocalyptic terminology, hinting at the idea that the *Shekinah* will return to God's future earthly Temple even as today the same Spirit indwells the bodily temple of believers.[54]

Paul's Concept of the Church as an Eschatological Temple

Thus far we have dealt with some of the arguments offered by proponents of the position that Paul taught that the church permanently replaced the Jerusalem Temple as the true institution of service on earth. Yet another argument used to demonstrate that Paul promoted this view is based on Galatians 4:25-26. This passage, though beset with interpretive difficulties,[55] is thought by many commentators to equate the heavenly Jerusalem with the church and teach that it has eclipsed the old earthly Jerusalem. Here we can see that Paul accepts the concept of an eschatological Jerusalem, hence an eschatological Temple, however, a careful examination of the text reveals that his concern in Galatians is not with the eschatological age, but with an apologetic concern facing the Galatian church. Paul, as we will see, keeps separate his two images of the heavenly and earthly Jerusalem, and in fact does not confuse or equate the heavenly Jerusalem with the church on earth.

The epistle to the Galatians was probably written to the church in South Galatia prior to the Jerusalem Council (Acts 15) (although a North Galatian destination sometime after is also possible[56]). Paul's purpose was to write an apologetic defense of his position on Christian liberty (see Galatians 2:4; 5:1,13).[57] A polemical tone is evident in the book, first in answering charges against his apostleship (chapters 1–2), then in arguing the theological position on justification by faith (chapters 3–4), and again in contending against the theological position of his opponents on circumcision (chapter 5:1-12). The most irenic section appears in Galatians 5:13–6:18, which, following the pattern of his other epistles, concludes with practical admonitions. It is within the section comprising chapters 3–4 that Paul, to reinforce his case on justification by faith, appeals to the Old Testament and adds a midrash on the story of Abraham, which he concludes with what he terms an "allegory" (Greek, *allagoreō*), although the idea is more "figurative" than "allegorical."[58]

Paul introduces the figure of Abraham first in Galatians 3:6 with a citation from Genesis 15:6 concerning Abraham's reception of God's promise by faith. This forms the theological foundation of his discussion of the nature of the relationship between promise (the Abrahamic covenant) and Law (the Mosaic covenant). Underscoring the conditional nature of the Mosaic covenant, Paul cites Deuteronomy 27:26 (see Galatians 3:10) as evidence that legal obligation results in a curse upon all who violate its commandments, thus removing those people from the sphere of promise (verse 14; see Galatians 5:4).

With verse 16 Paul returns to his context in Genesis 15 with an allusion to Genesis 15:5, using its singular reference (over against a collective interpretation) to "seed" (Greek, *spermati* = Hebrew, *zera*) to define the spiritual limitations of the inheritors of the promises to Abraham. The argument is that relationship to God, rather than physical descent, determined the individual inheritance of the promises. This relationship was established by faith in Jesus, who as Messiah, was intended as the sole "seed" of Abraham. Therefore Jesus' followers share in His inheritance as the only Israelite capable of fulfilling the Abrahamic covenant for the Nation. However, the point here is that the inheritance was originally granted freely through faith, not on the basis of legal obligation, so Paul returns to answer the question of the relationship between promise and the Law in verse 17.

Although historically Law followed promise, Paul maintains that the conditions of the Mosaic covenant did not vitiate the unconditional promise of the Abrahamic covenant. Rather, the Law was a necessary, though temporary, custodian of the promises until the Messiah was born (Galatians 3:19-23; 4:4). The Messiah, then, took upon Himself the curse of the Law, thereby freeing men to receive the promise by faith (Galatians 3:13,26). With this Abrahamic midrash as background, we are prepared for Paul's analogical use of the figures of Abraham's wives Hagar and Sarah in Galatians 4:21-31 (taken from Genesis 16 and 21).[59]

Paul's introduction of the Abraham midrash was in view of the polemical nature of his defense. This continues to be the explanation for his typological/ analogical use of the Hagar-Sarah stories, and especially the unique clash between type and antitype here, since, as Barrett has pointed out, his exegetical method here was determined not by his own choice, but by his opponents' use of the Pentateuchal traditions.[60] Apparently Paul's opponents derived their theological position of spiritual inheritance by physical descent from these same accounts in Genesis,[61] and while the literal interpretation of the text conveys this thought, Paul brings to surface the greater spiritual intentions of the texts (based on the Abrahamic-faith paradigm which includes these wives) to establish his refutation.[62] His selection of only two of Abraham's wives with only their children (verses 22-23) followed the contrast introduced by his opponents to defend their child of flesh = child of promise thesis. However, Paul forcibly inverts his opponents' exegesis by use of his typological/analogical method in Galatians 4:24-26: "This is allegorically speaking: for these women are two covenants, one proceeding from Mount Sinai bearing children who are to be slaves; she is Hagar. Now Hagar is Mount Sinai in Arabia, and corresponds to the present Jerusalem, for she is in slavery with her children. But the Jerusalem above is free; she is our mother."

In Paul's contrast here, the focus is on the mothers rather than the children.[63] This change in focus is due to his new direction of argumentation, using the two women to typify the Abrahamic and Sinaitic covenants, a focus that nevertheless is consistent in the context because it is continued by extension from the Abrahamic promise/Mosaic Law contrast of the previous Abraham midrash.[64] While it is difficult to understand the textual basis of Paul's equation of Hagar with Mount Sinai and the Law,[65] the slavery motif provides the literary justification for the analogy, since the Jews, and not only them but their spiritual center, Jerusalem, are in a state of bondage to the Mosaic Law, just as Hagar and her children were in bondage.

The other side of the contrast is unexpected, for Paul does not set in antithesis the equations Sarah/free woman = Abrahamic covenant = New Jerusalem as anticipated. Instead, he relegates the first two elements of the equation to an ellipsis, making explicit only the last element (verse 26a), in which he describes the "Jerusalem above" as "free." Thus, in contrasting "the present Jerusalem" of the Hagar equation with "the Jerusalem above" in the antithetical equation, Paul juxtaposes temporal and spatial categories, which although unusual, has a precedent, as we have seen in chapter 3, in the biblical theology of the *tabnit* or the heavenly Temple pattern reproduced on earth.[66]

Paul now adds to his parallelism between the two women and the two cities, the qualifying words "she is our mother," basing the contrast upon a *Zion as the mother of the faithful* motif.[67] His use of this motif is apparently conditioned by his opponent's assumption that "the present Jerusalem" served as the mother city and therefore as the center of faith for both Judaism and the church.[68] Paul's argument by this inclusion is that, while he acknowledges that earthly Jerusalem is the spiritual center, it is not now, nor has it ever been, the true mother. Since, as

Paul argued, faith, not Law, is what establishes the true relationship with God, then "the Jerusalem above," which was not part of the legal system (imposed because of human sin), is the true center for believers, whether Jew or Gentile.[69]

However, we should *not* see here Paul's rejection or replacement of "the Jerusalem below" (or its Temple) by "the Jerusalem above,"[70] but, like Jesus' "cleansing" of the Temple, Paul is attacking a contemporary Judaism that threatened the freedom of faith. From Paul's perspective, the Mosaic system, as interpreted by the Judaizers, was not compatible with the independent nature of "the Jerusalem above."[71] The literary context does not imply that the earthly Jerusalem would be destroyed and replaced by the heavenly Jerusalem, but simply sets up a positive correspondence in its position as "the mother" of the Christian faith. Whereas the Judaizers put Christianity within the sphere of Judaism, Paul argued that two separate realms existed, both properly subsumed within the true mother. However, one cannot have a "citizenship" in both cities—one must either be born in bondage to the Law in "the present Jerusalem," or born to freedom as a child of faith in "the Jerusalem above." If that is the case, then no regulatory authority can be exercised by the former upon the latter. This is clearly stated in Galatians 4:27 (citing Isaiah 54:1): "For it is written, 'Rejoice, barren woman who does not bear; break forth and shout, you who are not in labor; for more are the children of the desolate than of the one who has a husband.'"[72]

In Isaiah 54:1 the barren woman is used as a restoration motif for Jerusalem after the exile. But here, Paul applies it to Sarah, who, as the matriarch of faith, was given the promise of the inheritance.[73] Paul's deliberate use of irony here shifted the promise from the historical Jerusalem, the city of the Law, to the heavenly Jerusalem, or the city of faith, again showing that the promise given unconditionally was proscriptive of the freedom of faith, not the bondage of the Law.[74] Paul then returns to the Pentateuch to conclude his argument from the patriarchal context in Genesis. In Galatians 4:28, in typological fashion, he links Isaac with Christians (Jew or Gentile) as children of the promise, and then in verse 29 he forges the link between the present situation and the Pentateuchal tradition with the Isaac-Ishmael struggle.[75] The source of the persecution Paul alluded to in verse 29 was explained in later rabbinic tradition as Ishmael's idolatry,[76] or as a challenge for inheritance based on submission to voluntary circumcision.[77] Whether or not Paul had such an extrabiblical tradition in mind, he used the connection to facilitate a last ironic thrust for his argument from Genesis 21:10, for with this text Paul calls for the expulsion of the Judaizers on the basis of the very law they claimed for their support.

Paul's Affirmation of a Traditional View

We have seen that in this context Paul does in fact distinguish between an earthly and heavenly Jerusalem, and it is this very distinction that argues against any idea of replacement. The Temple symbolized the legal system of Judaism, which, in Paul's view, was now being used to discredit the faith of Gentiles who had not undergone ritualistic proselytism (that is, circumcision). This system was seen as subordinate to the greater promise made to Abraham, which was apart from and prior to the Mosaic covenant. Christ is the ultimate seed of Abraham, fulfilling the spiritual aspects of the promise for those who believe. The earthly Temple was at present in bondage to this inferior system. However, the heavenly Jerusalem (with its heavenly Temple) existed to fulfill this spiritual function for those who are now related to Christ by faith. Paul does not deal eschatologically with the Temple in this analogy, and does not equate the mother Jerusalem in heaven with the church on earth. While Paul may have held to the view that the heavenly Jerusalem was the counterpart of the earthly Jerusalem, he polemically presents them as separate realms in his analogy. Nothing in this text cancels respect for the present Temple, nor mitigates against an ultimate fulfillment for the Temple in terms of restoration (Ezekiel 40–48; see also Revelation 11:19). Therefore, while not implied here, this understanding leaves open an earthly fulfillment of function by the Messianic Temple under the New Covenant in the Millennium.

Our conclusion, then, is that the apostle Paul, as both a Jewish theologian and a missionary to the Gentiles, respected the traditional understanding of the Temple as God's holy place and, based on this established concept, derived the analogy of the believer's body, and by extension the body of all believers united in Christ, the church, as a spiritual temple in which the holy presence of God dwells through the Spirit. In the same way, Paul referred to the ritual purification in the Temple as a metaphor for the priestly consecration and spiritual service of believers to God through Christ. Nowhere in Paul's epistles do we find him speaking negatively of the Temple or its services; rather, in warning passages concerning personal (immorality) or corporate defilement (idolatry), Paul borrowed from the language of divine retribution against Temple desecration. Given this positive portrayal of the Temple and Paul's recognition of the severity of Temple desecration, we are justified in reading Paul's statements concerning the Temple in 2 Thessalonians 2:3-4 as a future violation of the Jerusalem Temple's sanctity. This conclusion will be further validated as we move in the next chapter to see how the apostle John predicted similar events for the Temple in his Apocalypse.

CHAPTER 14

Predictions in the Apocalypse

The Last Days Temple in the Book of Revelation

The figurative interpretation [of the Temple in the book of Revelation] fails for a number of reasons. . . . The only way out of this entanglement of internal contradictions is to understand this as a literal Temple that will exist in actuality during the future period just before Christ returns. The false messiah will desecrate it and turn it into a place for people to worship him. . . . A distinct hope of Christians is for the future repentance of Israel. This requires a re-institution of the national life of this people, including its Temple.[1]

—Robert Thomas

From John's first vision in the book of Revelation to his last, the Temple is in view. Indeed, the Temple makes more appearances in Revelation than in any other single book in the New Testament and in the Synoptic Gospels combined. Here we see the entire history of the Temple in John's references to the Tabernacle, Tent, Temple, and the Heavenly Temple in the New Jerusalem—the final reality of the divine purpose for the Sanctuary. Its presentation of the Temple employs multiple parallels to Genesis, completing the circle between first things and last things (protology and eschatology). The concept of a Sanctuary, which appeared in Genesis in a symbolic form, is developed in Revelation to its full and final extent. The divine ideal revealed in the first chapters of Genesis are viewed as a reality in the final chapters of Revelation. As the latest of the New Testament compositions, the book of Revelation stands at the end of the biblical corpus to reveal God's future and ultimate teaching concerning the Last Days Temple.

The Interpretation of the Book of Revelation

The literary genius G.K. Chesterton once quipped, "Though St. John the Evangelist saw many strange monsters in his vision, he saw no creatures so wild as one of his own commentators."[2] The widely varied conjectures of various commentators is one reason many people simply give up on trying to understand John's vision in Revelation, for they conclude that if the scholars cannot agree on how to interpret the book's prophetic language, then how could a layman? If you find yourself in this company, take heart, for the book has always challenged the best of saints and scholars. While this fact may end up adding to many people's confusion and tempt them to abandon the search for meaning, it is important to recognize that for the most part, only four major interpretations of the book have arisen through time. Once we understand these four viewpoints, we will gain a better perspective of why the Temple, one of the central subjects of the book, is so often misunderstood. Let us briefly consider the four principal prophetic positions held by historic Christianity[3] in order to understand the problems presented by John's prophecies concerning the coming Temple.

1. *The Historicist interpretation.* Historicism views the book of Revelation as a prewritten record of the course of history (hence, "historicists")—from the apostolic period to the world's end (which for this interpretation means the entire church age). The fulfillment of its prophecies began shortly after its writing during the reign of the Roman emperors and has continued for the last 2,000 years. This view, therefore, allows for the setting of dates for prophetic fulfillment both in the past and the present, although modern adherents, except for

Seventh-Day Adventists, have usually refrained from this practice. Therefore, according to this view, the prophecies concerning the Temple are interpreted as having had their fulfillment in the ancient past, ending with the events associated with its destruction by Rome in A.D. 70.

2. *The Preterist interpretation.* Preterism, like historicism, interprets the fulfillment of the prophecies of Revelation as past, but it differs in that it interprets this fulfillment as having most, if not all, of its fulfillment during the Roman war against the Jews (A.D. 66–70), culminating with the Roman destruction of Jerusalem in A.D. 70. *Extreme* (or consistent) *preterists* hold that *complete* fulfillment of all the prophetic events (including the second coming of Christ) occurred in the first century by the time of the Roman destruction of Jerusalem (the end of the generation of Jews who killed Christ). *Moderate* (or inconsistent) *preterists* agree that an *incomplete* fulfillment of the prophetic events occurred by the time of this destruction, including a return of Christ to judge the Jews, but also hold that Christ's coming is still future. Preterists argue that the book of Revelation was written before the fall of Jerusalem; therefore they contend that the Temple described in Revelation 11:1-2 was the Second Temple, whose destruction completely fulfilled all of the prophecies concerning it.

3. *The Futurist interpretation.* Futurism shares with historicism and preterism a belief that the prophetic events described in the book of Revelation will have a historical fulfillment. It differs in that it holds that these events await fulfillment in future history, after the present age of the church, in the end time. For this reason, consistent futurists insist that there are no prophecies being fulfilled today, but that current events are preparing (or setting the stage) for fulfillment in the future. Futurism (the view adopted in this book) understands Jesus' prophecy of the destruction of the Second Temple to have already been fulfilled when John received his vision on the Isle of Patmos. Therefore, the Temples described in Revelation are the Heavenly Temple and the earthly Tribulation Temple that will be rebuilt in the end time.

4. *The Idealist interpretation.* Idealism, unlike any of the other views, does not believe that visions in the book of Revelation will be fulfilled literally at any particular point in history. Rather, idealists hold that the interpretation of this book is symbolic or spiritual, depicting an ongoing drama of spiritual conflict between Christ and Satan. There is no specific fulfillment of any individual prophecy, but rather, there are representative expressions of them in historical events throughout the age (the conflict), or they are fulfilled within people's own experiences. The Temple, according to this view, is symbolic of other spiritual

realities (such as representing the community of the redeemed), and therefore has no historical fulfillment.

One of the factors affecting a person's decision to follow a specific interpretation of Revelation, especially with respect to the question of the Temple, has to do with the time at which one believes the book was written.

The Date of the Book of Revelation

Dating the book of Revelation is significant to our examination of the Temple because the interpretation of prophetic references to the Temple may be affected by whether or not they can be ascribed to the time of the Roman destruction. If the book is considered to have been written *before* the destruction of the Temple, its predictions concerning the Temple are generally thought to be descriptive of that event. Thus, all references to the Temple would be fulfilled *ipso facto* at the A.D. 70 date. For preterism there is no prophecy related to Israel beyond the Roman destruction, since this event ended Israel's purpose, as a nation, in the plan of God. In harmony with this, works such as the Jewish apocalyptic literature are also interpreted according to the past-fulfillment (A.D. 70) scheme of these Christian commentators.[4]

However, external and internal evidences lead to the conclusion that the book of Revelation is to be dated well *after* the fall of Jerusalem, in which case the events described are future from the standpoint of the Temple's destruction, and therefore are strictly eschatological in nature. The following summary supports a late date for the book:[5]

1. The external evidence for the date of Revelation comes primarily from the testimony of Irenaeus (A.D. 120–202), who was the disciple of the apostolic father Polycarp (A.D. 70–155), who was himself a disciple of the apostle John, the traditional author of Revelation. Irenaeus' statement is as follows:

> We will not, however, incur the risk of pronouncing positively as to the name of Antichrist; for if it were necessary that his name should be distinctly revealed in the present time, it would have been announced by him who beheld the apocalyptic vision. For that was seen not a very long time since, but almost in our day, towards the end of Domitian's reign.[6]

This comment refers to a date of approximately A.D. 90–95. This testimony may also be bolstered by the almost universally held chiliastic interpretation by the first- to-third-century ante-Nicean church fathers (e.g., Polycarp, Clement of Rome, Ignatius, Papias of Hierapolis, Justin Martyr, Tertullian, Commodianius,

Cyprian, Hippolytus, Nepos, Lactantius, Victorinus of Petau, Methodus, and Apollinaris of Laodicea). Their interpretations depended on a futurist perspective of the book of Revelation.

2. The internal evidence is of several kinds: (a) a comparative investigation of motifs between Revelation and Statius' *Silvæ* reveals that the former contains sufficient circumstantial parallel to identify the polemics of the Revelation within the religio-political milieu of emperor worship around A.D. 95;[7] (b) the use of the name "Babylon" for "Rome," which is a common nomen for the second destroyer of Jerusalem, patterned after that of the first, in Jewish literature. If it was adopted from Jewish tradition by the author of Revelation, it necessitates a date after A.D. 70; (c) the condition of the seven churches described in the first three chapters of Revelation accord well with the Domitian persecution.[8]

Therefore, based on the above data, there is adequate evidence to prefer the traditionally accepted date for the Apocalypse as circa A.D. 95, well after the destruction of the Jerusalem Temple. The late date does not in and of itself eliminate the view that Temple texts in Revelation might be theologically reminiscent of the Temple's pre-destruction glory, and thus could have reference to the Second Temple, but it makes the future interpretation of a Third Temple possible, and agrees best with the prophetic restoration texts of Isaiah, Ezekiel, Daniel, and Zechariah, which are cited or alluded to throughout the book.

Interpreting Revelation Literally

While most of the interpretive views may interpret statements in the book of Revelation literally, only futurists do so consistently. During the first three hundred years of Christianity the school of interpretation that adopted this consistently literal approach was known in Greek as Chiliasm or in Latin as Millenarism.[9] This view today is known as Premillennialism, based on the generalized definition that it places the second coming of Christ before the time of the Millennium. According to some researchers, it was considered the dominant view among the early church fathers.[10] For example, Irenaeus (A.D. 136–203) gives testimony to this in his citation from a fragment of Papias, one of the apostolic fathers in his discussion of the Millennial kingdom:

> Then creation, reborn and freed from bondage, will yield an abundance
> of food of all kinds from the heaven's dew and the fertility of the earth
> (Gen. 27:28), just as the elders recall. Those who saw John, the Lord's

disciple [tell us] that they heard from him how the Lord taught and spoke about these times....[11]

The premillennial system[12] seeks to interpret the apocalyptic genre in a literal fashion while recognizing the symbolic imagery of visionary discourse. While it accepts a soteriological (salvation) orientation, it argues that the scope of the divine purpose in redemptive history is too varied to reduce it to one category—i.e., the church. Since the redemptive program in the Old Testament was in nationalistic terms, consistency of interpretation would require that eschatological and apocalyptic texts in the New Testament be understood from this perspective. In the interpretation of Revelation,[13] premillennialism maintains that the presence of a literal succession of events implies a historical succession of events,[14] and that the imagery employed depends upon prior contextual usage in the Old Testament, where literal historical events were understood. This agrees with the interpretive method employed by the Jewish writers of apocalyptic literature during the Second Temple period, "who understand the words of the prophets [concerning the end of days and the redemption] as alluding to their own era."[15] In this regard premillennialism is consonant with Jewish eschatology, which affirms that the "Messiah...and the Messianic kingdom will appear within history."[16] Therefore, the constituent elements of the kingdom in Jewish eschatology—the return from exile, the coming of Messiah, and the rebuilding of the Temple[17]—are also accepted by premillennialists as indispensable to Israel's national prophetic program. Premillennialists further argue for a consistency in grammatical historical interpretation, following the normal use of words in context, which allows for figurative use where the context dictates such. Even where this is found in the context, we must still distinguish between the use of Temple symbolism and any attempt to make the Temple symbolic. However, where Temple symbolism is used, it is used in connection with the Heavenly Temple, whose structures and service have always been the basis for earthly comparison.

Temple Symbolism in Revelation

The one use of Temple symbolism occurs in Revelation 3:12, where we read, "He who overcomes, I will make him a pillar in the temple of My God, and he will not go out from it anymore." Since people here are called "pillars," the interpretation is obviously metaphorical, as the comparison of a living being to a non-living structure would require. The whole phrase "a pillar in the temple of My God" is the figure. The pillar metaphor is used elsewhere in the New Testament

(Galatians 2:9; 1 Timothy 3:15); however, these uses do not mention the Temple, so this verse serves as the only indisputable example of a Temple pillar metaphor. The speaker who refers to this Temple as His own is Christ (Revelation 1:12-20), through the Spirit (Revelation 3:13), and although His Temple is the Heavenly Temple, the metaphor here is not of place but position. While the New Jerusalem, which is a place, is mentioned later in the verse, it is mentioned in the same sense as the "pillars in the Temple." It is the city's "name" that is metaphorically written on these persons, indicating their position. That no literal association between the Temple and the New Jerusalem is in view can be seen by the fact that the New Jerusalem will not have such a Temple (Revelation 21:22).

This figure of pillars in the Temple can be variously understood. Such pillars were architecturally designed to serve as supports for the Temple façade on account of frequent earthquakes. The reference to pillars conveys the future secure position of believers now removed from the troubles and temptations of life. Coupled with this idea of stability may be the promise of remaining within the Temple—something that no priest, not even the high priest, was permitted to do for an extended duration of time, although being able to do so was the height of eschatological hope (see Psalm 23:6; 92:12-15).

Another meaning for the metaphor draws upon the geographical setting of this statement, which was written to the church in the Roman colony of Philadelphia (Revelation 3:7). In the background may be the ancient Roman custom of honoring a magistrate by placing a pillar, in his name, in one of the pagan temples of the city. If this is the proper meaning, the "temple" symbolism here has nothing to do with any Jewish Temple past, present, or future. Regardless of the specific setting for this figure, it can be understood as a promise of future blessing to overcoming church-age believers (probably in the New Jerusalem, see Revelation 21:2-3; 22:3-4). In this sense it accords with later passages that depict the Tribulation saints as being secured and honored in the Heavenly Temple (Revelation 6:9; 6:13-17), although here the interpretation is literal rather than figurative. Our point again is that the use of Temple symbolism ("pillars in the temple") cannot be the basis for arguing that the Temple, throughout the book of Revelation, is to be viewed symbolically.

The Literal Temple in Revelation

In order to understand whether a reference to the Temple (in the book of Revelation) is meant to be interpreted figuratively or literally, it is necessary to consider each mention of the Temple in its context to determine its specific meaning. While this cannot be done here in a comprehensive manner, I have attempted to group the pertinent passages of the two major forms of the Temple that are presented: the earthly Temple of Daniel's seventieth week (the Tribulation Temple) and the Heavenly Temple. There are, however, no direct references to the Millennial Temple. This at first seems surprising given the emphasis of the Old Testament prophets on this Temple; however, the focus of Revelation is the visible control and victorious conclusion of history through Christ. Therefore, one would expect a greater emphasis on the Heavenly Temple and Heavenly Jerusalem, as in the epistle to the Hebrews (see 9:23-24; 12:22-24), and on the earthly (Tribulation) Temple prior to the coming of Christ, as it recapitulates and culminates the prophetic program as presented by Christ in the Olivet Discourse. Although the Millennial Temple is placed chronologically within Revelation 20:1-9, these verses do not mention the traditional restoration events, but rather, they assume them. These verses provide a sweeping summarization of those in the Millennial kingdom who will reign (20:4-6) and those who will rebel (20:7-9). Let's begin by studying the setting and significance of the Tribulation Temple in Revelation 11:1-2.

The Literal Setting of the Tribulation Temple

A literal interpretation of Revelation yields a literal future earthly Temple. Futurists interpret the events described in association with this Temple (Revelation 11:1-2) as identical with the seventieth week in Daniel's 70 weeks prophecy (Daniel 9:24-27). Significant to the interpretation of the earthly Temple in Revelation is an acceptance of this setting. Non-futurists, however, contend that:

> ...a major feature of the Tribulation expected by futurists is its seven-year duration, divided in the middle by the Antichrist's violating a treaty he had made with Israel and setting up an image of himself in the rebuilt Jewish temple in Jerusalem. Yet none of these elements can be discovered from the literal interpretation of any passage in Revelation.[18]

While there is no specific mention of "the Tribulation" by this term, the splitting of a seven-year period divided in the middle is indicated in Revelation 11:2; 12:6 and 13:5. And, as in Daniel's seventieth week, the midpoint is distinguished by reference to the Temple in Revelation 11:2. Furthermore, Daniel's prophecy of the seventieth week (Daniel 9:27) may be seen to have significantly informed not only the sequence and main themes of the accounts in the Olivet Discourse, but also to have influenced the structure of the judgment section of the book of Revelation (chapters 4-19). In this section in particular, Daniel 9:27 may be seen to have, in part, shaped the genre, motifs, and language. An analysis reveals that the structure of the judgment section contains linguistic and thematic parallels with the Olivet Discourse that reflect an amplification of Jesus' reference to Daniel's prophecy (Matthew 24:15; Mark 13:14).[19] This might have been expected because Revelation is the final message of Jesus (Revelation 1:1,17-19; 22:16) on the future events He mentioned in His Sermon on the Mount. From this analysis (see chart below), the first five seals (chapter 6:1-11) are seen to be the midpoint in the seventieth week, and to correlate directly with the preliminary signs of the Olivet Discourse. Further, Revelation 7–19 is an expansion of the Discourse within the framework of Daniel 9:27. This is particularly evident in John's incorporation of the three-and-a-half-year division of the seventieth week, and the development of the Abomination of Desolation motif through the various beasts of chapters 12, 13, and 17. Finally, the third section (the Great Tribulation) of Revelation's six major sections[20] develops into four subsections (4:1–5:14; 6:1-17; 8:1–18:24; 19:1-21) shaped by the seal, trumpet, and bowl septet judgments. These septet judgments are structured according to the seventieth week:

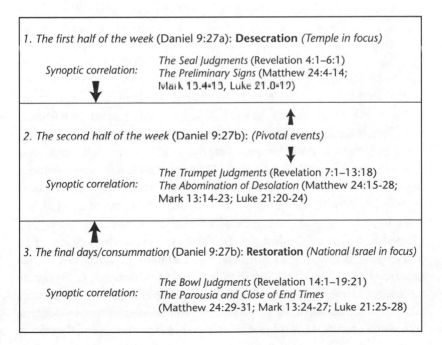

1. *The first half of the week* (Daniel 9:27a): **Desecration** *(Temple in focus)*

    Synoptic correlation: *The Seal Judgments* (Revelation 4:1–6:1)
                                    The Preliminary Signs (Matthew 24:4-14; Mark 13:4-13, Luke 21:0-19)

2. *The second half of the week* (Daniel 9:27b): *(Pivotal events)*

    Synoptic correlation: *The Trumpet Judgments* (Revelation 7:1–13:18)
                                      The Abomination of Desolation (Matthew 24:15-28; Mark 13:14-23; Luke 21:20-24)

3. *The final days/consummation* (Daniel 9:27b): **Restoration** *(National Israel in focus)*

    Synoptic correlation: *The Bowl Judgments* (Revelation 14:1–19:21)
                                      The Parousia and Close of End Times (Matthew 24:29-31; Mark 13:24-27; Luke 21:25-28)

The use of Daniel 9:27 as a paradigm for the structure of both the Olivet Discourse and the Apocalypse ties these apocalyptic discourses together, and argues that the unifying motif is that of desecration/restoration. In this regard it is significant that the subject of Temple desecration and the Abomination of Desolation in Daniel 9:27 finds further exposition in the judgment section (see Revelation 11:1-2; Revelation 13:4-18). Here we see that the pivotal events of the bowl judgments include the desecration of the earthly Temple (Revelation 11:1-2) and the announcement of judgment proceeding forth from the Heavenly Temple (Revelation 11:19)—which parallel the pivotal event of the Olivet Discourse, the Abomination of Desolation. Therefore, far from being absent in a literal interpretation of Revelation, as non-futurists contend, these events reveal that Revelation represents the final development of Daniel's seventieth week.

The Significance of the Tribulation Temple in Revelation

Since the Temple of Daniel's seventieth week may be identified with the Tribulation Temple seen in the earthly Temple of Revelation 11:1-2, it is important to consider this text concerning the details of its prediction. This chapter has been called "one of the most difficult and most important in the entire Apocalypse."[21] One reason for this difficulty is that the opening verses deal with the subject of a Temple on earth that is not only measurable (verse 1), but also seen to be desecrated for three-and-one-half years (verse 2). That a literal earthly Temple is in mind here is considered problematic because of the assumption that the use of symbolism in Revelation requires that the references to the Temple are also symbolic,[22] as one writer observes: "The literal Jerusalem had already been in ruins for over twenty years at the time John wrote, and everyone everywhere knew it. When told that the temple was to be measured, they sensed immediately that an allegorical sense was intended."[23] According to this interpretation, then, "the temple of God" is said to represent the church in harmony with similar usages in the Pauline epistles (1 Corinthians 3:16-17; 6:19; 2 Corinthians 6:16-18; Ephesians 2:20-21). Other arguments advanced in support of the symbolic interpretation generally run along theological rather than exegetical lines. For example, this Temple is said to be symbolic of the church because the literal Temple was abandoned by Christ and the Spirit transferred to the church.[24] Furthermore, it is argued the church has, in previous chapters, been symbolized by the 12 tribes, the seven golden lampstands, and the priests, so it is not unlikely that it should also be symbolized by the Temple. Another problem opponents raise with the presence of an earthly Temple in Revelation deals with the question of the date. Historicists, who acknowledge the literal Jerusalem Temple is in view and yet date the Apocalypse after A.D. 70, invariably assume that this is either a pre-A.D. 70 Temple tradition that has been incorporated at this point or take the references as merely symbolic of other realities. Conversely, preterists, who also see a literal Temple, use this very fact (in a form of circular reasoning) to support a pre-A.D. 70 date for the book, assuming the vision must depict only the events surrounding the Roman destruction of the Second Temple.[25]

Arguments for a Literal Tribulation Temple

Despite these arguments, the literal view held by premillennial futurists view is preferred for the following reasons: 1) While some New Testament passages use the Temple as a metaphor for the spiritual composition of the church and the Christian, all other references to the Temple in the New Testament, taken in their normal sense, refer to the literal Temple of the Jews (or its archetype in heaven);[26] 2) the noun describing the Temple is definite: "*the* Temple of God," i.e., the Jerusalem Temple, which is never used to symbolize Christians or the church[27] (although the church and Christians may be symbolically called "a temple," drawing an analogy from the structural and spiritual aspects of the Temple); 3) the Temple here is described as the Jewish Temple in Jerusalem, rather than as God's dwelling place (which would lend itself more to a symbolic usage), and therefore, would not be a suitable representation of the church, which is predominantly Gentile;[28] 4) the "altar" has no corollary to the church nor to the church age, and therefore would make no sense as a symbol of anything Christian. On the other hand, it *is* a literal and essential part of a functioning Temple, and is supported by Daniel's references (9:27; 12:11) mentioning the sacrifice and oblation, which presupposes the existence of the Temple;[29] 5) John speaks of the outer precinct being "trodden down by Gentiles" (verse 2), which would better suit an earthly Temple than a heavenly one;[30] 6) John's use of the terms "altar," "outer court," "Gentiles," and "the Holy City" all indicate that the context is Jewish, not Christian;[31] 7) the outer court and the entire city are trampled by the Gentiles, signaling that the Temple and the city must be something in contrast to the Gentiles—i.e., something Jewish;[32] 8) John's interests in this book are wholly eschatological, and since predictions of the restoration of the Temple were part of Jewish end-time expectations, he is showing how these earlier expectations of the end are to be fulfilled;[33] 9) the reference to "forty-two months" is clearly a reference to Daniel's seventieth week (Daniel 9:27; 12:11), which is divided into two divisions of 42 months (3 1/2 years) each. In addition, the context of the vision here is the end of the sixth trumpet judgment, which would corroborate this being the middle of the seventieth week;[34] 10) if the Temple here represents the church, then who is represented by the worshipers in the Temple? It would be inconsistent to make the Temple the church and then identify the church as these worshipers.[35] Since the worshipers are measured in addition to the Temple, they must be seen as distinct from it, or else John has been told to measure a group of people whose being is only a part of themselves.[36] The distinction between the Temple, the altar, and its worshipers is best explained as between the rebuilt physical Temple, its renewed sacrificial system, and a Jewish remnant who are true to God and the Temple service;[37] 11) the measurement here of the Temple is like that in Ezekiel 42:2, which probably informs this passage. If Ezekiel measured a literal earthly Temple, the Temple here should be understood in the same manner.[38]

Measuring the Tribulation Temple

If we interpret this Temple in context, we find that it and its (brazen) altar are measurable; however, so also are those who worship in it. Therefore, this measurement indicates a "spiritual" measurement or evaluation of the legitimacy of the earthly (Tribulation) Temple service, and for this reason no actual dimensions are recorded.[39] The purpose for this command to "measure" has been thought to be for "the acquisition of information disclosed later in this section,"[40] or as "an indication of judgment,"[41] but it must first be seen in opposition to the prohibition against measuring the outer court, which was accessible to the Gentiles. This qualification to "leave out" this outer court indicates exclusion in contrast to inclusion in the spiritual evaluation. This contrast implies, then, that the Temple, its sacrificial system, its furniture and vessels, and its worshipers are considered "holy" and in God's favor, while the Gentile nations, represented by the outer court, are "profane" and thus incur God's disfavor. Following this perspective, Robert Thomas has observed:

> John's future revelations will distinguish between God's favor toward the Sanctuary, the altar, and the worshipers associated with them, and His disapproval of all that is Gentile in orientation because of their profanation of the holy city for half of the future seventieth week. The immediate outcome of this measurement is the information about the

two witnesses whose orientation is toward the sanctuary and the altar and who consequently enjoy God's favor, and about the Gentile foes who will oppose them and eventually kill them in conjunction with their trampling of the holy city.[42]

The fact that divine favor is displayed toward the Tribulation Temple does not likewise imply divine protection. Indeed, the Temple's court and the city of Jerusalem will be given over, by divine command, to Gentile domination "for forty-two months" (Revelation 11:2c), the final half of Daniel's seventieth week in fulfillment of the prophecies of Jewish tribulation (Deuteronomy 4:30; Jeremiah 30:7). This predicted period coincides with the period of Great Tribulation set forth in the Olivet Discourse, which is characterized by Gentile persecution of the Jewish remnant. This is the pivotal period in the middle of the seventieth week, in which the Temple is desecrated by the Antichrist prior to and leading up to the trampling of Jerusalem (Revelation 11:2c). If we can supply the details of other prophetic texts touching upon this period, we can plot the course of desecration paralleling this text: 1) The cessation of the daily sacrifices polluting the altar (Daniel 9:27; 12:11);[43] 2) the Abomination of Desolation in the Holy of Holies (2 Thessalonians 2:4); and 3) the inordinate and defiling worship commanded by the Antichrist (Revelation 13:4,8).

This series of events provides a further reason for the exclusion of the Gentile court, which represents the Gentile nations, at the time of measurement. During the first half of the seventieth week Jerusalem appears to enjoy a time of pseudopeace under Jewish control because of the covenant with the Roman leader (the Antichrist). The evidence of this is the rebuilding of the Jewish Temple and the restoration of the sacrifical system (Revelation 11:1-2). By contrast, the second half of the seventieth week sees the assertion of Gentile control over Jerusalem (Revelation 11:2c) and a Gentile presence on the Temple Mount at the court of the Gentiles, leading to the interruption of sacrifices and the desecration caused by the Abomination of Desolation.

The Two Witnesses and the Tribulation Temple

The measurement of the Temple as God's single *place* of witness on earth and its ill treatment by the Gentiles serves to introduce God's "two witnesses," who likewise receive hostile treatment from the Antichrist, the head of the Gentile nations (11:7-10). That they have a direct relation to the Temple and represent the remnant is seen by the relationship of verses 1-2 to verse 3, which shows the time and purpose of their activity to be parallel to that of the

Temple's desecration. In the first half of the Tribulation they apparently are among the worshipers in the Temple (11:4), although some, supposing them to be Elijah and Enoch, have suggested them to be priests. This identification has problems (as a long history of competitive views reveals), and it seems unlikely that these two, who are apparently Jewish believers (note the words in verse 8: "where also their Lord was crucified") could carry out this function under an Orthodox Jewish administration. Nevertheless, the Temple was a place of protected Jewish assembly and worship, their presence as believers in God and their performance as witnesses would be expected there. Moreover, this duplicates the place of apostolic witness in the Second Temple as commanded by the Lord: "Go your way, stand and speak to the people in the temple the whole message of this Life" (Acts 5:20; see also Acts 2:43-47; 3:1; 4:1; 5:21). The description of the two witnesses as "clothed in sackcloth" fits the proper Jewish response to tragedy, especially with respect to a desecration Temple (see Lamentations 2:10). For example, in Zechariah 3:3-4 the high priest Joshua appears dressed in "filthy garments" because of "iniquity." This clothing most likely refers to sackcloth and ashes, the customary clothing for those in mourning.[44] His mourning because of "iniquity" refers to the "evil ways and evil deeds" mentioned in Zechariah 1:4 that had prevented the Lord's "return" in restoration (verse 3), which was symbolized by the Temple's lack of completion and interruption of the sacrificial service. During the Tribulation this will be epitomized by the Antichrist's invasion of the Temple and its ultimate desecration through the abomination of desolation. Therefore, the wearing of sackcloth by the witnesses is conditioned by these circumstances.[45]

During the last half of the Tribulation (the 42 months of verse 2 = the 1,260 days of verse 3), when the Temple has been desecrated and after the majority of the Israelites have fled from the Antichrist's persecution (Revelation 12:6, 14; compare Matthew 24:16-20; Mark 13:15-18), the two witnesses' prophetic activity serves to counter the prophetic "signs" of the false prophet (verses 5-6) and to oppose his campaign to deify the Antichrist and force the reception of worldwide worship (Revelation 13:11-17). The witnesses' subsequent death and resurrection in Jerusalem (Revelation 11:7-11), accompanied by the reaction of Gentile terror (Revelation 11:11) and the experience of a devastating and clearly divinely sent earthquake (Revelation 11:13), serves to signal the coming of Christ to deliver the city from Gentile domination (see Luke 21:26-28; see also Zechariah 14:2-9; Revelation 19:17-21) and leads to the final phase of divine vengeance on the nations of the world (Revelation 11:18). Thus, the desecration of the Temple in verse 2 and the murder of its two witnesses function together as the catalysts that provoke the divine judgment of the Great Tribulation (Revelation 11:14) as well as the advent of the Messiah (Zechariah 14:4; Revelation 19:11-16).

The Heavenly Temple in the Revelation

The Heavenly Temple, the heavenly pattern for all past and future earthly Temples,[46] is explicitly pictured in Revelation 7:15; 11:19; 14:15,17; and 15:5,6,8. Implicit references may also be seen in Revelation 4:3 and 6:16. In these passages the Heavenly Temple appears both as the place where the righteous are rewarded and from which divine judgment on the wicked goes forth. In Revelation 7:15, as in 15:5,6, not only is the Temple present, but also the Tabernacle, since the heavenly pattern was the same for both. The Tabernacle's inclusion is also fundamental to the restoration motif, since, as Craig Koester has observed, "some [New Testament] authors also associated the tabernacle with hopes for a restoration and unity in Israel. According to Acts the growth of the Jewish Christian community marked the restoration of David's tent, and in Revelation the church of the new age appears as the tabernacle-city."[47]

In Revelation 15:5 the author combines all of the earthly sanctuaries into one as typifying the ideal heavenly model: "After these things I looked, and the temple of the tabernacle of testimony [Ark] in heaven was opened." From the other references of the Heavenly Temple in Revelation we learn that the Heavenly Temple houses an altar (6:9; 8:3,5; 9:13; 14:18; 16:7), God's throne (16:17), and the heavenly Ark of the Covenant (11:19). In addition, J. Webb sees the veil which separated the Holy Place from the Holy of Holies present in those texts, which depicts an "opening" to the heavenly throne-room/Temple through which angelic beings or John himself passes immediately into the divine presence (see Revelation 4:1-3; 6:14-17; 15:5; 16:1,17).[48]

Priestly Service in the Heavenly Temple

Revelation 7:15 says, "they are before the throne of God; and they serve Him day and night in His temple; and He who sits on the throne shall spread His tabernacle [presence] over them." The previous verse notes that these are those "who come out of the great tribulation, and they have washed their robes and made them white." In verse 16 their service is said to be "before the throne of God" and verse 17 adds that "the Lamb in the center of the throne shall be their shepherd." Although the focus here is upon the martyred Tribulation saints, it is clear from the parallel language used in verses 9-10 that they are part of the "great multitude" made up "from every nation and all tribes and peoples and tongues" which share this position of service "before the Lamb, clothed in white robes." Therefore, the Heavenly Temple is here identified as the place of service for all of the redeemed. The language here of the Tabernacle being "upon them," as well as the shepherd metaphor, appears also in Ezekiel 37:27, is a central passage concerning the eschatological Temple.

The shared use of Temple terminology here for the earthly and Heavenly Temples has led non-futurist interpreters to argue that John is applying the Old Testament promise of Israel's restoration to the church. As one commentator concluded, "Ezekiel 37 was a prophecy uniquely applicable to ethnic or theocratic Israel in contrast to the nations, yet now John understands it as fulfilled in the church."[49] However, shared terminology does not require us to make one thing the fulfillment of the other, as we saw in Paul's use of "temple" for both the church (the universal body) and the Christian (the individual body).[50] Such complementary language might be expected when dealing with like subjects (the eschatological and Heavenly Temples) in a similar setting (universal testimony, see verses 9-10), but the contrasts between these two texts make "fulfillment" improbable. In Ezekiel 37:25 it is clearly the geographical Land of Israel that is to be the place of future fulfillment. In addition, the promise to "multiply them" (verse 26) is restoration terminology for an increase of the physical population (compare Ezekiel 36:29-30—of produce; Ezekiel 37–38—of people). This is hardly appropriate language for heaven (see Luke 20:35). Ezekiel 37:28 says that the event of the Sanctuary's return and God's presence sanctifying a newly reunited and redeemed Israel (see verses 16-23,28) will be a witness to the Gentile nations. Yet in Revelation 7:15 the nations are already a part of those who are in heaven and have a share in the Heavenly Temple. How, then, could the church, which is a composite of Jews and Gentiles, fulfill this distinction?

The Heavenly Temple as the Center for Divine Judgment

The Heavenly Temple is also depicted by John as the command center for the angelic orders to mediate God's judgment on the earth. The release of the plagues of Revelation 15:5-8, which will descend on the "wicked worldlings" (or "earth-dwellers"), follows the covenant paradigm of Exodus 15 and 32, in which the Re[e]d Sea punished those who persecuted God's people. In Revelation 15:6-8 the Temple serves as the setting of judgment from which emerge angels bearing golden bowls of wrath, representing earthly plagues. The movement continues from the Heavenly Temple to the earth, with the glory of God filling the Temple as a cloud that obscures the Heavenly Sanctuary from beholding the defilement produced by the plagues. In Revelation 15:1-4 there is recorded a heavenly celebration of the victory of God's judgment by both Israel and the church (note: "the song of Moses and...the song of the Lamb"), focusing on the deliverance of the Re[e]d Sea experience (Exodus 15) as well as the subduing of the Gentile nations to acknowledge God's sovereignty. The citation in verse 4c, which is from Isaiah 66:23—"all the nations will come and worship before Thee," prepares the reader to anticipate the fulfillment of one of the prophetic goals of Israel's national restoration in the Millennial kingdom, namely, the conversion of the Gentiles (see, for example, Isaiah 2:2-4; 19:21-25; 26:9; 56:6-7; 60:5-14; Haggai 2:7; Zechariah 6:15; 14:16-19). If the New Jerusalem consists of the Holy of Holies of the Heavenly Temple, then the references in Revelation 21:24,26 to the glory and honor of the nations being brought into it may also be part of the fulfillment of this restoration mandate.[51]

The Millennial Temple in Revelation?

Acording to most non-futurist eschatological interpretations, the promise of a Messianic kingdom was fully fulfilled in the past. For example, D. James Kennedy has written: "With the ascension of Christ, God established the Messianic kingdom. This kingdom has existed ever since Jesus was received back into heaven and granted the Davidic throne (Revelation 3:7; 5:5-9). All the rulers of the earth are now accountable to Christ (Revelation 1:5)."[52] In Revelation 20:1-15 premillennial futurists see the Messianic kingdom as the fulfillment of the Jewish expectation of a restored kingdom on earth during the future reign of Christ after the second advent. The references here to "thrones, and they [who] sat on them" (verse 4a), those who "reigned with Messiah" (verse 4c), and those who were made "priests of God" (verse 6b) are typical apocalyptic features found both in the Gospels and Jewish apocalyptic literature concerning the reign of Messiah and the restoration of the 12 tribes of Israel. The use here of "thrones" may be derived from the royal thrones of Daniel 7:9-10,22, where a divinely judicial process is in view, thus indicating a combination of ruling and judging. This is comparable to Jesus' prophecy of a coming age characterized by Jewish rule over the nations—"the regeneration" (Greek, *palingenesia*) (Matthew 19:28). In addition, the occupancy of these thrones occurs at the same time as that of Satan's binding (20:1-3). Thus, the picture is of a period of unthreatened holiness during which Israel enjoys a theocratic government. The apocalyptic overthrow of the nations ("Gog and Magog") opposed to the Messiah, with the attack centered on Jerusalem (called here "the beloved city") is also a familiar theme in Jewish apocalyptic literature. For this reason the present age could not fulfill the prophecies of the Messianic kingdom because the age is one of spiritual conflict with Satan (Ephesians 6:10-12; 1 Peter 5:8-9; 1 John 5:19), and the nations continue in rebellion against God and the Jewish people (Matthew 24:6-9).

Following the chronological pattern established in the Olivet Discourse and the Apocalypse, after the Messiah returns, He will build the Millennial Temple of Ezekiel's vision (Zechariah 6:12-13). Although the book of Revelation does not explicitly deal with the Millennial Temple but rather reserves its application of the ideal representation of the Temple to the New Jerusalem (chapters 21–22), it is implicitly present by virtue of its association with these events (just as in parallel restoration texts). It is impossible that Israel's national program could exist without a Temple. The conditions described here in Revelation 20 parallel those described in Ezekiel 40–48, during which the Millennial Temple exists (see Ezekiel 43:7; 44:3,24; 45:8-10), with the understanding that the informed reader would fill in the missing details from his knowledge of these well-known sources. However, if, as some premillennialists see it, Revelation 21:9-27 describes the Millennial age, then when the Gentile nations bring their glory into the New Jerusalem (see verses 24 and 26)—an act stated in the Old Testament as bringing tribute into the Temple (Psalm 72:10-11; Isaiah 60:3,10-12; 66:12)—there may be grounds for seeing a Millennial Temple over which the New Jerusalem is suspended.

From Prophecy to Preparation

We have now surveyed much of what Scripture teaches about the symbols of the Temple in Genesis and specific details provided by the prophets. Although the Temple is absent during the church age and its worship and service are conducted "spiritually," there is no depreciation of the Temple and its ritual from which these "spiritual" references are drawn. Rather, there is included for this period prophetic revelation concerning the presence of the Temple during the time of Gentile judgment and Jewish repentance and readiness for restoration (the Tribulation). Finally, as the book of Revelation has demonstrated, the Temple will occupy a prominent role in the Tribulation; its desecration will usher in the Messiah to rule and reign on the earth. In the next few chapters we will shift our focus from the *Word* of the Bible to the *world* of the Bible, where today a modern movement led by Israeli Jews and Orthodox Jews worldwide is in the midst of preparing to rebuild the coming Last Days Temple. This will take us on an exciting journey that connects the biblical past with our technological present to reveal the preparations being made today to rebuild the Last Days Temple.

PART III

The Preparations for the Last Days Temple

"This is the statute of the law which the LORD has commanded, saying, 'Speak to the sons of Israel that they may bring you an unblemished red heifer in which is no defect, and on which a yoke has never been placed. Now a man who is clean shall gather up the ashes of the heifer and deposit them outside the camp in a clean place, and the congregation of the sons of Israel shall keep it as water to remove impurity; it is purification from sin.'"

—Numbers 19:2,9

"If the blood of goats and bulls and the ashes of a heifer sprinkling those who have been defiled, sanctify for the cleansing of the flesh, how much more will the blood of Christ, who through the eternal Spirit offered Himself without blemish to God, cleanse your conscience from dead works to serve the living God?"

—Hebrews 9:13-14

CHAPTER 15

Searching for the Sacred Site

Preparing a Place
for the Temple

Once the site for the Miqdash ["Sanctuary"] was fixed in the days of Shemuel ["Samuel"] and King David, it is immutable. All that remains to do at a time such as the present is to rebuild the physical structure, and reinstitute the Temple Service....

(MISHNEH TORAH, BETH HA'BEHIRA 1:3, 4)

All these theories only do damage... because then the Arabs can say, "You yourselves are arguing about it. The Temple wasn't even on the Temple Mount."

—DAN BAHAT, CONSULTING ARCHAEOLOGIST,
WESTERN WALL TUNNEL EXCAVATION

Jesus said, "Upon this rock I will build My church…" (Matthew 16:18). Ever since He stated those words, "the church" has been debating what "rock" Jesus was referring to. In a similar way the Temple was once built on a rock, the top of Mount Moriah, but exactly what "rock" that was is being vigorously debated by Jewish researchers, rabbis, and archaeologists. As Rabbi Reznick puts it, "The Dome of the Rock is a shrine built to protect the treasure within—the rock. But what, exactly, is that rock?"[1] Answering this, and a host of related questions, has made the search for the location of the ancient Temple the most controversial subject engaging students of the Temple today. It is considered a top priority, for if the prophecy concerning the rebuilding of the Temple is to be fulfilled by the efforts of Israeli Jews, then the exact spot of the sacred site must be determined.

Rabbi Nahman Kahane of the Young Israel Synagogue and head of the Institute for Talmudic Commentaries contends that the lack of certainty in identifying the proper location is one of the major obstacles to rebuilding today: "We have to know where the original place of the altar was. Since no one knows where the altar was, no one is going anywhere on the Temple now.… The Temple now…is off limits to everybody. All of the different opinions…all of the discrepancies…surround only one question: Where is the place of the altar? That's the whole problem." This problem, facing all who attempt to investigate the original location of the Temple, is caused by a lack of sufficient, objective, material evidence. However, if the Jews gained sovereignty over the Temple Mount in 1967, and consider this of utmost importance, then why are they unable to verify the exact location? To understand this, we need to consider the present-day situation concerning the Temple Mount.

The Problems at Present

When the Jews returned from the Babylonian exile they were able to rebuild the Temple not only because they had access to the site, but because significant ruins remained and there were many people still alive who remembered the locations of the buildings of the former Temple. More important, as the Talmud notes, they were able to excavate and expose the foundations of the previous structures so as to know exactly where to rebuild (see Mishneh Torah, *Beth Ha'behira* 1:4). However, no archaeological remains of Solomon's or Zerubbabel's Temples are known to have survived Herod's extensive rebuilding program,[2] and all the actual structures connected with the Herodian Temple itself appear to have been completely erased by the Roman destruction of A.D. 70 and subsequent attempts to further desolate the area (see chapter 5). So apart from deductions that can be made from the extant surface structures of the Second Temple period, such as walls, stairs, and underground structures such as tunnels and cisterns, we are dependent upon biblical and extrabiblical descriptions of the building procedures (both Israelite and comparative regional temples),[3] topographical details, and the ceremonial ritual.[4] Even then, it has been difficult to pinpoint the location of this place.

The Temple Mount platform, built to support the Temple and its courts, has been preserved down through the centuries. While this has helped to limit the area of the search, it is impossible to resolve the matter until there can be more definite archaeological confirmation. Hoever, access to the site for archaeological excavation or even the use of non-invasive high-tech devices that could reveal underground structures is firmly prohibited. The reasons for this restriction fall into two categories: political and religious.

Political Problems

The Islamic occupation of the entire 35-acre Temple Mount platform (called by Muslims *Haram es-Sharif*—"the Noble Enclosure") for most of the past 1,360-plus years has forced Israel to make a political concession of this site for the prospect of peace. The Islamic Wakf, the governing authority of the Temple Mount since 1967, prevents any incursion whatsoever onto the premises regarded as strictly for Muslims. If prayer at this site by non Muslims is fervently fought against, how much more would excavations in search of a rival holy site be prohibited! The Wakf has consistently stated that the only purpose for Israeli archaeological excavations is to destroy the sacred structures of Islam in order to rebuild the Jewish Temple. However, most Israeli archaeologists are secular and have no religious agenda for building a Temple. What's more, Muslims have no interest in any archaeological discoveries related to the Temple Mount because they have continually denied that the site has any connection with the Jewish people or their ancient Temples. They find the archaeological evidence around the site unconvincing because they interpret the data in conformity with their preconception that nothing Jewish is there. For example, in summarizing the Israeli excavations from 1968 to 1978 at the southwestern and southern walls of the Temple Mount and the excavation of the Western Wall Tunnel begun in the early 1980s, Adnan Husseini, Executive Director of the Islamic Wakf, stated: "They [Israeli archaeologists] have done 4 to 5 attacks on the mosque from their diggings under it. What they found under the Haram [Temple Mount] is 90% Islamic and 10% pre-Islamic. Now they are digging a long tunnel [the Western Wall Tunnel] along the wall [of the Al-Aqsa compound] under the Moslem Quarter. Already seven buildings owned by Moslems have collapsed due to these diggings."[5]

This same authority, along with Yasser Arafat, accused the Israeli government of actually attacking the mosques on the Temple Mount when it opened an exit to this Western Wall Tunnel in 1995. The investigations of former Jewish holy sites are interpreted by them as attempts to further a Zionist program to replace them on the Temple Mount. For this reason, the Israeli *Protection of Holy Places Law* supports their position, and makes it a crime to in any way desecrate or restrict access to the Muslim holy sites, which would certainly occur if archaeological excavation took place. For these reasons, no archaeological excavations have ever been, or are likely to be, conducted on the Temple Mount. At the same time, archaeological excavations are the only way anyone can decisively resolve the question of the Temple's original location.

Religious Problems

As we have already seen in chapter 6, the Rabbinate has forbidden any Jew from setting foot on the *'Azarah*, the sacred precinct or enclosure of the ancient Temple. This was decided because it is held that the Ark of the Covenant, which is still believed to be attended by the divine presence, remains hidden somewhere beneath the Holy of Holies. Since all Jews today are in a state of ritual defilement, to inadvertently tread on this area would violate the sanctity of the entire Temple Mount. Therefore, observant Jews refrain from even entering the Temple Mount for fear they might happen to tread upon the site of the Holy of Holies. Many of those who have done extensive research in connection with the Temple's location would never transgress by actually going to the places they have proposed. For example, Orthodox Jew Tuvia Sagiv, though zealous for rightly identifying the site of the Temple, and even so bold as to say that the revered Western Wall was actually connected to Hadrian's Temple of Jupiter, insists that Jews must remain below the Temple Mount until the Messiah comes. From this viewpoint, archaeologists, like tourists who daily defile the site, have no business on the Temple Mount, even if their efforts could unravel the mysteries of the Temple's location.

Why Not Build Somewhere Else?

Given these problems, many people often ask, "If the Jews want a Temple so badly, and the attempt to wrest the ancient site from the Arabs would provoke a war, why couldn't they just build the Temple somewhere else in Jerusalem?" This may seem reasonable to those outside of Orthodox Judaism, but those within deem it absolutely necessary that the Third Temple be rebuilt *exactly* where the former two Temples stood. As Temple movement writer Yirmiyahu Fischer affirms: "Certainly, understanding the true placement of the *Beit HaMikdash* ["Temple"] is of utmost importance. The *Beit HaMikdash* must be built not just where there is room for it, but on the exact original place. When King Shlomo ["Solomon"] sanctified the *Beit HaMikdash* and the altar, he sanctified the place for all generations, and it is hence forbidden to erect an altar any place other than where the original altar stood."[6]

One reason for this is because it is argued that the site for the Temple was divinely appointed. If one follows the chain of commands from the first appearance of Mount Moriah as the site of the *Akedah* ("Binding of Isaac"), a pivotal prophecy that is believed to have revealed God's choice for the Temple (Genesis 22:2-14), to the Red Sea miracle where another prophecy to Moses concerning the "mountain of My inheritance" (Exodus 15:17) is seen as the place ordained for Israel's worship and clarified even more by Moses before his death (Deuteronomy 12:5-19), to the final realization of the site through David's purchase of the place and erection of the altar (2 Samuel 24:18-25; 1 Chronicles 21:18-29), and Solomon's construction (1 Kings 6-8; 2 Chronicles 3-7), it is evident that a prophetic path led to only one spot. While this may give a biblical priority to the site, other explanations from history and Jewish oral tradition also support this conviction.

The Reasons for the Temple Mount

Historically, the continuity between Temples was always preserved by building each one with its Holy of Holies enclosing the same rock protrusion of Mount Moriah known as *Even ha-Shetiyyah* ("The Foundation Stone"). This was the expected place for rebuilding, as Daniel's prayer in Babylon reveals (Daniel 9:16) and according to the Lord's command to Haggai to "rebuild the ruins" of the former Temple (Haggai 1:2-4,8-9,14). The Jewish sages followed this understanding and codified it in Jewish tradition: "Once the site for the *Miqdash* ["Sanctuary"] was fixed in the days of Shemuel ["Samuel"] and King David, it is immutable. All that remains to do at a time such as the present is to rebuild the physical structure, and reinstitute the Temple Service..." (Mishneh Torah, *Beth Ha'behira* 1:3, 4).

Another reason the exact site is so important is that it was upon the Foundation Stone that the Ark of the Covenant had been set and the *Shekinah* (divine presence) had descended (1 Kings 8:6-11), and from which it had later departed (Ezekiel 8:4; 11:23). Therefore, the place had a distinct sanctity that no other place ever had, and as Orthodox Jews believe, it still has that sanctity today. In addition, the literal fulfillment of the prophecies of the Temple's restoration require that it be rebuilt at the historic site. First, Bible prophecy says that the *Shekinah* that had departed in the past will return by exactly the same route that it departed from the Mount of Olives ("the way of the east") to the inner court to the Holy of Holies (Ezekiel 43:1-7). Second, how could any prophecy of the last days that spoke of going up to the "house of the Lord" (Temple) on the "mountain…of the Lord" or "My holy mountain" (Isaiah 2:2-3; 56:7) be understood other than by reference to the historic Temple Mount?

However, the primary reason given by Orthodox Jews to this question is that the building of the Temple and its service must be governed by Jewish Law as received throughout the generations. This precedent was established during the time of the Second Temple period, when the sect known as the Saduccees (who believed their interpretation of the Torah was more correct than the accepted oral tradition) gained control of the Temple and its service. Despite this fact, the high priest, whom they appointed, was required to take an oath that he would still perform the service according to tradition, without changing anything. This was affirmed by one of the greatest of the codifiers of Jewish Law, the Rambam (Rabbi Moshe Maimonides). Concerning the location of the Temple, he wrote, "The altar is in a very precise location, which may never be changed." He then went on to say that the altars that Avraham ["Abraham"], Noach ["Noah"], Kayin ["Cain"], Hevel ["Abel"], and Adam used for sacrifices were all on this exact location. Offering a sacrifice on any other location is considered to be a grave sin and a desecration (*Hilchot Beit HaBechirah* 2:1). In like manner, a rabbi writing in one of the journals published by a Temple movement organization wrote, "We are not required to build the *Beit HaMikdash* ['Temple'] according to Yechezkel's ['Ezekiel's'] vision. Even the prophets who lived in his time, Chagai ['Haggai'], Zechariah, and Malachi, did not build the *Beit HaMikdash* like Yechezkel. Rather, unless a prophet instructs us otherwise, we are to build according to the tradition that we have received, and only in its proper place."[7] For these reasons no other place can be substituted, which means that barring the coming of the prophet Elijah or the Messiah Himself, those who plan to rebuild the Temple intend to follow the time-honored tradition and rebuild it at the same location as the two previous Temples.

The Reason of the Temple Itself

Another reason (as implied in the quote above) it is imperative that this exact site be recovered and then thoroughly explored is because Jews must not only build on the same spot, but they must also build the same Temple. According to the Rambam, the returning exiles decided not to build the Second Temple according to Ezekiel's plan because it was "neither clear or explicit," so they built the Second Temple "according to the outlines of Solomon's Temple, but with some modifications based on the book of Ezekiel" (Mishneh Torah, *Hilchot Beit HaBechirah* 1:4). When the Maccabees and later Herod the Great renovated the Second Temple, they did so without altering its basic form. The convictions about this were so strong that the Tosefot Yom Tov declared that even in the Messianic age the basic structure of the Temple will follow the vision originally revealed to King David. This means the Third Temple will have to be built according to the same pattern as well as upon the same place as the Second (Herodian) Temple.

Unfortunately, material evidence for the location of Second Temple cannot be obtained through archaeological research, so the only sources for information we can look to are historical writings and traditional Jewish sources. Yet there are many significant discrepancies among these sources. For example, the earliest recorded description of the Temple site is that given by Josephus. His measurements of the area conflict in many respects with those given in the Mishnah's tractate *Middot* ("Measurements"), which was composed at least 100 years later. In addition, one of the most detailed sources about the Temple Mount of the fifth-century A.D., *Nehemiah's Jerusalem Atlas*, has provided vital clues to archaeologists, yet its accuracy has been questioned, especially in its identification of surviving remains and the location of certain landmarks. To make matters worse, the second-century B.C. document known as the *Temple Scroll* (found in the caves above the Wadi Jaffet-Zaben and dating to the time of the Second Temple itself), which gives detailed patterns for the rebuilding of the Temple, differs dramatically from the patterns recorded in Scripture or any of the extrabiblical sources.[8] The only way to resolve these discrepancies is by actually uncovering and measuring the site itself. Although every trace of the Temple itself has been removed, much that pertains to its placement and the courts around it could be discerned from knowing where on the platform it actually resided and which underground structures were actually associated with it.

Despite the present-day inability of archaeologists to excavate on the Temple Mount (in the nineteenth century some limited excavation was permitted), since 1967 Israeli archaeologists have been able to dig in the shadow of the

Temple Mount outside and below the huge supporting platform. Before we move on to the various theories about the Temple's location, let's look at some of the discoveries that have greatly advanced our knowledge of the Temple—discoveries that tempt us to imagine what greater secrets could be revealed on and under the Temple Mount itself.

What Archaeology Has Discovered

Back in 1887 J.L. Porter wrote pessimistically that "the Temple is gone. Not a stone, not a trace, remains."[9] In the middle of the twentieth century Dame Kathleen Kenyon, a British archaeologist who has excavated extensively in the vincinity of the Temple Mount, concluded: "Absolutely nothing survives of the Temple built by Herod."[10] Even the famous Israeli historian and archaeologist Michael Avi-Yonah stated, "The location of the actual Temple, the central problem, cannot yet be ascertained...."[11] This, of course, is true concerning the Temple's actual structure, the destruction of which Jesus accurately predicted would "not one stone here shall be left upon another" (Matthew 24:2; see also Mark 13:2; Luke 19:44).

Archaeological Research on the Second Temple

In the area of the esplanade on which the Temple had once stood, over a century ago extensive probes and tunneling excavations were conducted by British explorers. Though restricted by Moslem sensitivities, they were able to discover important structural remains that form the basis of our knowledge of the site today.[12] For example, in 1873–74 the Frenchman Charles Clermont-Ganneau, who had developed good relations with the Muslim Kadi in charge of the Temple Mount, was permitted to examine in detail the Dome of the Rock during a time of Muslim restoration work. When the ceramic tiles covering the floor were removed he was able to study the Crusader-period masonry, and was even able to look beneath the flagstone covering the Rock itself.

One of the greatest explorers to study the Temple Mount was Charles Warren, whose surveys and archaeological reports are indispensable primary sources for those seeking the Temple's location. Warren conducted extensive probes at the Eastern Gate and at the area below the Western Wall, revealing evidence of one of the five ancient gates to the Temple Mount (now known as Warren's Gate). These probes, as well as his extensive tunnelling, corrected earlier estimates of the true height of the Temple Mount's retaining walls, located the lost Tyropoeon (or Cheesemakers) Valley, and investigated many of the subterranean cisterns and passageways beneath the southern and central areas of the Temple platform. One of Warren's helpful contributions to determining the Temple's location was his discovery that the platform on which the Second Temple had stood was not identical with the original square platform which was thought to have supported the First Temple, but had been extended by King Herod's engineers. He also proved that the southwest corner of the platform had been artificially constructed, a fact that has assisted later researchers in determining the history of structural changes on the Temple Mount.[13]

When excavation became possible around the outer perimeters of the Temple Mount in the twentieth century, Dame Kathleen Kenyon, who had earlier stated "no trace of the Temple remains," revised her verdict and declared, "Much of Herod's work can still be traced in the great platform that supports the Dome of the Rock, so from the present structure back to Solomon there is no real break."[14] After the Six-Day War, Israeli excavations were conducted in the City of David by Yigael Shiloh and revealed the extent and location of the original palace complex of David and Solomon. Closer to the Temple Mount, excavations at its southwestern and southern walls—first directed by Benjamin Mazar and then by Meir Ben-Dov—and those in the Western Wall Tunnel (directed by Dan Bahat) have greatly improved our understanding of the Temple's location. For example, Mazar discovered clues to the original square Temple Mount (dating to the time of Solomon) and revealed the location of important bridges, gates, and staircases leading from ground level to the area of the Temple above. More recently, Ronny Reich uncovered the original Herodian street that stretched alongside the lower west side of the Temple Mount, along with the merchants' shops that lined the street.[15] In addition, the examination of old pictures of the site, such as German World War I reconnaissance photographs, have revealed structural elements no longer visible on and around the Temple Mount because of destruction or concealment by the Arabs.

Archaeology has also supplied from other cultures comparative examples of the form and design of the Temple. Archaeological examples of Solomonic-type temples have been found, such as the eighth-century long-room tripartite temple from Tel Tainat in the Amuq Valley at the northern Orontes in Syria, four other temples at two sites (Tel Munbaqa and Tel Emar), a poorly preserved temple at En Dara, two long-room temples of this type from the Middle Bronze IIB Period (1750–1550 B.C.) at Shechem and Megiddo, and an Israelite temple (from Solomon's time) within the Israelite fortress at Tel Arad (in the Negev).[16] And there's another recently excavated site in the Samaria region that promises to provide additional information about the Second Temple's structure; let us consider it briefly.

An Archaeological Replica of the Second Temple

From all indications, the Second Temple, originally built by Zerubbabel, was built according to the same plan and dimensions as the First Temple. While the later reconstruction by Herod completely erased all traces of this Temple, an extraordinary find in Samaria has opened up the possibility of recovering an exact duplicate of this Temple. The discovery was made by Israeli archaeologist Yizhak Magen on Mount Gerizim, the site sacred to the Samaritans as the place where their ancient temple once stood. According to the first-century historian Flavius Josephus, the Samaritan Temple was destroyed by John Hyrcanus in 113 B.C. It was this temple that the Samaritan woman referred to as the place where her "fathers worshiped" in her dialogue with Jesus (John 4:20). What has been found are the remains of the Samaritan Temple, including its six-foot thick walls, gates. and altars complete with sacrificial ashes and bones. In addition, two adjacent edifices, thought to be a royal residence and administrative building, were discovered. These buildings resemble the plan of the First Temple complex (1 Kings 7:1-12), which had a palace proper, throne room, House of Pharaoh's Daughter, Hall of Columns, and House of the Forest of Lebanon. The Samaritan Temple was found beneath the floor of the fifth-century Byzantine church of Mary Theotokos, which was uncovered in excavations in the 1920s. The temple's northern gate matches that of the Temple described in the *Temple Scroll*, a Dead Sea Scroll document written when the Second Temple of Zerubbabel was still standing. That the Samaritan Temple was most likely a replica of Zerubbabel's Temple is implied by Josephus' account of its origin.

According to his record, Menachem, a priest in the Jerusalem Temple, fell in love with a woman named Nikaso, the daughter of the Samaritan leader Sanballat. Because she was not Jewish, Menachem was told to choose between Nikaso and his priesthood. Menachem chose Nikaso, and Sanballat built his new son-in-law a rival temple on the sacred Mount Gerizim and made him its high priest. The only reference for this temple would have been the one served by Menachem in Jerusalem. Yitzhak Magen believes this implication from Josephus is correct, noting that second-century B.C. inscriptions discovered at the site confirm that "the Samaritans adopted everything from the Jewish prayers to sacrificial ritual."[17]

At present, attention is being focused on the excavation of the two adjacent buildings, whose remains are more complete than those of the temple itself. However, when all is finally excavated, not only will our knowledge of this longest-lived phase of the Jerusalem Temple be immensely improved, but the dimensions of this temple may contribute to better discerning through comparison of the exact location of the Jerusalem Temple. With this in mind, let us now proceed to examine the various theories that have been proposed concerning the Temple's location.

Theories on the Temple's Location

In the past two decades, the subject of the Temple's location has become a matter of intense investigation and debate. Meir Ben-Dov, one of the premier archaeologists of the Temple area, has noted: "...hardly a month goes by without at least one research paper being published on one aspect or another of the Temple Mount."[18] Bar-Ilan University archaeologist Aren Maeir adds, "'If you ask 100 scholars, you'll get 101 opinions' on the Temple's precise location, but 'those who are dealing with the facts in a responsible manner' don't vary by more than 20 meters one way or another."[19]

The three leading theories among researchers today and their main proponents are 1) the Southern Location (Bellarmino Bagatti, Tuvia Sagiv); 2) the Northern Location (Asher Kaufman); 3) the Central Location (Rabbi Shlomo Goren, Leen Ritmeyer, David Jacobson, and most archaeologists). There are also variations on some of these theories, such as the far-Southern Location (Nathan Kaplan—below the Al-Aqsa Mosque at the southern wall), and the farther-Southern Location (Ernest Martin) of Solomon's and Ezra's Temples—just above the Gihon Spring on the southeast ridge of Jerusalem.[20] These scholarly theories vie for acceptance today as answers to the questions about the original site of the First and Second Temples.

While each of these proposed sites respect the dimensions of the Muslim *Haram*, which generally follows the square outer perimeters of the Temple complex (as given by Josephus and the Mishnah tractate *Middot*), and maintain the same east-west orientation, they differ significantly in their placement within this enclosure. Due to limited space I will discuss only the three main theories (south, north, central) and each proponent's major arguments without critique or the objections of the other positions. For these the reader should refer to the bibliography provided in the footnotes for each of the theorists.[21]

The Southern Location
Father Bellarmino Bagatti

A Franciscan scholar, Father Bellarmino Bagatti, published his work *Recherches sur le Site du Temple de Jerusalem* in Jerusalem in 1979.[22] He concluded

Three Suggested Locations for the Site of the Temple
(All Temples are arranged in an east/west orientation)

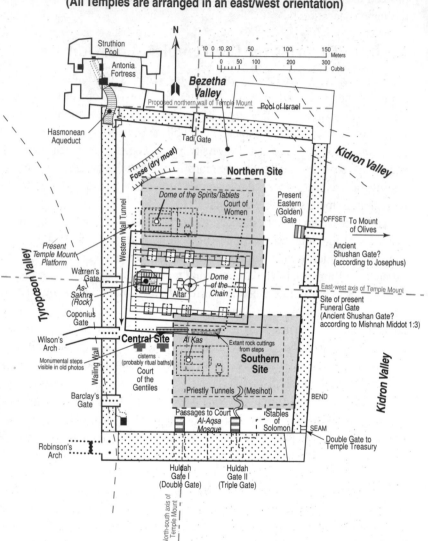

Proposed Temple Sites—Three proposed sites for the location of the ancient Temple according to Tuvia Sagiv, Leen Ritmeyer, David Jacobson, and Asher Kaufman. The Holy of Holies is indicated in each site by the Al Kas Foundation (southern), As-Sakhra "the [Sacred] Rock" (central), and the Dome of the Spirits/Tablets (northern). The location of the ancient Temple Mount gates are based on Mishnah (*Middot* 1:3), Joesphus (*Antiquities* 15:401), and modern excavations.

from his study of the ancient documents and his personal exploration and measurements that the ancient Temple must have occupied a site to the south, somewhere between the Dome of the Rock and the Al-Aqsa Mosque. This is not a new view, for it had been implied in the works of earlier researchers; however, Bagatti's arguments were supported with new and original data. His theory for the southern location of the Temple is based on several considerations. First, the ancient topography of the Temple Mount, as gleaned from historical sources, suggests that the Temple was situated at a lower elevation on the Temple Mount, rather than at the supposed highest point, the Rock under the Golden Dome. Included in this question of topography was Bagatti's contention that the rock face, which now has its boundary in the northwest corner of the Haram, originally extended further south and was cut back to its present line of scarp by either the Romans or the Arabs.

Second, in order to determine the square area that composed the huge platform upon which the Temple had stood, he measured the length of the southern Herodian wall beginning at the southeastern corner. Moving northward 920 feet, he came to a point in the eastern wall where the original line of the rampart ends and from which another wall, a short distance from the former wall, begins its northerly course towards the northeastern corner of the enclosure. This junction in the wall seemed to determine the course of an east-west wall, the northern boundary of the Temple. Looking across the present Haram in this direction, he saw that the ground revealed a definite depression along the supposed wall line. The fact that the area had been planted with trees by the Muslims further confirmed the absence of solid rock at this level. Apparently the area had been filled in by the seventh-century builders of the Muslim Dome of the Rock. Since this wall line was south of the present Eastern or Golden Gate, this gate was excluded from the Temple area, a fact which agrees with Josephus' description of the eastern Temple enclosure.

Third, Bagatti read in an account of a pilgrimage to the Temple site in A.D. 438—by a Christian named Barsauma—that the Jews gathered together to venerate their ruined Temple. While the exact place that they prayed was not given, Bagatti interpreted the statement "at the gates which lead to Siloam"[23] to refer to the Huldah Gate entrance at the southern wall (adjacent to the present Al-Aqsa Mosque), which indeed leads downward to the Pool of Siloam. From this he concluded that the Temple was situated nearby at this southern location.

Fourth, Bagatti claims that the Dome of the Rock had no real historical significance, neither being venerated by Israel during Temple times nor by Jews or

Christian pilgrims from the time of the Temple's destruction to the early Islamic period. In his opinion, the Rock beneath the Dome received its sacred character in the seventh-century only because of a political-religious rivalry between Jerusalem and Mecca. If the Rock had no prior religious importance, he reasons, it could not have been the site of the Holy Temple.

Two other lines of evidence have been advanced to support Bagatti's Southern theory. First, the presence of numerous underground reservoirs in the proximity of the Al-Aqsa Mosque agree with descriptions that such reservoirs were made to support the enormous amount of water needed for the Temple rituals. Too, many of these reservoirs were built using masonry and designed with vaults, suggesting that earlier they were used as secret escape tunnels or hidden chambers. The historical sources speak plainly of such hidden passageways and rooms, which were used by the Temple priests. The presence of these underground features at this site lends credence to a southern location for the Temple.

Tuvia Sagiv

In recent years a Tel Aviv architect named Tuvia Sagiv (see photo section) has vigorously championed the southern theory and added significant new arguments for its support. He began by looking at the topography of the Temple Mount from the perspective of his architectural expertise. He found that, according to the Mishnah, the main entrance to the Temple area from the south and the Holy of Holies had a difference in height of about 10 meters with about 39 meters between the entrance to the Temple Mount and the Temple above. Yet when he compared these dimensions to the Dome of the Rock, the traditional site of the Holy of Holies, he discovered the difference was 20 meters and 80 meters respectively. This led him to the conviction that the Temple had to have been located at a lower, more southern position.[24]

Moreover, according to Sagiv, the fosse (dry moat) that once existed north of the Temple Mount was also *north* of the Antonia Fortress. Based on this reasoning, he locates the Antonia Fortress where the Dome of the Rock is today. Sagiv further found that Josephus had stated that the Bezetha Hill, north of the Temple Mount, obscured the view of the Temple from the north. But if the Temple was located where the Dome of the Rock stands this would not be the case; therefore, the Temple would have to be lower (south) to be obscured by this hill.[25] Similarly, he discovered in his reading of Josephus that when King Herod Agrippa looked out the window of his palace (near the present Jaffa Gate), he was able to see the sacrifices on the altar outside the Second Temple.

However, if the Temple was located at the site of the Dome of the Rock, Agrippa's palace would have had to have been 75 meters high in order to see into the sacred precinct. Since no building is recorded to have been built to this height, the location of the Temple must have been lower.[26] One item of evidence that Sagiv finds particularly impressive is the remains of a water conduit (located in the side of the embankment near the southern stairs that ascend to the Jewish Quarter) that supplied water to the high priest's *miqveh* (ritual bath) situated above the Water Gate and to the Temple Mount for the purpose of rinsing sacrificial blood from the area. But a survey of the level of this aqueduct proved to him that if the Temple had been at the level of the Dome of the Rock, it would have been 20 meters too low to serve these sites. Again, the Temple would have had to be lower in elevation (to the south) for this to have worked.[27]

Sagiv has added to his research by non-invasive ground-penetrating radar probes (conducted in 1990) and thermal infrared fly-by scans (conducted 1993–1995) of the Western Wall, the open area behind the Wall toward the Al-Aqsa Mosque, and the Temple platform.[28] These revealed pentagon-shaped ruins beneath the Dome of the Rock, which Sagiv believes was a high place of Ashtoreth during the First Temple period, then became a part of Strabo's Tower in the Hasmonean period, and finally was incorporated into the Antonia Fortress in the Herodian period. He then assumes that the Muslims were either confused or deceived by the Jews into believing these remains were those of the Temple and built the Dome of the Rock over them.[29] In addition, Sagiv conjectured that if Hadrian's temple of Jupiter had been built over the ruins of the Second Temple, and the Temple was to the south, then perhaps the plans of the similarly built second/third century A.D. temple of Jupiter at Baalbek (modern Lebanon) would line up with this southern area.[30] It did, and proved to him that the Arabs had built both the Dome of the Rock and the Al-Aqsa Mosque over the remains of Hadrian's Roman temple. Based on this evidence, combined with the subterranean lines discernable in this area on the infrared scans, Sagiv was able to determine the Temple's exact location. This he places in the open area directly behind the Western Wall and between the present-day Al-Aqsa Mosque and the Dome of the Rock in the area of Al Kas, a sacred Muslim fountain that today sits on a north-south axis through the Dome and the Al-Aqsa Mosque. According to Sagiv's orientation, the Al Kas fountain would mark the site of the Temple's Holy of Holies (see diagram on page 338). Furthermore, passing down the length of this site, and possibly forming its axis, is the main east-west line of the Roman-period street known as the *decumanus*, which stretched eastward from the Jaffa

Gate along the line of the ancient first wall of David's city. East of the Temple Mount, in the Kidron Valley, the terminus of this line is marked by the prominent, 45-foot-tall monument popularly credited as Absalom's Tomb, but most likely built in the Herodian era toward the end of the first century B.C. The distance from the corner of the tower at the Jaffa Gate to Absalom's Tomb is 2000 cubits, measured by a cubit of 1.728 feet (0.526694 metres), the same as that by which the Temple was built.

The Northern Location

The theory of a northern location has been proposed by Asher Kaufman (see photo section), a Scottish immigrant who is a professor of physics at the Hebrew University of Jerusalem's Rachah Institute. In 1977 he published his defense of the northern theory in his paper, "New light upon Zion: the plan and precise location of the Second Temple," followed in later years by additional articles in numerous Israeli journals and American archaeological magazines.[31] His initial inquiry was stimulated by Ezekiel 8:16, where the prophet's view of the Jerusalem Temple gave an indication of the Temple's orientation. According to this text Ezekiel saw a vision of "about twenty-five men, with their backs to the temple of the LORD and their faces toward the east; and they were prostrating themselves eastward toward the sun." This indicated that the Temple was orientated eastward, directly facing the Mount of Olives.

Kaufman found another clue in Numbers 19, which describes the ceremony of the Red Heifer that took place on the Mount of Olives (for more on this ceremony, see chapter 16 of this book). At a special spot directly across from the Eastern Gate the high priest sprinkled the blood of the heifer directly before the tabernacle of the congregation seven times before burning the carcass to ashes. The Rambam records that all the walls of the Temple were high except the wall to the east, which was lower. "Thus, the priest [who offered the Red Heifer] could see the opening of the Temple when he sprinkled its blood, while standing on the Mount of Olives" (Mishneh Torah, *Hilchot Beit HaBechirah* 6:6). Therefore, this place must have been on the eastward extension of the Temple's axis, near the summit of the Mount of Olives. By further study of archaeological records and relics, Kaufman was able to identify the probable site of the Red Heifer ritual, to fix the line of the Temple's axis, and to discover the original ground plan of the building.[32] According to his measurements, a straight line runs from this point on the Mount of Olives through the Eastern Gate and to the top of a small cupola at the northwestern end of the Temple platform. This eastern orientation had also been suggested by the Mishnah tractate *Middot*, and led Kaufman to conclude that this alignment removed the Dome of the Rock from consideration as the site of the Temple.

To support his theory Kaufman sought physical evidence from possible structural remains above and below the ground at this site on the Temple platform. While his only access to the evidence beneath the Temple Mount consisted of reports written by British explorers a century ago, his survey on the enclosed platform produced some relevant new discoveries. Of special merit was a bedrock mass near the northeastern steps leading up to a small Muslim cupola on the Temple Mount. He compared these remains and others shown on old German World War I reconnaissance photos and photos he took of rock outcroppings now concealed by the Arabs. Based on a study of these remains, which he concluded were originally the northwest corner of the Court of the Priests, he determined that the Temple was formerly at the place marked by a small, open, domed and pillared sixteenth-century Muslim cupola that covered a flat patch of outcropping bedrock (see photo section). Further confirmation of this seemed to emerge upon a closer examination of the nature of this cupola. The bedrock inside the cupola (and extending a little outside) is the only such bedrock appearing on the Temple Mount esplanade. Was it the *Even Shetiyyah* ("Foundation Stone") had that portruded in the ancient Holy of Holies? Significantly, this bedrock appears to be pitted, a detail that agrees with the description by the fourth-century Bordeaux pilgrim of the Foundation Stone—called in his account the "Pierced Stone"—because it had numerous imprints of the hobnails of soldiers' boots. Adding to this identification was Kaufman's discovery of the Arabic names for this cupola: *Qubbat al-Arwah* ("the Dome of the Winds or Spirits") and *Qubbat el-Aloah* ("the Dome of the Tablets"). We know that Arabic titles often preserve original place names; were these dual titles reminiscent of the divine presence that accompanied the Ark that once occupied the Temple? Kaufman believes that they are, and that this further confirmed that this cupola had been built over the spot of the ancient Holy of Holies.

Based on this evidence, Kaufman placed the location of the first two Temples approximately 330 feet north of the Dome of the Rock. As a result of this northern placement of the Temple, the Western Wall is no longer adjacent to the holy precinct but merely a supporting wall for the Court of the Gentiles. Concerning the historical identification of the Dome of the Rock with the Temple, Kaufman argues that the exact knowledge of that location was unknown to the Muslim Caliph who erected the Dome in A.D. 691 and that the sources identifying the

Rock under the Dome as the site of the Temple lack historical validity.[33] This agrees with an old story that the guide who directed the Caliph to the site of the Rock was a Jew who, knowing the original location, deliberately deceived him so that a Muslim mosque would not be built over the site of the holy Temple.[34] In Kaufman's view the Rock beneath the Dome is part of the Hadrianic temple of Jupiter, which this pagan emperor chose to place in the Second Temple's Court of the Gentiles because its central location on the platform followed the pagan placement of temples. Therefore, the Rock within served as a speaker's platform, as did Mars Hill in the Areopagus in Athens (see Acts 17:19-22). When Queen Helena, the mother of Christian emperor Constantine the Great, came to the Holy Land in A.D. 326 to restore the Christian holy places, she, Kaufman contends, was not interested in archaeological authenticity. Rather, she wanted to eradicate the existing pagan temples and shrines and replace them with Christian structures. Accordingly, she turned the temple of Jupiter into a monastery dedicated to Saint Jacob. When the Muslims conquered the city in A.D. 638, it was this monastery they turned into a mosque.

Kaufman's view has attracted the attention of prophecy-minded evangelical Christians who believe his theory removes the major obstacle for the rebuilding of the Temple today.[35] If, they say, the Temple could be built alongside the Dome of the Rock,[36] then the only obstacle preventing the construction of the Temple is negotiations with the Arabs to share the Temple Mount. Those who argue this position believe they have scriptural support for their view in Revelation 11:2, a passage that mentions leaving out "the court which is outside the Temple"— where, according to Kaufman's theory, the Dome of the Rock today stands. Because in Revelation this court is left out of the Third Temple's measurements ("for it has been given to the nations"), it is argued that it has been reserved for the "nation" of Islam, leaving the area to the north for Israel to rebuild the Temple. The objection raised to this interpretation is that simply moving the location of the Temple to the northwest for Jewish worship while leaving an area only 100 yards away for Muslim worship would not resolve the problem of the sanctity necessary for the rebuilding the Temple. Orthodox Jews believe that such a compromise would go against the commandment of not having other gods before the Lord (Exodus 20:3), which the presence of the Islamic deity Allah and his worshipers would represent. This would defile the Temple Mount and prevent Jewish worship, which requires ceremonial purity. Kaufman himself rejects this Christian interpretation and in fact distances himself from any speculation about the rebuilding of the Third Temple.

The Central Location

The tradition that has come down through the ages from the reports of the earliest pilgrimages to the Temple has been of a central location for the Temple on the enclosed platform, almost always at the site of the Muslim Dome of the Rock. Because the central theory was also accepted and passed down by Torah sages, their rulings have largely settled the question of location for most Orthodox Jews, as one such writer explains:

> Those faithful to the branches of Torah do not change the clear ruling of the Radbaz, on which the entire Jewish People has relied on all questions of the Temple and sacrifices. Once the Radbaz has sanctioned the central opinion, it is there, it was there, and it will be there until there is a Prophet in Israel or, alternatively, until another location is proven for sure to be the site—not different versions, not questions, and not estimates. Therefore, the Rock at the center of the Dome of the Rock is the center of the Holy of Holies, and it is the corner stone to all measurements—the locations of the inner and outer courtyard, the location of the altar, the *chel* ["rampart"], and the entire Mount, which is today three times as large as the original Sanctified Temple Mount (see Tractate *Middot*) G-d willing, when we will be able to dig and reveal our dear coveted glory in the depths of the Mount, we will be able to discuss whether it is the correct place. Until then, a judge can only rule based upon what his eyes see—the *halacha* is not in Heaven and not overseas. Since one can execute based on an established status, one should use the established status accordingly, whether regarding the sanctity of the location and the *mitzvot* of the *Mikdash* ["commandments of the Temple"].[37]

Archaeologists have generally agreed on the central theory and that the Dome of the Rock marks the site of the Temple. There has been, however, considerable debate as to whether the Rock within the Dome was very significant to the Temple itself. David Jacobson (more on this in a momnet) has argued that the Temple was built over the Rock but that it lay between the Sanctuary floor and played no part in the Temple. Most Orthodox Jews in the Temple movement believe otherwise. They argue that the Rock protruded above the floor of the Holy of Holies and served as the site for the Holy Ark. On the other hand, the late Ashkenazi Chief Rabbi Shlomo Goren argued that the Rock was the site of the Altar of Sacrifice. In his opinion, if the Rock was the *Even Shetiyyah* ("The Foundation Stone"), and the Holy of Holies rested upon it, then the entire Temple would have to be shifted to the east to accommodate the amount of room at the back of the Temple as is indicated by the historical sources. If the Rock is the site of the Temple's altar (as the legitimate successor of David's altar),[38] then the Holy of Holies would be located west of the Dome of the Rock, on or near the present fifteenth-century *Sebil of Qaitbai.*

Because of the importance of this debate, let's consider these two theories concerning the Temple's location at the center of the Mount with respect to the Rock within the Dome of the Rock, and examine some new evidence from experts based on their personal investigations and excavations.

The Theory of the Rock as the Site of the Altar

Many Orthodox Jewish scholars follow Rabbi Goren's conclusions and identify the Rock as the base of the great Altar of Sacrifice. Jewish tradition also lends support to this theory. For example, in the *Midrashim* it is written that the rock is the *Even Akedah* ("the Stone of Binding") and marks the place where Abraham bound his son Isaac and laid him on an altar, but that the Holy of Holies was built over the place where the ram was caught in the thicket, a short distance away. Such tradition further identifies the Rock as not only the escarpment of Mount Moriah where the offering of Isaac was attempted, but also as the threshing floor of Arunah the Jebusite, which King David purchased and upon which he pitched the Tabernacle. Using figures of the *Shiltai HaGiborim*, based on tractate *Middot*, one scholar has sought to prove that the Dome of the Rock is over the place of the Altar.[39] Structural features that seem to argue for the Rock being the place of the Altar of Sacrifice are the bored hole for the drainage of blood and fluids; the cave directly below this perforation, which was said to collect the ash and drainage from above; and extensive reservoirs and aqueducts beneath the floor, including a canal running north that would carry away the refuse and water used in the rituals. How else, it is argued, can these features be explained if this is not the site of the Altar?

The material evidence for this view came immediately after the liberation of the Temple Mount in 1967, when Rabbi Goren assembled a team to carefully measure the distances from the outer walls (assumed to be the compound enclosure of the Second Temple) to the place of the inner walls (the Inner Court or '*Azarah*) within which stood the Temple. These measurements were compared against the standard of those given in Talmudic sources (principally *Middot* and *Shekalim*), and found to agree. Based on this survey, the location of the Temple, the Altar, and the Holy of Holies could be calculated. Rabbi Goren thus concluded: "The Holy of the Holies is not within, or beneath, nor is it located within the Dome of the Rock. The Moslems are mistaken. I made the measurements right after the Six-Day War, and I came to the conclusion, and it is one hundred percent [certain], that the Holy of the Holies is outside the Dome of the Rock, to the west side."[40]

Even though Goren was positive of his findings, he still believed it was necessary to await the prophet of the last days who would come and "confirm" his survey by personally identifying the exact locations. Therefore, the only use others have made of his survey has been to determine the boundaries of sanctity for those Jews wishing to pray on the Temple Mount. Even so, Goren's conclusion has been the basis of the Temple Mount Faithful's (see chapter 19) claim that the Temple could be built "tomorrow," since its exact location is known. However, some Israeli archaeologists, such as Dan Bahat, do not accept the accuracy of Goren's survey.

The Theory of the Rock as the Site of the Holy of Holies

The most-recognized site of the Temple by Jews, Muslims, and Christians is the Dome of the Rock. As Rabbi Chaim Richman says, "We have a tradition that has been passed down in an unbroken chain from our fathers that the Rock, the stone underneath the Dome of the Rock, is the 'foundation stone.'"[41] While some have argued that Jews deceived the Arabs in the seventh century A.D. as to the true location of the Temple (as well as the Tomb of the Patriarchs in Hebron), the Caliph Omar who first came to the stone had almost 700 years of Christian witness to confirm his choice. For all that length of time the stone had become the dumping place for refuse and garbage as a result of Christianity having adopted replacement theology. Thus, unless Christians themselves were deceived as to the ruins of the Temple, the Muslims identified the same spot but with the intent to revere it as the former site of Solomon's Temple. This was in keeping with Arab policy, as Yirmiyahu Fischer notes:

> It is the custom of Moslems to erect shrines and mosques in places that other religions regard as holy. In Israel, this has been the case at the Machpela Cave (where the patriarchs and matriarchs are buried), at the Prophet Shemuel's ["Samuel's"] grave site, at the prophets Gad and Natan's grave site, etc. Even in India, Moslems have built mosques on the sites of Hindu temples. The fact that Moslems do keep a shrine there is a proof that this was considered to be the placement of the *Beit HaMikdash* ["Temple"].[42]

There was even a belief in the early Muslim period that the builder of the Dome of the Rock, the Umayyad Caliph 'Abd al-Malik, like the Persian king Cyrus, was prophesied to build this as a Temple for the Jewish people. As one Jewish researcher has noted:

> Another work...attributed to the Jewish convert Ka'ab al-Ahbar, declares that he found a verse in one of the books saying, "Be it known to you, Jerusalem, *Bayt al-Maqdis* [Arabic term for Jerusalem = Temple], and *al-Sakhra* [Arabic term for the Dome of the Rock], and there are those who call it the Sanctuary. I will send you my servant, Abdel Malik and he will build you and decorate you. And I will return Jerusalem's government to her as it once was and...I will...place my Throne of Glory on *al-Sakhra*...." In these verses the Sanctuary is identified with the Dome of the Rock. Its construction by Abdel Malik was perceived as a fulfillment of this prophecy: ["I shall send you from your descendants kings and prophets of Mecca that his nation will build the Temple of Jerusalem..."].[43]

Israeli archaeologists, for the most part, agree that the First and Second Temples were on the site of the Dome of the Rock. This was stated as the official position of the Israeli Antiquities Authority when they sided against Asher Kaufman (in support of the Wakf!) in a legal dispute over the question of Islamic destruction of ancient remains on the Temple Mount.[44] For example, Dan Bahat, former district archaeologist for Jerusalem and consulting archaeologist for the Western Wall Tunnel excavation, has stated:

> I will say right now that the Temple was standing exactly where the Dome of the Rock is today on the Temple Mount. I want to say explicitly and clearly that we believe that the Rock under the Dome is the *precise site* of the Holy of Holies. [To be more accurate], the Temple extended *exactly* to the place where the Dome is. The "Foundation Stone" [= Rock within the Dome] is actually that stone which comprised the Holy of Holies....
>
> If this site were not the site of the Temple, we would not have the sanctity that has been bestowed upon that stone for centuries. The church fathers describe how the Jews were coming every year to that place, and the Moslems chose to build their sanctuary on the very same stone because they were aware of the Jewish tradition....Omar, the Moslem conqueror of Jerusalem, was brought by a Jew straight to that stone and

not to another one. So the tradition is quite clear about the tradition of this place.[45]

However, a theory needs more than verbal affirmations for its support, and this theory has impressive evidence in its favor.

One of the best-known proponents of this view, Leen Ritmeyer, spent 22 years in Israel and 16 years in Jerusalem excavating below the Temple Mount with Benjamin Mazar and served as the archaeological architect to the expedition until its end in 1978. He then pursued a doctorate at the University of Manchester, completing his dissertation on the location of the Temple. Today he heads Ritmeyer Archaeological Design in England and has published his research in a number of publications and materials related to the Temple.[46]

Ritmeyer's research has weighed more heavily upon known archaeological evidence and deductions from identifiable remains than upon the historical sources. His approach was to first establish the original dimensions of the Temple platform, starting with an archaeological clue he discovered at the base of today's Muslim platform, and then work systematically from this evidence to pinpoint the Temple's location. He says of the superiority of this approach: "There are two other proposals for the location of the Temple…and both start their research in the Temple Mount by saying the Holy of Holies is here, or it is in another place. I don't think that it is the right approach, unless you could find definite archaeological evidence that this was the place where the Temple stood. It's a wrong methodology to start saying here is the Holy of Holies and then try to plot a Temple and then the courts around it. My methodology was completely the opposite."

Ritmeyer realized that although the Bible does not describe the shape of Solomon's Temple platform, it does refer to the large court set around the Temple and the Royal Palace (1 Kings 7:2). The plan of a royal residence and court in connection with a Temple edifice has parallels at other sites in Israel and may be patterned after the First Temple plan.[47] Such parallels reveal *square-shaped* enclosures for their sacred precincts. Moreover, the Mishnah tractate *Middot* (2:1) clearly specifies the square dimensions of the Temple platform, and records its measurements as 500 cubits (861 feet) on a side.[48] It also provides a crucial comparative ratio of the spacial dimensions on each side of the Temple. *Middot* most likely preserves details about the rebuilt Second Temple, which in its pre-Herodian form did not differ from the First Temple plan, since the returning exiles were in no position to create new walls. Rather, they simply repaired those originally destroyed by the Babylonians.

If the precise measurements of the Temple platform can now be ascertained, then the location of the Temple itself can be successfully deduced according to this plan. Ritmeyer's evidence may be summarized as follows:

1. The original 500 cubit square platform has been determined after eliminating later extensions added during the Hasmonean period (second century B.C.) and the Herodian period (20 B.C.–A.D. 70). These reductions to the present platform, along with archaeological clues to the direction of the original walls, indicate that the Solomonic First Temple walls enclosing the Temple platform were on the *west* from step/wall remains at the northwest corner to approximately Barclay's Gate; on the *south* from Barclay's Gate to a bend in the present eastern wall north of the straight joint; on the *east* from this bend to an offset in the wall just north of the present Eastern Gate; and on the *north* from this offset back to the step/wall remains (see diagram on page 338).

2. *Middot* 2:1 states that the Temple was situated so that the surrounding courts all had different dimensions. The largest open space was on the *south*, the next largest on the *east*, the next on the *north*, with the least space on the *west*. Kaufman had contended that this plan for the Temple ruled out the placement of the site at the Dome of the Rock; however, he was assuming that the present dimensions of the Herodian platform were original. Ritmeyer's demonstration that a substantial area of the Herodian platform to the north was a Herodian extension, and that to the south there was both a Hasmonean extension and a Herodian, has changed significantly the basis for this assumption. Ritmeyer utilized his expertise as an architect to draw the Temple to scale according to the measurements given in tractate *Middot*. In doing so he observed that in order to fulfill the requirements of the dimensional ratios with the southern court as the largest and the other parts diminishing in a counterclockwise direction, the Temple had to be built around *es-Sakhra* ("the Rock"). Thus, Ritmeyer reached his conclusion not by starting at *es-Sakhra*, but by working from the outside (the platform) toward the center (the Dome of the Rock).

3. Topographic studies have shown that *es-Sakhra* is a natural rock mass that constitutes the top of the middle part of the eastern hill of Jerusalem. As we have noted, Josephus records that the Temple was built on the top of the mountain, and this precludes any spot other than that encompassed by the Dome of the Rock. Ritmeyer finds confirmation of this fact in Warren's plans. While *es-Sakhra* today stands about five to six feet above the floor of the Dome of the Rock, a short distance outside, in cisterns to the immediate north and south-

east, Warren had measured the difference in height from the top of *es-Sakhra* to be between 13–15 feet. Ritmeyer observed that this bedrock gently sloped upwards from the points measured by Warren to the base of *es-Sakhra*, and determined that in relation to the immediately surrounding bedrock, *es-Sakhra* actually stands some ten feet above it. *Middot* specified that the height of the Temple foundations were six cubits (ten feet)[49], which accords exactly with Ritmeyer's measurements. It appears that these foundations of 6 cubits height were necessary to bury *es-Sakhra* in order to create a level platform on which to build the Temple.

4. If the Temple remains are located on the site of the Dome of the Rock, then all of the underground cisterns (with one eastern exception) in the vicinity of *es-Sakhra* would fall outside the Sanctuary. This is to be expected, since no one would be drawing water within the Sanctuary itself. In addition, a large cistern in the southeastern corner of the square would ideally be situated in proximity to the Brazen Altar next to the site of the ancient Water Gate. This would have provided a convenient source for the water necessary for the service of the Temple.

5. A location of the Temple at *es-Sakhra* would correlate well with the historical and archaeological evidence of priestly exit tunnels. *Middot* 1:3 records that priests officiating in the Temple who happened to have a nocturnal seminal emission (and thus would become ceremonially defiled) would leave the Temple by means of a subterranean passageway that wound around until it reached a ritual immersion room (where he would become ceremonially pure again). The Tanaitic sage Rabbi Eliezer ben Jacob said, "He goes out by the passage which leads below the rampart, and so he came to the Tadi Gate." This same text refers to the Tadi Gate as being located *north* of the Temple and describes it as "serving no purpose at all." Ritmeyer's research has clarified this statement by showing that the northern extension of the Temple platform by Herod buried access to this gate, rendering it useless, although the underground passageway leading to this gate continued to be used by the priests. The British explorers Warren and Conder concluded that if two cisterns immediately north and west of *es-Sakhra* were extended farther north they would meet exactly at a point where the Tadi Gate was located. Ritmeyer has concluded that the northern cistern was probably the passageway reached by descending from the Chamber of the Hearth (one of three gates on the north of the inner court of the Temple), while the western cistern was the immersion room itself. In fact, the northern cistern is

directly in line with the Rock under the Dome of the Rock and with the passageways of the southern Double Gate, which also may have passed between other immersion rooms.[50] Ritmeyer finds great architectural importance in this alignment, since pilgrims approaching from either the north (the Tadi Gate) or the south (the Huldah Gates), would always see *first* whatever was built on that Rock—by his reckoning, the Temple (and especially the Holy of Holies).

Further investigation of the Rock within the Dome of the Rock led Ritmeyer to the conclusion that he could not only identify indications of some of the walls of the Holy of Holies within the structure, but also the actual spot where the Ark of the Covenant had once rested on the Rock. Ritmeyer explains how he came to this determination:

> It took me 20 years to figure it out. I was convinced that the Temple must have stood somewhere here. I started to look at the measurements of the Rock and the interior measurements of the Temple. We know that the interior measurements of the Temple were 20 cubits wide. The Holy [Place] was 40 cubits long and the Holy of Holies was 20 by 20 cubits. If you use the measurements of the 500 cubits measurements from the Mishnah it would measure 10.5 meters thereabouts. Comparing that with the size of the Rock, the Rock is larger than the Holy of Holies. Yet, the Mishnah [*Yoma* 5:2] says that this stone is called '*Even Ha-Shetiyyah*, "the Foundation Stone." Why would they call it the Foundation Stone? Because if the Holy of Holies was smaller than the Rock, then the Rock would have served as a foundation for at least one of the Temples. With that information in mind, I started looking closer at the Rock looking for a foundation.[51]

Ritmeyer's look at the Rock began first by eliminating the signs of Crusader quarrying on the Rock, which in A.D. 1099 had been captured from the Muslims and converted into a Christian church called *Templum Domini* ("the Temple of the Lord"). He attributed cuts in the Rock on the north, south, and west sides to their actions. The Crusaders thought that the rock disfigured the Temple of the Lord and so shaped it into a more acceptable size and built an altar on top of the Rock. In 1187, when the Caliph Saladin recaptured the Dome of the Rock, they found it covered with marble slabs. Once they had removed the slabs they found that the Rock had been mutilated. This mutilation also affected the cave, and deep tunnels dug beneath the Rock may indicate attempts by the Crusaders to locate the suspected hiding place of the Ark. The natural cave below the Rock was identified by the Crusaders as the Holy of Holies; there, they commemorated the angel's visit to Zacharias (Luke 1:11-20). They enlarged this cave in order to use it as a sanctuary. Because they burned candles and incense in the cave, it was necessary for them to cut a vertical shaft for ventilation (the present hole in the Rock).

Before the Crusaders, the upper level would have been larger and flatter and filled most of the Holy of Holies. Ritmeyer measured the flat areas at the southern part of the Rock, which formed foundation trenches, and found their combined dimensions agreed perfectly with the known thickness of the walls of the Second Temple (six cubits, or ten feet and four inches). This established the site of the southern wall of the Holy of Holies, with its back wall resting against the unchangeable natural rockscarp along the west. The northern wall would have been adjacent to the northern end of the Rock itself. The placement of these walls also agreed with Ritmeyer's earlier identification of the placement of the original Temple platform. He found that the direction of the western scarp was virtually identical to that of the step remains and of the eastern wall of the Temple Mount. Therefore, the First and Second Temples would have had the same orientation—the longitudinal axis of the Temple at right angles with the eastern wall. This axis is also aligned with the highest point on the Mount of Olives, where the sacrifice of the Red Heifer (necessary for ritual purification) took place (see next chapter). This became a further confirmation to Ritmeyer of his location of the Temple.

Having identified these structures, Ritmeyer began looking for additional clues that would help to position the Holy of Holies. He tells the story of how this happened:

> Once I began to research this problem in the spring of 1994, the secrets of the *Sakhra* revealed themselves to me in such rapid succession that it was sometimes breathtaking. While flying to Israel, 30,000 feet high in the air, I got my first glimpse of the most spectacular of all the discoveries, namely that of the former location of the Ark of the Covenant! Averting my gaze from the in-flight video, I took out a large photograph of the *Sakhra* from my briefcase and tried to trace again those flat areas, which of course, were familiar to me as foundation trenches....I sketched over the flat areas on the photograph of the *Sakhra* the line of the southern wall of the Holy of Holies....I drew the western edge of the Rock and the northern wall at the northern end of the exposed rock....I also drew a dotted line where the veil, which separated the Holy of Holies from the Holy, would have hung. I did not expect to find any remains there as no wall existed there. I then suddenly noticed in the middle of

this square a dark rectangle! What could it be? The first thing that came to mind was, of course, the Ark of the Covenant, which once stood in the centre of the Holy of Holies in Solomon's Temple. But that surely could not be true, I thought. . . . [However,] according to my plan, it falls exactly in the centre of the Holy of Holies. The dimensions of this level basin agree with those of the Ark of the Covenant, which were 1.5 x 2.5 cubits (2'7" x 4'4" or 79 cm. x 131 cm.), with the longitudinal axis coinciding with that of the Temple. Its location is rather unique, as it could only have been the place where the Ark of the Covenant once stood. It is clear that without such a flat area the Ark would have wobbled about in an undignified manner, which would not conceivably have been allowed.[52]

Therefore, according to Ritmeyer, this rectangular depression served as an incised base to secure the Ark within the Holy of Holies (see photo section). It could not have been a creation of the Crusaders because they covered the Rock with slabs to hide it. Moreover, they still would not have used it; they would have placed a statue in the middle of the Rock, but not in such a base at the north of the Rock (where the depression would have been at that time).[53] Only archaeological excavation will be able to conclusively confirm Ritmeyer's hypotheses, but his observations have added significantly to the theory that the Dome of the Rock is the site of the Temple.

The Theory of the Rock Beneath the Site of the Holy Place

Another theory, advanced by David M. Jacobson, who holds a doctorate in materials science from the University of Sussex (England), also centrally locates the Temple on the present *Haram es-Sharif,* but differs from Ritmeyer in that his positioning of the Temple places the Rock within the main hall of the Holy Place, known as the *Hekhal.* However, he argues that the Rock lay beneath this floor of the Temple and therefore it, as other existing structures on the Temple platform, offers no help in the search for the Temple's true location. Thus, he sought to deduce the ancient site based on the large-scale features of the expanded platform, or *temenos* (enclosure), that Herod constructed around the Temple. Jacobson's published research[54] has led him to several conclusions:

1. The shape of the Herodian Temple Mount enclosure was a trapezium (like a rectangle) and therefore is not coextensive with the present shape of the *Haram es-Sharif* platform as an irregular quadrilateral. The original outline is preserved in the present boundaries of the *Haram* on three sides (east, west, and

The Temple Mount Today

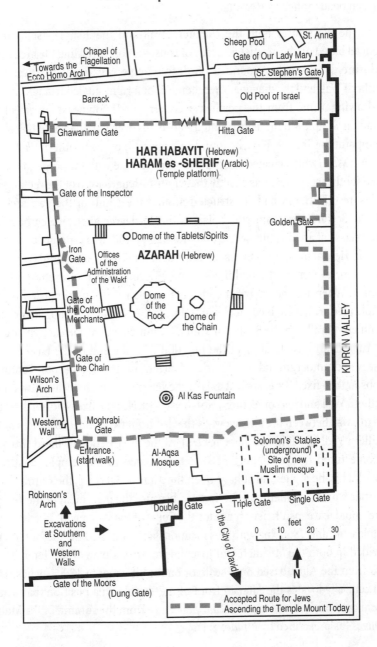

south), but not on the north, where only the present northwestern corner of this wall can be identified as Herodian.

2. The position of both the Northern Wall and the Temple itself can be deduced based on the geometric order of construction governing the area of the enclosure. Jacobson first found a 60-degree angle was formed between the Southern Wall and the diagonal (hypotenuse) of a right-angled triangle created by drawing a line from the northwest corner to the southeast corner of the Herodian Temple Mount. This resulted in two discoveries that enabled Jacobson to pinpoint the Temple. First, he found that the ratio of the Southern Wall to the Western Wall (which created the right-angled triangle with the 60-degree angle at the southeast corner) was exactly the width-to-length ratio of the rectangular enclosure that Herod had constructed around the Tomb of the Patriarchs in Hebron. Second, the geometrical plan of the 60-degree angle, which had governed classical architecture in the early Roman period, was especcially a signature of Herodian architects, as examples in buildings at Masada and the Herodium, as well as the building's mosaic decoration (the rosette pattern), confirm. When this geometrical construction plan was superimposed on the Temple platform, it enabled Jacobson to locate the Northern Wall in its original alignment parallel to the Southern Wall as commencing at the eastern edge of the Antonia and terminating at the junction with the end of the Eastern Wall (discovered underground by Charles Warren in the nineteenth century). Jacobson then fixed the east-west axis of the Temple Mount halfway between the Southern Wall and his conjectured Northern Wall. Next he fixed the north-south axis midway between the passageways that led from two tunnel entrances at the Southern Wall (Double and Triple Gates). At the intersection of these two axes he conjectured that an important structure related to the Temple must have existed. This, he argues, must have been the Altar of Sacrifice, the central focus of public worship, rather than the Temple, because the placement of the Temple there would leave insufficient space for the Court of the Women to the east of the Temple's entrance. Starting with this location, Jacobson used the measurements provided in both the Mishnah and Josephus to draw a plan of the Temple outward from the Altar, based on a scale of one cubit equal to 18.55 inches. This plan centrally locates the Altar in front of the Temple, in a position that would have allowed visibility of the Sanctuary entrance from the summit of the Mount of Olives (as prescribed by *Middot* 2:4).

3. The spots Jacobson identified for the Temple and the Altar are today occupied by the Muslim Dome of the Rock and the Dome of the Chain, a large cupola that sits directly east of the Dome of the Rock, sharing with it a raised inner asymmetrical platform. His measurements form the center of the Dome of the Chain to that of the Dome of the Rock were found to correspond almost exactly with those given in the Mishnah (*Middot* 4:6-7) for the distance between the Altar and the Temple. In addition, the dimensions of these two structures themselves almost precisely match those of the Temple and the Altar. Believing this indicated that the seventh-century Muslim Arabs who conquered this site intentionally preserved the memory of the original sacred construction, he found that other features of the present Islamic platform also duplicate elements of the Herodian Temple Mount and confirm the location of the Holy of Holies within the Temple. Measurements from the center of the Dome of the Chain to the northern and western edges of the inner platform produce a square whose dimensions (426 cubits) fall between the sets of measurements of the sacred square of the Temple precinct given by Josephus (400 cubits) and the Mishnah (500 cubits). Moreover, a terrace wall situated 121 feet south of the inner platform apparently marked the *Soreg* (boundary) of the Herodian Temple precinct. This was based on photographs from the early 1870s, which clearly revealed a flight of four monumental steps (no longer extant) ascending to a southern terrace that ran parallel to the Herodian monumental staircase at the Southern Wall. Jacobson identifies these steps with the *crepiodoma*, a set of monumental steps found in classical temple design that symbolized the entry into the sacred precinct. Furthermore, Israeli archaeologist Ronny Reich had identified two underground structures immediately south of the *crepiodoma*, originally thought to be cisterns, as *miqva'ot* (ritual immersion pools). Jacobson believes that these pools, oriented on the same east-west axis as the Temple mount and parallel to the staircase at the Southern Wall, represented the last opportunity for those coming to the Temple to ritually purify themselves, thereby confirming his location of the Temple.

4. Aligning the Holy of Holies along a common axis with the Altar placed it a little to the west of the Rock within the Dome of the Rock, yet still within the Sanctuary itself. This coincides with Josephus' testimony that the Temple was built on top of the mountain (*Antiquities* viii.97), and agrees with the tradition that identifies the Dome of the Rock with the Temple. However, based on the remains of a pilaster course found near the northern end of the Western Wall, the Herodian enclosure was at the same level as the present *Haram es-Sharif*. In

this case, the floor of the Temple, which would be still higher than the floor level of the outer court of the enclosure by an ascent of some 31 steps (about 24 feet), would completely bury the Rock within the present Muslim Dome of the Rock. Therefore, this underground Rock would not correspond to any feature of the Herodian Temple but simply mark the center of Mount Moriah, upon which the Temple was erected. According to Jacobson, the Rock's tradition as site of the Holy of Holies was due to its proximity to the original site and its identification by Christian pilgrims as the "Pierced Stone," a condition created as a result of the extensive construction efforts of Hadrian on the Temple Mount and the misidentification of the first Muslim conquerors. Consequently, though Jacobson diminishes the Rock's significance within the Temple, it serves for him as an additional confirmation of the site of the Temple at the summit of Mount Moriah, which underlay the Temple proper.

Conflicting Consequences of the Search for the Site

Ironically, the search for the exact location of the Temple has resulted in problems for those whose ambition is to ascend the Temple Mount in preparation for the rebuilding of the Temple. For example, Michael Ben-Ari complains:

> And now comes Sagiv and attempts to prove that "there is no way to know," for in his opinion, the location of the Temple was on the southern end of the Mount. Thus, today one must be wary of entrance to the Temple Mount at all. Indeed, in answer to the query why the Chief Rabbinate forbids entrance to the Temple Mount, the Office of the Chief Rabbinate relied on Sagiv's theory to "prove" and say "there is no way to know," and that there are "various opinions," etc.[55]

These various opinions have also created problems for those Israelis whose professional work (especially archaeology) requires them to avoid political and religious conflicts. Significantly, these theories are not treated as academic and theoretical but are taken quite seriously, and when used to support political activity, have the potential to overturn the present status quo on the Temple Mount itself! The problem here concerns both the Muslims, who do not want a Jewish presence on the Temple Mount, and the Jews, who are present daily at the Western Wall at the foot of the Temple Mount. Concerning the Muslim problem, Dr. Dan Bahat, a lecturer in the Land of Israel Studies Department of Bar Ilan

University and the consulting archaeologist for the Western Wall Tunnel excavation, has stated:

> All these theories only do damage...because then the Arabs can say, "You yourselves are arguing about it. The Temple wasn't even on the Temple Mount." [For example] I once participated in a television show with Ziad Abu-Ziad [a prominent Palestinian public figure] and he said that Jerusalem is not the city of the Temple....Look, the connection of the Jews to Jerusalem is beyond all doubt. An observant Jew mentions Jerusalem three times a day [in the daily prayers]....the entire Bible talks about Jerusalem...[how] the Temple of the city symbolizes the presence of God....[56]

Bahat's concern is quite real. Since the Palestinian usurpation of the Temple Mount from the Jordanians, they have publicly charged that Israel has no right to their sacred site because it never had a connection to the Jews. They insist that there never was a Temple at this site and therefore no access should be granted Jews to pray at the holy places of Islam. Every competing view only increases the Palestinians' conviction that the Jews have no idea where their Temple was and strengthens their justification for keeping Jews off of the Temple Mount.

The Jewish problem has been created as a result of the archaeological data uncovered in researching the ancient location: The Western Wall (the famous "Wailing Wall," or the *Kotel*) to which Judaism has looked as the only remnant of the destroyed Temple and to which it longed to return for centuries, never was a part of the Temple complex at all! On the other hand, the evidence from archaeological research has confirmed that the eastern wall of the Temple Mount is the same wall that was present during the time of the Temple. Yet when the original measurements of the Temple Mount (500 cubits x 500 cubits) are considered, and when one measures the distance from the eastern wall, the Western Wall is not reached. It is parallel to the western wall of the original Temple Mount, but it is still further west of the sacred precinct. Again Dan Bahat comments:

> With this supposition we present a problem for the observant Jew at the Western Wall. Why does he pray where he prays? Because he believes it is a part of the Holy Temple. Now we are showing him that he is really standing above a street that was built by Herod the Great. This was never a part of the sacred precinct. We are actually telling him that it does not even follow the line of the boundary of the ancient sanctified

Temple precinct, which was further to the east. In this sense, we are moving him away from his holy area.[57]

This fact is not in dispute among those who debate the various theories of location. Every view has demonstrated in their findings that the present Western Wall could not have had any relationship to the sacred area beyond it. The ramifications for this, as Bahat has stated, are that the Jewish people, and especially the Orthodox and ultra-Orthodox in Israel, who practically live at the Western Wall, no longer have a holy site accessible to them. In 1967, when Israel captured the Temple Mount, the alternative to continuing Israeli control of the Temple Mount was to abandon it in favor of the Western Wall, since it had become traditionally established as the focal point of prayer and pilgrimage. But what will happen if these observant groups can be convinced that the Western Wall is in fact not holy and therefore not the God-ordained place for prayer? The conclusion is obvious—they will unanimously demand the Temple Mount! On the one hand this could cause greater problems—for Israel politically and for the secular Israelis' hope of peace in the Middle East—but on the other hand, it could be the very catalyst to bring resolution to the current question of the Temple's location. If the site were once again in Jewish hands, the location of the Temple could be confirmed archaeologically, and if this were to occur, how far behind would be the rebuilding of the Temple?

The answer to this somewhat rhetorical question is more complicated than it may at first appear. In the next chapter I will explain why, and reveal little-known "insider" information about what is being done to make possible a Jewish presence on the Temple Mount in preparation for the Last Days Temple.

CHAPTER 16

The Hunt for the Holy Heifer

Purification for the Temple

In truth the fate of the entire world depends on the Red Heifer. For God has ordained that its ashes alone is the single missing ingredient for the restatement of biblical purity—and thereafter, the rebuilding of the Holy Temple.

—RABBI CHAIM RICHMAN

Nine Red Heifers were born during the time of the Tabernacle and the two Temples. The tenth, according to this tradition, will be born in the end-times for the Third Temple. Since the destruction of the Second Temple and in the time of the exile over the last 2000 years no Red Heifers have been born.... [But] now they are coming one after another, in Israel and on the ranches of friends of Israel.... It is a clear message from G-d to His people, Israel, that the time for the rebuilding of the Temple has come.

—GERSHON SALOMON

The majority of Orthodox rabbis forbid Jewish entrance upon the Temple Mount on the grounds that someone might inadvertently tread upon the site of the Holy of Holies, which has retained its sanctity despite the loss of the Temple itself. Let us suppose, however, that all of the obstacles we have considered thus far were suddenly to be removed. The Muslims decided they were tired of the constant conflict with Jews and agreed to dismantle their mosques and go back to Mecca. The Israeli government encouraged Jews everywhere to ascend the holy hill and approved the rebuilding of the Temple. The archaeologists were able to excavate on the Temple Mount and resolve all questions as to exactly where the Temple stood. Could the Temple then be rebuilt?

Surprisingly the answer most rabbis give is no.[1] The reason for this may be illustrated simply: Someone may have use of the best recipe in the world, but if there is one ingredient missing, he cannot begin to cook. Leaving out even one essential would ruin the whole meal! In the same way, there is one essential in the mix of items necessary to rebuild the Temple that, if it is missing, prevents the project from ever getting started. Why is this missing ingredient so necessary?

The Problem of Impurity

Israel's calling by God as a priestly Nation and the fact that God dwelt in the Nation's midst required the people to maintain a level of sanctity that made them distinct from the surrounding Gentile nations. The physical part of this distinction was ceremonial separation from all that represented sin and would render them unholy, thus disqualifying them from the divine service.

When it comes to sanctity, there are two Hebrew words that described the two opposite ends of the scale. At the top of the scale sanctity was *qadosh* ("holy"), and at the bottom of the scale was *tame'* ("unclean").[2] The term *qadosh,* the highest expression of holiness, is taken to the superlative degree with the place of God's presence—the Holy of the Holies (Hebrew, *Qodesh Qodeshim*) within the innermost part of the Temple. By contrast, the highest expression of unholiness also has a superlative level with corpse impurity, which is called "the father of fathers of impurity" (Hebrew, *'av 'avot ha-tumah*).[3] It is true that yet another Hebrew term, *ḥôl* ("profane"), in fact constitutes the ultimate unholiness, but this is only because it *causes* corpse impurity to be incurred by the entire Nation of Israel, which results in destruction and exile (see this cause-and-effect relationship in Ezekiel 36:17-19). Therefore, as corpse impurity is experienced on a national level it affects the Temple, forcing the holy presence of God to depart from the Holy of Holies and therefore from the Nation of Israel (Lamentations 4:13-16). It was this possibility that concerned the prophets when they leveled invectives against Israel's corrupt social and political life. Rather than abide by God's holy standards, Israel sought to imitate the surrounding nations, and consequently invited foreign invasion and the end of that which distinguished Israel's separateness: the Temple and its service. God had called the Land of Israel to be separated to Him and remain holy, and warned that any uncleanness would bring desecration. Therefore Israel was to remain clean by a constant adherence to God's own prescribed regulations for holiness (as given in the book of Leviticus). For this reason it was imperative that contact with the dead be limited, since such contact brought corpse impurity and made one unable to perform any holy service (Numbers 9:5-7). When a person died, he had to be buried immediately so as to limit the number of persons who could possibly incur this defilement, since contact with such persons brought ritual contamination that could spread to others. To be ceremonially cleansed from most kinds of ritual impurity one had to be immersed in spring water at a *miqveh* (ritual bath). But to be purified from defilement caused by contact with the dead, ritual immersion was not enough. Something special is required—something that is found in the 113th of the 613 Mandatory Commandments in Judaism. This commandment states: "The ashes of the Red Heifer are to be used in the process of ritual purification." According to Numbers 19, from which this commandment came, the only way to be cleansed from corpse impurity (including the case of unknown homicide, Deuteronomy 21:1-9) is to be sprinkled with water containing the ashes of a Red Heifer, and this water has to be handled by someone who is ceremonially clean.

Herein lies the problem: The state of corpse impurity has attached itself to every Jew in the whole Nation of Israel because all Jews have lived outside the Land among Gentile nations, where they have all incurred this defilement without the means of the ceremonial system to restore their purity. Therefore, there does not exist today one single ceremonially clean person who can sprinkle everyone else with water containing the Red Heifer ashes. And there is another difficulty: There are no longer any Red Heifer ashes. After the destruction of the Temple no more Red Heifer ashes could be made,[4] making purification from corpse impurity harder and harder to do as the supply of ashes became depleted and the number of priests ritually qualified to perform the service diminished. Jewish tradition records that until the end of the period of the *Amoraim* there were still *Chaverim* (the name given to those who were very strict about avoiding defilement and who purified themselves from defilement by the dead) remaining in Israel. But with the cessation and destruction of Jewish settlement in the country at the beginning of the Arab period, the ability to offer purification from corpse impurity died out completely. So today, with no means to ceremonially purify those who enter the Temple Mount area so that they don't defile the still-sanctified site of the Holy of Holies, there can be no Temple, priesthood, or sacrificial system. This, however, creates a catch-22, for in order to rebuild the Temple and restore the priesthood and sacrifices, Jews *must* be able to walk and work upon the Temple Mount!

The requirement to have a ceremonially clean priest on hand creates a problem in light of Exodus 25:8, which obligates the Jewish nation to rebuild the Temple whenever it becomes possible to do so. Activists in the Temple movement believe that despite the human condition, the Nation has sinned by not obeying this divine command. They argue that no Temple was ever built without human preparation (1 Kings 5-6; Ezra 3:7-11), and that this effort had divine approval (1 Chronicles 22:14; 23:4). They say that the Jews cannot simply wait for heaven to send the prophet Elijah and the Messiah as a sign of redemption, because this will not be done until there is national repentance and a willingness to begin the task of rebuilding (see *Yalkut Shimoni Samuel* 106). Neither Elijah nor the Messiah showed up at the previous rebuildings of the Temple. The only difference between then and now is that the Jews then had the ashes of the Red Heifer. Since the ashes are the means to reversing the present impurity of the Nation, those in the Temple movement have given top priority to restoring these ashes and reviving the ceremony of the Red Heifer.

What is the Red Heifer?

Numbers chapter 19 specifies that only an unblemished Red Heifer (Hebrew *parah adumah*, "red cow") can be used for the ceremony—a Red Heifer without defect and on which a yoke has never been placed. The English translation of *heifer* denotes the animal as a young cow which has just reached maturity—the age (three years) at which it would be yoked for labor (see 1 Samuel 6:7). This is the age at which it be can slaughtered and burned and its ashes mixed with spring water to make the liquid used in the purification ceremony. The red color specified for the animal may symbolize blood, the agent of atonement. This symbolism was accepted by the rabbis, however, only as related to another calf—the golden calf—which had caused Israel to sin at the foot of Mount Sinai (Exodus 32:1-10). Rabbi Chaim Richman explains this connection: "It was this single event [sin of the golden calf] which introduced the concept of the impurity of death into the world....In the same way, the red heifer serves to atone for the spiritual chaos brought into the world through the golden calf." Through this symbolic association the rabbis also explained other details concerning this animal that were left unexplained in the biblical text. For example, the prohibition against the animal having a yoke symbolizes the yoke of God's Law, which Israel threw off in the sin of the golden calf. The red color connects in this case with Israel's sin, atoned for by the heifer's ashes as described in Isaiah 1:18: "Though your sins are as scarlet, they will be white as snow; though they are red as crimson, they will be like wool." The rabbis explained that the Red Heifer's "red" must be perfect in its redness (no hairs of a different color), as Israel was faultless in its devotion to God before it sinned with the golden calf. Further explanation in connection with Mount Sinai, the incident of the golden calf, and especially the death of the high priest's sons, has been offered by Martin Greenberg:

> What can be the reasoning behind this seemingly arcane set of rules?...I suggest the following: The third-day sprinkling is intended to recall to the unclean person the three days of cleansing by the Israelites prior to the giving of the Ten Commandments....The red heifer represents the golden calf....The burning of the red heifer is equal to the grinding of the golden calf. The ashes mixed with water and the sprinkling of the water is equal to the drinking imposed by Moses (Message: Eradicate idols and their worship.)...Aaron's two oldest sons, Nadab and Abihu, then make an offering using "strange" (unauthorized) incense; fire comes forth from the Lord and consumes them. Thus, the burning of the red heifer also represents the burning of the wrongdoers, representative of violating the rules of worship. The sprinkling with the "waters of purification" on the seventh day of impurity is to impress on the individual the need for strict adherence to the rules of the sanctuary and need for preparation....After the two sons are struck dead by "fire from the Lord," Moses orders their dead bodies to be carried out of the camp by two of the Levite brethren (Lev. 10:4). The carriers became ritually unclean by reason of contact with the dead. Thus the burning of the red heifer and the use of the ashes for ritual purification is intended to recall for us the Nadab and Abihu event, and its lessons....The statement of Moses to Aaron right after Aaron's sons are struck dead, that God said, *Through those near to me will I be sanctified,* is memorized and carried out in the ritual of the red heifer. God and Moses did their utmost to bring some good out of this tragedy.[6]

While these explanations offer a biblical background for many mysterious aspects of the commandment concerning the Red Heifer, they do not explain them all. The unexplained nature of the command and its ceremony has spurred many stories in Jewish tradition in an attempt to perpetuate the inexplicable value of the Red Heifer not only in the present age, but also for the Messianic age to come.

The Value of the Red Heifer

How much is a Red Heifer worth? Considering the fact that the Mishnah records that only nine of them were ever sacrificed in all of Israel's past history, they appear to be very rare. However, their value for the spiritual service they perform cannot be overvalued, and for this reason their incalculable worth became the subject of rabbinic midrash. In one story a Gentile in whose herd a Red Heifer was born wanted to deceive the Jews who wanted to buy it. He placed a yoke on it (which disqualified it), but then he presented it to the Jews as having never been yoked. However, the Jews discovered the deception and did not buy the animal. Because of the great loss, the Gentile committed suicide. Another story is told about a Gentile in Ashkelon named Dama ben Netina. He received messengers from the Temple who came to him to buy from his father a precious stone for the breastplate of the high priest. However, because his father was asleep and his father's legs were upon the chest which contained the precious stone, he chose to relinquish the deal rather than wake his aged father. Therefore, the Almighty repaid him by causing, in the following year, a Red Heifer to be born in his herd.

The point in these two stories is the lesson that the value associated with the Red Heifer should not be measured materially, but spiritually, since it is attached to the higher order of things in the heavenly realm.

The Red Heifer and the Coming of Messiah

This explains the vital connection between the Red Heifer and the coming of the Age of Redemption. As already mentioned, the more than 1,500 years between the time Moses offered the first Red Heifer (Numbers 19:2) and the destruction of the Second Temple ended the possibility of continuing the practice, only nine Red Heifers (some say seven) had been necessary to produce the ashes sufficient for the needs of purification. The question for this age, as in all of the intervening ages, has been this: Will there be another Red Heifer, and if so, what should be expected of its appearance?

This was answered by the Jewish sage Maimonides when he wrote in his commentary on the Mishnah: "The tenth Red Heifer will be accomplished by the king, the Messiah."[7] It is believed that Maimonides, as an expert on Jewish Law, was making reference to an ancient tradition that the tenth Red Heifer will be associated with the Messianic era, during which the Messiah will officiate at its preparation (See Talmud, tractates *Parah*, Yad, *Parah Adummah* 3:4). Moreover, by tradition, only the son of David will be able to purify Israel with the ashes of a Red Heifer. According to Stephen Yulish, a former professor at the University of Arizona and former director of the Jewish Federation of Phoenix, "the Red Heifer is but another piece in the prophetic timetable which is moving us closer to the end of the age and the return of Messiah." This belief, coupled with the resurgence of the Temple movement and its own preparations for the Messianic era, led Rabbi Richman to say, "We cannot help but wonder and pray: If there are now Red Heifers, is ours the era that will need them?"[8]

The Importance of the Red Heifer

The obscure requirements connected with the Red Heifer ritual have been a problem for Jewish interpreters throughout the ages. As a ritual it was unique among all the ordinances given to Israel. It was the only sacrifice that required that the animal be a particular color. It was the only sacrifice that had to be offered outside the camp of Israel (later, outside the Temple precinct on the Mount of Olives). It was the only sacrifice in which the ashes were to be preserved after the sacrifice was burned.

What was the reason and purpose for these requirements? No explanation is provided at all for these rules or for how the ashes can clean the unclean. Many Jewish interpreters believe these mysteries will not be understood until all men attain to a higher plane of awareness. Otherwise, God expected Israel to implicitly obey this command with no questions asked, and by this to demonstrate to God how much they believe and obey all His commandments.

So mysterious is this ritual that a Jewish midrash observed: "Solomon was wiser than all men, but when he came to the section of the red cow, he admitted, 'I said, I will get wisdom, but it was far from me'" (*Qohelet Rabbah* 7:23). Some scholars have found parallels to the Red Heifer ceremony in the Mesopotamian *namburi* ritual, which had a concern over corpse contamination and a Hittite cleansing ritual that involved water to remove impurity. However, while there are similarities, these other rituals shed little light on the Israelite ritual.

Even though the particulars of the Red Heifer ritual are not given, the importance of the ordinance can be understood by examining the contexts in which it appears. According to Numbers 19:1-22, the practice of sacrificing a Red Heifer was begun in the wilderness of Sinai during the time of Israel's wandering. This wandering was a divine discipline, the result of Israel's sinful rebellion at Kadesh Barnea (Numbers 14–15). Further rebellion by some priests (the sons of Korah) resulted in their deaths and the divine destruction of nearly 15,000 others (Numbers 16). Because of this judgment, the Israelites became greatly fearful about approaching the Tabernacle, where God's presence was manifested (Numbers 17:12-13). As a remedy, the Levites were appointed as the sole ministers of the Sanctuary, but they too would die if they defiled it through ritual uncleaness (Numbers 18:1,22-23,32). Consequently, a provision for the priest's purity had to be made, and it was provided in the ritual of the Red Heifer (Numbers 19). It is in this context of death and destruction that the Red Heifer ordinance was given. Sin had made the approach to a holy God impossible, and only a process of ceremonial sanctification could change the people's unclean status to one that enabled the priests to resume their job of intercession for Israel before the altar.

Islam and the Red Heifer

Given the significance of the Red Heifer in Judaism, it is interesting that there is a similar understanding of the heifer's role in Islam. Vendyl Jones, who has been searching for an ancient vessel containing the last of the Red Heifer ashes since the 1960s, once made this statement in a Christian radio interview:

> The first book in the Muslim Bible, the Koran, is called *Parah*, "the calf," and it pertains to the ashes of the Red Heifer. The Muslims believe whoever finds this will rule the world. So this could have political implications as well. This could settle the *jihad*, "the holy war."[9]

Such an allegation goes to the heart of Muslim fears about Judaism—that it promotes a conspiracy to take over the world and enslave the other religions. But does the Qur'an, the Muslim holy book, actually contain statements that could be construed to teach this?

The second Surah (chapter two) of the Qur'an is indeed called *al-Baqarah* ("the Heifer") and is based on Numbers 19 in *Parashat Chukat* (the Red Heifer chapter in the Torah). In this Surah, verses 67-71 refer to the characteristics required for a cow to be a legitimate "Yellow Cow" (the Muslim equivalent of the

Red Heifer). And verses 72-73 deal with the sacrifice of the Yellow Heifer in order to identify the killer when a dead body is found (see Deuteronomy 21:1-9 in *Parashat Shoftim* of the Torah). However, in these verses there is no mention of ashes, because in reference to the murdered man (verses 72-73), it states that he was resurrected from the dead when his body was touched with "a part of the cow." Unlike the purification from corpse impurity symbolized by the Jewish ritual, the Islamic belief was that an actual reversal of death took place—yet "a part of the cow" is not the same as "the ashes of the cow." Nevertheless, it is apparent that Muslim teaching concerning the Yellow Cow (Red Heifer) gives the impression that the heifer possessed supernatural qualities.

As to the origin of the statement that the discoverer of the ashes would rule the world, Islamic Imam Professor Abdul Hadi Palazzi of Rome acknowledges that the Qur'an does not support this idea. He suspects that it was invented by Muslim activists and circulated as anti-Israel propaganda to convince unlearned Muslims that the Jews' search for the Red Heifer's ashes is to acquire magical power for world domination.[10] This may be the case, yet such a statement is in harmony with the kinds of things said by Orthodox and ultra-Orthodox Jews in the Israeli and foreign press reports about the birth of a Red Heifer. In these reports they claimed that the Red Heifer would usher in the Messianic era, the age of Jewish dominance in the world. Perhaps such statements by Jews, along with the supernatural character of the Qur'an account and misinformation by Muslim extremists, could have created this belief on the popular level.

The Red Heifer and the New Testament

The New Testament epistle to the Hebrews recognizes the historical validity of the Red Heifer ceremony when it asks, "For if…the ashes of a heifer, sprinkling the unclean, sanctifies for the purifying of the flesh, how much more shall the blood of Christ, who through the eternal Spirit offered Himself without spot to God, cleanse your conscience from dead works to serve the living God?" (Hebrews 9:13-14). The author of Hebrews is making a contrast here by means of a *Qal va-homer* (or *a fortiori*) argument that states, "If 'A,' then how much more 'B.'" However, in regard to replacement theology, it should be noted that there is no concept here of Jesus' work removing or replacing that of the Red Heifer's. Rather, there is a concession that its work of ceremonial purification was effective: "sanctif[ies] for the purifying of the flesh" (verse 13).[11] The contrast here is between two *different kinds* of purification—external and temporary (the Red Heifer's), and internal and permanent (Jesus')—both of which are considered necessary (see more on this in chapter 23). Therefore, the New Testament bases the efficacy of Christ's sacrifice on the efficacy of the existing sacrificial system,[12] and in this case on the efficacy of the Red Heifer.

The Ceremony of the Red Heifer

In order to produce the mixture of water and ash required for the cleansing of those contaminated by a corpse, a Red Heifer must be slaughtered by the high priest[13] in a special ceremony on the Mount of Olives. In the time of the Second Temple an arched bridge stretched from the Eastern Gate (Shushan Gate) to a "clean place outside the camp" (Numbers 19:9) (see photo section). The specific spot for the sacrifice on the Mount of Olives was known as the "Mount of Anointment." This bridge was also used on Yom Kippur to lead the scapegoat out of the Temple, over the Mount of Olives, and into the Judean desert. The spot of the sacrifice on the Mount of Olives faced the Eastern Gate and was aligned directly with the entrance to the Sanctuary where the purification ceremony with the ashes was performed. The heads of the Sanhedrin, the heads of the priests and Levitical shifts, and all the prominent people in Israel were present at the ceremony. The priests who participated in this ceremony had to be ritually pure, as the act of sacrificing the Red Heifer and the ingredients used in making the mixture rendered them ceremonially unclean. The animal was led to an altar and placed—with its head facing the Temple—on bundles of wood (cedar, pine, cypress, and fig) in order to increase the quantity of the ashes. Once the unblemished and unyoked Red Heifer was slaughtered, its blood was collected in the left hand of the high priest and sprinkled with his right index finger toward the entrance of the Temple seven times. Then the entire carcass was burned with a mixture of cedar wood, hyssop, and scarlet-dyed wool. The ashes obtained from this burning were ground to a fine texture (including the wood and all parts of the animal) and divided into three parts. A mixture was then made from these ashes and blended with water flowing from a natural source (either a spring or running stream) and used as a ceremonial cleansing agent. One third of the ashes was preserved in the Temple precincts within a wall in front of the Women's Court, a second third was given to the attendant priests so they could purify anyone who incurred impurity, and the third portion was deposited at the site of the altar on the Mount of Olives to be used by the priests who burned the next Red Heifer.

The Red Heifer Ashes

In Temple times, the ashes of the Red Heifer were stored in the "House of Stone"—in a stone jar called, in Hebrew the *klal* (see photo section). Even after the Temple was destroyed, a supply of the ashes was still available near the Eastern Gate and continued to be used as late as the Amoraic period (A.D. 200–500).[14] For water, the priests went to the Gihon spring at the base of the Temple Mount. The water was put in a stone jar that the Mishnah describes as having a thin neck. The vessels were made out of stone because, according to Jewish *halakha*, stone does not transmit ritual impurity (*tumah*). It should be remembered that the ashes themselves were not sprinkled, but the water containing the ashes. It was possible, then, to put only a speck of the ashes in a huge quantity of water for use in sprinkling. In this way a minute amount of ashes could be used to purify tens of thousands of people. Then a priest would dip a bundle of three stalks of hyssop into the mixture and sprinkle it onto a person on two different occasions (on the third day after having become defiled and then again on the seventh day), thus allowing him or her to enter the Temple in a state of ritual purity (*tahara*). This water mixture was also sprinkled on the clothing and vessels that became ritually impure as a result of being in the same house with a person who was impure. While this water "purified" the person or object that it touched, at the same time, the priests who officiated at this ceremony and their garments became ritually impure as a result of handling the waters of purification! This is one of the mysteries of this ritual—that the very agent that brings purity to those without it can make impure those who have it!

According to the biblical command, this ritual purification is still considered a prerequisite for any Jew today: "So it shall be a perpetual statute for them" (Numbers 19:21). How can modern-day Israel obey this command if it does not possess a Red Heifer? Because no one at present is qualified to begin the rebuilding of the Temple or to engage in priestly functions without the Red Heifer's ashes, considerable effort has been expended on researching the ancient ceremonies and seeking a solution to the problem of ceremonial impurity that prevents Jewish access to the Temple Mount. In fact, one of the most controversial projects underway today in Israel involves an attempt to produce a qualified Red Heifer and reinstate the Red Heifer and purification ceremonies.

Raising the Red Heifer and Restoring the Land

When I visited the Temple Institute in 1990 and spoke with Director of Public Affairs Rabbi Chaim Richman, he showed me photographs of Red Heifers recently received from a Gentile Pentecostal minister named Clyde Lott. This man bred Red Angus cattle by trade and had come to the Institute seeking to know if anyone in Israel was interested in obtaining them for purification purposes. According to Lott, the project to export Red Heifers to Israel had been developing since 1989, "when the Holy Ghost began to inspire [him] to research and contact Israel about the Red Heifer located in Numbers chapter 19." As the rabbis of the Temple Institute began studying the issues involved with actually possessing a qualified Red Heifer, they began to see that importing hundreds of Red Angus cattle to Israel could help to restore both livestock and agriculture throughout the entire Land of Israel. They saw the importation as contributing to the total economic advancement of the State, and, because the one offering the heifers was named "Lott" (like the biblical "Lot"), Rabbi Richman considered it "an allusion to the fact that he, as a Gentile, could play an important role."[15]

On November 11, 1994, Rabbi Richman traveled to Canton, Mississippi to personally inspect the Red Heifers on Lott's ranch. The other reason for his trip, as he explained it, "was to enable me to carry the message of what is happening in Israel, and the prophecies concurring the rebuilding of the Holy Temple, to audiences in the United States."[16] Rabbi Richman inspected four Red Heifers and was drawn to one in particular which Lott's daughter had named Dixie. After he studied it for 10 minutes from the tip of its nose to the tip of its tail, he declared, "This is the heifer that will change the world." According to Rabbi Richman this was the first Red Heifer in 2,000 years that met the biblical requirements in Numbers 19 as verified by a rabbi.

The original agreement with Lott was to provide 200 pregnant red heifers that would be shipped via ocean liner to Israel. Statistically, these pregnant heifers would produce 100 bulls and 100 heifers. The resultant 100 heifers would become the "potential" sacrifical stock. Time went by, and this event did not occur. However, Lott's plan has now reached a much grander scale. The goal now is to repopulate the herds of Israel with Lott's breed of cattle stock. So instead of 200 heifers, he is planning to ship thousands of heifers. Currently, however, neither Rabbi Richman nor the Temple Institute are working with Clyde Lott, although "the Temple Institute is maintaining contacts with a number of cattle producers, [both] Jewish and Gentile, and will do whatever is necessary to produce [qualified] cows."[17]

Another organization in the Temple movement seeking to obtain a Red Heifer is the Temple Mount Faithful. Gershon Salomon describes his organization's attempts in this regard:

> One year ago a perfect Red Heifer was born on a ranch in Texas of a member and friend of The Temple Mount and Land of Israel Faithful movement. A few years ago when I used to speak in the area about the vision and activities of the movement for the rebuilding of the Temple and the need to renew the life of Israel as it was in the biblical times, this rancher used to come and take part in these meetings. Immediately, he and his family were very special to me. Their love for the G-d and people of Israel and the vision of the rebuilding of the Temple moved my heart. In the meetings I felt a deep need to ask him whether a Red Heifer had already been born on his ranch. It was G-d who pushed me to ask the question again and again. I knew, and it was a deep feeling in my heart which only G-d could have put there, that on his ranch a Red Heifer would soon be born. One day about a year ago when I was back in my lovely city, Jerusalem, I received a letter from this wonderful rancher and the exciting message was that "a Red Heifer has been born on my ranch." In what exciting and special ways G-d is acting! At the same time, I received a phone call from another member and friend, Sam Peak, who also brought me this joyful message. He also asked how to handle the heifer and how to raise her according to the godly Jewish law. A Red Heifer needs to be raised and handled in a very special way like a holy thing which is completely dedicated to G-d. It has to be raised in a very special, clean stall and to be fed with special food, and even to be spoiled. She cannot be raised with other calves and especially not with males. It is forbidden to use her for any work or any other needs of the rancher. I gave them all the details and I thanked G-d for His kindness towards His people, Israel, and those who are fighting for the rebuilding of the Temple.[18]

Once Red Heifers became available in the United States and the proper authorities in the Department of Agriculture in both countries were contacted and permissions were received, the problem became how to finance the purchase of the cattle as well as the cost of transporting them all to Israel.

Financing the Red Heifer

The organizations promoting Red Heifers to Israel have posted their needs on the Internet at some 100 million dollars. The main support for their project is expected to come from Christians; however, Jewish donors have also been approached. In a letter to potential supporters, the organization (see below) leading the way toward making it possible to transport the Red Heifers to Israel announced:

> On March 7, 1998 Rev. Clyde Lott, Rev. Guy Garner, Jr., and Rev. Al Bishop met in Ripley, Mississippi to form a nonprofit/not-for-profit organization named Canaan Land Restoration of Israel, Inc. for the purpose of livestock and agricultural restoration according to biblical understanding located in the books of Isaiah, Ezekiel, and Joel. A division of this organization was also formed and named *Emmet Bet Sheroot* (Faithful House of Service) for the purpose of exchanging biblical knowledge and perspective of the Bible to further develop the relationship between the Orthodox Jew and the apostolic Christian that will facilitate the ultimate reconciliation of mankind, fulfilling God's divine plan for this time period.

Clyde Lott, the Pentecostal Gentile rancher who has raised the Red Heifers, serves as the president of Canaan Land Restoration of Israel, Inc., an organization established for the purpose of bringing together the Red Heifers and the Israelis and advancing the fulfillment of Bible prophecy. The suggested donation for bringing one Red Heifer is $1000, one-half a Red Heifer $500, one-fourth a Red Heifer $250, and $341 for the airfare of each individual animal. The original schedule for shipment was to have been on August 11, 1998, with 500 registered Red Angus Heifers going to Israel. Rabbi Richman told me that a new date has been set, but that it is not being publicly disclosed at the present time.[19]

Cloning the Red Heifer

With the existence of qualified Red Heifers, it is now possible to produce a Red Heifer in Israel without the cost of shipping cattle and waiting for a qualified offspring to be born. New advances in the science of cloning have made it possible to produce genetic duplicates of as many qualified Red Heifers as desired, anywhere and at any time. Cattle have been cloned since 1994, but at that time the scientists didn't know what traits these clones would have because of the mix of genes from a father and mother mixing with the genetic material of the cattle they were trying to clone. In 1998 researchers in Edinburgh, Scotland successfully cloned an exact duplicate of an adult sheep named Dolly. The scientists did this by taking an unfertilized egg, removing the egg's DNA, and then putting a full set of DNA from the animal to be cloned into the egg (embryonic growth begins once this full set of DNA is added to the egg). However, the donor cell must first be treated with chemicals to trick the cells into resetting the biological clock so that the DNA can begin initially to divide anew. Next, a spark of electricity is added to the egg to enable it to start dividing into an embryo. After a few days in the culture dish, the embryo is placed into the womb of the surrogate mother of the animal being cloned. The result is a clone that is genetically identical to the parent animal.[20] While Israel has set a five-year ban on research that involves cloning humans, nothing prevents the cloning of animals.

Whether actual herds of Red Heifers are transported to Israel or select Red Heifers are used as donor parents to produce genetic duplicates, the day in which Red Heifers are again on the scene and being readied for ritual use is possible at any time.

The Tale of the Birth of Israel's First "Red Heifer"

In order to fulfill the biblical mandate as well as the prophetic one, the next Red Heifer that provides the ashes for the cleansing of the priesthood must be born in the Land of Israel. The problem with Clyde Lott's Red Heifers is that they must first be imported to Israel, then bred or genetically cloned. Only after a perfect Red Heifer is produced and is raised according to the strict standards required could it be accepted for the Red Heifer ceremony. The preference would be for a Red Heifer to be native-born, but up until 1997, that had not happened for two millennia. Then on March 16, 1997 a Red Heifer was said to have been born on the religious kibbutz Kfar Hassidim, near the northern Israeli port of Haifa.[21] It was immediately hailed by religious Jews as a sign from God that work can soon begin on the Third Temple in Jerusalem.[22]

That the Red Heifer was born to a black-and-white mother and a dun-colored bull was seen as a miracle by many in the Temple movement. Rabbi Yehuda Etzion, director of Chai veKaiyam, was quoted as saying: "We have been waiting 2,000 years for a sign from God, and now He has provided us with a Red Heifer."[23] The Red Heifer was named Melody, and its birth and the rabbis' startling claim sent shock waves around the world. Some euphoric rabbis rejoiced that God's will had been fulfilled and were excited that Messiah's appearance could be imminent. The news media at once descended upon the kibbutz, all anxious to see what they had dubbed "the Holy Heifer from Haifa." Not everyone was glad, however, and some people believed Melody was a threat to the peace process and threatened to kill her. Still others thought she was the Antichrist's abomination of desolation since the words *Melody, Israel,* and *Temple* each have six letters—hence "666."

Melody was closely guarded and all were waiting for her to reach her sacrificial age (in August 1999) when the unthinkable happened: Melody sprouted a few white hairs in her tail. Some came to her defense with a rabbinical loophole: She would continue to be qualified so long as no two white hairs proceeded from the same pore! Others claimed that the white hairs actually had red roots! However, in the end, the decision was made by her keepers at the kibbutz to reject Melody and hope for a successor:

> Residents of the northern community of Kfar Hassidim announced with sorrow recently that the Red Heifer that they had been raising had become unfit for ritual use. Hairs on its tail were found to be whitening, rendering it not totally red, and therefore unfit to be used in the purification process for service in a future Holy Temple. The residents are hopeful that the cow will bear red calves that will be able to be used for this purpose.[24]

Red Heifers in Israel Today

While the kibbutz members waited for Melody to become pregnant, new Heifers were announced to have been born in Israel. As with the birth of Melody, the birth of each of these heifers is considered a miracle and a sign that the Temple is about to be rebuilt. In 1998 the Temple Mount Faithful movement reported news of a Red Heifer that had been born in the Ayalon Valley, a site near Jerusalem famous for the biblical account of David's defeat of Goliath. Again in 1999 another Red Heifer was reported born in northern Israel. Gershon Salomon inspected the heifers and stated with elation, "The Red Heifer which was born in Israel I named *Tsiona*—to Zion—the name of the Temple Mount, which is Mount Moriah. We are really living in very exciting days. It is such a privilege for this generation."[25] These two Red Heifers were dedicated by The Temple Mount Faithful to be used for the preparation of the Red Heifer ashes when they are three years old—that is, if they continue to be perfect Red Heifers. As Salomon says: "We want to be ready for this moment, and we feel and know that time is short and all the events are leading us to this moment. When G-d started to send these Red Heifers it was also a message from Him that time is short." Even so, not everyone in the Temple movement agrees with Saloman's assessment concerning the heifers. Rabbi Chaim Richman stated to me at the Temple Institute in August 1999 concerning Saloman's claim: "No Red Heifers have been born in Israel!"

However, Salomon is also involved with the Texas rancher who has reported the birth of a Red Heifer. Salomon expects to receive this Red Heifer from him to be raised exclusively by The Temple Mount Faithful movement. Concerning this Red Heifer and The Temple Mount Faithful's plans, Salomon has written:

> My friend of the Faithful Movement, Ze'ev bar Tov and I had the privilege of seeing and checking for ourselves this special Red Heifer in Texas. She really looked perfect. Although we had not planned it, our visit to the ranch coincided with the week in which the Parasha Hukkat which deals with the law of the ashes of the Red Heifer was read in the synagogues. It was again a clear [sign] for us that the birth of the Red Heifer on this ranch was not an accident—even the timing was a godly timing. It was one of the most exciting moments in my life and I felt the presence of the G-d of Israel on this ranch and in this family. I immediately knew that G-d had brought me to the United States and to that place to see His miracles and these wonderful friends and lovers of the God and people of Israel whom I had met so often in various places in the United States. He wanted to show me in which wonderful miraculous ways He is fulfilling the prophecy of Isaiah 49:22-23; 66:18-24; Zechariah 8:20-23 and other prophecies of Isaiah and other prophets. So when the rancher and Sam Peak asked what name should be given to the heifer, the name *Geula*—"redemption"—immediately came to my mind. I really felt that this special event represents one of the most exciting events of the redemption of Israel at this prophetic end-time which we are now experiencing.[26]

According to Salomon, when this Red Heifer from Texas is ready, it will be brought to Israel and handed over to the Temple Mount Faithful in a special ceremony. Salomon believes that it is no accident that after 2,000 years without a single Red Heifer that in only a few short years Red Heifers have appeared in Israel and the United States in numerous places. For him there is no question that these appearances are prophetic signs that the time of redemption is near and with it the Messianic era and the rebuilding of the Third Temple:

What I wonder is how so many people are too blind to see what G-d is doing with Israel at this exciting time and even try to stop G-d from acting together with Israel to fulfill and accomplish His prophetic end-time plans together with His people, Israel. In Israel in the secular press and in other places in the world, articles have been published which stated that the birth of a Red Heifer is a big danger like an atom bomb because it will open the door and the ability for millions of Jews to purify themselves and to walk on the Temple Mount and in this way liberate it from the Islamic occupation and rebuild the Temple. I can only wonder how they can differentiate between day and night if they see so poorly and how they cannot see the appearance of G-d and His Word before their eyes at this exciting time. None of them or any of the enemies of G-d and Israel can stop the determined decision of G-d to accomplish His prophetic end-time plans with Israel, to very soon rebuild His house and to bring Mashiach ben David in our lifetime. The process of the redemption of Israel will continue and soon be accomplished....It is a clear message from G-d to His people, Israel, that the time for the rebuilding of the Temple has come and G-d is no longer prepared to wait. More than this, He cannot wait. It is no accident that for almost 2,000 years no Red Heifers were born and now they are coming one after another, in Israel and on the ranches of friends of Israel.[27]

Whether Red Heifers have been born in Israel (or will soon be) or shipped from abroad, the possibility that one will be qualified as suitable for producing the ashes needed for the "waters of purification" grows nearer every day. When this finally occurs the Temple movement will at last have all the necessary ingredients for the recipe of rebuilding the Third Temple. In harmony with the day in the near future when a priesthood could be ritually purified to begin their work, numerous organizations have been actively preparing such a priesthood. In the next chapter we will reveal some of these little-known preparations that are moving the world closer to the prophetic reality of the Last Days Temple.

CHAPTER 17

Preparing a Priesthood

Securing the Sacred Service
for the Sanctuary

A kohen ["priest"] is a reminder of the Holy Temple in Jerusalem and what it means to us. They were employees of the sacred Temple who are temporarily laid off.[1]

—RABBI YISROEL MILLER

If it were not for Jews studying the laws of Temple sacrifices, Heaven and Earth would lose their right to exist.

—RABBI YAAKOV BAR ACHA

When the Romans stormed the Temple Mount in A.D. 70, burning the Temple and slaughtering its priests, they destroyed in one moment not only the stored records of ancestral genealogy and of the secrets of reproducing certain priestly items, but also those who had the knowledge to pass these facts on to future generations. Although some essential priestly information was preserved and passed on through later rabbinic writings, many of the details described in these texts were already obscure to the rabbis who wrote them. After the Temple's destruction, even though priests no longer performed the traditional religious duties, the heritage continued to be preserved within families of priestly descent. But with the worldwide dispersion and cultural assimilation that took place afterward, no one could actually be *certain* of having a priestly lineage. Outside of Israel it was not possible to observe the festival calendar nor the prescribed rituals of *halakha,* which depend upon the presence of a Temple and functional priesthood. Therefore, the only hope that remained for Orthodox Jews was that a future generation of Jews might somehow revive a legitimate priesthood.

Over the last few decades, as Jewish people have returned to the land of the Bible in increasing numbers, many of them have become convinced that the time has arrived for a return to a more biblical lifestyle. At the same time, many technological breakthroughs have taken place that have provided the means to do the extensive research necessary to rediscover the lost knowledge about the priestly heritage. As a result, the pieces of the puzzle have been coming back together again, making it possible for the priesthood to be restored when the Temple is rebuilt in the future.

The Purpose of the Priesthood

The purpose of the priesthood was to represent Israel before God at the Sanctuary (2 Chronicles 29:11; 35:2). Because God's presence was in the midst of the Nation at the Tabernacle and then the Temple, the priests' responsibility was to preserve the people in a state of ceremonial purity so that God's presence could remain and bless the Nation. The importance of God's presence, as well as the intricate nature of the ceremonial service, required that a separate class of people devote their constant attention to performing the required functions with careful precision. The Levite tribe was chosen to fulfill this role. They were not included in the national census (which was taken for military purposes) because they belonged to God and to the service of the Tabernacle and Temple

(Numbers 1:47-51). However, their priestly function was as necessary to Israel's security as were the Nation's soldiers, for their work of maintaining sanctity protected Israel from God's wrath being unleashed on a sinful society (Numbers 1:53).

A number of different functions comprised this performance:

1. The priests carried out the daily, festival and Sabbath offering of sacrifices on the altar in the Temple's court of the priests. Once a year on the Day of Atonement, the high priest would offer the burnt offering and take the blood of the sin offering into the inner Temple (the Holy of Holies—Leviticus 4:3-21; 16:3-25).

2. The priests blessed the people in the divine name (Deuteronomy 10:8; 21:5). One of these priestly blessings or benedictions is recorded in Numbers 6:22-26, with verse 27 stating, "They shall invoke My name on the sons of Israel, and then I will bless them."

3. The priests blew the *shofar* (ram's horn) or trumpet on certain occasions such as festivals and new moons (Numbers 10:10), the Day of Atonement in a Jubilee year (Leviticus 25:9), and on the first day of the seventh month (Leviticus 23:24; Numbers 29:1).

4. The priests, and especially a designated division known as the Kohathites, were responsible for transporting the Ark of the Covenant during times of war and previously when the Nation moved from place to place during the time of the Tabernacle (Exodus 25:14-15; Numbers 3:30-31; 4:1-15; 7:9). Once the Ark was installed permanently within the Temple, it was not moved except on one occasion—when King Manasseh placed an idol in the Temple (2 Chronicles 33:7; 35:3).

5. The priests were responsible for the daily care of the Sanctuary, which included the burning of incense on the altar of incense (Exodus 30:7-9), refilling the oil in the lamps (Exodus 27:20-21; Leviticus 24:1-4; Numbers 8:1-3), and setting out fresh shewbread on the Table of Shewbread (Exodus 25:30; Numbers 4:7).

6. The high priest received divine revelation from the Lord under certain circumstances. To accomplish this he consulted the Urim and the Thummim (Numbers 27:21), dark- and light-colored stones that were located in a pouch underneath the breastplate on the ephod (Exodus 28:30; Leviticus 8:8). These were used when a *yes* or *no* answer was needed to discern between two opposing options.[2] Lots were employed in more complex situations (Isaiah 34:17; Ezekiel 24:6; Micah 2:5) and in the Temple court for decisions of national

importance (Numbers 26:55-56; Joshua 7:13-18; 14:21; Judges 1:3; 20:9-10) and on the Day of Atonement (Leviticus 16:7-10).

7. The priests were responsible for verifying the presence or absence of impurities or diseases that brought ceremonial defilment. Very specific instructions had to be communicated to those who were infected or suspected of impurity (Deuteronomy 21:5; 24:8; Ezekiel 44:23). This included special preparation of the ashes of the Red Heifer and their use in the ceremonial purification of the priestly personnel and the sacred vessels used in the ritual service (Numbers 19:4).

8. The priests were involved in judging and instructing the Nation. Litigants were to appear before the priests in appointed cities (Deuteronomy 17:8-13; 21:5; see also Ezekiel 44:24). Priests would also resolve doubtful legal cases through ceremonial means, such as the cases of those accused of adultery (Numbers 5:11-31).

The People of the Priesthood

Some believe that originally, all the first-born Israelite males were to be set apart to God as priests (Exodus 13:2; Numbers 3:40; see also Judges 17:5). However, the more certain origin stems from the incident involving the golden calf at the foot of Mount Sinai. Because of the loyalty the Levites exhibited to Moses in this encounter, this tribe was accorded the unique privilege of priestly service (Exodus 32:26-29; Numbers 3:41,45; Deuteronomy 10:8-9). The biblical instructions concerning the priesthood are unequivocal in stating that the only legitimate source for priestly service are descendants from the tribe of Levi: "Aaron then shall present the Levites before the LORD as a wave offering from the sons of Israel, that they may qualify to perform the service of the LORD.... Thus you shall separate the Levites from among the sons of Israel, and the Levites shall be Mine" (Numbers 8:11,14; see also Exodus 28:1; Hebrews 7:11).

Apparently one family within the tribe of Levi, the family of Aaron, was designated as *kohanim* ("priests") and was to be assisted in the maintenance work of the Sanctuary by those from other families among the tribe designated as *leviim* ("Levites") (Numbers 3:6-9). The office of high priest was derived only from the Aaronic priesthood (Numbers 3:10), although with the advent of the First Temple the legitimate priestly heritage was identified thereafter with the Aaronide high priest Zadok, who had faithfully served King David (2 Samuel 8:17; 15:24; see also Ezekiel 43:19). With the loss of the Temple the priesthood immediately ceased to have a practical service, and those of priestly descent, which in the time of the Second Temple were from the sect of "the Sadducees," were forced to assume other functions.

How to Prove a Priest

Modern-day Israelis who have wanted to restore the priesthood have been confronted with one basic problem: With the loss of the genealogical records and the dissolution of the priesthood, how could the priestly order ever be reclaimed?

One answer, according to rabbinic tradition, is that even though the genealogical records of the Temple were lost and the Jews became scattered throughout Gentile lands, those of priestly descent were forbidden to change their names (which connoted their priestly heritage)—even when they assimilated into foreign cultures. Thus, we continue to this day to have *Levis* and *Cohens* (the Hebrew words for "priest") and many derivatives of these names that were slightly altered as priestly families adopted different languages and cultures. For example, variations of the name Cohen appear as Kohen, Kohn, Kone, Cone, Kahn, Cahn, Kahane, Kagan, Kogen, Cogan, Kaplan, Katz, Katzman, Kaganoff, Kaganovitch, Cohan, and Coen. In addition, names like Mazeh, Adler, Rappaport and Shapiro are acronyms for or have associated meanings with a priestly heritage.

However, not all people with these names are of priestly descent. Many Gentiles also bear some of these surnames, such as the former U.S. Secretary of Defense William Cohen.

In the past, the traditional method of passing on the knowledge of this patrilineal connection within priestly families has been by word of mouth. From generation to generation, fathers of priestly descent have told their sons about their special priestly inheritance. It is estimated that about 5% of the 7 million Jewish males alive in the world today (some 350,000) are of priestly descent.[3] Up until recent times this was the way in which Jewish males understood that they were *cohanim* ("priests").[4] Furthermore, owing to the multiple restrictions placed upon those of the priestly line (no marriage to certain persons, no attendance at funerals except family members), there was no advantage to admitting one was of such descent if, in fact, it were not so. Those who are thought to be priests are distinguished in Orthodox and some conservative Jewish circles and given the right to pronounce over the synagogue congregation the *birkat kohanim* ("priestly blessing"), also known as the ancient rite of

Duchan, which involves holding the hands with the fingers spread between the middle and ring fingers to form the Hebrew letter "shin" (the first letter in the word *Shaddai*, "Almighty," one of the names of God). They are also given the honor of being called up first to read from the Torah during a service, as well as presiding over the traditional ceremony for firstborn boys....Still, most of Judaism today has believed that the *kohanim* and *leviim* are of...doubtful lineage. Reform Judaism has abandoned any consideration of priesthood entirely, and conservative Judaism has done the same to a lesser degree. The general consensus has been that ultimately, only the Messiah can determine who is and who is not a true Aaronide. However, thanks to science, it appears that Jews won't have to wait for the Messiah's return in order to prove a priest.

The Role of Genealogy and Genes

Determining the Priestly Lineage

Recently, a scientifically controlled test to verify those of priestly lineage has been devised. The first published research on priestly identification appeared in 1996 and was based on a genetic comparison of 68 men who claimed priestly descent with 120 non-priestly Jews. This first test group included only men of priestly descent rather than just Levites (ostensively because they represent a different and more genetically diverse priesthood). However, the next year a more comprehensive study included 306 Jewish men (including 106 from Israel, Canada, and England) who claimed priestly descent.[5] This time the test included 81 self-identified Levites. The method of DNA testing used on these men had previously been employed to link criminals to their crimes, to link fathers to babies in paternity cases,[6] and even to link together various fragments of Dead Sea scroll manuscripts (based on the unique DNA code of each sheep whose hide was used to make the scroll parchment). Because the common heritage of priestly descent linked all Jewish claimants to the office, they were the perfect candidates for this type of testing. Knowing that a bit of a man's identity is transmitted strictly from father to son by the Y chromosome (which carries the gene for maleness), and that this is the only chromosome that does not cross over and recombine, it was selected in the search for any unique genetic marker that might appear.[7] After scraping a few cells from inside each volunteer's cheek, the genetic analysis was performed. The result was the discovery that as a group, those who claimed priestly descent carried a dominant type of Y chromosome that marked them on the genetic level as distinct from the rest of the Jewish population.[8] One of the researchers, David B. Goldstein of Oxford University, said, "Most had the same version of the Y chromosome or close variants that differ because of random mutations." That shows there has been "reasonable adherence to the policy of father-son inheritance." Since each person's DNA is as individual as a fingerprint, this characteristic linked these men together as a separate and identifiable group that must be traced back to an original ancestor. Unfortunately, the study could not confirm with certainty those who identified themselves as Levites. The Levites showed too much variety in their Y chromosomes. According to Goldstein, "That could mean that non-Levite Jews took up the designation in the past, or that the original Levites had a lot of variety in their Y chromosomes."

With respect to the verifiable priestly sampling, Dr. Goldstein believes that the fact that the genetic marker existed in Jews of both the Ashkenazi (European) and Sephardi (Spanish and Portuguese) groups led researchers to conclude that the shared genes predated the split of world Jewry into these separate ethnic groups more than 1,000 years ago. Furthermore, he observed that the fact that there was variation in the shared dominant Y chromosome proved that the genetic link was ancient rather than recent. He estimated that based on these variations the *kohanim* line began no later than 700 years ago but could go back as much as 10,000 years. The average came out to about 3,000 years, a period that dates to the time of the Exodus.[9]

In support of this conclusion, the original research team's leader, Dr. Karl Skorecki, head of molecular medicine at the Technion Institute of Technology in Haifa (and of priestly lineage himself), stated that "the simplest, most structured explanation is that these men have the Y chromosome of Aaron [the first high priest]."[10] Was this genetic marker placed in Aaron's gene pool by divine design so that as the time for the rebuilding of the Temple and the re-constitution of the priesthood neared, there would be no doubt as to who would be qualified to serve? Whether or not it is of divine design, individuals at Biosciences West at the University of Arizona have designed a self-test kit whereby Jewish men who so desire (and test positive) can now prove their priestly status.[11]

Cataloging the Priestly Descendants

Now that there is a scientifically verifiable method of tracing a person's legitimate ancestry back 3,200 years, it is possible to test all those who today claim priestly descent and catalog them for future service. An early attempt at this can be traced back to *Agudat Anshei Emunim* (Society of Faithful Men), who in 1979 founded an international organization known as the *Shmirat Hamikdash Society* ("Guardians of the Holy Place") with the goal of developing a computerized registry of qualified *Cohanim* and *Leviim* from around the world and assigning them a time of guard duty *(shmira)* to maintain the sanctity of the Temple Mount, which they believed would "hasten the establishment of the *Beit Hamiqdash*" (the Temple).[12]

This has also been the longtime goal of Rabbi Nachman Kahane, head of the Young Israel Synagogue (the synagogue closest to the Western Wall, located in the Muslim Quarter) and The Institute for Talmudic Commentaries. For many years before the discovery of the genetic marker, Rabbi Kahane, a priest himself, has sought to register all self-identified priests living in the Land of Israel. He has maintained a computerized database of known candidates, which now reaches into the thousands. Rabbi Kahane told me that he is keeping this list so that when the Messiah finally arrives he can go to his computer, print out the list, and say, "Here, Mr. Messiah, are your priests!" Recently, a new organization called Keter Kehuna Shevet Levi has been established by reputable Jewish leaders from around the world to begin to register all qualified priests and Levites on an international scale. This effort goes beyond the work of Rabbi Kahane in its attempt to make possible the universal ingathering of the priesthood in the event that the Third Temple becomes a reality.

With a test that can establish the identity of the priesthood and with a registration process underway whereby these individuals can be summoned for service, it would seem that the personnel for the Temple could be assembled without much difficulty. But as we learned in the previous chapter, without the ashes of the Red Heifer it is impossible for any priests to carry out their functions, for, like all Jews today, they are not yet in a proper state of ceremonial purity. However, the solution to this problem has also been worked out.

The Need for a Pure Priesthood

The problem of recovering a pure Jewish *Kohanim* is not new. In the Tosefta, Rabbi Yehuda records that when the Jews returned to Israel from the Babylonian captivity at the beginning of the Second Temple period, there was no one among them who had not been defiled by contact with the dead (corpse impurity).[13] How did they solve the dilemma of procuring a purified priest who could purify others? The Jewish sages explain that those returning from the exile constructed buildings whose foundations were raised off the ground to create a hollow space between the floor and the Land of Israel. This prevented contact with any impurity that might rise from hidden graves underneath and defile those inside. It was necessary to build an entire complex of "courtyards," as the sages called them, in this special manner. It is said that these specially constructed buildings housed selected pregnant wives of the *Kohanim* so they could give birth to pure children. This follows, in a sense, the precedent set by Hannah, who presented her young son, Samuel, to Eli, the high priest, to be raised for the priesthood (1 Samuel 1:24-28). These women were brought before they gave birth in order to provide them with the appropriate medical treatment and to take the proper precautions in case a death occurred during birth and the whole system was defiled.

The children born to these women continued to stay at the courtyard after birth, and were raised by their mothers (who were supported by the Temple treasury) until they could perform the duty of producing the ashes of the Red Heifer and sprinkling the defiled remnant. Isolation might seem a likely problem in this arrangement, but it wasn't, for these courtyards could accommodate a large number of children. The number of children raised at any one time was based on the contingency of illness or death, so that there would always be a sufficient number present. Priestly education and health services were provided, but the children were not permitted to leave the courtyards, and rigid restrictions were placed on their families.

When these young priests had reached a sufficient age, preparations were made for them to perform the purification process with the ashes of the Red Heifer. The sages say that these ceremonially undefiled children were being transported on "doors" to the Pool of Siloam (the Shiloach spring). These "doors" were actually flat boards that were laid across the broad backs of oxen. They rode on the boards in such a way as to prevent any part of their bodies from touching the oxen, which served as a partition between them and the ground, in case they passed over any place where a grave was present. At the Pool of Siloam, the young priests dismounted from the oxen and filled special stone containers (which do not absorb defilement)[14] with the pure spring water. Once the vessels were filled, the children remounted the oxen and rode to the Temple Mount, where they could dismount from the oxen without fear of defilement because the platform that held the Temple complex was built with chambers of empty space underneath, like the courtyards in which the priestly children were brought up. They took some of the ashes stored in the Temple and, after sanctifying the water for use in the sin-offering, were ready to sprinkle those who were defiled. However, if no ashes were available, it was also necessary for one of these priestly children to slaughter the Red Heifer, since this work can only be performed by an undefiled priest.[15] Otherwise, they mixed the water with the existing ashes and sprinkled the mix onto the high priest to purify him as he prepared the Red Heifer.

Producing a Purified Priesthood Today

Surprising as it may seem, plans to produce a purified priesthood in this ancient manner are moving ahead today. Rabbi Yosef Elboim (see photo section), who directs the Movement for Establishing the Temple, has sought 20 couples to dedicate their unborn male children with the goal of raising a purified priesthood. Rabbi Elbom wants to raise newborn babies of Levitical descent in isolation from contact with ritual defilement. In November of 1998 I met with Rabbi Elbom to discuss his planned work. He explained that 95 percent of the observances performed in the Temple can't be carried out because of ritual impurity. His project would resolve this deficiency by taking the wives of *Kohanim* who volunteered to live at a secluded compound in the Jerusalem hills so their children could be brought up in the same kind of specially constructed buildings described by the sages of the Second Temple period. As in ancient times, this is thought important because the ground could contain unmarked graves which could cause defilement. Corpse-impurity is a ceremonial contamination that prevents the priesthood from functioning today. Daily contact with the dead (people, animals, or insects) as well as with those people or things in contact with them (such as workers in hospitals) has put every Jew today into a state of ritual defilement. The special compound necessary to help keep the children free from such defilement has already been donated by the ultra-Orthodox Jewish Idea Yeshiva. Too, four priestly families connected with the Kach movement have volunteered their unborn children for the purification project. According to Rabbi Elbom, his project will reverse the impediment that affects the present priesthood. When the boys reach their thirteenth birthdays, they will be qualified to collect water from the Pool of Siloam, burn the Red Heifer, and distribute its ashes. Members of Elbom's group were reported in the Israeli daily, *Ha-Aretz*, as saying, "The Temple is one of the central parts of our ideology; we view its rebuilding as part of Jewish experience, and its restoration is near at hand."

Protecting the Purity of the Priesthood

Even though the priesthood cannot perform its purpose without a Temple, the expectation of a coming Temple requires each generation of those who are of Levitical descent to preserve the original restrictions laid down in the Bible in order to maintain their qualification for the priestly office. One of these restrictions is that one who is of priestly lineage is prohibited from marrying a widow, divorcee, or harlot (Leviticus 21:14). Rabbinic tradition adds the prohibition of marriage to a "convert." The application of this requirement to Jewish men today demonstrates the strength of the desire to safeguard the priesthood. In one 1994 case,[16] an Israeli couple's 1982 marriage was ruled invalid because it was discovered that the wife, Shoshana Hadad, a Tunisian immigrant who had married Masoud Cohen, of priestly descent, was found to have had a relative who illegally married a divorcee in the year 580 B.C. Even though this sin was committed by the wife's distant relative 2,574 years before, the Ministry of Religious Affairs said that Masoud Cohen could face criminal charges for misleading the rabbi who authorized their marriage. Because the transgression marked the entire family, the rabbinical court ruled that no daughter for succeeding generations, including Shoshana Hadad, could legitimately marry someone in the priestly line, such as a Cohen. Masoud's act of marriage only became "criminal" when he claimed he was qualified to serve in the future Temple. This ruling shows the serious intent of the modern-day Israeli authorities who are preparing a priesthood for the anticipated Third Temple.

Training the Priesthood

Today the training of priests for the Temple service is being conducted in Jerusalem, the city of the priests. The *yeshiva* (Hebrew, "sitting") or college founded for this purpose is known as *Yeshiva Ateret Cohanim* (Hebrew, "Crown of the Priests"). It was founded in 1978 by Rabbi Motti Dan HaCohen in the Old City of Jerusalem near the western walls of the Temple Mount. The school trains its students in the order of priestly service, and posts a sign that it is not interested in activist attempts to enter the sacred precincts. Rather, their focus is on purely educational instruction. This instruction is for those identified as priests and who will commit to an eight-year program that includes courses in the ancient rites and regulations of the priesthood known as the "Order of the Sacrifices of the Temple." It is, of course, remarkable that young men would spend so many years acquiring skills for a profession that does not yet exist! But this commitment is motivated by faith, not finances, and the young men in training earnestly believe that they will have jobs in their lifetime in the rebuilt Third Temple.

For Rabbi HaCohen, the motivation is Messianic. He contends that unless the Jewish People in Israel act proactively with respect to the coming of the Messiah and the rebuilding of the Temple, the event will continue to be postponed: "If the Jewish People are not prepared, both physically and spiritually, for the coming of the Messiah, then they are in no position to demand of God that He should send the Messiah at all."[17] Although firm in his conviction, Rabbi HaCohen was surprised when more than 350 students showed initial interest in his school. Since the school began the enrollment has stood at a steady 200 students. They spend their days studying the large volumes of talmudic and midrashic texts on the sacrifices as well as newly written textbooks authored by Temple movement researchers who have gained extensive knowledge about the duties of the ancient Temple priests.

Yeshiva Ateret Cohanim is not only dedicated to academic study; with its sister organization *Atara Leyoshna*, it is involved in aggressive acquisitions of Arab properties in the Muslim Quarter next to the Temple Mount (as well as in the Arab Silwan village that occupies the western bank of David's City). Even though such purchases have countered Israeli government policies and put Arab sellers at risk of being punished by death, they have continued because of the overwhelming desire to establish a Jewish presence at the Temple Mount in preparation for the rebuilding of the Temple (see chapter 20).

The Preparation of the Levites

During the time of the First and Second Temples, a number of the Levites played on two types of harps, singing arcane melodies that no one else was permitted to learn. This knowledge was passed from father to son, until the destruction of the Second Temple. Since that time the special knowledge of this music has been said to be "hidden." Because of the sacredness of the music of the Temple instruments, most Orthodox Jewish communities do not use any instrumental music in their synagogues. They do this as a sign of mourning over the destruction of the Temple.

However, Rabbi Yisrael Ariel, founder and director of the Temple Institute, has established a school of art and music which has restored the instruction of Levitical craftsmanship and music. The school, known as *Yeshivat D'vir*, has been designed as a high-school yeshiva "to educate youth who are faithful to the Torah, to the nation, and to the Land."[18] The school is looking for students who have artistic and musical inclinations or abilities that can be developed and pursued as a holy endeavor. The course offerings include study of the Bible (chapters on the Land, Tabernacle, offerings, commandments dependent on the Temple), the Mishnah (*Seder Zra'im, Kodshin*), the Talmud (Gemara: Tractates *Brachot, Shabbat, Pesachim, Shekalim, Yoma, Succa, Ta'anit, Megilla, Hagigah, Tamid*), and the Judaic arts (playing, singing, instruments, drawing, architecture, woodworking, jewelry), with examinations in their chosen field(s) of emphasis. When I met with Rabbi Ariel and the principal of this school, Danny Zakaria, they stated that this school for youth was but a first step toward establishing a yeshiva of higher learning in the studies of the holy writings and art. As Rabbi Ariel explains:

> The D'vir Yeshiva is a school with students for all kinds of professions that are connected with the Temple. The students learn from those talmudic books that explain the details and plans of the Temple, what priests and Levites did all day, all year, and especially on the holidays. The students also learn the skills in connection with the Temple, such as developing music and learning in-depth about the music in the times of the Temple....The students learn these subjects so that when the day will come, they will be able to produce these instruments and objects for the Temple exactly as they were in the First and Second Temple.[19]

The Performance of Priestly Service

If members of the priesthood are being trained with a view to offering sacrifices in the future, is it possible that some of the individuals could offer sacrifices today? This question has been thoroughly examined by those in the Temple movement, with some giving an affirmative answer. For example, Rabbi Shlomo Moshe Scheinman wrote in an article entitled "It Is a *Mitzva* ["commandment"] to Attempt to Offer Sacrifices at This Time" that "there is a precedent in the history of our Nation for the offering of sacrifices upon an altar on the Temple Mount at a time that the Temple is not built." This was the case when the Jews returned from the Babylonian captivity before the Second Temple was constructed: "From the first day of the seventh month they began to offer burnt offerings to the LORD, but the foundation of the temple of the LORD had not yet been laid" (Ezra 3:6). Just as sacrifices were offered after the destruction of the First Temple, so sacrifices were attempted after the destruction of the Second Temple. This is documented in the book *Torat Habayit* ("Laws of the Temple"), which records in the name of the Kaftor VaPherach that more than 1,100 years after the destruction of the Second Temple Jews tried to offer sacrifices, even though at that time the control of the Temple Mount was in the hands of the Gentiles and there was no Temple there: "My teacher, my rabbi Boruch Z.L., said to me that Rabbeinu Chananel [according to Rabbi Bar-Chaim it should be Yechiel and not Chananel] from Paris Z.L. sought to come to Jerusalem and he was in year 17 of the sixth millennium and he sought to offer sacrifices in this time" (1.6:7, page 15).[20] Likewise, in this same source are recorded the words of the author of the Chafetz Chaim and Mishna Brura: "And we sacrifice, even though there is no Temple."

Shlomo Moshe Scheinman explains why sacrifices should be performed today in the absence of the Temple: God will permit the Temple to be rebuilt only when a portion of the Jewish people return spiritually "to the table of our Father" (the sacrificial altar).[21] The enthusiasm of this portion will influence others who are uncommitted to do the same.

A Modern Passover Sacrifice

In order to fulfill the commandment to offer sacrifices, several organizations today have revived ancient sacrificial ceremonies and practices in anticipation of the rebuilding of the Temple. For several years the Temple Mount and Land of Israel Faithful movement, together with the Chai va'Kaiyam organization, have sought to perform a Passover sacrifice on the Temple Mount on an altar which they have prepared.[22] One reason for this, Gershon Salomon says, is because "Major rabbis during the time after the destruction of the Temple, especially Rabbi Tucochinsky in Jerusalem in the 1930s, stated that the first Passover sacrifice which will be made on the Temple Mount will bring about the coming of Mashiach ben David and the rebuilding of the Temple."[23] These groups each year have appealed directly to the Prime Minister and government of Israel for permission to conduct this service, claiming that the future of Israel itself is at stake:

> The G-d of Israel returned Jerusalem and the Temple Mount to us through major miracles. Now He expects us to renew this sacrifice immediately, even before the Temple is rebuilt. Our tradition teaches us that once the sacrifice is reintroduced the redemption of Israel will be accomplished, the Third Temple will be built and Mashiach ben David will come. This was and is the dream of all the generations of Israel since the destruction of the Second Temple as well as so many people all over the world. We are not allowed to disappoint the G-d of Israel and all those. We are not allowed to neglect what G-d commanded us to do especially at this time of redemption in Israel.... The day when the

Passover sacrifice is performed will be a big day in the eyes of G-d and in the life of the people and land of Israel and many people all over the world.[24]

Although permission has never been granted for the groups to enter the Temple Mount, the sacrifice has been performed each year in the City of David before the Southern gates of the Temple Mount, the main gates used by the Israelites to enter the Temple Mount during the time of the First and Second Temples. Even though *halakha* requires the Passover sacrifice to be performed on the Temple Mount, the sacrifice in the City of David can be symbolic of this because, according to the Temple Mount Faithful, "King David was the greatest king of Israel, who liberated Jerusalem, bought the Temple Mount, built an altar to God on Mount Moriah, and prepared it for the building of the First Temple by King Solomon."[25]

This was considered as a first step toward the fulfillment of the commandment and a prelude to the rebuilding of the Third Temple. However, according to Gershon Salomon, it would be possible for Jews to perform the rite on the Temple Mount even if the Temple is not rebuilt since the Pesach sacrifice had been offered long before the time of the First Temple. When I was taken by Yehuda Etzion to this place in the courtyard of a former monastery belonging to the Greek Orthodox Church in the Abu Tor quarter of Jerusalem, I stood on the ancient promontory overlooking the Temple Mount known as the Hill of Hannania, named after a high priest who lived there in biblical times. It was obvious that from this point those offering the Passover sacrifice could also look onto the place where the Holy of Holies had been in the days when the high priest would enter that sacred spot carrying the blood to the Mercy Seat of the Ark. So, in their own symbolic way, those offering this present-day sacrifice are aligning themselves with the site of future fulfillment, awaiting the day when they themselves can follow the priests to the proper place of the altar.

The group offering this Passover sacrifice usually consists of about a dozen members with about twice that number of small children. They sacrifice a male goat and roast it over a wood fire in a large outdoor metal oven, according to biblical and traditional laws. Gershon Salomon explains the details of the sacrifice and its significance for the future:

> The sacrifice was brought from one of the settlements in Samaria to symbolize the eternal link between Samaria, Judea, Gaza and Jerusalem and the Temple Mount as an undivided part of the promised land of Israel. During this special event the priest prayed the prayers and com-

mandments from the Torah which are connected to the Pesach sacrifice. A special oven which was built according to the godly Law was used to roast the sacrifice and while that was happening all the members who took part in this unique event sang songs and thanked the G-d of Israel, who gave all of us the privilege to perform the exciting Pesach sacrifice after 2000 years of destruction and exile, after so many generations of Jews dreamed and prayed to be a part of such a prophetic end-time event. During the history of the exile, many Jews have tried to come to Jerusalem and secretly perform the sacrifice on the Temple Mount which was controlled by their enemies but they could not do it, but here, in 1999, in the free State of Israel, the continuance of the Biblical Israel, a Pesach sacrifice was performed which was the biggest prophetic redemptional dream of the Jewish People. We could feel the significance of this godly, prophetic, exciting moment. It moved our hearts and the hearts of many Israelis who heard of this event through the media. One day soon, when the Pesach sacrifice will be performed in the Third Temple, G-d and history will not forget those who opened the door to an event which is one of the most significant events in the life of the people of Israel. Everyone of those who participated in the event received a part of the sacrifice and used it at their own Seder tables that every family held that evening and ate it before midnight and did not break any of the bones exactly as G-d commanded. For the first time everyone of them ate a real Pesach sacrifice, exactly as it has to be done in the Seder. In this way we renewed a deep and significant link between us and all the generations before us since the generation of Moses and the Exodus when the first Pesach sacrifice was held.[26]

Even though this Passover sacrifice was conducted by one small group, the event itself was carried by the international media around the world and via the Internet. And although the sacrifice itself was only symbolic because no Temple yet exists, its symbolism reminds us that a priesthood is alive and well and that there are some who are looking to the future when another great exodus will change the status quo and return them to the Temple.

In order to bring the performance of the priesthood to reality, several organizations are busily preparing the equipment that will be needed by the future priests. In the next chapter we will visit these sometimes public but most times private institutions and discover what they are doing to hasten the coming of the Last Days Temple.

CHAPTER 18

Provisions for the Priesthood

Furnishing the Tools
for the Temple

We are working for the Temple-in-the-making just as we did for Zionism-in-the-making. Just as they did not establish a Jewish state right after the first Zionist Congress [1896], but built an organization that led to its establishment, so with the building of the Temple.[1]

—RABBI YISRAEL ARIEL

E very job has its tools of the trade. The doctor needs his medical equipment, the lawyer his law books, the farmer his machinery for planting and harvesting, the painter his rollers and brushes, and the bricklayer his trowel. Likewise, the priests who will function in the coming Last Days Temple will need certain tools to carry out their work.

According to estimates by those who have the hope of rebuilding, the Third Temple is expected to employ some estimated 28,000 priests and 4,000 Levites, all of whom must have the proper equipment to carry out their respective tasks in the service of the Sanctuary. For every other profession in the world the necessary tools can be purchased, but not so for the priests. Where does one go to buy tools for a Temple that has not existed for 2,000 years? What store would manufacture and supply tools for a profession that today cannot even use them? While there is no shop to which prospective priests can go, the tools of their trade nevertheless now exist and are being produced in increasing quantity. They represent the provisions for the future worship that is a vital part of the preparation for the Last Days Temple. In this chapter, we will look at the organizations responsible for making these tools, the items they are making, and the practical use to which they are being put in advance of the Temple itself.

Restoring the Tools of the Temple

Shlomo Moshe Scheinman, in an article addressing the commandment to offer sacrifices even before the Temple is rebuilt, asked, "Why should we prepare all the needs of the Temple and certainly all the more so of the sacrificial service immediately even though currently the government of Israel disturbs us from our efforts to offer sacrifices?"[2] In other words, is it good sense to manufacture products that have no present purpose? It may not seem good sense, but Mr. Scheinman beieves it is good scripture. He points out the precedent, in the Bible, of King David, who although told by God that he could not build the Temple and that it would not be built in his lifetime (2 Samuel 7:5, 12-13; 1 Kings 5:3-5), prepared all the materials for building and all the furnishings of the structure. This preparation by David included his charge to his son to build the Temple (1 Chronicles 28:10,20) and came with detailed plans for its construction (1 Chronicles 28:11-19). In addition, David started a building fund and lavishly provided out of his own royal resources the precious metals and other materials needed for the production of the Temple's adornment and ritual vessels (1 Chronicles 29:2-5).[3] Moreover, he directed a fundraising program among his subjects that resulted in even greater amounts being donated (1 Chronicles 29:1, 6-8).[4]

Based on this example, Mr. Scheinman explains: "If King David...prepared all the construction needs for the building of the Temple that were in his capacity to prepare, even though he received an explicit prophecy that the Temple would not be built in his days, how much more so is it fitting that we prepare all the needs of the Temple, when there is a possibility that the Temple will be rebuilt in our days."[5] Furthermore, just as King David's example motivated the Jewish people in his time to join in the preparations, the hope is that the enthusiasm of those in the Temple movement will influence "middle of the road" Jews to desire the same things.

Preparing the Priestly Apparel

The priests who officiate in the future Temple will be required to wear garments that conform to the biblical specifications for representative purity. Unfortunately, both the exact method of weaving these sacred garments and the procedure for producing the special blue dye used for the garments had been lost to time. This made it necessary to do extensive research in the hope of recovering this ancient knowledge. Some of the research began before the Second World War, but it wasn't until the 1980s that the discoveries were able to be put to use. One of the first discoveries involved that of recovering the biblical blue dye.

The Rediscovery of Biblical Blue

God commanded that the Tabernacle be constructed with a veil that included material dyed the colors of "blue and purple and scarlet" (Exodus 26:31). The same colors were prescribed for the garments of the high priest, including a sash of "fine twisted linen, and blue and purple and scarlet, the work of the weaver" (Exodus 39:29), and a "blue cord" fastened to the mitre or crown (Exodus 39:31). God also commanded that this blue be a part of the garment of every Israelite: "The LORD also spoke to Moses, saying, 'Speak to the sons of Israel, and tell them that they shall make for themselves tassels [Hebrew, *tzitzit*] on the corners of their garments throughout their generations, and that they shall put on the tassel of each corner a cord of blue'" (Numbers 15:37-39). Since this command applies to all observant Jewish males, just as the former command applies to the priests, it was necessary for this exact blue color to be found if the commandment was to be obeyed. The problem was that the origin and manner of producing this biblical blue (Hebrew, *techelet*) had been completely lost; such a statement is recorded in the Midrash: "And now we have only white, for the *techelet* has been hidden" (*Numbers Rabbah* 17:5). This loss occurred with the Muslim conquest of Israel in A.D. 638, when the oppression forced the Jewish dye industry underground and the process became obscured. Although the exact source for the biblical blue was unknown, the sages had left a name for it: *Hilazon*. But what was it? Some guessed it was a squid, and others a type of plant. But in the end, one rabbi unlocked the secret.

This was the Hasidic Rebbe and former Chief Rabbi of Israel, Isaac Herzog. He took seriously the comment in a letter written by Rabbi Gershon Hanokh Leiner, the Radzyner Rebbe, which declared: "It is obligatory for all who are capable to search for it [the *Hilazon*] to merit Israel with this commandment, which has been forgotten for the last several centuries. And he who succeeds in this will surely be blessed by God."[6] Rabbi Herzog's extensive investigation concluded that the biblical blue came from a sea snail known scientifically as *Murex Trunculus*.[7] Traces of this rare dye showed up in archaeological discoveries and confirmed his research. One sample of the stain was on a 3,200-year-old Bronze Age pottery shard found at Tel Shikmona, and another from the first century A.D. was found on a piece of clothing discovered at Masada. Archaeological excavations at Tel Dor on the Mediterranean coast have also revealed mounds of *Murex* shells dating from the biblical period. These shells were broken in the exact spot necessary to obtain the dyestuff. In addition, chemical analysis of the stains on ceramic vats from 1,200 B.C. have matched the modern-day *Trunculus*. The actual secret of producing the dye was rediscovered by professor Otto Elsner of the Shenkar College of Fibers. When he examined the snail that Rabbi Herzog had identified, he found that the hypobranchial gland, from which the dye was produced, held a clear liquid which, when exposed to the air, turned purple. But purple was not the correct color; where had the blue come from? Then he realized that those who worked at crushing the shells to extract the dye had done their work right on the seashore because the enzyme within the gland that turns into the dye material decomposes within minutes. Perhaps it had something to do with the bright Mediterranean sunlight. It did! In a cloudy climate the dye remains purple, but under Middle Eastern conditions it turns a brilliant blue.

Because of the rarity of the snails that produced this dye, the dyeing industry came under imperial control. The Romans issued edicts that only royalty could wear garments colored with this dye. Perhaps this was for the best, for one source written in A.D. 300 tells us that one pound of blue-dyed silk sold for the modern-day equivalent of $96,000. So prestigious was this dye that the use of this color on a single thread of the fringed garment of the common man gave him a touch of royalty.

The Hope Promised by the Blue Dye

That this dye developed such special connections with nobility is interesting, for God had said that Israel was to be a kingdom of priests, a status greater than that of any king on earth. According to the Talmud (*Menahot* 44a), the shores of Israel are inundated with these snails only once every 70 years. Many thought this to be exaggeration, but in late October 1990, *Trunculus* snails in huge quantities were found all along beaches on the coast of Israel. This was hailed by some of the ultra-Orthodox as a sign of the imminent coming of the Messianic age and with it the revival of the priesthood and the building of the Temple. The same expectation was expressed long ago: "The revelation of the *Hilazon* is a sign that the redemption is shining near" (*Divrey Menakhem* 25). Today this hope is being communicated by an organization based on the research and work of Rabbi Eliyahu Tavger of Jerusalem, who applied the entire process of producing the techelet according to the traditional prescribed ritual. This organization, known as Amutat P'Til Tekhelet, with offices in both Jerusalem and New York, now produces after 1,300 years *tzitzit* with the elusive biblical blue-colored thread.

Furnishing the Priesthood

In anticipation of the possibility of rebuilding the Temple in this generation, there are now organizations dedicated to furnishing the sacrificial requirements of the priesthood. One of these, known as Yeshivat Torat HaBayit ("School of the Laws of the Temple"), was founded, according to their own issued statement, "with the encouragement of the sages of the generation to train Torah scholars in the laws of rebuilding the Temple and the Temple sacrifices—*halacha lema'ase* ("applied Jewish law")…and the design and manufacture of the priestly garments and service vessels, all of them kosher for use according to *halacha* and ready to be handed over for the Temple Service."[8] So far they have made the four priestly garments, the Menorah, incense utensils, the *mizrak* (a sacrificial vessel), the *kiyor* ("sink"), silver trumpets, and measurement vessels. The organization has sought support from the Jewish community through donations made in remembrance of the annual half-shekel tax paid to the

Temple treasury in Temple times. Since this practice ended with the destruction of the Temple in A.D. 70, Jewish custom has been to donate to another worthy cause "in commemoration of the commandment of the half-shekel" (Hebrew, *Zecher leMachatzit HaSheqel*). Because the work of this organization is closer to the original purpose of the half-shekel donation than any other modern cause, they feel they are entitled to receive it. However, convincing other Jews of this could prove a more difficult task than rebuilding the Temple itself!

The Temple Institute

Since 1986 a group of rabbinical scholars, researchers, designers, artisans, and craftsmen under the direction of Rabbi Yisrael Ariel have been involved in raising the awareness of and educating the Jewish public concerning the importance of the Temple to their heritage and hastening the building of the Third Temple. In 1988 they created, in the Jewish Quarter of the Old City of Jerusalem, what they call a "Temple-in-waiting"[9] in order to fulfill the biblical commandment of Exodus 25:8 to make God a sanctuary (Temple)." Known as The Temple Institute (Hebrew, *Machon HaMikdash*), this organization, located within view of the Temple Mount itself, has been at the forefront of the publication of Third Temple research. Rabbi Ariel and those connected with The Temple Institute believe that there is a direct correlation between the problems Israel has faced and the lack of a Temple. In fact, they contend that the problems that the world is suffering result as well from the Temple's absence. Therefore, even though the time has not yet arrived to rebuild the Temple, the efforts of The Temple Institute are viewed as hastening that day and the coming of the Messiah.

The Temple Institute's Founder

Rabbi Ariel, who founded The Temple Institute, drew his inspiration from his involvement as part of the paratroop unit that captured the Temple Mount in the Six-Day War. The men in this unit were among the first Israelis to reach the Western Wall, and Rabbi Ariel was given the unique responsibility of guarding the Dome of the Rock the day after its capture. When Moshe Dayan returned custody of the Temple Mount to the Muslims, Rabbi Ariel decided to dedicate himself to reversing this "traitorous" decision and help prepare for the rebuilding of the Temple, which, from his perspective, had only been temporarily delayed. As Rabbi Ariel recounts:

> The [Temple] Institute was founded after the Six Day War. From the moment that the Israeli soldiers took over the holy place about 30 years

ago, the need to find the exact location of the Temple, how the priests worked there, what the Levites sang and what kind of vessels were there, was revived.[10]

For this reason Rabbi Ariel moved to the Jewish Quarter, which at the time was in the process of restoration, and began studies with Rabbi Shlomo Goren, the former Ashkenazi Chief Rabbi (see chapter 19) whose teaching further fueled these ambitions. Rabbi Ariel became a biblical and Talmudic scholar and has paid special attention to the subject of the sanctity of the Land of Israel in connection to the Temple. In two published volumes (of a projected four-volume set) on this subject,[11] he argues that the original boundaries of the Land promised to Abraham (Genesis 15:18-21) and never yet fulfilled in history[12] extend west to east from a point near the present Suez Canal to the Persian Gulf, and north to south from northern Syria along the Euphrates River to a boundary line running from Eliat on the Red Sea to the border with Persia. Within these boundaries today fall the countries of Egypt, Jordan, Lebanon, Syria, and portions of Iraq and Saudi Arabia. Rabbi Ariel's understanding is that when the Temple is rebuilt and all Jews presently resident outside the Land return, these lands will be necessary for the greater population of restored Israel. Moreover, he recognizes that while in 1967 the main spiritual center of Israel had been restored to the Jewish people, its treasures, believed to be hidden beneath the Temple Mount, had not. Ariel believes that the restoration of the objects used in the Temple service will cause Jews throughout the world to revive their desire for a Temple and ultimately will lead to its rebuilding.

Activity on the Mount

Not all of Rabbi Ariel's pursuits with respect to the Temple have been scholarly. He was the chief organizer of a zealot group known as Tzfia, whose stated objective is regaining control of the Temple Mount. In March of 1983 Rabbi Ariel, with 38 of his yeshiva students and a group of Israel Defense Forces soldiers from Kiryat Arba and Jerusalem, organized a plan to tunnel beneath the Al-Aqsa Mosque for the purpose of holding Passover prayers.[13] Part of their plan may have been to create a settlement in this area of the Temple Mount in order to establish a Jewish presence at the site. The plans were never realized because the group was turned back before reaching the Temple Mount. However, in April of 1989 Rabbi Ariel and Joel Lerner, Director of the Sanhedrin Institute, were successful in gaining entrance to the Temple Mount. This time they hoped to offer a Passover sacrifice on the Temple Mount, an act that they believed would begin the process of redeeming the site for the rebuilding of the Temple. The act would have great significance, since this particular offering historically *ceased* with the destruction of the Temple in A.D. 70, although the other Passover rites and ceremonies were continued as before. Their hope was that the first *korban Pesach* offered in 2,000 years on the Temple Mount would announce the imminent rebuilding of the Temple, which requires the return of the sacrificial system, and inaugurate the Messianic era that Jewish people anticipate each year at Passover in the hopes that the prophet Elijah will appear as the messenger of the Messiah (Malachi 4:5-6; see also Matthew 17:10-11). Behind these actions is the conviction that they can influence God to respond.[14] They believe that if there is to be a restoration of the Passover in all its fullness from heaven, then it can be hastened by taking the initiative on earth. However, on this occasion in 1989 Rabbi Ariel and his group were prevented from completing the ritual. Even so, their actions, joined six months later by those of the Temple Mount Faithful's attempt to lay a cornerstone for the Third Temple (see chapter 19), have been cited as the cause for the Arab riot of the following year, which left 17 Palestinians dead.

These "setbacks" have not led Rabbi Ariel to hide behind the walls of the Temple Institute nor the Institute of Talmudic Commentaries, where he also spends time. On Tisha B'Av in 1997, in an event sponsored by The Temple Institute but unreported by the media, thousands of religious Zionists, including rabbis and students from mainstream yeshivas, silently gathered in the vaulted, tunnel-like entrance to the Temple Mount's "Cotton Gate," intending to pray on the Mount.[15] They were blocked by a tight row of police officers. Undaunted, the mostly young men and some women prayed where they stood, and asked God to "undo Israel's shame and restore the Temple: 'Just as we've seen it in ruins, let us merit seeing its rebuilding.'" The dark tunnel was filled with piercing, brassy sounds when a man concluded the service by blowing one of the silver trumpets created by The Temple Institute for use in the Third Temple.

Educating a New Generation

The Temple Institute has been credited with changing the attitude of Orthodox youth raised by a generation for whom the Temple was of little interest. Tens of thousands of religious Zionists—including students in state-sponsored religious high schools—have attended lectures and slide presentations by organizations like The Temple Institute. Today, as the result of years of educational outreach and exposure to the history of the Temple, a new generation of Orthodox Jews has arisen for whom the goal of realizing the Third Temple is a major concern. The Temple Institute was begun for this very purpose, and today is visited by more than 100,000 people each year. Over the last decade it has developed affiliate organizations, including The Institute for Temple Studies, The Exhibition of Temple Vessels or Treasures of the Temple (a Jerusalem museum and gallery), The Academy of Temple Studies (a traveling branch of the Institute), and several Jerusalem area based schools: Yeshivat Bet Habehira, Beit Hauman Ha'ivri, and Yeshivat D'vir (a school of Judaic Arts). It also has published numerous books and produced films in Hebrew and other languages about the Second Temple, the Temple ritual, and the Third Temple. These include titles such as *The Odyssey of the Temple* (1995) and a revised and updated edition entitled *The Light of the Temple* (1999), the *Temple Haggadah* (1996), which is a guide for the Passover seder, new versions of various tractates of the Mishnah which deal with the Temple service, and a series of *Machzorim* (holiday prayer books), all depicting observance in the days of the Temple through lavish illustrations and photos of the Institute. In addition, the institute publishes the newsletter *On the Altar,* which reports on the progress of their work.

Creating the Vessels of the Temple

However, the most highly profiled work of The Temple Institute, and the one for which it has gained notoriety,[16] is its authentic recreation of the 93 sacred Temple vessels necessary for resumption of the Temple services (see photo section). In addition, it has produced computerized visualizations and blueprints for building the Third Temple as well as created a scale model of the Temple (on display at the Institute's visitors' center). One of the first items created was a special computerized loom to manufacture the priestly garments that must be woven as a single piece in a complex "garment of six" pattern (in which each individual thread consists of six separate threads spun into one). Among the more than 60 items that have been, or are in the process of being created, are the eight garments of the High Priest—four of woven white flax (inner robe or ephod, belt, turban, pants) and four of various materials—a golden crown with words "Holy to the Lord," a jeweled breastplate bearing the names of the tribes of Israel, an outer robe decorated with bells, and an apron. Additional items include the silver trumpets (for assembling Israel to worship at the Temple), the blue-purple dye (*techelet*) for the *tzitzit*, ritual and sacrificial items such as the barley altar, the eleven sacrificial incense spices, urns, ewers, incense pans, forks, shovels, and carts (for burnt offerings), the gold and silver *mizraqot* (vessels used to catch and dispense the sacrificial blood on the altar), a copper laver or basin (for priestly purification), copper flasks and measuring cups (used in the libation offerings), vessels for the meal offerings, lottery boxes (for the Day of Atonement), the mortal and pestle and stone vessels (*kelal*) for grinding and holding the purifying ashes of the Red Heifer, the six-foot tall gold Menorah (lampstand),[17] the cleaning instruments, and oil pitchers for replenishing the oil for its light. In addition, the golden Altar of Incense and the Table of Shewbread were completed as of the Jewish New Year 5760 (September 1999). While a miniature replica of the Ark of the Covenant is prominently on display in the audio-visual presentation room of The Temple Institute's visitors' center, spokesmen for the institute publicly state that they will not need to reproduce the Ark as the original is believed to still exist only meters away in a secret chamber under the Temple Mount beneath the site of the Holy of Holies.[18] When access to this site is possible, and all the other ritual requirements have been met, they expect the Ark to be recovered and take its place within the restored Third Temple.[19]

On display as well in the institute's public exhibition is a growing collection of over 100 framed oil paintings by a Russian immigrant artist depicting various scenes of the Tabernacle and Temple's history and services. These paintings, as well as many of the ritual vessels listed above, can be viewed at the Temple Institute's web site (www.temple.org.il), which also publishes articles about various aspects of Temple-related research.

In recent years The Temple Institute was involved in creating a full-size working model of the Temple's outer altar, known as the Altar of Sacrifice, that stood in the inner courtyard of the Sanctuary. This reconstructed altar, about the size of a two-story building, was made along the shore of the Dead Sea on the grounds of the Dead Sea Works. It was constructed out of scrap metal by plant workers during their free time on the orders of Avi ben Nun, former CEO of the Dead Sea Works. Its purpose, as Raphaella Tabak (the Temple Institute's Educational Director) says, "is to learn the steps of the daily service [offering the *tamid*] in the Temple by walking through it."[20] It had been used to teach the functions of the Temple service to select groups of priestly students by helping them follow the course of those making the offerings through illustrated handouts. In November 1998 I met with Rabbi Ariel to discuss the altar and was able to take photographs of him and others ascending its ramp. However, that spring, The Temple Institute's Director, Menachem Mackover, reported that it had been dismantled. According to Rabbi Chaim Richman, Director of Public Affairs for the Temple Institute, the successor of Avi ben Nun had it "plowed under completely."[21]

Yeshiva Beit Habechira

The Judean settlement of Carmei Tzur currently serves as the location of Yeshiva Beit Habechira ("School of the House of the Choice"), one of the schools founded by The Temple Institute to do research on the Third Temple. The Yeshiva bases its purpose on a statement in the Talmud, which accords special merit to those who will dedicate themselves to this work: "Torah scholars that are involved with the *halachas* of the sacrificial service, the scriptural passage accounts them as if the Temple was built in their days" (*Menachot* 110). In particular, the task of the yeshiva is to raise up a generation of Torah scholars, lecturers, researchers, and experts on the Temple and its service in the hopes of hastening the hour of the building of the Temple. This work is done in accordance with the words of the sages: "Great is study that brings to action" (*Kedushin* 40b). The yeshiva is supported by private donations based on the teaching that it is an obligation to support Torah scholars that deal in-depth with the *halachas* ("laws") of the Temple and thereby bring nearer the hour of its rebuilding. The scholars of the yeshiva have already written many articles (published on the Internet) on various topics, such as how sacrifices can resume before a Temple is rebuilt.

Micah and Shoshanna Harrari

After a 2,000-year absence, the sound of the biblical harp has returned to Jerusalem. With the return of the Jewish people to Israel, and the recognition that they were on the threshold of the days of the Messiah, Micah and Shoshanna Harrari (see photo section) reintroduced the harp to their Land. It began while the Harraris were in California, building and repairing stringed instruments and studying harpmaking. Planning to immigrate to Israel, they heard that Teddy Kollek, then mayor of Jerusalem, had said, "Jerusalem needs a harpmaker." Answering this need, the Harraris decided to research the biblical harp. They discovered that the ten-stringed harp of King David was considered a symbol of Israel (Psalm 144:9), and believed that its recreation would serve as a symbol of the future of Israel as foretold by the prophets of old. A story is told that when they had first made their replica of the ten-stringed harp of David and tuned it to the ancient Hebrew mode, a rabbi came by to see it. When he saw and heard it, he exclaimed that this was a fulfillment of prophecy, for the Talmud said that this harp was a symbol of "The World to Come," and that when this harp again was sounded in Jerusalem that the Messiah would come!

The Harraris met with Messianic believers when they first moved to Israel, but soon joined with the Orthodox and now share their beliefs. With this background they are perhaps the most able at conversing with Christians among those in the Temple movement. They believe that they are part of the divine plan in ushering in the days of the Messiah and world peace, for it is also written of this harp that the *Shir Hadash*, or New Song, whose main theme is a world of no more war, will be sung upon it. They believe that it is the *Asora*, the mythical harp spoken of in Jewish literature "whose song will rise on the day when the world that is to be will be recreated in one harmonious whole."[22] They work in concert with most of the Temple movement organizations and are frequently a part of their demonstrations and activities. The ten-stringed harps manufactured by the Harraris are included among the vessels on display at The Temple Institute, and along with other models, are offered for sale at the House of Harrari, a shop located near Zion Square in the center of Jerusalem's new city.

House of Levi

The *Kohanim* ("priests") and *Leviim* ("Levites") have traditionally been regarded as the spiritual and royal guides of the Jewish people. One organization known as the House of Levi believes that the future development of the Jewish people will not be guaranteed until all of those who are members of these divisions of the priesthood are fully aware of their priestly lineage and duties. Their call is for Levites the world over to join "the royalty of Keter Kehuna Shevet Levi, whose aim is to unify the people throughout the world." They base this call on new genetic research (see chapter 17), which they believe has confirmed that they are the only authentic royal line in human history, "dating back 3,300 years when it was first established in Sinai by divine decree." The organization's particular concern is the need to stem the rising tide of cultural assimilation, which has distanced the *Kohanim* and *Leviim* from their unique heritage and significance as descendants of Levi. Because they do not know of their duties to the Nation of Israel, they and the Nation are suffering. The organization's mission statement describes their purpose and their plan for assembling and educating those who will comprise the future priesthood in the Third Temple:

> The House of Levi is an organization aiming to raise the consciousness of today's *Kohanim* and *Leviim*. We intend to make this exclusive group a cohesive and unified family of royal *Kohanim* and *Leviim*, fully aware of their traditions dating back to the days of the Temple—and beyond,

to their origins in the desert. Our purpose is to foster Jewish pride and unity among the Jewish people. We plan to issue informative booklets on historical aspects and contemporary customs of *Kohanim* and *Leviim*. We will establish chapters of *Kohanim* and *Leviim* around the world, complete with seminars, study groups and conferences.[23]

The organization's founding chairman, Abraham Yakov Hirschfeld Halevi, is joined in this mission by such notable Israeli Kohanim as the Chief Rabbi of Efrat, Rabbi Shlomo Riskin, Ron Nachman, the Mayor of Ariel, and a member of the Israeli Knesset as well as a host of other directors from the United States and Canada. Their first attempt at uniting the international community of *Kohanim* and *Leviim* has been through the official registry at the organization's website.[24] The education this organization offers is a vital part of the process to equip a priesthood, since those who serve must first understand the complex laws of the sacrificial service. If this knowledge is not precisely understood and followed, each priest and Levite risks incurring, even inadvertently, ceremonial impurity, the effect of which can disrupt their service and defile the Temple.

Yeshivat Ateret Cohanim
Training Future Priests for Religious Rites

In 1978 Rabbi Matiyahu Dan HaCohen founded the Yeshivat Ateret Cohanim ("Crown of the Priests Seminary") for the purpose of educating those of the priestly order in the religious rites and regulations. In the beginning this organization was simply a yeshiva dedicated to instructing their students in the proper method of preparing the ritual vestments, using the sacred vessels, and how to sacrifice a menagerie of kosher animals. When I visited the yeshiva in 1995 I was told the coursework involved study of the various tractates of the Mishnah given to descriptions of the priestly service, Maimonides' *Laws of the Temple*, and various works by present-day scholars researching the priestly *halachic* requirements. Students have also built models of the Temple and the Ark of the Covenant for study. When the school was first advertised by Rabbi HaCohen, 350 prospective students came to the first meeting. Since then the school has boasted a resident student body of between 50 and 75 individuals who live in buildings in the area, with as many as 200 men overall in active preparation for the priesthood.

Although Ateret Cohanim received much publicity when the Temple movement was first discovered by the media,[25] it has had a lower profile in the last decade, with people's attention diverted by the more activist organizations. One reason for this is because Ateret Cohanim's position on the Temple Mount has followed the strict rabbinic ban, discouraging their students from entering the Mount area. However, both Rabbi HaCohen and the spiritual leader of the yeshiva, Rabbi Shlomo Aviner, Chief Rabbi of Beit-El, a settlement in biblical Judea, are proponents of purchasing properties in the Muslim Quarter of the Old City which are situated adjacent to the Temple Mount. They share with leaders of the Gush Emunim a common heritage as students of Rabbi Tzvi Yehuda Kook, who was the father of the modern settlement movement.

The Ateret Cohanim has argued that control of the area next to the Temple Mount is necessary to ensure the safety of Jews who worship at the Western Wall. They also say that the proximity to the Temple Mount makes these properties sacred, and as such they should be in the possession of the Jewish people. Moreover, they believe that it is imperative to conquer and hold this area and to establish an exclusive Jewish presence so that when the Messiah arrives Israel will be in a position to immediately rebuild the Third Temple. Another reason for their desire to acquire property rights has to do with concern over the present ritual impurity of the Temple Mount. In order to eventually cleanse the site in preparation for the rebuilding of the Third Temple, priests must establish residence near the site so they can perform the necessary purification work.

Purchasing Property for the Priesthood

Ateret Cohanim was quite active in purchasing Muslim properties with the help of both Jewish and Christian contributions until the Rabin/Perez administrations froze all such activities and branded as terrorists Messianic Jewish organizations that attempted to upset the political status quo with the Arabs. This policy was relaxed somewhat by the Netanyahu government (though not officially), but Yasser Arafat and his Mufti Sheik Ikrama Sabri threatened a death sentence on any Arab (Muslim or Christian) who sold any property to a Jew. Since this sentence has been carried out in quite a number of instances, even when it was merely *rumored* that such a sale was under consideration,[26] the Ateret Cohanim was prevented from acquiring the property. Nevertheless, in recent years they have made significant purchases (with great controversy) and settled students in buildings acquired in the City of David and on the Mount of Olives. Although they keep a lower profile than many of the more activist organizations (see chapter 19), they do join with these organizations, particularly the Temple Mount Faithful, for special services and demonstrations.

Atara Leyoshna

Another organization that shares in the education and settlement work with Yeshivat Ateret Cohanim is Atara Leyoshna. Its name means "restoring the crown to its original form," which has reference to reestablishing the royal priesthood to the Temple. The connection with Ateret Cohanim goes back to 1981, when the two organizations were one and met with Rabbi Nachman Kahane of the Young Israel Synagogue (located in the Muslim Quarter near the Temple Mount). In this same year they separated into independent but ideologically aligned groups. The group maintains an educational study and tourist center that houses their Temple Model Museum in the Jewish Quarter near The Temple Institute. Visitors to the center are offered a tour of the exhibits and asked to view a video presentation of the progress made by the group's settlement activity. The museum's guides explain the organization's goals of creating a Jewish environment near the Temple Mount, the return of the property of Old Jerusalem to its rightful Jewish ownership through the process of legal purchase, and the ultimate goal of rebuilding the Third Temple. On display in the museum are model replicas of the First and Second Temples, replicas of various pieces of Temple furniture, including a full-scale Ark of the Covenant, a Menorah, a collection of incense spices, a model of Noah's Ark (which includes dinosaurs!), and other items relating to Jewish tradition. The largest model, occupying center stage, is one clearly labeled "The Third Temple" (see photo section). Its placement is such that through the window behind the model one can look out upon the Temple Mount and catch a glimpse of the Dome of the Rock, the prospective site for this new Temple. Unlike most Temple movement models, this one is not based on the Second Temple but on the dimensions of Ezekiel's Temple, and is accompanied by references to relevant Scripture passages from the book of Ezekiel.

Beged Ivri

Another Temple-related organization is a nonprofit outfit in Jerusalem by the name of Beged Ivri (literally, "Hebrew clothing" or "Israelite garments"). The organization is the brainchild of Reuven Prager, an Orthodox immigrant from Miami, Florida. Of himself Prager says, "I am a Levite, my father is a Levite, my father's father is a Levite, and I've been serving for the last 15 years as a Levite on duty. The tribe of Levi did not receive a portion of the Land of Israel, we received a duty. Our duty was to prepare the physical vessels that were necessary for the spiritual well-being of the people. And for the last 15 years we've been working

20 hours a day bringing back the physical vessels that will pave the way for the rebuilding of the Third Temple."[27]

The Clothing

Prager's shop, now in his flat in a business tower in the Harredi community of *Mea Shearim*, creates tailor-made "clothing for the Third Temple era." This clothing, made by Prager as a levitical function, is designed according to biblical and historical sources, and purports to be authentically patterned after the dress worn in biblical times. As Prager says, "It is our attempt to recreate a native Israelite's dress so that those of us who have returned to the Land can begin to dress and look like we live here. Now that we're back in the Land we should be making them magnificent as our ancestors did as a free people upright in our Land."[28]

Prager's purpose for manufacturing the clothing is not simply economical, but spiritual—to revive Temple consciousness and pave the way for the establishment of the Third Temple: "This generation is different from the past one. Look at the creation of Israel. There are signs that ancient prophecies will be fulfilled, [of] the Jews returning from the four corners of the earth to Jerusalem, and [of] the rebuilding of the Temple."[29]

Beged Ivri has been producing fringed garments (*tzit-tzit*) as an outer garment as opposed to the small four-cornered undergarment that Orthodox Jews hid underneath their Gentile apparel during the 1,900 years of their exile. These garments, which have a twist of blue on the fringes of each corner, fulfill the biblical commandment to make such fringes on an outer garment (Numbers 15:37-41). However, it was the Temple, not simply a desire to adopt a more biblical lifestyle, that motivated Prager. In a 1989 interview, *Hadassah* magazine reported of Prager, "It is the image of the rebuilding of the Third Temple which led Prager to wonder at the appearance of Jews when they came to Jerusalem to pray during the days of the First and Second Temples. Prager believes that Jews should start dressing that way again in preparation for the Third Temple."[30] It was Prager's vision of seeing people coming to pray at the Third Temple that inspired him to create his fashions in the hopes of advancing that day.

The Biblical Incense

Beged Ivri has also assisted in the research and restoration of the incense (Hebrew, *ketoret*) used in the Temple service. Various types of incense were essential to the sacrificial offerings, but the knowledge of what some of them were and exactly how they were mixed was lost in antiquity. Prager explains their importance and use as well as the way they can exist today apart from a functioning Temple and priesthood:

> In the Temple there were two altars; an outer sacrificial altar and an inner altar that was the altar of the incense. The inner altar was small and it was a golden altar. It was made of acacia wood overlaid with gold. Upon that altar they would burn an incense everyday that was a compound of eleven different ingredients. During the course of the last fourteen years we have identified and made once again available the eleven original ingredients that were compounded into the incense that was burnt daily in the Temple. We have made available as essential oils, each of the eleven individual ingredients. There is a biblical prohibition against preparing the incense in powder form the way it was done in the Temple. But by presenting it as an essential oil, as a pure sap liquid that comes directly out of the tree, it was never used in the Temple in that form, and, therefore, there is no prohibition against using them for either educational purposes or whatever.[31]

Although the powder form of the incense exists in locked cabinets at The Temple Institute and the offices of The Temple Mount Faithful, the liquid form is available not only from Beged Ivri, but also from gift shops throughout Jerusalem as well as in select kibbutzim throughout the Land.

The Biblical Marriage Customs

Other items made by Beged Ivri are connected with the restoration of the ancient biblical marriage ceremony. One is the "Jerusalem of Gold Bridal Crown," a golden crown depicting the walls of Jerusalem. According to Prager, it was the custom of the Jewish people from the time of the exodus up until the early second century A.D. that every bride in Israel on her wedding night wore this crown:

> Between the First and Second Temple period, there existed an ancient marriage ceremony which was performed primarily in Jerusalem. This beautiful and colorful event fell into disuse after the destruction of the Second Temple and the loss of the Land. With the return of the Jewish people to the Land of Israel, preparations are paving the way for the establishment of the Third Temple and with them, the revival of Temple consciousness—hence the...proposal for the reinstitution of the ancient Jewish marriage ceremony.[32]

In Song of Solomon 3:9-10 there is given a description of the ancient royal wedding litter (Hebrew, *Apiryon*) that King Solomon had made. It was comprised of the cedars of Lebanon, and had pillars of silver and drapings of gold with an "interior canopy" (Hebrew, *chupat chatanim*) of purple. Beged Ivri has recreated this royal wedding litter for the first time in over 1,928 years and it has been in service for several years. At weddings patterned after the ancient ceremony, the Israelite bride is carried through the streets of Jerusalem on the litter to the accompaniment of shofar blowers and harp players (see photo section).

The Holy Half-Shekel

Beged Ivri's latest project, which Prager finished in 1998 and which required 15 years of research and more than 71,000 man hours of work, was the restoration of the half-shekel coins used to fulfill the ancient requirement of redeeming the firstborn. According to Exodus 30:11-16, every male aged 20–50 was commanded to give a pure silver half-shekel to the Temple every year "to atone for one's soul." This traditionally was done on the holiday of Purim (a postbiblical celebration of divine protection recorded in the book of Esther). Since the age range of 20–50 years is the same for those involved in military service, the sages taught that this donation was primarily intended for Israelite soldiers as an atonement for the potential liability of taking people's lives (in battle). However, it was also understood that anyone who so desired could give this donation. And, in fact, it was the almost universal payment of this as a Temple tax that unified the Jewish Nation in Israel with those in the Diaspora for 1,425 years. This practice continued annually even after the destruction of the Temple (except for some interruptions) until the Roman Emperor Hadrian banned it in A.D. 135. The reason the emperor did this, says Prager, is "because he realized that as long as the Jews donated the half-shekel, they had a sense of sovereignty over Jerusalem."[33] Another reason the Jews continued to collect the half-shekel tax was to rebuild a new Temple. In addition, there are other situations in which there was a need to use shekels to pay either a ransom or to fulfill a commandment, such as the commandment to redeem the firstborn with five shekels or ten half-shekels. Even though coinage was not introduced to the world until the sixth century B.C. with the Persians, prior to that stone weights were put on a scale and the equivalence in silver bullion was paid against their weight. Prager's new half-shekel coins are based on originals in his possesion from A.D. 45, which reflect a Hellenistic influence. His coins, however, have been modified to conform to a Jewish standard, with one set minted for military personnel and another for Jews in and outside the Land (see photo section). He has also constructed a gilded half-shekel chest that must be transported by the *Leviim* (Levites). This chest resides in the Herrari's harp shop in Jerusalem.

Concerning these items and their relationship to the Temple, Prager says:

> For the first time in 1,928 years, we have minted in Jerusalem a pure silver holy half-shekel, which we can use to fulfill the commandment from the book of Exodus. We've prepared this magnificent set of shekels as a set for the redemption of the firstborn. Congregations all over the world donated the means to create the master dies to mint the coins. People donated hundreds of ounces of silver that we used for the minting of the coins. [In ancient times as again today] the coins were produced in Jerusalem and distributed worldwide. People would then receive the coins and then contribute them back to Jerusalem. The coins were collected in Jerusalem in a special chest from the Temple court-yard that was used to collect the half-shekels. It was called the Chest for New Shekels (Hebrew, *Aron LeShekilim Hadashim*). Three times this last year we performed the *Trumat HaLishkah* ("separation of the office") ceremony by which the coins were removed from the golden chest and actually became the property of the Third Temple. As a result of the restoration of the giving of the holy half-shekel, the Third Temple now has a budget. The restoration of the half-shekel is but the latest sign that we're getting much, much closer to a period where we can actually begin to speak about rebuilding the Temple. In the last 15 years many, many things from the ancient days have been restored: biblical harps, biblical garments, biblical weddings, gold and silver vessels of the Temple, the spices of the incense, the biblical blue fringe, the Red Heifer. And, now, perhaps the theologically most significant occurrence in the last 50 years, the giving of the holy half-shekel.[34]

Prager's excitement over the reinstitution of the *Trumat HaLishkah* ceremony stems from his belief that this has reversed two long-standing problems that have existed in Judaism with respect to the Temple. The first has to do with the apathy of the Jewish people toward the rebuilding of the Temple. The problem here, according to Prager, "is a *Galut* mentality"—that is, a way of thinking that opposes changes to the status quo (assimilated or Diaspora Judaism) rather than being willing to return to a more authentic form of Judaism. But with his re-creation of the holy half-shekel he says, "With the sound of this coin dropping, the exile officially ends!"[35] Evidence of this has been made by two public donations of the half-shekel coins collected from Jewish congregations around the world and brought by representatives to Jerusalem for deposit in his half-shekel chest. The first of these collections was presented in Zion Square in Jerusalem by members of a European congregation on March 26, 1998, and the second by Temple Beth-El in Anniston, Alabama (although collected from sources in Washington, Colorado, and Michigan as well) at the House of Harrari on September 17, 1998 (where the chest remains today).[36]

The second problem has to do with possession of Temple property without a Temple. Once this money was donated to God at the *Trumat HaLishkah* ceremony, it became *hekdesh* (property sanctified to the Holy Temple) and could be used for no other purpose. However, goods imported into Israel are subject to a 17-percent "value added tax" (VAT). The coins are God's property; can the Israeli government tax God? To resolve this dilemma, Prager had the *hekdesh* sent to the Chief Rabbinate, transported to their offices by two levitical-descended Brinks armored car guards. Prager explains his plan in this transfer to the religious authorities:

> By delaying the delivery of the coins until after the *Trumat HaLishkah* ceremony, we are forcing the hands of the Rabbanim to demand from the tax authorities to amend the law, to make *hekdesh* exempt from VAT. From the moment that the VAT laws are amended to recognize *hekdesh* as exempt from VAT, we have established the Temple in law. Who would have imagined that we would create the Temple in law, not by blowing up mosques, and not by sacrificing animals, but through the laws of VAT?[37]

Prager, however, had already experienced the elation of this moment some time earlier. Of this he says, "On February 26 [1998] I faxed a copy of the check [that paid for the master dies for minting the coins] to Jerusalem to the offices of the minter, and asked that he please meet me in his office on March 23, on Purim, because I knew I needed to begin production on that date for historical reasons. As I handed over the check and received the receipt...I knew deep in my being that I had just founded the Third Temple. The same feeling Herzl had exactly 100 years ago when he left the first Zionist conference in Basel and knew he had just founded the Jewish State, I had that day."[38] Whether or not the rabbinic authorities agree with Prager that the Temple has been legally established, Beged Ivri continues to mint the holy half-shekels, which sell for about ten dollars (U.S.), with the belief that his reviving this ancient tradition will eventually, as one writer put it, "buy admission to the Third Temple Era."[39]

Architectural Plans of the Temple

Until recent times there were no known models of the Temple. The etchings and paintings of those who depicted Jerusalem usually were either based on the architectural style of their day or were entirely romantic or imaginative representations. This is especially true of King Solomon's First Temple. A special exhibit at the Bible Lands Museum in Jerusalem entitled "Royal Cities of the Biblical World" makes this point for visitors who view both a model of Jerusalem in First Temple times as well as a superbly detailed computer visualization of the First Temple by three different designers. A disclaimer with these models emphasizes that "every model of the Solomonic Temple is theoretical, since no actual remains of the Temple have survived its destruction in 586 B.C." This was once also true for the Second Herodian Temple, but that changed after 1967 when Israelis were able to begin archaeological excavations at the foot of the Temple Mount. Today, the Holyland Hotel, the Temple Model Museum, the Ateret Cohanim, and The Temple Institute have all created models of the Temple. The model of Rabbi Zalman Koren occupies a prominent place underground within the Western Wall Tunnel, and Catriel Sugarman, a Jerusalem artist, has created the latest (and some say greatest) model to date. There is also a computer-generated 3-D Temple available on CD-ROM in Hebrew and English that offers an interactive virtual reality "fly-through" tour of the Temple in four different directions as well as the opportunity to view its furniture and vessels and computer simulations of its services.[40] Most all of these models are of the Second Temple, the only Temple for which we have access to preserved records of the architectural details. The sources of these details include the Mishnayot of *Middot, Tamid, Yoma,* parts of *Sukkah, Shekalim,* and many others along with the appropriate Gemarot, the classic commentaries: Rashi, Rambam, Bartenura, Tosafot Yom Tov, Tiferet Yisrael, the Chanukat HaBayit, the writings of Josephus, the New Testament, Roman annals, the archaeological surveys of the nineteeth century, and thousands of articles in archaeological journals and journals of biblical studies. In most cases the archaeologists, architects, engineers, or rabbis who created these models spent significant quantities of time studying these sources in preparation for their work.

The result has been a phenomenal increase in the knowledge of the architecture of the Second Temple. In many cases the written sources were ambiguous about exact locations or silent concerning certain minor features or functions. With the help of these models, key questions have now been resolved and have made it more possible for the construction of the next Temple to begin. The general consensus among those in the Temple movement is that the Second Temple must serve as the basis for the Third Temple if the Messiah does not arrive with plans for a different design. This is because in the succession of Temples built in Israel's history, each appears to have followed the basic structural outline of the former, beginning with the pattern that was given to Moses by divine revelation. The other reason is that the design preserved by the prophet Ezekiel is generally agreed to be for the eschatological age. While many are hopeful that the signs of the times indicate that the Messianic advent is near and that the Third Temple will be the Temple of Ezekiel, obedience to the command to rebuild requires the building of an interim Temple whenever possible. At this time, then, if it becomes possible to rebuild the Temple, the construction plans used will be those of the last Temple, the Second (Herodian) Temple. Do these construction plans already exist? When Rabbi Chaim Richman served as the executive director of The Temple Institute, he acknowledged (in 1995) that architectural plans for the Third Temple had then been ready for some time.[41]

Drawing Closer to the Day

The plans and the artifacts produced by these various Temple groups have made it possible to provide the basic equipment priests will need in order to function when the Temple Mount is purified and the site of the altar discovered. The big problem, of course, is acquiring the Temple site so that all of these groups can realize their goals. In the next chapter we will get an inside look at some organizations endeavoring to liberate the Temple Mount so that the Third Temple can be built. Come join me as we march in step with these movements in order to see how they plan to get possession of the site of the Last Days Temple!

The Temple Through Time

Top left—Artist's depiction of Moses at the Tabernacle at Mt. Sinai when God's presence descended to the Ark, 1446 B.C.

Top right—The future site of the Temple in the days of King David—the barren hill above the city is Mount Moriah, where Solomon built the First Temple (10th century B.C.).

Above—Artist's depiction of the First Temple, showing bronze pillars of Jachin and Boaz (in front), bronze sea (right), and brazen altar (left). Used by permission of The Temple Institute.

Left—Artist's depiction of the Second Temple, constructed by Herod the Great for the Jews in the first century A.D., from the west looking toward the Temple entrance.

The Temple Through Time

Right–This photo from the nineteenth century shows the narrow area of the Western Wall open to Jews during the Muslim period (until 1948).

Above–The Western Wall plaza being expanded for Jewish worship. At this time (July 1967) control of the Temple Mount had not yet been returned to the Muslims.

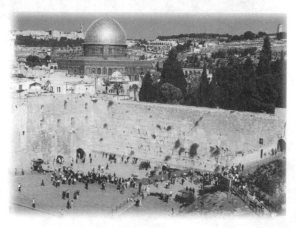

Right–The Dome of the Rock, as the site of the Temple, looms in the background as Israelis gather at the Western Wall in 1999.

Discovering
the
Temple
Today

Below– The Herodian construction and architecture of the 2,000-year-old Tomb of the Patriarchs in Hebron resembles the walls of the Herodian Temple.

Below–The author shows a group one of the large "foundation stones" of the Temple–42 feet long, 11 feet high, 14 feet deep, and weighing more than 600 metric tons–discovered within the Western Wall tunnel, some 50 feet below the present ground level.

Right–June 7, 1967: Israeli Colonel Motta Gur, at the command post on the Mount of Olives, gives the order to attack the Temple Mount.

The *Temple Mount Is in Our Hands!*

Above–Israel Defense Forces liberate the Temple Mount and enter the Temple site at the Muslim Dome of the Rock for the first time in 1,324 years.

Below–Israel Defense Forces Chaplain Rabbi Shlomo Goren blows the shofar and pronounces the first prayer at the liberated Western Wall in 2,000 years.

Above–Israeli paratroopers hoist the Israeli flag on an iron fence on a wall of the Temple Mount. Rabbi Ariel, founder of the Temple Institute, was a member of this paratrooper division.

Left—Inside the Dome of the Rock: An Arabic sign reading "Allah" hangs above the rock itself, demonstrating Islamic possession of the site. Below—A Muslim prayer niche was built in the cave beneath the rock.

Muslims
on the
Temple Mount

Left—Palestinian Mufti of Jerusalem Ikrama Sabri, chief cleric in charge of Islam's holy places on the al Haram al-Sharif (the Temple Mount).

Right—Muslims at prayer during Ramadan. They face toward Mecca—away from the Dome of the Rock.

Below—A Hamas poster advocates defending the Muslim holy places with live weapons and removing the Zionist occupiers. (Photo by Zvika Israeli)

October 8, 1990—Palestinian Arabs hurl stones and molotov cocktail bombs at Israeli police in response to news that the Temple Mount Faithful planned to bring the cornerstone of the Third Temple to the Western Wall area.

August 23, 1969—The Al-Aqsa Mosque burns with a fire set by a Christian cultist who wanted to see the Temple rebuilt.

Trouble
on the
Temple
Mount

September 26, 1996—Israeli police prepare to quell the Arab riot on the Temple Mount that erupted in response to the opening of an exit tunnel **(below)** to the Western Wall Tunnel. The Muslims claimed Israelis opened this tunnel to destroy the mosques on the Temple Mount to rebuild the Temple.

May 1997—An anti-Arab demonstration in downtown Jerusalem organized in response to multiple bus and city bombings.

Preparing
to
Rebuild:
The Temple Institute

Clockwise, from top right–1. The six-foot-high *Menorah* of pure gold used in the Holy Place of the Temple. 2. *The pure gold crown, or mitre,* worn by the high priest. The Hebrew inscripture reads "Holy to the Lord." Attached to the crown are two blue threads dyed in the ancient manner. 3. *The jeweled breastplate* worn by the high priest. The 12 stones are inscribed with the names of the 12 tribes of Israel. 4. *Firepans and shovels* used by the priests in making burnt offerings in the Temple. 5. A closeup of the *mitzraq,* the vessel used to transport the blood of the sacrificial offering. 6. *Silver trumpets* used by the Levites to call worshipers to the Temple at festival times. 7. The *copper wash-basin, or laver,* used by the priests for ritual purification prior to officiating in the Temple.

Preparing *to* Rebuild:
The Temple Institute

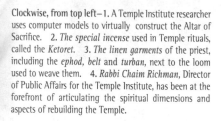

Clockwise, from top left—1. A Temple Institute researcher uses computer models to virtually construct the Altar of Sacrifice. 2. *The special incense* used in Temple rituals, called the *Ketoret*. 3. *The linen garments* of the priest, including the *ephod*, *belt* and *turban*, next to the loom used to weave them. 4. *Rabbi Chaim Richman*, Director of Public Affairs for the Temple Institute, has been at the forefront of articulating the spiritual dimensions and aspects of rebuilding the Temple.

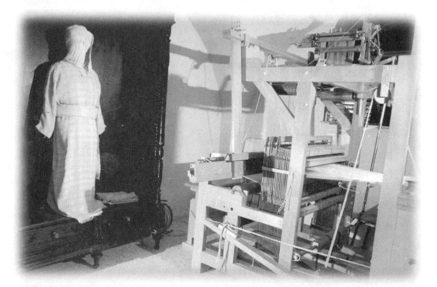

Preparing
to
Rebuild:
Other Organizations

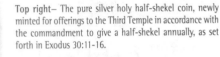

Top right– The pure silver holy half-shekel coin, newly minted for offerings to the Third Temple in accordance with the commandment to give a half-shekel annually, as set forth in Exodus 30:11-16.

Below–Shoshanna Harrari with a *kinnor,* or 10-string lyre, much like the one King David played. Her husband, Micah, a Levite and master craftsman, makes authentic biblical harps for the levitical priests who will officiate at the Third Temple. His designs are based on the information found in the Bible, Talmud, and archaeology.

Top left–Yeshiva Ateret-Cohanim, located in the Old City of Jerusalem, where priests are being trained to perform their duties in the Third Temple.

Above–The chambers of the Sanhedrin, constructed near the Temple Mount by the late Rav Shlomo Goren. The Sanhedrin are priests who handle legal matters concerning the Temple, but have not not convened since A.D. 70.

Preparing
to
Rebuild:
Other Activities

Counterclockwise, from top right—1. A Jewish-believer musician stands giving witness to the Messiah in levitical dress and playing the *nevel*, a 22-string harp.   2. Bank security guards who also have a priestly heritage transport the *hekdel*, or half-shekel offering, for the Temple in its deposit box to the offices of the Rabbinate in Jerusalem. 3. A *wedding litter*, or *aperion*, like those used during Temple times. This one was made by Reuven Prager, of Beged Ivri.   4. In a biblical wedding ceremony, levitical priests carry the bride in the *aperion*.

Preparing the Sacrifice

Top—Artist's rendition of the Red Heifer ceremony on the Mount of Olives. A bridge for the priests connects the mount with the Eastern Gate of the Temple. Used by permission of The Temple Institute.

Middle—Stone vessels made by the Temple Institute for the preparation and storage of the ashes of the Red Heifer.

Right—Mississippi rancher Clyde Lott, president of Canaan Land Restoration of Israel, Inc., with a ritually qualified Red Heifer of the kind that will be shipped to Israel.

Locating
the
Holy Site

Left—Leen Ritmeyer, chief architect for the Temple Mount excavations, places the Temple at the site of the Muslim Dome of the Rock. According to Ritmeyer's calculations, the Holy of Holies is inside the Dome of the Rock. Outlined in the photo is an indentation in the rock where he believes the Ark of the Covenant once rested.

Below—Asher Kaufman, retired Hebrew University (Jerusalem) physicist. He places the Temple north of the Dome of the Rock with the Holy of Holies located at the site of the Dome of the Tablets/Spirits (foreground), north of the Dome of the Rock.

Below—Tuvia Sagiv, a Tel-Aviv architect who places the Temple in the open area between the Al-Aqsa Mosque and the Dome of the Rock. A computer reconstruction shows the placement of the Temple in relation to the Dome of the Rock and Al-Aqsa Mosque according to the Sagiv's theory.

Faces
in the
Temple
Movement

Left–Rabbi Yisrael Ariel, founder and director of The Temple Institute, whose efforts to change the status quo on the Temple Mount began in 1967.

Above–Rabbi Yosef Elboim, director of the Movement for Establishing the Temple. He has spearheaded Jewish ascent of the Temple Mount and is seeking to raise a purified priesthood from infancy.

Left–Yehuda Etzion, head of Chai Ve Kaiyam, an organization that seeks Jewish access to the Temple Mount through activist means. He has been arrested and indicted by Israeli authorities more than 20 times.

The
Temple Mount Faithful:
Ready to Rebuild

Top—The flag of the Temple Mount and Land of Israel Faithful Movement carries a Star of David with a picture of the rebuilt Temple in its center.

Above and Right—Priest Yehuda Cohen at the water-drawing ceremony performed annually by the Temple Mount Faithful at the Pool of Siloam.

The
Temple Mount Faithful:
Ready to Rebuild

Below—Gershon Salomon, founder and director of the Temple Mount Faithful, stands with the 4½-ton cornerstone prepared for the Third Temple.

Right—The Temple Mount Faithful march to the Dung Gate entrance with the cornerstone for the Third Temple at the Feast of Tabernacles (April 1998). Gershon Salomon, seated in front of the cornerstone, addresses the group (top, middle) while a priest holds sacrificial vessel *(mitzraq)* and *lulav* (middle), and a member blows the ceremonial ram's horn, or *shofar* (bottom).

The
Future
of the
Temple

Above–An artist's conception of the Temple, made by super-imposing a picture of a model of the Second Temple on a photo of the present Temple Mount in modern Jerusalem.

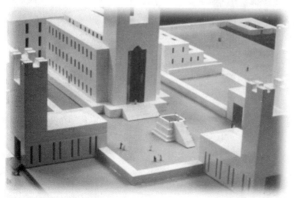

Above–An artist's conception of the Ultra-Orthodox view of the Third Temple descending out of heaven upon the waiting Temple Mount.

Left–A scale model of Ezekiel's Temple, constructed by John Schmidt of Messianic Temple Ministries.

CHAPTER 19

Liberating the Temple Mount

The Campaign to Control
the Sacred Site

The first nail in the Temple would start World War III . . . [to rebuild the Temple] you have to have the political background, you have to have the capability, but this could happen tomorrow.[1]

—RABBI NAHMAN KAHANE

The mission of the present generation is to liberate the Temple Mount and to remove—I repeat, to remove—the defiling abominations there. . . . The Jewish people will not be stopped at the gates leading to the Temple Mount. . . . We will fly our Israeli flag over the Temple Mount, which will be minus its Dome of the Rock and its mosques and will have only our Israeli flag and our Temple. This is what our generation must accomplish.[2]

—GERSHON SALOMON

I had been in the office of the Temple Mount Faithful movement for only a few minutes when a shiny red, white, and blue-colored card caught my eye. Seeing that I was interested, Gershon Salomon, the movement's director, proudly handed me one, saying, "These are our new bumper stickers! We want to get them all over Israel!" The Hebrew message on the stickers boldly declared, Yeshuchrar Har-Habayit ("Liberate the Temple Mount!"). These words are literally a battle cry (in Hebrew, the verb is used to speak of military action), and recall the momentous events on June 7, 1967, when then-Colonel Mordecai Gur led his 55th Paratroop Brigade into the Old City and up the steps of the Dome of the Rock to radio to General Uzi Narkiss the famous words, "The Temple Mount is in our hands. Repeat: The Temple Mount is in our hands!" That event is still referred to historically by Israelis as the "liberation of the Temple Mount."

The liberation of the Old City was especially significant to Jerusalemites who well remembered the date of May 25, 1948, when the Old City had fallen to the Jordanians. After weeks of desperate fighting, the defenders of the Jewish Quarter—local residents, Etzel members, and about 80 Haganah soldiers—found themselves outnumbered and outgunned by the Arab Legionnaires. They decided to surrender in order to save the more than 2,000 elderly Jews who still lived in that part of the city. For the next 18 years, Jews were forbidden to travel to the Temple Mount or even to the Western Wall. However, the depth of their loss in the Jewish Quarter was not realized until Israel's return in the Six-Day War. Only then was the rampant desecration and destruction of everything Jewish revealed. Although Israel retained access to the Jewish Quarter and the Western Wall, it relinquished religious access to the Temple Mount on the condition that the Islamic Wakf would resume custody of the site, thus ending the brief "liberation of the Temple Mount." Although the Israeli government could have changed the status of the Temple Mount at any time over the past 30-plus years, there has never been the will to do so. And with each passing year, its authority to exercise any executive decision on the Temple Mount continues to diminish.

Today the Islamic Wakf (Muslim Supreme Council) has declared its sovereignty over the site and acts independent of the Israeli government in its activities (especially construction) on the Temple Mount. To Orthodox Israelis who fought in the 1967 war to bring about the liberation of the Temple Mount, this is an intolerable situation. Gershon Salomon, head of The Temple Mount Faithful movement, has well expressed the feelings of many of his generation who fought for but failed to keep the Temple Mount: "We have lost the Temple

Mount....after we heard, 'The Temple Mount is in our hands,' the situation is that it is not in our hands. Feisal Husseini [Palestinian Authority Minister of Jerusalem Affairs] orders the Israeli Police to close off the Mount [to Jews] and it is closed. We simply allow our sovereignty to disintegrate, and this is a terrible disgrace for the Jewish people."[3] Although Salomon (and others in the Temple movement) is an Orthodox Jew, it did not help matters that Moshe Dayan's decision to return control of the Temple Mount to the Muslims was supported by the Chief Rabbinate of Israel, or that they ruled in July of 1967 (just one month after the capture of the Temple Mount) that Jews were forbidden onto the Temple Mount for fear that they would desecrate the Holy of Holies.[4] Even more distressing was the report that when Dayan returned custody of the site to the Wakf, the Wakf said it would have readily settled for only the area around the Al-Aqsa Mosque. However, once the Wakf was given control of the entire site, they immediately annexed the whole of the Temple Mount, claiming it was all part of the Al-Aqsa Mosque![5]

Since then, many activist organizations—like the Temple Mount Faithful—have been formed to counter what they believe is a government that has betrayed God and the Israeli people. The common goal of these groups is to work toward once again liberating the Temple Mount so that the Temple can be rebuilt.

The Key to Liberating the Temple Mount

Without a Prayer

The first step these activists have taken toward liberation is regaining Jewish access to the Temple Mount. It is difficult for those outside of Israel to relate to the experience of the Jew who daily goes to the Western Wall for prayer but cannot ascend a few hundred meters to pray on the Temple Mount. Imagine holding one place on earth as holy for over 3,000 years, living in that place, and even gaining political sovereignty over that place, yet still being unable to physically go to that place simply to pray. Even worse, imagine that your government, who protects the worship of 300,000 Muslims (as at the annual feast of Ramadan, see photo section), will not permit a single Jew to enter for religious purposes. This is remarkable considering that the Jews have suffered so many deprivations among the nations of the world for so many centuries, and here they are denied a privilege in their own land! Even under the British Mandate, Jews in Palestine were permitted to mumble their prayers at the Temple Mount.

Israel is the Jewish homeland, the sole refuge in the world from Jewish persecution, the only democratic country in the Middle East, and by law guarantees residents the freedom of religion and access rights to the holy places of those religions. Yet in the holy city of Jerusalem, the capital of the Jewish State, observant Jews three times a day face toward the Temple Mount for prayers with the knowledge that they cannot go there to offer them! One reason for this is that Muslim authorities do not recognize the Jewish claims on the Temple Mount: "There's no mention at all in Islam that this was the original site of the Temple," says Adnan Husseini, director of the Wakf. "If Jews were allowed up here to pray," warns Hassan Tahbub, the Palestinian Authority's minister of religion, "of course there'd be violence."[6] As a result, it has always been understood by the Muslims that a government ban existed against Jewish prayers at the site of their holy places.

However, it may be that the Israeli government never has officially forbidden Jews to pray on the Temple Mount! In August of 1967, just two months after the Six-Day War, when the Western Wall plaza was opened for thousands of anxious Jewish worshipers, the government denied a specific request by Rabbi Shlomo Goren to pray on the Temple Mount on Tisha B'Av. The government's decision mentions Rabbi Goren by name in the first two clauses, and only his followers in the third clause. Yehuda Etzion of the Chai V'Kayam organization has provided evidence that then-Jerusalem District Police Chief Aryeh Amit "blanked out the first two clauses, thus giving the impression that the decision was applicable for every request of Jews to pray on the Mount, for all time."[7] Ever since, this decision has been cited as binding, even by Israel's Supreme Court, and has served as the legal ground for preventing Jewish access to the Temple Mount for prayer. However, according to an official protocol from a meeting held a few weeks after the decision was first issued, when one minister cited it as grounds for preventing Jewish prayer, then-Minister Menachem Begin objected, saying, "I was the one who suggested the original proposal then, and the decision applied only to that specific case. We never made a decision to forbid Jewish prayer on the Temple Mount."[8]

The reason the government and the courts give for upholding this ban over the past 30 years is because allowing Jewish prayers at the Muslim holy places poses too great a security risk. However, according to Jerusalem Magistrate's Court Justice Shimon Feinberg, Jewish prayer on the Temple Mount would not constitute a significant danger to the well-being of the public.[9] Even so, the courts have argued that the problem is that the Temple Mount police are not able to guarantee the safety of the Jews praying there. However, according to Public Security Minister Avigdor Kahalani, "The police can do it, but the courts forbid Jews to pray on the Temple Mount."[10] Despite this confusion over political precedence, there has been no confusion on how the police act when Jewish activists have attempted to exercise their right to pray. Arrests have occurred when Jews under police escort have requested to visit the site but have pulled out prayer shawls en route and attempted to pray.[11] These arrests are said to be for unruly behavior in a public place, disorderly conduct, incitement to riot, and disturbing the peace, and have resulted in those charged being permanently restricted from entering the site for even nonreligious purposes.

What is the real reason behind this enforced denial of Jewish access to the Temple Mount for prayer? To understand this, we need to review the history of this problem. When the Jewish people were under the British Mandate from 1918 to 1948, they were allowed to mumble prayers on the Temple Mount. The only period in modern times when Jews were prevented from praying freely in Jerusalem was 1948–1967, when the late King Hussein of Jordan controlled the holy sites. In violation of the Israel-Jordan Armistice Agreement of 1949, which granted freedom of access to the holy sites by all religions, the Jordanians strictly prohibited Jewish access even to the Western Wall. In 1967, when Moshe Dayan returned day-to-day control over the Haram al-Sharif, it was with the condition that though Jews would be allowed to *visit* the site, they would be forbidden to *pray*. When the Palestinian Authority under Yasser Arafat (Abdul Raouf al-Codbi al-Husseni) nullified the Jordanian jurisdiction of the Temple Mount and moved the office of the Grand Mufti to the Temple Mount, the demand that religious Jews be kept off the site grew stronger than ever before. This was demonstrated after the signing of the Wye Memorandum (which had promised significant additional territory to the Palestinians), when during a visit to Nablus, Yasser Arafat declared (on November 14, 1998): "Our guns are ready, and we are ready to use them against whoever would prevent us from praying in Jerusalem."[12] Had such a declaration been made by the Israelis it would have been nothing short of an international incident. This, then, reveals the nature of the problem for Israel. Not only is there the threat of Arab retaliation, but there is also the political intimidation of a world that is largely supportive of the Arab agenda and suspicious of anything that appears as Israeli intolerance or imperialism. The Jewish passion to pray on the Temple Mount, then, has brought an added tension to the current conflict on the Temple Mount.

Fighting to Pray

On June 17, 1967 then-defense minister Moshe Dayan removed his shoes and sat on a prayer rug in the silver-domed Al-Aqsa Mosque and told Muslim officials they would retain control of the Mount. By offering exclusive Muslim rights over the Mount, Dayan hoped to prevent the Arab-Israeli conflict from degenerating into a Muslim-Jewish holy war over the region's most sensitive ground. The condition for acceptance was a government compromise allowing Jews to have access to the Mount, but not to conduct prayers or religious activities. This was confirmed when, 12 days later, the Israeli Knesset (Parliament) declared the reunification of East and West Jerusalem. Because this act officially made the Temple Mount part of modern Israel, the Israeli leadership was being careful to assure the various religious groups of their good intentions. With that in mind, government officials met with both Muslim and Christian authorities to place the administration of the city's holy places under their respective jurisdictions.

Although the majority of religious Jews were content to pray at the Western Wall, others sought to establish a Jewish presence on the Temple Mount, now that it was officially owned by Israel. However, from the outset it was clear that the Muslims expected the Jews to abide by Dayan's pledged conditions and would not accept a religious Jewish presence. Between August 1-8 of 1967, Israeli police were repeatedly petitioned by the Wakf to enforce public order at the Temple Mount due to "improper visitor conduct." A temporary ban restricting Jewish entrance to the site was issued for "security reasons," and the Israeli Ministry of Religious Affairs committee was given oversight of holy places to maintain the status quo. However, at that time it was not imagined that this ban was meant to be binding or to apply to Jews going to the Mount for the purpose of prayer. Therefore, only a week later (on August 15, 1967), Israel Defense Forces Chief Chaplain Rabbi Shlomo Goren led a group of people, including army chaplains, up to the Temple Mount to pray. The Chief Rabbinate, however, wanted to enforce the ban for religious reasons in order to prevent the desecration of the unknown site of the Holy of Holies. So on August 22, 1967 signs were posted at a ramp leading to the Mughrabi Gate, the only Jewish entrance, that forbid "everyone" from entering the site "owing to the sacredness of the place." And so the fight was on for "Redemptionist Jews," who could not expect support from either their government nor their Chief Rabbinate, to save Israel from itself.

Despite government restrictions which limited prayer to the Western Wall, the first attempt by a nationalistic Jewish group to offer prayer on the Temple Mount took place a year and a half after the Six-Day War, on December 19, 1968.

The prayers were made at Hanukkah, in keeping with the celebration of the Temple's rededication, but the police stopped the service and arrested the members of the group. This resulted in a court action on April 15, 1969 as the Temple Mount Faithful brought suit against the arresting officers and petitioned the Lower Court for legal recognition of the rights of Jews to conduct Jewish prayer services on the Temple Mount. Before a decision could be reached, another incident took place on the Temple Mount—this time, an attack on the Al-Aqsa Mosque. As a result of the months of Arab rioting that followed, the court decided not to change the ruling and continued the restriction. In protest of the court's action, on March 11, 1971 Gershon Salomon of the Temple Mount Faithful led a group of students to pray on the Temple Mount, which resulted in some minor disruptions with the Muslims. Then on August 8, 1973, Knesset member Binyamin Halevi and Rabbi Louis Rabinowitz attempted to pray on the Temple Mount—also in protest of the ban.

A reversal of the ban came on January 30, 1976 when the Lower Court (Magistrate) acquitted several Betar youths who were arrested for holding a prayer service on the Temple Mount. This resulted in a ruling that Jews were permitted to pray there. Arab residents reacted to this, however—the very next week, Arab schools and shops closed in East Jerusalem, and riots occurred in the West Bank area. The result was over 100 arrests. Matters worsened on March 4 when United Nations Secretary Kurt Waldheim pledged to introduce Islamic contentions against Israel's interference with Muslim holy places. On March 8, Gershon Salomon and Rabbi Rabinowitz attempted to test the ruling in light of the Arab reactions and led a group to the Temple Mount. They were turned back by the Israeli police. Then, three days later, Muslim councils in Ramallah, El Bireh, and Nablus protested the police action that had been taken against Arabs who had demonstrated against the Lower Court ruling. Consequently, on March 17 the Lower Court overturned its ruling, although the District Court upheld "the historical and legal right of Jews to pray on the Temple Mount if the Ministry of Religious Affairs could regulate such activity to maintain public order." Using this proviso, the Ministry thereafter persistently has denied access to Jews who want to pray on the Temple Mount, stating that it did not have the ability to guarantee their safety or control Muslim protests.

The next conflict over prayer erupted on March 25, 1979, based on rumors that ultra-right-winger Meir Kahane, the leader of the Kach movement, and a group of yeshiva students would hold a prayer service on the Temple Mount. This provoked a general strike among West Bank Arabs, and 2,000 Arab youths brandishing stones and staves rioted at Temple Mount. Then on August 3, several Jewish nationalist groups attempted to conduct a prayer service on the Temple Mount. They were not allowed to enter the site. This led the Israeli High Court to consider, a year later, an appeal to revoke the ban on prayer on the Temple Mount. This appeal was based on a law guaranteeing freedom of access to religious sites that was enacted with the formal annexation of East Jerusalem that same year. However, only four days later, the activist group *Gush Emunim* ("Bloc of the Faithful"), with over 300 supporters, attempted to forcibly enter the Temple Mount and were dispersed by the police.

Throughout the 1980s some alternative measures were taken for prayer, such as the September 17, 1983 prayer service conducted *beneath* the Temple Mount by Rabbi Shlomo Goren and Israel Defense Forces Chief of Staff Moshe Levy (this took place within the Western Wall Tunnel). Yet the desire to be on the Mount continued to drive activists. For example, on January 8, 1986 several members of the Knesset, led by Geula Cohen, attempted to hold a prayer service in the Temple area. As expected, the incident provoked an Arab riot and led to an altercation with the Arabs on the site. And the 1990s saw even more violent attempts by Jewish activists to take over the Temple Mount—all of which has kept the prayer issue deadlocked within the courts and kept the police constantly wary of individuals who might do something to stir up conflict.

In 1996, activists again sought to force the issue when Benjamin Netanyahu appeared to champion Jewish prayer on the Temple Mount. Netanyahu's one-time Justice Minister Ya'acov Ne'eman vowed legal support for the move. Although forced to resign following allegations of wrongdoing, Ne'eman was the first serving minister ever to participate in prayers on the Temple Mount, joining a private afternoon prayer group on Tisha B'Av in the Makhkema, a building at the southern entrance to the Mount that serves as the headquarters for the border police. Afterwards, activists attempted to test the government's resolve by openly ascending the Temple Mount for prayer. However, the danger of inciting the Arabs during a delicate time for the peace process—which is under the watchful eye of the United States and other allies—made it impossible for them to implement their stated intentions. As a result, the status quo continues today, with Jews wearing *kippot* (head coverings) allowed entrance for nonreligious visits only after registering their names with the Wakf guards and remaining under constant police escort. There are special Islamic officials posted throughout the area whose sole task is to ensure that any Jewish visitors are not moving their lips in prayer. The Jews regard this not only as a restriction of their religious freedom, but an infringement on their basic dignity and human freedom as well as a violation of their civil rights.

Given the state of affairs on the Temple Mount, we need to ask an important question: Why do the Jews feel so strongly about praying on the Temple Mount? What compels them even in the face of so much resistance from their own government and the Muslim authorities?

Prayer Changes Things

There is an old Christian slogan that says "prayer changes things." Those who continue to force the issue of public praying on the Temple Mount are quite aware that prayer is the battleground for changing the status quo of a Muslim presence at the site. They know that it would be intolerable, and in fact impossible, for Islamic and Israeli worship to be conducted side by side on the Temple Mount. Even if some Islamic scholars can show that the Koran does not forbid it,[13] and even though there were brief periods where such coexistence under Muslim domination occurred, today the site is under Israeli sovereignty, not Islamic, and Muslims will not allow themselves to be ruled by non-Muslims or coexist on non-Muslim terms, since this would be considered a betrayal of Islam. The Jewish activists realize that gaining access to the Temple Mount for prayer would be a huge step forward in the direction of their goals of redemption. Since prayer is worship, all that would remain once it is approved would be to erect an altar, revive the sacrificial system, and rebuild the Temple. The activists see prayer as the war that must be won if they want to make progress toward rebuilding the Temple.

History of Attempts
to Liberate the Temple Mount

After 1,330 years in non-Israeli hands, the Temple Mount came back under Israeli sovereignty as a result of military action. For this reason Jewish activism understands that the only way to take back control will be by force. Therefore, within a short time after Jewish sovereignty was relinquished, activists began plans to remove Arab occupation. Ironically, the first act of aggression against the Muslim structures on the Temple Mount did not come from Jews, but from an Australian member of a Christian cult. In the early morning hours of August 23, 1969, Dennis Rohan, believing that his actions would hasten the return of Christ, set fire to the Al-Aqsa Mosque (see photo section). The fire ravaged parts of the inner and outer structure, completely destroying a rare sixth-century A.D. wooden pulpit that had stood in the mosque. The Arab reaction, however, was not pitted against the psychologically unstable young perpetrator nor Christianity, but against the State of Israel. Wakf officials blamed the Israeli government and accused it of being behind a plot to destroy the Islamic holy places in order to make room for building the Third Temple. Four days later the Wakf closed the Temple Mount to non-Muslims for two months while thousands of angry Muslims in the Old City called for *Jihad* (holy war) against Israel. Even after the Israeli government denounced the action and swore it had no designs on the Temple Mount, the conclusions of an official Muslim inquiry continued to hold the government responsible and suspect. In light of this reaction and in fear of future repercussions, on September 9, 1970 the Israeli High Court decided not to take on the case brought forward by the Temple Mount Faithful and instead, allowed the government restriction against prayer to remain.

On August 28–30, 1981, Chief Rabbi Shlomo Goren and workers of the Ministry of Religious Affairs traced the trail of a leaking cistern and discovered one of the original entrances to the Temple Mount—an entrance known as Warren's Gate. Over the next 18 months Rabbi Goren, who was joined by Rabbi Yehuda Getz, dug a secret tunnel through this gate and underneath the Muslim Dome of the Rock in search of a hidden chamber containing the Ark of the Covenant. When news of the dig and its purpose was leaked by the media, the Arabs rioted in protest and sealed the cistern shut, preventing any further access to the tunnel. On September 2–4 some yeshiva students, under orders from Rabbi Getz, broke down the wall that sealed the tunnel. This led to a clash with the Arabs, and subsequent arrests by the police. On September 4 the Supreme Muslim Council ordered a general strike of all Arab schools and shops in East Jerusalem to protest the excavation efforts under the Temple Mount, and on September 10 the Wakf and the Israeli authorities jointly sealed the entrance.

The next attack came on April 11, 1982, when an American immigrant in the Israeli army named Alan Goodman opened fire on the Temple Mount as he said, "To liberate the spot holy to the Jews!" Although he was ruled mentally unstable by the Israeli courts and sentenced to life imprisonment, the incident set off week-long Arab riots in Jerusalem, the West Bank, Gaza, and even drew international criticism against Israel. Only two weeks later, Kach Party member Yoel Learner (later head of the Sanhedrin Institute, which seeks to return the government to a theocracy) attempted to sabotage a mosque on the Temple Mount. He too was arrested and sentenced to two-and-one-half years in prison. (However, Jewish activists are not the only ones who have been taking weapons to the Temple Mount. On December 9, 1982, Geula Cohen, a member of Israel's Knesset, raised the charge that the Muslims had caches of ammunition sequestered on the Temple Mount in preparation for the next war.

On March 10, 1983, Rabbi Yisrael Ariel and a group of more than 40 followers sought permission to pray on the Temple Mount at the Solomon's Stables area adjacent to the Al-Aqsa Mosque. However, after four youths connected with Yamit Yeshiva were caught breaking into the area, weapons and diagrams of the Temple Mount were recovered in a police search of Rabbi Ariel's base of operations, and many arrests made. Then on January 27, 1984, Temple activists were again arrested for attempting to blow up the mosques when a cache of explosives was discovered by a Temple Mount guard. Three years later, the Palestinian *Intifada* ("uprising") began, and the Temple movement developed organizationally to oppose the threat this uprising posed to the Temple Mount. In October 1989 the Temple Mount Faithful began carrying out demonstrations at the Temple Mount. And on October 8 of the following year, the Temple Mount Massacre occurred, in which 17 Palestinian Arabs were killed.

The *Intifada* precipitated the "peace process" negotiations, which raised hopes that a peace like that with Egypt could be negotiated with those Arab countries bordering Israel (Lebanon, Jordan, Syria) and with the Palestinian Arabs in the West Bank and Gaza. However, from the outset it became clear that the price of this peace would be too high, for the Arabs demanded the redivision of Jerusalem and the return of the Temple Mount. This was first stated on October 31, 1991 at the Middle East Peace Conference in Madrid, Spain, when Syrian Foreign Minister Farouk Al-Shara accused Israel of attempting to blow up the Al-Aqsa Mosque and proclaimed that there would be no free access to the religious sites on the Temple Mount unless Israel returned all of East Jerusalem to the Arabs. This same rhetoric was proclaimed in all of the speeches made by Yasser Arafat and his representatives.[14] Evidence of this Arab attitude revealed itself violently in September 1995 when the Israeli government opened an exit for the Western Wall Tunnel. The Wakf and Yasser Arafat publicly charged Israel with attempting to destroy the Islamic holy places and rioted on the Temple Mount and throughout the West Bank, leaving some 58 people dead. By 1998, the peace process negotiations drew toward a standstill. So the tension had already been building when conditions in the peace process, on May 14, 1998, an arsonist set fire to one of the heavy wooden gates surrounding the Temple Mount. Internal Security Minister Avigdor Kahalani reported that a firebomb had been hurled at the door, setting it ablaze and damaging several stones surrounding the gate.[15] In 1999, Ehud Barak was elected to replace Benjamin Netanyahu and lead Israel into the new century. And the Wakf continues to view all attempts by Jews to pray on the Temple Mount as invasions of sovereign Arab territory, vowing that bloodshed will be the final result.

Let's look now at the religious leaders and groups who have been and continue to be involved in clashes with the Muslims over ultimate control of the Temple Mount.

Groups Working to Liberate the Mount

The Chai VeKayam Movement

The *Chai VeKayam* movement is an activist organization dedicated to reversing the lack of Jewish access to the Temple Mount for prayer as part of its overall plan to liberate the Temple Mount. Their vision is in keeping with the process of the redemption of the Land, begun in 1887 with the Zionist movement and actualized with the founding of the State of Israel in 1948. This group sees itself as the catalyst for a Jewish renaissance: a return to the Torah of Israel as the guide for the people, the kingdom, and the lifestyle in the Land of Israel. The organization publishes a magazine called *Labrit,* which deals with ideological discussions related to the Third Temple's culture and form of government. The organization has issued a public declaration expressing their intention to establish an alternative leadership and bring about a revolution that will lead towards the re-establishment of the kingdom of Israel and the building of the Last Days Temple:

> ...Now that the present leadership has agreed to recognize the liberation organization of the enemy which comes "to liberate" this country from us and in practice establishes its state, something has happened in Israel: With a handshake, with a light movement of a pen, the leadership, in whose hands the Zionist command and vision lies, brought us to the end of Zionism.... In opposition to this tendency of betrayal and rejection, we are raising the flag of the Hebrew revolution: a value-conceptual moral revolution which is intended to define and reform the aims of the return to Zion and the establishment of the State in the spirit of the Torah of Israel and the morality of the patriarchs and the prophets, while fitting the commandment and the dream to the understanding of our immediate obligation.... We are making this proclamation in order to publicize to the general public and to the political

leadership of the people that we are now standing up and taking responsibility for the cultural, political, new event: the culture of the Third Temple...to take responsibility to form a new leadership, to form ranks as soldiers of the kingdom of the house of David, that fell and that shall arise again....When it is completed, the future political event in the leadership and government and the new institutions shall express the kingdom of the house of David and all its ancillary functions, the Supreme Court in the hewn stone chamber in the Temple Mount and the presence of the Almighty shall exist over the whole people and its inheritance from the heart to the body, from the center—the Temple, which shall be rebuilt as in former days in its place—to the State and the entire Land which the Lord gave us, to be preserved....we shall decide from now on which laws and regulations [of the present Israeli government] we shall no longer observe. The Torah of Israel shall be our guiding light, while constantly attempting to understand which things we are obligated to do....We are coming to build a future leadership, to change the government in the State and the overall system, fundamentally, from inside and to remove them by means of developments and revolutions....[16]

The founder and director of *Chai VeKayam* is Yehuda Etzion (see photo section), who was one of the organizers of the Macteret Yehudit, an underground "liberation" organization. The Macteret began in 1978 largely in reaction to Israel's giving away of the Sinai Peninsula to Egypt in the Camp David Accords—an act Etzion and others viewed as a threat to the process of redemption. Etzion viewed this act as a divine punishment for Israel's having permitted the Muslim presence or "abomination" to continue on the Temple Mount. He helped form the Macteret with the express purpose of destroying the Muslim structures of the Dome of the Rock and the Al-Aqsa Mosque while preserving the integrity of the Temple Mount for the rebuilding of the Temple. A motivating factor for Etzion was his relationship with the late Shabatai Ben-Dov, a leading promoter of "active redemption."[17] On his deathbed, Shabatai Ben-Dov is said to have charged Etzion (a distant relative) with the mission, saying, "If you want to act in a way that would solve all the problems of the people of Israel do this thing! [destroy the Dome of the Rock]."[18]

In 1984, after four years of planning (1978–1982), Etzion, in association with members of the settlement movement known as *Gush Emunim* ("Bloc of the Faithful"), set out to liberate the Temple Mount by forming a group of eight demolition experts and acquiring sufficient explosives to carry out the task. The explosives were taken from a cache belonging to the Israeli Defense Forces. However, the plot was never carried out because the group could not persuade a rabbi to give them *halakhic* sanction. Etzion was later imprisoned for seven years for his role in the attempt. While in prison, he stated to reporters, "No...ownership claim, that is not made in the name of Israel and for the rebuilding of the Temple, is valid. The expurgation of the Temple Mount will prepare the hearts [of the Jewish people] for the understanding and further advancing of our full redemption. The purified Mount be—if G-d wishes—the hammer and anvil for the future process of promoting the next holy elevation."[19] Because he made such statements during his prison term, he has still been regarded as "a member of the Jewish terror underground"[20] even though he claims to no longer have ties with his former associates since his release from prison. Moreover, because of his attempt to destroy the Muslim religious structures on the Temple Mount, he was banned by the Israeli government from ever entering the Old City, in which the Temple Mount is located.

On a windy day in November of 1998 I met with Etzion on the northern slope of the Mount of Olives, which overlooks the Temple Mount. As we talked about his concerns for the Temple Mount, he related to me his involvement in the effort to destroy the mosques (these are documented in the video *The Coming Last Days Temple*). He still believes that one day these structures will be done away with. Here he explains his understanding of prophecies related to the Temple Mount and why he feels it is imperative to continue the efforts to liberate the site:

> Without the Temple Mount we [the Jewish people] don't have any center, we don't have any core. We have only separate individuals spread throughout the world. But we are speaking as the prophets said to us that in the future all the Jews will come together to pray and three times a year they have to come to this place [Temple Mount]. And in this place, the Temple Mount, we all believe that if we shall build, and when we shall build, our center in all its glory, it will be like a man and a woman who we meet after many years apart. This means the God of Israel and the nation of Israel will be here together like a couple. Then all the other nations will come and share with us in this experience. This meeting will not only be for the future of Israel, but for the future of all the world and all mankind.[21]

Later he took me to a site where he and other groups, such as the Temple Mount Faithful, have regularly offered sacrifices in token of the time when they will again be offered on the Temple Mount. From my limited observation, Etzion seems genuinely motivated by his cause and has obviously paid a price for his convictions (whether justifiable or not). At our meeting his appearance was disheveled, his clothing ragged, and his vehicle old and in need of repairs. His activities in recent years have been focused on forcing the Israeli government to concede that Jews have rights on the Temple Mount, and to this end he has taken his case before the Israeli Supreme Court and won their support for Jewish prayers at the site. Yet despite such achievements, no practical gains have been experienced because of the threat of Arab riots by the Mufti and the Wakf, and because of the unchanged attitude secular Israeli leaders have toward achieving peace with their enemies.

HaTenu'ah LeChinun HaMikdash

This organization, whose name means "Returning the Jewish People to the Holy Temple," organizes mass group demonstrations to arouse consciousness among the people, the leaders, the Chief Rabbis, and the Government of Israel to rebuild the Temple and return the priests to their places of service.[22] One of the group's purposes is to conduct national and regional conferences, such as the recent Temple Conference, and organizes ascents to the Temple Mount— ascents open to individuals, groups, and the public at large. They also put out a publication called *Yibane HaMikdash* ("Build the Temple") and *Mikdash-Build*, the abridged English Internet version. This publication serves as a forum of Jewish law and thought on subjects relating to the Temple Mount, the Temple, and renewing the Temple service. The group also sponsors rabbis and others who have taken upon themselves the task of teaching about the Temple Mount, its boundaries, its sanctity, and the laws related to entering it in holiness and purity. In its early years the organization was known as The Society for the Preparation of the Temple and stated that its goal was the establishment of a religious Jewish presence on the Temple Mount as "a preparatory step to the erection of the Third Temple."[23]

This goal has continued to be a guiding purpose, and is put into effect by organizing groups of Jews to daily ascend the Temple Mount, thus creating a continual Jewish presence. This has not been the problem it has been in the past when the rabbinical ban was almost universally supported. Today, however, some of the most respected rabbinic authorities, including former chief rabbis Mordechai Eliyahu and Avraham Shapira, have allowed followers to go up to the Mount, provided they do so without provocation or demonstrations and they avoid the Dome of the Rock (the place acknowledged as the former site of the Temple). While the current Ashkenazi chief rabbi Yisrael Meir Lau has not officially endorsed these ascents of the Mount, he will not condemn them, but only cautions against entering forbidden areas. Among those *HaTenu'ah LeChinun HaMikdash* who have assisted with this action are rabbis, heads of religious academies (Hebrew, *roshei yeshivot*) and their students, and classes from half a dozen *hesder* (military schools). The procedure for making the ascent requires a strict adherence to *halakha*: after immersion in a *mikva* (a ritual immersion pool) to purify themselves from physical impurity, and after learning the rules of the permissible areas in which to walk, and other *halakhot* ("laws") about the Temple Mount, Jews go up every day (when the area is open to Jews: 8:00–11:30 A.M. and 1:30–3:00 P.M. except on Friday, the Muslim holy day) via the Mughrabi Gate. In the time of the Temple the priests used to walk on the Temple Mount and especially in the Temple itself without shoes. In similar fashion, no leather shoes (because the act of tanning involves death) may be worn today by Jews walking in the permitted areas. Moreover, they are to enter with an attitude of prayer and dirge in their hearts. In this way they express their attachment to the Temple Mount, and demonstrate that the Temple Mount belongs to the Jewish people.

The point of these ascents of the Temple Mount is to prove that Jews can enter the area for religious purposes (since the very act of ascent is an act of worship), and to announce that such acts will eventually lead to a reclamation of the site and the rebuilding of the Temple. This purpose is well understood by the Palestinians who have taken charge of the area. As one of their representatives stated when Benjamin Netanyahu was Prime Minister and once pledged to restore Jewish prayer on the Temple Mount despite Muslim opposition:[24] "If he insists on praying here, he is just getting on the nerves of the Arabs and the Muslim world. And at that point there is no such thing as peace. The peace process that has been formed will be destroyed in a second."[25] Such threats, however, have no effect on Temple Mount movement organizations that actually welcome an end to the peace process. One such organization, whose demonstrations seek to provoke an end to the Muslim domination and bring about renewed liberation of the Temple Mount for Jews, is the Temple Mount Faithful.

The Temple Mount Faithful Movement

The most visible activist organization today is the Temple Mount and Land of Israel Faithful movement, or simply The Temple Mount Faithful (Hebrew, *Ne-*

Emanei Har Habayit). The central goal of this organization is "to liberate again the Temple Mount from Arab occupation, and then to rebuild again the Third Temple in its right place, on the Rock in the center of the Temple Mount, a Temple that will be again a center of religious, national, spiritual and moral life for Israel."[26] More than any other activist organization, The Temple Mount Faithful has developed an outreach among not only Israelis and Jews outside the Land, but also a supportive network among Christians, some of whom are involved with the organization's outreach through newsletters, a web site, and lecture tours. In fact, the Temple Mount Faithful has recently been joined by a group of women (predominately Christian) in the United States (headquartered in Texas) which calls itself "The Battalion of Deborah." This name was chosen because of the biblical Deborah, one of the Israelite judges in the book of Judges who was also a prophetess and general of the Israelite army. She saved the Israelites at a very dangerous time when the enemy tried to destroy them. In like manner, "these women decided to be like Deborah and to give themselves for the rebuilding of the Temple in Jerusalem, the re-liberation of the Temple Mount, for Jerusalem as the capital of Israel and for the people and Land of Israel at a critical time of the redemption of the people and Land of Israel."[27]

The founder and leader of the Temple Mount Faithful is Gershon Salomon, a charismatic figure who by profession is an Orientalist and lecturer in Middle Eastern studies, specializing in the history of the national movement of the Kurdish people. Salomon is a tenth-generation Jerusalemite. Two hundred years ago, the first of his forefathers came to Israel as a pioneer to redeem the land and the people of Israel and Jerusalem. One of his descendants was Rabbi Avraham Solomon Zalman Zoref, who settled in Jerusalem in 1811. Rabbi Zoref was one of the first Jewish pioneers in Jerusalem to start the redemptive process of the people and the Land in preparation for the coming of the Messiah on the Temple Mount. He was stabbed to death by Arabs in the Old City who were trying to prevent Jewish expansion. Solomon, who is still an officer in the Israel Defense Force, has witnessed or fought in most of Israel's wars. He was involved as a youth in the War of Independence and arrested at age 11 by the British Mandatory police. Later when he joined the Israel Defense Forces, he led a company in the Golan Heights. In 1958, during a battle with the Syrian army, he was injured when he was run over by a tank. Salomon says he was miraculously rescued from death by angelic intervention; he relates that when he was approached by Syrian soldiers, who are trained to shoot to kill wounded Israeli soldiers, they all suddenly ran away. Later, he says, these Syrians soldiers reported to United

Nations officials that they had fled because they had seen thousands of angels around Salomon. It was at this time that Salomon says he also heard the voice of God speaking to him and telling him that He was not yet finished with him. Salomon understood this as a divine call to consecrate himself to the work of the Temple Mount.

Salomon feels that his calling was confirmed when, during his service in the Six-Day War, he was among the soldiers who participated in the liberation of the Temple Mount. He believes that at that moment the circle was closed between his generation and the generation that was alive during the destruction of the Temple in A.D. 70. But the Temple Mount, as we know, was returned to Muslim control, and Salomon says his calling is to reverse this action (through the Temple Mount Faithful). According to his published statement of purpose, "he has dedicated himself to the vision of consecrating the Temple Mount to the Name of G-d, to removing the Muslim shrines placed there as a symbol of Muslim conquest, to the soon rebuilding of the Third Temple there, and the G-dly redemption of the people and the Land of Israel."[28]

Gershon Salomon and many other members of the Temple Mount Faithful movement are students of Rabbi Zvi Yehuda Kook, the son of Rabbi Avraham Kook, the first chief rabbi of Israel in the early part of the twentieth century. He was the spiritual father of the religious Zionist redemption movement of Israel. Following in his footsteps, Rabbi Zvi Yehuda Kook founded and defined the ideology of the *Gush Emunim* movement. This religious Zionist movement helped resettle the Land of Israel, but also was dedicated to bringing about the end-time redemption of the prophets. Salomon credits him as his inspiration for rebuilding the Temple and for liberating the Temple Mount, Jerusalem, and the Land of Israel. In keeping with this philosophy of religious Zionism, Salomon interprets current events in Israel and the nations in the light of what he understands as prophetic fulfillment in process. This can be seen by his exposition of three "signs of the times:"

> We are now living in the most exciting time in the history of the Chosen People of G-d....All His prophetic promises to Israel are becoming a reality. According to the Word of G-d, three major events will occur in the end-times prior to the coming of Mashiach ben David. The first is the re-establishment of the State of Israel in the land of Israel. The second is the regathering of the Jewish people to the Promised Land from all over the world. The third is the rebuilding of the Temple on the Temple Mount in Jerusalem on the same place as the First and Second

Temples. The first condition has been fulfilled although not completely to the boundaries which G-d promised to Abraham. In the Six-Day War, G-d brought Israel to the Jordan River. The rest is soon going to be fulfilled. This is the Land which He chose for Himself and for His people....The second condition is in the process of being fulfilled.... Everyday more Jews return home. Even lost tribes of Jews from the far corners of the world are being regathered by G-d. Parts of the ten lost tribes have also started to return. Groups like the Ethiopian Jews from the tribe of Dan and Jews from Asia who belonged to the tribe of Manasseh and others have returned. The third condition is soon to be fulfilled. As a result of the miraculous events of the Six-Day War of 1967, G-d brought Israel back to the Temple Mount, the whole of Jerusalem and the biblical areas of Judea, Samaria, Gaza, the Golan Heights and the Sinai peninsula. This was not an accidental event. G-d brought us back to the Temple Mount to build His House and to open another end-time era in the life of Israel. The terrible, sinful mistake of the then-Defense Minister, Moshe Dayan, did not cancel G-d's plans [but they] were merely delayed to [that] generation....[Now] a new generation has emerged...[and] the time is ripe for the Temple to be rebuilt. This is the climax of all the events before the coming of Mashiach ben David. G-d wants to again dwell in the midst of His beloved people, Israel.[29]

As Salomon's statement reveals, although the present secular government has prevented the immediate rebuilding of the Temple since 1967, he believes that the present generation will be the one to finally realize the prophetic dreams of his forefathers.

Laying the Third Temple Cornerstone

In the previous chapter, we learned about the vessels being prepared by the Temple Institute—vessels that have been made with a rebuilt Temple in mind. The Temple Mount Faithful have also made preparations for the coming Temple in the form of a cornerstone. The Temple Mount Faithful brought this cornerstone to Jerusalem from Mitzpe Ramon in the Negev (a desert area to the south of Israel). It is one of the few places in the Land of Israel where the character and color of the stone are similar to that from which the First and Second Temples were made. There was also a symbolic reason for bringing the stone from this area: The Torah was given to the people of Israel in the desert at Mount Sinai, which today is in Egypt, but geographically is not far from Mitzpe Ramon. Because the divine instructions for building the First Temple forbade the use of iron implements for shaping its stones, a flint rock that in Hebrew is called *even tzor* (also referred to by the special name of *Shamir*) was used to cut the soft limestone. However, no tools were used on the Temple Mount Faithful's cornerstone, for it was already adequate in its natural state. As Salomon puts it: "We brought it as is, as we found it. It was also a miracle. It was like it was ready and waiting for us!"[30]

The stone is not typical limestone but a harder marble and weighs almost four tons. When carried each year at Succot to the Siloam Pool, and then around the walls of the Old City, it is transported on a flatbed truck. In this way the stone is thought to bring a testimony to the rebuilding of the Temple and the coming of Messiah Ben-David (the ruling or King Messiah). According to Salomon, "This is a godly stone and it will begin the accomplishment of the end times in which we are living right now."[31]

Despite the "sanctity" of this stone, it lies today in one of the busiest traffic circles in the city, being soiled daily by exhaust fumes and littered by people walking the crosswalk next to it. It remains in this spot due to the police, who refuse to allow the stone to be brought inside the walls of the Old City for fear of another disaster like the "Temple Mount Massacre" that took place on October 8, 1990. The stone is located in a central square not far from the Temple Mount, so it's not far from its future resting place. From Salomon's perspective, this central square is a very historical place close to the third wall of Jerusalem and the memorial stone honoring the Israeli soldiers who died in the battle for the liberation of the Temple Mount. He also thinks it providential that the American consulate can be seen from the front of the stone, and suggests, "Maybe this is also a message for the American people, but mainly for the American administration, for the president to support the godly event [the process of redemption] that is taking place in the Land...to rebuild the Third Temple for Israel and for all the nations." Even so, the stone is even closer to the Christian sites of the Dominican Catholic École Biblique and the Protestant Garden Tomb.

Salomon, undaunted in his dream for the stone's future, declares:

> The cornerstone is lying here temporarily.... We shall continue to bring it to the Temple Mount ....In the right day—I believe it is very soon— this stone will be put on the Temple Mount, and will be worked and polished...and will be the first stone for the Third Temple.... It will be laid on the Temple Mount not far from the rock of Abraham and Isaac in the same line and location where the First and Second Temples were located.... Just now this stone lies not far from the Temple Mount, very

close to the Walls of the Old City of Jerusalem, near Shechem [Damascus] Gate….and this stone watches over the Temple Mount. But the day is not far that this stone will be in the right place—it can be today…or tomorrow, we are very close to the right time.[32]

Until the right time comes, the cornerstone will play its part in the demonstrations carried out by the Temple Mount Faithful in and around the Temple Mount.

The Demonstrations of the Temple Mount Faithful

The Controversy Surrounding the Demonstrations

My first encounter with Gershon Salomon and the Temple Mount Faithful was at their first demonstration during the Feast of Tabernacles on October 16, 1989. I was present with the group when Gershom Salomon and Yehoshua Cohen, dressed in the priestly garments, led the group's members and supporters in an attempt to lay the cornerstone for the Third Temple at the entrance to the Temple Mount. A protest at an Arab school earlier in the day led police to rescind previously received permission to conduct the ceremony at the site, and the stone had to be left at a location near, but outside, the Old City. The next year (1990) the Temple Mount Faithful announced they would repeat the previous year's ceremony and attempt to lay the cornerstone. Although police had assured the Muslim authorities that the group would be prevented from entering the Dung Gate, which leads to the Western Wall plaza, rumors among the Arabs stated that the group was coming to pray on the Temple Mount, thus provoking a major riot. On the morning of October 8, during the opening of the Feast of Tabernacles celebrations, when more than 20,000 Jews were assembled for Kol Ha-Moed services at the Western Wall, more than 3,000 Palestinian Arabs on the Temple Mount above began to pelt the crowd with stones (see photo section). Official inquiry later found that this event had been orchestrated by Faisal Husseini, who is now the Jerusalem Administrator for the Palestinian Authority. He used the Temple Mount Faithful's march as an opportunity to attack the Western Wall worshipers and provoke a conflict.[33] As loudspeakers on the Temple Mount sounded a call for Muslims to come and kill the Jews who were "trying to take their holy places," the Israeli police first fired tear gas to dispel the rioters, then rubber bullets, and finally, live ammunition. When the fighting was over, some 17 Arabs were dead.[34] The United Nations, including the United States, voted to condemn Israel for the incident. However, Israeli investigators uncovered the fact that the Palestinian provocation had been part of a plot masterminded by Iraqi dictator Saddam Hussein. In August of that year, in an attempt to unite the Arab league against the United States and their allies opposed to his invasion of Kuwait, Hussin called for the Arabs to start an incident on the Temple Mount in the hopes of inciting a pan-Arab *Jihad* against Israel. This was intended by Saddam Hussein as the beginning of a Middle-East war that he would lead on behalf of all Arabs.[35] But for the restraint Israel showed—brought in part by the intense pressure and assurances of the United States—the Jewish Nation would have retaliated when Hussein bombed them with scud missiles. Had that happened, the entire region, if not the world, could have plunged into what the secular media fearfully predicted as "Armageddon." Such is the potential of the Arab reaction to Jewish activism at the Temple Mount.

The Prophetic Significance of the Demonstrations

The Temple Mount Faithful continue to hold annual demonstrations during the key Temple-related festivals on the Jewish calendar. Although the Temple does not exist today, it continues to overshadow aspects of the various commemorative feasts which also have Messianic or eschatological significance.[36] The group's effort to lay the cornerstone each year is scheduled during Succot, one of the major feasts of the High Holy Days or Days of Awe (Hebrew, *Yamim Nora'im*), which occurs in Tishri, the seventh month of the Jewish calendar (September/October). Gershon Salomon explains the significance of this date for their action:

> We brought the cornerstone to the City of David very close to the gates of the Temple Mount, to the same place where King David brought the Ark of Covenant and anointed it to be in the first Temple. In the same place where King Solomon decided to start the process of the building of the Temple we brought the cornerstone. A priest…was on this place and anointed the cornerstone. Levis with music instruments that were reconstructed also…played music. And we brought also the vessels that we reconstructed for the third Temple to this place. And the purpose was to say to everyone, we are ready for the rebuilding of the Temple.[37]

On each day of the month preceding the month of Tishri, the shofar is sounded at the Western Wall of the Temple Mount. At this time of national preparation for repentance, the reminder that God once revealed Himself at Mount Sinai points to His promised return to Jerusalem to reveal Himself again at the end of days (Zechariah 8:3). The first day of Tishri, known as the Feast of

Trumpets, signals the beginning of a solemn occasion of national repentance and spiritual return to the Lord. The shofar, a ram's horn that long ago was used to assemble the Israelite troops for battle, is sounded to issue a call for spiritual preparation. In Temple times, the shofar was blown (Leviticus 23:24) by a priest from the southwestern corner of the retaining wall surrounding the Temple. The people then offered a burnt offering at the Temple in token of their spiritual preparation. This points prophetically to the time of Daniel's seventieth week (Daniel 9:27; 12:1), during which the Jewish remnant is prepared for national repentance through the persecution of the Antichrist at the close of this period (Zechariah 12:1-9; Matthew 24:31).

Immediately following the Feast of Trumpets, on the tenth day of Tishri, is the holiest day in the Jewish calendar, Yom Kippur (Day of Atonement). This is the day on which Israel historically made atonement for their national sin. In ancient times both the act and fact of forgiveness was dependent upon a series of sacrifices in the Temple that were performed by the high priest on behalf of the people. The climax of the act of atonement was when the high priest entered into the Holy of Holies (the innermost and most sacred chamber within the Temple) with a sin offering and sprinkled its blood on the mercy seat of the Ark of the Covenant. On Yom Kippur, Jews fast as in Temple times, incorporate the high priest's sacrificial service into the synagogue ritual, and sing at the conclusion of the service: "Next Year in Jerusalem" (Hebrew, *Lashanah haba'ah birushalayim*). Prophetically, Yom Kippur looks forward to the great day of national redemption and spiritual cleansing that is to follow her repentance at Messiah's coming to the Mount of Olives (Zechariah 12:10-13:1; Matthew 24:30; Romans 11:27).

The conclusion of this spiritual period of preparation for national repentance and spiritual cleansing comes only with the final day of the seven-day Feast of Succot (Tabernacles or Booths), also known as the Feast of Ingathering (Exodus 23:15-16). In ancient times, all Jewish men were required to go to the Temple for this celebration, where 70 sacrifices were offered in atonement for the sins of the nations that had come from the sons of Noah. The final day (seventh day) of this feast is known as *Hoshana Rabbah* (The Day of the "Great Hosanna")—taken from liturgical passages recited throughout the feast which begin with the Hebrew imperative *hoshana* ("save now"). At this time the people waved their lulavs, or palm branches, while the Levites chanted the *Hallel* (Psalms 113-118). The name of this day—*Hosanna*—comes from the closing words of Psalm 118, which reads: "O LORD, do save, we beseech Thee.... Blessed is the one who comes in the name of the LORD." This prayer for the speedy advent of Messianic redemption accompanied a special ceremony known as the "water-drawing festival" (Hebrew, *simhat bet hassoevah*). At this ceremony water was drawn from the Pool of Siloam and poured on the corner of the altar in the Temple as a libation offering. This water was poured in connection with prayers for the annual rains, but it also had Messianic significance as well. It was here at the Siloam (Hebrew, *Shiloach*, "He sent") that the fullers had washed their clothing (Isaiah 7:3), a figure drawn upon by the prophets to illustrate the Messianic purification of the Millennial Temple's servants (see Malachi 3:2-3). Here, too, the prophet Isaiah challenged Ahaz to trust God, not man, and revealed a Messianic sign (Isaiah 7:7-14). Succot also celebrates God's provision of refuge in the wilderness, recalls His prophetic promise of rescue at the time of Jacob's trouble (Jeremiah 30:7), and affirms His promise of restoration in the future kingdom of Messiah.

The water for Succot was taken to the Temple and poured over the corner of the altar, a ritual based on an oral tradition that dated to the time of Moses (*Ta'anit* 3a, *Succot* 44b, 44a). This pouring out of water was both *symbolic* and *prophetic*. Its *symbolic* purpose was that it served as a prayer for rain, since summer was about to end and the rainy season would soon begin. This prayer for rain demonstrated Israel's dependence upon the Lord, an act of faith that will be required of all the nations who observe this ceremony in the Millennial Temple (Zechariah 14:16-19). Its *prophetic* purpose was Messianic, looking forward to the outpouring of the *Ruach Ha-Kodesh* ("the Holy Spirit") upon Israel and the nations under the new covenant in the kingdom age (Ezekiel 36:27; Joel 2:28).

This ceremony forms the backdrop for the New Testament account of Jesus' arrival at Succot as described in Matthew 21:9 and John 7:37-39, when He rode through the Eastern Gate and entered the Temple precincts greeted by shouts of "Hosanna," and then proclaimed to the crowds that He was the true giver of the "water" and the "light" of the world (John 7:37-38; 8:12). On this day during Temple times, willow branches were beaten against the pavement next to the Great Altar to symbolize the casting away of the Nation's sins. In the future, the nations of the world will join with Israel in the ongoing celebration of Succot (Zechariah 14:16-19). It is also significant that the Scripture passage read in the synagogue on the Shabbat during Succot is Ezekiel chapter 38, which deals with the future battle of Gog and Magog, a last-days war in which the Lord miraculously preserves Israel.

These details help give some insight into why the Temple Mount Faithful, at the conclusion of Succot, take their cornerstone to the Pool of Siloam. There they draw some water in a libation vessel (*mizraq*), pronounce the *shehehianu* blessing (thanksgiving for having reached a special occasion), and pour out the water as an offering on the cornerstone in lieu of the Altar, since it is considered the only existing part of the Third Temple. For the Temple Mount Faithful, this ceremony proclaims the prophetic promise that the Temple will soon be built and the water will then be able to be poured on the restored altar.

The Temple Mount Faithful announce these demonstrations via their web site, e-mail messages, and printed newsletter, often attracting international attention. For example, their announced intention to attempt to lay the cornerstone on October 6, 1998 brought a flurry of Internet and radio speculations of apocalyptic proportions. In one report of the WorldNetDaily, writer Kaye Corbett penned the headline: "Temple plan could ignite WWIII: Cornerstone to be laid today on explosive real estate."[38] He then went on to suggest that "a small religious group known as the Temple Mount and Land of Israel Faithful movement, could bring this planet to the brink of World War III...."[39]

What Does the Future Hold?

The day the Roman Tenth Legion stormed the Temple Mount and set fire to the Sanctuary ended Jewish sovereignty over the site. From that time onward the names of the conquerors of Holy Jerusalem have changed, and control has remained in foreign hands. In 1967 Motta Gur proclaimed the Mount's liberation to recoup history's 2,000-year-old debt. Abraham Rabinovitch, author of *The Battle for Jerusalem*, recalls that Colonel Gur had been hoping for a chance to attack the Old City and regain the Temple Mount at the very outset of the threat of war in May. Being a man under command he refused to act independent of orders, even when then-Chief Army Chaplain Rabbi Shlomo Goren pleaded with him to "ignore orders" and goaded him by saying, "You're not afraid to take chances? We could fix it up afterwards!" Nevertheless, Rabinovitch writes, "Gur said no, but he had in fact been thinking of that very thing. What would history say, he wondered, if Israel turned away from this moment? What would history say about him as the commander who failed to seize this historic opportunity?"[40] On June 7 Colonel Gur got the chance to seize his opportunity, and the Temple Mount finally fell into Israel's hands. Today it remains in Israeli hands, but it is Islamic hands that hold it, and new liberators again wonder what history will record of them in this moment and with this opportunity. Whether or not these present-day activists will realize their hopes, we can know for certain that there is a future Jewish Commander who will at last liberate the Temple Mount and prevent it from ever being lost again. But be warned—you must prepare yourself for war!

CHAPTER 20

The Coming War

The Battles over the Last Days Temple

The time has come to rebuild the Jewish Temple destroyed two millenniums ago. We came to say to the whole world that the Arab occupation of the Temple Mount is finished forever!

—GERSHON SALOMON, DIRECTOR,
TEMPLE MOUNT FAITHFUL MOVEMENT

The principle of negotiation on this piece of property is not acceptable in the Arab Islamic world. They can negotiate on East and West Jerusalem. But when it comes to the Temple Mount, there is no such negotiation—even if its going to get us into World War III.[1]

—JERIES SOUDAH,
LEADER IN THE PALESTINIAN PARTY

It is universally conceded that there is no more volatile acreage on earth than that of the Temple Mount. If the Temple Mount is dynamite, and the Temple movement has lit the fuse, how long will it be until an explosive situation is reached? There is no doubt as to the reaction of Islam. Sheik Ahmed Yassin, the Islamic spiritual leader of the terrorist Palestinian organization Hamas, has declared that any attempt by Jewish militants to seize control of the Temple Mount or to destroy Islamic shrines would lead to a bloodbath. He said, "They will start a fire in which they shall perish."[2] We have seen that Temple activism has raised the tension in the battle for the Temple Mount to a height never before realized in the past 1,362 years and Islamic reaction has followed suit. Whenever Temple groups act, they are regarded by the Muslims as agents of the Israeli government seeking to destroy their holy places. Although the Israeli government repeatedly denies any association, Adnan Husseini, the executive director of the Islamic Wakf, still contends, "We [in the Wakf] see no difference between these two groups [The Temple Mount Faithful and Ateret Cohanim] and the government. We consider the government and these two groups as one body. The government leaves these persons working. What we can see today started in 1967 immediately after the occupation, when Jews cleaned the Wailing Wall plaza.... What the Jews want there is a pure Jewish country. If they want to fight us, they will have to fight Islam.... We are here because God sent us here. We cannot change. If they want to fight us, they have to fight God. But we are blaming the government...."[3] In like manner, when two Israelis were detained in 1998 for allegedly plotting to throw a pig's head into the Muslim compound, Palestinian leader Yasser Arafat said, "We have always warned of this; many times, we have warned of the attempts of Israeli extremists to defile Al-Aqsa and destroy it."

On the other hand, the Islamic Wakf have destroyed ancient remains of the Temple around the Haram and in unauthorized construction projects for building new mosques inside the Huldah Gates and Solomon's Stables.[4] They say of any Jewish interference: "There will be massacres if there is any attempt to stop the opening of the mosque."[5] Yet the Jewish proposal to build a synagogue on the Temple Mount (presented by Knesset member Rabbi Benny Elon and Rabbi Yisrael Ariel, head of The Temple Institute), based on evidence from archaeologists and historians that such a synagogue once occupied the site,[6] was violently opposed by the Wakf as an attempt to subvert their sovereignty over the site. But on this issue the Wakf is clearly in error. The Temple Mount is still under Israeli sovereignty and Israel can do whatever needs to be done at this site when necessary. This was demonstrated in 1998 when Palestinian terrorists, who escaped from Israeli security forces in Jerusalem, ran to the Temple

Mount and received refuge from the Wakf who tried to prevent the Israeli police from catching them. However, Islamic jurisdiction did not stop the police from entering the site and arresting them—demonstrating Israel's sovereign status and its ability to assert itself on the Temple Mount when it so chooses.

The Battle Begins

The Conquest of the Mount

When Israeli forces captured the Old City of East Jerusalem on June 7, 1967, the world watched in wonder. What would happen next? Would Israel annex East Jerusalem, demolish the Muslim mosques, and rebuild the Temple? Would the surrounding Arab nations retaliate and stage a massive invasion of Jerusalem to retrieve control of their holy places? Israel did indeed annex East Jerusalem, but returned jurisdiction of the Temple Mount to the Muslims and denied any government-approved intention to rebuild the Temple. Thus, at least for the time, a war was averted with the Muslim countries in the Arab League and Jerusalem could learn to respect the multiplicity of religions that had historically occupied its most holy site. But on the day Israel entered the Temple Mount after being exiled from it for a quarter century, Jewish expectations were for permanent possession of the site. The comments of Colonel Motta Gur, commander of the Reserve Paratroop Brigade which captured the Old City on the day they took the Temple Mount, represented the feelings of what is now described as a deprived generation: "I feel at home here. The object of all the yearnings. The Temple Mount! Mount Moriah. Abraham and Isaac. The Temple. The Zealots, the Maccabees, Bar-Kokhba, Romans and Greeks. A confusion of thoughts. But there is one feeling that is firmer and deeper than everything. We're on the Temple Mount! The Temple Mount is ours!... We are in Jerusalem to stay."[7] Interestingly, no less sentiments were voiced by General Moshe Dayan, commander of the Israeli forces, who joined Colonel Gur's paratroopers at the newly won Western Wall: "We have united Jerusalem, the divided capital of Israel. We have returned to our holiest of holy places, never to part from it again...."[8] He went on to assure Muslims and Christians that the Israelis would safeguard the holy places and grant free access to them, because no one imagined at that time that they would ever again be controlled by anyone other than Israel.

Nevertheless, Dayan, who had led in the Mount's capture, felt that Israel could not justify maintaining Jewish sovereignty over the site in view of the greater threat from the Arab world. While Dayan believed the West Bank and Sinai, which had also been captured in the war, should be held in view of future bargaining with the Muslims for peace, Jerusalem, and especially the Temple Mount, held a unique religious status for Muslims and would invite only war if Jews asserted their rights there. Dayan expressed his opinion within hours of the first day of conquest when he ordered the Israeli flag to be taken down from the Dome of the Rock, where triumphant soldiers had placed it earlier. In the days that followed, Dayan heard of religious Jews who wanted to destroy the Dome of the Rock and saw Teddy Kollek, Jerusalem's Jewish mayor, give the order to bulldoze all the Arab buildings in the Moghrabi Quarter to clear an area for the thousands of estatic Jews who were streaming to the Western Wall for prayer. Dayan also saw the Israel Defense Forces Chief Rabbi Shlomo Goren open a synagogue on the Temple Mount itself.

Fearing that all of this would provoke Muslim hostilities, Dayan decided to take a controversial action of his own. Just ten days after Jews had recovered access to their Temple Mount for the first time in 2,000 years, Dayan entered the Al-Aqsa Mosque, sat on the Muslim prayer carpets in stocking feet with the Wakf (the Islamic trust responsible for managing their religious places on the Temple Mount) and returned to them control of the site. When I interviewed Goren in 1994, he told me that Dayan had acted on his own authority, but that no one in the government dared to oppose his action or attempted to reverse his decision. Only Rabbi Goren, as Dayan ordered him to remove the Jewish prayer books from the Temple Mount, reminded him of the gravity of his deed: "You gave away the Holiest of the Holies to the enemies of yesterday and tomorrow!" In time Goren's words proved true, for as Lawrence Wright, a writer for *The New Yorker* has pointed out, "Since then, the Temple Mount has been an Islamic island in an increasingly Jewish, and increasingly Orthodox city—and, as such, it has become a flashpoint for religious extremists of both faiths."[9]

Blow Up the Dome of the Rock!

On June 7, 1967, Colonel Gur's belief that Israel had providentially won the Temple Mount was taken a step farther by Rabbi Shlomo Goren, Chief Rabbi of the Israel Defense Forces. When Goren blew the shofar and recited the first Jewish prayers heard at the newly recovered Western Wall in nearly a quarter of a century, he stated that he believed the taking of Jerusalem had begun the Messianic era. This belief motivated him to undertake a plan of action that would return Jewish worship to the Temple Mount and one day see the Temple rebuilt. Because Rabbi Goren was the military's Chief Rabbi, he was given complete authority over the Temple Mount in the first month after its capture. Therefore, he immediately ordered a team of army engineers to survey the Mount, in order to establish the perimeters of access without violating the rabbinic injunction against violating the holiness of the site by inadvertently treading upon the holy precincts, below which some people believe the Ark of the Covenant is still preserved within a secret chamber.

In May 1998 it was revealed for the first time that only hours after Israeli soldiers had captured the Temple Mount, Rabbi Goren had urged that the Dome of the Rock be blown up. Goren's remarks were quoted in an interview with retired Major General Uzi Narkiss, who led Israel's capture of Jerusalem's Old City.[10] Narkiss stipulated that nothing be published until everyone involved in the discussion had died.[11] According to the interview, Rabbi Goren said, "Uzi, now is the time to put 100 kilograms of explosives into the Mosque of Omar so that we may rid ourselves of it once and for all." When Narkiss rebuked him, Goren persisted: "Uzi, you will go down in history if you do this!" When Narkiss again refused, Goren is said to have pleaded: "You don't grasp what tremendous significance this would have. This is an opportunity that can be taken advantage of now, at this moment. Tomorrow it will be too late!" At this point Narkiss said he told Goren that if he kept on persisting, Narkiss would put him in jail. Upon hearing that, Goren turned and walked away in silence.

Goren's former aide, Rabbi Menahem Hacohen, who was present at this discussion, gave a slightly different account of the story to Israel's Army radio. According to him, "The rabbi told Uzi that if, during the course of the war a bomb had fallen on the mosque and it would have, you know, disappeared, that would have been a good thing. Uzi said, 'I am glad that did not happen.'" Furthermore, Hacohen said Goren "did not suggest using explosives," and "Uzi never told him not to do it." Nevertheless, the Army radio played a tape of a speech Goren made in 1967 at a military convention, in which he called it a "tragedy" that Israel had left the Temple Mount in control of the Muslims. On the tape, Goren also said, "I told this to the Defense Minister (Moshe Dayan) and he said, 'I understand what you are saying, but do you really think we should have blown up the mosque?' and I said, 'Certainly we should have blown it up. It is a tragedy for generations that we did not do so....I myself would have gone up there and wiped it off the ground completely so that there was no trace that there was ever a Mosque of Omar there.'"

Dave Dolan, a CBS radio correspondent in Jerusalem, has personally observed the major conflicts on the Temple Mount over the past two decades. He shares his thoughts concerning blowing up the Dome of the Rock, as well as other options for its removal:

There are those who are so extreme that they want to go and literally blow up the Dome of the Rock, which I don't advocate nor think is very wise....but I do know that we are in a season today of wars and rumors of wars. I have been here for 21 years and I've seen the SCUD missiles flying over. Who's to know what could possibly happen and how destruction could come and clear the area? Something else could go up in its place. [Also] Jerusalem experiences a major earthquake every 50 years. The last major earthquake was in 1927. When I arrived here in 1977, we were told that we were already maxed out on the 50 years and that a major earthquake should hit Jerusalem any day now. Well, it never happened. Now it's much beyond [that time] and now we are looking to the [new] millennium and there still hasn't been a major earthquake. It wouldn't take much to shake the very foundations of the structures all around Jerusalem, including the mosques. I think God has His ways and when His time is right, the way will be made and God will take care of it and will show the people exactly when and how they can build this Temple.[12]

If a destruction of the Muslim structures would not make possible the rebuilding of the Temple, then could not the site be peaceably negotiated in view of preventing an inevitable war?

Is the Temple Mount Negotiable?

Although peace proposals, plans, agreements, and accords have all been considered and tried, a formal, lasting peace between the present parties in the Middle East is an impossibility. The reason for this is religious, not political. If Israel withdrew from all of the disputed "occupied territory" it captured in the 1967 Six-Day War, peace could still not be secured with the Palestinians, since, according to its charter, the PLO was founded to liberate the lands occupied by the Jews *before* 1947! However, even if Israel were to abandon all the territory it occupied as a result of the war in 1948 and occupy only the territory allocated to it by United Nations Resolution 181 (section 2), there would still be no peace, since the Arab League rejected that original partitioning of Palestine and went to war in 1948 for the sole purpose of eradicating the very existence of a Jewish State in their midst. In every case the decisions of the Arabs were based on the inflexible dictates of their religion. Nothing has changed nor can change in the Islamic agenda because the Koran has commanded the faithful to *Jihad* ("holy war") with the world of non-Muslims, and once any land has been conquered by Islam, it is forever the possession of Islam, regardless of whether or not it is lost again to non-Muslims. It is for this reason alone that the Temple Mount, all of

Jerusalem, and all of Israel will remain on the Islamic agenda and why peace can never come to the region short of the Islamic threat being removed.

From time to time, except for offers in the past by Jewish groups or Freemasons to buy the Temple Mount from the Arabs (offers the Arabs have been quick to reject), the proposal has been put forth that the Temple Mount could be shared in some way by both the Jews and Muslims. However, such proposals fly in the face of the basic tenets of each of these religions—exclusivism. For Judaism, the Temple Mount must be under Jewish control in order to fulfill the prophecies that "many peoples will come and say, 'Come, let us go up to the mountain of the LORD [the Temple Mount], to the house of the God of Jacob [the Temple]; that He may teach us concerning His ways, and that we may walk in His paths" (Isaiah 2:3). According to this passage, the whole world is to one day come to a rebuilt Jewish Temple situated on the Temple Mount in order to learn the truth of the Jewish God and follow His laws.

For Islam, the great Day of Judgment will take place before the seat of justice on Jerusalem's Mount Moriah, where today the *al-Mizan* (the Balances)—pillars and arches on the Temple Mount—await the scales that will weigh the deeds of resurrected souls.[13] According to Islam, the whole world is to be subjugated to Allah and the Koran universally revered as the final revelation of God. This is why the chairman of the Islamic endowment in Jerusalem, Adnan Al Husseini, warned that Islam will never, under any circumstances, agree to allow Jews to pray on the Temple Mount. In an interview with Voice of Palestine Radio, Husseini threatened to use violence against any Jews who dare to pray on the Temple Mount. He accused the rabbis of Judea, Samaria, and Gaza of being responsible for past attempts by Jews to pray on the Mount. This basic Islamic theology also explains why the sheikh in the Al-Aqsa Mosque publicly attacked the Israeli Supreme Court's decision to allow Yehuda Etzion to pray on the Temple Mount. In his Friday sermon broadcast live on Voice of Palestine Radio, he said, "We will not stand idly by." He later added, "We refuse to obey the decisions of this racist court. The rabbis will not enter the Al-Aqsa mosque, not over our dead bodies and shrouds."[14] If the differences in these religions make it is impossible to negotiate even *prayer* on the Temple Mount, how can we ever expect that a Temple could be negotiated?

Can the Sacred Site Be Shared?

For the same reason that neither peace nor prayer can be negotiated, it is also impossible that a Temple could be built anywhere on the Temple Mount alongside the Islamic Dome of the Rock or Al-Aqsa Mosque. Before the Temple could be rebuilt the entire Temple Mount would have to be ritually purified. Foreign structures, especially pagan structures, such as the mosques and shrines of Islam, are considered abominations that have to be removed before the ceremonial system could function. In like manner, Muslims cannot allow non-Muslims to corrupt their worship by their presence. In light of this it is strange that rumors of deals being struck between the Muslims and Israelis continue to crop up. For example, Rabbi Simcha Pearlmutter published an article that reported that the Palestinians, in 1993, had offered to allow the Jews to build their Temple north of the Dome of the Rock in exchange for recognition of legal status in East Jerusalem.[15] But if the mosques on the Temple Mount are holy to all Muslims everywhere, no single Muslim, not even an Imam or a sheik, and certainly not someone like Arafat, whose political clout is barely recognized in the Arab world, could authorize such a compromise of Islamic principles with the enemy of the entire United Arab Emirates! This point has been made clear by one of Arafat's own Palestinian leaders, Jeris Soudah: "Everybody in Saudi Arabia has a one-hundred percent right to vote yes or no about what happens on the Temple Mount, and they are not going to vote yes. All the Muslim world is involved here.... The Arabs and the Palestinians have no problem with dividing the city [of Jerusalem] between the east and the west. The east was the Arab side and the west was the Israeli side.... the Temple Mount is in the east side and that is why we cannot negotiate on this."[16] Adding the Egyptian voice to this issue, Mohammed Abdul Koddus, a well-known Egyptian writer and prominent member of the Muslim Brotherhood (an Islamic political group), has said, "There can be no peace so long as the Jewish state occupies Jerusalem."[17] Even though Egypt has had a formal peace with Israel since 1979, it can still hold out the prospect of war if Jews do not abandon their claims to the Holy City and the Temple Mount.

The Politics of the Temple

The issue of rebuilding the Temple has been at the forefront (though often downplayed) of the Arab-Israeli conflict. The Islamic authority (called in Arabic the *Wakf*) who maintains rigid control of the Temple Mount, blamed the Israeli government for starting a fire in the Al-Aqsa Mosque in 1969 in order to destroy the structure and rebuild the Temple—despite the fact that a mentally unstable member of a "Christian" cult actually set the blaze! Ever since, the Muslims have assumed that every incursion in or near the area, whether for archaeological or religious purposes, has had negative intentions. For this reason riots followed an excavation to uncover the subterranean Western Wall tunnel in 1982. Riots also followed a demonstration by the Temple Mount Faithful in 1990 (in which 17 were killed), excavations to reveal the Herodian street next to the Western Wall in 1995, and the opening of an exit tunnel to the Hasmonean tunnel in September 27, 1996 (in which 58 were killed). In March of 1997 Yasser Arafat was shown in a photograph, distributed internationally by the Associated Press, holding up an artist's rendering of a restored Jewish Temple and telling his people to "get ready for the next battle" (for Jerusalem). Similar calls for conflict were also issued from loudspeakers on the Temple Mount to Arabs in East Jerusalem during each of the aforementioned riots.

Scripture tells us we can expect a future war over the Temple Mount. When will it take place, and what will be its outcome? Let's look at that next.

The Last-Days Battles for the Temple Mount

We know that observant Jews desire to take back the Temple Mount, but would the secular Israeli public also support a conflict on the Temple Mount? Secular Zionists might cringe at the thought, but the very word *Zion*, from which their political movement took its name, is a reference to the Temple that was built on Mount Zion.[18] Even so, Carrie Hart, an experienced news commentator and Israeli believer living in Jerusalem, contends that the present passion for peace has so consumed secular Israeli society that these people will make any concession to secure it:

> There are some Israelis living here who will not be content until they go through the completed process of the peace accords. They will not be satisfied until they have tried every human effort to keep their sons from fighting and being killed on the battlefield. They will not be quiet, or hold their voices, until they see the outcome of their demands for two lands, two peoples, two flags, two anthems, peace within their borders, peace with their Arab neighbors. Even if it takes an internationalization of Jerusalem, they will not stop pushing their concept of peace...at all costs.[19]

Could the Temple Mount be taken and the Temple rebuilt by the minority of Orthodox Jews who support such a cause today? It seems that something will have to happen to change the attitude of the Israeli public so that both peace and possession of the Temple Mount is possible. Could a war occur in such a way that even the secular populace would be moved to acknowledge it was time for a Temple? The answer may be found by studying the biblical prophecies concerning the Last Days Temple. They indicate that Israel will survive a great invasion from the north (Ezekiel 38–39)—completely unscathed in such a way that even the greatest of skeptical secularists will acknowledge it was a miracle of God. These prophecies also indicate that at least three more future battles are to be expected (Revelation 11:2 with Daniel 11:45a; Zechariah 12–14; Revelation 20:7-9), each relating to the Temple Mount and each setting in motion events that lead to the ultimate fulfillment of Israel's destiny. Let's consider these coming wars for the Temple Mount.

The Battle of Gog and Magog

The "Battle" or "War of Gog and Magog"[20] appears between two Temple texts in Ezekiel (37:26-28 and 40–48) and therefore has some relationship to the Last Days Temple. The Temple described in these texts is the Final or Restoration Temple of the Millennial age. The placement of the Gog and Magog account in Ezekiel 38–39 could either relate to this Temple (in which case it would accord with the Millennium—see Revelation 20:8) or precede it (in which case it could be pre-Tribulational, Tribulational, or post-Tribulational). Without question this matter of chronological placement is one of the most difficult issues in prophetic interpretation.[21] There is no doubt that it belongs to the eschatological period, for the text makes this explicit: It will come about in the "latter years....last days..." (Ezekiel 38:7-8,16). It is also clear that the stage is the Land of Israel (Ezekiel 38:9-12,14,16,18-19; 39:11), and specifically northern Israel: "the mountains of Israel" (Ezekiel 38:8,21; 39:2-3,17-19). The reference to "unwalled villages" may also indicate a northern location (since Jerusalem, to the south, is a walled city),[22] as does the geography of the invaders "out of the remote parts of the north" (Ezekiel 38:6,15), and scene of the battle: "you shall fall on the mountains of Israel" (Ezekiel 39:4). There may also be an indication of this in the identification of the lands of the primary invaders (Ezekiel 38:2-3): Magog (after Josephus) with the land of the Scythians, and Meshech and Tubal with modern Turkey, as well as most of their allies (Ezekiel 38:5-6) all located north of Israel.

The Context

Problems with a Millennial Context

The text further indicates that at the time of this invasion the people of Israel "have been gathered from many nations" (Ezekiel 38:8), inhabit the waste places (Ezekiel 38:12), have become prosperous ("gathered cattle and goods," Ezekiel 38:12-13), and live securely (Ezekiel 38:8,11,14). While this description of Israel uses restoration language, the very fact that Israel is surrounded by hostile enemies prevents this time from being the time of the Restoration or the Millennial kingdom, when all of Israel's enemies (the nations) have been subdued and brought to honor Israel and her God (Isaiah 2:3-4; 19:16-25; 61:6; 66:18-20; Zechariah 8:20-23; 9:10; 14:16-19). In fact, in the Millennium, some of the very enemies listed here as attackers against Israel (Tarshish, Put, Meshech, Rosh) will receive a witness from converted nations of God's glory and come to the Millennial Temple to worship (Isaiah 66:19-20). Moreover, while the time of security described in this text seems to agree with the conditions of the Millennium, the reference to "unwalled villages" presents a condition opposite to that described for this period. For example, in Isaiah 26:1 we read, "In that day this song will be sung in the land of Judah: 'We have a strong city; He sets up walls and ramparts for security.'" The feeling of security that results from a lack of walls must be of a different kind than that which depends on their presence. This security seems to be connected with Israel's military existence in the Land, rather than reliance upon the Lord.[23] If this is the case, then Israel is here depicted as having returned to the Land and established a State in unbelief. This is confirmed by the fact that the outcome of the war appears to bring about for Israel a new understanding of God (Ezekiel 39:7), yet it is only afterward that Israel comes to "know" the Lord (Ezekiel 39:22) and His Spirit is poured out on them (Ezekiel 39:29). This argues that this war must take place before the Millennium.

Problems with a Tribulational Context

This text also uses language that appears to fit the Tribulation period—such as the mention of God's "fury," and "wrath," "anger" (Ezekiel 38:18-19a; see also Revelation 6:17; 14:10; 15:1,7; 19:15)—as well as terrestrial judgments, such as "a great earthquake" (Ezekiel 38:19; see also Revelation 6:12; 11:13; 16:18) effects on fish and animal life (Ezekiel 38:20a; see also Revelation 8:8-9), "mountains thrown down" (Ezekiel 38:20b; see also Revelation 6:14; 16:20), "pestilence... blood...hailstones, fire, and brimstone" sent by God on His enemies (Ezekiel 38:22; 39:6; see also Revelation 6:8; 9:17; 11:6; 16:3-9, 21; 18:8), and scavenger birds and beasts called to feast on the corpses of the slaughtered dead (Ezekiel 39:4, 17-20; see also Revelation 19:17-18). Despite these similarities, which can be explained by the common use of apocalyptic "Day of the Lord" language (compare the use of these same elements in past divine intervention/retribution contexts: Exodus 9:15-34; Numbers 16:31-35; Joshua 10:11; Ezekiel 5:12-17; 14:21; Joel 1:15-2:11; Amos 1:7,10,12,14; 4:10-11), there are significant differences. For one, the judgments during the Tribulation, except for the campaigns of Armageddon, are universal (affect all of mankind) and global (affect all physical environs) and not specific to a particular place, enemy, or battle as is the case with this war in Ezekiel 38–39. Furthermore, while in the Tribulation Period the armies of the world assemble for war in the northern part of Israel (Mount Megiddo, Revelation 16:14,16), the biblical text does not say that they will fight there. Rather, according to Zechariah 12–14, the scene of this final battle is Jerusalem. By contrast, Gog and his allies meet their doom "on the mountains of Israel" (Ezekiel 39:4). In addition, in Ezekiel 38–39 there are a definite number of allied nations that attack Israel in a time of "rest" to capture its "wealth" (Ezekiel 38:11-13), whereas at the battle of Armageddon it is "all nations" allied with Antichrist against Jerusalem to destroy the Jewish people, who are in distress (Zechariah 12:3; 14:2). Such differences argue against this war being the same as or a part of that battle of Armageddon at the end of the Tribulation.

The Chronological Context for the War

My preference is to place this battle *before* the Tribulation,[24] during the present-day period when Israel is experiencing the first phase of physical restoration—a period to which this restoration language could apply (see Ezekiel 36:24; see also Isaiah 11:11).[25] There is nothing in the description of Israel in Ezekiel 38–39 that does not fit the reality of the modern State of Israel today. This time frame also resolves the problem of how Israel disposes of the captured weapons and the slain bodies of Gog and his allies (Ezekiel 39:9-16). According to Jewish law, the dead must be buried immediately because exposed corpses are a source of ritual contamination. However, because of the vast number of corpses this will take "seven months" (Ezekiel 39:12). Furthermore, the destruction of the weapons will take "seven years" (Ezekiel 39:9). If this battle were to take place at any point during the Tribulation the Jews would run out of time to complete this task, for they will be persecuted during the last half of the Tribulation and most will have fled to the wilderness (Revelation 12:6) or remained in Jerusalem (Zechariah 12:7-8; 13:1; 14:2). But if this battle occurs before the Tribulation begins, there would be ample time for this job.

The other question concerns the conditions described for Israel at this time as "living securely." Whether the "security" Israel feels at this time is the result of a negotiated pseudopeace in which Israel imagines itself "at rest...liv[ing] securely" (Ezekiel 38:11) or because Israel truly is secure, we can be certain this peace occurs at a time *before* Israel faces persecution *in her Land*, such as it will experience from the midpoint of the Tribulation until the end (Matthew 24:16-22; Revelation 12:6, 13-17). It's possible the peace here refers to peace through military strength, which the Hebrew term *betach* ("security") can imply. Whatever the case, what we see in Ezekiel 38–39 does fit Israel's present conditions.

It is also significant that the word "peace" does not appear in the context, since it is clear from the fact of the invasion that Israel does not have peace in the sense of a cessation of hostilities or absence of war. Israel's setting in this text is one of confidence, even though it is apparently surrounded by enemies (as the geographical locations of these invading nations reveal).[26] However, the outcome of this war results in at least a temporary peace, as the nations are forced to reckon with the divine protection uniquely afforded Israel, as well as the consequences for any nation that goes against her (Ezekiel 38:23; 39:7). By contrast, the Tribulation begins with Antichrist's diplomatic conquest of the nations (Revelation 6:1-3), which results in a pseudopeace for the first half of the Tribulation period. The last half of the Tribulation will be marked by a series of wars, which will end with the climactic advent of the Messiah as a divine warrior (Zechariah 14:3-4; Revelation 19:11-15).

The Specifics

The Connection with the Temple

Real and irreversible peace is one of the distinguishing characteristics of the Millennial kingdom (Isaiah 2:4; 9:7; 11:6-9; Micah 5:4-5) and as such contrasts with the conditions in Ezekiel 38–39. But, in my opinion, it is just such a contrast that Ezekiel has in mind with his placement of this passage between the two Millennial Temple texts. In Ezekiel 37:25-28 he has described the "covenant of peace" and promised that it will be "an everlasting covenant" (verse 26). The symbol of God's promise will be His presence, which will be realized through the Millennial Temple (verses 26-27), which is also promised "forever" (verse 28). However, Israel had been promised restoration and a Temple before, but the former was not realized in full and the latter was eventually destroyed. What assurance is there that this promise will be different? The reason this unspoken concern needs to be addressed is because before Israel receives the Restoration Temple promised in Ezekiel 37, it will go through the Tribulation. In the first half of the Tribulation Israel will see the rebuilding of the Temple and probably experience a time of national revival and regathering of Jews from among the nations. If the Temple is rebuilt through the covenant made with the Antichrist (Daniel 9:27), who will be a global Gentile ruler, Israel may indeed experience an unparalleled period of peace and international respect. Since these conditions would appear to fulfill the restoration expectations of the prophets, many Jews will undoubtedly be deceived into believing that the era of the Redemption has finally arrived. Yet, at the midpoint of the Tribulation the Temple will be desecrated and the Jewish people persecuted, ending this illusion of restoration.

Before Israel comes to this time of trouble in which all of God's promises could be called into question, rendering the Jewish remnant more susceptible to the worldwide delusion of the signs and wonders of the Antichrist and his false prophet (see Matthew 24:24; 2 Thessalonians 2:9-12; Revelation 13:3,13-14), God will leave them a lesson of His power and purpose in the fulfillment of Ezekiel 38–39. As they go back to the context of this Scripture text they will see the assurance God had in placing this account between the promise of the Restoration Temple and the plan for its realization. They will see that though an invasion of Israel by superior powers was still to be suffered in the last days—after the promise of the Restoration and its Temple were given—(Ezekiel 37:26-28), God would yet intervene to fight for Israel (Ezekiel 38:18-22; 39:2-6). Thus this future threat would not prevent the Nation from experiencing the promised fulfillment described in Ezekiel 40–48.

In addition, if the seven years during which Israel will burn the weapons of these nations is the seven years of the Tribulation (Daniel 9:27; Revelation 11:2), then this, along with the burial ground of Gog and the slain multitude[27] (Ezekiel 39:11-16), serves as a witness throughout the Tribulation that beyond this time of final Gentile judgment waits Israel's Restoration and the Lord's return to dwell with them and reverse the Antichrist's desecration of the Temple. And, if this battle took place under the first stage of Israel's restoration (return to the Land in unbelief), it would provide both a witness to the means by which the second stage (return to the Lord in belief) would be effected (divine intervention for Israel) and the goal of restoration (divine dwelling with Israel). This is, in fact, what Ezekiel 39:21-29 reveals as it pictures the promised Millennial fulfillment. In verse 21 the statement "I shall set My glory among the nations" may refer contextually backward to Ezekiel 37:26-28 and forward to Ezekiel 43:1-7 and the return of the divine presence to the Millennial Sanctuary.

Gog and Magog Today

We can rightly identify the modern nations listed in Ezekiel 38:2-6 as nations hostile to Israel and supportive of the Islamic Arab agenda and of the Palestinian plan in particular. This can be seen by a quick look at the modern-day nations that occupy the ancient locations mentioned in Ezekiel's prophecy. Today the Magog ruled by Gog (the ancient land of the Scythians) is comprised of the former Soviet republics of Kazakhstan, Kirghiza, Uzbekistan, Turkmenistan, and Tajikistan, and Gog's allies are Meshech and Tubal (territories in Turkey), Gomer (Germany), Togarmah (Turkey), Persia (Iran), Cush/Ethiopia (Sudan), and Put (Libya). Just as the modern Israeli State fits the description Ezekiel gave of the Israel that will experience this battle, so these modern countries fit the details of enemy peoples who can and have formed alliances and have economic incentives for invasion. If the Gog and Magog war was predicted for a time such as this, it accords well with present conditions as the balance of power has shifted to Europe (EEC), Russia has become economically dependent, and Islam has become the fastest-growing religion, dominating the Middle East (for example, six of the former Soviet republics to the north of Israel have become independent *Islamic* nations: Azerbaijan, Kazakhstan, Uzbekistan, Kirghizia, Turkmenistan, and Tajikistan). Russia could easily fulfill the role of Gog, for its current economic hardships and political instability have led Russia to forge military alliances with Islamic powers that continually call for Israel's destruction.[28] As *U.S. News & World Report* editor-in-chief Mortimer Zuckerman has observed:

> Russia is an economic free fall that threatens the coherence of the central state and the ability of the government to control its arsenal of nuclear, chemical, and biological weapons. Any time now they might become black-market items for rogue buyers....And if the state disintegrates altogether, we could face the apocalyptic scenario of ultranationalists or some other faction challenging the command and control of nuclear weapons spread over 39 different Russian districts....Russia is a tragedy on the way to a catastrophe that could envelop us all.[29]

Israel is without a doubt one of the most highly developed[30] and westernized countries in the Middle East, and its technological achievements (Israel is the Silicon Valley of the Middle East) and natural resources (water, chemicals in the Dead Sea, deep but vast untapped oil reserves) could meet the requirements of the "great spoil" Ezekiel 38:13 says these nations seek to steal. Today Turkey (Togarmah) has a military alliance with Israel and its million-man army is one of the factors keeping both Egypt and Syria (with whom it shares a border) at bay. However, even though Turkey is non-Arab and generally against militants, it is an Islamic country, and if it were called to an Islamic alliance at some future time against Israel, it could be expected to join. Middle-East analysts have already predicted political instability as a result of the August 1999 earthquake in the Istanbul region of Turkey, which may lead to such an alliance. At the present time an axis is believed to have been formed between Russia and the Middle Eastern countries of Iraq, Iran, Syria, Sudan, and Ethiopia with the goal of overthrowing the United States and its Zionist ally in the Middle East, Israel. Russia has already forged alliances with some of these countries and others: Iran, Syria, Pakistan, Libya, and Turkey. Moreover, the Central Asian Republics of Kazakhstan, Turkmenistan, Tadzhikistan, Uzbekistan, and Krygzstan have signed a military assistance pact with the Russian Federation. These countries are all Islamic and have been confirmed to possess nuclear weapons. Iran and Iraq have been arming themselves with weapons supplied by Russia and China, and Iraq continues to issue threats to the West and Israel. This has led Palestinian Authority "President" Yasser Arafat to believe that "a Palestinian victory over Israel and Iraqi victory over the United States are mutually dependent."[31] Whether or not the present alliances will have a role in the Gog and Magog war, we don't know, but something like them surely will be. It is interesting to hear how Orthodox Jews—and especially those in the Temple Movement, understand Ezekiel's prophecy.

Jewish Expectations of Gog and Magog

Orthodox Jews see the "Wars of Gog" as a series of three assaults of Gog against Jerusalem, as recorded in the prophecies of Ezekiel, Daniel, and Zechariah.[32] The details of this interpretation are found in Jewish commentaries that discuss the afflictions Israel will undergo before the beginning of the Messianic era (known as the birthpangs of Messiah). Concerning this future time when war would be rampant, the Jewish Midrash states, "If you see kingdoms rising against each other in turn, then give heed and note the footsteps of the Messiah" (Genesis Rabbah). The expression "kingdoms rising against each other" reminds us of Jesus' statement in the Olivet Discourse "nation will rise against nation, and kindgom against kingdom" (Matthew 24:7; see also Mark 13:8; Luke 21:10). This is an idiom for "world war," and in the time of the Tribulation will be climaxed by the advent of the Messiah: "I saw heaven opened; and behold, a white horse, and He who sat upon it is called Faithful and True; and in righteousness He judges and wages war" (Revelation 19:11).

According to Jewish interpretation, Targum Jonathan on the Prophets foretells that at the beginning of the Messianic era Israel will be punished for their transgressions by the oppressions of Armelus, followed by the wars of Gog. The result of these sufferings will be that Israel and the nations turn to God with perfect faith. Armelus in Jewish interpretation (see *Yoma* 10), is "the future wicked king of Daniel's fourth kingdom (Rome) [whose] Wicked Empire will have expanded its dominion over the entire world...during the era before the coming of the Messiah."[33] While this would imply that the war comes at the end of what Christians refer to as the Tribulation, Rashi seems to have viewed the time as earlier. Basing his interpretation on Ezekiel 38:8, he says: "After many days you will be summoned; in the latter years you will come into the land that is restored from the sword, whose inhabitants have been gathered from many nations to the mountains of Israel which had been a continual waste...." He also said, "Only shortly before Gog's coming have the People of Yisrael returned to their land; until then it has 'been continual waste' and desolate."

Rashi apparently understood that when the Jews returned to Israel from the Diaspora and replanted and rebuilt the Land (established a State), the war of Gog and Magog would soon follow. I have in my library a small book published in Hebrew in Tel-Aviv in 1973 entitled *The War of Russia and Israel: Gog and Magog*. In this book the Israeli author holds that this climactic conflict is imminent in Israel, and that the events of the Yom Kippur War set the process in motion. He teaches that a coming invasion of Israel will result in God's intervention and the final redemption of Israel. Following somewhat this same interpretation, Rabbi Rafael Eisenberg summarizes the corpus of Jewish tradition on this matter:

> Our prophets and sages have foretold that prior to the arrival of the Messiah, the Wicked Empire, Rome (which as we have already shown, is modern Russia), will regain its former greatness. In those pre-Messianic days, Russia will expand over and conquer the entire globe, and her ruler, "who will be as wicked as Haman," will arise and lead the nations of the world to Jerusalem in order to exterminate Yisrael....At that time, the overt miracles which will bring about the great retribution against Yisrael's enemies and the final destruction of the Wicked Empire, will convince the world that God, alone, is the Judge and Ruler of the Universe.[34]

Orthodox Jews in the Temple movement in Israel generally agree that the war of Gog and Magog is to be the next of Israel's wars, and believe that it will be fought over possession of Jerusalem and the Temple Mount. For example, Gershon Salomon, the leader of Israel's Temple Mount Faithful, writes concerning the imminency of this war:

I consider it my duty to warn my people and all the friends of Israel that a terrible war, the most terrible war of all the seven wars of Israel, is going to be perpetrated in this land against the people of Israel as a direct result of these terrible agreements and the giving away to the enemies of G-d our Holy Temple Mount and the most holy and important biblical areas of Israel....[35]

The prophet Ezekiel prophesied that in the end times of the redemption of the people of Israel, a terrible war will break out in the land when Gog and Magog with many other nations come to the land of Israel and try to destroy the people and State of Israel (Ezekiel 38–39). G-d said that He would bring this enemy from the far north against the mountains of Israel. The prophet Zechariah also spoke about the same event (Zechariah 12–14)....We have tried to understand how G-d would accomplish His end-time plans for Israel. The questions that arose were: Why, from the first moment of the redemptional process of Israel, would Israel be attacked again and again? Why, close to the end of this process, would the Gog and Magog war break out? Why could this wonderful process not be accomplished without wars? Why, as in biblical times, is Israel again surrounded by so many enemies who want to destroy her? Why does the small David, armed only with a small rock, again need to fight against giants? As we come closer and closer to the accomplishment of the redemption process we can begin to give answers to these questions. We only need to read Ezekiel and Zechariah carefully to gain understanding. The G-d of Israel will use this means to finally defeat all those many enemies of Israel who have continually tried to destroy the State and people of Israel and push them into the Mediterranean. Now...they prepare to destroy Israel with terrible weapons. Iran, with Russian help, has started to build an atomic capability with long-range missiles directed at Israel. Syria, Egypt and the other Arab countries are also preparing for an atomic, chemical and biological war against Israel....Russia is doing all it can to renew her political and military ties with the Arab countries around Israel. After helping Iran to become a nuclear power and also helping Iraq to develop her non-conventional arsenal, Russia is now doing the same with Syria. Are Russia and her Arab allies the enemy of the North that the prophets spoke about?! The Palestinian Authority has also started to prepare for a war against Israel. They have brought in weapons from every direction to arm their forces. These are the forces that the former government of Israel, in a terrible and sinful mistake, helped to create....The coming war will be the final war undertaken against

Israel by her enemies. In it G-d will terribly defeat them. The prophet Zechariah describes the way G-d will defeat and punish them and it makes us think of a nuclear, chemical and biological war (Zechariah 14:13). After this war the new (G-dly) era will start. The Third Temple will be the House of G-d, the only building on the Temple Mount. Mashiach ben David will be the King of Israel and all mankind. We can see how the black clouds are coming closer and closer to Jerusalem and to the mountains of Israel. The march of Gog and Magog and all their allies has started in the direction of Jerusalem and Israel....The time of judgment is close at hand. Israel will survive this war and become the nation which G-d and all the prophets dreamed about.[36]

Although Salomon (as other Jewish interpreters) in my opinion incorrectly equates the war of Gog and Magog with the end-time battle for Jerusalem in Zechariah 12–14, he correctly understands that if this war results in the miraculous deliverance of the Israeli Nation, it will have far-reaching consequences for its status among the nations. Rabbi Rafael Eisenberg explains this well when he writes, "The miraculous defeat of Gog (Russia) and her satellites in Jerusalem will reveal that it is God who guides the universe, punishing the wicked, and upholding His promise to His servant Yisrael."[37] While it is not clear that the war of Gog and Magog takes place in Jerusalem, I propose that it might be the catalyst that brings about the Jerusalem covenant of Daniel 9:27, which seems to result in the rebuilding of the Third Temple.

A Possible Scenario with Gog and Magog

If the next war is that of Gog and Magog, it may be the war that cripples Islamic control and begins the process of re-ordering the world powers. Daniel 7:23-24 indicates that a one-world government will first arise, which will then be divided into ten governments. If the war of Gog and Magog occurs first and puts down the Islamic power base, it is possible that a new world alliance—on the order of a United Nations, NATO-like organization—could assume control for global stability. However, because this occurs before the Antichrist's rise to power, there will be no central figure to sustain this government, and it will be re-organized into the ten allied nations. This ten-nation confederacy will continue up to the middle of the Tribulation, and then the Antichrist will declare war on its ten kings (Daniel 11:40-45), killing three of them (Daniel 7:24; Revelation 17:12-13). However, during the time of this re-organization (before the Tribulation begins), there may be a time of relative peace. This will be short-lived, as the Antichrist's rise to power comes with war on a global scale (Revelation 6:2).

The Antichrist and Israel

Sometime at the beginning of this period of war the Antichrist will seek to negotiate directly with Israel for normalized relations. In light of the situation created by Israel's stunning victory over the Russian-Arab alliance, the Jewish Nation will be perceived as a force to be reckoned with by all nations. This would mean that the Antichrist's global policy will have to include concessions to Israel. The Islamic powers will not protest, for having suffered a decisive loss at "the hand of God," they will wisely capitulate based on Israel's perceived (and the Antichrist's apparent) superior strength. The Antichrist's purpose in making a treaty (Daniel 9:27) with Israel may simply be part of a deceptive scheme to politically position himself in order to later carry out the Satanic goal of Jewish genocide (Revelation 12:13). However, the motivation may also be good strategic planning, since Israel will have gained a position of worldwide respect as a result of the "miraculous" victory in the Gog and Magog war. Any move the Antichrist makes to consolidate his leadership would be improved with Israel in his pocket. Therefore, like a mobster running a protection racket, the Antichrist may offer by this covenant a special guarantee of security that would enable Israel to act with an independence never previously known.

From the Israeli side, without the threat of Islam (the secular political objection to Israel asserting itself on the Temple Mount), and with the war's victory as evidence to Israel's leaders of the opening of a new spiritual era (which would resolve the religious rabbinic objection to a Jewish presence on the Temple Mount), nothing would prevent Orthodox Jews from successfully arguing for a rebuilding of the Temple. If the Antichrist's covenant confirms that the nations also support the rebuilding effort, most Jews in the Temple movement would likely believe that they were seeing the fulfillment of the prophecy of the Messianic age.

The Jewish basis for this belief are prophecies made in the Oral-Torah (the Talmud), one of which says, "Jews will not have to fight a war against the non-Jewish custodians [of the Temple Mount] in order to take possession of it from them."[38] It is also stated in these sources that the Arabs will seek to destroy the Jews and that all the nations of the world will help Israel establish its state and rebuild its Temple. Many believe that today's generation will see the fulfillment of these prophecies "because this century has been the only time that Arab countries have ever tried to destroy all the Jews of Israel,"[39] and the State of Israel came into being through the support of the United Nations. In accord with these expectations, the Gog and Magog war will be the first war that Israel wins without a fight, leading the nations to acknowledge the power of Israel's God (Ezekiel 38:16,23; 39:7). It will also be the first time in modern history that Israel will be able come away from the international negotiating table *getting* something instead of *giving up* something! And what Israel will appear to receive may be the freedom to build the Third Temple. Even if only a minority of Jews come to view the Temple as a place of worship, under these circumstances secular Israelis would probably not object to the rebuilding effort and might accept it as a national monument to Israel's sovereignty as well as a fitting religious tribute to God for the victory over Gog and Magog..

This rebuilding of the Temple by the Israelis most likely will be tolerated by the world's major powers because they will be preoccupied with the Antichrist's rise to power and their own problems stemming from various worsening conditions around the globe (Revelation 6:2-4). By contrast, during this period of three-and-one-half years (the first half of the Tribulation) Israel may appear as an "oasis of peace" in a world where material and environmental conditions will be rapidly deteriorating (Revelation 6:1-17). Since the Antichrist's covenant will protect Israel from Gentile incursion, it may be that Israel, or at least Jerusalem, will experience only a marginal Gentile presence. This seems to be implied in John's measurements of the Temple site in Revelation 11:1-2, where he is told to leave out the Gentile court. The exclusion of the Gentile court indicates that it was being reserved, along with the city of Jerusalem, for later Gentile invasion in the second half of the Tribulation, probably beginning with the Antichrist's desecration of the Temple (Daniel 9:27; Matthew 24:15; Mark 13:14; 2 Thessalonians 2:4).

The Antichrist's First Assault on the Temple Mount

Another battle that will take place on the Temple Mount will be for possession of the Temple at the midpoint of the Tribulation (this battle will be covered in more detail in the next chapter). As we already know based on Daniel 9:27, Matthew 24:15, Mark 13:14, and 2 Thessalonians 2:4, the Antichrist will drive out the Temple priesthood, stop the sacrificial system, and seat himself in the Holy of Holies. We can be certain that when this takes place, some kind of a battle will be waged. This battle is implied in Revelation 11:2, which depicts the troops of the Antichrist "treading underfoot" the city of Jerusalem, which, based on the reference to the Temple in verse 1, must include the Temple Mount. Another passage that mentions this invasion by the Antichrist is Daniel 11:44-45, where in verse 45 we read, "He will pitch the tents of his royal pavilion between the seas at the beautiful Holy Mountain." This tells us the Antichrist will set up his military and political base in Jerusalem (between the Mediterranean Sea and the Dead Sea), and particularly on the Temple Mount ("beautiful Holy Mountain"). It seems to me that this act will occur suddenly and without warning. The Antichrist may come to Jerusalem on a pretext—perhaps an inspection tour—but, of course, with his usual military entourage. Then, one day while the priests are carrying out their daily tasks, a unit of the Antichrist's soldiers will invade the Temple Mount, expel the priests and Levites, and secure the area.

While everyone is in a state of confusion and protesting the action to the government, the Antichrist will parade onto the Temple Mount and into the Temple's Holy of Holies. In an act of desecration that historically identifies him as a conqueror, but that he knows will disrupt the further functioning of the Temple, he will go beyond all previous conquerors and seat himself in the place of deity (2 Thessalonians 2:4). He may then indicate his continued presence there by installing a statue of himself (Revelation 13:14-15). Jewish believers, who will have been forewarned of the significance of this act by the New Testament words of Jesus and Paul (Matthew 24:15; Mark 13:14; 2 Thessalonians 2:4), will attempt to flee from the city and take refuge in the wilderness (Revelation 12:14). Thus, the "Abomination of Desolation" (the act of rendering the Temple ritually defiled)—and the priests' inability to remove the idol and reconsecrate the site—will end the sacrificial system and inaugurate the final period of Gentile domination over Jerusalem, which will be marked through the last half of the Tribulation by widespread persecution of Jews and battles for control of the city (Zechariah 12–14).

The Antichrist's Final Assault on the Temple Mount

The end-time battle for the Temple Mount that occurs in the last half of the Tribulation—in two separate invasions—is recorded in Zechariah 12–14. In harmonizing the events here with those in the book of Revelation, it appears that as the Antichrist moves his troops to join his international allies in the Valley of Jezreel (Revelation 16:14-16) his enemies will launch an attack against his commercial center, Babylon, and destroy it (Revelation 18:1-24). Rather than move against these enemies who will have already finished their work, the Antichrist will move against Jerusalem with all of his allied nations (Zechariah 12:1-3; 14:1). Perhaps his attack will be motivated by a Satanic hatred of the Jews as the people of God, or because Jewish forces will have re-taken control of the city, possibly with the help of the two witnesses (Revelation 11:4-9). Because the

Antichrist set up his base on the Temple Mount (Daniel 11:45a), his attack will include the attempted recovery of this site. Because God will strengthen the Jewish fighters (Zechariah 12:5-9; see also Micah 4:11-5:1), the Antichrist will be able to recapture only half of the city (Zechariah 14:2). At this point Jerusalem will again be a divided city, and although the text does not explicitly state which section of the city this part of the Jewish remnant (the "one third" of Zechariah 13:8b ="all Israel" of Romans 11:26)[40] will control, it is possible to deduce this from the events associated with the final phase of this battle. I suggest it will be eastern Jerusalem and the Temple Mount for several reasons: 1) because of the presence of the Temple, this area might receive the greatest protection and may be the last to fall; 2) the fact that the part of the Mount of Olives specified in the text is that "which is in front of Jerusalem on the east" directly across from the Temple Mount; and 3) the Mount of Olives will split in two, with each side of the mountain moving north and south, creating an east-west escape route for the Jews (Zechariah 14:5). This east-west escape route would go directly from the eastern side of the city (and probably directly from the Temple Mount) across the Kidron Valley and through the Mount of Olives toward the Judean desert. Since the most direct access to this route would be from the eastern part of the city, it seems reasonable that this is the area that would be in the possession of the Jewish remnant.

The language of the original Hebrew text in Zechariah also implies that it may be the Temple Mount area where the Jewish remnant will be rescued. In Zechariah 14:3 we read that the Lord will "fight against those nations, as when He fights on a day of battle." The Hebrew verbal form used here (Niphal infinitive construct) suggests a customary or traditional way of fighting as "on a day of battle"—that is, in the same way God fought for His people in the past.[41] There were many battles in the Old Testament in which God directly and miraculously intervened, but a Hebrew reader of the next verse would know exactly which one was meant here. In this verse we read that when the Lord's feet stand upon the Mount of Olives, it will "split" (Hebrew, *baqa'*). This is the same verb used of the first—and most famous—of Israel's deliverances: when God "split" the Red Sea (Exodus 14:16,21; see also Nehemiah 9:11; Psalm 78:13; Isaiah 65:12). The use of this exodus motif fits the situation precisely. Just as the children of Israel were surrounded by the armies of Pharaoh (a type of Antichrist), so here they are surrounded by the armies of the Antichrist (the antitype). Just as the situation in Exodus seemed hopeless, so will this future scene of a small remnant of Jews enveloped by "all the nations" in the Kidron valley seem hopeless. Just as God fought the Egyptians and then led the ancient Israelis safely through the protective valley of the waters He created, so the Messiah will lead His remnant to safety through the valley of rock He will create (Zechariah 14:4-5). This guidance imagery implies that the Messiah may rescue His people on the Temple Mount and escort them Himself from Jerusalem across the Kidron to the Mount of Olives. Just as God blocked the Egyptians from reaching the Israelites and destroyed them in the Red Sea, so will it be that when the Lord's feet touch the mountain, it will both open a way of escape for israel (see also Joshua 3:6-17), and block the Antichrist's armies from escaping to the north or the south, leaving them alone in the Kidron Valley (also known as the Valley of Jehoshaphat—"God will judge") to be destroyed (Zechariah 14:12-15; see also Isaiah 14:3-21; Joel 3:12-13; Revelation 19:11-16). All this will occur when the Lord comes with His armies to bring judgment not only in Jerusalem, but throughout the world (Zechariah 14:5). Again, the language used of this judgment (Zechariah 14:6; see also Joel 2:28-32) parallels that of the divine warrior at the exodus and elsewhere (Isaiah 13:6-16; Amos 5:18-20; Zephaniah 1:14-18; Matthew 24:29-31; Mark 13:8; 2 Peter 3:16), which Zechariah has previously described (Zechariah 9:1-7; 10:4-5; 12:1-9).[42]

This event will fulfill Jesus' promise that the Temple would be desolate and the leaders of Jerusalem would not see Him until they said, "Blessed is He who comes in the name of the Lord!" (Matthew 23:39). When Israel beholds the Messiah coming in glory to rescue them, they will be moved to repentance in fulfillment of this prophecy (Zechariah 12:8-14; Matthew 24:30-31; Revelation 1:7). Upon the conclusion of this battle for the Temple Mount, the Lord will enthrone Himself in a new Temple (Zechariah 14:9,16; see also Jeremiah 3:17) on a greatly restored Temple Mount (Zechariah 14:10; see also Isaiah 2:2-3). From there He will rule the world throughout the Millennial age (Isaiah 24:23). Yet there is still one more battle for the Temple Mount that awaits the culmination of history.

The Final Battle for the Temple Mount

In Revelation 20:7-9 a more universal "Gog and Magog" appears as a symbol of the collective enemies of the Lord. It is obvious that a different "Gog and Magog" are depicted, for in Ezekiel's text the allied army was from neighboring countries, whereas here it is comprised of those from "the four corners of the earth" (Revelation 20:8). Also, in Ezekiel's text the attack was launched from and fought in the north, but here the attack is in the south (Jerusalem). The setting for the war that follows is at the conclusion of Israel's time of restoration. For 1,000 years the Millennial Temple will have been recognized as the Lord's throne, and the world will have made annual pilgrimages to it in worship of the Messiah who reigns within. Peace will have prevailed on the earth, and Israel and the nations will have forgotten both the art and the horror of war (Isaiah 2:4). Satan will have been bound throughout this period, but God will release him for a short time of deception before the close of earth's history. Knowing that the source of war is the evil still resident within mankind (James 4:1-3), Satan will gather to himself all of those who have conformed outwardly to the New Covenant, but not inwardly. These people will be the children born to the regenerate races that first populated the Millennial kingdom after the judgment of Jews (Ezekiel 20:33-38) and Gentiles (Matthew 25:31-46) in the Kidron Valley (Valley of Jehoshaphat—Ezekiel 34:17-24; Joel 3:2,12).

It may be that God's purpose in this is to reveal that even in the most perfect environment—with a clearly visible manifestation of the Lord's own presence and 1,000 years of instruction in God's Word—the heart of unregenerate man will remain unchanged. Whatever the reason, Satan, in the guise of Gog, will lead his worldwide allied army against the Millennial Temple. The text identifies this place as "the broad plain of the earth...the camp of the saints and the beloved city" (Revelation 20:9). According to Zechariah 14:10, this broad plain was the result of the divine transformation of the topography around Jerusalem "from Geba [10 miles north of the city] to Rimmon [35 miles southwest of the city]." Isaiah 2:2 implies that this land was flattened in order to elevate and distinguish the Temple Mount in its center (see Ezekiel 48:21). Ezekiel 48:10-22 describes the "camp of the saints" as the divisions of land around the Sanctuary where the priests, Levites, and workers of the holy city will dwell. It is clear from these descriptions, then, that this attack will be upon the Temple Mount—the place of the Messiah and those who serve Him.

Just as Ezekiel's war of Gog and Magog revealed to the whole world God's protection of Israel before the great deception of the Tribulation, so its example will serve in the Millennium's final hour to prove this point to a generation equally deceived and in need of defense. And just as the defeat of the enemies in Ezekiel's Gog and Magog battle bore evidence of divine intervention, so here those deceived are dispatched by "fire [that] came down from heaven" (Revelation 20:9). In like manner, the devil, the deceiver, is also judged by fire, joining the Antichrist and false prophet for eternity (Revelation 20:10). Therefore, even at the end of the world, the Temple remains intact and the Lord's presence remains with Israel, fulfilling the promise made in Ezekiel 37:28 that both would be in Israel's midst "forever."

The War Is Coming!

The Jewish Midrash states, "If the nations of the world had only known how much they needed the Temple, they would have surrounded it with armed forces to protect it" (*Numbers Rabbah* 1:3). Yet the nations of the world have not known this and will not know until they are brought under Messiah's reign in the Millennial kingdom (Zechariah 14:16). Until that time, they will increasingly view the Temple Mount as a source of international controversy and conflict, and in the end times they will launch attacks against it. In fact, in 1998 some 5,000 Hamas supporters gathered in Gaza's Shati refugee camp to mark the eleventh anniversary of the founding of the Islamic opposition movement. The Hamas' spiritual leader, Sheikh Ahmad Yassin, delivered the main address, promising that Israel would survive no more than three more decades: "It is our people's right to oppose this and wage *Jihad* until our rights are restored and we establish our state."[43] In a similar way, Palestinian leader Jeris Soudah has predicted that Israeli intransigence over East Jerusalem and the Temple Mount has made war inevitable:

> When it comes to that sensitive point—Jerusalem, I think there will be another war. The Islamic and the Arab world just cannot compromise concerning Jerusalem. They just can't....[44]

> United Nations Resolution 242, which states that Israel has to pull out from the occupied territories, from the West Bank and Jerusalem, has to be taken into consideration. If this will not happen or if they will not at least negotiate about Jerusalem, another Civil War, another *Intafada*, will start....This time the entire Arab world will participate in that *Intafada*. It will be Arabs, Muslims, Christians—a huge *Intafada* that Israel cannot resist. Arabs are not going to give up the holy place that easily. Palestinians and the whole Arab world are ready to go for a new civil war....But talking about the Temple, Israelis say that it has to be built on the site of the Dome of the Rock. The Muslim community will not allow anything to happen to the Dome [of the Rock]....[45]

No one in the Arab world is waiting to see what will happen to the Dome of the Rock. They are preparing now to prevent Israel from ever changing the status quo on the Temple Mount by changing Israel's status quo in the Middle

East. This can be seen in the inflammatory words of a sermon delivered in the Al-Aqsa Mosque on September 10, 1999:

> Oh Muslims, do you want glory? Do you want to remove the corruption around you? Do you want victory? Do you want to be able to carry Islam to the whole world? Do you want to please Allah?...The Islamic state that the Prophet (may peace be upon him) established was able to carry Islam to the world by *Jihad*. Allah says, "And fight them until there is no more tumult or oppression, and there prevails justice and faith in Allah together and everywhere" (al-Anfal 8:39)....Islam says about the Jews that they are enemies. Islam says about the Jews: "Fight them," "Kill them," "Drive them out." Islam says about the Jews that they are infidels....I swear by Allah that the Islamic state is close and it will overthrow their thrones [and] it will overthrow this alleged peace process....And we say to the rulers in the Muslim world, to the Jews, and to the rulers of the whole world, "We are coming to the promise of Allah about you!"[46]

The evidence to support such a contention is published regularly by Jewish organizations such as FLAME (Facts and Logic About the Middle East). Their reports of the current Islamic agenda reveals that the coming war for the Holy Land closely parallels the conditions described for the world and the Middle East in the last days:

> The Arab countries (and Iran) are frantically arming themselves with the most dreadful weapons of mass destruction. As the world knows, it is for one purpose only—their only political objective and their relentless obsession—namely, the destruction of Israel. Two or three nuclear weapons would wipe Israel off the map once and for all. Retaliation by Israel, the destruction of major Arab cities, and millions of Arab casualties would not deter the Muslim fanatics from pursuing their goal. For them, it would be a small price to pay. With Israel dismembered, with five or six Arab states poised to attack with weapons of mass destruction, with 40,000 Palestinian "police" armed to the teeth in Israel's midst, can anybody really doubt that a second Holocaust, even more terrible than the first one, is just about upon us?[47]

Is it really as bad as this? Are we on the brink of unparalleled days of trouble for the Jewish people in the Middle East? Recently I attended a secular conference in Washington, D.C., to learn inside information about the problems facing the Middle East. The speakers were some of the world's leading political analysts. One of the men who lectured that day was Israeli Yohanan Ramati, who serves as Director of the Jerusalem Institute for Western Defense. I was so impressed by Ramati's comments that I decided to interview him myself a few months later in Jerusalem. Ramati, who served in the British Army during the Second World War and has witnessed from his home in Jerusalem every war fought in Israel over the past half century, and who has known personally Israel's past and present leaders, is an expert on the Muslim world. If anyone could accurately perceive the situation in the Middle East, I felt he would be the one. Ramati not only confirmed the worst for Israel, but warned that the western world shares the same threat:

> Well, if I'm allowed to hope, I want to hope that we have at least as many years in front of us as we have behind us. [But] I'm not sure of that at all. If I'm allowed to hope, let me hope that western civilization will survive another 30 or 40 years, which at the moment I rather doubt. That is so much for hopes. I'm not giving any scenarios. All the scenarios I can see are too pessimistic to give. One thing I promise you: There is not going to be any peace here [in Israel]. There may be peace treaties [but] there will not be peace because the Arabs do not want peace with us. They are using the peace treaties as a means to create a situation in which they can wage a victorious war....I don't know whether the Temple movement in Israel has any future. I can visualize an imaginary situation in a war where things could happen, but if that is to be we have to be in a situation to win a war....[However,] everyone concerned, not only the Arabs, but [also] the [international] powers, seem to be determined to put us in a situation in which we cannot win a war. Obviously this cannot have a good end.[48]

Such a statement may seem extreme to some, but according to the prophecies of the days to come and the wars to come, it is not only realistic, but reserved by comparison. In the next chapter we will take a closer look at those coming days of trouble for the Temple Mount, and the Tribulation that will come upon all of the Jewish people and the world. It will not be an easy journey but it is a necessary one, for we will not see the light of dawn until we've passed through the darkness that precedes it. So let us take a step into the darkness of the Last Days Temple that we may better see the light.

PART IV

The Program for the Last Days Temple

"For just as the new heavens and the new earth which I make will endure before Me," declares the LORD, "so your offspring and your name will endure....All mankind will come and bow down before Me," says the LORD.

—Isaiah 66:22-23

I saw the holy city, new Jerusalem, coming down out of heaven from God....And I heard a loud voice from the throne, saying, "Behold, the tabernacle of God is among men, and He shall dwell among them, and they shall be His people, and God Himself shall be among them."...And I saw no Temple in it, for the Lord God, the Almighty, and the Lamb, are its Temple.

—Revelation 21:2-3,22

CHAPTER 21

Trouble in the Temple

The Temple in the Tribulation

I find that Christians have almost a morbid view of the Temple. Most of them view it from the standpoint that the Antichrist is coming, and personally, I find the Antichrist to be repulsive. I find it repulsive that you believe he will kill so many people, especially Jews. . . this coming is something I find very difficult to accept.[1]

—RABBI CHAIM RICHMAN

Today the headline news from Jerusalem frequently includes accounts of trouble on the Temple Mount. At a time and a place where rival religions vie for control of sacred space, such is the inevitable heritage. As today, every past age has had its own set of circumstances affecting the outcome of events within it.

The First Temple was built by an Israelite king who lived at a time when his culture was surrounded by idolatry and forced to make political compromises with it. And with every idolatrous high place he constructed and every offering he burned to foreign gods (1 Kings 11:7-8), he sowed the seeds of the Temple's destruction.

The Second Temple was built at a time when most of Israel was captive and those left in the Land were still subject to foreign domination. In this era, the attempt to rebel and regain lost freedom doomed the Temple to invasion and destruction (see Daniel 8:9-13; John 11:48; Luke 19:43-44).

The Third Temple of the coming age will also follow the path of its predecessors. However, unlike any previous age, this one will be a time unparalleled in both idolatry and Gentile domination (Matthew 24:21-24). Built in such a time, there is certain to be trouble *for* the Temple, but surpassing this, the Bible predicts, also trouble *in* the Temple. This trouble will be the Antichrist's usurpation of the place of God within the Holy of Holies, bringing about the Temple's desecration and the outpouring of God's wrath upon the earth. This teaching is often misunderstood by Christians, which may result in an even greater misunderstanding of Christians among Jews in the Temple movement (for example, see Rabbi Richman's statement on page 473). In order to better grasp what the Old and New Testament texts actually say concerning this pivotal event in the Temple's future, let us consider the nature and role of the Antichrist in relation to the Temple, examine in detail the biblical accounts of his act (known as the "Abomination of Desolation"), and then discuss the legitimacy of the Tribulation Temple as a holy Temple and a place of worship.

The Antichrist and the Temple

During the period of the Second Temple a host of actual and would-be desecrators of the Temple marched into Jerusalem and onto the stage of history. The Syrian-Greek ruler Antiochus IV Epiphanes erected an "abomination" in the area of the Temple near the Altar of Sacrifice; the Greek world-conqueror Alexander the Great attempted to approach the Temple, and the Roman emperor Pompey actually entered the Holy of Holies. The Roman emperor

Gaius Caligula attempted to place Roman images in the court of the Temple, while the Roman emperor Vespasian and his general son Titus succeeded in destroying the Temple itself. All of these desecrators were types of the greater antitype to come. The designation "Antichrist," appearing only in the epistles of John (1 John 2:18,22; 4:3; 2 John 7), is made up of the Greek words *anti* ("against, in place of") and *christos* ("Christ," "Messiah"), and indicates any agent of the evil one (Satan) who acts contrary to or seeks to usurp the place of God's Anointed who is destined to rule the world (Psalm 2:2, 6-8; 110:1-2; Isaiah 9:6-7, et al.).[2] The figure identified with "the prince who is to come" (Daniel 9:26), who will make a covenant with the Jewish leaders in Jerusalem (see chapter 11) may be understood as the Antichrist and connects him with the activity of rebuilding and desecrating the Tribulation Temple. Daniel also presents other portraits of the Antichrist as an insolent, despicable, self-willed king (Daniel 8:23; 11:21, 36-45) also known as the "little horn" (Daniel 7:8, 24-27). In addition, Jesus' reference to the Abomination of Desolation (Matthew 24:15; Mark 13:14), and Paul's reference to the "man of sin," "lawlessness," and "son of destruction" who will defile the Temple (2 Thessalonians 2:3-4), further support the identification of this "prince" with the Antichrist.[3]

Many have wondered how the Antichrist will be able to make a covenant with the Jewish leadership that will result in the rebuilding of the Temple. Some have proposed that the Antichrist will be Jewish and will be accepted by the Jews as the Messiah. What does Scripture tell us? The Old Testament predicts that the Messiah will build the Temple (Zechariah 6:12); therefore, many prophetic teachers believe that the Antichrist will seek to counterfeit this Messianic activity. Elwood McQuaid, Executive Director of The Friends of Israel Gospel Ministry, explains this position:

> The building of [the Tribulation Temple] will be, I think, in the spirit of what Herod did on the Temple Mount. We call it Herod's Temple [because] he refurbished that Temple; he embellished that Temple, [and] enlarged the Temple Mount. He was building something that was ostensibly for the Jewish people, but in actuality it was for himself. I think the Antichrist may participate in the building of the Temple for that very reason....He is not really having that building constructed for the Jewish people and for Jewish worship, he is having it constructed for himself, because in the midpoint of the Tribulation period, he's going to go to that Temple and raise the Abomination of Desolation and there declare himself divine.[4]

In line with this, other prophecy teachers, pointing to the worship of the Antichrist by the world (Revelation 13:4,16) think that he will head a world religion and that the Jewish religious leaders will have apostatized from Judaism and joined his ecumenical faith. However, if the Jews who have control of the Temple area at this future time have departed from the Jewish law, they would not care about rebuilding the Temple because the very purpose of rebuilding the Temple is to fulfill the Orthodox observance of Jewish law!

A number of prophetic teacchers also believe that because the Antichrist will build the Temple he must be Jewish. The matter of the Antichrist's ethnic background and whether or not he will be accepted as the Messiah by his action in relation to the Temple is more complicated; however, it can be resolved by a careful study of his nationality.

The Nationality of the Antichrist

Three basic arguments seek to establish the national or ethnic identity of the Antichrist. The first is the logical argument. It states that since the Jewish people claim that the definitive way the Messiah will be identified by the Jewish Nation is by his building of the Temple—that when the Antichrist makes possible the rebuilding of the Third (Tribulation) Temple, the Jewish people will accept him as the Messiah. Consequently, if the Antichrist is accepted as the Messiah, and the Messiah is Jewish, then the Antichrist must also be of Jewish origin. Would the Jewish people allow a non-Jew to be involved in rebuilding the Jewish Temple? A second argument is the lexical argument, a deduction drawn from the biblical text. In this case evidence of Jewish origin is said to be found in the words of Daniel 11:37 in the King James version: "And he will not regard the God of his fathers...." Since the context of this verse describes the character of the Antichrist, and since the term "God of the fathers" is used elsewhere to refer to the God of Abraham, Isaac, and Jacob (the Jewish patriarchs or fathers), some Bible teachers believe this must indicate that the Antichrist is an apostate Jew.[5] Finally, the linguistic argument contends that because of the Greek preposition *anti* in Antichrist, the Antichrist is a counterfeit of Jesus Christ, and since He was Jewish, so must the Antichrist be Jewish in order to claim this identity.

These arguments, however, need to be scrutinized in the light of other scriptural and historical factors. One reason for this, aside from the desire for biblical accuracy, is that this view, to a Jewish person, is tantamount to the blood libel under which generations of Jews were persecuted by Christians. In fact, in the spring of 1999 Dr. Jerry Falwell was accused of anti-Semitism by the American Jewish Committee in New York for holding this view. He quickly became the target of pundits on national television talk shows, political commentary programs, and was widely denounced in newspaper editorials throughout the country.[6]

Few realize the history behind this view, which caused a major uproar when Falwell openly espoused it. One early proponent of this view was the church father John Crysostom (fourth century A.D.). He said that the Antichrist would be a Jewish dictator from the cursed tribe of Dan[7] and called the Jews inveterate murderers, destroyers, men possessed by the devil. The blood libel is based on this idea and claims such as these: that the Jews had sold themselves to Satan, that they had grown horns as a result of their pact with the devil, and that they are the architects of a worldwide scheme to enslave the non-Jewish races.

Because of the terrible history of anti-Semitism by Christians, it is incumbent for Christians who believe that the Antichrist is Jewish to thoroughly study their view. However, as we examine the arguments given earlier, we will find that this view is, in fact, quite doubtful. Let's consider the arguments one by one.

The Logical Argument

Does the person who rebuilds the Temple have to be considered the Messiah? Note that neither the Jewish governor Zerubbabel nor the Judean king Herod—both of whom rebuilt the Second Temple—were thought by the Jewish people to be the Messiah. They understood that interim Temples could be rebuilt at any time before the final restoration and the erection of the Temple by Messiah in Zechariah's vision. Futhermore, the Jews have, in the past, accepted Gentile rulers as messiahs. One example was the Gentile Persian emperor Cyrus, who made possible the rebuilding of the Second Temple through his edict and provision of materials and funds (2 Chronicles 36:22-23; Ezra 1:1-11). A notable modern example was the French general Napoleon Bonaparte. In fact, the very character of a covenant, such as that in Daniel 9:27, implies that it is with a foreign (Gentile) power. Jewish-Christian author Zola Levitt explains:

> It is an outsider who has to sign a legal covenant with the Jewish people, not one of their own. If, for example, Prime Minister Benjamin Netanyahu or David Bar-Illan of Israel came up with some idea for a seven-year peace plan, the Jews could adopt it or not. They wouldn't need a special covenant drawn up between them and one of their own citizens.[8]

The Lexical Argument

As for Daniel 11:37, the verse could easily be translated "the gods of his fathers," which is how it's rendered in more modern translations (for example, the New American Standard and New International versions). Even so, the focus of Daniel 11:36-39 is upon the Antichrist's usurption of deity and blasphemous actions against the true God. The only "god" he reveres is military power. His attack on the Holy Land, which includes Israel (verse 41), makes it clear that he has no special kinship with the Jews, but intends to control and ultimately destroy this Nation. Such actions are not usually taken against one's own people. In this light, since the object of Satan's attacks during the Tribulation are all ethinic Jews (Revelation 12:13), it would seem unlikely that the one Satan empowers would also be Jewish (Revelation 13:2). What's more, the description in Daniel 11:36-39 parallels the description given of a series of historical Gentiles who have persecuted the Jewish people (Pharaoh, Nebuchadnezzar, Antiochus IV Epiphanes, Titus, Hadrian, and other Roman, Muslim, and European rulers, such as Adolph Hitler, down through the centuries.[9]

The Linguistic Argument

There is nothing in the use of the word *anti* in *Anti*christ that linguistically requires the Antichrist to be "a counterfeit Christ." The word *anti* is a preposition that can have the possible meanings of 1) equivalence—one object set over against another as its equivalent (Matthew 5:38; 1 Corinthians 11:15); 2) exchange—one object opposing or distinct from another, or one object given or taken in return for the other (John 1:16; Romans 12:17); and 3) substitution—one object given or taken instead of the other (Matthew 2:2; Luke 11:11).[10] While the idea of *replacement* is denoted by these possible meanings, the idea of *counterfeit* is not. It must be derived from the context. But does any context indicate that the purpose or program of the Antichrist is to counterfeit Christ? It is stated that their will be "false christs" (Matthew 24:23-24), but this does not mean that the Antichrist will be one of these. His role seems to surpass these in both degree of deception and designated destruction (2 Thessalonians 2:8-12). Rather, the very spirit of the Antichrist is that he rejects and opposes Christ as an adversary (1 John 4:3; Revelation 17:14). It is not that the Antichrist seeks to copy and reflect Christ, but to conquer and replace Him. In addition, passages such as Revelation 19:19 and Daniel 11:36-39 affirm that the Antichrist will war *against* both Christ *and* the Jewish people. This would be a strange incongruity if he were a Jew seeking to counterfeit the Jewish Messiah.

Perhaps one of the most significant arguments against this view is the fact that the Antichrist's rule takes place during the period of time known as the "times of the Gentiles" (Luke 21:24), indicating that this one who is the final ruler of this period and epitomizes domination over Israel will be a Gentile. It would be contrary to the prophetic sequence revealed in Daniel to have a Jew rise to the status of a world ruler before the appointed time for the Jewish kingdom (Daniel 2:32-45; Romans 11:25). Furthermore, the Antichrist appears as the final ruler of this "times of the Gentiles." "If this is so," asks Arnold Fructenbaum, "how can a Jew be the last ruler at a time when only Gentiles can have the preeminence? To say the Antichrist is to be a Jew would contradict the very nature of the time of the Gentiles."[11]

We also need to remember that the Antichrist will lead a European alliance of Gentile nations (Daniel 7:8-24). In Daniel 2 and 7, all of the Gentile rulers mentioned come from within the boundaries of their empires. Would not the Antichrist, whose roots appear in the Roman empire (Daniel 2:40; 7:23-26; especially 9:26), also be circumscribed by his empire's ethnic Gentile boundaries? Moreover, the self-willed king and his actions, as described in Daniel 11:36-45, have remarkable similarities with the final remnant of the last Gentile kingdom of Daniel 2:42-45 and the fourth beast with its little horn in Daniel 7:8,19-27. These figures attack the God of Israel, the Jewish people, and the saints, and are interpreted as having an identity with the Roman empire. This fits Gentile action and origin better than Jewish. The same time period also seems to be described in Revelation 6-19, and the desecration of the Temple, described in Daniel 9:27, has parallel passages in Matthew 24:15, Mark 13:14, and 2 Thessalonians 2:4.[12]

Furthermore, it would be out of character for a Jew to lead the nations against his own people when the Tribulation is, by nature, a time of Jewish distress (Jeremiah 30:7; Daniel 12:1). This period is distinguished by the Gentile nations' persecution of the Jewish Nation (especially Jewish believers, Daniel 7:25; Matthew 24:9; Luke 21:12,17), even though there will clearly be Jewish defection (Matthew 24:10; Luke 21:16) and Jewish false prophets (Matthew 24:11,23-24; Revelation 13:11-17). In addition, in Revelation 13:1,11, two different beasts are described as arising from the "sea" and the "earth." The "sea" is a literary image that often indicates the "Gentile nations" (Daniel 7:2-3). This would mean that its opposite term here, "earth," would refer to "the Jews." There is support for this in that the Greek word can be used as a technical expression for "the Land of Israel." If this is so, then the first beast, which is from the sea, the Antichrist, is Gentile. And the second beast, the false prophet, is Jewish.

Finally, even if the Antichrist does play a key role in rebuilding the Temple, it is not necessary that he be considered the Messiah because in Orthodox Jewish thinking, the obligation to rebuild the Temple rests on the Jewish *people*, not the Messiah. The Jerusalem Talmud, along with other authoritative Jewish sources, holds that the Temple can be rebuilt before the coming of the Messiah. Therefore, while the Antichrist's association with the rebuilding of the Temple could be a means of identifying him as the Messiah, it need not be. While Zechariah 6:12 indicates that the Messiah ("the Branch") will build the Temple, Zechariah is referring to the Millennial Temple. This allows for the Third (Tribulation) Temple to be built by someone else. Moreover, the text in Revelation 11:2 that identifies the Antichrist with the Temple in its desecration does so in terms of Gentile occupation of the site. This would imply that the leader of this action of "trampling the holy city" would also be of "the nations" (i.e., a Gentile).

The Jewish View of the Antichrist During the Tribulation

In the final analysis, Scripture does not show the Antichrist to be Jewish or to have been accepted by the Jewish people as Messiah. He is simply regarded by them as another Gentile ruler who, like past Gentile rulers (for example, Cyrus), will be instrumental in effecting the conditions that enable the Jewish people to comply with their standing order to rebuild the Temple. For this the Antichrist will be given no greater acclaim than the previous pagans, who were considered unwitting agents of the Almighty (see Isaiah 44:28; 45:4-5). This is in line with the Jewish expectation for the future time of rebuilding. The Jewish sage Tosafot Yomtov, in a description of the Land of Israel at the end of days, says this in his commentary to the Mishnah: "It comes out that until the Davidic Kingdom, our enemies will have a little bit of rule over us, as was in the beginning of the Second Temple period" (*Ma'aser Sheni* 5:2). Temple activist Yirmiyahu Fischer explains that "here is where he deals with the rebuilding of the *Beit HaMikdash* ["Temple"]...and according to this a limited Jewish kingdom, even though not fully independent, is good enough to rebuild the *Beit HaMikdash* ["Temple"], as was the case in the time of Ezra [under Persian rule]."[13] Therefore, under the covenant of Antichrist, the Jewish people will be allowed a greater (though still limited) national sovereignty sufficient to rebuild the Temple—and there is no evidence that he will be regarded by them with any religious affection. This fits with what we know about the first half of the Tribulation, during which the Antichrist has not yet "tread under foot the holy city" (Revelation 11:2) or performed miraculous "signs" (2 Thessalonians 2:9; Revelation 13:3, 13-15) to prove his religious status.

One reason that Orthodox Jews will probably reject the Antichrist when he reveals his true identity at the midpoint of the Tribulation is that their own rabbinic literature, as well as their scriptures (Tanach), has prepared them for such a figure. In the *Jerusalem Talmud, Targum pseudo-Jonathan*, and the later Jewish apocalyptic *midrashim* (commentaries), a Jewish equivalent of the Antichrist appears by the name of Armilus. Works such as *Sefer Zerubbavel* and those by Saadiah Gaon reveal his characteristics in striking detail. According to these Jewish sources, Armilus will deceive the whole world into believing he is God and will reign over the whole world. He will come with ten kings and together they will fight over Jerusalem. Armilus is expected to persecute and banish Israel to the wilderness and it will be a time of unprecedented distress for Israel: There will be famine conditions, and the Gentiles will expel the Jews from their lands, and these Jews will hide in caves and towers. Then at the end, God will war against the host of Armilus, there will be a great deliverance for Israel, and the kingdom of heaven will spread over all the earth.

Other references further describe Armilus as arising from the Roman empire, having miraculous powers, and being born to a stone statue of a virgin (because of which he was called "the son of a stone"). It is also interesting that he makes this statue "the chief of all idolatry," with the result that "all the Gentiles will bow down to her, burn incense and pour out libations to her." This resembles Daniel's wicked "king" and "coming prince" and his "abomination of desolation" (Daniel 11:1-31, 36-37), and especially the book of Revelation's statue of the beast which is brought to life and made an object of worship (Revelation 13:4, 15). So even though Orthodox Jews are unbelievers from the Christian viewpoint, they believe their own Bible and have an "Antichrist" in their own traditions. For this reason, as Rabbi Richman states in the quote at the beginning of this chapter, they will be as opposed to the Antichrist's pagan program and religious demands for worship, as will be the Tribulation saints.

The Desecration of the Temple

The Antichrist's desecration of the Temple—especially its Holy of Holies—will render the Temple inoperative due to ritual impurity, an act symbolized by the cessation of the sacrificial system (Daniel 9:27). To understand why his future act will have such a consequence, let's consider what the Bible has in mind when it speaks of the Temple's desecration.

According to the usage of the words that speak of ritual impurity, the Temple can be the object of both "desecration" (Hebrew, *tame'*) and "defilement" (Hebrew, *chalal*).[14] The *defilement* of the Temple implies that a transgressor is in a persistent and deliberate condition of defiling. In Leviticus 15:31 the people of Israel are warned not to incur uncleanness lest they die in this state (having neglecting purification) and thereby "defile My tabernacle." The same is said for the person who incurs corpse impurity and fails to obtain purification (Numbers 19:13,20). And, idolatry indirectly defiles the Temple by directly defiling the idolater (2 Chronicles 36:14; Ezekiel 23:38-39). The presence of idols within the Temple can also bring defilement (Jeremiah 7:30; 16:18; 32:34). In each of these cases we have a deliberate act (called in Numbers 15:30 "the soul that acts with a high hand").

The chief agent of *desecration* is the invasion of a foreign element into the Temple. The Bible does not unambiguously support the notion that foreigners were intrinsically unclean;[15] however, the idea developed during the intertestamental period and appears in various forms in the first century A.D.[16] Regardless of whether a foreigner was considered to be unclean or not, his presence in the Temple was viewed as a form of desecration (see Ezekiel 25:3 of the Babylonians). We see this expressed in Ezekiel 7:21-24, where "foreigners" (verse 21) and "the worst of the nations" (verse 24) are pictured as "robbers" (verse 22) invading the Temple and entering into the Holy Place (called here "My secret place").[17] As a result, three times in these verses the Temple is the object of "defilement" (*chalal*). In like manner, in Psalm 74:7, the Temple, connected here with the divine name, is considered "defiled" by the invading Babylonians. While God Himself is sometimes seen as the *causative* agent of desecration (see Ezekiel 24:21), He is not the *responsible* agent, since He employs secondary agents (foreigners) to execute His judgment, and holds them accountable for any arrogance displayed in being so used (see Isaiah 14:4-6; Habakkuk 1:6; 2:4-5).

These descriptions indicate that the Temple is defiled by a descending degree of violations—from the highest degree (intentional acts that culminate in rebellion and the permanent presence of idols) to the least degree (the negligent acts of individual Israelites). The Antichrist's act, of course, will be of the highest order: an invasion of the Temple and the setting up of himself as an object of worship (2 Thessalonians 2:4). It is this act that is called, by Daniel and

Jesus, "the abomination of desolation." In order to make the proper connection between this act and the horrific meaning this term has to Orthodox Jews, it is necessary that we first survey the use of the term "abomination" in the Bible.

The Language of "Abomination"

"Abomination" language refers to a group of related terms all translated by the general word "abomination." Members of this word group include 1) "abomination, detestable thing" (Hebrew, *piggûl*), used only four times (Leviticus 7:18; 19:7; Isaiah 65:4; Ezekiel 4:14) for edible meats that had become detestable (probably "rotten") and were not to be eaten;[18] 2) "detestable, offensive, repulsive" (Hebrew, *to'ebah*) always used negatively to refer to acts that were foreign to Israelite ethical standards (see Genesis 43:32; 46:34) or of that which was repugnant to God, including the illegitimate use of "unclean animals" for sacrifice (Leviticus 14:3), pagan deities (2 Kings 23:13), idolatrous images (Deuteronomy 27:15), (cultic) prostitution (Deuteronomy 23:18), "false weights" (i.e., inaccurate accounting—Proverbs 11:1), perverse attitudes (Proverbs 11:20), lying speech (Proverbs 12:22), illegitimate sacrifices (Proverbs 15:8; Isaiah 1:13), sorcery (Deuteronomy 18:12), sexual deviations (often cultic—Leviticus 18:22; 20:13), and anything associated with Canaanite cultic activity (Leviticus 18:26; see also frequent uses in Ezekiel); and 3) "abominable act, wicked device" (Hebrew, *zimah*, from the root *zaman*), used of acts of lewdness such as unchastity and incest (Leviticus 18:17; 19:29; Jeremiah 13:27; Ezekiel 16:36,43,58; 22:9; 23:27-29,35,48-49; 24:13; Hosea 2:10), lustful crime (Judges 20:6), immorality (Leviticus 20:14), and evil machinations, plans (Psalm 140:8).

The term directly associated with the term "abomination" in the book of Daniel is a form of the Hebrew root *shaqatz*. Two nouns (*sheqetz* and *shiqqûtz*) are derived from this root—the first always related to unclean animals (for dietary purposes), especially loathsome creatures such as "swarming things" (Leviticus 11:10) and "creeping things" (Isaiah 66:17),[19] and the second for idols as "detestable things" and the idolatrous practices associated with them[20] (Deuteronomy 29:17; 1 Kings 11:5,7; 2 Kings 23:13,24; 2 Chronicles 15:8; Isaiah 66:3; Jeremiah 4:1; 7:30; 13:27; 16:18; 32:34; Ezekiel 5:11; 7:20; 11:18,21; 20:7-8,30; 37:23; Nahum 3:6; Zechariah 9:7). The root *shaqatz* appears 45 times in the Old Testament primarily as a technical term denoting animals and other things that rendered the Israelite "unclean." The term is used of any detestable thing (Hosea 9:10; Nahum 3:6; Zechariah 9:7), but predominately in connection with idolatrous practices. In Jeremiah 7:30-32 the prophet decries the desecration of the

Temple by the erection of "abominations" (*shiqûtzim*) in the Holy Place. Here the reference must be to the images of idols, referred to by hypocatasasis as "detestable, or horrible things." In its verbal form (occurring only in the Pi'el as *shiqqetz*) it appears seven times (Leviticus 7:18; 19:7; Isaiah 65:4; Ezekiel 4:14) with the factitive meaning of "abhor, detest," but since what is detested is that which defiles, it has a causative connotation of "contaminate" or "make abominable."[21]

From this technical survey of terms it can be seen that acts of ritual impurity and especially the threat of foreign invasion of the Temple were viewed by the Israelites as ultimate violations of sanctity and as a sign of judgment. For this reason, they were extremely careful to prevent such acts, and in the time of the Second Temple had erected a boundary fence, the *Soreg*, between the Court of the Gentiles and the Court of the Israelites, with a warning inscription promising death to any non-Israelite who passed beyond it into the Court of the Israelites. The New Testament (Acts 21:27-28) records a Jewish crowd's violent reaction to Paul when they mistakenly believed that he had taken a Gentile proselyte (Titus) into the Temple to offer sacrifice. The specific accusation against Paul was that he had "defiled this holy place" (the Temple—verse 28).

Knowing this, we can understand why the Antichrist's act of desecration will be such a climatic event and why the desecration of the Temple appears as the signal event bringing the intensification of God's wrath in the second half of the Tribulation (Matthew 24:15; Mark 13:14). However, these multifaceted elements of desecration were loaded into a single phrase by Daniel (and repeated in the New Testament by Jesus and Paul) to epitomize the highest expression of desecration—"abomination of desolation"—and to embody it in an eschatological Desecrator.

The Meaning of the Phrase "Abomination of Desolation"

The phrase "abomination of desolation" or "desolating abomination" (Hebrew, *shiqqûtz m^eshomem*) occurs in Hebrew only in Daniel (9:27; 11:31; 12:11). The form of the Hebrew term for "desolation" in this phrase is the *Pol'el* participle *shomem* or *m^eshomem*, which has a range of verbal meanings: "devastate, desolate, desert, appall," with nominal derivatives: "waste, horror, devastation, appallment." Hermann Austel, in his study of this term, says that "basic to the idea of the root is the desolation caused by some great disaster, usually as a result of divine judgment."[22] Perhaps for this reason it has also been used to describe an attitude of appalling horror due to criminal and barbaric acts of idolatry.[23] The *Pol'el* here has a causative (or better, factitive) force similar to the use of the *Hiphil*, except that the *Hiphil* generally involves a physical devastation, while the *Pol'el* seems to put more stress on the fact that someone has caused (active) the Sanctuary or altar to be desecrated, thus rendering it unfit for the worship and service of God. In Daniel, two nuances of the term "desolation due to war" and "desolation due to idolatry" are combined in Daniel 8:13, which describes the condition of Jerusalem under foreign domination: "How long will the vision about the regular sacrifice apply, while the transgression *causes horror*, so as to allow both the holy place and the host *to be trampled?*"[24] This is very similar to the description of Jerusalem in Daniel 12:11, where a foreign invader has both abolished the regular sacrifice and substituted it with "the abomination of desolation." When combined with the Hebrew term for "abomination" (*shiqqûtz*), the idea of the forcible intrusion of idolatry into a place of sanctity in order to defile it is significantly intensified.

In the New Testament, the expression "abomination of desolation" appears in Greek as *bdelugma tes eremōseōs* (Matthew 24:15; Mark 13:14; Luke 21:20). The first part of this phrase, the word *bdelugma* ("abomination"), is used in the New Testament four times (Luke 16:15; Revelation 7:4-5; 21:27), and in the Septuagint (Greek translation of the Old Testament) 17 times to translate the Hebrew *shiqqûtz*.[25] The term *bdelugma* comes from a root term with the meanings "to make foul" and "to stink." Thus it has the basic idea of something that makes one feel nauseous, and thus by transference, is psychologically or morally abhorrent and detestable. As with the Hebrew meaning in the Old Testament, the Greek term is applied particularly to idols or associated with idolatrous practices,[26] and in the Septuagint some usages are paralleled by the word "lawlessness" (Greek, *anomia*). This supports the allusion to the abomination of desolation in 2 Thessalonians 2:3, which describes the same figure using the phrase "man of lawlessness."[27] In this regard *bdelugma* appears as an expression of antithesis between the divine and human wills, as well as denoting the repugnance of the ungodly to the will of God.[28] It is also used in Luke 16:15 to speak of God's repugnance toward human pride (i.e., to things highly esteemed by men, which is tantamount to idolatry).[29]

The word "desolation" (Greek, *eremōseōs*) is the genitive feminine singular of a root which signifies "to lay waste, make desolate, bring to ruin" (see Matthew 12:25; Luke 11:17; Revelation 17:16; 18:17,19). It is used most commonly in the Septuagint for *meshomem* or its cognates (see Leviticus 26:34-35; Psalm

73:19; 2 Chronicles 30:7; 36:21; Jeremiah 4:7), generally in reference to the desolation of the Land as a result of desecration and exile. Most likely this is the concept we see described in the Septuagint's use of *eremōseōs* in Daniel 9:27.

The form of the expression "abomination of desolation" (both in Hebrew and Greek) has been considered an anomalous construction in grammatical terms. A number of theories have been offered to explain this,[30] however, the literary and theological linkage of both the terms *shiqqûtz* ("abomination") and *meshomem* ("desolation") in the prophetic writings of Jeremiah and Ezekiel[31] appear to provide the best explanation. These texts, especially with their promise of a resolution of the dilemma for the Temple, which in part governed Daniel's concern (Jeremiah 25:11-12; Daniel 9:2), may well have influenced this. Thus we may find it helpful to do a brief survey of the usage of these terms in Jeremiah and Ezekiel.

In both Jeremiah and Ezekiel, frequent mention is made of "abominations" and "desolations" (Jeremiah 4:1,27; 7:10; 44:22; Ezekiel 5:11,14-15; 7:20),[32] idolatry that has desecrated the Holy Place, and foreign invaders who will further desecrate and destroy the Temple (see Jeremiah 4:6-8; Ezekiel 6:11; 7:20-23). Jeremiah 44:22 in particular states that Israel's "abominations" have caused the desolation of the Land and made it "an object of horror" (see Ezekiel 5:11,15; 7:20-24; 36:19-21). Jesus' message was a continuation of what the biblical prophets proclaimed, and His frequent citations from Jeremiah and Zechariah make it certain that He and the disciples were evaluating their generation in light of the prophecies found in those books. As we saw in chapter 12, the background for Jesus' "cleansing of the Temple" was most likely Jeremiah's Temple sermon, and it was in this context that He made His predictions about the destruction of the Temple. The Olivet Discourse contains striking resemblances to the prophetic warnings of judgment found in Ezekiel and Jeremiah. If these are then linked with the citation from Daniel, we see a pattern of dependence upon collections of prophetic texts that were themselves dependent upon one another.

The "Abomination of Desolation" in Daniel 9:27

In Daniel 9:27 we read that "on the wing of abominations will come one who makes desolate." This wording is the basis for the term "abomination of desolation" that we find in the New Testament. Since we have already examined the meanings of the words for "abomination" and "desolation," let's look carefully at the meaning of this new term, "wing." It is clear that this term (Hebrew, *kᵉnaf*) has a direct association with the "abomination of desolation" and most likely describes the *place* where it will occur in relation to the Temple. The word has been the subject of extensive controversy and fanciful interpretation in both ancient and modern commentaries. Among Jewish commentators, Abarbanel simply translated it as "because" (leaving the derivation of the term unexplained) and applying "abominations" to the sins of the Jewish Nation: "because of the abomination of the Jews, the city and the Temple are desolate." On the other hand, Rabbi Avraham bar Chiya attributed the cause of "abomination" and "desolation" to the Gentile nations, rendering the clause "*to the corners of the world* they [the nations ruling the world after the destruction of the Temple] will spread abomination and desolation." In a similar fashion, Radak interprets the term metaphorically as "spread" (after the imagery of "wings," compare Ruth 2:12 with 3:9), but applies it loosely and thus avoids interpreting the cause of "abomination" and "desolation," paraphrasing the clause as "the spread of abominations will cause people to be astonished" (*mᵉshomem*).

Christian scholars have exhibited no less diversity in their explanations for the form suggesting emendations to read "and in its place," "on their base," "lord of wing," or "winged one" (on the model of "horned one," a title of the Syrian god of heaven, see Daniel 8:6,20).[33] Other interpretations have ranged from the poetic "rapid flight" (see "wings of the dawn," Psalm 139:9),[34] "shall rise up" (taking *kᵉnaf* as figurative of an image of an eagle which was placed above[35] and "over spreading" (KJV), to the literal "pinnacle [of Temple]," the "horns [of the altar]," or as a "winged [statute or solar disk]." One plausible theory proposes that *shiqqûtz mᵉshomem* ("abomination that makes desolate") is a word play on a foreign deity, and if so, it would be consistent to see *kᵉnaf* ("wing") having a similar connotation—in this regard the idea of "winged" statues,[36] or as in the Syriac version, which adds to the term "abomination" the word "standard" or "emblem."[37] The comparative Ugaritic term *B'l Knp* ("lord of the wing") may support this since the image of the Syrian *Ba'al Shamin* was generally represented on monuments in the form of an eagle.

Along this line of interpretation I suggest that *kᵉnaf* might suggest the location where the "abomination of desolation" is placed: in the Holy of Holies in relation to the winged cherubim of the Ark of the Covenant. The Septuagint (followed by the Vulgate) translated the Hebrew word *kᵉnaf* to the Greek word *pterugion* to designate any projecting extremity or "wing-like projections." In addition, in the text of Daniel, the mention of "sacrifices" just before this term may imply a ritual association. For this reason it is often connected with the "pinnacle" of the Temple (see Matthew 4:5; Luke 4:9) or the "horned" altar of the Temple.[38] However, Paul's statement in 2 Thessalonians 2:4 that the "man of law-lessness" will seat himself in the innermost part of the Temple (*naos*) may suggest another possibility. If the Antichrist follows the precedent of previous desecrators, such as Manasseh, who replaced the Ark of the Covenant with an idolatrous image of Asherah (see 2 Kings 21:7; 2 Chronicles 33:7; 35:3), such an action might be expected. Christian commentator Frederick Tatford proposed this when he wrote: "Evidently the audacious rebel will blasphemously take his seat in the *sanctum sanctorum* itself."[39] In addition, if the Antichrist is enthroning himself to proclaim that he is deity, there is no better place for him to do this than between the wings of the cherubim atop the Mercy Seat of the Ark, where the God of Israel's divine presence was manifested in ages past. Indeed, Paul states in 2 Thessalonians 2:4 that he "seats himself *in the Temple of God, showing himself as God*" (emphasis added). In the days of the Tabernacle and the First Temple, the throne of the Lord was said to be "seated above or between the cherubim" (Psalm 80:1; 99:1),[40] and numerous archaeological reliefs portray rulers sitting on winged thrones. Therefore, for the Antichrist to usurp "the throne of the Lord" as his own would certainly be the height of blasphemy, desecration, and defilement for God and the Temple.

Some say that this would be possible only if the Ark of the Covenant were recovered. However, the Antichrist could create his own version of an Ark-throne and install it in the Holy of Holies. Whatever the case, if the Antichrist were to enter the Holy Place and approach the Ark without suffering physical consequences, he would be, in effect, declaring his superiority over the God of Israel. To those who believe the Temple is inviolable and the Ark an untouchable object of divine power, such a feat will prove to a strong delusion, and those who accept the Antichrist's claim of divinity will have sealed their spiritual doom (2 Thessalonians 2:10-12).

The Identification of the Abomination of Desolation

Most critical scholars have dismissed the eschatological interpretation of the Temple desecrator in Daniel 9:27 by claiming it refers to Antiochus IV Epiphanes, who in December (25 Kislev) 167 B.C. committed a desolation in the Temple by setting up an idolatrous image and sacrificing an unclean animal on the altar. Preterists seek to see the abomination of desolation and the figure of the desolator in Daniel 9:27 as fulfilled in the events of the Roman invasion of Jerusalem and the destruction of the Temple in A.D. 70. However, the Roman invasion, though a defiling act, does not match the idolatrous dimensions and specific nature of placement in the Temple as defined by the passages in Daniel, the Gospels, and 2 Thessalonians. The Roman conqueror Titus did not seat himself in the Temple as 2 Thessalonians 2:4 describes (some historical sources even record that he did not want to destroy it!), nor was he destroyed as described in Daniel 9:27. Rather, as the Arch of Titus' Triumph in Rome today still reveals, he paraded even the Temple vessels through the streets of Rome and lived on to enjoy the rewards of his victory.

The figure and activities of the "little horn," Antiochus IV Epiphanes, which were predicted in Daniel 8:9-25 and 11:5-20, contain much that is typical of the description of the "little horn" Antichrist of Daniel 8:8-13 and the agent of destruction in Daniel 11:31. And, the Roman conquest predicted in the Gospels (Luke 21:20-24) certainly has parallels to both previous and yet future invasions of Jerusalem. However, if we are seeking exact correspondences leading to a *complete* fulfillment in these events, we have no historical support for our identification.[41]

Other scholars have said, "As far as the use of *shaqatz* in Daniel is concerned, the meaning of the 'abomination of desolation' seems to go beyond the idea of idol with an eschatological dimension....To limit its interpretation to Antiochus Epiphanes...seems to contradict the [New Testament] use of the text in an eschatological perspective."[42] Rather, Antiochus IV Epiphanes is but another figure in a succession of anti-theocratic rulers whose acts of desecration move toward a climax of fulfillment in the last days.

Still other scholars have offered their interpretations for the "abomination of desolation" as a past fulfillment. I will simply list these with a brief observation about each: 1) *The Statue of Titus erected on the side of the desolated Temple* (popular in Patristic times) is more likely a tradition that developed from the memory of Roman standards erected in the Temple area by order of Titus. 2) *Statues erected by Pilate and Hadrian.* All we know for certain is that Pilate brought Roman standards into the Temple, which had medallions with an image of the emperor. As to the site of the equestrian statue, John Wilkinson argues that it would not have been at the site of the Temple itself, but that this area would have remained free of such objects so that the site could later be rebuilt by the Jews as a show of Roman benevolence.[43] 3) *Caligula's attempted desecration*. The events of A.D. 33–40 are believed to have created a fear that although Caligula had attempted to erect a pagan statue in the Temple and failed, another might succeed. However, this whole theory has been shown to be implausible on textual and historical grounds.[44] 4) *The invading Roman army of* A.D. 70. If the Roman invasion that desecrated and destroyed the Temple in A.D. 70 was the fulfillment of the abomination of desolation, we are left without a complete correspondence with Daniel 9:27, for both the covenant is missing and the destruction of the desolator would have to be construed differently.

The Eschatological Alternative

The only other alternative is that of an *eschatological* (future) desolator, identified by other texts as the Antimessiah or Antichrist.[45] In eschatological contexts, both Jesus and Paul refer to Daniel 9:27.[46] Jesus references the passage in Matthew 24:15 and Mark 13:14 in proclamations about future events (see chapter 12), and almost all of the details of Daniel 9:27 are explicitly or implicitly alluded to by Paul in his explanation of the Day of the Lord in 2 Thessalonians 2:3-9. With all the other views, we are left with unresolved details that either must be harmonized by reading the Bible in other than a literal, historical manner or by dismissing details altogether. One factor in favor of the eschatological view is that it has the precedence of types that await their antitype to ultimately fulfill them. Furthermore, John McLean, in his doctoral dissertation[47] at the University of Michigan, has demonstrated that Daniel's "seventieth week"—and especially the concept of the "abomination of desolation"—influenced the literary structure of the Olivet Discourse in the Synoptic Gospels and the judgment section of the book of Revelation.[48] Jesus' interpretation of the order of the events of the seventieth week, in the context of prophetic history, appears to confirm an eschatological interpretation for Daniel 9:27. In Matthew 24:7-14 Jesus predicts that persecution, suffering, and wars would continue to the end of the age, climaxing in a time of unparalleled distress (verses 21-22— i.e., "the time of Jacob's distress," see also Daniel 12:1; Jeremiah 30:7). Only *after* these events does Jesus make reference to Daniel 9:27 (see Matthew 24:15), or the abomination of desolation.

If the 70 weeks are supposed to run sequentially, without interruption, then why does Jesus place this intervening period *before* the fulfillment of the events of the seventieth week? Matthew in particular reveals that Jesus' preview of the future was in the context of answering His disciple's questions about His second coming and the end of the age (Matthew 24:3). Jesus here explains why His coming is necessary (for divine intervention and national repentance, verses 2/-31; see also Zechariah 12:9-10) and when it will occur ("after the Tribulation of those days," verse 29). According to Matthew,[49] the events described in this period prior to the Messianic advent could *not* have been fulfilled in A.D. 70 with the destruction of Jerusalem, since these events usher in and terminate with the coming of Messiah.[50] In the New Testament, Paul presents the most detailed treatment of Daniel's prophecy related to the Temple. Let's look to what Paul says, and see if he can shed further light on the desecration of the Temple.

Paul's Prophecy of Trouble in the Temple

Paul's second epistle to the Thessalonians has been called "the tale of the two *parousias*," because in it is contained both the "appearance" (Greek, *parousia*) of Christ and of the Antichrist.[51] Paul most likely wrote this epistle in response to a report he received[52] in response to his first epistle to the Thessalonians. In particular, word came to him of a group of Christian "negligents" who had abandoned the normal affairs of life because they understood that Paul had said Christ's return was imminent (2 Thessalonians 2:6-15). Their erroneous application (not erroneous understanding) of Paul's teaching about preparation for the last days (1 Thessalonians 5:1-11) was evidence of prophetic confusion. Apparently some were teaching that the end times were already at hand (2 Thessalonians 2:2), and therefore justified negligence in the normal affairs of life. In this epistle Paul offers a correction to this misunderstanding, explaining that before the appearance of the Messiah must come the appearance of the Antichrist (2 Thessalonians 2:3-9). The setting for the discussion about "the apostasy" (verse 3a), "the man of lawlessness" (verse 3b), "the son of destruction" (verse 3c), and "that lawless one" (verse 8) is unquestionably eschatological, as are the references to the "coming" of Christ (verse 1—rapture of church; verse 8—revelation of Christ) and "the Day of the Lord" (verse 2b).[53] Further, the eschatological events Paul describes in verses 3b-12 clearly precede this "Day of the Lord" at which time the Antichrist will be destroyed (verse 8).

The Nature of the Temple Desecrator

The nature of the Temple desecrator (Antichrist) is developed in Paul's text by the phrases[54] "the man of lawlessness" and "the son of destruction" (2 Thessalonians 2:3). The term "lawlessness" (Greek, *anomias*) describes his opposition to the divine order (demonstrated in verse 4), while the term "destruction" (Greek, *apoleias*) refers to his destiny—namely, destined for "destruction" or "perdition" (see verse 8). The fact that this one is "revealed" *(apokaluphte)* in verse 3, and that the verb is in the emphatic position, may parallel Matthew 24:15 and Mark 13:14 in their announcement of the Temple's desecration as a signal event. It is by this act that the nature of the Antichrist is manifested to the world, although some argue that the term "revealed" could also imply the supernatural (satanic) character of the Antichrist's coming as in a "revelation" or "manifestation" like that of Christ (verse 9).[55] In this light Frank Hughes notes, "Obviously the Man of Lawlessness ...is a quasi-divine figure, a kind of evil 'divine man,' some intermediate figure between God and humanity."[56] The Antichrist's nature is further qualified by the term "[he] who opposes" (Greek, *antikeimenos*) in verse 4. The Septuagint uses this root in rendering the Hebrew noun *satan* ("adversary") in 1 Kings 11:25, and the Hebrew verb *satan* ("prosecute") in Zechariah 3:1. Elsewhere Paul uses this term to denote Satan as the supreme adversary of God and the saints (see 1 Timothy 5:14). A similar idea is expressed here in 2 Thessalonians 2:9 when it states that the Antichrist's coming is "in accord with the activity of Satan."[57] This offers another parallel to the Olivet Discourse and Jesus' prediction that false prophets and false messiahs would arise before the advent of the true Messiah, showing "signs and false wonders" that lead people into deception (compare 2 Thessalonians 2:9-10 with Matthew 24:24; Mark 13:22).

An Analysis of Temple Desecration

The act of Temple desecration is introduced in verse 4 by the use of the middle voice with its reflexive nuance to emphasize the autonomy of action: "exalts himself." The sphere of the Antichrist's self-elevation is specified as "over every so-called god or object of worship" (verse 4). Since the setting is Jerusalem during the Tribulation, this may mean that he not only ranks himself superior to every false messiah that has appeared in the first half of that period, but also to all the supreme beings worshiped by the various religions of the world ("so-called gods"). Yet the phrase "object of worship" may be pointing us to the Temple and its sacred vessels. The Antichrist's ultimate offense, however, is that of elevating himself above the only true God by enthroning himself in the place of deity within "the Temple of God" to "display himself" (Greek, *apodeiknunta*) as God (Greek, literally, "that he is God"). This act fulfills Daniel's prediction that the Antichrist "will exalt and magnify himself above every god, and speak monstrous things against the God of gods" (Daniel 11:36), and has allusions to Isaiah 14:13-14 and Ezekiel 28:2, where we read about figures who seek to "raise [their] throne above the stars of God," "make [themselves] like the Most High," and declare, "I am a god; I sit in the seat of the gods."

The Literal Nature of Temple Desecration

It is significant to observe that Paul calls the Tribulation Temple "the Temple *of God*" (2 Thessalonians 2:4). Apparently this future Temple will be recognized as legitimate otherwise it could not be desecrated. John Townsend stated in his Harvard dissertation on this point: "Since Paul sets the desecration of the Temple beside the ultimate blasphemy of proclaiming oneself to be God and since he regards these acts as the climax of the evil which is to precede the *parousia* [Christ's second coming], there can be no doubt of Paul's veneration for this Temple."[58] Furthermore, this phrase cannot be interpreted as metaphorical of the church, with the "man of lawlessness" as an apostate "Christian" or "Christianity" in the present age, as some have suggested.[59] Matthew and Mark are clearly speaking of a literal Temple when they write that the "abomination of desolation" will be "standing in the holy place" (Matthew 24:15) "where it should not be" (Mark 13:14).[60] To Mark's first-century audience, this could only mean one place; the Jewish Temple in Jerusalem.

There are additional reasons for rejecting the symbolic interpretation of 2 Thessalonians 2:4 and accepting the fact that Paul is talking about a literal Temple: 1) In the few places where Paul used the Greek word *naos* ("temple") to mean something other than the actual Holy Place within the Jerusalem Temple, he always explained his special meaning so that his readers would understand his metaphorical usage.[61] 2) The word "temple" is preceded by a definite article ("the temple"), which stands in contrast to Paul's analogical usage, where "temple" is almost always anartharous ("a temple").[62] For this reason George Milligan states: "...the nature of the context, the use of such a local term as καθίσαι ["sits down"] and the twice-repeated def. art. (τὸν ναὸν τοῦ θεοῦ) ["the temple of God"] all point to a literal reference in the present instance...."[63] 3) "The temple of God" is the direct object of the verb "sits down" (Greek, *kathisai),* a verb suggesting a definite locality, not an institution. Another verb for "enthronement" or "usurpation" would have been used to express the symbolic sense had it, rather than the literal act of "taking a seat," been intended. 4) Second Thessalonians 2:4 reflects a dependence upon Daniel (Daniel 9:27; 11:31-36; 12:11),[64] and the only Temple that could have been understood in Daniel was the Jerusalem Temple. This would also be the case in Jesus' use of Daniel 9:27 (see Matthew 24:15; Mark 13:14), with which Paul was undoubtedly familiar and which most likely informed Paul's eschatology on this point. 5) The ante-Nicene church fathers interpreted "the temple of God" in 2 Thessalonians 2:4 to mean the Jerusalem Temple, as well as to refer to a literal seating of the Antichrist. For example, in A.D. 185 Irenaeus wrote, "when this Antichrist shall have devastated all things in this world, he will reign for three years and six months, and sit in the Temple at Jerusalem; and then the Lord will come from heaven in the clouds, in the glory of the Father, sending this man and those who follow him into the lake of fire; but bringing in for the righteous the times of the kingdom." By contrast, the symbolic or "spiritual" use of the church for the Temple does not appear in developed form until the third century A.D. with Origen, who was influenced by the allegorical interpretations of the Hellenistic idealist school of Philo.

In like manner, just as 2 Thessalonians 2:4 must be understood to be speaking of a literal Temple, so must the Antichrist's action of seating himself and displaying himself as being God be understood as literal. The impossibility of taking this verse in a metaphorical sense can be demonstrated with two points: First, if part of the clause is literal (the phrase "the temple of God"), it would be inconsistent with the structure of the verse to make the whole clause figurative.[65] Second, the historical figures who desecrated the Temple in the First and Second Temple eras committed *physical* acts against a *material* Temple. If the Antichrist is the antitype of these previous desecrators, then his actions would need to precisely parallel theirs in order to adequately fulfill the correspondence.

The Antichrist as Temple Desecrator

In Revelation 13:1-10 the ascent of the Antichrist and his usurpation of divine prerogatives is described with allusions drawn from the career of Daniel's "little horn" (Daniel 7:8,24-25).[66] The blended qualities of insolent blasphemy toward God and seductive religious influence over men are seen as traits common to both figures and characterize the Antichrist, like Satan, as "the god of this world" (2 Corinthians 4:4; see also John 12:31). Some scholars believe there is a reference to the Antichrist's desecration of the Temple in Revelation 13:6, where an epexegetical clause develops the Antichrist's blasphemy against God: "...to blaspheme His name and His tabernacle, [and or that is] those who dwell in heaven." In that citation of Revelation 13:6 I have deliberately included the variants the original manuscripts give for this text to reveal the problem of how the phrase "His tabernacle" is to be understood. If we take the majority reading with the conjunction "and" included (which has extensive support in the versions), "His tabernacle" becomes another in the list of the objects blasphemed by the Antichrist: God's name, God's dwelling place, *and* God's heavenly dwellers. In this case "His tabernacle" might have reference to the earthly Temple, and "His name" in apposition to "His tabernacle" might have reference to the *Shekinah*. If we take the witness of the "better manuscripts," which omit "and"[67] (following the *UBS4* Greek text), the clause "those who dwell in heaven" is in apposition to "His tabernacle" as the place those in heaven occupy—namely, the heavenly Temple. In this case the Antichrist is pictured as attacking heaven as the source of the authority he is usurping on earth. Even so, this might imply that the next step from the desecration of God's name and His heavenly Temple (by blasphemy) would be the actual desecration of the earthly Temple (by usurpation).

The Degree of the Antichrist's Desecration

The desecration (*chalal*) of the Temple does not necessarily *render* the Temple unholy (by the addition of the element of uncleanness), but only *deprives* it of holiness.[68] But desecration usually precedes defilement (*tame'*), which not only is the acquisition of a state of uncleanness, but also implies an alienation requiring a purification. The Sanctuary (as the representative place of God's name), like the Land of Israel, remains holy even when desecrated and defiled because it, like the Land, is non-tangible and ultimately God's possession. However, the vessels within the Temple and the physical structure of the Temple itself can become defiled.

Foreigners who enter the Temple generally bring about only desecration, not defilement, and for this reason the Second Temple could be rebuilt after its desecration and destruction by the Babylonians without requiring a purification ceremony (Ezra 3:2-13). However, the Second Temple later required purification (*channukah*, "dedication") because an apostate Israelite priest sacrificed an unclean animal (a sow) on the altar (under orders of the Seleucid king Antiochus IV Epiphanes) and thereby brought defilement. In addition, the presence of idols or idolatrous practices is an "abomination" (*shiqqûtz*) that brings both desecration and defilement to the Temple and the Land, which has harbored such abominations. This is the ultimate loss, since now both the Temple and Land are rendered common (*chôl*) and can be violated as any other place.[69]

When the Antichrist enters the Holy of Holies, blasphemously establishes himself as god (an idol), and accepts worship (an idolatrous practice), then the Temple complex and the entire Land of Israel will be put into a state of ritual defilement. It is the immense gravity of the Antichrist's act that demands restoration and ritual purification, and which results in the Messiah's advent to destroy the desecrator (Daniel 9:27; Zechariah 14:3-4,12-13; Revelation 19:17-21), restore the Land (Zechariah 14:10), and rebuild and consecrate the Temple (Zechariah 6:12; Daniel 9:24).

Building the Tribulation Temple

The restoration of the earthly Temple mentioned in Revelation 11:1 apparently will take place *prior* to the mid-point of the seventieth week, since at that point the "abomination of desolation" will have taken place in its Holy Place (see Daniel 9:27; Matthew 24:15; Mark 13:14; 2 Thessalonians 2:4). Accordingly, this interpretation envisions the building of the Third Temple and the reinstitution of the sacrificial service (note "the altar" in Revelation 11:1) at a time prior to the Messianic era, since these events are associated with the advent of the Messiah and the restoration of national Israel. If the attitude of that time is the same as that of Orthodox Jews in the Temple movement today, this Temple could simply be built in obedience to the standing command to "construct a sanctuary for Me" (Exodus 25:8), taking advantage of the pact made possible by the Antichrist, the Gentile world leader. As we saw earlier, the ability of the Jewish leaders to rebuild the Temple does not require that the Antichrist be accepted by them as the Messiah. Since the Temple and those who worship in it appear to have God's favor, and the two witnesses seem to be associated with it, it is also probable that this Third Temple will serve as a meeting place for Jewish believers just as the Second Temple did (Acts 2:46; 3:1).

On the other hand, based on the unparalleled deception predicted for this period (2 Thessalonians 2:9-12), it is also possible that those who build the Temple will have been deceived to believe that the covenant made with the "prince that shall come" (Antichrist) will have ushered in the Messianic era, since one of the signs of this era's arrival is the rebuilding of the Temple through Gentile assistance (Zechariah 6:12-13). We may add to this the works of the false prophet (Revelation 13:11-15), whose "great signs" (Revelation 13:13) may initially convince many Jews that their Messiah has arrived. This accords with the prediction of false messiahs who make their appearance during the first half of the seventieth week (see Matthew 24:5,11; Mark 13:5-6). However, the work of this false prophet will be to lead the unbelieving world to worship the Antichrist as a god (Revelation 13:15). Despite the tremendous deception of this day, it appears that the Orthodox Jewish worshipers at the Temple (and especially Jewish believers) will reject the false prophet's claims, and this may be what prompts the Antichrist to invade and desecrate the Temple and trample down the Holy City (Revelation 11:2; see also Zechariah 12:2; 14:2). Jewish believers will recognize this as the sign of the "abomination of desolation" predicted by Daniel, Jesus, and Paul (Daniel 9:27; Matthew 24:15; Mark 13:14; 2 Thessalonians 2:4) and will flee the city (Matthew 24:16-20), except for the two witnesses, who remain to oppose the Antichrist and give a worldwide demonstration of God's power (Revelation 11:5-6, 11-12). Later, at the climax of the seventieth week, the Antichrist will be destroyed as the true Messiah appears, and ultimately restores the Temple (Revelation 19:11-21; see also Daniel 9:27d; Zechariah 14:3-11).

Will the Tribulation Temple be Sanctioned by God?

If the Temple is rebuilt by unbelieving Jews who reject Jesus as their Messiah, is rebuilt during the time of worldwide delusion and Israel's judgment, and is destined to be desecrated by the Antichrist, will not this Temple be rejected by God and rightly called "Antichrist's temple"? Those who answer this question affirmatively may be critical of believers who have any relationship with Orthodox Jews in the Temple movement because they believe that such "support" endorses the false system of deceptive worship that will prevail in the Tribulation (as today) and thus prevent Jews from believing in Jesus as the Messiah. Scriptural endorsement for this view is argued from Isaiah 66:1-6, where, in the context of the dedication of the Temple (verses 1-2a), the Lord declares:

> He who kills an ox is like one who slays a man; he who sacrifices a lamb is like one who breaks a dog's neck; he who offers a grain offering is like one who offers swine's blood; he who burns incense is like the one who blesses an idol. As they have chosen their own ways, and their soul delights in their abominations, so I will choose their punishments, and I will bring on them what they dread....A voice of uproar from the city, a voice from the temple, the voice of the LORD who is rendering recompense to His enemies (verses 3-4,6).

In chapter 10 we saw that the passages preceding and following this section (Isaiah 65:17-25; 66:7-24) are set in the Millennial kingdom. However, the reference to Israel's rebirth in verses 7-9 requires the present section, verses 3-6, to be

Tribulational.[70] If the Tribulation Temple is in view, the setting for this verse would be the completion of the Temple probably during the first quarter of the Tribulation (verse 1). While these verses pronounce a divine verdict against worshipers in the Temple, there is clearly a contrast indicated between the *kinds* of worshipers. In verse 2 the Lord commends "him who is humble and contrite of spirit, and trembles at My word," but in verses 3-4 He condemns those who "have chosen their own ways" (verse 3). Careful scrutiny of this context reveals that the condemnation here is not related to building the Temple or the offering of sacrifices. That these are legitimate acts is seen in the previous chapter, where those condemned are the ones who "forsake the LORD, who forget [His] holy mountain" (Isaiah 65:11). Moreover, in the previous chapter of Isaiah we read the laments, "Our holy and beautiful house, where our fathers praised Thee [through scrifices], has been burned by fire," and we are further told that God Himself is properly incensed by this desecration (Isaiah 64:11-12).

The condemnation in Isaiah 66:3-4 is directed at self-reliant worshipers who presumptuously perform the Temple ritual in the belief that righteous acts are sufficient. But, the Lord desires worshipers who approach His Temple in humble, God-fearing dependence upon the promises of His Word (verse 2c-d). The text also reveals that the believing group is ostracized by the unbelieving group (verse 5), which would be expected if Jewish believers in Jesus joined with Orthodox Jews at the Tribulation Temple as the only place on earth where God was legitimately acknowledged and worshiped (as in the first-century—see chapter 7). Such a conflict is also mentioned in Jewish apocalyptic literature, which speaks of a final rebellion in the last day by "the wicked" in Israel against "the righteous" in Israel (see Jubilees 23:14-23; IV Ezra 4:26-42; 6:18-28).[71] The result for the unbelieving Jewish group, according to Isaiah, will be severe disappointment, for they will be confronted by "a voice of uproar from the city, a voice from the temple, the voice of the LORD who is rendering recompense to His enemies" (verse 6).

When will this judgment from the city and Temple come upon Israel? According to Matthew 24:15-21, Mark 13:14-19, and Revelation 11:1-3, it will occur when the abomination of desolation desecrates the Temple and the Antichrist begins persecuting the Jewish people. The believing Jewish community, forewarned by Jesus (in the prohecy) to flee, will be spared, but the unbelieving Jewish people who remain to preserve a Jewish presence there will suffer in an earthquake (Revelation 11:13) as well as the Antichrist's assault on the city (Zechariah 14:1-2). These judgments, however, may lead many of the unbelieving Jews to repent and receive the Messiah at His return (Zechariah 14:4-5; see also 12:10–13:9). Yet despite this understanding that we see a group of true worshipers in Isaiah 66, there are still doctrinal concerns about whether the Temple in the Tribulation is sanctioned by God.

Is the Tribulation Temple a Legitimate Temple?

Those who believe that the Tribulation Temple will be built with the help of the Antichrist and serviced by Christ-rejecting Jews deny that this Temple is a Temple of God. Among those in Israel and abroad who adopt this perspective are Messianic Jews,[72] or Jews who believe in Jesus (Yeshua) as their Messiah. Although they are part of the church, they prefer to emphasize their Jewish identity and often express themselves in distinctively Jewish forms of worship. They share with Gentile Christians an evangelical faith as well as the same spectrum of perspectives on prophecy. However, being both Jewish and a believer makes the subject of the Temple more complicated. On the one hand there is a natural identification with Israel and its institutions, especially in the celebration of the biblical feasts that historically focused on the Temple. On the other hand, the Jewish community ostracizes Jewish believers because they view the latter as having converted to another religion and as being no longer Jewish. This is especially true of the Jews in Israel who are seeking to rebuild the Temple. As Orthodox Jews they have rejected Jesus as Messiah, and they consider Jewish believers to be traitors. In fact, one of the Temple movement's most prominent leaders said to me that he felt Jews who believed in Jesus were "worse than terrorists"! In addition, those in the Temple movement see the Temple as the means for bringing all Jews home to Judaism (as well as making Gentiles proselytes to Judaism). Rejecting any sense of a Messiah atoning for sins, they seek to revive the sacrificial system for this purpose. So on both theological as well as practical (and emotional) grounds, the Messianic believer struggles with the concept of building a Third Temple.

The Problem of a Third Temple

Among Messianic Jews who adopt a consistently literal interpretation of the Scriptures there is a belief in both a Third (Tribulational) and Final (Messianic) Temple. The final (Messianic) Temple is viewed as sanctioned by God and offers no real problems, except for the question of the purpose of the sacrifices in this Temple (more on this in chapter 24). This Temple is accepted as the legitimate Temple of God for the coming Millennial kingdom. However, there is an overwhelming rejection of the Third Temple as a legitimate Temple, and there is usually a negative reaction to the subject of rebuilding (except as a fulfillment of prophecy). This is particularly the case in Israel, where congregational leaders often disavow any interest in the Temple movement, even though Gentile believers in the Land and Christian tourists (such as those who annually gather in Jerusalem for the Feast of Tabernacles) often express great interest. The Messianic Jews who maintain a consistently literal interpretation of prophecy and feel negatively about the Third Temple have two biblical objections to its legitimacy.

The Spiritual Nature of New Covenant Worship

First, if a Temple is rebuilt during the church age it would seem to be in conflict with the form of spiritual worship predicted by Jesus as part of the New Covenant: "An hour is coming when neither in this mountain [Mount Gerizim], nor in Jerusalem [the Temple Mount], shall you worship the Father....But an hour is coming, and now is, when the true worshipers shall worship the Father in spirit and truth; for such people the Father seeks to be His worshipers" (John 4:21,23). If Jesus' words here are interpreted to mean that Christians are to worship in *spiritual* rather than in *material* ways, this could forbid not only icons and crucifixes (which evangelicals reject), but also church buildings, hymn books, and bulletins (which evangelicals accept), and especially for messianic believers, kippot, prayer shawls, shofars, Torah arks and scrolls. However, Jesus' point has nothing to do with this. As Christian commentator Rudolf Schnackenburg points out: "A spiritualistic understanding, as though Jesus was contrasting the material place of worship with a purely interior worship of God in the mind of man, is excluded by the concept of *pneuma*, which according to v. 24 can only mean the Spirit of God, as it mostly does in the Johannine writings."[73] Rather, in harmony with Jesus' connection of "spirit" with "truth" and His words "an hour is coming," His meaning is that the prophetic Spirit will be, and now is, active. This is in accord with the use of similar expressions in the texts of the Dead Sea Scrolls (whose community believed the prophetic Spirit had not ceased with the close of the Old Testament canon) and with Samaritan theology, which awaited the *Taheb*, a prophet like Moses who would prophetically declare all things (see John 4:25). Jesus is the long-awaited prophet (verse 26) and is the way to the worship of God the Father. He demonstrates (particularly in this context) that the prophetic Spirit is active in Himself (see John 4:18-19).

But does Jesus' statement about worship in Jerusalem indicate that worship in the Temple is wrong? If so, Jesus' actions contradict His words, for just before saying the preceding words He and His disciples had gone to Jerusalem to observe Passover at the Temple (John 2:13–3:21), and after saying these words they again went back to Jerusalem to observe a feast (John 5:1). Evidently, Jesus' disciples, the early church, and Paul did not understand His words in this manner either, for they continued to pray and even offer sacrifices in the Temple. What Jesus was saying is that the *place* of worship is not as important as the *procedure* in worship—a principle that is in accord with the Old Testament concept that "to obey is better than sacrifice" (1 Samuel 15:22; see also Psalm 40:6-8; 51:16-17; Isaiah 1:11-15; Jeremiah 7:22-23; Hosea 6:6; Micah 6:6-8). Although Jesus made it clear that "salvation is from the Jews" (John 4:22), His emphasis in verse 21 here is that through Him, worship may be offered to God in any place by any person. This does not exclude the Temple of God as a place of worship any more than it excludes at the present time a Messianic synagogue or church building. I believe that during the Tribulation the true church (composed of both Jew and Gentile) will have been removed and that the Holy Spirit will again work in believers' lives (both Jew and Gentile) in the same way as He did in the lives of the Old Testament saints. They worshiped in a Temple and were filled with the Spirit; it should not be any different in the Tribulation.

Even so, the early Jewish church—before the destruction of the Temple— was indwelt, sealed, and filled with the Spirit and yet *continued* to worship in the Temple! This would imply that a Third Temple could be built during the church age and even sacrifices commenced without there being a necessary conflict with "spiritual worship." However, it seems to me that both the conditions for the rebuilding of that Temple (the covenant of Daniel 9:27a), as well as the nature of worship depicted in Revelation 11:1, would require a Tribulation setting.

The Third Temple as the Tribulation Temple

A second reason that Messianic Jews may reject the legitimacy of the Third Temple is because it will be built by unbelieving Jews or even by the Antichrist and is destined to be occupied by the Antichrist at the midpoint of the Tribulation. Therefore, as the "Tribulation Temple," how could it be something that believers, much less God Himself, would accept?

It is perfectly understandable that the Messianic community would not support the efforts of the Temple movement given their unbelief and hostile attitude toward the gospel of the Messiah and Jewish believers. However, according to the New Testament, we should not be surprised that unbelieving Jews express this attitude toward believers in Jesus (Romans 11:28). Moreover, this has not prevented believing Jews from supporting unbelieving Jews in Zionist issues such as *aliyah* (returning to the Land) or developing and defending the State of Israel. Are not these things as much a part of the eventual fulfillment of the prophesied restoration of Israel as the rebuilding of the Third Temple? Therefore, with respect to the matter of the character of the Tribulation Temple and its association with the Antichrist, the following points should be considered:

1. The Tribulation Temple is called "the Temple of God" (2 Thessalonians 2:4; Revelation 11:1) in harmony with references to previous earthly Temples that were understood to have been "holy" as valid places of legitimate worship (Matthew 21:12; 26:6). While it may be objected that this designation was used to distinguish the Jerusalem (or Jewish) Temple from pagan temples for Gentile readers, it is unlikely that such a distinction was necessary since there was only one historic and legitimate Temple of God and that was the one in Jerusalem. But distinction in this manner cannot be defended in light of the fact that Paul and John also use the term "the Temple" (without distinction) in their writings to Gentile churches (1 Corinthians 9:13; Revelation 14:15,17; 15:8). Rather, Paul and John appear to use this term to distinguish the Temple as a place of special sanctity because it houses the presence of God (1 Corinthians 3:16-17; 2 Corinthians 6:16; see also Ephesians 2:21; Revelation 3:12; 11:19). Therefore, the implication of this term for the Tribulation Temple is that it, as a Third Temple, is as approved and legitimate a Temple as the previous two Jewish Temples in Israel's history.

2. The Tribulation Temple is regarded as an illegitimate place of worship because it will be built by unbelievers and have an idol (the abomination of desolation) placed in its Holy of Holies. However, both the First and Second Temples also knew false worship, unbelieving priests, idolatrous kings, and the rejection of God's prophets. The Judean king Manasseh built idolatrous altars in the First Temple and placed an idolatrous image in the Holy of Holies (2 Kings 21:4-7; 2 Chronicles 33:4-7). Zechariah, son of Berechiah and grandson of Jehoiada the priest, was stoned in the Temple precincts for seeking to turn Israel away from idolatry (2 Chronicles 24:20-22; Matthew 23:35). In the Second Temple (built by Zerubbabel), which had none of the sacred objects of the First (such as the Ark of the Covenant), swine had been offered as sacrifices and an idol of Zeus Olympias was erected under the command of Antiochus IV Epiphanes. In this Temple there was a politically appointed, non-Zadokite (ille-

gitimate), and generally corrupt Hasmonean priesthood. The Herodian Second Temple had been built by the same unbelieving Judean king who sought to murder Jesus at his birth (Matthew 2:13-18) and who had permitted the placement of symbols of Roman domination on its façade and in its precincts. In addition, Jesus had been rejected in this Temple and threatened with a stoning (John 10:23,31-33). Note too that Jesus had pronounced God's judgment on Israel and the destruction of the Second Temple (Matthew 24:1-2; Mark 13:1-2; Luke 21:5-6), just as Jeremiah (and other prophets) had prophesied the same for the First Temple (Jeremiah 7:1–8:3; Isaiah 39:6; Ezekiel 8-10). However, despite this history, Zacharias the father of John the Baptizer served in this same Temple as a priest and the angel of the Lord appeared to him there (Luke 1:11-20); Joseph and Mary dedicated Jesus there (Luke 2:22); and believers such as Simeon, Nicodemus, and all those in the early church worshiped and prayed there. If our Lord and these godly saints entered and worshiped in these Temples of the past, which had their own problems with unbelievers and desecration, then why should the Third Temple of the Tribulation be rejected as any less legitimate?

3. Why should not the Tribulation-period Jerusalem, which will be occupied by the Antichrist and used as his headquarters (Daniel 11:45), also be considered as rejected by God? Especially if the city hosts the Tribulation Temple. In fact, this appears to be the point of Revelation 11:1-2, where the Tribulation Temple is called "the temple of God" and Tribulation Jerusalem is likewise denoted as "the holy city." Ironically, those who reject the Tribulation Temple as a holy Temple accept Tribulation Jerusalem as a holy city. This, of course, they must do, since prophecy makes it plain that it is the city God has sworn to jealously protect (Zechariah 2:8-13; 8:2-23) and defend against the nations (Zechariah 12:8-9; 14:3,12) and that Messiah will return to redeem (Zechariah 14:4; see also Luke 21:28) and turn into the throne of His millennial government (Isaiah 2:2-3; Jeremiah 3:17; Zechariah 8:2-3; 14:9-11). We need to recognize that Tribulation Jerusalem and the Tribulation Temple will both share the same desecration and destiny. Tribulation Jerusalem will be invaded by foreign desecrators (Zechariah 14:2; Revelation 11:2). In the same way the Tribulation Temple will be invaded by foreign desecrators (the Antichrist and the abomination of desolation—Daniel 9:27; Matthew 24:15; Mark 13:14; 2 Thessalonians 2:4). Each, in turn, shares the destiny of restoration: Tribulation Jerusalem is rescued from the onslaught of the Antichrist (Zechariah 14:3-5; Revelation 19:11,19-20; 20:1-3), and the Tribulation Temple is rebuilt to give universal access to a regenerate world of worshipers (Isaiah 2:2-3; 56:6-7; Zechariah 14:16-21). Therefore, if "the city of God" that

Messiah is coming to restore is holy, then "the Temple of God" that Messiah is coming to rebuild should also be holy.

4. The Tribulation Temple is depicted as being "defiled" or "desecrated" by the presence of the Antichrist (2 Thessalonians 2:4), the invasion of Jerusalem and the Temple Mount by Gentile nations (Revelation 11:2), and the abomination of desolation (Daniel 9:27; Matthew 24:15; Mark 13:14). This is inferred not only from the fact that the sacrificial service is disrupted (Daniel 9:27), but from the obvious contrast that is being made in these texts: "the abomination of desolation…in the holy place" (Matthew 24:15), "where it should not be" (Mark 13:14), "man of lawlessness…who opposes and exalts himself above every so-called god…takes his seat in the temple of God" (2 Thessalonians 2:3-4), and "the Temple of God….they will tread under foot" (Revelation 11:1-2). Yet how can the Temple be considered desecrated if in fact it is already rejected by God as an unholy institution? If it were itself an abomination, why object that an abominaiton of desolation should be placed within it? Why are the believing prophets of God, the two witnesses (see chapter 14), wearing sackcloth as a sign of mourning over this desecration (Revelation 11:3)? They should rather be rejoicing that the false sacrificial system has been ended.

In response to some of these concerns CBS radio correspondent Dave Dolan, who has lived in Jerusalem for over 20 years, worships in a Messianic congregation, and is author of several books on the Middle East and Bible prophecy, has observed:

> The Tabernacle in the midst of the people as they wandered in the desert was an opportunity for them to see the presence of God and always have His presence with them. A Temple in Jerusalem was also a recognition of God's presence. Therefore, such a thing is going to draw people's attention to the centrality and the necessity of the worship of God in a form that they understand as Jews, and, trying to keep faithful to what we call the Old Testament they have certain performances and prerequisites. It is not necessarily going to take them away from God, but would perhaps bring them to the place in God where they would see a greater need. I find the apostle Paul never stopped going into the Temple. He never stopped sacrificing. He never changed anything that he was doing even though he saw Jesus as his Messiah and the Messiah of Israel. Because the functions and the practices of the Temple were prerequisites that God had required of His people and led them to an understanding of the need for a salvation that went beyond it but cer-

tainly didn't distract them....I think the Scriptures are clear that a Temple will be built....the Antichrist himself says he places his image [there] and defiles the Temple. Well, if he *defiles* the Temple, then it must be a *holy* place which is defiled.

Based on these arguments, it is preferable to view the Third Temple as a legitimate Temple in the succession of Temples for the Jewish nation. Its desecration by the Antichrist is a sign of his rejection of God (as represented by the Temple) and war against Israel (and especially the believing remnant), who brought forth the Messiah and to whom He will return (Revelation 12:5-6,13-17). The cessation of the sacrificial offerings (Daniel 9:27) is to be viewed not only as the result of this desecration but a violation against the sanctity of the Temple itself. This last point understands that the sacrificial system was for the maintenance of ritual purification—not for personal salvation—and therefore did not (and will not, in the future Temple) conflict with the atoning sacrifice of Jesus (see chapter 24). Even though the Tribulation Temple will be invaded by the Antichrist, it is not the Antichrist's Temple, but God's, which is what makes the invasion such an abomination and a clear sign to believing Jews that they need to flee the city of Jerusalem (Matthew 24:15-22). And, the Tribulation Temple will be replaced by Ezekiel's significantly greater Temple (the Fourth Temple) not because the Tribulation Temple is unholy, but because it is inferior (Haggai 2:9). The dimensions of the Millennial Temple, as well as the topographical changes that will prepare Millennial Jerusalem to be the throne of the Lord (Isaiah 2:2; Zechariah 14:10), will require that the previous Temple—and even the Temple Mount—be changed to accommodate the new situation and structures.

The Tribulation Temple in Summary

In this chapter we have seen that the Tribulation Temple will be a Temple sanctioned by God. In Scripture, it is called the "temple of God" (2 Thessalonians 2:4; Revelation 11:1), even though it will be desecrated by the most sinister figure ever to appear on this planet. Ultimately this will call for a divine retribution, which will come with the coming of the Lord (Zechariah 13:3-4,12; 2 Thessalonians 1:6-10; 2:8-9; Revelation 19:17-21). Once the Messiah has returned to His city of Jerusalem, the desecrated Tribulation Temple will be replaced by a Temple unlike any ever seen in the past. It is this Final Temple in the divine program of the last days that we now want to explore.

CHAPTER 22

Measuring the Future

Ezekiel's Vision of the Messianic Temple

This incomparable prophecy...concludes with a description of the glory of the Lord in the glorified city of Jerusalem...with God dwelling with man in holiness and glory. Beyond this there is no greater goal of history and God's dealings with man.[1]

—CHARLES LEE FEINBERG

The Greek tragedies are considered to be the most pitiable of human dramas in the literature of the past. But there is an even greater tragedy tucked away within the books of the Old Testament. While the Greek tragedies dealt with the loss of a lover or a life, this Hebrew horror story dealt with the loss of God. And for a people whose entire existence was defined by their relationship with God, no greater tragedy could be imagined. The name of this Israelite tragedy was called, in Hebrew, *Ichabod* ("The Departed Glory"). The book that records this drama is the book of Ezekiel. Ezekiel was a Temple priest and prophet who lived through the last dark days of Israel's slide into judgment, crying out his message of doom to an already deafened race.

As a priest, Ezekiel's primary focus in life was the service of the Temple, and in this time of inward defection and outward invasion, the desecration that threatened the Temple became his consuming passion. He personally experienced God's judgment against Jerusalem when in 597 B.C. he was taken captive with thousands of other Judean hostages in the second deportation to Babylon. Afterward, in exile from his native land, he served to deliver God's word of correction and comfort to his fellow exiles.[2] As a prophet he saw beyond the gloom of decay and devastation to the brightness of return and restoration. In the twenty-fifth year of his exile and the fortieth chapter of his book, he received a vision of victory that turned his story's tragedy of *Ichabod* ("The Departed Glory") into the triumph of *Chabod* ("The Glory [Restored]"). In Ezekiel's vision, the Angel of the Lord appeared with an object in his hand. It was not what one might expect for such a majestic figure—not a sword nor a scroll, but a measuring rod (Ezekiel 40:3). But with this simple tool Ezekiel was shown and assured of all God's promises for his people, for with it he measured the future.

Measuring Ezekiel's Message

Ezekiel's plight as a priest was to have served in a day when both the kingdom and people's consciences were corrupted and his priestly role compromised. In chapters 8–11, he chronicled just how wicked these worst of times had become. In the Holy Place of the Temple, where his priestly duties were performed, he was shocked to find every form of foreign idolatry and abomination (Ezekiel 8:5-16). If Ezekiel was disgusted by what he saw, imagine how much more so God felt, for it was His house that had been polluted and profaned! The desecration of His holy house was the final act of human injustice, forcing Him to enact the curses of His covenant and withdraw His presence. This had long been the great fear that had faced Israel—to be a Nation without God—yet, by Ezekiel's time, the divine departure didn't seem a matter of concern to a sin-focused society. God's departure was shown to have occurred in stages, going from the cherubim upon the Ark, to the entrance of the east gate, to the midst of the city, and finally, over the Mount of Olives (Ezekiel 10:18-19; 11:22-23). Because the people were away from God, they had not noticed that *He* went away. But God soon got their attention, for when His protective presence was gone, their enemies came calling.

After the fall of the Temple and the city of Jerusalem in 586 B.C., the prophet Ezekiel wrote of Israel's future restoration with a conviction equal to that which he had expressed when he penned word of their destruction. In Ezekiel 40–48, Ezekiel addressed the theological problem that resulted from the Temple's desecration and destruction, the sign of which was the abandonment of the Sanctuary by God's divine presence. Steven Tuell, author of a study on the laws of Ezekiel, has summarized well the theological purpose of this vision when he writes:

> Though city, king, Temple, and cult be destroyed, this vision is a promise of YHWH's continuing presence—a concrete demonstration of YHWH's promise to be a sanctuary for Judah's exiles (11:16). As the Jerusalem sanctuary had become, for Ezekiel, totally and irredeemably defiled, the perfect archetypal Temple of his vision is a place guarded from defilement, defended by massive fortified gates. Indeed, the gate by which the divine enters the Temple is sealed for all time. The glory [of God] will never leave again; the Temple will never again be defiled.[3]

That this theological restoration comes to be fulfilled is generally accepted by most interpreters, but *when* (past or future) and *how* (literally or figuratively) this is to be applied has remained the subject of much interpretive debate and resulted in at least five different views.

Interpreting Ezekiel's Prophecy

Interpreting Ezekiel's prophecy has never been an easy task. The Talmudic rabbis struggled with the numerous textual difficulties and discrepancies from the Torah. Most decided that it was best to wait for the prophet Elijah, at the final Redemption, to explain them (Babylonian Talmud, *Menahoth* 45a). However, one rabbi named Chanina ben Hezekiah accepted the challenge and, sequestered in an upper chamber, expended over 300 jars of oil in his lamps before successfully reconciling them. Had he not, we are told, the entire book of Ezekiel might have

Ezekiel's Temple

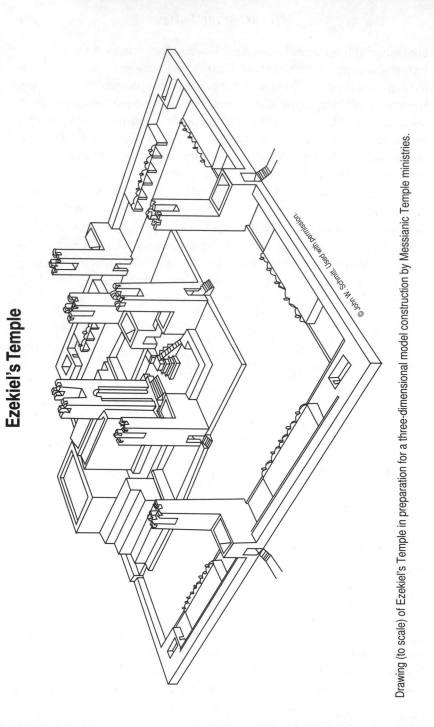

Drawing (to scale) of Ezekiel's Temple in preparation for a three-dimensional model construction by Messianic Temple ministries.

© John W. Schmitt. Used with permission.

been excluded from the Hebrew canon![4] Despite the obvious problems in interpretation, we should not despair at seeking to interpret these chapters, nor should the importance of the pursuit be underestimated. As Charles Feinberg advised, "Some may think it not germane to enter upon such a discussion...[but] great issues are at stake; good and sincere men differ widely in their interpretation; wisdom would dictate that time be allotted to some discussion of the views which are so determinative for such a long section of the Word of God."[5] In addition, whether there will be a future Temple and how it could be built depends in large measure on how these chapters are understood. For example, the most generally accepted interpretation of this prophecy by critical scholars and non-futurists is that it was a literal description of the Temple (but described in hyperbolic or exaggerated language) of the past or of the Temple built shortly after the Jews' return from exile, or conversely, that it was intended to be understood and find fulfillment in a non-literal manner, as a spiritual ideal or as symbolic of some other spiritual reality (the church, heaven, or the eternal state). But if the literal interpretation is rejected, there remains no portion of Scripture which supplies the instructions for construction of the future Temple and its service, and the way is open for the spiritualization of all the restoration prophecies (including those concerning the coming of the Messiah!).

Therefore, let us survey these interpretations in order to see why there is such a lack of concensus in the belief of a coming Last Days Temple. We will first consider two interpretations of past fulfillment and then two interpretations of symbolic fulfillment.

A Look Back to Solomon's Temple

While the exiles were in captivity, those who remembered the Temple wept over its destruction, but those who were born in Babylon had no connection with the Temple of old. Some interpreters contend, then, that Ezekiel's vision of the Temple was a *literary* look back to these glorious days. Ezekiel's role, they argue, was to share his priestly memories of the Israelite monarchy in order to preserve the memory of the Temple and its services and to comfort the Jews with a message that God was still with them.

This view, however, runs into several problems: First, the prayers of the exiles, as illustrated by Daniel in Babylon, were for a *future rebuilding* of the Jerusalem Temple (see Daniel 9:3-19). Although the Jews did weep over the loss of Solomon's Temple, the only reference to this, outside of Jeremiah's lament, is when a comparison is made with the rebuilt Temple of Zerubbabel (Ezra 3:12-13;

Haggai 2:3). Second, a description of the First Temple had already been preserved in the books of Kings and Chronicles. And third, the description that Ezekiel preserves differs radically from the description of Solomon's Temple, with unprecedented divergences in structure, style, and ceremony. Because Ezekiel's description also had immensely larger dimensions; some have objected that Ezekiel's Temple is too large to have fit on Solomon's (or even the present) Temple Mount site. For example, according to Ezekiel 48:9-10, the sacred area set apart for the Temple is 25,000 cubits (8.75 miles square) on each side;[6] according to Ezekiel 48:35 the city of Jerusalem measures 18,000 cubits (some 6 miles); and according to Ezekiel 42:20 the overall size of the Temple itself is "500 cubits" (875 square feet, or the equivalent of about three football fields).

The answer to this objection is provided by both Ezekiel and several of the other prophets, who report that extraordinary topographical changes will take place in the Land of Israel to accommodate these increased dimensions of the Temple. During the Tribulation period the earth will experience violent changes as earthquakes alter both cities and terrain. One of the cities that will be hardest hit is Jerusalem (Revelation 11:13), which will also suffer a mountain-splitting earthquake at the end of the Tribulation when the Messiah sets foot again upon the Mount of Olives (Zechariah 14:4). Zechariah also speaks of the flattening of huge portions of land and elevating the Temple Mount (Zechariah 14:4-10). Other prophets also say the Temple Mount itself will be raised up above all other mountains (see Isaiah 2:3; 60:14; 61:6). Ezekiel notes the enlarged territory for the tribal allotments (Ezekiel 47:13-23; 48:1-14, 23-29) and changes in the southern part of the country (Ezekiel 47:1-12). According to Jeremiah 3:17 the entire city of Jerusalem will become "the Throne of the LORD" and be a dedicated holy place. This means that Ezekiel's Temple will occupy a newly elevated and expanded Temple Mount that will include the former city of Jerusalem itself (Ezekiel 48:10). To the north of this will be the place of the priests (Ezekiel 48:11-12), to the south of the Temple will be the place of the Levites (Ezekiel 48:13-14), and to the south of this a new city will be built for workers out of the Israelite tribes (Ezekiel 48:18-19). To the east and west will be an administrative center for the prince (Ezekiel 48:21-22). Given the extensive topographical expansion that is predicted to take place, the new boundaries and dimensions of the Sanctuary are realistic.

A Plan for the Post-Exilic Temple

Other interpreters argue that Ezekiel's description was a visionary plan for the rebuilding of the post-exilic Second Temple. This view says that since the returning exiles expected to rebuild the Temple, these detailed instructions were provided by their priest-in-exile, Ezekiel, to enable them to erect the structure and properly perform its service. Typical of this view are the words of one Christian commentator: "With the exception of the Messianic section in chapter 47:1-12, the fulfillment of all the rest of the prophecy belongs to the times immediately after the return from the Chaldean exile. So must every one of its first hearers and readers have understood it."[7] Although it is reasonable to assume that the builders of Zerubbabel's Temple would have employed these plans, it is obvious that they did not. The fact is that none of those who led the rebuilding of Jerusalem—Ezra, Haggai, nor Nehemiah—made any reference to Ezekiel's Temple. This is quite inexplicable if the purpose of the prophecy was to provide the exiles with a description that would enable them to start up the Temple and its services. Remember, Zerubbabel's Temple was smaller than the Solomonic Temple, and the services were reinstituted strictly in accordance with Mosaic law (Nehemiah 8:1-18; 10:28-39). That Ezekiel resided with the exiles in Babylon and personally communicated to them his prophecy only strengthens this conclusion. Why would they ignore it?

While some have sought to find some areas of compatability, the greater differences in Ezekiel's topography, dimensions, details, and priestly performance with that of the Second Temple argue that an alternate pattern was followed by Ezra and Zerubbabel when they rebuilt the Temple. In addition, the Land was never divided among the tribes, as Ezekiel's prophecy required. And, many of the instructions given to Ezekiel contradict what was earlier stated in the Torah, and some even think Ezekiel spoke of the giving of a new Torah (see Ezekiel 43:12).[8] Some of the departures from the Mosaic law have been listed as the absence of the Ark of the Covenant in the Holy of Holies, no mention of the table for the shewbread or the lampstand in the outer Holy Place, no anointing oil within the Temple or its court, and no mention of the high priesthood. However, the most compelling objection is that the *Shekinah* glory failed to return to the Second Temple—and it is this *Shekinah* glory that is the focal point of Ezekiel's Restoration Temple.

A Symbol of a Spiritual Reality

Non-futurists hold that Ezekiel's Temple is symbolic and not physical or literal. This view argues that because a literal fulfillment did not occur after the exile, the fulfillment must have been other than literal. However, the first advent of Messiah (Jesus) did not historically fulfill all that was prophesied about the coming Messiah, either. The lack of Israel's political and spiritual redemption, the destruction of the Gentile nations, and His reign over a restored city in perfect, universal peace and undefilable holiness, was, and continues to be, a major stumbling block for Jews. Yet if these events will yet be fulfilled literally at His second advent, as were those at His first advent, then a prophetic postponement until the future, rather than a resolution to spiritual fulfillment in the past or present, is to be understood.

Regardless of one's interpretive stance, all evangelical interpreters still accept a literal return of Christ and resurrection of the dead, yet these are as inseparable from Israel's prophetic promises as those concerning the restoration of its Temple. Moreover, those who interpret Ezekiel's Temple symbolically do not agree on what these symbols signify. Therefore, Ezekiel's vision has been said to represent variously the returned Israelite Nation,[9] Jesus, the church, Christ and His community of believers, the new heavens and the new earth, and heaven. However, those who support a symbolic interpretation of this passage must also deal with the detailed architectural and geographical measurements, and the intricate instructions concerning priestly dress and the preparation of the sacrifices and offerings. Jon Levenson, a University of Chicago Divinity School professor of Hebrew Bible, makes this observation:

> The highly specific nature of the description of the Temple, its liturgy and community bespeaks a practical program, not a vision of pure grace. For example, when the text says that eight steps led up to the vestibule of the inner court (Ezek. 40:31), can this be other than a demand that the new Temple be constructed just so?...What Ezekiel was shown is the divinely constructed model, the *tabnit*, like the one David showed Solomon (1 Chron. 28:11-19).[10]

How would one go about building a symbol? Yet, the "plan" (Hebrew, *tabnit*) and "design" (Hebrew, *tzurat*), the words used for this in Ezekiel 43:10-11 of this Temple, can be understood just as well as architectural language that expects the activity of literal construction. Moreover, the claim that Ezekiel is here using figurative language does not explain why his measurements differ so radically from those of the only Temple (Solomon's Temple) with which he and all the exiles were familiar. This detail alone has led prophetic authors such as Elwood McQuaid to state:

> I believe that the Ezekiel Temple is a literal Temple that will be built during the millennial reign of Jesus Christ. One of the reasons is

because the description that is given in the book of Ezekiel about this Temple has aspects to it that were not resonant in any of the other Temples: Solomon's Temple, Zerubbabel's Temple, nor the Herodian refurbishing of Zerubbabel's Temple. None of them had the dimensions and none of them lined up exactly. For that reason, among many others that could be mentioned, I think that without a doubt this is something that is in the future [as it is] unprecedented at any time in the past.[11]

The returning exiles were indeed familiar with the priestly language used by Ezekiel—which was based on the descriptions of the Sanctuary and its service in Exodus and Leviticus—and would have expected to fulfill these instructions literally in continuity with these previously revealed commands. Unless one is already predisposed to see the church in the Old Testament and view ritual language as spiritually anticipating the "New Israel," there is nothing in Ezekiel's prophecy that corresponds to the New Testament church. Furthermore, if Ezekiel only intended to convey a spiritual truth through visionary symbols, why did he diverge from accepted ritual standards and established Jewish law? For these reasons, as one scholar has observed, Ezekiel 40–48 "really gives no textual clues that it is to be interpreted symbolically as other visions in the book should be by virtue of their unrealistic characters (e.g., ch. 1)."[12]

In fact, Ezekiel's early chapters represent one of the greatest use of symbols among the prophets. Beside the vision of chapter 1:4-28, Ezekiel is called upon by God to perform symbolic acts (concerning the seige and destruction of Jerusalem) such as eating a scroll (Ezekiel 2:8–3:3), writing on a brick and setting up an iron plate (Ezekiel 4:1-3), lying on his side (Ezekiel 4:4-8), cooking strange bread (Ezekiel 4:9-15), shaving his head and beard and burning the hair (Ezekiel 5:1-4), carrying baggage (Ezekiel 12:1-7), eating and drinking with trembling (Ezekiel 12:17-18), and restraint in mourning for his dead wife (Ezekiel 24:15-17). In addition, the book has a number of parables (chapters 15–17, 23–24, 34, 37). When one attempts to understand the many details symbolically, they invariably have no control in their interpretation, and the meaning of the text varies from interpreter to interpreter. This results in many details in the text being assigned arbitrary meanings or becoming completely meaningless. Yet, this is the opposite of what Ezekiel himself states: "Then I said, 'Ah LORD GOD! They are saying of me, "Is he not just speaking parables?" ' " (Ezekiel 20:49). His concern was that they did not understand the literal interpretation of his symbolic acts, but only understood them as symbols, which would spell their doom. However, later the people came to their senses and asked for the literal meaning: "And the people said to me, 'Will you not tell us what these things that you are doing mean for us?' " (Ezekiel 24:19). Therefore, while Ezekiel could have continued his symbolic imagery in chapters 40–48, and still had in mind a literal structure, the absence of such language emphasizes the intention that this section not be misunderstood as anything but a literal promise for the future.

A Preview of the Eternal State

One of the of symbolic views mentioned earlier sees Ezekiel 40–48 as figurative of the eternal state of the righteous in heaven. This argument is based on a number of correspondences (they would say parallels) that exist between this text and Revelation 21–22—texts which depict the New Jerusalem. While indeed there are a number of impressive correspondences, there are more differences than there are similarities.[13] The greatest of these are with the nature of the cities described. Ezekiel's reconstruction of the earthly Jerusalem is quite ordinary, with its shape being square (Ezekiel 40:47) and built of common wood and stones.[14] The New Jerusalem, by contrast, is cubical and built of precious metals, pearls, and rare gemstones (Revelation 21:16-22). The most significant contrast is that Ezekiel's city has a Temple that dominates the center, while the New Jerusalem has no such constructed Temple at all (Revelation 22:21). Finally, the reinstitution of blood sacrifices "for atonement" (Ezekiel 43:19-20) in Ezekiel's Temple should alone be a sufficient contrast to preclude any identification with the eternal state. The similarities that exist are those that should be expected between the Millennial kingdom (during which Ezekiel's Temple exists) and the Heavenly Temple and the eternal state, since these reflect the divine ideal: a restoration of what was lost in the Garden of Eden.

The Promise of a Future Restoration Temple

Given the objections against the four views presented above, the only remaining option is to take the text literally and its application as eschatological—that is, to see it as describing the future restoration of national Israel during the Millennial reign of the Messiah. The late Jewish-Christian scholar Charles Lee Feinberg underscored the importance of adopting the literal view against all others when he wrote:

> The concluding chapters of Ezekiel form a kind of continental divide in
> the area of biblical interpretation....It is one of the areas where the lit-
> eral intepretation of the Bible and the spiritualizing or allegorizing

method diverge widely....When thirty-nine chapters can be treated detailedly and seriously as well as literally, there is no valid reason *a priori* for treating this large division of the book in an entirely different manner....The literal [view] declares that the prediction speaks of the restoration and establishment of the people of Israel in their own land in the last days of their national history, their conversion to the Lord through faith in their long-rejected Messiah, and the manifest presence and glory of the Lord in their midst.[15]

There are a number of arguments that support the literal interpretation of this passage as a promise for the future:

1. *The literary unity of the book requires that a literal Temple be understood throughout its chapters.* Chapters 40–48 form an inseparable literary conclusion to the book. Although these chapters constitute a new vision in the prophecy, they are linked with chapters 1–39 because they repeat earlier themes in a more detailed fashion. This linkage may be seen in the fact that the beginnings of chapters 1 and 40 share a number of similar features. For example, Ezekiel's vision of the presence of God in Babylon (Ezekiel 1:1; compare 8:1) finds its complement and completion in the vision in the Land of Israel (Ezekiel 40:2). In like manner, the problem created by the departure of God's presence in chapters 8–11 finds its resolution with the return of His presence in this section (see Ezekiel 43:1-7).[16] In fact, the concern for the presence of God could be argued as "the uniting theme of the entire text of Ezekiel."[17] Without chapters 40-48 there is no answer to the outcome of Israel, no resolution to their history of sacred scandal, and no grand finalé to the divine drama centered from Sinai on the Chosen Nation.

Ezekiel's prophecy of the future Temple is the means to restoring the presence of God to Israel. Its focus in the book falls into three divisions: 1) prophecies of the Temple's desecration and destruction (Ezekiel 4:1-24,27); 2) prophecies of Israel's return and restoration (Ezekiel 33:1–39:29); and 3) prophecies of the Temple's rebuilding and ritual (40:1-48:35). Since it was a *physical* First Temple's desecration and destruction Ezekiel described in the first section of the book, the last section's discussion of a Temple's restoration would also expect a structure of the same kind. In view of the exilic understanding of a return from captivity necessitating a rebuilding of the Temple (Daniel 9:20; 2 Chronicles 36:22-23; Ezra 1:2-11; Haggai 1:2–2:9; Zechariah 1:16; 6:12-15; 8:3), would Ezekiel (or God) have attempted to comfort his people's loss with anything other than the literal restoration of a physical Temple to which the divine presence would return?

The literary structure of the book of Ezekiel argues against the possibility that chapters 40–48 are a spiritual vision. All interpreters are in agreement that in chapters 8–11 the literal Solomonic Temple in Jerusalem is in view. Ezekiel's description of its desecration is the basis for his explanation to the exiles about why God would have to remove His presence and destroy the structure. Also, we need to remember that Ezekiel wasn't physically present in Jerusalem when he reported these things, but in Babylon with the Judean exiles. It was "in the visions of God" that he was spiritually transported to Jerusalem (Ezekiel 8:3). Everything he mentions there concerning the Temple, its "inner court" (8:3), "porch" (8:16), "altar" (8:16), "threshold" (9:3), and "east gate" (10:19) were all seen in a vision. Yet they are considered to have been a vision of the literal Temple. Why, then, when in a vision of the Temple (Ezekiel 40:2) in chapters 40–48 he mentions the exact same places—"inner court" (40:27), "porch" (40:48), "altar" (43:18), and "the gate facing toward the east" (43:4)—are they now only spiritual symbols? In summary we can say this in regard to the literary unity of the book: If the presence of God left a literal Temple and will return, it should return to a literal Temple. If the desecration and destruction of a literal Temple were described in a vision, then the vision of the restoration and reconsecration of a Temple should also be understood as literal.

2. *The context of the Temple's restoration requires a literal interpretation.* These chapters open with a contextual note concerning the specific date of Ezekiel's vision—on "the tenth of the month [of Tishri]" (Ezekiel 40:1). The Jewish sages saw this as setting an eschatological context, since the tenth of Tishri is reckoned as a Jubilee year (Hebrew, *yovel*), and the date of Ezekiel's vision was determined to be the first Day of Atonement (Hebrew, *Yom Kippur*) of the Jubilee year. Together, this date prefigured Israel's Day of Redemption in both its physical (Land) and spiritual aspects, as Rabbi Joseph Breuer notes: "On that day, which summoned the subjugated and estranged among God's people to accept freedom and called upon all the sons of Israel to return to their God, on that day it was given to the prophet to behold a vision of the rebuilt, eternal Sanctuary of the future and to receive the basic instructions for the establishment of the State of God that would endure forever."[18] Therefore, from the very first verse, the rabbis considered the passage's context to be both literal and eschatological.

Daniel had also predicted that the Temple would be reconsecrated in the future as the climatic fulfillment of six eschatological restoration goals (see chapter 11). The reconsecration of Ezekiel's Temple by the restored presence of

God appears as the climatic event in the restoration context of Ezekiel 37:25-28, which serves as an introductory summary of chapters 40–48:

> They shall live on the land that I gave to Jacob [Israel] My servant, in which your fathers lived; and they will live on it, they, and their sons, and their sons' sons, forever; and David My servant shall be their prince forever. And I will make a covenant of peace with them; it will be an everlasting covenant with them. And I will place them and multiply them, and I will set My sanctuary [Hebrew, *miqdash*] in their midst forever. My dwelling place [Hebrew, *Mishkan*] also will be with [over] them; and I will be their God, and they will be My people. And the nations will know that I am the LORD who sanctifies Israel, when My sanctuary [Hebrew, *miqdash*] is in their midst forever.

These verses reveal that the future restoration of the Nation will be in the same place (Israel) and in the same form (a Temple) as in the past. The geographical context for this prophecy is "the land that I gave to Jacob My servant, in which your fathers lived." The mention of Jacob, whose name was changed to Israel, along with the historical habitation of "the fathers," clearly distinguishes this place as the Land of Israel. Notice, too, that the covenant made between God and Israel is "a covenant of peace" (verse 26). No such covenant of security and well-being (the idea of the Hebrew *shalom* translated here as "peace") was ever made with God during any time in Israel's past, nor will it be made during the Tribulation period (the covenant of Daniel 9:27 is not stated to be a "*peace* covenant"). According to Ezekiel 34:25-29, this covenant is Land-centered, completely eliminating harmful animals, guaranteeing security from any foreign invasion, and bringing unparalleled agricultural renewal accompanied by divinely sent seasonal rains (see Zechariah 14:17). In addition, this covenant, unlike those of the past, is said to be "everlasting" (Ezekiel 37:26).

In Ezekiel 37:25-28 the Temple is described in terms that can only be realized in the future. First, the Temple is called a *mishkan*, the Hebrew word used formerly for the Tabernacle, and it is said to be "with [over] them" (Hebrew, *'alîhem*).[19] This pictures God's "sheltering presence" as being protective in the same way that the Tabernacle was when Israel was in the wilderness. One of the false hopes the people had was that the Temple was inviolable and that it would preserve the Nation even in times of disobedience simply because it existed. In the future, however, the Nation will not sin and the Temple, with the *Shekinah*, will serve as the source of the Nation's—and the world's—prosperity and peace. The Temple is also called *miqdash* ("Sanctuary"), emphasizing its holiness, and is said to be, like the covenant and the restoration of God's presence, "everlasting" (verses 26-28). Again, such a Temple could only find its fulfillment in the Millennial kingdom, where the protective "glory-cloud" of God will return to fulfill this concept of the Temple (see Isaiah 4:5-6). This Temple, presented as part of the eternal covenant, is that which is the same one that we see described in greater detail in the prophecy of chapters 40-48.[20] Professor Moshe Greenberg of the Hebrew University of Jerusalem offers this explanation:

> The fivefold repetition of "forever" stresses the irreversibility of the new dispensation. Unlike God's past experiment with Israel, the future restoration will have a guarantee of success; its capstone will be God's sanctifying presence dwelling forever in the sanctuary amidst his people. The vision of the restored Temple (and God's return to it) in chapters 40-48 follows as a proleptic [anticipatory] corrobation of these promises.[21]

Based on the nature of the promised restoration as revealed in Ezekiel 33-37, the returning exiles surely must have recognized that the nature of Ezekiel's future Temple in chapters 40-48 was also eschatological. Therefore, those who rebuilt the Temple after the Babylonian captivity did not attempt to implement Ezekiel's architectural design or priestly instructions. Their assessment of the kind of restoration they were experiencing had to be weighed against several factors: 1) The larger proportion of the Jewish population had chosen to remain in Persia and Egypt; 2) the fact that only a paltry 49,897 Jews had returned to Judah (Ezra 2:64-65); and 3) the low level of spiritual life evident among the resident Jews in the Land (Ezra 5:16; 9:1-4; Haggai 1:2-6). These realities must have indicated that their return and rebuilding was not the fulfillment of the final restoration described in Ezekiel. This was probably most apparent when the foundation of Zerubbabel's Temple had been laid and the older people wept because it did not measure up to Solomon's Temple (Ezra 3:12-13; Haggai 2:3), much less to the Temple envisioned by Ezekiel. Therefore, it must have been understood that Ezekiel's Temple awaited the more complete promise of restoration, which included the coming of the Messiah (Ezekiel 34:11-31), a full regathering of the entire Jewish remnant (Ezekiel 36:24,28), and a national spiritual regeneration (Ezekiel 36:25-27; 37:1-14).

If Ezekiel's readers were interpreting his restoration program as being for a future age, then they would have understood the interruption of Ezekiel's "Gog and Magog" battle (Ezekiel 38-39) between the discussions of the Temple in Ezekiel 37:25-28 and 40-48. This literary placement not only helped the readers understand an eschatological context for the Temple prophecy, but added the assurance that, unlike the foreign invasions of the past, even this greatest of foreign invasions in the future would not disturb God's plans for the final Temple.

3) *The description of the Temple indicates that it is to be a literal construction.* This is the impression a reader gets as he reads about the Temple's measurements, structures, courts, pillars, galleries, rooms, chambers, doors, ornamentation, vessels, priests, and offerings. Yet one of the leading commentators on the book of Ezekiel has contended, "The description of the temple is not presented as a blueprint for some future building to be constructed with human hands," and that "nowhere is anyone commanded to build it."[22] However, in Ezekiel 43:10-11 we read, "As for you, son of man [Ezekiel], describe the temple to the house of Israel…and let them measure the plan. And if they are ashamed of all that they have done, make known to them the designs of the house, its structure, its exits, its entrances, all its design, all its statutes, and all its laws. And write it in their sight, so that they may observe its whole design and all its statutes, *and do them*" (emphasis added). These verses indicate that those Jews who are alive at the time that Ezekiel's prophesied restoration is fulfilled are the ones who are to build the Temple. Later in this context (43:13-27), when the same kind of architectural measurements and detailed instructions are given for the altar, it is stated that the altar will be built by "the house of Israel" (verse 10). If the altar of the Temple is to be built, then why not the Temple itself? This is in fact the case, for it is this same "house of Israel" to whom Ezekiel is commanded to "declare…all that you see" (Ezekiel 40:4). The command in Ezekiel 43:11 to "observe its whole design and all its statutes, and do them" is parallel in expression to God's original command to build a Sanctuary (given at Mount Sinai in Exodus 25:8-9). If the house of Israel interpreted the original command to Moses literally and thus built the Tabernacle and ordained the priesthood, why would they not likewise interpret the restatement by Ezekiel? This is the expectation of those involved in the Temple movement, who believe that while human hands will be employed, the command to build will be issued by the Messiah at His coming (Zechariah 6:12-13).

If we consider the detailed description of the Temple, we discover that the plans communicated to Ezekiel are so precise that blueprints could be drawn and a building constructed from them. In fact, a three-dimensional model of this Temple has already been made by John Schmitt, the executive director of Messianic Temple Ministries[23] (see the diagram on page 510). When a comparison is made between Ezekiel's details for the construction of the Temple buildings and the sacrificial system and the details recorded elsewhere for the construction of the Tabernacle and First Temple and their service, there is no reason to take Ezekiel's instructions as less literal or historical. Would Ezekiel have been given such elaborate and practical instructions if only spiritual or symbolic realities were intended? Would the house of Israel be expected to interpret the details in a manner other than that which was consistent with God's revelation regarding previous structures—especially in the absence of any guidelines for an alternate (symbolic) interpretation?

Although it is possible that symbolical and spiritual significance can be discovered in the details of the Tabernacle and Temple's construction and ceremonies, it is interesting that such symbolism is not directly revealed in the Bible. Of course, there is an analogous use of ritual language in relation to the spiritual service of the believer (Romans 12:1-2; 1 Corinthians 3:16-17; 6:19) and to the Spirit-filled church (Ephesians 2:21-22), but this is not the same as typology, where a type is fulfilled by an antitype. Even in a book such as Hebrews, in which a comparison is made between Israel's liturgical system and the believer's gracious access in Christ, and where such a symbolic significance might be expected, only a description of the Tabernacle and its furniture is given (Hebrews 9:1-5). This passage does refer to the "outer Tabernacle" as a "symbol" (or "figure, illustration"—Greek, *parabole*) for "the present time" (verses 8-9). The interpretation of these verses is much debated,[24] but their main point is that the Levitical system was weak in that it offered only limited and exclusive access to God's presence. But, as one writer has noted, "This does not mean that the Levitical system was bad or that it did not accomplish the purpose for which God instituted it."[25] However, even if the Scriptures were replete with symbolical and spiritual uses of the entire Levitical system and the Sanctuary, this would in no way affect their literal interpretation. John Whitcomb, longtime professor of Old Testament at Grace Theological Seminary, makes this point when he says:

> The fact that its structure and ceremonies will have a definite symbolical and spiritual significance cannot be used as an argument against its literal existence. For the Tabernacle was a literal structure in spite of the fact that it was filled with symbolic and typical significance. Such reasoning might easily deny the literality of Christ's glorious second coming on the basis that the passages which describe His coming are filled with symbolical expressions (see Matthew 24 and Revelation 19).[26]

Therefore, even if one could impute symbolic meaning to the description of the Temple and its ritual service in Ezekiel 40–48 (in the Old Testament there is no precedence for this and in the text there is no guide for understanding the symbolism), there is no reason why the fulfillment should not be as literal as for every Temple and priesthood of the past.

4. *The eschatological interpretation of Ezekiel 40–48 is in harmony with other Old Testament prophetic passages.* The same text that commands the house of Israel to build the Temple also states the time when the people are to build it: after "they are ashamed of all that they have done" (Ezekiel 43:10-11). The time of this national repentance accords with the eschatological period previously described in the restoration text of Ezekiel 36:22-38, in which Israel has been made "ashamed" as part of the regenerative work of the Spirit (verse 32). Just because the exilic community expected restoration does not mean that what they experienced upon their return was what Ezekiel (and other prophets) had prophesied. Even the commentator cited earlier—who sought to place this prophecy's fulfillment in the return of 538 B.C. and rebuilding of the Temple in 516 B.C.—still postponed the fulfillment of Ezekiel 47:1-12 to the time of the Messiah. But why should only this portion of the prophecy be considered as having its fulfillment in the Messianic age? The same question must be posed to those who believe that the form of government seen in these chapters reflects the religious polity of the restoration community under the Persian administration of Darius I.[27] This is unwarranted, for in other prophetic texts, this kind of restoration government is clearly reserved for the eschatological kingdom of Israel.[28]

If Ezekiel's prophecies were meant to be fulfilled historically in the Second Temple, then they must be considered a failure. Any attempt to make the Second Temple fulfill these restoration prophecies forces us to either abandon literal interpretation (which, as we have seen, the details of the text do not allow) or admit that the Word of God itself has failed (which orthodox theology cannot allow). For this reason, Jewish interpreters have concluded that the Second Temple was not built according to Ezekiel's plan because the people knew it was not yet time to build this Temple. Rashi, one of the greatest medieval Jewish commentators, explained this when he wrote:

> The return to Israel in the days of Ezra could have been like the first time the Jewish people entered Israel in the days of Joshua....However, sin prevented this, for their repentance was imperfect. Since they were not worthy, they did not have permission to build the Temple which was designated as the Temple for the eternal redemption, for when it will be

built according to this design, the [divine] glory will rest upon it forever.[29]

One objection to the eschatological interpretation of chapters 40–48 is the alleged absence of eschatological language—such as the phrase "on that day" and "in the latter days," which appear in chapters 34–37 and especially 38–39. However, as noted above, the literary linkage to these chapters establishes an eschatological setting, as does the description of the transformation of the Land, the city of Jerusalem, the Temple, and the priesthood. The unprecedented change from the laws of the past, the return of the glory of God (Ezekiel 43:1-12), the extended holiness of the Temple Mount, the physical changes in the Land of Israel (Ezekiel 47:1-12), the enlarged boundaries of the Land (Ezekiel 47:13-23), and God's presence dwelling in an enlarged Jerusalem (Ezekiel 48:35) all serve to indicate that the time of fulfillment is eschatological. This is clearly seen when these details are compared with similar Old Testament accounts of a future Temple, a raised Temple Mount, and restored conditions—most of which happen to include these eschatological time markers (such as Isaiah 2:2-4; 56:6-7; 60:10-22; Jeremiah 3:16-17; 31:27-40; 33:14-18; Joel 3:18-21; Micah 4:1-8; Haggai 2:7-9; Zechariah 6:12-15; 14:16,20-21. Specifically, we may categorize those related only to the Temple and its ceremonies as follows:

Prophecies of a Millennial Temple	Prophecies of Sacrifices in a Future Temple
Joel 3:18	Isaiah 56:6-7
Isaiah 2:3	Isaiah 60:7
Isaiah 60:13	Jeremiah 33:18
Daniel 9:24	Zechariah 14:16-21
Haggai 2:7,9	

When we consider Ezekiel's remarks about the restoration of the Levitical priesthood, we find that not only do the other prophetical books agree in terms of the details, but that Ezekiel's prophecy provides the most complete statement. In fact, the ancient promises to the Levitical priesthood cannot have a literal fulfillment unless Ezekiel's prophecy is eschatological. God promised to Zadok, (the Aaronide high priest at the time of David and Solomon—1 Kings 1:34); and his descendants an everlasting priesthood (1 Samuel 2:35; 1 Kings 2:27,35). This promise was the reconfirmation of similar promises made to Zadok's ancestor Phinehas (Numbers 25:13) and Phinehas' grandfather Aaron, the progenitor of the Israelite priesthood (Exodus 29:9; 40:15). The Zadokite priesthood was the dominant priesthood up until the time of the Maccabean revolt, after which the office became corrupted and the Hasmonean dynasty appointed the high priests with political purposes in mind. Thus, the priests serving in the Temple in the time leading up to its destruction in A.D. 70 were not of the legitimate Zadokite line. Jewish sects like those at Qumran, which had members claiming to be Zadokite priests (1QS 5:2, 9; 1Qsa 1:2, 24; 2:3; 1Qsb 3:22), rejected the Jerusalem Temple and its corrupt priesthood and expected their priesthood to regain its position of service in a future Temple that would be built after a climactic end time war in which the Hasmonean priests would be punished (1 QpHab 9:4-7; 4QpNah 1:11).[30] Only Ezekiel unequivocally states the fulfillment of God's promise that the Zadokite priesthood was eternal by stating that it is the Zadokites who will serve in the Millennial Temple (Ezekiel 40:46; 44:15). Ezekiel's contemporary Jeremiah linked the perpetuity of the Levitical priesthood with the perpetuity of the Davidic dynasty and guaranteed it by comparing it to the perpetuity of the earth's rotation on its axis (Jeremiah 33:17-22). If we allow Ezekiel's prophecy of a future Zadokite priesthood to be spiritualized, then, according to the linkage in Jeremiah's prophecy, the promises of the Davidic covenant (2 Samuel 7:13,16) could also be spiritualized. This would put all Messianic fulfillment in jeopardy (including anything fulfilled in Jesus)! So, if we accept a literal and eschatological fulfillment for the Levitical priesthood, then we must also accept it for the Temple in which these priests will serve. In addition, if 12,000 individuals from the tribe of Levi can be sealed during the Tribulation period (Revelation 7:7), then a literal restoration of the Levitical priesthood after the Tribulation is certainly plausible. In harmony with other prophets, then, Ezekiel depicts an eschatological restoration—of which the Temple and its priesthood are an essential part.

The Millennial Temple: From Ichabod to Chabod

If Ezekiel 40–42 presented the "blueprint" for building, and Ezekiel 43:10-11 gave the "building permit," Ezekiel 43:1-7 describes the "on-site inspection." Since these verses on the return and restoration of God's glory to the new Temple are one of the strongest evidences for the eschatological interpretation of chapters 40–48, it is important to give closer attention to this event. Nowhere in Scripture nor in extrabiblical Jewish literature is it stated that the divine presence filled the Second Temple as it did the Tabernacle (Exodus 40:34-35) and the

First Temple (1 Kings 8:10-11; 2 Chronicles 5:13-14; 7:13). Rather, Jewish sources made a point of its absence (see *Tosefta Yom Tov*) and relegated such a hope to the eschatological period known as "the period of restoration of all things" (Acts 3:21). That the Divine presence, or *Shekinah*, will only return in this future time of redemption is evident from the description of its return in Ezekiel's 43:1-7:

> Then he [the angelic guide of 40:4] led me to the gate, the gate facing toward the east [Eastern Gate]; and behold, the Glory of the God of Israel was coming from the way of the east. And His voice was like the sound of many waters; and the earth shone with His glory....And the glory of the LORD came into the house [Temple] by the way of the gate facing toward the east. And the Spirit lifted me up and brought me into the inner court; and behold the glory of the LORD filled the house. Then I heard one [God] speaking to me from the house, while a man [the angelic guide] was standing beside me. And He said to me, "Son of man, this is the place of My throne and the place of the soles of My feet, where I will dwell among the sons of Israel forever. And the house of Israel will not again defile My holy name...."

Ezekiel here presents the reversal of the *Shekinah's* previous departure, carefully describing the order of return to match the order of abandonment detailed in chapters 9–11: *departure*—Holy of Holies to Inner Court to Eastern Gate to east; *return*—east to Eastern Gate to Inner Court to Holy of Holies. Notice, too, that this return fulfills the divine ideal of the Creator dwelling with His creation as first shown at Eden and then at Mount Sinai. In this respect note that the elements of God's approaching presence in the Garden of Eden (see Genesis 2:8; 3:8) are repeated: an eastward orientation (verses 2,4) and the sound of God's voice (verse 2), and the reference to "the glory of the God of Israel" (verse 2) reminding the reader of His original return (the Tabernacle in Sinai) and of His prophetic promise to return His glory (in the same way) to the Final Temple (Haggai 2:5,7,9). The last aspect of this description that confirms this is the future Messianic age is that the "sons of Israel" will be not be able to again defile the Temple as in the past (verse 7). This will be because they have been constitutionally changed to prevent this possibility (Ezekiel 36:25-27; 37:14,23).

With the return of the *Shekinah* to the Millennial Temple, the condition of "no glory" (*ichabod*) became one of "glory" (*chabod*). The greater restoration of God's glory to the Temple described by Ezekiel distinguishes the Jerusalem of the Millennial Kingdom and its recreated Temple Mount from that of any other in history. Not only will it be physically elevated above all other mountains in the Land (Isaiah 2:2; 40:4-5; Micah 4:1; Zechariah 14:10), but it will shine out as a beacon to all the nations as the place where divine revelation now resides on earth (Isaiah 2:2-3; 49:6; Jeremiah 3:17; Zechariah 8:20-23).[31] So pervasive will the Presence of God be in the city (Ezekiel 43:12; see also Zechariah 8:3) that the city will be renamed YHWH *Shammah* ("the Lord is there"). This divine presence will also endue the city with perpetual holiness (Ezekiel 48:35; see also Zechariah 14:20-21). Isaiah describes in greater detail this holiness and the awesome appearance of God's glory dwelling at the Temple Mount:

> In that day the Branch of the LORD will be beautiful and glorious, and the fruit of the earth will be the pride and the adornment of the survivors of Israel. And it will come about that he who is left in Zion and remains in Jerusalem will be called holy....Then the LORD will create over the whole area of Mount Zion and over her assemblies a cloud by day, even smoke, and the brightness of a flaming fire by night; for over all the glory will be a canopy. And there will be a shelter to give shade from the heat by day, and refuge and protection from the storm and the rain (Isaiah 4:2-3,6).

In view of the glory-cloud's provision, Ezekiel 48:1-34 arranges the tribal territories around the Temple in such a way as to place it at the center (Ezekiel 48:15). Because of the sanctity of the site, even the king's palace was not to be placed too close to the Temple complex lest it serve as a reminder of the past history of the apostate kings and idolatrous deeds of Israel, which were considered as abominations (Ezekiel 43:7-9). Likewise, the gradations of the Temple's sacred space is greater than in previous Temples, allowing no uncircumcised foreigner to partake of Passover and no ordinary Israelite to enter the inner courtyard (Ezekiel 44:17-19; 46:20).

One of the most distinguishing elements of Ezekiel's Temple is that the restoration of the rest of Land of Israel appears to be sourced out of the Temple. In Ezekiel 47:1-12 (see Joel 4:18) we read that fructuous waters will flow from beneath the Sanctuary, transforming the Dead Sea into a body of water teeming with aquatic life. That, in turn, could possibly renew all of the Land so that it becomes like the Garden of Eden (Ezekiel 36:35). As an interesting aside it should be noted that archaeological confirmation of such a subterranean water source that has occasionally erupted on the Temple Mount in past history was given by Edward Robinson based on his discovery of the Fountain Ash-Shafa, whose waters came from a spring 80 feet below the Rock of the Dome. The same

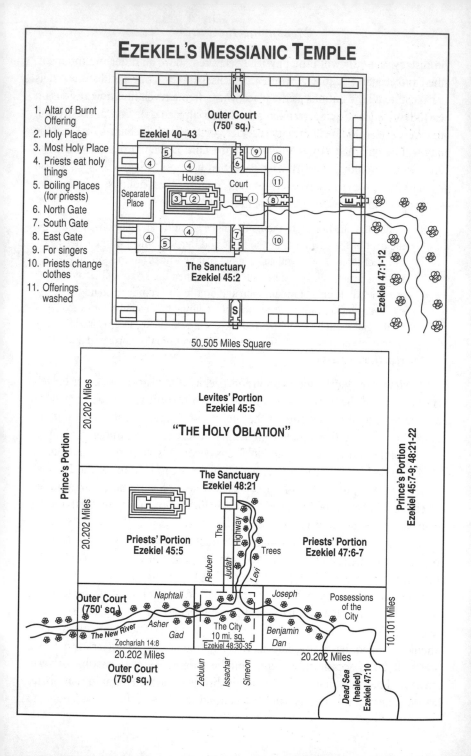

EZEKIEL'S MESSIANIC TEMPLE

1. Altar of Burnt Offering
2. Holy Place
3. Most Holy Place
4. Priests eat holy things
5. Boiling Places (for priests)
6. North Gate
7. South Gate
8. East Gate
9. For singers
10. Priests change clothes
11. Offerings washed

Outer Court (750' sq.)

Ezekiel 40–43

House

Court

Separate Place

The Sanctuary
Ezekiel 45:2

Ezekiel 47:1-12

N

E

S

50.505 Miles Square

Levites' Portion
Ezekiel 45:5

"THE HOLY OBLATION"

20.202 Miles

20.202 Miles

Prince's Portion

Prince's Portion
Ezekiel 45:7-9; 48:21-22

The Sanctuary
Ezekiel 48:21

Priests' Portion
Ezekiel 45:5

Priests' Portion
Ezekiel 47:6-7

The Highway

Reuben

Judah

Levi

Trees

Outer Court
(750' sq.)

Naphtali

Joseph

Possessions of the City

The New River
Zechariah 14:8

Asher

Gad

The City
10 mi. sq.
Ezekiel 48:30-35

Benjamin

Dan

10.101 Miles

20.202 Miles

Outer Court
(750' sq.)

Zebulun

Issachar

Simeon

20.202 Miles

Dead Sea
(healed)
Ezekiel 47:10

source of water is mentioned in the Mishnah *(Tamid* 1:1; *Middot* 1:6-9) and today is thought to be located not far from cistern # 30 *(Shakib Ka-it-Bey)* near the Western Wall.[32] In the spring of 1999 rumors abounded of a water flow on the Temple Mount, seemingly the result of the new construction on the Muslim mosque at the Southern Wall, but also reported near the Eastern Gate and Western Wall.

Ezekiel's Prophecy Regarding the Eastern Gate

Every visitor to Jerusalem looks forward to seeing the famous Golden Gate situated proudly on the eastern wall of the Old City at the Temple Mount. It has been sealed shut for hundreds of years—since the Saracens conquered Jerusalem in 1187. Long ago a Muslim graveyard was placed across the gate's entrance in the hopes that the graveyard's defiling influence will prevent a Jewish Messiah from returning through this gate to reclaim Jerusalem and rebuild the Temple. Many Christians believe that the blocking of the Golden Gate is a fulfillment of Ezekiel 44:1-3, which reads:

> He brought me back by the way of the outer gate of the sanctuary, which faces the east; and it was shut. And the LORD said to me, "This gate shall be shut, it shall not be opened, and no man shall enter in by it, for the LORD God of Israel, has entered in by it; therefore it shall be shut. [It is] for the prince, he shall sit in it as prince to eat bread before the LORD; he shall enter by way of the porch of the gate, and shall go out by the same way."

This passage's association with this gate has a long tradition. Since the early days of the church Christians have believed that the path of Jesus' last journey to Jerusalem and onto the Temple Mount was through this gate, which lies on a direct east-west axis with the Church of the Holy Sepulcher, the traditional place where Jesus was crucified and buried. One of the last Christian monarchs said to have walked through the Golden Gate was the Emperor Heraclius, who, in A.D. 631, brought back to Jerusalem fragments of the supposed True Cross, which he had recovered from the Persians. When the Crusaders took over Jerusalem, they kept the gate shut except for Palm Sunday, during which they would allow processions. According to Muslim prophecy, on the Day of Judgment the angel Gabriel will sound three blasts on a ram's horn to announce the resurrection, all the peoples of the world will assemble on the Mount of Olives, and Abraham, Moses, Jesus, and Mohammed will stand beside the scales of justice located on the Temple Mount. The souls of those who have been granted eternal life will then pass along a tightrope stretched across the Kidron Valley and through the Golden Gate, which Muslims call in Arabic *Bab el-Dahabiveh* ("Eternal Gate"), but also by the names for each of its two arches, the northern *Bab el-Tobeh* ("Gate of Repentance"), and the southern *Bab el-Rahmeh* ("Gate of Mercy").

Based on a similar theology, many evangelical Christian groups believe that Jesus, upon His return, will enter through this present-day gate. Such an understanding has caused one group, the end-time organization Daystar International Ministry, to provide continuous camera coverage of the Golden Gate in the event the Messiah might arrive and enter the gate at any moment. Internet users can access the current status of "Golden Gate news" from the "MessiahCAM" at www.olivetree.org/webcam.htm.[33]

However, there is no conclusive evidence that the present Golden Gate is even the same gate as the ancient Eastern Gate (or Shushan Gate) which opened onto the Temple Mount in the time of Christ. According to Leen Ritmeyer, there are stones in the wall beside the gate that may date to the time of Nehemiah, and the inside of the gate contains pillars from the Second Temple period. However, the Golden Gate that people see today was constructed by a fifth-century A.D. Byzantine emperor. It was known to have been in ruins by A.D. 629, when it was rebuilt by Emperor Heraclius. It was first closed by the Arabs in A.D. 810, reopened by the Crusaders in A.D. 1102, and walled up again by the Saracens in A.D. 1187. Apparently it was opened again during reconstruction work done by the Ottoman Turkish Sultan Suleiman the Magnificent, who rebuilt the present-day walls of the Old City. However, he closed it for the last time in A.D. 1546. As these facts reveal, its closing had nothing to do with prophecy, and despite popular stories to the contrary, there was nothing in the past—nor is there anything at the present—that would prevent it from being reopened by whatever power controlled the area.

A careful look at the context of Ezekiel's prophecy, however, makes it clear that the sealing of the Eastern Gate will occur in the end times with the return of the *Shekinah* to the topographically altered Temple Mount and rebuilt Temple (Ezekiel 43:1-7). Therefore, Ezekiel's prophecy cannot be interpreted to have been fulfilled during the Second Temple period at the time of Jesus' so-called "Triumphal Entry" into Jerusalem (Luke 19:28-38), even if this were the gate He used. The plain meaning of this passage is that the gate will be shut only after the *Shekinah* has reentered the Holy of Holies in the Temple—an act signifying the Lord's uniquely holy status and perhaps the fact that He will never again depart, but remain forever (Ezekiel 37:28; 43:7; 48:35). This is in keeping with the Near Eastern custom of showing special honor to a dignitary by restricting others from using the same gate the dignitary had used (see Exodus 19:9-23 and especially verse 24).

The "prince" who is mentioned here as sitting in this gate "to eat bread [a meal] before the LORD" (Ezekiel 44:3) is also prohibited from using this gate for entry. The rabbis identified him as the Messiah, but because he is not a priest, has no priestly rights, has sons (Ezekiel 46:16), and needs to offer a sin offering (Ezekiel 45:22), it is preferable to view him as someone of Davidic lineage who represents the Messianic government on earth.[34] The fulfillment of this passage will take place at the Eastern Gate of the new Millennial Temple, not the present-day Golden Gate, which will probably end up being torn down and reconstructed when the Third Temple is built during the Tribulation period, and the gate will certainly be leveled by the earthquake that accompanies the Messiah's advent to the Mount of Olives (Zechariah 14:4) and the topographical changes that follow (Zecahriah 14:10).

In this chapter I have attempted to present the arguments for a literal interpretation of the future Temple described in Ezekiel 40–48. While the support for the Last Days Temple does not depend on this prophecy alone, it is the major text providing the details of its construction in the Millennial kingdom. However, one of the major objections against a literal interpretation is that Ezekiel's description mentions the revival of animal sacrifices in the Millennial Temple. How does this fit in with all that we've considered so far? In the next chapter I will present this problem and its proposed solutions; join me as we seek the answers from Scripture.

CHAPTER 23

Blasphemy or Blessing?

Sacrifices in the Last Days Temple

Jesus Christ is the only Mediator, His blood the final sacrifice. There can be no going back. If there is a way back to the ceremonial law, to the types and shadows of what has now become the bondage of legalism, then Paul labored and ran in vain—more than that, Christ died in vain.[1]

—EDMUND P. CLOWNEY

Is it heretical to believe that a Temple and sacrifices will once again exist? . . . Ezekiel himself believed it was a reality and the future home of Messiah. Then, it becomes not heresy to believe that a Temple and sacrifices will exist; rather, it is almost a heresy to not believe this, especially because it is a part of God's infallible word. The burden on us is to determine how it fits—not its reality.[2]

—JOHN SCHMITT

W hen the Temple was standing, its most central function was to serve as a site for sacrificial worship. Every Jew we read about in the Bible offered sacrifces—from Abraham, the father of the Jewish Nation, to Jesus, the founder of Christianity.[3] When the Temple was destroyed in A.D. 70 the sacrificial system came to an end. Despite this loss, Jewish liturgy preserved the ancient Temple services, recounting the sacrifices verbally in accord with Hosea 14:3: "So we shall render for bullocks the offering of our lips." In the words of the Talmud, "The prayers were instituted in correlation to the tamid sacrifices." The tamid, or *olat ha-tamid,* was a twice-daily offering, morning and evening, of a male lamb. Even though the sacrifices were continued in symbol only, Jewish orthodoxy maintained the belief that they would return in substance with the Third Temple. One basis for this belief has been the references to this practice in the prophecies of Jewish restoration and the Last Days Temple. In the last chapter we argued that Ezekiel's prophecy of the future Temple will be a literal structure. If so, how should we understand the instructions in this prophecy prescribing blood sacrifice? After 2,000 years in which Judaism has gotten along perfectly well without sacrifice, and after which Christianity has been built on a finished sacrifice, is the return of sacrifices to be interpreted as a religious blasphemy or a restored blessing? Will there really be literal sacrifices in the Last Days Temple? Before we attempt to answer these questions, let's survey the struggle both Christians and Jews have had with this issue.

The Problem of Sacrifices for Christianity

The early Jewish Christians faced the problem of continuing life in the Jewish culture, which required offering sacrifices for acceptability. Initially there appears to have been little difficulty with this because such sacrifices were being made in faith to the true God and were not seen as conflicting with one's faith in Christ. We read in Acts 21:20 concerning the testimony of the Jerusalem church that there were "many thousands...among the Jews of those who have believed, and they [were] all zealous for the Law" (which included sacrifices as a part of Temple worship). Furthermore, this same text shows that they considered sacrifices at the Temple as an evidence of fidelity as a Jew, and that even the apostle Paul complied with this practice (Acts 21:22-26). The Jewish Christians' most significant problem with sacrifices was how to fellowship with their Gentile brethren, who were not required to offer sacrifices, but with whom they shared an equal access to God through faith in Jesus (Acts 15:11). Working through this problem enabled Jewish Christians to make the spiritual adjustment to life without sacrifices after the destruction of the Temple.

By contrast, Gentile Christians who had no history in or access to the sacrificial rites in the Jerusalem Temple, faced a different problem. As Gentiles they lived in the cultural context of pagan sacrifices—from which they as Christians had to make an immediate break because these sacrifices represented offerings to idols (false gods—see Acts 14:15; 1 Corinthians 12:2; 1 Thessalonians 1:9; 1 John 5:21). Their problem with sacrifices was reflected in the major concern they had about buying meat that had first been offered to idols as a sacrifice (see 1 Corinthians 8:1-13; see also Romans 14:13-23). Moreover, abstinence from eating sacrificial meat had been imposed as a social requirement for maintaining good relations with the Jewish Christians (Acts 15:20). Even though the Gentile Christians' lives had formerly been regulated by the pagan sacrificial system, and they must likely have faced immense pressure from relatives and business associates to continue this practice culturally, they adapted to spiritual worship without sacrifice by understanding that Jesus had made them acceptable to the true God by offering the ultimate sacrifice on their behalf.

Not until after the destruction of the Temple and the onslaught of Roman persecution against non-pagan religions did both Jewish and Gentile Christians find themselves facing a common problem in relation to sacrifices. Roman officials demanded that Christians living in Roman colonies offer sacrifices to Rome's pagan gods as a demonstration of loyalty to the emperor and the empire. No Christian could do this because to do so was to make a public acknowledgment of another god, which was tantamount to renouncing Christ.

It is interesting, then, that when Christianity became the official religion of the Roman empire, its institutional form that became Roman Catholicism renewed the practice of sacrifice on an altar at each celebration of the mass. Since the Roman Catholic view of transubstantiation results in viewing the sacrifice as literal rather than strictly symbolic, it continues the sacrificial work of Christ and would not find a conflict with the idea of sacrifice per se. Rather, its rejection of a restoration of Israel and its sacrificial system is based on its doctrine of replacement theology.

It is Protestant and evangelical Christianity that has the greatest difficulty with the return of animal sacrifices in a future Temple. Here it is popularly assumed to be equivalent to a denial of the finality and sufficiency of Christ's sacrifice. For example, Edmund Clowney, past president of Westminster Theological Seminary, a leading Reformed institution, has declared, "Jesus Christ is the only

Mediator, His blood the final sacrifice. There can be no going back. If there is a way back to the ceremonial law, to the types and shadows of what has now become the bondage of legalism, then Paul labored and ran in vain—more than that, Christ died in vain."[4] In like manner, but more to the point, author Archibald Hughes affirmed that "to restore these things today…would be apostasy."[5] These statements reflect the common contention that a resumption of the sacrificial system would contradict Hebrews chapters 7–10, which is interpreted to teach that all animal sacrifices were temporary types fulfilled by Christ's ultimate sacrifice. If Christ's sacrifice was the final sacrifice, it is argued, then the need for animal sacrifices ended at the cross, and any resumption of this system is a return to the Mosaic legislation which repudiates the completed work of Christ (see John 19:30). In Hebrews 10 we read that "the Law" is only "a shadow," and that the "sacrifices" it prescribes "can *never*…make perfect" those who offer them (verse 1), nor "take away sins" (verses 4,11). Furthermore, it goes on to say—in relation to the sacrifices of the old covenant—that "He [Christ] *takes away the first* in order to establish the second," that He "offered *one sacrifice for sins for all time*" and consequently, "we have been sanctified through the offering of the body of Jesus Christ *once for all*" (verses 8-12, emphasis added). Therefore, "where there is forgiveness of these things, there is *no longer any offering for sin*" (verse 18). Jesus is "the Lamb of God who takes away the sin of the world" (John 1:29), and it was at His sacrificial death that the veil in the Temple was rent (Matthew 27:51; Luke 23:45). These passages appear to teach the irreversible cessation of the sacrificial system so clearly and plainly that any thought of future sacrifices is seen as scandalous. For this reason, it is thought, a return to sacrifices in the future can only be interpreted as a return to Judaism and a renunciation of Christianity.

The Problem of Sacrifices for Judaism

Like Christianity, post-Temple Judaism also struggled with the concept of sacrifices. In the time of the Second Temple it is estimated that as many as 600,000 sacrifices took place annually. Therefore, when the Temple was destroyed, the issue of the loss of the sacrificial system was paramount for the Jews. As one Jewish writer explains:

> How can we possibly sense the terror that must have gripped a person who had to atone for his sins but was unable to do so? The Jew who lived at the time of the Temple's destruction did not have other methods of

atonement developed by generations of halakhic legislation....That generation of Jews had to grapple with a new reality which appeared to deny any possibility of religious wholeness: An individual who sinned would have to continue to live with his sin. This factor contributed to the doubts which assailed many Jews of this period as to whether there was any point—or indeed any possibility—of maintaining a religious way of life.[6]

Some Jews, and even Jewish proselytes,[7] attempted to offer sacrifices even after the Temple's destruction, but this practice was eventually outlawed by the Romans. Even though Traditional or Orthodox Judaism continued the spiritual principle of worship (see Hosea 6:6) according to the modifications of Judaism by the Ta'anaitic Rabbi Yohanan ben Zakkai, it has never adequately resolved the problem of handling the many commandments related to sacrifice. Over one-third of the 613 commandments, obligatory for observant Jews, are connected to the Temple and sacrifices. So central are these commands to Jewish life that modern Temple activist Binyamin Ze'ev Kahane declares, "While everyone understands that there is no Judaism without *mitzvot* ['commandments'] many do not grasp the fact that the Temple and sacrifices are also essential to Judaism, and without them, there really is no Judaism."[8]

But how would it be possible for Jews to perform sacrifices today? On the one hand the chief rabbinate of Israel has held that Jews who enter the Temple Mount in their present state of ritual impurity are liable for the punishment of *Kareit* ("cutting off") or banishment from the Jewish community. On the other hand, an equal risk of liability results from *not* entering the Temple Mount to perform the Passover sacrifice, for the same sentence is pronounced upon a ritually pure person who intentionally does not bring the Passover lamb on the fourteenth day of Nisan (even when the entire Nation is impure from the contact with the dead).

Partly because of such seemingly irreconcilable difficulties, but mainly because of a denial of the binding nature of the Written and Oral Laws, the liberal branches of Judaism, the Reform and Reconstructionist movements, long ago abandoned the idea of attaching any significance to the matter of sacrifices. For them the sacrificial system was part of the primitive religion that more enlightened mankind has outgrown. In like manner, Conservative Judaism, though retaining Hebrew references to sacrifices in its old Conservative Siddur, meticulously omitted the translations in the prayer book. However, its newest Conservative Siddur, *Sim Shalom* (1985) has almost entirely rewritten, in alternative versions, the festival Musaf liturgy, which explicitly recounts the sacrificial ritual and has put sacrificial references in the past tense. The reason for this, says conservative rabbi Elliot Dorf, rector of the University of Judaism in Los Angeles, is because "the sacrifices were one stage in the development of Jewish ritual practice, and not something God wants us to do in the future. According to this view, God merely 'tolerated' sacrifices as a stage in religious development." In general, four objections have been offered by Judaism to animal sacrifices:[9]

1. *The sacrifices seem mechanistic and meaningless.* The instructions in the Torah give this impression by providing little explanation of their significance. The instructions tend to emphasize what is being done rather than why it is being done or what is thought or felt by the one giving the offering. While the biblical condemnation of offering sacrifices mechanistically with an improper intent or in an unrighteous way implies that "a contrite spirit" (Psalm 51:19; Isaiah 66:2) and "obedient heart" (1 Samuel 15:22; Psalm 40:6) was to accompany sacrifice, if this was all that God really wanted, then why were sacrifices ever necessary?

2. *The depictions of the sacrifices emphasize gore, not grandeur.* The sacrificial system essentially turned the Temple into a slaughterhouse, with the priests standing knee-deep in entrails and suet while pouring huge quantities of blood over the altar, sacred objects, and each other. What other image is possible when we read, for example, in 1 Kings 8:63 that at the dedication of the Temple Solomon offered "22,000 oxen and 120,000 sheep"! Such a scene in our aesthetically clean, nonviolent, culture is not only alien, but offensive, and its vulgar and earthy image of a bloodthirsty God runs counter to the modern-day emphasis of God as a high and lofty figure filled with grandeur and glory.

3. *The notion that God "smells" and "eats" the sacrifices seems pagan.* When the Bible describes the sacrifices in respect to God it often uses anthropomorphic language to show His acceptance or rejection of them. Accordingly it is said that "the LORD smelled [the sacrifice]" (Genesis 8:21), or that the sacrifices are His "bread" (Leviticus 21:6), "the food" of God (Leviticus 22:25), "a soothing aroma" (Numbers 28:2), or that God was "filled...with the fat of...sacrifices" (Isaiah 43:24). Even though the Bible makes it clear that such terminology does not imply a pagan sense of God having need—"If I [God] were hungry, I would not tell you...shall I eat the flesh of bulls, or drink the blood of male goats?" (Psalm 50:12-13)—the imagery still conveys to the reader a sense that seems to conflict with the concept of God as a noncorporeal Being.

4. *It is morally wrong to kill an animal as an expression of religious feeling.* Perhaps the greatest objection to a restoration of the sacrificial system is that it represents the wanton, senseless killing of innocent and useful animals. Israeli society, like Western society, has its animal-rights advocates, who feel that the superfluous slaughter of animals is needless, abusive and criminal. For example, a daughter of one of the leading figures in the Temple movement (whose organization supports the return to sacrifices and even offers sacrifices on occasion) told me that she rejects the idea of returning to sacrifices because she views it as wrong to treat animals with such cruelty. Once the sacrifices are separated from worship and viewed as expendable, their ceremonial use appears not only as impractical, but immoral.

These objections, however, all disregard the fact that animals as sacrifices serve a higher purpose than man's convenience. As sacrifices they function in the service of their Creator to preserve sanctity and restore the divine order. Furthermore, they were not offered capriciously out of a desire to harm animals or for personal pleasure, since financial loss is incurred by their sacrifice, but in obedience to God's commandments and to please Him. For this reason, such objections are of no consequence to ultra-Orthodox (or Hasidic) and many Orthodox Jews. They accept Maimonides' 13 Articles of Faith and his legal code, which envision a return to animal sacrifice and the literal building of the Third Temple on Mount Zion. Not willing to bow to modern convention, and seeking to preserve the hope that sacrifices can once again be resumed (even though in the case of the ultra-Orthodox it is interpreted through a maze of mysticism), the Jews developed a custom in the Middle Ages of killing a chicken on the afternoon before the beginning of Yom Kippur ("Day of Atonement") and raising the bleeding carcass over their heads while saying a prayer for the atonement of their family's sins. And, as we have seen in a previous chapter, some in the Temple movement today have resumed the *korban Pesach* ("Passover sacrifice") overlooking the Temple Mount with a prayer that they soon will be able to offer sacrifices on the Temple Mount itself.

Ezekiel's Statements on Sacrifices

Regardless of one's views on sacrifices, every interpreter of the last chapters of Ezekiel must wrestle with the fact that there is a statement concerning the sacrificial system in all of the nine chapters but one (chapter 47). These references include "new moons," "sabbaths," and "all the appointed feasts" (Ezekiel

44:24; 45:17; 46:3,11-12), "daily offerings" (Ezekiel 46:13-14), "burnt offerings," "grain offerings," and the "libations" (Ezekiel 45:17; 46:2,4,11-15), "blood sacrifices" (Ezekiel 43:20), "an altar for the burnt offerings" (Ezekiel 40:47; 43:13-27), "an altar for the incense offerings" (Ezekiel 41:22), "boiling places" to "boil the sacrifices of the people" (Ezekiel 46:23-24), a Zadokite priesthood to "offer...the fat and the blood" (Ezekiel 40:46; 42:13-14: 43:19; 44:15-16; 48:11), and a Levitical priesthood to slaughter the burnt offerings (Ezekiel 44:10-11; 48:22). Furthermore, the offerings are stated to be for "a sin offering" (Ezekiel 43:22,25; 44:24,29) and to "make atonement" (Ezekiel 43:20; 45:25). Since the sacrifices and sacrificial personnel are so prominent throughout these chapters, the treatment of the sacrifices cannot be avoided as incidental.

Therefore, the first question we must answer is this: Were these references to sacrifice intended as symbol or substance? These options are not merely academic concerns, but have significant theological implications. As the late German prophetic scholar Erich Sauer stated, "We stand here really before an inescapable alternative: *Either* the prophet himself was mistaken in his expectation of a coming temple service, and his prophecy in the sense in which he himself meant it will never be fulfilled; *or* God, in the time of Messiah, will fulfill literally these prophecies of the temple according to their intended literal meaning. There is no other choice possible."[10] However, the option most commonly resorted to by interpreters is to abandon a literal interpretation of all of Ezekiel's prophecy in chapters 40–48 in preference of the symbolic (see chapter 22). This is at least a consistent interpretation, since we can hardly spiritualize the sacrifices and then literalize the Temple.[11] In the previous chapter I discussed the issue of symbolic and spiritual interpretations of the Temple, so let's now consider the spiritual interpretation of the sacrifices.

The Spiritual Interpretation of the Sacrifices

After the destruction of Jerusalem in A.D. 70, Judaism had no ritual access to the site of the Temple Mount, which prohibited the people from rebuilding the Temple and resuming the sacrificial system. Judaism was thus forced to prioritize the spiritual aspects of worship and reinterpret or abandon other commands that required a functioning priesthood. Jewish-Christianity historically faced the same situation, but had already adopted a spiritual priority that permitted them to function without sacrifices. This was because it understood Jesus' prediction that a day would come when worship in Jerusalem would be removed (John 4:23-24) and because Paul had taught that the Holy Spirit was spiritually building their community (with Gentile believers) into a holy temple in Messiah (Ephesians 2:21-22). Rabbinic Judaism, which realized that the sacrifices were essential but unattainable, likewise reconciled this difficulty by substituting the study of the sacrifices for the sacrifices themselves. The Talmudic passage that teaches this presents the argument of Rabbi Yaakov Bar Acha, who wrote:

> If it were not for Jews studying the laws of Temple sacrifices, heaven and earth would lose their right to exist, as the Torah states, "And he said, 'How will I know that I will inherit it?' " (Genesis 15:8). Avraham said to G-d, if Jews sin, will You destroy them like the Generation of the Deluge or the Generation of the language separation? He meant, tell me with what merit shall my children inherit. G-d answered, "Take for yourself a calf" (meaning that the merit of Temple Sacrifice will sustain and atone the Jewish People). Avraham answered that this will suffice as long as the *Beit HaMikdash* [Temple] is standing, but when the *Beit HaMikdash* is destroyed, what will be? He answered, I have established the laws of the sacrifices. When you study them, I will consider it as if you performed the sacrifices, and I will forgive you (Talmud, *Ta'anit* 27b).

The spiritualization of sacrifices within Gentile Christianity arose because of several factors: the bitter encounters with pagan sacrifice, the theological interpretation of judgment on the sacrificial system with the Temple's destruction, and the disappearance of Nazarene Jewish-Christianity in the fourth century. After this time the Christian interpretation of sacrifice became reduced to the concept of "forfeiture" and was embodied in religious "acts of sacrifice" such as personal piety: vows of abstinence, self-abnegation, renunciation of the world (monasticism), and even martyrdom. As a result, the only physical sacrifice that was necessary, or relevant, was the last and final sacrifice of Christ, which had forever ended the sacrificial system of the Jews. Even though this system had not actually ended with the sacrifice of Christ, but had continued for another 40 years, it was believed that from the divine perspective it had in fact ended along with His rejection of the Temple as demonstrated by the tearing of the veil in the Temple at the time of the crucifixion (Matthew 27:51; Mark 15:38; Luke 23:45).[12] According to this interpretation of the symbolism of this event, what was torn was the *inner* veil that separated the Holy Place from the Holy of Holies (Exodus 26:33), since this was the place where the atoning sacrifice was made. Even if this were the case, it need only symbolize that the *spiritual* (not ritual) barrier between God and man had been removed. However, there are three arguments against this meaning for the symbolism in this event:

1. A better case can be made for the veil that was torn being the *outer* veil that hung at the entrance doors to the Temple.[13] One reason for this is that Mark's account links this event with the response of the Roman centurion who watched Jesus die (Mark 15:39). While the text certainly links the soldier's confession of Jesus as "the Son of God" (verse 39b) to the *way* he saw Jesus die (in full command of His spirit, verse 37; see also Luke 23:46-47), Mark nevertheless mentions the tearing of the Temple curtain *in between* his statements about Jesus' final breath and the centurion's declaration. If the centurion's awestruck response includes his witnessing the rending of the veil, the only veil he could have seen "standing right in front of Jesus" (verse 39a) was the outer veil, since the inner veil was completely hidden from public view.

2. If we study this outer veil we have another clue as to what was symbolized by this event. The first-century Jewish historian Flavius Josephus tells us that this outer curtain was an 80-foot-high embroidered Babylonian tapestry that depicted "a panorama of the entire heavens" (*Jewish Wars* 5.5.4 §§212-14).[14] The significance of this for the symbolism here is unmistakable, especially in view of the fact that both the Matthean and Markan accounts specify that the direction of the tear in this curtain was "from top to bottom." This has been recognized by almost all commentators to symbolize the divine reaction "from heaven to earth." Therefore, we have the Temple itself[15] (which represented God's presence) dramatically symbolizing heaven's (the divine) response to the death of Jesus.[16]

3. While other motifs of "rending" have been suggested,[17] the Jewish context suggests that the one most common and universally recognized by a Jewsih audience was the rending of garments as an official expression of extreme emotion such as grief or outrage (Judges 11:35; 2 Kings 19:1; Job 1:20; 2:12; Acts 14:14; 16:22). And, because of the nature of the garment, the specific direction of tearing in this custom is from the "top to the bottom."[18] It is significant that in this very same context of the Passion narrative, during Jesus' trial, the high priest "tore his garment" in response to Jesus' self-confession (which the high priest called "blasphemy") as the divine "Son of Man" of Daniel 7:13 (see Matthew 26:64-65; Mark 15:62-63).[19] Putting together these details, I suggest that the rending of the veil symbolized the Temple's (heaven's) response to the blasphemy of the Jewish leadership who delivered Jesus to the Gentiles ("wicked

men who crucified the Lord of glory," see Acts 2:23; see also 3:15; 7:52). As such, it serves as an ironic contrast to the high priest (who represented the Temple), as does the Gentile Roman soldier's statement of belief (Luke 23:47) to that of the Jewish high priest's statement of blasphemy. Accordingly, the very Temple that the Temple establishment claimed Jesus wanted to destroy and that formed their accusation (along with His divine confession) for His condemnation (Mark 14:58), stood against them as a witness to Jesus.

If this interpretation is valid, it excludes any negative idea of "the rending of the veil" as a divine attack on the institution of the Temple or a rejection of the sacrificial system which it embodied. Therefore, the fact that the evening sacrifice (3:00 P.M.) took place in the Temple at the very moment the veil was rent did not symbolize a rejection of the sacrificial system. Rather, it revealed that this divine demonstration, evidenced by the tearing of the outer curtain, concerned Christ's *sacrifice*. Without this additional witness of the Temple's sacrifice to Christ's sacrifice it would have been unclear as to what this event specifically pointed.

Nevertheless, those who adopt the non-literal, symbolic interpretation of the sacrifices have said that the literal interpretation of the sacrifices of Ezekiel's Temple is an "embarrassment"[20] to the consistently literal view, and that "it shows how *completely* this view misinterprets the significance of God's dealings with mankind."[21] This leads us to ask: What support is offered in favor of a literal interpretation? Though in the past consistent literalists have often had as difficult a time explaining these references as have the spiritualizers,[22] recent studies have produced some convincing arguments in support of the literal interpretation.

The Literal Interpretation of the Sacrifices

Those who employ the literal method have responded to the spiritualizers' accusations by noting that theirs (the literalists') is the only system able to interpret the references to sacrifices in a manner that is consistent with the uses of these terms throughout the Old Testament. Where else in the Old Testament is the priesthood, the altar, the feasts, the offerings, and the sacrifices made typical or symbolic of any other truth? If the New Testament is suggested as the key to interpreting the sacrifices symbolically, then how did Jews, for whom the Old Testament was written, manage to understand and practice sacrifice for thousands of years without this key? But even if the New Testament suggests a spiritual pattern for interpreting the sacrificial system, it provides no specific pattern that enables one to interpret the sacrificial references in Ezekiel. For this reason, there can be no consistent interpretation of this text by the symbolic method and therefore, no clear understanding of its message. Moreover, the symbolic approach has to deal not only with the references in Ezekiel, but with numerous other references to sacrifices within eschatological contexts (see, for example, Isaiah 56:6-7; 60:7; 66:20-21; Jeremiah 33:18; Zechariah 14:16-21; Haggai 2:7; Malachi 1:11). In Jeremiah 33:17-23 we find this prophecy: "Thus says the LORD, 'David shall never lack a man to sit on the throne of the house of Israel; and the Levitical priests shall never lack a man before Me to offer burnt offerings, to burn grain offerings, and to prepare sacrifices continually'....Thus says the LORD, 'If you can break My covenant for the day, and My covenant for the night, so that day and night will not be at their appointed time, then My covenant may also be broken with David My servant that he shall not have a son to reign on his throne, and with the Levitical priests, My ministers. As the host of heaven cannot be counted, and the sand of the sea cannot be measured, so I will multiply the descendants of David My servant and the Levites who minister to Me.' "

Can this prophecy be spiritualized to find fulfillment in David as Christ and the Levites as Christians? This is not possible because the fulfillment of the prophecy in Jesus depends upon a literal fulfillment as the "son of David" by physical lineage (see Matthew 1:1), which the symbolical school accepts. Now it would be hermeneutically inconsistent to take the prophecy to David literally and the prophecy to the Levites as spiritual, especially since they are bound together in a dual promise of perpetuity with a fulfillment that is divinely guaranteed. Therefore, in the same way, the fulfillment of this prophecy for the Levites depends upon their being the physical descendants of Levi. To take this other than literally would be to remove it (in the case of David) from the rank of Messianic prophecy, yet it is also obvious that to find a literal fulfillment in any time but the future would be to admit that this prophecy has failed. The fulfillment, then, must take place with Christ reigning on the throne of David in the Millennial Jerusalem and the Levites ministering through the sacrifices in a rebuilt Temple.

It is also remarkable, from the symbolic point of view, that the main passages dealing with the sacrifices in Ezekiel (the altar of burnt offerings, the priests and Levites, the sacrificial offerings) are introduced immediately after Ezekiel 43:1-12, in which the glory of God returns to the Temple Mount to restore its sanctity and bring a new, extended spiritual dimension to Israel (verse 12). The contrast with the old defiled order is described in terms of there no longer being any of the former abominations in the Temple (verses 8-9), and it is only on the condition that Israel is truly "ashamed of all that they have done" (verses 10-11) that the design of the Temple is to be made known and its statutes able to be performed (verse 11). If, according to the symbolic school, the old sacrificial system had truly been fulfilled by Christ's sacrifice, which, in the symbolic view, would be represented by the coming of the glory of the Lord into the Temple, then why would sacrifice symbolically follow as part of this new design? By this interpretation it should have been part of the old order of abominations for which Israel should have been ashamed.

Some have argued that Isaiah 66:3-4 depicts a condemnation of sacrifice itself, or else in its eschatological context, of future Temple sacrifices (see chapter 21). But in this passage, is it the reinstitution of the sacrificial system which is rejected? Rather, it is the attitude of unbelief, characterized by self-sufficiency and the arrogance of self-merit, that is condemned. This attitude, which is properly addressed at the rebuilding of the Temple and the reinstitution of the sacrificial system (verses 1-2), was also condemned at previous Sanctuaries (1 Samuel 3:22-35; 4:3-11; 6:19; 13:12-13; 2 Samuel 6:6-8; 2 Kings 15:5 and 2 Chronicles 26:16-23). This verse is saying what the prophet Samuel said to Saul about selective obedience based on one's own way: "Has the LORD as much delight in burnt offerings and sacrifices as in obeying the voice of the LORD? Behold, to obey is better than sacrifice, and to heed than the fat of rams" (1 Samuel 15:22). It is saying the same thing as Solomon said when he wrote, "The sacrifice of the wicked is an abomination..." (Proverbs 21:27), and, "He who turns away his ear from listening to the law, even his prayer is an abomination" (Proverbs 28:9). Therefore, such biblical condemnations of ritual violations in sacrifice cannot be used as examples of a divine rejection of the sacrificial system. Instead, the importance attached to keeping the ritual pure only strengthens its significance for proper worship.

But was not Christ's sacrifice the end of all sacrifices? The answer to this requires us to consider the purpose of the Old Testament sacrifices as well as the nature of Christ's redemptive work (see below). However, whatever our conclusion for the present age, it should be remembered that "just because animal sacrifices and priests have no place in Christianity does not mean that they will have no place in Israel after the rapture of the church...."[23] The problem this statement raises is the failure to discern the distinction between the ages preceding and subsequent to the present age of grace. As Clive Thompson notes:

The basic error in this question is the assumption, usually unconscious, that the conditions which prevail in this age of grace must necessarily be the same in all future ages, that the relations between God and man which exist now must continue to the end of time.... He will again bring forward His people Israel, the only nation He has ever recognized (Amos 3:2), and deal with them and with the Gentiles on a basis of law, although necessarily modified by grace as in the Mosaic dispensation. This follows for at least three reasons: 1) The age or dispensation of grace ends at the rapture and is never to be repeated. 2) In all other ages God deals with man on a law relationship. 3) All left on earth are God's enemies and must therefore be dealt with by law. Law is, and must be, accompanied by sacrifice. A repentant Israel must join in such sacrifices; and repentant Gentiles must conform and join therein also.[24]

The dispensation of the church is an eschatological interregnum that, by its nature of Jew and Gentile baptized by the Holy Spirit equally into position with Christ (1 Corinthians 12:13), could not fulfill the distinct restoration prophesies for Israel and the nations. The church age is not simply the *incorporation* of Gentiles (Romans 11:11-24,30) into the place of privilege (the "olive tree" of Romans 11:17-24) but the *integration* of Gentile and Jew in one body under the law of Christ (1 Corinthians 9:21; Galatians 6:2; Ephesians 2:14-16). By contrast, the Millennium is an eschatological extension of the Jewish age, which involves the *inclusion* of Gentiles into an earthly Jewish economy (Isaiah 2:2-3; 56:6-7; 66:18-21) under the theocratic laws of the New Covenant, which includes physical sacrifices at a physical Temple (Isaiah 66:20-21; Zechariah 14:16-18). Therefore, in the present age the church serves as a "spiritual temple" (Ephesians 2:20-21) with "spiritual sacrifices" (Romans 12:1; Hebrews 13:15-16) and spiritual access through Christ to the Heavenly Temple (Hebrews 4:14-16; compare 12:22-24). However, once the church age has run its predetermined course (Romans 11:26), the spiritual temple will be replaced by the physical Temple, in conformity with the return of national Israel to the divine program (Romans 11:27). Accompanying this return will be many of the former physical elements that are essential to Israel's functioning as a theocratic Nation. The reason for this is that the church age is set between the failure of Israel under the Old Covenant and the restoration of Israel under the New Covenant. Unlike the church, which is governed indirectly by Christ through the Spirit and was not promised an earthly kingdom, Israel was governed directly by God (theocracy), and will be governed through the Messiah, and was promised an earthly kingdom. Israel's promised restoration in the last days will not take place within the church, but within the New Covenant. It is not the place of privilege promised to national Israel, the Temple or the sacrificial system that has been set aside by this New Covenant, but the unattainable legal requirements of the old Mosaic Covenant. Even though this covenant had included this promise and sacrificial institution, by design these were pre-Mosaic, being included respectively in the Abrahamic Covenant (Genesis 12:2-3) and the divine design.

Moreover, this replacement was prophesied not in the New Testament but in the Old Testament. The two principal prophecies of the New Covenant in the Old Testament are in Ezekiel (Ezekiel 36:25-28) and Jeremiah (Jeremiah 31:31-34). According to the literal interpretation of these texts, national Israel will realize the spiritual and physical (Land) blessings of the New Covenant only in the eschatological age (Ezekiel 36:29-36; see also 34:25-29; 37:25-28; Jeremiah 31:31,33). The restoration the Nation will enjoy under this covenant will involve all Israel—the house of Judah and the house of Israel (Ezekiel 36:22,32; see also Ezekiel 37:19-23; Jeremiah 31:31,37), with the corporate Nation experiencing individual spiritual regeneration (Jeremiah 31:33-34; Ezekiel 36:26-27).

One example of Jesus' own understanding of this is His promise to His disciples at their last Passover together in the upper room. In each of the Synoptic Gospels, we read that Jesus takes the cup and pledges that He will drink it again with them in the Kingdom age (Matthew 26:29; Mark 14:25; Luke 22:18).[25] This implies that the Jewish festival of Passover will again be celebrated in the future Kingdom.[26] This implication is made explicit in Ezekiel 45:21: "In the first month, on the fourteenth day of the month, you shall have the Passover...." It should be obvious that if the Passover will be celebrated in the Millennium, then the Passover sacrifice, the central feature of the feast, must also be resumed. Until then, even the church may celebrate the feast in its spiritual dimensions (without a sacrifice), as Judaism does today, since "Christ our Passover...has been sacrificed" (1 Corinthians 5:7-8).

The problem with the Mosaic Covenant was not its ritual but its requirements. Israel could not keep its conditional regulations, and therefore a superior and unconditional covenant was necessary that could guarantee the fulfillment of its requirements. The New Covenant's provision of spiritual regeneration makes possible the spiritual obedience that was lacking under the Mosaic economy, thereby preventing any further loss of relationship with God, the Land, or the Temple. That certain ritual aspects of the Mosaic Covenant remain under the New Covenant is to be expected, since the divine ideal is for the Creator to dwell with His creatures in an uninterrupted relationship (see Zechariah

2:10-11 and 3). Even so, the significant legal differences in the ritual under the New Covenant confirms it is not a repetition of the Mosaic Covenant. This ritual, the focus of which was the regulation of a relationship between God and man through sacrifice, as already mentioned, was initiated with Adam and Eve (see Genesis 3:20; 4:3-7),[27] and continued on in the Abrahamic Covenant (Genesis 15:1-18)—long before the Mosaic legislation was enacted.

The physical nature of life in the Millennial kingdom will require that there still be a regulation in this relationship (the Temple and ceremonial system), but the spiritual conditions of this period (a theocratic government, a regenerate populace, universal peace, no threat from the nations, etc.) will have made all other aspects of the Mosaic Covenant unnecessary and obsolete.[28] For example, Ezekiel 43:17 states that the altar of burnt offering in the Millennial Temple will have eight steps facing east. Under the Mosaic Law this altar would have been illegitimate, because its stipulations prohibited both going "up by steps to My altar" (Exodus 20:26) and an eastward orientation. That is why the altars in previous Temples were constructed with a ramp for priestly ascent (see Mishnah, *Middot* 3:4) and with a north-south orientation. The reason for this prohibition (as well as the commandment in Exodus 28:42 concerning the priests wearing linen underwear) was because of Israel's proximity to the Canaanite culture, whose priests ascended stepped altars in order to reveal their nakedness during their sacrificial rituals, which involved the worship of nature and fertility deities. In addition, the Canaanites worshiped the god Shamash, who represented the sun, which rises in the east. The need for Israel to be separate both spatially and spiritually from Canaanite and other similar pagan cultures and rituals resulted in many of the requirements found in the Mosaic legislation. However, in the Millennial kingdom, there will be no foreign countercultures such as the Canaanites (see Zechariah 14:9). All the nations will worship the Lord (see Zechariah 14:16-19), and Jerusalem will be holy and beyond contamination (see Zechariah 14:20-21). Therefore, there will be no need to continue observing these types of regulations from the Mosaic economy.

In addition, it has been suggested that the reason for Ezekiel's eastward orientation of the altar was so that the priests will be able to face in the direction of the Messiah, who will be enthroned in the Temple.[29] Incidentally, this reveals how radically the Millennial sacrificial system deviates from that prescribed under the Mosaic Covenant.[30] It was for this reason that post-exilic Judaism did not attempt to employ these new ritual commandments, because they understood them not as a reinstitution of the Mosaic system, but as functioning under Jeremiah's prophesied New Covenant in the Millennial kingdom. This remains the best solution to resolving the contradictions with Mosaic Judaism in Ezekiel's text.

With this understanding, let's consider the two ways in which the consistently literal school of interpretation has explained the nature of the Millennial sacrifices in light of the New Testament sacrifice of Christ.

Sacrifices as Millennial Memorials

The majority of those who hold a consistently literal interpretation of this text maintain that the sacrifices will be memorials of the sacrifice of Christ. For example, John F. Walvoord, Chancellor of Dallas Theological Seminary, says, "The Scriptures also tell us that in the Millennial Kingdom, which begins with the Second Coming of Christ, there will be a huge Temple built as described in Ezekiel chapters 40–48....And we learn here that there will be animal sacrifices offered. The question is often asked why this is necessary, and the answer is simply that it is a memorial, a reminder of the death of Christ, just like the Old Testament sacrifices were in anticipation of it."[31] As Walvoord's statement implies, this view finds scriptural precedent in the Lord's Supper, which was done "in remembrance" of Christ (Luke 22:19; 1 Corinthians 11:24). Since this ordinance is only "until He [Christ] comes" (1 Corinthians 11:26), another such reminder of Christ's redemptive work will be necessary for the generation that populates the Millennium.[32] Therefore, in contrast to the Old Testament sacrifices, which were *prospective* (looking forward to the fulfillment of the cross), these millennial memorials will be *retrospective* (looking back at the accomplishment of the cross). Some have added that since the Lord's Supper also proclaimed the future coming of Christ (1 Corinthians 11:26) and the kingdom (Matthew 26:29; Mark 14:25; Luke 22:18), these sacrifices will warn of future wrath at the coming Great White Throne judgment, especially for those who will rebel at the end of the Millennium and join in the satanic attack on the Temple Mount (Revelation 20:7-11).[33]

In line with this interpretation is the understanding that Old Testament sacrifices were only symbolic. The late commentator Charles Lee Feinberg states: "...the function of Old Testament sacrifices...were never efficacious; they were never meant to be expiatory, that is to care for the penalty of sin; they were never meant to be anything but symbolic of the forfeiture of life for sin...."[34] While the memorial view has much to commend it, it does not adequately address the fact that Ezekiel (Ezekiel 43:20,26; 45:15,17,20), under the New Covenant, clearly says that the blood sacrifices are for "atonement" in just the same way that Leviticus (Leviticus 4:20,26,35; 16:27; 17:11, et. al) does under the Mosaic

Covenant. Furthermore, nowhere in Ezekiel's prophecy concerning the sacrificial system is it ever implied that the sacrifices are "memorial" in nature. For this reason, another literal view has been advanced which attempts to incorporate the concept of atonement in its interpretation of the millennial sacrifices.

The Atonement View of Millennial Sacrifices

This view argues that it is insufficient to say that the animal sacrifices of the Old Testament were only symbolic of the final sacrifice of Christ. First, it is apparent that when a worshiper in Old Testament times offered a sacrifice on the altar, he came away believing that something happened that was immediately and personally significant for his relationship with God. Second, there is simply no evidence in the presentation of the sacrificial worship of the Old Testament that indicates each and every Israelite offerer throughout the entire span of Old Testament times understood that his offering was anticipatory of a sacrificed Messiah. To argue this is to deny the nature of progressive revelation that unfolded the redemptive program throughout the ages. While God always had the death of Christ in view as the basis of eternal salvation, the faith of the Israelites rested on God their Savior, who promised life for life in the substitution of an animal's life-blood for their own (see Genesis 22:8,13-14). Third, living so long with the historical loss of sacrifice has diminished the importance of the concept of sacrifice for us today. As E. P. Sanders, Oxford University Professor of Exegesis, reminds us: "Modern people so readily think of religion without sacrifice that they fail to see how novel that idea is."[35] Therefore, in order to understand Ezekiel's concept of sacrifice, it is necessary to understand the purpose of sacrifice as it was presented in the Old Testament.

Making Sense of the Sacrifices

Both ceremonial purification and substitution is at the heart of the concept of sacrifice. The English word *sacrifice* hints at this dual idea in its original derivation. As Jewish scholar Joshua Berman, author of a major Jewish study on the Temple, explains:

> The [English] word *sacrifice* is a conjunction of two Latin words, *sacer* —holy—and *facere*—to make. When one offered a sacrifice in the Greco-Roman world, it was viewed as the process of making something holy by offering it to the gods....Sacrifice called upon the owner of the animal to *renounce* his ownership of the animal so that the gods could *receive* the animal in his place.[36]

When an Israelite in Old Testament times dedicated an animal as an offering, it was no longer his for personal use but was considered as *hekdesh* ("something made holy"). The primary Hebrew word used for offering is *korban*, which, coming from the root meaning of "close," has the connotation of bringing something close to God. In the process of offering an animal as a *korban* the first step involved is an act of transference whereby the owner lays his hands upon the head of the animal (Hebrew, *semikhah*, "leaning"). This rite symbolized an investiture of identity (understood from transfers of human authority—see Numbers 8:5-11; 27:18-23) so that the animal now stood representatively in the place of the owner himself (see Leviticus 8:14,18,22). The Jewish sage Nachmanides explained this act as something of an "execution in effigy," for the burning of each body part of the animal and the sprinkling of the blood is reckoned as if it were the person's own. In his commentary on Leviticus 1:9 he then goes on to express the penal nature of the substitution involved:

> All these acts should be performed in order that when they are done, a person should realize that he has sinned against God with his body and his soul, and that "his" blood should really be spilled and "his" body burned, were it not for the loving-kindness of the Creator, Who took from him a substitute and a ransom, namely this offering, so that its blood should be in place of his blood, its life in place of his life....[37]

Here, according to Nachmanides' interpretation, the sacrificial rite should be understood as the punishment the owner should have rightly received and viewed by him as a punitive act against his own body. This idea of substitution is strenthened by the fact that blood is shed as part of the sacrifice—especially the burnt offering (see below). Leviticus states that blood is required because "the life of the flesh is in the blood...for it is the blood by reason of the life that makes atonement" (Leviticus 17:11). The term "the life of the flesh" is literally "the soul of the flesh" (Hebrew, *nefesh habasar*). It has been understood to mean that "it is not merely that the animal's blood represents the blood of its owner, but because the *soul* of the animal represents the owner's *soul*."[38] While penal substitution lies at the heart of the sacrificial act, the purposes for which this substitution is made only becomes clear as we consider the five categories of the offerings (*korbanot*), all of which appear in Ezekiel 40–48 (see, for example the lists in Ezekiel 40:39; 45:25).

The first offering mentioned in our Ezekiel text is the "burnt offering" (Hebrew, *korban 'olah*—Ezekiel 40:38-39,42; 43:18,24,27; 44:11; 45:15,17,23,25; 46:2,4,12-13,15). The word in Hebrew for this offering is *'olah*, which means "one that rises," which is literally depicted by the smoke of the totally incinerated animal rising upward toward God (see Leviticus 7:8). This offering portrayed the complete devotion of the one making the offering, since the animal, which represented the person, was consumed entirely (Leviticus 1:3). The purpose of this offering was "that it may be accepted for him to make *atonement* on his behalf" (Leviticus 1:4; see also Ezekiel 45:15,17). The burnt offering is also the first offering mentioned in the book of Leviticus, where the details of the sacrificial system are enumerated, although this sacrifice was commanded for Abraham in relation to his son Isaac (Genesis 22:2). In Jewish tradition, "the binding of Isaac" (Hebrew, *Akedah*) was one of the most significant acts in the Bible, for on the exact spot of the future Temple it was demonstrated that the animal sacrifice (ram) substituted for the human sacrifice (Isaac).

The second offering that appears in Ezekiel is the "sin offering" (Hebrew, *korban chatat*—Ezekiel 40:39; 42:13,19,21-22,25; 44:27,29; 45:17,19,22-23,25; 46:20). The translation as "*sin* offering" suggests a derivation from the Hebrew word for sin (*chatat*); however, it is likely that it is derived from the Hebrew infinitive *lechatei,* which means "to purify through ablution."[39] The support for this understanding is seen in Leviticus 4:1–5:13, where the sin offering is described not as overt "sin," but as an inadvertent (unintentional) violation of a transgression due to ceremonial inattention. While this was an individual act (Leviticus 4:27-35), the whole community could be liable (Leviticus 4:13-21), as also in the case of a priest whose act brought guilt on the entire Nation (Leviticus 4:3-12), since he represented the people before God (Exodus 28:12,29,38). The primary purpose for this offering was the ritual purification or ceremonial cleansing of sacred objects on behalf of the person(s) who caused their contamination.[40] Even where people are the object, the idea is of a "cleansing of the spiritual defilement that their sin has engendered."[41] In Ezekiel it is said, in relation to the altar, "to purify and make atonement…cleanse" (Ezekiel 43:20,22), "make atonement…purify…consecrate" (Ezekiel 43:26), and for the "house of Israel" "to make atonement" (Ezekiel 45:17).

The third listed offering is the "guilt offering" (Hebrew, *korban 'asham*— Ezekiel 40:39; 42:13; 44:29; 46:20). The word "guilt" in the sense understood by the original Hebrew text is "liable to pay," and according to its usage in Leviticus 5–6 looks at a legal reparation payment for the restoration of damages. This obligatory restitution was necessary for acts that violated sacred objects, transgressions against God's commandments, and for offenses against fellow Israelites. Ezekiel always groups this offering with the sin offering, but gives no explanation for the function of this offering, so its purpose is apparently assumed from Leviticus. Here it is seen as an inadvertent action (like that which required the sin offering), such as a person deriving benefit from resources dedicated to the Temple and therefore with his restitution a guilt offering must be made (Leviticus 5:14-16).

A fourth category of offering is the "grain offering" (Hebrew, *korban minchah*—Ezekiel 42:13; 44:29; 45:15,17,24-25; 46:5,7,11,14-15,20). The Hebrew term *minchah* literally means "gift," but technically a gift given in recognition of the stature of the recipient (inferior to superior). This offering, in Leviticus, is always offered with the burnt offering, and less often with a peace offering (Leviticus 2:1-14). Whereas the burnt offering represented a complete dedication to God of the person, this offering represents a total dedication of the person's possessions. And like the burnt offering, it will occupy a significant place in the ritual service of the Temple.

The final category of offering is the "peace offering" (Hebrew, *korban shelamim*—Ezekiel 43:27; 45:15,17; 46:2,12). This offering was strictly voluntary and is never mentioned in relation to transgression. Therefore the "peace" it represents is not one made with God, but an expression that one was already at peace with God. For this reason it is the only offering in which the owner of the animal offered partakes of the meat (Leviticus 3:17) and even shares it with others. In offering the animal to God, this communal meal symbolizes a "breaking bread with God" or a covenant partnership (see Exodus 18:12; 24:10-11; Deuteronomy 12:7,18; 14:23,26; 15:20). In the context of Ezekiel it is found offered by the prince (Ezekiel 45:17) and as part of the festivals and feasts (Ezekiel 46:11).

Summarizing these five offerings which make up the sacrificial system, we can see that they were offered by those who were in a covenant relationship with God that required obedience as part of its stipulations and especially the maintenance of ceremonial purity so that the relationship (or fellowship) could continue between a Holy God and a sinful people. In addition, it is clear that while the offerings *symbolized* something, they also *accomplished* something that was more than symbolic. They had a particular efficacy in either rendering the worshiper or the sacred objects of worship as ceremonially acceptable. In the Millennial kingdom they will also prove useful in the divine instruction of both Israel (Ezekiel 44:23) and the nations (Isaiah 2:3). In order to understand the nature of this efficacy and how it can be reconciled with the sacrifice of Christ, we need to look at the meaning of *atonement*, the word that most often is identified with the purpose of sacrifice.

The Meaning of Atonement

The basis of the atonement view of the Millennial sacrifices is the proper understanding of the word *atonement*. Since Ezekiel states that these offerings "make atonement," and it has been seen that these offerings actually *did* something, the question that now must be answered is this: Just what did atonement accomplish in the Old Testament, and what will be its function in the Millennial economy?

Two recent Christian studies of this word in the Old Testament—one with a concentration on its meaning in the book of Leviticus,[42] and the other paying special attention to Ezekiel's usage in chapters 40–48[43]—have offered a re-evaluation of its meaning in the context of a theocratic government. Their research has determined that the understanding of the Hebrew term for atonement, *kipper*, should be "to purify" or "cleanse," based on the Akkadian cognate *kuppuru*, rather than the traditionally understood meaning of "to cover," borrowed from the cognate Arabic *kapara* or the ransom/propitiation view, which is based on the noun form *kopper* and sees atonement as the "averting of divine wrath by the payment of a ransom."[44] The idea of "cover over," which has been popularly expressed in Christian books treating this subject for over a century, is that the blood "covered up" or "hid" the offenses from the sight of God so that in not seeing them He would not exact punishment for them. In this light the Mercy Seat of the Ark of the Covenant, called in Hebrew the *kipporet* (from *kipper*, "to atone"), has been explained as a box containing objects connected with Israel's past sins—which needed to be hidden from the presence of the Lord enthroned above the cherubim on either side of the Mercy Seat.[45] The concepts of divine wrath and payment are certainly present in the act of atonement, but the explanation of propitiation/ransom does not take into account the wider range of usage in Leviticus nor the syntax and synonyms of the verb *kipper*. For example, in Leviticus, where the meaning of the term is established, God never appears as the direct object of atonement, but only objects and persons (indirectly) that have become ceremonially impure. Therefore, contrary to the idea of propitiation and ransom, the act of "atonement" is not exercised on God nor something that directly affects Him. This is consistent with the purpose of "atonement" as it is used in Ezekiel 40–48. As Hebrew University professor Moshe Greenberg, author of a scholarly three-volume commentary on Ezekiel, explains:

> This is done by purgation and whole offerings whose function is to *kipper* (purge), *hitte'* (decontaminate), and *tihher* (purify) the altar so as

to make it fit for the regular worship (43:20,22,26). These rites have…to do with…the very ancient idea that all pollutions…contaminated the sanctuary.[46]

According to this view, sacrifice accomplished the removal of ritual impurity in order to restore a worshiper's ability to approach God. This concept understands that ritual violations (such as those specified in Leviticus) result in a ceremonial condition of uncleanness that not only interrupts and restricts the worship of the one who has committed the offense, but by its contagious nature is able to contaminate other people and objects, disrupting the required service of God. The possibility then exists that not only could the entire Nation suffer uncleanness, but that also the Temple itself could be defiled. This would create a situation such as that reported by Ezekiel in chapters 8–11, which resulted in the departure of the *Shekinah* (divine presence) from the Temple. If this occurred, the promise of restoration would be reversed and the people would again suffer exile. However, the promise of the Millennial restoration is that this reversal will never again occur (Isaiah 2:4; 51:22; Jeremiah 31:34,40; Ezekiel 36:25-30; 37:23-28; Daniel 2:44; Joel 3:17,20; Zechariah 8:11-15). Therefore, to protect the holiness of the divine presence and to prevent problems associated with the human condition (unholiness), the safeguards of the New Covenant include both the external requirements necessary to create a sanctified status (Jeremiah 33:18; Ezekiel 44:23 25) and the internal provision of a new heart necessary to maintain it (Jeremiah 31:33; Ezekiel 36:26-27; Zechariah 13:1).

In this light it is necessary to remember three facts about life in the Millennial kingdom. First, the presence of God will dwell literally in the midst of the people. As in the time of the Tabernacle and First Temple, God's manifest glory will be on earth (Ezekiel 43:1-7), but unlike those days, the glorified Christ will be resident in the Temple (Zechariah 2:10-11; 14:9), extending an unparalleled degree of sanctity to the entire city of Jerusalem (Isaiah 4:5; Jeremiah 3:17; Zechariah 2:5; 14:11, 20-21) and requiring sanctified conditions for the entire earth (Isaiah 11:9; Habakkuk 2:14; Zechariah 14:9,16-18). Second, the unglorified human population will be capable of incurring ritual defilement and polluting the earthly Sanctuary. Even though those who initially enter the Millennial kingdom are all regenerate (Jews—Ezekiel 20:33-38; Gentiles—Matthew 25:31-46), they are still mortal beings who intentionally or unintentionally can violate ceremonial standards. Furthermore, they will produce children who may or may not become spiritually regenerate and receive a new heart (see Revelation 20:7-8), and therefore lack the inward restraint of sin. Third, the Millennial population will be under the New

Covenant and will be regarded as a holy and priestly Nation just as they were under the Mosaic Covenant. Whether or not this is individually so, it was and will be corporately required. Just as by grace the understanding of a penal substitution and faith in God as Savior resulted in personal spiritual salvation for the individual Israelite under the Mosaic system, so under the New Covenant grace through faith based on the universal and undeniable knowledge (Jeremiah 31:34) of the past work of the now resident and ruling resurrected and glorified Messiah (Jeremiah 33:15-16) will save in the Millennial kingdom. Even so, in both Jewish ages the Nation (and in the future, also the nations) must maintain a status of ceremonial purity. As argued above, this kind of sacrificial "atonement" is not for salvation nor for inward sanctification, but to preserve outward *corporate "sanctification"* (or ceremonial purification) so that a holy God can remain in the midst of an unholy people. Since every member of this theocratic kingdom will be required to conform to the ceremonial requirements, the sacrificial system will be necessary in order to sustain corporate sanctity.

Millennial Sacrifices and Christ's Sacrifice

Based on this discussion, then, it should be apparent that the act of offering sacrifices after the sacrifice of Christ does not present a contradiction. However, having said this it is now necessary to understand the relationship between these future sacrifices and the once-for-all sacrifice of Christ. First, it is important to note the contrasts between these two kinds of sacrifices, particularly as revealed in the book of Hebrews. While the Old Testament sacrificial system was *effective,* it was not *expiatory.* In the words of Hebrews, it was effective for temporary ritual restoration, the "cleansing of the flesh" (Hebrews 9:13; see also 9:10), but it could not permanently expiate guilt by "tak[ing] away sins" (Hebrews 10:4) or "cleans[ing] the conscience" (Hebrews 9:14). The ceremonial system was never meant to have this purpose; rather, it was to help the Nation (Exodus 19:6) outwardly conform to its holy status (Leviticus 11:44-45; 19:2; 20:7). This will be even more necessary when the glorified Lord returns to earth and establishes the Jewish people as a Nation of priests in the Millennial kingdom (Isaiah 61:6; see also 66:21). However, the penal substitution that was inherent in the nature of sacrifice and demanded an inward identification with sin and its punishment looked forward to an ultimate realization of this in God the Savior. Since this was only possible through substitution, the Savior offered Himself in place of guilty sinners to both *expiate* (remove guilt of sin) and *pro-*

pitiate (appease the righteous wrath of God against sin). Therefore, the outward and earthly character of the ceremonial sacrifices and the internal and spiritual character of Christ's sacrifice are of two different kinds, operated in two different spheres, and were for two different purposes. Under the present administration of grace—in which Christ is absent from the earth and our approach is in the heavenly realm—sanctification is possible under the spiritual provisions of the New Covenant (the Holy Spirit, the new heart). However, under the coming administration of the kingdom in which Christ will be present on the earth and the approach will be at the Temple in Jerusalem, outward corporate "sanctification" (or ceremonial purification) will be necessary, as well as inward personal sanctification, under the full terms (spiritual and physical) of the New Covenant.

Therefore, the literal interpretation of the sacrifices of the Temple of Ezekiel and their resumption during the Millennium have not been found to be blasphemous, but rather, to be the God-ordained means to blessing in the theocratic kingdom. And though this Final Temple and its priestly service will be at the center of the blessings of this Messianic age, its course will conclude when the 1,000-year reign of Christ over a restored Israel is complete (Revelation 20:7) and the eternal state has begun with the creation of a new heavens and earth (Isaiah 66:22; Revelation 21:1).

Yet this will not be the final chapter for the Temple. There's still more to come, as we will discover in the Temple beyond time.

CHAPTER 24

The Temple Beyond Time

The Final Fulfillment of the Future Temple

The Temple embodies Judaism's attempt to sanctify the material world: Just as Shabbat and the holidays are intended to create sacred time, so was the Temple meant to create sacred space. According to tradition, the Temple was the place where God violated His remoteness and revealed Himself to human beings. The yearning for the Temple is a longing for the renewal of the dialogue between God and Israel.

—HANAN PORAT,
HEAD OF THE TEMPLE MOUNT LOBBY IN THE KNESSET

I t has often been said that "without a heavenly hope man is of no earthly good." The great hope of every good man, therefore, is of heaven—not because he loathes earth, but because he loves God, and heaven is where God dwells. From the beginning, when the Maker created man in His image (Genesis 1:26-27), He made him for a relationship with Himself. The Temple, in time, symbolized God's dwelling with man, which made possible to a limited degree the experience of a relationship that was something more than merely spiritual. And just as the Millennium and its Temple will be a fulfillment of the divine ideal for the Nation of Israel, so the eternal state and the heavenly New Jerusalem will be the fulfillment of the divine ideal for all redeemed mankind. The first had its inception at Mount Sinai, but the second goes back to the beginning of God's revelation of Himself in the Garden of Eden (see chapter 9). Even so, the historical Temples (Temples in time) all reflected something of the original divine ideal, the Heavenly Temple (Temple before time) although limited by the circumstances of the Fall and violations of the Mosaic Covenant. For this reason, under the New Covenant the description of the Temple of Ezekiel has parallels with Genesis just as does the New Jerusalem depicted in Isaiah and Revelation. These parallels establish the continuity in God's purpose to dwell with man, yet only the ultimate relationship of man with God in the eternal state (the Temple beyond time) completes this purpose.

Looking Beyond Time

Revelation 21–22 pictures a period *after* a new heavens and a new earth have been created (see also Isaiah 65:17; 66:22; 2 Peter 3:13) and a new state of existence will have begun. After the restoration has been fulfilled with the Millennial kingdom, there will come a new creation that better fits the divine design. That a re-creation, rather than a renovation, is in view appears evident from the language employed: "the first heaven and the first earth passed away, and there is no longer any sea....No longer...any death...making all things new....No need of the sun or of the moon...no night there...no longer any curse" (see Revelation 21:1,4-5,23,25; 22:3,5).[1] This is also apparent in the context of Isaiah 66 (from which this re-creation language is borrowed), where the theme of the restoration of Jerusalem is immediately associated with the theme of re-creation.[2] While this terminology is reminiscent of the original creation in the Garden of Eden (with its Edenic Sanctuary where God was able to dwell with man), it is because we have now been transported to its archetypal setting, the heavenly Jerusalem, with its divine Sanctuary.

The debate over Revelation 21:9-27 being a chronological recapitulation to the Millennium or kept in the chronological progression of 19:11–22:6 as the eternal state is unnecessary for this discussion.[3] In Revelation 21:10 (see also 21:2, first appearance), the New Jerusalem is assumed by the text to have already been in existence. In Revelation 21:9-27, as far as the focus on the description of the city goes, whether it appears in the Millennium or the eternal state is not an issue (although verses 24-26 require a decision). Rather, because John centers on the *place* (descriptively) rather than its *position* (chronologically), the reference point is "beyond time." In other words, the reality of which John is speaking is timeless and eternal—regardless of the time in which it appears. However, before we look in particular at the Temple in this New Jerusalem, let us look at the broader concept of the city as presented in the Old and New Testaments as well as in Judaism.

Understanding the New Jerusalem

The New Jerusalem in the Old Testament

The Book of Hebrews declares that those who follow God are headed toward the destination of a heavenly city (Hebrews 13:14). Hebrews indicates that this has been the aim of the faithful going all the way back to the fathers of the faith, beginning with Abraham: "By faith Abraham, when he was called, obeyed by going out to a place which he was to receive for an inheritance; and he went out, not knowing where he was going" (Hebrews 11:8). Abraham, like all of the patriarchs, was nomadic and wandered the land, as do modern Bedouin, without respect to borders. The patriarchs lived a life of constant motion, always looking for a better place to live. The point in Genesis 12:1-3—where Abraham's call was first given—is that God had a place prepared, and He would show it to the one who in faith obeyed (verse 1). That place was the place of promise, where ultimately all the families of the earth would be blessed (verses 2-3). Therefore, even though it's not expressed in the text of Genesis, Abraham was looking for the city which had foundations, "whose architect and builder is God...a better country, that is a heavenly one" (Hebrews 11:10,16). As God later revealed, this would be the place shown to Moses (Exodus 25:9,40) and David (1 Chronicles 28:11-19)—the place where the Heavenly Temple was found. This could only have been the heavenly Jerusalem, since the structures on earth were copied after the heavenly (Exodus 25:9,40; Hebrews 9:23), and the divinely designated site of the Temple (progressively revealed) was Jerusalem (see Genesis 22:2,14; Exodus 15:17; Deuteronomy 12:11; 2 Samuel 7:10,13; 1 Kings 8:16-21).

When the psalmist refers to "the LORD, who dwells in Zion" (Psalm 9:11; compare 48:2; 74:2; 76:2), he is employing the language of heaven, the true dwelling place of God (1 Kings 8:30,39,43; 2 Chronicles 6:21,30,33,39) to describe the reality of God's presence at His chosen place on earth (2 Chronicles 6:41). Since the Old Testament prophets clearly predicted that neither the present earth nor heaven would continue (Isaiah 34:4) but would one day pass away (Isaiah 65:17), Judaism projected the understanding of the earthly Jerusalem as God's "dwelling place" heavenward (as the early Jewish-Christian epistle to the Hebrews reveals), forming the hope of an eternal Jerusalem where, in further contrast, there would be fullness of the presence of God (Isaiah 66:22). Whereas the earth was God's footstool, heaven was His throne and the place where each of His subjects longed to be (see Psalm 23:6; 27:4).

Therefore, while the New Jerusalem is not *explicit* in the Old Testament, the concept of it is *implicit* in some passages—especially in those that proclaim the eternality and inviolability of Jerusalem. When the psalmist gives the assurance that "those who trust in the LORD are as Mount Zion, which cannot be moved, but abides forever" (Psalm 125:1), his ultimate reference must be the New Jerusalem, since only it will abide forever. In the same way, when Ezekiel 37:28 promises that "My sanctuary" will be "in their midst forever" it can be understood as until the end of time, yet the focus is upon God dwelling in such a way that the ideal covenant relationship—"I will be their God, and they will be My people" (verse 27)—will be realized without interruption. This is exactly what the book of Revelation sees as fulfilled in the eternal state in the New Jerusalem: "And I saw the holy city, New Jerusalem, coming down out of heaven....And He shall dwell among them, and they shall be His people, and God Himself shall be among them" (Revelation 21:2-3). Although this understanding is the result of progressive revelation, surely the Old Testament saints must have reasoned (in light of the unseen city which Abraham sought) that if the old Jerusalem they knew was to remain "forever," a New Jerusalem needed to exist to fulfill such prophecies. This is what is meant to be understood when Isaiah joins his eschatological description of a restored Jerusalem to passages that describe the new heaven and new earth:

> Behold, I create new heavens and a new earth; and the former things shall not be remembered or come to mind. But be glad and rejoice for-

ever in what I create; for behold, I create Jerusalem....My holy mountain Jerusalem....I will also take some of them for priests and Levites.... For just as the new heavens and the new earth which I make will endure before Me...so your offspring and your name will endure (Isaiah 65:17; 66:20-22).

The association here of Millennial Jerusalem with the Jerusalem of the new creation, the heavenly Jerusalem, in the same contexts, may make the chronology of the passage seem ambiguous, but the point is to reveal future fulfillment. In Isaiah 65:17-25 and 66:10-21 the contexts reveal that in the Millennial kingdom—where there is still death, decay, and giving birth (Isaiah 65:20,22-23) as well as judgment and sacrificial offerings (Isaiah 66:14c-17, 20)—this fulfillment is partial, even though it has been realized on earth as promised (Genesis 12:3). However, with the new heavens and earth (the eternal state), every aspect of God's promise will be fully performed, both in the guarantee of an untarnished future (Isaiah 65:17) and the execution of eternal punishment (Isaiah 66:24). This foundational concept of the heavenly Jerusalem was developed in later Judaism, both between the testaments and in the Talmudic period, into a more elaborate eschatological hope.

The New Jerusalem in Judaism

The first development of the concept of the New Jerusalem appears in the Jewish apocalyptic literature and the Jewish midrashim of the post-exilic Second Temple period. In these extrabiblical documents the heavenly Jerusalem, perfect in every respect, either replaces or transforms the imperfect earthly Jerusalem as the final fulfillment of the restoration period.[4] For example, in the apocalyptic writings of the Dead Sea Scrolls, a document preserved in several fragmentary copies (1Q32, 2Q24, 4Q554-555, 5Q15, 11Q18) presents a vision of the New Jerusalem. It is comparable to Ezekiel's vision of Jerusalem and the Temple in Ezekiel 40–48 as well as that of John's in the Apocalypse (Revelation 21–22), but differs in significant details. Like these familiar apocalyptic texts, the dimensions of the New Jerusalem are much greater than those of the ancient city, and we read a description of the 12 gates of the city, each named for one of the 12 tribes. This document also understands that the setting for this New Jerusalem is the eschatological period, after the final end-time battle in which Israel emerges victorious over the Gentile nations and Israel has been restored in glory.[5] This would place it, in our terms, in the Millennium and eternal state.

In postbiblical rabbinic Judaism, the sages faced the need to preserve the hope of Jewish restoration within the contradictory experience of losing the earthly Jerusalem, which the Jewish scriptures had said could not be lost or destroyed. To resolve this dilemma, the sages went back to the nascent concept of the New Jerusalem in the Old Testament and developed the idea of "Jerusalem the Lower" (Hebrew, *Yerushalaim Shel Matta*)—the earthly Jerusalem, and "Jerusalem the Upper" (Hebrew, *Yerushalaim Shel Maalah*)—the heavenly Jerusalem. Yitzhak I. Hayutman, Dean of Research and Development at the Academy of Jerusalem, explains the meaning of this dualism for Judaism:

> In these legends the heavenly Jerusalem is the archetype of the good to come, which will be revealed to all at the redemption of the world. At present she hovers above the earthly Jerusalem, even when the latter lies in ruin or sin, but only the most righteous can see her, in moments of grace. In Christian tradition, she is described at the end of the New Testament as descending out of heaven perfect and complete at the consummation of history, while Jewish legends emphasize the building from below to actualize the heavenly Jerusalem.[6]

The consummation of history of which Dr. Hayutman speaks is known in Judaism as "the World to Come" (Hebrew, *ha 'Olam habba'*) and is distinguished from "the days of the Messiah" (Hebrew, *Yemot ha-Mashiach*) and "the Redemption" (Hebrew, *Ge'ulah*), both terms for the Millennium, since in this age there will be "no eating and drinking, no begetting of children, no bargaining, no jealousy and hatred, and no strife; but the righteous sit with their crowns on their heads enjoying the effulgence of the *Shekinah*" (*Bab. Berakot* 17a). The Jewish Talmud states that the heavenly Jerusalem, although belonging to the World to Come, could already be seen in moments of grace by the righteous, who could receive heavenly inspiration from it. In some places the Talmud implies that the heavenly Jerusalem is not to be regarded as above the earthly Jerusalem. This was probably stated in reaction to disputations with Christianity where it had been argued that the heavenly Jerusalem (the church) had replaced earthly Jerusalem (Israel).

The heavenly Jerusalem also appears in the Zohar, the extrabiblical text revered by Kabbalistic (mystical) Judaism. It views the heavenly Jerusalem as the place created by God to house the souls of the righteous. It also makes a distinction between earthly Jerusalem, which it identifies with the kingdom[7] in which the *Shekinah* (the presence of God) is again present, and the heavenly Jerusalem which it identifies with the higher *Shekinah,* the *sefira* of *binah* ("level of understanding") of the World to Come. From this we can see that Judaism came to recognize that the New Jerusalem presently existed as the heavenly counterpart of the earthly Jerusalem, and would be realized in the ultimate age by the righteous as they collectively worked to effect its appearance by their spiritual and moral attainments in this world.

The New Jerusalem in the New Testament

In the Bible, the use of the term "New Jerusalem" is exclusive to the book of Revelation. However, other New Testament writers were quite familiar with the *concept* of the New Jerusalem, although they preferred to use alternate expressions. In Galatians 4:26 the apostle Paul speaks of "the Jerusalem above" in distinction to "the present Jerusalem" (verse 25). Even though this is an analogical (not allegorical) use for the sake of comparison (see chapter 13), the concept clearly is present in Paul's thinking. The author of the epistle to the Hebrews, in using the term "heavenly Jerusalem," accepts it as a concept readily understood by his Jewish-Christian audience. He provides a description of the heavenly Jerusalem when he contrasts it as the place of grace with the earthly Mount Sinai, the place of the law: "You have come to Mount Zion and to the city of the living God, the heavenly Jerusalem, and to myriads of angels, to the general assembly and church of the first-born who are enrolled in heaven, and to God, the Judge of all, and to the spirits of righteous men made perfect, and to Jesus, the mediator of a new covenant" (Hebrews 12:22-24).

According to this description, the inhabitants of the heavenly Jerusalem are the angelic host ("myriads of angels"), the church ("the general assembly of the first-born who are enrolled in heaven"), God ("the Judge of all"), the Old Testament saints ("spirits of righteous men made perfect"), and Jesus ("the mediator of a new covenant"). This agrees with the descriptions of the heavenly court and the New Jerusalem found in Revelation. In addition, the Hebrews passage places this New Jerusalem in the eternal state when it says, "Yet once more I [God] will shake not only the earth, but also the heaven" (Hebrews 12:26). The expression "yet once more" denotes the removal of those things which can be shaken, as in created things, in order that those things which cannot be shaken may remain. "Therefore, since we receive a kingdom which cannot be shaken, let us show gratitude...for our God is a consuming fire" (Hebrews 12:28). That the eternal state is in view is made certain by the references to a new heavens and earth and the removal of the old created order (both the earth and the heavens) by fire and its replacement by an indestructible kingdom. This follows the general outline of Isaiah 65–66 and also harmonizes with the same cosmic dissolution spoken of by Peter as the climax of the Day of the Lord, which results in "new heavens and a new earth" (see 2 Peter 3:10-13). Therefore, the "kingdom which cannot be shaken" must be the eternal state.

Because the most significant text for the study of the New Jerusalem is the book of Revelation, let us now consider it as a prelude to the specific study of the Temple which it is said to "contain."

The New Jerusalem in the Book of Revelation

Although the heavenly Jerusalem, and specifically the Sanctuary-court of God, appears at significant intervals throughout the judgment section (Revelation 6–19) to show the response of heaven to events on earth (see chapter 14), the most complete description of the New Jerusalem is in Revelation 21–22. John calls it "the bride, the wife of the Lamb" (Revelation 21:9), and through the words that introduce this expression he explains to the discerning reader his intent. His words, "Come here and I will show you…" set up a direct contrast to this same introduction in Revelation 17:1 of the "great harlot." The contrast then is between the city of Babylon, which, though a real place, symbolized the absence of God (Revelation 17:2-7), and the New Jerusalem, also a real place, which symbolized the presence of God (Revelation 21:3; 22:3-5).

Those of the symbolic school reject the New Jerusalem as a place and identify it as a person (God's true people, the church).[8] They find it incredible that anyone could interpret the description of the New Jerusalem literally because it would result in it being "a city from outer space"! They point to its immense size, its cubical shape, its jeweled adornment, and its supernatural source of illumination all as symbols of the church (either as the redeemed on earth or in heaven). However, it is no less incredible to accept that heaven and hell are literal places, and this reference is most likely the use of an object for what it contains (the saints in the city), since in Revelation 22:3 the "bond-servants" of the Lamb (the saints) are separate from the city itself (so it cannot be a symbol of them). Moreover, despite its unusual features, this city qualifies in every sense as a *physical* reality, with measurable architectural structures, planned design, building materials, rivers, trees, and human inhabitants.

What appears to us as an incredible description is due to our present inability to grasp such future realities. As an eternal city for an eternal people, it is not of earth, but from heaven; the handiwork of an infinite God that should not be expected to conform in every respect to our conventional concepts (see Revelation 21:5). The city is laid out as a square with connecting planes of equal size that form a cube. Its gates are inscribed with the names of the 12 tribes of Israel and the foundation stones of its wall with the names of the 12 apostles (Revelation 21:12-14). Even though these are all Jewish, they represent the two dispensations of Israel and the church (or the Old and New Testament saints, as in Hebrews 12:23). This accords with the fact that the church's "foundation of the apostles and prophets" (Ephesians 2:20) was Jewish, and reminds Gentiles who are grafted into the place of privilege or blessing (mediated to the nations through the Abrahamic Covenant) that they must not be arrogant toward the Jews, who are the natural branches (Romans 11:18-23). As such, it is fitting that it was still during the dispensation of Israel when Jesus, as the Jewish Messiah, announced to His Jewish disciples that He was going away (to heaven) to prepare a place (this city) for them as His bride (John 14:2). Part of that preparation may be His entrance into the heavenly Holy of Holies as a High Priest in order to bring His saints there to serve the living God (see Hebrews 9:11-14; Revelation 22:3).

The brilliant splendor of the inner city described by John—with iridescent stones of every color and hue, streets of pure gold like transparent glass—is again the language of accommodation in harmony with the vision of God's presence. In Exodus 24, when Moses and the elders of Israel were permitted to see the God of Israel, their vision was of His heavenly court, where the street was described as "a pavement of sapphire, as clear as the sky" (verse 10). John had described the New Jerusalem as "having the glory of God" (Revelation 21:11), and it is this that John emphasizes in his description of the city. The supernatural illumination of the city is also the result of the presence of God, and the reason why where can be no night there (Revelation 21:5; 22:5). The archetype of the Garden of Eden is also present in the city, complete with the tree of life and a river of the water of life (Revelation 22:1-2).

Because the presence of God is the chief concern of the New Jerusalem passages, let's consider this in greater detail.

The Presence of God in the New Jerusalem

In Revelation 21:3, reference is made to the Tabernacle of God: "Behold, the tabernacle of God is among men, and He shall dwell among them, and they shall be His people, and God Himself shall be among them." Interpreting this text literally, it is a fulfillment of the prophetic text from which it was taken, Ezekiel 37:27: "My dwelling place also will be with them; and I will be their God, and they will be My people." Again, the presupposition of the symbolic school of interpretation is that such apocalyptic description must be hyperbolic imagery.[9] Under this system Revelation 21:3 is interpreted as the church—either the church on earth in its universal dominion (postmillennialists), or the church in heaven (amillennialists). Based on the assumption that only the Christian community is in view, this meaning is read back into the Old Testament with the result being that Ezekiel 37:27 and 40–48 (its larger expansion) were originally intended to be typological descriptions of the church. This means that every nationalistic promise made to Israel (as a subservient part of the covenantal format) in an eschatological context is primarily soteriological in nature, and therefore applies spiritually (or soteriologically) to the church as the elect of God who inherits the covenant blessings.

However, if we take the New Jerusalem symbolically, there is no reason we should not likewise interpret symbolically "the new heavens and new earth" (Revelation 21:1), or for that matter, Christ as the "Alpha and Omega" who makes "all things new" (Revelation 21:5-6). Also, while the symbolic view has argued from Pauline usage that the church is the Temple, John here states that "the Lord God, the Almighty, and the Lamb are its temple" (Revelation 21:22). How can the church and God symbolize the same thing? Interpreted literally, this text would understand the New Jerusalem as an eschatological city distinct from the terrestrial Jerusalem (since the New Jerusalem is said to have no Temple). Those who take Revelation 21:9-27 as Millennial would see this text supporting the idea that the New Jerusalem will be suspended over the earthly Jerusalem during the Millennial kingdom (Revelation 21:10). This understanding could explain how the "nations shall walk by its light" (Revelation 21:24)—as it illumines the earthly city and turns it into the Throne of God (Jeremiah 3:17), how the *Shekinah* fills the earthly Temple while also being the source of light in the New Jerusalem (Revelation 21:23), and how the Lamb can be with His resurrected saints above and His Millennial saints below. In the context of the eternal state it seems to have replaced the former Jerusalem as the abode of all the people of God (Revelation 21:3-8);[10] however, it may also be the conduit between the new heavens and the new earth, allowing God's redeemed creatures, for whom this new world will be made, to enjoy its recreated wonders while dwelling securely in the place promised and prepared by the Savior (John 14:2).

While Revelation 21:2, as described in verses 9-27, is a literal structure, it is also a spiritual one, as this verse declares: God dwelling among His people. The correspondences between Revelation 21:11-21 and Ezekiel 40–48 (the eschatological Temple) are the result of the common source—the pattern of the Heavenly Temple—from which Ezekiel also drew its structure, which as the courts of the Lord and His hosts, is itself a Temple, not needing to contain a separate complex. This may, in part, explain why John reports he saw no Temple there (verse 22—more on this in a moment).

It is the unique language of Ezekiel 37:27 which was the basis of the selection of this text for application to the ultimate manifestation of the Lord among men in Revelation 21. In addition to the usual term "sanctuary," Ezekiel uses here and nowhere else the term *mishkan* ("dwelling place"). The association of these terms tied together all of Lord's the "sanctuaries" throughout time (including the eschatological Temple of Ezekiel 40–48), because all were in some way linked to the *Shekinah*, the divine immanence.[11] Thus the terminology pointed to the divine ideal of an ultimate dwelling, which in John's vision, best suited the final stage of divine manifestation. This prepares us for the concept of the Temple of the New Jerusalem.

The Temple of the New Jerusalem

With Revelation 21:22 we finally come to a specific mention of the Temple in the New Jerusalem. As we have just seen, the city is described as having the *Shekinah* glory of God (Revelation 21:11), so the expectation is that a Temple is present. However, the opening words of this verse are, "And I saw no temple in it.…" Such a statement would have been startling to those accustomed to viewing the Temple as the place of the divine presence. For this reason, Ezekiel used historic detail in keeping with the *Shekinah's* manifestation in the Tabernacle (Exodus 19:9; Leviticus 16:2) and the First Temple (1 Kings 8:10-13; 2 Chronicles 5:13–6:2; 7:1-3) to depict the return of the *Shekinah* glory to the Millennial Temple (Ezekiel 43:1-7). Although John's description of the New Jerusalem has allusions to Ezekiel, probably for ceremonial continuity (since the New Jerusalem is a "Temple-city"),[12] his declaration, intended for dramatic contrast, that there will be no Temple there, must be understood.

As we saw in chapter 9, when man as a creature dwelt with God the Creator in the Garden of Eden, even though there was no Temple, there was still a sanctuary structure. Rabbi Mordecai Kornfeld explains that the recognition of the Creator by the creature and the relationship that should follow is the purpose for God's desire to "dwell" with man:

> The root of the Hebrew word "Shechinah" is the word "SHaCHaN," or "dwell." It appears to be based on the words of the verse, (Shemos 25:8),

"Let the Jewish people make for me a Mikdash ["Sanctuary"], and I will
dwell ("v'SHaCHaNti) amongst them." This verse itself leaves much
to explain. If Hashem [God] fills all of creation, how can He be said to
"dwell" in one particular place? The *Sefer ha'Chinuch* (Mitzvah #95)
explains the reasoning behind the Mitzvah ["commandment"] to build
Hashem a Temple. It is not in order to provide a place of dwelling for
Hashem that we built the Holy Temple, he explains, but it is for our own
benefit. The point of our prayers and sacrifices in the Temple (at least on
a simple plane of meaning) is in order that we may bring ourselves
closer to the service of Hashem. The magnificent Temple, the purity in
which it is kept, the dedicated service of the priestly Kohanim
["priests"], all combine to instill in those who witness them the awe of
the Almighty in a most tangible manner. This, he explains, is what is
meant by saying that Hashem "rests his Shechinah" in the Temple. That
is, the Temple is a place which "arouses us" to recognize our Creator.
When we encounter places where Hashem's presence is made more
obvious to us, we may say that "Hashem's Shechinah" rests there.[13]

After the Fall and its curse on mankind, there was no possibility that God
could dwell with man without destroying man. The Temple was necessary for
man to be protected from the glory of God, which is described as "a consuming
fire" (see Deuteronomy 4:24; 9:3; Isaiah 33:14; Hebrews 12:29; see also Exodus
19:18-24 for Israel's experience). In the New Jerusalem, where the curse no
longer exists and men will exist in glorified resurrection bodies, God is able to
dwell with them face to face without any means of separation. This idea is
drawn from the understanding in Revelation 21:3 (based on Ezekiel 37:26-28)
that God would "tabernacle" or "dwell among" them. But because verse 22 says,
"I saw no temple in it," some commentators see here the passing away of
"symbol for reality," and "the breaking away of the author from dependence
upon Ezekiel."[14] While it is proper to observe the differences between the
description of the New Jerusalem and Ezekiel's Temple, this difference is not an
exchange of symbol for reality, since Ezekiel's Temple was not symbolic, but an
earthly Restoration Temple. One must further take exception with the contention that the model of Ezekiel's eschatological Temple has been discarded.
For almost the whole of the chapter, John has been building his description
from allusions to Ezekiel, and completes his description in verses 24-27 with
both the worship of the nations being brought to the New Jerusalem (verses 24-
26) and cultic exclusions to maintain absolute ritual purity (verse 27)—all patterned after Zechariah 14:16-21 (a previous allusion to Zechariah 14:7 appears in

verse 25). It is this use of the language of Ezekiel that continues the Sanctuary connection with the New Jerusalem and helps identify it as a Temple-city.

But how can the New Jerusalem be considered a Temple-city if there is no Temple in it? Remember that when John first introduced the New Jerusalem in Revelation 3:12, he used an illustration of honoring overcoming believers in the New Jerusalem as "a pillar in the temple of My God." This statement refers to the ancient Grecian custom of placing a pillar in a temple in order to honor a dignitary. This is not in contradiction to the later statement omitting a Temple, but perhaps an implication that the New Jerusalem is something of a Temple itself. This is, in fact, what is stated in the very next words of Revelation 21:22—that there *is* a Temple, but it is *more* than any Temple envisioned through time. By comparison with all earthly Temples, including the Millennial Temple, the New Jerusalem is unique. It has no Temple in the sense that it contains one, yet it has a Temple in the sense that it is a part of one, namely "the Lord God, the Almighty, and the Lamb" which "are its temple" (Revelation 21:22). All former Temples were the construction or reconstruction of an earthly structure, ritually restricted (even to the priests), and concealing the *Shekinah* from the view of man in its unlit innermost chamber. This New Temple, by contrast, has none of these former limitations, and goes beyond them in the same way that the archetype exceeds the model. These unique features are depicted as follows:

1. *An absence of ritual restrictions for the righteous.* In Revelation 21:7 "he who overcomes" is the individual (in opposition to the group, see Revelation 2–3) who will inherit or partake of eternal life (see verses 4,6) and especially the covenantal status of the "people of God" reflected in the phrase: "I will be his God and he will be My son" (see verse 3 for the group). What is particularly exceptional is the degree of this access: "and they shall see His face" (Revelation 22:4). This clearly indicates a new access without the former restrictions, in light of Exodus 33:20: "You cannot see My face, for no man can see Me and live!" The text explains that the reason this is possible is because the New Jerusalem cannot be defiled *from within* because the curse is past (Revelation 22:3), nor *from without*, since all possible desecrators have been confined in the lake of fire (Revelation 21:8, 27). Thus, as one commentator has pointed out: "In the eternal state God will dwell among His people in a direct unmediated communion."[15]

2. *A transference from heaven to earth.* In Revelation 21:2,10 (see also Revelation 3:12) the New Jerusalem is described as descending out of heaven from God. The present participle in these verses indicates the city as being in the

process of descent, thereby characterizing it as a "descending from heaven" kind of city. This is further emphasized by the Greek prepositions *ek,* indicating origin (heaven), and *apo,* indicating the originator (God). This city is not of an earthly construction, but is a structure transferred from heaven. From the parallels between the description of this city and the Garden of Eden and Ezekiel's Temple, we may conjecture a common source—namely, the archetypal Heavenly Temple, which John has previously depicted in his heavenly throne visions. Thus, we may have here a transference of the Heavenly Temple to the new earth to constitute a new Temple where the divine ideal of the Creator among His creation, lost at Eden (see Genesis 3:8), can be realized.

3. *A constitution as the Sanctuary par excellence.* In the previous descriptions of the descending city, it is stated that this city is "the holy city" (Revelation 21:2), "having the glory of God" (Revelation 21:11). These phrases indicate respectively the supernal holiness of the New Jerusalem and the presence of the *Shekinah.* This is reinforced by the announcement in 21:3: "Behold, the tabernacle of God is among men, and He shall dwell among them, and they shall be His people, and God Himself shall be among them." This "tabernacle of God" is the *heavenly* Tabernacle that has previously appeared (see Revelation 7:15; 13:6; 15:5) and has in view the Holy of Holies, as indicated by both "the tabernacle" and the verb "dwell." I suggest this implies that the Holy of Holies in the Heavenly Temple/Tabernacle may have been separated from its courts[16] and now constitutes the New Jerusalem. The intensive phrase "God Himself" emphasizes the presence of God without mediation or representation, because priestly performance within the courts and the Holy Place are no longer required.

This supposition may be supported by Revelation 21:16, which reveals the dimensions of the city as "laid out as a square, and its length is as great as the width." Here is a city said to be 1,500 miles in measurement, yet with all the measurements equal.[17] Since the Holy of Holies in the earthly Temples were built according to this design (see 1 Kings 6:19-20), it has been well recognized that what this depicts is the *entire city* as a Sanctuary, or rather, an immense Holy of Holies.[18] The original design of the Tabernacle was to allow God to dwell among His people (Exodus 25:8). This was also stated as the goal of the Restoration Temple (Ezekiel 37:27; Zechariah 2:10; 8:8). Here then is the Sanctuary *par excellence,* epitomizing the realization of the Temple's most ideal function, the communion of God and man. Within this Temple is what has always constituted a holy place—the true Temple, God Himself. As Revelation 21:22 says, "for the Lord God, the Almighty, and the Lamb, are its temple." Thus the divine presence as Lord and Lamb (God and Messiah) in the midst of the New Jerusalem as the Holy of Holies constitutes it as the true and ultimate Temple.

This ultimate communion between God and man was the goal of the divine ideal for the eternal state. Although this concept appears in the Christian apocalypse, it is not an exclusively Christian concept. This has been pointed out by Hebrew University Professor Emeritus David Flusser, who has suggested that it reflects a Jewish concept.[19] He shows that a Jewish midrash on Isaiah 60:19 (which was fused with a midrash on Psalm 132:17) presents an almost identical parallel to this text (Revelation 21:22-23):[20] These parallel elements may be illustrated as follows:

Revelation 21:22-23	The Midrash
v. 22—"And I saw no temple in the city"	"In the world to come there will be no need of the light of the Temple"
v. 23—"The glory of God has illumined it"	"God will be the everlasting light of Jerusalem"
v. 23—"And its lamp is the Lamb"	"The Messiah is compared to a lamp"

This concept is also evident in this statement from Hanan Porat, who heads the Knesset's Temple Mount lobby and helped conquer the Mount, as a paratrooper, in 1967:

> The Temple embodies Judaism's attempt to sanctify the material world: Just as Shabbat and the holidays are intended to create sacred time, so was the Temple meant to create sacred space. According to tradition, the Temple was the place where God violated His remoteness and revealed Himself to human beings. The yearning for the Temple is a longing for the renewal of the dialogue between God and Israel.

While Porat's comment was directed to the future Third Temple, it reveals that the understanding of the Temple as the place where all is holy and man meets God is paramount in the Jewish concept. If this can be understood as the goal of the earthly Temple, how much more and to what greater degree can it be imagined for the Temple beyond time?

With this final view of the fulfillment of the divine design and man's own dreams, John ends his vision of the last days with a holy city and Temple—as did the prophet Ezekiel, whose Millennial Temple set the precedent for the indwelling presence of God in the Temple beyond time with the closing words "the name of the city from that day shall be, 'the LORD is there'" (Ezekiel 48:35). This is precisely what John sees when he describes the New Jerusalem as the place where the saints not only "see His face," but they also have "His name…on their foreheads" and with him they "shall reign forever and ever" (Revelation 22:4-5).

The New Jerusalem Today

Many scholars believe that the city of New Jerusalem exists right now, but that it won't descend to the earth until the Millennium or the beginning of the eternal state. If the New Jerusalem (as Hebrews 12:22 suggests with its wording "you *have come* to…the heavenly Jerusalem") does exist, I have already implied that this city of the saints may be that place presently being prepared for believers by Jesus in fulfillment of His promise, "In my Father's house are many dwelling places; if it were not so, I would have told you; for I go to prepare a place for you. And if I go and prepare a place for you, I will come again, and receive you to Myself; that where I am, there you may be also" (John 14:2-3). It is important to note that there is no conception here of individual dwellings *apart* from the Lord, as if He lived on top of a hill and we all had mansions (in ascending order of size and proximity) somewhere on His land. There is only one house— "the Father's house"—and all of the rooms are in it. This could give the impression of a gigantic apartment complex; however, because the function of believers will be to "serve Him day and night *in His temple*" (Revelation 7:15, emphasis added; see also 22:3), it is best to view "the Father's house" in its normal usage here as "His temple."[21] In the Jerusalem Temple there were many dwelling chambers for the priests within the Temple precincts; this was necessary because the priests were on duty day and night. In Ezekiel's Millennial Temple the chambers for the priests and workmen surround the Temple-city (Ezekiel 48:11-20) and the throne of the Lord (Jeremiah 3:17), over which is God's canopy of protection (Isaiah 4:5-6). In the same way, in the New Jerusalem there will be places prepared for the saints so that all will be in the presence of the Lord, whose presence will abolish night forever (Revelation 22:5), making possible the unceasing service of the saints as priests. We are also told that the home of the saints will be "the holy city, New Jerusalem, coming down out of heaven from God" and that, as a result, "the tabernacle of God [will be] among men, and He shall dwell among them, and they shall be His people, and God Himself shall be among them" (Revelation 21:2-3). This is the same "Mount

Zion...the city of the living God, the heavenly Jerusalem" in which reside believers of both the Old and New Testament times (Hebrews 12:22-24).

Therefore, the New Jerusalem as the Holy of Holies, with God Himself constituting "the temple," offers us some startling contrasts with the old Jerusalem and its Temple in time. Rather than one man serving as a high priest for the people of God, all of God's people are priests. Unlike the earthly high priest, who could rarely enter the old Holy of Holies, the priests in this new Temple will ever remain there. Their service is not once a year on the Day of Atonement, but continuously and forever. The presence of God does not dwell within the Holy of Holies away from man, but God and the Lamb (Christ) dwell among all of the redeemed. This is the great and heavenly hope of all who "seek His face" (Psalm 17:15; 27:8; 42:2; 105:4), and the prophetic promise of a Temple beyond time.

Before this day of ultimate fulfillment comes to pass, however, there must first be the fulfillment of other yet future prophecies for the Temple. In our concluding chapter, we will consider just how ready Israel is to rebuild...and begin the final drama of the Last Days Temple.

PART V

The Progression Towards the Last Days Temple

"Behold, your House [Temple] is left to you desolate! For I tell you,...'"

—Haggai 1:2,4,8

[We should] probe the issue not as an exercise in apocalyptic forecasting, but with an eye toward those aspects of the Temple's rebuilding that may contribute to 'the fear of God and the love of Him.'"

—Joshua Berman

CHAPTER 25

Ready to Rebuild

Significant Sign of the End Times

What are the next steps of this process? How do we get from where we are to that which we pray for several times a day—the rebuilding of the Temple?

—JOSHUA BERMAN

We must. . . openly and unabashedly, over and over, declare the simple truth that the entire Temple Mount is ours. It is the site of the two destroyed Holy Temples, and is the place upon which the Third Temple will be rebuilt—soon, with the help of G-d. We have not given up on the Temple Mount, we have no authority to do so, and we will never do so. It is the heart of Jerusalem, of the Land of Israel, of the world—and it is the heart of the people of Israel.[1]

—RABBI ZALMAN MELAMED

efore he entered office, former Prime Minister Benjamin Netanyahu wrote to one Temple activist, "The right of the Jewish people to its holy place—the Temple Mount—cannot be questioned."[2] This statement from Netanyahu, though considered sensational by the press, could be made by any of Israel's prime ministers, for to deny it would be tantamount to denying the Jewish heritage itself. The real statement that those in the Temple movement are waiting to hear is one that does not repeat old assurances about "rights" that have no reality, but one that declares, "We are ready to rebuild."

As Orthodox Jews continue to prepare for the Third Temple, and Israel continues to be threatened by enemies within and without, a growing sense of readiness is filling the Land. More than ever before, voices are asking, "Are these signs of the end time? How near are we to these days? How much longer before Messiah comes?" With Israel tottering on the edge of decision, answering such questions while keeping a proper balance is the challenge of the day. For such a time as this the example of Rabbi Kook, the spiritual father of many people involved in the Temple movement, should be recalled:

> Rabbi Kook's perfect faith that the revealed End was indeed at hand in no way contradicts the notion that we may, heaven forbid, miss the mark....We must act in full awareness of the mighty messianic potential of our era....There is, however, a fine line between appropriate faith and false confidence, between true reverence that knows how great is the gulf separating it from its Creator and the arrogant certainty that presumes to know the mind of the Most High....And we bear an exalted responsibility to see that the potential is realized.[3]

The words are fitting for those who eagerly expect redemption but are warned that they may be in their final hour. When people are ready, it is hard to wait!

Restlessness on the Temple Mount

As the Millennial countdown began with the turn of the Gregorian calendar to its final year, fears of apocalyptic fever erupted in Israel. According to Jerusalem police commander Yair Yitzhaki, Israeli police were preparing for the possibility that messianists would attempt some violent action on the Temple Mount in the hopes of forcing the last days to come. Their fears were realized when on January 3, the Israeli government arrested and deported eight American members of a doomsday cult known as "Concerned Christians." Linda

Menuhin, a spokeswoman for the Jerusalem police department, said the members were part of an apocalyptic sect based in Denver, Colorado. The sect's leader, Monte Kim Miller, a former marketing executive, claimed he could speak in God's voice. He prophesied that the world would end at the close of 1999, that he would die in Jerusalem and be resurrected three days later, and that only he and members of his flock would be saved in the Holy City. The group had sold all their belongings before going to Israel in November of 1998 and moving into a house in the Meveseret Zion neighborhood.

The police said that cult experts advised them that the members "intended to commit extreme, violent activity in Jerusalem['s] streets and possibly commit suicide on the Temple Mount towards the end of 1999 in order to initiate a procedure to bring back Jesus."[4] After the deportation of this group, more unsettling activity took place on the Temple Mount in that month and the next. During that time the police prevented five attacks on the Temple Mount by Jews and others.

As police commander Yitzhaki says, "There is nothing more sensitive than the Old City. We have invested unprecedented manpower and resources to secure it."[5] But it is just such an assurance that flies in the face of Temple Mount activists. Their response is, "Rather than investing in manpower and resources to secure the Temple Mount *from* Jews, they should be doing this *for* Jews!" For this reason, they would say, what the police fear most is still going to happen again and again—violence on the Temple Mount.

When Israel made its formal peace treaty with Jordan, U.S. President Bill Clinton, in an address to the Jordanian Parliament (which was half-empty due to Arab opposition to the treaty), said, "The conflict between fear and hope is the problem of the Middle East today. Extremists who clothe themselves in religion…seek to destroy the progress of this peace….You are the past, not the future."[6] But Clinton was speaking here as a politician, not a prophet. The path of the future will include religious extremists, for there will be no other way to move the moderates of this age to make the necessary changes. That is why the activists adhere to the motto "Make it happen!"

Taking Action over the Temple Mount

The current generation leading the Temple movement is comprised largely of those who believe in "active redemption." It is not the individual Jew's responsibility to *wait* for the Temple, but to *work* for the Temple. The precedent for this may be seen in the example set by King David, who took action even when circumstances did not yet permit him to build the Temple: "The king said to Araunah, 'No, but I will surely buy it from you for a price, for I will not offer burnt offerings to the LORD my God which cost me nothing.' So David bought the threshing floor and the oxen for fifty shekels of silver. And David built there an altar to the LORD, and offered burnt offerings and peace offerings. Thus the LORD was moved by entreaty for the land, and the plague was held back from Israel" (2 Samuel 24:24-25).

Shlomo Moshe Scheinman believes that there is a principle here that can be applied to the present day:

> I suggest that we learn from David how to make an effort on behalf of the Temple and the sacrificial service in our days. I suggest that we donate fifty shekels to create the vessels that are needed for the sacrificial service, without waiting for national repentance, or the Messiah, or peace, etc. It should be plainly understood, that we donate the money without putting upon the money the sanctity of Hekdesh ("consecrated"). For we build in a state where holiness is lacking and afterwards we sanctify.

The imperative of doing this now has been well stated by Temple movement activists:

> There is but one way to redeem the Temple Mount and but one way to renew the sacrifices and build the Temple. Action! Sitting in a state of atrophy will not only allow the status quo to continue, it will cause needless and unimaginable suffering to the Jewish people. Just as we witnessed the destruction of six million Jews because of inaction concerning the return to Zion, so will we endure terrible tragedy should we opt for the same inaction concerning the Temple Mount. The fate and destiny of the Jewish people and their redemption are in the hands of each and every Jew. All that is required is will and faith of Jews to enter the Temple Mount until we have the numbers to demand its return to its rightful owners. If every one would make the commitment needed to redeem the Mount it will surely be speedily in our hands.[7]

However, most Jews have not yet felt the imperative to commit to redeeming the Temple Mount. Binyamin Ze'ev Kahane summarizes why this need has not been felt, and adds a note of censure for those who are observant of the Torah but will observe nothing for the Temple:

There are no shortages of excuses, each camp offering its own explanation why we can't build the Temple today. Some say: "The Temple will fall from the sky, and it is none of our business." Others claim: "The Temple is a project for the Messiah." And then there is this gem: "We are on too low a level to deal with such a lofty topic." And there are more. For all these excuses, there are clear and powerful answers.... But there really is no need to, since the rebuilding of the Temple is one of the 613 commandments. That closes the case. Have you ever heard anyone say that eating *matzoh* [unleavened bread] on Passover is a job for the Messiah? Has anyone ever said: Family purity? *Mikveh* [ritual immersion]? What for?! Family purity will descend from the heavens! Or how about: Study Torah [Bible]!? A lowly sinner like me should study the holy Torah!?... Did G-d allow us to conquer the Temple Mount thirty years ago just so that the Arabs can continue to desecrate His name on our holiest site, this time under Jewish sovereignty? Shouldn't we feel that this is the very last *mitzvah* [commandment] we should choose to ignore? [8]

For those who feel they should make it happen, the next question is this: How should they make it happen? On this there continues to be significant differences of opinion. Some believe that war is the only course, while others still cling to the hope for peace. This has resulted in two different approaches to reversing the status quo on the Temple Mount and rebuilding the Temple.

Perspectives on Reclaiming the Temple Mount

In the following discussion I am not attempting to be a prophet, but am simply showing the options that are presently being discussed within Israel and the Temple movement. From my prophetic perspective I can only see that the Third Temple will be rebuilt, according to the Scripture, and that terrible times of war and Tribulation must precede the better blessings of the Messiah and the Millennium. However, both ages will have a Temple, and in going from here to there, what is stated in the following paragraphs may surely happen, only some of it may happen in the Tribulation and some in the Millennium. Nevertheless, from the Orthodox Jewish perspective today, it is certain that something will happen soon.

The Mosques Will Be Moved to Rebuild

If the Muslim mosques are in the way of the Jewish Temple, then one option is that they be moved. Yohanan Ramati, Director of the Jerusalem Institute for

Western Defense, while not in the Temple movement and certainly not advocating the destruction of the Muslim holy places, nevertheless argues for Israel's *right* to do so in light of the historical situation in which Islam has already done this to Israel:

> If you allow your enemy to destroy synagogues and churches and build these mosques on top of them, then you must be allowed to do the same. And the fact that they are going to kick up God knows how much noise about this, should be disregarded. Because if you don't you are eventually going to cede them the right, and we are already ceding them the right. I'm not talking about Israel now. We're not intending to pull down any Muslim holy places. What I'm talking about is the world that regards it as perfectly normal and acceptable that the Muslims should build mosques where churches previously stood, but thinks it an outrage if Christians do it to Muslims. That sort of double standard only serves the people who are the enemies of your religion. The atheists and the agnostics are a growing part of the population all over the Christian and Jewish world.[9]

Gershon Salomon, director of the Temple Mount Faithful, does not want to continue a double standard either, but wants Israel to act as the independent and sovereign Nation it is supposed to be. His perspective is that if the Muslims don't like Israel changing the status quo on the Temple Mount, they should move back to where they have their own independent and sovereign state—and take their mosques with them! He says:

> What must be done now is to take the Mosque and the Dome of the Rock, and with all respect, to move them from the Temple Mount. We live now in a time when we have very progressive mechanical systems and we could do it very easily, stone by stone, to take it and move it from the Temple Mount and rebuild it again in the right place, where [it ought] to be, in Mecca. This will be a place where every Arab, if they want, can come and pray in these buildings, in Mecca. The Temple Mount must be only a place for one thing, the Third Temple, as it was for the First and Second Temple. All...buildings that were built on this place [the Temple Mount] by strange occupiers, like the Arabs, must be moved....And as a vision of the prophets which spoke in the name of God, the Temple Mount will be—and very soon—the place for only one thing, the Third Temple.[10]

Christians, even those sympathetic to Salomon's cause, usually hold to yet another perspective, preferring to look to some other means of the inevitable being brought to pass. Sharing this conviction is CBS Radio Correspondent and author David Dolan, whom I quoted earlier with these words.

> I have been here for 21 years; I've seen the SCUD missiles flying over. Who's to know what could possibly happen and how destruction could come and clear the area?...Jerusalem experiences a major earthquake every 50 years. The last major earthquake was in 1927....we are already maxed out on the 50 years [schedule] and there still hasn't been a major earthquake....I think God has His ways. And when His time is right... God will show the people exactly when and how they can build this Temple.[11]

However, Clarence Wagner, International Director of Bridges for Peace in Jerusalem, believes it won't be natural disasters that destroy the mosques. Like David Dolan, he believes that God will take care of the matter, in harmony with the end-time plan that He has revealed:

> There's a lot of speculation that radical Israeli groups might destroy the mosques that are up on the Temple Mount and that would open the way for the Temple to be rebuilt. There's a big problem with that, however. The Muslims consider the entire Temple Mount a mosque, not just the buildings on it, but the site itself. Even if those building were destroyed in an earthquake, which is a possibility, or bombed out, they would still insist on rebuilding them. This leads me to the conclusion that it has to be a greater power that would impose a Temple on the Muslims and possibly on many Israelis who are ambivalent about a Temple being rebuilt. I myself believe that it will be the Antichrist who will rebuild this building. The Temple is mentioned in [2] Thessalonians [2:4], in Daniel [9:27], and in Revelation [11:1-2] in connection with this man of sin....I believe this is a hint as to who will build it. And politically speaking, only some great world power that was greater than the Muslims in the region, and even many Israelis, would be able to build such a thing and impose it, as it were, on the different peoples here. That's the scenario that I see unfolding. I think it will happen in time, but I don't think it will likely be at the hands of the Israelis and I certainly don't see the Muslims ever willingly giving up their claims to the entire Temple Mount or acceding to a Jewish Temple going up on the Temple Mount.[12]

While many are accustomed to see activism as the mark of the Temple movement, there are also those whose activism is couched in the hope that a God who could send an earthquake to move the Muslim mosques could also send a revival to move the Muslims minds to rebuild the Temple.

The Muslims Will Be Moved to Rebuild

Haifa Chief Rabbi Sh'ar-Yashuv Cohen has emphasized that the Temple will not rise as a result of expulsion of the Arabs and the destruction of their mosques. In his view, it will be quite the opposite: The Temple will be rebuilt as a result of the fulfillment of Zephaniah 3:9: "For then I will give to the peoples purified lips, that all of them may call on the name of the LORD." His view is that the nations of the world, including the Arabs, will invite the Jews to go up and build the Temple. Rabbi Cohen contends that anyone who has convinced himself that it is possible to speak of actually rebuilding the Temple under the prevailing circumstances without a miraculous change of heart on the part of the nations will be proven wrong. He argues that the Temple movement's goal of liberating the Temple Mount from Islam is not the way God intends to work. Rather, drawing an analogy from the text of Genesis 26:15-31, he claims that the Temple will be built when Israel understands its mission to develop a different attitude toward the nations and, as a result, there will be peace and a cooperative rebuilding of the Temple:

> The Jewish rabbis and interpreters have not overlooked this vision [of rebuilding the Temple]. [Take] for example, the Rambam's (Nachmanides) interpretation of the conflict over the wells that the patriarch Isaac had with the Philistines and the king of Gerar. Each well, according to his exegesis, is analogous to one of the Temples. The first two wells were destroyed by them just like the first two Temples were destroyed. The third well—Rehovot , about which Abraham said "for now the Lord has made room for us, and we shall be fruitful in the land"—parallels the Third Temple. There was already an evident cooperation between the Children of Abraham and the people of the land (or, more specifically if you like, with the Philistines). And lastly, there is a point in remembering who was the "Messiah" who gave the order to build the Second Temple: the Persian emperor Cyrus (who saw himself as given "all the kingdoms of the earth" by the Lord God of heaven who chose Jerusalem). When all the peoples, including the Moslems, under-

stand the global benefit for building the Temple in Jerusalem, they will ask Israel to build it.[13]

From a similar perspective, Reuven Prager of Beged Ivri believes that the problem with activism is that it too often neglects the spiritual element. Such militaristic Jews do not look for God to bring about a change in those with whom they have problems in this world (the Arabs). Prager argues that God will instead change the Arabs at the appointed time:

> People often ask me, How are we going to build the Temple? There's a mosque standing on the Temple Mount. Now normally I don't deal with political issues, but I do feel the need to respond. The only voice that we've heard for the last 50 years towards rebuilding the Temple has been the voice of let's take down the mosques and by force build the Temple. Or those who are waiting for an earthquake to come for the mosque to be tumbled down off the Temple Mount. Or some kind of miracle with the Temple falling down from the sky completely built. The Muslim world is not preventing us from rebuilding the Temple. If anything, it is we ourselves that are holding ourselves back. We have to keep in mind that a Muslim believes in God. And I know there is a popular movement right now to say that the Muslims don't serve God, they serve Allah.... [But] when a guy wraps himself with explosives and blows himself up screaming, Allah Ackbar ["God is great!"] or grabs a wheel of a bus and drives it off a cliff screaming, "God is great," these guys are crazy about serving God. They're [just] being misdirected towards how God wants them to serve.... [but] when God makes it manifestly clear that the time is come that He wants His house to be rebuilt, do you think a Muslim is going to stand before God and say, "No"? Can't be! Islam is in submission before God.... [So] it is not the Muslim world that's holding us back from rebuilding the Temple; it's our own fear of taking responsibility for beginning the work to prepare for rebuilding the Temple.[14]

As I mentioned at the beginning of this section, both of these proposals for dealing with the mosques and rebuilding the Temple may well take place; however, the biblical means and timing must be discerned. There will be war on the Temple Mount in the future (see chapter 20), so the activists are correct in understanding that the Muslims will not surrender their holy sites anytime soon. However, once all war is past, and the Messiah has come and restored all things, the non-Jewish peoples will willingly come and ask to be a part of the rebuilding of Messiah's Temple. So, those who hope for a spiritual change in the world are also correct. The prophetic confusion that has produced these two viewpoints reminds us that in light of the rapid development of the prophetic program in our day, we must be discerning of the times, and especially the times for the Temple.

Discerning the Times for the Temple

Rabbi Chaim Richman, Director of Public Affairs for the Temple Institute and director of Light to the Nations, believes that despite the world's opinion that Israel might not survive the current Middle East crisis, the Nation's present problems are but the preparation for prophetic fulfillment:

> There are those of us who feel more strongly than ever that the appearance of Messiah is near. I would go further than that and tell you that, although there are those of us who are upset about the direction of things in Israel, this is not a cause for despondency or depression. On the contrary, the fact that things are going the way they are going here in Israel with this government, with the leadership, with the false peace, with the treachery, and with the terrorism, its nothing but another indication of the fact that God in His great mercy is bringing about all that which He from the beginning had in mind for His people and for His world. We feel that we are blessed to be living in this time. Perhaps this is more of a pivotal generation than any that has ever existed, and we feel that we, in fact, are seeing things that our fathers only dreamed of, and that we will be blessed to see the culmination of these things.[15]

However, before the Messiah appears, the Jewish people must find this "great mercy" of God of which Rabbi Richman speaks. Today, the day of redemption is nearer than ever before, but so is the time of Tribulation ("pangs of the Messiah"). Jews who look for the *Shekinah* must also remember that the *Sitra Ahra* looks for them. The *Sitra Ahra* (literally, "the Other Side") is a term used to describe the force of evil, sent by Satan, which according to Jewish legend, stands ready to pounce upon a Jew as soon as he sets foot on sacred soil. This was often used to dissuade Jews from immigrating to Israel, since the force would be more virulent there than in the foreign land from which they came. If setting foot on the sacred soil of the Holy Land was thought to be dangerous, what of setting foot on the soil of utmost sanctity, the holy Temple Mount?

The problem is deeper than the need for a ritual purification in order to serve God; it is a need for a righteous position in order to see God. Though the Lord declared, "No man can see me and live!" (Exodus 33:20), David longed to "dwell in the house of the LORD all the days of [his] life, to behold the beauty of the LORD, and to meditate in His temple" (Psalm 27:4). The Temple for which David longed was the Heavenly Temple, where, no longer being a mortal man, he could behold the Lord in all His beauty. In like manner Moses beseeched the Lord, "I pray Thee, show me Thy glory!" (Exodus 33:18), yet the prophet Isaiah proclaimed, "Then the glory of the LORD will be revealed, and all flesh will see it together" (Isaiah 40:5). How can these things be? What is needed is more than a promise; what is needed is a position. Though one may have a position in this life as a child of Abraham, a son of the Covenant, one of the Chosen People, there is still the need for a position like this in heaven. The Prophets have said that what is needed for any Jew or Gentile is *teshuvah* ("repentance") toward God and toward His Messiah (Yeshua="Jesus"). The prophet Hosea made this future act by national Israel the key to experiencing the promised Redemption in Hosea 3:5: "Afterward the sons of Israel will return and seek the LORD their God and David their king; and they will come trembling to the LORD and to His goodness in the last days." The interpretation of this text in Yalkut Shimoni Samuel 106 understood that this Restoration in the last days included the Temple:

> In the future, Israel is destined to show disdain for three things: the kingdom of Heaven, the kingdom of David, and the building of the Temple....Rabbi Simon ben Menasiah said: "Israel will never see a sign of redemption until they once again desire all three. This is what the verse [Hosea 3:5] states: 'And afterwards the Children of Israel will return and seek out the Lord their God'—this is the Kingdom of Heaven, 'and David their King'—This is the kingdom of David—'And they shall come trembling to the Lord and His goodness in the Latter Days'—This is the Holy Temple.

What we learn from this is that the things most sought after, including the Last Days Temple, will only come as Israel returns to the Lord in national repentance in the last days. Clarence Wagner of Bridges for Peace reminds us that the One who will come and restore all things and reveal His glory to all flesh in the Temple will be none other than the Messiah Himself:

> In Revelation 19–20 we read how in this area [of the Mount of Olives], He [Jesus] will come back on a white horse. He will come back into the city and the elders will be with Him and He will be judging from Jerusalem. Where is He going to be sitting? I'm sure [it will be] in His Temple. He will be worshiped in Jerusalem and be the central focus. Except this time instead of the Holy Spirit's presence in the Holy of Holies, it will be Yeshua [Jesus] Himself who will be ruling and reigning

from Zion. There is no doubt in my mind that the place He will do this from is not the City Hall but will be the rebuilt Temple of God, sanctified for Him.[16]

Beyond the Point of No Return?

We have come to a turning point on the prophetic path from which we will not likely turn back. The determination among Israeli Jews, and Jews worldwide, to see the coming of the Messiah and the rebuilding of the Temple is resolute. To those of us who are able to see the future Temple in Scripture, we should see these activities of the Jewish people to prepare for the Temple as a present sign—in fact, one of the most significant signs of the end times.

The French General Napoleon Bonaparte once passed a synagogue on the ninth of Av and heard the Jews weeping. "What's this weeping?" he asked. When told that the Jews were weeping about the destruction of their Temple, Napoleon said, "A people that longs so much for its city and its Temple are bound to restore them one day!" As weeping for the Temple has today turned to working for the Temple, may we not believe that the day of restoration is near? Clarence Wagner believes that the signs point to the nearness of that day:

> It's so exciting living just a mile south of the Mount of Olives because, of course, Zechariah told us, Jesus Himself told us, that this would be the spot that He'll return to in the last days. And I believe that's very, very soon. His feet will stand again on the Mount of Olives. And then He'll go over to the Temple Mount, He'll cleanse it, He'll restore it, and of course the Scriptures tell us that water will flow from under the Temple out into the Kidron Valley down here and down towards the Dead Sea in the Millennial age. One thing we're really lacking in Jerusalem today is water. We have no streams even; no rivers, no lakes, no oceans close by. But in that day it's going to come from right here on the Temple Mount. And the Temple that will accompany that has got to be something fantastic. We have some description of it in the Bible. But it's hard to even imagine. But sometimes as I drive along the ridge here south of the Temple Mount, I think about that and I try to picture what it might be like when the Lord returns and when that new Temple is here. I can't even, frankly, imagine it. But I believe it will occur and all the signs are there that the Temple's time is near. And the main sign is that this city is once again a thriving metropolis—over 500,000 people and the capital of a rebuilt, restored Jewish State, just as the prophet said it would be in the last days. So the day of His return has got to be drawing very, very near.[17]

Those in the Temple movement believe that the process of Israel's redemption began with the reunification of Jerusalem and the retaking of the Temple Mount in the Six-Day War. How well many of them remember that afternoon on June 7, 1967, when the leaders of Israel began to assemble at the foot of the newly won Western Wall and Defense Minister Moshe Dayan issued both a pronouncement and a prediction: "We have returned to the holiest of our holy places, never to part from them again."[18] They have returned, but not yet to the Temple Mount. The process begun on that day is deemed irreversible and will eventually culminate in the rebuilding of the Third Temple. All that remains, they say, is for the Israeli government to realize the terrible mistake made in returning custody of the site to the Muslims and to act in keeping with the historical reality of Jewish sovereignty over the Temple Mount. They are now ready to rebuild, and wait only for their Nation to catch up with them.

The Final Steps of the Ascent

The goal to rebuild the Temple appears to be a mountainous task, and it literally is that! The Temple Mount is indeed a mountain with the Temple at the very top of its summit. In the days of the Temple a person who ascended the mountain began with a climb up the monumental staircase at the southern entrance, and then went up through an underground tunnel to the level of the Temple complex. Coming out the top of the tunnel, that person entered a large pavilion from which could be seen the Temple, high in the distance. The ascent to the Temple itself involved a series of steps that moved a person progressively upward from the Women's Court to the Israelite Court to the Inner Court, and finally, to the point where the Temple itself stood at the highest point.

In like manner, as we consider the ascent of modern Israeli Jews toward the goal of rebuilding the Temple today, there are also a series of steps that will move them toward their goal. The first step of this ascent was completed when they captured the Temple Mount in 1967. As a result, Israelis were able to actually unearth the ancient monumental staircase, but could not enter the underground tunnel because it is in the area controlled by the Muslims. Nevertheless, Jews have taken the next step and ascended to the pavilion. This occurred as Orthodox Jews began to walk a circuitous path on this level of the Temple Mount at the close of the 1990s.

The next step, and the most challenging, will be reached only when Israel regains full control of the Temple Mount itself. Only then will it be possible to ritually purify the area and make it possible for sacrifices to be resumed at the place of the altar. However, once this has occurred, the summit will have been surmounted, and the next step of rebuilding the Temple assured.

What does this say to you and me? It says that not only have the Jews already begun the ascent to their goal, but they are only one step away from accomplishing it! As this book has shown, the current conflict over the Temple Mount and the resolve of Jewish activists to prepare for the conclusion of this conflict have provided the momentum for the short distance that remains of the climb. We live in a day that is on the brink of the rebuilding effort, and with it the beginning of the fulfillment of the prophecies that will move the world rapidly to see as a reality the coming Last Days Temple.

> In ancient times the Temple stood
> Clothed in stone and gilded wood;
> A symbol of the Maker's plan
> To dwell on earth with sinful man.
>
> Though fallen long and desolate
> Its fall did not decide its fate,
> In days to come it will arise
> Though by the nations still despised.
>
> Till when Messiah comes at last
> Its desolation will be past,
> Rebuilt in splendor it will shine
> In all the earth through all of time.
>
> Then beyond time—the world to come
> Will need no Temple, moon, or sun,
> For greater Temple there will be
> The Lord, through all eternity!

A Chronology
of the Temple
in History and Prophecy

A chronological presentation of the major events associated with the Temple Mount and the preparations for the earthly Sanctuaries in history and prophecy:

The Temple in History

The Ancient Period

Before the Temple

After Creation   Prototypical "sanctuary" revealed to Adam and Eve in the Garden of Eden as part of the divine ideal (Genesis 2–3).

C. 2000 B.C.   Abraham and Isaac offer a ram on Mount Moriah, which tradition identifies with the Temple Mount (Genesis 22:1-19).

1446 B.C.   Moses receives the earthly pattern for the earthly Sanctuary based on a divine revelation on Mount Sinai of the heavenly Temple archetype (Exodus 24:15-18; 25:8-22,40).

C. 1400 B.C.   Moses describes service to be performed at the future central Sanctuary (Temple) (Deuteronomy 12:5-21; 15:19-20). Tabernacle at Shiloh destroyed, Ark taken (Psalm 78:60-61; Jeremiah 7:12; 26:6; 1 Samuel 4:10-11,22).

996 B.C.   David makes Jerusalem his capital and moves the Ark to a site adjacent to Temple Mount (2 Samuel 5:6-12; 6:1-17; 1 Chronicles 11:4-9; 15:1–16:38).

993 B.C.	David desires to build the Temple; Solomon designated as builder (2 Samuel 7:1-13; 1 Chronicles 17:1-14).
990 B.C.	David purchases threshing floor of Araunah the Jebusite as site for the First Temple (2 Samuel 24:18-25; 1 Chronicles 21:18-26).
961 B.C.	David reveals plans of archetypal Sanctuary to Solomon (1 Chronicles 28:11-19) and makes Levitical and material preparations for the First Temple (1 Chronicles 22–26; 29:1-21).

The First Temple

960–950 B.C.	Solomon builds the First Temple (1 Kings 5-8).
910 B.C.	Temple treasures taken by Egyptian Pharaoh Shishak (1 Kings 14:25-28; 2 Chronicles 12:1-11).
835 B.C.	Jehoash (Joash), King of Judah, and Jehoiada repair damaged parts of Temple (2 Kings 12:5-14; 2 Chronicles 24:12-14).
826 B.C.	Jehoash (Joash), King of Israel, attacks Judah, breaks down the walls of Jerusalem, and plunders the Temple, removing the Temple treasury to Samaria (2 Kings 14:13-14).
742–735 B.C.	Jotham, son of Uzziah, builds the upper gate of the Temple (2 Kings 15:35; 2 Chronicles 27:3).
720 B.C.	Ahaz closes Temple, empties Temple treasury, breaks up Temple furnishings and vessels to pay tribute to the Assyrian king Tiglath-Pileser, and defiles Temple with a pagan Syrian altar (2 Kings 16:8-18; 2 Chronicles 28:21, 24).
715 B.C.	Hezekiah opens Temple doors, cleanses Temple, returns Temple vessels, restores ritual and Passover, and builds storehouses for Temple contributions (2 Chronicles 29:3-19; 30:1-27; 31:11-12).
711 B.C.	Hezekiah is forced to give up Temple treasuries and strip gold off Temple doors to pay tribute to the Assyrian king Sennacherib (2 Kings 18:15-16).
700 B.C.	King Hezekiah foolishly shows the treasures of the Temple treasury and of the king's house to Berodach-baladan, a prince of Babylon and his envoys; an act the prophet Isaiah predicted would lead to the eventual plunder of the Temple by the Babylonians (2 Kings 20:12-21; 2 Chronicles 32:31).

695–642 B.C.	King Manasseh of Judah places idols within the Temple, including the Holy Place and the Holy of Holies. The Ark and the other Temple treasures were probably removed by the faithful Levites, whom Manasseh deposed, to prevent their defilement. Manasseh later repents, but does not restore these treasures to the Temple (2 Kings 21:4-7; 2 Chronicles 7–9, 15).
622 B.C.	King Josiah of Judah, grandson of Manasseh, in restoring the Temple, recovers one of the Temple treasures, the Torat Moshe (autograph of the Pentateuch) that once was placed beside the Ark and was apparently hidden in the Temple in the time of Manasseh (2 Kings 22:8; 2 Chronicles 34:14-18) and commands the Levites to return the Ark to the restored Temple (2 Chronicles 35:3).
605 B.C.	Babylon's King Nebuchadnezzar pillages the Temple, taking articles and depositing them in the Babylonian temple at Shinar (2 Chronicles 36:7).
598/7 B.C.	King Nebuchadnezzar returns and further plunders the treasures of the Temple (2 Kings 24:13; 2 Chronicles 36:7).
586 B.C.	King Nebuchadnezzar invades Jerusalem a third time and destroys the Temple.
573 B.C.	Ezekiel, in Babylonian exile, has vision of Millennial Temple (Ezekiel 40–48).
538 B.C.	Daniel prayed concerning Jerusalem's and the Temple's restoration and received prophecy of the seventy weeks concerning the Messiah's death in Jerusalem, the destruction of the Second Temple, and its future rebuilding and desecration by Antichrist (Daniel 9:1-27). Daniel also receives vision of the defiling of the future Second Temple (Zerubbabel's) by Antiochus Ephiphanes' placement of a statue of Zeus in the Holy Place (Daniel 11:31).

The Second Temple

539 B.C.	On October 11–12, Babylonian king Belshazzar desecrates Temple vessels at a pagan feast (Daniel 5:1-4) and Persian monarch Cyrus the Great conquers Babylon.
538 B.C.	Cyrus issues decree allowing Jews in exile to return to Jerusalem and rebuild the city and the Temple (2 Chronicles

36:22-23; Ezra 1:1-4; 6:3-5) and returns Temple vessels taken by Nebuchadnezzar (Ezra 1:7-11; 6:3-15).

520–515 B.C.	Zerubbabel, a descendant of David, rebuilds and dedicates the Temple and restores the sacrificial system with assistance of the Persian king Darius (Ezra 3:1-13; 5:1-17; 6:1-18).
445 B.C.	Nehemiah returns to Jerusalem from Persia to rebuild the walls of the city and protect the Temple Mount (Nehemiah 1-7:4).
332 B.C.	Alexander the Great conquers Jerusalem and, according to Josephus, prostrates himself before the high priest and offers sacrifice in the Temple *(Antiquities* xi. 392-339). This is probably an embellished account given to explain why Alexander spared the Temple.
175–165 B.C.	Antiochus IV (Epiphanes), Seleucid king of Syria, pillages Temple; soldiers of Antiochus defile Temple; the king stops Jewish sacrifices and institutes worship of Olympian Zeus in Temple (1 Maccabees 1:10-63; 2 Maccabees 5:1ff).
165 B.C.	On December 25, Judas Maccabaeus restores Jewish ritual by cleansing and rededicating the Temple (first Hanukkah) after successful revolt against Seleucids (1 Maccabees 4).
168 B.C.–A.D. 73	The Jewish apocryphal, apocalyptic, and pseudepigraphical writings, including the Dead Sea Scrolls (such as the *Temple Scroll,* 11QT), are produced and include prophecies about the restoration of the Temple.
67 B.C.	Aristobulus besieges Jerusalem and substitutes pig for sheep in attempt to end Temple sacrifices (which were stopped on the 17th of *Tammuz*). The result of this fratricidal war between Aristobulus and his brother Hyracanus led to the intervention of Rome and the end of Jewish independence.
63 B.C.	Roman emperor Pompey conquers Jerusalem and enters Holy of Holies.
20 B.C.	Herod the Great begins work to totally rebuild and expand dimensions of Second Temple; work continues on the Temple until about A.D. 64 (Matthew 24:1; Mark 13:1; Luke 21:5; John 2:20).

5/4 B.C.	In the winter season, Jesus is dedicated in Herod's Temple; recognized there as Messiah by Simeon and Anna the prophetess (Luke 2:22-38).
9 A.D.	On April 29, Jesus (age 12) makes pilgrimage to Temple at Passover and remains there three days to talk with Jewish teachers (Luke 2:41-51).
29 A.D.	In the summer or autumn, Jesus, at the commencement of His ministry, is tempted by Satan by being taken to the pinnacle of the Temple (Matthew 4:5; Luke 4:9); Jesus drives money-changers from outer courts of Temple in the 46th year of its building (John 2:13-17,20).
32 A.D.	September 10–17, Jesus comes to the Temple at Succot (John 7:2, 10).
32 A.D.	On December 18, Jesus comes to Temple courts at Hanukkah (John 10:22-23).
33 A.D.	On Monday, March 30, Jesus enters Temple Mount through Eastern Gate (Matthew 21:1-11; Luke 19:37-44); casts out money-changers a second time (Matthew 21:12-13; Luke 19:45-46); teaches and heals daily in Temple (Matthew 21:14,37; Luke 19:47).
33 A.D.	Tuesday, March 31, Jesus predicts destruction of Second Temple (Matthew 23:37-38; 24:2; Mark 13:2; Luke 21:6,20-24) and defiling of Third (Tribulation) Temple in His Olivet Discourse (Matthew 24:15; Mark 13:14).
33 A.D.	Friday, April 3, outer veil (curtain) of the Holy of Holies is torn at death of Jesus (Matthew 27:51).
33 A.D.	On Sunday, May 24, Peter preaches in Court of the Gentiles in Temple at *Shavuot* (Pentecost—Acts 2); Peter heals lame man at the Nicanor Gate leading from Court of Gentiles to Court of Women in Temple (Acts 3:1-11).
c. 26–34 A.D.	Saul Paulus (Paul) is educated as a Pharisee under Rabbi Gamaliel on southern entrance steps to the Temple (Acts 22:3; 26:4-5).
40 A.D.	Roman emperor Caligula fails in his attempt to defile Temple by erecting a statue of himself.

56 A.D. Paul goes to Temple with men completing Nazirite vow and is wrongly accused of defiling the Temple by taking a Gentile there (Acts 21:26-28).

70 A.D. Roman General Titus destroys Second (Herodian) Temple and carries off Temple treasures to Rome.

After the Temple

C. 75–85 A.D. Jewish general, and later historian, Josephus Flavius (Joseph ben Matthias) writes his famous *Jewish Wars* and *Jewish Antiquities,* which contain valuable eyewitness descriptions of the Temple.

130 A.D. Roman emperor Publius Aelius Hadrianus reneges on promise to rebuild Temple for Jews and has Temple Mount plowed by Tinneis (Turnus) Rufus, Roman governor of Judea on the ninth of *Av* (some say fulfilling the prophecy of Micah 3:12) to signify the utter destruction of the Jewish city and signal the birth of Jerusalem as the Roman colony *Aelia Capitolina.*

132 A.D. Bar Kokhba rebellion; possible rebuilding of Second Temple by Bar Kokhba.

135 A.D. Hadrian retakes Jerusalem, destroys Bar Kokhba Temple, rebuilds Jerusalem according to Roman city plan, and desecrates Temple Mount by erecting statute of himself at site of the Holy of Holies.

326 A.D. Byzantine emperor Constantine builds Church of Holy Sepulchre to overlook Temple ruins as example of Christianity as new spiritual center.

333 A.D. The Pilgrim of Bordeaux visits Jerusalem and records details of the Temple site.

337–380 A.D. Visits to Jerusalem by Eusebius, bishop of Caesarea (337) and pilgrim nun Aegeria (380) result in further accounts of Temple area.

363 A.D. Pagan emperor Julian (the Apostate) allows Jews to attempt rebuilding of Temple to counter Byzantine Christianity; effort fails as earthquake destroys building materials stored in Solomon's Stables.

443 A.D.	Hopes that Empress Eudoxia would permit a rebuilding of Temple prompts letter calling for Jewish return and Messianic revival.
C. 500 A.D.	*Jerusalem Talmud* completed by rabbinic academies in Galilee, preserving valuable information about the Temple and its ritual.
565 A.D.	Mosaic map is created in Madaba (today in Jordan) depicting walled Jerusalem and the Western Wall.
614 A.D.	Jewish support of Persian conquest of Jerusalem leads to favored status of Jews and hopes for rebuilding Temple.
622 A.D.	The Islamic prophet Mohammed is believed to have made a night journey (*Hejirah* = to Year 1 on Islamic calendar) to Jerusalem, and to have ascended to the seventh heaven from the site of the holy Rock *(as-Sakhra)—Koran*, Surah xv2.
637 A.D.	Muslims conquer Jerusalem and Caliph Omar Ibn el-Khattab is shown Temple Mount and site of Temple (Rock) by Jerusalem Patriarch Sophronios, and finds it covered in centuries of dung and debris.
640 A.D.	Kalif Omar Ibn-Chatub cleans and repairs the Temple Mount, allows seven Jews to settle there and build a yeshiva.
691 A.D.	Muslim Caliph Abd al-Malik Ibn-Marwan completes Dome of the Rock on the Temple Mount 72 years after Mohammed's *Hejirah* (flight from Mecca to Medina).
701 A.D.	The Muslim Caliph al-Walid completed the Al-Aqsa Mosque on the site of a Byzantine church (on southern portion of Temple Mount). This is the Al-Aqsa *el-Qadimeh* ("eastward") underneath the present structure.
921 A.D.	Rabbi Aharon ben Meir (Gaon of Israel) writes that Jews continue to worship from the Mount of Olives toward the Temple Mount.
940 A.D.	The Karaite writer, Solomon Ben-Yerucham, writes about a synagogue on the southern side of the Temple Mount and the arguments between the Rabbis and Karaites that caused the Jews to lose their foothold on the Mount.

1000 A.D.	Rabbi Avraham Berachia writes about a synagogue and yeshiva that the Jews built on the Temple Mount, and Rabbi Shemuel ben Paltiel records Jewish prayer services at the *Kotel Maaravi*.
1099–1118 A.D.	Crusaders capture Jerusalem and transform Muslim Dome of the Rock into Christian church (*Templum Domini*, "the Temple of the Lord") and the Al-Aqsa Mosque into headquarters of the Order of the Knights Templar.
1100 A.D.	Rabbi Abraham ben Chiyah Hanassi writes that Jewish worship occurred all around the Temple Mount walls before Crusader conquest.
1165 A.D.	The Rambam visits Jerusalem and prays on the Temple Mount.
1173 A.D.	Rabbi Benjamin of Tudela describes his visit to the Temple Mount in A.D. 1167.
1187 A.D.	Saladin recaptures Jerusalem for Muslims and converts *Templum Domini* and Al-Aqsa to mosques.
1193 A.D.	King Afdal, son of Saladin (who captured Jerusalem in 1187), constitutes area in front of Western Wall (Burak) as holy property (Wakf) to Muslims.
1215 A.D.	Rabbi Menachem ben Peretz of Hebron writes that the Western Wall still exists and that Jews live near it.
1264 A.D.	Mamlukes under Sultan Baybers capture Jerusalem and repair Dome of the Rock and Temple Mount.
1267 A.D.	The Rambam (Nachmanides) moves to Jerusalem to establish Jewish institutions and describe Temple Mount.
1287 A.D.	The Meiri writes that he heard that the custom is to enter the Temple Mount.
1322 A.D.	Rabbi Estori Haparchi (of Florence) describes the Temple Mount in his work *Kaphtor Vaferach*.
1350 A.D.	Rabbi Isaac Halevi Asir Hatiqvah founds a yeshiva near the Western Wall.
1476 A.D.	Jews enter Al-Aqsa for a hearing about the Rambam.
1487 A.D.	Rabbi Ovadiah of Bertinoro founds yeshiva near Western Wall.

1538–9 A.D.	Sultan Suleiman I "The Magnificent" embellishes Dome of the Rock and builds present perimeter walls and gates around Jerusalem (today's Old City) and designates the Western Wall as the official place for Jewish worship.
1541 A.D.	The Golden Gate is sealed to bar Jesus (or the expected Jewish Messiah), who, according to tradition (based on prophecy in Ezekiel 44:2-3), is to enter the gate and rule Jerusalem.
1662 A.D.	The false Messiah Shabatai Zvi arrives in Jerusalem, producing hopes that the Temple would be rebuilt.
1777 A.D.	Venetian Jewish prayers at Western Wall for Arab pogroms in Jerusalem.
1799 A.D.	The French emperor Napoleon Bonaparte invades Palestine and announces that he would restore Jerusalem to the Jews, but is defeated at Acre (on the northern Mediterranean coast).
1827 A.D.	Egyptians, under Muhamad Ali, conquer Jerusalem and forbid repair of Western Wall pavement.
1838 A.D.	Edward Robinson discovers arch in the outer Western Wall of the Temple that belonged to the monumental staircase to the Temple area described by Josephus.
1854 A.D.	Crimean War (Turkey, France, England, Russia) fought to resolve guardianship of Jerusalem's holy places (especially the Temple Mount).
1855 A.D.	Duke of Brabant becomes first non-Muslim to tour Dome of the Rock since 1187 expulsion of the Crusaders.
1865 A.D.	Charles Wilson discovers another arch a little further north of Robinson's arch in the western wall of the Temple; probably of Hasmonean origin and enlarged by Herod the Great.
1866 A.D.	Jews become majority in Jerusalem for first time since A.D. 614 and Sir Moses Montefiore makes renovations at Western Wall.
1867–70 A.D.	Sir Charles Warren, on behalf of the Palestine Exploration Fund, conducts first archaeological excavations in the area of the Temple Mount (above and below ground).
1873–74 A.D.	Discovery of Temple inscription forbidding Gentile entrance to the Temple courts.

1883 A.D.	Attempt by General Charles Gordon to locate site of Calvary and the Garden Tomb; proposal of "skeleton plan" with Temple.
1887 A.D.	Baron Edmund de Rothschild attempts to purchase yards in front of the Western Wall.
1891 A.D.	Report on clearance of Eastern Gate by Ottoman authorities.
1897 A.D.	Theodore Herzl holds First Zionist Congress and establishes that Israel must be the Jewish homeland, sparking the first waves of *Aliyah* (immigration) to the Land.

The Modern Period

1913	Anglo-Palestine Bank attempts to buy site to build a synagogue at the Western Wall.
1917–1948	Jerusalem is conquered by British; continual struggles and riots between Arabs and Jews over access and control of Western Wall of Temple Mount; Israeli independence granted May 14, 1948 but no access to Western Wall or Temple Mount; both Dome of the Rock and Al-Aqsa Mosque damaged by bombs in War of Independence.
May 25, 1948	Old City falls to the Jordanians and Jews are forbidden access to the Western Wall of the Temple Mount for the next 18 years. Jordan destroys 58 synagogues in the Jewish Quarter.
1951	King Abdullah of Transjordan is assassinated by Muslims at the Al-Aqsa Mosque; succeeded by King Hussein of Jordan.
1958–1964	Egypt, Jordan, and Saudi Arabia underwrite extensive repairs to the Dome of the Rock.
1961–1967	British archaeologist Dame Kathleen Kenyon conducts excavation at southwest corner of Temple Mount.
June 7, 1967	Israel, during Six-Day War, liberates Temple Mount; hopes of rebuilding Temple revive, and Rabbi Goren suggests blowing up mosques on the Temple Mount, but later Defense Minister Moshe Dayan orders Israeli flag removed from atop the Dome of the Rock.
June 8, 1967	IDF Chief Chaplain Rabbi Shlomo Goren and team carefully measure the dimensions of the Temple Compound based on

available archaeological remains compared with measurements recorded in Josephus, Mishnah tractates *Middot* and *Shekalim*, Maimonides, and Sa'adia Gaon.

June 17, 1967	Moshe Dayan meets with leaders of Supreme Muslim Council in Al-Aqsa Mosque and returns Temple Mount, especially site of the Temple, to sovereign control of the Muslim Wakf as a gesture of peace; agrees that Jews can have access to Mount, but cannot conduct prayers or religious activities.
June 28, 1967	Israeli government officals meet with Muslim and Christian authorities and place administration of Jerusalem's holy sites under control of religious leaders.
June 29, 1967	Israeli Knesset (parliament) declares the reunification of East and West Jerusalem, making the Temple Mount part of modern Israel.
August 1–8, 1967	Israeli police are asked to regularly enforce public order at Temple Mount and other religious sites in Jerusalem after reports of improper visitor conduct; Ministry of Religious Affairs committee given oversight of holy places.
August 15, 1967	Rabbi Shlomo Goren leads group, including army chaplains, to pray on Temple Mount. Based on his measurements taken on the Mount in June, he contends that he knows where the Holy of Holies is located and that rabbinic ban against entering the Temple Mount is no longer applicable.
August 22, 1967	Chief Rabbinate seeks to enforce religious ban on entrance to Temple Mount by posting signs at ramp leading to Temple Compound.
February 29, 1968	Israeli archaeologist Benjamin Mazar begins extensive excavations south and southwest of the Temple Mount 100 years after first British excavation. Significant finds relating to the Temple include the original entrance to the Temple Mount through the Huldah Gates and Temple priest's tunnels.
July 15, 1968	Muslim Court of Appeals rejects $100 million offer by American Masonic Temple Order to build their "Temple of Solomon" on the Mount.
December 19, 1968	Prayers are offered on Temple Mount at Hanukkah by nationalistic Jewish group.

April 15, 1969	Temple Mount Faithful file legal action against Police Minister Shlomo Hillel to allow Jewish prayer services on Temple Mount; Israeli State Attorney upholds police enforcement of government prohibition of prayer on basis of national security and political concerns.
August 23, 1969	Australian Christian cultist Dennis Michael Rohan sets fire to the Al-Aqsa Mosque; Arab demonstrators, and later Muslim legal representatives, accuse Israel of deliberately setting the blaze in order to rebuild the Temple.
August 27, 1969	Wakf closes Temple Mount to non-Muslims for two months.
September 9, 1970	Israeli high court decides not to ajudicate in Jewish prayer on Temple Mount case brought by the Temple Mount Faithful and allows government restriction to remain.
March 11, 1971	Gershon Salomon of Temple Mount Faithful leads group of students to pray on Temple Mount; this results in minor disruption.
August 8, 1973	Knesset member Binyamin Halevi and Rabbi Louis Rabinowitz pray on Temple Mount in protest of government ban.
January 30, 1976	Lower court (magistrate) acquittal of Betar youths arrested for holding prayer service on Mount effects ruling that Jews are permitted to pray on Temple Mount; Police Minister Shlomo Hillel rejects court ruling.
February 9–23, 1976	Schools in Arab East Jerusalem protest the lower court ruling, resulting in over 100 arrests; Arab shops close in strike, riots in West Bank; court ruling is appealed (February 11).
March 4, 1976	U.N. Secretary Kurt Waldheim pledges to introduce Islamic contentions against Israel's interference with Muslim holy places.
March 8, 1976	Gershon Salomon and Rabbi Rabinowitz attempt to lead group to Temple Mount but are turned back by police.
March 11, 1976	Muslim councils in Ramallah, El Bireh, and Nablus protest police action against Arabs who demonstrated against the lower court ruling permitting Jewish prayers on the Mount.
March 17, 1976	Lower court ruling is overturned by district court but upholds the historical and legal right of Jews to pray on the Temple

Mount if the Ministry of Religious Affairs can regulate such activity to maintain public order.

August 14, 1977 — Gershom Salomon leads 30 members of *El Har Hashem* ("To the Temple Mount of God") in an attempt to conduct a *TishaB'Av* service on the Temple Mount, but is turned away by police.

March 25, 1979 — Rumors that Meir Kahane and yeshiva students would hold prayer service on Temple Mount provoke a general strike among West Bank Arabs; 2,000 Arab youths brandishing stones and staves riot at Temple Mount and are dispersed by Israeli police.

August 3, 1979 — Several Jewish nationalist groups are prevented from holding prayer service on Temple Mount.

August 6, 1980 — Israeli high court considers appeal to revoke ban on prayer on Temple Mount based on recent law guaranteeing freedom of access to religious sites.

August 10, 1980 — Ultra-right activist group, *Gush Emunim* ("Bloc of the Faithful") with 300 supporters, attempts to force entrance to the Temple Mount and is dispersed by police.

August 28–30, 1981 — Chief Rabbi Shlomo Goren and workers of the Ministry of Religious Affairs trace a leaking cistern to discover one of the original entrances to the Temple (Warren's Gate); Goren closes dig; Yigael Yadin condemns the dig as quasiarchaeological; Arabs seal the cistern, thus preventing entrance to the tunnel.

September 2–4, 1981 — Yeshiva students, under orders from Rabbi Getz, break down Arab wall-seal; Getz claims that the treasures of the Temple, including the Ark of the Covenant, are hidden within a lower chamber accessed by the tunnel; Arabs clash with Jewish students and police intervene; gate entrance is sealed due to rioting Wakf protests (September 3); Supreme Muslim Council orders general strike of all Arab schools and shops in East Jerusalem (September 4) to protest excavation under Temple Mount.

September 10, 1981 — Wakf seals tunnel from Muslim side to prevent future Israeli entrance.

September 15, 1981	Gershon Salomon and the Temple Mount Faithful attempt another prayer service on the Mount, but are again stopped by police.
April 11, 1982	Alan Goodman, an American immigrant in the Israeli army, opens fire on the Temple Mount "to liberate the spot holy to the Jews." Though ruled mentally unstable by the Israeli courts, and later sentenced to life imprisonment, the incident set off week-long Arab riots in Jerusalem, the West Bank, and Gaza, and drew international criticism against Israel.
April 25, 1982	Kach Party member Yoel Learner attempts to sabotage a mosque on the Temple Mount. He is arrested and later sentenced to two-and-one-half years in prison.
December 9, 1982	Geula Cohen, a member of Israel's Knesset, raises the charge that Muslim Arabs have caches of ammunition sequestered on the Temple Mount.
March 10, 1983	Rabbi Israel Ariel and a group of more than 40 followers, plan to pray on the Temple Mount (via the Solomon's Stables adjacent to the Al-Aqsa Mosque) after four youths connected with Yamit Yeshiva are found breaking into the area. Weapons and diagrams of the Temple Mount are recovered in a police search, and numerous arrests are made.
April, 1983	The *Jerusalem Post* prints an "Open Letter to the Prime Minister and the People of Israel," drafted by an "evangelical Christian" group, condemning the arrests made by the police.
May 11, 1983	Israel's high court reverses a police refusal to grant a license for prayer at the entrance to the Temple Mount to members of the Temple Mount Faithful.
May 22, 1983	Physicist Lambert Dolphin of SRI International in California and his team attempt to use scientific equipment within the Western Wall tunnel area to determine the Temple's location. Israeli police stop the project as a result of pressure from Muslim officials.
September 17, 1983	Rabbi Shlomo Goren and IDF Chief of Staff Moshe Levy conduct a prayer service within the Western Wall tunnel beneath the Temple Mount.

January 27, 1984	Temple activists are arrested for attempting to "attack" the Temple Mount.
January 3, 1985	It is revealed that a secret airlift of 3,000 Ethiopian Jews to Israel was successfully accomplished the previous month. Temple activist groups contend it is a sign of the nearness of the Messiah and the rebuilding of the Temple.
January 8, 1986	Several members of the Knesset, led by Geula Cohen, seek to hold a prayer service in the Temple area. The incident provokes a riot and an altercation with Arabs on the Mount.
February 1987	The Temple Institute opens a visitor's center for the exhibition of their Temple artifacts on the second floor of a building in the Jewish Quarter.
1988	Jordan's King Hussein officially announces that Jordan relinquishes its claim to the West Bank territories, except for the holy sites, including the Temple Mount.
October 16, 1989	Gershom Salomon, Yehoshua Cohen (dressed in the priestly garments), and members of the Temple Mount Faithful attempt to lay a cornerstone for the Third Temple at the entrance to the Temple Mount during the Feast of Tabernacles. A protest at an Arab school earlier in the day led police to rescind previously granted permission to conduct the ceremony.
October 16, 1989	*Time* magazine runs Richard Ostling's article "Time for a New Temple?" describing the Temple controversy and current preparations for rebuilding.
October 1989	Israel's Ministry of Religious Affairs sponsors the First Conference on Temple Research at Shlomo (The Great Synagogue).
May 1990	Lubavitcher Hassids proclaim their leader Rabbi Menachem Mendel Schneerson as "King Messiah," and predict that he will move from Crown Heights in Brooklyn to Kfar Habad (near Tel-Aviv) and rebuild the Temple.
October 8, 1990	Preannounced plans by the Temple Mount Faithful to repeat their previous year's ceremony and attempt to lay a cornerstone for the Third Temple provoke a riot on the Temple Mount. At the Western Wall where more than 20,000 Jews are assembled for Feast of Tabernacle services, 3,000 Muslim Palestinian Arabs pelt the crowd with stones from above. The result of the mêlée

with Israeli police leaves 17 Arabs dead and brings condemnation from the United Nations and the United States.

July–August 1991   Gershom Salomon and members of the Temple Mount Faithful come to the United States for an extended lecture tour, including a television appearance on Pat Robertson's "700 Club" and numerous other radio, television, and public meetings.

September 24, 1991   The Temple Mount Faithful conduct their third attempt to lay a cornerstone and to pray on the Temple Mount. Met by opposition from *harredim* who fear a repetition of the 1990 Arab riot and official restraint, the attempt to lay the cornerstone is aborted.

September–
October 1991

A house is purchased in Muslim Quarter for *Ateret Cohanim* (which manages a school for the training of Third Temple priests), and Jewish settlers purchase and occupy houses in the strictly Arab Silwan Village (site of the ancient City of David); Israeli Housing Minister Ariel Sharon announces desire of the government to assist continued Jewish settlement of East Jerusalem (where Temple Mount is located).

October 31, 1991   At the Middle East Peace Conference in Madrid, Spain, Syrian Foreign Minister Farouk Al-Shara accuses Israel of attempting to blow up the Al-Aqsa Mosque and proclaims that there will be no free access to the religious sites on the Temple Mount unless Israel returns all of East Jerusalem to the Arabs.

March 1993   Kach activist Rabbi Baruch ben Yosef founds *Yeshivat Har HaBayit* (Temple Mount Seminary) to work toward the liberation of the Temple Mount. After the assassination of Prime Minister Yitzhak Rabin, all Kach-related organizations are declared illegal as terrorist organizations and go underground.

Spring 1994   Yasser Arafat launches first challenge to Jordanian jurisdiction over Islamic holy sites in Jerusalem and appoints his own Palestinian Mufti, Sheik Sabri, to counter the authority of the established Jordanian Mufti on the Temple Mount.

Fall 1994   Rabbi Chaim Richman travels to Canton, Mississippi to the ranch of Rev. Clyde Lott to examine his Red Heifers. He is convinced that one is a perfect Red Heifer and that it will someday "change the world."

1995–1998	Extensive repairs are made to the dome of the Dome of the Rock by an Irish construction company; repairs are financed by King Hussein of Jordan.
March 1995– September 1996	The Herodian-era street running at the foot of the Western Wall is uncovered by archaeologist Ronny Reich in time for the 3,000th anniversary of Jerusalem; Arabs protest that the excavations are an attempt to destroy Arab history in the city and rebuild the Temple.
August 1996	The first Red Heifer born in the Land of Israel in 2,000 years is born at Kfar Hassidm near Haifa). Some Orthodox Jews claim it is a sign that the coming of the Messiah and the rebuilding of the Temple are imminent. However, the heifer, named Tzlil (or Melody), later sprouts 10 white hairs and is disqualified.
September 25, 1996	Temple Mount riot occurs when Israeli government opens an exit tunnel to the Hasmonean aqueduct at the end of the Western Wall Tunnel and 58 deaths result in Jerusalem and the territories.
1997	At the beginning of the year two Red Heifers are born—one in northern Israel and the other in Ayalon Valley, as well as another on a ranch in Texas—and dedicated by the Temple Mount Faithful for use in the purification ceremony to prepare for the rebuilding of the Temple and priestly service.
February 17, 1997	A record crowd of 1,000 people take part in a dinner in honor of the Jerusalem Temple and a Jewish presence on the Temple Mount.
September 1997	Israeli Orthodox Jew Yehuda Etzion is arrested for attempting to pray on the Temple Mount; he appealed to Supreme Court, which upheld his right (and Jewish right) of access to the Temple Mount for worship. However, attempts by his organization Chai veKayam continued to be rebuffed by police fearing Arab riots.
October 1997	Conflict over construction of Yeshiva Ateret Cohanim settlement at the Mount of Olives (Ras el-Amud) property acquired by Dr. Irving Moskowitz.

March 7, 1998	Mississippi rancher and Pentecostal preacher Clyde Lott, Rev. Guy Garner, and Rev. Al Bishop form the organization Canaan Land Restoration of Israel, Inc., with Rabbi Chaim Richman as director. The aim of the organization is to raise money to send Red Heifers to Israel for both sacrificial and economic purposes.
May 14, 1998	An arsonist throws a firebomb at the wooden gate leading to the Temple Mount.
May 24, 1998	The Temple Mount Faithful commemorate this day marking the liberation of Jerusalem by demonstrating against a Palestinian State. Members carry a coffin on which is written "The Oslo Agreements" and "The Palestinian State" and a Trojan horse to the American Consulate, the Orient House, and the Temple Mount.
August 2, 1998	On Tisha B'Av, members of the Temple Mount Faithful march to the Temple Mount wearing chains and sackcloth and ashes to lament the destruction of the Temple.
September 1998	Orthodox Jews begin regularly ascending the Temple Mount, through the assistance of the organization HaTenu'ah LeChinun HaMikdash, by walking a prescribed course while guarded by Temple Mount police and Islamic attendants.
September 15, 1998	Annual Temple conference/convention is held at the Binyanei HaUma in Jerusalem, with a record number attending to demonstrate their plans to build the Third Temple.
October 1998	Reports are published of an estimated 200 cultists living on the Mount of Olives (opposite the Temple Mount) awaiting the return of Christ with the new millennium.
October 7, 1998	The Temple Mount Faithful march to the Temple Mount with their cornerstone, only to be rebuffed by police. International news reports warn in advance that this action could "ignite World War III."
November 1998	Israeli police detain and later deport 14 members of the Concerned Christians cult, fearing they will attack the Temple Mount in an attempt to force the end of days.

Muslims destroy remains of Second Temple Huldah Gate architecture as work begins on construction of a new mosque within Solomon's Stables.

November 14, 1998   PLO Chief Yasser Arafat threatens war if Palestinians are prevented from praying in Jerusalem while, at the same time, the Palestinian Mufti prevents Jews from praying on the Temple Mount.

December 1998   Palestinian Mufti moves office onto Temple Mount, stating that the area is only for Islam.

December 2, 1998   The U.N. General Assembly passes a resolution declaring Israeli sovereignty over Jerusalem illegal and calling for Israel to give the right of self-determination to the Palestinians, who want Jerusalem as their capital, and forbidding any Jewish presence on the Temple Mount.

December 20, 1998   The Temple Mount Faithful, on the seventh day of Hanukkah, carry the torch of the Maccabees from the Maccabean tombs in Mod'in to the Temple Mount, calling for the liberation and rededication of the site of the Temple, but Arabs close the gates before they can enter.

March 31, 1999   Members of the Temple Mount Faithful and Chai veKayam join Gershon Salomon and Yehuda Etzion to perform a symbolic Passover sacrifice on a hill overlooking the Temple Mount.

April 1999   Reports circulate worldwide about water mysteriously flowing from beneath Dome of the Rock on the Temple Mount. The Temple Mount Faithful proclaim it is preparation for the fulfillment of Ezekiel 47. The water turns out to be from the Solomon's Stable area, where the new mosque is being constructed.

July 22, 1999   The Temple Mount Faithful march to the Temple Mount on Tisha b'Av and demonstrate for the rebuilding of the Temple by reading from the book of Lamentations.

August 9–11, 1999   Wakf opens door at Southern Wall in anticipation of Muslims entering the new mosque inside the Hulda/Solomon's Stable area. Israeli government seals the door over Muslim protests claiming the act affects the status quo of the Temple Mount.

September 27, 1999   The Temple Mount Faithful conduct the Nisuch haMaim
                        ("water-drawing") ceremony at the Pool of Siloam and anoint
                        the cornerstone and attempt to lay it on the Temple Mount.

December 11, 1999   The Temple Mount Faithful carry the Torch of the Maccabees at
                        Hanukkah from the Maccabean tombs at Modi'in to the site for
                        the rebuilding of the Temple.

The Temple in Prophecy

The Tribulation Temple (The Tribulation Period—7 years)

First Half of the Tribulation (3½ years)

In the first quarter of the first half of the Tribulation, the Jewish
Temple is rebuilt in Jerusalem, perhaps as a part of the provi-
sions of the covenant made with the Antichrist (Daniel 9:27;
Revelation 11:1).

The sacrifices are resumed and Jews worship in the Temple
daily, apparently joined by the Two Witnesses (Revelation 11:1).

Midpoint of the Tribulation

The Antichrist breaks his covenant with Israel by desecrating
the Jerusalem Temple with the abomination of desolation and
stopping the sacrificial system (Matthew 24:15; Mark 13:14;
2 Thessalonians 2:4).

The Antichrist invades Jerusalem and tramples the Temple
Mount (Daniel 11:40-48; Isaiah 28:14-22; Revelation 11:1-2).
During this time the abomination of desolation takes place in
the Temple (Daniel 9:27; 12:11; Matthew 24:15-16; 2 Thessalonians 2:3-4, 8-12; Revelation 13:11-15) and the Antichrist forces
his godless worship on Jerusalem and the world (Daniel 11:36-
39; Revelation 13:1-18).

Last Half of the Tribulation

The two witnesses don sackcloth in public mourning for the
Temple's desecration and then remain to oppose the Antichrist's

persecution of Jews in Jerusalem and permit the remnant to flee (Revelation 11:3-6).

Jews flee Jerusalem after the Antichrist ends his pseudopeace, knowing that the abomination of desolation in the Temple signals the escalation of the Tribulation judgments (Matthew 25:16-22; Mark 13:14-20).

The Antichrist will move against Jerusalem in a satanically inspired desire to destroy the Jews (Zechariah 12:1-3; 14:1). Briefly, Jewish forces will control the city (Zechariah 12:4-9; Micah 4:11–5:1), possibly with the help of the two witnesses. But, ultimately half the city will be taken (Zechariah 14:2) and the two witnesses killed and their bodies put on display in the street of Jerusalem (Revelation 11:7-10). A Jewish remnant apparently occupies the eastern part of the city with the Temple Mount.

Jesus the Messiah will return, defend the remnant of Israel, bring deliverance to Jerusalem, and will come to His Temple, bringing judgment to the nations (Isaiah 37:32,35; Zechariah 12:4,9; 14:2; Malachi 3:1; Revelation 19:11-21).

In the battle for Jerusalem, Messiah will triumphantly ascend the Mount of Olives on the east of Jerusalem (Zechariah 14:3) and a great earthquake will split Jerusalem, creating a valley leading from the Temple Mount to the desert—a valley through which the Jews will flee to safety (Joel 3:14-17; Zechariah 14:4-5; Revelation 16:18-19).

Transition Between Tribulation and Millennium (75 days)

The interval between the end of the Tribulation and beginning of the kingdom age (Daniel 12:11-12) will include these events: the Antichrist will be removed (Revelation 19:20), the abomination of desolation will be removed (Daniel 12:11-12), the Gentiles will be judged (Joel 3:1-3; Matthew 25:31-46), the Old Testament and Tribulation saints will be resurrected (Daniel 12:2; Isaiah 26:19; Revelation 20:4).

The Millennial Temple (Millennial Kingdom Period—1,000 years)

The topography of the Temple Mount will be transformed and rise above its present height (Zechariah 14:9-10; Isaiah 2:2-4; Micah 4:1).

Jerusalem will be constituted as "the throne of the LORD" (Psalm 48:1-3; Jeremiah 3:17) and the Messiah will build the Millennial Temple (Ezekiel 40:5–43:27; Zechariah 6:12-15) and reign on Mount Zion (Isaiah 24:23).

The Temple area will be free from the physical harm of the old order (Isaiah 11:9; Zechariah 14:20f).

The Temple area will be holy and free from ritual contamination (Zechariah 14:20-21).

A river will flow east and west from beneath the altar of the Temple (Zechariah 14:8), bringing new freshness and life to the Dead Sea (Ezekiel 47:1-12).

The *Shekinah* glory will return to the Millennial Temple (Ezekiel 43:1-7) and the entire city will be a place of holiness, righteousness, and justice (Isaiah 1:26-27; 2:2-4; 65:17-25; Micah 4:1-5; Zechariah 14:20-21).

The glory of the Lord will be revealed from Jerusalem and, by implication, from the Temple (Isaiah 40:5), which will become the center of joy and rejoicing for the world (Isaiah 65:17-25).

The nations of the world will come to the Temple Mount to find justice and learn God's law (Psalm 147:15,19-20; Isaiah 2:2-4) and Jerusalem will become the center for universal peace (Haggai 2:9; Zechariah 6:13), prayer (Isaiah 56:6-7; Zechariah 8:22), and worship (Isaiah 27:13, 56:8; 66:20; Ezekiel 20:40-41; Micah 4:1-2; Zechariah 8:20-23; 14:14-16).

Offerings and sacrifices will continue in the Millennial Temple without interruption (Jeremiah 33:18).

The New Jerusalem may descend and be suspended above the earthly Jerusalem, possibly aligned with the earthly Holy of Holies in the Millennial Temple, providing a heavenly illumination in which the nations will walk when they bring their tribute to the city (Revelation 21:23-24).

At the end of the Millennium the Temple Mount (where Messiah is resident) will be attacked by Satan and a multitude of rebellious earthly unbelievers (Revelation 20:6-9).

The Eternal Temple (The Eternal State)

The Great White Throne judgment ushers in the Eternal State (Revelation 21:1-2) and is followed by the creation of the new heavens and new earth.

The New Jerusalem appears at the beginning of the Eternal State, coming down from the new heavens (Revelation 21:2-3). Its Eternal Temple will be the Lord God Himself (Revelation 21:22).

Directory of
Temple Organizations

The following is a list of key Jewish organizations (mostly in Israel) involved in preparations to rebuild the Temple. There are many yeshivot and organizations that aren't listed, which provide ancillary education opportunities and conduct research-oriented activities. These may be found as links at some of the organizational websites.

CHAI VEKAYAM MOVEMENT (Alive and Existing)
Purpose: To return the Jewish people to the Temple Mount and prepare Jewish society for the Third Temple era.
Chairman: Yehuda Etzion
Address: Ofra, D.N. Mizrach, Binyamin 90627, Israel
Phone: 972-2-997-3889 (Hebrew only)
Fax: 972-2-997-4833 (Hebrew only)
Cellular (Hebrew only): 050-706610
Website: www.chaivekayam.org
E-mail: Yehuda@chaivekayam.org

KETER KEHUNA SHEVET LEVI (The Crown of the Priesthood Rests [with] Levi)
Purpose: To register all qualified priests and Levites on an international scale.
Address: 328 East 61st Street, New York, NY 10021
Phone: 212-319-8594
Website: www.houseoflevi.org
E-mail: houseoflevi@juno.com

HATENU'AH LECHINUN HAMIKDASH (Returning the Jewish People to the Holy Temple)

Purpose: To gather en masse to arouse consciousness among the people, its rabbis, and its leaders to rebuild the Beit HaMikdash and return the Cohanim to their service.

Chairman: Rabbi Yosef Elboim

Address: P.O. Box 31336, Jerusalem, Israel

Phone: 972-2-5371904

Website: http://www.virtualjerusalem.co.il/orgs/orgs/temple/

E-mail: (subscriptions): listproc@virtual.co.il

Publications: *Yibaneh HaMikdash* (English: *Mikdash-Build*), newsletter about the pursuit of Jewish prayer on the Temple Mount and the possibility of rebuilding of the Holy Temple, and *Torat HaBayit* (three volumes).

Program: Wednesdays at 3:00 P.M. on Radio Kol HaEmet 105.7 FM in Jerusalem, 95.8 FM in the central region, 107.8 FM in the north.

YESHIVAT TORAT HABAYIT (Laws of the Temple Mount Seminary)

Purpose: To educate on the laws governing the Temple and its services.

Director: Rabbi Yirmiyahu Fischer

Address: P.O. Box 1797, Jerusalem 91000, Israel

E-mail: yirmi@shani.net

Program: On Arutz 7 Sundays at 3:00 P.M. for a short discussion about the *Beit HaMikdash* and every Tuesday 12:30 P.M. Jerusalem Standard Time at the Mugrabi Gate (near the Kotel) to ascend the Temple Mount (the Temple Mount is open to Jews 7:30–10:30 A.M. and 12:30–1:30 P.M., excluding Fridays and Muslim holidays).

NE-EMANEI HAR HABAYIT (Temple Mount and Land of Israel Faithful Movement)

Purpose: To prepare for the redemption of the Land of Israel and the rebuilding of the Temple (including the struggle for actualization of rights to ascend the Temple Mount, via the courts).

Director: Dr. Gershon Salomon

Address: P.O. Box 18325 Yochanan Horkanos 4, Jerusalem 91182, Israel

Phone: 972-2-625-1112

Voice Mail/Fax: 972-2-625-1113

Website: www.templemountfaithful.org

E-mail: gershon@templemountfaithful.org

Publications: Newsletter, "TMF Mailing List" from maillist@templemountfaithful.org

YESHIVAT ATERET COHANIM (Crown of the Priests Seminary)

Purpose: To educate in the laws governing the Temple, to train priests for future Temple service, and establish a Jewish presence in the Old City known as The Jerusalem Reclamation Project.

Founder: Rabbi Mota Dan HaCohen

Director: Rabbi Shlomo Aviner

Address: Muslim Quarter, Old City, Jerusalem, Israel

E-mail: tours@ateret.jer1.co.il

Publications: Torah journal *Iturei Cohanim* and monthly newsletter to students serving in the Israeli Defense Forces.

YESIVAT HAR-HABAYIT (Temple Mount Seminary)

Purpose: Seminary to educate students on the Temple and to bring about the full liberation of the Temple Mount.

Director: Rabbi Baruch ben Yosef

Address: P.O. Box 31336, 22 Misgav Ladach Street, Jewish Quarter, Old City, Jerusalem, Israel

ATARA LEYOSHNA (Restoring the Crown to Its Place)

Purpose: To purchase property and settle Jews in the Old City, especially the Muslim Quarter around the Temple Mount, and to educate people concerning the Temple.

Visitors' Center: *Dugmat HaMikdash* (Temple Model Museum)

Manager: Esther Schlisser

Address: Misgav Ladach Street, Jewish Quarter, Old City, Jerusalem, Israel

Phone: 972-2-689-4466

BEGED IVRI (Hebrew Clothing)

Purpose: To prepare Jewish society for the Third Temple era.

Director: Reuven Prager

Address: P.O. Box 28052, 111 Agrippas Street #16, Jerusalem, Israel

Phone: 972-2-625-8943

Fax: 972-2-625-5191

Website: www.israelvisit.co.il/beged-ivri

E-mail: Reuven@marksman.co.il

MACHON HAMIKDASH (The Temple Institute)

Purpose: To serve as a center of information and educational activity for youth and adults to increase knowledge of the Temple. Also engaged in research on the construction of the Third Temple, the preparation of usable vessels for its services, and education and training concerning the priestly services.

Director: Rabbi Yisrael Ariel

Visitors' Center and Offices: Treasures of the Temple Exhibition

Address: 24 Misgav Ladach Street, Old City of Jerusalem, 97500, Israel

Phone: 972-2-626-4545

Fax: 972-2-627-4529

Website: www.temple.org.il

E-mail: Temple@temple.org.il

Sister Organizations: Institute for Temple Studies, Exhibition of Temple Vessels, Yeshivat Bet Habehira, Yeshivat D'vir, and Beit Hauman Ha'ivri

MERKAZ HAHAR (The Temple Mount Center)

Purpose: To encourage Jews to visit the Temple Mount, maintain a team of trained guides to take visitors up in accordance with Jewish Law, and to create an awareness of the importance and centrality of the Temple Mount. To be a virtual learning center for all issues relating to the Temple Mount and the Temple.

Website: www.virtual.co.il/orgs/orgs/temple/

Publication: "The HarHabayit Connection" in the *The Har-Parsha List* is written by a panel of rabbis and Torah scholars and aims to provide a different and innovative insight into parshat ha-shavua. It is designed to explain briefly an inspiring idea from the *parsha* that can be given over at the Shabbat table, encouraging the connection to *Har Habayit* (the Temple Mount) and the Temple amongst *Am Yisrael* (the Nation of Israel).

LIGHT TO THE NATIONS

Purpose: To provide access to news of events happening in Israel and to provide biblical study and commentary from a traditional Jewish perspective.

Director: Rabbi Chaim Richman

Address: P.O. Box 31714, Jerusalem, Israel

Fax: 972-2-430-286-0453

E-mail: crlight@netvision.net.il

Publication: *The Restoration* newsletter

THE ACADEMY OF JERUSALEM

Purpose: Academic research and discussions on Temple-related subjects; organization proposes architectural-cybernetic model for Third Temple.

Director: Dr. Yitzhak Hayut-Ma'N

Address: P.O. Box 8115, Jerusalem 91080, Israel

E-mail: yrusalem@actcom.co.il

Publication: *Academy of Jerusalem Proceedings* (electronic publication)

HOUSE OF HARRARI

Purpose: To design and manufacture biblical harps for the Levites of the Third Temple and work in conjunction with the educational and demonstrative activities of other Temple organizations.

Directors: Michael & Shoshanna Harrari

Address: 7 Nachlat Shiva Street (off Jaffa [Yafo] Road near Zion Square), P.O. Box 1577, Jerusalem, Israel

Phone: 972-2-624-8496

Fax/Voice Mail: 972-2-625-5191

Website: www.virtual.co.il/arts/harrari/

E-mail: biblharp@netvision.net.il

Publication: On-line newsletter

CHABAD (C=*Chokmah*—"wisdom," B=*Binah*—"insight," D=*Da'at*—"knowledge")

Purpose: To present the teachings of the Lubavitcher Rebbe Menachem Mendel Schneerson on the halachot of the Temple.

Website: http://www.chabad.org/

AGUDAT EL HAR HASHEM (Together to the Mount of G-d)

Purpose: To defend Jewish rights to the Temple Mount.

Director: Yisrael Meidad

Phone: 972-2-994-2328

AGUDAT EL HAR HAMOR (Together to the Mount of Grief)
Purpose: To promote the study of the subject from a halakhic (Jewish Law) standpoint and from a scientific research standpoint. They give lectures on the halakhic issue of ascending the Temple Mount and encourage ascending the Temple Mount scrupulously following Halakha.
Phone: 972-2-997-5155

SOCIETY FOR THE ESTABLISHMENT OF THE TEMPLE
Purpose: To promote organized efforts to educate Jews concerning realizing the goals of rebuilding the Third Temple.
Address: 17 Ali Ha-Kohen Street, Jerusalem, Israel
Phone: 972-2-637-1904

Lectures on the Temple

Jewish Perspective

Lecturer: Rav Hagai Yekutiel
Program: Slide show presentations of the structure of the Temple Mount and its development, as well as the places where it's permissible to walk.
Phone: 972-2-993-1538

Lecturer: Rav Michael Ben Ari
Program: Lectures to both adults and youth. Slide show presentation of the Temple Mount from Torah, historical, and archeological perspectives.
Phone: 972-2581-2006, cellular 050-824161

Lecturer: Rav Chaim Richman
Program: Lectures to groups (Jewish and Christian) on the Temple from traditional Jewish sources.
Address: P.O. Box 31714, Jerusalem, Israel
Fax: 972-2-430-286-0453
E-mail: crlight@netvision.net.il

Lecturer: Dr. Gershon Salomon
Program: Lectures to both Jewish and Christian groups on rebuilding the Temple and the goals of the Temple Mount Faithful movement.
Address: P.O. Box 18325, Yochanan Horkanos 4, Jerusalem 91182, Israel
Phone: 972-2-625-1112
Voice Mail/Fax: 972-2-625-1113
Website: www.templemountfaithful.org
E-mail: gershon@templemountfaithful.org

Lecturer: Reuven Prager
Program: Lectures to both Jewish and Christian audiences on Levitical aspects of Temple preparation and accomplishments of his Beged Ivri organization.
Address: P.O. Box 28052, Jerusalem, Israel
Phone: 972-2-625-8943
Fax: 972-2-625-5191
Website: www.israelvisit.co.il/beged-ivri

Christian Perspective

Lecturer: John W. Schmitt
Program: Lectures to all audiences on the Messianic Temple of Ezekiel with slide presentation and scale model.
Address: Messianic Temple Ministries, 5812 N.E. Alton, Portland, OR 97213

Lecturer: Dr. Randall Price
Program: Lectures with slide presentations on the historical Temples, biblical prophetic texts, Temple movement, Ark of the Covenant.
Address: World of the Bible Ministries, Inc., P.O. Box 827, San Marcos, TX 78667-0827
Phone: (512) 396-3799
Fax: (512) 392-9080
Website: www.worldofthebible.com
E-mail: wbmrandl@itouch.net

Temple Models on Exhibit

Model of the Second Temple by Catriel Sugarman. For slide show schedule of this model contact Catriel Sugarman, 18 Shlomtzion HaMalka Street, Jerusalem. Phone: 972-2-624-5269, 972-2-652-4495, or E-mail: acatriel@intournet.co.il

Models of the First, Second, and Third Temples. On display at The Temple Model Museum of Atara Lesyoshna, Misgav Ladach Street, Jewish Quarter, Old City, Jerusalem.

Model of the Second Temple. On display at The Temple Institute's Visitor's Center, Misgav Ladach, Jewish Quarter, Old City, Jerusalem

Models of the stages of the development of the Temple Mount and of Second Temple by Rabbi Zalman Koren on display within the Western Wall Tunnel, next to the Western Wall, Jerusalem.

Model of the First Temple and Solomonic Jerusalem. On display at the Bible Lands Museum (lower floor), 25 Granot Street, Museum Row (across from Israel Museum on Mount Herzl), Jerusalem. Phone: 972-2-661-1066.

Model of Second Temple and the Herodian Temple according to Israeli historian Michael Avi-Yonah, exhibited in the yard of the Holyland Hotel on Mount Herzl, Jerusalem.

Model of Jerusalem in the First Temple period. Exhibited by The Jerusalem Foundation and Yad Izhak Ben-Zvi, Shonei Halachot St., corner of Pelugat Ha-Kotel, Jewish Quarter, Old City, Jerusalem.

Model of the Tabernacle (1:60 scale) by Moshe Levine. On display at the Beit Ya'acov Yeshiva, Tel-Aviv.

Model of the Second Temple by Leen Ritmeyer (11.5" x 1.75"). Available for purchase from Ritmeyer Archaeological Design, 50 Tewit Well Road, Harrogate, HG2 8JJ, England. Phone: 44 1423-530 143, Fax: 44 1423-504 921.

Model of the Tabernacle (full-size). On display at The Mennonite Information Center, 2209 Millstream Road, Lancaster, Pennsylvania. Phone: (717) 299-0954.

Model of the Tabernacle (full-size with dramatization). On display at The Great Passion Play (New Holy Land Tour), P.O. Box 471, Eureka Springs, Arkansas, 72632. Phone: (800) 882-7529, Website: www.greatpassionplay.com

Model of The Messianic Temple of Ezekiel by John Schmitt. Exhibited by special request by Messianic Temple Ministries, 5812 N.E. Alton, Portland, OR 97213, Phone: (513) 282-1507.

Model of the Second Temple (virtual). CD-ROM by Beit HaMikdash, AVIMedia Ltd., and N.G. Media Interactive, Ltd. Available from Quantum Link, Inc., 21218 St. Andrews Blvd., Suite 234, Boca Raton, FL 33433. Phone: 1-888-TEMPLCD.

Resources for
Further Study
of the Temple

The works included here represent those significant to a study of the Temple in history and eschatology. Because of the need to study all viewpoints on the subject, there has been no attempt to distinguish works that adopt the author's futurist perspective. For a complete bibliography of the sources used in this book see the references provided in the appropriate footnotes.

Primary Sources

Literary Sources

Babylonian Talmud. 30 volumes (English edition) *(Ketuvot, Yoma, Berakot, Ta'anit, Zevahim, et. al.)*.

Flavius, Josephus. *The Works of Josephus Flavius.* Translated by William Whiston. 2 vols. London: Chatto and Windus, n.d. See also the condensation of Josephus' *Antiquities* and *Wars* (written about A.D. 953) known as *Jossipon.* Ed. H. Hominer. Jerusalem, 1971.

Ginzberg, Louis. *The Legends of the Jews.* Philadelphia: Jewish Publication Society, 1913.

Greek and Latin Authors on Jews and Judaism. 3 vols. Ed. Menahem Stern. Jerusalem: The Israel Academy of Sciences and Humanities, 1976–1984.

Hayward, C. T. R. *The Jewish Temple: A Non-Biblical Sourcebook.* New York/London: Routledge, 1996.

Maimonides, Moses (Rambam). *Mishneh Torah (Hilchos Bais HaBechirah ["The Laws of God's Chosen House"]).* Trans. by Rabbi Eliyahu Touger. New York/Jerusalem: Maznaim Publishing Corp., 1986.

Midrashim (Midrashey Halachah: *Mechiltah, Sifrey, Sifra*, Midrashey Agadah: *Rabba* [as per books of the Bible–*Genesis Rabbah, Exodus Rabbi*, et. al, *Pesikta, Tanchumah, Pirke de-Rabi Eliezar, Yalkutim: Shimoni*, etc.).

Mishnah (tractates [primary]: *Middot, Tamid, Yoma, Sukkah, Shekalim, Parah*, [secondary]: *Mo'ed, Qodashim, Zevahim, Pesahim, Hagigah, Ta'anit, Rosh ha-Shanah, Shevuot, Menahot, Sheviit, Tamid, Bikkurim, Hullin, Hallah, Nazir, Nedarim*). Best edition is Jacob Neusner, *The Mishnah: A New Translation*. New Haven/London: Yale University Press, 1988.

Philo of Alexandria. *The Works of Philo: Complete and Unabridged*. Translated by C.D. Yonge. Peabody, MA: Hendrickson Publishers, 1993.

Tosefta (companion to the Mishnah, various tractates as above).

Vilnay, Zeev. *Legends of Jerusalem*. Philadelphia: The Jewish Publication Society, 1978.

See also: commentaries by Rashi, Bartenura, Yom Tov, Tiferet Yisrael, and the *Chanukat HaBayit*.

Pilgrim Reports (after A.D. 70)

Adler, Elkan N. *Jewish Travellers in the Middle Ages: 19 Firsthand Accounts*. New York: Dover, 1987.

Benjamin ben Yonah (A.D. 1173). *Sefer Hamassoth* (1840) and *The Itinerary of Benjamin of Tudela*. London, 1927.

Egeria's Travels to the Holy Land. Translated with notes by John Wilkinson. Revised edition. Jerusalem: Ariel Publishing House, 1981.

Estori Haparchi, Rabbi Isaac ben Moses (A.D. 1322). *Kaftor va-Ferach*. Venice, 1547.

Eusebius. *Ecclesiastical History*. Translated by Paul Meir. Grand Rapids: Kregel Publications, 1999.

Radbaz, Rabbi David ben Solomon Ibn Zimra (1470-1574). *Responsa*. English citations in Israel M. Goldman. *The Life and Times of Rabbi David I.A.Z.* New York, 1970.

The Library of the Palestine Pilgrims' Text Society. 13 vols. New York: AMS Press, Inc., 1971.

Wilkinson, John. *Jerusalem Pilgrims Before the Crusades*. Warminster: Aris and Phillips, 1977, p. 61.

Archaeological Sources (19th century)

Bagatti, Bellarmino. *Recherches sur le site du Temple de Jérusalem (Ier-VIIe siècle)*. Publications du "Studium Biblicum Franciscanum Collectio minor 22." Jerusalem: Franciscan Printing Press, 1979.

Bliss, F. J. and Macalister, R. A. S. *Excavations during the Years 1898-1900*. London: Palestine Exploration Fund, 1902.

Conder, C.R. "The High Sanctuary at Jerusalem." *Transactions of the Royal Institute of British Architects* 11 (1879): 25-60.

———. "Age of the Temple Wall: Pilasters of the Western Haram Wall." *Palestine Exploration Fund Quarterly Statement* 3 (1987): 135-77.

Robinson, Edward. *Biblical Researches in Palestine, Mount Sinai and Arabia Petraea.* 3 vols. Boston: Crocker & Brewster, 1841.

Sschck, Conrad. *Die Stifshütte, der Tempel in Jerusalem und der Tempelplatz der Jetztzeit.* Berlin: Weidmannsche Buchhandlung, 1896.

Warren, Charles. "The Tanks and Souterrains of the Sanctuary." *The Recovery of Jerusalem: A Narrative of Exploration and Discovery in the City and Holy Land.* Eds. by C.W. Wilson, et. al. London: R. Bentley, 1871.

——. "Note on the Souterrains in the Noble Sanctuary, Jerusalem." *Palestine Exploration Fund Quarterly Statement* 7 (1875): 96-97.

——. *Underground Jerusalem.* London: R. Bentley, 1876.

——. "The Site of the Temple of the Jews." *Transactions of the Society of Biblical Archaeology* 7 (1881): 1-22.

——. *Plans, Elevations, Sections, etc., Shewing the Results of the Excavations at Jerusalem, 1867-70.* London: Palestine Exploration Fund, 1884.

—— and Conder, C.R. *Survey of Western Palestine: Jerusalem Volume.* London: Palestine Exploration Fund, 1884.

Wilson, C.W. Ordinance Survey of Jerusalem Made in the Years 1864 to 1865. Southampton: Ordinance Survey Office, 1866.

——. "The Ordinance Survey of Jerusalem: 1864-5" in *The Recovery of Jerusalem: A Narrative of Exploration and Discovery in the City and Holy Land.* Eds. C.W. Wilson, et. al. :London: R. Bentley (1880): pp. 9-32.

——. "The Masonry of the Haram Wall." *Palestine Exploration Quarterly Fund Statement* 12 (1880): 9-65.

Archaeological Sources (20th century)

Avigad, Nachman and Geva, Hillel. "Jerusalem: Second Temple Period," in *New Encyclopedia of Archaeological Excavations in the Holy Land.* Ed. Ephraim Stern. Jerusalem: Israel Exploration Society, 1993. 2:717-757.

Ben-Dov, Meir. *In the Shadow of the Temple: The Discovery of Ancient Jerusalem.* Trans. by Ina Friedman. New York: Harper & Row, 1985.

Geva, Hillel, ed. *Ancient Jerusalem Revealed.* Jerusalem: Israel Exploration Society, 1994.

Kenyon, Kathleen, M. *Jerusalem: Excavating 3,000 Years of History.* New York: McGraw Hill, 1967.

——. *Digging Up Jerusalem.* New York: Prager, 1974.

——. "The Temple Mount." *Biblical Archaeology Today: Proceedings of the International Congress on Biblical Archaeology, Jerusalem, April 1984.* Jerusalem: Israel Exploration Society, 1985.

Mazar, Benjamin. *The Mountain of the Lord.* New York: Doubleday, 1975.

Secondary Sources

Books on Historical Temples

These sources include archaeological, historical, and theological studies on the First and Second Temples and the Temple service as well as on the Muslim Dome of the Rock.

Avigad, Nachman. *Discovering Jerusalem.* Jerusalem: Shokmona Publishing Company, 1983, pp. 120-50.

Bartlett, W.H. *Jerusalem Revisited.* Jerusalem: Ariel Publishing House, Reprint of 1855 edition.

Barrois, G.A. *Jesus Christ and the Temple.* New York: St. Vladimir's Seminary Press, 1980.

Ben-Dov, Meir and Aner, Z. *The Western Wall.* Jerusalem: Ministry of Defense, 1983.

————. *Jerusalem Man and Stone: An Archaeologist's Personal View of His City.* Trans. by Yael Guiladi. Tel-Aviv: Modan Publishing House, 1990.

Blackhouse, Robert. *The Kregel Pictorial Guide to the Temple.* ed. Tim Dowley. Grand Rapids: Kregel Publications, 1996.

Brown, J. R. *Temple and Sacrifice in Rabbinic Judaism.* The Winslow Lectures. Illinois: Seabury-Western Theological Seminary, 1963.

Busink, T. A. *Der Temple von Jerusalem von Salomo bis Herodes: Eine archäologischhistorische Studie unter berücksichtigung des westsemitischen Tempelbaus.* 2 vols. Leiden: E.J. Brill, 1980.

Charlesworth, James. *Jesus Within Judaism: New Light from Exciting Archaeological Discoveries,* The Anchor Bible Reference Library. New York: Doubleday, 1988, esp. pp. 103-30.

Chilton, Bruce. *The Temple of Jesus: His Sacrificial Program Within a Cultural History of Sacrifice.* Pennsylvania: The Pennsylvania State University Press, 1992.

Clements, R. E. *God and His Temple.* Oxford: Basil Blackwell, 1965.

Clifford, Richard J. *The Cosmic Mountain in Canaan and in the Old Testament,* Harvard Semitic Monographs 4. Cambridge: Harvard University Press, 1972.

Comay, Joan. *The Temple of Jerusalem.* London: Weinfeld & Nicolson, 1975.

Cohn, Robert L. *The Shape of Sacred Space: Four Biblical Studies.* New York University Press, 1981.

Congar, Yves M.-J. *The Mystery of the Temple.* Trans. R.F. Trevett. Westminster, MD: Newman Press, 1962.

Cornfeld, Gaalyah, *The Mystery of the Temple Mount: New Guidebook to Discovery.* Tel-Aviv/Jerusalem: Bazak Israel Guidebook Publishers, Ltd., n.d.

Domingo, Leon Munoz. *Gloria de la Shekinahen los Targumim del Pentateuco.* Madrid, 1977.

Duncan, Alistar. *The Noble Sanctuary.* London: Middle East Archive, 1972.

Edersheim, Alfred. *The Temple: Its Ministry and Services as They Were in the Temple in the Time of Jesus Christ.* Revised ed. Grand Rapids: Kregel Publishers, 1998.

Eisenberg, Rafael. *A Matter of Return: A Penetrating Analysis of Yisrael's Afflictions and Their Alternatives.* Jerusalem: Feldheim Publishers, 1980.

Flusser, David. *Judaism and the Origins of Christianity.* Jerusalem: Magnes Press, 1988.

Fox, Michael V., ed. *Temple in Society.* Winona Lake, IN: Eisenbrauns, 1988.

Gale, Herbert M. *The Use of Analogy in the Letters of Paul.* Philadelphia: Westminster Press, 1964.

Gammie, John G. *Holiness in Israel, Overtures to Biblical Theology.* Minneapolis: Fortress Press, 1989.

Garrard, Alec. *The Splendour of the Temple.* Norfolk, England: Moat Farm Publications, 1997.

Gärtner, Bertil. *The Temple and the Community in Qumran and the New Testament.* Cambridge: University Press, 1965.

Gaston, Lloyd. *No Stone Upon Another: Studies in the Significance of the Fall of Jerusalem in the Synoptic Gospels,* New Testament Supplements 23. Leiden: E. J. Brill, 1972.

Gutmann, Joseph. *The Temple of Solomon: Archaeological Fact and Medieval Tradition in Christian, Islamic, and Jewish Art,* Religion and the Arts 3.

Haran, Menahem. *Temples and Temple Service in Ancient Israel.* Oxford: Clarendon Press, 1978.

Heffern, Andrew D. *Apology and Polemic in the New Testament: The Bohlen Lectures, 1915.* New York: Macmillan Company, 1922.

Hildesheimer, Rabbi Azriel. *Middoth Beth Hamikdash shel-Hordos.* Jerusalem, 1974.

Hollis, Frederick J. *The Archaeology of Herod's Temple: With a Commentary on the Tractate Middoth.* London: Dent, 1934.

Horbury, William. *Templum Amicitiae: Essays on the Second Temple Presented to Ernst Bammel,* Journal for the Study of the New Testament Supplements 48. Sheffield: JSNT Press, 1991.

Hurowitz, Victor (Avigdor). "I Have Built You an Exalted House: Temple Building in the Bible in Light of Mesopotamian and Northwest Semitic Writings." *Journal for the Study of the Old Testament Supplements* 115. Sheffield: JSOT Press, 1992.

Isaacs, Ronald H. *The Tabernacle, the Temple, and Its Royalty.* New York: Jason Aronson, 1999.

Jenson, Philip Peter. *Graded Holiness: A Key to the Priestly Conception of the World.* JSOT Sup 106. Sheffield: JSOT Press, 1992.

Jeremias, Joachim. *Jerusalem in the Time of Jesus.* Trans. by F. H. and C. H. Cave. London: SCN Press, 1969.

Jones, O. R. *The Concept of Holiness.* New York: The Macmillan Company, 1961.

Juel, Donald. *Messiah and Temple: The Trial of Jesus in the Gospel of Mark.* Society of Biblical Literature Dissertation Series 31. Ed. Howard C. Kee and Douglas A. Knight. Missoula, MO: Scholars Press, 1977.

Klein, Mina C. and H. Arthur. *Temple Beyond Time.* New York: Van Nostrand Reinhold Company, 1970.

Knowles, Michael. *Jeremiah in Matthew's Gospel: The Rejected Prophet Motif in Matthaean Redaction,* Journal for the Study of the New Testament Supplements 68. ed. Stanley E. Porter. Sheffield: JSOT Press, 1993.

Koester, Craig R. *The Dwelling of God: The Tabernacle in the Old Testament, Intertestamental Jewish Literature, and the New Testament.* Catholic Biblical Quarterly Monograph Series 22. Washington, D.C.: The Catholic Biblical Association of America, 1989.

Landay, Jerry M. *Dome of the Rock.* Wonders of Man (series). Ed. by Joseph L. Gardner. New York: Newsweek Book Division, 1972.

Levenson, Jon. *Sinai and Zion: An Entry into the Jewish Bible.* New York: Harper & Row Publishing Co., 1985.

Lohmeyer, E. *Lord of the Temple: A Study of the Relations Between Cult and Gospel.* Trans. S. Todd. Richmond: John Knox Press, 1962.

Mare, W.H. *The Archaeology of the Jerusalem Area.* Grand Rapids: Baker Book House, 1987.

Mendels, Doron. *The Rise and Fall of Jewish Nationalism,* AB Reference Library. New York: Doubleday, 1992.

Milgrom, Jacob. *Studies in Levitical Terminology 1: The Encroacher and the Levite: The Term ʾAboda.* University of California Publications, Near Eastern Studies 14. Berkeley and Los Angeles: University of California Press, 1970.

Millgram, Abraham E. *Jerusalem Curiosities.* Philadelphia/New York: An Edward E. Elson Book, 1990, esp. pp. 91-134, 185-302.

Moore, George Foot. *Judaism in the First Centuries of the Christian Era.* 2 vols. Cambridge: Harvard University Press, 1930.

Nereparampil, L. *Destroy This Temple: An Exegetico-Theological Study on the Meaning of Jesus' Temple-Logion in Jn. 2:19.* Bangalore: Kharmarem Publications, 1987.

Neusner, Jacob. *A History of the Mishnaic Law of Holy Things. Part 6, The Mishnaic System of Sacrifice and Sanctuary.* Studies in Judaism in Late Antiquity 30. Leiden: E.J. Brill, 1980.

Ollenburger, Ben C. *Zion the City of the Great King: A Theological Symbol of the Jerusalem Cult.* Journal for the Study of the Old Testament 41 . Sheffield: JSOT Press, 1987.

Patai, R. *Man and Temple.* New York: KTAV, 1967.

Peters, Francis E. *Jerusalem and Mecca: The Typology of the Holy City in the East.* New York University Studies in Near Eastern Civilization 11. New York University Press, 1999.

Price, J. Randall. *Secrets of the Dead Sea Scrolls.* Eugene, OR: Harvest House Publishers, 1996, see esp. "The Temple and the Scrolls," pp. 235-63.

———. *The Stones Cry Out: What Archaeology Reveals About the Truth of the Bible.* Eugene, OR: Harvest House Publishers, 1997, esp. "The Temple: Political Propaganda or Proven Place," pp. 175-202 and "Archaeology and the Ark: Sacred Superstition or Ancient Artifact?" pp. 203-19.

Ritmeyer, Leen and Kathleen. *Reconstructing Herod's Temple Mount in Jerusalem,* BAR offprint. Washington, D.C.: Biblical Archaeology Society, 1991.

———. *The Temple and the Rock.* Harrogate, England: Ritmeyer Archaeological Design, 1996.

———. *The Archaeology of Herod's Temple Mount.* England: Ritmeyer Archaeological Design, 1967.

———. *Secrets of Jerusalem's Temple Mount.* Washington, D.C.: Biblical Archaeology Society, 1998.

———. *Worship and Ritual in Herod's Temple.* Harrogate, England: Ritmeyer Archaeological Design, 1999.

Rosenau, Helen. *Vision of the Temple: The Image of the Temple of Jerusalem in Judaism and Christianity.* London: Oresko Books, Ltd., 1979.

Sabourin, Leopold. *Priesthood: A Comparative Study.* Studies in the History of Religion 15. Leiden: E.J. Brill, 1973.

Safrai, Samuel. *Haaliyah La-Regel bi-Yemey Bayit Sheni.* Jerusalem, 1965 (Hebrew).

Sanders, E. P. *Jesus and Judaism.* Philadelphia: Fortress Press, 1985.

———. *Judaism: Practice and Belief 63 B.C.E.–66 C.E.* Philadelphia: Trinity Press International, 1992, esp. pp. 47-240.

Schaffer, Shaul and Asher, Joseph. *Israel's Temple Mount: The Jews' Magnificent Sanctuary.* English editor Rabbi Asher Feuchtwanger. Jerusalem: Achva Press, 1975.

Schmidt, M. *Prophet und Tempel.* Zollikon-Zürich: Evangelischer Verlag, 1948.

Schürer, Emil. *The History of the Jewish People in the Age of Jesus Christ.* 3 vols. Revised and ed., G. Vermes, F. Millar, M. Black. Edinburgh: T. & T. Clark, 1993.

Shanks, Hershel, ed. *In the Temple of Solomon and the Tomb of Caiaphas.* Washington D.C.: Biblical Archaeology Society, 1993.

Soltau, Henry W. *The Holy Vessels and Furniture of the Tabernacle.* Reprint. Grand Rapids: Kregel Publications, 1975.

Steckoll, Solomon H. *The Temple Mount: An Illustrated History of Mount Moriah in Jerusalem.* London: Tom Stacey, Ltd., 1972.

———. *The Tabernacle: The Priesthood and the Offerings.* 3d ed. Grand Rapids: Kregel Publications, 1976.

Van Dam, Cornelis. *The Urim and Thummim: A Means of Revelation in Ancient Israel.* Winona Lake, IN: Eisenbrauns, 1997.

Wilkinson, John. *Jerusalem as Jesus Knew It: Archaeology as Evidence.* London: Thames & Hudson, 1978.

Wise, Michael O. *A Critical Study of the Temple Scroll from Cave 11,* SAOC 49. Ed. by A. Holland. Chicago: The Oriental Institute of the University of Chicago, 1990.

Yadin, Yigael. *The Temple Scroll.* New York: Random House, 1985.

Zehr, Paul M. *God Dwells with His People: A Study of Israel's Ancient Tabernacle.* Scottdale, PA: Herald Press, 1981.

Zussman, L.A. *Jerusalem of Gold: The History of the First and Second Temples.* Trans. and ed. by Elimelech and Shoshana Lepon. Jerusalem: Hochma Books & Publishing, 1988.

Articles and Essays on the Historical Temples

Ådna, Jostein. "The Attitude of Jesus to the Temple: A Critical Examination of How Jesus' Relationship to the Temple Is Evaluated within Israeli Scholarship, with Particular Regard to the Jerusalem School [of Synoptic Research]." *Mishkan* 17-18 (2/1992–1/993): 65-81.

Andreasen, Niels-Erik. "The Heavenly Sanctuary in the Old Testament," *The Sanctuary and the Atonement*. Ed. A. V. Wallenkampf and W. Richard Lesher. (Washington, D.C., 1981): 67-86.

Avi-Yonah, Michael and Stern, Menahem. "Jerusalem: History of the Second Temple Period." *Encyclopedia Judaica* 9 (1978): 1379.

Baltzer, Klaus. "The Meaning of the Temple in the Lucan Writings." *Harvard Theological Review* 58 (1965): 263-77.

Barrett, C. K. "Allegory of Abraham, Sarah, and Hagar in the Argument of Galatians." *Rechterfertigung: Festschrift fur Ernst Kasemann*. Ed. J. Friedrich, W. Pohlmann, and P. Stuhlmacher. Tubingen: J. C. B. Mohr, 1976.

————. "Attitudes to the Temple in the Acts of the Apostles" in *Templum Amicitiae: Essays on the Second Temple presented to Ernst Bammel. Journal for the Study of the New Testament Supplements* 48. Ed. William Horbury. Sheffield: JSOT Press, 1991.

Baumgarten, Joseph, M. "Exclusions from the Temple: Proselytes and Agrippa I," *Journal of Jewish Studies* 33:1-2 (1982): 215-225.

————. "Sacrifice and Worship among the Jewish Sectarians of the Dead Sea (Qumran) Community." *Harvard Theological Review* 46 (1953): 141-57.

Bockmuehl, Markus N. A. "Why Did Jesus Predict the Destruction of the Temple?" *Crux* 25 (1989): 11-18.

Braun, "Solomon, The Chosen Temple Builder," *Journal of Biblical Literature* 83 (1964): 586-90.

Brodie, L. T. "A Temple and a New Law." *Journal for the Study of the New Testament* 5 (1979): 21-45.

Brownlee, W. H. "The Meaning of the Temple in the Lukan Writings," *Harvard Theological Review* 58 (1965): 236-77.

Büchler, A. "The Levitical Impurity of the Gentile in Palestine before the Year 70," *Jewish Quarterly Review* 17:2-4 (1926-27): 1-81.

Caldecott, A. "The Significance of the Cleansing of the Temple." *Journal of Theological Studies*, o.s., 24 (1923): 382-86.

Charlesworth, James H., ed. *The Messiah: Developments in Earliest Judaism and Christianity*. First Princeton Symposium on Judaism and Christian Origins. Minneapolis: Fortress Press, 1992.

Clark, K. W. "Worship in the Jerusalem Temple after A.D. 70," *New Testament Studies* 6 (1960): 269-80.

Clements, Ronald E. "Temple and Land." *Transactions of the Glasgow Oriental Society* 19 (1963): 16-28.

Cohen, Shaye, J.D. "The Temple and the Synagogue." In *The Temple in Antiquity*. Ed. T.C. Madsen. RSMS 9. Provo, Utah: Religious Studies Center, 1984, pp. 151-74.

Coppens, Joseph C. "The Spiritual Temple in the Pauline Letters and Its Background." *Studia Evangelica* 6 (1969): 53-66.

Cowley, A. "The Meaning of םוֹקָמ in Hebrew," *Journal of Theological Studies* 17 (1916): 174-76.

Cullmann, Oscar. "L'opposition contre le temple de Jerusalem, motif commun de la theologie johannique et du monde ambiant," *New Testament Studies* 5 (1958-59): 157-173.

Dawsey, James M. "The Origin of Luke's Positive Perception of the Temple," *Perspectives in Religious Studies* 18:1 (Spring, 1991): 5-21.

Day, J. "The Destruction of the Shiloh Sanctuary and Jeremiah vii 12, 14," *Studies in the Historical Books of the Old Testament*. Ed. J.A. Emerton. *Vetus Testament Supplements* 30. Leiden: E. J. Brill, 1979.

De Lacey, D. R. "οἵτινές ἐστε ὑμεῖς: The Function of a Metaphor in Paul." *Temple Amicitae: Essays on the Second Temple Presented to Ernst Bammel*. Ed. William Horbury. *Journal for the Study of the New Testament Supplements* 48. Sheffield: JTOS, 1991.

——. "The Jewish Religion in the Second Temple Period," s.v. "Interpretation (*P*e*shat* and *D*e*rash*) at the Time of the Second Temple," *World History of the Jewish People* First Series: Ancient Times, vol. 8: *Society and Religion in the Second Temple Period*. Eds. Michael Avi-Yonah and Zvi Baras. Jerusalem: Masada Publishing Ltd., 1977.

Delcor, Mathias. "Is the Temple Scroll a Source of the Herodian Temple?" In *Temple Scroll Studies*, ed. G.J. Brooke. Sheffield: JSOT Press, 1989, pp. 87-89.

Dubarle, A.M. "Lesegne du Temple." *Revue Biblique* 48 (January 1939): 21-44.

Elad, Amikan. "Why Did 'Abd al-Malik Build the Dome of the Rock? A Re-examination of the Muslim Sources." In *Bayt al-Maqdis, 'Abd al-Malik's Jerusalem*. Eds. Julian Raby and J. Johns. Oxford: University Press, 1992.

Eskenazi, Tamara C. and Richards, Kent H., eds. *Second Temple Studies. Journal for the Study of the Old Testament Supplement Series* 175. Sheffield: JSOT Press, 1994.

Eybers, I.H. "The Rebuilding of the Temple According to Haggai and Zechariah." In *Studies in Old Testament Prophecy*. Eds. W.C. Van Wyk. Potchefstroom: Pro Rege, 1975, pp. 21-23.

Fox, Michael V., ed. "Temple and Community in Ancient Israel," *Temple in Society*. Winona Lake, IN: Eisenbrauns, 1988.

——. Hurowitz, Victor Avigdor, Hurvitz, Avi, Klein, Michael, Schwartz, Baruch J., and Shupak, Nili, eds. *Texts, Temples, and Traditions: A Tribute to Menahem Haran* (Winona Lake, IN: Eisenbrauns, 1996), esp. pp. 3-64, 147-62, 187-94.

Fredriksen, Paula. "Jesus and the Temple, Mark and War." *Society of Biblical Literature Seminar 1990 Papers* 29. Ed. David J. Lull. New Orleans: Scholars Press, 1990.

Freedman, David Noel. "Temple Without Hands," *Temples and High Places in Biblical Times: Proceedings of the Colloquium in Honor of the Centennial of Hebrew Union College—Jewish Institute of Religion March 14–16, 1977*. Jerusalem: The Nelson Glueck School of Biblical Archaeology of Hebrew Union College, 1981, pp. 21-28.

Gafni, Isaiah. *Jerusalem to Jabneh: The Period of the Mishna and Its Literature*. Ramat-Aviv: Everyman's University, 1980.

Gaston, Lloyd. "Theology of the Temple: the New Testament Fulfillment of the Promise of Old Testament Heilgeschichte." In *Oikonomia*. Ed. F. Chript. Hamburg-Bergstedt: H. Reich Evangelische Verlag, 1967, pp. 32-41.

Gerhardsson, Birger. "Sacrificial Service and Atonement in the Gospel of Matthew." In *Reconciliation and Hope*. Ed. R.J. Banks. London: Paternoster Press, 1974, pp. 25-35.

Gibson, Shimon and Jacobson, David M. "The Oldest Datable Chambers on the Temple Mount in Jerusalem," *Biblical Archaeologist* 57:3 (1994): 150-60.

Hamilton, N. Q. "Temple Cleansing and Temple Bank." *Journal of Biblical Literature* 83 (1964): 368.

Harrelson, Walter. "Guilt and Rites of Purification Related to the Fall of Jerusalem in 587 B.C." *Numen* 15 (1968): 218-21.

Hasel, Gerhard. "Studies in Biblical Atonement I: Continual Sacrifices, Defilement/Cleansing and Sanctuary." *Sanctuary and Atonement: Biblical, Historical, and Theological Studies*. Ed. Arnold V. Wallenkampf and W. Richard Lesher. Washington, D.C.: Review and Herald Publishing Association, 1981.

Holmgren, Fredrick. "Before the Temple, the Thornbush: An Exposition of Exodus 2:11–3:12," *Reformed Journal* 33:3 (March, 1983): 9-11.

Holt, Else Kragelund. "Jeremiah's Temple Sermon and the Deuteronomists: An Investigation of the Redactional Relationship between Jeremiah 7 and 26," *Journal for the Study of the Old Testament* 36 (1986): 73-87.

Hurowitz, Victor. *I Have Built You an Exalted House: Temple Building in the Bible in the Light of Mesopotamian and Northwest Semitic Writings. Journal for the Study of the Old Testament Supplements* 115 (University of Sheffield, 1992), Appendix 7 ("The Cosmic Dimensions of Cities and Temples"), pp. 335-37.

Iersel, B.M.F. van. "The Finding of Jesus in the Temple." *Novum Testamentum* 4 (1960): 161-73.

Jacobson, D.M. "The Plan of Herod's Temple." *Bulletin of the Anglo-Israel Archaeological Society* 10 (1990-91): 36-66.

––––––. "Hadrianic Architecture and Geometry." *American Journal of Archaeology* 90 (1986): 71-75.

Japhet, Sara. "The Temple in the Restoration Period: Reality and Ideology." *Union Seminary Quarterly Review* 44:3-4 (1991): 195-252.

Jerusalem Perspective (Second Temple issue) 46-47 (September-December, 1994). Jerusalem: Jerusalem School for Synoptic Research.

Johnson, Ron. "The Centrality of the Jewish Temple in the Affairs of God, Israel, and the Nations— Part I—Historical Temples," *The Conservative Theological Journal* 1:1 (April 1997): 61-84.

Jones, Douglas. "The Cessation of Sacrifice after the Destruction of the Temple in 586 B.C." *Journal of Theological Studies*, n.s. 14 (1963): 12-31.

Kapelrud, Arvid S. "Temple Building, a Task for Gods and Kings." *Orientalia* 32 (1963): 56-62.

Kaufman, Asher. "Where the Ancient Temple of Jerusalem Stood." *Biblical Archaeology Review* 9:2 (March/April, 1983): 40-58.

Kim, Seyoon. "Jesus and the Temple." *ACTS Theological Journal* 3 (1988): 87-131.

Lampe, G.W.H. "A.D. 70 in Christian Reflection." In *Jesus and the Politics of His Day*. Ed. E. Bammel and C.F.D. Moule. Cambridge: University Press, 1984, pp. 153-71.

Liver, J. "The Half-Shekel Offering in Biblical and Post-Biblical Literature." *Harvard Theological Review* 56 (1963): 173-98.

Lundguist, John. "What is a Temple? A Preliminary Typology," *The Quest for the Kingdom of God: Studies in Honor of George E. Mendenhall*. Eds. H. B. Huffmon, F. A. Spina, and A. R. W. Green. Winona Lake, IN: Eisenbrauns, 1983, pp. 205-219.

Maier, Johannan. "The Architectural History of the Temple in Jerusalem in Light of the Temple Scroll," in *Temple Scroll Studies*, ed. George J. Brooke (*Journal for the Study of the Pseude-pigrapha Supplement Series* 7, 1987), pp. 23-62.

Matthews, Kenneth A. "John, Jesus and the Essenes: Trouble at the Temple." *Criswell Theological Review* 3:1 (Fall, 1988): 101-26.

Mazar, Benjamin. "The Royal Stoa in the Southern Part of the Temple Mount," *Recent Archaeology in the Land of Israel*. Ed. Herschel Shanks. Washington D.C.: Biblical Archaeology Society, 1985.

———. "Herodian Jerusalem in the Light of the Excavations South and Southwest of the Temple Mount." *Israel Exploration Journal* 28 (1978): 230-37.

Meyers, Carol L. "The Elusive Temple." *Biblical Archaeologist* (Winter 1981): 33, 41.

———. "Jerusalem Temple." *Anchor Bible Dictionary* 6 (1992): 360-69.

———. "David as Temple Builder." *Ancient Israelite Religion*. Eds. P. Miller, Jr., P. Hanson, and S. D. McBride (Philadelphia: Fortress Press, 1987).

Milgrom, Jacob. " 'Sabbath' and 'Temple City' in the Temple Scroll." *Bulletin of the American Schools of Oriental Research* 232 (1978): 25-27.

———. "Israel's Sanctuary: The Priestly 'Picture of Dorian Gray.' " *Revue Biblique* 3 (July, 1976): 393-94.

Miller, James E. "The Aetiology of the Tabernacle/Temple in Genesis." *Proceedings: Eastern Great Lakes and Midwest Bible Societies* 4 (1986): 152-57.

Moule, C.F.D. "Sanctuary and Sacrifice in the Church of the New Testament." *Journal of Theological Studies* new series 1 (1950): 29-41.

Mueller, James R. "The Apocalypse of Abraham and the Destruction of the Second Jewish Temple." *Society of Biblical Literature* 1982 *Seminar Papers* 21 (1982): 341-49.

Nereparampil, Lucius. "Biblical Symbolism of the Temple." *Journal of Dharma* 9:2 (April-June, 1984): 164-66.

Neusner, Jacob. "Money-Changers in the Temple: The Mishnah's Explanation." *New Testament Studies* 35 (1989): 287-90.

———. *A History of the Mishnaic Law of Holy Things: Studies in Late Antiquity* (Vol. 30, Part VI) from the collection of *The Mishnah*. Leiden: E. J. Brill, 1980.

————. "The Idea of Purity in Ancient Judaism." *Journal of the American Academy of Religion* 43:1 (March, 1975): 16-17.

Ouellette, Jean. "The Basic Structure of Solomon's Temple and Archaeological Research." *The Temple of Solomon.* Ed. J. Gutmann. Missoula: Scholars Press, 1976.

Parry, Donald W. *Temples of the Ancient World: Ritual and Symbolism.* Salt Lake City, UT: Deseret Book Company, 1994.

Parunak, H. Van Dyke. "Was Solomon's Temple Oriented Toward the Sun?" *Palestine Exploration Quarterly* 110 (1978): 28-33.

Patrich, Joseph. "Reconstructing the Magnificent Temple Herod Built," in *Archaeology and the Bible,* 2: *Archaeology in the World of Herod, Jesus and Paul.* Eds. H. Shanks and D. P. Cole. Washington, D.C.: Biblical Archaeology Society, 1990: 64-77.

Petersen, David L. "The Temple in Persian Period Prophetic Texts," *Biblical Theology Bulletin* 21:3 (Fall, 1991): 88-96.

Porten, Bezalel. "Temple: The Temple of Zerubbabel." *Encyclopedia Judaica* 15 (1972): 958.

Rabe, Virgil W. "Israelite Opposition to the Temple." *Catholic Biblical Quarterly* 29:2 (1967): 228-33.

Rigaux, B. "βδέλγυμα τῆς ἐρημώσεως." *Biblica* 40 (1959): 675-83.

Ritmeyer, Leen. "Locating the Original Temple Mount." *Biblical Archaeology Review* 18:2 (March-April, 1992): 24-45, 64-65.

Rodriguez, Angel Manuel. "Sanctuary Theology in the Book of Exodus." *Andrews University Seminary Studies* 24:2 (Summer, 1986): 127-45.

Roth, Cecil. "The Cleansing of the Temple and Zech. 14:21." *Novum Testamentum* 4 (1960): 174-78.

Rosen-Ayalon, Miriam. "The Early Islamic Monuments of al-Haram al-Sharif, an Iconographic Study." *Qedem* 28 (1989).

Rowland, "The Second Temple." *Temple Amicitiae: Essays on the Second Temple Presented to Ernst Bammel.* Ed. William Horbury. *Journal for the Study of the New Testament Supplements* 48. Sheffield: JSOT Press, 1991.

Runnels, D. "The King as Temple Builder: A Messianic Typology." In *Spirit Within Structure.* Ed. E.J. Furcha. Allison Park: Pickwick, 1983, pp. 15-37.

Schiffman, Lawrence. "Jewish Sectarianism in Second Temple Times." *Great Schisms in Jewish History.* Ed. R. Jospe (1981): 1-46.

Silberman, Neil A. "In Search of Solomon's Lost Treasures." *Biblical Archaeology Review* 6:4 (July/August, 1980): 30-32.

Simon, Marcel. "Saint Stephen and the Jerusalem Temple." *The Journal of Ecclesiastical History* 2 (1951): 127.

Snaith, Norman H. "Priesthood in the Temple." In *A Companion to the Bible,* ed. T.W. Manson. Edinburgh: T. & T. Clark, 1939, pp. 418-43.

Spencer, A. J. "The Brick Foundations of Late-Period Peripteral Temples and Their Mythological Origin" in *Glimpses of Ancient Egypt.* Eds. Fs. H. W. Fairman, John Ruffle et al. Warminster: Aris and Phillips, 1979.

Stone, Michael E. "Reactions to the Destruction of the Second Temple." *Journal for the Study of Judaism* 12 (1981): 195-204.

Sweet, J.M.P. "A House Not Made with Hands." *Templum Amicitiae: Essays on the Second Temple presented to Ernst Bammel. Journal for the Study of the New Testament Supplements* 48. Sheffield: JSNT, 1991: 387-406.

Sylva, Dennis D. "The Temple Curtain and Jesus' Death in the Gospel of Luke." *Journal of Biblical Literature* 105 (1986): 239-50.

"The Jerusalem Temple" (special issue). *Eretz* 46 (May-June, 1996): 5-74.

Townsend, John T. "The Jerusalem Temple in the First Century" in *God and His Temple: Reflections on Samuel Terrien's The Elusive Presence: Toward a New Biblical Theology.* Ed. Lawrence E. Frizzell. New Jersey: Department of Judeo-Christian Studies, Seton Hall University, 1979.

Van Buren, E. Douglas. "Foundation Rites for a New Temple." *Orientalia* 21 (1952): 293.

Wallace, David H. "The Essenes and Temple Sacrifice." *Theologische Zeitschrift* 13 (1957): 335-38.

Weinert, Francis D. "Luke, the Temple and Jesus' Sayings About Jerusalem's Abandoned House (Luke 13:34-35)." *Catholic Biblical Quarterly* 44 (1982): 68-76.

Weinfeld, Moshe. "Sabbath, Temple and Enthronement of the Lord—The Problem of the Sitz im Leben of Genesis 1:1-2:3." *Mélanges bibliques et orientaux en l'honneur de M. Henri Cazelles.* Ed. A. Caquot and M. Delcor. Butzon & Bercker Kevelaer, 1981: 501-06, 510.

Wenham, Gordon J. "Sanctuary Symbolism in the Garden of Eden Story," *Proceedings of the Ninth World Congress of Jewish Studies, Jerusalem, August 4–12, 1985.* Division A: The Period of the Bible. Jerusalem: World Union of Jewish Studies, 1986, pp. 19-25.

Wilcoxen, Jay A. "The Political Background of Jeremiah's Temple Sermon." *Scripture in History & Theology: Essays in Honor of J. Coert Rylaarsdam.* Ed. A.L. Merrill and T.W. Overholt. Pennsylvania: The Pickwick Press, 1977.

Williamson, H. G. M. "The Temple in the Book of Chronicles" in *Templum Amicitiae: Essays on the Second Temple Presented to Ernst Bammel.* Journal for the Study of the New Testament 48. Ed. William Horbury. Sheffield: JSOT Press, 1991.

Wilkinson, John. "Christian Pilgrims in Jerusalem During the Byzantine Period." *Palestine Exploration Quarterly* 108 (1976): 77.

Winkle, Ross E. "The Jeremiah Model for Jesus in the Temple." *Andrews University Seminary Studies* 24:2 (1986): 155-72.

Wise, Michael O. "The Eschatological Vision of the Temple Scroll." *Journal of Near Eastern Studies* 49:2 (1990): 155-72.

Wright, David P. "The Spectrum of Priestly Impurity" in *Priesthood and Cult in Ancient Israel.* Eds. Gary Anderson and Saul M. Olyan. *Journal for the Study of the Old Testament Supplements* 125. Sheffield: JSOT Press, 1991.

Wright, G. Ernest. "The Temple in Palestine-Syria." *The Biblical Archaeologist Reader* 3. Eds. David Noel Preedman and G. Ernest Wright, Anchor Books. New York: Doubleday, 1961.

————. "The Significance of the Temple in the Ancient Near East." *Biblical Archaeologist* 7 (1944): 65-77.

Young, Francis M. "Temple Cult and Law in Early Christianity." *New Testament Studies* 19 (1973): 325-38.

Zeitlin, S. "The Temple and Worship." *Jewish Quarterly Review* 51 (1961): 209-41.

————. "There Was No Court of Gentiles in the Temple Area." *Jewish Quarterly Review* 56 (1965): 88.

Zimmer, Robert G. "The Temple of God." *Journal of the Evangelical Theological Society* 18:1 (Winter, 1975): 41-46.

Zmijewski, J. "βδέλγυμα," *Exegetical Dictionary of the New Testament.* Eds. Horst Balz and Gerhard Schneider (Grand Rapids: William B. Eerdmans Publishing Co., 1978–1980) 1:210.

Unpublished Works on Historical Temples

Abegg, Robert Miles. "The New Testament Doctrine of the Church as the Temple of God." Th.M. thesis, Dallas Theological Seminary, 1981.

Amorim, Nilton Dutra. "Desecration and Defilement in the Old Testament." Ph.D. dissertation, Andrews University, 1985.

Braithwaite, Gilbert G. "The Doctrine of the Central Sanctuary in Deuteronomy." Th.D. dissertation, Dallas Theological Seminary, 1978.

Cunningham, Scott S. "The Temple Motif in Ephesians 2:19-22." Th.M. thesis: Dallas Theological Seminary, 1980.

Dowda, R.E. "The Cleansing of the Temple in the Synoptic Gospels." Ph.D. dissertation, Duke University, 1972.

Edwards, David D. "Jesus and the Temple: A Historico-Theological Study of Temple Motifs in the Ministry of Jesus." Ph.D. dissertation, Southwestern Baptist Theological Seminary, 1992.

Fujita, Shozo. "The Temple Theology of the Qumran Sect and the Book of Ezekiel: Their Relationship to Jewish Literature of the Last Two Centuries B.C." Th.D. dissertation, Princeton Theological Seminary, 1970.

Hart, John F. "The Purpose of the Laws of Purification." Th.M. thesis, Dallas Theological Seminary, 1976.

Hull, William E. "The Background of the New Temple Concept in Early Christianity." Ph.D. dissertation, Southern Baptist Theological Seminary, 1960.

Meisner, Lorne J. "The Temple Motiff—God's Witness Unto Himself." Th.M. thesis, Dallas Theological Seminary, 1977.

Ritmeyer, Leen. "The Architectural Development of the Temple Mount in Jerusalem." Ph.D. Thesis, University of Manchester, 1992.

Rose, Theodore S. "The Attitude of the Rabbis Toward the Destruction of the Second Temple." Ph.D. dissertation, Hebrew Union College, 1943 (microfilmed 1967).

Sage, David L. "The Figurative Use of the Word *Temple* in Paul's Epistles." Th.M. thesis: Dallas Theological Seminary, 1980.

Salmon, Marilyn. "Hypotheses About First-Century Judaism and the Study of Luke-Acts." Ph.D. dissertation, Hebrew Union College, 1985.

Schwartz, David R. "Priesthood, Temple, Sacrifices: Opposition and Spiritualization in the Late Second Temple Period." 2 vols. Ph.D. dissertation, Hebrew University, 1979.

Taylor, Theophilus Mills. "Uncleanness and Purification in Paul." Ph.D. dissertation, Yale University, 1956.

Townsend, John. "The Jerusalem Temple in New Testament Thought." Ph.D. dissertation, Harvard University, 1958.

Valentine, James. "Theological Aspects of the Temple Motif in the Old Testament and Revelation." Ph.D. dissertation, Boston University, 1985.

Weinert, F. "The Meaning of the Temple in the Gospel of Luke." Ph.D. dissertation, Fordham University, 1979.

Williams, Robert E. "The Post-Captivity Temple in Haggai." Th.M. thesis, Dallas Theological Seminary, 1956.

Books on Future Temples

Ariel, Yisrael. *The Odyssey of the Third Temple*. Trans. and adapted by Chaim Richman. Jerusalem: G. Israel Publications & Productions, Ltd., 1993.

Barclay, J. T. *The City of the Great King or Jerusalem As It Was, As It Is, and As It Is to Be*. Philadelphia: James Challen and Sons, 1858.

Beasley-Murray, *Jesus and the Future: An Examination of the Criticism of the Eschatological Discourse, Mark 13, with Special Reference to the Little Apocalypse Theory*. London/New York: Macmillan, 1954.

———. *Jesus and the Last Days: The Interpretation of the Olivet Discourse*. Peabody, MA: Hendrickson Publishers, 1993.

Brickner, David. *Future Hope: A Jewish Christian Look at the End of the World*. San Francisco: Purple Pomegranate Productions, 1999 (see esp. "The Abomination of Desolation: What Happens in the Temple?," pp. 55-66).

Campbell, Donald and Townsend, Jeffrey, eds. *A Case for Premillennialism: A New Consensus*. Chicago: Moody Press, 1992.

Chance, J. Bradley. *Jerusalem, the Temple, and the New Age in Luke-Acts*. Macon, GA: Mercer University Press, 1988.

Congar, Yves. *The Mystery of the Temple or the Manner of God's Presence to His Creatures from Genesis to the Apocalypse*. Trans. R.E. Trevett. Newman, 1962.

De Young, James Calvin. *Jerusalem in the New Testament: The Significance of the City in the History of Redemption and in Eschatology*. Amsterdam: J. H. Kok, N. V. Kampen, 1960.

Ford, Desmond. *The Abomination of Desolation in Biblical Eschatology*. Washington, D.C.: University Press of America, 1979.

Goren, Rav Shlomo. *Sepher Har-HaBayit: Meshiv Malachmah Heleq Rabi'i*. Tel Aviv/Jerusalem, 1992 (Hebrew).

Greenberg, Moshe. *Ezekiel 38-48: A New Translation with Introduction and Commentary*. The Anchor Bible. New York: Doubleday, forthcoming.

Ice, Thomas and Gentry, Kenneth L. *The Great Tribualtion: Past or Future?: Two Evangelicals Debate the Question*. Grand Rapids: Kregel Publications, 1999.

—— and Price, J. Randall. *Ready to Rebuild: The Imminent Plan to Rebuild the Last Days Temple*. Eugene, OR: Harvest House Publishers, 1992.

—— and Demy, Timothy. *The Truth About The Last Days' Temple*. Eugene, OR: Harvest House Publishers, 1996.

Kaplan, Rabbi Aryeh. *Jerusalem the Eye of the Universe*. New York: National Conference of Synagogue Youth/Union of Orthodox Jewish Congregations of America, 1984.

——. *Until the Mashiach*. Ed. Rabbi David Shapiro. Jerusalem: Breslov Research Institute, 1985.

Levenson, Jon. *Theology of the Program of Restoration of Ezekiel 40–48*. Ed. Frank Moore Cross, Jr., HSM 10. Missoula, MT: Scholars Press, 1976.

Martin, Ernest L. *The Place of the New Third Temple*. Portland, OR: Associates for Scriptural Knowledge, 1994.

McCaffrey, James. *The House with Many Rooms: The Temple Theme of Jn. 14, 2-3*. Analecta Biblica 114. Rome: Pontifical Biblical Institute, 1988.

McCall, Thomas and Levitt, Zola. *Satan in the Sanctuary*. Chicago: Moody Press, 1972.

McKelvey, R. J. *The New Temple: The Church the New Testament*. Oxford Theological Monographs. London: Oxford University Press, 1969.

Newberry, Thomas. *The Temples of Solomon and Ezekiel*. Glasgow, Scotland, n.d.

Payne, James. *The Millennial Temple of Ezekiel's Prophecy*. London, 1947.

Pentecost, J. Dwight. *Things to Come: A Study in Biblical Eschatology*. Grand Rapids: Dunham Publishing Co., 1958.

Price, J. Randall. *The Desecration and Restoration of the Temple as an Eschatological Motif in the Tanach, Jewish Apocalyptic Literature and the New Testament*. Ph.D. dissertation, University of Texas at Austin. Ann Arbor, MI: UMI, 1993.

——. *In Search of Temple Treasures: The Lost Ark and the Last Days*. Eugene, OR: Harvest House Publishers, 1994.

——. *Jerusalem in Prophecy: God's Stage for the Final Drama*. Eugene, OR: Harvest House Publishers, 1998, esp. "God Comes Home: The Rebuilding of Jerusalem's Temple," pp. 247-79.

Reznick, Rabbi Liebel. *The Holy Temple Revisited*. New Jersey: Jason Aronson Inc., 1990.

Richman, Chaim. *The Mystery of the Red Heifer*. Jerusalem: Chaim Richman, 1997.

——. *The Light of the Temple*. Jerusalem: The Temple Institute, 1998.

Rigaux, Béda. *L'Antéchrist: et l'Oppostion au Royaume Messianique dans l'Ancien et le Nouveau Testament.* Universitas Catholica Lovaniensis Dissertationes Seires ii. tomus 24. Pais. J. Gabalda et Fils, 1932.

Schmitt, John W. and Laney, Carl J. *Messiah's Coming Temple: Ezekiel's Prophetic Vision of the Future Temple.* Grand Rapids: Kregel Publications, 1997.

Steinberg, Shalom Dov. *The Third Beis HaMikdash: The Third Temple According to the Prophecy of Yechezkel Following Rashi and Tosafos Yom Tov.* Trans. Rabbi Moshe Leib Miller. Jerusalem: Moznaim Publications, 1993.

Stewart, Don and Missler, Chuck. *The Coming Temple.* Orange, CA: Dart Press, 1991.

Sulley, Henry. *The Temple of Ezekiel's Prophecy.* Birmingham, England, 1949.

Telford, William R. *The Barren Temple and the Withered Tree: A Redaction-Critical Analysis of the Cursing of the Fig-Tree Pericope in Mark's Gospel and its Relation to the Cleansing of the Temple Tradition.* JSNT Supplement 1. Sheffield: JSOT Press, 1980.

Tregelles, Samuel P. *The Man of Sin.* Reprint 1840. Ed. London/Aylesbury: Hunt, Benard & Co., 1930.

Tuell, Steven S. *The Law of the Temple in Ezekiel 40–48.* Harvard Semitic Monographs 49. Ed. Frank Moore Cross. Atlanta, GA: Scholars Press, 1992.

Urbach, Ephraim. *The Sages: Their Concepts and Beliefs.* Jerusalem: The Magnes Press, 1975.

White, F.H. *The City and the Temple of Israel in the Millennium, Ezekiel Chapters 40–48.* London: Patridge, n.d.

Articles and Essays on Future Temples

Adler, William. "The Apocalyptic Survey of History Adapted by Christians: Daniel's Prophecy of 70 Weeks" in *The Jewish Apocalyptic Heritage in Early Christianity. Compendia Rerum Iudaicarum ad Novum Testamentum 4.* Eds. James C. VanderKam and William Adler (Minneapolis: Fortress Press, 1996): 201-38.

Beal, Todd S. "The Abomination of Desolation: Past, Future, or Both?" Paper read at the Evangelical Theological Society Eastern Regional Meeting, April 5, 1991.

Bockmuehl, Markus. "Why Did Jesus Predict the Destruction of the Temple?" *Crux* xxv: 3 (September, 1989): 11-17.

Broshi, Magen. "The Gigantic Dimensions of the Visionary Temple in the Temple Scroll." *Biblical Archaeology Review* (Nov./Dec., 1987): 36-37.

Clowney, Edmund P. "The Final Temple," *Studying the New Testament Today. The New Testament Student 1.* Ed. John Skilton (Nutley, NJ: Presbyterian and Reformed Publishing Co., 1976), pp. 119, 129.

Dodd, C. H. "The Fall of Jerusalem and the 'Abomination of Desolation.'" *Journal of Roman Studies* 37 (1947): 51-63.

Doukhan, Jacques. "The Seventy Weeks of Dan. 9: An Exegetical Study." *Andrews University Seminary Studies* 17 (Spring, 1979): 8.

Feinberg, Charles L. "The Rebuilding of the Temple" in *Prophecy in the Making: Messages Prepared for the Jerusalem Conference on Biblical Prophecy*. Ed. Carl F. H. Henry (Carol Stream, IL: Creation House, 1971): 89-112.

Flusser, David. "The Hubris of the Antichrist in a Fragment from Qumran." *Immanuel* 10 (Spring, 1980): 31-37.

————. "No Temple in the City." *Judaism and the Origins of Christianity*. Jerusalem: The Magnes Press, 1988.

Ginsberg, Harold Louis. "Abomination of Desolation." *Encyclopedia Judaica* 1 (1972): 98.

Grabbe, Lester L. " 'The End of the Desolations of Jerusalem': From Jeremiah's 70 Years to Daniel's 70 Weeks of Years," *Early Jewish and Christian Exegesis: Studies in Memory of William Hugh Brownlee*. Eds. Craig Evans and William Stinespring (Scholars Press, 1987):68-74.

Gunther, John J. "The Epistle of Barnabas and the Final Rebuilding of the Temple." *Journal for the Study of Judaism* 7:2 (September, 1976): 143-51.

Hamerton-Kelly, R.G. "The Temple and the Origins of Jewish Apocalyptic." *Vetus Testamentum* 20 (1970): 1-15.

Hiers, Richard H. "Purification of the Temple: Preparation for the Kingdom of God." *Journal of Biblical Literature* 90 (1971): 90.

Himmelfarb, Martha. "Apocalyptic Ascent and the Heavenly Temple." *Society of Biblical Literature 1987 Seminar Papers* 26 (1987): 216.

Hooker, Morna D. "Traditions About the Temple in the Sayings of Jesus." *Bulletin of the John Rylands University Library of Manchester* 70:1 (Spring, 1988): 18-19.

Hullinger, Jerry M. "The Problem of Animal Sacrifices in Ezekiel 40–48." *Bibliotheca Sacra* 152:607 (July-September 1995): 279-89.

Johnson, Elliott. "Apocalyptic Genre in Literal Interpretation," *Essays in Honor of J. Dwight Pentecost*. Chicago: Moody Press, 1986.

Johnson, Ron. "The Centrality of the Jewish Temple in the Affairs of God, Israel, and the Nations—Part II—Future Temples." *The Conservative Theological Journal* 1:2 (August 1997): 119-39.

Kline, Meredith. "The Covenant of the Seventieth Week." *The Law and the Prophets: Old Testament Studies Prepared in Honor of Oswald Thompson Allis*. Ed. John H. Skilton. Nutley, NJ: Presbyterian & Reformed Publishing Co., 1974.

Kidder, S. Joseph. " 'This Generation' in Matthew 23-24." *Andrews University Seminary Studies* 21:3 (1983): 203-09.

Kolenkow, Anitra Bingham. "The Fall of the Temple and the Coming of the End: The Spectrum and Process of Apocalyptic Argument in 2 Baruch and Other Authors." *Society of Biblical Literature Seminar Papers* 21 (1982): 243-50.

Levenson, Jon. "The Jerusalem Temple in Devotional and Visionary Experience." *Jewish Spirituality 1: From the Bible Through the Middle Ages*. Ed. Arthur Green. New York: Crossroad Publishing Co., 1988, pp. 53-57.

MacRae, Allan A. "The Seventy Weeks of Daniel." Paper delivered at the Evangelical Theological Society, Deerfield, IL: Trinity Evangelical Divinity School, 1978, pp. 1-9.

McCall, Thomas. "How Soon the Tribulation Temple?—Part 1." *Bibliotheca Sacra* 128:510 (October-December, 1971): 341-51, Part II: "Problems in Rebuilding the Tribulation Temple." *Bibliotheca Sacra* 129:513 (January-March, 1972): 75-80.

McClain, Alva J. "The Parenthesis of Time Between the Sixty-Ninth and Seventieth Weeks." *Daniel's Prophecy of the Seventy Weeks*. Grand Rapids: Zondervan Publishing House, 1960.

McNichol, Alan J. "Eschatological Temple in the Qumran Pesher 4Q Florilegium 1:1-7." *Ohio Journal of Religious Studies* 5 (October 1977): 133-41.

Mitchell, John L. "The Question of Millennial Sacrifices." *Bibliotheca Sacra* 110 (October-December, 1953): 248-67, 342-61.

Murphy, Frederick J. "The Temple in the Syriac Apocalypse of Baruch," *Journal of Biblical Literature* 106:4 (1987): 671-83.

Price, J. Randall. "Prophetic Postponement in Daniel 9 and Other Texts," chapter 7 in *Current Issues in Dispensationalism*. Eds. Charles C. Ryrie, John R. Master, and Wesley R. Willis. Chicago: Moody Press, 1994.

————. "Old Testament Tribulation Terms." *The Return: Understanding Christ's Second Coming and the End Times*. Eds. T. Ice and T. Demy (Grand Rapids: Kregel Publishers, 1999): 27-53.

Sevener, Harold A. "The Temple: Where Did It Stand? Where Will It Be Rebuilt?" *The Chosen People* 99:4 (December, 1992): 1-14.

Showers, Renald E. "New Testament Chronology and the Decree of Daniel 9." *Grace Theological Journal* 11 (1970).

Thomson, Clive, A. "The Necessity of Blood Sacrifices in Ezekiel's Temple." *Bibliotheca Sacra* 123 (1966): 237-48.

Unger, Merrill F. "The Temple Vision of Ezekiel." *Bibliotheca Sacra* 105 (January-March, 1948): 418-32, 106 (April-June, 1949): 48-64, 169-77.

Walvoord, John. "Will Israel Build a Temple in Jerusalem?" *Bibliotheca Sacra* 125:497 (April 1968): 99-106.

Waterman, G. Henry. "The Sources of Paul's Teaching on the 2nd Coming of Christ in 1 and 2 Thessalonians." A Paper presented to the Midwest Regional meeting of the Evangelical Theological Society. Deerfield, IL: Trinity Evangelical Divinity School, March 21, 1975.

Weinfeld, Moshe. "Creation, Exodus and the Eschaton." *Recontre Astriologique Internationale* xxv (Berlin, July 3-7, 1978).

Wentling, Judith L. "Unraveling the Relationship Between 11QT, the Eschatological Temple, and the Qumran Community." *Revue de Qumran* 53:14:1 (June, 1989): 61-74.

Whitcomb, John C. "Daniel's Great Seventy-Weeks Prophecy: An Exegetical Insight." *Grace Theological Journal* 2:2 (Fall, 1981): 259-63.

————. "Christ's Atonement and Animal Sacrifices in Israel." *Grace Theological Journal* 6:2 (1985): 201-17.

Unpublished Works on the Future Temple

Carpenter, Eugene E. "The Eschatology of Daniel Compared with the Eschatology of Selected Intertestamental Documents." Ph.D. dissertation: Fuller Theological Seminary, 1978.

Chance, James B. "Jerusalem and the Temple in Lucan Eschatology." Ph.D. dissertation, Duke University, 1984.

De Santo, Pasquale. "A Study of Jewish Eschatology with Special Reference to the Final Conflict." Ph.D. dissertation, Duke University, 1957.

Eastman, Robert C. "A Correlation of the Three Accounts of the Olivet Discourse." Th.M. thesis, Dallas Theological Seminary, 1954.

Foos, Harold D. "Jerusalem in Prophecy." Th.D. dissertation: Dallas Theological Seminary, 1965.

Gaines, Elizabeth. "The Eschatological Jerusalem: The Function of the Image in the Literature of the Biblical Period." Ph.D. dissertation, Princeton Theological Seminary, 1980.

Hullinger, Jerry M. "A Proposed Solution to the Problem of Animal Sacrifices in Ezekiel 40–48." Th.D. dissertation, Dallas Theological Seminary, 1993.

Keist, John E. "Interpreting Christ's Prophecy Concerning the Fall of Jerusalem in Matthew 24 and Luke 21." Th.M. thesis, Dallas Theological Seminary, 1981.

Lane, William L. "Times of Refreshment: A Study of Eschatological Periodization in Judaism and Christianity." Ph.D. dissertation, Harvard University, 1962.

Martins, Elmer Arthur. "Motivations for the Promises of Israel's Restoration to the Land in Jeremiah and Ezekiel." Ph.D. dissertation, Claremont Graduate School, 1972.

Mayhue, Richard L. "The Prophet's Watchword: Day of the Lord." Th.D. dissertation, Grace Theological Seminary, 1981.

McLean, John A. "The Seventieth Week of Daniel 9:27 as a Literary Key for Understanding the Structure of the Apocalypse of John." Ph.D. dissertation, University of Michigan, 1990.

Mulholland, John H. "Principles of Eschatological Interpretation of the Apocalypse." Th.D. dissertation, Dallas Theological Seminary, 1959.

Price, J. Randall. "Theocratic Theodicy: The Eschatological Restoration of Israel in Ezekiel 36." Dallas Theological Seminary, 1981.

Scoggins, John M. "The New Jerusalem, The Bride of Christ." Th.M. thesis: Dallas Theological Seminary, 1976.

Scott, Malcolm M. "The Use of Daniel's Seventieth Heptad in the Apocalypse." Th.M. thesis: Dallas Theological Seminary, 1981.

Sit, Hong Chan. "The Eschatological Significance of the Post-Exilic Prophets," Th.D. dissertation, Northern Baptist Theological Seminary, 1957.

Wehmeyer, Donald A. "Toward Disaster in the Middle East: The Role of the Religious Futurists." Unpublished manuscript, Georgetown, Texas, 1987.

Williams, Richard A. "The Man of Sin in 2 Thessalonians 2:1-12." Th.D. disseration: Dallas Theological Seminary, 1966.

Sources for a Study of the Temple Movement

These sources include books, journal and magazine articles, essays, and unpublished theses on the personalities and plans of the Temple movement.

Andrews, Richard J. "The Political and Religious Groups Involved with Building the Third Temple in Jerusalem." M.A. thesis: Indiana University, 1995.

Ariel, Yisrael. *The Odyssey of the Third Temple*. Trans. and Adapted by Chaim Richman. Jerusalem: G. Israel Publications & Productions, Ltd., 1993.

Carmesund, Ulf. *Two Faces of the Expanding Jewish State: A Study on How Religious Motives Can Legitimate Two Jewish Groups Trying to Dominate Mount Moriah in Jerusalem*. Uppsala University Faculty of Theology Interdisciplinary Study, 1992.

Goren, Rav Shlomo. *Sepher Har-HaBayit: Meshiv Malachmah Heleq Rabi'i*. Jerusalem/Tel Aviv, 1992 (Hebrew).

Ice, Thomas and Price, Randall. *Ready to Rebuild: The Imminent Plan to Rebuild the Last Days Temple*. Eugene, OR: Harvest House Publishers, 1992.

Jerusalem Temple Conference. Lectures by prominent figures in the Temple movement in Israel recorded at the annual Temple conferences in Jerusalem (sponsored by Koinonia House/Chuck Missler). Set for each year (beginning in 1992) includes tape cassettes and assorted study notes, diagrams, and references. Koinonia House, P.O. Box D, Coeur d'Alene, ID 83816-0347.

Liebi, Roger. *Jerusalem–Hindernis für den Weltfrieden: Das Drama des jüdischen Tempels*. Schwengeler-Verlag, 1994.

McNeill, G. "An Unsettling Affair: Housing Conditions, Tenancy Regulations and the Coming of the Messiah in the Old City of Jerusalem" in *Arab Thought Forum. Occasional Research Papers*. Bir Zeit: Bur Zeit University, 1990.

Ostling, Richard N. "Time for a New Temple." *Time* 134:16 (October 16, 1989): 64-65.

Price, J. Randall. "Time for a Temple?: Jewish Plans to Rebuild the Temple." *Israel My Glory* (Temple issue) 55:6 (December/January 1997/98): 13-19.

———. *Jerusalem in Prophecy: God's Stage for the Final Drama*. Eugene, OR: Harvest House Publishers, 1998, esp. "God Comes Home: The Rebuilding of Jerusalem's Temple," pp. 247-79.

Ravitzky, Aviezer. *Messianism, Zionism, and Jewish Religious Radicalism*. Trans. Michael Swirsky and Jonathan Chipman. Chicago/London: University of Chicago Press, 1993.

Richman, Chaim. *The Mystery of the Red Heifer*. Jerusalem: Chaim Richman, 1997.

———. *The Light of the Temple*. Jerusalem: The Temple Institute, 1998.

Schmitt, John W. and Laney, Carl J. *Messiah's Coming Temple: Ezekiel's Prophetic Vision of the Future Temple*. Grand Rapids: Kregel Publications, 1997.

Shragai, Nadav. *The Temple Mount Conflict*. Jerusalem, 1995.

Spanier, Ehud, ed. *The Royal Purple and the Biblical Blue*. Jerusalem: Keter Publishing House, 1987.

Sprinzak, Ehud. *The Ascendance of Israel's Radical Right.* New York: Oxford University Press, 1991.

Stewart, Don and Missler, Chuck. *The Coming Temple.* Orange, CA: Dart Press, 1991.

"The Jerusalem Temple" (special issue). *Eretz* 46 (May–June, 1996): 5-74.

M'chon Harbotzas Torah, *The Pictorial Avodah Series* (various authors). Descriptive and pictorial guides to the sacrifices (as presented in the traditional Jewish texts): Korban Olah, Korban Mincha, Korban Chattas, Korban Shelamim, Laws of Tzoraas, Laws of Mitzora. Lakewood, NJ: C.I.S. Distributors.

Zuckerman, Mortimer B. "Should the Temple Be Rebuilt?" *Time* (June 30, 1967): 56.

Notes

Preface

1. Thomas Ice and Randall Price, *Ready to Rebuild: The Imminent Plan to Rebuild the Last Days Temple* (Eugene, OR: Harvest House Publishers, 1992).
2. Ibid., p. 15.
3. *The Desecration and Restoration of the Temple as an Eschatological Motif in the Tanach, Jewish Apocalyptic Literature and the New Testament* (Austin: The University of Texas, 1993) and (Michigan: University Microfilms Incorporated, 1994).
4. *In Search of Temple Treasures* (Eugene, OR: Harvest House Publishers, 1994).
5. "Prophetic Postponement in Daniel 9 and Other Texts," *Issues in Dispensationalism*, eds. Wesley Willis and John Masters (Chicago: Moody Press, 1992), pp. 132-65, "The Temple and the Scrolls," *Secrets of the Dead Sea Scrolls* (Eugene, OR: Harvest House Publishers, 1996), pp. 235-64, "The Temple: Political Propaganda or Proven Place," *The Stones Cry Out: What Archaeology Reveals about the Truth of the Bible* (Eugene, OR: Harvest House Publishers, 1997), pp. 175-202, "God Comes Home: The Rebuilding of Jerusalem's Temple," *Jerusalem in Prophecy: God's Stage for the Final Drama* (Eugene, OR: Harvest House Publishers, 1998), pp. 247-80, and "The Temple in the Book of Acts," *A Biblical Handbook to the Book of Acts*, ed. Mal Couch (Grand Rapids: Kregel Publishers, 1999).
6. *Dictionary of Premillennial Theology*. ed. Mal Couch (Grand Rapids: Kregel Publishers, 1997), pp. 109-118.
7. This first began as a newsletter in 1992 published by Biblical Awareness Ministries and in 1995 became a regular feature article in *The Messianic Times*, a leading messianic newspaper published in Ontario, Canada with an office and distribution in Jerusalem, Israel.

Chapter 1—Time for a Temple

1. Elise Ackerman, "Millennial madness, Jerusalem jitters," *U.S. News & World Report* (January 18, 1999): 33; for a comprehensive report with my commentary on these events see "Millennial Fever Threatens Temple Mount," *The Messianic Times* 9:4 (Winter 1999): 13.
2. As cited in "Millennial madness, Jerusalem jitters," by Elise Ackerman, *U.S. News & World Report* (January 18, 1999): 33.
3. Irving Greenberg, "Some Thoughts on the Meaning of the Restoration of Israel and Jerusalem for Days of Commemoration," in *Jerusalem: City of the Ages*, ed. Alice L. Eckardt (New York: American Academic Association for Peace in the Middle East, 1987), p. 281.
4. *Newsweek*, June 19, 1967, p. 30.
5. Cf. ad that appeared before the Six-Day War in the *Washington Post*, May 21, 1967, and statements of Rabbi Ginni Halb in stam, "The Beth Hamildosh," in *The Jewish Press*, August 2, 1968, pp. 19-20.
6. See Daniel Fuchs article in *Chosen People*, December, 1967, pp. 1-5; *The Christian and Christianity Today*, August 4, 1967, and articles in *Bibliotheca Sacra* by John Walvoord ("Will Israel Build a Temple in Jerusalem?" April, 1968, pp. 99-106); and Thomas McCall ("How Soon the Tribulation Temple?" October–December, 1971, pp. 341-51; and "Problems in Rebuilding the Tribulation Temple," January–March, 1972, pp. 75-80).
7. That is, all land west of the Jordan River, including Israel. Further testimony to this fact came in the January 1, 1991 statement by Salah Khalaf (Abu Iyad), the PLO's second-in-command, given at a Fatah Day celebration in Amman, Jordan: "Now we accept the formation of the Palestinian State in part of Palestine, in the Gaza Strip and West Bank. We start from that part and we will liberate Palestine, inch by inch."
8. Anne Marie Oliver and Paul Steinberg, "In the Forest of Symbols," *Jerusalem Post (Weekend Supplement)*, June 21, 1991, p. 22.
9. *Time* magazine (October 16, 1989), pp. 65-66.
10. Finding of the Zamir commission reported by David Bar-Illan in an article entitled, "Temple Mount Provocation," *Jerusalem Post International Edition*, August 10, 1991, p. 7.
11. This contention is supported by the investigation of the International Relations Task Force and the Mattus Heritage Institute in their report "Incident at the Temple Mount: Oct. 8, 1990."
12. Dr. Y.I. Hayutman, *HaYashan Yithadesh vehaHadash yitkadesh—he'arot leMashma'ut haMikdash* ("Let the Old be Renewed and the New Sanctified—insights into the Meaning of the Temple").
13. API interview reported in *Midland Times*, May 8, 1989.
14. As cited by Thomas S. McCall, "How Soon the Tribulation Temple?: Part 1," *Bibliotheca Sacra* 128:510 (April–June, 1971): 341.
15. Interview with Clarence Wagner, Mount of Olives, Jerusalem, November 12, 1998.
16. Richard N. Ostling, "Time for a New Temple?," *Time* magazine (October 16, 1989), p. 64.

17. As cited by Lee Underwood in "Israel in the News" (now "Tzemach News") (September 19, 1998), p. 1.

18. This interpretation depends on if this spiritual evaluation is setting these worshipers apart from other Jews who do not so worship, and not merely distinguishing them from the outer court given to the Gentiles, which is not measured.

19. Yirimayhu Fischer, "Editorial," *Mikdash-Build* 2:12 (April 21, 1998).

20. Interview with Elwood McQuaid, Lawrence Welk Resort, Escondido, California (September 21, 1998).

Chapter 2—The Purpose of the Temple

1. Rabbi Chaim Richman, *The Restoration* (Fall 1996), p. 3.

2. The Hebrew word *hekal* is derived from the root *ykl* or *kwl*, which has the basic meaning "to contain," cf. Brown, Driver, and Briggs, *Hebrew-English Lexicon of the Old Testament*, s.v. " ," p. 228. For further definition of the term see W. B. Kristensen, *The Meaning of Religion* (The Hague: Martinus Nijhoff, 1960), p. 369. If the literal idea of the root is retained in the noun *(hekal)*, it has been proposed that the term may connote the idea of the Temple as a "container" for the name of God, cf. Lorne Meisner, "The Temple Motif: God's Witness Unto Himself" (Th.M. thesis, Dallas Theological Seminary), p. 4.

3. In its most general sense, *hekal* sometimes was used to refer to a royal palace (1 Kings 21:1; 2 Chronicles 36:7), although its primary reference is to the "house of God." The more general word for "palace" is *'armon*, which signifies a *fortified* part of the royal complex (1 Kings 16:18; 2 Kings 15:25), but is never used with reference to the Temple. See Menahem Haran, *Temples and Temple Service in Ancient Israel* (Oxford: Clarendon Press, 1978), p. 13.

4. Cf. Anton Deimel, "Erdaufschuttung," *Sumerisch-Akkadisches Glossar Sumer-isches Lexikon* (Rome: Verlag Des Papstl. Bibelinstituts, 1934) 3/1, p. 206.

5. Liddell & Scott, *A Greek Lexicon*, p. 1774, refers specifically to a clearly marked area where a theophany once occurred and was again expected on the ground of tradition. Usually, it is a place distinguished by nature, e.g., the grotto of Zeus on Crete, the rock cleft at Delphi, or the holy grove at Olympia.

6. Haran concludes that the expression "arises from the basic concept of a divine residence and expresses the inherent, intrinsic nature of the institution, which primarily was conceived of as the god's dwelling place"—"Temples and Cultic Open Areas as Reflected in the Bible," *Temples and High Places in Biblical Times* (Jerusalem: The Nelson Glueck School of Biblical Archaeology of Hebrew Union College—Jewish Institute of Religion, 1977), p. 31.

7. The Hebrew term *mishkanot* (rendered in the English versions "tent," "dwellings") is used once in connection with shepherds (Song of Songs 1:8), and generally describes the dwellings of nomadic groups (Judges 6:3-5, cf. Ezekiel 25:4). The term is used in biblical poetry in parallelism with *'ohel* ("tent") Numbers 24:5; Isaiah 54:2; Jeremiah 30:18; Psalm 78:60; cf. Job 21:28, and also in the Ugaritic texts (though here as mythological residences of the gods, cf. 2 Aqht v. 31-3), C. H. Gordon, *Ugaritic Textbook* (Rome, 1965), p. 128, and Y. Avishur, *Semitics* [Pretoria] 2 (1971-2), pp. 19-20. Hillers has discovered the word *miskana'* in the Aramaic inscriptions of Hatra, D. R. Hillers, *Bulletin of the American Schools of Oriental Research* 206 (1972): 54-56, however, as Haran points out, *Temples and Temple Service*, p. 196, n. 12, its meaning in these inscriptions appears to be "abode," "dwelling place," rather than "tabernacle," or even "shrine."

8. The modern term apparently developed from the Mishnaic *beit miqdash* ("house of holiness"), the common phrase for the Temple, which has one biblical occurrence in 2 Chronicles 36:17.

9. The noun *miqdash* is not used exclusively of a temple, but also of any article or object possessing sanctity (e.g., the tithe, Numbers 18:29).

10. For example, Homeric usage in *Iliad* 1, 39; *Odyssey* 6, 10; 12, 346.

11. Moulton and Milligan, *The Vocabulary of the New Testament and Literary Papyri* suggests that *Koine* Greek, following classical usage, may have distinguished between the use of *heiron* (neuter of *heiron,* "holy [place]," used as a noun) and *naos*. The former may have had a wider and more general use, with reference to the entire edifice (i.e., the Temple complex with all of its courts), while the latter may have been restricted to the most sacred part of the Sanctuary (i.e., the *Devir)*—see Moulton and Milligan, *The Vocabulary of the New Testament and Literary Papyri,* s.v. "ναός," p. 422. This distinction may hold true for the New Testament, since the older term for the site of a "temple," τεμενός, is not used, cf. Otto Michel, *Theological Dictionary of the New Testament,* s.v. "ναός," p. 887. One example usually cited for support is Matthew 27:5, where ναός apparently refers to the Holy of Holies. However, this distinction is contested, since in other instances the two terms appear to be used interchangeably, e.g., John 2:20, where *naos* is here apparently used of the entire Temple, cf. Bauer, Arndt, Gingrich and Danker, *Greek-English Lexicon of the New Testament,* s.v. "ναός," p. 300.

12. See W. von Meding, *New International Dictionary of New Testament Theology,* s.v. "ναός," p. 783.

13. While *naos* can sometimes refer to both the Temple complex and the inner Sanctuary, it generally bears a technical distinction from *hieros*, which always appears to denote the general structure. The 45 occurrences of *naos* in the New Testament are divided among the historical books (9 times in Matthew; 3 in Mark; 4 in Luke; 3 in John; 2 in Acts), the

Pauline corpus (4 times in 1 Corinthians; 2 in 2 Corinthians; once each in Ephesians and 2 Thessalonians), and the Apocalypse (16 times in Revelation). For further discussion on this distinction, cf. Bauer, Arndt, Gingrich and Danker, *Greek-English Lexicon of the New Testament*, (1979), pp. 373.2, 535.1a, *Exegetical Dictionary of the New Testament*, s.v. "ναός," by U. Borse, p. 457, and A. T. Robertson, *Word Pictures in the New Testament* (Nashville: Broadman Press, 1932) 4:377; 5:38.

14. Note especially in Revelation 11:1-2 that the Temple is referred to as *ton naon tou theou*, and then in the next part of the verse reference is made to *ten aulen ten exothen tou naou* ("the court which is outside the Temple") as something separate. This outer precinct was thus outside the *naos*, but still within the *heiros*, indicating the specificity given to the terms.

15. Some English versions may use the translation "shrine" or "sanctuary" to distinguish pagan cultic installations.

16. Shaye J. D. Cohen, *From the Maccabees to the Mishna. Library of Early Christianity*, ed. by Wayne A. Meeks (Philadelphia: The Westminster Press, 1987), p. 106.

17. Ephraim E. Urbach, *The Sages: Their Concepts and Beliefs*, trans. Israel Abrahams, 2 vols. (Jerusalem: Magnes Press, 1975) 1:50.

18. Cf. R. E. Clements, *God and Temple* (Oxford: Basil Blackwell, 1965), pp. 63-78 (esp. 71, 83).

19. Cf. the brief discussion of this concept in Lucius Nereparampil, "Biblical Symbolism of the Temple," *Journal of Dharma* 9:2 (April–June 1984), pp. 164-66.

20. The reason for the specificity of Deuteronomy 12:9, the first such use of the Hebrew term *haminuchah* with a definite article, is that in Numbers 10:33 *minuchah* had described the *temporary* "resting places" where Israel was to camp during their wilderness sojourn, but with entrance to the Promised Land in view (Deuteronomy 12:10), *haminuchah*, a *permanent* resting place, is envisioned—i.e., a divine, God-given "rest."

21. Note in 1 Chronicles 22:9 that Solomon, before his birth, was appointed as a man of *minuchah* ("rest"), which in this text apparently parallels the bestowal of his name (cf. *shalom*, "peace"). The very next verse (verse 10) predicts Solomon's task as Temple-builder for the Lord's "name," thus connecting with the two passages discussed above.

22. For references to "rest" during the time of the conquest/judges cf. Joshua 21:43-45; 22:4-5; 23:1; Nehemiah 1:26-28. Second Samuel 7:10-11 cites the first promise of a central sanctuary made to Moses in Exodus 25:9, mentioning the temporary rest experienced during the period of the judges, and then linking the whole promise to fulfillment in the house of David. David appears to have believed that this rest was experienced in part during his reign (1 Chronicles 23:25-26), and Solomon recognized it as existing during his time with relation to the Temple (1 Kings 5:18 [5:4 in English]). Rest is also mentioned during the period of the monarchy during the reigns of Asa (2 Chronicles 14:4-6 [14:5-7 in English]; 15:15), Jehoshaphat (2 Chronicles 20:29-30), and Hezekiah (2 Chronicles 31:10).

23. Such a loss of rest was predicted in Deuteronomy 28:65 as a result of covenant unfaithfulness (cf. Psalm 95:10-11; Micah 2:7,10).

24. *Jerusalem to Jabneh: The Period of the Mishna and Its Literature* (Ramat-Aviv: Everyman's University, 1980), Unit I.3, p. 15.

25. Mishnah *Avodah Zarah* 8b and *Sanhedrin* 14b (the ruling is based on Deuteronomy 17:8).

26. All legal matters were decided by the Sanhedrin, who had their full prerogatives of office only when seated in the Temple, and only when the sacrificial system was operational.

27. Cf. for additional discussion on this concept, Jon. Levenson, "The Jerusalem Temple in Devotional and Visionary Experience," *Jewish Spirituality 1: From the Bible through the Middle Ages*, ed. Arthur Green (New York: Crossroad Publishing Co., 1988), pp. 53-57.

28. Cf. TP, *Berakot* 4, 5; cf. *Tosefta Berakot* 3, 15; *Pesiqta Rabbati* 149b.

29. TP, *Berakot* 4, 5.

30. While only a speculation, it may be that for a similar reason sacrifice was acceptable on the barren "Foundation Stone" within the Second Temple. Perhaps also because the Ark of the Covenant was thought to be buried in a hidden chamber directly below the Pen of Wood, and therefore directly below the Holy of Holies (cf. *Shekalim* 6:1-2), it thereby transferred sanctity to the region above, aligned with the true Ark in the heavenly Holy of Holies.

31. Cf. R. Aha, *Tanhuma*, Exodus; *Exodus Rabbah* 2:2; *Midrash*, Psalms 11:3.

Chapter 3—The Temple Before Time

1. Victor Aptowitzer, *The Celestial Temple As Viewed in the Aggadah* (Jerusalem: International Center for University Teaching of Jewish Civilization, 1980), p. 1.

2. This prayer should actually be called "The Disciple's Prayer," since it was taught by Jesus to His disciples at their request for a model prayer. Because it contains the words "forgive us our sins," it is doubtful that Jesus could ever have prayed

this prayer as the sinless Son of God. It was Jesus Himself who challenged the religious authorities (John 8:46), and the author of the book of Hebrews states that He was "tempted in all things as we are, yet without sin" (Hebrews 4:15).

3. For a listing and discussion of the relevant texts cf. Niels-Erik Andreasen, "The Heavenly Sanctuary in the Old Testament," *The Sanctuary and the Atonement*, ed. A. V. Wallenkampf and W. Richard Lesher (Washington, D.C., 1981), pp. 67-86.

4. The description in Ezekiel 1 is more of a throne-room than a temple; however, in the context, it appears that God has revealed Himself to Ezekiel in His Heavenly Temple as a dramatic contrast as He pronounces judgment upon the desecration of His earthly Temple (chapters 4–8).

5. J. Webb Mealy, "After the Thousand Years: Resurrection and Judgment in Revelation 20," *Journal for the Study of the New Testament Supplements* 70 (Sheffield: JSOT Press, 1993), pp. 143-62, 196-97.

6. For a separate study of this topic see C.T.R. Hayward, *The Jewish Temple: A Non-Biblical Sourcebook* (London and New York: Routledge, 1996).

7. Koehler-Baumgartner, s.v. "תבנית," *Lexicon in Vetevis Testament, Libros,* 3d ed. (Leiden: E.J. Brill, 1980), p. 1018.

8. The revelation of temples and cultic objects in dreams or visions is a well-known phenomenon. For biblical and extra-biblical sources, cf. J. Lindblom, *Prophecy in Ancient Israel* (Philadelphia: Fortress Press, 1962), pp. 173-82, according to Hurowitz, "Excursus," in "I Have Built You An Exalted House: Temple Building in the Bible in Light of Mesopotamian and Northwest Semitic Writings," *Journal for the Study of the Old Testament Supplements* 115 (University of Sheffield, Journal for the Study of the Old Testament, 1992), p. 168. Another way of revealing a plan of a cult object to its potential fashioner is by revealing a prototype. Hurowitz apparently views the revelation of the Temple in a distinct category from other revelatory experiences recorded in the Bible.

9. This view combines the idea of a replica with that of the actual heavenly Sanctuary, and was suggested by Umberto Cassuto, *A Commentary on the Book of Exodus* (Jerusalem: Magnes Press, 1970).

10. For a more detailed discussion of these interpretations cf. Richard M. Davidson, *Typology in Scripture* (Berrien Springs, MI: 1981), pp. 372-74.

11. *b. Men.* 29a, Rashi and Rambam to Exodus 25:9,40.

12. S. E. Loewenstamm, *Mishnah Encyclopedia Miqra 'it* V, col. 534, cites an incident from the Atrahasis myth in which Ea draws a picture of a boat for Atrahasis (who claims to have had no experience in boat making) as a parallel to the didactic function of the *tabnit,* cf. Lambert and Millard 1969: 128 DT 42 (W) 14-15: *[ina qaqlqari esir u[surtul [u.sur]tu Ilumurma giseeleppa [Iupus-]* "Draw the design on the ground that I may see [the design] and [build] the boat."

13. See V. Hurowitz, *op. cit.* pp. 168-70.

14. He cites these as references for uses of this meaning: Joshua 12:28; 1 Chronicles 28:18; cf. Ezekiel 8:3,10; 10:10: Deuteronomy 4:16-18; Psalm 106:20; 144:12; Isaiah 44:13.

15. Therefore, he sees two meanings for the term in Chronicles according to the context of its appearance. In verses 11, 12, and 19, it is the "blueprint" for what Solomon is to build, while in verse 18 it is the (earthly, yet to be constructed) replica of the heavenly dwelling. He also finds the word bears the same two meanings in 2 Kings 16:10, though simultaneously.

16. Angel Mañuel Rodríguez, "Sanctuary Theology in the Book of Exodus," *Andrews University Seminary Studies* 24:2 (Summer 1986): 142. From this understanding of the term, the *tabnit,* as a solid, three-dimensional object, could be either a miniature model or the real archetypal Sanctuary.

17. This view is also particularly popular today among scholars who utilize a comparative and tradition-history approach.

18. Paul Ellingworth, *The Epistle to the Hebrews: A Commentary on the Greek Text* (Grand Rapids: William B. Eerdmans Publishing Co., 1993), p. 408.

19. David Noel Freedman, "Temple Without Hands," *Temples and High Places in Biblical Times: Proceedings of the Colloquium in Honor of the Centennial of Hebrew Union College—Jewish Institute of Religion March* 14–16, 1977 (Jerusalem: The Nelson Glueck School of Biblical Archaeology of Hebrew Union College, 1981), p. 26. He bases his conclusion in this article on his exegesis of Exodus 15:1-18,21 and his connection of the divine sanctuary (made without hands) to Sinai, rather than as popularly associated, with Jerusalem and Mount Zion. He includes the insight of Benjamin Mazar on Exodus 3:5 that the expression *'adamat qadesh* ("holy ground") is not to be restricted to a few square meters on which Moses and the bush stood, but to the entire district which bore the name *Qadesh,* p. 24.

20. The Heavenly Temple also served as the archetype of the Edenic Sanctuary, as a comparison of Genesis 2 and Revelation 22 reveals (see chapter 9).

21. See Rodríguez, *op. cit.,* pp. 131-41, who develops this correspondence between Mount Sinai and the Tabernacle with the top of the mountain the Holy of Holies, the middle section as the Holy Place, and the base as the outer court (for graphic sketch, see p. 133). Cf. also Jacob Milgrom, *Studies in Levitical Terminology* 1 (Los Angeles, 1970), pp. 44-46, who also

identifies Mount Sinai as "the archetype of the tabernacle." We will expand on this correspondence in our discussion on the graded holiness of the Sanctuary in the next chapter.

22. The argument of the epistle of the Hebrews concerning the necessity of Jesus' heavenly priesthood is based on the premise that since He was descended from the tribe of Judah (cf. the genealogy through Joseph, Matthew 1:1-17; and through Mary, Luke 3:23-38), He was not qualified (Hebrews 8:4) to serve in the Aaronic priesthood in the earthly Sanctuary (Numbers 18:1-8,23; cf. Exodus 28:1). Therefore, His sphere of priestly service had to be in the heavenly Sanctuary, and His order of priesthood according to Melchizedek (Hebrews 5:4-10). The latter is based on an antitypical analogy drawn from Genesis 14:18-20. Melchizedekian traditions are also preserved in apocalyptic texts from Qumran, such as the Genesis Apocryphon (22:14) and the 11Q Melchizedek, in which Melchizedek, the heavenly figure of a divine redeemer, wrestles with Belial (lines 9–11). Cf. further, M. de Jonge and A. S. van der Woude, "11Q Melchizedek and the New Testament," *New Testament Studies* 12 (1966): 306; J. A. Fitzmyer, "Further Light on Melchizedek from Qumran Cave 11," *Essays on the Semitic Background of the New Testament* (London, 1971), pp. 245-67; and F.L. Horton, "The Melchizedek Tradition," *Society for New Testament Studies Monograph Series* 30 (Cambridge, 1976).

Chapter 4—The Temple Through Time

1. Mina C. Klein and H. Arthur Klein, *Temple Beyond Time: The Story of the Site of Solomon's Temple* (New York: Van Nostrand Reinhold Company, 1970), p. 23.

2. Carol L. Meyers, "The Elusive Temple," *Biblical Archaelogist* (Winter 1981), pp. 33, 41.

3. Explanation of Dan Bahat in an interview July 18, 1991, Jerusalem, Israel.

4. This is the traditional view of conservative scholarship. For a defense of the conservative position see Umberto Cassuto, *A Commentary on the Book of Exodus* (Jerusalem: Magnes Press, 1967), pp. 429-30. Critical scholarship, which views the entire narrative concerning the wilderness Sanctuary as an idealized portrayal (i.e., non-historical), sees the "Tent of Meeting" as evidence of a non-priestly source (JE) in contrast to the Tabernacle as a priestly source (P). They would see the "Tent of Meeting" as a more primitive structure used solely for revelation and the Tabernacle as a later tradition used strictly for cultic worship. The problems here are the references to bringing sacrifices to the "Tent of Meeting" (Leviticus 1:3, et. al.), but according to the Documentary Hypothesis this merely reflects the confusion of an editor attempting to insert conflicting sources. For an example of a higher-critical scholar who holds to the Documentary Hypothesis but does not believe the Tabernacle was a fictionalized projection of the Temple see Hebrew University professor Menahem Haran, *The Temple and Temple-Service in Ancient Israel* (Oxford: Oxford University Press, 1978), pp. 195ff.

5. For further discussion see my "The Tabernacle Beneath the Temple" in *In Search of Temple Treasures* (Eugene, OK: Harvest House Publishers, 1994), p. 193.

6. For a discussion on this see Richard E. Friedman, "The Tabernacle in the Temple," *Biblical Archaeologist* (Fall 1980): 241-42, and V. Rabe, *The Temple as Tabernacle* (Ph.D. dissertation, Harvard University, 1963), pp. 35ff.

7. David M. Levy, *The Tabernacle: Shadows of the Messiah, Its Sacrifices, Services, and Priesthood* (Bellmawr, NJ: The Friends of Israel Gospel Ministry, 1993), p. 19.

8. According to one Jewish source, the Tabernacle served in the desert for 39 years, in Gilgal for 14 years, as a roofless building in Shiloh for 369 years, and as interim structures in Nov and Giv'on for 57 years.

9. Mishneh Torah, *Hilchot Beit HaBechira* ("Laws of the Temple"), 7:11.

10. Because the building of the Temple in Jerusalem was seen to be inspired in the heart of David by God (Psalm 132:1-5; 1 Chronicles 12:13; 28:19; 2 Samuel 7:1-2), and thereby came to be seen as the historic choice of God Himself (1 Kings 11:32, 36; 14:21).

11. H. G. M. Williamson, "The Temple in the Book of Chronicles," *Templum Amicitiae: Essays on the Second Temple presented to Ernst Bammel,* Journal for the Study of the New Testament 48, ed. William Horbury (Sheffield, 1991), pp. 22-25, cites as reasons for the chronicler's connection of the site of the Temple with Mount Moriah as being: 1) "Moriah" may by a popular form of etymology be understood as "the vision of the Lord or the like, comparable to the appellative used of the mountain in Genesis 22:14"; 2) First Chronicles 21:22-25 patterns David's purchase of the threshing floor of Ornan (Araunah) the Jebusite after Abraham's purchase of the cave of Machpelah in Genesis 23:3-20; e.g., the grammatical parallels: the use of the expression *bekesef male'* ("at its full price"), Genesis 23:9/1 Chronicles 21:22; the use of the verb *natan* ("buy") Genesis 23:4, 9/1 Chronicles 21:22, and literary parallels: David, like Abraham, initiating the conversation (Genesis 23:3/1 Chronicles 21:22); the double emphasis in both accounts on the desire to "give" the site (Genesis 23:11/ 1 Chronicles 21:23); 3) perhaps based on this pattern, from the dispute over the cave as part of the field required in the purchase, the extension is made to include the threshing floor as part of the mountain in David's purchase; 4) according to the biblical text, the cave of Machpelah was the *only* piece of real estate secured by the patriarchs in the Promised

Land, a distinction which gave it a traditional significance and value; 5) Second Chronicles 3:1 connects these accounts by explicitly stating that Solomon built the Temple "on Mount Moriah, where [God] had appeared to his father David…on the threshing floor of Ornan the Jebusite." It is important in this respect to note that the Genesis 22 text does not explicitly say Abraham built his altar on the mountain, but, this was assumed by the chronicler, possibly with a polemical thrust against the Molech cult, which practiced human sacrifice in the area, since Genesis 22 was viewed as a statement against such practice; 6) the chronicler saw a need to provide a continuity between the site of the Temple as a new acquisition with the Nation's earliest history in the Land.

12. For a popular account of Phœnician influence see Clifford Wilson, "Solomon and Israel's Golden Age: Part 1—Solomon's Temple," *Bible and Spade* 1:2 (Spring 1972): 43-47.

13. For details of this Temple see the excellent article by Sara Japhet, "The Temple in the Restoration Period: Reality and Ideology," *Union Seminary Quarterly Review* 44:3-4 (1991): 195-252, which provides the most complete survey of material to date.

14. This may also be assumed from pottery models of temple-like shrines that have a porch supported by two pillars and a idol within. A good example is an Iron Age IIB model from Idalion, Cyprus.

15. See G. Ernest Wright, "The Archaeology of Solomon's Temple," *Biblical Archaeology* (Westminister/John Knox Press, 1962), p. 137.

16. See Victor Hurowitz, "Inside Solomon's Temple," *Bible Review* 10:2 (April 1994): 24-37.

17. This calculation is based on the royal cubit, which was about 20.9 inches.

18. For details on this inscription see P. Bordreuil, F. Israel, and D. Pardee, "King's Command and Widow's Plea: Two New Hebrew Ostraca of the Biblical Period," *Near Eastern Archaeology* 61:1 (1998): 3-7.

19. Arnaud Sérandour, "King, Priest, and Temple," *Near Eastern Archaeology* 61:1 (1998): 6.

20. These continual relapses into idolatry led the rabbis to interpret 2 Samuel 20:1 "Every man *to his tents*, O Israel" as if it had been originally read "Every man *to his gods*, O Israel" (Midrash on 2 Samuel, 42b § 4, and *Mechilta* 39a).

21. Cf. Herbert G. May, "The Departure of the Glory of Yahweh," *Journal of Biblical Literature* 56 (1937): 309- 21.

22. Cf. Martin Noth, "The Jerusalem Catastrophe of 587 B.C. and Its Significance for Israel," in *The Laws in the Pentateuch and Other Essays* (Philadelphia: Fortress Press, 1967): 260-80.

23. Josephus Flavius, *Antiquities of the Jews*, Book XI, ch. 1:2.

24. However, cf. the excellent article by Sara Japhet, "The Temple in the Restoration Period: Reality and Ideology," *Union Seminary Quarterly Review* 44:3-4 (1991):195-252, which provides the most complete survey of material to date.

25. Josephus Flavius, *Contra Apion* 2:23, sec. 193.

26. Tacitus, *Historiae* 5, 9: 1.

27. According to John 2:20, in the time of Jesus it was remarked that it had taken "46 years to build this Temple." Josephus, writing from a later period in the first century noted that additional work projects had continued at the site after the time mentioned in the Gospel of John and up until only a few years before the Temple's destruction in A.D. 70.

28. Remains of this exist today as the Western Wall, more than 1,000 feet of which are extant beneath the present Western Wall Plaza and Moslem Quarter. Some of the largest building stones in Israel have been discovered at this retaining wall, one of which is an estimated 458 tons. Such huge stones apparently were set as "shock absorbers" to stabilize the Temple platform in the instance of earthquakes, which are frequent in this area (from an on-site excavation report, July 1992, by excavation director Dan Bahat, Western Wall Heritage Foundation, Jerusalem).

29. For the most accurate description of the Second Temple cf. Leen and Kathleen Ritmeyer, *Reconstructing Herod's Temple Mount in Jerusalem* (Washington, D.C.: Biblical Archaeology Society, 1991); *A Model of Herod's Temple* (London: Ritmeyer Archaeological Design, 1993); and *Secrets of Jerusalem's Temple Mount* (Washington, D.C.: Biblical Archaeology Society, 1998).

30. Jacob Neusner, *First Century Judaism in Crisis* (Nashville/New York: Abingdon Press, 1975), p. 21.

31. As recorded by Eusebius, the Bishop of Caesarea in his *Ecclesiastical History* III.5.3.

32. Cf. Josephus, *Jewish Wars* 6:290ff; *TB*, Yoma 39b [cf. citations above]; *TJ*, Yoma 43c; Tacitus, *Historiae* 5, 13; Matthew 27:51/Mark 15:38/Luke 23:45.

33. Josephus, *Jewish War*, Loeb Classical Library 210, trans. H. St. J. Thackery (Cambridge: Harvard University Press, 1928), III:461-63.

34. Some commentators also have connected the reference in Acts 6:7b to Temple priests who "became obedient to the Faith [i.e., Christianity]" with this event, supposing that their faith in Jesus may have resulted from their witnessing the rent veil during their time of service.

35. Michael Avi-Yonah and Menahem Stern, "Jerusalem: History of the Second Temple Period," *EJ* 9:1379.

36. See Lawrence Schiffman, "Jewish Sectarianism in Second Temple Times," *Great Schisms in Jewish History,* ed. R. Jospe (1981), pp. 1-46.

37. Evidence of this army's presence has recently been located in the excavation of a camp of the Tenth Legion (which destroyed the city and Temple) outside Jerusalem. In addition, the Vespasian-Titus Inscription discovered in 1970 on a stone column near the Temple Mount commemorates the father emperor and son general of the Tenth Legion as well as Silva, the Roman commander of the Tenth Legion, who attacked the Jews who had fled to Masada in A.D. 73. See Benjamin Mazar, "Archaeological Excavations Near the Temple Mount," *Jerusalem Revealed,* ed. Yigael Yadin (Jerusalem: Israel Exploration Society, 1975), p. 33.

38. One evidence of this burning and slaughter has been uncovered in the present Jewish Quarter of the Old City of Jerusalem and is open to tourists—it is known as "the Burnt House."

39. For pictures and a discussion of this excavation with the Israeli director of the excavation, Ronny Reich, see my book *The Stones Cry Out: What Archaeology Reveals About the Truth of the Bible* (Eugene, OR: Harvest House Publishers, 1997), pp. 194-96.

Chapter 5—The Temple in Transition

1. Rambam, *The Laws of the Temple* 7:7.

2. See K.W. Clark, "Worship in the Jerusalem Temple After A.D. 70," New Testament Studies 6 (1960): 269-80.

3. F.E. Peters, *Jerusalem* (New Jersey: Princeton University Press, 1985), p. 122.

4. R.M. Smallwood, *The Jews under Roman Rule: From Pompey to Diocletian* (Leiden: E.J. Brill, 1976), pp. 434-36.

5. Rabbi Leibel Reznick, *The Mystery of Bar Kokhba: A Historical and Theological Investigation of the Last King of the Jews* (New Jersey: Jason Aronson, Inc., 1996).

6. Ibid., p. 73.

7. Rabbi Leibel Reznick, *The Holy Temple Revisited* (New Jersey: Jason Aronson Inc., 1990), p. 156.

8. Ibid., p. 157.

9. Rabbi Leibel Reznick, *The Mystery of Bar Kokhba: A Historical and Theological Investigation of the Last King of the Jews* (New Jersey: Jason Aronson Inc., 1996), pp. 77-79.

10. *Paschal Chronicle* P.G. 92, 613; cf. also, Benjamin Mazar, *The Mountain of the Lord* (New York: Doubleday & Co., 1975), p. 236.

11. Dio Cassius, *Roman History,* lxix: 12.

12. Jerome, *Commentary on Isaiah* 2:9.

13. John Wilkinson, "Christian Pilgrims in Jerusalem During the Byzantine Period," *Palestinian Exploration Quarterly* 108 (1976): 77.

14. St. Jerome, *Commentary to the Book of Zephaniah* (cited in: *The Forgotten Generations: Twenty Centuries of Jewish Life in the Holy Land,* ed. Dan Bahat (Jerusalem: *The Israel Economist,* 1975, p. 18).

15. Jeffrey Brodd, "Julian the Apostate and His Plan to Rebuild the Jerusalem Temple," *Bible Review* 11:5 (October 1995): 38. Julian makes the connection with Jewish sacrifices in the Jerusalem Temple in his Julian contra the Galilaeans, *The Works of the Emperor Julian,* trans. W.C. Wright (London: William Heinemann, 1913-1926), 3: pp. 404-7.

16. In Julian's letter *To the High-Priest Theodorus.*

17. *Letter to the Community of the Jews,* no. 51, 396-398 in W.C. Wright, *The Works of the Emperor Julian* (3 vols. 1913-1923).

18. As recorded by the sixth-century historian Lydus in his *De Mensibus;* as cited in Julian, *The Works of the Emperor Julian,* trans. W.C. Wright (London: William Heinemann, 1913-1926), 3: 301-2.

19. Ammianus Marcellinus in *Ammianus Marcellinus,* trans. John C. Rolfe (London: William Heinemann, 1939), 2: 23.1,2.

20. Jerusalem Talmud, *Ta'anim* 65a; *Hor.* 47c; *Yoma* 21b.

21. Jerusalem Talmud, *Ma'as. Shabbat* 56a.

22. Gregory of Nazianzus, Oratio V contra Julianum, 4, in *Julian the Emperor,* trans. C.W. King (London: George Bell & Sons, 1888).

23. Ephraem of Syria, *Hymni contra Julianum* 1.16 and 2.7.

24. Meir Ben-Dov, *In the Shadow of the Temple: The Discovery of Ancient Jerusalem* (New York: Harper & Row, Publishers, 1982), p. 219.

25. Philip C. Hammond, "New Light on the Nabateans," *Biblical Archaeology Review* (March/April, 1981), p. 23.

26. Ammianus Marcellinus in *Ammianus Marcellinus,* trans. John C. Rolfe (London: William Heinemann, 1939), 2: 23.1,3.

27. Reverend Warburton, *Julian or a Discourse concerning the Earthquake and Fiery Eruption which Defeated that Emperor's Attempt to Rebuild the Temple at Jerusalem* (London: J. & P. Knapton, 1750), pp. 156-59.

28. From a chronicle composed by the Syrian monk Bar-Yoma, published in *Revue de l'Orient Chretien* (1913-1914).

29. Avi-Yonah, *The Jews of Palestine: A Political History from the Bar Kokhba War to the Arab Conquests* (Oxford: Basil Blackwell, 1976), p. 266.

30. As quoted in *America and Palestine*, ed. Reuben Fink (New York: American Zionist Emergency Council, 1944), p. 88.

31. See "The Struggle for the Temple Mount" in *Mikdash-Build* 1:18 (16 Shvat 5757), translated from *Yibane HaMikdash* 110; originally in *Darchei Torah*.

32. Ibid.

33. Interview with Gershon Salomon, home in Jerusalem, October 19, 1994.

34. Israel Eldad, *Jerusalem: A Challenge*, as cited in *Mikdash-Build* 2:13 (April 1998): 1-2.

Chapter 6—The Holy Hope

1. *Guide to the Treasures of the Temple Exhibition* (Jerusalem: The Temple Institute), p. 3.

2. Ibid.

3. Krister Stendahl, *Bulletin of the Harvard Divinity School* (Autumn 1967).

4. The law enforcing this came in 1997 as the result of a bill sponsored by NRP MK Shaul Yahalom, chairman of the Constitution, Law and Justice Committee, after a Tel Aviv court canceled an existing municipal bylaw forbidding the opening of places of entertainment on the eve of the Tisha B'Av (as reported by Arutz-7 News, July 29, 1997).

5. Leo Trepp, *Judaism: Development and Life*. 3rd ed. (California: Wadsworth Publishing Co., 1982), p. 112.

6. Rabbi Abraham Isaac Kook as cited by Galtzer in *The Dynamics of Emancipation*, p. 54. For the full quotation see Trepp, *Judaism*, pp. 112-13.

7. Chaim Kramer, *Mashiach: Who? What? Why? How? Where? And When?* (Jerusalem/New York: Breslov Research Institute, 1994), pp. 53, 55, 56.

8. Dr. Morris Goldman, Tel Aviv in "Letters," *The Jerusalem Post International Edition* (April 9, 1999), p. 11.

9. Quoted in *Time* (October 16, 1989), p. 65.

10. Associated Press story by Paula Story, "Reform Judaism leaders urge return to traditional values," *San Antonio Express-News*, Thursday, May 27, 1999, p. 10A.

11. Ibid.

12. Interview with Chaim Richman, June 23, 1991.

13. Yitzhak I. Hayutman, "Why the Temple Is Not Being Rebuilt Today," website at http://numbers.tripod.com/TheHOPE/ACADEMY.htm.

14. Interview with Gershon Salomon, Office of the Temple Mount and Land of Israel Faithful Movement, Jerusalem, November 4, 1998.

15. This, of course, assumes a uniform rate of decline; however, there are forces at work today that threaten to rapidly accelerate this trend. One factor is the 52 percent rate of Jewish intermarriage, in which marriages three out of every four children are being raised outside of the Jewish faith or with no religion at all. This is contrasted to 1964, in which only 9 percent of all marriages were interfaith marriages. This trend, combined with a below-replacement birthrate, a rising tide of divorce, and a virtual end to immigration, is shrinking the Jewish community. A second factor is the resurgence of Nazi (not neo-Nazi) anti-Semitism in the United States, France, and Germany as well as other parts of Europe. The November 21, 1992 edition of the *Jerusalem Post* magazine featured the rise of German Nazi anti-Semitism with the by-line "Time to Leave Germany Again?" Other forms of anti-Semitism, particularly among professing Christian denominations and White Supremacy groups, as well as incipient anti-Semitism in current America's foreign policy toward Israel (Jerusalem, which is recognized as Israel's capital by Israel, is not considered a part of Israel by the U.S. State Department) further contributes to a growing ostracization of Jews in America.

16. *Newsweek* magazine, July 22, 1991, p. 48.

17. Irving Greenberg, "Some Thoughts on the Meaning of the Restoration of Israel and Jerusalem for Days of Commemoration," in *Jerusalem: City of the Ages*, ed. Alice L. Eckardt (New York: American Academic Association for Peace in the Middle East, 1987), p. 281.

18. *Jerusalem Post*, April, 1991.

19. This prohibition is not only for Jews, but extends to Gentiles as well. It includes not only entrance for prayers, but also for tourism and archaeological investigation.

20. HaRav David Bar Haim, "The Torah of Geula (Part III)," *Your Jerusalem* 12:4 (September-October, 1998): 2.

21. Yitzhak I. Hayutman, *HaYashan Yithadesh vehaHadash yitkadesh—he'arot leMashma'ut haMikdash* ("Let the Old Be Renewed and the New Sanctified—Insights into the Meaning of the Temple").

22. Excerpt from Yitzhak I. Hayutman, lecture in English at the Israel Center in Jerusalem, July 1990.

23. Ibid.

24. Interview in the *Jerusalem Post,* October 17, 1989.
25. Interview with Nahman Kahane, June 23, 1991.
26. As cited in Joan Comay's *The Temple of Jerusalem* (New York: Holt, Rinehart and Winston, 1975), p. 263.
27. Rabbi Yisrael Ariel, "A Heaven-Sent Temple: In Halakha a Heaven-Sent Temple," translated and ed. Israel Fuchs, senior editor, *B'tzedek,* in "Helping to Build the Holy Temple: The Third Temple in Jerusalem" from website www.btzedek.co.il.
28. Yirmiyahu Fischer, reply in explanation as to why the Orthodox do not begin to rebuild the Temple today, *Mikdash-Build* journal, October 1997.
29. Interview with Chaim Richman, June 25, 1991.
30. Interview with the *Jerusalem Post,* October 17, 1989.
31. Rabbi Yose in a Braita on tractate Sanhedrin 20b.
32. Rambam, in *Hilchot Melachim* 1:2, held that the coming of the Messiah and his appointing a Davidic king precedes the rebuilding of the Temple.
33. Yirmiyahu Fischer, Mikdash-Build 1:20 (February 14, 1997), pp. 6-7.
34. Interview with Gershon Salomon, Office of the Temple Mount and Land of Israel Faithful Movement, Jerusalem, November 4, 1998.
35. As cited by Yirmiyahu Fischer in *Mikdash-Build* 2:2 (October 12, 1998): 1.

Chapter 7—The Christian Connection

1. Irenaeus, *Against Heresies:* Book v, Chapter 30, Paragraph 4.
2. See Amborse commentary on Hebrews 8:2, and Gregory of Nazianus, *Ad Julianum,* also alluding to Hebrews 8:2.
3. Robert L. Wilken, "Jerusalem, Emperor Julian, and Christian Polemics" in *Jerusalem: City of the Ages,* ed. Alice L. Eckardt (Lanham, MD: University Press of America, 1987):242.
4. Ibid., p. 243.
5. Jeffrey Brodd, "Julian the Apostate and His Plan to Rebuild the Jerusalem Temple," *Bible Review* 11:5 (October 1995): 34.
6. I prefer not to classify one view as "Dispensational" and the other as "Reformed," because many of those in the dispensational camp hold to a reformed soteriology and ecclesiology, and in some cases even classic covenantalism, while some Reformed scholars may hold to a spiritual restoration of ethnic Israel distinct from the church (see John Murray, *The Epistle to the Romans,* New International Commentary on the New Testament, (Grand Rapids: Wm. B. Eerdmans Publishing Co., 1973), pp. 96-99. Nevertheless, the Reformed tradition has viewed biblical history based on theological convenants (redemption, works, grace), whereas the Dispensational tradition has viewed history within the revealed program of God in Scripture, which includes separate fulfillments for Israel and the church.
7. Edmund P. Clowney, "The Final Temple," *Prophecy in the Making: Messages Prepared for the Jerusalem Conference on Biblical Prophecy,* ed. Carl F. H. Henry (Carol Stream, IL: Creation House, 1971), p. 85.
8. David Chilton, *Paradise Restored: An Eschatology of Dominion* (Tyler: Reconstruction Press, 1985):224.
9. Gary DeMar, *Last Days Madness: Obsession of the Modern Church* (Atlanta, GA: American Vision, Ins., 1994), pp. 76, 8.
10. Hans Conzelmann, *The Theology of St. Luke* (London: SCM Press, 1982), p. 165.
11. See Markus Bockmuehl, "Why Did Jesus Predict the Destruction of the Temple?," *Crux* xxv: 3 (September, 1989), pp. 11-17. Holding to the same interpretation for Jesus' predictions, yet without the element of judgment, is E. P. Sanders, *Jesus and Judaism* (London: SCM Press, 1985), pp. 85-88, who notes "the naturalness of the connection between expecting a new temple and supposing that the old one will be destroyed" (p. 85).
12. See Joachim Jeremias, *Jerusalem in the Time of Jesus,* trans. F. H. & C. H. Cave (London: SCM Press, 1969), pp. 193-94, 377-78.
13. Those who argue that the Temple was of secondary importance do so with the thinking that the synagogue had replaced the Temple as the center of worship—see George Foot Moore, *Judaism in the First Centuries of the Christian Era* (Cambridge: Harvard University Press, 1930), 2: 13ff; and R. T. Herford, *Pharisaism* (New York: Putman, 1912), pp. 27ff. However, the two institutions were never in conflict, the synagogue arising from the Temple and during Second Temple times serving as a means for those outside Jerusalem to participate in the Temple cult. Synagogue services corresponded to the Temple liturgy, and were a constant reminder of the prominent place of the Jerusalem Temple both before and after its destruction. In later Jewish thinking the synagogue, and the home as well, served as a microcosm of the Temple, re-enforcing rather than replacing its importance in Jewish theology and worship.
14. E. P. Sanders, *The Historical Figure of Jesus* (New York: The Penguin Press, 1993), p. 262.
15. Scholarly consensus is that Luke-Acts, if even written by the same author, were composed by a Gentile writing outside of Palestine after A.D. 70. However, it will not do, as Dawsey *(op. cit.),* points out, to posit that a Gentile, writing after

A.D. 70, presumably to a Gentile audience (note address to "Theophilus," Luke 1:3; Acts 1:1) borrowed a positive view of the Temple from Judaism and incorporated it into both the gospel and the history of Christianity.

16. Based on the description of the site from the ancient sources, and especially Josephus, *Antiquities* 20.221, the Stoa of Solomon was a colonaded nave 667 feet long situated on the eastern side of the Temple complex at the deepest descent from Mount Moriah into the Kidron Valley.

17. Such specificity of purpose here must indicate the high esteem held by these for the Temple and not simply be incidental to the events which transpire as the drama of the story *contra* Calvin, who supposed that the reason for going to the Temple was because it offered the best opportunity for missionary work (incorrectly assumed by the command of Acts 5:20 to preach at the Temple). That prayer, and not missionary endeavor, was the purpose of the assembly is made clear by Acts 5:13, which indicates that "the rest" (λοιπῶν = ὁ λαός) "[did not] associate, join, with" (κολλᾶσθαι in the sense of spatial proximity) them out of esteem for their piety and the miracles they performed.

18. We must remember that at this time the early disciples of Jesus were all observant Jews. Peter is particularly revealed as such (see Acts 10:14; Galatians 2:7, 11-14). Even at the Jerusalem Council, still years away, the *kasrut* laws are still applied through the Noahic covenant to the Gentile converts to the Jewish Messiah (Acts 15:19-21; 28–29), a proviso that was agreed to by even the most observant among the group (Acts 15:5 with verse 22). It is very difficult to defend any position of these Jewish believers other than that they continued to reverence the Temple as the place designated by God for daily prayers. Just as Jesus' condemnation of the Jewish Nation had not led them to abandon their country, so Jesus' announcement of the Temple's destruction had not caused them to reject it as valid.

19. Later, in Acts 10:14, Peter's adherence to *kashrut* laws is presented in his denial: "I have never eaten anything unholy (κοίνον = חבר and חלל, 'profane, ceremonially unclean') and unclean (ἀκαθαρτόν, = טמא, 'ceremonially impure')."

20. This observation, at least, ought to balance the thinking of those like Sandmel, who regarded John as the most anti-Semitic of the Gospels.

21. W. O. E. Oesterley, *The Jewish Background of the Christian Liturgy* (Oxford: Clarendon Press, 1925), p. 96.

22. The text in Matthew 21:43 does not warrant this interpretation, especially in light of the subsequent parable of the wicked husbandman in 22:1-14, which it introduces. There is no reason to go outside a Jewish context for this idea of replacement. The better understanding of this pronouncement of Jesus is that those from whom "the kingdom will be taken away" are unbelieving Jews who controlled establishment Judaism. Verse 45 explicitly says, "And when the chief priests and the Pharisees heard His parables, they understood that He was speaking about them." Therefore, "the nation" to whom this kingdom will be given is the believing Jewish remnant. Certainly Jews "producing the fruit of it" (the Jewish Nation) fits more naturally with the context and accords with other New Testament texts (see Romans 11:11-15,26-27) which understand the restoration promises to Israel in the future of a spiritually revived remnant whose faith is in Jesus as their Messiah. This is more plausible than replacing Israel with the church, which has been predominantly Gentile throughout its history, as fulfilling promises made to the Jewish Nation.

23. Eusebius, *Ecclesiastical History*, trans. Kirshop Lake, Loeb Classical Library (New York: G. Putnam's Sons, 1926-1932), 2. xxiii.

24. This concept was of an earthly Messianic reign preceding the eternal state, sometimes of a thousand years duration, as at Revelation 20:4, but also of varying length—see J. W. Bailey, "The Temporary Messianic Reign in the Literature of Early Judaism," *Journal of Biblical Literature* 53 (July, 1934): 170-87. This literal hope of restoration was even shared by Philo, though accustomed to allegorization of Jewish religious beliefs) nevertheless could write: "The cities that now lay in ruins will be cities once more," *De Praemiis et Poenis*, p. 168. For the documentation of this view of an eschatological earthly kingdom at Qumran see Shemaryahu Talmon, *The World of Qumran from Within: Collected Studies* (Jerusalem: Magnes Press, 1989), pp. 300ff.

25. The terms in Acts 3:20-21 are drawn from the language of the prophetic discourses. The phrase in verse 20, καιροὶ ἀναψύξεως, is parallel with the phrase χρόνων ἀποκαταστάσεως in verse 21. The former use of ἀνάψυξις is attested in the LXX only in Exodus 8:15 where it must have the sense of "respite," following רוחה. The idea, then, is of a "respite" from Gentile oppression through the deliverance from Gentile domination accompanying the advent of the Messiah (see Zechariah 12–14). This domination was considered a judgment from God for past apostasy (see Deuteronomy 28:36,47-50) that would find a reversal with Israel's restoration (see Isaiah 11:11-12; see also Luke 21:24; Romans 11:25).

26. Robert H. Gundry, *Matthew: A Commentary on His Literary and Theological Arts*, p. 392.

27. The term in its New Testament usage and context clearly indicates an era yet future—see *Theological Dictionary of the New Testament*, s.v. "παλλιγγενέσια," by Friedrich Buschel, ed. G. Kittel (Grand Rapids: William B. Eerdmans, 1974) 1:686-89, and F. W. Burnett, "Palingenesia in Matt. 19:28: A Window on the Matthean Community?" *Journal for the Study of the New Testament* 17 (February, 1983): 60-72.

28. The role of the disciples would be governors functioning as tribal judges (see 2 Kings 15:5; Psalm 2:10; Isaiah 1:26), sim-
    ilar to the traditional role of the phylarchs, the princes of the 12 tribes, who would rule over Israel in the period of the
    restoration as depicted at Qumran (e.g., 1QM 3:3; 5:1-2), and the apocalyptic literature (e.g., Testament of the Twelve
    Patriarchs—Testament of Judah 25:1-2; Testament of Benjamin 10:7), see William Horbury, "The Twelve and the Phy-
    larchs," *New Testament Studies* 32 (1986): 503-27, esp. pp. 512, 524.

29. The temporal phenomenon parallels the condition that exists within the heavenly New Jerusalem (Revelation 22:1-2)
    because the restoration to the divine ideal is in this way shown to be fulfilled in the earthly Temple finally conformed to
    its heavenly archetype. That these two descriptions are not to be identified as the same may be seen in Ezekiel's
    emphasis on the Temple, called "the house" (Ezekiel 47:1) and "the sanctuary" (Ezekiel 47:12), contrasted with Revela
    tion's emphasis on "no temple" (Revelation 21:22).

30. Even though the early Jewish-Christian community expected Israel's restoration, they knew that it awaited the prede-
    termined time of God and that they were to spread the good news about Messiah from Jerusalem throughout the
    Roman empire (Acts 1:8). They did not know when the Temple would be destroyed or that the age of the church would
    stretch now to 2,000-plus years. They only knew that when national Israel finally repented that the Messiah and the
    Messianic kingdom would arrive. The imminent hope of the rapture was revealed to Paul and seen as belonging
    uniquely to the church apart from Israel. This was not in conflict with the hope of Israel's restoration but was an addi-
    tional hope that stabilized the early Jewish church in the midst of persecution.

31. E. P. Sanders, *Jesus and Judaism* (Philadelphia: Fortress Press, 1985), pp. 87, 103.

32. Luke, as a historian in the manner of Thucydides, has reported factual information based on the actual events,
    obtaining access to the details from Paul, who presided over Stephen's trial (Acts 7:58; 8:1-2) or perhaps from members
    of the Sanhedrin who later became Christians; see J. J. Scott, Jr., "Stephen's Speech: A Possible Model for Luke's Histor-
    ical Method?" *Journal of the Evangelical Theological Society* 17 (1974): 93; M. H. Scharlemann, "Stephen's Speech: A Lucan
    Creation?" *Concordia Journal* 4 (1978): 57. The speech probably was preserved in a fixed oral or written tradition, since it
    is not thought to be a verbatim account of the speech. This is revealed in an analysis of the speech, which reveals that in
    word choice, at least 23 words that do not occur elsewhere in Acts or any other New Testament book, and in Lucan con-
    structions, numerous typical literary forms peculiar to Luke-Acts are here absent—see J. Kilgallen, "The Stephen
    Speech: A Literary and Redactional Study of Acts 7, 2-53," *Analecta Biblica* 67 (Rome: Pontifical Biblical Institute Press,
    1976), p. 113; Simon J. Kistemaker, "The Speeches in Acts," *Criswell Theological Review* 5:1 (1990): 34-35.

33. A partial listing is as follows: verse 3 (Genesis 12:1); verse 5 (Genesis 48:4); verses 6-7 (Genesis 15:13-15); verse 7 (Exodus
    3:12); verse 14 (LXX, Genesis 46:27); verse 18 (Exodus 1:8); verses 27-28 (Exodus 2:14); verse 30 (Exodus 3:2); verse 32
    (Exodus 3:6); verse 33 (Exodus 3:5); verse 34 (Exodus 3:7-8, 10); verse 35 (Exodus 2:14); verse 37 (Deuteronomy 18:15);
    verse 40 (Exodus 32:1, 23); verses 42-43 (LXX, Amos 5:25-27); verses 49-50 (Isaiah 66:1-2).

34. Marcel Simon, "Saint Stephen and the Jerusalem Temple," *The Journal of Ecclesiastical History* 2 (1951), p. 127.

35. Simon again argues his position, in this case by reference to exploited Hellenistic diaspora Jews who, carrying the oppo-
    sition at Qumran from simply the present priesthood to the Temple itself, would see the very construction of a man-
    made building for worship as a violation of God's will—see *Saint Stephen and the Hellenists* (London: Longmans, 1958),
    pp. 84-94.

36. However, it is not accurate to say that the LXX uses only of idols, for in LXX Isaiah 16:12 we read εἰσελεύσεται εἰς τὰ
    χειροποίητα αὐτῆς, where the reference is to the מקדש ("Holy Place") or Temple proper.

37. There has been considerable debate over Luke's use of sources in Stephen's sermon as well as that of Paul at the Are-
    opagus (Acts 17). Because the literary style of the sermon appears to be non-Lucan, C.C. Torrey had early argued for a
    single Aramaic source, "The Translations Made from the Original Aramaic Gospels," *Studies in the History of Religions
    Presented to Crawford Howell Toy by Pupils, Colleagues, and Friends*, ed. D. G. Lyon and G. F. Moore (New York, 1912),
    pp. 269-317. C .K. Barrett, "Attitudes to the Temple in the Acts of the Apostles," *Templum Amicitiae: Essays on the Second
    Temple presented to Ernst Bammel, Journal for the Study of the New Testament* 48, ed. William Horbury (Sheffield, 1991),
    pp. 365-67; and *New Testament Christianity for Africa and the World, Essays in Honor of H. Sawyer*, ed. E. W. Fashole'-Luke
    (London: SPCK, 1974), pp. 69-77, revised Torrey's argument and posited instead Hellenistic Jewish sources, because he
    discovered that the Aramaisms in the speech can also be found in other Hellenistic writings not based on Aramaic or
    Semitic sources, see also H. J. Cadbury, "Luke—Translator or Author?" *American Journal of Theology* 24 (1920), pp. 436-
    55. While Foakes Jackson, *The Acts of the Apostles*, Moffatt New Testament Commentary (New York: Harper & Row, 1931),
    p. 65 has cited the apparent lack of Christian references, e.g. to Jesus. Others argue that it lacks affinity with other
    speeches in Acts and does not seem to fit well into the narrative (Acts 6:8–7:60). However, affinities can be drawn
    between Stephen's speech and other speeches in Acts, e.g. Peter's sermon in Acts 3:22f, which uses the same text in
    Deuteronomy 18:15f—see J. Dupont, "L'utilisation apologetique de l'Ancien Testament dans les discours des Acts," *Eph.*

Theol. Lov. 29 (1953), pp. 292-94; and John Townsend, "The Jerusalem Temple in New Testament Thought" (Ph.D. dissertation: Harvard University, 1958), pp. 141-43. That the Stephen speech contains little of Christian theology is answered by the fact that reference is made in verse 52 to "the Righteous One" (certainly an epithet of Jesus), and since Peter has already expounded the Christian position in his sermon, Luke may have felt no need to include a restatement here—see H. J. Cadbury, "The Speeches in Acts," *The Beginnings of Christianity, Part I: The Acts of the Apostles,* ed. F. J. Foakes Jackson and Kirsop Lake (London, 1920-1933), vol. 5, pp. 402-27 (especially p. 409).

38. See J. R. Brown, *Temple and Sacrifice in Rabbinic Judaism,* The Winslow Lectures 1963 (Illinois: Seabury-Western Theological Seminary, 1963), pp. 13-14, who says, "Stephen's speech...has found almost as many interpreters as it has commentators, but it is surely not a polemic against the Temple. In fact, the accusation that he was against the Holy Place is very carefully ascribed by the author to false witnesses. The *datam* of the speech is that the Jews have rejected Jesus...not an isolated case, but the culminating episode in a long history of disobedience....Very naturally he refers back to the building of the Temple...."

39. See J. Jervell, "The Acts of the Apostles and the History of Early Christianity," *Studia Theologica* 37 (1983): 24.

40. On the basis of these similarities, J. Finegan, *Die Überlieferung der Leidens-und Auferstehungsgeschichte Jesu* (Giessen, 1934), pp. 72-74 and H. Lietzmann, "Der Prozess Jesu," *Sitzungsber, Preuss, Ak Wissenschaft: Phil.—hist. Kl.*, 14 (1931), pp. 313-22 (in Townsend, dissertation, pp. 122-23), have argued that Jesus' trial before the Sanhedrin was a construction based on Acts 6:11-7:60. The opposite, however, is more likely. First, Luke alone of the Synoptic Gospel writers omits the accusation from his account of Jesus' trial. The explanation for this is his practice of including in Acts (actually the continuation of the Gospel, see Acts 1:1) material lacking in Luke (see Acts 1:7; 9:40; 12:4). Obviously, he has based Acts 7 on his Gospel sources. Second, the Stephen story has similarities with the whole Passion narrative and the Transfiguration account as well (Acts 6:15 = Matthew 17:2; Luke 9:29; see also Mark 9:3), not simply with the trial alone. It could hardly be argued that all of these traditions in the Gospels were influenced by Stephen's speech! Third, there is only one mention of a prophecy of the Temple's destruction in Stephen's sermon, while numerous traditions put such a prophecy on the lips of Jesus, and such a tradition is firmly fixed in two places in the Passion narrative. Therefore, it appears that Luke drew on the sources for the Passion account for allusions to Stephen's speech when he wrote Acts 6:11-7:60.

41. See the statement of Joseph Alexander: "The error here denied is that of Heathenism and corrupted Judaism, namely, that Deity could be confined or unchangeably attached to any earthly residence, not the genuine Old Testament doctrine of Jehovah's real and continued dwelling in the tabernacle and temple"—*Commentary on the Acts of the Apostles* (Grand Rapids: Baker Book House, 1983), p. 616.

42. The term χειροποιήτοις has the meaning in secular Greek of "human-made as opposed to natural," and while Philo uses it of idolatry, he also uses it in this sense to denote "calamities artificially provoked by man's destructive energy"—*Spec. Leg.* 1.184; 3.203; *Flacc.* 62.

43. J. M. P. Sweet, "A House Not Made with Hands," *Temple Amicitiae*, p. 387.

44. This argument depends upon adopting the variant reading Θεῷ in Acts 7:46 instead of the more difficult reading οἴκῳ. Indeed the best manuscripts have οἴκῳ and this is the preferred reading—see Bruce Metzger, *A Textual Commentary on the Greek New Testament* (Stuttgart: United Bible Societies, 1971), pp. 351-53. A reading of οἴκῳ would imply that Stephen differentiated the Tabernacle as for the "house" of Jacob, i.e., as a place where the people were to serve God, from Solomon's Temple, which was misunderstood as God's abode. This is the position of A. F. J. Klijn, "Stephen's Speech—Acts VII. 2-53," *New Testament Studies* 4 (1957-1958): 25-27, who by analogy with an alleged parallel in 1QS IX, 3-6 finds support for the οἴκῳ reading. However, the Qumran text deals with service to God in a purely spiritual "house," a sense not normative to Luke's non-spiritualizing treatment of the Temple and cult. Whether or not we admit that the use of the variant is a case of *lectio facilior*, in harmony with the citation from Old Testament, the shift to οἴκῳ is awkward, and would not be understood by any reader in Luke's day—see Haenchen, *The Acts of the Apostles: A Commentary,* trans. B. Noble and G. Shinn (Oxford: Basil Blackwell, 1971), p. 285, n. 2. Furthermore, the syntax in verses 46b-47 argues for Θεῷ, since it is the closest antecedent for αὐτῷ in verse 47 (rather than Θεους in verse 46a), and the last half of verse 46 stands parallel to the first half—see E. Richard, *Acts 6:1-8:4: The Author's Method of Composition* (Missoula: Scholars Press, 1978), p. 132.

45. F. Weinert, "The Meaning of the Temple in the Gospel of Luke" (Ph.D. dissertation, Fordham University, 1979), pp. 27, 84, 127.

46. By contrast is the typical approach of a writer who, while acknowledging Stephen's acceptance of the Temple as a divine institution, does so only for the past age: "Stephen is far from denying that the law and the temple were of God, but like the Lord Himself he was aware that a new dispensation had come which outmoded the old"—"The Attitude of the Primitive Church toward Judaism," *Bibliotheca Sacra* 113:450 (April 1956):136.

47. On the historical reliability of Paul in Acts, see F. F. Bruce, "Is the Paul of Acts the Real Paul?" *Bulletin of the John Rylands Library* 58 (1976), 282-305.

48. Paul was so intent on observing the feasts that at the end of his third journey he avoided the province of Asia in order to reach Jerusalem by Pentecost (Acts 20:16).

49. The Ephesian Jews who charged Paul had apparently seen this man in the city in the company of Paul. Believing the rumors that Paul had taught the Gentiles to forsake the Law, they assumed that Paul had no regard for Temple sanctity and that he therefore would have violated the prohibition against bringing his companion into the restricted area.

50. The *soreg* was a protective barrier that separated the inclusive Court of the Gentiles from the exclusive Court of Israel. Posted at regular intervals along this balistrade—in plain sight—was a Greek inscription warning of the death penalty for entering into the area prohibited to non-Jews. The remains of one of these "warning placards" was found in the Temple Mount excavations under Benjamin Mazar and is today on display in the Israel Museum, Jerusalem.

51. For more discussion of Paul's "offense" see Brian Rapske, "Paul on Trial in Acts," *The Book of Acts in Its First Century Setting: Palestinian Setting*, ed. Richard Bauckham (Grand Rapids: Wm. B. Eerdmans Pub. Co., 1994), pp. 135-49, 160-67.

52. It is such an understanding that must be applied to the interpretation of a passage such as Galatians 6:16, where reference is made to the "Israel of God." This could not have reference to the church *per se*, but only to a division within the church— i.e., Jewish Christians, who, while a part of the body of Christ, are nevertheless uniquely related to the chosen people whose calling preceded the formation of the church.

53. John Townsend, "The Jerusalem Temple in the First Century," p. 58.

54. There is no doubt that Paul's understanding of the Law and the Temple had been reformed (or perhaps informed) by his belief that Jesus was the Messiah; however, this new meaning need not have altered the old truths, but rather enhanced them in terms of an eschatological fulfillment, of which he saw the Christian community as the first and essential component (see Romans 9:4-6,27; 11:1-32; esp. verses 28-32).

55. E.P. Sanders, *Jesus and Judaism* (Philadelphia: Fortress Press, 1985), p. 268.

56. Ibid.

57. Markus Barth, *The People of God*, Journal for the Study of the New Testament 5 (Sheffield: JSOT Press, 1983), p. 72.

58. Reuven Doron, Founding Director, Embrace Israel Ministries, Inc., as cited in *An Intercessor's Guide to the Jewish World*, 2d ed. (Richmond, VA: YWAM Jewish-World Office, 1998), inside back cover.

59. *Time*, October 16, 1989, p. 64.

60. Steve Rodan, *Religious News Service* (as printed in *The Dallas Morning News*, October 28, 1989, p. 38A).

61. Wesley G. Pippert, *Land of Promise, Land of Strife* (Waco: Word Books, 1988), p. 152.

62. *Jerusalem Post*, September 30, 1983.

63. Yitzhak Hayutman, "A House of Prayer for All Nations," Academy of Jerusalem Proceedings (Jerusalem, 1998), pp. 4-5.

64. Ibid., p. 5.

65. Interview on the web with James Tabor of the Religious Studies Dept. of the University of North Carolina.

Chapter 8—Only for Islam

1. As cited in *Israel Today* 2 (February 1999): 11.

2. Ibid.

3. For more details on the Mufti's Nazi connection see, J.B. Schechman, *The Mufti and the Führer* (London: J.P. Mohr, 1965), and Yehuda Taggar, *The Mufti of Jerusalem and Palestine Arab Politics 1930–1937* (New York: Garland, 1986).

4. Hussein's forfeiture of the guardianship of the Al-Aqsa Mosque and the Dome of the Rock was a particular blow to him.

5. My wish is to avoid stereotyping all Arabs as enemies of the Jewish people. For example, Gershon Salomon of the Temple Mount Faithful has held meetings with a Jordanian Arab Christian minister who avidly supports his movement to rebuild the Jewish Temple!

6. *U.S. News & World Report*, August 26–September 2, 1991, p. 33

7. Gaalyah Cornfield, *The Mystery of the Temple Mount* (Jerusalem: Bazak Israel Guidebook Publishers, Ltd., n.d.), pp. 9-10.

8. George W. Braswell, Jr., *Islam: Its Prophet, Peoples, Politics and Power* (Nashville: Broadman & Holman Publishers, 1996), p. 44.

9. For a discussion of the historical events between Mohammed and the Meccans see W. Montgomery Watt, *What Is Islam?* Arab Background Series (New York: Frederick A. Prager, 1968), pp. 97-101.

10. For the tradition concerning David, see Fannie Fern Andrews, *The Holy Land Under Mandate* (Boston and New York, 1931), 1:165; for Jesus, see Ermete Pierotti, *Customs and Traditions of Palestine* (Cambridge, 1864), pp. 70-72.

11. These factions with well-known political representatives are: Sunnis (Egyptian president Hosni Mubarak), Shiites (Iranian leader Hashemi Rafsanjani), Sufis (Iraqi dictator Saddam Hussein), Alawites (Syrian dictator Hafez al Assad), Takfirs (Kuwait Emir Jaber al Ahmed), and Wahhabis (Saudi Arabian King Fahd).

12. Steve Runciman, *A History of The Crusades: The First Crusade* (Cambridge University Press, 1951), p. 3.

13. Shelomo Dov Goitein, "The Historical Background of the Erection of the Dome of the Rock," *Journal of the American Oriental Society* 70:2 (April-June, 1950), p. 107.

14. Miriam Ayalon, "Islamic Monuments In Jerusalem," in *Jerusalem: City of the Ages*, p. 82.

15. This explanation was offered by the historian Ya'qubi in A.D. 874, cf. G. Le Strange, *Palestine Under the Moslems*, reprint of the 1890 edition (Beirut: Khayats, 1965), p. 116. While repeated by later Muslim authors and acepted by most Western historians, the account suffers by virtue of the fact that no other contemporary historians are aware of Ya'qubi's story, but instead offer entirely different explanations.

16. Ibid., p. 83.

17. *Al-Muqaddasi: Description of Syria, including Palestine,* translated from the Arabic and annotated by G. Le Strange, Palestine Pilgrims Text Society 3, reprint of 1896 edition (New York: AMS Press, 1971), pp. 22-23, as cited in F.E. Peters, *Jerusalem*, p. 198.

18. For some of these Islamic associations from folklore see Abraham E. Millgram, *Jerusalem Curiosities* (Philadelphia and New York: The Jewish Publication Society, 1990), pp. 185-216.

19. Gershon Salomon, "Arabs Destroy Remains of the First and Second Temples," Newsletter of the Temple Mount and Land of Israel Faithful Movement (May 3, 1998).

20. Ibid.

21. For the quote by Yakut see Eliyahu Tal, *Whose Jerusalem?* (Tel-Aviv: International Forum for a United Jerusalem, 1994), p. 69.

22. As discussed by Professor Hava Lazarus [Yafeh] in her book *Some Religious Aspects of Islam* (Leiden: E.J. Brill, 1981).

23. As cited by Eliyahu Tal, *Whose Jerusalem?* (Tel Aviv: The International Forum for a United Jerusalem, 1994), p. 76.

24. As cited in the article "Sheik: Jerusalem is ours and not yours," in *Watch: Jerusalem* 2:7 (April 14, 1998), p. 1. Original source: MEMRI's Media Review of April 6, 1998.

25. As cited by Moshe Kohn in his column "View from Nov," in *The Jerusalem Post International Edition* (February 19, 1999), p. 30.

26. Gaalyah Cornfield, *The Mystery of the Temple Mount*, p. 10.

27. "The Arab Case for Palestine: Evidence Submitted by the Arab Office, Jerusalem, to the Anglo-American Committee of Inquiry, March 1946" in *The Israel-Arab Reader*, ed. Walter Laqueur (New York: Bantam, 1969), p. 92.

28. John Michell, *The Temple at Jerusalem—A New Revelation* (The Academy of Jerusalem: Gospels of the Temple, 1999), p. 5.

29. Interview with Jeris Soudah by Irwin Baxter, "Arafat and Jerusalem from a Palestinian Perspective," *Endtimes* magazine 7:5 (September/October 1997), pp. 9-10.

30. For a summary of the historical evidence see *Encyclopedia Judaica*, s.v. "Ishmaelites," by L. Nemoy (Jerusalem: Keter Publishing House, 1992), 9:87-90.

31. Abdul Hadi Palazzi, "No Authentic Theological Reason Why Moslems Should Not Recognize Jerusalem as the Capital of the Jewish State of Israel," Root & Branch Association, Ltd. (July 10, 1998), ftnt. 1.

32. David Bar-Illan, "Errors in Arabizing Jerusalem," *The Jerusalem Post International Edition*, November 27, 1993, p. 13.

33. Abdul Hadi Palazzi, "No Authentic Theological Reason Why Moslems Should Not Recognize Jerusalem as the Capital of the Jewish State of Israel," Root & Branch Association, Ltd. (July 10, 1998).

34. Asher Kaufman, "Locating the Site of the Temple," *Ariel* 43 (1997), pp. 63-99.

35 Hershel Shanks, "Ancient Remains on the Temple Mount Must Not Be Destroyed," *Biblical Archaeology Review* 9:2 (March/April 1983), p. 60.

36. Much of this report is based on personal conversation with Gershon Salomon and details he published on the web site of the Temple Mount Faithful in October 1998.

37. Arutz Sheva News Service, Friday September 6, 1996.

38. Arutz Sheva News Service, Thursday, December 26, 1996.

39. Arutz Sheva News Service, Wednesday, September 11, 1996.

40. Interview with Elwood McQuaid at the Lawrence Welk Resort in Escondido, California, September 22, 1998.

Chapter 9—Sanctuary Symbolism

1. Joshua Berman, *The Temple: Its Symbolism and Meaning Then and Now* (Northvale, NJ: Jason Aronson, Inc., 1995), p. 22.

2. For a more thorough explanation of these connections see Jon D. Levenson, *Sinai and Zion: An Entry into the Jewish Bible* (New York: Harper & Row Publishers, 1985), pp. 131-33.

3. The theological continuity of Genesis 1–11 with the rest of the Pentateuch based on a structural analysis of parallelism has been documented by Gary Smith, "Structure and Purpose in Genesis 1–11," *Journal of the Evangelical Theological Society* 20:4 (1977): 307-19.

4. I have discussed these symbols at length in *The Desecration and Restoration of the Temple As an Eschatological Motif in the Tanach, Jewish Apocalyptic Literature, and the New Testament* (University Microfilms, Inc., 1994), pp. 182-211. Other works that present a study of these symbols are referenced in these footnotes.

5. E.g. Umberto Cassuto, *A Commentary on the Book of Exodus*, translated by Israel Abrahams (Jerusalem: The Magnes Press, 1967), p. 476; cf. P. J. Kearney, "Creation and Liturgy: The P Redaction of Exod 25–40," *Zeitschrift für die Alttestamentliche Wissenschaft* 89 (1977): 375-87.

6. Donald W. Parry, "Garden of Eden: Prototype Sanctuary," *Temples of the Ancient World: Ritual and Symbolism,* ed. Donald W. Parry (Salt Lake City, UT: Deseret Book Company, 1994), p. 126. (Note: this book is a collection of scholarly Mormon studies on the temple with research that can be profitable for the discerning reader.)

7. Mircea Eliade, *Patterns in Comparative Religion* (London: Sheed and Ward, 1958), pp. 367-408.

8. For additional study see Ronald S. Hendel, "Getting Back to the Garden of Eden," *Bible Review* 14:6 (December 1998): 17, 47.

9. A Ugaritic parallel exist in the 15th-century B.C. text the Epic of Aqhat (3 Aqhat, obverse, lines 20, 31-32), e.g., "Over him [Aqhat] eagles will soar, there will hover a [flight of b]irds" (line 20). Here, Ugaritic *rachaf* ("hovers, soars") is associated with the subject *neshrim* ("eagles"), just as in Deuteronomy 32:11, and argues for a Hebrew verb describing the actions of birds, not winds.

10. Joshua Berman, *The Temple: Its Symbolism and Meaning Then and Now* (Northvale, NJ: Jason Aaronson, Inc., 1995), p. 27.

11. For the documentation and discussion see Gordon Wenham, *Genesis 1–15,* Word Biblical Commentary (Waco, TX: Word Books, 1987), 1:61.

12. James E. Miller, "The Aetiology of the Tabernacle/Temple in Genesis," *Proceedings: Eastern Great Lakes and Midwest Bible Societies* 4 (1986): 153-54. His examples include: 1) Genesis 13:8-13 uses Edenic imagery ironically to parallel the choice of Lot to live not only away from Abraham (with whom God had made covenant), but in "Sodom," a land of sinners that lay to the east of the mountains where he stood with Abraham. To reach this place, described as "like the garden of the Lord," Lot had to travel "east" (verse 11). This same terminology had been applied earlier in Genesis 11:2 to the eastward movement of the founders of the tower and city of Babel, which as the later "Babylon" becomes in literary imagery the antithesis and opponent of Zion (the center of covenantal dynasty). Thus, as the builders were driven from their desecrating project, so Lot was driven away from the desecrating valley. That the direction of his choice indicated a direction away from God appears to be indicated by God's nullification of his division, giving instead all of the four cardinal points to Abraham (Genesis 13:14); 2) Genesis 12:8 (cf. 13:3-4) contains the only cultic description in Genesis defined by cardinal points; the narrative presents Abraham establishing a worship center at Bethel. It is significant, however, that the altar Abraham erects is not in Bethel, but between Bethel and Ai, which etymologically as "heap, ruins, tell," and lying to the east, gives it a negative connotation. Moreover, Bethel as "house of God" and lying to the west, bears a positive connotation. By contrast, Cain and Abel's altars were on the east of Eden. At this point, a comparison can be drawn to the Tabernacle/Temple situated west of the altar, and to the east-west orientation of the Tabernacle/Temple in general; 3) Genesis 29:1, which describes Jacob's being sent away (perhaps in the drama of the event *driven* away) to the land of his uncle Laban. Here the place where Laban dwells is called "the land of the sons of the east." Since the journey was directionally away from the Promised Land and to the land originally abandoned by Abraham, "east" is employed to give this negative character to the event. When the negative direction is reversed, and restoration takes place, the return to God or to Eretz-Yisrael is described as a return from the east (Genesis 12:1 of Abraham's call; 14:17-20 of Lot's rescue and the return to the city of Salem = Jerusalem; 31:21 of Jacob's return from Laban).

13. The pronominal suffix *he* ("the") on both *'abar* ("work") and *shamar* ("keep") is feminine, while *gan* ("Garden") is masculine. This may simply be a case of variable gender in nouns denoting place (cf. Gesenius, Kautsch, Cowley, *Hebrew Grammar*, par. 122I) or, as I have opted, a reference to *'adamah* ("ground") or *'aretz* ("earth"), both of which are feminine. This seems the best option, since nowhere else is *gan* ("Garden") treated as feminine.

14. This is supported by the fact that the poetic synonym of *shamar* ("keep") is *nasar* ("to protect"), and that the same root is used in Genesis 3:24 of the action of the guardian cherubim: "…and stationed at the east of the Garden of Eden the cherubim…to guard the way to the tree of life," cf. this parallelism in Deuteronomy 33:9; Psalm 12:8 [English, verse 7]; 105:45; 119:34,55-56,145-146; 140:5 [English, verse 4]; 141:3; Proverbs 2:8,11: 4:6; 5:2; 27:18.

15. This translation has deliberately emphasized the more literal rendering of the terms in order to convey their cultic overtones. The normal meaning of 'avar is "to serve," while that of shamar is "to exercise great care over," or "to guard." A more stylized translation might be "to till and to tend," or the traditional "to dress and keep."

16. The desecration here would be the intrusion of sin, which would bring a curse on it—cf. Genesis 3:17: "cursed is the ground because of you...." Various views for the source of this sin include either men themselves (i.e., the extended family of Adam, cf. Genesis 5:4), Genesis 4:7: "sin is crouching at the door and its desire is for you," or evil powers, such as embodied by the serpent (Genesis 3:1-5,13-15).

17. Gordon Wenham, Genesis 1–15, Word Biblical Commentary, pp. 21-22. Another inference from this "clothing" is that with the desecration of the "Garden-sanctuary," it was now necessary to preserve the sanctity of divine worship by the exercise of human decency. The later requirement for priests approaching the altar was that they have their private parts decently covered: "And you shall not go up by steps to My altar, that your nakedness may not be exposed on it"—Exodus 20:23 [English, verse 26]; cf. 28:42. This was in contrast to the practice of Canaanite priests, who ascended the steps of their altars in order to expose their genitals to worshipers as a fertility rite. In this case, the prohibition may also have been to avoid association with pagan deities and a foreign cultus as well as to promote cultic and social purity. Common decency and modesty was also commanded of the average Israelite in Deuteronomy 23:12-14: "You shall also have a place outside the camp and go out there, and you shall have a spade among your tools and it shall be when you sit down outside [to relieve yourself], you shall dig with it and shall turn to cover up your excrement." This command to relieve oneself outside the camp was based on the presence of the holy God: "The Lord your God walks in the midst of your camp..." (Deuteronomy 23:14). Therefore, the general purpose expressed by the command is ritual purity to keep (or restore) the presence of the Lord, or ritual impurity to alienate His presence: "...therefore your camp must be holy; and He must not see anything indecent among you lest He turn away from you" (Deuteronomy 23:14). This latter concept of cultic activity in relation to the presence of God in the Sanctuary carries an implicit expression of the desecration/restoration motif. If this act of preservation of cultic purity is also in Genesis, then the Eden narrative may also bear examples of our desecration/restoration motif.

18. The people of Israel were represented by the high priest symbolically through the jewels on his breastplate—one for each of the 12 tribes of Israel (Exodus 39:14).

19. In Genesis 3, however, there is no return to the Garden and the Tree of Life through this act because of man's new dual knowledge of "good and evil" (Genesis 3:22). Such a return could only come after the world itself had been purified by the Flood and the disruption at Babel (cf. parallels between Genesis 6-9, 11).

20. The classic study of protology and eschatology is Hermann Gunkel, Schöpfung und Chaos in Urzeit und Endzeit (Göttingen: Vandenhoeck & Ruprecht, 1895).

21. See further Yamil Jimenez-Tabash, The Bible and Archetypes, translated by David Mathieson (San Isidro, Costa Rica: Casa del Banquete Ministries, 1998), pp. 19-24.

Chapter 10—Predictions in the Prophets

1. Jacob S. Golub, In the Days of the First Temple (Cincinnati: Union of American Hebrew Congregations, 1931), p. 319.

2. Elitzur Segal, "The Fast of the Tenth Shall Be for the House of Yehuda for Joy and Happiness" (Part 2 of 2), Yibane HaMikdash 75 (December 10, 1994).

3. On the social-ethical level this life was governed through hokmah ("wisdom," or better "a skill in living"), which took the legal outline of the cult and made it practical for life (see Israel's Wisdom Literature, but especially Proverbs 1–9).

4. For further discusion on the prophetic background of the Qumran community and the Dead Sea literature, see my book Secrets of the Dead Sea Scrolls (Eugene, OR: Harvest House Publishers, 1996).

5. The grammatical explanation for the defectively written cohortative 'ekaved (Ketib, "what is written") may be explained as apocapation ("dropping off") of the final he because of the following aleph in the word 'amar ("says")—see H.G. Mitchell, A Commentary on Haggai and Zechariah, International Critical Commentary (Edinburgh: T. & T. Clark, 1912), p. 52. However, Hans W. Wolff, Haggai: A Commentary, Biblischer Kommentar series (Minneapolis: Augsburg Publishing House), p. 30 argues that the shorter form 'ekaved is the older form and therefore most likely the original form. He also argues that the Qere is a Niphal cohortative and, following the imperative "build" (Hebrew, benu), has a permissive nuance. The Ketib he sees as a Niphal imperfect either passive ("I will be glorified") or reflexive ("I will glorify Myself"). The latter sense is favored by the lexicons and grammars (see F. Brown, S.R. Driver, and C.A. Briggs, Hebrew and English Lexicon of the Old Testament (Oxford University Press), p. 457; L. Koehler and W. Baumgartner, Lexicon in Veteris Testamenti Libros, 3d ed. (Leiden: E.J. Brill), p. 434; Gesenius, Kautzsch, Cowley, Hebrew Grammar, 2d ed. (Oxford University Press), 51c. However, Eugene Merrill, An Exegetical Commentary: Haggai, Zechariah, Malachi (Chicago: Moody Press,

1994), p. 28, noting the close connection between the *Ketib* and the preceding indicative *'ertzeh*, believes that the cohortative is to be construed also as indicative with the idea of purpose "that I may be glorified."

6. Eugene Merrill, *Haggai, Zechariah, Malachi*, An Exegetical Commentary (Chicago: Moody Press, 1994), p. 357.

7. For additional examples of this pattern and its contribution for understanding the eschatological interpretation of the Temple, see my published dissertation *The Desecration and Restoration of the Temple as an Eschatological Motif in the Tanach, Jewish Apocalyptic Literature, and the New Testament* (Ann Arbor, MI: UMI Dissertation Services, 1994).

8. For instance, prophets such as Jeremiah, Ezekiel, and Hosea depict Israel's failure as infidelity in terms of a marriage covenant (Jeremiah 2–3; 31; Ezekiel 16, 23; Hosea 1–10).

9. The dates for this period are reasonably precise owing to the Babylonian Chronicle—see Donald J. Wiseman, *Chronicles of the Chaldean Kings (626–556 B.C.)* (London: The British Museum, 1956), pp. 13-32. The address may have been occasioned by the political situation of Jehoahaz's usurpation by the Egyptian-backed rival anti-Josiah policy party of Jehoiakim. The assault, headed by Pharaoh Necho in September 609 B.C.E., enthroned Jehoiakim, who then imposed stringent punitive levies against the deposed king's supporters—see Jay A. Wilcoxen, "The Political Background of Jeremiah's Temple Sermon," *Scripture in History & Theology: Essays in Honor of J. Coert Rylaarsdam*, ed. A. L. Merrill and T. W. Overholt (Pennsylvania: The Pickwick Press, 1977), pp. 151-66.

10. The clause is literally translated "make good your ways and your doings," but since it is a view of cultic reform, I have provided the dynamic equivalent in my translation—see John Bright, *Jeremiah*, AB 21 (New York: Doubleday & Co., 1986), p. 52, who translates: "Reform the whole pattern of your conduct."

11. Compare A. Cowley, "The Meaning of מָקוֹם in Hebrew," *Journal of Theological Studies* 17 (1916), pp. 174-76; J. Gamberoni, "מָקוֹם," *Theologisches Wörterbuch zum Alten Testament*, 4 (1978), cols. 1113-24; see also on the reference here: Deuteronomy 12:11; 14:23; 1 Kings 8:29-30, 35 for "the place where the Lord causes His name to dwell," and the facts that the nearest antecedent is the threefold repetition of "Temple" in the next verse, and that verse 12 uses the same term to refer to the "house of Lord at Shiloh." Further support may be the parallel situation and statements in Ezekiel 10:4,18-19; 11:22-23, that the *Shekinah* departed from the Temple, because of the same form of idolatrous practices recorded here. Jon Levenson, *Sinai and Zion*, p. 166, n. 125 suggests that in the next verse (verse 4), the word הַמְּה be read as a scribal abbreviation for הַזֶּה הַמָּקוֹם ("this Sanctuary"). If this is so, it would add further support to הַזֶּה מָקוֹם as the Temple here. The alternative reference is "the Land," as clearly in verse 7, however, there is no need to make an artificial distinction between "the Land" and "the Temple," since they are joined in the concept of "sacred place." To desecrate and defile one is to simultaneously affect the other, with the same consequences of exile implied in verse 3.

12. The destruction here most likely is that which occurred under the Philistines (c. 1050 B.C.); see J. Day, "The Destruction of the Shiloh Sanctuary and Jeremiah vii 12, 14," *Studies in the Historical Books of the Old Testament*, ed. J. A. Emerton, *Supplements to Vetus Testament* 30 (Leiden: E. J. Brill, 1979), pp. 87-94. For the view that this referred to a recent destruction of Shiloh in Jeremiah's era, compare R. A. Pearce, "Shiloh and Jer. VII 12, 14, & 15," *Vetus Testament* 23 (1973): 105-8.

13. The literal rendering is "evil of My people," but 1 Samuel 3:13-14 indicates that God was talking about the cultic transgressions of Eli and his sons Hophni and Phinehas, which probably involved cult prostitution or some form of pagan sexual fertility rite (see 1 Samuel 2:22-24). Whatever the desecration, the Lord considered it worthy of capital punishment (1 Samuel 2:25; 4:17).

14. One reason for this heightened sensitivity with regard to proper ritual procedure in Nehemiah may be because "he, more than any other person, was responsible for the organization of the Temple cult" (see Nehemiah 13:30-31), Bezalel Porten, "Temple: The Temple of Zerubbabel," *Encyclopedia Judaica* (1972) 15:958.

15. Compare David L. Petersen, "The Temple in Persian Period Prophetic Texts," *Biblical Theology Bulletin* 21:3 (Fall, 1991), pp. 88-96. A preliminary draft of this paper was first published under the same title in *Second Temple Studies 1. Persian Period*, ed. Philip R. Davies, *Journal for the Study of the Old Testament Supplements* 117 (Sheffield: JSOT Press, 1991), pp. 125-44.

16. See for discussion of this term—and of post-exilic typology in general—Hong Chan Sit, "The Eschatological Significance of the Post-Exilic Prophets" (Th.D. dissertation, Northern Baptist Theological Seminary, 1957), pp. 50-66, 93-99.

17. The literal function of the term as "that which authenticates legal business and has a binding effect" stands behind the metaphorical use in this context. The function of the term in the ancient Near East was as a device to authenticate legal enactments, identify property, and authorize a proxy (see Jeremiah 32:10-44; 1 Kings 21:8). It is used literally of a ring used for signification or documentation (Genesis 41:42; Esther 3:10; Jeremiah 22:24), and in the metaphorical sense, of an identification of ownership in Song of Songs 8:6 or of high and unique identification (see Ezekiel 28:12).

18. Hans Walter Wolff, *Haggai: A Commentary*, trans. Margaret Kohl (Minneapolis: Augsburg Publishing House, 1988), pp. 106, 108. Wolff suggests that Haggai's use of the rare metaphor would have possibly been drawn from its similar use with his grandfather Jehoiachin (Jeremiah 22:24). Even though this connection might imply a promise of Zerubbabel as a

continuation of the Davidic dynasty, Wolff rejects this hypothesis because the context does not seem to "suggest a reminiscence of the Nathan prophecy," (p. 106).

19. See R. P. Carroll, *When Prophecy Failed: Cognitive Dissonance in the Prophetic Traditions of the Old Testament* (New York: Seabury, 1979), pp. 157-83.

20. For a study of the use of the term, see Richard L. Mayhue, "The Prophet's Watchword: Day of the Lord," *Grace Theological Journal* 6:2 (1985), pp. 231-46, and Walter K. Price, *The Prophet Joel and the Day of the Lord* (Chicago: Moody Press, 1976).

21. Joseph Blenkinsopp, *A History of Prophecy in Israel* (Philadelphia: Westminster Press, 1983), p. 236.

22. Pieter A. Verhoef, *The Books of Haggai and Malachi*, New International Commentary on the Old Testament (Grand Rapids: William B. Eerdmans Publishing Co., 1987), p. 36.

23. The primary support for this reading is the Greek Septuagint (LXX).

24. The primary support for this reading is the Latin Vulgate.

25. I have translated the Hebrew term ("precious things") as "wealth" in harmony with Zechariah 14:14. The term can also be translated as "desire" and could refer to the Messiah according to both Jewish tradition and early Christian interpretation. If it is "the Messiah" that is "the desire of all nations," then the "coming" here must be the second coming rather than the first coming, since the nations do not acknowledge Messiah or give God glory until God demonstrates His glory through Israel (see Ezekiel 36:23, 36; 37:27-28; 38:16; 39:7, 21; Revelation 15:4; 20:3). This interpretation would also support the identification of the "latter Temple" as the Millennial Temple.

26. On this point see Hans W. Wolff, *Haggai: A Commentary*, trans. Margaret Kohl (Minneapolis: Augsburg Publishing House, 1988), p. 77: "Here he is not talking about the entry of 'Yahweh's glory' (see 1 Kings 8:11; Exod. 40:34f; see also Hag. 1:8 אכבד, "'I will glorify myself'").

27. See Pieter Verhoef, *The Books of Haggai and Malachi*, New International Commentary on the Old Testament (Grand Rapids: Wm. B. Eerdmans Publishing Co., 1987), pp. 36-37, 150, who also sees the idea of fulfillment in stages, but adopts a strictly christological interpretation in which the stages are: 1) Zerubbabel, 2) Jesus, 3) the Christian church. For a study of this idea in the prophets see my "Prophetic Postponement in Daniel 9 and Other Texts," *Issues in Dispensationalism*, eds. W.R. Willis and J.R. Master (Chicago: Moody Press, 1994), pp. 133-66.

28. The possibility according to the MT is either a reading of כתיב: אֶכָּבֵד ("and I will honor Myself," or "and I will be honored"), a *Niphal* imperfect indicative, or קרי: אֶכָּבְדָה ("that I may honor Myself," or "that I may be honored"), a *Niphal* cohortative. Another alternative is that the original had a paragogic ה- which was dropped by the Massoretes because this ה- represented the fifth thing missing from the Second Temple; i.e., the *Shekinah* (see complete listing in earlier note).

29. The *Niphal* may be rendered either with a passive or a reflexive meaning. The passive nuance is widely preferred by translators to give the thought that the Lord will be honored as He should be by the rebuilding of the Temple, as with the command in verse 8a. However, the honor of the Lord has already been conveyed in this use in parallelism with אֶרְצֶה ("I will be pleased"), verse 8b. Others suggest adding a subjective element to the passive sense: "Lord will consider Himself honored" (when they have rebuilt). Yet, again, the honoring of the Lord will be an afterthought. Rather, with the previous verb אֶרְצֶה we have the active sense "I will take pleasure," indicating the acceptance of the action of rebuilding, and with אֶכָּבְדָה a continued active sense "I will reveal My glory."

30. Consensus of scholarly opinion is that verse 5a is to be considered as a gloss, since it is absent from the LXX, Vetus Latina, and Peshitta, and it breaks the connection between the two clauses in verses 4 and 5, viz., אֲנִי אִתְּכֶם ("I am with you"), verse 4, and רוּחִי עֹמֶדֶת בְּתוֹכְכֶם ("My Spirit will always remain among you"), verse 5, which apparently were meant to be parallel as in Exodus 29:44-45.

31. The use of the participle עֹמֶדֶת with רוּחִי is unusual, but makes better sense with the idea of the "glory cloud" than with a sense of "the guiding, sustaining presence of God" among the leadership and people (compare Isaiah 63:11-14). Also, if an interpretation of renewal, such as in Ezekiel 36:27, were in view, בְּקִרְבְּכֶם ("within you"), rather than בְּתוֹכְכֶם would have been expected. The participle further denotes continuous action and may include both past and present within its meaning, which also would have suggested the scribal connection with the exodus experience of the *Shekinah* abiding with the Israelites throughout their wilderness journey (with which the remnant might compare their return as a new exodus).

32. This is clearly indicated by the description of the Lord as "Lord of armies," and to the "glory" as "the silver" and "the gold." The use of "silver and gold" may be literal, or be used representatively of the quintessence of all material values (see also Hosea 2:8; Ezekiel 7:19; Proverbs 22:1; Ecclesiastes 2:8).

33. The LXX (Codex Alexandrinus) particularly sought to emphasize the Lord's sovereignty by their embellishment of verse 22 with the words: "and I will overturn their entire might and I will pull down their boundaries and strengthen My chosen one."

34. The syntactical use of the participle here functions as "a *futurum instans* after a specification of time," P. Joüon, *Grammaire de l'hébreu biblique*, reprint. (Rome: Pontifical Biblical Institute, 1965), par. 121.

35. See Verhoef, *op. cit.*, pp. 139-40.

36. Compare Elizabeth Gaines, *op. cit.*, p. 112, who notes the emphasis of K. Seybold, "Bilder zum Tempelbau: Die Visiionen des Propheten Sacharja," *Stuttgarter Bibelstudien* 70 (Stuggart: KBW, 1974):134-49, that the function of Zechariah's Temple vision was as a source of divine legitimization for the Second Temple; see also Bruce Halpern, "The Ritual Background of Zechariah's Temple Song," *Catholic Biblical Quarterly* 40 (1978): 167-90.

37. David Petersen, "The Temple in Persian Period Prophetic Texts," *Second Temple Studies*, pp. 136-37.

38. While in Psalms 26:8; 76:2 the phrase "His holy habitation" may refer to the *earthly* Temple, here the contrast is made between the Lord's permanent dwelling (in the heavenly Sanctuary) and the earthly Sanctuary to which He is about to come.

39. The term "top stone" (הָאֶבֶן הָרֹאשָׁה) has been interpreted to be a "foundation stone" rather than a "capstone," since no such top stone is evidenced in comparative Near Eastern texts. It is true that the pyramids had a capstone; however, it is not possible to make the connection between tomb and temple easily. The evidence for a foundation stone, on the other hand, is well attested (compare *Ancient Near Eastern Texts Relating to the Old Testament*, ed. James Pritchard. 3d ed. (Chicago: University of Chicago Press, 1974), pp. 340-41, and the evidence summarized by Albert Petitjean, *Les Oracles du Proto-Zacharie, Etudes Bibliques* (Paris: Librairie Lecoffre, 1969), pp. 243-51. The problem with a foundation stone in this context, however, is that the foundation of the Temple had already been laid (Zechariah 4:9), and the promise is that the edifice will be completed, not begun. It seems preferable to take this term as "completion stone" and to see the end of human work signaling the beginning of the divine accomplishment.

40. The Hebrew term *mophet* literally means "a marvelous or wondrous sign"—see German *Wünderzeichen*, since its original meaning is that of "marvel, wonder" (compare Psalm 71:7); however, its use in connection with אוֹת ("sign") is analogous to that which exist between τεράς and σημείον in Greek, and *prodigium* and *signum* in Latin. It is "wondrous" primarily because it foreshadows a future event. The construct with "men" is appositional, viz. "men [priests] are a marvelous sign."

41. There may be an allusion to Zerubbabel's name, which means "Shoot of Babylon," since the four-word phrase is without articles. The fit seems to be justified by the two both functioning as Temple builders (Zechariah 4:7-9; 6:12-13). I do not, however, agree that the figure crowned (6:14) was originally Zerubbabel, but prefer to leave it as the text states, with Joshua. However, this does not mean that there might not have been two crowns, or that the one crown could have been placed in turn on both heads.

42. The rendering of the phrase "and there shall be a priest upon his throne" has been questioned simply on the grounds of the unusual allocation of rule to a priest. Many commentators take the preposition עַל as "by," seeking to remove the difficulty; however, there seems to be no justification for this since the normal meaning is "on," and it has this use in the previous clause to which this clause is joined. The LXX, recognizing the use of "on," sought to correct the problem by substituting the phrase "on his right hand" for "on his throne."

43. The use of הוֹד as "majesty" or "royal honor" appears in 1 Chronicles 29:25; Psalm 21:2; 45:4; 96:6; 104:1; 111:3; Isaiah 30:30; Jeremiah 22:18; Daniel 11:21, where it signifies the special glory of the Lord, and the glorious distinction conferred by Him upon His representatives, such as kings. The term is appropriate here also because of its use to designate the "beauty" of the olive (Hosea 14:6), which may have a connection since the olive tree appeared in the vision (4:3) in which Zerubbabel was first presented as Temple-builder (4:6-10).

44. This term usually refers to a divine consignment to annihilation (as with the Canaanite cities during the period of the conquest, Joshua 6:17-18), but here has the lesser sense of desecration and deportation (see Isaiah 43:28).

45. For support for this view see Joyce G. Baldwin, *Haggai, Zechariah, Malachi*, Tyndale Old Testament Commentaries (Downers Grove, IL: InterVarsity Press, 1972), p. 201.

46. The use of this expression for universal manifestation of rule ("from east to west") is found in one of the Amarna letters: "Behold, the king, my lord, has set his name at the rising of the sun and at the setting of the sun"—see C. J. Mullo Weir, *Documents from Old Testament Times*, ed. D. Winton Thomas (New York: Harper & Row Publishers, 1958), pp. 43-44.

47. Some commentators, employing a strictly synchronic approach, argue that שׁוּב refers to a renewal of the social order, as this idea is more consistent with comparative ancient Near Eastern eschatology—see A. Jeremias, *Babylonisches im Neuen Testament* (Leipzig: Hinrichs, 1905), pp. 97-98. However, as Verhoef has pointed out, *op. cit.*, p. 342, the semantic domain of הֵשִׁיב is not so much the projected social order but the covenant relationship. Since the reference to שָׁנִים קַדְמֹנִיּוֹת ("former days") in this context refers to a return to covenant purity via the purification of the Levites

to perform a ritually pure service (Malachi 3:3-4), I would suggest that the particular focus of this covenant renewal is cultic.

Chapter 11—Predictions in Daniel

1. Rabbi Hersh Golwurm, Daniel: *A New Translation with Commentary Anthologized from Talmudic, Midrashic and Rabbinic Sources*. ArtScroll Tanach Series, eds. Rabbis Nosson Scherman and Meir Zlotowitz (New York: Mesorah Publications, Ltd., 1979), p. xiii.

2. Alva J. McClain, *Daniel's Prophecy of the Seventy Weeks* (Grand Rapids: Zondervan Publishing House, 1971), p. 6.

3. For a defense of the early date of Daniel see Appendix C: "Eschatological Interpretation and the Date of the Book of Daniel" in my work *The Desecration and Restoration of the Temple as an Eschatological Motif in the Bible and Jewish Apocalyptic Literature* (San Marcos, TX: World of the Bible Press, 1993), pp. 643-48; for the date of Daniel in light of the Dead Sea fragments see my *Secrets of the Dead Sea Scrolls* (Eugene, OR: Harvest House Publishers, 1995), pp. 157-63. For additional study see Gordon J. Wenham, "Daniel: The Basic Issues," *Themelios* 2 (1977): 49-52; Edwin M. Yamauchi, "Daniel and Contacts Between the Aegean and the Near East Before Alexander," *Evangelical Quarterly* 53 (1981): 37-47; Arthur Ferch, "The Book of Daniel and the Maccabean Thesis," *Andrews University Studies* 21 (1983): 129-41; Eugene E. Carpenter, "The Eschatology of Daniel Compared with the Eschatology of Selected Intertestamental Documents" (Ph.D. dissertation: Fuller Theological Seminary, 1978), pp. 97-109; Donald J. Wiseman, et. al., *Notes on Some Problems in the Book of Daniel* (London: The Tyndale Press, 1970); Bruce K. Waltke, "The Date of the Book of Daniel," *Bib Sac* 133:532 (October-December, 1976): 319-329; Gleason Archer, "The Aramaic of the 'Genesis Apocryphon' Compared with the Aramaic of Daniel," *New Perspectives on the Old Testament*, ed. J. Barton Payne (Waco, TX: Word Publishers, 1970).

4. Josephus is thought to have belonged to the sect of the Pharisees, possibly the School of Hillel, to whose canon he probably referred concerning Daniel, cf. Rudolf Meyer, "Bemerkungen zum literargeschichtlichen Hintergrund der Kanontheorie des Josephus," *Festschrift Otto Uschel*, eds. Otto Betz, Klaus Haacker, et. al. (Göttingen: Vandenhoeck und Ruprecht, 1974), pp. 285-99. This group considered Daniel as an important prophetic voice, whose visions held the key to the interpretation of world events, especially concerning the Romans. This was also the trend followed by first- and second-century rabbis, cf. discussion, R. Nosson Scherman, "Daniel—a Bridge to Eternity," in *Daniel*, by R. Hersh Goldwurm, ATS, eds. Rabbis N. Scherman and M. Zlotowitz (New York: Mesorah Publications, Ltd., 1989), pp. xlix-lv. The Jewish use of oracles taken from the Tanach is also recorded by the Roman historian Tacitus *(Historiae* V, 13) and Suetonius *(Divus Vespasianus* 4, 9).

5. Josephus, III: The Jewish War, Books IV-VII, trans. Henry St. John Thackeray. LCL (Cambridge: Harvard University Press, 1968), p. 467.

6. E.g., the expectation of Gentile domination, Israel's supersession and rule in the coming age is found in the other prophets besides Daniel (see chapter 4)—cf. also J. B. van Zijl, *A Concordance to the Targum of Isaiah*, SBL Aramaic Studies 3 (Missoula, MT: Scholars Press, 1979), pp. 142-43.

7. K. Koch, op. cit., p. 125. Koch observes that Daniel always employs a twofold sequence: 1) a vision, dream, or old prophecy is reported (e.g., Daniel 9:2); and 2) a succeeding interpretation (rvp) is revealed by an angel to Daniel (e.g., Daniel 9:21-22), or by Daniel, if the vision or dream was that of a king (chs. 2, 4). cf. also Koch, "Vom prophetischen zum apokalyptischen Visionsbericht," *Apocalypticism in the Mediterranean World and the Near East*, ed. David Hellholm (Tübingen: Mohr, 1983), in which he seeks to draw a connection between the genre of Daniel 7–12 and the prophetic visions of Zechariah.

8. Koch, "Is Daniel Also Among the Prophets?" p. 125 explains the point: There is here revealed an underlying and determinative conception of a two-stage revelation: The prophets like Isaiah, Jeremiah, and Ezekiel are indispensable but preliminary spokesmen of the Word of God; it is only with Daniel that the final stage begins.

9. This shift may also be representative of an altered approach that came to all of the prophets, in which they were conceived of more as preachers of social and religious repentance and less proclaimers of the age to come.

10. Such an allowance was permitted to the divisions of the Hebrew scriptures, but forbidden to the Torah. For this distinction in mashal interpretation between the Torah and the Prophets/Writings see the Lav Middot of R. Eleazar b. Jose of Galilee.

11. For failed calculations see Rabbi Akiva's proclamation of Bar Kokhba as Messiah in 132 C.E., and the prediction of the "pangs of Messiah," including the War of Gog and Magog to begin on 14 Nisan 4291 (A.D. 531). As a result, the coming of the Messiah was included among "three things that will come unawares" (Sanhedrin 97a), and strict prohibitions against attempts to calculate or predict the end were included in the Talmud. For example, Kethubim 111a put Jews under an oath "not to make known the end, and not forcibly to hasten the advent of the end," and Sanhedrin 97b warns: "May the bones of those who calculate the end rot." Nevertheless, we still find sages making such predictions (e.g.,

R' Saadiah Gaon in *twdw twnwma,* and even Rambam himself!). However, their conditions seemed to warrant apocalyptic polemics; i.e., whenever their generation suffered intense persecution (Christian and Muslim), were infiltrated by rival sects such as the Karaites (as was the Gaon), or faced oppression by imposter messiahs (such as Rambam with the Jews of Yemen).

12. See *Sefer Hasidim,* ed. J. Wistinetzki (1924), pp. 76-77, no. 212, which admonishes potential prognosticators: "If you see that a man has prophesied the advent of the Messiah, know that he is engaged either in sorcery or in dealings with devils....One has to say to such a man: 'Do not talk in this manner....Eventually he will be the laughingstock of the whole world.'"

13. The normal biblical usage of *shavua'* is "week" (of days), as is attested by every appearance of the noun itself in the Old Testament (Genesis 29:27-28; Exodus 34:22; Leviticus 12:5; Numbers 28:26; Deuteronomy 16:9 (2x),10,16; 2 Chronicles 8:13; Jeremiah 5:24; Ezekiel 45:21). However, an exception to this use is thought to be found in Daniel, where *shavua'* can mean "week" of years. This usage is found in the apocalyptic literature (e.g., the "Apocalypse of Weeks," 1 Enoch 91-104); however, it may have precedent in Daniel, since much of 1 Enoch draws its thematic material from Daniel—cf. Eugene E. Carpenter, "The Eschatology of Daniel Compared with the Eschatology of Selected Intertestamental Documents" (Ph.D. dissertation: Fuller Theological Seminary, 1978), pp. 274-75, 287. Whitcomb has demonstrated the validity of this usage on the basis of analogous Hebrew usage, comparative chronology, and the prophetic context, cf. John C. Whitcomb, "Daniel's Great Seventy-Weeks Prophecy: An Exegetical Insight," *Grace Theological Journal* 2:2 (Fall, 1981): 259-63. He argues first on the basis of analogous Hebrew usage that *shavua'* may be compared to *asor,* usually translated "ten days," but in Psalm 33:2; 92:4 [English, verse 3]; 144:9 must be translated "ten strings" or "ten-stringed instrument." This indicates that *asor* means literally a "decad" or "unit of ten," and that the distinction in numerical measure must be derived from the context. In like manner, *shavua'* literally means a "heptad," or "unit of seven," and has no intrinsic reference to time periods of any sort. Support for this may be seen in three appearances of *shavua'* with *yamim* ("days"), the addition indicating that *shavua'* alone was not sufficient to show that a period of seven days was meant (cf. Ezekiel 45:21; Daniel 10:2-3). The fact that two of these three combinations occur in Daniel 10, immediately following the "Seventy Weeks Prophecy," may be a signal to the reader that a different sense of *shavua'* is now intended. He next demonstrates based on comparative chronology that if the Seventy Weeks Prophecy refers to weeks (sevens) of years, then *shavu'im* indicates a time-span of "seventy sevens" of years, or 490 years (70 x 7 years). The comparative chronology for this determination are those given in the biblical texts, which explain the duration of the captivity as a sevenfold judgment based on the covenantal stipulation of exilic curse in Leviticus 26:34-35,43; cf. 25:2-5 (Jeremiah 25:11; 29:10 and 2 Chronicles 36:21). The time period given in these explanatory passages for the violation of Levitical sabbath-rest years is 490 years—cf. Robert C. Newman, "Daniel's Seventy Weeks and the Old Testament Sabbath-Year Cycle," *Journal of the Evangelical Theological Society* 16 (1973): 229-34. Since Daniel was studying Jeremiah to determine the conclusion of the captivity, and there he learned that 490 years of sabbath-rest violations had resulted in 70 years of punishment (captivity), would not the announcement of another corresponding period of "seventy sevens" be 490 years, rather than 490 days? Certainly the announcement of another destruction of Jerusalem and the Temple only a year and a half after the end of the exile could have been of little comfort, and of course, the Persian period texts reveal that the city was not rebuilt within this period of time. Whitcomb further argues from the context of biblical prophecy that in Daniel 7:25; 12:7 we read the prediction of a wicked person who will commit abominable acts "for a time, times, and half a time." This phrase is also used in Revelation 12:14, cf. verse 6, where it is paralleled with the phrase "one thousand two hundred and sixty days," (cf. also Revelation 11:3). This same period is mentioned in Revelation 11:2; 13:5 as being "forty [and] two months." Thus, "a time, times, and half a time," according to the New Testament apocalypse, = 1,260 days = 42 months, or in other words = "a year and two years and a half a year" (3½ years). We have a similar measurement of time given in Daniel 9:27 as "one week"..."half or middle of the week." If we interpret *shavua'* as a "week of years," then *shavua'* *'echad* ("one week") = 7 years, and *hetzi hashavua'* ("half of the week") = 3½ years, which agrees with the New Testament interpretation of the phrase.

14. This is one interpretation of the phrase *'eyn lo* ("will have nothing"); an alternate translation is "not for Himself," meaning that the Messiah's death was either not for Himself; i.e., it was substitutionary (for others), or that He was innocent (i.e., there was no guilt or criminal reason for His death). The former interpretation strengthens the eschatological argument, but the latter does not detract from it.

15. See Pasquale de Santo, "A Study of Jewish Eschatology with Special Reference to the Final Conflict" (Ph.D. dissertation: Duke University, 1957), p. 356, which has shown parallels in the Jewish apocalyptic literature to 2 Thessalonians 2 such as a final rebellion by "the wicked" in Israel against "the righteous" in Israel, who represent God and Torah sanctity, at the last day (cf. Jubilees 23:14-23; IV Ezra 4:26-42; 6:18-28), and the close parallel in Psalms of Solomon 17:13, 23-27, which describes "the son of David" delivering Israel by destroying "the lawless one" (cf. 2 Thessalonians 2:8a), by "the word of

his mouth" (cf. 2 Thessalonians 2:8b), the purging of Jerusalem and the restoring of the Promised Land to the Jews. Based on these parallels George Wesley Buchanan, "The Eschatological Expectations of the Qumran Community" (Ph.D. dissertation: Drew University, 1959), p. 269, concluded that the hopes expressed in 2 Thessalonians were clearly sunteleological. In a similar fashion, Jesus in the Olivet Discourse had predicted an "apostasy" in which many would defect from the true faith and betray one another to deceiving false prophets (Matthew 24:10-11). The close association of eschatological structure and thought of 2 Thessalonians 2 with the Olivet Discourse have led many commentators to see Daniel 9 as the common source, cf. G. Henry Waterman, "The Sources of Paul's Teaching on the 2nd Coming of Christ in 1 and 2 Thessalonians," a paper presented to the Midwest Regional Meeting of the Evangelical Theological Society (Deerfield, IL: Trinity Evangelical Divinity School, March 21, 1975), p. 8.

16. See John A. McLean, "The Seventieth Week of Daniel 9:27 as a Literary Key for Understanding the Structure of the Apocalypse of John" (Ph.D. dissertation: The University of Michigan, 1990).

17. For example many *hapax legomena* appear in this passage: *nechettak*, "determined" (9:24); *charutz*, "moat," (9:25); *tzoq*, "trouble" (9:25); usage uncharacteristic of Danelic idiolect, e.g., *berit*, "covenant" (9:24; cf. 9:4; 11:22,28,30, 32), [ha]*rabbim*, "the many" (9:27), and even the term *mashiach*, "anointed, Messiah" (9:26); as well as unexplainable grammatical constructions: *shiqutzim meshomem*, "desolating abominations" (9:27), and terms: *kenaf*, "wing" (9:27).

18. In Jerome's fourth-century commentary on Daniel, the oldest Christian source for patristic interpretations on the 70 weeks prophecy, Jerome lists nine exegetes with eleven interpretations: *Jerome's Commentary on Daniel*, trans. Gleason Archer, Jr. (Grand Rapids: Baker Book House, 1958), pp. 94-110; cf. Jay Braverman, *Jerome's Commentary On Daniel: A Study of Comparative Jewish and Christian Interpretations of the Hebrew Bible*, The Catholic Biblical Quarterly Monograph Series 7 (Washington D.C.: The Catholic Biblical Association of America, 1978), pp. 103-12.

19. For a critique of the theological debate between the various eschatological schools cf. Michael Kalafian, *The Prophecy of the Seventy Weeks of the Book of Daniel: A Critical Review of the Prophecy as Viewed by Three Major Theological Interpretations and the Impact of the Book of Daniel on Christology* (New York: University Press of America, 1991).

20. For my study of these differing views see "Prophetic Postponement in Daniel 9 and Other Texts," *Issues in Dispensationalism* (Chicago: Moody Press, 1995), pp. 144-46.

21. This view is called eschatological because it interprets at least part of the seventieth week to have its fulfillment at the eschaton. This interpretive method may be divided into two variant groups: a symbolic (or schematic) approach, and an apotelesmatic approach. The first view takes the seventieth week as heptads of time that are to be understood symbolically (the numbers 7 and 10 = perfection and completion) and which will only be experienced at the consummation of all things. This view, represented, for example, by C.F. Keil, *Biblical Commentary on the Book of Daniel*, trans. M.G. Easton (Grand Rapids: William B. Eerdmans Publishing Co., 1949), pp. 399-402; and H.C. Leupold, *Exposition of Daniel* (Columbus: Wartburg Publishers, 1949), pp. 423-33, sees three divisions of the 70 weeks: the 7 heptad: in which the decree of Cyrus returns the Jews to rebuild Jerusalem and Messiah appears, the 62 heptads: in which a spiritual Jerusalem is rebuilt, i.e., the Christian church, the 1 heptad: in which the Messianic purpose for the church appears to fail, since worship of Messiah is "cut off," due to the influence of Antichrist, who is destined to be destroyed, thus ending the third period (verse 27). The second view, the apotelesmatic approach, is the most widely held of the eschatological interpretations. It is called apotelesmatic because it sees an interval or parenthesis of time between the end of the first 69 weeks and the beginning of the seventieth week (which is fulfilled eschatologically). Several variations exist within this view: 1) The Sabbatical Year view, in which weeks are not years, but sabbatical cycles, the final sabbatical cycle being future. The interval is based on the reference to the destruction of the Temple in verse 26, but the cessation of ongoing sacrifices in verse 27, presupposing a rebuilt Temple in between—cf. Robert C. Newman, "Daniel's Seventy Weeks and the Old Testament Sabbath-Year Cycle," *Journal of the Evangelical Theological Society* 16 (Fall 1973): pp. 229-34. 2) The Double Internal view, in which a parenthesis occurs after both the first and second division of the 70 weeks. The first interval occurs after the return of the Jews to rebuild the Temple and city until about 436 B.C. The second interval follows the "cutting off" of Messiah, verse 26, until the appearance of the Antichrist, verse 27. This is the final week and it is eschatological; cf. Allan A. MacRae, "The Seventy Weeks of Daniel" (paper delivered at the Evangelical Theological Society, Deerfield, IL 1978), pp. 1-9; 3) The Solar Year and the Prophetic Year views. These views will be considered together inasmuch as they are essentially the same except for the type of year used in calculating the 70 weeks prophecy, (i.e., a 365-day "solar year" versus a 360-day "prophetic year"). Both views reject the pointing of the MT on the grounds that it is a tenth-century addition, the athnach is often put where it is unexpected, and does not always indicate a principal break in the sentence (Numbers 28:19; cf. Genesis 7:13; 25:20; Exodus 35:23; Leviticus 16:2; Isaiah 49:21; 66:19), and the understanding of passage is made more complicated (e.g., the "plaza and moat" of verse 25 would appear to take 434 years to build!). The events from the beginning of the 69 weeks until its close include the career of Messiah up to the destruction of Jerusalem and the Temple in A.D. 70. The seventieth week is then final and eschatological.

22. The 457 B.C. date is that of Ezra's return to Jerusalem in the seventh year of Artaxerxes; cf. Gleason Archer, *"Daniel,"* The Expositor's Bible Commentary (Grand Rapids: Zondervan, 1985) 7:114; L.A. Foster, "The Chronology of the New Testament," *Expositor's Bible Commentary* 1:598-599, 607. The date of 445 B.C. is that of the commission given to Nehemiah in the twentieth year of Artaxerxes; cf. Harold W. Hoehner, *Chronological Aspects of the Life of Christ* (Grand Rapids: Zondervan, 1977), pp. 116-28.

23. This was the conclusion drawn by Norman Porteous, *Daniel, Das Alte Testament Deutsch* 23 (Göttingen, 1962), translation: *Daniel, A Commentary. Old Testament Library* (Philadelphia: Westminster Press, 1965), p. 144: "...the end predicted by the author of the book of Daniel did not come true...." The reason for rejecting the Maccabean interpretation is that the events of that period simply do not fit Daniel's description. Neither the city nor the Temple were destroyed, nor was a covenant made between Antiochus and the Jews (even the renegade Jews). The Roman interpretation better fits the historical description of verses 26-27, however, details must again be pressed beyond the chronological and historical datum. For an example of the attempts to reconcile such difficulties cf. Rabbi Hersh Goldwurm, *Daniel: A New Translation with a Commentary Anthologized from Talmudic, Midrashic and Rabbinic Sources,* The ArtScroll Old Testament Series, eds. Rabbis Nosson Scherman and Meir Zlotowitz (New York: Mesorah Publications, Ltd., 1989), pp. 264-65. The Roman interpretation is accepted by some dispensationalists who argue for dual fulfillment, as well as by Seventh-Day Adventist scholar Desmond Ford, who argues for a nondispensational futurist interpretation for the seventieth week analogous to the Israel (church)/Rome (Antichrist) pattern of A.D. 70, cf. *Daniel* (New Castle: Desmond Ford Publications, 1980), p. 201.

24. Lester L. Grabbe, "The End of the Desolations of Jerusalem: From Jeremiah's 70 Years to Daniel's 70 Weeks of Years," *Early Jewish and Christian Exegesis: Studies in Memory of William Hugh Brownlee,* ed. C. Evans and W. Stinespring (Scholars Press, 1987), p. 69. Grabbe, in recognizing this difficulty, proposes a compromise interpretation which still argues for a Maccabean setting, but contends that Daniel 9:24-27 has made use of an older pre-existing oracle, and therefore represents one of several post-exilic attempts to reconcile the 70-year Jeremiah prophecy with the historical events (e.g., Zechariah 12:1; 2 Chronicles 36:22-23). In this way he attempts to reconcile the disparate Maccabean historical references, which are considered as post eventum, yet appear in Daniel too as *ex eventu* prophecy. For this reason, those who hold to the Hasmonean interpretation must postpone the destructive events of the seventieth week (verse 26) to the Roman period, even though they contend it was chronologically fulfilled earlier. This is also a problem for those who attempt to interpret "weeks" as "sabbatical-cycles," and make events fit the Maccabean period. Wacholder admits: "More problematical, however, is the inconsistency of the date of the placement of the 'abomination' in the Temple.... Although the difference between the two datings is only about fifteen or sixteen months, it does present a serious objection to the calculation, as it is too large an error for contemporaneous chronology. He adds concerning his approach: "This method would reduce Daniel's departure from the historical date to ten months, perhaps a permissible deviation in a chronomessianic book." Ben Zion Wacholder, "Chronomessianism: The Timing of Messianic Movements and the Calendar of Sabbatical Cycles," *Hebrew Union College Annual* 46 (1975): 208-9.

25. For a study of earlier classical dispensational discussions of this concept, cf. Alva J. McClain, "The Parenthesis of Time Between the Sixty-Ninth and Seventieth Weeks," *Daniel's Prophecy of the Seventy Weeks* (Grand Rapids: Zondervan Publishing House, 1960), pp. 23-40; H.A. Ironsides, *The Great Parenthesis* (Grand Rapids: Zondervan, 1940); J. Dwight Pentecost, *Things to Come* (Grand Rapids: Dunham, 1958), pp. 246-50; John F. Walvoord, *Daniel: The Key to Prophetic Revelation* (Chicago: Moody Press, 1971), pp. 228-37.

26. The Masoretes placed a disjunctive accent (*athnach*) under the word "seven," which might indicate that they interpreted the two sections as separate divisions. If so, three distinct periods of time are marked off, and the punctuation would imply the appearance of an "anointed" (*masiah*) at the end of both the seven and the 62 week periods (usually the former is Cyrus and the latter a different ruler). However, such accents are merely expressions of rabbinic commentary and in this case earlier textual traditions (Greek—LXX Theodotion, Latin Vulgate, Syriac Peshitta) testify to an ancient reading that combines the numerical elements seven and 62 to equal one unit (i.e., 69). These versions may well preserve a pre-masoretic reading of the text or an early Jewish or Christian oral tradition concerning the 70 weeks. Because the presence of the disjunctive at this point makes the Messianic or christological interpretation of this passage practically impossible, the tenth century A.D. addition of the accent here may well be the result of an anti-Christian bias. For additional reasons for the rejection of a division here see Alva J. McClain, "The Parenthesis of Time Between the Sixty-Ninth and Seventieth Weeks," *Daniel's Prophecy of the Seventy Weeks* (Grand Rapids: Zondervan Publishing House, 1960), pp. 23-40; H.A. Ironsides, *The Great Parenthesis* (Grand Rapids: Zondervan, 1940); J. Dwight Pentecost, *Things to Come* (Grand Rapids: Dunham, 1958), pp. 246-50; John F. Walvoord, *Daniel: The Key to Prophetic Revelation* (Chicago: Moody Press, 1971), pp. 228-37.

27. Cf. Robert Gundry, *The Church and the Tribulation* (Grand Rapids: Zondervan, 1973), pp. 189-90.

28. There is general agreement among scholars that Daniel should be divided as: chapters 1-6, consisting primarily of historical narration, and chapters 7-12, consisting of visions concerning the future kingdoms of the world and of God, cf. David W. Gooding, "The Literary Structure of the Book of Daniel and Its Implications," *Tyndale Bulletin* 32 (1981): pp. 48-51.

29. E.g., *hashomem* ("desolations"), verse 17-18, *marad* ("transgression"), verse 9, *'avin* ("iniquity"), verses 5,13,16, *chata'* ("sin"), verses 5,8,11,20, *miqdash* ("Sanctuary"), verse 17 (cf. verse 20), *'ir* ("city"), verse 19, *'am* ("people"), verses 19-20, and *torat Moshe* ("Law of Moses"), verses 11,13.

30. Daniel, as a member of the exilic community, would have been greatly affected by the writings of Ezekiel and Jeremiah. This fact is supported by the internal evidence of the book, which depicts Daniel studying Jeremiah's prophecy in order to determine the end of the desolations (Daniel 9:2).

31. Other language and themes in Daniel are also found in the prophets; e.g., Ezekiel the departure of the *Shekinah* (Ezekiel 10–11) signals the defilement of the Temple and its impending destruction. In Ezekiel 9:8 the prophetic judgments leveled against Jerusalem in the form of war, pestilence, and famine are such that Ezekiel fears that the whole remnant of Israel will utterly perish. Similar scenes are mirrored in Jeremiah (cf. 7:32-34), Lamentations (cf. 1:4-5,8-10,16; 2:6-10,20; 5:18), and some of the Psalms (cf. e.g., 74:1-7; 79:1-7). These were also reinforced by the historical and theological reviews and warnings of the post-exilic prophets, who likewise rehearsed the eschatological battle to come against Jerusalem (e.g., Zechariah 14:2).

32. Jacques Doukhan points this out when he states, "The seventy weeks' prophecy must be interpreted with regard to history in as realistic a way as Daniel did for the prophecy of Jeremiah." Jacques Doukhan, "The Seventy Weeks of Dan. 9: An Exegetical Study," Andrews University Seminary Studies 17 (Spring 1979): 8.

33. See John E. Goldingay, *Daniel,* Word Biblical Commentary 30, ed. John Watts (Dallas: Word Books, 1989), p. 258, who says, "It does not have a worldwide perspective; it is not speaking of the end of all history, or of the sin of the whole world. Daniel is returning to 'salvation history' from the secular history that dominated chaps. 7–8 and will dominate chaps. 10–12. His moving between these two reflects the fact that both are of God." Goldingay is correct in his limiting the stage of this fulfillment to Israel, however, if, as he says, the events concerning the goal of the 70 weeks are at once exclusively Israel's history, and yet also 'salvation history,' then how can this fulfillment be isolated from a universal effect? One of Daniel's primary interests is the future outcome of the kingdoms of the world, which have at their nexus the establishment of the Messianic Kingdom.

34. For the different eschatological interpretations of these goals cf. e.g., C.F. Keil, *Daniel in C.F. Keil and Franz Delitzsch,* Commentary on the Old Testament, reprint (Grand Rapids: Baker Book House, 1976), pp. 341-50, who sees the goals in a reciprocal relationship: the first three goals as negative (taking away sin), with the last three as positive (bringing in everlasting righteousness), and Robert A. Anderson, *Signs and Wonders: A Commentary on the Book of Daniel* (Grand Rapids: Baker Book House, 1984), pp. 113-14, who views the goals as parallel; Jacques Doukhan, "The Seventy Weeks of Daniel 9: An Exegetical Study," pp. 10-15, who views the goals as part of the chiastic structure of verses 25-27.

35. For this position see Todd S. Beall, "The Abomination of Desolation: Past, Future, or Both?" (a paper presented to the Evangelical Theological Society, November 18, 1995): 1-13.

36. The term *kala'* means to "terminate" or "complete," while *hatem* has the idea of "making whole," i.e., "completing." This is the end of a condition that is described by the objects as "the rebellion," i.e., the rejection of the Messiah (cf. Isaiah 53:1-9; Zechariah 12:10), and innate sin (*chata'*), i.e., sin which prevents ritual purity (cf. Isaiah 27:9; Ezekiel 36:25-27; 37:23; cf. Romans 11:27).

37. In line 51 we read: *sr tsml* ("to bring evil to an end"), cf. Robert Eisenman and Michael Wise, *The Dead Sea Scrolls Uncovered* (Massachusetts: Element, 1992), pp. 67-68.

38. Scherman and Zlotowitz, *Daniel,* The Artscroll Old Testament Series, p. 260. One reason for this interpretation is because these commentators believed that Jewish suffering would atone for their transgression. Abarbanel noted that the return to Jerusalem and even the rebuilding of the Second Temple did not bring the expected redemption nor atone for past sins, since it was itself a part of the exile and atonement. He held that the real and complete redemption was still far off in history, and thus not yet fulfilled according to Daniel's prophecy.

39. Some dispensationalists argue that each of these six elements are to be treated separately and not to be fixed or combined arbitrarily (e.g., John F. Walvoord, *Daniel: The Key to Prophetic Revelation,* pp. 220-21). They hold that the goals relating to sin and the atonement were fulfilled with the death of Christ, even though the application to Israel will be made in the future (i.e., the first three goals are Christ coming to redeem, the last three goals are Christ coming to reign). Other dispensationalists see Israel's transgression as brought to completion over the course of time at the end of the 70 weeks (e.g., J. Dwight Pentecost, *Things to Come* [Grand Rapids: Zondervan Publishing Co., 1971], p. 172). The problem for the position of a partial (or dual) fulfillment is the lack of hermeneutical control, for the text itself suggests

no chronological separations in fulfillment. Therefore, another approach is to take these six infinitives as representing a sixfold goal, treating them as a unit, rather than as individual goals partially or separately fulfilled at different times The options, then, are to take the sixfold goal as either completely fulfilled in the first century or in the eschatological future. J. Barton Payne, "The Goal of Daniel's Seventy Weeks," *The Journal of the Evangelical Theological Society* 21 (June 1978): 97-115, is an example of one who argues for the first option. The major weaknesses of Payne's argument are: 1) his use of *qds* for imputation does not fit the predominant use, especially in the exilic period, as "vindication," also as defined by Messianic restoration expectation; 2) he has not demonstrated that these events took place within the historically complete period; and 3) he does not explain the futuristic perspective of the New Testament allusions to Daniel 9. The second option gains support from an examination of the terminology of these goals in relation to Jewish apocalyptic literature (especially the Dead Sea literature), which appear to have employed the 70 weeks as an interpretive guide for their expectation of Messianic fulfillment at the eschaton (which they assumed was imminent). While such Jewish apocalyptic writers are not part of the inspired canon, they do present a useful comparative hermeneutical model.

40. Compare *tzedeq 'olamim* ("everlasting righteousness") 11QPsa col. xxii. Here in an apocryphal psalm addressed to Zion (Jerusalem) concerning the anticipated deliverance from Gentile domination (as in Daniel 9) it is written, "May you attain everlasting righteousness" (line 16).

41. This translation is in accord with restoration usage and, e.g., the parallelism with "salvation" in Isaiah 1:27; 46:13; and 51:1-8.

42. See The Artscroll commentary on Daniel (p. 261): " 'to bring in everlasting righteousness'—It will usher in the epoch of the Messianic king."

43. The "sealing of the prophetic vision" (*a hendiadys*), like the sealing of other documents in the ancient Near East, was for authentication or confirmation (see 1 Kings 21:8). The sense then is that of the fulfillment of prophecy, just as in goal number two the same infinitive (i.e., the *kethiv*) was used in relation to the fulfillment (or end) of sin (cf. the *keri*). This would also be the sense in Daniel 12:4, 9; cf. 6:17. The fulfillment of the restoration as prophesied by Jeremiah, then, could only be eschatological, since no such restoration was ever experienced by the nation. An alternate ancient view, found both at Qumran and in Sotah 48b, interprets this phrase as "the end of the era of prophecy" (i.e., the beginning of the Second Temple). This view, however, has difficulty reconciling with the context of Daniel 12:9: "the end time," i.e., the time of the resurrection (of Old Testament saints) (verse 13). An alternative interpretation sees the terms "vision" and "prophecy" as referring respectively to oral and written prophecy and views their function as being fulfilled or finished at the Second Advent.

44. Though the term for restoration was conditioned on the Mosaic covenant (Deuteronomy (as as) Jeremiah 9:10 1), the effecting of the restoration was based on the unconditional Abrahamic covenant (Genesis 17:7-8; Deuteronomy 4:30-31). The theological resolution is found in the national regeneration of Israel to spiritually fulfill these conditions (Ezekiel 36:24-31; 37:13-14,23).

45. See P. Grelot, "Soixante-dix semaines d'années," *Biblica* 50 (1969), pp. 180,184.

46. For further explanation of this chronology see my chapter "Prophetic Postponement in Daniel 9 and Other Texts" in *Issues in Dispensationalism*, eds. W. Willis and J. Master (Chicago: Moody Press, 1994), pp. 132-65, and my several articles on the interpretation of Daniel's 70 weeks prophecy in the *Dictionary of Premillennial Theology*, ed. Mal Couch (Grand Rapids: Kregel Publications, 1996), pp. 75-81.

47. Interview with John F. Walvoord, San Marcos, TX, September 20, 1998.

48. The word for "temple" here is the Greek word *naos*, which usually distinguishes the most sacred portion of the Temple from its less-sacred precincts (Greek: *hieros*).

49. Harold D. Foos, "Jerusalem in Prophecy," Th.D. dissertation, Dallas Theological Seminary, 1965, p. 230.

50. See *Daniel*, The Artscroll Old Testament Series, p. 264.

Chapter 12—Predictions in the Gospels

1. E.P. Sanders, *The Historical Figure of Jesus* (New York: The Penguin Press, 1993), p. 262.

2. In this regard note the words of New Testament scholar James Charlesworth: "I am convinced that we cannot re-present the New Testament documents, their theologies, and their tendencies without ultimately focusing on the challenge of one single life. Jesus is the power paradigm for all the New Testament writers. We must acknowledge that New Testament—perhaps all Christian—theology develops out of the tension between tradition and addition, between remembered history and articulated faith." *Jesus Within Judaism, The Anchor Bible Reference Library* (New York: Doubleday, 1988), p. 10.

3. Ibid.

4. The first to use this term was D. Winter, *The Search for the Real Jesus* (London, 1982): "But the last decade has seen an amazing transformation...historians and theologians have turned with gusto to the original documents, parallel historical records and the geographical sites, and at every turn have found a clearer and clearer picture emerging of Jesus of Nazareth. Hence, I call the new development 'Jesus Research' " (pp. 8-9). For a summary and assessment of this trend cf. J.H. Charlesworth, "From Barren Mazes to Gentle Rappings: The Emergence of Jesus Research," *The Princeton Seminary Bulletin* N.S. 7 (1986): 221-230. This shift in thinking has been the subject of at least one study, cf. Donald A. Hagner, *The Jewish Reclamation of Jesus: An Analysis & Critique of the Modern Jewish Study of Jesus* (Grand Rapids: Academie Books/Zondervan Publishing House, 1984).

5. One of the best early works by a Jewish scholar in this regard was that by Hebrew University professor David Flusser, *Jesus*, trans. R. Wallis (New York: Herder & Herder, 1969). For more recent studies see M. Wilcox, "Jesus in the Light of His Jewish Environment," *ANRW*, eds. W. Haase and H. Temporini (Berlin/New York) II, 25:1 (1984): 131-195; and in the same volume, J.H. Charlesworth, "The Historical Jesus in the Light of Writings Contemporaneous with Him," pp. 451-76, O. Betz, *What Do We Know About Jesus? The Bedrock of Fact Illuminated by the Dead Sea Scrolls*, trans. M. Kohl (London, 1986).

6. Doron Mendels, *The Rise and Fall of Jewish Nationalism*, Anchor Bible Reference Library (New York: Doubleday & Co., 1992), pp. 304-5.

7. These predictions are recorded by Josephus and in early rabbinic literature. For a listing of many of these with discussion, see Markus N. A. Brockmuehl, "Why Did Jesus Predict the Destruction of the Temple?" *Crux* 25 (September 1989): 3, pp. 12- 14. Doron Mendels notes that because the Temple had gradually lost its significance as a religio-political and spiritual symbol through the abuse of the priesthood, that by the end of the Second Temple period there emerged the idea that the priesthood and Temple should be destroyed (although he cites Paul as an example of this school of thought!), *op. cit.*, p. 305.

8. Luke, in making reference to this pilgrimage here and again in verse 43 with the reference to "fulfilling the days," i.e., "spent the full time," the Passover week, may have also implied another instance of the family's status as observant Jews, as the requirement was only for a stay of two days. It is possible that there is likewise a hint of further devotion to the pilgrimage in the route they would have taken, probably along the Jordan from Galilee to Jerusalem. S. Safrai, *Pilgrimage in Second Temple Times* [Hebrew], pp. 15, 48 indicates that such an alternate route might have been taken to escape the Samaritans (who acted hostile to families on such pilgrimages). The necessity of taking this longer and more arduous route might have discouraged those less devoted.

9. It was apparently a tradition that children accompany their fathers to the Passover at least a year prior to their reaching puberty (*M. Niddah* 5:7-9; cf. *M. Hagiga* 1:1; *Pirke Avot* 5:24). S. Safrai, "Home and Family," *JPFC* 2:771f, notes that *T. Hagiga* 1:2 indicates that a child was to keep whatever *mitzvot* he was capable of performing. The later concept of the *Bar Mitzvah* probably developed from this early tradition.

10. For example, in Luke 4:43 of His preaching of the gospel; 9:22 for His Passion and resurrection; 13:33 of His final journey to Jerusalem; 17:25 of His suffering; 19:5 for His ministry to Zacchaeus; 22:37 of His identification with criminals on the cross; 24:7 of His death and resurrection; 24:6 of His exaltation to glory; 24:44 for the fulfillment of Scripture.

11. For a survey of the various options and the support for supplying "house" in this phrase see Darrell L. Bock, *Luke Volume 1: 1.1–9:50*, Baker Exegetical Commentary on the New Testament (Grand Rapids: Baker Books, 1994), pp. 269-71.

12. The accounts are almost parallel except for Luke's reversal of the order of the last two temptations. The reason for Luke's change in order is probably for topographical reasons, and in the case of the second testing, possibly because he wanted to end this pericope with a reference to the kingdom—cf. Walter Liefield, "Luke," *Expositor's Bible Commentary* (Grand Rapids: Zondervan Publishing House) 8:864. Matthew's order is most likely the original. Mark makes only a brief reference to the event, but J. Duppont has shown that he was most certainly familiar with the larger account, "L'Arrière-fond Biblique du Récit des Tentations de Jésus," *New Testament Studies* 3 (1956-1957): 287-304.

13. For a thorough treatment of the use of the wilderness motif in this passage and the New Testament see Urich Mauser, *Christ in the Wilderness: The Wilderness Theme in the Second Gospel and Its Basis in the Biblical Tradition*, Studies in Biblical Theology 39 (Illinois: Alec R. Allenson, Inc., 1963).

14. This expression for Jerusalem is familiar from its use toward the end of the biblical period (Nehemiah 11:1; Isaiah 48:2; Daniel 9:24; see also Matthew 21:10; 27:53). Luke prefers to use "Jerusalem" because he is writing of the progress of the gospel from Jerusalem to the Gentile nations. It is not that the Jewish appellative "holy city" might be confusing to some Gentile readers; rather, it is the geographical, not only the spiritual, concept of the city that Luke wants to emphasize.

15. Some have thought that the reference must be to the entrance porch of the Temple, since at this place the building bears such a resemblance, extending outward beyond the breadth of the Temple. However, Josephus (*Antiquities* 15.11.5 §§ 411-12) describes the "royal stoa") located in the southern part of the Temple complex (Josephus says southern part of the court

of the Gentiles) as of such a great height that if anyone looked down from the top "he would grow dizzy, his eyes not being able to reach so vast a depth."

16. For instance, J. Andrew Kirk, "The Messianic Role of Jesus and the Temptation Narrative," *Evangelical Quarterly* 44 (1972): 91–95, would see in this a challenge for Jesus to prove His Messiahship by leaping from the Temple pinnacle, as in a late Jewish midrash, to prove Himself to the people as a new "David" who would rid Jerusalem of the "Jebusites" (i.e., Romans). However, the midrash makes no mention of spectators, and its lateness, as well as the Levitical consideration earlier stated, makes the hypothesis untenable. Equally wrong, to my mind, is the suggestion of N. Hyldahl, "Die Versuchung auf der Zinne Temples," *Studia Theologica* 15 (1961):113- 27, that Jesus was being tempted to voluntarily submit to the punishment for blasphemy by being thrown off the pinnacle of the Temple.

17. Darrell L. Bock, *Luke Volume 1: 1:1–9:50*, Baker Exegetical Commentary on the New Testament (Grand Rapids: Baker Books, 1994), p. 380.

18. While both Mark and Luke refer to the Tabernacle, only Matthew 12:5 makes the connection with the Second Temple. This inclusion is most probably because of the orientation of his Gospel toward Jewish-Christian readers. However, it is possible that the connection is implied in Luke 6:4, since the term used for the Tabernacle is the Greek *ton oikon tou Theou*, which is the equivalent of the Hebrew *beit 'elohim*, which can apply also, and perhaps more properly, to the Temple, cf. Robert H. Gundry, *Matthew: A Commentary on His Literary and Theological Arts* (Grand Rapids: Wm. B. Eerdmans, 1982), pp. 223-24.

19. The support for this view is based on an Arabic version of this event preserved in the testimony of early Jewish-Christians, which was discovered by Hebrew University professor Shlomo Pines.

20. The meaning of the Hebrew expression is literally "the light [Hebrew, *qal*] to the heavy" (Hebrew, *chomer* means literally, "substance, matter"). The words, however, are used in the sense of "less important" and "more important"—therefore the minor (*qal*) and the major (*chomer*) points of a case. The expression, then, may be understood, according to the Latin term, as an inference *a minori ad majus* (an argument from the minor premise to the major premise). The uses of *Qal va-homer* as a hermeneutical device in the Talmud and Mishnah reveal at least four distinct ways in which this reasoning device has been employed. The primary distinction appears in the manner in which the *major* and *minor* premises are assembled, though the act of inference remains the same after the relevant premises have been gathered. These four uses may be classified as argument by identity, argument by degree, argument by difference, and argument by opposition. Both Jesus and Paul frequently employed this form of argument (also known as an *a fortiori* argument) in their discussions of biblical and rabbinic *halakhah*. For further study see my paper "Midrashic Middot: A Study of the Use of the Hermeneutic Rule *Qal va-homer* in the Talmud and Mishnah" (available from World of the Bible Productions, P.O. Box 827, San Marcos, TX 78667-0827).

21. Rabbinic tradition suggested that this event took place on the Sabbath because the 12 loaves of shewbread had just been changed, a fact noted in 1 Samuel 21:5-6. If this is the case, it strengthens Jesus' analogy with David as a fellow Sabbath violator.

22. This "consecrated bread" was the 12 sacred loaves of shewbread (literally, "the bread of the setting forth" or "of the face" = "presence") found in the Holy Place of the Tabernacle and Temple (Leviticus 24:5-9). For details see Marvin R. Vincent, *Word Studies in the New Testament*, 4 vols. (Grand Rapids: William B. Eerdmans Publishing Co., reprint, 1975),1: 173-74.

23. A masculine variant does exist in some copies but is poorly attested in the manuscript evidence. Its appearance can be explained as a copyist "correction" of the text based on his presupposition that this referred to Jesus.

24. See Nigal Turner, *Syntax*, vol. 3 of J. H. Moulton, *A Grammar of the Greek New Testament* (Edinburgh: T. & T. Clark, 1965), p. 21. However, see arguments in *From Sabbath to Lord's Day*, ed. D. A. Carson (Grand Rapids: Zondervan Publishing Co., 1982), p. 67, which argue that the neuter is rather *quality*—the authority of Jesus in contrast with that of the priests.

25. R. Steven Notley, "Something Greater than the Temple," *Dispatch from Jerusalem* 24:3 (May-June, 1999), p. 15.

26. The rescue of a work animal would fit within the category of preserving a (human) life, since its loss would threaten life, especially in an agrarian culture (see Luke 14:5). Other permitted cases of "work" on the Sabbath in *halakhah* are the priority of giving birth or burying the dead.

27. Michael O. Wise, "Temple," *Dictionary of Jesus and the Gospels*, eds. Joel Green and Scot McKnight (Downers Grove, IL: InterVarsity Press, 1992), p. 816.

28. The same point is made in Isaiah 66:35b concerning Jerusalem, "the city of the great King" (see Psalm 48:2), and in verse 36 concerning changing the color of the "head" (hair), since the aging process is a divine prerogative and reflects His sovereign rule. The fact that Isaiah 66:1-2 contrasts "heaven [and] earth" with "a house you could build for Me" is meant to eliminate any presumption on behalf of Temple builders that God needed a Temple as the pagan gods did, who were localized by means of a temple-house where they were cared for by their worshipers. It is clear from Ezekiel 43:7 that the

Temple is "the place of My throne and the place of the soles of My feet, where I will dwell among the sons of Israel forever."

29. This "gold" is probably not the famous golden adornment of the Temple but the gold of individuals reserved for the service of the Temple by ascribing it as "Korban." This interpretation better understands the context of taking oaths by the Temple or its altar (Matthew 23:18), since the money would have been dedicated to the Temple as part of a vow.

30. The 45 occurrences of the Greek term *naos* in the New Testament are divided among the historical books (nine times in Matthew; three in Mark; four in Luke; three in John; two in Acts), the Pauline corpus (four times in 1 Corinthians; two in 2 Corinthians; once each in Ephesians and 2 Thessalonians), and the Apocalypse (sixteen times in Revelation). While *naos* can sometimes refer to both the Temple complex and the inner Sanctuary, it generally bears a technical distinction from ἱερός. It is significant that only *naos* is used metaphorically with reference to the church, since in these cases the emphasis is on the indwelling presence of God, not on the Temple itself as an institution. For further discussion on this distinction, see *BAGD* (1979), pp. 373.2, 535.1a; *EDNT* s.v. "ναός," by U. Borse, p. 457; and A. T. Robertson, *Word Pictures in the New Testament*, 6 vols. (Nashville: Broadman Press, 1932) 4:377; 5:38. A similar usage is found in John 2:14, where the money changers are shown to be within the Temple complex (*hieros*). However, Johannine usage appears to favor the term *naos*, the predominance being in the Apocalypse where the Holy of Holies is often indicated either by God's presence, incense, or the Ark of the Covenant (see 11:19; 15:8), and especially where the concept is figurative of the divine presence (see 21:22). Note especially in Revelation 11:1-2 that the temple is referred to in Greek as *ton naon tou Theou* ("the Temple of God"), and then in the next part of the verse reference is made to "the court which is outside the Temple" as something separate. This outer precinct was thus *outside* the *naos*, but still *within* the *heiron*, indicating the specificity given to the terms.

31. After the Exile one-third of a shekel was collected annually, and by the time of Jesus the amount had been restored to the original half-shekel (= two drachmas). This is well attested in both Josephus, *Antiquities* III, 193-196 [viii. 2]; XViii, 312 [ix. 1] and Mishnah *Shekalim*, (which deals with the obligation to support the Temple service).

32. The view of some commentators is that this deals with civil taxation in support of Rome. Their argument, in part, is in view of the references in verse 25 to "the kings of the earth" and "toll or poll tax" which they interpret as references to the Roman imperial practice belonging to the period after 70 A.D. when they suppose Matthew to have been written. In this case, they see Jesus' answer as anachronistic—the question being recast to address the concern of Christians under Roman law obligation to pay taxes to Rome cf. Richard Cassidy, "Matthew 17:24-27—A Word on Civil Taxes," *Catholic Biblical Quarterly* 41 (1979): 571-580. Though the Greek term *basileus* ("king") commonly refers in Hellenistic literature and the Greek papyri to the Emperor, it has been suggested by D. A. Carson, "Matthew," *EBC* 8 (Grand Rapids: Zondervan Publishing House, 1984), p. 394, that here it should not specifically refer to Rome because: 1) the generalized terminology "the kings of the earth" is inadequate to denote Caesar, and 2) in the context the "king" who collects the tax is Jesus' "Father," and comparison of Jesus' sonship in relation to an imperial king is unprecedented. A mediating position sees here both the Temple tax (verse 24) and the civil tax (verse 25), understanding, however, that verse 24 establishes the topic of the entire pericope, while verse 25 is parabolic. The point of Jesus' interrogation of His disciples, however, is to stress that as "sons of the [heavenly] Kingdom" they are exempt from the taxes of this world's kingdom.

33. However, *Berakot* 9:5 does not talk about the selling of animals within the Temple walls, but the prohibition against transporters using Temple grounds as a thoroughfare across the city. Most who argue from the prohibition in *Berakot*, however, fail to notice that Mark supports this view, adding in his narrative that Jesus also would not permit anyone to carry a vessel through Temple grounds, a detail that agrees much more closely with the Mishnaic legislation.

34. See B. Mazar, *op. cit.*, and Meir Ben-Dov, *In the Shadow of the Temple*, trans. Ina Friedman (New York: Harper & Row, 1985), esp. pp. 149-68; and more recently, Kathleen and Leen Ritmeyer, *Reconstructing Herod's Temple Mount in Jerusalem, Biblical Archaeology Review* offprint (New York: Biblical Archaeology Society, 1991).

35. The area uncovered is known as the *Hanuyot*, according to Talmudic sources (Sanhedrin 41:2; Aboda Zara 8:2), and is identified today with the three-level Southern Royal Portico (considered a sacred, or by some, semi-sacred area. In this place, east of the Double and Triple Huldah Gates (in what is now called "Solomon's Stables") where ramps led directly to the Temple Mount, there have been discovered evidence of troughs for animals, as well as dents for tethers. The presence of such animals, a source for impurity, so close to the Temple was considered a desecration by pious Jews. On the evidence for this discovery see Benjamin Mazar, *The Mountain of the Lord* (New York: Doubleday, 1975), p. 126 and also his report in *The Historical Jesus*, ed. Gaalyah Cornfield (New York: Macmillan Publishing Co., 1982), pp. 149-57.

36. Additional archaeological evidence for this location includes: 1) Similarities with the Caesarean structures of the Hellenistic city centers of Alexandria and Antioch, which formed the newly built additions of the Herodian complex; 2) the direct access from the Royal Stoa to the market quarter below (in the main street and around the corner) via the steps leading down from Robinson's Arch.

37. The term "cleansing" that has traditionally described this account is not an appropriate choice since it suggests purification rites or some similar ritual of sanctifying a desanctified site. Since neither Jesus' actions nor words imply any
such thing, the term *clearing* would be a better substitute. I have retained the customary terminology because of its
universal recognition, but have indicated my reservations by the use of quotation marks.

38. In the Synoptic Gospels the event is placed as the last public act of Jesus in order to use it to explain the Sanhedrin's plot
to arrest Jesus, while in John it is used to introduce Jesus' public ministry in the Temple. The varying positions of the
account is apparently a result of authorial purpose, which governs the selection and placement of historical material for
theological or dramatic emphasis. There are, however, significant differences between the Synoptic and Johannine
accounts, leading many to adopt the view that there were actually *two* "cleansings"—see D. A. Carson, *Matthew, EBC*
(Grand Rapids: William B. Eerdmans Publishing Co., 1984), p. 441; Leon Morris, *The Gospel According to John, New International Commentary on the New Testament* (Grand Rapids: William B. Eerdmans Publishing Co., 1971), pp. 190-92.

39. See William R. Telford, *The Barren Temple and the Withered Tree: A Redaction-Critical Analysis of the Cursing of the Fig-
Tree Pericope in Mark's Gospel and its Relation to the Cleansing of the Temple Tradition,* Journal for the Study of the New
Testament Supplements 1 (Sheffield: JSOT Press, 1980).

40. Those who hold to a Markan priority argue that Matthew's sequence is out of chronological order. See Craig S. Keener,
The IVP Bible Background Commentary: New Testament (Downer's Grove, IL: InterVarsity Press, 1993), p. 102.

41. See Jacob Neusner, "Money-Changers in the Temple: The Mishnah's Explanation," *New Testament Studies* 35 (1989): 287-
90; and recently, Jostein Ådna, "The Attitude of Jesus to the Temple: A Critical Examination of How Jesus' Relationship
to the Temple Is Evaluated Within Israeli Scholarship, with Particular Regard to the Jerusalem School [of Synoptic
Research]," *Mishkan* 17-18 (2/1992–1/1993): 65-81.

42. See David Flusser, "Jesu Prozess und Tod," *Entdeckungen im Neuen Testament, Band 1: Jesusworte und inre Uberlieferung*
(Neukirchen- Vluyn, 1987), p. 145; Benjamin Mazar, *The Mountain of the Lord* (New York: Doubleday & Co., 1975), p. 126;
"The Royal Stoa in the Southern Part of the Temple Mount," *Recent Archaeology in the Land of Israel,* ed. by Herschel
Shanks (Washington, D.C.: Biblical Archaeology Society, 1985), p. 147; and Shmuel Safrai, *Die Wallfahrt im Zeitalter des
Zweiten Tempels* (Neukirchen-Vluyn, 1981), p. 185.

43. The only difference between the form of the citations is that while Matthew has "you make," Luke has "you have made."

44. Of the ten occurrences in the LXX of the Greek term *lestes,* six are in Jeremiah literature (Jeremiah 7:11; 12:9; 18:22; cf. esp.
Jeremiah 13, 17, 57). The word is also found in Josephus (*Antiquities* 14.415, 421) describing literal bandit hideouts, and as
a loan-word in rabbinic literature. The New Testament employs it metaphorically (cf. Matthew 26:55/Mark 14:48/Luke
22:52; Matthew 27:38/Mark 15:27; Matthew 27:44; Luke 19:39, 36; John 10:1, 8; 18:40; 2 Corinthians 11:26). See further,
BAGD, p. 474.1; K. H. Rengstorf, s.v. "λῃστής," *Theological Dictionary of the New Testament* 4: 257-62.

45. Of course in the eschatological context of Zechariah 14 no *ethnic* Canaanites would still exist to defile the restored
Temple, which is Zechariah's point in describing the unparalleled ceremonial purity of Jerusalem and the Temple
Mount. But why single out the Canaanites? Their history of idolatrous and ritually contaminating acts resulted in a ban
of genocide being carried out against them from the time of Joshua through King David. Because of this, there would be
no reason to mention their absence in a time after they had long since disappeared. Some who accept this rendering
read it in light of the preceding verse (verse 20), which speaks of a sanctified Temple and city and see it referring generally to any defiling Gentile presence (for example, Charles Ryrie, *Ryrie Study Bible,* p. 1429: "Canaanite: Symbol of all
unscrupulous unbelievers"). However, since the previous verses (verses 16-19) refer to Gentile nations coming to worship annually at the Temple, this is unlikely. Eugene Merrill, understanding this problem, prefers the idea that "there will
no longer be a Canaanite" because in that day of ultimate redemption "all alike will be the people of YHWH"—Eugene
Merrill, *Haggai, Zechariah, Malachi,* An Exegetical Commentary (Chicago: Moody Press, 1994), p. 366. However, the concern of Zechariah is the extent of sanctity, not the equality of saints, as his words "no longer be... *in the house of the
Lord*" indicate. Therefore, a specific problem from the past is in view. This is addressed by John's understanding of
"trader" as those who need to guarantee pure sacrifices, which will be unnecessary in this future day of pervasive
purity.

46. Knowles has suggested that a Matthaean redaction borrowed the Rejected Prophet motif from Mark, and employed it in
light of prevailing Jeremiah traditions in first-century Judaism, for the typological, theodical, and apologetic concerns
of the Christian community—Michael Knowles, *Jeremiah in Matthew's Gospel: The Rejected Prophet Motif in Matthaean
Redaction, Journal for the Study of the New Testament* 68 (Sheffield: JSOT Press, 1993), Ross Winkle has noted the
instances in which Jeremiah is mentioned in the Gospel of Matthew, the only Gospel in which he is mentioned by
name—Ross E. Winkle, "The Jeremiah Model for Jesus in the Temple," *Andrews University Seminary Studies* 24:2 (1986):
155-72.

47. See further, B.T. Dahlberg, "The Typological Use of Jeremiah 1:4-9 in Matthew 16:13-23," *Journal of Biblical Literature* 94 (1975): 73-80.

48. See E. Schweizer, *The Good News According to Matthew*, trans. D. E.. Green (Atlanta, 1975), p. 340.

49. See further, C. K. Barrett, "The House of Prayer and the Den of Thieves," *Jesus und Paulus: Festschrift für Werner Georg Kümmel zum 70. Geburtstag*, eds. E. Earl Ellis and E. Gräßer (Göttingen: Vandenhoeck & Ruprecht, 1975), pp. 13-20.

50. See for a discussion of the violent fate of the prophets, including the above motif, D. R. A. Hare, *The Theme of Jewish Persecution of Christians in the Gospel According to Matthew*, Society for New Testament Studies Monograph Series 6, ed. Matthew Black (Cambridge: At the University Press, 1967), pp. 137-39.

51. The only explicit mention of the murder of prophets is that of Zechariah, the son of Jehoida the high priest, who was stoned to death in the Temple court because he announced that God had forsaken the people because they had forsaken the Temple (2 Chronicles 24:18-21). The other example is that of Uriah from Kiriath-Jearim, who was extradited from Egypt (where he had fled) and killed in Jerusalem, because, like Jeremiah, he had prophesied against the city, and probably also the Temple (Jeremiah 26:19-23). Also, from the apocryphal book of the Prayers of Manasseh, as well as Jewish tradition, we learn that Manasseh had Isaiah the prophet executed in Jerusalem. There were other prophets killed in other places outside Jerusalem for other reasons (see 1 Kings 18:4,13; 19:10,14; Nehemiah 9:26; Jeremiah 2:30), but these are irrelevant to this specific motif since it is qualified by the Temple as both cause and site of the murders.

52. See Theodore Zahn, *Das Evangelium des Matthäus*, Kommentar zum Neuen Testament (Leipzig: Deichert; Erlangen: Scholl, 1922), 1:624, 660 n. 89.

53. The terminology makes explicit that these are not another category of '*am haratez* ("common people") by a repetition of qualifiers. The force of these expresses something like: "non-Jewish foreigners, non-Israelites, from lands outside Israel." That they are directing their prayers toward the Temple, and therefore to YHWH, indicates that as "foreigners" they have turned from "foreign gods" and are considered as proselytes.

54. For these eschatological observations, see Kenneth A. Matthews, "John, Jesus and the Essenes: Trouble at the Temple," *Criswell Theological Review* 3:1 (Fall, 1988): 101-26.

55. The *soreg* was described by Josephus as being a low stone wall (1.5 meters/5 feet), located in the middle of the courtyard and surrounding the inner court, upon which were inscriptions in Greek and Latin warning Gentiles against entry upon pain of death. The first of these notices, engraved in limestone, was discovered in Jerusalem in 1871 and another in 1936.

56. See Morna D. Hooker, "Traditions about the Temple in the Sayings of Jesus," *Bulletin of the John Rylands Library* 70:1 (Spring, 1988): 18-19. Hooker suggests that perhaps the reason the Malachi 3:1-3 passage was not cited with reference to Jesus' activities was because in Malachi the cleansing of the Temple was seen as successful, and the refined sons of Levi once more offer acceptable offerings to the Lord, but the "cleansing" by Jesus was unsuccessful, since instead of the reform He, in the mantle of Jeremiah, requested, He met opposition, arrest, and death.

57. The imperative should be rendered as a concession—see *A Greek Grammar of the New Testament and Other Early Christian Literature*, eds. Blass DeBrunner and Funk (University of Chicago Press, 1973) §387(2). On the irony intended by the citation at this juncture in John's account, see P. D. Duke, *Irony in the Fourth Gospel* (Atlanta: John Knox Press, 1985), p. 87, who observes that "the succession of 'temples' is made possible because of the Jews themselves, who, by destroying the body of Jesus, doomed the Temple they sought to defend."

58. See D. A. Carson, "Understanding Misunderstandings in the Fourth Gospel," *Tyndale Bulletin* 83 (1982): 80, 90, who notes that it was not that the Jews *mis*understood so much as they *did* not understand.

59. This fact does not mean that the disciples were "dull witted," since apparently no one else understood Jesus' meaning either, but reflects the common experience of perceiving prophecy in retrospect (see, for example, 2 Kings 9:36-37). This was the interpretive method found in the Dead Sea Scrolls, especially as their "Teacher of Righteousness" revealed the true meaning of prophecies that had failed to be fulfilled as expected.

60. However, some argue that John changed the subject from the first person (as reflected in Jesus' opponents' quotes, "He said, 'I will destroy this Temple…,'" Matthew 26:60) in light of his insight into Jesus' true meaning—see E. P. Sanders, *Jesus and Judaism* (Philadelphia: Fortress Press, 1985), p. 73. Sanders also thinks that Jesus predicted the destruction of the Temple by God, in harmony with Jeremiah's similar actions (Jeremiah 7:12-14).

61. There is only one apocalyptic text to support his supposition, 1 Enoch 90:28-29, but the Messianic connection there is weak, and it is probably God who destroys the old Temple and builds the new through His agents (verse 28). However, it is instructive that the old house, viewed in the text as corrupt, must be torn down before the new house is built. Nevertheless, the later Jewish traditions concerning the rebuilding of the Temple by the Messiah do not have in view His destruction of an existing Temple, since for them the Temple was already in ruins.

62. For examples see E.P. Sanders, "New Temple and Restoration in Jewish Literature" (chapter 2) in *Jesus and Judaism*, pp. 77-119.

63. Commentary on John 2:19 in the *New English Translation* (Biblical Studies Press), p. 282.

64. David Flusser, "The Judean Desert Scrolls and the Beginning of Christianity," p. 2.

65. See James H. Charlesworth, "Reinterpreting John: How the Dead Sea Scrolls Have Revolutionized Our Understanding of the Gospel of John," *Bible Review* 9:1 (February 1993): 24.

66. See my book *Secrets of the Dead Sea Scrolls* (Eugene, OR: Harvest House Publishers, 1996), especially pp. 246-61.

67. This offers the best explanation of the statement in connection with Jesus' citations related to the eschatological restoration of the Temple, a position defended by E. P. Sanders against replacement theologians, *Jesus and Judaism*, pp.71-119.

68. See, for example, Lloyd Gaston, *No Stone Upon Another: Studies in the Significance of the Fall of Jerusalem in the Synoptic Gospels*, New Testament Supplements 23 (Leiden: E. J.. Brill, 1970); and James Calvin de Young, *Jerusalem in the New Testament: The Significance of the City in the History of Redemption and in Eschatology* (Amsterdam: J. H.. Kok N. VanKampen, 1960).

69. See Markus Bockmuehl, "Why Did Jesus Predict the Destruction of the Temple?," *Crux* XXV: 3 (September, 1989), pp. 11-17. Holding to the same interpretation for Jesus' predictions, yet without the element of judgment, is E. P. Sanders, *Jesus and Judaism* (London: SCM Press, 1985), pp. 85-88, who notes "the naturalness of the connection between expecting a new temple and supposing that the old one will be destroyed" (p. 85).

70. He gives the reason for this school of interpretation as twofold: 1) *Theological*. The first and most important reason was that the restoration promises of the biblical prophets had not been fulfilled. Prophecies about the exile and subsequent return to the Land under ideal conditions were obviously unfulfilled. This awareness is found already in the pre-Maccabean book of Tobit (13:16-18; 14:5), as well as in Daniel 9:17,26-27. The corruption and decline of the Hasmonean dynasty and subsequent occupation by Roman forces exacerbated doubts that a full restoration, much less a liberation, of the Jewish Nation would take place. In addition, there were doubts, by groups such as the Essenes, and those who frequented the Jewish Temple at Leontopolis, that the Maccabees had effected a complete cleansing of the Temple. If despite its Herodian-restored splendor it was not the eschatological Temple, and if the purity of the Zadokite priestly line was at all a matter of concern, then the only logical conclusion was that the present corrupt system would need to give way to a new one, 2) *Social and Political*. In addition, the degeneration of the priestly aristocracy invited comparison with the earlier prophetic oracles of judgment and destruction (the desecration motif). Of the 28 high priests between 37 B.C. and A.D. 70, all but two came from illegitimate non-Zadokite families. It became increasing clear to most Jews that the cultic center, which regulated all of Jewish life, was in the hands of a vast network of economic and religious oppression. The legitimate and necessary operation of the Temple was supported by a maze of intrigue, nepotism, and graft (Mishnah *Keritot* 1.7) such as that of the well-known priestly family of the house of Kathros (cf. *Baraita*, B.*Pesahim* 57a). Such social and political factors prompted many Jews to consider the theological perspective previously discussed.

71. *Historicism* is an eschatological school of interpretation that holds to the fulfillment of prophetic events in the Old and New Testaments, and especially those in the Olivet Discourse, while originally future at the time of their being revealed, took place in *past history* (usually sometime during the Roman empire, though some interpret events in later times).

72. *Preterism* is a subset of Historicism and holds in that either all (Extreme or Consistent Preterism) or most (Moderate Preterism) prophetic fulfillment, both in the Old and New Testaments (and especially the Olivet Discourse), took place by and in the event of the Roman destruction of Jerusalem in A.D. 70. Extreme Preterism sees the second coming of Christ as already fulfilled in the Roman invasion, while Moderate Preterism sees two second comings: one in the Roman invasion and a final one at the end of the age. For a defense of the position see, R.C. Sproul, *The Last Days According to Jesus: What the Bible Really Says About When Jesus Will Come* (Grand Rapids: Baker Book House, 1998).

73. That the scope cannot be limited to a present audience is obvious from the fact that such usage cannot mean only those who heard the message or who were currently part of the present generation, since others who were not present and who were yet to be born must be included, while some would certainly have died before the events were fulfilled and were no longer a part of that generation, especially since it is still *future* from the perspective of the speaker.

74. A comparison of the Greek texts of the three accounts reveals, for example, that while Matthew and Mark use the term "great tribulation," Luke uses the term "great distress." This is because "tribulation" may serve as a technical expression of "the time of Jacob's trouble," an eschatological event, while "distress" may refer to a less specific time of persecution, such as that attending a military conquest. See further on this Lukan distinction, J. Dwight Pentecost, *Things to Come: A Study in Biblical Eschatology* (Grand Rapids: Dunham Publishing Co., 1958), pp. 276-77. This permits Luke's chiastic structure to have both a historical series and an eschatological series, whereas Matthew and Mark's chiasm is strictly eschatological.

75. Desmond Ford, *The Abomination of Desolation in Biblical Eschatology* (Lanham: University Press of America, 1978), pp. 75-76, has purposed an alternative solution to the question. He argues that Jesus linked the destruction of Jerusalem with the end of the age and promised *both* to His generation. Was Jesus, therefore, wrong, for the end of that age (A.D. 70) did not bring the predicted coming of Messiah? Ford responds negatively, because he believes that Mark 13:30 can be understood as belonging to the same genre as Jonah's "Yet forty days and Nineveh will be overthrown" (p. 75). He says, "We submit that the exegesis of Mk. 13:30 is only complete if we allow for the possibility that Christ, as a Hebrew of the Hebrews, may have used an absolute statement with less than an absolute meaning, in harmony with those Scriptures He so implicitly trusted. It is possible that He believed that if the early church proved faithful to its missionary commission, and if the chastened Jewish nation repented, the end would transpire in that same Age. It is the linking of the gospel proclamation to the world with the end of the Age that provides the hint of the contingent element" (p. 76).

76. Luke's omission of this signal event is one of the reasons it is believed that at this point in his narrative he is presenting the fall of Jerusalem in A.D. 70 rather than the eschatological end of the age.

77. For this reason Consistent Preterists must interpret Christ's coming as having occurred in A.D. 70. To do so, however, requires the employment of a non-literal and historical hermeneutic, since the events cannot be reconciled with either the literal interpretation of the Old Testament citations and allusions in the Olivet Discourse or the actual events of the destruction.

78. Jesus' handling of the biblical text followed the exegetical methods common to Judaism and drew its perspective and presuppositions from Jewish backgrounds. Jesus' use of both quotations and allusions from the Old Testament reveal that He was skilled in these various forms of rabbinic exegesis that were normative in His day (literalist and midrashic)—E. Earl Ellis, *The Old Testament in Early Christianity: Canon and Interpretation in the Light of Modern Research* (Grand Rapids: Baker Book House, 1992), p. 121. Ellis, in a discussion of Jesus' method of interpretation, demonstrates examples in the Gospels of Jesus' use of Hillel's Rules, *proem* and *yelammedenu*-type midrash, see appendix I, pp. 130-38. Furthermore, because the Judaism of Jesus' day was Torah-centric, to gain a hearing among His people, Jesus' teaching had to also be Torah-centric. The distinctive difference in Jesus' methodology was His employment of a creative element in his hermeneutics that arose from His concept of the Old Testament as a pre-Messianic Torah, for examples of this Messianic interpretive paradigm in application to Jesus' parabolic style have been ably demonstrated by Robert H. Stein, *The Method and Message of Jesus' Teachings* (Philadelphia: The Westminster Press, 1978), pp. 112-47. In this regard, Jesus' eschatology, which followed the literalist approach of the Apocrypha, Pseudepigrapha, and Qumran in looking for a future fulfillment of the restoration of Israel in a millennial age, following the judgment of the Gentile nations, served as the basis for the Johannine, Pauline, and Peterine epistles—see E. Earl Ellis, *Prophecy and Hermeneutic in Early Christianity* (Grand Rapids: William B. Eerdmans Publishing Co., 1978), pp. 147-72, and Pasquale de Santo, *A Study of Jewish Eschatology with Special Reference to the Final Conflict* (Ph.D. dissertation, Duke University, 1957), pp. 397-402. We should add here the statement of Lamar Cope: "'To the Close of the Age': The Role of Apocalyptic Thought in the Gospel of Matthew," *Apocalyptic and the New Testament: Essays in Honor of J. Louis Martyn, JSNT Supplement Series* 24 (Sheffield, 1989), p. 123: "So it seems to me that we need to acknowledge that Christian faith did arise out of the seedbed of late Jewish apocalyptic movements, but we should also recognize that its finest insights about God, human life, and discipleship are anchored in a radical understanding of the grace of God which negates the dark side of apocalyptic." In response to Cope, I would say that the Christian faith, especially as reflected in the early Jewish-Christianity of the New Testament, is better recognized as a continuation of the eschatological thought of the biblical prophets, sharing with apocalyptic literature where it has also drawn from this same source. The "darker" side of apocalyptic—that is, divine retribution/punishment—is essential to the formation of the "grace" theology which Cole would have it eclipse. Both of these elements are part and parcel to the prophetic message, and thus indispensable ingredients to the eschatological faith of Christianity. Therefore, it is essential, in understanding Jesus' eschatological treatment of the Temple, to underscore his continuity with a Torah-centered Judaism whose eschatological hope was primarily drawn from the biblical prophets and whose influence governed the hermeneutical development of the early church.

Chapter 13—Predictions in Paul

1. John T. Townsend, *The Jerusalem Temple in New Testament Thought* (Ph.D. dissertation, Harvard Divinity School, 1958), pp. 32-33.

2. For example, in representing the Historicist position on Revelation 11:1, Steve Gregg writes "The Temple of God (v. 1) throughout the New Testament is always the church (1 Cor. 3:16; 6:19; 2 Thess. 2:4)"—*Revelation: Four Views—A Parallel Commentary* (Nashville: Thomas Nelson Publishers, 1997), p. 220. Note, however, that all of his examples are from the Pauline epistles.

3. One writer believes that Paul's imagery, at least in 1 Corinthians 3:16-17, was not the Temple at all, but the Tabernacle— see J. M.. Ford, "You Are God's 'Building'" (I Cor iii. 10-17)," *New Testament Studies* 21 (1973/74) pp 139-42; however, his alleged parallels are not convincing and go against the use of the desecration motif, which envisions the desecration/ destruction of the building itself, which means only the Jerusalem Temple could be understood as the source. William Hendriksen, *Exposition of Ephesians*, New Testament Commentary (Grand Rapids: Baker Book House, 1967), p. 145, argues that in Ephesians 2 the allusion must also be to the pagan Greek temple of Artemis (or Diana to the Romans), which was located in that city. He notes in support of this position that Paul's words in Acts 17:24 are applicable to any man-made temple, and that the temple of Artemis, as one of the seven wonders of the ancient world, could hardly have been eclipsed in Ephesian thought by the Jerusalem Temple, and that this temple and its service were at the center of conflict for Paul (Acts 19:23-41). While this suggestion has merit, we cannot read the mind of Paul beyond what he has directly or indirectly revealed in his texts, and these bear witness, it seems to me, only of the Jerusalem Temple. When we look for sources for Paul's theological treatises to Gentile audiences, he does refer to familiar Greek poets (Acts 17:28; Titus 1:12), religious objects (Acts 17:23), and notions (Acts 14:11-13), but he has not used them to communicate spiritual truths, even by analogy, but rather condemned such (I Timothy 1:3-4; 4:7). The fact that Paul in 1 Corinthians 3:16 and 6:19 introduced his Temple metaphor with the interrogative phrase *ouk oidate?* ("do you not know?") suggests that the image was assumed by Paul to already be a familiar one, and what temple would be more familiar to diaspora Jews living in Corinth (and fit for use as an analogy to the believing community) than the Jerusalem Temple? It is of further relevance to this argument that Paul did not have to explain his analogy or defend the appropriateness of its use, but expected it to be received without contention. Only the Jerusalem Temple could be expected to merit this uncontentious reception.

4. Ibid., p. 52.

5. J.M.P. Sweet, "A House Not Made with Hands," *Templum Amicitiæ: Essays on the Second Temple presented to Ernst Bammel*, Journal for the Study of the New Testament Supplements 48 (Sheffield: Journal for the Study of the New Testament , 1991), p. 388.

6. On the specific use of these metaphorical relationships in the respective texts see Herbert M. Gale, *The Use of Analogy in the Letters of Paul* (Philadelphia: Westminster Press, 1964), pp. 38-39, 64-75, 79-93.

7. One reason for this selection, as was mentioned earlier, is that the *naos* consisted of or was equivalent to the Holy of Holies in technical distinction, and therefore indicated the place of spiritual dwelling and of divine communion. We may add as support for this distinction the use of the plural, which occurs only in Acts 17:24 ("temples made with hands") and 19:24 ("silver shrines"), both with reference to pagan temples, where the focus seems to be on the presence of an idol. Whether or not the idol was placed within the pagan temple's inner sanctum, that was where the Ark of the Covenant and the *Shekinah* were located in the Jerusalem Temple, and only *naos* would draw attention to this comparison. Since Paul's point to his readers is that God now dwells in them and constitutes them a holy place, the best referent for his analogy would have been *naos*.

8. The German commentator Otto Michael argued for this distinction in his article on "ναός" in *Theological Dictionary of the New Testament* (Grand Rapids: Wm. B. Eerdmans Publishing Co., 1976), 4: 880-90 (especially p. 887), although he notes that this distinction cannot be strictly maintained in all of the Greek of the New Testament period. From the Gospel of Matthew (27:5) he cites what he considers an example (pp. 884-85) of *naos* referring to the Temple precincts when Judas is said to have thrown the 30 pieces of silver into the *naos*. But, the text does not say that Judas *entered* into the *naos*, which was something he, in fact, could not do—only that he *threw* the money there. Even if Michael is correct concerning the usage during the New Testament period, it is more likely that the usage in the Septuagint, where *heiron* is rarely used for the Temple (outside of 1 Esdras and Maccabees) may have influenced Paul—see *Theological Dictionary of the New Testament*, s.v. "ἱερον," 3:226, 233.

9. Unlike Paul, Peter refers to the Temple indirectly by reference to the church as *oikos* ("a [spiritual] house"). This is almost equivalent to *naos* (because he continues his analogy by referring to the actions of the Temple priesthood within the Holy Place by calling the church a "holy priesthood" that offers up spiritual sacrifices [1 Peter 2:5]).

10. Acts 15 is important to this argument because it shows that Paul not only recognized the authority of the Jerusalem Council (Acts 15:2,4—Paul reported to the Council concerning his ministry and to receive their verdict on the faith/works controversy), but that he was actually commissioned by them to communicate their theological position to the Gentile churches (Acts 15:22).

11. This is admittedly a complex interpretive matter; however, James is using the Amos passage not to demonstrate present fulfillment, but to show that a Gentile inclusion was predicted in God's program for Israel, and that "after these things" (verse 16a), i.e., after the present witness to the Gentiles, the program for Israel would be fulfilled. This served as an

assurance to the Jewish church that the many conversions of Gentiles reported by Paul would not be a threat to the promise of the prophets; rather, it would be part of the process leading to its ultimate fulfillment (see Romans 11:25-32).

12. This observation was made by R. J. McKelvey, *The New Temple: The Church in the New Testament* (London: Oxford University Press, 1969), p. 43. It should be noted, in exception of McKelvey, that even if such a substitution was made during the exile, it did not alter the belief in normative Judaism that the Temple was the central sanctuary or that the service was the only proper means of spiritual service to God.

13. Philo taught that the purified soul of man becomes the temple of God as a result of human achievement. The Stoics, while not directly making reference to man as a temple, indirectly taught the idea—e.g., as in Seneca's concept of man housing a part of the divine spirit. In contrast to Philo, the Stoics believed that the indwelling of God was by natural endowment.

14. Philo saw the *soma* as the prison of the soul and only allowed that it could have been the temple of God for Adam as the perfect man. Seneca, for example, contended that the *soma* was useless and perishable, a threat to the purity of the soul or spirit, which alone could glorify God. See J. N. Sevenster, *Paul and Seneca* (Leiden: E. J. Brill, 1961), p. 76.

15. Some modern Christian authors, especially those who accept a positive view of the Temple, have adapted this symbolic Hellenistic concept and used it to teach Christian truth. This approach must be reconsidered not only because it is a concept that misinterprets the Pauline concept, but also because it borders on Kabbalistic teaching, and appears in esoteric works—for example, see R. A. Schwaller de Lubicz, *The Temple and Man: Sacred Architecture and the Perfect Man*, trans. Robert Lawlor (New York: Inner Tradition International, 1977). For an example of evangelical usage without recognizing the distinction made here, see the note on 1 Corinthians 3:16 in *The Ryrie Study Bible* (Chicago: Moody Press, 1978), p. 1731.

16. Note that the development of the "in Christ" doctrine is presented in Corinthians (e.g., 1 Corinthians 12:12-13; see also 2 Corinthians 3:18) and Ephesians (e.g., Ephesians 2:6-7; see also 4:4-6; 5:23), the two books in which Paul employs the Temple metaphor in connection with *soma*.

17. Bertil Gärtner, *The Temple and the Community in Qumran and the New Testament* (Cambridge: University Press, 1965), pp. 55-56.

18. For my own comparison of Pauline theology and the Dead Sea Scrolls see my book *Secrets of the Dead Sea Scrolls* (Eugene, OR: Harvest House Publishers, 1996), pp. 179-83, 202-12, 323, 372-74, 442-43.

19. However, in 2 Corinthians 6:19 Paul's analogy of defilement introduced to the Temple via idols indicates that he is drawing his imagery from the Old Testament rather than Qumran, whose literature, though stating opposition to idolatry, never explicitly contrasts idols with the Temple. This is also consistent with Paul's dependence on the Old Testament in the remainder of 1 Corinthians 6. For the use of Temple imagery at Qumran see 1QS 2:11, 17; 4:5; 1QH 4:19; CD 20:9. Bertil Gärtner, *The Temple and the Community in Qumran and the New Testament*, pp. 100-105 provides a survey of comparisons and contrasts between the Dead Sea literature and Pauline usage. For further comparisons between the Qumran literature and Paul on the Temple, see Karl Georg Kuhn, "The Epistle to the Ephesians in the Light of the Qumran Texts," *NTS* 7 (1960-1961): 334-46; and Franz Mussner, "Contributions Made by Qumran to the Understanding of the Epistle to the Ephesians," *Neutestamentliche Aufsätze: Festschrift für J. Schmidt*, ed. J. Blinzler (Regensburg Verlag, 1968): 185-98.

20. Both the Qumran community, and, originally, the Christian community were considered sects of Judaism. Their similar allegiance to their sectarian teachers (the "Teacher of Righteousness" and Jesus), their belief that they were the elect, faithful to the Torah and the prophets, and their necessary separation from the established religious leadership, may well have caused a common identification between their community and the Temple as the embodiment of sanctification and especially the presence of God. Neither at Qumran, nor in Paul, was the "community" viewed as a *replacement* for the Jerusalem Temple, even though its service was considered corrupt. Paul and the Jewish-Christians worshiped in the Second Temple, and while the Qumran community separated itself from direct participation, they may have indirectly respected the institution by payment of the Temple tax.

21. David L. Sage, "The Figurative Use of the Word Temple in Paul's Epistles" (Th.M. thesis, Dallas Theological Seminary, 1980), pp. 8-9.

22. The correspondence between Christ's physical body and Christ's spiritual body, the Christian community, may have been drawn by Paul from his view of Jesus' resurrection (the subject of John 2:19-22), which made possible the indwelling of the believer individually and corporately by the Spirit. If so, then Paul's dependence for the use of the Temple metaphor is based directly on that of Jesus.

23. The idea of replacement, however, is axiomatic to many commentators—see Ralph P. Martin, *2 Corinthians*, Word Biblical Commentary 40 (Waco, TX: Word Books, 1986), p. 201: "Since, for Paul, the Temple of God in Jerusalem had been replaced in *Heilsgeschichte* by the Temple of God (the believing community). ..."

24. While we argue that Paul used the indefinite to avoid giving the sense of replacing the Temple with the church or Christians, we nevertheless believe that he had the literal Jerusalem Temple as a reference. For this reason Heinrich A. Meyer, *Critical and Exegetical Handbook to the Epistle to the Corinthians* (Winona Lake, IN: Alpha Publications, Reprint 1979), p. 78, and Alfred Plummer, *A Critical and Exegetical Commentary on the Second Epistle of St Paul to the Corinthians*, International Critical Commentary (Edinburgh: T & T Clark, Reprint 1970), pp. 67-68, believed that Paul intended to be definite here, since to use an indefinite would imply there was more than one Temple, which would not only be inconsistent with the Jewish conception of the "one Temple for the one God," but would distort the Christian conception of the one body of Christ. Since we will argue that Paul is using the Temple metaphorically, he could properly have used the definite article (and did in 1 Corinthians 3:17), since the figure is not confused with the literal object from which it is drawn. However, the indefinite sense avoids the paradox of only one "temple of God," and yet many churches and each Christian as a "temple."

25. Leon Morris, *The First Epistle of Paul to the Corinthians*, Tyndale New Testament Commentary (Grand Rapids: William B. Eerdmans Publishing Co., 1958), p. 69.

26. English versions translate the two anarthrous uses of *naos* in 2 Corinthians 6:16 as definite: "what agreement has the temple of God with idols? For we are the temple of the living God." But it would be more in keeping with their indefinite construction [and with Paul's meaning] to translate: "what agreement has God's Temple [the Jerusalem Temple] with idols? For we are a [spiritual] temple of the living God."

27. While in this verse the construction is lacking the article, definiteness might be intended if we apply Colwell's rule that anartharous predicate nouns preceding the verb are usually definite. The word order here is *naos theou este*, and even if not an illustration of the rule, probably still indicates definiteness by the emphatic position of *naos*—see BDF (1961): par. 273. Johannine usage of *naos* with the definite article seems to always indicate the Temple in Jerusalem as distinct from any symbolic usage. In this respect Isbon T. Beckwith, *The Apocalypse of John* (New York: Macmillan Publishing Co., 1919), p. 586, is bold to assert: "This is *the* temple at Jerusalem that is in view. The temple at Jerusalem is never used to symbolize Christians or the church."

28. This is the position of Gordon D. Fee, *The First Epistle to the Corinthians*. New International Commentary on the New Testament (Grand Rapids: William B. Eerdmans Publishing Co., 1987), p. 147.

29. I am indebted for the outline and some details of these elements to the theses by Robert Miles Abegg, "The New Testament Doctrine of the Church as the Temple of God" (Th.M. thesis: Dallas Theological Seminary, 1981), pp. 45-50; Lorne J. Meisner, "The Temple Motif—God's Witness Unto Himself," (Th.M. thesis: Dallas Theological Seminary, 1977), pp. 20-21; and David Sage, "The Figurative Use of the Word *Temple* in Paul's Epistles" (Th.M. thesis, Dallas Theological Seminary, 1980).

30. The arrangement of Greek temples also revealed this concept of the indwelling deity, for an image of the deity (service statue) was usually placed at the end of the *cella*—see *Oxford Classical Dictionary*, s.v. "temple" (Oxford: University Press). While Paul rejected any such notion for the Jerusalem Temple, the word was probably ideally chosen by the Septuagint to refer to the Holy of Holies for this very purpose.

31. For additional evidence from Greek constructions in this text, see Scott S. Cunningham, "The Temple Motif in Ephesians 2:19-22" (Th.M. thesis: Dallas Theological Seminary, 1980), pp. 56-64.

32. See 1 Corinthians 5:7—"Christ our Passover," and Romans 3:25—with most likely Yom Kippur in mind. It must be admitted, however, that Paul did not necessarily hold that because Christ had fulfilled the spiritual aspects of the sacrificial system (both for salvation and sanctification) that Christ thereby replaced the validity of the continuing Temple sacrifices. Because Paul, following the prophets (see 1 Samuel 15:22; Psalms 40:6-8; 51:16-17; Micah 6:6-8), saw that the sacrifices were never considered efficacious in themselves, nor the act of offering as meritorious in itself, he saw them simply as the ordained vehicle by which faith could be overtly demonstrated, and therefore valid as long as they could serve this purpose (i.e., while the Temple stood). This may explain the infrequent use of sacrificial terminology by Paul with respect to Jesus' crucifixion—only three times in his epistles (Romans 3:25; 1 Corinthians 5:7; Ephesians 5:2). However, some argue that Paul's use of the Greek prepositions *anti* and *huper* for substitutionary atonement (Romans 5:8; 8:3; Galatians 1:4; 4:20), and *peri* [*hamartias*] ("for [sin]" in Romans 8:3) which designates a "sin offering" in the Septuagint (Leviticus 7:37; 9:3; 14:13, 22, 31, etc.) should also be included.

33. The analogy from the holiness of the Temple is also implicitly seen in 2 Corinthians 6:14–7:1 (see also contrasts of verses 14-16 with the exhortation to separation in verse 17), and is perhaps behind other Pauline appeals to sanctification, since the appeal is often made in priestly language, and where else would holy priests serve but in the holy Temple?

34. See J. Shanor, "Paul as Master Builder," *New Testament Studies* 34 (1988), pp. 461-71.

35. It is also noteworthy that Paul, in 1 Corinthians 3:9, juxtaposes a gardening metaphor with a (Temple) construction metaphor: "You are God's garden, [you] are God's building." This relationship of husbandry to building was apparently

drawn from the Old Testament, where parallel examples may be seen, each in some connection to the Temple service (see Deuteronomy 16:21; Isaiah 61:3-6; Jeremiah 35:7-9,17; Ezekiel 28:26; 36:30-36). It is also quite possible that *oikodoma* could be used to express that part of the semantic range of *oikos* which approximates to "dwelling places" (see the phrase *tas oikodomas tou iepou* in Matthew 24:1, though the plural here may modify the semantic range). In like manner, Ignatius, *Epistle to the Ephesians* 9:1, refers to the cross as the *machana*, the instrument by which it is raised.

36. This is the usual focus in interpretation of this section—Gordon Fee, *op. cit.*, p. 140, though L. L. Welborn, "On Discord in Corinth: 1 Corinthians 1–4 and Ancient Politics," *Journal of Biblical Literature* 106 (1987): 85-111, argues that Paul has in mind the cosmic conflict between "the rulers of this age" and "the power of God" (see 1 Corinthians 2:5-8); however, the "rulers of this age" here are not cosmic, but earthly—the Roman rulers who crucified Jesus—and the "power of God" is (from the human viewpoint) the weak and humble manner in which the gospel has been presented (see 1 Corinthians 2:1-4). For a more prosaic and contextually satisfying alternative see the presentation of the view of D. R. de Lacey below.

37. The Temple was constructed of wood with straw for thatch for the roofing, then built up of stones, with Solomon's Temple in particular, said to be gilded with gold (the Holy of Holies) and its foundation laid with costly stones (see 1 Kings 6:17,20-22).

38. The use of fire in apocalyptic imagery is integral to Paul's gospel (2 Thessalonians 1:7) and was probably modeled after Malachi 4:1 as a Day of the Lord motif (compare Isaiah 66:15; Daniel 7:9) in terms of the appearance of God with fire (see Exodus 3:2; 19:18; Ezekiel 1:13).

39. The word *akrpgoniaios* ("cornerstone") has been variously interpreted as to its location in the Temple complex. It is used by the Septuagint to translate the Hebrew *pinnah* ("corner") at Isaiah 28:16, and Symmachus uses it to translate the Hebrew phrase *rosh pinnah* ("head of the corner") in Psalm 118:22. Since the Greek prefix *akros* intensifies the force of *goniaios*, it is taken to indicate either "height" or "priority," and was therefore either that stone which was first set by the builder and which determined the lie of the whole construction, i.e., a "foundation stone," or as Joachim Jeremias, *Theological Dictionary of the New Testament*, s.v. "ἀκρογωνιαῖος," 1 (1964): 792, originally suggested an *Abschlusstein* ("capstone"), or as Stig Hanson, *The Unity of the Church in the New Testament: Colossians and Ephesians* (Uppsala: Almquist & Wiksells Boktryckeri, 1946), pp. 131-32, a "final stone." This argument finds support in the Testament of Solomon 22:7 with "a great cornerstone (put) at the head of the corner completing the Temple of God," and from its other use in the Greek New Testament with *logeisthai* ("to fit") in Ephesians 4:16 *sunarmologoumenon* ("fitted together") to indicate an integration from above—i.e., high up on a building. Whether we take the sense as elevation or strategic position, the stone still remains part of the Jerusalem Temple and draws its importance from that fact.

40. D. R. de Lacey, "οἵτινές ἐστε ὑμεῖς: The Function of a Metaphor in Paul," *Temple Amicitae: Essays on the Second Temple Presented to Ernst Bammel*, ed. William Horbury, *Journal for the Study of the New Testament Supplements* 48 (Sheffield: JTOS, 1991), pp.406-8.

41. It seems to me that the construction of the Herodian Temple, lasting, with its continual additions and embellishments, through the lifetime of Paul, and almost until the A.D. 70 destruction, would have heightened the appropriateness of this analogy to any Jerusalemite, pilgrim, or visitor to Jerusalem. The Temple certainly was a central focus for Jesus' disciples during their trips to Jerusalem, and prompted Jesus' famous prophetic declaration of the Temple's destruction (see Matthew 24:1-2; Mark 13:1-2; Luke 21:5-6). It is also relevant that in each of these accounts the *stones* are the referent, both for the disciples and Jesus.

42. On this particular use of inverted order, see D. R. de Lacey, "Word-Order and Emphasis," *Bible et Informatique: Méthodes, outils, résultats*, ed. F. Poswick (Genève: Slatkine, 1989).

43. See Ernst Käsemann, "Sätze Heiligen Rechts im Neuen Testament," *New Testament Studies* 1 (1954-1955): 248-60; Gordon Fee, *op. cit.*, p.148.

44. See C. J. Roetzel, "The Judgment Form in Paul's Letters," *Journal of Biblical Literature* 88 (1969): 305.

45. See James C. Vanderkam, "The Dead Sea Scrolls and Early Christianity (Part 1): How Are They Related?," *Bible Review* (December 1991): 20.

46. See Ralph P. Martin, *2 Corinthians*, Word Biblical Commentary 40 (Waco, TX: Word Books, 1986), p. 204.

47. W. D. Davies, *The Gospel and the Land: Early Christianity and Jewish Territorial Doctrine* (Berkeley: University of California Press, 1974), p. 188.

48. Davies, *op. cit.*, pp. 193-204.

49. Some suggest that Paul's choice of the term was influenced by his rabbinic training, since in *Sifre Deuteronomy* 117 (on Deuteronomy 15:7-9) and *Sanhedrin* 111b the expression is explained as a pun: "having no yoke," i.e., "having thrown off the yoke of God."

50. Belial in the apocalyptic literature was represented as a personalized (*supra*human) force in opposition to God and His people, especially in the final battle of the last days (see *Jubilees* 1:20; *T. Reuben* 4:11; *T. Simeon* 5:3; *T. Levi* 19:1; *T. Daniel*

4:7; 5:1; T. *Naphtali* 2:6; 3:1; *Ascension of Isaiah* 3:11), and especially at Qumran, where the figure appears as an immoral force inspiring the "Wicked Priest" and causing the defilement in the Jerusalem Sanctuary (see 1QM 13:11; 1QS 1:18-24; 2:19; 1QM 1:1,5,13; 4:2; 11:8; 13:4,11; 14:9; 15:3; 18:1,3; 1QH 6:21; 4QFlor 1:8,9; 2:2). See further H. W. Huppenbauer, "Belial in den Qumrantexten," *Theologische Zeitschrift* 15 (1959): 81-89.

51. See 2 Thessalonians 2:5: "Remember that while I was still with you, I was telling you these things"—a reference to his frequent teaching on this subject.

52. If the provenance of 2 Thessalonians is the city of Corinth, as many conservative scholars affirm, then added weight is given to this argument, since Paul may well have been communicating the same message under different metaphors to these respective congregations.

53. See further Theophilus Mills Taylor, "Uncleanness and Purification in Paul" (Ph.D. dissertation: Yale University, 1956).

54. See R. Jewett, *Paul's Anthropological Terms: A Study of their Use in Conflict Settings* (1971), who insists that 1 Corinthians 7:1 stands in the Jewish apocalyptic tradition, so that *pneumatos* is God's *pneuma* ("spirit") given to man (see *T. Naphtali* 10:9: "Blessed is the man who does not defile the holy spirit of God which has been placed and breathed into him"). Such a usage would be similar to our previously studied context of 1 Corinthian 6:17-19.

55. For a survey of these difficulties see Gary Staats, "A Study of the Basic Interpretive Problems of Galatians 4:21-31" (Th.M. thesis, Dallas Theological Seminary, 1967).

56. On the theories concerning the provenance of the epistle (North or South Galatia), see for Southern destination theory Robert Jewett, "The Agitators and the Galatian Congregation," *New Testament Studies* 17 (1970-71), pp. 198-212. For a good survey of both positions, with a Southern Galatian preference defended, see F.F. Bruce, *Commentary on Galatians*, New International Greek Testament Commentary (Grand Rapids: William B. Eerdmans, 1982), pp. 3-32. Of equal difficulty is the identification of Paul's opponents in the epistle—see C. Berker, *Paul the Apostle: The Triumph of God in Life and Thought* (Philadelphia: Fortress Press, 1980), pp. 42-47, who argues for Jewish Judaizers of the circumcision party *contra* J. Munck, *Paul and the Salvation of Mankind,* trans. F. Clarke (London: SCM Press, 1959), pp. 87-134, who argues for Gentile-Christian Judaizers, and Walter Schmitals, *Paul and the Gnostics,* trans. John E. Steely (Nashville: Abingdon, 1972), pp. 13-64, who argues for opponents characterized by incipient Gnosticism.

57. The *theological* theme of the book is a treatise and defense of the Pauline position on justification by faith, which he illustrates by citations and allusions from the Old Testament. Yet the *practical* theme is Paul's defense of the accusations against his supposed compromising view on the Law and his alleged liberal position on Christian liberty. He must defend his apostleship in light of these renegade suspicions, and it may be that his presentation of justification by faith serves too as the theological ground for his defense of the freedom that results from this act.

58. We should perhaps not understand "allegory" in the classical sense. Although in the first century the term was acquiring a technical connotation (as in Plutarch and Herucleitus), it may not have had the same meaning that it was later given by the Alexandrian school of exegesis, and, in fact, none of the figures here are themselves "allegorized." His use, then, is a typological, or analogical one, and the term itself, *a hapax legomena* in the New Testament, conveys this thought in the literal translation of the verb *allagoreo* (*allo* + *agoreuo*—"to speak [to] another")—see the *New International Version's* dynamic equivalent translation: "these things may be taken figuratively." This may be demonstrated by an analysis of the analogical characteristics of the story, the principal one, which, according to Gale, *The Use of Analogy in the Letters of Paul*, pp. 67-68, is *fragmentariness*. Paul does not proceed from the story itself, showing how the various elements within it correspond to certain facts in the contemporary situation, but moves instead from one idea to another as these arise out of the present situation and applies some correspondence from the story. The absence of systematic development is seen in two ways: 1) in the way in which a single figure in the story is used at one moment to represent one thing or one idea and at the next moment to represent something quite different; 2) in the way in which even single points of correspondence are not developed or carried through to their full conclusions. While this usage is unique to the Pauline corpus, it was a common exegetical device in the first century—see A. T. Lincoln, *Paradise Now and Not Yet: Studies in the Role of the Heavenly Dimension in Paul's Thought with Special Reference to his Eschatology*, Society for New Testament Studies Monograph Series 43 (Cambridge: Cambridge University, 1981), pp. 12-15; and J. Bonsirven, *Exégèse Rabbinique et Exégèse Paulinienne. Bibliothéque de Theologie Historique* (Paris: Beauchesne, 1939), pp. 210-12, 309-11.

59. In this section Paul follows standard midrashic exegetical methodology, beginning with a citation from the Old Testament (verses 21-22), then developing his exposition around principal themes from the texts (verses 23-29), and then concluding with a final citation and application (verses 30-31)—see D. Patte, *Early Jewish Hermeneutic in Palestine*, Society of Biblical Literature Dissertation Series 22 (Missoula: Scholars Press, 1975), pp. 117-27.

60. C. K. Barrett, "Allegory of Abraham, Sarah, and Hagar in the Argument of Galatians," *Rechertfertigung: Festschrift für Ernst Käsemann*, ed. J. Friedrich, W. Pohlmann, and P. Stuhlmacher (Tübingen: J. C. B. Mohr, 1976), pp. 6-13.

61. That Paul is employing his opponent's own proof texts against them is evident from his introduction to this section with an ironic appeal: "Tell me, you who desire to be under the Law, do you not hear the Law?" This also accords well with Hellenistic diatribe literature, in which the use of an opening interrogation is a traditional device, and Pauline debate style, in which he invokes his opponent's argumentation against them with an initial question (see Romans 2:17–4:25; 6:1–7:25; 8:31-39; 9:1–11:36). Paul's method here is not to cite specific texts, though he does employ the normal Greek citation formula *gegraptai gar hoti* ("for/as it is written"), but summarizes select material from various chapters. His use of the citation formula also calls attention to the biblical basis for his opponent's arguments, with which he differs on the basis of the theological interpretation of the entire tradition.

62. Typology presupposes that *Heilsgeschichte* displays a recurring pattern of divine action. F.F. Bruce, *Commentary on Galatians*, p. 217, notes that just such a pattern was employed by the exilic prophets "when they portrayed their people's return from Babylon in terms of a second Exodus…[which] typology is particularly widespread in the NT period (Hebrews 3:7–4:11; Jude 5)."

63. For this reason Paul shifts from the use of the more specific term *huious* ("sons") to the more general term *teknow* ("children").

64. To do otherwise, such as importing the idea that Sarah is the new covenant, does violence to the literary *Sitz im Leben* of the allegory.

65. The phrase *to de Agar Sina oros estin en ta Arabia* ("now this Hagar is Mount Sinai in Arabia") in verse 25a is disputed. The problem arises textually because of manuscript variants: A,B,D,κ.τ.λ. read *to de Agar Sina oros estin en ta Arabia* ("Now Hagar is Mount Sinai in Arabia "), but א, C, G, κ.τ.λ. read: *to gar Sina oros estin en ta Arabia* ("For Sinai is a mountain in Arabia"). Other slightly different variants also exist. In favor of the first variant, the use of the neuter article *to* with Hagar, rather than the feminine *ha*, indicates that the reference is to the name of Hagar rather than to the woman herself. This does not mean that one has to accept that some peak on Mount Sinai may have been so designated, or that Hebrew *hagar*, Aramaic *hargara*, or Arabic *hadjar* ("crag," "cliff") is being used as a paranomasia based on the similar sounds—see G.I. Davies, "Hagar, El-Hegra and the Location of Mount Sinai," *Vetus Testament* 22 (1972), pp. 152-63, but that the copula *estin* means "signifies," or "represents," in harmony with the correspondence conveyed by *sustoichei*— see 2 Corinthians 3:17; and especially 1 Corinthians 10:4 (typologically): "and the rock was, i.e., 'signified,' Christ." In addition, in the second variant, א adds ου following Σινα, an insertion that would not have been necessary had Hagar not been the original reading. Thus, even א could be added in support of the first variant. Since so many variants exist in an attempt to clarify the text, the *lectio difficilior* should be preferred, even though it is the longer, and especially on the intrinsic grounds mentioned above, for how would a mere geographical statement (as in the second variant) contribute to the analogy? The more difficult problem is how this identification supports the analogical argument, though it is not crucial to its equation.

66. While the antithesis between Sinai and Zion developed in a number of directions from this early concept, and is contrasted in Hebrews 12:18-24 and in the later pseudo-Cyprianic anti-Jewish treatise *De montibus Sina et Sion* (*Oxyrhynchus Papyri* IV. 991-1000), it is deliberately avoided here so that the focus may be entirely on Jerusalem and the contrasts derived from its condition. Paul, from his lack of description, appears to assume that his audience is familiar with this concept of "the Jerusalem above."

67. This is a motif that has a history in biblical and extrabiblical Jewish tradition (see Isaiah 49:20f; 50:1; 54:1-13; Jeremiah 50:2; Hosea 4:5; 2 Barach 3:1-5; 2 Esdras 10:7, 17). Nevertheless, Paul does not employ it as an original theological argument, but only as an apologetic response to his opponents' presuppositions based on it.

68. This seems to have been the position of Paul's opponents based on his charges in Galatians 1–2. If they were insisting that Jerusalem, because of its unique sanctity, be the controlling factor for the Gentile-Christians, then the distinction removed by the ground of common access to God through faith (see Acts 15:11; Ephesians 2:11-22, Paul's other Temple-analogy) was obliterated.

69. Indeed, in Paul's thinking, the inviolability of Jerusalem was only rightly conceived in terms of the eschatological Jerusalem, which, "not made with hands," could not be desecrated by men. It was because such a true service center existed that hope could continue for a restored Temple and a resumed service center after the earthly house was desolated or destroyed. However, here Paul does not talk about a future descent of the heavenly Jerusalem, so we should not assume that his analogy is necessarily operating on the traditional apocalyptic model.

70. One must resist the temptation to define Paul's use of "the Jerusalem above" on the familiar grounds of Jewish apocalypticism and rabbinic notions of the heavenly Jerusalem, since here his analogical method is being determined by his polemical argument, and which has redefined these elements of the text.

71. The idea of *ano* ("above") does not mean "future," as though the Jerusalem depicted were coming in the eschaton. Rather, with its antithesis to *nun* ("present"), it has the idea of "eternal," having both a pre-existence and a future durative existence.

72. Isaiah 54:1 is here cited not only because it is a *locus classicus* for this theme, and a part of Isaiah 40–66, which served as a source for *testimonia* for the New Testament and the early church, but because the mother here congratulated is Jerusalem. The use of Isaiah in this fashion was preceded by the Qumran texts, where the authority for their wilderness retreat was adduced from Isaiah 40:3 (see 1QS 8.13; 4Q Is). Qumran also used parts of Isaiah 54 (e.g., verse 11) to refer to the elect community forming the nucleus of the restored Israel of the future. Paul apparently understood the Jerusalem above to be the community of the elect, but not necessarily with an eschatological restoration to Israel in view, even though Isaiah 54:1 was used this way in rabbinic literature. With Paul, the cities, not the women, are being again contrasted, so that the Jerusalem before the exile and the Jerusalem after the exile, but destined to be restored, are in view, and the two cities are distinct entities.

73. Elizabeth Gaines, *op. cit.*, p. 292, n. 20, maintains that this link was not original with Paul, but suggests antecedents in rabbinic literature, which probably preserved traditions of the first century (see *Pesiquim Rabbi* 32:2; *Haftorah* to Genesis 6:9–11:32). The originality in Paul's exegesis was not in his application of Isaiah 54:1 to Sarah, but in identifying Sarah with Gentile believers.

74. This does not require that Paul saw the church as fulfilling the Abrahamic promise, but that believing Jews and Gentiles had equal rights of inheritance in the spiritual promise of being Abraham's seed *spiritually*—through Christ. In harmony with Paul's statements in Romans 3:25-29, which I believe was directed to ethnic Jews only (physical inheritance versus spiritual relationship) in view of countering the same theological assumption as at Galatia, it is best to not posit that Paul did not also include a hope for the fulfillment of the Abrahamic covenant by a restored Israel (see Romans 11:25-27).

75. It is also an interesting suggestion that this persecution might be considered as a result of the Genesis 3:15 antagonism, since it was within the proto-Temple desecration context and carried Messianic overtones. Of course, no such linkage is implied in the text.

76. Haggadic literature frequently elaborated on this tradition. *Genesis Rabbah* 53:11 (on Genesis 21:9) based its conclusions that the struggle was over religious apostasy based on the more sinister connotations claimed for "sexual sporting," or "violent action." R. Ishmael charged that Ishmael was an idolater based on the use of the term in Exodus 32:6 in connection with the worship of the golden calf. In a similar manner, *Targum Neofiti I*, on the same text, says that Sarah saw Ishmael "doing unseemly things" which an added gloss explains as actions pertaining to a foreign service. R. Akiba likewise saw Ishmael's conduct as immorality on the basis of Genesis 39:17, where Potiphar's wife claimed that Joseph came "to lie with me," but literally "to play with me." R. Azariah in the name of R. Levi, expounding on 2 Samuel 2:14, where Hebrew *visachachu* (literally, "let them play," or "hold a contest") is used of the sport of shooting arrows, said that Ishmael used to shoot arrows in the direction of Isaac, while pretending to be playing. See further, J. Bowker, *The Targums and Rabbinic Literature* (Cambridge: University Press, 1969), pp. 204-6.

77. Rabbinic tradition makes mention of the rivalry between Ishmael and Isaac over the matter of inheritance based on circumcision, which is the context here. According to *Genesis Rabbah* 55:4 (on Genesis 22:1), Ishmael claimed the inheritance because he had accepted circumcision voluntarily at the age of thirteen (Genesis 17:25), whereas Isaac had received it involuntarily when he was but eight days old. If this were in the background, it would help make the connection with Paul's typology clearer.

Chapter 14—Predictions in the Apocalypse

1. Robert Thomas, *Revelation 8–22: An Exegetical Commentary* (Chicago: Moody Press, 1995), pp. 81-82.

2. As cited in *Revelation: Four Views—A Parallel Commentary,* ed. Steve Gregg (Nashville: Thomas Nelson Publishers, 1997), dust jacket.

3. For an overview of these systems, especially as categorized with respect to their views of the millennium (Amillennialism, Postmillennialism, Premillennialism), see *The Meaning of the Millennium: Four Views,* ed. Robert G. Clouse (Downers Grove, IL: InterVarsity Press, 1977).

4. For the arguments of such modern preterist interpreters see David Chilton, *Days of Vengeance* (Fort Worth, TX: Dominion Press, 1987).

5. See Adela Yarbro Collins, "Myth and History in the Book of Revelation: The Problem of Its Date," *Traditions in Transformation: Turning Points in Biblical Faith,* ed. Baruch Halpern and Jon D. Levenson (Winona Lake, IN: Eisenbrauns, 1981), pp. 402-3.

6. *The Ecclesiastical History of Eusebius Pamphilus*, trans. Isaac Boyle, reprint (Grand Rapids: Baker Book House, 1977), p. 188.

7. The first effort to investigate these parallels was that of Kenneth Scott, "Statius' Adulation of Domitian," *American Journal of Philology* 54 (1933): 247-59. The most recent is that of Deane James Woods, "Statius' 'Silvæ' and John's 'Apocalypse': Some Parallel and Contrastive Motifs" (Th.D. dissertation, Dallas Theological Seminary, 1990). Woods analyzes 11 motifs to validate that the literary motifs in the Apocalypse were common to those circulating in the Roman empire during the reign of Domitian.

8. However, the assumption of chronological indicators after chapter four, when the literary style changes from symbolic narrative to apocalyptic, must be cautioned. Whether one seeks the identity of the seven kings of Revelation 17 or the identification of persecutions is tendentious for any dating of the book. The rise of opposing kingdoms, persecutions, and battles are all more closely related to normative apocalyptic literature than to Roman history.

9. So-called because of the Greek or Latin word for "thousand" and their literal interpretation of the "thousand years" of Revelation 20.

10. See Joel Gregory, "The Chiliastic Hermeneutic of Papias of Hierapolis and Justin Martyr Compared with Later Patristic Chiliasts" (Ph.D. dissertation, Baylor University, May, 1983). This well-established historical view has recently been challenged by Charles Hill, *Regnum Cælorum: Patterns of Future Hope in the Early Church* (Oxford: Clarendon Press, 1992), whose revisionist historical analysis of the first 600 years of the church argues that a non-Chiliastic eschatology existed as recognized orthodoxy. Nevertheless, his own table summarizing his evidence indicates that the earliest patristic interpretation was "definitely Chiliastic" (his term). His evidence rather reveals a growing non and anti-Chiliasm as one moves forward in time. Others have argued from this evidence that the chiliastic interpretation lost ground as anti-Jewish polemics increased, and Greek philosophical thought became normative in the Christian hierarchy. Thus, a shift occurred from literalism (considered Jewish) to allegory (considered Christian), and a "spiritual" interpretation developed (via Clement and Origen), which was especially championed by Eusebius Pamphilius, Bishop of Caesarea, who said that Chiliasts should "go worship with the Jews" (see Walter Kaiser, "Response 3: An Evangelical Response," in *Dispensationalism, Israel and the Church: The Search for Definition*, eds. C.A. Blaising and D. Bock (Grand Rapids: Zondervan Publishing Co., 1992), pp. 360-76 (especially pp. 361-63). In addition, from the time of Constantine, the political merger with Christianity had deemed Chiliasm inadequate for the social order, and its "Christianizing" of the empire further polarized Jew and Christian. Chiliasm apparently began to revive after a return to literal interpretation with the Protestant Reformation (which had depended in large measure on Jewish exegetical methodology to counter the Roman Catholic mysticism and the doctrine of papal infallibility) and Puritan scholasticism, which revived the Christian study of Mishnah and Talmud, see Pinchas Lapide, *Hebrew in the Church* (William B. Eerdmans Publishing Co., 1989). For further discussion of chiliastic historical development see LeRoy E. Froom, *The Prophetic Faith of Our Fathers: The Historical Development of Prophetic Interpretation*, 4 vols (Washington, D.C.: Review and Herald, 1950), and J.N.D. Kelly, *Early Christian Doctrines*, 5th revised ed. (San Francisco: Harper & Row, 1978).

11. *The Apostolic Fathers: The Fragments of Papias*, trans. Joseph M.-F. Marique (New York: Fathers of the Church, 1947), p. 375.

12. For a biblical-theological overview of this system see C.C. Ryrie, *The Basis of the Premillennial Faith* (New York: Loizeaux Brothers, 1953), and for a recent exegetical defense see *A Defense of Premillennialism*, eds. D.K. Campbell and J. Townsend (Chicago: Moody Press, 1992). For a comparison of premillennialism with amillennialism (from a premillennial perspective) see C.L. Feinberg, *Premillennialism or Amillennialism?: The Premillennial and Amillennial Systems of Biblical Interpretation Analyzed & Compared*, 2nd ed. (New York: American Board of Missions to the Jews, Inc., 1961).

13. For further discussion, see Robert L. Thomas, *Revelation 1–7: An Exegetical Commentary* (Chicago: Moody Press, 1992); John F. Walvoord, *The Revelation* (Chicago: Moody Press, 1966); Stanley K. Fowler, "A Defense of the Futurist Interpretation of the Apocalypse" (Th.M. thesis, Dallas Theological Seminary, 1972).

14. See Harold W. Hoehner, "Evidence from Revelation 20," *A Case for Premillennialism: A New Consensus*, eds. D.K. Campbell and J.L. Townsend (Chicago: Moody Press, 1992), p. 262.

15. David Flusser, "The Jewish Religion in the Second Temple Period," s.v. "Interpretation (Peshat and Derash) at the Time of the Second Temple," *World History of the Jewish People* 8: *Society and Religion in the Second Temple Period*, eds. M. Avi-Yonah and Z. Baras (Jerusalem: Masada Publishing Ltd., 1977), p. 14.

16. "The Eschatology of Judaism" in Luther H. Harshbarger and John A. Mourant, *Judaism and Christianity: Perspectives and Traditions* (Boston: Allyn and Bacon, Inc., 1968), p. 337.

17. See Solomon Schechter, *Aspects of Rabbinic Theology* (New York: Schocken Books, 1969), p. 98: "The idea of the kingdom is accordingly often so closely connected with the redemption of Israel from the exile, the advent of the Messiah, and the restoration of the Temple, as to be inseparable from it."

18. *Revelation: Four Views—A Parallel Commentary,* ed. Steve Gregg (Nashville: Thomas Nelson Publishers, 1997), p. 41.

19. For an analysis of Revelation with regard to Daniel's prophecy, see John A. McLean, *The Seventieth Week of Daniel 9:27 As a Literary Key for Understanding the Structure of the Apocalypse of John* (Unpublished dissertation, University of Michigan, 1990), pp. 187-258.

20. The six sections of the book of Revelation according to McLean are: 1) Prologue (chap. 1); 2) Letters to the Seven Churches (chaps. 3-4); 3) God's Great Tribulation (chaps. 4-19); 4) Kingdom of God (chap. 20); 5) New Jerusalem (chaps. 21–22:5); 6) Epilogue (chap. 22:6-21).

21. Martin Kiddle, *The Revelation of St. John,* Moffatt New Testament Commentary (New York: Harper & Row, 1940), p. 174.

22. See, for example, G.V. Caird, *A Commentary on the Revelation of St. John the Divine,* Harper New Testament Commentary (New York: Harper & Row, 1966), p. 131: "In a book of symbols such as Revelation the last thing that the temple and the holy city could refer to was the physical temple and the earthly Jerusalem. A literal meaning would be inconsistent with his symbolism elsewhere." Caird, in order to maintain his idea of consistency, here makes the outer court = members of the church who have compromised with the world, and the holy city = the world outside the church (p. 132). However, there is no textual or hermeneutical control to justify this identification, and any such interpretation as this must therefore be arbitrary.

23. See M. Kiddle, *The Revelation of St. John,* pp. 178-79.

24. See Albert Barnes, *The Book of Revelation* (New York: Harper, 1851), pp. 268-69; Kiddle, *The Revelation of St. John,* p. 179; R.C.H. Lenski, *The Interpretation of St. John's Revelation* (Columbus, OH: Luther Book Concern, 1935), p. 328; Homer Hailey, *Revelation, an Introduction and Commentary* (Grand Rapids: Baker Book House, 1979), p. 250; G.R. Beasley-Murray, *The Book of Revelation,* NCB (Grand Rapids: William B. Eerdmans Publishing Co., 1978), p. 182.

25. See Chilton, *op. cit.*

26. John F. Walvoord, *The Revelation of Jesus Christ* (Chicago: Moody Press, 1966), p. 176.

27. Isbon T. Beckwith, *The Apocalypse of John* (New York: Macmillan Publishing Co., 1919), p. 586.

28. George E. Ladd, *A Commentary on the Revelation* (Grand Rapids: William B. Eerdmans Publishing Co., 1972), p. 152.

29. J.B. Smith, *A Revelation of Jesus Christ* (Scottsdale, PA: Herald Publishing House, 1961), p. 164.

30. Alan F. Johnson, *Revelation,* Expositor's Bible Commentary 12 (Grand Rapids: Zondervan Publishing Co., 1981), p. 500.

31. J.A. Seiss, *The Apocalypse,* 3 vols. (New York: Charles C. Cook, 1909), 2:159. This is the brazen altar of burnt offering in the outer court, rather than the golden altar of incense in the Holy Place, because the worshipers seem to be in proximity to it (and only priests could go into the Holy Place), and it may be observed that when an altar is spoken of in the text without further qualification it always means to indicate the brazen altar—see Beckwith, *The Apocalypse of John,* p. 597.

32. Ladd, *op. cit.*

33. M. Kiddle, *The Revelation of St. John,* pp. 179-80.

34. Robert L. Thomas, "The Argument of the Book of Revelation" (Th.D. dissertation, Dallas Theological Seminary, 1959), pp. 187-88; cf. A.T. Robertson, "Revelation," *Word Pictures in the New Testament,* 6 vols. (Nashville: Broadman Press, 1933), 6: 384.

35. Robert L. Thomas, *Exegetical Digest of Revelation 8–14* (1993), p. 155.

36. E.W. Bullinger, *The Apocalypse or "The Day of the Lord"* (London: Eyre and Spottiswoode, n.d.), p. 347.

37. See Ladd, *A Commentary on the Revelation,* p. 152.

38. A.T. Robertson, "Revelation," *Word Pictures in the New Testament,* 6:376.

39. Even though the act of measuring recalls Ezekiel's measurement of the Millennial Temple (Ezekiel 40:3–42:20), unlike the Ezekiel text, there are no measurements recorded. Therefore the symbolism must be of something that relates to both measuring (verse 1a) and non-measuring (verse 1b), since the act is to afford information about the inner and outer platforms of the Temple Mount.

40. This is the normal connotation of μετρέω, and assuming that 11:1 continues the Johannine commission begun in 10:11 of the obtaining of information is the proper sequel and expected function, cf. Henry Alford, "Revelation," *The Greek New Testament,* 4 vols. (London: Longmans, Green and Co., 1903), 4: 657.

41. Measurement can indicate such judgment (see 2 Samuel 8:2a; 2 Kings 21:13; Isaiah 34:11; Lamentations 2:8; Amos 7:7-9); cf. J. Massyngberde Ford, *Revelation,* Anchor Bible (Garden City: Doubleday & Co., 1975), p. 176.

42. Robert Thomas, *Exegetical Digest of Revelation 8–14,* p. 153. See also his *Revelation 8–22: An Exegetical Commentary* (Chicago: Moody Press, 1995), pp. 78-86.

43. In Daniel 12:11 the 1,290 days = 42 months based on a 360-day lunar calendar.

44. See *The Jerusalem Bible,* p. 1533 (margin note).

45. See James C. VanderKam, "1 Enoch, Enochic Motifs, and Enoch in Early Christian Literature," *The Jewish Apocalyptic Heritage in Early Christianity,* eds. J.C. VanderKam and W. Adler (Minneapolis: Fortress Press, 1996), p. 90.

46. John's vision of the Heavenly Temple, and especially his use of the phrase "the temple of God which is in heaven" (Revelation 11:19), reveals that he follows in the tradition of the Old Testament *tabnit* ("pattern") shared with the New Testament epistles and Hebrews (see 8:4-5). A similar development of the tradition also appears in early Judaism; see for rabbinic references H.L. Strack and P. Billerbeck, *Kommentar zum Neuen Testament aus Talmud und Midrasch* (München: C.H. Beck'sche Verlagsbuchhandlung, 1961), pp. 702-4.

47. Craig R. Koester, *The Dwelling of God: The Tabernacle in the Old Testament, Intertestamental Jewish Literature, and the New Testament*, Catholic Biblical Quarterly Monograph Series 22 (Washington, D.C.: The Catholic Biblical Association of America, 1989), p. 185.

48. J. Webb Mealy, *After the Thousand Years: Resurrection and Judgment in Revelation 20*, Journal for the Study of the New Testament Supplements 70 (Sheffield, NJ: JSOT Press, 1993), pp. 143-162, 196-97.

49. See Gregory K. Beale, *The Book of Revelation: A Commentary on the Greek Text*, The New International Greek Testament Commentary (Grand Rapids: Wm. B. Eerdmans Publishing Co., 1999), p. 440. For his "modified-idealist" interpretation of this passage see his discussion on pages 440-43.

50. There is also here the language of Isaiah 25:8 (alluded to also in 1 Corinthians 15:54 and Revelation 21:4), which is also part of a millennial restoration context. As with Ezekiel 37:25-28, the fulfillment for this verse is said to be on "the earth."

51. See my discussion of this point in *Jerusalem in Prophecy* (Eugene, OR: Harvest House Publishers, 1998), pp. 315-20.

52. D. James Kennedy, *Messiah: Prophecies Fulfilled* (Ft. Lauderdale, FL: Coral Ridge Ministries, n.d.), p. 99.

Chapter 15—Searching for the Sacred Site

1. Rabbi Leibel Reznick, *The Holy Temple Revisited* (Northvale, NJ: Jason Aronson, Inc., 1993), 2:142.

2. While it has been claimed that some remains of Solomonic masonry are extant in and around the Temple enclosure, notably at the southern and eastern walls (e.g., the "seam"), nothing directly connected to the Temple has yet been discovered. In conversation with Meir Ben-Dov, chief archaeologist for the Temple Mount excavations, he has stated that he believes the Second Temple, which completely erased all traces of the First Temple, stood at least three meters above the present *azurah*, and therefore, no remains of even the Herodian structure could be extant. However, subterranean structures connected with the Temple service may have been discovered—see, for example, Ronnie Reich, "Two Possible *Miqva'ot* on the Temple Mount," *Israel Exploration Journal* 39 (1989): 63-65; and the more comprehensive work by Meir Ben-Dov, *tybh rh twrypj* (Jerusalem: Keter Publishing House, 1982) (Hebrew), and English ed. trans. Ina Friedman, *In the Shadow of the Temple: The Discovery of Ancient Jerusalem* (New York: Harper & Row, 1985).

3. For a discussion of the various chronological, philological, textual, and architectural problems related to the study of the Temple of Solomon see Jean Ouellette, "The Basic Structure of Solomon's Temple and Archaeological Research," *The Temple of Solomon*, ed. J. Gutmann (Missoula: Scholars Press, 1976): 1-20. One of the crucial difficulties in reconstructing the Temple based on the historical sources is their lack of agreement in architectural details. This is also the case, for example, in western Asia, where it is rare to find an instance of the union of excavated Temple remains and texts which can be unequivocally related to the ritual practices of the Temple. In Egypt, however, some such examples can be found—see E. A. E. Reymond, *The Mythological Origins of the Egyptian Temple* (Manchester/New York: Manchester University Press/Barnes and Noble, 1969). For the most recent architectural research in relation to the Temple Mount, and especially the archaeological identification of the various historical additions to the *azurah*, its dimensions, and the most probable location of the First and Second Temples, see Leen Ritmeyer, "The Architectural Development of the Temple Mount in Jerusalem" (Ph.D. dissertation, University of Manchester, 1993) and *idem*. "Locating the Original Temple Mount," *BAR* 18:2 (March/April 1992), p. 45. To this should be added Asher S. Kaufman's detailed study *The Temple of Jerusalem: Tractate Middot* (Jerusalem: Har Yéra'eh Press, 1991) (Hebrew), which incorporates into the commentary the latest archaeological and scientific research on the Temple's location and construction (however, written from Kaufman's perspective that the Temple was situated north of the present Dome of the Rock).

4. In general, the word *cult* indicates the observable actions of a people, singly or in community, in which they engage in conjunction with their religion. We will use the term in this manner with reference to foreign (pagan) religious practices. Our primary usage, however, is with reference to the biblical form of Israel's worship, which included the Temple, its *sancta*, and its associated services. For the most recent and thorough description of the Temple cult see R. Chaim Richman, *The Odyssey of the Temple* (Jerusalem: Israel Publications and Productions, Ltd., 1993).

5. As cited by Ulf Carmesund, *Two Faces of the Expanding Jewish State: A Study on How Religious Motives Can Legitimate Two Jewish Groups Trying to Dominate Mount Moriah in Jerusalem* (Uppsala University, 1972), p. 86.

6. Yirmiyahu Fischer, *Mikdash-Build* 1:22 (Adar 5757).

7. See *Mikdash-Build* 1:30 (9 Tamuz 5757).

8. It is an idealized but *actual* Temple that might be described as a combination of Solomon's First Temple and Ezekiel's visionary Fourth or Millennial Temple. For further information on this Temple's plan see Lawrence H. Schiffman, *The Eschatological Community of the Dead Sea Scrolls* (Atlanta: Scholars Press, 1989), pp. 180-81, and his forthcoming commentary on the Temple Scroll.

9. J.L. Porter, *Jerusalem, Bethany, and Bethlehem* (London: Nelson, 1887), p. 52.

10. Kathleen Kenyon, *The Bible and Recent Archaeology* (London: The British Museum, 1978), pp. 85-86.

11. Michael Avi-Yonah, "Jerusalem of the Second Temple Period" in *Jerusalem Revealed*, ed. Yigael Yadin (New Haven: Yale University Press, 1976), p. 13.

12. See my book *The Stones Cry Out* (Eugene, OR: Harvest House Publishers, 1997), pp. 175-202 for a more comprehensive treatment of these excavations related to the Temple.

13. Two popular sources for additional information on early explorers and excavations are Neil Asher Silberman, *Digging for God and Country: Exploration, Archaeology, and the Secret Struggle for the Holy Land, 1799-1917* (New York: Alfred A. Knopf, 1982); and Naomi Shepherd, *The Zealous Intruders: The Western Rediscovery of Palestine* (San Francisco: Harper & Row, Publishers, 1987), pp. 193-227.

14. Kathleen Kenyon, *Jerusalem: Excavating 3,000 Years of History* (New York: McGraw-Hill, 1967), p. 55.

15. For a description of this and other recent excavations at the Temple Mount, see *The Stones Cry Out: What Archaeology Reveals about the Truth of the Bible* (Eugene, OR: Harvest House Publishers, 1997), pp. 175-220.

16. Yohanan Aharoni, "The Solomonic Temple, the Tabernacle and the Arad Sanctuary," H.A. Hoffner, ed., *Orient and Occident: The C.H. Gordon Festschrift* (Berlin: Neukirchen-Vluyn, 1973), pp. 1-8.

17. As cited in the article "Second Temple Replica Discovered," *Jerusalem Post*, April 8, 1995.

18. Meir Ben-Dov, *In the Shadow of the Temple* (New York: Harper & Row Publishers, 1982), p. 77.

19. As quoted in "What if this isn't the Western Wall?" *The Jerusalem Report* 9:15 (November 23, 1998): 70.

20. See Ernest L. Martin, "The Temples that Jerusalem Forgot: Secrets of Jerusalem Now Made Clear" (Portland, OR: Associates for Scriptural Knowledge, November 1996).

21. While each of the proponents have argued against their opponents' theories, one recently published against Tuvia Sagiv's Southern Option should be included here: Michael Ben-Ari, "The Temple Was Not Located on the Southern End" (trans. Yisrael Dubitsky), Mikdash-Build 1:2 (29 Ellul 5756).

22. Based on his two previously published articles: "Il 'Tempio di Jerusalemme' dal II all' VIII Secolo," *Biblica* 43 (1962): 1-21, and "La Posizione del tempio erodiano di Gerusalemme," *Biblica* 46 (1965): 428-44.

23. Citing Jerome (in Matt. 4:24; cf. J. Migne, ed., *Patrologia Latina*, 26, 180f; *Enchiridion*, no. 445), Bagatti, Il 'Tempio di Gerusalemme' dal II all VIII Secolo, *Biblica* 43 (1962). 13-14.

24. See Tuvia Sagiv, *The Hidden Secrets of the Temple Mount* (Tel Aviv: unpublished paper, n.d.), pp. 3-4.

25. Ibid., pp. 4-5.

26. Ibid., pp. 6-7.

27. Ibid., pp. 5-6.

28. For these see Tuvia Sagiv, *The Hidden Secrets of the Temple Mount* (Tel Aviv: unpublished paper, 1992), pp. 10-11, and especially *Penetrating Insights into the Temple Mount* (Tel Aviv: unpublished paper, n.d.), pp. 1-18.

29. See Tuvia Sagiv, *Penetrating Insights into the Temple Mount* (Tel Aviv: unpublished paper, n.d.), pp. 1-5.

30. See Tuvia Sagiv, *Temples on Mount Moriah* (Tel Aviv: unpublished paper, 1993), pp. 1-24.

31. *Niv Hamidrashia* 15 (1980): 115-130 (Hebrew); *Biblical Archaeologist* 44 (1981): 108-115; *Biblical Archaeology Review* IX:2 (1983): 40-59; *Proceedings of the Ninth World Congress of Jewish Studies*: Jerusalem, August 4-12, 1985 (Division B, Vol. 1), pp. 13-20 (Hebrew); *Har HaBayit ve'atriv* (1989), pp. 179-181 (Hebrew). He has recently published (in Hebrew) a critical edition of Mishnah tractate *Middot* (which gives the critical measurements of the Temple), which include notes based on his findings with accompanying charts and diagrams.

32. *Ariel* 43 (1977): 63-99.

33. Based on interview at Kaufman home (with Jimmy DeYoung), July 21, 1991.

34. This story was related to me (Randall) by Gershon Salomon who, as professor of Oriental Studies at the Hebrew University, is an expert on Arab legends connected with the Temple Mount.

35. Among those in the evangelical Christian community who early accepted Kaufman were academics such as Dr. John McRae, an established archaeologist, who published Kaufman's evidence as the preferred theory in his *Archaeology and the New Testament* (1991), pp. 112-114, 122 (however, McRae has since changed his view and has accepted the proposal of Ritmeyer, cf. "Locating the Original Temple Area Is a Source of Controversy," *Messianic Times* (Summer 1992), p. 10). The Southern Baptist Convention quarterly *Biblical Illustrator* (Summer 1991, pp. 38-41) published a diagram of the First Temple based exclusively on Kaufman's theory of location. Nearly every evangelical prophecy scholar joined in the

acceptance of this theory. Prominent among its popularizers were Dr. Hal Lindsey in his *Prophetic Walk Thru the Holy Land* (1983), Grant Jeffrey in his *Armaggedon: Appointment with Destiny* (1989), Chuck Missler & Don Stewart in their *The Coming Temple* (1991), and Harold Sevener in the November and December 1992 issues of *Chosen People* magazine, which featured a two-part series on the rebuilding of the Temple. Today, it continues to be the most popular view among evangelicals and charismatic Christians as demonstrated by the frequency with which it is cited on websites.

36. See "Mysteries on the Temple Mount," *Israel Today* 4 (April 1999): 15.

37. As cited in "From the Cutting Chamber" (Lishkat HaGazit) *Bein HaUlam LaMizbeach*, issue 10.

38. See 2 Samuel 24:25; 1 Kings 8:22,64; 9:25; 2 Kings 16:14-15.

39. Ibid., pp. 148-50.

40. Interview with Rabbi Goren (by Jimmy DeYoung), July 21, 1991.

41. Interview with Chaim Richman, June 26, 1991.

42. Yirmiyahu Fischer, Mikdash-Build 1:22 (Adar 5757).

43. As cited by Ofer Livne-Kafri, "Rock of Sages," *Eretz* 46 (May-June 1996), p. 52.

44. "Judgment on the Temple Mount," *Jerusalem Post,* Friday, June 21, 1991, p. 9

45. Interview with Dan Bahat (by Jimmy DeYoung), July 1991.

46. See (with Leen Ritmeyer), *Secrets of Jerusalem's Temple Mount* (Washington, D.C.: Biblical Archaeology Society, 1998); *The Temple and the Rock* (Harrogate: Ritmeyer Archaeological Design, 1996); *From Sinai to Sakhra* [Ark of the Covenant slide set and booklet] (Harrogate: Ritmeyer Archaeological Design, 1995), *The Archaeology of Herod's Temple Mount* [slide set & booklet] (Harrogate: Ritmeyer Archaeological Design, 1994); *Worship and Ritual in Herod's Temple* [slide set and booklet] (Harrogate: Ritmeyer Archaeological Design, 1999); *Jerusalem in 30 A.D.* [slide set and booklet] (Harrogate: Ritmeyer Archaeological Design, 1994); and a 11.5" x 7" x 1.75" hand-cast, high-quality resin model of Herod's Temple.

47. Professor Avraham Biran excavated such a parallel plan at Tel Dan. He uncovered a *temenos* (sacred enclosure) that was probably built by Jeroboam I (tenth century B.C.—the time of Solomon). This enclosure was much smaller than that of the Temple Mount; however, it was nearly *square* in shape.

48. Confirmation of the accuracy of this description may perhaps be seen in the plan of Ezekiel's visionary Temple (Ezekiel 40–48) whose combined dimensions of gates and two courts (Ezekiel 40) form a square of exactly 500 cubits to a side.

49. Based on Ritmeyer's verification that the Egyptian long cubit, also called the *royal* or *sacred* cubit, equalled 20.669257 inches and was that used in the layout of the Temple platform. Kaufman believed that the *medium* cubit was used, and calculated its length at 20.319 inches. Ritmeyer's measurements of the platform proved that the distance from the step/wall to the eastern wall equalled 500 cubits of 20.67 inches, according exactly with the measurements in *Middot*.

50. See Ronnie Reich, "Two Possible Miqva'ot on the Temple Mount," *Israel Exploration Journal* 39 (1989): 63-65.

51. Excerpt from recorded presentation given by Leen Ritmeyer at the annual meeting of the Near Eastern Archaeological Society, November 20, 1996 in Jacksonville, Mississippi.

52. Leen Ritmeyer, *The Temple and the Rock* (Harrogate, England: Ritmeyer Archaeological Design, 1996), pp. 24, 25, 41.

53. See further concerning Ritmeyer's views "The Ark of the Covenant, Where It Stood in Solomon's Temple," *Biblical Archaeology Review* (January-February 1996) and "Locating the Original Temple Mount," *Biblical Archaeology Review* (March/April 1992).

54. David M. Jacobson, "Ideas Concerning the Plan of Herod's Temple," *Palestine Exploration Quarterly* (January–June 1980), pp. 33-40; "Sacred Geometry: Unlocking the Secret of the Temple Mount (Part 1)," *Biblical Archaeological Review* 25:4 (July/August 1999), pp. 42-53, 62-64; (Part 2), *Biblical Archaeological Review* 25:5 (September/October 1999), pp. 54-63, 74,76.

55. Michael Ben-Ari, "The Temple Was Not Located on the Southern End" (trans. Yisrael Dubitsky), *Mikdash-Build* 1:2 (29 Ellul 5756).

56. Interview with Dan Bahat by Miriam Feinberg, *Eretz Magazine* 46 (May-June 1996), pp. 7-8.

57. Ibid., p. 9.

Chapter 16—The Hunt for the Holy Heifer

1. There are some rabbis who contend that although it is preferable that the Temple be built by those who have undergone the purification of the ashes of the Red Heifer, the Temple could still be built in a state of defilement. They argue this based on the understanding that public sacrifices, and the Passover sacrifice, may be brought in a state of defilement *in absence of the means of purification*. However, they agree that the Temple service would be significantly restricted. Private sacrifices could not be brought, many public sacrifices could not be consumed by the priests, and those who need

to bring an atonement sacrifice (such as a woman who gave birth) could not do so, and thus could not bring or eat the Passover sacrifice.

2. See Mary Douglas, *Purity and Danger* (London: Routledge & Kegan Paul, 1966), p. 159, who places *vdq* and *amf* at opposite poles in contradistinction to earlier scholars in this field, e.g., William Robertson Smith, *Lectures on the Religion of the Semites* (London: Adam and Charles Black, 1901), pp. 153-54, 446-54; M. Eliade, *The Sacred and the Profane*, trans. R. Willard (New York: Harcourt , Brace and Co., 1959), who proposed, on a primarily cultural-anthropological basis, that such a polarity did not exist.

3. For a more detailed explanation of the gradations of sanctification and desanctification within the semantic field see my work *The Desecration and Restoration of the Temple as an Eschatological Motif in the Tanach, Jewish Apocalyptic Literature and the New Testament* (Ann Arbor: University Microfilms Inc., 1994), pp. 137-56.

4. This was the case for Israel and also for the Qumran community, where the practice also seems to have existed, but not so with the Samaritan community on Mt. Gerizim, which apparently continued up until A.D. 1348.

5. Rabbi Chaim Richman, *The Mystery of the Red Heifer: Divine Promise of Purity* (Jerusalem: Rabbi Chaim Richman, 1997), p. 9.

6. Martin A. Greenberg, "The Red Heifer Ritual: A Rational Explanation," *Jewish Bible Quarterly* 25:1 (1997): 45-46.

7. Moses Maimonides, *Commentary on the Mishnah*. His exact statement reads: "...and the tenth Red Heifer will be accomplished [prepared?] by the king, the Messiah...." For more details on this subject see the *Mystery of the Red Heifer* booklet by Chaim Richman and my article "Red Heifer Born in Israel" in my regular column "Temple Times," *The Messianic Times* (Fall 1997).

8. Rabbi Chaim Richman, *The Mystery of the Red Heifer: Divine Promise of Purity* (Jerusalem: Rabbi Chaim Richman, 1997), p. 76.

9. *The Search for the Ashes of the Red Heifer*: Round Table Discussions featuring Vendyl Jones, with Noah Hutchings and Dr. Emil Gaverluk (Oklahoma: Southwest Radio Church, 1981), pp. 15, 20-21.

10. From "Root & Branch Association, Ltd." (<rb@rb.org.il>) Wednesday, January 27, 1999.

11. See William Lane, *Hebrews 9-13*, Word Biblical Commentary (Dallas, TX: Word Books, 1991), 47a:239.

12. See Paul Ellington, *The Epistle to the Hebrews: A Commentary on the Greek Text* (Grand Rapids: Wm. B. Eerdmans Publishing Co., 1993), p. 453, who thinks it paradoxical for this to be the grounds, since he contends that the latter removed the former.

13. Since in Numbers 19 it was Eleazar—the assistant of his father the high priest—who slaughtered the Red Heifer, it is assumed that any priest, not just the high priest, is able to do this. However, it is recorded that the privilege was such that the high priest jealously guarded the honor.

14. *Encyclopedia Judaica* 14:12.

15. For this story see Lawrence Wright, "Forcing the End," *The New Yorker* (July 20, 1998), pp. 44-45.

16. Ibid., p. 71.

17. Gershon Salomon, "Red Heifer Born in Israel," *Newsletter of the Temple Mount Faithful* (April 1999): 3.

18. Private correspondence from Rabbi Chaim Richman, September 1, 1999.

19. Rick Weiss, "Scientists Achieve Cloning Success" *Washington Post* (Feb. 24, 1997), p. A01.

20. Ibid.

21. Kendall Hamilton (with Joseph Contreras and Mark Dennis), "The Strange Case of Israel's Red Heifer," *Time* magazine (May 19, 1997), p. 16.

22. Reported in the *Sunday Telegraph* (London) March 16, 1997.

23. Ibid.

24. Arutz Sheva News Service, Sunday, January 25, 1998.

25. Gershon Salomon, "Red Heifer Born in Israel," *Newsletter of the Temple Mount Faithful* (April 1999): 3.

26. Ibid., p. 4.

27. Ibid.

Chapter 17—Preparing a Priesthood

1. Rabbi Yisroel Miller, rabbi of the Poale Zedek Orthodox synagogue in Squirrel Hill, as cited in *Israel Wire* (September 23, 1998), p. 4.

2. See further, Cornelis Van Dam, *The Urim and Thummim: A Means of Revelation in Ancient Israel* (Winona Lake, IN: Eisenbrauns, 1997).

3. "Jewish Priestly Line Maintains Legacy—and Genetic Marker," *Israel Wire* (September 23, 1998), p. 1.

4. It is instructive that since the tribal lineage is passed through the males only that this remains a witness to the biblical concept of Jewish identity being carried by the father. Contrary to this, rabbinic Judaism holds that the tribal ancestry is passed only through the mother.

5. *Nature* journal 9 (June 1998). The original report was apparently also published in *Nature* as well as in the journal *Lancet* (August 1997).

6. One famous DNA case was the revelation (after her death) that Anna Anderson, who had claimed throughout her life to be the Grand Duchess Anastasia, the lost daughter of the Russian Czar Nicholas II, was, in fact, genetically unrelated.

7. In the original report of the study published in the British scientific journal *Nature*, researchers studied two of the chromosome's genetic markers, or sections, of DNA, the double-stranded molecule that carries our encoded genetic material. Most chromosomes rearrange themselves randomly through succeeding generations, which increases genetic diversity. But these chromosomes were distinctly more homogeneous.

8. The discovery was of a preponderance of the YAP, DYS19B haplotype, unique as a genetic marker in 1.5% of the Cohanim as compared to 18.4% of the non-priestly Jews. Another marker appeared in 54% of the Cohanim, but only 33% of the non-priestly Jews. "This indicates that a large portion of the Kohain population carries common genes, perhaps inherited directly, through patrilineal descent from Aaron," Miryam Z. Wahrman, "Priestly Genes," *Roundup: Jewish Communications Network* (September 18, 1998), pp. 1-2.

9. See John Rivera, "Chromosome ties modern Jews to Aaron," *SunSpot* (June 9, 1998).

10. Ibid., p. 2.

11. The kit is available by writing for information to: Michael Hammer, Dept. of EEB, Biosciences West, University of Arizona, Tucson, AZ 85721, or by e-mail to David Sheinbin at Sheinbi@u.arizona.edu

12. *The Jewish Press*, Friday, October 14, 1983.

13. However, Rabbi Shim'eon disputes the matter with Rabbi Yehuda and says that, even amongst the Jews returning from the Babylonian captivity, there were pure people. This is because only during the Hasmonean period did the sages decree that foreign countries, called by the sages "the countries of the peoples," were unclean with the defilement from the dead. Therefore, those returning from the Babylonian captivity, in whose time the decree had not been made, could take ashes of the Red Heifer to Babylon and purify themselves there. They also did this when they returned to the country of Israel, so that there were pure people amongst them. Nevertheless, even Rabbi Shim'eon admits that those returning from the Babylonian captivity, used, for the purpose of making the ashes, the help of children who had never become ritually defiled.

14. The widespread use of stone containers has been authenticated by impressive archeological findings; see *The Stone Vessels Industry in Jerusalem in the Period of the Second Temple* (Tel-Aviv: The Society for Nature Preservation in Israel, 1996). In the period of the First Temple the stone vessel industry was well developed, but they were not aware of the connection between the stone vessels and the laws of defilement and purity because the Oral Law, in which this concept is taught, was not followed until the period of the Second Temple.

15. While any valid priest can slaughter the Red Heifer, the high priest usually did so and apparently preferred to do this instead of the other priests, whenever possible.

16. As reported in the *Daily Oklahoman*, December 17, 1994.

17. As cited by Ulf Carmesund, *Two Faces of the Expanding Jewish State: A study on how religious motives can legitimate two Jewish groups trying to dominate* (Uppsala University: Faculty of Theology/Interdisciplinary Study, 1992), p. 34.

18. Description of purpose from Temple Institute website, s.v. "Education."

19. Interview with Rabbi Yisrael Ariel, Temple Institute, Jerusalem, November 19, 1999.

20. This also appears in the *Laws of Beit Mikdash* 6:15: "Therefore, we may offer all the sacrifices [on the Temple site], even though the Temple itself is not built. Similarly, sacrifices of the most holy order can be eaten in the entire [area of the] courtyard, even though it is in ruin and not surrounded by a divider."

21. This is based on *Ohr Hachaim on Vayikra* (Leviticus) chapter 25 verse 25, which reads : "And the Redemption will be when the hearts of men are aroused and it will be said to them, is it good for you to be dwelling outside exiled from the Table of our Father? And what can be pleasant for your life in this world except the high company that you were reliant upon…about by the table of your Father, He is the Lord of the Universe blessed be He, for eternity. And he shall disparage in his eyes the desires that are imagined and he will arouse them with a longing for the spiritual ... until they improve their deeds and by this Hashem will redeem that which he has sold. And over this, in the future the masters of the Earth, the great men/the Gedolim of Israel will be brought to judgment and from them, Hashem will seek the disgrace of The disgraced House/Temple!"

22. "Temple Mount Faithful" mailing list news item, Monday, March 23, 1998.

23. Report by Gershon Salomon in the "Temple Mount and Land of Israel Faithful Newsletter," April 10, 1998.

24. Ibid.

25. Ibid.

26. Report by Gershon Salomon, "Temple Mount and Land of Israel Faithful Newsletter," April 3, 1999.

Chapter 18—Provisions for the Priesthood

1. As cited by Ehud Sprinzak, *The Ascendance of Israel's Radical Right* (New York: Oxford University Press, 1991), p. 268.

2. Shlomo Moshe Scheinman, "It Is a Mitzva to Attempt to Offer Sacrifices At This Time (Part 1)," p. 3.

3. The amount of David's donation, according to the text, amounted to 3.6 million ounces of gold and 8.4 million ounces of silver.

4. According to 1 Chronicles 29:7-8, the amounts given by King David's subjects were 6,045,000 ounces of gold, 12 million ounces of silver, 1.35 million pounds (675 tons) of brass, and 7.5 million pounds (3,750 tons) of iron., and precious stones.

5. Shlomo Moshe Scheinman, "It Is a Mitzva to Attempt to Offer Sacrifices At This Time (Part 1)," p. 3.

6. As cited in *Tekhelet: The Story of the Discovery of the Biblical Blue* (Jerusalem: P'Til Tekhelet, 1998), p. 5.

7. Dr. Isaac Herzog, *The Royal Purple and the Biblical Blue, Argaman and Tekhelet: The Study of Chief Rabbi Dr. Isaac Herzog on the Dye Industries in Ancient Israel and Recent Scientific Contributions* (Jerusalem: Keter Publishing House, 1989).

8. Description of Yeshivat Torat HaBayit by the Rosh Yeshiva ("head of the school") published in *Mikdash-Build* 3:6 (3 Adar 5759), p. 1.

9. Yisrael Ariel and Chaim Richman, *The Odyssey of the Third Temple* (Jerusalem: Israel Publications & Productions Ltd., 1994), p. 102.

10. Interview with Rabbi Yisrael Ariel, The Temple Institute, Jerusalem, November 19, 1999.

11. *Atlas of the Land of Israel: Its Boundaries According to the Sources* (Hebrew) (Jerusalem: Cana Publishing House), vol. 1 (1988), vol. 2 (1989).

12. The reference in 1 Kings 4:21 to Solomon's rule over boundaries that resemble these make it clear that though much of the land was possessed, it did not completely fulfill the extent of the land promised. Note that the reference in 1 Kings 4:21 is to the "border of Egypt," which is less than the reference in Genesis 15:8 to "the river of Egypt." Furthermore, under Solomon this territory was held for only 40 years. It is hardly feasible that possessing these boundaries for such a brief period during the first Israelite monarchy (which was less than God's design) could fulfill a promise for which Abraham's descendants had waited (to that time) for more than 1,000 years!

13. See Ehud Sprinzak, *The Ascendance of Israel's Radical Right* (New York: Oxford University Press, 1991), p. 283.

14. This is called, in Rabbinic terminology, *yediat ha-chetz* ("forcing the hand" [of Messiah]), and is built upon the belief that there is a cause-effect relationship between human acts (the masculine waters) and divine response (the feminine waters). A rabbinic Midrash observes that "the Red Sea did not part until the Israelites stepped into it." Following this principle, The Temple Mount Faithful argue that the Temple will not be rebuilt until men start making efforts to rebuild it.

15. See Yossi Klein Halevi, "Special Report: The Battle for the Temple Mount," *Mikdash-Build* 1:7 (5 Heshvan 5757), p. 3.

16. A full-color spread of some of these items was first introduced to the public through Richard Ostling's article "Time for a Temple?" in *Time* magazine (October 16, 1989), pp. 64-65. A framed copy of this article has graced the wall of the Temple Institute office ever since.

17. Haim Odem, a craftsman who immigrated to Israel from Soviet Georgia, constructed the present wax replica that stands in the exhibition center. According to *The Jerusalem Post International Edition* (August 31, 1991), the cost of constructing the actual Menorah, which will require 94.6 pounds of gold for the electroplating, has been estimated at $10 million.

18. For an explanation and the available evidence for this belief, see my book *In Search of Temple Treasures: The Lost Ark and the Last Days* (Eugene, OR: Harvest House Publishers, 1994), pp. 157-85, and the testimonies of Rabbi Shlomo Goren and Rabbi Yehuda Getz on my video by the same title (Harvest House, 1994).

19. I have discussed these plans and the possible prophetic purpose for the Ark of the Covenant in my book *In Search of Temple Treasures: The Lost Ark and the Last Days* (Eugene, OR: Harvest House Publishers, 1994).

20. Raphaella Tabak, "An 'Altarnative' Experience," *On the Altar* 1:2 (Spring 1998), p. 4.

21. Interview with Chaim Richman, The Temple Institute, Jerusalem, August 5, 1999.

22. Quoted from literature given by the Harraris concerning their harps.

23. From the homepage of the House of Levi website.

24. The address for registering with this group is: House of Levi, 328 East 61st Street, New York, NY 10021-8766; (212) 751-2424 or fax (212) 751-8574.

25. The school was featured by Hugh Downs in a 1985 segment of the popular "60 Minutes" television program in a feature entitled "One Step in Heaven." The school also featured in the October 16, 1989 issue of *Time* magazine and has appeared in a host of Christian prophesy-related television and radio productions as well as a number of publications.

26. Quite a number of reports of this have been published in Israeli newspapers, but I also have personally talked with Christian Arab friends who knew of those who were murdered for meeting with Jews who wished to buy properties, and who were themselves threatened because they owned acreage outside Bethlehem that was up for sale.

27. Interview with Reuven Prager, Beged Ivri, Jerusalem, November 15, 1998.

28. Ibid.

29. Interview reported in *Hadassah* magazine, January 1989, pp. 26-27.

30. Ibid.

31. Interview with Reuven Prager, Beged Ivri, Jerusalem, November 15, 1998.

32. Reuven Prager, *Proposal for the Revival of the Ancient Jewish Marriage Ceremony*, p. 3

33. As quoted by Illana Katz, "Coins and Kohan: 'Holy Half-Shekel' Buys Admission to Third Temple Era," *Heritage Southwest Jewish Press* 5759:19 (Friday, February 12, 1999), p. 9.

34. Interview with Reuven Prager, Beged Ivri, Jerusalem, November 15, 1998.

35. As cited by Tehiya Ripps, "Levites Called to Active Duty," *Your Jerusalem* 21:2 (April 1998).

36. For the published reports of these ceremonies see Tehiya Ripps, "Levites Called to Active Duty," *Your Jerusalem* 21:2 (April 1998), and Jonathan Lifland, "Reviving a Holy Tradition," *The Anniston Star* (Friday, September 18, 1998), p. 1D (Faith section).

37. As quoted by Tehiya Ripps, "Levites Called to Active Duty," *Your Jerusalem* 21:2 (April 1998).

38. Ibid.

39. Illana Katz, "Coins and Kohan: 'Holy Half-Shekel' Buys Admission to Third Temple Era," *Heritage Southwest Jewish Press* 5759:19 (Friday, February 12, 1999), p. 8.

40. The CD-ROM is sold in Israel under the title of *Beit HaMikdash* ("The Holy Temple") and in the U.S. as *The Ultimate Temple CD*. It is produced by Torah Software and Avimedia Ltd./NG Media Interactive Ltd. In Israel it is available from Torah Scholar, 8 Mea Shearim, 52 King George, Jerusalem (02-622-1792) and in the U.S. from Quantum Link Inc., 21218 St. Andrews Blvd., Suite 234, Boca Raton, FL 33433 (1-888-TEMPLCD).

41. Interview with Chaim Richman by Irwin Baxter, *Endtime* (July/August, 1995), p. 12.

Chapter 19—Liberating the Temple Mount

1. Interview with Nahman Kahane, June 23, 1991.

2. From a speech delivered by Gershon Salomon at the Temple Conference, Binyanei Ha'ooma, Jerusalem, September 15, 1998 as reported by Nadav Shragai, "Dreaming of a Third Temple," *Ha'aretz* (English edition), Thursday, September 17, 1998, p. 3.

3. Interview with Gershon Salomon, Office of the Temple Mount Faithful, Jerusalem, November 5, 1998.

4. Ehud Sprinzak, *The Ascendance of Israel's Radical Right* (New York: Oxford University Press, 1991), p. 279.

5. See Don Stewart and Chuck Missler, *The Coming Temple* (Orange, CA: Dart Press, 1991), pp. 85-87.

6. As cited by Yossi Klein Halevi, "Special Report: The Battle for the Temple Mount," *Mikdash-Build* 1:7 (5 Heshvan 5757), p. 4.

7. See *Arutz Sheva* News Service (Monday, October 13, 1997).

8. As reported in *Arutz 7*, March 2, 1997. The document was prepared by the Cabinet Assistant Secretary in 1986.

9. See Israel Wire, "Court Does Not Forbid Jewish Prayer on the Temple Mount," May 24, 1998.

10. As cited by Nadav Shragai, "A Jewish Right to the Temple Mount," *Ha'aretz*, February 2, 1998.

11. The case in mind was that of against right-wing activists Mordehai Karpel and Oded Lipshitz, who were arrested for these actions in 1994. Judge Feinberg, in his ruling, stated that the Temple Mount was empty of Muslim worshipers at the time of the incident, and there were only a small number of tourists, adding, "The defendants were attempting to pray in a secluded area and were not openly visible." In this case the defendants were acquitted of the charges.

12. As cited in the publication *Dispatch from Jerusalem* 24:1 (January/February 1999)· 6.

13. See the studied defense of this position by Shaykh Professor Abdul Hadi Palazzi, "Jerusalem: Threefold Religious Heritage for a Contemporary Single Administration," available from Root & Branch Association, U.S. Office: 860 Grand Concourse, Bronx, NY 10451. Professor Palazzi is Secretary Geneal of the Italian Muslim Association and Imam of the Italian

Islamic Community, and is also Muslim Co-Chairman of the Islam-Israel Fellowship, which encourages Muslims to have a positive attitude towards jews and Israel based on a re-examination of the teachings of Mohammed as revealed by the Koran and Hadith (Islamic Oral Tradition).

14. For my discussion of the content of these speeches with respect to Jerusalem and the Temple Mount, see my book *Jerusalem in Prophecy: God's Stage for the Final Drama* (Eugene, OR: Harvest House, 1998), pp. 145-47, 164, 278-79, 338-39.

15. See Joshua Brilliant, "Arsonist Targets Jerusalem Temple Mount," *Arutz Sheva* News Service (Friday, May 15, 1998).

16. Excerpted from the Chai VeKayam website: *www.chaivekayam.org.*

17. This concept teaches that all the conditions necessary for the redemption of Israel are already present and that the only thing lacking is the desire to take action and bring redemption to pass. Shabtai Ben-Dov advocated typical redemption ideals: the establishment of a Jewish theocracy, a Torah-centric government administered by the Sanhedrin, and the rebuilding of the Third Temple. For more information on Ben-Dov and his viewpoint see Ehud Sprinzak, *The Ascendance of Israel's Radical Right* (New York: Oxford University Press, 1991), pp. 94-95.

18. As cited in Ehud Sprinzak, Ibid., pp. 255-56.

19. Ibid., p. 257.

20. Kol Israel Radio, Daily News from Israel No. 251 (March 21, 1997).

21. Interview with Yehuda Etzion, Mount of Olives, Jerusalem, November 17, 1998.

22. For information on this organization or to receive a subscription to their publication, write to: Yirmiyahu Fischer, P.O. Box 31336, Jerusalem, Israel (telephone: 972-2-537-1904).

23. *Jerusalem Post*, Friday, October 13, 1989, p. 1.

24. See Bill Hutman and Evelyn Gordon, "Justice Minister Favors Temple Mount Worship," *The Jerusalem Post International Edition* (July 20, 1996).

25. Interview with Jeries Soudah by Irwin Baxter in "Arafat and Jerusalem," *Endtime* magazine 7:5 (September/October 1997), p. 11.

26. Statement by founder Gershon Salomon in first newsletter of the organization, October 1995.

27. As reported on the Temple Mount Faithful website, January 1999.

28. Informational brochure published by the Temple Mount Faithful, Jerusalem, p. 2.

29. As cited in the *Voice of the Temple Mount Newsletter* (May 19, 1998), pp. 1-2.

30. Interview with Gershon Salomon at the cornerstone, November 12, 1998.

31. Ibid.

32. Interviews with Gershom Salomon, June 24, 1991 and November 12, 1998.

33. The evidence for this is 1) only 20 Temple Mount Faithful members were marching to the Siloam, hardly constituting a threat; 2) Arabs had been stockpiling stones and weapons on the Temple Mount above the Western Wall since 3 A.M. the morning of the attack; 3) Wakf Security personnel were absent; and 4) the event was planned regardless of whether or not the Temple Mount Faithful made their march. For the documentation in connection with this see *The Real Story: The Attack on the Western Wall Plaza* (RTF Film Associates—Mattus Heritage Institute Productions, 1991), and Richard J. Andrews, "The Political and Religious Groups Involved with Building the Third Temple in Jerusalem" (Unpublished thesis, Indiana University, June 30, 1995), pp. 51-54.

34. The death toll varies according to the source. By Israeli reports the number was 17; by Palestinian reports it was 20.

35. Finding of the Zamir commission, reported by David Bar-Ilan in "Temple Mount Provocation," *Jerusalem Post International Edition* (August 10, 1991):7.

36. For the arguments about this significance the group and other activist groups have a "sacred timetable"—see Ulf Carmesund, *Two Faces of the Expanding Jewish State* (Uppsala University: Faculty of Theology/Interdisciplinary Study, 1992), pp. 133-40.

37. Interview with Gershon Salomon, Office of the Temple Mount Faithful, Jerusalem, November 5, 1998.

38. *WorldNetDaily Exclusive*, Tuesday, October 6, 1998, p. 1.

39. Ibid.

40. Abraham Rabinovitch, "Making History Happen," *The Jerusalem Post International Edition* (July 29, 1995): 21.

Chapter 20—The Coming War

1. Interview with Jeries Soudah by Irwin Baxter in "Arafat and Jerusalem," *Endtime* magazine 7:5 (September/October 1997), p. 11.

2. As cited in *Artifax* (Winter 1999): 8.

3. As cited by Ulf Carmesund, *Two Faces of the Expanding Jewish State: A Study on How Religious Motives Can Legitimate Two Jewish Groups Trying to Dominate Mount Moriah in Jerusalem* (Uppsala University, 1972), pp. 86-87.

4. See "Damage to Temple Mount 'Under Discussion,'" *Arutz Sheva* news service (Wednesday, May 26, 1999), pp. 1-3.

5. Statement by Hasan Tahboub, Head of Religious Affairs in the Palestinian Authority, as cited in Arutz-7 News: Sunday, October 13, 1996.

6. Arutz-7 News: Monday, October 14, 1996.

7. Mordecai Gur, *The Temple Mount Is in Our Hands* (Tel-Aviv: Defense Ministry Publishing House, 1968) as cited in Abraham E. Millgram, *Jerusalem Curiosities* (Philadelphia: The Jewish Publication Society, 1990), p. 291.

8. As cited by Martin Gilbert, *Jerusalem in the Twentieth Century* (New York: John Wiley & Sons, Inc., 1996), p. 287.

9. Lawrence Wright, "Forcing the End," *The New Yorker* (July 20, 1998), p. 46.

10. See "Rabbi Wants to Destroy Mosque; Wanted Mosque Leveled," *Ha'aretz* (December 31, 1997).

11. Rabbi Goren died in 1994, and Narkiss died December 17, 1998.

12. Interview with David Dolan, Mount of Olives, Jerusalem, November 15, 1998.

13. Zev Vilnay, *Legends of Jerusalem* (Philadelphia: Jewish Publication Society of America, 1973), pp. 42-43.

14. *Arutz Sheva* news service (August 4, 1998), p. 2.

15. "Has a Deal Been Made to Rebuild the Third Temple?" *Davar M'Tamar* (January 1994), pp. 2-3.

16. Interview with Jeries Soudah by Irwin Baxter in "Arafat and Jerusalem," *Endtime* magazine 7:5 (September/October 1997), pp. 11-12.

17. Mohammed Abdul Koddus, as cited by Amany Radwin, "Fundamentalism: God's Country," *Time* magazine (April 13, 1998): 203.

18. The Temple was built on Mount Moriah, and Mount Zion was originally the site of King David's city. However, when the Temple was built the name became attached to this site so that in the Psalms, Mount Zion becomes the place of God's presence.

19. From her report in the *Galilee Experience Update* 25, Friday, May 14, 1999, p. 3.

20. This would better be translated "Gog of Magog," since "Gog" is the name of a ruler and "Magog" the place of his rule. He is also the "chief ruler" (the meaning of "prince of Rosh") of the regions of Meshech and Tubal.

21. At least six different chronological placements have been suggested. For these see my book with H. Wayne House, *Charts on Biblical Prophecy* (Grand Rapids: Zondervan Publishing House, 1999).

22. The clause in Ezekiel 38:12, "who live at the center of the world," also refers idiomatically to Israel, e.g., *Tanhuma* 106: "Israel lies at the center of the earth, and Jerusalem lies at the center of the Land of Israel." Some have thought on the basis of Ezekiel 5:5: "This is Jerusalem; I have set her at the center of the nations, with lands around her," that the reference here is to the Holy City. There is no question that the literal Hebrew term here "navel of the earth" has been historically applied to Jerusalem. However, the words here are those of the enemy, who appear to be mocking Israel's confidence by this expression. Then the sense might be "it [Israel] thinks it is the best in the world." This accurately portrays the attitude of Israel's enemies today.

23. However, Rashi believes just the opposite: "Gog will come to them that feel peaceful and quiet and will see in what they place their trust. That is, when Gog comes to make war against Yisrael with his army of many nations, he will attempt to challenge their trust and confidence in God, his objective being to destroy their religious faith."

24. For additional discussion in support of this view see Arnold G. Fructenbaum, *The Footsteps of the Messiah: A Study of the Sequence of Prophetic Events* (Tustin, CA: Ariel Ministries, 1982), pp. 69-84; and Thomas S. McCall and Zola Levitt, *The Coming Russian Invasion of Israel* (Chicago: Moody Press, 1974). Prophetic teachers Thomas Ice, executive director of the Pre-Trib Research Center and Tim LaHaye, co-author of the popular *Left Behind* series of prophetic novels, also hold to this interpretation.

25. For my interpretation of two phases of restoration (physical to the Land, spiritual to the Lord) see my book *Jerusalem in Prophecy: God's Stage for the Final Drama* (Eugene, OR: Harvest House Publishers, 1998), pp. 203-20.

26. The Jewish commentator Rashi understands *betach* in this way: "The inhabitants of the unwalled villages are confident and unafraid; they feel no need to seek shelter in fortified cities."

27. Interpreters are divided as to whether the location for this will be the Mediterranean Sea or the Dead Sea. Rashi says that it is "the valley near the Sea of Galilee, which must be transversed in order to bring the fruits of Ginosar to the Land of Yisrael."

28. For details about Russia's longtime backing of Syria and its recent support of a Palestinian State see *The Jerusalem Post International Edition* (April 30, 1999).

29. Mortimer B. Zuckerman, "Coming to Russia's Rescue," *U.S. News & World Report* (February 8, 1999): 68.

30. Other significant technologies and industries, for example, are (with export figures for 1998) Israel Aircraft Industries ($1.44 billion), Teva Pharmaceutical Industries ($863 million), ECI Telecom ($780 million), and Formula Systems ($259

million). So significant are hi-tech firms in the Israeli economy that some have jokingly said that the Jaffa orange, which currently serves as the symbol of Israel's produce, should be changed to the micro chip!

31. Palestinian Authority daily newspaper *Al-Hayat Al-Jadida*, December 1, 1997. In this regard it should be noted that Louis Rene Beres, Professor of International Law, Department of Political Science, Purdue University has reported that the formation of a Palestinian State poses a threat to the systematic destruction of Israel's nuclear infrastructure, leaving Israel "weakened" in the eyes of other Arab powers and vulnerable to attack.

32. The support for this threefold invasion concept is based on Ezekiel 38:17: "Thus says the Lord God, 'Are you [Gog] the one of whom I spoke in former days through My servants the prophets of Israel who prophesied in those days for many years that I would bring you against them?'" Jewish interpreters understood these as the prophets Daniel and Zechariah; however, these prophets are both later than Ezekiel, not earlier. There are no specific references to Gog, and the best general reference would be Jeremiah's "foe from the north" (Jeremiah 25:9). However, it is possible that this expects a negative, rather than affirmative, response from Gog, although it is assumed his answer would be affirmative, showing his arrogance. For the support for this view see Daniel I. Block, *The Book of Ezekiel: Chapters 25-48* (Grand Rapids: Wm. B. Eerdmans Publishing Co., 1998), p. 456.

33. Rafael Eisenberg, *A Matter of Return: A Penetrating Analysis of Yisrael's Afflictions and Their Alternatives* (Jerusalem: Feldheim Publishers, 1980), pp. 104-5.

34. Ibid., p. 155.

35. Excerpted from the *Voice of the Temple Mount* newsletter (Autumn 1995), pp. 2, 7.

36. Excerpted from the *Voice of the Temple Mount* newsletter (May 19, 1998), pp. 4-6.

37. Rafael Eisenberg, *A Matter of Return: A Penetrating Analysis of Yisrael's Afflictions and Their Alternatives* (Jerusalem: Feldheim Publishers, 1980), p. 101.

38. As cited by Rabbi Nisan Aryeh Novick, *Fascinating Torah Prophecies Currently Unfolding* (Staten Island, NY: Netzach Yisrael Publications, Inc., 1997), p. 77.

39. Ibid., p. 191.

40. This remnant are those Jews who repent and cry out for the Lord's deliverance (Zechariah 12:10–13:1; see also Joel 2:28-32). However, this is not an isolated repentance, but a national one that extends also to the remnant that will have fled to Bozrah and to which the Messiah will apparently first appear (Zechariah 12:7; see also Isaiah 34:1-7; 63:1-6; Habakkuk 3:3). Antichrist's forces will have come to destroy this enclave of Jews after the first invasion of Jerusalem, but before the attack, he will be destroyed by the Messiah in the Kidron Valley (Zechariah 14:3,12-15).

41. See Eugene Merrill, *An Exegetical Commentary: Haggai, Zechariah, Malachi* (Chicago: Moody Press, 1994), p. 347.

42. See P. D. Miller, *The Divine Warrior in Early Israel* (Cambridge, MA: Harvard University, 1973), pp. 140-41.

43. Amira Hass, "Israel Won't Last More than 30 More Years," *Ha'aretz* (December 28, 1998).

44. Interview with Jeries Soudah by Irwin Baxter in "Arafat and Jerusalem," *Endtime* magazine 7:5 (September/October 1997), p. 11.

45. Ibid., p. 9.

46. Sermon on the Temple Mount, recorded Friday, September 10, 1999, at the Al-Aqsa Mosque and transmitted by Murray Kahl (kahl@gate.net), September 13, 1999.

47. Excerpt from an advertisement by Facts and Logic About the Middle East in *The Jerusalem Post International Edition* (March 26, 1999): 22.

48. Interview with Yohanan Ramati, Jerusalem, November 4, 1998.

Chapter 21—Trouble in the Temple

1. As cited in John W. Schmitt and J. Carl Laney, *Messiah's Coming Temple: Ezekiel's Prophetic Vision of the Future Temple* (Grand Rapids: Kregel Publications, 1997), p. 105.

2. The plural use of this term ("antichrists") allows for both a comprehensive and a concentrated expression of Antichrist, and ultimately the eschatological duo known as the "first Beast" (*the* Antichrist) and the "second beast" (the false prophet), who, with the "dragon" (Satan) as the origin of their "power" (authority), form a sort of counterfeit trinity (Revelation 13:1-2,11). While the specific term *Antichrist* is rarely used, the Bible is filled with descriptive terminology relating to his diabolical and desecrating nature. Among the more obvious epithets are "the little horn" (Daniel 7:8), "the insolent king" (Daniel 8:23), "the prince who is to come" (Daniel 9:26), "the one who makes desolate" (Daniel 9:27), "the despicable person" (Daniel 11:21), "the strong-willed king" (Daniel 11:36), "the worthless shepherd" (Zechariah 11:16-17), "the man of lawlessness" (2 Thessalonians 2:3), "the son of destruction" (2 Thessalonians 2:3), "the lawless one" (2 Thessalonians 2:8), "the beast" (Revelation 11:7; 13:1; 14:9; 15:2; 16:2; 17:3, 13; 19:20; 20:10). For additional information see my entries on "Antichrist" in the *Dictionary of Premillennial Theology*, ed. Mal Couch (Grand Rapids: Kregel Publishers, 1997).

3. Even though this individual is only called "the Antichrist" in 1 John 2:18, 22, this cognomen identifies him with a historic succession of antichrists, of which he is the last and climatic figure. It will be used as the best descriptive term, for this man will be so aligned with Satan as to share his common purpose and ultimate destiny (Revelation 13:2, 4; 19:20).

4. Interview with Elwood McQuaid, Lawrence Welk Resort, Escondido, California, October 23, 1998.

5. This was the identification of such conservative, dispensational commentators as J.N. Darby and Arno Gaebelein.

6. Dr. Falwell is, in fact, a strong supporter of Israel (see Merrill Simon's 1984 book *Jerry Falwell and the Jews* and denounces anti-Semitism in any form. He later retracted his statement. However, he also observed that he was simply stating the view of Pretribulational Premillennialism (this was stated on the political commentary program "Crossfire").This is, at best, a minority view among Pretribulational Premillennialists and is more widely espoused by Replacement theologians.

7. The early Church father Hippolytus (*Commentary on the Benedictions of Isaac and Jacob* [Gen. 49:14]) began the Christian tradition that the Antichrist originates from the Israelite tribe of Dan; he apparently made this connection from the Jewish *Testaments of the Twelve Patriarchs* (*T. Dan* 1:4-9; 5:6-7), which states that evil spirits would be active in the tribe (5:5), that "Satan" was "their prince" (5:6), and that they would be hostile in the future to the tribes of Levi and Judah (5:6-7). Support for the view is based on the absence of the mention of the tribe of Dan in the list of tribes in Revelation 7:4-8 from which the 144,000 will be selected. The argument is that Dan must have been left out for a reason and that reason must be because that tribe was cursed (see Genesis 49:17; Deuteronomy 33:22; Jeremiah 8:16) because it was destined to bring forth the Antichrist (Daniel 11:37). However, these verses do not warrant such a supposition and only Daniel 11:37 has any reference to the Antichrist. The Bible does not tell us why Dan was left out, but it is not unusual for names of tribes to be left out of listings for numeral balance (the assumption for the reader is that they are included). Dan, in fact, is included with the tribes that are in the Millennial Kingdom (Ezekiel 48:2), so there apparently was not a curse on the tribe.

8. *Levitt Letter* 21:2 (February 1999): 3.

9. For my discussion on the typology of the Antichrist see *In Search of Temple Treasures* (Eugene, OR: Harvest House Publishers, 1994), pp. 247-50.

10. *Dictionary of the New Testament Theology,* s.v. ajntiv, appendix, by M. J. Harris (Grand Rapids: Zondervan Publishing Co., 1978), 3:1179.

11. Arnold Fructenbaum, *The Nationality of the Antichrist* (Englewood Cliffs, NJ: American Board of Missions to the Jews, n.d.).

12. For a complete study of this question see Ed Hindson, *Is the Antichrist Alive and Well?* (Eugene, OR: Harvest House Publishers, 1998).

13. Yirmiyahu Fischer, *Mikdash-Build* 1:20 (February 14, 1997), p. 7.

14. For an extensive treatment of the defilement of the sanctuary, see Gerhard Hasel, "Studies in Biblical Atonement I: Continual Sacrifices, Defilement/Cleansing and Sanctuary," *Sanctuary and Atonement: Biblical, Historical, and Theological Studies,* eds. Arnold V. Wallenkampf and W. Richard Lesher (Washington, D.C.: Review and Herald Publishing Association, 1981), pp. 85-114.

15. The argument for Gentiles being considered unclean is derived from two principal texts: 1) Isaiah 52:1, which parallels "uncircumcised" with "unclean"—however, not explicitly with reference to Gentiles. The context would allow for the first reference to be Gentiles ("uncircumcised"), but the second ("unclean") might also refer to Israelites whose misconduct had also contributed to the fall of the city. In this case not one, but two different categories of people are in view. Even if it does refer to one group, it may only mean that "Gentiles" will no longer enter the city to establish "uncleanness" (i.e., idolatry) in it any longer. 2) Joshua 22:19; see also Ezra 9:11; Amos 7:17; Leviticus 18:24-27, where lands outside of Israel are considered to be unclean. However, upon careful examination of the texts, it is not the inhabitants (as "unclean" in themselves) of these lands which render them unclean, but the presence of idolatry (just as the presence of pagan altars in Israel defiled the Land).

16. See A. Büchler, "The Levitical Impurity of the Gentile in Palestine Before the Year 70," *Jewish Quarterly Review* 17:2-4 (1926-1927): 1-81. He concluded that the Levitical impurity of the Gentile was instituted by the rabbis about the year 1 as a novelty going beyond the law in Leviticus 15. Its first stage was the extension of the rules of the menstruous Jewish woman to the Gentile woman, and the communication of her impurity to her Gentile husband; and as she did not observe the purification rites, she remained permanently in the Levitical state of the menstruous woman. Later, the Hillelites attempted the same sort of extension based on corpse defilement, but failed due to the opposition of the Shammaites. Again, in A.D. 66, grave impurity was ascribed to the Gentile, but the outbreak of the Jewish Revolt prevented any practical application. The records show that such assumed Levitical impurity only affected the priest on duty in the Temple, and the ordinary Jew when purified for participation in the Temple in a sacrifical meal; it did not restrict pri-

vate or commercial relations, and the Gentile could even move freely about on the Temple Mount (until the first century, when the boundary was pushed back by the erection of the *Soreg.* Similarly, with respect to the case of Gentile prose-lytes, Joseph M. Baumgarten, "Exclusions from the Temple: Proselytes and Agrippa I," *Journal of Jewish Studies* 33:1-2 (1982): 215-25, concludes that "none of the [Jewish] sources we have considered provides decisive evidence that prose-lytes were actually excluded from the Jerusalem Temple. Rabbinic texts preserve *halakhot* which presuppose the entrance of 'proselytes' into the Temple courtyard. The Temple inscription, despite the possibility of taking non-Jews of alien descent, was not applied to proselytes. Thus, it would appear that the Qumran rulings…essayed to keep converts out of the sanctuary belonged to the realm of purest desiderata not realized in contemporary Temple practice" (p. 225).

17. It is also possible that there is another reference to the Temple in verse 24 with the word *meqadsheyhem.* The Massoretic text points this as a Pi'el participle ("they that sanctify them"); however, many commentators would suggest an emen-dation to read "their holy places," in which case the plural may refer to the various compartments of the Temple—see Walther Zimmerli, *A Commentary on the Book of the Prophet Ezekiel,* trans. Ronald Clements (Philadelphia: Fortress Press, 1979), I: 200.

18. This "rotten" condition applies to the "peace offering" in Leviticus and carcasses torn by animals in Ezekiel.

19. The Hebrew term *taqehes sheqetz* is related to *pigul* in that the latter refers to *dead* carcasses (see Isaiah 65:4), while the former only to *living* animals (see Leviticus 7:21; 11:10-13,20,23,41; Isaiah 66:17; Ezekiel 8:10).

20. See Herman J. Austel, "שׁקץ," *Theological Wordbook of the Old Testament* 2:955, who argues for both a reference to the "idols" and "something associated with the idolatrous ritual." He adds, "Not only are the idols an abomination, but they that worship them 'become detestable like that which they love' (Hosea 9:10), for they identify themselves with the idols."

21. This association is expressed in Leviticus 11:43; 20:25, where the root *shqtz* is paralleled with *tame'*, and in its close asso-ciation with the meanings of the Pi'el forms of both *tame'* ("make unclean") and *ta'ab* ("abhor"), see Bruce K. Waltke, "Abomination," *New International Standard Bible Encyclopedia I* (Grand Rapids: William B. Eerdmans Publishing Co., 1979), p. 14.

22. Hermann J. Austel, "שׁמם," *Theological Wordbook of the Old Testament* 2, eds. R. Harris, G. Archer, Jr., B. Waltke (Chicago: Moody Press, 1980): 936-37.

23. *BDB* s.v. "שׁמם," pp. 1030-31.

24. While *shomem* could here be translated as "the transgression *that causes horror*," expressing the psychological nuance as a result of the idolatrous act, it seems preferable to retain the idea of cultic or spiritual "desolation" as a result of idolatry, in keeping with the concept of *pasha'* as desecration, and allow *meremes* to carry the nuance of physical desolation.

25. Edwin Hatch and Henry A. Redpath, *A Concordance to the Septuagint,* 2 vols. (Graz: Akademische Druck-V Verlagsan-stalt, 1954), 1:215.

26. See BAGD, s.v. "βδέλυγμα," p. 134: 1) literally, anything that must not be brought before God because it arouses His wrath (see LXX Isaiah 1:13; Proverbs 11:1; Luke 16:15; Epistle of Barnabas 2:5); 2) as in the Old Testament of everything connected with idolatry (see LXX Deuteronomy 29:16; 1 Kings 11.6,33; 2 Kings 23:13; 2 Chronicles 28:3; Revelation 17:4f); also see X. Léon-Dufour, *Wörterbuch zum Neuen Testament* (1977), pp. 409-11.

27. W. Foerster, "βδέλυγμα," *Theological Dictionary of the New Testament* 1 (1964): 598. His references for the "abomina-tions" are LXX Jeremiah 13:27; 39:35; 51:22; Ezekiel 5:9, 11; 6:9, etc., and for the parallel with "lawlessness": LXX Jeremiah 4:1; Ezekiel 11:18; 20:30; Amos 6:8; Psalm 5:7; 13:1; 52:1; 118:163; Job 15.16.

28. See LXX Proverbs 29:27; Ecclesiasticus 1:25; 13:20.

29. J. Zmijewski, "βδέλυγμα," *Exegetical Dictionary of the New Testament,* eds. Horst Balz and Gerhard Schneider (Grand Rapids: William B. Eerdmans Publishing Co., 1978-1980) 1: 210.

30. It is not possible in the space of this treatment of the expression to deal with the unusual form of the construction. Much has been made of the grammatical peculiarities in the form in Daniel 9:27 and the theories are thoroughly dis-cussed in my *The Desecration and Restoration of the Temple as an Eschatological Motif in the Tanach, Jewish Apocalyptic Literature and the New Testament* (Ann Arbor, MI: UMI, 1994), pp. 360-67.

31. This association was first observed by Béda Rigaux, "βδέλυγμα τῆς ἐρημώσεως," *Biblica* 40 (1959): 675-83, and Charles Perrot, "Essai Sur Le Discours Eschatologique," *Recherches de Science Religion* 47 (1959): 481-514. More recently it has been championed by Desmond Ford, *The Abomination of Desolation in Biblical Eschatology* (Washington, D.C.: University Press of America, 1979), pp. 148-49, 172-75.

32. I have restricted my examples to those passages employing only the term *shiqqutz;* however, the number of references could be doubled if we included those containing the synonym *to'evah.*

33. If this latter emendation to the absolute with ב substituted for ו were accepted, it would make *ba'al kenaf* the subject of *yashvit* ("cause to cease").

34. Donald Glen & Kenneth Barker, "Notes for the Course: Problem Passages in the Old Testament" (Dallas Theological Seminary, 1977), s.v. "Daniel 9:24-27."

35. See A. Jeffrey, "Introduction and Exegesis of Daniel," *Interpreter's Bible* 4 (1956), p. 443.

36. A. Bentzen, *Daniel, Handbuch zum Alten Testament,* 2nd ed. (Tübingen, 1952).

37. G. R.. Beasley-Murray, *Jesus and the Future: An Examination of the Criticism of the Eschatological Discourse, Mark 13 with Special Reference to the Little Apocalypse Theory* (London: Macmillan & Co., 1954), pp. 255-56 (appendix).

38. First Maccabees 1:54 (see 2 Maccabees 6:2) uses the Greek term of the altar of burnt offerings within the Temple, where Antiochus had constructed an altar or statue to Zeus Olympios (see Josephus, *Antiquities* x.2, 5.4).

39. Frederick A. Tatford, *Paul's Letters to the Thessalonians* (New Jersey: Loizeaux Brothers, 1991), p. 90.

40. Whether or not this implies that the Antichrist would need to seat himself on the actual Ark of the Covenant, if it reappeared according to the apocalyptic legends, see 2 Maccabees 2:6-8, is not certain, since even without the Ark, the Holy of Holies retained its distinction as the place of the divine presence in the Second Temple.

41. For the historicists' perspective, see Frank Wilton Hardy, "A Historicist Perspective on Daniel 11," (M.A. Thesis, Andrews University, 1982), pp. 88-93.

42. Nilton Dutra Amorim, "Desecration and Defilement in the Old Testament," p. 266.

43. John Wilkinson, "Christian Pilgrims in Jerusalem During the Byzantine Period," *Palestine Exploration Quarterly* 108 (1976): 77.

44. See G. Beasley-Murray, *Jesus and the Future: An Examination of the Criticism of the Eschatological Discourse, Mark 13, with Special Reference to the Little Apocalypse Theory* (London/New York: Macmillian & Co., 1954).

45. The construction *ad sensum* in the masculine participle *estekota* linked to the neuter *bdeluga* and the obvious parallel found in Matthew 24:15 and 2 Thessalonians 2:3-8 constitute primary evidence for this interpretation.

46. Rigaux saw Daniel 9:27 as underlying Daniel 11:31 and 12:11 (see Beda Rigaux, *L'Antechrist: et l'Opposition au Royaume Messianique dans l'Ancien et le Nouveau Testament,* Universitas Catholica Lovaniensis Dissertationes Seires II Tomus 24 [Paris: J. Gabalda et Fils, 1932]), and Hendriksen follows this, observing, however, that it is upon the first reference to *shomem* ("abominations") in Daniel 8:13-14 that all later passages in Daniel and the New Testament are based (see William Hendriksen, *1 & 2 Thessalonians. Hendriksen New Testament Commentaries* [Grand Rapids: Baker Book House, 1955], p. 176]). Ford contends that Daniel 9:27 is therefore the source for Matthew and Mark, and makes the deciding factor the parallels between Daniel 7–9, 11–12, rather than on purely philological grounds (since linguistically, Matthew 24:15 and Mark 13:14 are closer to Daniel 11:31 and 12:11). He also suggests that Jesus' use of Daniel 9:27 (especially in Mark 13:14) may have in view a summary statement of the "abomination" material, and therefore include all of the parallel Danielic passages, including Daniel 8:13-14 (since Luke 21:24 cites this passage).

47. John A. McLean, "The Seventieth Week of Daniel 9:27 as a Literary Key for Understanding the Structure of the Apocalypse of John" (Ph.D. dissertation, University of Michigan, 1990), pp. 121-86.

48. For my treatment of this see "Prophetic Postponement in Daniel 9 and Other Texts," *Issues in Dispensationalism,* eds. W. Willis and J. Master (Chicago: Moody Press, 1994), pp. 157-58.

49. Luke's omission of this signal event is one of the reasons it is believed that at this point in his narrative he *is* presenting the fall of Jerusalem in 70 C.E. rather than the eschatological end of the age.

50. For this reason consistent preterists must interpret Christ's coming as having occurred in A.D. 70. To do so, however, requires the employment of a non-literal and historical hermeneutic, since the events cannot be reconciled with either the literal interpretation of the Old Testament citations and allusions in the Olivet Discourse or the actual events of the destruction.

51. See Ben Witherington III, *Jesus, Paul and the End of the World: A Comparative Study in New Testament Eschatology* (Downers Grove, IL: InterVarsity Press, 1992), p. 161.

52. While authorship is not necessarily a crucial factor in the tracing of our motif, I am assuming both of the Thessalonian epistles to be genuinely Pauline. The Corinthian correspondence appears to bear some significant theological parallels with 2 Thessalonians 2, which, in my opinion, argues for common authorship.

53. See B.B. Warfield, *Biblical and Theological Studies* (New Jersey: Presbyterian & Reformed Publishing Co., 1972), pp. 472-73, who insisted that this "was fulfilled in the terrible story of the emperors of Rome." However, as with the events of Daniel 9:27, upon which this text is most likely based, no actual historical event(s) can be found to match the literal description.

54. Each of these phrases contain an adjectival genitive which has been carried over into the *Koine* Greek of the LXX and New Testament in the form of a Semitic idiom.

55. See George Milligan, *St. Paul's Epistles to the Thessalonians: The Greek Text with Introduction and Notes* (Grand Rapids: William B. Eerdmans Publishing Co., 1953), p. 98.

56. Frank Witt Hughes, *Early Christian Rhetoric and 2 Thessalonians*, Journal for the Study of the New Testament Supple-
    ment; 30 (Sheffield: JSOT Press, 1989), p. 39. For further study of the character and career of the Antichrist figure in bib-
    lical and postbiblical literature see Béda Rigaux, *L'Antéchrist: et l'Oppostion au Royaume Messianique dans l'Ancien et le
    Nouveau Testament*, Universitas Catholica Lovaniensis Dissertationes Seires II, Tomus 24 (Paris: J. Gabalda et Fils, 1932);
    W. Bousset, *The Antichrist Legend: A Chapter in Christian and Jewish Folklore*, trans. A.H. Keane (London: Hutchinson
    and Co., 1896); Ernst Renan, *Antichrist*, trans. W.G. Hutchinson (London: W. Scott, 1899); and Samuel P. Tregelles, *The
    Man of Sin*, reprint of the 1840 edition (London/Aylesbury: Hunt, Benard & Co., 1930).

57. The Antichrist is somehow "energized" by, or as in apocalyptic literature, the incarnation of, Satan. This "energizing" of
    the Antichrist has its analog in Revelation 13:2, where the beast from the abyss receives "his power and his throne and
    great authority" from the great red dragon (a symbol of Satan). Again a counterfeit to Christ is intended, since these
    three substantives are all used in this order of the works of Jesus to authenticate his messiahship (see Acts 2:22).

58. John T. Townsend, *The Jerusalem Temple in New Testament Thought* (Ph.D. dissertation, Harvard Divinity School, 1958),
    p. 68.

59. See Henry Hamann, "A Brief Exegesis of 2 Thess. 2:1-12 with Guideline for the Application of the Prophecy Contained
    Therein," *Concordia Theological Monthly* 24:6 (June, 1953), pp. 427-28.

60. David Wenham, *The Rediscovery of Jesus' Eschatological Discourse*, Gospel Perspectives 4 (Sheffield: JSOT Press, 1984),
    p. 178, argues that in view of the synoptic references to "holy place," and "where it ought not to be," and the Danelic back-
    ground, the Jerusalem Temple is the preferred location.

61. For example: 1 Corinthians 3:16: "You are a temple of God"; 6:19: "Your body is a temple"; 2 Corinthians 6:16: "We are a
    temple"; Ephesians 2:19-21: "The household of God…grows into a holy temple in the Lord." This is not the language of
    equivalence, nor of replacement, but of analogy; otherwise we have three temples replacing the Jewish Temple: a uni-
    versal temple, a local temple, and an individual temple. If one is making this substitution because of a felt need to
    remove the old institution in favor of the new spiritual reality, why compound the old imagery?

62. An apparent exception to this grammatical pattern is 1 Corinthians 3:17; however, while "a temple" in verse 16 = the
    church, the reference to "the Temple" in verse 17 must mean "the Temple [at Jerusalem]" in order for the argument to
    make sense. There is here an almost *a fortiori* argument: "Do you not know that you are a temple of God? If anyone
    destroys the [Jerusalem] Temple, God will destroy him. For the [Jerusalem] Temple is holy as you are [holy]." In other
    words, if the Jerusalem Temple is holy and violators will be punished (the greater), what do you think will happen if you
    violate the church, which is a temple by analogy (the lesser)?

63. George Milligan, *St. Paul's Epistles to the Thessalonians*, reprint of the 1908 edition (Minneapolis: Klock & Klock, 1980),
    p. 100.

64. See Northrop Frye, *The Great Code: The Bible and Literature* (New York: Harcourt Brace Jovanovich, Publishers, 1982),
    p. 95: "The imagery here [2 Thessalonians 2:3-4] is clearly derived from Daniel's 'abomination.'"

65. See Wolfgang Trilling, *Der zweite Brief die Thessalonicher, Evangelisch-Katholisher Kommentar zum Neuen Testament*
    xiv, ed. J. Blank, R. Schnackenburg, E. Schweizer, and U. Wilckens (Benziger Verlag, 1990), p. 86.

66. See Isbon Beckwith, *The Apocalypse of John*, p. 636; George Ladd, *A Commentary on the Revelation of John*, p. 179.

67. For example, P⁴⁷, an early third-century Greek manuscript, and the earliest reading of this text, not only excludes the
    "and" but ends the verse with "His tabernacle in heaven." Therefore, the internal criteria of preferring the more difficult
    reading, and that which best explains the other variants results in the omission of the "and" as the best reading.

68. Like the desecration of the Sabbath and the divine name, the Sanctuary (in the sense of the place of the divine name),
    which has nontangible qualities, and is only affected in a subjective way so that it does not lose its intrinsic holiness, but
    remains permanently holy, beyond the contagion of *tame'*. Only tangible objects, such as the Temple implements, and
    the physical structure of the Temple itself, can be not only desecrated but also defiled, and thus acquire the pollution
    communicated by *tame'*. It should be noted that while holiness appears incompatible with uncleanness in persons, this
    is not necessarily the case with places. Still, while the condition may not be one of unholiness, it results in much the
    same affect with the withdrawal of the divine (holy) presence that gave it sanctity.

69. This may be the reason lesser acts of defilement, such as that committed by Nadab and Abihu (Numbers 5:2-3), or those
    that threatened to defile, such as the case of Joab (1 Kings 2:28, 31-34) and Queen Athaliah (2 Kings 11:15, do not have the
    same affect as a massive destruction, which would not only bring about an accumulation of dead corpses in the Sanc-
    tuary (see Psalm 79:1; Ezekiel 9:6-9), but would remove the Temple's *raison d'être*.

70. There is no clear argument for a chronological sequence here and the dedication of the Temple in verses 1-2 might apply
    to the dedication of the Millennial Temple and the judgment that will be experienced at the end of the Millennium
    (Revelation 20:7-9).

71. See Pasquale De Santo, "A Study of Jewish Eschatology with Special Reference to the Final Conflict" (Ph.D. dissertation: Duke University, 1957), p. 356.

72. This term simply means Jews who believe in Messiah. This can be confusing since both Orthodox and ultra-Orthodox Jews also believe in Messiah and the latter are called by this title in Israel. Jews in Israel who believe in Jesus as the Jewish Messiah are called *messachim* ("messianist") by one another, rather than *notzrim* ("Christian") because the latter term is used as a term of derision by unbelieving Jews and makes no distinction between Jewish and Gentile Christians. Those who speak English generally refer to them as "Israeli believers." In the Land, they worship in congregations (*keilot*) which may be called churches, but are usually just called "assemblies" due again to the anti-Semitic history of the term "church" for the Jewish People. Outside of Israel, Messianic Jews are Jews who believe in Jesus as the Jewish Messiah and assemble for worship in Messianic synagogues or congregations, usually with a uniquely Jewish form of praise, music, and biblical teaching from a Jewish perspective. They are also called by fellow believers "Completed Jews," "Jewish-Christians," "Hebrew Christians," or simply "Jewish believers."

73. Rudolf Schnackenburg, *The Gospel According to John* (New York: The Seabury Press, 1980), 1: 437.

Chapter 22—Measuring the Future

1. Charles Lee Feinberg, *The Prophecy of Ezekiel: The Glory of the Lord* (Chicago: Moody Press, 1969), p. 279.

2. Ezekiel's prophecy to the Babylonian exiles can be dated based on his internal chronology from 592–570 B.C. He served as the counterpart to Jeremiah, who gave the same prophetic message of caution and comfort first to the Judeans, and then to those Judeans who fled to Egypt to escape the Babylonian destruction.

3. Steven S. Tuell, *The Law of the Temple in Ezekiel 40–48*, Harvard Semitic Monographs 49, ed. Frank Moore Cross (Atlanta: Scholars Press, 1992), pp. 175-76.

4. Fisch, *Ezekiel*, Soncino Books of the Bible, ed. A. Cohen (London: The Soncino Press, 1973), p. 265.

5. Charles Lee Feinberg, *The Prophecy of Ezekiel: The Glory of the Lord* (Chicago: Moody Press, 1969), p. 233.

6. The text does not specifiy "cubits," and the unit of measurement in "reeds" could also be used here. Many English translations supply "cubits" here and I have followed the NASB version in its rendering. I have used the Egyptian long cubit of 21 inches, since this is thought to have been the royal cubit used in building the Temple. However, if the measurement is in reeds (10.50 feet), the size increases to 49.75 miles square.

7. E. W. Hengstenburg, *The Prophecies of Ezekiel* (Minneapolis: James Reprints, 1869), p. 348.

8. See Menahem Haran, "The Law-Code of Ezekiel XL–XLVIII and Its Relation to the Priestly School," Hebrew Union College Annual 50 (1979): 45-71.

9. See Raymond Abba, "Priests and Levites in Ezekiel," *Vetus Testament* 28 (1978): 2, who sees the vision as a symbolic representation of YHWH dwelling in holiness in the midst of His people. Jon Levenson, *The Theology of the Program of Restoration of Ezekiel 40-48*, Harvard Semitic Monographs 10, ed. Frank Moore Cross (Missoula, MT: Scholars Press, 1976), pp. 46, 116, 129, also views the restoration as purely ideal. Other adherents of this view include Moshe Greenberg, "The Design and Themes of Ezekiel's Program of Restoration," Int 38 (1984): 181-208; Walther Eichrodt, *Ezekiel: A Commentary*, OTL, eds. G. Ernst Wright, John Bright, James Barr, and Peter Ackroyd, trans. C. Quin (Philadelphia: Westminster Press, 1970), p. 542; John Weavers, *Ezekiel*. NCBC, eds. R. E. Clements and Matthew Black, reprint (Grand Rapids: William B. Eerdmans Publishing Co., 1982), p. 343; and George Berry, "The Composition of the Book of Ezekiel," JBL 58 (1939): 172.

10. Jon D. Levenson, *Theology of the Program of Restoration of Ezekiel 40–48* (Missoula, MT: Scholars Press, 1976), p. 45.

11. Interview with Elwood McQuaid, Escondido, California, September 21, 1998.

12. Jerry M. Hullinger, "A Proposed Solution to the Problem of Animal Sacrifices in Ezekiel 40–48" (Th.D. dissertation, Dallas Theological Seminary, 1993), p. 18.

13. For a list of these comparisons and differences see Daniel I. Block, *The Book of Ezekiel, Chapters 25-48*, The New International Commentary on the Old Testament (Grand Rapids: Wm. B. Eerdmans Publishing Co., 1998), pp. 502-3.

14. This is inferred from the lack of anything unusual being mentioned. The only reference point when discussing carved wood panels and stone walls and buildings is the earthly reference point of similar past constructions.

15. Charles Lee Feinberg, *The Prophecy of Ezekiel: The Glory of the Lord* (Chicago: Moody Press, 1969), pp. 233, 237.

16. See Jon Levenson, *Theology of the Program of Restoration of Ezekiel 40–48* (Missoula, MT: Scholars Press, 1976), p. 112 notes: "The immensely detailed vision of the restored community in Ezekiel 40–48 comes as no shock to the sensitive reader of chaps. 1–39."

17. Steven S. Tuell, *The Law of the Temple in Ezekiel 40–48*, Harvard Semitic Monographs 49, ed. Frank Moore Cross (Atlanta: Scholars Press, 1992), p. 175.

18. Rav Dr. Joseph Breuer, *The Book of Yechezkel: Translation and Commentary* (New York/Jerusalem: Philipp Feldheim, Inc., 1993), p. 333.

19. For the support of this translation rather than that which appears in most English versions ("with them") see Moshe Greenberg, *Ezekiel 21–37: A New Translation with Introduction and Commentary*, The Anchor Bible (New York: Doubleday, 1997), pp. 757-58.

20. For additional confirmation of this connection see Mark F. Rooker, "Evidence from Ezekiel," *A Case for Premillennialism: A New Consensus*, eds. Donald K. Campbell and Jeffrey L. Townsend (Chicago: Moody Press, 1992), pp. 128-29.

21. Moshe Greenberg, "The Design and Themes of Ezekiel's Program of Restoration," Interpretation 38 (April 1984): 182.

22. Daniel I. Block, *The Book of Ezekiel, Chapters 25–48*, The New International Commentary on the Old Testament (Grand Rapids: Wm. B. Eerdmans Publishing Co., 1998), p. 505.

23. For these details as well as pictures of the model see John W. Schmidt and J. Carl Laney, *Messiah's Coming Temple: Ezekiel's Prophetic Vision of the Future Temple* (Grand Rapids: Kregel Publications, 1997).

24. See Paul Ellingworth, *The Epistle to the Hebrews: A Commentary on the Greek Text*, The New International Greek Testament Commentary (Grand Rapids: Wm. B. Eerdmans Publishing Co., 1993), pp. 437-42 lists at least seven different points for debate along with the pertinent literature where such variant interpretations may be found.

25. Jerry M. Hullinger, "A Proposed Solution to the Problem of Animal Sacrifices in Ezekiel 40–48" (Th.D. dissertation, Dallas Theological Seminary, 1993), pp. 188-89.

26. John C. Whitcomb, "The Millennial Temple of Ezekiel 40–48" (unpublished paper, n.d.), pp. 1-2.

27. Steven S. Tuell, *The Law of the Temple in Ezekiel 40–48*, pp. 13-14.

28. Jon Levenson, *Theology of the Program of Restoration of Ezekiel 40–48*, Harvard Semitic Monographs 10 (Missoula, MT: Scholars Press, 1976): pp. 37-53.

29. As cited by Rabbi Shalom Dov Steinberg, *The Third Beit HaMikdash*, trans. Rabbi Moshe Leib Miller (Jerusalem: Moznaim Publications, 1993).

30. For more details see my book *Secrets of the Dead Sea Scrolls* (Eugene, OR: Harvest House Publishers, 1996), pp. 110-11, 235-63.

31. Jon Levenson, *Theology of the Program of Restoration of Ezekiel 40–48* (Missoula, MT: Scholars Press, 1976), pp. 33, 41.

32. See Ben Zion Luria, "And a Fountain Shall Come Forth from the House of the Lord," *Dor le Dor* 10 (1981): 48-58.

33. "Camera to Show Jesus' Arrival on the Internet," originally appearing in *Israel Today*, as cited in *The Spirit of Prophecy* 27:5 (September/October 1999): 6.

34. For further support for this conclusion see Charles Lee Feinberg, *The Prophecy of Ezekiel: The Glory of the Lord* (Chicago: Moody Press, 1969), pp. 257-58.

Chapter 23—Blasphemy or Blessing?

1. Edmund P. Clowney, "The Final Temple," *Prophecy in the Making: Messages Prepared for the Jerusalem Conference on Biblical Prophecy*, ed. Carl F. H. Henry (Carol Stream, IL: Creation House, Inc., Publishers, 1971), p. 85.

2. John Schmitt and Carl Laney, *Messiah's Coming Temple: Ezekiel's Prophetic Vision of the Future Temple* (Grand Rapids: Kregel Publications, 1997), p. 181.

3. I have made the point in chapter 13 that Jesus, not Paul, deserves this honor. Christians think of "founding" in the sense that the church, a unique organism consisting of Jew and Gentile in equal relationship to Messiah by faith (Ephesians 2:11-22), came into existence (Acts 1:4-5, 8; 2:1-4) as Jesus predicted (Matthew 16:18), although it had never before been previously revealed in the Old Testament (Romans 16:25-26; Ephesians 3:3-6). In another sense, Christianity continued the faith of the Old Testament saints, and as such, can be traced back to the beginning of the history of redemption (Genesis 3:15).

4. Edmund P. Clowney, "The Final Temple," *Prophecy in the Making: Messages Prepared for the Jerusalem Conference on Biblical Prophecy*, ed. Carl F. H. Henry (Carol Stream, IL: Creation House, Inc., Publishers, 1971), p. 85.

5. Archibald Hughes, *A New Heaven and a New Earth* (London: Marshall, Morgan & Scott, 1958), p. 157.

6. Yaron Tsur and Yeshayahu Gafni, *Jerusalem to Jabneh: The Period of the Mishnah and its Literature*, Units 3,4, s.v., "Destruction of the Second Temple: Aspects" (Tel-Aviv: Everyman's University Publishing House, 1980), p. 1.

7. In the Jerusalem Talmud, tractate *Megilla* (1:11 Vilna, 1:13 Venecia), it is told that a Gentile named Antuninus asked a rabbi if he could erect an altar to offer incense to God.

8. Binyamin Ze'ev Kahane, "A Time to Build," *Mikdash-Build* 3:7 (1 Nisan 5759): 1-2.

9. As given by Joshua Berman, *The Temple: Its Symbolism Then and Now* (New Jersey: Jason Aronson, Inc., 1995), pp. 112-14.

10. Erich Sauer, *From Eternity to Eternity* (Grand Rapids: William B. Eerdmans Publishing Co., 1954), p. 181.

11. See this criticism leveled against the inconsistency of consistent literalists by Anthony Hoekema, *The Bible and the Future* (Grand Rapids: Wm. B. Eerdmans Publishing Co., 1979), p. 204 against a statement in *The New Scofield Reference Bible* (New York: Oxford University Press, 1967), p. 888, n. 1 that spiritualizes the sacrifices within a literal Temple!

12. In addition, there is a tradition in both Jewish and Christian sources that a scarlet string which hung in the Second Temple, and which miraculously turned white on the Day of Atonement to show God's acceptance of the Nation, *failed* to change color for the last 40 years of the Temple's existence. Whether or not this actually occurred, it was used by Christian apologists in their disputations with Jewish opponents. The failure of the string to change color was understood by both Jews and Christians to have denoted divine disfavor and rejection. Yet, while Christians contended it symbolized the rejection of the Temple and its sacrificial system, the Jews argued it was a punishment of the Nation resulting from the rivalries between the Jewish religious factions of the time.

13. Jewish sources record that there were 13 veils or curtains in the Temple, although it is not stated where these were. See for details Alec Garrad, *The Splendour of the Temple* (Eye, Suffolk, UK: Alec Garrad, Moat Farm, Fressingfield, 1997), pp. 75-76. However, the outer veil was the only visible veil and therefore would naturally be the one whose rending would give a public demonstration of the heavenly response.

14. *Jewish Wars*, Loeb Classical Library, trans. H. St. James Thackeray (Cambridge: Harvard University Press, 1979), 3:265.

15. The Temple was considered a reproduction of the heavenly Temple on earth (the Hebrew *tabnit*, "pattern" of Exodus 25:9, 40), and as also the place of the divine presence (*Shekinah*), though absent at that time, could appropriately represent "heaven" or God's response.

16. "Heaven" or the "heavens" was a figure of speech (hypocatastasis) for the presence of God.

17. Some have also seen here a connection in Mark with the "tearing of the heavens" (Mark 1:10) at Jesus' baptism arguing that Mark used this "tearing metaphor" as a narrative device to signal the very beginning (baptism) and very end (crucifixion) of Jesus' public ministry. They find further support in the heavenly confession at Jesus' baptism that He was "the Son of God" with that of the Roman centurion's and the fact that the outer curtain symbolized the "heavens" which were rent. While this is possible, I prefer to find the contrast within the Passion narrative context, which as I have demonstrated, is obvious enough. For the case of the "tearing metaphor" see S. Motyer, "The Rending of the Veil: A Markan Pentecost," *New Testament Studies* 33 (1987): 155-57; and Howard M. Jackson, "The Death of Jesus in Mark and the Miracle from the Cross," *New Testament Studies* 22 (1987): 23-31. For the connection with the "heavenly" veil imagery see David Ulansey, "The Heavenly Veil Torn: Mark's Cosmic 'Inclusio,'" (revised paper) originally published in *Journal of Biblical Literature* 110:1 (Spring 1991): 123-25.

18. This is confirmed by the design of ancient tunics, which were ankle-length and had only one opening at the top (like a poncho). This design is the reason the inner garment ("the robe of the ephod") of the high priest had to be specially lined at the neck so it could not be torn (Exodus 28:32).

19. Because of the supernatural context of the Danielic reference, this "Son of Man" can be parallel to the "Son of God" in the Gospel context.

20. Oswald T. Allis, *Prophecy and the Church*, 2d ed. (Philadelphia: Presbyterian & Reformed Publishing Co., 1947), p. 243.

21. J.B. Taylor, *Ezekiel*, Tyndale Old Testament Commentaries (Downers Grove, IL: 1969), p. 252.

22. Surveys of the works of those holding to a literal interpretation of Ezekiel 40–48 have revealed an inconsistent tendency to spiritualize the sacrifices, making them a figure of speech (hypocatastasis) or symbolic of certain spiritual realities in the Christian life (though not of the church). For surveys and critiques of these interpretations see Jerry M. Hullinger, "A Proposed Solution to the Problem of Animal Sacrifices in Ezekiel 40–48" (unpublished Th.D. dissertation, Dallas, TX: Dallas Theological Seminary, 1993), pp. 1-13; and John Whitcomb, "The Millennial Temple of Ezekiel 40–48" (unpublished paper, Winona Lake, revised 1998), pp. 3-4.

23. Ibid., p. 6.

24. Clive A. Thompson, "The Necessity of Blood Sacrifices in Ezekiel's Temple," *Bibliotheca Sacra* 123:491 (July-September, 1966), p. 238.

25. Matthew has "My Father's Kingdom," Mark has "in the Kingdom of God," while Luke reads "until the Kingdom of God comes." Each one reflects a slightly different aspect of the Millennial kingdom, but together relate to the same eschatological age when Jesus has returned.

26. Some have suggested that what is here is the Messianic banquet of Isaiah 25:6-9; however, this is unnecessary, since Passover is the context of Jesus' promise and Ezekiel 45:21 states a Passover will be celebrated regularly in the kingdom.

27. The sages held that Adam offered sacrifices to God, although this is not stated in the Scriptures (*Shabbat* 28b, *Avoda Zara* 8a, *Chulin* 60a, Midrash, *Tehillim* 39).

28. For further explication of these points see John C. Whitcomb, "Christ's Atonement and Animal Sacrifices in Israel," *Grace Theological Journal* 6:2 (1985): 202-8.

29. See John W. Schmitt and Carl L. Laney, *Messiah's Coming Temple: Ezekiel's Prophetic Vision of the Future Temple* (Grand Rapids: Kregel Publications, 1997), pp. 113, 119. John Schmitt also suggests that the altar facing the direction of the Messiah in the Temple explains why the Hebrew word *ariel* ("Lion of God") is uniquely used of it. However, it is not certain that this should be the translation of *ariel* here. In addition, three different words for "altar" appear in this section. Either the types of altars or something about their particular descriptions may be intended in the different translations.

30. The deviations in sacrificial ritual are among the more than 20 differences between Ezekiel and the Torah that forced the prophecy of chapters 40–48 to either be spiritualized or interpreted for the Messianic Age when Elijah the prophet would come and resolve all the difficulties.

31. Interview with John F. Walvoord, San Marcos, Texas, September 20, 1998.

32. See Arno C. Gaebelein, *The Prophet Ezekiel: An Analytical Exposition* (New Jersey: Loizeaux Brothers, 1972), pp. 312-13.

33. For a defense of this purpose of the memorial sacrifices, see Gaebelein, *The Prophet Ezekiel*, pp. 239-48.

34. Charles Lee Feinberg, *The Prophecy of Ezekiel: The Glory of the Lord* (Chicago: Moody Press, 1969), p. 254.

35. E. P. Sanders, *The Historical Figure of Jesus* (New York: The Penguin Press, 1993), p. 262.

36. Joshua Berman, *The Temple: Its Symbolism and Meaning Then and Now* (New Jersey: Jason Aronson, Inc., 1995), p. 115.

37. Nachmanides, *Commentary on the Torah, Leviticus 1:9*, trans. Charles B. Chavel (New York: Shilo Publishing House, 1974) as cited by Berman, *ibid.*, p. 119.

38. Joshua Berman, *op. cit.*, p. 125.

39. For the arguments in favor of this suggestion, see Rabbi David Zvi Hoffman, *Sefer Vayikra* ["Book of Leviticus"], trans. Zvi Har Shefer and Aharon Lieberman (Jerusalem: Mosad Harav Kook, 1971-72), 1:150.

40. See Jacob Milgrom, "Sin Offering or Purgation Offering?" *Vetus Testamentum* 21 (1971): 238, and "Israel's Sanctuary: The Priestly Picture of Dorian Gray," *Revue Biblique* 83 (1976): 391.

41. See Joshua Berman, *The Temple: Its Symbolism Then and Now* (New Jersey: Jason Aronson, Inc., 1995), p. 121.

42. See Richard E. Averbeck, "An Exegetical Study of Leviticus 1:4 with a Discussion of the Nature of Old Testament Atonement" (unpublished M.Div. thesis: Winona Lake, IN: Grace Theological Seminary, 1977).

43. Jerry M. Hullinger, "A Proposed Solution to the Problem of Animal Sacrifices in Ezekiel 40–48" (unpublished Th.D. dissertation, Dallas, TX: Dallas Theological Seminary, 1993).

44. For a discussion of the lexical issues that determine this preference, see Hullinger, *ibid.*, pp. 39-56.

45. For my own presentation of this popular view see my book *In Search of Temple Treasures: The Lost Ark and the Last Days* (Eugene, OR: Harvest House Publishers, 1994), pp. 54-55.

46. Moshe Greenburg, "The Design and Themes of Ezekiel's Program of Restoration," *Interpretation* 38 (1984): 194.

Chapter 24—The Temple Beyond Time

1. The language of re-creation is expressed as "passed away" (Revelation 21:1), compare "fled away" (Revelation 20:11); "a new heaven and a new earth" (Revelation 21:1). N.B. here new replaces old rather than old being renovated; "[there] is no [longer any] sea" (Revelation 21:1) thus the removal of the archetypal connotations of evil personified by the sea; "[there] shall be no [longer any] death" (Revelation 21:4) "[there] shall be no night there" (Revelation 21:25; 22:5); "[there] shall no [longer] be [any] curse" (Revelation 22:3). These last three phrases, all which are suggestive of evil and the old order, reflect that this new order is entirely pervasive—see Revelation 21:5: "I am making all things new."

2. J. Webb Mealy, *After the Thousand Years: Resurrection and Judgment in Revelation 20*, Journal for the Study of the New Testament Supplement Series, No. 70 (Sheffield: JSOT Press, 1992), p. 192. Webb would see this as evidence that the re-creation attends the *parousia*; however, it is not necessary to see this re-creation as attendant, but proceeding as a result, from the new order initiated at the eschaton. The *parousia* rather sets in motion an irreversible sequence of events culminating in the new heavens and new earth.

3. For my treatment of this question see my book *Jerusalem in Prophecy* (Eugene, OR: Harvest House Publishers, 1998), pp. 315-18.

4. The following texts contain references to the New Jerusalem concept among those works considered as Jewish apocryphal or pseudepigraphical (and apocalyptic): Tobit 13:8-18; Testament of Dan 5:12-13; Sibylline Oracles 5:420-27; 1 Enoch 90:28-29; 2 Esdras 7:26; 10:25-28; 13:36; 2 Baruch 4; 32:1-4.

5. For the complete extant text of this document see Michael Wise, Martin Abegg, Jr., and Edward Cook, *The Dead Sea Scrolls: A New Translation* (San Francisco: HarperCollins, 1996), pp. 180-88.

6. Yitzhak I. Hayutman, *Realizing the Heavenly Jerusalem*, The Academy of Jerusalem Monographs #3 (March, 1995).

7. This follows the Hasidic understanding that present-day Israel, founded and governed by secular Zionists, and present-day Jerusalem, though retaining sanctity but liberated by Zionists and ruled by Arab Muslims, is not the fulfillment of

prophecy, but awaits a restored theocracy where spiritual enlightenment and a higher plane of morality will exist on a universal level. Only then will earthly Jerusalem be free and fulfill its destiny to again house the *Shekinah*.

8. See Greg K. Beale (an eclectic Idealist), *The Book of Revelation: A Commentary on the Greek Text*, The New International Greek Testament Commentary (Grand Rapids: Wm. B. Eerdmans Publishing Co., 1999), p.1066. However, this is not restricted to the symbolic school—see Robert H. Gundry (a post-tribulational Premillennialist), "The New Jerusalem: People, Not Place," *Novum Testamentum* 29 (1987): 254-64.

9. For example, commentators have assumed that the immense dimensions of the New Jerusalem require that it be symbolic, and have attempted various schemes to interpret these numerical measurements figuratively—see Louis Berkhof, *Systematic Theology*, 4th rev. ed. (Grand Rapids: William B. Eerdmans Publishing Co., 1949), p. 715; H. B. Swete, *The Apocalypse of St. John* (London: Macmillan and Co., Ltd., 1907), p. 289; Albert Barnes, "Book of Revelation," *Notes on the New Testament*, vol. 9 (London: Blackie and Son, n.d.), p. 481; P. W. Grant, *The Revelation of John* (London: Hodder & Stoughton, 1889), pp. 591-93.

10. John notes that this "holy city" was in heaven, but now has apparently descended to earth: "descending out of heaven from God" (verses 2,10), thus, transferring the celestial to the terrestrial. This may incidentally be equated with the rabbinic notion of the Temple descending from heaven in fire. For a discussion of the premillennial view as contrasting the amillennial view on this topic: Alan A. McNickle, "The New Jerusalem in Amillennial Theology" (Th.M. thesis, Dallas Theological Seminary, 1984).

11. This is how the Targum understood this verse, translating the Hebrew *shaken* ("dwell") here by *shekinah*; hence: "I will make My *Shekinah* dwell among them." This language allowed John, in the fourth Gospel, to speak of Jesus as the incarnate "Word tabernacled with us" (here the Greek *logos* is equivalent to the Hebrew concept of *davar* and the Greek verb *eskenosen* simply transliterates the Hebrew *mishkan*), John 1:6,14. Since in Christian interpretation the *Shekinah* is now resident in Christ, to be the Church = the body of Christ, as we have seen Paul explain, is to be a temple, corporately and individually localizing the divine presence.

12. It should also be noted that if the Temple-city is the Heavenly Temple descended to a restored earth, then the language displays the continuity between the Edenic Sanctuary and Ezekiel's Temple, both of which were patterned after the heavenly archetype and represented idealic realizations. Thus, the Millennial Temple (Ezekiel's) realized the earthly ideal, which was lost at Eden, and unrealized by the First and Second Temples, and the New Temple represents the ultimate realization in an uncursed (new Eden) world.

13. Mordecai Kornfeld, "The Shechinah in Exile," *Parashat Vayigash* (Jerusalem, January 7, 1998), p. 2.

14. See, for example, Robert Mounce, *The Book of Revelation*, New International Commentary on the New Testament (Grand Rapids: William B. Eerdmans Publishing Co., 1977), p. 383; M. Kiddle, *The Revelation of St. John*, p. 436.

15. George E. Ladd, *A Commentary on the Revelation of John* (Grand Rapids: William B. Eerdmans Publishing Co., 1972), p. 284.

16. As seen above, the purified condition of the peoples would not require outer courts, which formerly served to provide separation or gradations of holiness.

17. The predicate adjective *tetravgwno* ("foursquare"), describing the city, is from *tevtra* (Aeolic for *tevssare*) "four" and *gwvno* (a cognate of *gwniva*), "corner." This term was also used with reference to cube-shaped building stones—see BAGD, p. 821, and indicates here a quadrilateral quadrangle or tetragonal structure.

18. Some have suggested this mimics the city planning of Near-Eastern cities such as Babylon, which, according to Herodotus, was laid out as a square with each side 120 stadia in length, and Nineveh, which Diodorus Siculus described in a similar fashion. However, the adjective *i[sa* indicates the shape of a perfect cube, which, from the Jewish perspective, would have had reference to the Holy of Holies, as described in 1 Kings 6:19-20.

19. Flusser, denying the possibility of dependence by the Midrash upon the Apocalypse, concludes, "The idea that [scholars] have assumed that no corporeal temple will exist in the eschatological Jerusalem must be Christian in origin, because they imagine it to be unthinkable in Jewish Messianic expectations [is]...wrong." David Flusser, "No Temple in the City," *Judaism and the Origins of Christianity* (Jerusalem: The Magnes Press, 1988), p. 465.

20. Ibid., p. 459.

21. Since John alone records both of these promises from Jesus (John 14:2-3; Revelation 1:1; 22:16,20), it seems reasonable that he would have made this connection.

Chapter 25—Ready to Rebuild

1. Statement by Rabbi Zalman B. Melamed on Arutz-7 news program, September 26, 1996.

2. Letter to Yehuda Etzion, Director of Chai VeKayam from Benjamin Netanyahu, dated March 1995, as cited by Bill Hutman and Evelyn Gordon, "Justice Minister Favors Temple Mount Worship," *The Jerusalem Post International Edition* (July 20, 1996).

3. Rabbi David Henshke, "What Happened to Orot ha-Reiyah?," *Orot ha-Reiyah,* ed. Moshe Y. Zuriel (Sha'alabim, 1989), pp. 12-13.

4. As cited by Amy Klein, "Jerusalem Foil Five Attacks on Temple Mount," *The Jerusalem Post* (February 26, 1999), p. 5.

5. Ibid.

6. From the televised speech of Bill Clinton to the Jordanian Parliament, Amman, Jordan (October 26, 1994).

7. As cited in the article "The Issue of the Temple Mount" by Yeshivat Har HaBayit, originally published in *Yibane HaMikdash* 75 [Hebrew] and reprinted in the English version *Mikdash-Build* 3:3 (December 16, 1998): 5.

8. From the Judean Voice <http://www.kahane.org>

9. Interview with Yohanan Ramati, Jerusalem, November 4, 1998.

10. Interview with Gershon Salomon, Office of the Temple Mount Faithful, Jerusalem, November 6, 1998.

11. Interview with David Dolan, Jerusalem, November 14, 1998.

12. Interview with Clarence Wagner, Mount of Olives, Jerusalem, November 16, 1998.

13. As cited by Yitzhak Hayutman, "A House of Prayer for All the Nations," trans. Yitzhak Zuriel in *The Question of Rebuilding the Temple Today* (part 1) (Jerusalem: Academy of Jerusalem Proceeding, n.d.), p. 1. Rabbi Cohen's statement was given in August of 1989.

14. Interview with Reuven Prager, Beged Ivri, Jerusalem, November 14, 1998.

15. Interview with Chaim Richman by Irwin Baxter, *Endtime* magazine (July/August, 1995), p. 13.

16. Interview with Clarence Wagner, Mount of Olives, November 16, 1998.

17. Interview with Clarence Wagner, Mount of Olives, Jerusalem, November 16, 1998.

18. As cited by Mina C. Klein and H. Arthur Klein in *Temple Beyond Time: The Story of the Site of Solomon's Temple* (New York: Van Nostrand Reinhold Co., 1970), p. 20.

Subject Index

Scripture Index

Jewish Text Index

ABOUT THE AUTHOR

Randall Price is regarded as one of the leading evangelical authorities on biblical prophecy and is recognized as an expert on the Middle East. He holds a master of theology degree from Dallas Theological Seminary in Old Testament and Semitic Languages, a Ph.D. from the University of Texas at Austin in Middle Eastern Studies, and has done graduate study at the Hebrew University of Jerusalem in the fields of Semitic Languages and Biblical Archaeology. He has taught undergraduate and graduate courses on biblical archaeology at the University of Texas, biblical languages at the Central Texas Bible Institute, and biblical theology at the International School of Theology.

As President of *World of the Bible Ministries, Inc.*, a nonprofit organization dedicated to reaching the world with a biblical analysis of the past, present, and future of the Middle East, Dr. Price speaks to international audiences through conferences and lectureships each year. He also serves as director of the Qumran Plateau excavation project in Israel, is a certifed pilgrim tour guide in Israel, and through his tour company *World of the Bible Tours* has directed 45 tours to the Bible lands. Dr. Price has authored or co-authored some 20 books on the subjects of biblical archaeology and biblical prophecy, is General Editor of *The Messianic Prophecy Bible* (in progress), and is a contributor to the *New Eerdmans Dictionary of the Bible*.

He has appeared on numerous television documentaries, including the "Ancient Secrets of the Bible" series, the "Thief in the Night" series, and "Uncovering the Truth about Jesus," has been the executive producer and on-screen host of five video productions based on his books, and has featured regularly on television and radio talk shows. Dr. Price and his wife Beverlee have five children and reside in Texas.

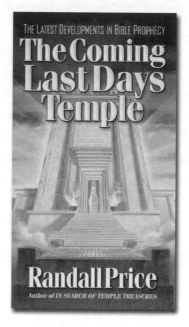

WORLD OF THE BIBLE MINISTRIES

World of the Bible Ministries, Inc., is a nonprofit Christian organization dedicated to bringing to the modern world the world of the Bible past, present, and future. By returning to the original context of the people and events of the Bible the Scriptures are better understood and their truths better applied. Three ministries comprise this organization to accomplish this practical purpose:

World of the Bible Productions—produces new books and documentary films on biblical backgrounds and biblical prophecy for international outreach through distribution and media, and publishes the *World of the Bible News & Views* newsletter.

World of the Bible Seminars—the speaking outreach ministry of Dr. Randall Price through conferences in churches, Christian organizations, and college, university, and seminary lectureships.

World of the Bible Tours—the Bible lands tour company, which offers customized annual pilgrimages and study tours that allow participants to experience the reality of the world of the Bible.

To find out more about our products, request a free subscription to our newsletter, contact Dr. Price about speaking, or ask for a brochure of current tours to the Bible lands, you can reach us at:

Website: www.worldofthebible.com
E-mail: wbmrandl@itouch.net
Address: World of the Bible Ministries, Inc.
P.O. Box 827
San Marcos, TX 78667-0827
Phone: (512) 396-3799
Fax: (512) 392-9080